# MANAGERIAL ECONOMICS
**Sixth Edition**

# MANAGERIAL ECONOMICS

**Sixth Edition**

**James L. Pappas**
University of South Florida

**Mark Hirschey**
University of Kansas

**THE DRYDEN PRESS**

Chicago  Fort Worth  San Francisco
Philadelphia  Montreal  Toronto
London  Sydney  Tokyo

Acquisitions Editor: Rebecca Ryan
Developmental Editor: Eric Elvekrog
Project Editor: Cathy Crow
Design Supervisor: Rebecca Lemna
Production Manager: Barb Bahnsen
Permissions Editor: Cindy Lombardo
Director of Editing, Design, and Production: Jane Perkins

Text and Cover Designer: Diane Hutchinson
Copy Editor: Judy Lary
Indexer: Leoni McVey
Compositor: Weimer Typesetting, Inc.
Text Type: 9½/12 Melior

**Library of Congress Cataloging-in-Publication Data**

Pappas, James L.
    Managerial economics / James L. Pappas, Mark Hirschey.—6th ed.
       p.    cm.
    Includes bibliographies and index.
    ISBN 0-03-031202-7
    1. Managerial economics.   I. Hirschey, Mark.   II. Title.
HD30.22.P37   1990
    658.15—dc20
                                                        89-35716
                                                          CIP

Printed in the United States of America
901-040-987654321
Copyright ©1990, 1987, 1983, 1979, 1976, 1972, by The Dryden Press,
a division of Holt, Rinehart and Winston, Inc.

Address orders:
The Dryden Press
Orlando, FL 32887

Address editorial correspondence:
The Dryden Press
908 N. Elm Street
Hinsdale, IL 60521

The Dryden Press
Holt, Rinehart and Winston
Saunders College Publishing

Cover Source: Spencer Grant/MGA, Chicago

To Bonnie, Kari, and Kristen—JLP
To Christine, Jessica, and Nicholas—MH

# The Dryden Press Series in Economics

# Preface

In the years since the first edition of *Managerial Economics* was published, successful management has become ever more complex and challenging. This complexity is a natural by-product of the dramatic change occurring in the economic environment. Uncertainty about resource prices and availability, rapid changes in technology, and increases in international competition have produced major transformations in the context and process of managerial decision making. In such an environment, sound economic analysis takes on even greater importance—regardless of whether the decision-making unit is an individual, household, firm, nonprofit organization, or government agency.

*Managerial Economics,* Sixth Edition, is designed to provide a solid foundation of economic understanding for use in managerial decision making. This text offers a comprehensive treatment of economic theory and analysis, using calculus throughout. It focuses on the use of managerial economics tools and techniques in specific decision-making settings. Examples and problems illustrate the application of economic thinking to a wide variety of practical situations. The nature of the decision process and the role that economic analysis plays in that process are emphasized throughout the text.

A key feature of this text is its attempt to depict the firm as a cohesive, unified organization. A basic valuation model is constructed and used as the underlying economic model of the firm. Each topic in the text is then related to an element of the value-maximization model. In this process, management is shown to involve an integration of the accounting (information), finance, marketing, production, and personnel (human resource), functions. This integrative process consolidates the materials covered and demonstrates that important business decisions are *interdisciplinary* in the truest sense of the word. Our students have found that the presentation of the business firm as a unified whole—rather than as a series of discrete, unrelated areas—is one of the most valuable aspects of the study of managerial economics.

Although both micro- and macroeconomic relations have implications for managerial decision making, this edition continues our concentration on microeconomic topics of particular importance. Following the development of the economic model of the firm, we examine the vital role of profits. Because demand for a firm's products plays a major part in determining its profitability and ongoing success, demand analysis is an essential area of study. We also explore production theory and cost analysis, which examine the economics of resource allocation and employment.

Another important topic is market-structure analysis, which provides a foundation for studying the external economic environment and for examining the pricing practices required for successful management. The effect of government activity on the business environment, including the constraints it imposes on management, requires an examination of regulation and the field of antitrust law. Capital budgeting, the keystone of an enterprise's long-range planning process, is also important to society because it involves the allocation of scarce capital resources. Finally, because managerial decision making involves attempts to optimize behavior under conditions of risk or uncertainty, this book describes a number of optimization and risk-analysis procedures that have been developed for use in economic analysis.

*Managerial Economics*, Sixth Edition, takes a problem-solving approach. Our focus is on the economics—not the mathematics—of the managerial decision process. Quantitative tools are introduced to give greater insight into the method of economic analysis, as well as to facilitate the practical use of economics in decision situations.

## CHANGES IN THE SIXTH EDITION

Just as the world in which managerial decisions are made is constantly changing, so, too, must a textbook be modified and updated to maintain its value as an educational resource. This revision of *Managerial Economics* contains a number of important additions and refinements that reflect recent developments in the field. Many of these changes are in response to the valuable suggestions we continue to receive from students and instructors. The following material highlights some of the changes in the sixth edition.

### Content

- A new Chapter 3, *Demand and Supply*, has been added to show how the basic forces of demand and supply interact to determine prices and quantities for all goods and services.

- Chapter 4, *Demand Analysis*, has been revised to include a brief but comprehensive introduction to the theory of consumer demand. This chapter now makes clear the basis of consumer demand to all students, including those with only modest previous coursework in economics.
- The material on interpreting regression equations and the use of regression statistics in Chapter 5, *Demand Estimation*, has been extensively revised and simplified.
- Chapter 7, *Production*, now develops the concept of optimal input combinations by emphasizing the relations among factor productivity, value of output, and resource employment. Practical examples show how these relations are equally valuable in analyzing the production of both goods and services.
- Chapter 8, *Cost Analysis*, demonstrates the practical relevance of economic analysis through expanded coverage of topics such as minimum efficient scale, economies of scope, and learning (or experience).
- Two new chapters provide expanded coverage of market-structure concepts. Chapter 11, *Market Structure I: Perfect Competition and Monopoly*, provides a framework for analysis of both perfectly competitive markets and monopoly markets. Imperfectly competitive markets are the focus of Chapter 12, *Market Structure II: Monopolistic Competition and Oligopoly*, which explores price and nonprice (e.g., advertising) methods of competition. We also discuss the market-structure data that are available from both private and public sources to illustrate how one can identify and analyze a firm's product markets.
- Chapter 13, *Pricing Practices*, includes a comprehensive discussion of markup pricing practices. Simple rules for determining the profit-maximizing markup on cost and markup on price are developed to aid in understanding optimal pricing practices.
- Chapter 14, *The Role of the Government in the Market Economy*, provides a thorough treatment of equity and efficiency issues involved in defining the scope of regulation—and, increasingly, the scope of deregulation. Questions of property rights and the government's role in both assisting and directing the private economy are fully examined.
- Chapter 15, *Decision Making under Uncertainty*, contains a more comprehensive treatment of techniques for evaluating the costs and benefits of managerial decisions when outcomes are not known with certainty. In particular, we expand on our previous use of the probability concept and game theory.

## Pedagogical Features

- Each chapter integrates extended real-world applications of chapter concepts. These simple numerical examples and solved problems emphasize the practical implications of the materials covered. A special symbol ▦ in the margin indicates the location of these solved problems and examples.

- Each chapter also includes several nonnumerical *Managerial Applications* boxes that show the usefulness of managerial economics in practical decision making. In total, more than 50 new *Managerial Applications* are provided to emphasize the practical use of the topics covered. Based on articles taken from business periodicals, this new feature illustrates how the concepts of managerial economics are relevant to many issues encountered in actual business practice.

- The text also incorporates many new regression-based problems and case studies that illustrate chapter concepts using data adapted from real-company situations. These illustrative problems and cases are self-contained and require only a basic understanding of regression statistics gained from an introductory statistics course or from a review of Chapter 5, *Demand Estimation*. Data diskettes and a computer supplement are now available to instructors who wish to more fully incorporate the use of regression analysis in their courses.

- End-of-chapter questions and problems have also undergone extensive revision and class testing. The problem sets cover a wide variety of decision situations and illustrate the role of economic analysis throughout the firm. End-of-chapter questions and problems emphasize economic intuition and are designed to assist students in acquiring a practical working facility with the tools and techniques of economic analysis.

# ANCILLARY PACKAGE

*Managerial Economics*, Sixth Edition, is supported by a comprehensive and expanded ancillary package designed to make the use of the text easier for both instructors and students.

## Instructor's Manual

The *Instructor's Manual* contains teaching suggestions as well as detailed answers and solutions for all chapter questions and problems.

## Study Guide

The *Study Guide* provides a summary of major concepts for each chapter, a detailed outline of the most important relations developed, and an expanded set of more than *150 solved problems*. This new edition has undergone extensive class testing and analysis. We believe that this revised *Study Guide* will prove to be an extremely valuable resource for students.

## Test Bank

A comprehensive *Test Bank* with more than 600 problems contains a variety of multiple-choice questions, as well as one-step and multi-step problems, for every chapter. Full solutions follow all problems. The *Test*

*Bank* was written by Louis Amato and Gaines Liner of the University of North Carolina–Charlotte.

### Computerized Test Bank

A *Computerized Test Bank* for IBM microcomputers is available to adopters of *Managerial Economics,* Sixth Edition.

### Computer Supplement

A printed supplement accompanied by a numerical data disk in ASCII format is available. This supplement allows instructors to fully integrate the use of spreadsheet and regression analysis in their courses. This ancillary also provides the means for analyzing the more complex systems of simultaneous equations and linear programming problems that are typical of real-world business situations.

# ACKNOWLEDGMENTS

We are grateful to the many people who aided in the preparation of *Managerial Economics,* Sixth Edition. Many helpful suggestions and valuable comments have been received from a great number of instructors and students who have used previous editions. Numerous reviewers have also provided insights and assistance in clarifying difficult presentations. Among those who have been especially helpful in the development of this edition are: Dean Baim, Pepperdine University; Coldwell Daniel II, Memphis State University; William Gunther, University of Alabama; Dean Hiebert, Illinois State University; Ann Horowitz, University of Florida; and James Truitt, Baylor University.

We would also like to give special recognition to Christine E. Hauschel, who did extensive manuscript reviewing and problem checking.

The University of South Florida, the University of Kansas, our students, and our colleagues provided us with a stimulating environment and general intellectual support. We are also indebted to The Dryden Press staff and would like to thank Cathy Crow, Eric Elvekrog, Rebecca Lemna, Becky Ryan, and Karen Shaw for their special efforts. Finally, we want to thank our wives, Bonnie and Chris, for their encouragement, support, and assistance.

Every effort has been made to provide an error-free package of text and ancillary materials. Should any errors have slipped through despite our efforts, we apologize. We invite readers to correspond with us directly concerning corrections, suggestions for further improvements in clarity, or related matters.

Finally, it is clear that today, more than ever, economic efficiency is an essential ingredient in the successful management of all private- and public-sector organizations. The field of managerial economics continues to undergo important changes in response to the challenges imposed by a rapidly changing environment. It is stimulating and exciting to participate in these developments. We sincerely hope that the sixth edition of *Managerial Economics* will contribute to a better understanding of the application of economic theory and methodology to managerial practice.


James L. Pappas
Mark Hirschey
October 1989

# About the Authors

**James L. Pappas,** Ph.D. (UCLA), is Dean and Lykes Professor of Banking and Finance in the College of Business Administration at the University of South Florida. He is a member of several professional organizations and has served as an officer of the Financial Management Association. Articles by Professor Pappas have appeared in *Decision Sciences, Engineering Economist, Financial Analysts' Journal, Journal of Business, Journal of Finance, Journal of Industrial Economics, Journal of Marketing Research, Southern Economic Journal,* and other leading academic journals. He has served on the editorial boards of *Financial Management* and *Managerial and Decision Economics,* and is co-author of *Fundamentals of Managerial Economics,* Third Edition, with Mark Hirschey. Active in executive education, Professor Pappas serves as Academic Dean of the Graduate School of Banking, which is offered by the Central States Conference of Bankers Associations and the University of Wisconsin–Madison.

**Mark Hirschey,** Ph.D. (University of Wisconsin–Madison), is a Professor in the School of Business at the University of Kansas, where he teaches undergraduate and graduate courses in managerial economics and finance. Professor Hirschey is president of the Association of Managerial Economists as well as a member of several professional organizations. He has published articles in the *American Economic Review, Journal of Accounting Research, Journal of Business, Journal of Business and Economic Statistics, Journal of Finance, Journal of Industrial Economics, Review of Economics and Statistics,* and other leading academic journals. He is editor of *Managerial and Decision Economics* and co-author of *Fundamentals of Managerial Economics,* Third Edition, with James Pappas.

# Contents

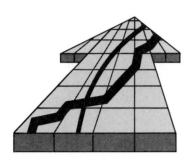

C H A P T E R · 3
# Demand and Supply                                                 85

C H A P T E R · 4
# Demand Analysis                                                   123

C H A P T E R · 8
# Cost Analysis                                                        339

CHAPTER · 14

# The Role of Government in the Market Economy    635

CHAPTER · 15

# Decision Making under Uncertainty    681

# The Nature and Scope of Managerial Economics

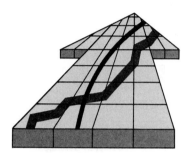

**E**ffective resource management is a continuing challenge to managers in all types of organizations. Managers must develop clear policies so that the objectives of the organization can be efficiently realized. Resources must be obtained and organized; employees need to be trained and motivated. Information systems have to be installed to ensure that ongoing performance is accurately reported and monitored. Extensive knowledge and a wide variety of skills are required to complete each of these important tasks so that appropriate decisions can be made. One of the most important requirements for a successful manager is the ability to make good decisions, and one of the most important tools used by successful managers is the methodology of managerial economics.

**managerial economics**
**Applies economic theory and methods to business and administrative decision making.**

**Managerial economics** applies economic theory and methods to business and administrative decision making. Because it uses the tools and techniques of economic analysis to solve managerial problems, managerial economics links traditional economics with the decision sciences to develop important tools for managerial decision making. This is illustrated in Figure 1.1.

We can appreciate the use and value of managerial economics by examining both its prescriptive and descriptive components. Managerial economics prescribes rules for improving managerial decisions. It tells managers how things should be done to achieve organizational objectives efficiently. Managerial economics also helps managers recognize how economic forces affect organizations and describes the economic consequences of managerial behavior.

Managerial economics can be used to identify ways to efficiently achieve virtually any of the organization's goals. For example, suppose a

■ Figure 1.1
## The Role of Managerial Economics in Managerial Decision Making

Managerial economics uses economic concepts and decision science techniques to solve managerial problems.

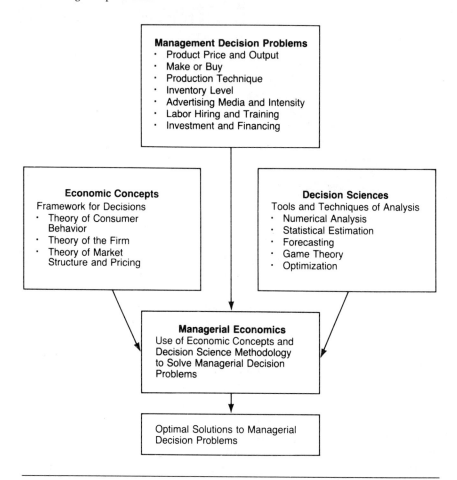

small business seeks rapid growth in order to reach a size that will permit efficient use of national media advertising. The firm's managers can use managerial economics to identify pricing and production strategies that will help meet this short-run objective as quickly and effectively as possible. Similarly, managerial economics provides pricing and output rules that will permit the company to maximize net profits once it has achieved its growth objectives.

Managerial economics also has prescriptive applications outside the for-profit sector of an economy. For example, an administrator of a nonprofit hospital strives to provide the best medical care possible given limited medical staff, equipment, and related resources. Using the tools and concepts of managerial economics, the administrator can determine the optimal allocation of these limited resources. In short, managerial economics helps managers arrive at a set of operating rules that aids in the efficient utilization of scarce human and capital resources. Following these rules enables businesses, nonprofit organizations, and government agencies to meet their objectives efficiently.

To establish appropriate decision rules, managers must thoroughly understand the economic environment in which they operate. Managerial economics describes how economic forces affect and are affected by managerial decisions. For example, a grocery retailer may offer consumers a highly price-sensitive product, such as milk, at an extremely low markup over cost—say, 1 or 2 percent—while offering less price-sensitive products, such as nonprescription drugs, at markups as high as 40 percent over cost. Managerial economics describes the logic of this pricing practice with respect to the goal of profit maximization. Similarly, managerial economics reveals that imposing auto import quotas reduces the availability of substitutes for domestically produced cars, raises auto prices, and creates the possibility of monopoly profits for domestic manufacturers. It does not tell us whether or not imposing quotas is good public policy; it only describes the predictable *economic* consequences of such actions.

With its prescriptive and descriptive components, managerial economics provides a comprehensive application of economic theory and methodology to managerial decision making. Managerial economics is just as relevant to the management of nonbusiness, nonprofit organizations, such as government agencies, cooperatives, schools, hospitals, museums, and similar institutions, as it is to profit-oriented businesses. Thus, while this text focuses primarily on business applications, it also includes examples and problems from the government and nonprofit sectors to illustrate the broad relevance of managerial economics concepts and tools.

## THEORY OF THE FIRM

A useful way to begin our study of managerial economics is to consider the broad framework within which we analyze managerial decision making. A business enterprise is a combination of people, physical and financial assets, and information (technical, marketing, coordinative, and so on). People directly involved include stockholders, management, labor, suppliers, and customers. In addition, all of society is affected by a firm's activity, because businesses use resources that would otherwise be available for other purposes, pay taxes if operations are profitable, provide employment, and produce most of society's material and services output.

## 1.1  **Managerial Application**

Is Value Maximization Relevant?

During the mid-1980s, Dennis B. Levine, a managing director of mergers and acquisitions for Drexel Burnham Lambert, Inc., admitted to stealing material nonpublic information from his employer and using it to amass millions of dollars in illegal stock market trading profits. The scandal broadened when the Securities and Exchange Commission announced that Levine had cultivated a mutually profitable relationship with Ivan Boesky, a stock market speculator. Levine supplied Boesky with tips concerning pending merger announcements in return for a share of any trading profits Boesky realized. Both Levine and Boesky, along with others implicated in this insider trading scandal, were forced to give up ill-gotten profits, paid additional millions of dollars in fines, served time in federal prison, and were barred from the securities business for life.

In an unrelated development, *Business* *Week* ran an exposé concerning Robert Buckley, chief executive officer (CEO) of Allegheny International, Inc. In its investigation of the company, *Business Week* uncovered lavish spending on executive perks, conflicts among "independent" members of the board of directors, and limited disclosures to stockholders. Other benefits for top executives included frequent nonbusiness use of corporate aircraft, personal loans at below-market interest rates, and placement of children of senior executives on the corporate payroll. *Business Week* asked, "What is going on here?"

What indeed! Clearly, these instances of self-dealing on the part of employees and corporate executives simply cannot be regarded as being consistent with the long-run interests of stockholders, and, therefore, they are inconsistent with expected value maximization. However, before we reject the value maximization theory of the firm on the

*continued*

See: William C. Symonds and Pete Engardino, "Big Trouble at Allegheny," *Business Week*, August 11, 1986; and Christopher Farrell, "Suddenly, Blue Chips are Red-hot for ESOPs," *Business Week*, March 20, 1989, 144.

**theory of the firm**
Recognizes expected value maximization as the primary objective of a business.

Firms exist because they are useful in the process of producing and distributing goods and services. They are basically economic entities. As such, their activities can best be analyzed in the context of an economic model.

The basic model of the business enterprise is derived from what is called the **theory of the firm.** In its earliest version, the firm was thought to have *profit maximization* as its primary goal; that is, the firm's owner-

**Managerial Application** *continued*

grounds that it doesn't describe real-world behavior, we must ask if self-dealing behavior is common business practice. If employee and managerial self-dealing is typical, the value maximization theory will have little descriptive relevance. On the other hand, if such instances are relatively rare, the value maximization model can provide useful descriptive insight concerning real-world business practice.

Fortunately, the types of behavior typified by the Levine/Boesky and Allegheny International scandals are quite rare. Far from being an industry riddled with corruption, the securities business is one in which scandal occurs infrequently. Every business day on Wall Street, thousands of transactions, some involving billions of dollars, are made on the basis of a simple phone conversation. One's word is one's bond. If honesty and trust didn't pervade Wall Street, the ability of the securities business to operate would be more than hampered; it would founder. It is interesting that the Levine/Boesky relationship came to light within only eighteen months of its inception. Apparently, keeping such a lucrative and intricate scheme hidden was impossible in light of typical industry practice and regulation. Similarly, given current reporting requirements, it was impossible to keep quiet the apparent self-

dealing of top executives at Allegheny International. Indeed, Buckley was forced to resign as CEO in the aftermath of the *Business Week* disclosures. Although highly regrettable and obviously costly to affected stockholders, the Levine/Boesky and Allegheny affairs were of relatively short duration and appear to be rather atypical. Neither can be regarded as examples of "business as usual."

Finally, it is interesting to note the growing trend among large companies to adopt employee stock ownership plans (ESOPs) in an effort to minimize the problems sometimes caused by a separation of management and control. Both company performance and stockholder returns seem to improve when top executives and a broad range of other employees hold a substantial equity interest in a firm. The current popularity of ESOPS, and the growing trend toward ESOP adoptions, suggests a strong and growing motive for value maximization in corporate America. Therefore, even though instances of business practice that are inconsistent with value maximization do arise from time to time, these instances are relatively rare. As a result, value maximization can be regarded as a useful description of the fundamental motivation for everyday business decision making.

**expected value maximization**
An emphasis on profit maximization that includes uncertainty and the time dimension.

manager was assumed to be striving to maximize the firm's short-run profits. Later, the emphasis on profits was broadened to encompass uncertainty and the time dimension. In this more complete model, the primary goal of the firm was viewed as **expected value maximization** rather than short-run profit maximization. The goal of expected value maximization is now considered the *primary* objective of business in the economic model of firm behavior.

## Defining Value

Since the basis of the economic model is maximizing the value of the firm, we should clarify the meaning of *value*. Actually, many concepts of value are found in economics and business—book value, market value, liquidating value, going-concern value, and so on. For our purposes, the **value of the firm** is defined as the present value of the firm's expected future net cash flows. If we equate cash flows to profits for simplicity, the value of the firm today—its **present value**—is the value of expected future profits, discounted back to the present at an appropriate interest rate.[1]

**value of the firm**

The present value of the firm's expected future net cash flows.

**present value**

The value of an expected future amount, discounted back to the present at an appropriate interest rate.

The essence of this model, which we use throughout the book, can be expressed as follows:

$$\text{Value of the Firm} = \text{Present Value of Expected Future Profits}$$

$$= \frac{\pi_1}{(1+i)^1} + \frac{\pi_2}{(1+i)^2} + \cdots + \frac{\pi_n}{(1+i)^n}$$

$$= \sum_{t=1}^{n} \frac{\pi_t}{(1+i)^t}. \qquad \textbf{1.1}$$

Here $\pi_1$, $\pi_2$, and so forth represent the expected profits in each year, $t$, and $i$ is the appropriate interest, or discount, rate. The final form for Equation 1.1 is simply a shorthand expression in which sigma ($\Sigma$) stands for "sum up" or "add together." The term

$$\sum_{t=1}^{n}$$

simply says, "Add together as $t$ goes from 1 to $n$ the values of the term to the right." For Equation 1.1, the process is as follows: Let $t = 1$ and find the value of the term $\pi_1/(1+i)^1$, the present value of year 1 profit; then let $t = 2$ and calculate $\pi_2/(1+i)^2$, the present value of year 2 profit; continue until $t = n$, the last year included in the analysis; then add up these present-value equivalents of yearly profits to find the value of the firm.

Since profits ($\pi$) are equal to total revenues (TR) minus total costs (TC), Equation 1.1 can be rewritten as:

$$\text{Value} = \sum_{t=1}^{n} \frac{TR_t - TC_t}{(1+i)^t}. \qquad \textbf{1.2}$$

---

[1]Discounting is required because profits obtained in the future are less valuable than profits earned presently. To understand this, one needs to recognize that $1 in hand today is worth more than $1 to be received a year from now, because $1 today can be invested and, with interest, grow to a larger amount by the end of the year. If we had $1 and invested it at 10 percent interest, it would grow to $1.10 in one year. Thus, $1 is defined as the present value of $1.10 due in one year when the appropriate interest rate is 10 percent. For the reader who is unfamiliar with the concepts of present value and compound interest, we have included a detailed treatment of the subject in Appendix A.

We can use this expanded equation to examine how the expected value maximization model relates to a firm's various functional departments and activities. The marketing department of a firm has major responsibility for sales (*TR*); the production department has a major responsibility for costs (*TC*); and the finance department has a major responsibility for acquiring capital with which to support the firm's activities and, hence, for the discount factor (*i*) in the denominator. There are many important overlaps among these functional areas. The marketing department, for example, can help reduce the costs associated with a given level of output by influencing customer order size and timing. The production department can stimulate sales by improving quality and reducing delivery lags. Still other departments—for example, accounting, personnel, transportation, and engineering—provide information and services vital to both sales growth and cost control. Thus, the determination of *TR* and *TC* is a complex task that requires recognizing the important interrelations among the various areas of firm activity. Further, all of these activities affect the firm's risks and thereby the discount rate used to determine present values. An important concept in managerial economics is that managerial decisions throughout the firm should be analyzed in terms of their effects on the various determinants of value as expressed in Equations 1.1 and 1.2.

## Constraints and the Theory of the Firm

Most managerial decisions are made in light of constraints imposed by technology, resource scarcity, contractual obligations, and government restrictions. To make decisions that will maximize value, managers must consider both short- and long-run implications as well as how various external constraints affect their ability to achieve organizational objectives.

Although a tremendous variety of constraints can arise in managerial decision problems, most fall within three broad categories. These are resource constraints, output quantity or quality constraints, and legal constraints. To clarify the important role that constraints play in managerial decision making, we will briefly examine some examples of constrained decision problems.

Firms and other organizations frequently face limited availability of essential inputs, such as skilled labor, key raw materials, energy, machinery, and warehouse space. Managers also often face capital constraints that are limitations in the amount of capital resources available for a particular project or activity.

Managerial decisions can also be constrained by contractual requirements. For example, labor contracts limit flexibility in employee scheduling and job assignment, sometimes even affecting whether labor costs are fixed or variable. Constraints often require that a minimum level of output be produced to meet delivery requirements. In other instances, output must meet certain minimum quality requirements. Some common examples of output quality constraints are nutritional requirements for feed mixtures, audience exposure requirements for marketing promotions, reliability requirements for electronic products, and requirements for minimum customer service levels.

Legal restrictions that affect both production and marketing activities can also play an important role in managerial decisions. Laws that define minimum wages, health and safety standards, pollution emission standards, fuel efficiency requirements, and fair pricing and marketing practices all limit managerial flexibility.

The role constraints play in managerial decision making makes the topic of *constrained optimization* a basic element of managerial economics. In later chapters, we will consider important economic implications of both self-imposed and societal constraints on firms. This analysis is important because both value maximization and productive and allocative efficiency in society depend on the efficient use of scarce (limited) economic resources.

## Limitations of the Theory of the Firm

Some critics have questioned why the profit or wealth maximization criterion is used as a foundation for the study of firm behavior. Are not the firm's managers interested, at least to some extent, in power, prestige, leisure, employee welfare, community well-being, and society in general? Further, do managers really try to *maximize,* or do they *satisfice*— that is, do they seek *satisfactory* rather than *optimal* results? Would the manager of a firm really seek the *sharpest* needle in a haystack (maximize), or would he or she stop upon finding one sharp enough for sewing (*satisfice*)?

It is extremely difficult to determine whether managers try to maximize firm value or merely attempt to satisfy owners while pursuing other goals. How can one tell whether a community activity undertaken by a firm leads to long-run value maximization? Are high salaries and substantial perquisites really necessary to attract and retain managers who can keep the firm ahead of the competition? When a risky venture is turned down, can one say whether this reflects conservatism or inefficient risk avoidance on the part of management or whether it, in fact, reflects an appropriate decision from the standpoint of value maximization given the venture's risks compared with its potential return?

It is impossible to give definitive answers to questions like these, and this has led to the development of numerous alternative theories of firm behavior. Some of the more prominent alternatives are models in which size or growth maximization is the assumed primary objective of management, models that assume managers are most concerned with their own personal utility or welfare maximization, and models that treat the firm as a collection of individuals with widely divergent goals rather than as a single, identifiable unit.

Each of these theories, or models, of managerial behavior has added to our knowledge and understanding of the firm. Still, none can supplant the basic microeconomic model of the firm as a basis for analyzing managerial decisions. Examining why will provide additional insight concerning the value of managerial economics for managerial decision making.

The theory of the firm states that managers maximize the value of the firm subject to constraints imposed by resource limitations, technology, and society. The theory does not explicitly recognize other goals, including the possibility that managers might take actions that would benefit parties other than stockholders—perhaps the managers themselves or society in general—but *reduce* stockholder wealth. Thus, the model seems to ignore the possibilities of satisficing, managerial self-dealing, and voluntary social responsibility on the part of business.

Given that firms assert the existence of multiple goals, engage in active "social responsibility" programs, and sometimes exhibit what appears to be satisficing behavior, is the economic model of the firm really adequate as a basis for our study of managerial decision making? Based on the evidence, the answer is *yes*.

First, research has shown that the typically vigorous competition both in product markets, where firms sell their output, and in the capital market, where they acquire the funds necessary to engage in productive enterprise, forces managers to seek value maximization in their decisions. Stockholders are, of course, interested in value maximization, because it affects their rates of return on common stock investments. Managers who pursue their own interests instead of stockholders' run the risk of being replaced. Buyout pressure from unfriendly firms ("raiders") has been considerable during recent years. Unfriendly takeovers are especially unfriendly to inefficient management, which is usually replaced. Further, recent studies of managerial compensation indicate a strong correlation between firm profits and managers' salaries. Thus, managers appear to have a strong economic incentive to pursue value maximization through their decisions.

Second, managers must consider the costs as well as the benefits of any action before they can make a reasoned decision. This applies to a decision to satisfice rather than to maximize. Before a firm can decide on a satisfactory level of performance, management must examine the costs of such an action. Would it be wise or profitable to seek out the "best" technical solution to a problem if the costs of finding this solution would greatly exceed resulting benefits? Of course not. Indeed, what often appears to be satisficing on the part of management can be interpreted as value-maximizing behavior once the costs of information gathering are considered. Similarly, short-run growth maximization strategies often can be seen as being consistent with long-run value maximization when production, distribution, or promotional advantages of large firm size are better understood.

Finally, the value maximization model provides insight into a firm's voluntary social responsibility activities, though at first glance the model may seem to preclude this possibility. The criticism that the neoclassical theory of the firm emphasizes profits and value maximization while ignoring the issue of social responsibility is important enough to warrant a somewhat extended discussion, and we shall return to it later in this chapter. It will prove useful, however, to examine first the concept of profits, which is central to the theory of the firm.

# PROFITS

In order to understand the theory of firm behavior and the role of the firm in a free enterprise economy, one must understand the nature of profits. Indeed, profits are such a key element in the free enterprise system that it would fail to operate without profits and the profit motive. Even in planned economies, where state ownership rather than private enterprise has been typical, the profit motive is increasingly being used as a spur to efficient resource use. In China, the Soviet Union, Yugoslavia, and other countries, profit incentives for managers and workers have led to increasing product quality and cost efficiency. Thus, profits and the profit motive play a key and growing role in the efficient allocation of economic resources on a worldwide basis.

## Business versus Economic Profit

The general public and the business community typically define profit using an accounting concept. Here profit is the residual of sales revenue minus the explicit (accounting) costs of doing business. It is the amount available to the equity capital or ownership position after payment for all other resources the firm uses. This definition of profit is often referred to as accounting or **business profit.**

**business profit**

Sales revenue minus the explicit (accounting) costs of doing business.

The economist also defines profit as the excess of revenues over the costs of doing business. To the economist, however, the inputs provided by the firm's owner(s), including entrepreneurial effort and capital, are resources that must be paid for if they are to be employed in that use rather than some other. Thus, the economist includes a normal rate of return on equity capital and an opportunity cost for the effort of the owner-entrepreneur as costs of doing business, just as the interest paid on debt and wages paid to labor are considered costs in calculating business profit. The normal rate of return on equity is the minimum return necessary to attract and retain investment for a particular use. Similarly, the opportunity cost of owner effort is determined by the value that could be received in an alternative activity. To an economist, profit is business profit minus the implicit costs of equity and other owner-provided inputs used by the firm. This profit concept is frequently referred to as **economic profit** to distinguish it from the business profit concept.

**economic profit**

Business profit minus the implicit costs of equity and other owner-provided inputs used by the firm.

The concepts of business profit and economic profit help sharpen our focus on the issue of why profits exist and what their role is in a free enterprise economy. The concept of economic profit recognizes a required payment for the use of owner-provided inputs. There is a normal rate of return, or profit, for example, that is necessary for inducing individuals to invest funds in one activity rather than investing them elsewhere, or spending them for current consumption. This normal profit is simply a cost for capital; it is no different from the cost of other resources, such as labor, materials, and energy. A similar price exists for the entrepreneurial effort of a firm's owner-manager and for other resources owners bring to the firm. These opportunity costs for owner-provided inputs offer a primary explanation for the existence of business profits.

What explains the difference between the economist's concept of normal profits as a cost of equity capital and other owner-provided inputs and the actual business profits earned by firms? In equilibrium, economic profits would be zero if all firms operated in perfectly competitive markets. All firms would report business profit rates reflecting only a normal rate of return on equity investment and payment for other owner-supplied inputs. We know, however, that reported profit rates tend to vary widely among firms. Recent profit rates have ranged from very low in, for example, the agricultural equipment and savings and loan industries, to very high, such as in the pharmaceutical, office equipment, and other high-technology industries. While we can explain some of this variation in business profits as risk premiums (higher profits) necessary to compensate investors if one business is inherently riskier than another, many firms do earn significant economic profits (or experience economic losses) at any given point in time. Examining several theories used to explain the existence of economic profits will provide further insight into their critical role in a market economy and in managerial decision making.

**Frictional Theory of Economic Profits.**   One explanation of economic profits (or losses) is the frictional theory. It states that markets often are in disequilibrium because of unanticipated changes in product demand or cost conditions. Shocks occur in the economy, producing disequilibrium conditions that lead to either positive or negative economic profits for some firms. For example, the emergence of a new generation of user-friendly computer software might lead to a marked increase in the demand for microcomputers, which could cause profits of microcomputer manufacturers to rise above the normal level for a period of time. Alternatively, a rise in the use of plastics or aluminum in automobiles might drive down the profits of steel manufacturers. Over time, barring impassable barriers to entry and exit, resources would flow into or out of the microcomputer and steel manufacturing industries, driving rates of return back to normal levels. But during interim periods, profits might be above or below normal because of frictional factors that prevent instantaneous adjustment to new market conditions.

**Monopoly Theory of Economic Profits.**   A second explanation—the monopoly theory—is an extension of the frictional theory. It asserts that some firms, because of such factors as economies of scale, high capital requirements, patents, or import protection, can build monopoly positions that allow them to keep their profits above normal for extended periods. Monopoly, a most interesting topic, is discussed at length in Chapters 11, 12, and 14, where we consider its causes and consequences and how society attempts to mitigate its potential costs.

**Innovation Theory of Economic Profits.**  A third theory of economic profits—the innovation theory—is also related to frictions. Under the innovation theory, above-normal profits can arise as a result of successful innovation. For example, the theory suggests that Xerox Corporation, which historically earned a high rate of return because it successfully developed, introduced, and marketed a superior copying device, continued to receive these supernormal returns until other firms entered the field to compete with it and drive these high profits down to a normal level. Similarly, McDonald's Corporation earned above-normal rates of return as an early innovator in the fast-food business. With increased competition from Burger King, Wendy's, and a host of national and regional competitors, however, McDonald's, like Xerox, has seen its above-normal returns decline. As in the case of frictional or disequilibrium profits, profits that are due to innovation are susceptible to the onslaught of competition from imitating competitors.

**Compensatory Theory of Economic Profits.**  The compensatory theory of economic profits holds that above-normal rates of return may simply be a reward to firms that are extraordinarily successful in meeting customer needs, maintaining efficient operations, and so forth. For example, if firms that operate at the industry's average level of efficiency receive normal rates of return, it is reasonable that firms that operate at above-average levels of efficiency will earn above-normal rates of return. Similarly, inefficient firms can be expected to earn relatively unsatisfactory (below-normal) rates of return.

This theory also recognizes economic profit as an important reward to the entrepreneurial function of owners or managers. Every firm and product starts as an idea for better serving some established or perceived need of existing or potential customers. This need remains unmet until an individual takes the initiative to design, plan, and implement a solution. The opportunity for economic profits is an important motivation for such entrepreneurial activity.

## The Role of Profits

Each of the preceding theories describes economic profits obtained for different reasons. In some cases, several might apply. To illustrate, a very efficient manufacturer may earn an above-normal rate of return in accordance with the compensatory theory, but during a strike by a competitor's employees, already above-average profits may be augmented by frictional profits. Similarly, Xerox's profit position might be partly explained by all four theories: The company certainly benefited from successful innovation; it is well managed and has earned compensatory profits; it earned high frictional profits while 3M, Kodak, Canon, and other firms were tooling up in response to the rapid growth in demand for office copiers; and it has earned monopoly profits, because it is protected to some extent by its patents.

Economic profits play an important role in a market-based economy. Above-normal profits serve as a valuable signal that firm or industry output should be increased. Indeed, expansion by established firms or entry by new competitors often occurs quickly during periods of high profit. Just as above-normal profits provide a signal for expansion and entry, below-normal profits provide a signal for contraction and exit. Economic profits are one of the most important factors affecting the allocation of scarce economic resources. Also, above-normal profits can constitute an important reward for innovation and efficiency, just as below-normal profits can serve as a penalty for stagnation and inefficiency. Thus, profits play a critical role both in providing an incentive for innovation and productive efficiency and in allocating scarce resources.

An understanding of how profits affect business behavior provides important insight into the relationship between the firm and society. We turn now to an examination of the firm's role in society and to a further look at the social responsibility of business.

## ROLE OF BUSINESS IN SOCIETY

As suggested earlier, an important element in the study of managerial economics is the interrelationship between the firm and society. Managerial economics can clarify the vital role firms play in society and point out ways of improving their benefits to society.

The evidence that business in the United States has contributed significantly to social welfare is both clear and convincing. The economy has sustained a notable and unprecedented rate of growth over many decades, and the benefits of that growth have been widely distributed. Suppliers of capital, labor, and other resources have all received substantial returns for their contributions. Consumers have benefited from both the quantity and the quality of goods and services available for consumption. Taxes on the business profits of firms, as well as on the payments made to suppliers of labor, materials, capital, and other inputs, have provided the revenues government needs to increase its service to society. All of these contributions to social welfare stem directly from the efficiency of businesses that serve the economy.

Does this mean that firms do not or should not exercise social responsibility in a broader, perhaps more philanthropic sense? Not necessarily. Firms exist by public consent to serve the needs of society. Only through the satisfactory execution of this mandate will business survive and

## 1.2 **Managerial Application**

Do Profits Serve a Social Purpose?

Corporations can be rightly criticized for toxic waste handling and disposal policies when careless dumping occurs because they have failed to install common safeguards. Similarly, a company with a policy of firing older, and higher salaried, workers can be criticized for age discrimination. However, by focusing on the higher short-term profits sometimes earned by companies with socially misguided policies, the broader and highly beneficial role of profits in the economy can be obscured.

Perhaps Karl Marx is most responsible for popularizing the view of the foundations of capitalism as being morally deficient. According to his view, profits serve no useful social purpose. Rather than reflecting superior operating performance by firms or individuals, they simply reflect the amount of resources taken out of the economic system and converted from social to private use. Although this point of view is losing credibility and support, even in Communist bloc countries, there are still those who regard profits as evil. For example, in their 1986 pastoral letter on the economy, U.S. Catholic bishops described the profit motive as a "vexing" moral problem. To be sure, this view remains controversial among Catholics and others. Still, the fact that some people regard *all* profits as immoral suggests that profits and the profit motive remain misunderstood.

It is reasonable to condemn the abuses previously cited, because they are immoral, *and* because they are inconsistent with our profit-based system. It is important to recognize, however, that not all profits, including above-normal or economic profits, are immoral or unwarranted. Firms cannot operate outside the law nor outside the common bounds of morality. They must operate within the bounds that society imposes. This follows from the fact that the economy is part of the larger political, economic, and moral system. Firms that needlessly pollute

*continued*

See: Michael Novak, "How About Obscene Losses?", *Forbes*, March 6, 1989, 76–77.

prosper. As the needs and social requirements placed on our economic system change, business must adapt and respond to its changing environment.

If social welfare could be measured, business firms might be expected to operate in a manner that would maximize some index of social well-being. Maximization of social welfare requires answering such impor-

**Managerial Application** *continued*

or discriminate in their employment practices face the very real prospect of legal sanctions leading to long-run costs that far exceed any short-run benefits from such action. Apart from the effects of regulation, market forces themselves often act to correct such abuses. For example, a company that discriminates in its hiring policies will find it difficult to attract and retain valued employees. Thus, any above-normal profits earned through such antisocial behavior tend to be fleeting.

What critics fail to realize is the important role that profits and the profit system have played in the long-term betterment of much of humankind. Before the time of Adam Smith, an 18th century Scottish political economist and philosopher, human poverty was commonplace. The wealth of nations was measured in terms of the amount of precious goods enjoyed by nobility. Smith argued that, in contrast, the wealth of nations is best measured in terms of the level of well-being enjoyed by the common worker. The fundamental characteristic of a profit-based system is that it has as its underlying objective the enhancement of the wealth of nations, not just the wealth of a few. The U.S. economy's demonstrated capacity to lift successive generations of poor immigrants out of poverty is testimony to the power of the profit motive to do good.

Today, industrialists in the United States and in other countries with market-based economies continue to build factories to exploit profit-making opportunities. The millions of jobs that result create buying power necessary to fuel more factories, more jobs, and continued economic betterment. It is perhaps ironic that firms and individuals whose objective is to do well (earn profits) end up doing good (causing economic betterment) in the process. Far from being abhorrent, enlightened self-interest is the means by which all benefit.

From a social perspective, many have found most troubling what philosopher Michael Novak calls the "obscene losses" of poorly run private and state enterprises. In some countries, governments and worldwide organizations underwrite unprofitable activities that drain economies of vital economic resources. These losses are tragic in that they deprive these developing nations of the means by which they might otherwise greatly enhance the basic material well-being of the general populace. In such instances, one might reasonably argue that establishing or reenforcing the profit motive is the most effective means available for reducing the waste of economic resources and thereby increasing the economic welfare of the world's truly poor.

tant questions as: What combination of goods and services (including negative by-products, such as pollution) should be produced? How should goods be produced? And how should goods and services be distributed? These are some of the most vital questions faced in a free enterprise system, and, as such, they are important issues in managerial economics.

In a market economy, the economic system produces and allocates goods and services according to the forces of demand and supply. Firms determine what consumers desire, bid for the resources necessary to produce these products, and then make and distribute them. The suppliers of capital, labor, and raw materials must all be compensated out of the proceeds from the sale of output, and competition (bargaining) takes place among these groups. Further, each firm competes with other firms for the consumer's dollar.

Although this process of market-determined production and allocation of goods and services is for the most part highly efficient, there are potential difficulties in a totally unconstrained market economy that can prevent maximization of social welfare. Society has developed a variety of methods for alleviating these problems through the political system.

One possible difficulty with an unconstrained market economy is that certain groups could gain excessive economic power, permitting them to obtain too large a share of the value created by firms. To illustrate, the economics of producing and distributing electric power are such that only one firm can efficiently serve a given community. Further, there are no good substitutes for electric lighting. As a result, electric companies are in a position to exploit consumers; they could charge high prices and earn excessive profits. Society's solution to this potential exploitation is direct regulation. Prices charged by electric companies and other utilities are controlled and held to a level that is thought to be just sufficient to provide stockholders with a fair rate of return on their investment. The regulatory process is simple in concept; in practice it is costly, difficult to implement, and in many ways arbitrary. It is a poor substitute for competition, but sometimes it is necessary.

A second problem in a market economy occurs when because of economies of scale or other conditions, a limited number of firms serve a given market. If the firms compete with one another, no difficulty arises. However, if they conspire with one another in setting prices, they may be able to restrict output, obtain excessive profits, and thereby reduce social welfare. Antitrust laws are designed to prevent such collusion as well as the merging of competing firms when the effect of merger would be to substantially lessen competition. Like direct regulation, antitrust laws contain arbitrary elements and are costly to administer, but they too are necessary if economic justice, as defined by society, is to be served.

A third problem is that under certain conditions, workers can be exploited. As a result, laws have been developed to equalize the bargaining power of employers and workers. These labor laws require firms to submit to collective bargaining and to refrain from unfair practices. The question of whether labor's bargaining position is too strong in some instances also has been raised. For example, can powerful national unions such as the Teamsters use the threat of a strike to obtain "excessive" increases in wages, which may in turn be passed on to consumers in the form of higher prices and thus cause inflation? Those who believe this is the case have suggested that the antitrust laws should be applied to labor unions, especially to those bargaining with numerous small employers.

A fourth problem a market economy faces is that firms can impose external costs on society through their production activities. For example, they can dump wastes into the air or water or deface the earth, as in strip mining. If a factory pollutes the air, causing people to paint their houses every three years instead of every five or to suffer lung ailments or other health impairments, the factory imposes a cost on society in general. Failure to shift these costs back onto the firm—and, ultimately, to the consumers of its output—means that the firm and its customers unfairly benefit because the firm does not pay the full costs of its activities. This results in an inefficient allocation of resources between industries and firms. Currently, much attention is being directed to the problem of internalizing social costs. Some of the practices used to internalize social costs include setting health and safety standards for products and production systems, establishing emissions limits on manufacturing processes and on products that pollute, and imposing fines on or closing firms that do not meet established standards.

All of these measures—utility regulation, antitrust laws, labor laws, and direct regulation of products and operations—are examples of actions taken by society to modify the behavior of business firms and to make this behavior more consistent with broad social goals. As we shall see, these constraints have an important bearing on the firm's operations and, hence, on managerial decision making.

What does all this mean with respect to the value maximization model of the firm? Is the model adequate for examining issues of social responsibility and for developing rules for business decisions that sufficiently reflect the role of business in society? Business firms are *primarily* economic entities and, as such, can be expected to analyze social responsibility in the context of an economic model of the firm. This is an important consideration in examining the set of inducements that can channel the efforts of business in directions that society desires. Similar considerations should also be taken into account before imposing political pressures or regulations on firms to constrain their operations. For example, from the consumer's standpoint it is desirable to pay low rates for gas, electric, and telephone services. If public pressures drive rates down too low, however, utilities' profits will fall below the level necessary to provide an adequate return to investors. Capital will not flow into the regulated industries, innovation will cease, and service will deteriorate. When such issues are considered, the economic model of the firm provides useful insights. The model emphasizes the close interrelation between the firm and society. This, in turn, indicates the importance to business of participating actively to develop and formulate its role in helping achieve society's goals.

# 1.3 **Managerial Application**
Capitalism and Democracy

Capitalism is based on voluntary exchange between self-interested parties. Given that the exchange is voluntary, it becomes necessary that both parties perceive benefits in order for market transactions to take place. If only one party were to benefit from a given transaction, then there would be no incentive for the other party to cooperate. No voluntary transaction would take place. Thus, a self-interested capitalist must also have in mind the interest of others. In contrast, a truly selfish individual is only concerned with himself or herself, without regard for the well-being of others. As such, selfish behavior is inconsistent with the capitalistic system. Self-interested behavior leads to success under capitalism; selfish behavior does not.

Like any economic system, capitalism has far-reaching political and social consequences. Similarly, democracy has far-reaching economic consequences. What is sometimes not understood is that capitalism and democracy are mutually reenforcing.

Some philosophers have gone so far as to say that capitalism and democracy are intertwined. Without capitalism, democracy is impossible. Without democracy, capitalistic systems fail. To better understand the relation between capitalism and democracy, it becomes necessary to consider the fundamentally attractive characteristics of a decentralized exchange economy.

Capitalism is socially desirable because of its decentralized and customer-oriented nature. The menu of products to be produced is derived from market price and output signals originating in free and competitive markets, not from the output schedules of a centralized planning agency. As such, production is freely directed by self-interested producers seeking to meet the demands of individual customers. Resources and products are impartially allocated through market forces. They are not allocated on the basis of favoritism due to social status or political persuasion. Any producer able to meet customer demands is allowed

*continued*

See: Ronald Bailey, "The Right Path," *Forbes*, January 23, 1989, 80–81; and Robert J. Dowling, "Communism in Turmoil," *Business Week*, June 5, 1989, 34–37.

**Managerial Application** *continued*

to compete. Similarly, through their purchase decisions, customers are able to shape the quantity and quality of products brought to market.

A freely competitive market gives customers a broad choice of goods and services, and gives all producers the opportunity to succeed. As such, capitalism reenforces the individual freedoms protected in a democratic society. In democracy, government does not grant individual freedom. Instead, the political power of government emanates from the people. Similarly, the flow of economic resources originates with the individual customer in a capitalistic system. It is not centrally directed by government.

Competition among producers is also a fundamentally attractive feature of the capitalistic system in that it tends to keep costs and prices as low as possible. By operating efficiently, firms are able to produce the maximum quantity and quality of goods and services possible, given scarce productive resources. Even though efficiency in resource allocation is an often recognized virtue of capitalism, the egalitarian nature of capitalistic production methods is sometimes overlooked. Mass production is, by definition, production for the masses. By its nature, capitalism seeks to satisfy a broad rather than narrow constituency. Competition by entrant and nonleading firms typically undermines the concentration of

economic and political power. When economic forces tend to reduce rather than increase the number of viable competitors, antitrust or regulation policy is sometimes used to avoid potentially harmful consequences. On balance, and especially when compared to centrally planned economies, competitive processes in a capitalistic system tend to further the principles of individual freedom and self-determination. From this perspective, capitalism and democracy are seen to be mutually reenforcing. Strong market forces tend to undermine the economic favoritism that tends to occur under totalitarian systems of government. Similarly, the democratic form of government is inconsistent with concentrated economic influence and decision making.

As we enter the 1990s, communism and totalitarian forms of government are in turmoil around the globe. China has experienced violent upheaval as the country embarks on much-needed economic and political reforms. In the Soviet Union, years of economic failure have forced the government to dismantle entrenched bureaucracy and install economic incentives. Economic and political unrest is evident because rising living standards and political freedom has made life in the West the envy of the world. Given this backdrop, the future appears bright for both capitalism and democracy.

# STRUCTURE OF THIS TEXT

## Objectives

This text should help you accomplish the following objectives:

1. Develop a clear understanding of economic theory and methods as they relate to managerial decision making;
2. Acquire a framework for understanding the nature of the firm as an integrated whole as opposed to a loosely connected set of functional departments;
3. Recognize the interrelation between the firm and society and the key role of business as an agent of social and economic welfare.

## Development of Topics

The value maximization model provides a basis for the study of managerial economics. It establishes a framework for developing prescriptive rules for optimal managerial decisions. Similarly, the model helps us understand observed economic relationships. The basic test of the value maximization model—indeed, of any theory—is its ability to explain behavior in the real world of managerial decision making. Therefore, as we introduce the basic elements of managerial economics, we will provide examples of how it explains real-world practice. This text highlights the complementary relation between theory and practice. Theory is used to improve managerial decision making, and practical experience leads to the development of better theory.

In Chapter 2, we begin by examining the basics of economic analysis. There we introduce the concept of optimization and the important role that marginal analysis plays in this process. We explore the balancing of marginal revenues and marginal costs to determine the output level at which profits will be maximized, and we consider other fundamental relationships that help organizations effectively employ scarce resources. The concepts of demand and supply are basic to our understanding of the effective use of economic resources. Therefore, the general overview of demand and supply in Chapter 3 provides a framework for the analysis that follows. In Chapter 4, we turn our attention to a more detailed consideration of demand. The successful management of any organization requires a thorough understanding of the demand for its products. The demand function relates the sales of a product to such important factors as the price of the product itself, prices of other goods, income, advertising, and weather. The role of demand elasticities, which measure the strength of the relations expressed in the demand function, is an important emphasis of this chapter. We expand on demand topics in Chapter 5, where we examine demand estimation, and in Chapter 6, where we study the methodology of economic forecasting.

In Chapters 7, 8 and 9, we examine supply issues and develop production and cost concepts. The economics of resource employment in the manufacture and distribution of goods and services is the focus of this material. These chapters present economic analysis as a basis for developing operating and planning rules for improved managerial decisions as well as a context for understanding the underlying logic of managerial decisions. The role of cost considerations in managerial decision making is fully explored.

In the remainder of the book, we build on the foundation provided in Chapters 1 through 9 to examine a variety of topics in the theory and practice of managerial economics. In Chapter 10 we introduce linear programming, a tool from the decision sciences that can be applied to many important optimization problems. This technique offers managers highly useful input for short-run operating decisions as well as information helpful in the long-run planning process. In Chapters 11 and 12, we explore market structures and their implications for the development and implementation of effective competitive strategy. Here we integrate our earlier analyses of demand and supply to examine the dynamics of economic markets. In Chapter 11, we study perfect competition and monopoly to gain a perspective on how product differentiation, barriers to entry, and the availability of information interact to determine the vigor of competition. In Chapter 12, we consider "competition among the few" in partly competitive, partly monopolistic industries in which monopolistic competition and oligopoly prevail. In Chapter 13, we analyze pricing practices commonly observed in business to show how they reflect the predictions of economic theory. In Chapter 14, we focus on the role of government in the market economy by considering how conditions in the external economic environment affect the managerial decision-making process. We investigate how interactions among business, government, and the public result in antitrust and regulation policies with direct implications for the efficiency and fairness of an economic system. In Chapters 15 and 16, we consider the final elements necessary for an effective planning framework for managerial decision making. In Chapter 15, we examine risk analysis as a basis for managerial decision making under conditions of uncertainty. In Chapter 16, we explore capital budgeting decisions and how firms combine demand, production, cost, and risk analyses—in a context that recognizes societal constraints—to effectively make the strategic long-run investment decisions that shape their futures and the material well-being of society in general.

## SUMMARY

We began this chapter by defining *managerial economics* as the application of economic theory and methods to the practice of managerial decision making. As a first step in our analysis of managerial decision making, we examined the *theory of the firm* as the basic model of how a firm operates. This model is based on the premise that managers seek to maximize the value of their firms subject to a variety of constraints. Although we briefly discussed alternative models, including satisficing and multiple-goal models, we stressed the *expected value maximization* model, which has proved to be most useful for analyzing firm behavior.

An important element in the model is the firm's profit stream. The value of the firm is the present value of expected future profits. Because profits are so critical to understanding both the theory of the firm and the firm's role in a free enterprise economy, the nature of profits, including both theories used to explain their existence and problems encountered in defining and measuring them, received our attention. We also examined the role of business in society and concluded that the interaction of the firm with society is an important aspect of managerial decision making. Understanding how business activities support the goals of society is a key component of managerial economics.

The use of economic theory and methods to analyze and improve the managerial decision-making process combines the study of theory and practice to gain a useful and practical perspective. In taking from both economics and the decision sciences, managerial economics provides an integrative and comprehensive framework for solving managerial decision problems. Although the logic and consistency of managerial economics are intuitively appealing, its primary virtue lies in its usefulness.

## Questions

1.1 Why is it appropriate to view firms primarily as economic entities?

1.2 Explain how the valuation model given in Equation 1.2 could be used to describe the integrated nature of managerial decision making across the functional areas of business.

1.3 In terms of the valuation model discussed in the chapter, explain the effects of each of the following:
  A. The firm is required to install new equipment to reduce air pollution.
  B. The firm's marketing department, through heavy expenditures on advertising, increases sales substantially.
  C. The production department purchases new equipment that lowers manufacturing costs.
  D. The firm raises prices. Quantity demanded in the short run is unaffected, but in the longer run, unit sales are expected to decline.
  E. The Federal Reserve System takes actions that lower interest rates dramatically.
  F. An expected increase in inflation causes generally higher interest rates, and, hence, the discount rate increases.

1.4 It is sometimes argued that managers of large, publicly owned firms make decisions in order to maximize their own welfare as opposed to that of stockholders. Would such behavior create problems in using value maximization as a basis for examining managerial decision making?

1.5 How is the popular notion of business profit different from the economic profit concept described in the chapter? What role does the idea of normal profits play in this difference?

1.6 Does the business profit concept or the economic profit concept provide the more appropriate basis for evaluating the operations of a business? Why?

1.7 What factors should one consider in examining the adequacy of profits for a firm or industry?

1.8 Why is the concept of self-interest important in economics?

1.9 "In the long run, no profit-maximizing firm would ever knowingly market unsafe products. However, in the short run, unsafe products can do a lot of damage." Discuss this statement.

1.10 Is it reasonable to expect firms to take actions that are in the public interest but that are detrimental to stockholders? Is regulation always necessary and appropriate to induce firms to act in the public interest?

## Selected References

Aaron, Henry J. "Politics and the Professors Revisited." *American Economic Review* 79 (May 1989): 1–15.

Akerlof, George A., and Janet L. Yellen. "Rational Models of Irrational Behavior." *American Economic Review* 77 (May 1987): 137–142.

Boardman, Anthony E., and Aidan R. Vining. "Ownership and Performance in Competitive Environments: A Comparison of the Performance of Private, Mixed, and State-Owned Enterprise." *Journal of Law and Economics* 32 (April 1989): 1–33.

Boudreaux, Donald J., and Randall G. Holcombe. "The Coasian and Knightian Theories of the Firm." *Managerial and Decision Economics* 10 (June 1989): 147–154.

Dyl, Edward A. "Corporate Control and Management Compensation: Evidence on the Agency Problem." *Managerial and Decision Economics* 9 (March 1988): 21–25.

Eisner, Robert. "Divergences of Measurement and Theory and Some Implications for Economic Policy." *American Economic Review* 79 (March 1989): 1–13.

Furtado, Eugene P. H., and Michael S. Rozeff. "The Wealth Effects of Company Initiated Management Changes." *Journal of Financial Economics* 18 (March 1987): 147–160.

Hirschey, Mark. "Mergers, Buyouts and Fakeouts." *American Economic Review* 76 (May 1986): 317–322.

Jarrell, Greg A., James A. Brickley, and Jeffry M. Netter. "The Market for Corporate Control: The Empirical Evidence Since 1980." *Journal of Economic Perspectives* 2 (Winter 1988): 49–68.

Jensen, Michael C., and William H. Meckling. "Theory of the Firm: Managerial Behavior, Agency Costs and Ownership Structure." *Journal of Financial Economics* 3 (October 1976): 305–360.

Jensen, Michael C., and Jerold B. Warner. "The Distribution of Power among Corporate Managers, Shareholders and Directors." *Journal of Financial Economics* 20 (January/March 1988): 3–24.

Lewellen, Wilbur, Claudio Loderer, and Kenneth Martin. "Executive Compensation and Executive Incentive Problems: An Empirical Analysis." *Journal of Accounting and Economics* 9 (December 1987): 287–310.

Morck, Randall, Andrei Shleifer, and Robert W. Vishny. "Management Ownership and Market Valuation: An Empirical Analysis." *Journal of Financial Economics* 20 (January/March 1988): 293–315.

Navarro, Peter. "Why Do Corporations Give to Charity?" *Journal of Business* 61 (January 1988): 65–93.

Poirier, Dale J. "Frequentist and Subjectivist Perspectives on the Problems of Model Building in Economics." *Journal of Economic Perspectives* 2 (Winter 1988): 121–144.

Scherer, F. M. "Corporate Takeovers: The Efficiency Arguments." *Journal of Economic Perspectives* 2 (Winter 1988): 69–82.

Shepherd, William B. "Self-Interest and National Security." *American Economic Review* 78 (May 1988): 50–54.

Shleifer, Andrei, and Robert W. Vishny. "Value Maximization and the Acquisition Process." *Journal of Economic Perspectives* 2 (Winter 1988): 7–20.

Weisbach, Michael S. "Outside Directors and CEO Turnover." *Journal of Financial Economics* 20 (January/March 1988): 431–460.

Winn, Daryl N., and John D. Shoenhair. "Compensation-Based (DIS) Incentives for Revenue-Maximizing Behavior: A Test of the 'Revised' Baumol Hypothesis." *Review of Economics and Statistics* 70 (February 1988): 154–157.

# Economic Optimization

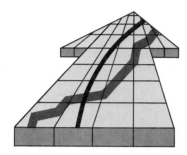

**optimal decision**

The action that produces the result most consistent with the decision maker's objectives.

**M**anagerial decision making is the process of determining the best possible solution to a given problem. If only one solution or action is possible, no decision problem exists. If a number of alternative courses of action are available, however, the **optimal decision** is the alternative that produces a result most consistent with the decision maker's goal. Managers use the tools of managerial economics to assist in the process of finding this best action or decision.

A major challenge associated with the decision-making process is defining alternatives in terms of the goals or objectives of the decision maker. Not only must decision makers be able to recognize the available options in any given situation, they must also be able to specify those options in terms of the appropriate decision variables and relevant costs and benefits. This delineation of available alternatives, often the most difficult facet of the decision-making process, is enhanced through application of the principles of managerial economics.

Analyzing and evaluating the alternatives available in a decision situation are additional requirements for decision making. Here the concepts and methodologies of economic analysis are applied to the set of feasible alternatives to aid in selecting the optimal course of action given the decision maker's objective.

In this chapter we introduce a number of basic economic concepts and fundamental principles of economic analysis. These fundamental relations are essential to our understanding of managerial economics. In addition to providing an introduction to the tools and techniques of optimization, the material provides further insight into the theory of the firm and the complexities of goal-oriented managerial activities.

# MAXIMIZING THE VALUE OF THE FIRM

In managerial economics the primary objective of management is assumed to be maximization of the firm's value. This objective, which was introduced in Chapter 1, is expressed in Equation 2.1:

$$\text{Value} = \sum_{t=1}^{n} \frac{\text{Profit}_t}{(1+i)^t} = \sum_{t=1}^{n} \frac{\text{Total Revenue}_t - \text{Total Cost}_t}{(1+i)^t}. \qquad \textbf{2.1}$$

Maximizing Equation 2.1 is a complex task, involving the determinants of revenues, costs, and discount rates in each future year of some unspecified time horizon. Revenues, costs, and discount rates are interrelated, complicating the problem even more. A closer inspection of the associations in Equation 2.1 should help clarify both the concept and the complexities.

A firm's total revenues are directly determined by the quantity of products sold and the prices received. This is nothing more than a recognition that total revenue (TR) is the product of price (P) times quantity (Q); that is, $TR = P \times Q$. For managerial decision making, the important considerations relate to factors that affect prices and quantities and to the interrelations among them. These factors include the choice of products the firm designs, manufactures, and sells; the advertising strategies it employs; the pricing policy it establishes; the general state of the economy; and the nature of the competition it faces in the marketplace. In short, the revenue relation encompasses both demand and supply considerations.

Cost relations involved in producing a firm's products are similarly complex. An analysis of costs requires examination of alternative production systems, technological options, input possibilities, and so on. The prices of factors of production play a primary role in cost determination, and thus factor supply considerations are important.

Finally, there is the relation between the discount rate and the company's product mix, physical assets, and financial structure. These factors affect the cost and availability of financial resources for the firm and ultimately determine the discount rate used by investors to establish a value for the firm.

To evaluate the choices available to management and to determine the optimal course of action, marketing, production, and financial decisions—as well as decisions related to personnel, product distribution, and so on—must be combined into an integrated system, one that shows how any action affects all parts of the organization. The theory of the firm provides a basis for this integration, whereas the principles of economic analysis enable one to analyze the important interrelations.

The complexity involved in integrated decision analysis typically limits its use to major planning decisions. For many day-to-day operating decisions, much less complicated partial optimization techniques are employed. Partial optimization concentrates on more limited objectives within the firm's various operating departments. For example, the marketing department is usually required to determine price and advertising policies that will achieve a given sales goal, given the firm's product line and constraints on marketing expenditures. The production department is expected to minimize the cost of producing a specified quantity of output of a stated quality level. Here again, the fundamentals of economic analysis provide the basis for optimal managerial decisions.

The decision process, regardless of whether it is related to fully integrated or to partial optimization problems, takes place in two steps. First, economic relations must be expressed in a form suitable for analysis. Generally, this means expressing the problem in analytical terms. Second, various techniques are applied to evaluate alternatives and determine the optimal solution to the problem at hand. In the material that follows, we first introduce a number of concepts useful for expressing decision problems in an economic framework. Then, several economic relations frequently used to evaluate decision alternatives are examined.

# METHODS OF EXPRESSING ECONOMIC RELATIONS

Equations, tables in which data are enumerated, and graphs in which data are plotted are all frequently used to express economic relations. A table or graph is sufficient for many decision problems. When the problem is complex, however, equations are useful because the powerful tools of mathematical analysis and computer simulation may be used.

### Functional Relations: Equations

Perhaps the easiest way to examine various means of expressing economic relations and, at the same time, gain insight into the economics of optimization is to consider several functional relations that play key roles in the basic valuation model. Consider first the relation between output, $Q$, and total revenue, $TR$. Using functional notation, we can express the relation in general terms with the following **equation**:

**equation**
An explicit statement of the relation between dependent and independent variables.

$$TR = f(Q). \qquad \textbf{2.2}$$

Equation 2.2 is read, "Total revenue is a function of output." The value of the dependent variable—total revenue—is determined by the independent variable—output. In an equation such as this one, the variable to the left of the equal sign is called the *dependent variable*, as its value *depends* on the size of the variable or variables to the right of the equal sign. The variables on the right-hand side of the equal sign are called *independent variables*, because their values are assumed to be determined outside, or *independently*, of the model expressed in the equation.

Equation 2.2 does not indicate the specific relation between output and total revenue; it merely states that some relation exists. A more specific expression is provided by the equation:

$$TR = P \times Q, \qquad \textbf{2.3}$$

## 2.1  **Managerial Application**

Entrepreneurship: Creating the Spark

Sometimes it is easy to overlook the fact that firms are made up of people. Indeed, firms often are started by a single individual with no more than an idea for a better product or service—the entrepreneur. Taken from the Old French word *entreprendre,* meaning "to undertake," the term *entrepreneur* refers to one who organizes, operates, and assumes the risk of a business venture.

Until recently, there appeared to be little academic or public policy interest in this key function or in the entrepreneur's role in the economy's overall performance. The entrepreneur's skill was simply considered part of the labor input in production. Now, we are beginning to better understand the critical role of the entrepreneur, partly because entrepreneurship has become a formal field of study at many leading business schools.

As a catalyst, the entrepreneur brings economic resources together in the risky attempt to meet consumers' needs and desires. This process often leads to failure—in fact, the odds against success are long. Seldom do more than one in ten start-up businesses enjoy even minimal economic success. Even those select few that see their product or service reach a national market find stable long-term success elusive. Once established, they in turn become targets for future entrepreneurs.

Given the long odds against success, you might wonder why so many willingly embark on ventures (adventures?) that appear doomed to fail. One reason is that one-in-a-million chance of developing "the" truly revolutionary product that will fundamentally change how people live, work, or play. Chester Carlson, the founder of xerography,

*continued*

See: Zachary Schiller, "Doing Well by Doing Good," *Business Week,* December 5, 1988, 53–57; and Roger Ricklefs, "Schools Increase Courses to Help Entrepreneurs," *The Wall Street Journal,* February 6, 1989, B1–B2.

where $P$ represents the price at which each unit $Q$ is sold. Here, the manner in which the value of the dependent variable is related to the independent variable is more precisely specified. Total revenue is equal to price times the quantity of output sold. If, for example, price is constant at $1.50 regardless of the quantity sold, then the relation between quantity sold and total revenue is precisely stated by the function:

$$TR = \$1.50 \times Q. \qquad \textbf{2.4}$$

**Managerial Application** *continued*

made hundreds of millions of dollars following the introduction and rapid acceptance of the Xerox machine. While the opportunity for such wealth is surely an important motivation, the impact and recognition that come with creating a truly unique good or service often are equally important to entrepreneurs. Many simply want to "make a difference."

What about the entrepreneur's role from the standpoint of society in general? We all benefit from the innovative products, services, delivery systems, and so on that result from entrepreneurs' efforts. Consider the benefits resulting from the efforts of such entrepreneurs as Thomas Edison, Chester Carlson, and Steve Jobs. Their fame and fortune only partly reflect the benefits we enjoy from phonography, electric lighting, photography, xerography, the "graphic desktop," and "user-friendly" computers. Like all entrepreneurs, they have played an important role in determining the types of goods that become available in the marketplace and when they become available.

In addition, entrepreneurship plays an important role in what economist Joseph Schumpeter called the "creative destruction of capitalism." This is the process of replac-

ing the old with the new, the inefficient with the efficient, and low quality with a superior product. An important recent role of the entrepreneur has been what is called *intrapreneurship,* in which the entrepreneur works within the overall framework of an existing organization. Many firms, such as the 3M Company, have come to recognize the importance of the intrapreneur. 3M's encouragement of its researchers to explore new ideas resulted in Art Fry's brainchild, Post-It Notes. Thus, entrepreneurship plays a key role in both the initial development and the ongoing revitalization of firms and the economic system.

In understanding the role of profits in a market-based economy, it is important to recognize the part the entrepreneur plays. The opportunity to earn a normal business profit plus an attractive salary or wage is the realistic objective of every entrepreneur. The hope of above-normal economic profits is the dream that spurs this "bottom-up" method of economic development.

## Functional Relations: Tables and Graphs

In addition to equations, tables and graphs are often used to express economic relations. The data in Table 2.1, for example, express exactly the same functional relation specified by Equation 2.4, and this same function is graphically illustrated in Figure 2.1. All three methods of expressing relations play an important role in presenting and analyzing data for managerial decision making.

■ Table 2.1
### Relation between Total Revenue and Output:
### Total Revenue = $1.50 × Output

| Total Revenue | Output |
|---|---|
| $1.50 | 1 |
| 3.00 | 2 |
| 4.50 | 3 |
| 6.00 | 4 |
| 7.50 | 5 |
| 9.00 | 6 |

■ Figure 2.1
### Graph of the Relation between Total Revenue and Output

When P = $1.50, a one-unit increase in the quantity sold will increase total revenue by $1.50.

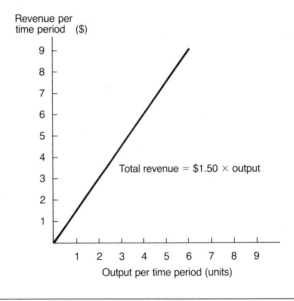

# TOTAL, AVERAGE, AND
# MARGINAL RELATIONS

**marginal**

The change in the dependent variable of a function associated with a unitary change in one of the independent variables.

Total, average, and marginal relations are very useful in optimization analysis. The definitions of totals and averages are too well known to warrant restating, but it is perhaps appropriate to define the term *marginal*. A **marginal** is defined as *the change in the dependent variable of a function associated with a unitary change in one of the independent* *variables.* In the total revenue function, marginal revenue is the change in total revenue associated with a one-unit change in output.

Because the essence of the optimizing process involves analysis of changes, the *marginal concept* is of critical importance. Typically, we analyze an objective function by changing the independent variables to see what effect these changes have on the dependent variable. In other words, we examine the *marginal* effect of changes in the independent variables on the dependent variable. The purpose of this analysis is to identify that set of values for the independent, or decision, variables that optimizes the objective function.

## Relation between Totals and Marginals

Table 2.2 shows the relation between totals, marginals, and averages for a hypothetical profit function. Columns 1 and 2 show the output and profit relation; column 3 shows marginal profits for one-unit changes in output; and column 4 gives the average per-unit profit at each level of output.

Marginal profit refers to the change in profit associated with each one-unit change in output. The marginal profit of the first unit of output is $19. This is the change from $0 profits related to an output of 0 units to the $19 profit earned when one unit is produced. Likewise, the $33 marginal profit associated with the second unit of output is the increase in total profits ($52–$19) that results when output is increased from one to two units.

*The importance of the relation between marginal and total values in decision analysis lies in the fact that when the marginal is positive, the*

■ Table 2.2
## Total, Marginal, and Average Relations for a Hypothetical Profit Function

| Units of Output $Q$ (1) | Total Profits $\pi^a$ (2) | Marginal Profits $\Delta \pi^b$ (3) | Average Profits $\bar{\pi}^c$ (4) |
|---|---|---|---|
| 0 | $ 0 | $ 0 | — |
| 1 | 19 | 19 | $19 |
| 2 | 52 | 33 | 26 |
| 3 | 93 | 41 | 31 |
| 4 | 136 | 43 | 34 |
| 5 | 175 | 39 | 35 |
| 6 | 210 | 35 | 35 |
| 7 | 217 | 7 | 31 |
| 8 | 208 | −9 | 26 |

[a]*The Greek letter $\pi$ (pi) is frequently used in economics and business to denote profits.*
[b]*The symbol $\Delta$ (delta) denotes difference or change. Thus, marginal profit is expressed as $\Delta \pi = \pi_Q - \pi_{Q-1}$.*
[c]*Average profit ($\bar{\pi}$) equals total profit ($\pi$) divided by total output (Q):$\bar{\pi} = \pi/Q$.*

*total is increasing, and when the marginal is negative, the total is decreasing.* The data in Table 2.2 can be used to illustrate this point. The marginal profit associated with each of the first seven units of output is positive, and total profits increase with output over this range. Since the marginal profit of the eighth unit is negative, however, total profits decline if output is raised to that level. Maximization of the profit function—or any function, for that matter—occurs at the point where the marginal is zero (as it shifts from positive to negative). This important relation is examined again later in the chapter.

## Relation between Averages and Marginals

The relation between average and marginal values is also important in some decision analyses. Since the marginal represents a change in the total, it follows that when the marginal is greater than the average, the average must be increasing. For example, if a firm operates five retail stores with average sales of $350,000 per store and it opens a sixth store (the marginal store) that generates sales of $400,000, the average sales per store will increase. Conversely, if sales at the new (marginal) store are less than $350,000, average sales per store will decrease.

The data in Table 2.2 can be used to illustrate the relation between marginal and average values. In going from four units of output to five, marginal profit, $39, is greater than the $34 average profit at four units; hence, average profit increases—to $35. The marginal profit associated with the sixth unit, however, is $35, the same as the average for the first five units, so average profit remains unchanged between five and six units. Finally, the marginal profit of the seventh unit is below the average profit at six units, causing average profit to fall.

## Graphing Total, Marginal, and Average Relations

Knowledge of the geometric relations between totals, marginals, and averages can also prove useful in managerial decision making. Figure 2.2a presents a graph of the profit-to-output relation given in Table 2.2. Each point on the curve represents an output–total profit combination, as do columns 1 and 2 of Table 2.2. The marginal and average profit figures from Table 2.2 have been plotted in Figure 2.2b.

Just as there is an arithmetic relation between the totals, marginals, and averages in the table, so too is there a corresponding geometric relation. To see this, consider first the average profit per unit of output at any point along the total profits curve. The average profit figure is equal to total profit divided by the corresponding number of units of output. Geometrically, this relation is represented by the slope of a line from the origin to the point of interest on the total profits curve. For example, consider the slope of the line from the origin to point *B* in Figure 2.2a.

**slope**

The marginal change in height (*Y*) for a one-unit change in distance (*X*).

**Slope** is a measure of the steepness of a line, and it is defined as the increase (or decrease) in height per unit of distance along the horizontal axis. The slope of a straight line passing through the origin is determined

■ Figure 2.2
## Geometric Representation of Total, Marginal, and Average Relations: (a) Total Profits; (b) Marginal and Average Profits

(a) Marginal profit is the slope of the total profit curve; it is maximized at Point C. More importantly, total profit is maximized at Point E, where marginal profit equals zero. (b) Average profit rises (falls) when marginal profit is greater (less) than average profit.

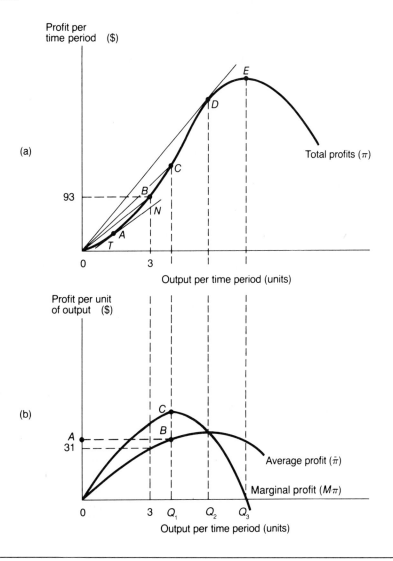

by dividing the $Y$ coordinate at any point on the line by the corresponding $X$ coordinate. That is, using $\Delta$ (read delta) to denote change, slope $= \Delta Y/\Delta X = (Y_2 - Y_1)/(X_2 - X_1)$. Since $X_1$ and $Y_1$ are zero for any line going through the origin, slope $= Y_2/X_2$ or, more generally, slope $= Y/X$. Thus, the slope of the line $0B$ can be calculated by dividing \$93 (the $Y$ coordinate at point $B$) by 3 (the $X$ coordinate at point $B$). Notice, however, that in this process we are dividing total profits by the corresponding units of output. This is the definition of average profit at that point. *Thus, at any point along a total curve, the corresponding average figure is given by the slope of a straight line from the origin to that point.* These average figures can also be graphed directly, as in Figure 2.2b. There, each point on the average profit curve is the corresponding total profit divided by the output quantity.

The marginal has a similar geometric association with the total curve. In Table 2.2 each marginal figure was shown to be the change in total profit associated with the last unit increase in output. This rise (or fall) in the total profit associated with a one-unit increase in output is the *slope* of the total profit curve at that point.

Slopes of nonlinear curves are typically found geometrically by drawing a line tangent to the curve at the point of interest and determining the slope of the tangent. (A tangent is a line that touches but does not intersect the curve.) In Figure 2.2a, for example, the marginal profit at point $A$ is equal to the slope of the total profit curve at that point, which is equal to the slope of the tangent labeled *TAN.* Therefore, *at any point along a total curve, the corresponding marginal figure is given by the slope of a line drawn tangent to the total curve at that point.* These slope, or marginal, figures can also be graphed directly, as shown by the marginal profit curve in Figure 2.2b.

Several important relations between the total, marginal, and average figures may now be examined. First, note that the slope of the total profit curve is increasing from the origin to point $C$. That is, lines drawn tangent to the total profit curve become steeper as the point of tangency approaches point $C$, so marginal profit is increasing up to this point. This is also illustrated in Figure 2.2b, where the marginal profit curve increases up to output $Q_1$, corresponding to point $C$ on the total profit curve. At point $C$, called an *inflection point,* the slope of the total profit curve is maximized; thus, marginal (but not average or total) profits are maximized at that output. Between points $C$ and $E$, total profit continues to increase because marginal profit is still positive even though it is declining. At point $E$, the total profit curve has a slope of zero and thus is neither rising nor falling. Marginal profit at this point is zero, and total profit is maximized. Beyond $E$ (output $Q_3$ in Figure 2.2b), the total profit curve has a negative slope, indicating that marginal profit is negative.

In addition to the total-average and total-marginal relations, the relation between marginals and averages is also demonstrated in Figure 2.2b. At low output levels, where the marginal profit curve lies above the average, the average is rising. Although marginal profit reaches a maximum at output $Q_1$ and declines thereafter, the average curve continues to rise so long as the marginal lies above it. At output $Q_2$, marginal and average profits are equal, and here the average profit curve reaches its maximum value. Beyond $Q_2$, the marginal curve lies below the average, and the average is falling.

### Deriving Totals from Marginal or Average Curves

Just as we can derive marginal and average profit figures from the total profit curve in Figure 2.2a, we can also determine total profits from the marginal or average profit curves of Figure 2.2b. Consider first the derivation of total profits from the average curve. Total profit is simply average profit times the corresponding number of units of output. The total profit associated with $Q_1$ units of output, for example, is average profit, $A$, times output, $Q_1$, or equivalently, total profit is equal to the area of the rectangle $0ABQ_1$. This relation holds for all points along the average profit curve.

A similar relation exists between marginal and total profits. Recall that the total is equal to the sum of all the marginals up to the specified output level. Thus, the total profit for any output is equal to the sum of the marginal profits up to that output quantity. Geometrically, this is the area under the marginal curve from the $Y$ axis to the output quantity under consideration. At output $Q_1$, total profit is equal to the area under the marginal profit curve, or the area $0CQ_1$.

Because these average/marginal/total relations are the basis for many important managerial economics principles, they should be thoroughly understood. The most widely known example of their use is in short-run profit maximization: Marginal cost and revenue curves are derived from average or total figures, and profits are maximized where marginal profit (equal to marginal revenue minus marginal cost) is zero. Thus, profit is maximized where marginal revenue is equal to marginal cost. This is only one illustration of the use of these concepts; we will encounter many others in our study of managerial economics.

First, however, we will consider the use of some elementary calculus, which is extremely valuable for finding optimal solutions to economic problems. The calculus concepts will help to further clarify the relations between marginals, averages, and totals and the importance of these relations in the optimization process.

# MARGINALS AS THE DERIVATIVES OF FUNCTIONS

Although tables and graphs are useful for explaining concepts, equations are frequently better suited for problem solving. One reason is that the powerful analytical technique of differential calculus can then be employed to locate maximum or minimum values of an objective function. In addition, basic calculus concepts are easily extended to decision problems in which the options available to the decision maker are lim-

ited by one or more constraints. Thus, the calculus approach is especially useful for the constrained optimization problems that often
characterize managerial decision making.

## Concept of a Derivative

Earlier, we defined a marginal value as the change in the value of the
dependent variable associated with a one-unit change in an independent
variable. Consider the general function $Y = f(X)$. Using $\Delta$ (read delta) to
denote change, we can express the change in the value of the independent variable, $X$, by the notation $\Delta X$ and the change in the dependent
variable, $Y$, as $\Delta Y$.

The ratio $\Delta Y/\Delta X$ provides a very general specification of the marginal
concept:

$$\text{Marginal } Y = \frac{\Delta Y}{\Delta X} \qquad \textbf{2.5}$$

The change in $Y$, $\Delta Y$, divided by the change in $X$, $\Delta X$, indicates the
change in the dependent variable associated with a one-unit change in
the value of $X$.

Figure 2.3, which is a graph of a function relating $Y$ to $X$, illustrates this relation. For values of $X$ close to the origin, a relatively small

■ Figure 2.3
## Illustration of Changing $\Delta Y/\Delta X$ over the Range of a Curve

The ratio $\Delta Y/\Delta X$ changes continuously along a curved line.

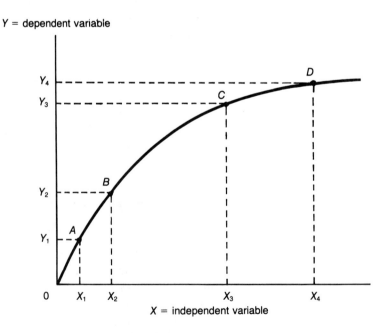

change in $X$ provides a large change in $Y$. Thus, the value of $\Delta Y/\Delta X = (Y_2 - Y_1)/(X_2 - X_1)$ is relatively large, showing that a small increase in $X$ induces a large increase in $Y$. The situation is reversed farther out along the $X$ axis. A large increase in $X$, say from $X_3$ to $X_4$, produces only a small increase in $Y$, from $Y_3$ to $Y_4$, so $\Delta Y/\Delta X$ is small.

It is clear that the marginal relation between $X$ and $Y$, as shown in Figure 2.3, changes at different points on the curve. When the curve is relatively steep, the dependent variable $Y$ is highly responsive to changes in the independent variable, but when the curve is relatively flat, $Y$ does not respond as notably to changes in $X$.

**derivative**
The marginal value of a function at a given point.

A **derivative** is a precise specification of the general marginal relation, $\Delta Y/\Delta X$. Finding a derivative involves finding the value of the ratio $\Delta Y/\Delta X$ for extremely small changes in $X$. The mathematical notation for a derivative is:

$$\frac{dY}{dX} = \lim_{\Delta X \to 0} \frac{\Delta Y}{\Delta X},$$

which is read: "The derivative of $Y$ with respect to $X$ equals the limit of the ratio $\Delta Y/\Delta X$, as $\Delta X$ approaches zero."[1]

This concept of the derivative as the limit of a ratio is precisely equivalent to the slope of a curve at a point. Figure 2.4 presents this idea, using the same curve relating $Y$ to $X$ shown in Figure 2.3. Notice that in Figure 2.4 the *average* slope of the curve between points $A$ and $D$ is measured as:

$$\frac{\Delta Y}{\Delta X} = \frac{Y_4 - Y_1}{X_4 - X_1},$$

and it is shown as the slope of the chord connecting the two points. Similarly, the average slope of the curve can be measured over smaller and smaller intervals of $X$ and shown by other chords, such as those connecting points $B$ and $C$ with $D$. At the limit, as $\Delta X$ approaches zero, the ratio $\Delta Y/\Delta X$ is equal to the slope of a line drawn tangent to the curve—for example, at point $D$. *The slope of this tangent is defined as the derivative, dY/dX, of the function at point D; it measures the marginal change in Y associated with a very small change in X at that point.*

For example, the dependent variable $Y$ might be total revenue, and the independent variable might be output. The derivative $dY/dX$ shows

---

[1]A limit can be explained briefly. If the value of a function $Y = f(X)$ approaches a constant $Y^*$ as the value of the independent variable $X$ approaches $X^*$, then $Y^*$ is called the limit of the function as $X$ approaches $X^*$. This is written as follows:

$$\lim_{X \to X^*} f(X) = Y^*.$$

For example, if $Y = X - 4$, then the limit of this function as $X$ approaches 5 is 1; that is,

$$\lim_{X \to 5} (X - 4) = 1.$$

This says that the value of $X$ approaches but does not quite reach 5; the value of the function $Y = X - 4$ comes closer and closer to 1. This concept of a limit is examined in detail in any introductory calculus textbook.

■ Figure 2.4
## Illustration of a Derivative as the Slope of a Curve

The derivative of $Y$ with respect to $X$ identifies the slope of a curve.

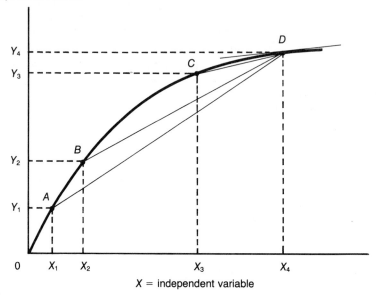

precisely how revenue and output are related at a specific output level. Because the change in revenue associated with a change in output is defined as the marginal revenue, the derivative of total revenue provides a precise measure of marginal revenue at any specific output level. A similar situation exists for total cost: the derivative of the total cost function at any output level indicates marginal cost at that output.

Derivatives provide information useful in managerial economics. Illustrations developed in the remainder of this chapter will indicate their value both for problem solving and for clarifying some fundamental managerial economics concepts.

## MARGINAL ANALYSIS IN DECISION MAKING

Managerial decision making frequently requires one to find the maximum or minimum value of a function. For a function to be at a maximum or minimum, its slope or marginal value must be zero. The *derivative* of a function is a very precise measure of its slope or marginal value at a particular point. Thus, maximization or minimization of a function oc-

■ Figure 2.5
## Profit as a Function of Output

Total profit is maximized at 100 units, where marginal profit equals zero. Beyond that point, marginal profit is negative and total profit decreases.

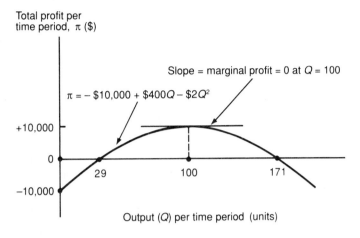

Total profit per
time period, $\pi$ ($)

Slope = marginal profit = 0 at $Q$ = 100

$\pi = -\$10,000 + \$400Q - \$2Q^2$

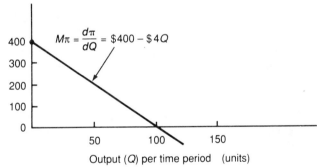

Marginal profit
per unit of output ($)

$M\pi = \dfrac{d\pi}{dQ} = \$400 - \$4Q$

Output ($Q$) per time period (units)

curs where its derivative is equal to zero. To illustrate, consider the following profit function:

$$\pi = -\$10,000 + \$400Q - \$2Q^2. \qquad \textbf{2.6}$$

Here $\pi$ = total profit and $Q$ is output in units. As shown in Figure 2.5, if output is zero, the firm incurs a $10,000 loss (fixed costs are $10,000), but as output rises, profit also rises. Breakeven points (output levels where profit is zero) are reached at 29 and 171 units of output. Profit rises as output expands to 100 units of output, where profit is maximized at $10,000, and declines thereafter.

The profit-maximizing output could be found by calculating the value of the function at a number of outputs, then plotting these as is done in

## 2.2 **Managerial Application**
The Relevance of Theory to Practice

Have you ever been a spectator at a golf, tennis, or racquetball tournament when a particular athlete's play became the center of attention? As people admired the performance, some questions inevitably arose. Have you ever heard people ask, "Where did that athlete study physics?" or "Who was her geometry instructor?" or "Boy, who taught that guy physiology?" Chances are you didn't. Instead, the discussion probably centered on the players' skill, finesse, or tenacity. Natural talent developed through long hours of dedicated training and intense competition is commonly regarded as the chief prerequisite for becoming an accomplished amateur or professional athlete. But if you think about it, an accomplished racquetball player must also know a great deal about angles, speed, and acceleration. Likewise, a successful tennis competitor must fully understand his or her physical limits as well as the competition's.

While success in these games requires that one understand the basic principles of geometry, physics, and physiology, most athletes develop their "feel" for these subjects on the tennis court, golf course, baseball diamond, or gridiron. In fact, successful athletes may have had little or no formal textbook instruction in these subjects. Their understanding more often is based, for example, on the "applied physics" courses offered daily on campus racquetball courts.

Similarly, some very successful businesses are run by people with little or no formal training in accounting, finance, management, or marketing. This is especially true of older executives who "came up through the ranks" before the post–World War II college education boom. These executives' success testifies to their ability to develop a "feel" for business in much the same way that the successful athlete develops a "feel" for his or her sport. Although the term

*continued*

See: Dyan Machan, "Taking Charge," *Forbes*, March 6, 1989, 154–156.

Figure 2.5. The maximum can also be located by finding the derivative, or marginal, of the function, then determining the value of $Q$ at which the derivative (marginal) is equal to zero.[2]

$$\text{Marginal Profit } (M\pi) = \frac{d\pi}{dQ} = \$400 - \$4Q.$$

[2]Basic rules for finding the derivative of a function are found in the Math Analysis for Managers appendix to this chapter.

**Managerial Application** *continued*

*optimization* may be foreign to such individuals, the methodology of optimization is familiar to each of them in terms of their everyday business practice. Adjusting prices to avoid stockout situations, increasing product quality to "meet the competition," and raising salaries to retain valued employees all involve a basic, practical understanding of optimization concepts.

The behavior of both the successful athlete and the successful executive can be described, or modeled, as being consistent with a process of optimization. In the case of, say, the tennis player, the pursuit of on-the-court success can be described as being consistent with performance maximization, given his or her skill and other capabilities. In the case of the successful business executive, the day-to-day activities incorporated into ongoing business practice typically are quite consistent with long-term value maximization. The fact that some successful sport and business practitioners learn their "lessons" through hands-on experience rather than in the classroom doesn't diminish the value of formal educational experience. In the classroom, one can discuss and analyze the basic lessons and themes that emerge in the business practice of successful managers and firms. When described in model form, such as in the value maximiza-

tion model, the generality of these lessons and themes becomes apparent, thereby enhancing the classroom experience.

The usefulness of economic models and optimization analysis in the study of managerial decision making arises from their provision of a logical framework for organizing and characterizing the wealth of institutional knowledge gained through practical business experience. This is not to say that only quantitative factors are important in successful management. For example, some successful security analysts focus on the "numbers"—that is, data such as the firm's return on investment, cash flow per share, price/earnings ratio, and so on. Others adopt a more qualitative approach, favoring the company with the best management tradition, or "bloodlines." Both approaches can be successful, but those who combine quantitative *and* qualitative considerations in their investment decision making often earn the greatest returns. Similarly, the optimization framework typically is best used when combined with the insights that seasoned business judgment provides. In short, the task of successful business management is made easier through the careful combination of theory and practice.

Setting the derivative equal to zero results in:

$$\$400 - \$4Q = 0$$
$$\$4Q = \$400$$
$$Q = 100 \text{ units.}$$

Therefore, when $Q = 100$, marginal profit is zero and total profit is at a maximum. Beyond $Q = 100$, marginal profit is negative and total profit is decreasing. Even in this simple illustration, it is easier to locate the profit-maximizing value by calculus than by graphic analysis; had the function been more complex, the calculus solution might have been the only efficient means of determining the profit-maximizing output level.

## Distinguishing Maximums from Minimums

A problem can arise when derivatives are used to locate maximums or minimums. The first derivative of the total function provides a measure of whether the function is rising or falling at any point. To be maximized or minimized, the function must be neither rising nor falling; that is, the slope as measured by the first derivative must be zero. However, since the marginal value or derivative will be zero for both maximum and minimum values of a function, further analysis is necessary to determine whether a maximum or a minimum has been located.

This point is illustrated in Figure 2.6, where we see that the slope of the total profit curve is zero at both points *A* and *B*. Point *A*, however, locates the output that minimizes profits, whereas *B* locates the profit-maximizing output.

The concept of a *second derivative* is used to distinguish between maximums and minimums along a function. The second derivative is simply the derivative of the original derivative; it is determined in precisely the same manner as a first derivative. If total profit is given by the equation $\pi = a - bQ + cQ^2 - dQ^3$, as in Figure 2.6, then the first derivative defines the marginal profit function as:

$$\frac{d\pi}{dQ} = M\pi = -b + 2cQ - 3dQ^2. \qquad \textbf{2.7}$$

The second derivative of the total profit function is the derivative of the marginal profit function, Equation 2.7:

$$\frac{d^2\pi}{dQ^2} = \frac{dM\pi}{dQ} = 2c - 6dQ.$$

Just as the first derivative measures the slope of the total profit function, the second derivative measures the slope of the first derivative or, in this case, the slope of the marginal profit curve. We can use the second derivative to distinguish between points of maximization and minimization, because the second derivative of a function is always *negative* when evaluated at a point of *maximization* and *positive* at a point of *minimization*.

The reason for this inverse relation can be seen in Figure 2.6. Note that profits reach a local minimum at point *A* because marginal profits, which have been negative and therefore causing total profits to fall, suddenly become positive. Marginal profits pass through the zero level from below at point *A* and hence are increasing or positively sloped. The reverse situation holds at a point of local maximization; the marginal value is positive but declining up to the point where the total function is maximized, and it is negative after that point. Thus, the marginal

■ Figure 2.6
## Locating Maximum and Minimum Values of a Function

The second derivative of a function is always negative when evaluating at a point of maximization and positive at a point of minimization.

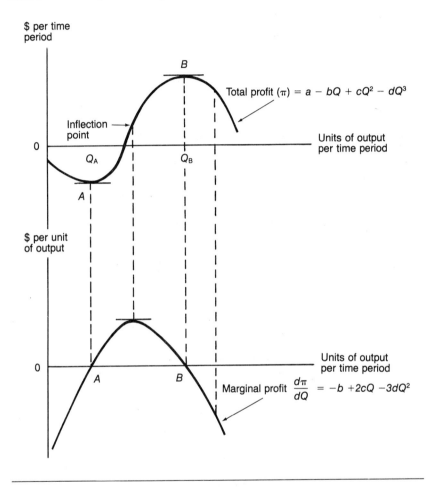

function is negatively sloped (that is, *its* derivative is negative) at the point of maximization of the total function.

Another example should help clarify this concept. Assume that the total profit function illustrated in Figure 2.6 is given by the following equation:

$$\text{Total Profit} = \pi = -\$3{,}000 - \$2{,}400Q + \$350Q^2 - \$8.333Q^3. \qquad \textbf{2.8}$$

Marginal profit is given by the first derivative of the total profit function:

$$\text{Marginal Profit} = \frac{d\pi}{dQ} = -\$2{,}400 + \$700Q - \$25Q^2. \qquad \textbf{2.9}$$

Total profit is either maximized or minimized at the points where the first derivative (marginal profit) is zero; that is, where:

$$\frac{d\pi}{dQ} = -\$2{,}400 + \$700Q - \$25Q^2 = 0.$$    **2.10**

Output quantities of 4 and 24 units satisfy Equation 2.10 and are therefore points of either maximum or minimum profits.[3]

Evaluation of the second derivative of the total profit function at each of these output levels will indicate whether they are minimums or maximums. The second derivative of the total profit function is found by taking the derivative of the marginal profit function, Equation 2.9:

$$\frac{d^2\pi}{dQ^2} = \frac{dM\pi}{dQ} = \$700 - \$50Q.$$

For example, at output quantity $Q = 4$:

$$\frac{d^2\pi}{dQ^2} = \$700 - \$50(4) = \$500.$$

Since the second derivative is positive, indicating that marginal profits are increasing, total profit is *minimized* at 4 units of output. In other words, total profit at 4 units of output corresponds to point $A$ in Figure 2.6.

Evaluating the second derivative at 24 units of output, we obtain:

$$\frac{d^2\pi}{dQ^2} = \$700 - \$50(24) = -\$500.$$

Since the second derivative is negative at 24 units, indicating that marginal profit is decreasing, the total profit function has reached a

---

[3]Any equation of the form $Y = aX^2 + bX + c$ is a quadratic, and its two roots can be found by the general quadratic equation:

$$X = \frac{-b \pm \sqrt{b^2 - 4ac}}{2a}.$$

Substituting the values from Equation 2.10 into the quadratic equation, we obtain:

$$X = \frac{-700 \pm \sqrt{700^2 - 4(-25)(-2{,}400)}}{2(-25)} = \frac{-700 \pm \sqrt{490{,}000 - 240{,}000}}{-50}$$

$$X = \frac{-700 \pm \sqrt{250{,}000}}{-50} = \frac{-700 \pm 500}{-50}.$$

The plus root is:

$$X_1 = \frac{-700 + 500}{-50} = \frac{-200}{-50} = 4 \text{ units},$$

and the minus root is:

$$X_2 = \frac{-700 - 500}{-50} = \frac{-1{,}200}{-50} = 24 \text{ units}.$$

*maximum* at that point. This output level corresponds to point *B* in Figure 2.6.

## Use of Marginals to Maximize the Difference between Two Functions

**profit maximization**

The output level of greatest profit, where marginal revenue equals marginal cost, and marginal profit is zero.

Another example of the importance of the marginal concept in managerial economics is provided by the important and well-known microeconomic corollary that marginal revenue equals marginal cost at the point of **profit maximization.** It stems from the fact that the distance between revenue and cost functions is maximized at the point where their slopes are the same. Figure 2.7 illustrates this point; there hypothetical revenue and cost functions are shown. Total profit is equal to total revenue minus total cost and is, therefore, equal to the vertical distance between the two curves at any output level. This distance is maximized at output level $Q_B$, where the slopes of the revenue and cost curves are equal. Because the slopes of the total revenue and total cost curves measure marginal revenues, $MR$, and marginal costs, $MC$, where these slopes are equal, $MR = MC$.

The reason that $Q_B$ is the profit-maximizing output level can be seen by considering the shapes of the two curves to the right of point $Q_A$. At $Q_A$, total revenue equals total cost, and we have a breakeven point—that is, an output quantity where profits are zero. At output quantities just beyond $Q_A$, total revenue is rising faster than total cost, so profits are increasing and the curves are spreading farther apart. This divergence of the curves continues as long as total revenue is rising faster than total cost, or in other words, as long as $MR > MC$. Once the slope of the total revenue curve is exactly equal to the slope of the total cost curve—in other words, where marginal revenue equals marginal cost—the two curves will be parallel and no longer diverging. This occurs at output quantity $Q_B$. Beyond $Q_B$ the slope of the cost curve is greater than that of the revenue curve (marginal cost is greater than marginal revenue), so the distance between them is decreasing and total profits decline.

An example will help to clarify this use of marginals. Consider the following revenue, cost, and profit functions:

$$\text{Total Revenue} = TR = \$41.5Q - \$1.1Q^2.$$
$$\text{Total Cost} \quad = TC = \$150 + \$10Q - \$0.5Q^2 + \$0.02Q^3.$$
$$\text{Total Profit} \quad = \pi \ = TR - TC.$$

The profit-maximizing output can be found by substituting the total revenue and total cost functions into the profit function, then analyzing the first and second derivatives of that equation:

$$
\begin{aligned}
\pi &= TR - TC \\
&= \$41.5Q - \$1.1Q^2 - (\$150 + \$10Q - \$0.5Q^2 + \$0.02Q^3) \\
&= \$41.5Q - \$1.1Q^2 - \$150 - \$10Q + \$0.5Q^2 - \$0.02Q^3 \\
&= -\$150 + \$31.5Q - \$0.6Q^2 - \$0.02Q^3.
\end{aligned}
$$

■ Figure 2.7
## Total Revenue, Total Cost, and Profit Maximization

The difference between the total revenue and total cost curves is greatest when their slopes are equal. At that point, marginal revenue equals marginal cost, marginal profit equals zero, and profit is maximized.

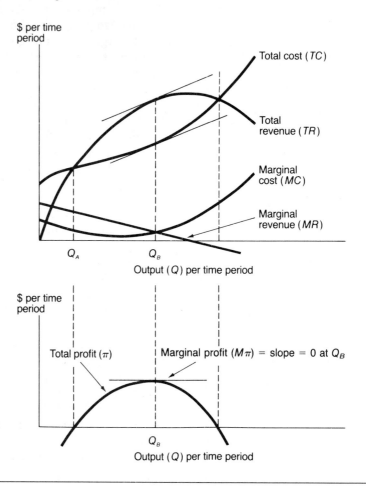

Marginal profit, the first derivative of the profit function, is:

$$M\pi = \frac{d\pi}{dQ} = \$31.5 - \$1.2Q - \$0.06Q^2.$$

Setting marginal profit equal to zero and using the quadratic equation to solve for the two roots, we obtain $Q_1 = -35$ and $Q_2 = +15$. Since negative output quantities are not possible, $Q_1$ is an infeasible output level and can be rejected.

An evaluation of the second derivative of the profit function at $Q = 15$ will indicate whether this is a point of profit maximization or profit minimization. The second derivative is given by:

$$\frac{d^2\pi}{dQ^2} = \frac{dM\pi}{dQ} = -\$1.2 - \$0.12Q.$$

Evaluating this derivative at $Q = 15$ indicates a value of $-\$3$; therefore, $Q = 15$ is a point of profit maximization.

The relations of marginal revenue and marginal cost to profit maximization can also be demonstrated by considering the general profit expression $\pi = TR - TC$. Marginal profit, the derivative of the total profit function is:

$$M\pi = \frac{d\pi}{dQ} = \frac{dTR}{dQ} - \frac{dTC}{dQ}.$$

Given that $dTR/dQ$ is by definition the expression for marginal revenue, $MR$, and that $dTC/dQ$ represents marginal cost, $MC$, we have:

$$M\pi = MR - MC.$$

Because maximization of any function requires that the first derivative be equal to zero, profit maximization will occur where:

$$M\pi = MR - MC = 0,$$

or where:

$$MR = MC.$$

Continuing with our numerical example, marginal revenue and marginal cost are found by differentiating the total revenue and total cost functions:

$$MR = \frac{dTR}{dQ} = \$41.5 - \$2.2Q.$$

$$MC = \frac{dTC}{dQ} = \$10 - Q + \$0.06Q^2.$$

At the profit-maximizing output level, $MR = MC$; thus,

$$MR = \$41.5 - \$2.2Q = \$10 - Q + \$0.06Q^2 = MC.$$

Combining terms, we obtain:

$$\$31.5 - \$1.2Q - \$0.06Q^2 = 0,$$

which is the same expression obtained when the first derivative of the profit function is set at zero. Solving for the roots of this equation (again using the quadratic formula) results in $Q_1 = -35$ and $Q_2 = 15$, the same values found previously. This confirms that marginal revenue equals marginal cost at the output level where profit is maximized. This ex-

■ Figure 2.8
## Profit-Maximizing Output Conditions

Profit is maximized at $Q = 15$, where $MR = MC = \$8.50$, and $M\pi = 0$.

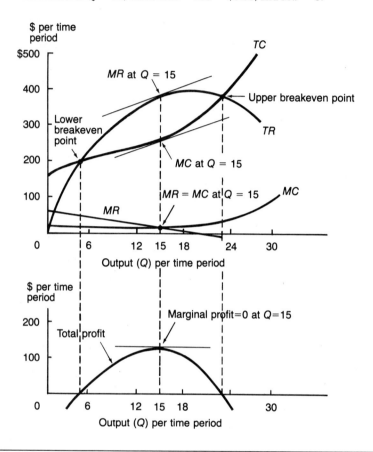

ample also illustrates that although $MR$ must equal $MC$ at the profit-maximizing activity level, the converse does not hold. Profits are not necessarily maximized at any point where $MR = MC$, as for example at $Q = -35$ in the current problem.

To conclude the example, Figure 2.8 presents graphs of the revenue, cost, and profit functions. The upper section of the graph shows the revenue and cost functions; at 15 units of output, the slopes of the two curves are equal, and $MR = MC$. The lower section of the figure shows the profit function, and the profit-maximizing output is shown to be 15 units, at which output $d\pi/dQ = 0$ and $d^2\pi/dQ^2 < 0$.

# MULTIVARIATE OPTIMIZATION

**multivariate optimization**

Finding the optimal point on a function involving three or more variables.

Because many economic relations involve more than two variables, it is useful to examine the concept of **multivariate optimization** for equations with three or more variables. Consider the demand function for a product where the quantity demanded, $Q$, is determined by the price charged, $P$, and the level of advertising expenditure, $A$. Such a function would be written as follows:

$$Q = f(P,A). \qquad \textbf{2.11}$$

When analyzing multivariable relations, such as the one in Equation 2.11, we need to know the marginal effect of each independent variable on the dependent variable. In other words, optimization in this case requires an analysis of how a change in each independent variable affects the dependent variable, *holding constant the effect of all other independent variables.* The partial derivative is the concept used for this type of marginal analysis.

Using the demand function of Equation 2.11, we can examine two partial derivatives:[4]

1. The partial of $Q$ with respect to price = $\partial Q/\partial P$.
2. The partial of $Q$ with respect to advertising expenditure = $\partial Q/\partial A$.

The rules for determining partial derivatives are essentially the same as those for simple derivatives. Since the concept of a partial derivative involves an assumption that all variables except the one with respect to which the derivative is being taken remain unchanged, those variables are treated as constants in the differentiation process. Consider the equation:

$$Q = 3{,}200 - 50P + 39A + 0.25PA - 0.1A^2. \qquad \textbf{2.12}$$

In this function there are two independent variables, $P$ and $A$, so two partial derivatives can be evaluated. To determine the partial with respect to $P$, note that the function can be rewritten as:

$$Q = 3{,}200 - 50P + 39A + (0.25A)P - 0.1A^2. \qquad \textbf{2.12a}$$

Since $A$ is treated as a constant, the partial derivative of $Q$ with respect to $P$ is:

$$\frac{\partial Q}{\partial P} = 0 - 50 + 0 + 0.25A - 0$$

$$= -50 + 0.25A.$$

---

[4]The symbol $\partial$, called *delta*, is used to denote a partial derivative. In oral and written expressions of this concept, the word *derivative* is frequently omitted. That is, reference is typically made to the *partial* of $Q$ rather than the *partial derivative* of $Q$.

In determining the partial of $Q$ with respect to $A$, $P$ is treated as a constant, so we can write:

$$Q = 3,200 - 50P + 39A + (0.25P)A - 0.1A^2, \qquad \textbf{2.12b}$$

and the partial with respect to $A$ is:

$$\frac{\partial Q}{\partial A} = 0 - 0 + 39 + 0.25P - 0.2A$$

$$= 39 + 0.25P - 0.2A.$$

## Maximizing Multivariate Functions

The requirement for maximization (or minimization) of a multivariate function is a straightforward extension of that for single variable functions. All first-order partial derivatives must equal zero.[5] Thus, maximization of the function $Q = f(P,A)$ requires:

$$\frac{\partial Q}{\partial P} = 0,$$

and

$$\frac{\partial Q}{\partial A} = 0.$$

To illustrate this procedure, let us reconsider the function given previously,

$$Q = 3,200 - 50P + 39A + 0.25PA - 0.1A^2,$$

whose partial derivatives are

$$\frac{\partial Q}{\partial P} = -50 + 0.25A,$$

and

$$\frac{\partial Q}{\partial A} = 39 + 0.25P - 0.2A.$$

To maximize the value of Equation 2.12, each partial must be set equal to zero:

$$\frac{\partial Q}{\partial P} = -50 + 0.25A = 0,$$

and

$$\frac{\partial Q}{\partial A} = 39 + 0.25P - 0.2A = 0.$$

---

[5]Because the second-order requirements for determining maxima and minima are somewhat complex and are not necessary for the materials that follow in this text, they are not developed here. A full discussion of these requirements can be found in any elementary calculus text.

■ Figure 2.9

## Finding the Maximum of a Function of Two Variables: $Q = 3,200 - 50P + 39A + 0.25PA - 0.1A^2$.

All first-order partial derivatives are set equal to zero to find the maximum of a multivariate function.

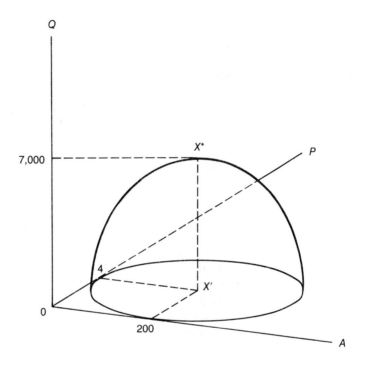

Here we have two equations in two unknowns. Solving them simultaneously, we find that the values $P = 4$ and $A = 200$ maximize the function.[6] Inserting these values for $P$ and $A$ into Equation 2.12, we find the value of $Q$ to be 7,000; therefore, the maximum value of $Q$ is 7,000.

The process involved here can perhaps be clarified by referring to Figure 2.9, a three-dimensional graph of Equation 2.12. Here we see that for positive values of $P$ and $A$, Equation 2.12 maps out a surface with a peak at point $X^*$. At the peak, the surface of the figure is level. Alternatively stated, a plane that is tangent to the surface at point $X^*$ will be parallel to the $PA$ plane, meaning that the slope of the figure with respect to either $P$ or $A$ must be zero; this is the requirement for locating a maximum of a multivariate function.

[6]Since $-50 + 0.25A = 0$, $0.25A = 50$ and $A = 200$. Substituting this value for $A$ into $39 + 0.25P - 0.2A = 0$, we obtain $39 + 0.25P - 0.2(200) = 0$, which implies that $0.25P = 1$ and $P = 4$.

# CONSTRAINED OPTIMIZATION

In many decision problems faced by managers, there are constraints imposed that limit the options available to the decision maker. For example, a production manager may be charged with minimizing total cost, subject to the requirement that specified quantities of each of the firm's products be produced. At other times the production manager may be concerned with maximizing output from a particular department, subject to limitations on the quantities of various resources (labor, materials, or equipment) available for use.

**constrained optimization**

Optimization in light of input or output limitations.

Other functional areas of the firm also face **constrained optimization** problems. Marketing managers are often charged with the task of maximizing sales, subject to the constraint that they not exceed a fixed advertising budget. Financial officers, in their efforts to minimize the cost of acquiring capital, must frequently work within constraints imposed by investment financing needs and cash balance requirements, and by creditor restrictions.

Constrained optimization problems may be solved in several ways. In some cases, where the constraint equation is not complex, one can solve the constraint equation for one of the decision variables, then substitute for that variable in the objective function—the function that the firm wishes to maximize or minimize.[7] This procedure converts the problem to one of unconstrained maximization or minimization, which can be solved by the methods outlined previously.

This procedure can be clarified by examining its use in a constrained minimization problem. Suppose a firm produces its product on two assembly lines and operates with the following total cost function:

$$TC = \$3X^2 + \$6Y^2 - \$1XY,$$

where $X$ represents the output produced on one assembly line and $Y$ the production from the second. Management seeks to determine the least-cost combination of $X$ and $Y$, subject to the constraint that total output of the product must be 20 units. The constrained optimization problem can be stated as follows:

Minimize

$$TC = \$3X^2 + \$6Y^2 - \$1XY,$$

subject to

$$X + Y = 20.$$

[7]In this section we examine techniques for solving constrained optimization problems in those cases where the constraints can be expressed as equations. Frequently, constraints impose only upper or lower limits on the decision maker and, therefore, may not be "binding" at the optimal solution. Constraints of this second, more general, type are properly expressed as inequality relations, and in these cases another optimizing technique, mathematical programming, is often used to analyze the problem. Mathematical programming is discussed in Chapter 10.

Solving the constraint for $X$ and substituting this value into the objective function results in:

$$X = 20 - Y,$$

and

$$
\begin{aligned}
TC &= \$3(20 - Y)^2 + \$6Y^2 - \$1(20 - Y)Y \\
&= \$3(400 - 40Y + Y^2) + \$6Y^2 - \$1(20Y - Y^2) \\
&= \$1{,}200 - \$120Y + \$3Y^2 + \$6Y^2 - \$20Y + Y^2 \\
&= \$1{,}200 - \$140Y + \$10Y^2.
\end{aligned}
$$

**2.13**

Now we can treat Equation 2.13 as an unconstrained minimization problem. Solving it requires taking the derivative, setting that derivative equal to zero, and solving for the value of $Y$:

$$
\begin{aligned}
\frac{dTC}{dY} = -\$140 + \$20Y &= 0 \\
20Y &= 140 \\
Y &= 7.
\end{aligned}
$$

A check of the sign of the second derivative evaluated at that point will insure that a minimum has been located:

$$\frac{dTC}{dY} = -\$140 + \$20Y$$

$$\frac{d^2TC}{dY^2} = +\$20.$$

Since the second derivative is positive, $Y = 7$ must indeed be a minimum.

Substituting 7 for $Y$ in the constraint equation allows us to determine the optimal quantity to be produced on assembly line $X$.

$$X + 7 = 20$$

$$X = 13.$$

Thus, production of 13 units of output on assembly line $X$ and 7 units on line $Y$ is the least-cost combination for manufacturing a total of 20 units of the firm's product. The total cost of producing that combination will be:

$$
\begin{aligned}
TC &= \$3(13)^2 + \$6(7)^2 - \$(13 \cdot 7) \\
&= \$507 + \$294 - \$91 \\
&= \$710.
\end{aligned}
$$

## Lagrangian Multipliers

Unfortunately, the substitution technique used in the preceding section is not always feasible; constraint conditions are often too numerous or too complex for substitution to be employed. In these cases, the technique of *Lagrangian multipliers* can be used.

**Lagrangian technique**

A popular method for solving constrained optimization problems.

The **Lagrangian technique** for solving constrained optimization problems is a procedure that calls for optimizing a function that combines the original objective function and the constraint conditions. This combined equation, called the Lagrangian function, is created in a way that insures (1) that when it has been maximized (or minimized), the original objective function will also be maximized (minimized), and (2) that all the constraint requirements will have been satisfied.

A re-examination of the constrained minimization problem illustrated previously will clarify the use of this technique. Recall that the firm sought to minimize the function $TC = \$3X^2 + \$6Y^2 - \$1XY$, subject to the constraint that $X + Y = 20$. Rearranging the constraint to bring all the terms to the right of the equal sign, we obtain:

$$0 = 20 - X - Y.$$

This is always the first step in forming a Lagrangian expression.

Multiplying this form of the constraint by the unknown factor $\lambda$ and adding the result to the original objective function creates the Lagrangian expression.[8]

$$L_{TC} = \$3X^2 + \$6Y^2 - \$1XY + \lambda(20 - X - Y). \qquad \textbf{2.14}$$

$L_{TC}$ is defined as the Lagrangian function for the constrained optimization problem under consideration.

Because it incorporates the constraint into the objective function, the Lagrangian function can be treated as an unconstrained optimization problem. The solution to the unconstrained Lagrangian problem will *always* be identical to the solution of the original constrained optimization problem. To illustrate this, consider the problem of minimizing the Lagrangian function constructed in Equation 2.14. At a minimum point on a multivariate function, all the partial derivatives must be equal to zero. The partials of Equation 2.14 can be taken with respect to the three unknown variables, $X$, $Y$, and $\lambda$, as follows:

$$\frac{\partial L_{TC}}{\partial X} = 6X - Y - \lambda,$$

$$\frac{\partial L_{TC}}{\partial Y} = 12Y - X - \lambda,$$

$$\frac{\partial L_{TC}}{\partial \lambda} = 20 - X - Y.$$

Setting these three partials equal to zero results in a system of three equations and three unknowns:

$$6X - Y - \lambda = 0, \qquad \textbf{2.15}$$

$$-X + 12Y - \lambda = 0, \qquad \textbf{2.16}$$

[8]$\lambda$ is the Greek letter *lambda*, which is typically used in formulating Lagrangian expressions.

and

$$20 - X - Y = 0. \qquad \textbf{2.17}$$

Notice that Equation 2.17, the partial of the Lagrangian function with respect to $\lambda$, is the constraint condition imposed on the original optimization problem. This result is not mere happenstance. The Lagrangian function is specifically constructed so that the derivative of the function taken with respect to the Lagrangian multiplier, $\lambda$, will always give the original constraint. So long as this derivative is zero, as it must be at a local extreme (maximum or minimum), the constraint conditions imposed on the original problem will be met. Further, since under such conditions the last term in the Lagrangian expression must equal zero—that is, $0 = 20 - X - Y$—the Lagrangian function reduces to the original objective function, and thus the solution to the unconstrained Lagrangian problem will always be the solution to the original constrained optimization problem.

Completing the analysis for our example will clarify these relations. We begin by solving the system of equations to obtain the optimal values of $X$ and $Y$. Subtracting Equation 2.16 from Equation 2.15 gives:

$$7X - 13Y = 0. \qquad \textbf{2.18}$$

Multiplying Equation 2.17 by 7 and adding Equation 2.18 to this product allows us to solve for $Y$:

$$
\begin{aligned}
140 - 7X - \phantom{1}7Y &= 0 \\
7X - 13Y &= 0 \\
\hline
140 \phantom{XXX} - 20Y &= 0 \\
140 &= 20Y \\
Y &= 7.
\end{aligned}
$$

Substituting 7 for $Y$ in Equation 2.17 yields $X = 13$, the value of $X$ at the point where the Lagrangian function is minimized.

Since the solution of the Lagrangian function is also the solution to the firm's constrained optimization problem, 13 units from assembly line $X$ and 7 units from line $Y$ will be the least-cost combination of output that can be produced subject to the constraint that total output must be 20 units. This is the same answer that we obtained previously by using the substitution method.

The Lagrangian technique is a more powerful technique for solving constrained optimization problems than the substitution method; it is easier to apply to a problem with multiple constraints, and it provides the decision maker with some valuable supplementary information. This is because the Lagrangian multiplier, $\lambda$, has an important economic interpretation. Substituting the values of $X$ and $Y$ into Equation 2.15 allows us to determine the value of $\lambda$ in our example:

$$6 \cdot 13 - 7 - \lambda = 0$$
$$\lambda = +\$71.$$

Here we can interpret $\lambda$ as the marginal cost of production at 20 units of output. It tells us that if the firm were required to produce only 19 instead of 20 units of output, total costs would fall by approximately $71. Similarly, if the output requirement were 21 instead of 20 units, costs would increase by that amount.[9]

Since $\lambda = +\$71$ can be interpreted as the marginal cost of production, an offer to purchase another unit of output for $100 would be accepted because it would result in a $29 marginal profit. Conversely, an offer to purchase an additional unit for $50 would be rejected because a marginal loss of $21 would be incurred. From this we see that $\lambda$ can be thought of as a planning variable, since it provides valuable information concerning the effects of altering current activity levels.

Another example will provide additional perspective on the value of the Lagrangian method. Recall from our discussion of Equation 2.6 and Figure 2.5 that the profit function,

$$\pi = -\$10,000 + \$400Q - \$2Q^2,$$

where $\pi$ is total profit and $Q$ is output in units, is maximized at $Q = 100$ with $\pi = \$10,000$. The impact of constraints in the production process, and the value of the Lagrangian method, can be further illustrated by considering the situation in which each unit of output requires 4 hours of skilled labor, and a total of only 300 hours of skilled labor is currently available to the firm. In this instance, the firm will seek to maximize the function $\pi = -\$10,000 + \$400Q - \$2Q^2$, subject to the output constraint $Q = 75 \, (= 300/4)$. Rearranging the constraint to bring all the terms to the right of the equal sign, we obtain:

$$0 = 75 - Q.$$

Multiplying this form of the constraint by $\lambda$ and adding the result to the original objective function creates the Lagrangian expression:

$$L_\pi = -\$10,000 + \$400Q - \$2Q^2 + \lambda(75 - Q), \qquad \textbf{2.19}$$

with the following partials:

$$\frac{\partial L_\pi}{\partial Q} = 400 - 4Q - \lambda,$$

$$\frac{\partial L_\pi}{\partial \lambda} = 75 - Q.$$

Setting these two partials equal to zero results in a system of two equations and two unknowns. Solving provides the values $Q = 75$, $\lambda = +\$25$, and, from the objective function, $\pi = \$8,750$. The constraint on skilled labor has reduced output from 100 to 75 units and has reduced

---

[9]Technically, $\lambda$ indicates the marginal change in the objective function solution associated with an infinitesimally small change in the constraint. Thus, it provides only an approximation of the change in total costs that would take place if one more (or less) unit of output were required.

total profits from $10,000 to $8,750. The value λ = +$25 indicates that should a one-unit expansion in output become possible, total profits would rise by $25. This information indicates that the maximum value of additional skilled labor is $6.25 per hour, since each unit of output requires four hours of labor. Thus, assuming there are no other costs involved, $6.25 per hour is the most the firm would pay to expand employment.

The effects of relaxing the constraint as progressively more skilled labor becomes available are illustrated in Figure 2.10. If an additional 100 hours of skilled labor, or 400 hours in total, were available, the output constraint would become $0 = 100 - Q$ and solved values $Q = 100$, $λ = \$0$, and $π = \$10,000$ would result. The value $λ = \$0$ indicates that skilled labor no longer constrains profits when 400 hours are available. Profits are maximized at $Q = 100$, which is the same result obtained in our earlier unconstrained solution to this profit maximization problem.

In this instance, the output constraint becomes *nonbinding* because it does not limit the profit-making ability of the firm. Indeed, in our example the firm would not willingly employ more than 400 hours of skilled labor. To illustrate this point, consider the use of 500 hours of skilled labor and the resulting constraint $0 = 125 - Q$. Solved values are $Q = 125$, $λ = -\$25$, and $π = \$8,750$. The value $λ = -\$25$ indicates that one additional unit of output, and the expansion in employment which results, would *reduce* profits by $25. Conversely, a one-unit reduction in

■ Figure 2.10

## The Role of Constraints in Profit Maximization

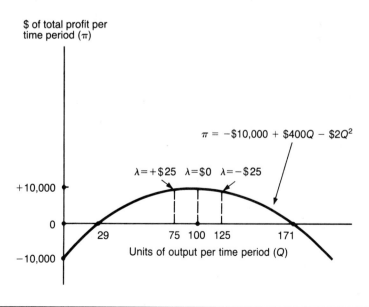

the level of output would *increase* profits by \$25. Clearly, in the situation in which $\lambda < 0$, the firm has an incentive to reduce input usage and output, just as $\lambda > 0$ provides an incentive for growth.

**Lagrangian multiplier, λ**
The effect on the objective function of a one-unit change in the constraint.

To generalize, a **Lagrangian multiplier, λ,** indicates the marginal effect on the objective function of decreasing or increasing the constraint requirement by one unit. Often, as in the previous examples, the marginal relation described by the Lagrangian multiplier provides economic data that help a manager evaluate the potential benefits or costs of relaxing a constraint. This use of the Lagrangian variable is further examined in Chapter 10, where the linear programming approach to constrained optimization is introduced.

# THE INCREMENTAL CONCEPT IN ECONOMIC ANALYSIS

The marginal concept introduced earlier is a key component of the economic decision-making process. It is important to recognize, however, that marginal relations are limited for managerial decision making by the fact that they measure only the impact associated with *unitary changes*. In many managerial decision situations, one is interested in the effect of changes or differences resulting from alternatives of a much broader nature. For example, one might be interested in analyzing the effects on revenues, costs, and profits of doubling a firm's production level. Or, one might want to analyze the profit impact of introducing a new product or to assess the cost impact of changing the production system used to produce the firm's current products. In all managerial decision making, *differences* or *changes* are the key elements in the selection of an optimal course of action. The marginal concept, although correct for analyzing unitary changes, is too narrow to provide a general methodology for evaluating alternative courses of action.

**incremental change**
The change caused by a given managerial decision.

The incremental concept is the economist's generalization of the marginal concept. Incremental analysis involves examining the impact of alternative courses of action on revenues, costs, and profit. It focuses on changes or differences between the available alternatives. The **incremental change** is defined as the total change resulting from a decision. For example, the incremental revenue associated with adding a new item to a firm's product line would be measured as the difference between the firm's total revenue with the product and without the product.

**incremental profit**
The change in profit caused by a given managerial decision.

The fundamental relations of incremental analysis are essentially the same as those with marginal analysis. Total profit increases so long as **incremental profit** is positive; with a negative incremental profit, total profit declines. Similarly, incremental profit is positive (and total profit increases) if the incremental revenue associated with a decision exceeds the incremental cost. The incremental concept is so intuitively obvious that it is easy to overlook both its significance in managerial decision making and the potential complexity of correctly applying it.

For this reason, the incremental concept is often violated in practice. For example, a firm may refuse to sell excess computer time for $500 an hour because it figures its cost as $550 an hour, calculated by adding a standard overhead cost of $250 an hour to an incremental operating cost of $300 an hour. The relevant incremental cost of computer usage, however, is only $300, so the firm would forgo a $200-per-hour contribution to profit by not selling its excess time. Any firm that adds a standard allocated charge for *fixed* costs and overhead to the true incremental cost of production runs the risk of turning down profitable sales.

On the other hand, care must be exercised to insure against incorrectly assigning a low incremental cost to a decision when a higher cost actually exists. An example that came to the authors' attention involved a heat-treating plant where metal parts were hardened prior to final assembly in various products. At the time, the economy was depressed and the plant had unused capacity. A major steel company offered the firm a five-year contract to treat certain products, but at a price well below the normal charges. The price offered exceeded operating expenses but was not sufficient to cover all overhead and provide a normal profit margin. That is, the offered price covered out-of-pocket costs but not full costs plus profits. The heat-treating company accepted the contract, believing that it would cover incremental costs and still have a little left over to contribute to total overhead expenses, which would not be affected by the decision.

A few months later the economy picked up, and other customers, who paid a higher price, began to bring in additional business. The plant was soon operating at full capacity, and the firm faced the prospect of being forced to turn away profitable business. At this point, the plant manager realized his mistake—he had misjudged demand and thereby miscalculated his costs. He had assumed that plant and equipment costs would be unaffected by the new contract, but in fact the contract forced him to expand at some considerable cost. If expansion had not been possible, the incremental costs of taking on the steel firm's business would have included the opportunity cost (lost profits) of the forgone regular business.

As another example of the comprehensive nature of the incremental concept, consider the measurement of the incremental revenue resulting from adding a new product to a firm's product line. Incremental revenue in this case would include not only the revenue received from sale of the new product but any change in the revenues generated by the remainder of the firm's product line. Thus, the incremental revenues would include any revenue resulting from increased sales of another product, where that increase was the result of adding the new product to the firm's line. Similarly, if the new item took sales from another of the firm's products, the loss in revenue on sales of those products would have to be accounted for in measuring the incremental revenue of the new product.

 Another interesting illustration of the incremental concept is found in the financing decision often associated with purchasing real estate.

## 2.3  **Managerial Application**

The Descriptive Power of Economics

The methodology of economics is based on the underlying presumption that individuals make economic decisions to further their own "self-interest." This means that firms will bring their products to market only when doing so is profitable. These profits, and the dividends and other benefits derived from them, motivate firms to provide goods and services that customers want and are willing to purchase. Similarly, buyers make purchase decisions on the basis of furthering their own self-interest. Only when the price and other terms of sale for a particular good or service are judged attractive will one make a purchase decision. Market transactions occur only when both parties derive some positive marginal benefit. Therefore, the voluntary nature of our market-based system insures that both producers and consumers obtain benefits through market transactions.

This self-interest view of economic motivation is based on an underlying theory of rational decision making by both firms and consumers. It presumes that producers will expand output so long as doing so increases profits and consumers will increase their purchases of goods and services so long as doing so enhances their well-being or sense of satisfaction. Even if this underlying theory were proven invalid, the methodology of economic optimization could still provide a useful prescription for improving economic performance, but it would have only limited value in terms of describing how producers and consumers actually behave.

Economists have found strong support for the hypothesis that market participants act in a rational fashion in case studies of suc-

*continued*

See: Jerry E. Bishop, "Lab Experiments Test Old Economic Rules Raising New Questions," *The Wall Street Journal,* November 25, 1986, 1, 25.

Consider a small business whose $100,000 purchase offer recently was accepted by the seller of a small retail facility. The firm must now obtain financing to complete the transaction. The best rates it has found are at a local financial institution offering a renewable five-year mortgage at a 9 percent interest rate for a loan up to 80 percent of the purchase price and a 9½ percent interest rate for a loan up to 90 percent of the purchase price. Both loans require only interest payments during the five years. After five years, either note is renewable at then-current interest rates and will be structured with monthly payments designed to amortize the

**Managerial Application** *continued*

cessful firms and extensive empirical studies of aggregate market activity by both firms and consumers. Unfortunately, these real-world, or field, data are sometimes contaminated by extraneous factors beyond the researcher's control. As a result, economists have devised new and interesting ways of learning more about the motivations underlying economic behavior using experimental methods borrowed from psychology and other social sciences.

Professor Vernon Smith, an economist at the University of Arizona, was an early pioneer in the field of experimental economics. During the last 30 years, Professor Smith and other economists have conducted over 100 experiments in a laboratory setting in order to learn the role of the profit motive in so-called *double oral* auction markets. A double oral auction market is one in which a buyer and seller confront each other and bargain directly until the buyer's bid price and the seller's asked price converge and a sale transaction occurs. Perhaps the most famous double oral auction market in existence today is the New York Stock Exchange. Interestingly—and as economist Adam Smith predicted over 200 years ago—the laboratory subjects Professor Smith and

his colleagues studied strove to maximize their own profits. Yet, without so intending, the subjects consistently arrived at prices that gave the greatest profit to the greatest number of participants. In other words, the laboratory traders acted as though guided by an "invisible hand" to arrive at prices that produced the maximum overall benefit.

The consistency of these experimental results has encouraged economists to adopt the laboratory approach in studying additional topics. For example, economists have found that when shipping rates are widely publicized they tend to stabilize at higher prices than when left to private negotiation. These findings have led the Department of Transportation to regard unfavorably the railroads' request to widely publicize or "post" rates. Similarly, Professor Smith is trying to predict what would happen if airports sold the landing rights for convenient "time slots" to airlines and the airlines were then allowed to trade these time slots as commodities. Therefore, in addition to providing added support for the basic hypotheses underlying economic methodology, experimental economics is proving to be a valuable tool for designing and implementing public policy.

loan over 20 years. An important question facing the firm is: What is the incremental financing cost of the additional funds borrowed when 90 versus 80 percent of the purchase price is financed?

Since no principal payments are required, the annual financing cost under each loan alternative can be easily calculated. For the 80 percent loan, the annual financing cost in dollar terms is:

$$\text{Financing Cost} = \text{Interest Rate} \times \text{Loan Percentage} \times \text{Purchase Price}$$
$$= (0.09)(0.8)(\$100,000)$$
$$= \$7,200.$$

Similarly, for the 90 percent loan, the annual financing cost is:

$$\text{Financing Cost} = (0.095)(0.9)(\$100,000)$$
$$= \$8,550.$$

To calculate the incremental cost of the added funds borrowed under the 90 percent financing alternative, the firm must compare the additional financing costs to the additional funds borrowed. In dollar terms, the incremental annual financing cost is:

$$\text{Incremental Cost} = 90\% \text{ Loan Financing Cost} - 80\% \text{ Loan Financing Cost}$$
$$= \$8,550 - \$7,200$$
$$= \$1,350.$$

In percentage terms, the incremental cost of the additional funds borrowed under the 90 percent financing alternative is:

$$\text{Incremental Cost in Percentage Terms} = \frac{\text{Incremental Financing Costs}}{\text{Incremental Funds Borrowed}}$$
$$= \frac{\$8,550 - \$7,200}{\$90,000 - \$80,000}$$
$$= \frac{\$1,350}{\$10,000}$$
$$= 0.135, \text{ or } 13.5\%.$$

Careful analysis indicates that the true incremental cost of funds for the last $10,000 borrowed under the 90 percent financing alternative is 13.5 percent, not the 9.5 percent interest rate quoted for the loan. While this high incremental cost of funds is perhaps surprising, it is not unusual. It results from the fact that with a 90 percent loan, the higher 9.5 percent interest rate is charged on the entire loan, not just on the incremental funds received.

The incremental concept is important for managerial decision making, because it tells us to focus our analysis on changes or differences between the available alternatives. Likewise, it tells us that revenues and costs unaffected by the decision are irrelevant and should not be included in the analysis. The incremental concept is examined in somewhat greater detail in Chapters 8 and 13.

## Case 2.1

# Miami Devices, Incorporated: Optimization in Product Reliability Design

Miami Devices, Incorporated (MDI), is one of several manufacturers producing electrical switching equipment for petroleum refining plants. MDI's management is currently examining one standard switch, model

MDI–5, with the objective of optimizing its market position and maximizing the profit earned on this product. Management believes that, given the nature of the market within which the MDI–5 is sold, price competition would be an ineffective way to increase profits. The standard price of $200 is well established. Previous attempts to raise the price of similar products have resulted in substantial declines in market share, whereas attempts to increase market penetration by lowering price have always led to retaliatory price reductions by competing firms.

On the basis of discussions with its sales representatives, MDI's management believes that product reliability holds the key to increasing profits on the MDI–5. MDI's sales force has long claimed that there is an important relation between product reliability and sales volume. Although top management had considered this proposition indirectly in the past, no effort was made to determine the true parameters of this relation. Now, James "Sonny" Crockett, president of MDI, has requested such an analysis as part of the review of the MDI–5 product strategy. Specifically, he has requested that Ricardo Tubbs, an administrative assistant, prepare a report that will answer the following questions:

- What relation exists between sales volume and the reliability level of the product?
- What is the relation between product costs and reliability?
- Assuming that the current $200 price is to be maintained, what reliability level results in maximum profits for the MDI–5?

Tubbs began his analysis by examining the relation between demand and reliability. Reliability problems with an earlier design of the MDI–5 provided data on reliability and sales for a number of years. Because of the stability of price and the lack of growth in the total market for the MDI–5 switch during the period covered by the data, Tubbs thought that these data accurately reflected the effect of variation in reliability on demand.

The data are shown in the following table. A graph of the data indicated a curvilinear relation, and Tubbs fitted a quadratic equation to it, using the least squares regression technique. (This statistical method is discussed in Chapter 5.) The resulting equation was:

$$Q(000) = 42 - 2.25F - 0.092F^2. \qquad R^2 = .99$$

| Reliability Level | Sales Volume |
|---|---|
| ($F$ = percentage failure per year) | $Q$ |
| 1 | 39,700 |
| 3 | 34,400 |
| 5 | 28,450 |
| 7 | 21,750 |
| 9 | 14,250 |

Tubbs also sought help from MDI's engineering staff to determine the production cost/reliability relation for the MDI–5 switch. Engineering personnel determined that total costs should be separated into three relevant categories for the analysis:

1. *Per unit product costs* $(C_p)$, which are defined as all costs that remain constant (per unit) regardless of the reliability level of the product. These production costs were estimated at $75 per unit, and this cost figure is not expected to vary significantly with respect to the quantity produced over the output range that appears relevant to MDI's decision problem—15,000 to 40,000 units.

2. *Per unit warranty costs* $(C_w)$. The model MDI–5 switch is warranted for five years. On the basis of past service costs, it is estimated that warranty repair or replacement costs will average $100 for each failure. Thus, the per unit warranty costs can be expressed as a function of the annual failure rate $(F)$ by the following equation:

$$C_w = \text{Cost per Failure} \times \text{Number of Years Warranted} \\ \times \text{Failure Rate per Year}$$
$$= (\$100)(5)(F/100)$$
$$= \$5F.$$

3. *Per unit reliability costs* $(C_f)$. An extensive study by the engineering department of engineering alternatives that would provide different levels of product reliability as measured by the failure rate resulted in the following data:

| Engineering Alternative | Failure Rate $(F)$ | Reliability Costs per Unit $(C_f)$ |
|:---:|:---:|:---:|
| 1 | 1 | $117 |
| 2 | 3 | 103 |
| 3 | 5 | 87 |
| 4 | 7 | 73 |
| 5 | 9 | 57 |

A graphic plot of these data indicated that a linear expression of the relation between $C_f$ and $F$ would be acceptable for the decision problem at hand. Estimation of the linear regression equation resulted in the following relation:

$$C_f = \$125 - \$7.5F \qquad R^2 = .99$$

Tubbs received these cost equations from the engineering department and was preparing to calculate the optimal reliability level when Crockett called with an invitation to join his Friday afternoon golf foursome. Tubbs could not refuse this offer, but since he knew that the completed report would be needed for a Monday morning meeting of the executive committee, he asked you, a new management trainee, to complete the analysis. The following questions should be answered in your work:

A. What is the profit-maximizing reliability level?
B. What sales volume is expected to result from that reliability level?
C. Given an optimal reliability level, what are expected total profits from the MDI–5 switch?

# SUMMARY

Managerial decision making is the process of finding the best solution to a given problem. Managerial economics plays an important role in this process. In this chapter, we first introduced a number of methods used to express economic relations, then proceeded to examine several fundamental principles of economic optimization.

Economic relations can be expressed in tables, graphs, or equations. The key concepts involve totals, averages, and marginals, which are interrelated in a unique manner. Knowledge of these interrelations provides valuable insights for managerial decision making.

Frequently, optimality analysis involves locating the maximum or minimum value of a function. Values for the function could be calculated and entered in a table or plotted on a graph, and the point where the function is maximized would be observed directly. It is often more convenient, however, to use the marginal concept to locate the optimum point. The total value of a function will be increasing when the marginal is positive and decreasing when the marginal is negative. The marginal value will be zero at the point where the function is maximized or minimized.

A function may have several values at which the marginal is zero, with some points representing maximums and others minimums. To determine whether a maximum or a minimum has been found, the second derivative is calculated. If the second derivative is negative, a maximum has been found; if it is positive, a minimum has been located.

If a function contains more than two variables, partial differentiation is used, and the process of finding partials is examined. To maximize a function of two or more variables, the partial with respect to each variable must be calculated, and these partials must be simultaneously set equal to zero.

The topic of constrained optimization, the process of maximizing or minimizing a function subject to a set of constraints, was also examined. Here we introduced the Lagrangian technique and demonstrated how it is used to solve constrained optimization problems. We also noted the interpretation of the Lagrangian multiplier as the marginal change in the objective function associated with a unit change in the constraint.

Finally, the incremental concept was introduced as a generalized basis for structuring the economic analysis of decision alternatives. The incremental concept stresses the importance in managerial decision making of focusing on an analysis of change or differences. One needs to analyze those factors that are affected by a decision. Factors that do not change, or that are invariant across the alternatives available to the decision maker, will not have any impact on the outcome and are irrelevant to the decision.

The tools developed in this chapter are used in all types of economic analysis, especially in managerial economics. Accordingly, they are employed throughout the remainder of the text.

## Questions

2.1  Describe the relation between the total and marginal value of a function, and explain why this relation is so important in economic analysis.

2.2  Why must a marginal curve always intersect the related average curve at either a maximum or a minimum point?

2.3  Would you expect total revenue to be maximized at an output level greater or less than the profit-maximizing output level? Why?

2.4  Does the point of minimum long-run average costs always represent the optimal activity level?

2.5  Explain why marginal profit is zero, and, hence, why total profit is maximized at the output level at which marginal revenue equals marginal cost.

2.6  Economists have long argued that if you want to tax away excess profits without affecting allocative efficiency, you should use a lump-sum tax instead of an excise or sales tax. Use the concepts developed in the chapter to support this position.

2.7  Describe the objective function and constraint in each of the two broad classes of constrained optimization problems. How will both lead to the same efficient use of economic resources?

2.8  When profit is being maximized subject to a capital constraint, what is the economic interpretation of $\lambda$, the Lagrangian multiplier?

2.9  "It is often impossible to obtain precise information about the pattern of future revenues, costs, and interest rates. Therefore, the process of economic optimization is futile." Discuss this statement.

2.10 Distinguish the incremental concept from the marginal concept.

## Problems

2.1   A. Given the output (Q) and price (P) data in the following table, calculate the related total revenue (TR), marginal revenue (MR), and average revenue (AR) figures:

| Q | P | TR | MR | AR |
|---|----|----|----|----|
| 0 | $10 | | | |
| 1 | 9 | | | |
| 2 | 8 | | | |
| 3 | 7 | | | |
| 4 | 6 | | | |
| 5 | 5 | | | |
| 6 | 4 | | | |
| 7 | 3 | | | |
| 8 | 2 | | | |
| 9 | 1 | | | |
| 10 | 0 | | | |

    B. Graph these data using "dollars" on the vertical axis and "quantity" on the horizontal axis. At what output level is revenue maximized?

    C. Why is marginal revenue less than average revenue at each price level?

2.2   A. Fill in the missing data for price ($P$), total revenue ($TR$), marginal revenue ($MR$), total cost ($TC$), marginal cost ($MC$), profit ($\pi$), and marginal profit ($M\pi$) in the following table:

| Q | P | TR | MR | TC | MC | $\pi$ | $M\pi$ |
|----|------|------|------|------|------|------|------|
| 0 | $160 | $ 0 | $ — | $ 0 | $— | $ 0 | $ — |
| 1 | 150 | 150 | 150 | 25 | 25 | 125 | $125 |
| 2 | 140 | | | 55 | 30 | | 100 |
| 3 | | 390 | | | 35 | 300 | 75 |
| 4 | | | 90 | 130 | | 350 | |
| 5 | 110 | 550 | | 175 | | | |
| 6 | | 600 | 50 | | 55 | 370 | |
| 7 | | 630 | | 290 | 60 | | −30 |
| 8 | 80 | 640 | | 355 | | 285 | |
| 9 | | | | | 75 | | −85 |
| 10 | | 600 | | 525 | | | |

    B. At what output level is profit maximized?

    C. At what output level is revenue maximized?

    D. Discuss any differences in your answers to Parts B and C.

2.3  Characterize each of the following statements as *true* or *false*, and explain your answer:

    A. If marginal revenue is less than average revenue, the demand curve will be downward sloping.

B.  Profits will be maximized when total revenue equals total cost.
C.  Given a downward-sloping demand curve and positive marginal costs, profit-maximizing firms will always sell less output at higher prices than will revenue-maximizing firms.
D.  Marginal cost must be falling for average cost to decline as output expands.
E.  Marginal profit is the difference between marginal revenue and marginal cost and will always equal zero at the profit-maximizing activity level.

2.4  Kari Christensen is a regional sales representative for Dental Laboratories, Inc. Christensen sells alloy products created from gold, silver, platinum, and other precious metals to several dental laboratories in Maine, New Hampshire, and Vermont. Christensen's goal is to maximize her total monthly commission income, which is figured at 7.5 percent of gross sales. In reviewing her monthly experience over the past year, Christensen found the following relations between days spent in each state and monthly sales generated:

| Maine | | New Hampshire | | Vermont | |
|---|---|---|---|---|---|
| Days | Gross Sales | Days | Gross Sales | Days | Gross Sales |
| 0 | $ 4,000 | 0 | $    0 | 0 | $ 2,500 |
| 1 | 10,000 | 1 | 3,500 | 1 | 5,000 |
| 2 | 15,000 | 2 | 6,500 | 2 | 7,000 |
| 3 | 19,000 | 3 | 9,000 | 3 | 8,500 |
| 4 | 22,000 | 4 | 10,500 | 4 | 9,500 |
| 5 | 24,000 | 5 | 11,500 | 5 | 10,000 |
| 6 | 25,000 | 5 | 12,000 | 6 | 10,000 |
| 7 | 25,000 | 7 | 12,500 | 7 | 10,000 |

A.  Construct a table showing Christensen's marginal sales per day in each state.
B.  If administrative duties limit Christensen to only 10 selling days per month, how should she spend them?
C.  Calculate Christensen's maximum monthly commission income.

2.5  Climate Control Devices, Inc., estimates that sales of defective thermostats cost the firm an average of $25 each for replacement or repair. An independent engineering consultant has recommended hiring quality control inspectors so that defective thermostats can be identified and corrected before shipping. The following schedule shows the expected relation between the number of quality control inspectors and the thermostat failure rate, defined in terms of the percentage of total shipments that prove to be defective.

| Number of Quality Control Inspectors | Thermostat Failure Rate (percent) |
|:---:|:---:|
| 0 | 5.0 |
| 1 | 4.0 |
| 2 | 3.2 |
| 3 | 2.6 |
| 4 | 2.2 |
| 5 | 2.0 |

The firm expects to ship 250,000 thermostats during the coming year, and quality control inspectors each command a salary of $30,000 per year.

A. Construct a table showing the marginal failure reduction (in units) and the dollar value of these reductions for each inspector hired.

B. How many inspectors should the firm hire?

C. How many inspectors would be hired if additional indirect costs (lost customer goodwill, etc.) average 30 percent of direct replacement or repair cost?

2.6 Desktop Publishing Software, Inc., develops and markets software packages for business computers. Although sales have grown rapidly during recent years, the company's management fears that a recent onslaught of new competitors may severely retard future growth opportunities. Therefore, it believes that the time has come to "get big or get out."

The marketing and accounting departments have provided management with the following monthly demand and cost information:

$$P = \$1,000 - \$1Q. \qquad TC = \$50,000 + \$100Q.$$

A. Calculate monthly quantity, price, and profit at the short-run revenue-maximizing output level.

B. Calculate these same values for the short-run profit-maximizing level of output.

C. When would short-run revenue maximization lead to long-run profit maximization?

2.7 Inventory management is an area in which the calculus of optimization is a valuable technique for decision making. Assume that usage of a specific inventory item is evenly distributed over time and that delivery of additional units is instantaneous once an order has been placed. Under these conditions, annual costs for acquisition and inventory of the item are as follows:

$$\text{Purchase Costs} = P \cdot X,$$

$$\text{Order Costs} \quad = \Theta \cdot \frac{X}{Q},$$

$$\text{Carrying Costs} = C \cdot \frac{Q}{2},$$

where $P$ is the purchase price per unit, $X$ is the total quantity used per year, $\Theta$ is the cost of placing an order, $Q$ is the quantity of the item ordered at any one point in time, and $C$ is the per-unit inventory carrying cost (insurance, storage, investment cost, etc.). Thus, annual total costs associated with this inventory item are given by the expression:

$$TC = P \cdot X + \Theta \frac{X}{Q} + C \frac{Q}{2}.$$

Inventory costs can be minimized by selecting an optimal order quantity, $Q$, sometimes called the economic order quantity, or EOQ. Develop an expression for determining the optimal EOQ by minimizing the preceding total cost function with respect to $Q$, the order quantity.

2.8  Giant Screen TV, Inc., is a San Diego–based manufacturer and distributor of customized 50-inch high-resolution television monitors for individual and commercial customers. Revenue and cost relations are:

$$TR = \$5,100Q - \$0.25Q^2.$$
$$TC = \$7,200,000 + \$600Q + \$0.2Q^2.$$

A.  Calculate output, marginal cost, average cost, price, and profit at the average cost-minimizing activity level.
B.  Calculate these values at the profit-maximizing activity level.
C.  Compare and discuss your answers to Parts A and B.

2.9  Gopher Customized Vans, Inc., installs a variety of conversion packages in vans manufactured by the major auto companies. Gopher has fixed capital and labor expenses of $1.2 million per year, and variable materials expenses average $2,000 per van conversion. Recent operating experience suggests the following annual demand relation for Gopher products:

$$Q = 1,000 - 0.1P,$$

where $Q$ is the number of van conversions (output) and $P$ is price.
A.  Calculate Gopher's profit-maximizing output, price, and profit levels.
B.  Using the Lagrangian multiplier method, calculate profit-maximizing output, price, and profit levels in light of a parts shortage

that limits Gopher's output to 300 conversions during the coming year.

C. Calculate and interpret λ, the Lagrangian multiplier.

D. Calculate the value to Gopher of having the parts shortage eliminated.

2.10 Bellview Health Center, Ltd, (BHC) is a nonprofit foundation providing medical treatment to emotionally distressed children. BHC has hired you as a business consultant to aid the foundation in the development of a hiring policy that would be consistent with its overall goal of providing the most patient service possible given scarce foundation resources. In your initial analysis, you have determined that service (Q) can be described as a function of medical (M) and social-service (S) staff input as follows:

$$Q = M + 0.5S + 0.5MS - S^2.$$

BHC's staff budget for the coming year is $1.2 million. Annual employment costs are $30,000 for each social-service staff member and $60,000 for each medical staff member.

A. Construct the Lagrangian function that you would use to determine the optimal or service-maximizing social-service/medical staff employment combination.

B. Determine the optimal combination of social-service and medical staff for BHC.

C. Solve for and interpret the Lagrangian multiplier in this problem.

D. Calculate the expected average cost per service unit during the coming period. Are average costs rising, falling, or constant?

## Selected References

Baumol, William J., and Jess Benhabib. "Chaos: Significance, Mechanism, and Economic Applications." *Journal of Economic Perspectives* 3 (Winter 1989): 77–106.

Bouldin, Richard. *Calculus With Applications to Business, Economics and Social Sciences.* New York: Saunders College Publishing, 1985.

Buede, Dennis. "Structuring Value Attributes." *Interfaces* 16 (March–April 1986): 52–68.

Burton, Richard M., John S. Chandler, and H. Peter Holzer. *Quantitative Approaches to Business Decision Making.* New York: Harper and Row, 1985.

Cook, William P. *Quantitative Methods for Management Decisions.* New York: McGraw-Hill, 1985.

Cooper, Robin. "You Need a New Cost System When . . ." *Harvard Business Review* 67 (January–February 1989): 77–82.

Diamond, Jay and Gerald Pintel. *Applied Business Arithmetic.* Englewood Cliffs, NJ: Prentice-Hall, 1985.

Eastman, Byron D. *Interpreting Mathematical Economics and Econometrics.* New York: St. Martin's Press, 1985.

Graham, Robert J. " 'Give the Kid a Number': An Essay on the Folly and Consequences of Trusting Your Data." *Interfaces* 12 (June 1982): 40–44.

Harris, D. J. *Mathematics for Business, Management and Economics.* New York: John Wiley, 1985.

Hausman, Daniel M. "Economic Methodology in a Nutshell." *Journal of Economic Perspectives* 3 (Spring 1989): 115–128.

Lapin, Lawrence L. *Quantitative Methods for Business Decisions,* 3d ed. New York: Harcourt Brace Jovanovich, 1985.

Markland, Robert E., and James R. Sweigart. *Quantitative Methods: Applications to Managerial Decision Making.* New York: John Wiley, 1987.

McFarland, Henry. "Evaluating q as an Alternative to the Rate of Return in Measuring Profitability." *Review of Economics and Statistics* 70 (November 1988): 614–622.

Morgan, Theodore. "Theory versus Empiricism in Academic Economics: Update and Comparisons." *Journal of Economic Perspectives* 2 (Fall 1988): 159–164.

Nalebuff, Barry. "Puzzles: The Other Person's Envelope Is Always Greener." *Journal of Economic Perspectives* 3 (Winter 1989): 171–182.

Powell, Warren B., Yoseff Sheffi, Kenneth S. Nickerson, Kevin Butterbaugh, and Susan Atherton, "Maximizing Profits for North American Van Lines' Truckload Division: A New Framework for Pricing and Operations." *Interfaces* 18 (January–February 1988): 21–41.

Saffran, Bernard. "Recommendations for Further Reading." *Journal of Economic Perspectives* 3 (Winter 1989): 183–188.

Simon, Herbert A., et al. "Decision Making and Problem Solving." *Interfaces* 17 (September–October 1987): 11–31.

Smith, Vernon L. "Theory, Experiment and Economics," *Journal of Economic Perspectives* 3 (Winter 1989): 151–170.

APPENDIX · 2A

# Math Analysis for Managers

This appendix is designed to provide a brief, selective treatment of mathematical terms and methods commonly employed in managerial economics. The first section covers basic properties of real numbers that will help us understand how to solve equations. It is followed by an explanation of the use of exponents and radicals. The next section describes the fundamentals of equations, their different forms, and the operations used to manipulate them. The following section explains the use of logarithms. The final section covers some basic rules for differentiating a function to find its marginal.

# PROPERTIES OF REAL NUMBERS

In this section, we will review some important properties of real numbers. These properties are basic to our understanding of how to manipulate numerical values.

## Transitive Property

If $X$, $Y$, and $Z$ are real numbers, then:

$$\text{if } X = Y \text{ and } Y = Z, X = Z.$$

This means that if two numbers are both equal to a third number, they are equal to each other. For example, if $X = Y$ and $Y = 5$, then $X = 5$.

## Commutative Properties

If $X$ and $Y$ are real numbers, then:

$$X + Y = Y + X \text{ and } XY = YX.$$

This means that we can add or multiply numbers in any order. For example, $2 + 3 = 3 + 2 = 5$ and $2(3) = 3(2) = 6$.

## Associative Properties

If $X$, $Y$, and $Z$ are real numbers, then:

$$X + (Y + Z) = (X + Y) + Z \text{ and } X(YZ) = (XY)Z.$$

This means that for purposes of addition or multiplication, numbers can be grouped in any convenient manner. For example, $3 + (4 + 5) = (3 + 4) + 5 = 12$ and $3(4 \cdot 5) = (3 \cdot 4)5 = 60$.

## Distributive Properties

If $X$, $Y$, and $Z$ are real numbers, then:

$$X(Y + Z) = XY + XZ \text{ and } (X + Y)Z = XZ + YZ.$$

This means that within the context of an equation, the order of addition or multiplication is immaterial; that is, we can first multiply and then add, or vice versa. For example, $3(4 + 5) = 3(4) + 3(5) = 27$ and $3(4 + 5) = 3(9) = 27$.

## Inverse Properties

For each real number $X$, there is a number $-X$, called the *additive inverse* or *negative* of $X$, where:

$$X + (-X) = 0.$$

For example, since $5 + (-5) = 0$, the additive inverse of 5 is $-5$. Similarly, the additive inverse of $-5$ is 5. For each real number $X$, there also is a unique number, $X^{-1}$, called the *multiplicative inverse* or *reciprocal* of $X$, where:

$$X \cdot \frac{1}{X} = \frac{X}{X} = 1.$$

The expression $1/X$ can be written $X^{-1}$, so $X(1/X) = X \cdot X^{-1} = X/X = 1$. For example, $4(1/4) = 4 \cdot 4^{-1} = 4/4 = 1$. This property holds for all real numbers except 0, for which the reciprocal is undefined.

## EXPONENTS AND RADICALS

Exponents and radicals can be thought of as abbreviations in the language of mathematics. Consider, for example, the following product:

$$X \cdot X \cdot X = X^3.$$

In general, for a positive integer $n$, $X^n$ is an abbreviation for the product of $n$ $X$s. In $X^n$, the letter $X$ is called the *base* and the letter $n$ the *exponent* (or *power*). If $Y = X^n$, $X$ is called the $n$th root of $Y$. For example, $2 \cdot 2 \cdot 2 = 2^3 = 8$ and 2 is the third root of 8. Any number raised to the first power is itself, $X^1 = X$ (for example, $7^1 = 7$), and any number raised to the zero power is one—that is, $X^0 = 1$ for $X \neq 0$ ($0^0$ is not defined). Some numbers do not have an $n$th root that is a real number. For example, since the second power, or square, of any real number is nonnegative, there is no real number that is the second, or square, root of $-9$.

We also write:

$$\underbrace{\frac{1}{X \cdot X \cdot X \ldots \cdot X}}_{n \text{ factors}} = \frac{1}{X^n} = X^{-n}.$$

This implies that $1/X^{-n} = X^n$. In general, whenever we move a number raised to a power from the numerator (top) to the denominator (bottom) of an expression, the sign of the exponent, or power, is multiplied by $-1$, and vice-versa. For example, $1/(2 \cdot 2 \cdot 2) = 1/2^3 = 2^{-3} = 0.125$.

The symbol $\sqrt[n]{X}$ is called a *radical*. Here $n$ is the *index*, $\sqrt{\phantom{X}}$ is the *radical sign*, and $X$ is the *radicand*. For convenience, the index is usually omitted in the case of principal square roots, and we write $\sqrt{X}$ instead of $\sqrt[2]{X}$. Therefore, $\sqrt{16} = \sqrt[2]{16} = 4$. If $X$ is positive and $m$ and $n$ are integers where $n$ is also positive, then:

$$\sqrt[n]{X^m} = X^{m/n}.$$

For example, $\sqrt{2^4} = 2^{4/2} = 2^2 = 4$. Similarly, $\sqrt{9} = 9^{1/2} = 3$.

The basic rule for multiplication is $X^m \cdot X^n = X^{m+n}$ and for division is $X^m/X^n = X^{m-n}$. For example, $3^3 \cdot 3^2 = 3^{3+2} = 3^5 = 243$, and $3^3/3^2 = 3^{3-2} = 3^1 = 3$.

# EQUATIONS

A statement that two algebraic expressions are equal is called an *equation*. The two expressions that make up an equation are called its *members* or *sides*. They are separated by the symbol =, which is called an *equality* or *equal sign*. In solving an equation or finding its roots, we often manipulate the original equation in order to generate another equation that will be somewhat easier to solve.

## Equivalent Operations

There are three operations that can be performed on equations without changing their solution values; hence the original and subsequent equations are called *equivalent*. These operations are:

**Addition (Subtraction) Operation.** Equivalence is maintained when adding (subtracting) the same variable to (from) both sides of an equation, where the variable is the same as that occurring in the original equation. For example, if $6X = 20 + 2X$, subtracting $2X$ from both sides gives the equivalent equation $4X = 20$.

**Multiplication (Division) Operation.** Equivalence is maintained when multiplying (dividing) both sides of an equation by the same nonzero constant. For example, if $4X = 20$, dividing both sides by 4 gives the equivalent equation $X = 5$.

**Replacement Operation.** Equivalence is maintained when replacing either side of an equation with an equivalent expression. For example, if $X(X - 4) = 3$, replacing the left side with the equivalent expression $X^2 - 4X$ gives an equivalent equation $X^2 - 4X = 3$.

It is worth emphasizing that each of these operations can be applied to any equation with the effect that the resulting equation will be mathematically identical to the original.

Equations may take a wide variety of functional forms. Three of the more frequently encountered are described next.

## Linear Equations

An equation *linear* in the variable $X$ can be written:

$$aX + b = 0,$$

where $a$ and $b$ are constants and $a$ is called the slope *coefficient* and $b$ the *intercept*.

A linear equation is sometimes referred to as a *first-degree equation* or *equation of degree one*. To solve the linear equation $2X + 6 = 14$, we apply the subtraction and division operations to find $2X = 8$ and $X = 4$.

## Quadratic Equations

An equation *quadratic* in the variable $X$ can be written:

$$aX^2 + bX + c = 0,$$

where $a$, $b$ and $c$ are constants and $a \neq 0$. Here $a$ and $b$ are slope coefficients and $c$ is the intercept.

A quadratic equation is sometimes referred to as a *second-degree equation* or *equation of degree two*. Whereas linear equations have only one root, quadratic equations sometimes have two different roots. The solutions to quadratic equations are easily found through application of the *quadratic* formula. If $aX^2 + bX + c = 0$ and $a$, $b$, and $c$ are constants where $a \neq 0$, then:

$$X = \frac{-b \pm \sqrt{b^2 - 4ac}}{2a}.$$

The solutions for the values of $X$ are called the *roots* of the quadratic equation. For example, if $2X^2 - 15X + 18 = 0$, then $X = \left( +15 \pm \sqrt{225 - 4(2)(18)} \right)/2(2) = (15 \pm 9)/4 = 6$ and $1.5$. In many instances, one or both of the solved values for a quadratic equation will be negative. If the quadratic equation is a profit function and $X$ is output, for example, any root $X < 0$, implying negative output, will be mathematically correct but meaningless from an economic standpoint. Therefore, when applying the quadratic formula to problems in managerial economics, we must use judgment to identify those solution values that are both mathematically correct and economically relevant.

## Multiplicative Equations

An equation *multiplicative* in the variables $X$ and $Z$ can be written:

$$Y = aX^{b_1}Z^{b_2},$$

where $a$ is the constant and $b_1$ and $b_2$ are exponents.

For example, $Y = 5X^2Z^3$, where $X = 3$ and $Z = 4$, has the solution $Y = 5(3^2)(4^3) = 5(9)(64) = 2,880$. Multiplicative equations are often employed in managerial economics, particularly in demand, production, and cost analyses.

## Exponential Functions

Certain multiplicative functions are referred to as *exponential functions*. The function $Y = b^X$, where $b > 0$, $b \neq 1$, and $X$ is any real number, is referred to as an *exponential function to the base b*. Exponential functions often are constructed using $e$, the Naperian Constant $(= 2.71828\cdots)$ as a base. Thus, for example, the equation $Y = e^2$ means $Y = (2.71828\cdots)^2$. Although $e$ may seem a curious number to adopt as the base in an exponential function, it is usefully employed in economic studies of compound growth or decline.

## Logarithmic Functions

For the purposes of economic analysis, multiplicative or exponential relations often are transformed into a linear *logarithmic form*, where:

$$Y = \log_b X \text{ if and only if } X = b^Y.$$

Here $Y$ is a *logarithmic function to the base b*. We say that $Y = \log_b X$ is the logarithmic form of the exponential $X = b^Y$. For example, $\log_{10} 1{,}000 = 3$ is the logarithmic equivalent of the exponential $10^3 = 1{,}000$. For much of the work in managerial economics, logarithms are written using either the base 10, called *common logarithms*, or the base $e$ (= Naperian Constant = 2.71828···), called *natural logarithms*. Natural logarithms typically are denoted by the notation "ln" rather than "$\log_e$."

Some important basic properties of logarithms are:

**Product Property.**   The logarithm of a product is the sum of logarithms:

$$\ln XY = \ln X + \ln Y.$$

For example, $\ln 6 = \ln(3 \cdot 2) = \ln 3 + \ln 2 = 1.099 + 0.693 = 1.792$. It is important to note that the logarithm of a sum is *not* the sum of logarithms.

**Quotient Property.**   The logarithm of a quotient is the difference of logarithms:

$$\ln \frac{X}{Y} = \ln X - \ln Y.$$

For example, $\ln 1.5 = \ln 3/2 = \ln 3 - \ln 2 = 1.099 - 0.693 = 0.406$. Here note that the logarithm of a quotient is *not* the quotient of logarithms.

**Power Property.**   The logarithm of a number $X$ raised to the exponent $n$, $X^n$, is the exponent times the logarithm of $X$:

$$\ln X^n = n \ln X.$$

For example, $\ln 9 = \ln 3^2 = 2 \ln 3 = 2(1.099) = 2.198$.

Using the properties of logarithms, we see that there is a simple logarithmic transformation for any multiplicative or exponential function. For example, the logarithm transformation of the multiplicative equation $Y = 5X^2Z^3$ can be written $\ln Y = \ln 5 + 2 \ln X + 3 \ln Z$. Here we have used the natural logarithm of $X$, although the transformation would be the same using common logs or logs to any other base.

It is important to recognize the symmetry between the logarithmic and exponential functions. It is an important property of each that:

$$\ln e^X = X \text{ and } e^{\ln X} = X,$$

that is, the logarithm to the base $e$ of the number $e$ raised to the power $X$ equals $X$. Similarly, the number $e$ raised to the power $\ln X$ equals $X$. For example, $\ln e^1 = 1$ and $e^{\ln 1} = 1$. This means that any number or equation transformed into logarithmic form through use of logarithms can be converted back into original form through exponential transformation. For example, recall from our earlier discussion that the multiplicative equation $Y = 5X^2Z^3$ has the logarithmic equivalent $\ln Y = \ln 5 + 2 \ln X + 3 \ln Z$. It follows that if $X = 3$ and $Z = 4$, then $Y = 5(3^2)(4^3) = 5(9)(64) = 2,880$ and $\ln Y = \ln 5 + 2 \ln 3 + 3 \ln 4 = 1.609 + 2.197 + 4.159 = 7.965$. Equivalence requires that $\ln 2,880 = 7.965$ and $e^{7.965} = 2,880$, which is indeed the case.

The practical relevance of this symmetry between logarithms and exponential functions is that, for example, a multiplicative demand relation can be analyzed in linear logarithmic form using widely available computer-based regression packages and converted back into original form through exponential transformation for purposes of numerical evaluation.

# RULES FOR DIFFERENTIATING A FUNCTION

Determining the derivative of a function is not a particularly difficult task; it simply involves applying a basic formula to the function. This section presents the basic formulas or rules for differentiation. Proofs are omitted here, but they can be found in any introductory calculus textbook.

## Constants

The derivative of a constant is always zero; that is, if $Y$ is a constant,

$$\frac{dY}{dX} = 0.$$

This situation is graphed in Figure 2A.1 for the example $Y = 2$. Since $Y$ is defined as a constant, its value does not vary as $X$ changes and, hence, $dY/dX$ must be zero.

## Powers

The derivative of a power function such as $Y = aX^b$, where $a$ and $b$ are constants, is equal to the exponent $b$ multiplied by the coefficient $a$ times the variable $X$ raised to the $b - 1$ power:

$$Y = aX^b$$

$$\frac{dY}{dX} = b \cdot a \cdot X^{(b-1)}.$$

For example, given the function:

$$Y = 2X^3,$$

then

$$\frac{dY}{dX} = 3 \cdot 2 \cdot X^{(3-1)}$$

$$= 6X^2.$$

■ Figure 2A.1
## Graph of a Constant Function: *Y* = Constant; *dY/dX* = 0

If the value of $Y$ does not vary with changes in $X$, then $\Delta Y/\Delta X = 0$.

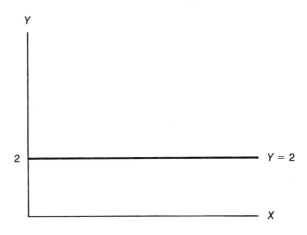

Two further examples of power functions should clarify this rule. The derivative of the function $Y = X^3$ is given as:

$$\frac{dY}{dX} = 3 \cdot X^2.$$

The exponent, 3, is multiplied by the implicit coefficient, 1, and in turn by the variable, $X$, raised to the second power.

Finally, the derivative of the function $Y = 0.5X$ is:

$$\frac{dY}{dX} = 1 \cdot 0.5 \cdot X^{1-1} = 1 \cdot 0.5 \cdot X^0 = 0.5.$$

The implicit exponent, 1, is multiplied by the coefficient, 0.5, times the variable, $X$, raised to the zero power. Since any number raised to the zero power equals 1, the result is 0.5.

A graph may help clarify the power function concept. In Figure 2A.2, the last two power functions given previously, $Y = X^3$ and $Y = 0.5X$, are graphed. Consider first $Y = 0.5X$. The derivative of this function, $dY/dX = 0.5$, is a constant, indicating that the slope of the function is a constant. This can be readily seen from the graph. The derivative measures the *rate of change*. If the rate of change is constant, as it must be if the basic function is linear, the derivative of the function must be constant. The second function, $Y = X^3$, rises at an increasing rate as $X$ increases. The derivative of the function, $dY/dX = 3X^2$, also increases as $X$ becomes larger, indicating that the slope of the function is increasing or that the rate of change is increasing.

■ Figure 2A.2
## Graphs of Power Functions

The derivative of the linear function $Y = 0.5X$ is constant. The derivative of the nonlinear function $Y = X^3$ rises as $X$ increases.

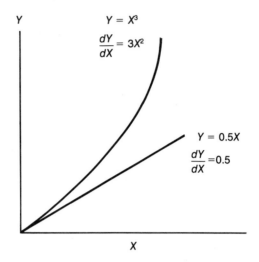

## Sums and Differences

The following notation is used throughout the remainder of this section to express a number of other important rules of differentiation:

$U = g(X)$: $U$ is an unspecified function, g, of $X$.

$V = h(X)$: $V$ is an unspecified function, h, of $X$.

The derivative of a sum (difference) is equal to the sum (difference) of the derivatives of the individual terms. Thus, if $Y = U + V$, then:

$$\frac{dY}{dX} = \frac{dU}{dX} + \frac{dV}{dX}.$$

For example, if $U = g(X) = 2X^2$, $V = h(X) = -X^3$, and $Y = U + V = 2X^2 - X^3$, then:

$$\frac{dY}{dX} = 4X - 3X^2.$$

Here the derivative of the first term, $2X^2$, is found to be $4X$ by the power rule; the derivative of the second term, $-X^3$, is found to be $-3X^2$ by that same rule; and the derivative of the total function is the sum of the derivatives of the parts.

Consider a second example of this rule. If $Y = 300 + 5X + 2X^2$, then:

$$\frac{dY}{dX} = 0 + 5 + 4X.$$

The derivative of 300 is 0 by the constant rule; the derivative of 5X is 5 by the power rule; and the derivative of $2X^2$ is 4X by the power rule.

## Products

The derivative of the product of two expressions is equal to the sum of the first term multiplied by the derivative of the second *plus* the second term times the derivative of the first. Thus, if $Y = U \cdot V$, then:

$$\frac{dY}{dX} = U \cdot \frac{dV}{dX} + V \cdot \frac{dU}{dX}.$$

For example, if $Y = 3X^2(3 - X)$, then, letting $U = 3X^2$ and $V = (3 - X)$, we get:

$$\frac{dY}{dX} = 3X^2 \left(\frac{dV}{dX}\right) + (3 - X) \left(\frac{dU}{dX}\right)$$

$$= 3X^2(-1) + (3 - X)(6X)$$

$$= -3X^2 + 18X - 6X^2$$

$$= 18X - 9X^2.$$

The first factor, $3X^2$, is multiplied by the derivative of the second, $-1$, and added to the second factor, $3 - X$, times the derivative of the first, $6X$. Simplifying the expression results in the final expression shown above.

## Quotients

The derivative of the quotient of two expressions is equal to the denominator multiplied by the derivative of the numerator *minus* the numerator times the derivative of the denominator, all divided by the square of the denominator. Thus, if $Y = U/V$, then:

$$\frac{dY}{dX} = \frac{V \cdot \dfrac{dU}{dX} - U \cdot \dfrac{dV}{dX}}{V^2}.$$

For example, if $U = 2X - 3$ and $V = 6X^2$, then:

$$Y = \frac{2X - 3}{6X^2}$$

and

$$\frac{dY}{dX} = \frac{6X^2 \cdot 2 - (2X - 3) 12X}{36X^4}$$

$$= \frac{12X^2 - 24X^2 + 36X}{36X^4}$$

$$= \frac{36X - 12X^2}{36X^4}$$

$$= \frac{3 - X}{3X^3}.$$

The denominator, $6X^2$, is multiplied by the derivative of the numerator, 2. Subtracted from this is the numerator, $2X - 3$, times the derivative of the denominator, $12X$. The result is then divided by the square of the denominator, $36X^4$. Algebraic reduction results in the final expression of the derivative.

## Logarithmic Functions

The derivative of a logarithmic function $Y = \ln X$ is given by the expression:

$$\frac{dY}{dX} = \frac{d \ln X}{dX} = \frac{1}{X}.$$

This also implies that if $Y = \ln X$, then $dY = (1/X)dX = dX/X$. Since $dX$ is the change in $X$ by definition, $dX/X$ is a percentage change in $X$. Derivatives of logarithmic functions have great practical relevance in managerial economics given the prevalence of multiplicative (and hence linear in the logarithms) equations used to describe demand, production, and cost relations. For example, the expression $Y = aX^b$ has an equivalent logarithmic function $\ln Y = \ln a + b \ln X$, where $d \ln Y/d \ln X = dY/Y/dX/X = b$. Here $b$ is called the *elasticity* of $Y$ with respect to $X$, since it reflects the percentage effect on $Y$ of a 1 percent change in $X$. The concept of elasticity is introduced and extensively examined in Chapter 3 and used throughout the remaining chapters.

## Function of a Function (Chain Rule)

The derivative of a function of a function is found as follows: If $Y = f(U)$, where $U = g(X)$, then:

$$\frac{dY}{dX} = \frac{dY}{dU} \cdot \frac{dU}{dX}.$$

For example, if $Y = 2U - U^2$ and $U = 2X^3$, we find $dY/dX$ as follows:

**Step 1:**

$$\frac{dY}{dU} = 2 - 2U.$$

Substituting for $U$, we have:

$$\frac{dY}{dU} = 2 - 2(2X^3)$$

$$= 2 - 4X^3.$$

**Step 2:**

$$\frac{dU}{dX} = 6X^2.$$

**Step 3:**

$$\frac{dY}{dX} = \frac{dY}{dU} \cdot \frac{dU}{dX}$$

$$= (2 - 4X^3) \cdot 6X^2$$

$$= 12X^2 - 24X^5.$$

Further examples of this rule should indicate its usefulness in obtaining derivatives of many functions.

**Example 1:** $Y = \sqrt{X^2 - 1}$.

Let $U = X^2 - 1$. Then $Y = \sqrt{U} = U^{1/2}$.

$$\frac{dY}{dU} = \frac{1}{2}U^{-1/2}$$

$$= \frac{1}{2U^{1/2}}.$$

Substituting $X^2 - 1$ for $U$ in the derivative results in:

$$\frac{dY}{dU} = \frac{1}{2(X^2 - 1)^{1/2}}.$$

Since $U = X^2 - 1$,

$$\frac{dU}{dX} = 2X.$$

Using the function of a function rule, $dY/dX = dY/dU \cdot dU/dX$, so:

$$\frac{dY}{dX} = \frac{1}{2(X^2 - 1)^{1/2}} \cdot 2X$$

$$= \frac{X}{\sqrt{X^2 - 1}}.$$

**Example 2:** $Y = \dfrac{1}{X^2 - 2}$.

Let $U = X^2 - 2$. Then $Y = 1/U$, and, using the quotient rule, we find:

$$\frac{dY}{dU} = \frac{U \cdot 0 - 1 \cdot 1}{U^2}$$

$$= -\frac{1}{U^2}.$$

Substituting $(X^2 - 2)$ for $U$, we obtain:

$$\frac{dY}{dU} = -\frac{1}{(X^2 - 2)^2}.$$

Since $U = X^2 - 2$,

$$\frac{dU}{dX} = 2X.$$

Therefore;

$$\frac{dY}{dX} = \frac{dY}{dU} \cdot \frac{dU}{dX} = -\frac{1}{(X^2 - 2)^2} \cdot 2X$$

$$= -\frac{2X}{(X^2 - 2)^2}.$$

**Example 3:**   $Y = (2X + 3)^2$.

Let $U = 2X + 3$. Then $Y = U^2$ and

$$\frac{dY}{dU} = 2U.$$

Since $U = 2X + 3$,

$$\frac{dY}{dU} = 2(2X + 3)$$

$$= 4X + 6$$

and

$$\frac{dU}{dX} = 2.$$

Thus,

$$\frac{dY}{dX} = \frac{dY}{dU} \cdot \frac{dU}{dX} = (4X + 6)2$$

$$= 8X + 12.$$

# Demand and Supply

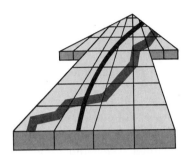

**S**uccessful operation of any economic organization requires a thorough understanding of demand and supply conditions for its products. In economic terms, demand refers to the amount of a product that people are willing and able to buy under a given set of conditions. Need or desire is a necessary component but must be accompanied by financial capability before an economic demand is created. Thus, economic demand requires potential buyers with a desire to use or possess something and the financial ability to acquire it.

Similarly, supply is the amount of a good or service that firms will make available for sale under a given set of conditions. Just as demand requires a desire to purchase combined with the economic resources to do so, supply requires a desire to sell along with the economic capability to bring a product to market.

Combining the concepts of demand and supply allows us to develop a framework for analyzing the interaction of buyers and sellers. Using that framework, we examine the determination of price and activity levels in economic markets and the conditions required for market equilibrium—a state in which the quantities demanded and supplied of a good or service are in perfect balance.

Comparative statics analysis is used in our study of economic markets. This analysis involves comparisons of market equilibrium conditions before and after a change in one or more factors underlying demand or supply. Comparative statics analysis provides a very useful framework for evaluating the consequences of changes in market demand and supply conditions.

The concepts of demand, supply, and equilibrium provide a basis for analyzing the interactions of buyers and sellers in the markets for all goods and services. The overview presented in this chapter provides a useful framework for our more detailed study of demand and supply concepts in Chapters 4 through 12.

The study of demand and supply is also important because together they determine the market structure and level of competition in an industry. In Chapters 11, 12, 13, and 14, which examine market structure, pricing, and the role of government in the market economy, the importance of demand and supply as determinants of business practice and public policy is considered.

# THE BASIS FOR DEMAND

**demand**

**The total quantity customers are willing and able to purchase.**

**Demand** is the quantity of a good or service that customers are willing and able to purchase during a specified period under a given set of conditions. The time frame might be an hour, a day, a year, or any other period. The conditions that must be considered include the price of the good in question, prices and availability of related goods, expectations of price changes, consumer incomes, consumer tastes and preferences, advertising expenditures, and so on. The amount of the product that consumers are prepared to purchase, its demand, depends on all these factors.

For managerial decision making, the primary focus is on market demand. Market demand, however, is merely the aggregate of individual, or personal, demands, and insight into market demand relations is gained by understanding the nature of individual demand.

Individual demand is determined by two factors: (1) the value associated with acquiring and using the good or service and (2) the ability to acquire it. Both are required for effective individual demand. Desire without purchasing power may lead to want but not to demand.

**direct demand**

**Demand for consumption products.**

**utility**

**Value.**

There are two basic models of individual demand. One, known as the theory of consumer behavior, relates to the **direct demand** for personal consumption products. This model is appropriate for analyzing individual demand for goods and services that directly satisfy consumer desires. In this model the value or worth of a good or service, its **utility,** is the prime determinant of individual demand. Individuals are viewed as attempting to maximize the total utility or satisfaction provided by the goods and services they acquire and consume. This optimization process requires that consumers consider the marginal utility (gain in satisfaction) of acquiring additional units of a given product or of acquiring one product as opposed to another. Product characteristics, individual preferences (tastes), and the ability to pay are all important determinants of direct demand.

Other goods and services are acquired not for their direct consumption value but because they are important inputs in the manufacture and distribution of products. The output of engineers, production workers, salespersons, managers, lawyers, consultants, office business machines, production facilities and equipment, natural resources, and commercial airplanes are all examples of goods and services demanded not for direct final personal consumption but rather for their use in providing other goods and services. We say that their demand is *derived* from the demand for the products they are used to provide. Thus, the demand for all inputs used by a firm is **derived demand.**

**derived demand**

Demand for inputs used in production.

The demand for mortgage money is an example. The quantity of mortgage credit demanded is not determined directly; rather, it is derived from the more fundamental demand for housing. Similarly, the demand for air transportation to major resort areas is not a direct demand but rather is derived from the demand for recreation. The demand for all producers' goods and services used in the manufacture of products for final consumption is derived. The aggregate demand for consumption goods and services determines demand for the capital equipment, materials, labor, and energy used to manufacture them. For example, the demands for steel, aluminum, and plastics are all derived demands, as are the demands for machine tools and labor. None of these producers' goods are demanded because of their direct value to consumers but because of the role they play in the production of final goods and services.

As one would expect, the demand for producers' goods and services is closely related to the demand for the final products they make. Therefore, an examination of final product demand is an important part of the demand analysis for intermediate, or producers' goods.

For products whose demand is derived rather than direct, the theory of the firm provides the basis for analyzing individual demand. Demand for these goods stems from their value in the manufacture and sale of other products. They have value because their employment has the potential to generate profits. Key components in the determination of derived demand are the marginal benefits and marginal costs associated with employing a given input or factor of production. The amount of any good or service employed will rise when its marginal benefit, measured in terms of the value of resulting output, is greater than the marginal costs of employing the input, measured in terms of wages, interest, raw material costs, or related expenses. Conversely, the amount of any input employed in production will fall when the resulting marginal benefits are less than the marginal cost of employment. In short, derived demand is related to the profitability of employing a good or service.

Regardless of whether a good or service is demanded by individuals for final consumption (direct demand) or as an input factor used in providing other goods and services (derived demand), the fundamentals of economic analysis provide a basis for investigating the characteristics of demand. For final consumption products, utility maximization as developed by the theory of consumer behavior explains the basis for direct demand. For inputs used in the production of other products, profit maximization provides the underlying rationale for derived demand. Since both demand models are based on optimization (they differ only in the nature of their objectives), it should come as no surprise that, while various characteristics that affect demand may differ, the funda-

## 3.1 **Managerial Application**
Demand and Supply in the Soviet Economy

Perhaps the most important characteristic of a market-based economy is the decentralization of production and operating decisions. No centralized government agency or industry trade association makes decisions about what types of products should be produced or the quantity or quality of output. Instead, these decisions are made by individual firms based on their perceptions of consumer preferences and market opportunities. The price consumers are willing to pay for established goods and services is a signal to which firms respond through their production and operating decisions. Firms that are able to offer goods and services in a relatively attractive fashion in terms of price, quantity, and quality tend to grow and prosper. Similarly, firms that successfully anticipate changes in consumer preferences reap substantial economic rewards. Those that

do not tend to fall by the wayside. In other words, a market-based economy relies only on the profit motive as a means for assuring the production of the types and quantities of goods and services that consumers want and need (demand). As economist Adam Smith said more than 200 years ago, by acting in their own self-interests, individuals are moved as if by an "invisible hand" to promote the common welfare.

At first, a market-based economy might appear to be a risky and costly means for organizing economic activity. When compared to the cost and risk of centralized economic planning, however, the virtues of the market system become readily apparent. In recognition of these advantages, the Soviet Union has recently made substantial efforts to modify its form of state planning to include some of the features of a market system.

*continued*

See: Peter Galuszka, "The Paradox of *Perestroika*: A Raging Black Market," *Business Week*, June 5, 1989, 66–70.

mental relations are essentially the same. This means that the principles of managerial economics, and particularly the principles of optimal resource use, provide a basis for understanding demand by both firms and consumers.

## THE MARKET DEMAND FUNCTION

**demand function**

The relation between demand and all factors that influence its level.

The market **demand function** for a product is a statement of the relation between the aggregate quantity demanded and *all* factors that affect this quantity. Written in general functional form, the demand function may be expressed as:

**Managerial Application** *continued*

The Soviet economy is apparently in a grave state because oil revenues from the 1970s and early 1980s were used primarily to fund purchases of grain and other consumer products rather than to finance factories, plant and equipment, and other productive investments. As a result, the country appears to have few economic resources to fund the retooling of its factories that is necessary before high-quality consumer products can be made widely available.

According to Leonid Abalkin, principal economic advisor to Soviet prime minister Mikhail Gorbachev, high rates of economic growth have often been achieved in the Soviet Union by making larger volumes of products that no one wanted to purchase. He called this "working for the storehouse." Of course, the value of such economic growth is questionable. A significant challenge for Soviet leaders is to create means by which the preferences of Soviet consumers for high-quality products more readily influence production and operating decisions.

As a first step in building their economic capabilities, the Soviets plan on a more extensive use of the pricing system. In an effort to limit demand and expand supplies,

prices will be allowed to rise for such scarce and highly valued commodities as meat and dairy products. The intent is to establish for Soviet consumers the links between greater demand, higher prices, and more plentiful supply. On the supply side, the economic returns to Soviet enterprises and their employees are to be more closely linked to performance measured in terms of satisfying customer demand for quality products and cost efficiency. In fact, Abalkin has even argued that Soviet enterprises must face the very real threat of bankruptcy as an incentive to operate more efficiently

Of course, the human disruption caused by bankruptcy, along with other economic costs, is often substantial. Economic losses associated with lost production because of work stoppages, retraining and relocation costs for managers and other workers, and expenses associated with factory retooling are obvious social costs incurred when bankruptcy takes place. What the Soviets have come to realize, however, is that the economic costs of bankruptcy are less than the costs of production errors made when the forces of demand and supply are ignored.

$$\begin{matrix}\text{Quantity of} \\ \text{Product } X \\ \text{Demanded}\end{matrix} = Q_X = \begin{matrix}f(\text{Price of } X, \text{ Prices of Related} \\ \text{Goods, Expectations of Price} \\ \text{Changes, Consumer Incomes, Tastes} \\ \text{and Preferences, Advertising} \\ \text{Expenditures, and So On}).\end{matrix} \qquad \textbf{3.1}$$

The generalized demand function expressed in Equation 3.1 lists variables that influence demand. For use in managerial decision making, the demand function must be made explicit. That is, the relation between quantity and each of the demand-determining variables must be clearly and explicitly specified. To illustrate what is involved, assume that we are analyzing the demand for automobiles and that the demand function has been specified as follows:

$$Q = a_1 P + a_2 Y + a_3 \, Pop + a_4 \, i + a_5 \, A. \qquad \textbf{3.2}$$

This equation states that the number of automobiles demanded during a given year, $Q$, is a linear function of the average price of cars, $P$; average per capita disposable income, $Y$; population, $Pop$; average interest rate on car loans (in percent), $i$; and advertising expenditures, $A$. The terms $a_1, a_2, \ldots, a_5$ are called the *parameters* of the demand function. We will examine procedures for estimating parameter values, together with indicators of our confidence in these estimates, in Chapter 4. For now we will simply assume that we know these parameters and that the demand function accurately indicates the quantity of the product demanded.[1] Substituting a set of assumed parameter values into Equation 3.2 we obtain:

$$Q = -2{,}500 \, P + 1{,}000 \, Y + 0.05 \, Pop - 1{,}000{,}000 \, i + 0.05 \, A. \qquad \textbf{3.3}$$

Equation 3.3 states that automobile demand falls by 2,500 units for each $1 increase in the average price charged; it increases by 1,000 units for each $1 increase in per capita disposable income; it increases by 0.05 units for each additional person in the population; it decreases by 1 million units for every 1-percent rise in interest rates; and it increases by 0.05 units for each $1 spent on advertising.

If we multiply each parameter in Equation 3.3 by the value of the related variable and then sum these products, we will have the estimated demand for automobiles for a given year. Table 3.1 illustrates this process, showing that the estimated demand for autos will be 10 million units, assuming the stated values of the independent variables.

## Industry Demand Versus Firm Demand

Market demand functions can be specified for an entire industry or for an individual firm, though somewhat different variables would typically be used in each case. Most importantly, variables representing competitors' actions would be stressed in firm demand functions. For example, a firm's demand function would include competitors' prices and advertising expenditures. Demand for the firm's product would be negatively related to its own price but positively related to the prices charged by competing firms. Similarly, demand for the firm's products would typically increase with its own advertising expenditures, but it could increase or decrease with additional advertising by other firms.

---

[1] If all the variables that influence demand are not included in the demand function, or if the parameters are not correctly specified, the equation will not predict demand accurately, sales forecasts will be in error, and incorrect expansion and operating decisions are likely. Obviously, the more accurate the firm's demand estimates, the lower its risk. Thus, a close relation exists between risk and the ability to estimate the demand function accurately. These points are elaborated on in Chapter 5, where techniques for estimating demand functions are developed.

■ Table 3.1
## Estimating Industry Demand for Automobiles Using a Hypothetical Demand Function

| Independent Variable (1) | Parameter (2) | Estimated Value of the Variable for the Coming Year (3) | Estimated Total Demand (4) = (2) × (3) |
|---|---|---|---|
| Average price (P) | −2,500 | $12,000 | −30,000,000 |
| Disposable income (Y) | 1,000 | $23,500 | 23,500,000 |
| Population (Pop) | 0.05 | 230,000,000 | 11,500,000 |
| Average interest rate (in percent) (i) | −1,000,000 | 10% | −10,000,000 |
| Advertising expenditures (A) | 0.05 | $300,000,000 | 15,000,000 |
| | | Total demand = | 10,000,000 |

In most instances, the parameters for specific variables also differ in industry versus firm demand functions. To illustrate, consider the positive influence of population on the demand for Ford automobiles as opposed to automobiles in general. While the effect is positive in each instance, the parameter value in the Ford demand function will be smaller than that in the industry demand function. Only if Ford had 100 percent of the market—that is, if Ford *was* the industry—would we expect the parameters for firm and industry demand to be identical.

Since firm and industry demand functions differ, different models, or equations, must be estimated for analyzing these two levels of demand. This matter need not concern us here, however, because the demand concepts developed in this chapter apply to both firm and industry demand functions.

## THE DEMAND CURVE

**demand curve**

The relation between price and quantity, holding constant the effects of other demand-determining variables.

The demand function specifies the relation between the quantity demanded and all variables that determine demand. The **demand curve** is the part of the demand function that expresses the relation between the price charged for a product and the quantity demanded, *holding constant the effects of all other variables.* Frequently, a demand curve is shown in the form of a graph, and all variables in the demand function except the price and quantity of the product itself are held fixed at specified levels. In the automobile demand function given in Equation 3.3, for example, we must hold income, population, interest rates, and advertising expenditures constant to identify the demand curve with which to examine the relation between automobile prices and the quantity demanded.

To illustrate this process, consider the relation depicted in Equation 3.3 and Table 3.1. Assuming that income, population, interest rates, and advertising expenditures are all held constant at their Table 3.1 values, we can express the relation between the quantity demanded and price as:

$$Q = -2,500P + 1,000(23,500) + 0.05(230,000,000)$$
$$-1,000,000(10) + 0.05(300,000,000)$$
$$= 40,000,000 - 2,500P. \hspace{2cm} \textbf{3.4}$$

Equation 3.4, which represents the demand curve for automobiles given specified values for all of the other variables in the demand function, is presented graphically in Figure 3.1. As is typical, we see that a reduction in price increases the quantity demanded and, conversely, an increase in price decreases the quantity demanded. The slope coefficient in Equation 3.4 ($-2,500$) means that a $1 increase in the average price of automobiles would reduce the quantity demanded by 2,500 units. Similarly, a $1 decrease in the average price of automobiles would increase quantity demanded by 2,500 units.

## Relation between Demand Curve and Demand Function

The relation between the demand curve and the demand function is important and worth considering in somewhat greater detail. Figure 3.2 shows three demand curves for automobiles. Each curve is constructed in the same manner as that represented in Equation 3.4 and then graphed in Figure 3.1. In fact, $D_2$ is the same automobile demand curve depicted in Equation 3.4 and Figure 3.1. If $D_2$ is the appropriate demand curve, then 10 million automobiles can be sold at an average price of $12,000, and 15 million automobiles can be sold at an average price of $10,000, but only 5 million automobiles can be sold at an average price of $14,000. This variation is described as a **change in the quantity demanded,** defined as a movement along a given demand curve. As average price drops from $14,000 to $12,000 to $10,000 along $D_2$, we say that the quantity demanded rises from 5 million to 10 million to 15 million automobiles. A change in the quantity demanded refers to the effect on sales of a change in price, holding constant the effects of all other demand-determining factors.

**change in the quantity demanded**

Movement along a given demand curve reflecting a change in price and quantity.

**shift in demand**

Movement from one demand curve to another following a change in a nonprice determinant of demand.

A **shift in demand,** or shift from one demand curve to another, reflects a change in one or more of the nonprice variables in the product demand function. In the automobile demand-function example, a decrease in interest rates causes an increase in automobile demand, because the interest rate parameter of $-1,000,000$ indicates that demand and interest rates are inversely related—that is, they change in opposite directions. When demand is inversely related to a factor such as interest rates, a reduction in the factor leads to rising demand and an increase in the factor leads to falling demand.

$D_1$ is another automobile demand curve; the sole difference between it and $D_2$ is that it assumes an interest rate of 5 percent rather than the

■ Figure 3.1
## A Hypothetical Automobile Demand Curve

The slope coefficient of this demand curve reveals that a $1 increase in the price of automobiles reduces the quantity demanded by 2,500 units, holding constant the effects of all other variables.

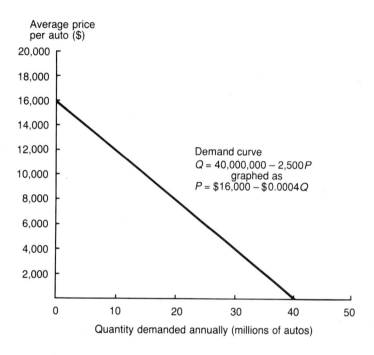

NOTE: *The dependent variable (quantity demanded) is plotted on the horizontal axis and the independent variable (price) on the vertical axis. Ordinarily, we would expect to see the dependent variable on the vertical scale and the independent variable on the horizontal scale. This point can be confusing, because it is easy to write a demand equation as in Equation 3.4, then to incorrectly graph it by treating the 40,000,000 as the Y-axis intercept instead of the X-axis intercept and, similarly, to misspecify the slope of the curve.*

*The practice of plotting price on the vertical axis and quantity on the horizontal axis originated many years ago with the theory of competitive markets. Here firms have no control over price but can control output, and output, in turn, determines market price. Hence, in the original model, price was the dependent variable and quantity (supplied, not demanded) was the independent variable. For that reason, price/quantity graphs appear as they do.*

10 percent rate used to construct $D_2$. Since the interest-rate parameter is negative, a decrease in interest rates causes an increase in automobile demand. Holding all else equal, a 5-percent reduction in interest rates leads to a 5-million-unit $[= -1,000,000 \times (-5)]$ increase in automobile demand. Therefore, a 5-percent decrease in average interest rates will lead to an upward or rightward shift in the original demand curve $D_2$ to

■ Figure 3.2
## Hypothetical Automobile Demand Curves

A shift in the original demand curve from $D_2$ to $D_1$ reveals that a 5-percent decline in average interest rates increases automobile demand by 5 million units at every price level. A 5-percent increase in interest rates will decrease demand by 5 million units, from $D_2$ to $D_3$.

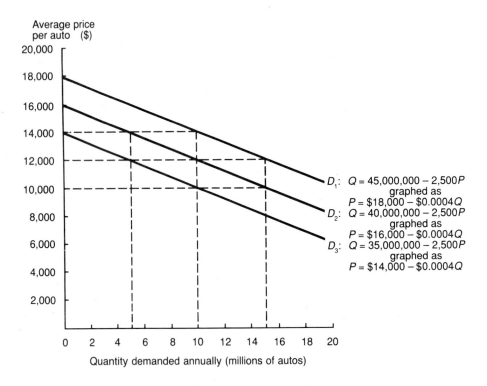

the new demand curve $D_1$. This means that a 5-percent interest rate reduction will increase automobile demand by 5 million units at each price level. At a price of $12,000, for example, a 5-percent reduction in interest rates increases automobile demand from 10 million to 15 million units per year. We also see from $D_1$ that 10 million automobiles could be sold at the higher price of $14,000 rather than the 5 million units indicated on demand curve $D_2$.

On the other hand, a 5-percent *increase* in interest rates, from 10 to 15 percent, would cause an inward or leftward shift in the original demand curve $D_2$ to the new demand curve $D_3$. A 5-percent increase in interest rates reduces automobile demand by 5 million units at each price level. At a price of $12,000, a 5-percent increase in interest rates reduces automobile demand from 10 million cars, the $D_2$ level, to only 5 million units. With interest rates at 15 percent, demand for 10 million cars would only arise at the lower average price of $10,000, again holding all else constant.

From the advertising parameter of 0.05, we infer that demand and advertising are positively related. Falling demand will follow reductions in advertising, and rising demand will follow increases in it. The shift from $D_2$ to $D_1$ in Figure 3.2, for example, could have resulted from a $100,000,000 increase in advertising rather than a 5-percent reduction in interest rates, or it could be the result of a $50,000,000 increase in industry advertising coupled with a 2.5-percent reduction in interest rates. In each case, the resulting demand curve is given by the equation $Q = 45,000,000 - 2,500P$, or $P = \$18,000 - \$0.0004Q$.

The distinction between changes in the quantity demanded, which reflect movements along a given demand curve, and changes in demand, which reflect shifts from one demand curve to another, is extremely important. Failure to understand the causes of changes in demand for a company's products can lead to costly, even disastrous, mistakes in managerial decision making. The task of demand analysis is made especially difficult by the fact that under normal circumstances, not only prices but also income, population, interest rates, advertising, and most other demand-related factors vary from period to period. Sorting out the impact of each factor makes demand analysis one of the most challenging aspects of managerial economics. We will return to this topic in Chapters 4 and 5.

## THE BASIS FOR SUPPLY

**supply**
**The total quantity offered for sale.**

The term **supply** refers to the quantity of a good or service that producers are willing and able to sell during a specific period and under a given set of conditions. Conditions, or factors, that must be specified include the price of the good in question, prices of related goods, the current state of technology, levels of input prices, weather, and so on. The amount of product that producers bring to the market—the supply of the product—depends on all these factors.

The supply of a product in the market is merely the aggregate of the amounts supplied by individual firms. The theory of the firm provides the basis for analyzing factors related to both individual firm and market supply. The supply of products arises from their value in terms of the firm's value-maximization objective. Key components in this supply determination are the marginal benefits and marginal costs associated with expanding output. The amount of any good or service supplied will rise when the marginal benefit to producers, measured in terms of the value of output, is greater than the marginal costs of production. The amount of any good or service supplied will fall when the marginal benefit to producers is less than the marginal costs of production. Thus individual firms will expand or reduce supply based on the expected profits of each action.

Among the factors influencing the supply of a product, the price of the product itself is perhaps the most important. Higher prices increase the quantity of output producers want to bring to market. Holding marginal production costs constant, higher output prices increase the marginal benefits of added production and make expansion profitable. As a result, firms will increase supply to earn the greater profits associated with expanded levels of output. Higher prices also allow the firm to afford the higher production costs (e.g., employee overtime rates and higher material prices) sometimes associated with expansions in output. Conversely, lower prices for their products will typically cause producers to supply a lower quantity of output. At the margin, lower prices can have the effect of making previous levels of production unprofitable.

The prices of related goods and services can also play an important role in determining supply of a product. If a firm employs limited resources that can be used to produce several different products, it can be expected to switch production from one product to another depending on market conditions for each. For example, the supply of gasoline typically declines in autumn when the price of heating oil rises. On the other hand, gasoline supply typically increases during the spring with the seasonal decline in heating oil prices.

Whereas the substitution of one output for another can cause an inverse relation between the supply of one product and the price of a second, complementarities in production can result in a positive relation between supply and the price of a related product. For example, ore deposits containing lead often also contain silver. An increase in the price of lead can therefore lead to an expansion in both lead and silver production.

Technology is a key determinant of product supply. The current state of technology refers to the manner in which inputs are transformed into output. An improvement in the state of technology, including any product invention or process innovation that reduces production costs, increases the quantity and/or quality of products offered for sale at a given price.

Changes in input prices also affect supply in that an increase in input prices will raise costs and reduce the quantity that can be supplied profitably at a given market price. Alternatively, a decrease in input prices will increase profitability and the quantity supplied at a given price.

For some products, especially agricultural products, weather can play an important role in determining supply. Temperature, rainfall, and wind all influence the quantity that can be supplied. Heavy rainfall in early spring, for example, can delay or prevent the planting of crops, significantly limiting supply. Abundant rain during the growing season, on the other hand, can greatly increase the available supply at harvest time. Finally, an early freeze that prevents full maturation or heavy rain or snow that limits harvesting activity can again reduce the supply of agricultural products.

Managerial decision making requires understanding both individual firm supply and market supply conditions. Market supply is the aggregate of individual firm supply, so it is ultimately determined by factors affecting firm supply. We examine firm supply in greater detail in Chapters 7 and 8. For now, substantial insight can be gained by understanding the nature of market supply.

# THE MARKET SUPPLY FUNCTION

**supply function**

**The relation between supply and all factors influencing its level.**

The market **supply function** for a product is a statement of the relation between the quantity supplied and all factors affecting that quantity. Written in general functional form, the supply function can be expressed as:

$$\begin{array}{l}\text{Quantity of} \\ \text{Product } X \\ \text{Supplied}\end{array} = Q = \begin{array}{l} f(\text{Price of } X, \text{ Prices of Related} \\ \text{Goods, Current State of Technology,} \\ \text{Input Prices, Weather, and So On}).\end{array} \qquad \textbf{3.5}$$

The generalized supply function expressed in Equation 3.5 lists variables that influence supply. As is true with the demand function, the supply function must be made explicit to be useful for managerial decision making. To illustrate, let us continue with our previous automobile example and assume that the supply function has been specified as follows:

$$Q = b_1 P + b_2 P_T + b_3 P_L + b_4 i + b_5 T. \qquad \textbf{3.6}$$

This equation states that the number of domestic plus foreign automobiles supplied during a given period, $Q$, is a linear function of the average price of cars, $P$; average price of trucks, $P_T$; average price of labor (wages), $P_L$; average interest rate (price of capital), $i$; and government taxes (tariffs) on imports, $T$. The terms $b_1, b_2, \ldots, b_5$ are the parameters of the supply function. Note that no explicit term describes technology, or the method by which inputs are combined to produce output, in the industry supply function. This reflects the fact that the current state of technology is an underlying or implicit factor in the supply function.

Substituting a set of assumed parameter values into Equation 3.6, we obtain:

$$Q = 2,000 P - 500 P_T - 180,000 P_L - 400,000 i - 1,000 T. \qquad \textbf{3.7}$$

Equation 3.7 indicates that automobile supply increases by 2,000 units for each $1 increase in the average price charged; it decreases by 500 units for each $1 increase in the price of trucks; it decreases by 180,000 units for each $1 increase in wage rates; it decreases by 400,000 units if interest rates rise 1 percent; and it decreases by 1,000 units with each $1 increase in the tax on imported cars. Thus, each parameter indicates the effect of the related factor on supply from domestic plus foreign manufacturers. For example, although a tax on imports will limit the supply of foreign cars, such a tax can increase supply from domestic manufac-

## 3.2  **Managerial Application**
Demand and Supply in the U.S. Auto Industry

The U.S. auto industry is an interesting case study of the dynamics of changing demand and supply conditions. In contrast to just a few years ago, when the Big Three auto makers dominated the industry, today there are six major companies that have a substantial share of the market and a handful of other companies that have been able to profitably exploit important market niches.

Despite a significant reduction in market share, General Motors remains by far the largest company in the U.S. auto market. GM's current market share is in the 30- to 35-percent range, followed by the Ford Motor Company with roughly a 20-percent market share, Chrysler with 10 to 12 percent, Honda with 8 to 10 percent, Toyota with 6 to 8 percent, Nissan with 5 percent, and other companies with a total market share of 10 to 15 percent. On an overall basis, domestically manufactured autos ac-count for roughly 65 to 70 percent of the U.S. market, with imports accounting for the remainder.

Even with its recent prosperity, there is widespread concern in the industry that a possible economic downturn in the early 1990s will cause a sharp drop in the demand for automobiles and trucks. As a result, a continuing flood of new products is emerging as the companies fight for market share with innovative new products. Many of these new products are aimed at market segments that didn't even exist during the mid-1970s, when the industry suffered its last major downturn. Chrysler, for example, was able to return from the edge of bankruptcy to record profits largely on the basis of its amazing success with minivans. By the early 1990s, however, there will be at least a dozen new vehicles aimed at this market, some with highly popular four-wheel drive.

*continued*

See: Joseph B. White, "Auto Makers Cheer '88, Worry About '89," *The Wall Street Journal*, January 6, 1989, B1; and Joseph B. White, Melinda Grenier, and Edwardo Lachica, "Despite Record Profits, Big Three Auto Firms Seek More Protection," *The Wall Street Journal*, January 24, 1989, A1, A8.

turers, as was the case during the mid-1980s in the United States. On balance, however, an import tax can be expected to have a negative overall effect on the total supply of automobiles since its direct impact on foreign manufacturers is greater than its indirect impact on domestic firms.

If we multiply each parameter in Equation 3.7 by the value of its respective variable and then sum these products, we will have the esti-

**Managerial Application** *continued*

To counter this attack on its most profitable market segment, Chrysler promises to introduce a new generation of minivans in the 1991 model year.

To gain entry into a large number of important market niches, some companies are entering into joint ventures. Mazda Motor Corporation and Ford, for example, work closely together in both automobile and truck segments of the industry. Ford has long been recognized as an innovative industry leader in trucks and has agreed to share its expertise with Mazda. Meanwhile, Mazda designs and builds cars for Ford. Ford will also begin to market minivans made with Nissan during the early 1990s. Mitsubishi Motors Corporation makes cars with Chrysler, and three Japanese companies and one Korean company make cars marketed by GM. Interestingly, each of the three largest U.S. manufacturers has taken important equity interests in a number of foreign producers. As a result, the distinction between foreign and domestic producers has begun to blur.

One important difference that remains between domestically produced and imported autos and trucks stems from the tariff protection that domestic manufacturers have been able to obtain from Congress. Despite record profits, the Big Three auto companies have been able to sustain significant protection from foreign competition. Not satisfied with voluntary quotas on Japanese auto imports, during the late 1980s domestic manufacturers successfully fought to extend a 25 percent tariff on hot-selling imported vans and sport-utility vehicles. Although vans and sport-utility vehicles account for only 15 percent of all vehicles sold in the United States, and imports enjoyed only a 10 percent share of this market segment, such vehicles are among the most profitable in the industry. Chrysler chairman Lee Iacocca argued to the Bush administration that his support for the 25 percent tariff was based on a concern for the nation's trade and federal budget deficits. However, in a letter to Chrysler dealers in which he asked for their support, Iacocca pointed out that such a tariff would result in a $2,000 per vehicle penalty for import competitors. A tariff-induced benefit of this magnitude will have a dramatic positive effect on the profits of U.S. manufacturers, and the supply of domestic vans and sport-utility vehicles. Unfortunately, the consumer is an obvious loser in this trade-off between domestic and import supply.

mated supply of automobiles during the coming period. Table 3.2 illustrates this process, showing that the supply of autos, assuming the stated values of the independent variables, will be 10 million units.

## Industry Supply versus Firm Supply

Just as in the case of demand, supply functions can be specified for either an entire industry or an individual firm. Even though the factors affecting supply would be highly similar in industry versus firm supply functions, the relative importance of these influences can differ dramatically.

■ Table 3.2

## Estimating Industry Supply for Automobiles Using a Hypothetical Supply Function

| Independent Variable (1) | Parameter (2) | Estimated Value of the Variable for the Coming Year (3) | Estimated Total Demand (4) = (2) × (3) |
|---|---|---|---|
| Average·price | 2,000 | $12,000 | 24,000,000 |
| Average price of trucks | −500 | $ 9,000 | −4,500,000 |
| Average price of labor (per hour) | −180,000 | $25 | −4,500,000 |
| Average interest rate (in percent) | −400,000 | 10% | −4,000,000 |
| Tariff on imported cars | −1,000 | $ 1,000 | −1,000,000 |
| | | Total supply = | 10,000,000 |

At one extreme, if all firms used identical production methods and identical equipment, had salaried and hourly employees who were equally capable and identically paid, and had equally skilled management, then individual firm and industry supply functions would have an obvious and close relation. We would expect each firm to be similarly affected by changes in the factors underlying supply. Each parameter in the individual firm supply functions would be smaller than in the industry supply function, however, and would reflect each firm's relative share of the market.

More typically, firms within a given industry will adopt somewhat different production methods, use equipment of different vintages, and employ labor of varying skills and compensation levels. In such cases, individual firms' supply levels can be affected quite differently by various factors. Japanese and Korean automakers, for example, may be able to offer subcompacts profitably at industry prices as low as $7,000 per automobile. On the other hand, U.S. auto manufacturers, who have historically operated with a labor cost disadvantage, may only be able to offer supply at average industry prices in excess of $8,000. This means that at relatively high average prices, say $9,000 per unit, both foreign and domestic auto manufacturers would be actively engaged in subcompact production. At relatively low prices, below say $8,000, only foreign producers would offer subcompacts. This would be reflected by different parameters describing the relation between price and quantity supplied in the individual firm supply functions for Japanese, Korean, and U.S. automobile manufacturers.

It is worth emphasizing that individual firms will supply output only when doing so is profitable. When industry prices are high enough to cover the marginal costs of increased production, individual firms will expand output, thereby increasing total profits and the value of the firm.

To the extent that the economic capabilities of industry participants vary, so too will the scale of output supplied by individual firms at various industry prices.

Similarly, supply will be affected by the production technology of various firms. Firms operating with highly automated facilities incur large fixed costs and relatively small variable costs. The supply of product from such firms is likely to be relatively insensitive to price changes when compared to less automated firms, for which variable production costs are higher and thus more closely affected by production levels. Relatively low-cost producers can and will supply output at relatively low market prices. Of course, both relatively low-cost and high-cost producers will be able to supply output profitably when market prices are high.

# THE SUPPLY CURVE

**supply curve**

The relation between price and the quantity supplied, holding constant the effects of other supply-determining variables.

The supply function specifies the relation between the quantity supplied and all variables that determine supply. The **supply curve** is the part of the supply function that expresses the relation between the price charged for a product and the quantity supplied, *holding constant the effects of all other variables.* As is true with demand curves, supply curves are often shown graphically, and all independent variables in the supply function except the price of the product itself are assumed to be fixed at specified levels. In the automobile supply function given in Equation 3.7, for example, we must hold constant the price of trucks, the price of labor, interest rates, and import taxes in order to examine the relation between automobile price and the quantity supplied.

To illustrate this process, consider the relation depicted in Equation 3.7. Assuming that the price of trucks, the price of labor, interest rates, and import taxes are all held constant at their Table 3.2 values, we can express the relation between the quantity supplied and price as:

$$Q = 2{,}000P - 500(9{,}000) - 180{,}000(25) - 400{,}000(10)$$
$$- 1{,}000(1{,}000)$$
$$= -14{,}000{,}000 + 2{,}000P. \qquad \textbf{3.8}$$

Equation 3.8, representing the supply curve for automobiles given the specified values of all other variables in the supply function, is presented graphically in Figure 3.3. When the supply function is graphed with price as a function of quantity, or as $P = \$7{,}000 + \$0.0005Q$, the industry price must increase by 1/2,000 or $0.0005 to cause a one-unit increase in the supply of automobiles. Thus, industry supply will increase by 2,000 units for each $1 increase in the average price of automobiles above $7,000 per unit. The $7,000 intercept in this supply equation means that the industry would not supply any cars at an average price below $7,000.

■ Figure 3.3
## A Hypothetical Automobile Supply Curve

For prices above $7,000, the slope coefficient of the supply curve reveals that a $1 increase in the average price of automobiles increases industry supply by 2,000 units.

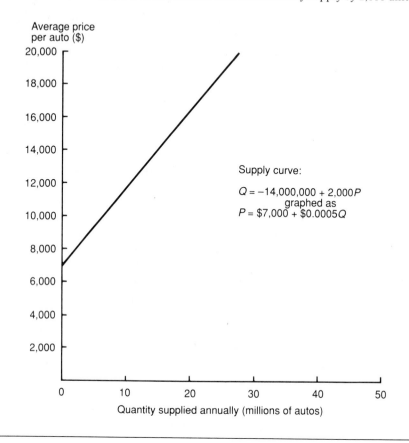

Supply curve:

$$Q = -14,000,000 + 2,000P$$
graphed as
$$P = \$7,000 + \$0.0005Q$$

*Average price per auto ($)* — vertical axis: 2,000; 4,000; 6,000; 8,000; 10,000; 12,000; 14,000; 16,000; 18,000; 20,000

*Quantity supplied annually (millions of autos)* — horizontal axis: 0, 10, 20, 30, 40, 50

## Relation between Supply Curve and Supply Function

Like the relation between the demand curve and the demand function, the relation between the supply curve and the supply function is very important in managerial decision making. Figure 3.4 shows three supply curves for automobiles: $S_1$, $S_2$, and $S_3$. $S_2$ is the same automobile supply curve determined by Equation 3.8 and shown in Figure 3.3. If $S_2$ is the appropriate supply curve, then 10 million automobiles would be offered for sale at an average price of $12,000, only 6 million automobiles would be offered for sale at an average price of $10,000, and 14 million automobiles would be offered for sale at an average price of $14,000. This is

■ Figure 3.4
## Hypothetical Automobile Supply Curves

A shift in the original supply curve from $S_2$ to $S_3$ reveals that a 5-percent increase in the cost of capital will reduce automobile supply by 2 million units at every price level. A 5-percent decrease in the cost of capital will increase supply by 2 million units, from $S_2$ to $S_1$.

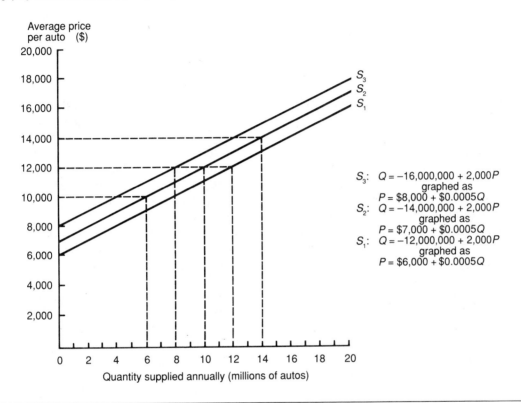

change in the
quantity supplied

Movement along a given
supply curve reflecting a
change in price and
quantity.

described as a **change in the quantity supplied,** defined as a movement along a given supply curve. As average price rises from $10,000 to $12,000 to $14,000 along $S_2$, we say that the quantity supplied increases from 6 million to 10 million to 14 million automobiles.

Supply curves $S_1$ and $S_3$ are similar to $S_2$. The differences are that $S_1$ is based on a 5-percent interest rate, whereas $S_3$ assumes a 15-percent interest rate. Recall that $S_2$ is based on an interest rate of 10 percent. Since the supply function interest rate parameter is $-400,000$, a 5-percent rise in interest rates will lead to a 2-million-unit ($= -400,000 \times 5$) reduction in automobile supply at each automobile price level. This reduction is described as an upward or leftward shift in the original supply curve $S_2$ to the new supply curve $S_3$.

## 3.3  **Managerial Application**

The Boom in CDs

Consumer acceptance of the compact disc (or CD) has been a marketing phenomenon. CD players use lasers to convert digital information on computer-encoded discs into music. CDs have gained rapid acceptance as a result of the product's high-quality sound resolution. Although prerecorded cassette tapes still account for about one-half the recording industry's total revenues, CD sales have grown rapidly. By the late 1980s, only a few years after their introduction, CD sales had begun to outstrip those of the more familiar 12-inch long-playing records in terms of the total number of units sold. Go into any record store today and compare the bustle of activity surrounding CD displays with the relative lack of interest in LPs.

Customer acceptance has been so complete that the CD threatens to send the 12-inch LP record the way of the now obsolete 78-rpm platter. In early 1987, for example,

RCA Records announced that it was shutting down its last vinyl-record pressing facility. The Indianapolis plant no longer made economic sense when vinyl-record sales had fallen to less than 25 percent of total sales (including CDs and tapes). Although the company will still offer vinyl records, it will simply put its label on records pressed by other firms.

The rapid growth of the CD market is expected to continue, if not accelerate, during the late 1980s and into the 1990s. The number of CD players sold exploded from 1 million before 1985 to 3 million in 1986 to roughly 4.25 million in 1987. This led to an exponential rate of growth in the number of CDs purchased, since a buyer of a CD player often must purchase a whole new collection of recorded music. Thus, while the price of CD players has plunged to as low as $200 in many areas, consumers often end up spend-

*continued*

See: Jack Eagan, "The Stunning Success of CD's," *U.S. News & World Report*, February 23, 1987, 41–42; and Francesca Z. Lunzer, "The Little Compact Disk Grows Up," *U.S. News & World Report*, January 2, 1989, 114.

At a price of $12,000, for example, a 5-percent rise in interest rates reduces automobile supply from 10 million units, the $S_2$ level, to 8 million units, the $S_3$ level. This reduction in supply reflects the fact that previously profitable production no longer generates a profit because of the increase in capital costs. On the other hand, a 5-percent reduction in interest rates leads to a 2-million-unit $[= -400,000 \times (-5)]$ increase in automobile supply at each automobile price level, holding all else constant. This increase is described as a downward or rightward shift in the original supply curve $S_2$ to the new supply curve $S_1$. At a price of

**Managerial Application** *continued*

ing between $400 and $600 on CDs during the first year they own CD players. CD sales of 23 million units in 1985 more than doubled to roughly 50 million in 1986 and doubled again to over 100 million during 1987. So rapidly have CD sales grown that CBS Records, the largest U.S. record company, found that CD sales represented more than 50 percent of the company's 1987 total dollar volume of sales.

The booming market for CDs provides an interesting basis for considering how the dynamic forces of demand and supply work together to influence the price and production of a product over time. In the product's very early years, prices were high and output quantities were limited. This combination resulted in high profits for firms in the industry. The large profit margins and recognized growth potential of the CD industry attracted new competitors.

Until mid-1986, the only CD pressing facility in the United States was Sony's Digital Audio Disk plant in Terre Haute, Indiana. By early 1987, the number of U.S. plants had grown to four, with half a dozen or more on the drawing boards. The biggest of these, with a projected annual capacity of 60 million CDs, is the Philips and Du Pont Optical

Company in Kings Mountain, North Carolina. This actual and projected expansion in supply substantially affected CD prices. Although some imported CDs cost as much as $20, mail order and regional promotions have reduced some retail prices to $11.99 and lower. CBS projected that price pressure in the industry will continue over the next few years, with the $14.99 average retail price in 1987 falling to $10 or less by the early 1990s. All of this suggests an industry with excess supply, a surplus situation.

According to industry sources, variable costs per unit are in the neighborhood of $7.50, composed of studio production, $3; artist's royalties, $2.25; promotion and advertising, $1.25; and packaging expenses, $1.

Even at today's lower prices, profits remain quite attractive in the industry. The CD industry's rapid rate of growth during the next few years seems sure to continue as increasing supply works to eliminate the large profits enjoyed by record companies and retailers during the late 1980s. Of course, consumers obviously benefit from this expanding supply and industry trend toward lower prices.

---

$12,000, a 5-percent reduction in interest rates increases automobile supply from 10 million units, the $S_2$ level, to 12 million units, the $S_1$ level. Supply rises following this decline in interest rates since, given a decline in capital costs, producers find that they can profitably expand output at the $12,000 price level.

**shift in supply**

Movement from one supply curve to another following a change in a nonprice determinant of supply.

A **shift in supply,** or a movement from one supply curve to another, indicates a change in one or more of the nonprice variables in the product supply function. In the automobile supply-function example, an increase in truck prices will lead to a decrease in automobile supply, since the truck price parameter of $-500$ indicates that automobile supply and truck prices are inversely related. This reflects the fact that as truck prices rise, holding all else constant, auto manufacturers will have an incentive to shift from automobile to truck production. When automobile supply is inversely related to a factor such as truck prices, rising truck prices lead to falling automobile supply and falling truck prices lead to rising automobile supply. From the negative parameters for the price of labor, interest rates, and taxes, we infer that automobile supply is inversely related to each of these factors.

For some products, a positive relation between supply and other factors such as weather is often evident. This is especially true for agricultural products. If supply were positively related to weather, perhaps measured in terms of average temperature, then rising supply would follow rising average temperature and falling supply would accompany falling average temperature. Weather is not included in the automobile supply function described here, meaning that there is no close relation between automobile supply and weather.

The distinction between changes in the quantity supplied, which reflect movements along a given supply curve, and a shift in supply, which reflects movement from one supply curve to another, is important, as was the distinction between changes in the quantity demanded and a shift in demand. Since the prices of related products, input prices, taxes, weather, and other factors affecting supply can be expected to vary from one period to the next, assessing the individual importance of each factor becomes a challenging aspect of managerial economics. We will return to this topic in Chapters 7 and 8.

# MARKET EQUILIBRIUM

**equilibrium**
Perfect balance in demand and supply.

Integrating the concepts of demand and supply establishes a framework for understanding how they interact to determine market prices and quantities for all goods and services. When the quantity demanded and the quantity supplied of a product are in perfect balance at a given price, the market for the product is said to be in **equilibrium.** An equilibrium is stable when the factors underlying demand and supply conditions remain unchanged in both the present and the foreseeable future. In those instances in which the factors underlying demand and supply are dynamic rather than constant, a change in current market prices and quantities is likely. A temporary market equilibrium of this type is often referred to as an unstable equilibrium. To understand the forces that drive market prices and quantities either up or down to achieve equilibrium, we must introduce the concepts of surplus and shortage.

## Surplus and Shortage

**surplus**
Excess supply.

A **surplus** is created when producers supply more of a product at a given price than buyers demand. Quite simply, surplus describes a condition of excess supply.

**shortage**
**Excess demand.**

Conversely, a **shortage** is created when buyers demand more of a product at a given price than producers are willing to supply. Shortage describes a condition of excess demand. Neither surplus nor shortage will occur when a market is in equilibrium, since equilibrium is defined as a condition in which the quantities demanded and supplied are exactly in balance at the current market price. Surplus and shortage describe situations of market disequilibrium because either will result in powerful market forces being exerted to change the prices and quantities offered in the market.

To illustrate the concepts of surplus and shortage and, in the process, the concept of market equilibrium, let us return to our automobile industry example and consider the demand and supply curves in Figure 3.5.

■ Figure 3.5
## Surplus, Shortage, and Market Equilibrium

At a market price of $14,000, the resulting surplus exerts downward pressure on both price and output levels. Similarly, excess demand at a price of $10,000 exerts upward pressure on both prices and output. Equilibrium is achieved when price equals $12,000.

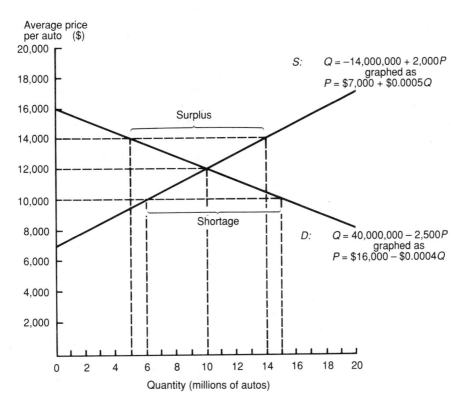

$S: \quad Q = -14,000,000 + 2,000P$
graphed as
$P = \$7,000 + \$0.0005Q$

$D: \quad Q = 40,000,000 - 2,500P$
graphed as
$P = \$16,000 - \$0.0004Q$

Note that the demand curve is the same hypothetical curve shown in Figure 3.1 (it is also $D_2$ in Figure 3.2). The supply curve shown is the one illustrated in Figure 3.3 (it is also $S_2$ in Figure 3.4). To clarify the concepts of surplus, shortage, and market equilibrium, it becomes useful to focus on the relation of the quantity supplied and the quantity demanded at each of three different hypothetical market prices.

At a market price of $14,000, we see that the quantity demanded is 5 million units. This is easily derived from Equation 3.4, the market demand curve; $Q_D = 40,000,000 - 2,500 \times 14,000 = 5,000,000$. The quantity supplied at a price of $14,000 is derived from the market supply curve, Equation 3.8, which indicates that $Q_S = -14,000,000 + 2,000 \times 14,000 = 14,000,000$. At an average automobile price of $14,000, the quantity supplied greatly exceeds the quantity demanded. This difference of 9 million units per year ($= 14,000,000 - 5,000,000$) constitutes a surplus.

An automobile surplus will result in a near-term buildup in inventories and pressure for a decline in market prices and production. This is typical for a market with a surplus of product. Prices tend to decline as firms recognize that consumers are unwilling to purchase the quantity of product available at prevailing prices. Similarly, producers cut back on production as inventories build up and prices soften, reducing the quantity of product supplied in future periods. The automobile industry has used rebate programs and dealer-subsidized low-interest-rate financing on new cars to effectively combat the problem of periodic surplus automobile production in the United States during recent years.

A different type of market imbalance is also illustrated in Figure 3.5. At a market price of $10,000, the quantity demanded rises to 15 million units ($= 40,000,000 - 2,500 \times 10,000$). At the same time, the quantity supplied falls to 6 million units ($= -14,000,000 + 2,000 \times 10,000$). This difference of 9 million units per year ($= 15,000,000 - 6,000,000$) constitutes a shortage. This shortage, or excess demand, reflects the fact that, given the current productive capability of the industry (including technology, input prices, and so on), producers cannot profitably supply more than 6 million units of output per year at an average price of $10,000, despite buyer wishes for more output.

Shortages exert a powerful upward force on both market prices and output levels. In our example, with only 6 million automobiles supplied, buyers would be willing to pay an average price of $13,600 ($= $16,000 - $0.0004 \times 6,000,000$). Consumers would bid against one another for the limited supply of automobiles and would thereby cause prices to rise. The resulting increase in price would cause manufacturers to increase production while reducing the number of buyers willing and able to purchase cars. The resulting increase in the quantity supplied and reduction in quantity demanded would work together to eventually eliminate the shortage.

The market situation at a price of $12,000 and a quantity of 10 million automobiles per year is shown graphically to be a balance between the

■ Table 3.3
## Surplus, Shortage, and Market Equilibrium

| Average Price per Auto ($) (1) | Quantity Supplied ($Q_s$) (2) | Quantity Demanded ($Q_D$) (3) | Surplus (+) or Shortage (−) (4) = (2) − (3) |
|---|---|---|---|
| $16,000 | 18,000,000 | 0 | +18,000,000 |
| 14,000 | 14,000,000 | 5,000,000 | +9,000,000 |
| 12,000 | 10,000,000 | 10,000,000 | 0 |
| 10,000 | 6,000,000 | 15,000,000 | −9,000,000 |
| 8,000 | 2,000,000 | 20,000,000 | −18,000,000 |
| 6,000 | 0 | 25,000,000 | −25,000,000 |

quantity demanded and the quantity supplied. This is a condition of market equilibrium. There is no tendency for change in either price or quantity at a price of $12,000 and a quantity of 10 million units. The graph shows that any price above $12,000 will produce a surplus. Prices in this range will create excess supply, a buildup in inventories, and pressure for an eventual decline in prices to the $12,000 equilibrium level. At prices below $12,000, shortages will occur, creating pressure for price increases. With prices moving up, producers are willing to supply more product and the quantity demanded declines, thus reducing the shortage.

Only a market price of $12,000 will bring the quantity demanded and the quantity supplied into perfect balance. This price is referred to as the market equilibrium price, or the market clearing price, since it just clears the market of all supplied product. Table 3.3 shows the surplus of quantity supplied at prices above the market equilibrium price and the shortage that results at prices below the market equilibrium price.

In short, surplus describes an excess in the quantity supplied over the quantity demanded at a given market price. A surplus results in downward pressure on both market prices and industry output. Shortage describes an excess in the quantity demanded over the quantity supplied at a given market price. A shortage results in upward pressure on both market prices and industry output. Market equilibrium describes a condition of balance in the quantity demanded and the quantity supplied at a given price. In equilibrium, there is no tendency for change in either price or quantity.

## Comparative Statics

Managers typically can control a number of the factors that affect the demand for or supply of their products. To make appropriate decisions concerning those variables, it is often useful to know how altering them will change market conditions. Similarly, the direction and magnitude of changes in demand and supply that are due to uncontrollable external factors, such as income or interest rate changes, need to be understood

## 3.4  **Managerial Application**

### Demand and Supply Conditions for Economists

Demand and supply exert powerful influences on the market for consumer products, as well as on the markets for labor and other inputs. An interesting case in point is the economics industry itself.

The demand for economists originates in the private sector, where they are employed in business—usually in staff rather than line positions—as consultants and commentators; in government, where economic analysis often guides public policy; and in academia, where economists are employed in teaching capacities, primarily at the college and university levels.

During recent years, financial economists have made quite a splash on Wall Street, offering their services in the pricing and marketing of complex financial instruments. Although perhaps no more than 500 to 1,000 economists are actually employed in this capacity, the rapid growth of the industry, and

bonus-based compensation plans that run into the several hundred thousand dollars per year for a handful of stars, has made this business highly visible. Many more economists, perhaps a few thousand, are employed in industry for their forecasting input concerning trends in macroeconomic conditions, as well as for their microeconomic advice concerning pricing, output, and other decisions. The National Association of Business Economists, for example, counts roughly 3,000 members in a wide variety of industries. Consulting and speech making, while a fairly small segment, is the glamour end of the business. Stars such as Lester Thurow, Dean of the Sloan School of Management at the Massachusetts Institute of Technology, have the capacity to earn hundreds of thousands of dollars per year in fees for consulting, speaking engagements, and publishing. The earnings of celebrity

*continued*

See: Augustine Hedberg, "Lights! Camera! Economists!" *Money,* October 1987, 148–169; and *Job Openings for Economists,* December 1989.

so that managers can develop strategies and make decisions that are consistent with the market conditions they face.

One relatively simple but quite useful analytical technique involves examining the effects on market equilibrium of changes in economic factors underlying the demand for and supply of a given product. This is called **comparative statics analysis.** In comparative statics analysis, the role of factors influencing demand is often analyzed while holding supply conditions constant. Similarly, the role of factors influencing supply can be analyzed by studying changes in supply while holding

**comparative statics analysis**

The study of changing demand and supply conditions.

economists such as Milton Friedman, John Kenneth Galbraith, Robert Heilbroner, Arthur Laffer, Paul Samuelson, and Lester Thurow are high in large part because they are so rare. The supply of such "superstars" is severely limited.

In terms of sheer numbers of jobs, perhaps the best employment opportunities for economists are in academia, especially for those who hold the doctoral degree. According to *Job Openings for Economists*, a publication of the American Economic Association, roughly 80 to 90 percent of the total number of job opportunities in economics are in four-year colleges and universities. An overwhelming majority of the roughly 20,000 members of the AEA hold academic jobs.

Since the mid-1970s, the number of new PhDs in economics has held steady at roughly 750 to 800 per year. This means that the supply of new academic economists is quite high when compared to the number of new PhDs in related disciplines like accounting, finance, management, and marketing. In fact, each year the number of new PhDs in economics is roughly equivalent to the number of PhDs granted in all of the functional areas of business administration

combined. Thus, academic job-market candidates from leading programs in economics may count themselves lucky to receive two or three attractive job offers after graduation, whereas similar candidates from leading business programs often enjoy two or three times as many job opportunities and typically at substantially greater salaries.

New PhDs in accounting, for example, total no more than 100 to 150 per year. At that pace, it will take 20 years to fill current vacancies in accounting. Therefore, it is perhaps not surprising that salaries for new academic PhDs in economics are in the $40,000 per year range, but they are in excess of $60,000 per year in accounting. What is surprising is how slowly the supply of accounting PhDs from high-quality doctoral programs has grown during recent years. Apparently, employment opportunities in the private sector are so attractive that talented accounting undergraduates do not find the PhD sufficiently rewarding to encourage them to pursue advanced degrees. Although this might explain the failure of accounting students to pursue advanced degrees, why economics PhD students don't switch to accounting remains a mystery.

demand conditions constant. Comparing market equilibrium price and output levels before and after various hypothetical changes in demand and supply conditions can yield useful predictions of expected changes.

Figures 3.6 and 3.7 illustrate the comparative statics of changing demand and supply conditions. Figure 3.6a combines the three automobile demand curves shown in Figure 3.2 with the automobile supply curve $S_2$ of Figure 3.4. Here we can illustrate the demand-related effects of changes in interest rates on the market price and quantity of automobiles. Given the supply curve $S_2$, *and assuming for the moment that*

■ Figure 3.6

## The Comparative Statics of (a) Changing Demand or (b) Changing Supply Conditions

(a) Holding supply conditions constant, demand will vary with changing interest rates. (b) Holding demand conditions constant, supply will vary with changing interest rates.

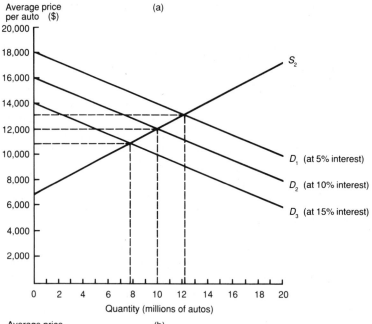

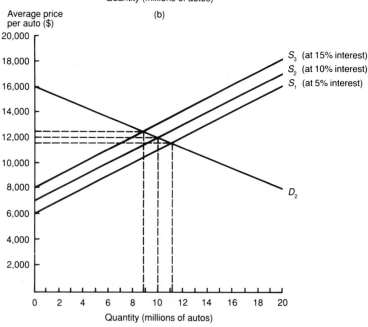

*supply does not change in response to changes in interest rates*, the intersections of the three demand curves with the supply curve indicate the market price and quantity combinations we would expect at different interest rates.

Along $D_1$, which corresponds to a 5 percent interest rate, supply and demand will be equal at a price of $13,111 and quantity of 12.22 million units. This result is obtained by simultaneously solving the equations for $D_1$ and $S_2$ to find the single price and quantity that satisfies both:

$$D_1 : Q_D = 45,000,000 - 2,500P.$$

$$S_2 : Q_S = -14,000,000 + 2,000P.$$

Demand and supply will be equal at a price of $13,111 because:

$$Q_D = Q_S$$

$$45,000,000 - 2,500P = -14,000,000 + 2,000P$$

$$4,500\,P = 59,000,000$$

$$P = \$13,111.$$

The related quantity can be found by substituting a price of $13,111 into either the demand curve $D_1$ or the supply curve $S_2$:

| Quantity Demanded when $P = \$13,111$ | Quantity Supplied when $P = \$13,111$ |
|---|---|
| $Q_D = 45,000,000 - 2,500P$ | $Q_S = -14,000,000 + 2,000P$ |
| $= 45,000,000 - 2,500 \times 13,111$ | $= -14,000,000 + 2,000 \times 13,111$ |
| $= 45,000,000 - 32,777,500$ | $= -14,000,000 + 26,222,000$ |
| $= 12,222,500 \approx 12.22$ million | $= 12,222,000 \approx 12.22$ million |

Using the same procedure to find the market clearing price–quantity combination for the intersection of $D_2$ (the demand curve for a 10-percent interest rate) with $S_2$, we obtain a price of $12,000 and quantity of 10 million units. With interest rates at 15 percent (curve $D_3$), the market clearing price and quantity would be $10,889 and 7.78 million units. Clearly, the level of interest rates plays an important role in the buyer's purchase decision. With higher interest rates, car buyers will purchase fewer automobiles and only at progressively lower prices. In part, this reflects the fact that most car purchases are financed, and at higher interest rates the cost of purchasing an automobile is greater.

Figure 3.6b combines the three automobile supply curves shown in Figure 3.4 with the automobile demand curve $D_2$ of Figure 3.2. Here we see the market equilibrium price and quantity effects of changing inter-est rates, holding demand conditions constant *and, in particular, assum-ing that demand does not change in response to changes in interest rates*. Given the market demand curve $D_2$, a fall in interest rates would

■ Figure 3.7

## The Comparative Statics of Changing Demand and Changing Supply Conditions

The market equilibrium price–output combination reflects the combined effects of changing demand and supply conditions.

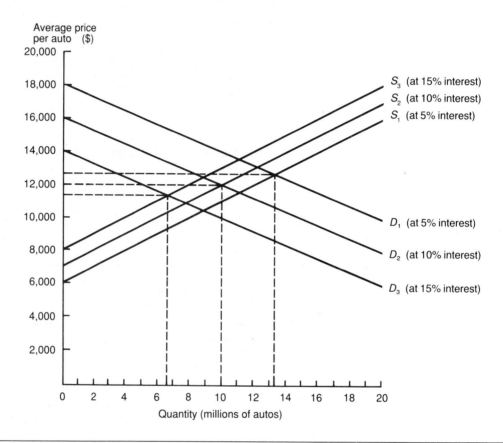

cause quantity to rise from 8.89 million units and a price of $12,444 (at 15 percent) to 10 million units and a price of $12,000 (at 10 percent) and to 11.11 million units and a price of $11,556 (at 5 percent). As interest rates fall, producers find that they can profitably supply more output, even as average price falls, given the capital cost savings that would accompany lower interest rates. These effects of lower interest rates on supply are dramatic, and they reflect the highly capital-intensive nature of the automobile industry.

We see from our analysis of these hypothetical automobile demand and supply relations that interest rates are an important factor influencing both demand *and* supply. This is a typical circumstance: Factors related to overall economic activity often have important influences on demand and supply. Figure 3.7 illustrates the comparative statics of changing demand *and* changing supply conditions by showing the net effects of changing interest rates. Here $S_1$ and $D_1$, both of which assume a 5-percent interest rate, yield an equilibrium price–output combination of $12,667 and 13.33 million units; $S_2$ and $D_2$, which assume a 10-percent interest rate, yield an equilibrium combination of a $12,000 price and output of 10 million units; $S_3$ and $D_3$, which assume a 15-percent interest rate, result in a price–output equilibrium of $11,333 and 6.67 million units. These price–output combinations reflect the joint effects of changing interest rates on demand and supply.

## SUMMARY

A fundamental understanding of demand and supply concepts is essential to the successful operation of any economic organization. The concepts introduced in this chapter provide the structure for the more detailed analysis of demand and supply in subsequent chapters and therefore contribute to the foundation for our study of managerial economics. In addition to providing a basis for understanding demand and supply relations, this chapter also illustrates how these forces combine to establish the prices and quantities observed in the markets for all goods and services.

The first topic introduced in this chapter was *demand*. Demand refers to the quantity of a good or service that consumers are willing and financially able to buy during a specified time period. Economic demand for a product requires individuals or organizations with both the need or desire and the means for acquisition. *Direct demand* is demand for personal consumption. This demand stems from the satisfaction or utility associated with consumption of a good or service. *Derived demand* relates to demand for a product used in the production of some other good or service demanded by consumers.

A *demand function* is a relation that identifies all factors having an important influence on the demand for a product, including price of the product itself, prices of related goods, income, advertising, and so on. The *demand curve* specifies the relation between the quantity demanded and the price of the product, holding constant the effects of all other factors in the demand function. A *shift in demand* relates to the movement of a demand curve that occurs when a demand factor other than the price of the product itself changes. A *change in the quantity demanded* describes the upward movement along a given demand curve that occurs when the price of a product increases or the downward movement along the demand curve that occurs when its price decreases.

The term *supply* refers to the quantity of goods or services that producers are willing and able to sell during a specified period. The supply of products is determined by the value they provide to the firm in terms of their effect on the value maximization objective. Individual firms will expand or reduce supply, based on the profitability of doing so. In general, firms will supply a product so long as the marginal revenues generated exceed the marginal costs of production.

The *supply function* is the relation that identifies factors having an important influence on the supply of a product, including the price of the product itself, prices of related goods, input prices, resource availability, weather, and so on. The *supply curve* specifies the relation between the quantity supplied and the price of a product, holding constant the effects of all other influences in the supply function. A *shift in supply* describes the movement of the supply curve that is due to a change in some supply factor other than product price. A *change in the quantity supplied* describes the movement along a given supply curve as a result of a change in the price of a product, holding constant the effects of all other supply determining factors.

*Market equilibrium* occurs when the quantity of a product demanded and the quantity supplied balance perfectly at a given price and under a given set of market demand and supply conditions. *Surplus* describes a situation of excess supply, whereas *shortage* describes excess demand. Implications of changing demand and supply conditions for market equilibrium are often considered using *comparative statics analysis*. This approach is useful for identifying the predictable consequences of changing market demand and supply conditions.

## Questions

3.1  What key ingredients are necessary for the creation of economic demand?

3.2  Describe the difference between direct demand and derived demand.

3.3  Explain the rationale for each of the demand variables in Equation 3.1.

3.4  Distinguish between a demand function and a demand curve. What is the difference between a change in the quantity demanded and a shift in the demand curve?

3.5  What key ingredients are necessary for the creation of economic supply?

3.6  Explain the rationale for each of the supply variables in Equation 3.5.

3.7  Distinguish between a supply function and a supply curve. What is the difference between a change in the quantity supplied and a shift in the supply curve?

3.8  "Dynamic rather than static demand and supply conditions are typically observed in real-world markets. Therefore, comparative statics analysis has only limited value." Discuss this statement.

3.9  Contrast the supply and demand conditions for new PhDs in economics and accounting. Why do such large differences in starting salaries seem to persist over time?

3.10 "A famous economist once argued, 'Supply creates its own demand'. It would have been more accurate to argue 'Demand creates its own supply'." Discuss this statement.

## Problems

3.1 The following relations describe demand and supply conditions in the lumber/forest-products industry:

$$Q_D = 80,000 - 20,000P, \qquad \text{(Demand)}$$

$$Q_S = -20,000 + 20,000P, \qquad \text{(Supply)}$$

where $Q$ is quantity measured in thousands of board feet (one square foot of lumber, one inch thick) and $P$ is price in dollars.

A. Complete the following table:

| Price (1) | Quantity Supplied (2) | Quantity Demanded (3) | Surplus (+) or Shortage (−) (4) = (2) − (3) |
|---|---|---|---|
| $3.50 | | | |
| 3.00 | | | |
| 2.50 | | | |
| 2.00 | | | |
| 1.00 | | | |
| .50 | | | |

3.2 The following relations describe monthly demand and supply relations for dry cleaning services in the metropolitan area:

$$Q_D = 500,000 - 50,000P, \qquad \text{(Demand)}$$

$$Q_S = 100,000 + 100,000P, \qquad \text{(Supply)}$$

where $Q$ is quantity measured by the number of items dry cleaned per month and $P$ is average price in dollars.

A. At what average price level would demand equal zero?

B. At what average price level would supply equal zero?

C. Calculate the equilibrium price/output combination.

3.3 The demand for housing is often described as being highly cyclical, and it is very sensitive to housing prices and interest rates. Given these characteristics, describe the effect of each of the following in terms of whether it would *increase* or *decrease* the *quantity demanded* or the *demand* for housing. Moreover, when price is expressed as a function of quantity, indicate whether the effect of each of the following is an *upward* or *downward movement* along a given demand curve or instead involves an *outward* or *inward shift* in the relevant demand curve for housing. Explain your answers.

A. An increase in housing prices;

B. A fall in interest rates;

C. A rise in interest rates;

D. A severe economic recession;

E. A robust economic expansion.

3.4 Demand and supply conditions in the market for unskilled labor are important concerns to business and government decision makers. Consider the case of a federally-mandated minimum wage set above the equilibrium or market-clearing wage level. Some of the following factors have the potential to influence the *demand* or *quantity demanded* of unskilled labor. Influences on the *supply* or *quantity supplied* may also result. Holding all else equal, describe these influences as *increasing* or *decreasing*, and indicate the direction of the resulting *movement along* or *shift in* the relevant curve(s).

A.  An increase in the quality of secondary education;
B.  A rise in welfare benefits;
C.  An increase in the popularity of self-service gas stations, car washes, and so on;
D.  A fall in interest rates;
E.  An increase in the minimum wage.

3.5  The Creative Publishing Company (CPC) is a coupon-book publisher with markets in several southeastern states. CPC coupon books are either sold directly to the public, sold through religious and other charitable organizations, or given away as promotional items. Operating experience during the past year suggests the following demand function for CPC's coupon books:

$$Q = 5,000 - 4,000P + 0.02Pop + 0.5I + 1.5A,$$

where $Q$ is quantity, $P$ is price ($), $Pop$ is population, $I$ is disposable income per household ($), and $A$ is advertising expenditures ($).

A.  Determine the demand curve faced by CPC in a typical market in which $P = \$10$, $Pop = 1,000,000$ persons, $I = \$30,000$, and $A = \$10,000$. Show the demand curve with quantity expressed as a function of price and price expressed as a function of quantity.
B.  Calculate the quantity demanded at prices of $10, $5, and $0.
C.  Calculate the prices necessary to sell 10,000, 20,000, and 30,000 units.

3.6  The Eastern Shuttle, Inc., is a regional airline providing shuttle service between New York and Washington, D.C. An analysis of the monthly demand for service has revealed the following demand relation:

$$Q = 26,000 - 500P - 250P_{OG} + 200I_B + 5,000S$$

where $Q$ is quantity measured by the number of passengers per month, $P$ is price ($), $P_{OG}$ is a regional price index for other consumer goods (1967 = 1.00), $I_B$ is an index of business activity (1980 = 100), and $S$, a binary or dummy variable, equals 1 in summer months and zero otherwise.

A.  Determine the demand curve facing the airline during the month of January if $P = \$100$, $P_{OG} = 4$, $I_B = \$250$, and $S = 0$.
B.  Calculate the quantity demanded and total revenues during the summer month of July if all price-related variables are as specified previously.

3.7 A review of industry-wide data for the jelly and jam manufacturing industry suggests the following industry supply function:

$$Q = -59{,}000{,}000 + 500{,}000P - 250{,}000P_L$$
$$- 500{,}000P_K + 2{,}000{,}000W,$$

where $Q$ is cases supplied per year, $P$ is the wholesale price per case ($\$$), $P_L$ is the average price paid for unskilled labor ($\$$), $P_K$ is the average price of capital (in percent), and $W$ is weather measured by the average seasonal rainfall in growing areas (in inches).

A. Determine the industry supply curve for a recent year when $P = \$60$, $P_L = \$4$, $P_K = 10$ percent, and $W = 20$ inches of rainfall. Show the industry supply curve with quantity expressed as a function of price and price expressed as a function of quantity.

B. Calculate the quantity supplied by the industry at prices of $\$50$, $\$60$, and $\$70$ per case.

C. Calculate the prices necessary to generate a supply of 4 million, 6 million, and 8 million cases.

3.8 Information Technology, Inc., is a supplier of math coprocessors (computer chips) used to speed data processing on desktop and portable personal computers. Based on an analysis of monthly cost and output data, the company has estimated the following relation between its marginal cost of production and monthly output:

$$MC = \$100 + \$0.004Q.$$

A. Calculate the marginal cost of production at 2,500, 5,000, and 7,500 units of output.

B. Express output as a function of marginal cost. Calculate the levels of output at which $MC = \$100$, $\$125$, and $\$150$.

C. Calculate the profit-maximizing level of output if wholesale prices are stable in the industry at $\$150$ per chip and, therefore, $P = MR = \$150$.

D. Derive the company's supply curve for chips assuming $P = MR$. Express price as a function of quantity and quantity as a function of price.

3.9 Cornell Pharmaceuticals, Inc., and Penn Medical, Ltd., supply generic drugs to treat a wide variety of illnesses. A major product for each company is a generic equivalent of an antibiotic used to treat postoperative infections. Proprietary cost and output information for each company reveal the following relations between marginal cost and output:

$$MC_C = \$10 + \$0.004Q_C. \qquad \text{(Cornell)}$$
$$MC_P = \$8 + \$0.008Q_P. \qquad \text{(Penn)}$$

The wholesale market for generic drugs is vigorously price-competitive, and neither firm is able to charge a premium for its products. Thus, $P = MR$ in this market.

A. Determine the supply curve for each firm. Express price as a function of quantity and quantity as a function of price. (Hint: Set $P = MR = MC$ to find each firm's supply curve.)

B. Calculate the quantity supplied by each firm at prices of $8, $10, and $12. What is the minimum price necessary for each individual firm to supply output?

C. Determine the industry supply curve when $P < \$10$.

D. Determine the industry supply curve when $P > \$10$. To check your answer, calculate quantity at an industry price of $12 and compare your answer with Part B.

3.10 Sunbest Orange Juice is a product of California's Orange County Growers' Association. Both demand and supply of the product are highly sensitive to changes in the weather. During hot summer months, demand for Sunbest and other beverages grows rapidly. On the other hand, hot, dry weather has an adverse effect on supply by reducing the size of the orange crop.

Demand and supply functions for Sunbest are as follows:

$$Q_D = -4{,}000{,}000 - 2{,}500{,}000P + 3{,}000{,}000P_S$$
$$+ 4{,}000Y + 200{,}000T, \qquad \text{(Demand)}$$

$$Q_S = 15{,}500{,}000 + 2{,}000{,}000P - 1{,}000{,}000P_L$$
$$- 500{,}000P_K - 100{,}000T, \qquad \text{(Supply)}$$

where $P$ is the average price of Sunbest ($ per case), $P_S$ is the average retail price of canned soda ($ per case), $Y$ is income (GNP in $billions), $T$ is the average daily high temperature (degrees), $P_L$ is the average price of unskilled labor ($ per hour), and $P_K$ is the average cost of capital (in percent).

A. When quantity is expressed as a function of price, what are the Sunbest demand and supply curves if $P = \$10$, $P_S = \$5$, $Y = \$6{,}000$ billion, $T = 75$ degrees, $P_L = \$6$, and $P_K = 12$ percent?

B. Calculate the surplus or shortage of Sunbest when $P = \$5, \$10$, and $15.

C. Calculate the market equilibrium price/output combination.

## Selected References

Alpern, Steve and Dennis J. Snower. " 'High-Low Search' in Product and Labor Markets." *American Economic Review* 78 (May 1988): 356–362.

Berkovec, James, and Don Fullerton. "The General Equilibrium Effects of Inflation on Housing Consumption and Investment." *American Economic Review* 79 (May 1989): 277–282.

Blomqvist, Hans C. "A Note on the Predictive Power of a Simple Demand-Supply Model of Unemployment." *Applied Economics* 21 (February 1989): 219–223.

Carson, Richard, and Peter Navarro. "A Seller's (and Buyer's) Guide to the Job Market for Beginning Academic Economists." *Journal of Economic Perspectives* 2 (Spring 1988): 137–148.

Davis, Steven J. "Allocative Disturbances and Specific Capital in Real Business Cycle Theories." *American Economic Review* 77 (May 1987): 326–332.

Drazen, Alan. "Self-Fulfulling Optimism in a Trade-Friction Model of the Business Cycle." *American Economic Review* 78 (May 1988): 369–372.

Fama, Eugene F., and Kenneth R. French. "Business Cycles and the Behavior of Metals Prices." *Journal of Finance* 43 (December 1988): 1075–1093.

Farber, Henry S. and Max H. Bazerman. "Why Is There Disagreement in Bargaining?" *American Economic Review* 77 (May 1987): 347–352.

Feldstein, Martin. "Supply-Side Economics: Old Truths and New Claims." *American Economic Review* 76 (May 1986): 26–30.

Hall, Christopher D. "A Dutch Auction Information Exchange." *Journal of Law and Economics* 32 (April 1989): 195–213.

Heston, Alan, and Robert Summers. "What We Have Learned about Prices and Quantities from International Comparisons: 1987." *American Economic Review* 78 (May 1988): 467–473.

Jaffe, Adam B. "Demand and Supply Influences in R&D Intensity and Productivity Growth." *Review of Economics and Statistics* 70 (August 1988): 431–437.

Krugman, Paul R. "Is Free Trade Passé?" *Journal of Economic Perspectives* 1 (Fall 1987): 131–144.

Levin, Richard C. "Appropriability, R&D Spending, and Technological Performance." *American Economic Review* 78 (May 1988): 424–428.

Long, John B., Jr., and Charles I. Plosser. "Sectoral vs. Aggregate Shocks in the Business Cycle." *American Economic Review* 77 (May 1987): 333–336.

Montgomery, Edward, and William Wascher. "Creative Destruction and the Behavior of Productivity over the Business Cycle." *Review of Economics and Statistics* 70 (February 1988): 168–172.

Portes, Richard, Richard E. Quandt, and Stephen Yeo. "Tests of the Chronic Shortage Hypothesis: The Case of Poland." *Review of Economics and Statistics* 70 (May 1988): 288–297.

Poterba, James M. "Are Consumers Forward Looking? Evidence from Fiscal Experiments." *American Economic Review* 78 (May 1988): 413–418.

Shapiro, Matthew D. "Are Cyclical Fluctuations in Productivity Due More to Supply Shocks or Demand Shocks?" *American Economic Review* 77 (May 1987): 118–124.

Varian, Hal R. "The Arbitrage Principle in Financial Economics." *Journal of Economic Perspectives* 1 (Fall 1987): 55–72.

# Demand Analysis

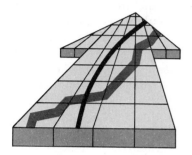

In many respects the most important determinant of a firm's profitability is the demand for its products. No matter how efficient its production processes and regardless of the skill of its financial officer, personnel director, and other managers, the firm cannot operate profitably unless a demand for its products exists or can be created, or unless it can find new products for which a demand exists.

Because of the critical role of demand as a determinant of profitability, a firm must have good information about the demand for its products to make effective long-run planning decisions and short-run operating decisions. For example, to price the firm's products effectively, management must know how changing prices will affect the quantity demanded. Similarly, management must know how credit terms affect demand to appraise the desirability of a proposed credit policy. Good estimates of the sensitivity of demand to both population and income changes will help a firm analyze future growth potential, which is important for establishing successful long-range programs.

Production decisions are profoundly influenced by the demand characteristics of the firm's products. Relatively stable demand allows for long, continuous production runs. If demand fluctuates, either flexible production processes must be employed or sizable inventories must be carried. Demand conditions in the product market also affect the firm's labor and capital requirements. If product demand is strong and growing, the financial manager must arrange to finance the firm's growing capital requirements and the personnel director must arrange to recruit and train a work force sufficient to produce and sell the firm's products.

Product demand also plays an important role in determining the market structure in which a firm will operate and, hence, the nature of its competition. Demand characteristics such as the number of potential buyers and the willingness of consumers to accept substitute products are important in determining the level of competition in a particular market. This topic is developed in Chapters 11 through 14, where market structure, pricing practices, and the role of the government in the market economy are examined.

Demand is a complex subject, but it must be thoroughly understood if managers are to effectively reach their goals. In this chapter, we first examine the basis for consumer demand. This provides the framework for our study of the elasticity concept, a useful means for quantifying the sensitivity or responsiveness of demand to changes in underlying conditions. We discover that separate elasticities characterize the effects of changes in prices, income, advertising, and any other factor with an important influence on the demand for a company's products. In the following chapter, we use the concepts developed here to formulate models that can be used to estimate demand functions and we consider the means by which firms measure various demand elasticities.

# THE BASIS FOR CONSUMER DEMAND

The ability of goods and services to satisfy consumer wants is the basis for consumer demand. Chapter 3 introduced the utility concept as a measure of satisfaction or well-being derived from consumption. In this section, we explore the basis for consumer demand further by developing the rationale for consumer purchases.

### Utility Functions

**utility function**

A descriptive statement that relates satisfaction or well-being to the consumption of goods and services.

A **utility function** is a descriptive statement that relates total utility, meaning satisfaction or well-being, to the consumption of goods and services. Utility functions are shaped both by the tastes and preferences of consumers and by the quantity and quality of available products.

The concept of a utility function can be illustrated using a simple two-product example. These two products can be closely related, such as basketball and football tickets, or relatively unrelated, such as clothing and medical care. The only requirement is that each can satisfy consumer wants—that is, each provides utility. Such a utility function can be written in the following general form:

$$\text{Utility} = f(\text{Goods, Services}). \qquad \textbf{4.1}$$

Table 4.1 is a tabular representation of such a two-product utility function. Each element in the table shows the amount of utility derived from the consumption of each respective combination of goods ($Y$) and services ($X$). For example, consumption of 3 units of $X$ and 3 units of $Y$ provides 68 utils (or 68 units of satisfaction), consumption of 1 $X$ and 10 $Y$ provides 80 utils, and so on. Each product is measured in terms of the *number* of dresses, *hours* of financial planning services, *days* of vacation, and so on.

■ Table 4.1
## Utility Derived from Consumption of Various Combinations of Goods and Services

| Goods (Y) | Services (X) | | | | | | | | | |
|---|---|---|---|---|---|---|---|---|---|---|
| | 1 | 2 | 3 | 4 | 5 | 6 | 7 | 8 | 9 | 10 |
| 1 | 25 | 36 | 46 | 55 | 63 | 70 | 76 | 81 | 85 | 88 |
| 2 | 37 | 48 | 58 | 67 | 75 | 82 | 88 | 93 | 97 | 100 |
| 3 | 47 | 58 | 68 | 77 | 85 | 92 | 98 | 103 | 107 | 110 |
| 4 | 55 | 66 | 76 | 85 | 93 | 100 | 106 | 111 | 115 | 118 |
| 5 | 62 | 73 | 83 | 92 | 100 | 107 | 113 | 118 | 122 | 125 |
| 6 | 68 | 79 | 89 | 98 | 106 | 113 | 119 | 124 | 128 | 131 |
| 7 | 73 | 84 | 94 | 103 | 111 | 118 | 124 | 129 | 133 | 136 |
| 8 | 77 | 88 | 98 | 107 | 115 | 122 | 128 | 133 | 137 | 140 |
| 9 | 79 | 90 | 100 | 109 | 117 | 124 | 130 | 135 | 139 | 142 |
| 10 | 80 | 91 | 101 | 110 | 118 | 125 | 131 | 136 | 140 | 143 |

The utility derived from consumption is intangible. However, consumers reveal their preferences through purchase decisions and thus provide tangible evidence of the utility they derive from various products.

The utility function depicted in Table 4.1 can also be displayed graphically, as in Figure 4.1. The height of the bar associated with each combination of goods and services indicates the level of utility provided through its consumption.

## Marginal Utility

**marginal utility**

The added utility derived from increasing consumption of a particular product by one unit.

Whereas total utility measures the consumer's overall level of satisfaction derived from consumption activities, **marginal utility** measures the added satisfaction derived from a one-unit increase in consumption of a particular good or service, *holding consumption of all other goods and services constant.* Marginal utility will tend to diminish as consumption of a product increases within a given time interval.

For example, suppose Table 4.2 illustrates the utility that Paul Daniels, a big eater, derives from hamburger consumption. From the table, we see that Daniels' marginal utility from consuming an initial hamburger is 5 units ($MU_{H=1} = 5$). Marginal utility is 4 units for a second hamburger, 3 units for a third, and so on.

If each hamburger costs $1, the cost per unit (util) of satisfaction derived from consuming the first hamburger is 20¢ (= $1/5 utils). A second hamburger costing $1 produces 4 utils of additional satisfaction at a cost of 25¢ per unit. Note that a diminishing marginal utility for hamburgers increases the cost of each marginal unit of satisfaction. Consequently, if Daniels had alternative consumption opportunities providing one additional unit of utility for 20¢ each, he would be willing to

■ Figure 4.1
## Representative Utility Function for the Consumption of Goods and Services

Total utility increases with a rise in the consumption of goods and services.

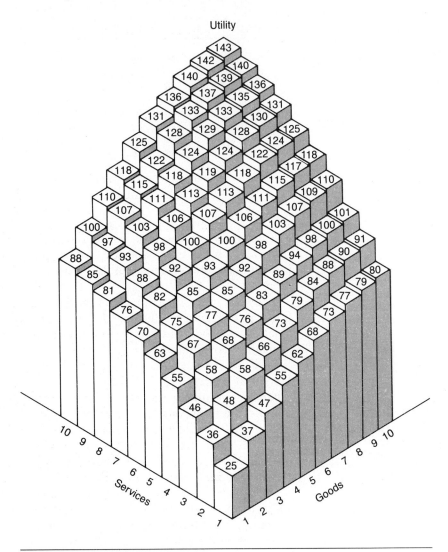

increase the quantity of hamburgers purchased only if hamburger prices were to fall. If Daniels' required price–marginal utility tradeoff for hamburgers is 20¢ per util (because this is the cost per unit of utility available from other products), then he would pay a price of $1 for a single hamburger. However, a hamburger price of 80¢ (= 20¢ × 4 utils) would be necessary to induce Daniels to buy a second hamburger, 60¢ for a

■ Table 4.2

## Total and Marginal Utility Derived from Hamburger Consumption

| Hamburgers per Meal, H | Total Utility, U | Marginal Utility $MU_H = \Delta U/\Delta H$ | Maximum Acceptable Hamburger Price at 20¢ per $MU_H$ |
|---|---|---|---|
| 0 | 0 | — | — |
| 1 | 5 | 5 | $1.00 |
| 2 | 9 | 4 | 0.80 |
| 3 | 12 | 3 | 0.60 |
| 4 | 14 | 2 | 0.40 |
| 5 | 15 | 1 | 0.20 |
| 6 | 15 | 0 | 0.00 |

third, 40¢ for a fourth, and so on. This gives rise to the downward-sloping demand curve shown in Figure 4.2.[1]

### The Law of Diminishing Marginal Utility

**law of diminishing marginal utility**

As consumption of a given product increases, the added benefit derived diminishes.

In general, the **law of diminishing marginal utility** states that as an individual increases consumption of a given product, the marginal utility gained from consumption will eventually decline. This law gives rise to a downward-sloping demand curve not only for hamburgers but also for all other goods and services. The law of diminishing marginal utility is illustrated in Table 4.3, which is derived from the data in Table 4.1. There we see that when service is held constant at 4 units, the marginal utility derived from consuming goods falls with each successive unit of consumption. Similarly, the consumption of services is subject to diminishing marginal utility. Holding goods consumption constant at one unit, the marginal utility derived from consuming services falls continuously. The added benefit derived through consumption of each product grows progressively smaller as consumption of one increases, holding the other constant.

## CONSUMER CHOICE

The decision to consume an individual product is seldom made in isolation. Instead, products are consumed as parts of a "market basket" of goods and services. To a greater or lesser degree, goods and services can be substituted for one another. For example, an executive may own several suits and dry clean each suit only occasionally or instead may own

---

[1]The demand curve in Figure 4.2 assumes that a consumer is free to purchase the quantity desired at each price. It does not represent the case in which a seller can force an all-or-nothing purchase decision at each price.

■ Figure 4.2
# Downward-Sloping Demand Curve for Hamburgers

The demand curve for hamburgers is downward sloping.

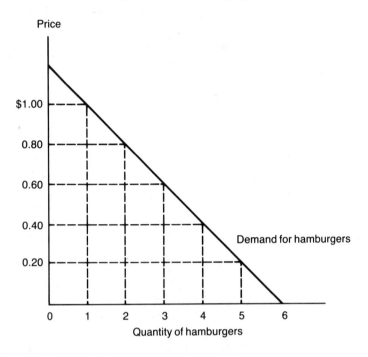

■ Table 4.3
# Total and Marginal Utility of Goods and Services

| Quantity | Goods (Y) | | Services (X) | |
|---|---|---|---|---|
| | Total Utility | Marginal Utility ($MU_y\|X = 4$) | Total Utility | Marginal Utility ($MU_x\|Y = 1$) |
| 1 | 55 | — | 25 | — |
| 2 | 67 | 12 | 36 | 11 |
| 3 | 77 | 10 | 46 | 10 |
| 4 | 85 | 8 | 55 | 9 |
| 5 | 92 | 7 | 63 | 8 |
| 6 | 98 | 6 | 70 | 7 |
| 7 | 103 | 5 | 76 | 6 |
| 8 | 107 | 4 | 81 | 5 |
| 9 | 109 | 2 | 85 | 4 |
| 10 | 110 | 1 | 88 | 3 |

only a few and dry clean each suit more frequently. In the first instance, the executive has bought a market basket with a high proportion of total expenditures devoted to suits (goods) and relatively little devoted to dry cleaning services. In the latter case, a market basket weighted less toward goods and more toward services has been purchased.

### Indifference Curves

**indifference curve**

A curve that identifies all combinations of goods and services that provide the same utility.

With the wide variety of alternative combinations of goods and services that are typically available, a large number of market baskets can be created that provide the same level of utility to the consumer. An **indifference curve** represents all market baskets among which the consumer is indifferent.

To illustrate, Figure 4.3 shows two indifference curves based on the data contained in Table 4.1. Note that 100 units of satisfaction can be

■ Figure 4.3
### Representative Indifference Curves from Table 4.1

Indifference curves show market baskets of goods and services that provide the same utility.

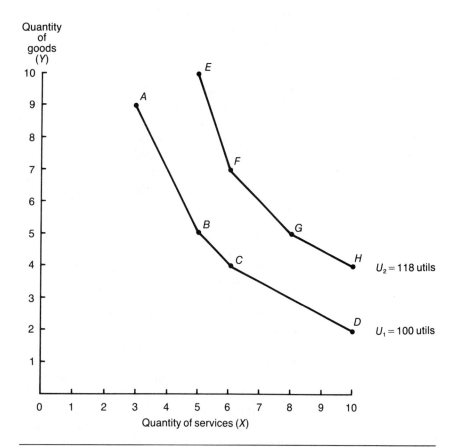

derived from the consumption of 3 $X$ and 9 $Y$ (Point $A$), 5 $X$ and 5 $Y$ (Point $B$), 6 $X$ and 4 $Y$ (Point $C$), and 10 $X$ and 2 $Y$ (Point $D$). Therefore, each of these points lies on the $U_1 = 100$ indifference curve. Similarly, 118 units of satisfaction are derived from consumption of 5 $X$ and 10 $Y$ (Point $E$), 6 $X$ and 7 $Y$ (Point $F$), 8 $X$ and 5 $Y$ (Point $G$), and 10 $X$ and 4 $Y$ (Point $H$). Therefore, all these points lie on the $U_2 = 118$ indifference curve.

An indifference curve is constructed by connecting all the points representing consumption baskets that provide the same level of utility. This construction assumes that consumption can be split between consumption baskets. For example, the line segment between Points $A$ and $B$ on the $U_1 = 100$ indifference curve represents a combination of market baskets $A$ and $B$. The midpoint of this line segment represents consumption of one-half of market basket $A$ plus one-half of market basket $B$. Similarly, the midpoint of the $GH$ line segment represents a 50/50 combination of the $G$ and $H$ market baskets.

The discrete utility-function data used to derive the indifference curves shown in Figure 4.3 (see Table 4.1 and Figure 4.1) can be generalized by assuming that the consumption of goods and services can be varied continuously rather than incrementally, as was assumed in the previous example. With the resulting utility function, indifference curves will have the smooth shapes shown in Figure 4.4. The slope at each point along such indifference curves measures the consumer's rate of substitution between products.

## Marginal Rate of Substitution

**marginal rate of substitution**

The amount of one product that must be substituted for another if utility is to remain unchanged.

In Figure 4.4 the slope of each indifference curve equals the change in goods ($dY$) divided by the change in services ($dX$). This relation, called the **marginal rate of substitution,** is simply the change in consumption of $Y$ (goods) necessary to offset a given change in the consumption of $X$ (services) if the consumer's overall level of utility is to remain constant. This can be stated algebraically:

$$MRS = \frac{dY}{dX} = \frac{\Delta Y}{\Delta X} = \text{Slope of an indifference curve.} \qquad \textbf{4.2}$$

The marginal rate of substitution is usually not constant but diminishes as the amount of substitution increases. For example, in Figure 4.3, as more goods are substituted for services, the amount of services necessary to compensate for a given loss of goods will continue to fall. Alternatively, as more services are substituted for goods, the amount of goods necessary to compensate for a given loss of services will continue to fall. This means that the negative slope of each indifference curve tends to approach zero as we move from left to right.

The product substitution relation indicated by the slope of an indifference curve is directly related to the concept of diminishing marginal utility introduced earlier. This is because the marginal rate of substitution is equal to $-1$ times the ratio of the marginal utility derived from the consumption of each product ($MRS = -1(MU_X/MU_Y)$. To see this,

■ Figure 4.4
## Indifference Curves with Continuous Substitution of *X* and *Y*

Indifference curves have smooth U shapes when *X* and *Y* can be continuously substituted for each other.

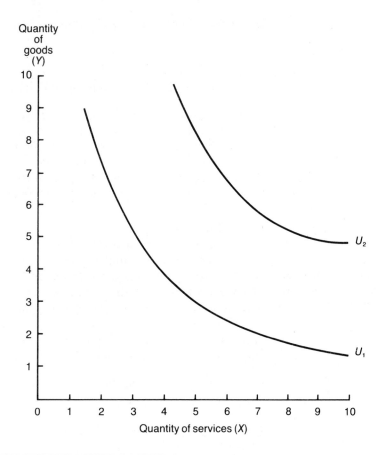

remember that the loss in utility associated with a small reduction in *Y* is equal to the marginal utility of *Y*, $MU_Y$, multiplied by the change in *Y*, $\Delta Y$. Algebraically:

$$\Delta U = MU_Y \times \Delta Y. \qquad \textbf{4.3}$$

Similarly, the change in utility associated with a change in the consumption of *X* is:

$$\Delta U = MU_X \times \Delta X. \qquad \textbf{4.4}$$

Along an indifference curve, the absolute value of $\Delta U$ must be equal for a given substitution of *Y* for *X*. In other words, since utility is held constant along an indifference curve, the loss in utility following a reduction in $Y$ must be fully offset by the gain in utility associated with an increase in $X$. Thus, $\Delta U$ in Equations 4.3 and 4.4 must be equal in size and have opposite signs for a given $\Delta Y$ and $\Delta X$. Therefore, along an indifference curve:

$$-(MU_X \times \Delta X) = MU_Y \times \Delta Y. \qquad \textbf{4.5}$$

Transposing the variables in Equation 4.5 produces:

$$-\frac{MU_X}{MU_Y} = \frac{\Delta Y}{\Delta X} \qquad \textbf{4.6}$$

$$MRS_{XY} = \text{Slope of an indifference curve.}$$

Thus, the slope of an indifference curve, shown in Equation 4.2 to be equal to $\Delta Y/\Delta X$, is determined by the ratio of marginal utilities derived from each product. In Figure 4.4, the slope of each indifference curve goes from a large negative number toward zero as we move from left to right. As seen in Equation 4.6, this implies that $MU_X$ decreases relative to $MU_Y$ as we progressively increase the relative consumption of $X$.

## Budget Lines

**budget line**

All combinations of products that can be purchased for a fixed dollar amount.

To fully understand consumer decisions, the concept of a budget line must be introduced. A **budget line** represents all combinations of products that can be purchased for a fixed dollar amount. To derive a budget line, we need only add up the amount of spending on goods and services that is feasible with a given budget. The amount of spending on goods is equal to the product of $P_Y$, the price of goods, times $Y$, the quantity purchased. Similarly, total spending on services is $P_X \times X$. When these amounts are added together, the budget line formula is derived:

$$\text{Total Budget} = \text{Spending on Goods} + \text{Spending on Services}$$

$$B = P_Y Y + P_X X.$$

Solving this expression for $Y$ so that it can be graphed as in Figure 4.5a results in:

$$Y = \frac{B}{P_Y} - \frac{P_X}{P_Y} X. \qquad \textbf{4.7}$$

Note that the first term in Equation 4.7 is the $Y$-axis intercept of the budget line. It indicates the quantity of Product $Y$ that can be purchased with a given budget, *assuming that zero units of Product X are purchased.* The slope of the budget line is equal to $-P_X/P_Y$ and, therefore, is a measure of the relative prices of the products being purchased. From this it follows that a change in the budget level $B$ leads to a parallel shift in the budget line, whereas a change in the relative prices of the items being purchased will result in a change in the slope of the budget line.

For example, if the price for goods is \$250 per unit and for services is \$100 per unit, the relevant budget line can be written as:

■ Figure 4.5

## Consumption Effects of Changes in Budget and Relative Prices

(a) An increase in budget results in a parallel outward shift in the budget line. (b) A price cut allows purchase of a greater quantity with a given budget.

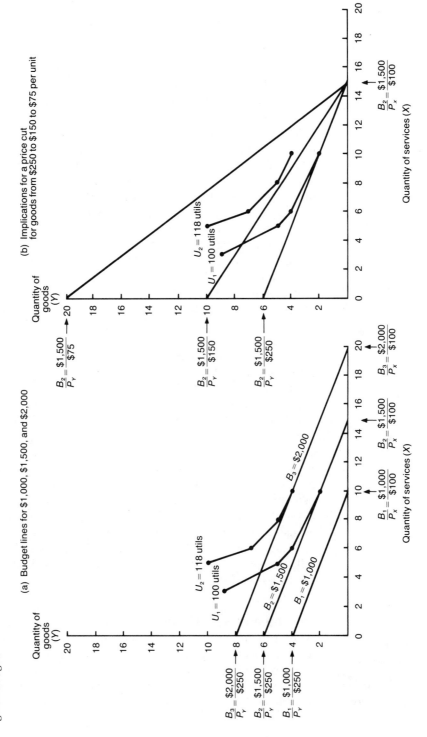

(a) Budget lines for $1,000, $1,500, and $2,000

(b) Implications for a price cut for goods from $250 to $150 to $75 per unit

$$B = \$250\,Y + \$100\,X$$

or

$$Y = \frac{B}{\$250} - \frac{\$100}{\$250}X.$$

Given a $1,000 budget, a maximum of 4 units of goods ($Y = \$1,000/\$250$) could be purchased. This assumes, of course, that the entire $1,000 is spent on goods and none on services. If all $1,000 is devoted to the purchase of services, a maximum of 10 units of services ($X = \$1,000/\$100$) could be purchased. These market baskets, ($0X$, $4Y$) and ($10X$, $0Y$), represent the endpoints of the $B_1 = \$1,000$ budget line shown in Figure 4.5a. This budget line identifies all combinations of goods and services that can be purchased for $1,000. Notice that $1,000 is insufficient to purchase any market basket lying on the $U_1 = 100$ or $U_2 = 118$ indifference curves. A minimum expenditure of $1,500 is necessary before the $U_1 = 100$ level of satisfaction can be achieved, and a minimum of $2,000 is necessary before the $U = 118$ level can be reached.

Again, the effect of a budget increase is to shift a budget line outward and to the right. The effect of a budget decrease is to shift a budget line inward and to the left. So long as the relative prices of goods and services remain constant, budget lines will remain parallel, as is shown in Figure 4.5a. This follows from the fact that so long as relative prices remain constant, the slope of this budget line also remains constant.

The effect of a change in relative prices is shown in Figure 4.5b. Here the budget of $1,500 and the $100-per-unit price of services remain constant while the price of goods falls progressively from $250 to $150 to $75 per unit. As the price of goods falls, a given budget will purchase more goods. Thus, a maximum of 6 units of goods can be purchased at a price of $250 per unit, 10 units at a price of $150, and 20 units at a price of $75.

In general, a fall in the price of goods or services permits an increase in consumption and consumer welfare. If both prices fall by a given percentage, a parallel rightward shift in the budget line will occur that is identical to the effect of an increase in budget. For example, the increase in consumption made possible by an increase in budget from $B_2 = \$1,500$ to $B_3 = \$2,000$ as shown in Figure 4.5a could also be realized following a decrease in the price of goods from $250 to $187.50 and for services from $100 to $75.

## Income and Substitution Effects

**income effect**

Shift to a new indifference curve following a change in aggregate consumption caused by a price change.

When product prices change, the consumer is affected in two ways. The **income effect** of a price change is the increase in overall consumption made possible by a price cut or the decrease in overall consumption made necessary by a price increase. The income effect results in a shift to a higher indifference curve following a price cut or a shift to a lower

■ Figure 4.6
# Income and Substitution Effects Following Reduction in the Price of Goods

A price change will result in both income and substitution effects.

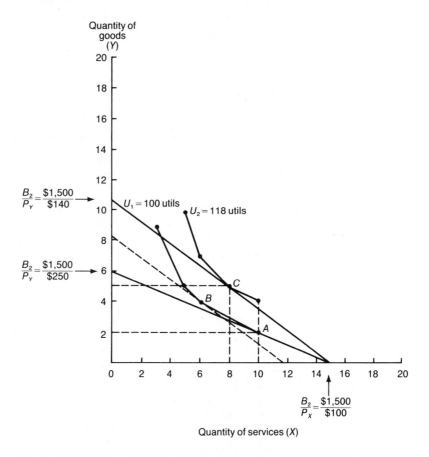

substitution effect

Movement along an indifference curve reflecting the substitution of cheaper products for more expensive ones.

indifference curve following a price increase. The **substitution effect** of a price change describes the change in relative consumption that occurs as consumers substitute cheaper products for more expensive products. The substitution effect results in an upward or downward movement along a given indifference curve. The total effect of a price change on consumption is the sum of the income and substitution effects.

Using our earlier example, the total effect of a change in the price of goods is shown in Figure 4.6. When $P_Y = \$250$ and $P_X = \$100$, $U_1 = 100$ is the highest level of satisfaction that can be achieved with a $1,500 budget. This involves consumption of 10 units of service and 2 units of goods. Following a cut in the price of goods from $P_Y$ = \$250 to $P_Y$ = \$140, consumption of the $X$ = 8 and $Y$ = 5 market basket becomes possible, and consumer welfare rises from $U$ = 100 to $U$ = 118. This change in consumption involves two components. The leftward movement along the $U_1$ = 100 indifference curve to point $B$, a tangency with the dashed hypothetical budget line representing the new relative prices for goods and services *but no income gain*, is the substitution effect. It reflects the substitution of now lower-priced goods for the relatively more expensive services. The upward shift from point $B$ on the $U_1$ = 100 indifference curve to point $C$ on the $U_2$ = 118 indifference curve is made possible by the income effect of the price reduction for goods.

# OPTIMAL CONSUMPTION

We can now integrate our analysis of the marginal rate of substitution, prices, and budget considerations to determine the optimal combination of products for consumption. This involves combining the consumer preference information provided by indifference curves with the cost considerations incorporated in budget lines.

## Utility Maximization

The optimal market basket is the one that maximizes a consumer's utility for a given budget expenditure. To allocate expenditures efficiently among various products, we must consider both the marginal utility derived from consumption and the prices for each product. Utility will be maximized when the marginal utility derived from each individual product is proportional to the price paid. This is illustrated graphically in Figure 4.7, which shows multiple indifference curves and multiple budget lines. Optimal market baskets of goods and services are indicated for each budget level by the points of tangency between respective indifference curves and budget lines. To see this, assume that an individual has the funds indicated by budget line $B_1$. In this case, the optimal consumption combination occurs at point $A$, the point of tangency between the budget line and indifference curve $U_1$. At that point, goods ($X$) and services ($Y$) are combined in proportions that maximize the utility attainable with budget expenditure $B_1$. No other combination of $X$ and $Y$ that can be purchased along budget line $B_1$ will provide as much satisfaction, or utility. All other $X$, $Y$ combinations along the budget line $B_1$ must intersect indifference curves representing lower levels of utility. Alternatively stated, the combination $X_1Y_1$ is the lowest-cost consumption market basket that provides the $U_1$ level of utility. All other $X$, $Y$ combinations on the $U_1$ indifference curve lie on higher budget lines. Similarly, $X_2Y_2$ is the lowest-cost combination of goods and services that provides utility at the $U_2$ level, $X_3Y_3$ is the lowest-cost market basket that provides a $U_3$ level of utility, and so on. All other market baskets providing $U_1$, $U_2$, and $U_3$ levels of utility are intersected by higher budget lines and, therefore, require a higher level of expenditure.

■ Figure 4.7
## Optimal Market Baskets for Consumption

The optimal path for consumption is found when $P_X/P_Y = MU_X/MU_Y$.

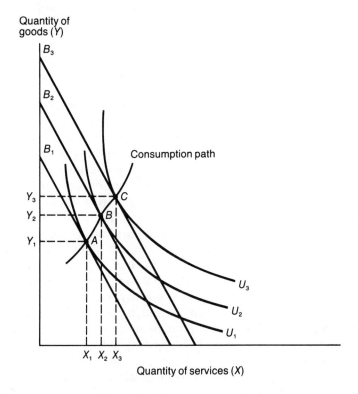

The fact that optimal consumption combinations occur at points of tangency between budget lines and indifference curves leads to a very important economic principle. The slope of a budget line was shown to be $-1$ times the ratio of the product prices, $-P_X/P_Y$. Recall also that the slope of an indifference curve was shown to be equal to the marginal rate of substitution of one consumption item for the other when utility is held constant at a given level. The marginal rate of substitution was shown in Equation 4.6 as $-1$ times the ratio of the marginal utilities for each product. Thus, the slope of an indifference curve equals $-MU_X/MU_Y$.

At each point where goods and services are combined optimally, there is a tangency between the budget line and the indifference curve; hence, their slopes are equal. Therefore, for optimal consumption combinations, the ratio of the prices of the goods and services must be equal to the ratio of their marginal utilities:

Slope of an Indifference Curve $=$ Slope of a Budget Line

$$-\frac{MU_X}{MU_Y} = -\frac{P_X}{P_Y}$$

$$\frac{MU_X}{MU_Y} = \frac{P_X}{P_Y}. \qquad\qquad \textbf{4.8}$$

or

$$\frac{MU_X}{P_X} = \frac{MU_Y}{P_Y} \qquad\qquad \textbf{4.8a}$$

*Utility will be maximized when products are purchased at levels such that relative prices equal the relative marginal utility derived from consumption.* The alternative statement of this principle, given by Equation 4.8a, shows that with optimal consumption proportions, an additional dollar spent on a given consumption item adds as much to total utility as would a dollar spent on any other such item. Any combination of goods and services violating this rule is suboptimal in the sense that a change in the consumer's market basket could result in greater utility being obtained for the same budget expenditure.

In Figure 4.7, Point A represents an optimal allocation, since $X_1$ and $Y_1$ will provide the highest possible utility for the $B_1$ expenditure level. Similarly, Points B and C represent efficient allocations for the $B_2$ and $B_3$ expenditure levels. By connecting all points of tangency between indifference curves and budget lines (such as Points A, B, and C), we identify a **consumption path,** which depicts optimal market baskets for consumption as the budget expenditure level grows.

**consumption path**

**Optimal combinations of products as consumption increases.**

To summarize, the demand for consumer goods and services is based on the utility or satisfaction derived from consumption. This utility will be maximized at each budget level when the relative marginal utility derived from consumption of each product is proportional to the price paid. Only then will each product be an attractive purchase in the sense of providing the same marginal utility per dollar of expenditure. Therefore, the effective allocation of a consumer's budget requires a consideration of both relative prices and the relative marginal utility derived from consumption.

With this background, we have the framework for a detailed analysis of the important roles played by prices, advertising, income, and other factors in determining the level of demand for a firm's products. Our analysis will focus on the sensitivity of demand to *changes* in important demand-determining factors.

# DEMAND SENSITIVITY ANALYSIS: ELASTICITY

For managerial decision making, the firm must know how sensitive demand is to changes in the underlying factors in demand functions. Factors such as price and advertising that are within the control of the firm

**endogenous variables**
Those factors controlled by the firm.

**exogenous variables**
Those factors outside the control of the firm.

are called **endogenous variables.** It is important for management to know the effects of altering these variables when making decisions. Other important factors that are outside the control of the firm such as consumer incomes, competitor prices, and the weather, for example, are called **exogenous variables.** Understanding the effects of both types of influences is important for effective managerial decision making.

The effects of changes in both types of influences must be understood if the firm is to respond effectively to changes in the economic environment. For example, a firm must understand the effects on demand of changes in both prices and consumer incomes in order to determine the price cut necessary to offset a decline in sales caused by a business recession (fall in income). Similarly, the sensitivity of demand to changes in advertising must be quantified if the firm is to respond appropriately with price or advertising changes to an increase in competitor advertising. Determining the effects of changes in both controllable and uncontrollable influences on demand is the focus of demand analysis.

**elasticity**
The percentage change in a dependent variable resulting from a 1-percent change in an independent variable.

One measure of responsiveness employed not only in demand analysis but throughout managerial decision making is **elasticity,** defined as the percentage change in a dependent variable, $Y$, resulting from a 1-percent change in the value of an independent variable, $X$. The equation for calculating elasticity is:

$$\text{Elasticity} = \frac{\text{Percentage Change in } Y}{\text{Percentage Change in } X}. \qquad \textbf{4.9}$$

The concept of elasticity is quite general. It simply involves the percentage change in one variable associated with a given percentage change in another variable. In addition to demand analysis, the concept is used in finance, where the impact of changes in sales on earnings under different production levels (operating leverage) and different financial structures (financial leverage) is measured by an elasticity factor. Elasticities are also used in production analysis to evaluate the effects of output changes on costs.

## Point Elasticity and Arc Elasticity

**point elasticity**
Measures elasticity at a given point on a function.

Elasticity can be measured in two different ways, called point elasticity and arc elasticity. **Point elasticity** measures elasticity at a given point on a function. The point elasticity concept is used to measure the effect on a dependent variable $Y$ of a very small or marginal change in an independent variable $X$. Although the point elasticity concept can often give accurate estimates of the effect on $Y$ of small (less than 5-percent) changes in $X$, it is not used to measure the effect on $Y$ of large-scale changes, because elasticity typically varies at different points along a function. In order to assess the effects of large-scale changes in $X$, the arc elasticity concept is employed. **Arc elasticity** measures the average elasticity over a given range of a function.

**arc elasticity**
Measures the average elasticity over a given range of a function.

Using the lower-case Greek letter $\epsilon$ (epsilon) as the symbol for point elasticity, the point elasticity formula can be written:

$$\text{Point Elasticity} = \epsilon_X = \frac{\text{Percentage Change in } Y}{\text{Percentage Change in } X}$$

$$= \frac{\Delta Y/Y}{\Delta X/X}$$

$$= \frac{\Delta Y}{\Delta X} \times \frac{X}{Y}. \qquad \textbf{4.10}$$

The $\Delta Y/\Delta X$ term in the point elasticity formula is the marginal relation between $Y$ and $X$, and it shows the effect on $Y$ of a one-unit change in $X$. Point elasticity is determined by multiplying this marginal relation by the relative size of $X$ to $Y$, or the $X/Y$ ratio at the point being analyzed.

At the limit, where $\Delta X$ is very small, $\Delta Y/\Delta X = \partial Y/\partial X$ (the partial derivative of the function taken with respect to $X$). We use the partial derivative $\partial Q/\partial X$ because we are concerned with the response of quantity demanded to changes in one independent variable, $X$, *holding all other variables constant*. This precise marginal relation at a specific point on the function is frequently used in the equation for point elasticity, providing the following alternative equation:

$$\text{Point Elasticity} = \epsilon_X = \frac{\partial Y}{\partial X} \times \frac{X}{Y}. \qquad \textbf{4.10a}$$

The point elasticity is determined by multiplying the partial derivative of the demand function at a given point by the ratio $X/Y$ at that point.

Point elasticity measures the percentage effect on $Y$ of a percentage change in $X$ at a given point on a function. If $\epsilon_X = 5$, a 1-percent increase in $X$ will lead to a 5-percent increase in $Y$, and a 1-percent decrease in $X$ will lead to a 5-percent decrease in $Y$. Thus, when $\epsilon_X > 0$, $Y$ changes in the same positive or negative direction as $X$. Conversely, when $\epsilon_X < 0$, $Y$ changes in the opposite direction of changes in $X$. For example, if $\epsilon_X = -3$, a 1-percent increase in $X$ will lead to a 3-percent decrease in $Y$, and a 1-percent decrease in $X$ will lead to a 3-percent increase in $Y$.

An example will illustrate the calculation and use of a point elasticity estimate. Assume we are interested in analyzing the responsiveness of movie-ticket demand to changes in advertising for the Buckeye Cinema Corporation, a regional chain of movie theaters. Also assume that analysis of monthly data for six outlets covering the past year suggests the following demand function:

$$Q = 6,600 - 5,000P + 3,500P_{\text{VCR}} + 50I + 1,000A, \qquad \textbf{4.11}$$

where $Q$ is the quantity of movie tickets, $P$ is average ticket price (in dollars), $P_{\text{VCR}}$ is the movie rental price at VCR outlets in the area (in dollars), $I$ is average disposable income per household (in thousands of dollars), and $A$ is monthly advertising expenditures (in thousands of dollars). If for a typical theater $P = \$5$, $P_{\text{VCR}} = \$2$, and income and advertising are $\$28,000$ and $\$20,000$, respectively, the demand for movie tickets at a typical theater can then be estimated as:

$$Q = 6,600 - 5,000(5) + 3,500(2) + 50(28) + 1,000(20)$$
$$= 10,000.$$

(Note that $I$ and $A$ are expressed in thousands of dollars in the demand function.)

The numbers that appear before each variable in Equation 4.11 are called coefficients or parameter estimates. They indicate the expected change in movie-ticket sales associated with a one-unit change in each relevant variable. For example, the number 5,000 indicates that the quantity of movie tickets demanded will fall by 5,000 units with every $1 increase in the price of movie tickets, or $\partial Q/\partial P = -5,000$. Similarly, a $1 increase in the price of video-cassette rentals will cause a 3,500 unit increase in movie-ticket demand, or $\partial Q/\partial P_{VCR} = 3,500$. In terms of advertising, the expected change in demand following a one-unit ($1,000) change in advertising, or $\partial Q/\partial A$, is 1,000. With advertising expenditures of $20,000, the point advertising elasticity at the 10,000 unit demand level is:

$$\epsilon_A = \text{Point Advertising Elasticity}$$

$$= \frac{\text{Percentage Change in Quantity } (Q)}{\text{Percentage Change in Advertising } (A)}$$

$$= \frac{\partial Q/Q}{\partial A/A}$$

$$= \frac{\partial Q}{\partial A} \times \frac{A}{Q}$$

$$= 1,000 \times \frac{\$20}{10,000}$$

$$= 2. \qquad \qquad \textbf{4.12}$$

Thus, a 1-percent change in advertising expenditures results in a 2-percent change in movie-ticket demand. The elasticity is positive, indicating a direct relation between advertising outlays and movie-ticket demand; that is, an increase in advertising expenditures leads to an increase in demand, and, conversely, a decrease in advertising expenditures leads to a decrease in demand.

For many business decisions, managers are concerned with the impact of substantial changes in a demand-determining factor, such as advertising, rather than with the impact of very small (marginal) changes. In these instances the point elasticity concept suffers a conceptual shortcoming.

To see the nature of the problem, consider the calculation of the advertising elasticity of demand for movie tickets when advertising increases from $20,000 to $50,000. Assume for this example that all other demand-influencing variables retain their previous values. With advertising at $20,000, demand is 10,000 units. Changing advertising to

## 4.1  **Managerial Application**

Using Sports Advertising to Sell Your Products

Advertising effectiveness is a major concern of managers in a wide variety of industries. During recent years, many have come to the conclusion that nothing sells like sports. The high and growing popularity of college and professional sports has influenced many firms to emphasize sports programming, especially in TV advertising. During 1986, for example, the top ten advertisers spent over one-half billion dollars sponsoring network sports telecasts. Anheuser-Busch was the advertising leader with $96.1 million in spending, followed by General Motors ($95.1 million), Philip Morris ($89.4 million), and Ford ($45.5 million). Interestingly, the U.S. Armed Forces rounded out the top five with $44.1 million in spending.

In addition to sponsoring regularly scheduled sporting events such as the National Football League games and Monday Night Baseball, companies spend millions of dollars in order to gain the endorsements of popular sports personalities. A sports personality with one of the highest endorsement incomes is golf pro Arnold Palmer, who earns a reported $6 million per year from Hertz, Pennzoil, Rolex, Paine Webber, and other sponsors. Tennis pro Boris Becker earns an estimated $5 million per year in endorsement income from Deutsche Bank, Puma, Coca-Cola, Polaroid, and other sponsors. Close behind is basketball star Michael Jordan, who earns an estimated $4 million per year endorsing products by Nike, Wilson, Coca-Cola, Johnson Products, and McDonalds. Other leading athletes with

*continued*

See: Michael Oneal and Peter Finch, "Nothing Sells Like Sports," *Business Week*, August 31, 1987, 48–53; and Jeffrey A. Trachtenberg, "Does Sports Marketing Make Sense?" *The Wall Street Journal*, April 19, 1989, B1.

$50,000 ($\Delta A = 30$) results in a 30,000-unit increase in movie-ticket demand, so total demand at that level is 40,000 tickets. Using Equation 4.10 to calculate the point advertising elasticity for the change in advertising from $20,000 to $50,000, we find that:

$$\text{Advertising Elasticity} = \frac{\Delta Q}{\Delta A} \times \frac{A}{Q} = \frac{30,000}{\$30} \times \frac{\$20}{10,000} = 2.$$

The point advertising elasticity is 2, just as we found previously. Consider, however, the indicated elasticity if we move in the opposite direction—that is, if we decrease advertising from $50,000 to $20,000. The indicated point elasticity is:

substantial endorsement incomes include golf pro Greg Norman ($4 million), football star Jim McMahon ($4 million), and America's Cup skipper Dennis Conner ($1.8 million). While expensive and risky, given the fleeting nature of many sports careers, the power of athlete endorsements is aptly illustrated by Jordan, whose "Air Jordan" basketball shoe, with a retail price in excess of $100 per pair, became an instant sensation with teenagers across the country.

An important new trend in sports advertising is the move toward event sponsorship. Rather than just buying time on network telecasts, more than 3,400 companies spent roughly $1.5 billion to sponsor entire sporting events during 1987. That represents a four-fold increase since 1983. Along with ads and promotions tied directly to sponsorship, the total advertising expenditure will soon reach $3.5 billion, or roughly double the total spent on network TV sports advertising. The Equitable Old-Timers' Baseball Games, the Coors International Bicycle Classic, the Sunkist Fiesta Bowl, and the American Telephone & Telegraph Co. Pebble Beach National Park Pro-

Am Golf Tournament are but a few examples. In many instances, event sponsorship has proved to be successful in allowing advertisers to create a cost-effective, stable, long-term marketing image in the minds of consumers. However, the approach is not without its problems. When AT&T took over sponsorship of the Pebble Beach Pro-Am, for example, it had to haggle with the Bing Crosby family and other officials over the right to affix its name to the tournament. Not only did the company suffer some negative publicity for its "over-commercialization" of the tournament, but many continue to refer to the tournament as "the Crosby" or the "Pebble Beach."

Despite high costs and other problems, event sponsorship in particular and sports marketing in general are sure to grow in importance during coming years. As Equitable Financial Co. has discovered, a little sales pitch mixed in with the old-timers' slow pitches is an effective means of generating an enormous amount of favorable publicity and goodwill.

$$\text{Advertising Elasticity} = \frac{\Delta Q}{\Delta A} \times \frac{A}{Q} = \frac{-30{,}000}{-\$30} \times \frac{\$50}{40{,}000} = 1.25.$$

We see that the indicated elasticity is quite different. This problem stems from the fact that elasticities are not typically constant but differ at different points along a given demand function. The advertising elasticity of 1.25 is the point advertising elasticity when advertising expenditures are $50,000 and the quantity demanded is 40,000 tickets.

To overcome the problem of changing elasticities along a demand function, the arc elasticity formula was developed to calculate an average elasticity for incremental as opposed to marginal changes. The arc elasticity formula is:

$$E = \text{Arc Elasticity} = \frac{\dfrac{\text{Change in } Q}{\text{Average } Q}}{\dfrac{\text{Change in } X}{\text{Average } X}} = \frac{\dfrac{Q_2 - Q_1}{(Q_2 + Q_1)/2}}{\dfrac{X_2 - X_1}{(X_2 - X_1)/2}}$$

$$= \frac{\dfrac{\Delta Q}{(Q_2 + Q_1)}}{\dfrac{\Delta X}{(X_2 + X_1)}} = \frac{\Delta Q}{\Delta X} \times \frac{X_2 + X_1}{Q_2 + Q_1}. \qquad \textbf{4.13}$$

Again we divide the percentage change in quantity demanded by the percentage change in a demand-determining variable, but here the bases used to calculate the percentage changes are averages of the two data points rather than the initially observed value. The arc elasticity equation eliminates the problem of the elasticity measure depending on which end of the range is viewed as the initial point. This yields a more accurate measure of the *average* relative relation between the two variables over the range indicated by the data. The arc advertising elasticity over the $20,000-to-$50,000 range of advertising expenditures can be calculated as:

$$\text{Arc Advertising Elasticity} = \frac{\text{Percentage Change in Quantity } (Q)}{\text{Percentage Change in Advertising } (A)}$$

$$= \frac{(Q_2 - Q_1)/(Q_2 + Q_1)}{(A_2 - A_1)/(A_2 + A_1)}$$

$$= \frac{\Delta Q}{\Delta A} \times \frac{A_2 + A_1}{Q_2 + Q_1}$$

$$= \frac{30,000}{\$30} \times \frac{\$50 + \$20}{40,000 + 10,000}$$

$$= 1.4.$$

Thus, a 1-percent change in the level of advertising expenditures in the range of $20,000 to $50,000 will result, on average, in a 1.4-percent change in movie-ticket demand.

To summarize, it is important to remember that point elasticity is a marginal concept. It measures the elasticity at a specific point on a function. Proper use of point elasticity is limited to analysis of very small changes, say 0 to 5 percent, in the relevant independent variable. Arc elasticity is a better concept for measuring the average elasticity over an extended range. It is the appropriate tool for incremental analysis.

**price elasticity of demand**

Measures the responsiveness of the quantity demanded to changes in the price of the product, holding constant the values of all other variables in the demand function.

# PRICE ELASTICITY OF DEMAND

The most widely used elasticity measure is the **price elasticity of demand**, which measures the responsiveness of the quantity demanded to changes in the price of the product, holding constant the values of all other variables in the demand function.

Using the formula for point elasticity, price elasticity of demand is found as:

$$\epsilon_P = \text{Point Price Elasticity} = \frac{\text{Percentage Change in Quantity } (Q)}{\text{Percentage Change in Price } (P)}$$

$$= \frac{\partial Q/Q}{\partial P/P}$$

$$= \frac{\partial Q}{\partial P} \times \frac{P}{Q}, \qquad \textbf{4.14}$$

where $\partial Q/\partial P$ is the marginal change in quantity following a one-unit change in price, and $P$ and $Q$ are price and quantity at a given point on the demand curve.

The concept of point price elasticity can be illustrated by referring to Equation 4.11:

$$Q = 6{,}600 - 5{,}000P + 3{,}500P_{VCR} + 50I + 1{,}000A.$$

The coefficient for the price variable indicates the effect on quantity demanded of a one-unit change in price:

$$\frac{\partial Q}{\partial P} = -5{,}000, \text{ a constant.}$$

At the typical values of $P_{VCR} = \$2$, $I = \$28{,}000$, and $A = \$20{,}000$, the demand curve can be calculated as:

$$Q = 6{,}600 - 5{,}000(P) + 3{,}500(2) + 50(28) + 1{,}000(20)$$
$$= 35{,}000 - 5{,}000P.$$

Now let us calculate $\epsilon_P$ at two points on the demand curve: (1) where $P_1 = \$5$ and $Q_1 = 10{,}000$, and (2) where $P_2 = \$6$ and $Q_2 = 5{,}000$:

$$(1)\ \epsilon_{P_1} = -5{,}000 \times \left(\frac{\$5}{10{,}000}\right) = -2.5.$$

$$(2)\ \epsilon_{P_2} = -5{,}000 \times \left(\frac{\$6}{5{,}000}\right) = -6.$$

Thus, a 1-percent increase in price from the $5 movie-ticket price level results in a 2.5-percent reduction in the quantity demanded, but at the $6 price level, a 1-percent increase results in a 6-percent reduction in the quantity demanded. This reflects the fact that movie-ticket buyers, like most consumers, become increasingly price sensitive as average price increases. This example illustrates how price elasticity can vary along a demand curve, with $\epsilon_P$ increasing in absolute value at higher prices and lower quantities. We will show in a later section that price elasticity always varies along a linear demand curve. Under certain conditions, however, it can be constant along a curvilinear demand curve.

Note also that the previously calculated price elasticities are negative numbers. This is typical and follows from the fact that the quantity demanded for most goods and services is inversely related to price. Thus, in the example, at a $5 price, a 1-percent *increase* in price leads to a 2.5-percent *decrease* in the quantity of movie tickets demanded. Conversely, a 1-percent decrease in price would lead to a 2.5-percent increase in the quantity demanded.[2]

Using the arc elasticity concept, the equation for price elasticity is:

$$E_P = \text{Arc Price Elasticity} = \frac{\text{Percentage Change in Quantity } (Q)}{\text{Percentage Change in Price } (P)}$$

$$= \frac{(Q_2 - Q_1)/(Q_2 + Q_1)}{(P_2 - P_1)/(P_2 + P_1)}$$

$$= \frac{\Delta Q}{\Delta P} \times \frac{P_2 + P_1}{Q_2 + Q_1}. \qquad \textbf{4.15}$$

This form is especially useful for analyzing the average sensitivity of demand to price changes over an extended range. For example, the average price elasticity over the range from $5 to $6 is:

$$E_P = \frac{\Delta Q}{\Delta P} \times \frac{P_2 + P_1}{Q_2 + Q_1}$$

$$= \frac{-5,000}{1} \times \frac{\$6 + \$5}{5,000 + 10,000}$$

$$= -3.67.$$

This means that, on average, a 1-percent change in price leads to a 3.67-percent change in quantity demanded when price is between $5 and $6 per ticket.

## Price Elasticity and Total Revenue

One of the most important features of the price elasticity concept is that it provides a useful summary measure of the effect of a price change on revenues. Depending on the degree of price elasticity, a reduction in price can increase total revenue, decrease it, or leave it unchanged. If we have a good estimate of price elasticity, we can estimate quite accurately the change in total revenue that will follow a price change.

**Elastic, Unitary, and Inelastic Demand**    For decision-making purposes, three specific ranges of price elasticity have been identified. Using $|\epsilon_P|$ to

---

[2]In some texts the equation for price elasticity is multiplied by $-1$ to change price elasticities to positive numbers. We do not follow this convention, although it creates no problem so long as one remembers the inverse relation between price and quantity. We alert the reader to this possible construction because price elasticities are sometimes reported as positive numbers.

denote the absolute value of the price elasticity, the three ranges can be classified as:

(1) $|\epsilon_P| > 1.0$, defined as elastic demand.
    *Example:* $\epsilon_P = -3.2$ and $|\epsilon_P| = 3.2$
(2) $|\epsilon_P| = 1.0$, defined as unitary elasticity.
    *Example:* $\epsilon_P = -1.0$ and $|\epsilon_P| = 1.0$
(3) $|\epsilon_P| < 1.0$, defined as inelastic demand.
    *Example:* $\epsilon_P = -0.5$ and $|\epsilon_P| = 0.5$

**elastic demand**

A situation in which a price change leads to a more than proportionate change in quantity demanded.

**unitary elasticity**

A situation in which price and quantity changes exactly offset each other.

**inelastic demand**

A situation in which a price change leads to a less than proportionate change in quantity demanded.

With **elastic demand** (that is, $|\epsilon_P| > 1$), the relative change in quantity is larger than that of price, so a given percentage increase in price causes quantity to decrease by a larger percentage, decreasing total revenue. Thus, if demand is elastic, a price increase will lower total revenue and a decrease in price will raise total revenue. Now consider **unitary elasticity,** a situation in which the percentage change in quantity divided by the percentage change in price equals $-1$. Since price and quantity are inversely related, a price elasticity of $-1$ means that the effect of a price change is *exactly* offset by the change in quantity demanded. The result is that total revenue, the product of price times quantity, remains constant. Finally, with **inelastic demand,** a price increase will produce a less than proportionate decline in the quantity demanded, so total revenues will rise. These relations are summarized in the following table:

| The Case of | Implies | Following a Price Increase | Following a Price Decrease |
|---|---|---|---|
| 1. Elastic demand, $\|\epsilon_P\| > 1$ | $\%\Delta Q > \%\Delta P$ | Revenue decreases | Revenue increases |
| 2. Unitary elasticity, $\|\epsilon_P\| = 1$ | $\%\Delta Q = \%\Delta P$ | Revenue unchanged | Revenue unchanged |
| 3. Inelastic demand, $\|\epsilon_P\| < 1$ | $\%\Delta Q < \%\Delta P$ | Revenue increases | Revenue decreases |

**The Limiting Cases**   Price elasticity can range from 0 (completely inelastic) to $-\infty$ (perfectly elastic). To illustrate, consider first the case in which the quantity demanded is independent of price so that some fixed amount, $Q^*$, will be demanded regardless of price.

When the quantity demanded of a product is completely insensitive to price, the partial derivative $\partial Q / \partial P$ equals zero and, therefore, price elasticity will also equal zero. The demand curve for such a good or service is perfectly vertical, as shown in Figure 4.8.

The other limiting case, that of infinite price elasticity, describes a product that is completely sensitive to price. The demand curve for such

■ Figure 4.8

## Completely Inelastic Demand Curve: $\epsilon_P = 0$

With perfectly inelastic demand, a fixed level of output is demanded irrespective of price.

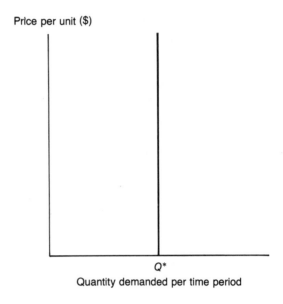

a good or service is perfectly horizontal, as shown in Figure 4.9. Here the partial derivative $\partial Q/\partial P = -\infty$ and $\epsilon_P = -\infty$ regardless of the value of $P/Q$.

The economic as well as mathematical properties of these limiting cases should be understood. A firm faced with a vertical, perfectly inelastic demand curve could charge any price and still sell $Q^*$ units. Thus, it could, theoretically, appropriate all of its customers' income or wealth. Conversely, a firm facing a horizontal, perfectly elastic demand curve could sell an unlimited amount of output at the price $P^*$, but it would lose all sales if it raised prices by even a small amount. Such extremes are rare in the real world, but monopolies selling necessities (for example, water companies) have relatively inelastic demand curves, whereas firms in highly competitive industries (for example, grocery retailing) face highly elastic demand curves.

## Varying Elasticity at Different Points on a Demand Curve

All linear demand curves, except perfectly elastic or perfectly inelastic ones, are subject to varying elasticities at different points on the curve. In other words, any given linear demand curve will be price elastic at

■ Figure 4.9
## Completely Elastic Demand Curve: $\epsilon_P = -\infty$

With perfectly elastic demand, all output is sold at a fixed price.

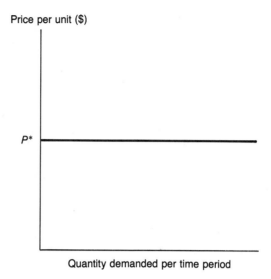

some output levels but inelastic at others. To see this, recall again the definition of point price elasticity expressed in Equation 4.14.

$$\epsilon_P = \frac{\partial Q}{\partial P} \times \frac{P}{Q}.$$

The slope of a linear demand curve, $\partial P/\partial Q$, is constant, and thus so is its reciprocal, $1/(\partial P/\partial Q) = \partial Q/\partial P$. However, the ratio $P/Q$ varies from 0 at the point where the demand curve intersects the horizontal axis (where price = 0) to $+\infty$ at the vertical (price) axis intercept (where quantity = 0). Since we are multiplying a negative constant by a ratio that varies between 0 and $+\infty$, the price elasticity of a linear curve must range from 0 to $-\infty$.

Figure 4.10 illustrates this relation. As the demand curve approaches the vertical axis, the ratio $P/Q$ approaches infinity, and $\epsilon_P$ approaches minus infinity. As the demand curve approaches the horizontal axis, the ratio $P/Q$ approaches 0, causing $\epsilon_P$ also to approach 0. At the midpoint of the demand curve $(\partial Q/\partial P) \times (P/Q) = -1$; this is the point of unitary elasticity.

## Price Elasticity and Revenue Relations
We can further clarify the relation between price elasticity and total revenue and emphasize its importance in demand analysis by examining

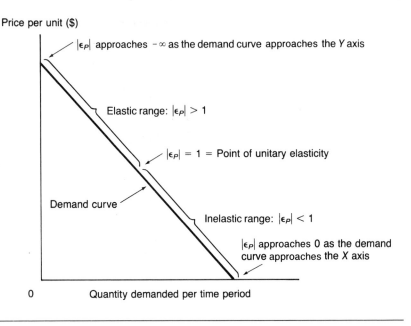

■ Figure 4.10
## Elasticities along a Linear Demand Curve

The price elasticity of demand will vary from 0 to $-\infty$ along a linear demand curve.

Price per unit ($)

$|\epsilon_P|$ approaches $-\infty$ as the demand curve approaches the Y axis

Elastic range: $|\epsilon_P| > 1$

$|\epsilon_P| = 1$ = Point of unitary elasticity

Demand curve

Inelastic range: $|\epsilon_P| < 1$

$|\epsilon_P|$ approaches 0 as the demand curve approaches the X axis

0        Quantity demanded per time period

Figure 4.11 and Table 4.4. Figure 4.11a reproduces the demand curve shown in Figure 4.10, but it adds the associated marginal revenue curve. The demand curve shown in Figure 4.11 is of the general linear form:

$$P = a - bQ, \qquad \textbf{4.16}$$

where $a$ is the intercept and $b$ is the slope coefficient. It follows that total revenue (TR) can be expressed as:

$$
\begin{aligned}
TR &= P \times Q, \\
&= (a - bQ) \times Q, \\
&= aQ - bQ^2.
\end{aligned}
$$

By definition, marginal revenue (MR) is the change in revenue following a one-unit expansion in output, $dTR/dQ$, and can be written:

$$MR = dTR/dQ = a - 2bQ. \qquad \textbf{4.17}$$

The relation between the demand (average revenue) and marginal revenue curves becomes clear when one compares Equations 4.16 and 4.17. Each equation has the same intercept $a$. This means that both curves begin at the same point along the vertical price axis. However, the marginal revenue curve has twice the negative slope of the demand curve. This means that the marginal revenue curve will intersect the horizontal

■ Figure 4.11
## Relations among Price Elasticity and Marginal, Average, and Total Revenue: (a) Demand (Average Revenue) and Marginal Revenue Curves; (b) Total Revenue

In the range where demand is elastic with respect to price, marginal revenue is positive and total revenue increases with a reduction in price. In the inelastic range, marginal revenue is negative and total revenue decreases with price reductions.

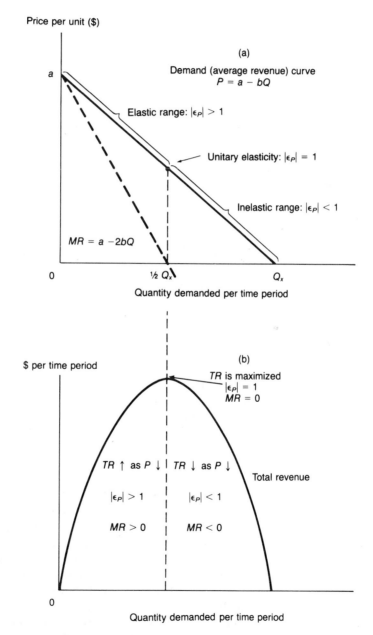

■ Table 4.4

# Price Elasticity and Revenue Relations: A Numerical Example

| Price P | Quantity Q | Total Revenue TR = P · Q | Marginal Revenue MR = ΔTR | Arc Elasticity[a] E_P |
|---|---|---|---|---|
| $100 | 1 | $100 | — | — |
| 90 | 2 | 180 | $80 | −6.33 |
| 80 | 3 | 240 | 60 | −3.40 |
| 70 | 4 | 280 | 40 | −2.14 |
| 60 | 5 | 300 | 20 | −1.44 |
| 50 | 6 | 300 | 0 | −1.00 |
| 40 | 7 | 280 | −20 | −0.69 |
| 30 | 8 | 240 | −40 | −0.47 |
| 20 | 9 | 180 | −60 | −0.29 |
| 10 | 10 | 100 | −80 | −0.16 |

[a]*Since the price and quantity data in the table are discrete numbers, the price elasticities have been calculated using the arc elasticity equation:*

$$E_P = \frac{Q_2 - Q_1}{P_2 - P_1} \times \frac{P_2 + P_1}{Q_2 + Q_1}.$$

axis at ½ $Q_X$, given that the demand curve intersects at $Q_X$. From Figure 4.11a we can also see that marginal revenue is positive in the range where demand is price elastic, zero where $\epsilon_P = -1$, and negative in the inelastic range. Thus, there is an obvious relation between price elasticity and both average and marginal revenue.

As shown in Figure 4.11b, price elasticity is also closely related to total revenue. Total revenue increases with price reductions in the elastic range (where $MR > 0$) because the increase in quantity demanded at the new lower price more than offsets the lower revenue per unit received at that reduced price. Total revenue peaks at the point of unitary elasticity (where $MR = 0$), since the increase in quantity associated with the price reduction exactly offsets the lower revenue per unit. Finally, total revenue declines when price is reduced in the inelastic range (where $MR < 0$). Here the quantity demanded continues to increase with reductions in price, but the relative increase in quantity is less than the percentage decrease in price, and thus it is not large enough to offset the reduction in revenue per unit sold.

The numerical example in Table 4.4 illustrates these relations. It shows that for one to five units of output, demand is elastic, $|\epsilon_P| > 1$, and a reduction in price increases total revenue. For example, decreasing price from $80 to $70 increases output from three units to four. Marginal revenue is positive over this range of output, and total revenue increases from $240 to $280. For output above six units (price below $50), demand is inelastic, $|\epsilon_P| < 1$. Here price reductions result in less total revenue, because the increase in quantity demanded is not large enough to offset the lower price per unit. With total revenue decreasing as output expands, marginal revenue must be negative. For example, reducing price from $30 to $20 results in revenue declining from $240 to $180 even though output increases from eight to nine units. Marginal revenue is −$60.

## Price Elasticity and Optimal Pricing Policy

Firms use price discounts, specials, coupons, and rebate programs to test the price sensitivity of demand for their products. As a practical matter, firms tend to maintain current and detailed information concerning the price elasticity of demand, even though they may not have the data necessary to completely derive the underlying demand function. The availability of price elasticity estimates, along with relevant cost data, is by itself sufficient to allow managers to set a pricing policy consistent with value maximization objectives. This is because a relatively simple mathematical relation holds between marginal revenue, price, and the point price elasticity of demand that, when combined with relevant cost data, can be used as the basis for an optimal pricing policy.

The relation between marginal revenue, price, and the point price elasticity of demand follows directly from the mathematical definition of a marginal relation developed in Appendix 2A. Using this relation, marginal revenue is the derivative of the total revenue function. That is, $MR = dTR/dQ$. Since total revenue equals price times quantity ($TR = P \times Q$), marginal revenue is found by taking the derivative of the function $P \times Q$ with respect to $Q$:

$$MR = \frac{d(P \times Q)}{dQ}.$$

Because price and quantity are interdependent in the typical demand situation, the rule for differentiating a product must be employed in taking the preceding derivative:

$$MR = \frac{dTR}{dQ} = \frac{d(P \times Q)}{dQ} = P \times \frac{dQ}{dQ} + Q \times \frac{dP}{dQ}$$

$$= P \times 1 + Q \times \frac{dP}{dQ}$$

$$= P + Q \times \frac{dP}{dQ}.$$

This relation is a completely general specification of marginal revenue, which, if $P$ is factored out from the right-hand side, can be rewritten as:

$$MR = P\left(1 + \frac{Q}{P} \times \frac{dP}{dQ}\right).$$

Note that the term $Q/P \times dP/dQ$ in the preceding expression is the reciprocal of the definition for point price elasticity, $\epsilon_P = dQ/dP \times (P/Q)$:

$$\frac{Q}{P} \times \frac{dP}{dQ} = \frac{1}{\dfrac{dQ}{dP} \times \dfrac{P}{Q}} = \frac{1}{\epsilon_P}.$$

Thus, marginal revenue can be rewritten as:

$$MR = P\left(1 + \frac{1}{\epsilon_P}\right) \qquad\qquad \textbf{4.18}$$

This simple relation between marginal revenue, price, and the point price elasticity of demand may well be one of the most useful pricing tools managerial economics has to offer. To illustrate the usefulness of Equation 4.18 as a practical pricing tool, consider the pricing problem faced by a profit-maximizing firm. Recall from Chapter 2 that profit maximization requires operating at the activity level where marginal cost equals marginal revenue. Most firms have extensive cost information and can estimate marginal costs reasonably well. By equating marginal costs with Equation 4.18, and given relevant point price elasticity of demand information, the profit-maximizing price level can easily be determined.

For example, suppose Walt's Sport Shop offered a 2-percent discount on "Bass Master" fishing reels and subsequently enjoyed a 6-percent increase in weekly sales. The point price elasticity of demand for Walt's fishing reels is:

$$\epsilon_P = \frac{\text{Percentage Change in } Q}{\text{Percentage Change in } P}$$

$$= \frac{6}{-2}$$

$$= -3.$$

What is the optimal price for fishing reels if Walt's relevant marginal costs per unit for purchase plus display and marketing are $10? From Equation 4.18, and employing the previous information, we set:

$$MC = MR$$

$$= P\left(1 + \frac{1}{\epsilon_P}\right),$$

which implies that the optimal or profit-maximizing price, $P^*$, equals:

$$P^* = \frac{MC}{\left(1 + \dfrac{1}{\epsilon_P}\right)}. \qquad\qquad \textbf{4.19}$$

With marginal costs of $10 and $\epsilon_P = -3$, the profit-maximizing price is:

$$P = \frac{\$10}{\left(1 + \dfrac{1}{-3}\right)}$$

$$= \$15.$$

Therefore, the profit-maximizing price on Walt's fishing reels is $15.

■ Table 4.5
## Price Elasticity and Optimal Pricing Policy

| Point Price Elasticity | Marginal Cost | Profit-Maximizing Price |
|:---:|:---:|:---:|
| − 1.25 | $10 | $50.00 |
| − 1.50 | 10 | 30.00 |
| − 2.50 | 10 | 16.67 |
| − 5.00 | 10 | 12.50 |
| − 10.00 | 10 | 11.11 |
| − 25.00 | 10 | 10.42 |

To see how Equation 4.19 can be used for planning purposes, suppose Walt's can order reels through a different distributor at a wholesale price that reduces marginal costs by $1 to $9 per unit. Under these circumstances, the new optimal retail price is:

$$P = \frac{\$9}{\left(1 + \dfrac{1}{-3}\right)}$$

$$= \$13.50.$$

Thus, the optimal retail price would fall by $1.50 because of a $1 reduction in Walt's relevant marginal costs.

Equation 4.19 can serve as the basis for calculating profit-maximizing prices under current cost and market-demand conditions, as well as under a variety of potential circumstances. Table 4.5 shows how profit-maximizing prices vary for a product with a $10 marginal cost as the point price elasticity of demand varies. Note that the less elastic the demand, the greater the difference between price and marginal cost. Conversely, as the absolute value of the price elasticity of demand increases (that is, as demand becomes more price elastic), the profit-maximizing price gets closer and closer to marginal cost. This important demand relation will be examined further in Chapter 13, where pricing practices are analyzed.

## Determinants of Price Elasticity
**Industry Demand**   Why is the price elasticity of demand high for some products and low for others? In general, there are three major causes of differential price elasticities: (1) the extent to which a good is considered to be a necessity, (2) the availability of substitute goods to satisfy a given need, and (3) the proportion of income spent on the product. A relatively constant quantity of a good such as electricity for residential lighting will be purchased almost irrespective of price, at least in the short run within price ranges customarily encountered. For this good there is no close substitute. Other goods—designer jeans, for example—while desir-

able, face considerably more competition, and the demand for them depends more on price.

Similarly, the demand for high-priced goods that account for a large portion of purchasers' incomes will be relatively more sensitive to price. Demand for less expensive products, on the other hand, will not be so sensitive to price, since the small percentage of income spent on these goods means that worrying about their prices simply would not be worth the time and effort it would require. Accordingly, the elasticity of demand will typically be higher for major items than for minor ones. Thus, the price elasticity of demand for automobiles is higher than that for automobile tires.

**Firm Demand**    Are the price elasticities of an individual firm's demand curve the same as its industry demand curve? In general, the answer is an emphatic no. The reason for this is discussed in detail in Chapters 11 and 12, which deal with market structure, but an intuitive explanation can be given here.

In pure monopoly, the firm's demand curve is also the industry's demand curve, so obviously the firm's elasticity at any output is the same as that of the industry. Consider the other extreme—pure competition, as approximated by wheat farming. The industry demand curve for wheat is downward sloping: the lower its price, the greater the quantity of wheat that will be demanded. However, the demand curve facing any individual wheat farmer is essentially horizontal. A farmer can sell any amount of wheat at the going price, but if he raises the price the smallest fraction of a cent he can sell nothing. The wheat farmer's demand curve—or that of any firm operating under pure competition—is therefore perfectly elastic. Figure 4.9 illustrated such a demand curve.

**Derived Demand**    As was explained in Chapter 3, the demand for producer goods and services is indirect, or derived from their value in use. Because the demand for all inputs is derived from their usefulness in producing other products, we say that their demand is derived from the demand for final products. In contrast to the term final product or consumer demand, we use the term *derived demand* to describe the demand for all producer goods and services. Although the demand for producer goods and services is related to the demand for the final products they are used to make, this relation is not always as close as one might suspect.

In some instances, the demand for intermediate goods is less price sensitive than is demand for the resulting final product. This is because intermediate goods sometimes represent only a small portion of the cost of producing the final product. For example, suppose the total cost to build a small manufacturing plant is $1 million, and $25,000 of this cost represents the cost of electrical fixtures and wiring. Even a doubling in electrical costs from $25,000 to $50,000 would have only a modest effect on the overall costs of the plant—which would increase by only 2.5 percent from $1 million to $1.025 million. Rather than being highly price sensitive, the firm might make its electrical contractor selection based on the timeliness and quality of service provided. In such an instance, the firm's price elasticity of demand for electrical fixtures and wiring will be quite low, even if its price elasticity of demand for the overall project is quite high.

In other situations the reverse might hold. Continuing with our previous example, suppose that steel costs represent $250,000 of the total $1 million cost of building the plant. Because of its relative importance, a substantial increase in steel costs will have a significant influence on the total costs of the overall project. As a result, the price sensitivity of the demand for steel will be close to that for the overall plant. If the firm's demand for plant construction is highly price elastic, the demand for steel is also likely to be highly price elastic.

Therefore, while the derived demand for producer goods and services is obviously related to the demand for resulting final products, this relation is not always close. When intermediate goods or services represent only a small share of overall costs, the price elasticity of demand for such inputs can be much different than that for the resulting final product. The price elasticity of demand for a given input and the resulting final product only have to be similar in magnitude when the costs of that input represent a significant share of overall costs.

## Uses of Price Elasticity

Price elasticity is useful for a number of purposes. First, firms need to be aware of the elasticity of their own demand curves when they price their products. For example, a profit-maximizing firm would never choose to lower its prices in the inelastic range of its demand curve; such a price decrease would decrease total revenue and at the same time increase costs, since output would be rising. The result would be a dramatic decrease in profits. Even over the range where demand is elastic, a firm will not necessarily find it profitable to cut price; the profitability of such an action depends on whether the marginal revenues generated by the price reduction exceed the marginal cost of the added production. Price elasticities can be used to answer questions such as these:

1. What will be the impact on sales of a 5-percent price increase?
2. How great a price reduction is necessary to increase sales by 10 percent?
3. Given marginal cost and price elasticity information, what is the profit-maximizing price?

The energy crisis that developed following the OPEC oil embargo also illustrates the importance of price elasticity. First, electric utility companies were forced to raise prices dramatically because of rapid increases in fuel costs. The question immediately arose: How much of a cutback in quantity demanded and, hence, how much of a reduction in future capacity needs would these price increases cause? In other words, what is the price elasticity of electricity? In view of the long lead times

## 4.2 **Managerial Application**

The Price Positioning Puzzle

Perhaps the most important element in defining an effective product pricing and promotion strategy is correct product positioning vis-à-vis the competition. Among the most important considerations in this effort is the price perception held by consumers. For many products, promotional pricing is a key element in the firm's overall promotional strategy. By definition, generic products are sold on the basis of low prices rather than superior quality, image enhancing advertising, and so on. Plain black-and-white labels emphasize the no-frills identity of these goods and appeal to frugal consumers who are highly price sensitive. Indeed, the marketing of generic products is designed to create an image in sharp contrast with the brand-name advertising adopted by major companies such as Procter & Gamble, General Mills, General Foods, and so on. Both methods of promotion continue to be successful because they effectively target different segments of the consumer population.

Of course, generic goods marketing is just an extreme example of the relative emphasis on price positioning as a marketing strategy. To a greater or lesser degree, identifying an appropriate product price, and therefore developing an appropriate product price perception, is an important consideration for all firms. The rapidly developing market for calorie-controlled frozen entrees provides an interesting example of the strategies that firms employ to establish consistent pricing images in the minds of consumers.

Stouffer's Lean Cuisine brand is an industry leader in the market for 300-calorie-or-less frozen entrees. Just since its creation in 1982, the brand had generated estimated annual sales in the $375 to $400 million per year range by mid-1987. This early success propelled the company past H. J. Heinz's Weight Watchers brand, with estimated 1987 sales of $150 to $200 million. Lean Cuisine's success can be attributed in part to its ability to establish itself as a line of high-quality products that appeal to men and

*continued*

See: George Lazarus, "Lean Cuisine's Sales Get a Little Bit Leaner," *Chicago Tribune*, August 3, 1987, 4; and Alix M. Freedman, "Glamour of Upscale Frozen Foods Fades as Buyers Return to Basics," *The Wall Street Journal*, December 15, 1987, 29.

required to build electric-generating capacity and the major economic dislocations that arise from power outages, this was a critical question for both consumers and producers of electricity.

Similarly, price elasticity has played a major role in the debate on a national petroleum policy since that same period. Some industry and government economists believed that the price elasticities for petroleum products were sufficiently large that the rather substantial oil price increases that occurred in 1974 and 1979 would reduce the quantity de-

women alike. Despite its continued success, Lean Cuisine's dramatic rate of sales growth stalled during mid-1987 in the face of new competition. At that time, Lean Cuisine ran into trouble in the form of Kraft, Inc.'s Budget Gourmet brand.

Budget Gourmet's marketing thrust is toward high quality at a bargain price. Its products, which usually sell in a range between $1.69 and $1.89, generally cost less than those offered by Lean Cuisine. Moreover, Budget Gourmet has made this price difference the main focus of major advertising campaigns. For example, ads placed by Budget Gourmet during late 1987 carried the message, "One bite and you may wonder why you've been paying such a fat price for Lean Cuisine." Budget Gourmet's objective was to exploit Lean Cuisine's average price of around $2.50, with some as high as $4. While Lean Cuisine maintained that its products were superior in quality to those offered by the competition, it was vulnerable on the price issue. Product quality, not price, had been the focus of Lean Cuisine advertising. Indeed, Budget Gourmet was not only successful in convincing consumers that Lean Cuisine's prices were high relative to the competition, but consumers came to perceive greater price differences than actually existed.

Budget Gourmet's price-comparison advertising brought an immediate response as Lean Cuisine initiated its own price advertising campaign. In an effort to stem the loss in sales to Budget Gourmet, Lean Cuisine's ads showcased 7 of its 25 entrees that sell for less than $2 with the message, "Would you believe Lean Cuisine entrees for around $1.99?" With this new strategy, Lean Cuisine was attempting to convince consumers that it featured not only high-quality products but also ones that were price-competitive.

While it is still too early to predict the ultimate success of the Budget Gourmet price positioning campaign and of Lean Cuisine's response, these strategies illustrate the difficulties firms face as they attempt to position their products in the marketplace. Lean Cuisine's quality emphasis contributed to its vulnerability on the price issue. Similarly, Budget Gourmet's ads might backfire by increasing Lean Cuisine's name recognition and association with high product quality. The fact that Budget Gourmet felt compelled to adopt the risky advertising strategy of attacking Lean Cuisine head-on illustrates the importance of price positioning in overall marketing strategy.

manded sufficiently to remove the imbalance between supply and demand. Others argued that the price elasticities were so low that only unconscionable price increases could reduce the quantity demanded sufficiently to overcome the supply shortfall, and therefore a rationing system was needed as a replacement for market allocation of petroleum products. The collapse of oil prices in the late 1980s raised many of these same elasticity questions because of fear that lower oil prices would increase demand enough to return the U.S. economy to heavy dependence on imported oil. These same issues have been a focal point of the controversy concerning deregulation of natural gas prices in the

United States.[3] These strongly interrelated energy issues continue to have important implications for all sectors of the economy, and price elasticity analysis is playing an increasingly important role in the search for solutions.

Yet another example of the importance of price elasticity in managerial decision making relates to the widespread discounting or reduced fares introduced in the airline industry following price deregulation by the Civil Aeronautics Board. Many of the discounts were in the range of 30 to 40 percent off the standard fare. The question of whether the reduced fares would attract enough additional travelers to offset the lower revenues per passenger was directly related to the question of the price elasticity of demand for air travel.

Additional uses of price elasticity are examined in later chapters. We now shift to an introduction of several other key demand relations.

## CROSS-PRICE ELASTICITY OF DEMAND

The demand for most products is influenced by the prices of other products. For example, the demand for beef is related to the price of a close substitute, chicken. As the price of chicken increases, so does the demand for beef; consumers substitute beef for the now relatively more expensive chicken. On the other hand, a price decrease for chicken will lead to a decrease in the demand for beef as consumers substitute chicken for the now relatively more expensive beef. In general, a direct relation between the price of one product and the demand for a second product holds for all **substitute products.** A price increase for a given product will increase demand for its substitutes; a price decrease for a given product will decrease demand for its substitutes.

Other goods and services (for example, cameras and film or computers and software) exhibit a completely different relation. Here price increases in one product typically lead to a reduction in demand for the other. Goods that are inversely related in this manner are known as **complements;** they are used together rather than in place of each other.

The concept of **cross-price elasticity** is used to examine the responsiveness of demand for one product to changes in the price of another. Point cross-price elasticity is given by the following equation:

**substitute products**

Related products for which a price increase for one leads to an increase in demand for the other.

**complements**

Related products for which a price increase for one leads to a reduction in demand for the other.

**cross-price elasticity**

A measure of the responsiveness of demand for one product to changes in the price of another.

$$\epsilon_{PX} = \frac{\text{Percentage Change in Quantity of } Y}{\text{Percentage of Change in Price of } X}$$

$$= \frac{\partial Q_Y / Q_Y}{\partial P_X / P_X}$$

$$= \frac{\partial Q_Y}{\partial P_X} \times \frac{P_X}{Q_Y}, \qquad \qquad \textbf{4.20}$$

---

[3]In the debate on energy policy, the relation between price and quantity supplied—the price elasticity of supply—is also an important component. As with most economic issues, both sides of the marketplace (demand and supply) must be analyzed to arrive at a rational decision.

where $Y$ and $X$ are two different products. The arc cross-price elasticity relationship is constructed in the same manner as was previously described for price elasticity.

$$E_{PX} = \frac{\text{Percentage Change in Quantity of } Y}{\text{Percentage of Change in Price of } X}$$

$$= \frac{(Q_{Y2} - Q_{Y1})/(Q_{Y2} + Q_{Y1})}{(P_{X2} - P_{X1})/(P_{X2} + P_{X1})}$$

$$= \frac{\Delta Q_Y}{\Delta P_X} \times \frac{P_{X2} + P_{X1}}{Q_{Y2} + Q_{Y1}}. \qquad \textbf{4.21}$$

The cross-price elasticity for substitutes is always positive; the price of one good and the demand for the other always move in the same direction. Cross-price elasticity is negative for complements—price and quantity move in opposite directions. Finally, cross-price elasticity is zero, or nearly zero, for unrelated goods; variations in the price of one good have no effect on demand for the second.

We can illustrate the concept of cross-price elasticity by considering the demand function for monitored in-the-home health care services provided by Home Medical Support, Inc. (HMS):

$$Q_Y = f(P_Y, P_D, P_H, P_T, i, I).$$

Here $Q_Y$ is the number of patient days of service per year; $P_Y$ is the average price of HMS service; $P_D$ is an industry price index for prescription drugs; $P_H$ is an index of the average price of hospital service, a primary competitor; $P_T$ is a price index for the travel industry; $i$ is the interest rate; and $I$ is disposable income per capita. Assume that the parameters of the demand equation have been estimated as follows:

$$Q_Y = 25,000 - 5P_Y - 3P_D + 10P_H + 0.0001P_T - 0.02i + 2.5I.$$

The effects on $Q_Y$ caused by a one-unit change in the prices of the other goods are:

$$\frac{\partial Q_Y}{\partial P_D} = -3.$$

$$\frac{\partial Q_Y}{\partial P_H} = +10.$$

$$\frac{\partial Q_Y}{\partial P_T} = 0.0001 \approx 0.$$

Since both prices and quantities are always positive, the ratios $P_D/Q_Y$, $P_H/Q_Y$, and $P_T/Q_Y$ are also positive. Therefore, the signs of the three cross-price elasticities in the example are determined by the sign of each relevant parameter:

$$\epsilon_{PD} = (-3)(P_D/Q_Y) < 0$$
(HMS service and prescription drugs are complements.)

$$\epsilon_{PH} = (10)(P_H/Q_Y) > 0$$
(HMS service and hospital service are substitutes.)

$$\epsilon_{PT} = (0.0001)(P_T/Q_Y) \approx 0,$$

so long as the ratio $P_T/Q_Y$ is not extremely large.
(Demand for travel and HMS service are independent.)

The concept of cross-price elasticity serves two main purposes. First, it is important for the firm to be aware of how the demand for its product is likely to respond to changes in the prices of other goods; this information is necessary for formulating the firm's own pricing strategy and for analyzing the risk associated with various products. This is particularly important for firms with extensive product lines, where significant substitute or complementary relations exist among the various products. Second, cross-price elasticity allows managers to measure the degree of competition in the marketplace. For example, a firm might appear to dominate a particular market or market segment completely if it is the only supplier of a particular product. If, however, the cross-price elasticity between this firm's product and products in related industries is large and positive, the firm, though it may be a monopolist in a narrow sense, will not be able to raise its prices without losing sales to other firms in related industries.[4] The importance of the cross-price elasticity of demand concept is explored further in Chapters 11 and 12, where market structures are examined, and in Chapter 13, where its role in multiple product pricing is analyzed.

# INCOME ELASTICITY OF DEMAND

For many goods, income is another important determinant of demand. Income is frequently as important as price, advertising expenditures, credit terms, or any other variable in the demand function. This is particularly true of luxury items such as sports cars, country club memberships, elegant homes, and the like. On the other hand, the demand for such basic commodities as salt, bread, and milk is not very responsive to income changes. These goods are bought in fairly constant amounts regardless of changes in income. Of course, income can be measured in many ways—for example, on a per capita, per household, or aggregate basis. Gross national product, national income, personal income, and disposable personal income have all served as income measures in demand studies.

**income elasticity**

A measure of the responsiveness of demand to changes in income, holding constant the effect of all other variables.

The **income elasticity** of demand measures the responsiveness of demand to changes in income, holding constant the effect of all other variables that influence demand. Letting $I$ represent income, income point elasticity is defined as:

---

[4]This argument has been raised in connection with antitrust actions. In banking, for example, even though relatively few banks may exist in a given market, banks compete with savings and loan associations, credit unions, commercial finance companies, and the like. The extent of this competition has been gauged in terms of cross-elasticities of demand between various banking services and competing institutions.

$$\epsilon_I = \frac{\text{Percentage Change in Quantity } (Q)}{\text{Percentage Change in Income } (I)}$$

$$= \frac{\partial Q/Q}{\partial I/I}$$

$$= \frac{\partial Q}{\partial I} \times \frac{I}{Q}. \qquad \qquad \textbf{4.22}$$

**inferior goods**

Products for which consumer demand declines as income rises.

**normal or superior goods**

Products for which demand is positively related to income.

Income and the quantity purchased typically move in the same direction; that is, income and sales are directly rather than inversely related. Therefore, $\partial Q/\partial I$ and hence $\epsilon_I$ are positive. For a limited number of products termed **inferior goods,** this does not hold. For products such as beans and potatoes, for example, individual consumer demand can decline as income increases, because consumers replace them with more desirable alternatives. More typical products, whose individual and aggregate demand is positively related to income, are defined as **normal** or **superior goods.**

To examine income elasticity over a range of incomes rather than at a single level, we use the arc elasticity relation:

$$E_I = \frac{\text{Percentage Change in Quantity } (Q)}{\text{Percentage Change in Income } (I)}$$

$$= \frac{(Q_2 - Q_1)/(Q_2 + Q_1)}{(I_2 - I_1)/(I_2 + I_1)}$$

$$= \frac{\Delta Q}{\Delta I} \times \frac{I_2 + I_1}{Q_2 + Q_1}. \qquad \qquad \textbf{4.23}$$

Again, this provides a measure of the average relative responsiveness of demand for the product to a change in income in the range from $I_1$ to $I_2$.

In the case of inferior goods, individual demand will actually rise during an economic downturn. As workers get laid off from their jobs, for example, they tend to substitute potatoes for meat, hamburgers for steak, bus rides for automobile trips, and so on. As a result, demand for potatoes, hamburger, and bus rides can rise during recessions, so demand for them is countercyclical.

For most products, income elasticity is positive, however, indicating that as the economy expands and national income increases, demand for the product will also rise. The actual size of the elasticity coefficient is also important. Suppose, for example, that $\epsilon_I$ for a particular product is 0.3. This means that a 1-percent increase in income will cause demand for this product to increase by only 3/10 of 1 percent—the product would not maintain its relative importance in the economy. Another product might have an income elasticity of 2.5; demand for it will increase 2½ times as fast as income. We see, then, that if $\epsilon_I < 1.0$ for a particular good, producers of the good will not share proportionately in increases in national income. On the other hand, if $\epsilon_I > 1.0$, the industry will gain more than a proportionate share of increases in income.

**noncyclical normal goods**
Products for which demand is relatively unaffected by changing income.

**cyclical normal goods**
Products for which demand is strongly affected by changing income.

Goods for which $0 < \epsilon_I < 1$ are often referred to as **noncyclical normal goods,** since demand is relatively unaffected by changing income. Sales of most convenience goods, such as toothpaste, candy, soda, movie tickets, and so on, account for only a small share of the consumer's overall budget, and spending on such items tends to be relatively unaffected by changing economic conditions. For goods having $\epsilon_I > 1$, referred to as **cyclical normal goods,** demand is strongly affected by changing economic conditions. Purchase of "big ticket" items such as homes, automobiles, boats, and recreational vehicles can be postponed, and they tend to be put off by consumers during economic downturns. As a result, housing demand, for example, can collapse during recessions and skyrocket during economic expansions. These relations between income and product demand are summarized in the following table:

| Description | Income Elasticity | Examples |
| --- | --- | --- |
| 1. Inferior goods (countercyclical) | $\epsilon_I < 0$ | Basic foodstuffs, generic products, bus rides |
| 2. Noncyclical normal goods | $0 < \epsilon_I < 1$ | Toiletries, movies, liquor, cigarettes |
| 3. Cyclical normal goods | $\epsilon_I > 1$ | Automobiles, housing, vacation travel, capital equipment |

These relations have important policy implications for both firms and government agencies. Firms whose demand functions have high income elasticities will have good growth opportunities in expanding economies, so forecasts of aggregate economic activity will figure importantly in their plans. Companies faced with low income elasticities, on the other hand, are not so sensitive to the level of business activity. This may be good because such a business is harmed relatively little by economic downturns, but since the company cannot expect to share fully in a growing economy, it may seek to enter industries that provide better growth opportunities.

Income elasticity can also play an important role in the marketing activities of a firm. If per-capita or household income is found to be an important determinant of the demand for a particular product, this can affect the location and nature of sales outlets. It can also have an impact on advertising and other promotional activities. For example, many firms that provide products or services with high income elasticities direct significant promotional efforts at young professionals in such areas as business, law, and medicine, primarily because of the potential for substantially increased future business from these people as their incomes increase.

At the national level, the question of income elasticity has figured importantly in several key areas. Agriculture, for example, has had problems for many years, partly because the income elasticity of many food products is less than 1.0. This fact has made it difficult for farmers' incomes to keep up with those of urban workers, a problem that, in turn, has caused much concern in Washington and national capitals throughout the world.

A somewhat similar problem arises in housing. Congress and all presidents since the end of World War II have stated that improving the U.S. housing stock is a primary national goal. If, on the one hand, the income elasticity for housing is high (in excess of 1.0), an improvement of the housing stock will be a natural by-product of a prosperous economy. On the other hand, if housing income elasticity is low, a relatively small percentage of additional income will be spent on houses; as a result, the housing stock will not improve much even if the economy is booming and incomes are increasing. In this case direct governmental actions such as public housing or rent and interest subsidies are necessary to bring the housing stock up to the prescribed level. In any event, not only has the income elasticity of housing been an important issue in debates on national housing policy, but these very debates have also stimulated a great deal of research into the theory and measurement of income elasticities.

## OTHER DEMAND ELASTICITIES

The elasticity concept is simply a way of measuring the effect of a change in an independent variable on the dependent variable in any functional relation. The dependent variable in this chapter is the demand for a product, and the demand elasticity of any variable in the demand function may be calculated. We have emphasized the three most common demand elasticities—price elasticity, cross-price elasticity, and income elasticity—but examples of other demand elasticities will reinforce the generality of the concept.

Advertising elasticity plays an important role in marketing activities. A low advertising elasticity means that a firm will have to spend substantial sums to shift demand for its products through advertising. In such cases alternative marketing approaches are often more productive.

In the housing market, mortgage interest rates are an important determinant of demand; accordingly, interest rate elasticity has been used in analyzing and forecasting the demand for housing construction. Studies indicate that the interest rate elasticity of residential housing demand is about $-0.15$. This indicates that a 10-percent rise in interest rates decreases the demand for housing by 1.5 percent, provided that all the other variables remain unchanged.[5] If Federal Reserve policy is expected

---

[5] Actually, this elasticity coefficient varies over time as other conditions in the economy change. Other things are held constant when measuring elasticity, but in the real world other things do *not* typically remain constant over time.

## 4.3  **Managerial Application**

Robert Giffen and the Potato Paradox

After graduation and successful job searches, it is common for former students to increase their rate of spending dramatically on consumption goods and services. Early purchases might include new clothes, a new or used car, furniture, a vacation trip, and so on. This is a typical response to the rapid increase in income one enjoys when assuming a new job. Conversely, if a downturn in economic conditions causes one to be temporarily laid-off, it is natural to expect a change to a conservative spending pattern. Movies might be substituted for more expensive dinner dates, new clothes purchases might be put on hold, and travel plans might be postponed. Newly unemployed workers just don't rush out and buy new cars, for example. In general, it is reasonable to expect that consumer spending will rise during economic expansions and fall during business downturns. Indeed, so typical is this pattern that economists define a "normal" good as one for which demand rises and falls with changes in overall economic conditions.

Theoretically, it seems plausible that the aggregate demand for some goods and services might be countercyclical, actually rising during a business recession and falling during an economic boom. After all, if individual consumers shift from hamburger to steak as incomes rise, wouldn't it seem reasonable to expect hamburger demand to rise with a fall in income?

The answer appears to be yes and no. Yes, as incomes rise, demand from high-income individuals seems to decline for "inferior" goods like hamburger, bus rides, and blue jeans as these consumers switch to more desirable substitutes such as steak, automobiles, and designer clothing. However, as incomes rise, other low-income consumers

*continued*

See: Gerald P. Dwyer, Jr. and Cotton M. Lindsay, "Robert Giffen and the Irish Potato," *American Economic Review*, March 1984, 188–192.

to cause interest rates to rise from 10 to 12 percent, a 20-percent increase, we can project a 3-percent decrease ($-0.15 \times 20 = -3$) in housing demand.

Public utilities calculate the weather elasticity of demand for their services. They measure weather using degree days as an indicator of average temperatures. This elasticity factor is used, in conjunction with weather forecasts, to anticipate service demand and peak-load conditions.

**Managerial Application** *continued*

also move up the economic ladder. Perhaps for the first time, they are now able to afford hamburger, bus rides, and blue jeans. As a result, aggregate or economywide demand for so-called inferior goods may actually rise as income levels increase, albeit at a much slower pace than demand for other, more desirable products.

Still, the possibility of an inverse relation between aggregate product demand and income continues to intrigue economists. This interest was originally created by an anomaly called the "potato paradox." As legend has it, a Victorian economist named Robert Giffen discovered that the potato crop failure of 1845 so depressed Irish incomes that the poor had to actually increase their consumption of the now higher-priced potatoes. Because they had to spend so much on potatoes, a necessary staple, the poor couldn't afford meat or other substitutes and became even more dependent than before on potatoes. Thus, potatoes became known as the classic case of the inferior or "Giffen" good.

However, recent evidence casts serious doubt on the credibility of such a chain of events. After studying the historical record, economists Gerald Dwyer and Cotton Lindsay found little evidence that the consumption of potatoes in Ireland increased during this period. So widespread were the effects of the fungus *Phytophthora infestans* that it destroyed roughly one-half of the 1845 potato crop in Ireland after inflicting serious damage in America, in England, and on the Continent. After September 1846 and until harvest time in August of the following year, few potatoes could be bought at any price. Without imports and with a decrease in domestic supply, how could potato consumption by the poor possibly have risen during the Irish potato famine? Moreover, there is no evidence that low potato prices during good years had a depressing effect on potato consumption by the poor, as would be necessary to classify potatoes as an inferior good.

Therefore, we can only conclude that the increase in potato prices and the decrease in income caused by the Irish potato famine resulted in a decline in the aggregate consumption of potatoes. As is typical for goods in general, a positive relation between potato demand and economywide income seems to hold. Despite the legend of the potato paradox, concrete evidence of an inverse relation between aggregate demand and income remains elusive.

We return to the topic of elasticities in the following chapter, where we examine empirical techniques used in estimating demand. First, however, we must consider some additional demand concepts useful for managerial decision making.

## TIME IMPACT ON ELASTICITY

Time is an important factor in demand analysis. One of the important time characteristics of demand relates to the lack of instantaneous response in the marketplace.

Consumers often react slowly to changes in prices and other demand conditions. To illustrate this delayed or lagged effect, consider the demand for electric power. Suppose that an electric utility raises its rates by 30 percent. How will this affect the quantity of electric power demanded? In the very short run, the effect will be slight. Customers may be more careful to turn off unneeded lights, but total demand, which is highly dependent on the appliances owned by the utility's residential customers and the equipment operated by their industrial and commercial customers, will probably not be greatly affected. Prices will go up and quantity demanded will not fall very much, so total revenue will increase substantially. In other words, the short-run demand for electric power is relatively inelastic.

Over the longer run, however, the increase in power rates has more substantial effects. Residential users will reduce their purchases of air conditioners, electric heating units, and other appliances, and those appliances that are purchased will be more energy efficient. These actions will reduce the demand for power. Similarly, industrial users will tend to switch to other energy sources, will employ less energy-intensive production methods, or will relocate to areas where electric costs are lower. Thus, the ultimate effect of the price increase on demand may be substantial, but it will take a number of years before its full impact is felt.

In general, opportunities to respond to price changes tend to increase with time as consumers obtain more information or better perceive the price effects and as more substitutes are made available. There is a similar phenomenon with income changes. It takes time for consumers' purchasing habits to respond to changed income levels. For these reasons, long-run elasticity tends to be greater than short-run elasticity for most demand variables.

## SUMMARY

The demand for a firm's products is a critical determinant of its profitability, and demand forecasts enter as key considerations in virtually all managerial decisions. To make a reliable demand forecast, one must thoroughly understand demand analysis.

Consumer demand is based on the ability of products to satisfy consumer wants—that is, to provide *utility*. *Marginal utility* is the increase in consumer well-being or satisfaction made possible through an increase in consumption. The *law of diminishing marginal utility* states that, as an individual increases consumption within a given time interval, the marginal utility derived will eventually decline. This gives rise to a downward-sloping demand curve for all goods and services. The optimal consumption basket of goods and services is obtained when the relative prices paid are proportional to the relative marginal utility derived from consumption:

$$\frac{MU_X}{MU_Y} = \frac{P_X}{P_Y}.$$

When this condition holds, the total utility derived from consumption is maximized.

This chapter also introduces the key concept of *elasticity*, defined as the percentage change in product demand caused by a 1-percent change in any of its various determinants. *Price elasticity* ($\epsilon_P$ and $E_P$, denoting *point* and *arc* elasticity, respectively) relates changes in the quantity demanded to changes in a product's own price. If $|\epsilon_P| > 1.0$, demand is said to be *elastic*, and a price reduction will lead to an increase in total revenue. If $|\epsilon_P| < 1.0$, demand is *inelastic*, and a price reduction will decrease total revenue. If $|\epsilon_P| = 1.0$, demand exhibits *unitary elasticity*, and price and quantity changes will exactly offset each other, resulting in no change in total revenue.

Price elasticity has a precise relation to marginal revenue and plays an important role in the setting of pricing policy. The profit-maximizing price of a product, $P^*$, is related to price elasticity by the following equation:

$$P^* = \frac{MC}{\left(1 + \dfrac{1}{\epsilon_P}\right)}.$$

*Cross-price elasticity*, $\epsilon_{PX}$ or $E_{PX}$, relates the demand for Product Y to the price of Product X. If $\epsilon_{PX} > 0$, an increase in $P_X$ causes an increase in $Q_Y$, and the goods are *substitutes*. Producers of substitute goods are competitors. If $\epsilon_{PX} < 0$, the goods are *complements*. When complementary relationships are especially strong, firms sometimes offer the related products together. If $\epsilon_{PX} \approx 0$, the goods are said to be *independent*, and price changes in one will have virtually no effect on demand for the other.

*Income elasticity*, $\epsilon_I$ or $E_I$, relates the demand for a product to various measures of income. Ordinarily, $\epsilon_I$ is positive, meaning that higher incomes cause greater demand. The relative size of the income elasticity coefficient is very important. If $\epsilon_I > 1.0$, demand increases more than in proportion to changes in income and demand is said to be *cyclical*. If $\epsilon_I < 1.0$, demand will tend to vary less than changes in overall income, and demand is said to be relatively *noncyclical*. Products with high income elasticities of demand tend to prosper with growth in the overall economy.

These are but a few of the important demand elasticities studied by firms. Many other types of elasticity are commonly calculated for use in demand analysis, including the demand elasticity of advertising, weather, interest rates, and so on.

Time can play an important role in demand analysis. Frictions in the marketplace typically restrain short-run effects on demand; the full impact of changes in demand-determining factors is felt only after extended periods, during which more complete adjustments in the forces of demand and supply are possible.

## Questions

4.1 Is the economic demand for a product solely determined by its usefulness?

4.2 "The utility derived from consumption is intangible and thus unobservable. Therefore, the utility concept has no practical value." Discuss this statement.

4.3 Is an increase in total utility or satisfaction following an increase in income inconsistent with the law of diminishing marginal utility? Explain.

4.4 What would an upward-sloping demand curve imply about the marginal utility derived from consuming a given product?

4.5 Describe the income, substitution, and total effects on consumption following a price increase.

4.6 Define each of the following terms, giving both a verbal explanation and an equation.
   A. Point elasticity
   B. Arc elasticity
   C. Price elasticity
   D. Cross-price elasticity
   E. Income elasticity

4.7 When is use of the arc elasticity concept valid as compared to use of the point elasticity concept?

4.8 What is likely to be the sign of the cross-price elasticities of demand for the following products:
   A. Movie cameras and video cameras? Why?
   B. Movie cameras and film? Why?
   C. Movie cameras and milk? Why?

4.9 Is the price elasticity of demand typically greater if computed for an industry or for a single firm in that industry? Why?

4.10 How could the cross-price elasticity concept be used in an analysis of the degree of competition in an industry?

## Problems

4.1 A. Complete the following table that describes the demand for "goods":

| Price | Units | Total Utility | Marginal Utility | Price/Marginal Utility |
|-------|-------|---------------|------------------|------------------------|
| $10 | 1 | 25 | — | — |
| 9 | 2 | 45 | | |
| 8 | 3 | 60 | | |
| 7 | 4 | 70 | | |
| 6 | 5 | 75 | | |

B. How does an increase in consumption affect marginal utility and the price/marginal utility ratio?
C. What is the optimal level of goods consumption if the marginal utility derived from the consumption of services costs 50¢ per util?

4.2  Consider the following data:

| Goods (G) | | Services (S) | |
|---|---|---|---|
| Units | Total Utility | Units | Total Utility |
| 0 | 0 | 0 | 0 |
| 1 | 100 | 1 | 70 |
| 2 | 160 | 2 | 124 |
| 3 | 210 | 3 | 175 |
| 4 | 250 | 4 | 220 |
| 5 | 275 | 5 | 250 |

A. Construct a table showing the marginal utility derived from the consumption of goods and services. Also show the trend in marginal utility per dollar spent (the $MU/P$ ratio) if $P_G$ = \$20 and $P_S$ = \$15.
B. If two units of goods are consumed, what level of services consumption would an optimal market basket contain?
C. If five units of services are consumed, what level of goods consumption would an optimal market basket contain?
D. What is the optimal allocation of a \$100 budget? Explain.

4.3  Alex P. Keaton is an ardent baseball fan. The following table shows the relation between the number of games he attends per month and the total utility he derives from baseball game consumption:

| Number of Baseball Games per Month | Total Utility |
|---|---|
| 0 | 0 |
| 1 | 50 |
| 2 | 90 |
| 3 | 120 |
| 4 | 140 |
| 5 | 150 |

A. Construct a table showing Keaton's marginal utility derived from baseball game consumption.
B. At an average ticket price of \$10, Keaton is able to justify attending only one game per month. Calculate his cost per unit of marginal utility derived from baseball game consumption at this activity level.

C.  If the cost–marginal utility tradeoff found in Part B represents the most Keaton is willing to pay for baseball game consumption, calculate the prices at which he would attend two, three, four, and five games per month.

D.  Plot Keaton's baseball game demand curve.

4.4  The demand for personal computers can be characterized by the following point elasticities: price elasticity $= -5$, cross-price elasticity with software $= -4$, and income elasticity $= 2.5$. Indicate whether each of the following statements is *true* or *false*, and explain your answer.

A.  A price reduction for personal computers will increase *both* the number of units demanded and the total revenue of sellers.

B.  The cross-price elasticity indicates that a 5-percent reduction in the price of personal computers will cause a 20-percent increase in software demand.

C.  Demand for personal computers is price elastic, *and* computers are cyclical normal goods.

D.  Falling software prices will definitely increase revenues received by sellers of *both* computers and software.

E.  A 2-percent price reduction would be necessary to overcome the effects of a 1-percent decline in income.

4.5  KRMY-TV is contemplating a T-shirt advertising promotion. Monthly sales data from T-shirt shops marketing the "Eye Watch KRMY-TV" design indicate that:

$$Q = 1,500 - 200P,$$

where $Q$ is T-shirt sales and $P$ is price.

A.  How many T-shirts could KRMY-TV sell at $4.50 each?

B.  What price would KRMY-TV have to charge to sell 900 T-shirts?

C.  At what price would T-shirt sales equal zero?

D.  How many T-shirts could be given away?

E.  Calculate the point price elasticity of demand at a price of $5.

4.6  In an effort to reduce excess end-of-the-model-year inventory, Harrison Ford offered a 2.5-percent discount off the average list price of Mustangs sold during the month of August. Customer response was enthusiastic, with unit sales rising by 10 percent over the previous month's level.

A.  Calculate the point price elasticity of demand for Harrison Ford Mustangs.

B.  Calculate the profit-maximizing price per unit if Harrison Ford has an average wholesale cost of $9,000 per unit, and also incurs marginal selling costs of $375 per unit.

4.7  Recently, the Irvine Cinema reduced ticket prices for afternoon "early bird" shows from $5 to $3 and enjoyed an increase in sales from 60 to 180 tickets per show. Buttered popcorn sales per show also increased from 30 to 150 cups.

    A. Calculate the arc price elasticity of demand for movie tickets.

    B. Calculate the arc cross-price elasticity of demand between buttered popcorn and ticket prices.

    C. Holding all else equal, would you expect an additional ticket price decrease to $2.50 to cause both ticket and popcorn revenues to rise? Explain.

4.8 Tucson Industries, Inc., is a leading manufacturer of tufted carpeting. Demand for Tucson's products is closely tied to the overall pace of building and remodeling activity and, therefore, is highly sensitive to changes in national income. The carpet manufacturing industry is highly competitive, so Tucson's demand is also very price-sensitive.

    During the past year, Tucson sold 15 million square yards of carpeting at an average wholesale price of $7.75 per yard. This year, GNP per capita is expected to surge from $17,250 to $18,750 as the nation recovers from a steep recession. Without any price change, Tucson's marketing director expects current-year sales to rise to 25 million yards.

    A. Calculate the implied arc income elasticity of demand.

    B. Given the projected rise in income, the marketing director believes that current volume of 15 million yards could be maintained despite an increase in price of 50¢ per yard. On this basis, calculate the implied arc price elasticity of demand.

    C. Holding all else equal, would a further increase in price result in higher or lower total revenue?

4.9 B. B. Lean is a catalog retailer of a wide variety of sporting goods and recreational products. Although the market response to the company's spring catalog was generally good, sales of B. B. Lean's $140 deluxe garment bag declined from 10,000 to 4,800 units. During this period, a competitor offered a whopping $52 off its regular $137 price on deluxe garment bags.

    A. Calculate the arc cross-price elasticity of demand for B. B. Lean's deluxe garment bag.

    B. B. B. Lean's deluxe garment bag sales recovered from 4,800 units to 6,000 units following a price reduction to $130 per unit. Calculate B. B. Lean's arc price elasticity of demand for this product.

    C. Calculate the further price reduction necessary for B. B. Lean to fully recover lost sales (i.e., regain a volume of 10,000 units).

4.10 Checkers' Pizza recently decided to raise its regular price on large pizzas from $9 to $12 following increases in the costs of labor and materials. Unfortunately, citywide sales dropped sharply from 16,200 to 9,000 pizzas per week. In an effort to regain lost sales, Checkers' ran a coupon promotion featuring $5 off the new regular price. Coupon printing and distribution costs totaled $500 per week and represented a substantial increase over the typical advertising budget of $3,250 per week. Despite these added costs, the promotion was judged to be a success, as it proved to be highly popular with consumers. In the period prior to expiration, coupons were used on 40 percent of all purchases and weekly sales rose to 15,000 pizzas.

A. Calculate the arc price elasticity implied by the initial response to Checkers' price increase.

B. Calculate the effective price reduction resulting from the coupon promotion.

C. In light of the price reduction associated with the coupon promotion, and assuming no change in the price elasticity of demand, calculate Checkers' arc advertising elasticity.

D. Why might the true arc advertising elasticity differ from that calculated in Part C?

## Selected References

Boskin, Michael J. "Consumption, Saving and Fiscal Policy." *American Economic Review* 78 (May 1988): 401–407.

Caves, Richard E., and Peter J. Williamson. "What Is Product Differentiation, Really?" *Journal of Industrial Economics* 34 (December 1985): 113–132.

Cespedes, Frank V., Stephen X. Doyle, and Robert J. Freedman. "Teamwork for Today's Selling." *Harvard Business Review* 67 (March–April 1989): 44–58.

Christiano, Lawrence J. "Is Consumption Insufficiently Sensitive to Innovations in Income?" *American Economic Review* 77 (May 1987): 337–341.

Clarke, Darral G. *Marketing Analysis and Decision Making: Text and Cases with Lotus 1,2,3.* Redwood City, CA: The Scientific Press, 1987.

Collins, Julia M. "Images and Advertising." *Harvard Business Review* 67 (January–February 1989): 93–97.

Dwyer, Gerald P., and Cotton M. Lindsay. "Robert Giffen and the Irish Potato." *American Economic Review* 74 (March 1984): 188–192.

Eckard, E. Woodrow, Jr. "Advertising, Concentration Changes, and Consumer Welfare," *Review of Economics and Statistics* 70 (May 1988): 340–343.

Edell, Julie A., and Kevin Lane Keller. "The Information Processing of Co-ordinated Media Campaigns." *Journal of Marketing Research* 26 (May 1989): 149–163.

Fuhrer, Jeffrey C. "On the Information Content of Consumer Survey Expectations." *Review of Economics and Statistics* 70 (February 1988): 140–144.

Hagerty, Michael R., James M. Carmen, and Gary J. Russell. "Estimating Elasticities with PIMS Data: Methodological Issues and Substantive Implications." *Journal of Marketing Research* 25 (February 1988): 1–9.

Hirschey, Mark. "Intangible Capital Aspects of Advertising and R&D Expenditures." *Journal of Industrial Economics* 30 (June 1982): 375–390.

Hoch, Stephen J., and John Deighton. "Managing What Consumers Learn from Experience." *Journal of Marketing* 53 (April 1989): 1–20.

Leamer, Edward E. "Let's Take the Con Out of Econometrics." *American Economic Review* 73 (March 1983): 31–43.

Marquez, Jaime and Caryl McNeilly. "Income and Price Elasticities for Exports of Developing Countries." *Review of Economics and Statistics* 70 (May 1988): 306–314.

Poterba, James M. "Are Consumers Forward Looking? Evidence from Fiscal Experiments." *American Economic Review* 78 (May 1988): 413–418.

Reddy, Jack, and Abe Berger. "Three Essentials of Product Quality." *Harvard Business Review* 61 (July–August 1983): 153–159.

Thomas, Lacy Glenn. "Advertising in Consumer Goods Industries: Durability, Economies of Scale, and Heterogeneity." *Journal of Law and Economics* 32 (April 1989): 163–193.

Thompson, R. S. "Circulation versus Advertiser Appeal in the Newspaper Industry: An Empirical Investigation." *Journal of Industrial Economics* 37 (March 1989): 259–271.

Train, Kenneth E., Daniel L. McFadden, and Andrew A. Goett. "Consumer Attitudes and Voluntary Rate Schedules for Public Utilities." *Review of Economics and Statistics* 69 (August 1987): 383–391.

# Demand Estimation

In Chapters 3 and 4 we introduced several useful demand concepts and indicated the key role that product demand plays in most business decisions. To use these important demand relations in decision analysis, one must often estimate the parameters of the demand function. In this chapter we examine procedures used to estimate and analyze demand relations.

In some cases it is relatively easy to obtain accurate estimates of demand relations, especially those necessary for short-run demand or sales forecasting. For example, if a company has a substantial backlog of formal purchase orders, accurate estimating of future sales is relatively easy. In other situations it is difficult to obtain even the information needed to make short-run demand forecasts, and still more difficult to determine how changes in specific demand variables—price, advertising expenditures, credit terms, prices of competing products, and so on—will affect demand.

The underlying variability of general economic conditions is one factor that affects demand estimation for many products. As we saw in Chapter 4, when the income elasticity of demand is high, demand for a product will tend to vary more than the concurrent change in overall economic activity. This is true for cyclical goods, such as autos, housing, and steel, the demand for which tends to be highly variable and follows the always-difficult-to-predict changes in aggregate economic conditions. The demand for goods and services also can be highly sensitive to changes in competitor prices and advertising, interest rates, or the weather. Unexpected changes in these important underlying variables constitute a considerable challenge to accurate short-run demand estimation.

The estimation of long-run demand involves all of the difficulties encountered in short-run demand estimation, but they tend to be magnified. In the long run, it is especially difficult to predict changes in the nature and scope of competition from established competitors. When competitors have years instead of just weeks or months to develop effective pricing, promotion, and product-development strategies, the sensitivity of demand to changes in any of these factors can be much more significant than during the short run. Moreover, the effects of unanticipated changes in technology, foreign competition, and government regulation will have an important influence on the firm's future demand. As a result, demand estimation, particularly long-run demand estimation, constitutes a compelling challenge to managers.

In this chapter, we consider three primary methods used by successful managers to estimate demand relationships. First, the consumer interview or survey method is often used to estimate potential demand for new products or to test the potential reaction to prospective changes in the prices or advertising for established products. Second, just as physical scientists conduct laboratory experiments, managers and market researchers use market experiments to evaluate customer reactions to new or improved products in a controlled setting. Like the consumer survey method, market experiments are well-suited to demand estimation problems involving new or improved products. A third method for demand estimation involves the use of historical market data and the powerful analytical technique of regression analysis. Given the rapid rate of improvement in the capabilities of relatively inexpensive desk-top computers and user-friendly software, already popular regression-based techniques are bound to become even more widespread in the years ahead. As a result, we devote a fair amount of attention in this chapter to the regression method of demand estimation. In later chapters, we shall draw on this tool extensively.

## THE IDENTIFICATION PROBLEM

One reason it is sometimes difficult to obtain accurate estimates of demand relations is that close interrelations exist among most economic variables. To see why this poses a difficulty, consider the problem of estimating the demand curve for Product X. If we have data on the price charged and the quantity purchased at several points in time, a logical first step might be to plot this information as in Figure 5.1. Can the line AB be interpreted as a demand curve and points 1, 2, and 3 as various combinations of price and quantity demanded on the demand curve? The curve connecting the points is negatively sloped, indicating the typical inverse relation between the price charged for a product and the quantity demanded, and each data point represents the quantity of X purchased at a particular price. Nevertheless, the available data is insufficient to allow us to conclude that AB is in fact the demand curve for X.

Let us consider why this is so. For each of several observations, we have the price charged for X and the quantity purchased. But this will not necessarily trace out a demand curve. In the previous chapter we stated that the demand curve shows the relation between the price charged for a good and the quantity demanded, *holding constant the*

■ Figure 5.1
## A Price/Quantity Plot for Product *X*

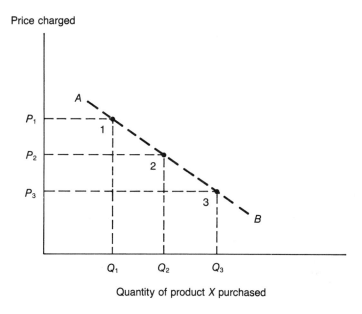

Quantity of product *X* purchased

*effects of all other' variables in the demand function.* Thus, to plot the demand curve, we must obtain data on the price/quantity relation, keeping constant the effects of all factors in the demand function other than price.

The price/quantity data used to construct Figure 5.1 are insufficient to develop a demand curve because the effects of all other demand-related variables may or may not have changed. The line *AB* might be a demand curve, but then again, it might not be. To see this, consider Figure 5.2, in which the price/quantity data are again plotted, along with hypothesized actual supply and demand curves for Product *X*. There we see that the data points indicate nothing more than the simultaneous solution of supply and demand relations at three points in time. The price/quantity data that we observe are the result of the interplay between the quantity of *X* supplied by producers and the quantity demanded by consumers. The intersection of the supply and demand curves at each point in time results in the plotted price/quantity points, but the line *AB* is *not* a demand curve.

In Figure 5.2 we see that nonprice variables in both the supply and demand functions have changed between the data points. Suppose, for example, that new and more efficient facilities for producing *X* are completed between observation dates, and as a result, the quantity supplied at any given price is larger. This causes a shift of the supply curve from $S_1$ to $S_2$ to $S_3$. Similarly, the price of a complementary product may have

■ Figure 5.2
## Supply and Demand Curves

*Price/quantity data sometimes reflect the intersection of several different demand and supply curves.*

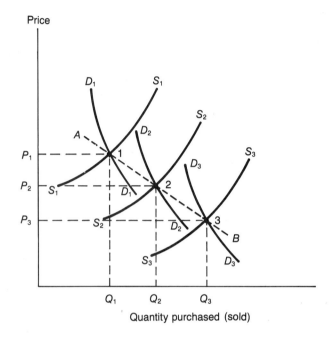

fallen or consumer incomes may have risen, so at any given price, larger quantities of $X$ are demanded in the later periods. This second phenomenon results in a shift of the demand curve from $D_1$ to $D_2$ to $D_3$.

Now observe what has occurred. Both the supply curve and the demand curve have shifted over time. This has resulted in a declining price and an increasing quantity purchased. The three intersection points of the supply and the demand curves in Figure 5.2—points 1, 2, and 3—are the same points plotted in Figure 5.1. But these are not three points on a single demand curve for Product $X$. Each point is on a *different* demand curve—the demand curve is shifting over time—so connecting them does not trace out the product demand curve for $X$.

Observe the effect of incorrectly interpreting the line $AB$ (which connects the points 1, 2, and 3) as a demand curve. If a firm makes this mistake, it might assume a high price elasticity for the product and also assume that a reduction in price from $P_1$ to $P_2$ would increase the quantity demanded from $Q_1$ to $Q_2$. An expansion of this magnitude might well justify the price reduction. Such a price cut, however, would actually result in a much smaller increase in the quantity demanded; the true demand curve, $D_1$, is much less elastic than the line $AB$.

■ Figure 5.3
## Shifting Supply Curve Tracing Out Stable Demand Curve

A demand curve is revealed *if* prices fall while demand conditions are held constant.

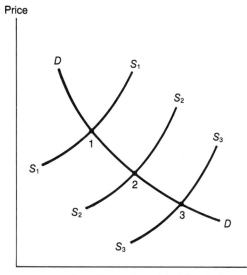

Thus, a price reduction would be much less desirable than implied by the line *AB*.

Given the interrelation between demand and supply curves, can data on prices and quantities purchased ever be used to estimate a demand curve? They can, but only under two conditions: (1) the demand curve has *not* shifted, but the supply curve *has* shifted; or (2) we have enough information to determine just how each curve has shifted between data observations. For example, if a technical breakthrough occurs in the manufacture of a product so that industry costs fall while demand conditions are stable, the situation depicted in Figure 5.3 may arise. The demand curve, which initially was unknown, is assumed to be stable. The supply curve shifts from $S_1$ to $S_2$ to $S_3$. Each price/quantity point represents the intersection of the supply and the demand curves. Because the demand-determining factors other than price are assumed to be stable, points 1, 2, and 3 must all be on the same demand curve, so the demand curve *DD* can be estimated by connecting the three points. Although relatively rare, such a situation occurred in the electronics industry, where rapid innovation allowed prices for watches, hand-held calculators, and related products to fall markedly within a short time.

It is clear from this example that the problem of simultaneous relations in demand analysis can be overcome only if one has enough infor-

**identification problem**

The problem of estimating a demand function when both supply and demand relations vary simultaneously.

mation to *identify* the interrelated functions so that shifts in a curve can be distinguished from movements along it. For this reason, the problem of estimating one function when simultaneous relations exist is known as the **identification problem**. To separate shifts in demand from changes in supply, we must have more information than just price/quantity data. Information about which curve is shifting, and to what extent it is shifting, is necessary to identify and estimate the demand relation. Frequently this information is unavailable. In these cases, statistical techniques of demand estimation, such as regression analysis, cannot provide reliable estimates of the demand function parameters. When the identification problem cannot be solved, techniques such as consumer interviews and market experiments can sometimes be used to obtain information about important demand relations. These techniques are also useful for providing data for use in statistical demand analysis when the identification problem can be resolved.

# CONSUMER INTERVIEWS

The consumer interview, or survey, method requires the questioning of customers or potential customers in an attempt to estimate the relation between demand for a firm's products and a variety of variables perceived to be important for marketing and profit-planning activities. The technique can be applied naively by simply stopping shoppers and asking questions about the quantity of the product they would purchase at different prices. At the other extreme, trained interviewers may present sophisticated questions to a carefully selected sample to elicit the desired information.

Consumer surveys can provide excellent information on many important demand relations. A firm might question each of its customers (or take a statistical sample if the number of customers is large) about projected purchases under a variety of different conditions relating to price, advertising expenditures, prices of substitutes and complements, income, and any number of other variables in the demand function. Then, by aggregating data, the firm could forecast its total demand and estimate some of the important parameters in the demand function for its product.

Unfortunately, this procedure does not always work smoothly in actual practice. The quantity and quality of information obtainable by this technique are sometimes limited. Consumers are often unable, and in many cases unwilling, to provide accurate answers to hypothetical questions about how they would react to changes in key demand variables.

Consider the problem of attempting to determine the effect of just two variables, price and advertising expenditures, on the demand for automobiles. If an interviewer asked how you would react to a 1, 2 or 3 percent increase (or decrease) in the price of a specific model of car, could you respond accurately? What if the question related to the effect of shifting the emphasis in the firm's advertising campaign from fuel efficiency to safety or of changing the advertising media? Could you tell how this action would affect your demand for the car? Because most people are unable to answer such questions—even for major items such as automobiles, appliances, and housing—it is obviously difficult to use such a technique to estimate the demand relations for most consumer goods.

We do not wish to imply that consumer survey techniques are not valuable in demand analysis. Using subtle inquiries, a trained interviewer can extract useful information from consumers. For example, an interviewer might ask questions about the relative prices of several competing goods and learn that most people are unaware of existing price differentials. This is an indication that demand may not be highly responsive to price changes, so a producer would not attempt to increase demand by reducing price—consumers would probably not notice the reduction. Similar questions can be used to determine whether consumers are aware of advertising programs, what their reaction is to the ads, and so on. Thus, useful information is obtainable by surveys, and the quality of the results is adequate for some decision purposes.

Also, for certain kinds of demand information there is no substitute for the consumer interview. For example, in short-term demand or sales forecasting, consumer attitudes and expectations about future business conditions frequently make the difference between an accurate estimate and one that misses by a wide margin. Such subjective information can often be best obtained through interview methods.

## MARKET STUDIES AND EXPERIMENTATION

An alternative technique for obtaining useful information about a product's demand involves market experiments. One market experiment technique entails examining consumer behavior in actual markets. The firm locates one or more markets with specific characteristics, then varies prices, packaging, advertising, and other controllable variables in the demand function, with the variations occurring either over time or between markets. For example, Del Monte Corporation may have determined that uncontrollable consumer characteristics are quite similar in Denver and Salt Lake City. Del Monte could raise the price of sliced pineapple in Salt Lake City in relation to that in Denver, then compare pineapple sales in the two markets. Alternatively, Del Monte could make a series of weekly or monthly price changes in one market, then determine how these changes affected sales. With several markets, the firm might also be able to use census or survey data to determine how demographic characteristics such as income, family size, educational level, and ethnic background affect demand.

Market experiments, however, have several serious shortcomings. They are expensive and are therefore usually undertaken on a scale too small to allow high levels of confidence in the results. Related to this is the problem of short-run versus long-run effects. Market experiments are seldom run for sufficiently long periods to indicate the long-run effects

## 5.1  **Managerial Application**
Estimating the Demand for Safety

"You won't hear any more beef from me," Chrysler chairman Lee Iacocca announced in a 1989 advertising campaign, as he pledged that air bags would be installed in all U.S.-produced Chrysler automobiles by the early 1990s. After years of saying that safety didn't sell, and after outspoken resistance to the air bag technology, Chrysler switched sides to become a strong advocate of air bags as a means for increasing automobile safety. At the same time, General Motors formed an in-house medical team dedicated to crash-injury research. Meanwhile, both Chrysler and GM raced to keep up with Ford Motor Company in the design and installation of advanced braking systems. It appears that the three major U.S. auto companies have simultaneously discovered that "safety sells."

More than 25 years ago, Ralph Nader wrote a book titled *Unsafe at Any Speed*, which made automobile safety a national concern. Over the years, consumers have been presented with more and more information from consumer groups, government agencies, insurance companies, and the manufacturers themselves about the safety of various models. Based on the results of crash tests and insurance company records on crash worthiness, consumers are now able to judge the relative costs and benefits of the various safety features offered on any given model. In addition, extensive press coverage of sudden acceleration problems with the Audi 5000 luxury sedan and suspected rollover problems with the Suzuki Samurai brought the safety issue to the forefront in the late 1980s.

Although it is clear to the industry that safety sells, what isn't clear is the price that

*continued*

See: Joseph B. White, "U.S. Auto Makers Decide Safety Sells," *The Wall Street Journal*, August 24, 1988, 15.

of various price, advertising, or packaging strategies. The experimenter is thus forced to examine short-run data and to attempt to extend it to a longer period.

Difficulties associated with the uncontrolled parts of the market experiment also hinder its use as an estimating tool. A change in economic conditions during the experiment is likely to invalidate the results, especially if the experiment includes the use of several separated markets. A local strike or layoffs by a major employer in one of the market areas, a severe snowstorm, or the like may well ruin the experiment. Likewise,

**Managerial Application** *continued*

consumers are willing to pay for various safety features. Unlike Chrysler, for example, GM doesn't plan to introduce air bags in all of its cars. GM doesn't believe that consumers are willing to pay the high costs of air-bag technology, and it cites the poor sales record of its $850 air-bag option to support this contention. What GM does think will sell is its new anti-lock brake system, a feature that allows a driver to stop on wet or icy roads without skidding. GM projects that millions of consumers will order the anti-lock brake system on their cars during the early 1990s, but dealers appear to be skeptical that a $900 brake system on a $10,000 car will be an easy sell. From a marketing perspective, the auto safety issue presents the industry with an intriguing demand-estimation problem. How does one estimate the demand for various auto safety features that are brand new and hence have never been marketed on a wide scale to consumers?

In the absence of reliable market data, the auto companies have turned to consumer surveys to estimate the demand for new auto safety features. Based on a poll of 200 large fleet buyers, GM found that 33 percent were willing to buy the air-bag option only if the cost were $50 or less, an additional 28 percent were willing to pay as much as $100, 19 percent more were willing to pay up to $150. Only 20 percent were willing to pay more than $200 for the air-bag option. These findings greatly tempered GM's enthusiasm for air bags as a safety option and caused the company to make air bags available on only 20 percent of its models.

As an alternate approach to estimating the demand for new safety features, Ford conducted a market experiment by introducing the anti-lock brake system as standard equipment on Scorpio models sold in Europe during the 1985 model year. This feature made the car become more expensive than the GM Opel Omega, its prime competitor, and Ford's German market share declined by 1.8 percentage points. As a result, Ford decided to introduce the anti-lock brake system in the United States as standard equipment only on high-priced Thunderbird, Mercury Cougar XR-7, and Lincoln Continental models.

As the auto makers continue to work on high-tech safety features for the cars of tomorrow, they are certain to rely on consumer surveys and market experiments to estimate potential demand.

a change in a competing product's promotion, price, or packaging may distort the results. There is also the danger that customers lost during the experiment as a result of price manipulations may not be regained when the experiment ends.

A second method uses a controlled laboratory experiment wherein consumers are given funds with which to shop in a simulated store. By varying prices, product packaging, displays, and other factors, the experimenter can often learn a great deal about consumer behavior. The laboratory experiment, while providing information similar to that of field experiments, has the advantages of lower cost and greater control of extraneous factors.

The consumer clinic or laboratory experiment technique is not without shortcomings. The primary difficulty is that the subjects invariably know that they are part of an experiment, and this knowledge may distort their shopping habits. They may, for example, exhibit considerably more price consciousness than is typical in their everyday shopping. Moreover, the high cost of such experiments necessarily limits the sample size, which makes inference from the sample to the general population tenuous at best.

### Demand for Oranges: An Illustrative Market Experiment

During the 1960s, a well-designed market experiment was conducted in Grand Rapids, Michigan, by researchers from the University of Florida. The purpose was to examine the competition between California and Florida Valencia oranges. The experiment was designed to provide estimates of the price elasticities of demand for the various oranges included in the study as well as to measure the cross-price elasticities of demand among varieties of oranges.[1]

The researchers chose Grand Rapids because its size, economic base, and demographic characteristics are representative of the midwestern market for oranges. Nine supermarkets located throughout the city cooperated in the experiment, which consisted of varying the prices charged for Florida and California Valencia oranges daily for 31 days and recording the quantities of each variety sold. The price variations for each variety of orange covered a range of 32¢ a dozen ($\pm 16$¢ around the price per dozen that existed in the market at the time the study began). More than 9,250 dozen oranges were sold during the experiment.

The price and quantity data obtained in this study enabled the researchers to examine the relation between sales of each variety of orange and its price, as well as the relations between sales and the price charged for competing varieties. The results of the study are summarized in Table 5.1, where the elasticities of these price variables are reported. The numbers along the diagonal represent the price elasticities of the three varieties of oranges, whereas the off-diagonal figures estimate the cross-price elasticities of demand.

The price elasticity for all three varieties was quite large. The $-3.07$ price elasticity for Florida Indian River oranges means that a 1-percent decrease in their price resulted in a 3.07-percent increase in their sales. The other Florida orange had a similar price elasticity, whereas the price

[1]See Marshall B. Godwin, W. Fred Chapman, Jr., and William T. Hanley, *Competition between Florida and California Valencia Oranges in the Fruit Market*, Bulletin 704, December 1965, Agricultural Experiment Stations, Institute of Food and Agricultural Services, University of Florida, Gainesville, Florida, in cooperation with the U.S. Department of Agriculture, Florida Citrus Commission.

■ Table 5.1
## Demand Elasticities for California and Florida Valencia Oranges

| | Percentage Change in the Sales of | | |
|---|---|---|---|
| A 1-Percent Change in the Price of | Florida Indian River | Florida Interior | California |
| Florida Indian River | − 3.07 | + 1.56 | + 0.01 |
| Florida Interior | + 1.16 | − 3.01 | + 0.14 |
| California | + 0.18 | + 0.09 | − 2.76 |

elasticity of the California orange was somewhat lower, indicating that demand for California oranges is less responsive to price changes than is demand for the Florida varieties.

The cross-price elasticities of demand reveal some interesting demand relations among these three varieties of oranges. First, note that cross-price elasticities of demand between the two Florida varieties are positive and relatively large. This indicates that consumers view these two varieties as close substitutes and therefore switch readily between them when price differentials exist. The cross-price elasticities of demand between the Florida and California oranges, on the other hand, are all very small, indicating that consumers do not view them as close substitutes. That is, the market for California oranges in Grand Rapids is quite distinct from the market for Florida varieties.

This market study provided estimates of two important demand relations, the price elasticity of demand for Florida and California oranges and their cross-price elasticities of demand. The researchers were able to identify and measure these relations because the 31-day study period was brief enough to prevent changes in incomes, tastes, population, and other variables that would influence the demand for oranges; and they were able to insure that adequate quantities of the various Valencia oranges were available to consumers at each experimental price.

### Summary of Market Experiments
The market-experiment demand-estimation technique can provide valuable demand information, as was indicated by the example of estimating demand for Florida and California oranges. The drawback of high costs associated with maintaining a controlled setting tends to limit experiments' use to those situations in which the information needed for statistical demand estimation cannot be obtained from historical records. Market experiments are sometimes used to develop some of the data required for more detailed statistical analysis of demand relations.

# REGRESSION ANALYSIS

**regression analysis**

A statistical method used to estimate a variety of managerial economics relations.

The statistical method most frequently employed in demand estimation is **regression analysis.** There are limitations to this technique, but regression analysis can often provide good estimates of demand functions at relatively low cost.

## Specifying the Variables

The first step in regression analysis is specification of the variables that are expected to influence demand. Product demand, measured in physical units, is the dependent variable. The list of independent variables, or those that influence demand, always includes the price of the product and generally includes such factors as the prices of complementary and competitive products, advertising expenditures, consumer incomes, and population of the consuming group. Demand functions for expensive durable goods, such as automobiles and houses, include interest rates and other credit terms; those for ski equipment, beverages, or air conditioners include weather conditions. Demand determinants for capital goods, such as industrial machinery, include corporate profitability, output-to-capacity ratios, interest rates, and wage-rate trends.

## Obtaining Data on the Variables

The second step in regression analysis is obtaining accurate estimates of the variables: measures of price, credit terms, output/capacity ratios, advertising expenditures, incomes, and the like. Obtaining estimates of these variables is not always easy, especially if the study involves data for past years. Further, some key variables, such as consumer attitudes toward quality and their expectations about future business conditions—which are quite important in demand functions for many consumer goods—may have to be obtained by survey (questionnaire and interview) techniques, which introduces an element of subjectivity into the data, or by market or laboratory experiments, which can produce biased data.

## Specifying the Form of the Equation

**linear model**

A function that is a straight line.

Once the variables have been specified and the data gathered, the next step is specifying the form of the equation or the manner in which the independent variables are assumed to interact to determine the level of demand. The most common specification is a **linear model** such as the following:

$$Q = a + bP + cA + dI. \qquad \textbf{5.1}$$

Here $Q$ represents the quantity of a particular product demanded, $P$ is the price charged, $A$ represents advertising expenditures, and $I$ is per-capita disposable income. The quantity demanded is assumed to change linearly with changes in each of the independent variables. For example, if $b = -1.5$, demand will decline by 1½ units for each 1-unit increase in the price of the product. The demand curve for a demand function such as that shown in Equation 5.1 is linear; that is, it is a straight line.

Linear demand functions have great appeal in empirical work for two reasons. First, experience has shown that many demand relations are in fact approximately linear over the range for which data are typically encountered. Second, a convenient statistical technique, the method of least squares regression analysis, can be used to estimate the parameters *a, b, c,* and *d* for linear equations. More will be said about least squares later, but first it is useful to examine another popular form of demand function.

**multiplicative model**
A power function.

The second most commonly used demand function is the **multiplicative model:**

$$Q = aP^bA^cI^d. \qquad\qquad 5.2$$

This equation is popular primarily because of two features. First, the multiplicative equation is frequently the most logical form of the demand function, assuming as it does that the marginal effects on demand of each independent variable are not constant but, rather, depend on the value of the variable as well as on the value of all other variables in the demand function. This can be easily seen by considering the partial derivative of Equation 5.2 with respect to income, $\partial Q/\partial I = adP^bA^cI^{d-1}$, which includes all the variables in the original demand function. Thus, the marginal effect of a change in per-capita disposable income on the product demand specified in Equation 5.2 depends on the level of income, as well as on advertising expenditures and the price charged for the product.

This changing marginal relation is often far more realistic than the implicit assumption in a linear model—namely, that the marginal is constant. For example, as incomes increase from a low level to a higher level, the demand for sirloin steak might increase continuously. However, it is unlikely that the increase in demand will be linear. Instead, it will probably be more rapid at lower income levels, then gradually taper off at higher levels. A similar relation probably holds for advertising expenditures. At low to moderate levels of spending, the marginal impact on sales of an additional dollar of advertising is likely to be quite large. With very high spending levels, however, there may well be a saturation effect and a resultant decrease in the marginal effect on demand of each added advertising dollar. In such situations, use of a nonlinear demand function, such as a power function, is indicated.

The second reason for the popularity of the multiplicative demand function is that Equation 5.2 is an algebraic form that can be transformed into a linear relation using logarithms (see Appendix 2A) and then estimated by the least squares regression technique. Thus, Equation 5.2 is equivalent to:

$$\log Q = \log a + b \cdot \log P + c \cdot \log A + d \cdot \log I. \qquad\qquad 5.3$$

Equation 5.2 is linear in logarithms, and when it is written in the form of Equation 5.3, the coefficients of the equation (log $a$, $b$, $c$, and $d$) can be estimated by least squares regression analysis.

An interesting and useful feature of a multiplicative model, such as the one specified in Equation 5.2, is that demand functions of this form have constant elasticities. Further, these elasticities are given by the coefficients estimated in the regression analysis. For example, consider the price elasticity of demand for the product whose demand function is represented by Equation 5.2. It was shown in Chapter 4 that point price elasticity is obtained by taking the partial derivative of the demand function with respect to price, then multiplying that partial derivative by the ratio of price to quantity demanded:

$$\epsilon_P = \frac{\partial Q}{\partial P} \cdot \frac{P}{Q}. \qquad\qquad\textbf{5.4}$$

Differentiating Equation 5.2 with respect to price, we obtain:

$$\frac{\partial Q}{\partial P} = abP^{b-1}A^cI^d. \qquad\qquad\textbf{5.5}$$

Therefore,

$$\epsilon_P = abP^{b-1}A^cI^d \cdot \frac{P}{Q}. \qquad\qquad\textbf{5.6}$$

Substituting Equation 5.2 for $Q$ in Equation 5.6 gives:

$$\epsilon_P = abP^{b-1}A^cI^d \cdot \frac{P}{aP^bA^cI^d}. \qquad\qquad\textbf{5.7}$$

Combining terms and canceling where possible in Equation 5.7, we obtain:

$$\epsilon_P = \frac{abP^{b-1}A^cI^d}{1} \cdot \frac{P}{aP^bA^cI^d}$$

$$= \frac{abP^bA^cI^d}{P} \cdot \frac{P}{aP^bA^cI^d}$$

$$= b.$$

Thus, the price elasticity of demand is equal to the exponent of price in the multiplicative demand function given as Equation 5.2. Since the elasticity is simply equal to $b$, it is not a function of the price/quantity ratio and hence is constant. This constant elasticity relation holds for *all* the variables in a multiplicative demand function.

Constant elasticities, when they occur, provide useful information for demand estimation. As an example, if the income elasticity of demand for housing is constant, then increases in income can be expected to produce proportionate changes in the demand for housing over wide ranges of income. If this does not hold—and recall that elasticity *always* changes along a linear demand curve—decision makers concerned with housing demand have to worry about differing elasticities at different income levels. We cannot force a demand curve into the multiplicative form of Equation 5.2. When appropriate, however, demand functions of this form have the useful property of constant elasticities.

To summarize, multiplicative demand functions imply a changing absolute effect on demand of changes in the various independent variables. This is a highly attractive property of the multiplicative form for demand analysis because the marginal effect of a dollar spent on advertising, for example, will often vary according to overall levels of advertising, prices, income, and so on. The changing marginal effect implicit in the multiplicative demand-function form contrasts with the constant marginal effect of independent factors in linear demand functions. A further important difference between the two most common approaches to demand estimation is that multiplicative demand functions imply constant demand elasticities, whereas along linear demand functions elasticity varies.

The algebraic form of the demand function—linear, multiplicative, or other forms—should always be chosen to reflect the true relation among variables in the system being studied. That is, care should be taken to insure that the structural form chosen for an empirical demand function is consistent with the underlying theory of demand. In practice, however, there is often no a priori basis for specifying the appropriate form for the demand relation being analyzed. In such cases, several conceptually appropriate forms may be tested, with the one that best fits the data selected as being most likely to reflect the true relationship. Methods of fitting regression equations are described in the following section.

##  Estimating the Regression Parameters

Regression equations are typically fitted—that is, the coefficients $a$, $b$, $c$, and $d$ of Equation 5.1 or 5.2 are estimated—by the method of least squares. Using a simple two-variable case, we can demonstrate the method as follows. Assume that data on Datacom Corporation's sales of Product $Y$ and the advertising expenditures on this product have been collected over the past seven years. The data are given in Table 5.2. If a linear relation between sales of $Y$ and advertising expenditures, $A$, is hypothesized, the regression equation will take the following form:

$$\text{Sales } Y = a + bA. \qquad \textbf{5.8}$$

The method of least squares is then applied to select the values of $a$ and $b$ that best fit the data in Table 5.2 to the regression equation. The procedure is presented graphically in Figure 5.4. Here each point represents the advertising expenditure and sales of $Y$ in a given year. In terms of Equation 5.8, each point can be specified by the relation

$$\text{Sales}_t = Y_t = a + bA_t + u_t, \qquad \textbf{5.9}$$

where u is a residual term that includes the effects of all determinants of sales that have been omitted from the regression equation, as well as a

■ Figure 5.4
## Relation between Sales and Advertising Expenditures for Datacom Corporation

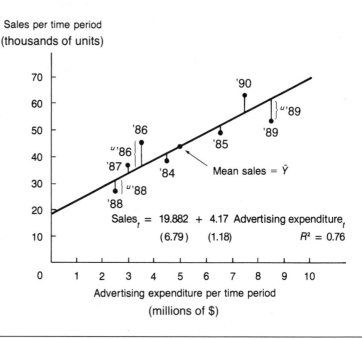

Sales per time period
(thousands of units)

$$Sales_t = 19.882 + 4.17\ Advertising\ expenditure_t$$
$$(6.79)\qquad(1.18)\qquad\qquad\qquad R^2 = 0.76$$

Advertising expenditure per time period
(millions of $)

---

stochastic or random element, and $t$ is used to denote the year of the observation.[2] Notice that in this regression equation, $a$ is the intercept of the regression line with the sales axis, $b$ is the slope of the line, and $u_t$ is the error term or residual, which measures the vertical deviation of each $t$th data point from the fitted regression line. The sum of the squares of these error terms is minimized by the choice of $a$ and $b$ through the least squares technique.[3]

The least squares process for fitting a regression equation is nothing more than an application of the optimization procedure developed in Chapter 2 to the problem of minimizing the sum of the squared deviations from the fitted line. We can demonstrate this by continuing with

---

[2] When time-series data are being examined, as they are in our example, the term $t$ is used for the subscript. However, if cross-sectional data are being examined—for example, if we are examining the sales of Product $Y$ during a given year in different markets in which advertising expenditures had varied—we would designate the various markets with the subscript $i$.

[3] Error terms are squared because the deviations are both positive and negative, and, hence, many different lines can be fitted that will result in the sum of the actual deviations being zero. By squaring the deviations, we are summing a set of positive numbers, and the line that minimizes this sum most accurately depicts the relationship between the dependent and the independent variables.

the sales/advertising example for Datacom Corporation. Solving Equation 5.9 for the error term, $u_t$, results in:

$$u_t = Y_t - a - bA_t.$$

Thus, the expression for the sum of the squared error terms is:

$$\sum_{t=1984}^{1990} u_t^2 = \sum_{t=1984}^{1990} (Y_t - a - bA_t)^2.$$

**5.10**

The least squares regression technique is a procedure for minimizing Equation 5.10 by choice of the two decision variables $a$ and $b$, the coefficients of the regression equation. Such minimization is accomplished by differentiating Equation 5.10 with respect to $a$ and $b$, setting the partial derivatives equal to zero, and solving the resulting two-equation system for $a$ and $b$:

$$\frac{\partial \sum_{t=1984}^{1990} u_t^2}{\partial a} = -2 \sum_{t=1984}^{1990} (Y_t - a - bA_t) = 0.$$

**5.11**

$$\frac{\partial \sum_{t=1984}^{1990} u_t^2}{\partial b} = -2 \sum_{t=1984}^{1990} A_t(Y_t - a - bA_t) = 0.$$

**5.12**

Equations 5.11 and 5.12 are called the *normal equations*, and when solved for $a$ and $b$ they result in:

$$b = \frac{\sum_{t=1984}^{1990} (A_t - \overline{A})(Y_t - \overline{Y})}{\sum_{t=1984}^{1990} (A_t - \overline{A})^2}$$

**5.13**

and

$$a = \overline{Y} - b\overline{A},$$

**5.14**

where $\overline{A}$ and $\overline{Y}$ are the mean values for the advertising and sales observations, respectively. Inserting the data from Table 5.2 into Equations 5.13 and 5.14 results in estimates of 19.882 for $a$ and 4.717 for $b$, so the sales/advertising regression for Datacom Corporation is estimated to be:

$$\text{Sales}_t = \hat{Y}_t = 19.882 + 4.717A_t.$$

Notice that we have dropped the error term, $u_t$, at this point because its expected value is always zero.

Although the previously developed relations are important for understanding regression analysis, it is not necessary that one actually perform the calculations. Virtually all personal computers and even many hand-held calculators can be equipped with regression software programs. All one need do is input data similar to those given in Table 5.2 and run the regression software to obtain the coefficients of the equation.

■ Table 5.2

## Sales and Advertising Data for Datacom Corporation

|  | 1984 | 1985 | 1986 | 1987 | 1988 | 1989 | 1990 | Mean |
|---|---|---|---|---|---|---|---|---|
| Sales (thousands of units) | 37 | 48 | 45 | 36 | 25 | 55 | 63 | $\overline{Y} = 44.1$ |
| Advertising expenditures (millions of dollars) | $4.5 | $6.5 | $3.5 | $3.0 | $2.5 | $8.5 | $7.5 | $\overline{A} = \$5.1$ |

In fact, if the problem is small enough for the equation to be conveniently fitted by hand, a freehand graphic fit is generally accurate enough, and the least squares estimating technique is unnecessary. If many data points are involved, or if two or more independent variables are included in the equation, however, computer solutions are the only practical means for implementing the least squares technique. Accordingly, rather than dwelling on the mathematical process itself, our discussion focuses on setting up regression problems for computer solution and on the interpretation of regression output.

### Interpreting the Regression Equation

Once we have estimates of the regression equation, how do we interpret the values of the coefficients? First, $a$, the intercept term, frequently has no economic meaning. Caution must always be exercised when interpreting points outside the range of the observed data, and typically the intercept lies far outside this range. In our present example, the intercept cannot be interpreted as the expected level of sales if advertising is completely eliminated. It *might* be true that the level of sales with zero advertising would equal the intercept term, $a$, but since the current example includes no observations of sales at zero advertising expenditures, we cannot safely assume that 19,882 units can be sold with no advertising. Similarly, it would be hazardous to extend the sales/advertising curve very far upward from the range of observed values. For example, we could not extrapolate the sales curve out to advertising expenditures of $15 or $20 million and have much confidence in the predicted level of sales (recall the previous discussion about the possible saturation of advertising's impact on demand). In summary, it is important that we restrict our interpretation of regression relations to within the range of data observations.

The slope coefficient, $b$ gives us an estimate of the change in sales associated with a one-unit change in advertising expenditures. Since advertising expenditures were measured in millions of dollars for the regression estimation, whereas sales were in thousands of units, a $1-million increase in advertising will lead to a 4,717-unit expected increase in sales; a $2-million advertising increase will lead to 9,434 additional units sold; and so on. Again, caution must be used when extending the analysis beyond the range of observed values in the data used to estimate the regression coefficients.

The results of this simple two-variable regression model can easily be extended to multiple-variable models. To illustrate the extension, suppose that we also have information on the average price, P, charged for Product Y in each of the seven years. This new information can be added to the linear model given in Equation 5.9, resulting in the following regression equation:

$$\text{Sales } Y_t = a + bA_t + cP_t + u_t. \qquad \textbf{5.15}$$

Again, computer programs using the method of least squares can be used to fit the data to the model and to estimate the parameters $a$, $b$, and $c$. When this is done, we interpret the coefficients as follows: $a$ is again an intercept term that may or may not have economic significance, depending on the range of sample values; $b$ is the expected change in sales related to a one-unit change in advertising expenditure, *holding constant the price of* Y; and $c$ is the expected change in sales related to a one-unit change in price, *holding constant advertising expenditures*. The coefficients of a multiple regression model are, therefore, equivalent to the partial derivatives of the function:

$$\frac{\partial \text{ Sales } Y}{\partial \text{ Advertising}} = b, \text{ and } \frac{\partial \text{ Sales } Y}{\partial \text{ Price}} = c.$$

Graphic representations of multiple regression models are not generally feasible, but Figure 5.4 can be used to gain insights into the process. Note that actual sales in 1989 were well below the value predicted by the regression line, so $u_{89}$ was large and negative. Similarly, note that actual sales exceeded the predicted level in 1986, so $u_{86}$ was large and positive. Now suppose that our new information on prices reveals that the average price of Y was relatively low in 1986 but high in 1989. Further, high prices prevailed in 1984, 1985, and 1988, whereas prices were low in 1986, 1987 and 1990. Thus, the price data seem to explain the deviations in the graph. Accordingly, we would expect that when the price data are added to the regression equation, the error terms, $u_t$, will be reduced; that is, the average absolute value of u in Equation 5.15 should be less than that of u in Equation 5.9, because more of the variation in sales can be explained by variables included in the model and, therefore, less need be absorbed by the error terms. Given that the sum of the squared error terms will be lower, Equation 5.15 is said to provide a better fit or explanation of the observed data.

## REGRESSION STATISTICS

When we use the least squares technique for estimating the parameters of a demand model, several available statistics greatly increase the value of the results for decision-making purposes. These statistics, which are

## 5.2 **Managerial Application**

Even a "Genius" Makes Mistakes

During the late 1960s and early 1970s, Fred Alger was one of the heros or "gurus" of the "go-go era" of mutual fund management. However, following a couple of years of poor investment performance, Alger disappeared from public view. He was forgotten until 1986, when a booming stock market encouraged Alger, along with a host of others, to introduce new mutual funds to satisfy the growing appetites of investors. During late 1986, a media blitz on television and in national magazines and newspapers encouraged consumers to request sales literature on a new family of mutual funds offered by the Alger Investment Management Company. Bold full-page ads in major newspapers asked investors, "Do you have a genius for a money manager?" One television spot even likened Alger to Leonardo da Vinci.

Both the scale and theme of the ad campaign stimulated criticism. Several members of the financial community criticized Alger's widespread consumer-response approach to mutual fund advertising. Without a broker to explain potential pitfalls, they contended, many consumers would be led to buy into funds with unsuitable risk characterics. The genius theme was similarly questioned by the Securities and Exchange Commission, who contended that descriptions of some aspect of Alger's historical investment record may have been misleading. Alger contended that consumer-response marketing is a proven means for reaching investors and that the complaints of the financial community only reflected the brokers' displeasure at being cut out of lucrative brokerage commissions derived from selling their in-house mutual funds. Alger also argued that the genius theme merely

*continued*

See: Laura Saunders, "Go for the Gray, Forget the Pickup Trucks," *Forbes*, September 7, 1987, 134–135.

included in the regular output of most computer regression routines, are described in the next section.

### Measures of Overall Explanatory Power

**coefficient of determination ($R^2$)**

The proportion of the total variation in the dependent variable that is explained by the full set of independent variables included in a regression model.

**Coefficient of Determination**   The **coefficient of determination**, indicated by the symbol $R^2$, shows how well the entire regression model explains changes in the value of the dependent variable.[4] It is defined as

[4]In simple regression—that is, regression models with only one independent variable—the *correlation coefficient*, r, measures the goodness of fit. In multiple regression, R, the coefficient of multiple correlation, is used similarly. The square of the coefficient of multiple correlation, $R^2$, is called the coefficient of determination.

**Managerial Application** *continued*

represented an attempt to personalize his marketing effort and to assure investors that a concerned individual would be managing their mutual fund dollars.

How did the ad campaign do? Not very well. Despite a roaring bull market and a highly receptive attitude on the part of investors to new mutual funds, the Alger genius promotion failed miserably. After spending an astonishing $13 million, huge even by the standards of industry giant Fidelity Investment Management Company, the campaign brought in only $9 million in new money. Even with Alger's steep 1-percent per year investment management charge, $9 million will generate only $90,000 per year in fees. At that rate, it will take more than a century for Alger to recoup his initial advertising outlay.

How could so successful a money manager so severely miscalculate the advertising response rate of mutual fund investors? What about the statistics showing that 40 percent of all consumers buy mutual funds through consumer-response marketing? Alger found out too late that most mutual fund sales generated by mail solicitation are from the funds' *current* customers, not new ones. Apparently, consumer-response marketing

is only an effective marketing tool when investors already have a positive disposition to a particular fund based on personal experience or past performance.

Alger's difficulty in estimating the effect of advertising on sales is not unique. Advertising effectiveness varies widely according to the media employed and the volume of expenditures. In many instances, a minimum or threshold level of advertising must be reached to achieve a meaningful effect on customer awareness. Very low levels of advertising may have no perceptible influence. Conversely, at very high rates of expenditure, advertising effectiveness may diminish as consumers become overwhelmed by the sheer volume of information. These saturation effects can rapidly diminish the effectiveness of the last or marginal dollars spent on advertising.

Of course, it is not only media choice and dollar volume that help to determine advertising effectiveness; differing levels of product price, income, and other factors are also important. As Alger Management discovered, the multiplicity of factors affecting advertising effectiveness made forecasting the success of an individual advertising campaign a risky endeavor indeed.

the proportion of the total variation in the dependent variable that is explained by the full set of independent variables included in the model. Accordingly, $R^2$ can take on values ranging from 0, indicating that the model provides no explanation of the variation in the dependent variable, to 1.0, indicating that all the variation has been explained by the independent variables. The coefficient of determination for the regression model illustrated in Figure 5.4 was 0.76, indicating that 76 percent of the total variation in Datacom Corporation's sales of Product Y are explained by variation in advertising expenditures. If the coefficient of determination is high, the deviations about a regression line, such as that shown in Figure 5.4, will be small; the actual observations will be close to the regression line, and the values of $u_t$ will be small.

This relation can be clarified by examining the algebraic formulation of $R^2$. The total variation in Y, the dependent variable in a regression model, can be measured by summing the squares of the deviations about the mean of that variable:

$$\text{Total Variation in Y} = \sum_{t=1}^{n}(Y_t - \overline{Y})^2. \qquad \textbf{5.16}$$

The deviations of each observed value, $Y_t$, from the mean value, $\overline{Y}$, are squared; then these squared deviations are summed to arrive at a measure of the total variation in Y. If Y were a constant, $Y_t$ would equal $\overline{Y}$ for all observations, and there would be no variance in Y. In this case, Equation 5.16 would equal 0. The greater the variability in Y, the larger the value of Equation 5.16.

Regression analysis breaks this total variation in the dependent variable into two parts: the variation explained by changes in the independent variables and the variation that cannot be explained by the regression model. This breakdown is illustrated in Figure 5.5. The total variation at a given data observation is seen to be $Y_t - \overline{Y}$. The predicted value of Y at each data point, $\hat{Y}_t$, can be calculated as:

$$\hat{Y}_t = a + bX_t. \qquad \textbf{5.17}$$

Using $\hat{Y}_t$ as derived in Equation 5.17, we define the value $\hat{Y}_t - \overline{Y}$ as the explained variation at point $t$, and the total variation explained by the regression equation is:

$$\text{Explained Variation} = \sum_{t=1}^{n}(\hat{Y}_t - \overline{Y})^2. \qquad \textbf{5.18}$$

The unexplained variation is simply the sum of the squared deviations about the regression line:

$$\text{Unexplained Variation} = \sum_{t=1}^{n}(Y_t - \hat{Y}_t)^2 = \sum_{t=1}^{n}u_t^2. \qquad \textbf{5.19}$$

The total variation must equal the sum of the total explained and unexplained variations, so we can write:

Total Variation = Explained Variation + Unexplained Variation,

or

$$\sum(Y_t - \overline{Y})^2 = \sum(\hat{Y}_t - \overline{Y})^2 + \sum u_t^2.$$

The coefficient of determination, $R^2$, is defined as the proportion of the total variation that is explained by the regression model. Thus:

$$R^2 = \frac{\text{Explained Variation}}{\text{Total Variation}} = \frac{\sum(\hat{Y}_t - \overline{Y})^2}{\sum(Y_t - \overline{Y})^2}. \qquad \textbf{5.20}$$

■ Figure 5.5
## Explained and Unexplained Variation of the Dependent Variable in a Regression Model

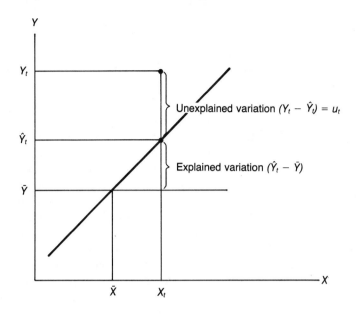

---

An $R^2$ of 1.0 indicates that all the variation has been explained. In this case, $\Sigma(\hat{Y}_t - \overline{Y})^2$ must exactly equal $\Sigma(Y_t - \overline{Y})^2$ or, alternatively stated, each predicted value for the dependent variable must exactly equal the corresponding observed value; that is $\hat{Y}_t = Y_t$ for all observations. Each data point will lie on the regression curve, and all residuals or error terms will be zero. It follows that $u_t = 0$ for all $t$'s.

As the size of the deviations about the regression curve increases, the coefficient of determination will fall. At the extreme, the sum of the squared error terms will be equal to the total variations in the dependent variable, and $R^2$ will equal zero. In this case, the regression equation has been totally unable to explain variation in the dependent variable.

In an actual regression study, the coefficient of determination will seldom be equal to either 0 or 1.0. For work in empirical demand estimation, values of $R^2$ of about 0.80, indicating that about 80 percent of the variation in demand has been explained, are quite acceptable. For some types of goods, $R^2$s as high as 0.90 to 0.95 are obtainable; for others, we must be satisfied with considerably less explanation of variation in demand.

Generally speaking, analyzing demand for a given firm or industry over time (time-series analysis) will lead to higher levels for $R^2$ than will similar analyses across firms or industries at a given point in time (cross-sectional analysis). This is because most economic phenomena are closely related to the overall level of economic activity and thus have an important trend element, whereas such exogenous factors are held constant in cross-section analyses. Therefore, in judging whether or not $R^2$ is sufficiently high, one must consider the type of analysis conducted and the anticipated use of statistical results. A low coefficient of determination indicates that the model is inadequate for explaining the demand for the product. The most general cause for this problem is the omission of some important variable or variables from the model.

**corrected coefficient of determination ($\overline{R}^2$)**

The proportion of explained variation after $\overline{R}^2$ is adjusted (corrected) for sample size and the number of coefficients estimated.

**Corrected Coefficient of Determination $\overline{R}^2$.**    As stated previously, an $R^2$ of 1.0 will result when each data point lies exactly on the regression curve. Even though one might think that any regression model with an $R^2 = 1$ would prove to be highly reliable as a forecasting device, this is not always the case. The coefficient of determination for any regression equation can be made artificially high if too small a sample is used to estimate the model's coefficients. At the extreme, $R^2$ will always equal 1.0 when the number of data observations is equal to the number of estimated coefficients, because each data point (observation) can be placed exactly on the regression function.

To conduct meaningful regression analysis, the data sample used to estimate the coefficients of the regression equation must be sufficiently large to accurately reflect the important characteristics of the underlying true relation. This suggests that we need a substantial number of data observations to adequately fit a regression model. More precisely, what is needed is a substantial number of degrees of freedom ($df$). **Degrees of**

**degrees of freedom ($df$)**

The number of data observations beyond the minimum necessary to calculate a given regression coefficient or statistic.

**freedom** is defined as the number of data observations beyond the minimum necessary to calculate a given regression coefficient or statistic. For example, to calculate an intercept term, we need at least one observation; to calculate an intercept term plus one slope coefficient, we need at least two observations; and so on. Since a regression's $R^2$ always approaches 1.0 as the $df$ approaches zero, statisticians have developed a method for correcting $R^2$ to account for the number of degrees of freedom. The corrected coefficient of determination, denoted by the symbol $\overline{R}^2$, is given by

$$\overline{R}^2 = R^2 - \left(\frac{k-1}{n-k}\right)(1 - R^2), \qquad \textbf{5.21}$$

where $n$ is the number of observations (data points) and $k$ is the number of estimated coefficients (intercept plus the number of slope coefficients). From Equation 5.21 it is obvious that the adjustment to $R^2$ will be large when $n$, the sample size, is small relative to $k$, the number of coefficients being estimated, and the adjustment to $R^2$ will be small when $n$ is large relative to $k$. Our confidence in the reliability of a given regression model will be high when both $R^2$ and degrees of freedom are substantial.

**The *F*-Statistic**    Another useful statistic for measuring the overall explanatory power of the regression equation is the **F-statistic**. As with the coefficient of determination, $R^2$, and corrected coefficient of determination, $\overline{R}^2$, the F-statistic relates to the relation between the explained and unexplained variation in the dependent variable. Whereas $R^2$ and $\overline{R}^2$ provide evidence on whether the proportion of explained variation is high or low, the F-statistic provides evidence on whether or not a statistically significant proportion of the total variation in the dependent variable has been explained. Like $\overline{R}^2$, the F-statistic is adjusted for degrees of freedom and is defined as:

$$F = \frac{\text{Explained Variation}/(k-1)}{\text{Unexplained Variation}/(n-k)}.$$

The F-statistic can be calculated in terms of the coefficient of determination as:

$$F = \frac{R^2/(k-1)}{(1-R^2)/(n-k)}. \qquad \textbf{5.22}$$

The F-statistic is used to test whether a significant proportion of the total variation in the dependent variable has been explained by the estimated regression equation. The hypothesis actually tested is that the dependent variable is statistically *unrelated* to all of the independent variables included in the model. If this hypothesis cannot be rejected, the total explained variation in the regression will be quite small. At the extreme, the F-statistic will take on a value of zero when the regression equation taken as a whole provides absolutely no explanation of the variation in the dependent variable (that is, if $R^2 = 0$, then $F = 0$). As the F-statistic increases from zero, the hypothesis that the dependent variable is not statistically related to one or more of the independent variables in the regression equation becomes easier to reject. At some point the F-statistic will become sufficiently large to enable one to reject the independence hypothesis and substitute an assumption that at least some of the variables in the regression model are significant factors in explaining the variation in the dependent variable.

The F-test is used to determine whether the F-statistic associated with a specific regression equation is large enough to enable one to reject the hypothesis that the regression model does not explain significant variation in the dependent variable. Performing this test involves comparing the F-statistic for a regression equation with a critical value from a table of the F-distribution. If the F-statistic for the regression *exceeds* the critical value in the F-distribution table, one can reject the hypothesis of independence between the dependent variable and the set of independent variables in the regression. One can then conclude that the regression equation, taken as a whole, explains significant variation in the dependent variable.

Tables of critical values of the $F$-distribution are constructed for various levels of statistical significance. The $F$-tables in Appendix C at the end of this text, for example, provide critical $F$-values at the 10-percent, 5-percent, and 1-percent significance levels; if a regression equation's $F$-statistic exceeds the $F$-value in the table, we can be 90, 95, or 99 percent certain that the model significantly explains the variance of the dependent variable. These 90-, 95-, and 99-percent confidence levels are "popular" levels for hypothesis rejection, because they imply that a true hypothesis will be rejected only one out of ten, one out of twenty, or one out of one hundred items, respectively. Such error rates are quite small and typically quite acceptable.

Critical values in an $F$-distribution depend on two degrees of freedom, one related to the numerator and one associated with the denominator. In the numerator, the degrees of freedom equal one less than the number of coefficients estimated in the regression equation ($k - 1$). The degrees of freedom for the denominator of the $F$-statistic equal the number of data observations minus the number of estimated coefficients ($n - k$). Thus, the critical value of $F$ can be denoted as $F_{f1,f2}$, where $f1$, the degrees of freedom for the numerator, equals $k - 1$, and $f2$, the degrees of freedom for the denominator, equals $n - k$.

The following example should clarify the use of the $F$-statistic. Assume that a regression analysis has been completed with the following results:

$F = 6.89$.
$k$ = number of estimated coefficients (including intercept) = 6.
$n$ = number of data observations = 20.

The relevant critical $F$-value would be denoted as $F_{5,14}$, since $f1 = k - 1 = 5$ and $f2 = n - k = 14$. The table of $F$-values in Appendix C indicates the critical $F$-values:

$F_{5,14} = 2.31$ for the 10-percent significance (90-percent confidence) level.
$F_{5,14} = 2.96$ for the 5-percent significance (95-percent confidence) level.
$F_{5,14} = 4.69$ for the 1-percent significance (99-percent confidence) level.

Since the $F$-statistic for the sample regression ($F = 6.89$) is larger than the critical $F$-value for the 1-percent significance level, we can reject the hypothesis of independence between the dependent and independent variables. We conclude that the regression model explains a statistically significant proportion of the total variation in the dependent variable. Since the $F$-statistic for the regression exceeds the critical $F$-value for the 1-percent significance level, there is less than a 1-percent probability that we are wrong in rejecting the independence hypothesis.

**standard error of the estimate**

Determines a range within which we can predict the dependent variable with established degrees of statistical confidence.

**Standard Error of the Estimate**    Yet another useful measure for examining the accuracy of the regression model as a whole is the **standard error of the estimate**. This measure provides a means of estimating a confidence interval for predicting values of the dependent variable *given*

■ Figure 5.6

## Illustration of the Use of the Standard Error of the Estimate to Define Confidence Intervals

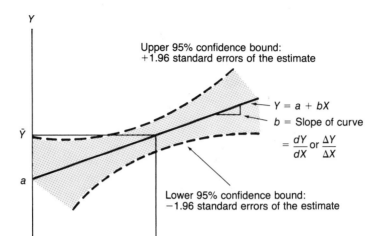

values for the independent variables. That is, the standard error of the estimate is used to determine a range within which we can predict the dependent variable with varying degrees of statistical confidence. Thus, although our best estimate of the *t*th value for the dependent variable is $\hat{Y}_t$, the value predicted by the regression equation, we can use the standard error of the estimate to determine just how accurate a prediction $\hat{Y}_t$ is likely to be.

If we can assume that the error terms are normally distributed about the regression equation, as would be true when large samples of data are analyzed, there is a 95-percent probability that future observations of the dependent variable will lie within the range $\hat{Y}_t \pm 1.96$ standard errors of the estimate. The probability that some future observation of $\hat{Y}_t$ will lie within 2.576 standard errors of its predicted value increases to 99 percent.[5] It is clear, then, that greater predictive accuracy is associated with smaller standard errors of the estimate.

This concept is illustrated graphically in Figure 5.6. Here we see the least squares regression line and the upper and lower 95-percent confidence limits. Ninety-five percent of all actual data observations will lie

[5]The standard error is, in effect, equivalent to a standard deviation; it is the standard deviation of the dependent variable about the regression line. We should note that the standard error of the estimate provides only an approximation to the true distribution of errors. Actually, the confidence band widens as observations deviate from the mean values, as is shown in Figure 5.6.

within ± 1.96 standard errors of the regression line. Thus, given the value of $X$, we can use the interval between the upper and lower confidence bounds to predict the value of $Y$ with a 95-percent probability that the actual outcome ($Y$ value) will lie within that confidence interval. Notice that the confidence bounds are closest to the regression line in the vicinity of the mean values of $X$ and $Y$—that is, at the center of the scatter diagram; then they diverge from the regression line toward the extremes of the observed points. This underscores a point made earlier: not too much confidence can be put in the predictive value of a regression equation beyond the range of observed values.

## Measures of Individual Variable Explanatory Power

**The *t*-Statistic**   Just as the standard error of the estimate indicates the precision with which the regression model can be expected to predict the dependent variable, the standard error of the coefficient provides a measure of the confidence we can place in the estimated regression parameter for each independent variable. When the standard error of a given estimated coefficient is relatively small, a strong relation between $X$ and $Y$ is suggested, and we can assume with a high level of confidence that the estimated coefficient accurately describes the relation between $X$ and $Y$. On the other hand, when the standard error of a coefficient is relatively large, the underlying relation between $X$ and $Y$ is typically weak, and we would not place as much confidence in the coefficient estimate.

A wide variety of tests can be conducted based on the size of a given estimated coefficient and its standard error. These tests are known as *t*-tests. Generally speaking, a *t*-test is performed to test whether the estimated coefficient $\hat{b}$ is significantly different from some hypothesized value, $b^*$. The *t*-statistic is given by:[6]

$$t = \frac{\hat{b} - b^*}{\text{Standard Error of } (\hat{b} - b^*)}.$$   **5.23**

**t-statistic**

Used to measure the confidence we can place in the estimated regression parameter for each independent variable.

Thus, the **t-statistic** measures the number of standard errors between an estimated regression coefficient, $\hat{b}$, and the hypothesized value for the true parameter, $b^*$. A *t*-test consists of comparing the calculated *t*-statis-

---

[6]The standard error of $(\hat{b} - b^*)$, typically denoted as $\sigma_{(\hat{b} - b^*)}$, is calculated as:

$$\sigma_{(\hat{b} - b^*)} = \sqrt{\sigma^2_{\hat{b}} + \sigma^2_{b^*} - 2\sigma_{\hat{b}, b^*}}.$$

Here $\sigma_{\hat{b}}$ and $\sigma_{b^*}$ are the standard errors of $\hat{b}$ and $b^*$, respectively, and $\sigma_{\hat{b},b^*}$ is the covariance of $\hat{b}$ and $b^*$. All of these regression statistics are typically provided by computerized regression analysis programs. It should be noted that when $b^*$ is a known constant rather than an estimated value, the standard error of $b^*$ and covariance between $\hat{b}$ and $b^*$ are both zero. Thus, the standard error of $(\hat{b} - b^*)$ in this instance reduces to just the standard error of $\hat{b}$, and the *t*-statistic is given by the expression $t = (\hat{b} - b^*)/\sigma_{\hat{b}}$.

tic with an appropriate critical $t$-value, $t^*$. If we find the calculated $t$ to be greater than the critical $t^*$, we reject the hypothesis that $b^*$ is the true parameter value. Conversely, if $t$ is not greater than $t^*$, we are unable to reject the $b^* = $ true value hypothesis.

**Two-Tail *t*-Tests**  There are two general types of hypothesis tests commonly undertaken using the $t$-statistic. Most common are simple tests of the size or magnitude of a given coefficient estimate. Should we want to know if a given variable, $X$, has an effect on $Y$, it is appropriate to test the null hypothesis that $b^*$ is equal to zero. That is, we test to determine whether $X$ is *unrelated* to $Y$. If we can reject this hypothesis, we can infer that $Y$ does indeed appear to be affected by $X$. If we cannot reject the hypothesis that $b^*$ is equal to zero, however, we have no statistical evidence that $Y$ is affected by $X$. *Tests of an effect of X on Y are* **two-tail t-tests.**

**two-tail *t*-tests**

Tests for a significant effect of an independent variable, *X*, on the dependent variable, *Y*.

The use of two-tail $t$-tests in demand analysis can be examined by reconsidering Equation 5.15,

$$\text{Sales } Y_t = a + bA_t + cP_t + u_t,$$

where $Y_t$ is unit sales, $A_t$ is advertising, and $P_t$ is the average price of $Y_t$. Questions a manager might be concerned about that could be answered using two-tail $t$-tests include the following:

| Question | Hypothesis | Two-Tail *t*-Test |
|---|---|---|
| 1. Does advertising affect sales? (Is $b^* \neq 0$?) | Sales are unaffected by advertising (i.e., $H_0{:}b^* = 0$) | $\lvert t \rvert = \dfrac{\hat{b} - 0}{\sigma_{\hat{b}}} > t^*$ |
| 2. Are sales sensitive to "own" price? (Is $c^* \neq 0$?) Note: Here $t^* > 0$. | Sales are unrelated to the price charged (i.e., $H_0{:}c^* = 0$) | $\lvert t \rvert = \dfrac{\hat{c} - 0}{\sigma_{\hat{c}}} > t^*$ |

Questions such as these are not answered directly. Rather, by rejecting the alternative case or hypothesis, we can answer each question by inference. For example, we cannot *prove* that advertising has an effect on sales. However, if we can reject as unlikely the hypothesis that there is no effect, we can *infer* there is evidence suggesting that advertising does have an effect on sales. Each of the tests described previously is a two-tail test because we can reject the null hypothesis that the true value for the parameter $b$ or $c$ is zero with a $t$-statistic that is either large and positive or very small (large negative number). In other words, the parameter estimate could be either positive or negative, and with a significant $t$-statistic, we would reject the hypothesis that the true parameter is zero.

Relatively simple two-tail $t$-tests, such as those relating to questions 1 and 2 in the table, are highly popular because they offer direct and

important evidence on the demand for a firm's products. Since the
*t*-statistic for these types of tests is simply the ratio of the estimated
coefficient divided by its standard deviation, we often look for coefficient estimates that are two or three times as large as the coefficient
standard deviation as an indication of a significant underlying relation.
For relatively large samples and relatively simple models, $df = (n - k)$
$> 30$, *t*-statistics as large as 2 or 3 will allow us to reject the hypothesis
of no effect with 95- or 99-percent confidence. That is, in a large sample
it would be extremely unlikely to find a coefficient estimate in a simple
demand relation that is more than two or three times as large as its
standard deviation if the underlying true parameter value were equal to
zero. For small samples or unusually complex demand relations ($df =
(n - k) < 30$), critical *t*-values can be found by consulting a *t*-table, such
as that found in Appendix C.

**One-Tail *t*-Tests**  Many managerial questions go beyond the simple matter of whether or not X influences Y. In some instances, it is interesting
to determine whether a given variable, X, has a positive or a negative
effect on Y, or whether the effect of variable $X_1$ is greater or smaller than
the effect of variable $X_2$. Tests of direction (positive or negative) or comparative magnitude are **one-tail *t*-tests.**

Questions a manager might ask could lead to some of the following
one-tail *t*-tests:

**one-tail *t*-tests**

Tests of direction (positive
or negative) or comparative
magnitude for the influences
of the independent variables
on Y.

| Question | Hypothesis | One-Tail *t*-Test |
|---|---|---|
| 1. Does advertising increase sales? (Is $b^* > 0$?) | The true parameter relating sales to advertising is nega-tive (i.e., $H_0:b^* < 0$) | $t = \dfrac{\hat{b} - 0}{\sigma_{\hat{b}}} > t^*$ |
| 2. Do price increases reduce sales? (Is $c^* < 0$?) | Price increases increase sales (i.e., $H_0:c^* > 0$) | $t = \left\|\dfrac{\hat{c} - 0}{\sigma_{\hat{c}}}\right\| > t^*$ and $\hat{c} < 0$ |
| 3. Is the effect of advertising on sales greater than the price effect? (Is $\|b^*\|>\|c^*\|$?) | The effect of price on sales is greater than the effect of advertising (i.e., $H_0:\|b^*\| < \|c^*\|$, or $H_0:\|b^*\| - \|c^*\| < 0$) | $t = \dfrac{\|\hat{b}\|-\|\hat{c}\|}{\sigma_{(\hat{b}-\hat{c})}} > t^*$ |

Although one-tail *t*-tests are somewhat less commonly employed than
two-tail tests, the usefulness of regression-based demand analysis is
greatly enhanced when both tests are understood.

**The *t*-Distribution**  To better understand the difference between one-
and two-tail *t*-tests, it is useful to consider the nature of the *t*-distribu-
tion. The *t*-statistic has what statisticians call an approximately normal
distribution. That is, for large sample sizes, the *t*-statistic, as given by

■ Figure 5.7
## The *t*-Distribution

For large samples, the *t*-statistic is normally distributed with a mean of zero and a standard deviation of one.

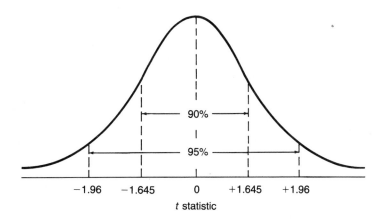

Equation 5.23, is normally distributed. From the *t*-distribution shown in Figure 5.7 we see that 90 percent of the total area beneath the bell-shaped curve is between $t = -1.645$ and $t = +1.645$, and 95 percent of this total area is between $t = -1.96$ and $t = +1.96$. Therefore, the probability of a *t*-value greater than $+1.645$ is only 5 percent, which is equal to the area in the one tail of the distribution beyond $t = +1.645$. A *t*-value greater than $+1.96$ has a probability of only 2.5 percent, again equal to the area in the *t*-distribution above a *t* of $+1.96$. The probability that the *t*-statistic will be *either* larger than $+1.645$ *or* smaller than $-1.645$ is 10 percent, equal to the combined areas in the *two* tails of the *t*-distribution outside $t = \pm 1.645$. Similarly, the probability of a *t*-statistic with an absolute value greater than 1.96 (i.e., larger than $+1.96$ or smaller than $-1.96$) is 5 percent, equal to the combined areas in the two tails beyond $t = \pm 1.96$. The difference between one- and two-tail tests relates to the "tails" of the *t*-distribution. In a two-tail *t*-test, we reject the null hypothesis with a finding that the *t*-statistic is not in the *region around zero*. That is, we want a *t*-statistic that is in *either* tail of the distribution. In a one-tail *t*-test, we reject the null hypothesis with a finding that the *t*-statistic is in one specified tail of the distribution.

It is interesting to note that given an appropriate positive or negative sign on the relevant coefficient, one-tail tests result in higher confidence levels. For example, with an estimated $t = -1.70$ for $\hat{b}$, we can reject the two-tail hypothesis $b^* = 0$ with 90-percent confidence ($|t| > 1.645$) but can reject the one-tail hypothesis that $b^* > 0$ with 95-percent confidence ($t < -1.645$). Similarly, with an estimated $t = +1.96$ for $\hat{b}$, we can reject the two-tail hypothesis that $b^* = 0$ with 95-percent confidence but can reject the one-tail hypothesis that $b^* < 0$ with 97.5-percent confidence. We must remember, however, that the choice between making one- and two-tail hypothesis tests is never made on the basis of which type of test can most easily yield statistically significant results. It depends instead on which is most appropriate for the economic question being analyzed.

## Multicollinearity Problems in Regression Analysis

We have seen the usefulness of the coefficient of determination, $R^2$, and the standard errors of the slope coefficients, but additional information may be gained by comparing these statistics. Suppose that the coefficient of determination for a regression model is large, near 1.0, indicating that the model as a whole explains most of the variation in the dependent variable. However, assume also that the standard errors of the coefficients for the various independent variables are also quite large in relation to the size of the coefficients, so little confidence can be placed in the estimated relation between any *single* independent variable and the dependent variable. This condition indicates that, although the regression model demonstrates a significant relation between the dependent variable and the independent variables as a group, the technique has been unable to separate the effects between each independent variable and the dependent variable. This is the problem of **multicollinearity** among the independent variables. It means simply that the independent variables are not really independent of one another but have values that are jointly or simultaneously determined.

**multicollinearity**

High correlation or interdependence among independent variables.

Home ownership and family income provide an example of this type of difficulty. A firm might believe that whether a given family will buy its product is dependent on, among other things, the family's income and whether the family owns its home or rents. Because families who own their homes tend to have relatively high incomes, these two variables are highly correlated.

This problem can be troublesome in regression analysis, at the extreme resulting in arbitrary values being assigned for the coefficients of the mutually correlated variables. For example, if two independent variables move up and down together, the least squares regression technique *can* assign one variable an arbitrarily high coefficient and the other an arbitrarily low coefficient, with the two largely offsetting each other. In such a case, neither coefficient would have any correspondence to the true relations of the system being investigated. When this problem occurs, it is sometimes best to remove all but one of the correlated independent variables from the model before the parameters are estimated using a single-equation regression model. Even then, the resulting regression coefficient assigned to the remaining variable can be used only for forecasting purposes rather than for explaining demand. That is, the coefficient of the remaining variable indicates its own effect on demand along with that of the removed correlated variable. Thus, the model is still unable to separate the effects of the two mutually correlated variables. The coefficient is not arbitrarily assigned in this case, however, and so long as the relation between the correlated independent variables does not change, it can be used for predictive purposes.

## Other Problems in Regression Analysis

**residuals**
**Error terms in least squares regression analysis.**

In addition to the assumption of independence among the independent variables or the problem of multicollinearity, least squares regression analysis requires four assumptions about the error terms, $u_t$, or **residuals,** as they are often called:

1. Residuals are assumed to be randomly distributed.
2. Residuals are assumed to follow a normal distribution.
3. Residuals are assumed to have an expected value of zero.
4. Residuals are assumed to have a constant variance.

A violation of any one of these assumptions reduces the validity of the ordinary least squares technique for estimating demand relations.

The residuals are typically calculated and printed as part of the output by most regression software programs, and one can examine the residuals in a number of ways to determine if any of the assumptions have been violated. For most cases a graphic method is quite revealing and easy to use. Three basic graphs of the residuals will indicate most violations of the basic assumptions.

**Frequency Distribution**   Plotting the residuals on a linear scale, as in Figure 5.8, provides a frequency distribution of the residuals. This distribution can be examined to determine whether the residuals appear to be normally distributed and whether the mean of the residuals is equal to zero. In most cases the frequency plots will not form a perfect bell-

■ Figure 5.8
## Frequency Distribution of the Residuals

Residuals are assumed to be normally distributed.

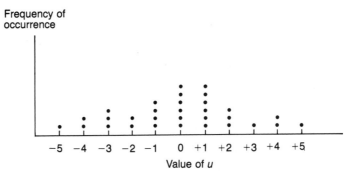

shaped (normal) curve, but any serious deviation from this shape will be readily indicated.

**Sequence Plot**   A plot of the residuals in order of occurrence provides another useful means for detecting violations of the regression assumptions. This plot is most beneficial for time series models, in which the sequence of the data has an economic interpretation. In plotting the residuals over time (or, more generally, in their order of occurrence), we expect them to be randomly distributed about a mean of zero. Reviewing the complete graph of the residuals plotted in sequence, we hope to see a horizontal band centered about the value zero, as is true of the dots in Figure 5.9. Within that band there should be no systematic patterns, which would indicate that the residuals are not occurring randomly, as is true of the x's in the figure; that is, any repetitive sequence in this plot, such as the x's, indicates that the residuals are not independent of one another but are serially correlated.

**serial correlation**

A condition that exists when the residuals are not independent of one another.

**Durbin-Watson statistic**

Used to measure the extent of serial correlation in the residuals.

   The problem of **serial correlation** (or autocorrelation, as it is called in time-series regression) occurs frequently and is not always easily detected by the graphic technique discussed here. For this reason the **Durbin-Watson statistic** is often calculated and used to measure the extent of serial correlation in the residuals.[7] A value of approximately 2 for the Durbin-Watson statistic indicates the absence of serial correlation; deviations from this value indicate that the residuals are not randomly distributed.

   When serial correlation exists, it can often be removed by making a transformation of the data. Taking first differences is one such transformation. For example, in demand analysis, serial correlation of the residuals is often caused by slowly changing variables such as consumer tastes or the development of new competing or complementary products. Because these are difficult if not impossible to measure, they cannot be included in the statistical analysis. Specification of the demand model

[7]The Durbin-Watson statistic, $d$, is calculated by the equation:

$$d = \frac{\sum\limits_{i=1}^{n}(u_i - u_{i-1})^2}{\sum\limits_{i=1}^{n}u_i^2}.$$    **5.24**

Essentially, the sum of the squared first differences of the residuals, $(u_i - u_{i-1})^2$, is divided by the sum of the squared residuals. Equation 5.24 can be rewritten as:

$$d = \frac{2\sum\limits_{i=1}^{n}u_i^2 - 2\sum\limits_{i=1}^{n}u_iu_{i-1}}{\sum\limits_{i=1}^{n}u_i^2} = 2(1 - \rho),$$

where $\rho$ is the correlation coefficient between successive residuals. Thus, if $\rho = 0$, indicating that the residuals are serially independent, $d$ will equal 2. As $\rho$ approaches $+1$, indicating positive serial correlation, $d$ will fall toward 0; and if $\rho$ is negative, indicating negative serial correlation, $d$ will increase, with an upper limit of $+4$ being associated with perfect negative serial correlation ($\rho = -1$).

■ Figure 5.9
## Sequence Plot of the Residuals

Residuals are assumed to be randomly distributed around a mean of zero.

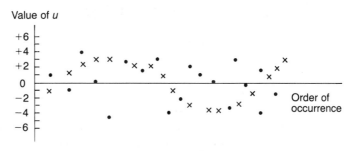

in terms of first differences—that is, in terms of the change in each variable from one period to the next—frequently overcomes this problem. Thus, in demand studies one often encounters regression models of the form:

$$\Delta \text{ Demand} = f(\Delta \text{ Price}, \Delta \text{ Income}, \Delta \text{ Advertising, and so on}).$$

Returning to the sequence plot of the residuals, three general patterns indicate violation of one or more of the regression assumptions. These three patterns are illustrated in Figure 5.10(a), (b), and (c). The pattern shown in Figure 5.10(a) occurs frequently in time-series regression where a trend variable has not been included in the model. In other words, the demand function is slowly changing over time (perhaps because of changing tastes, styles of living, and other factors). The model can be improved by explicitly accounting for this trend by including time as one of the variables explaining demand for the product. Sometimes the trend effect is not constant over time but rather indicates an increasing or a decreasing rate of change. When this is the case, a sequence plot of the residuals might appear as in Figure 5.10(b). Inclusion of time variables in quadratic terms will correct this problem.

A sequence plot such as that illustrated in Figure 5.10(c) indicates a somewhat more serious problem. There, the plotted points indicate that the variance of the residuals about their expected value is not constant over the range of observation. This will invalidate many of the statistics used to determine the usefulness of the regression coefficients.

**Plots against the Regression Variables**  The third useful kind of plot of the residuals is against the variables of the regression model. In each case the desired pattern would appear as in Figure 5.9, a horizontal band centered on zero with a constant dispersion, or variance.

Plots similar to those in Figure 5.10 all indicate difficulties of one form or another. A band that is positively (or negatively) sloped, as in

## 5.3 **Managerial Application**
Demand Estimation with Interactive Data

State-of-the-art demand estimation in the 1970s and 1980s typically involved relatively simple regression-based estimation of demand functions. Firms often relied on a combination of proprietary, company-supplied data plus publicly available industry and market-based data from government sources. Given limited data availability, the accuracy of resulting estimates of potential demand tended to vary considerably. Even though the approach led to the discovery of important and useful insights about the determinants of demand for many products, the potential of computer-based demand estimation was still limited by the relatively poor quality of available data.

To be most useful, data for market demand estimation must isolate demand characteristics for specific products based on relevant price and product-quality information. It also pays to focus on data pertaining to actual market transactions, given the lim-

ited reliability of data from surveys in which potential customers are asked to speculate on their reaction to a variety of possible market circumstances. Of course, when historical market data are relied on, the demand analyst must be careful to control for the effect of extraneous factors. However, it is often very difficult to adequately control for changes in product quality, consumer income, competitor advertising and prices, and other such factors. As a result, demand analysts have often been forced to restrict their analysis to relatively modest sets of data.

During the early 1990s, some of the problems relating to the quality of data available for demand estimation will be largely a thing of the past for many firms. For the first time, companies will have available so-called "interactive data" that is generated as a byproduct of the firm's telemarketing activities. At the heart of marketing methods

*continued*

See: Gary Slutsker, "Relationship Marketing," *Forbes*, April 3, 1989, 145–147.

Figure 5.10(a), indicates an error in the regression calculations when the residuals have been plotted against one of the independent variables in the model. Essentially, the linear effect of that variable has not been properly accounted for. If such a pattern appears in a plot of the residuals against the dependent variable, it indicates either an error in calculation as described previously or else a misspecification of the regression model, such as omitting a key variable from the analysis or suppressing the intercept term in the regression model.

**Managerial Application** *continued*

based on interactive media is a combination of the touch-tone telephone and computers capable of automatically responding to thousands of telephone calls per hour. Today, use of touch-tone telephones is widespread in the United States, and most people feel comfortable in using them. As such, they are a user-friendly means for consumer transactions and for companies to obtain a large amount of relevant market data. In turn, highly sophisticated (and now low-cost) computers are able to capture and analyze data on actual market transactions.

The technology to make this system possible was developed by First Data Resources (FDR) Interactive Technologies, a subsidiary of American Express, Inc. The main problem that needed to be addressed was that available systems that were set up to respond to incoming toll-free 800 numbers simply were not capable of handling large numbers of calls during a short time period. Truly large national promotions simply are not possible using live operator services. FDR Interactive's new systems for 800 or 900 touch-tone dialing are capable of handling 30,000 simultaneous calls and taking detailed messages. The FDR Interactive system collects a broad range of data that can be entered by touch-tone dialers and, with the aid of a large clerical staff, can record name and address information as well. Only when the technology of computer voice recognition is perfected will the FDR Interactive system be fully automated. Still, despite its limitations, the system is capable of handling up to 300,000 phone calls in a half-hour, as might be necessary to meet demand for a popular item advertised on a prime-time TV program. For example, a major retailer could use this system to move a warehouse full of surplus toaster ovens using a single national TV ad.

Perhaps just as important, the technology allows firms to develop highly sophisticated relational data bases. Marketing efforts can be narrowly focused on groups of customers with a detailed set of desired characteristics. In fact, it permits what some marketers call "one-on-one" marketing. Computer programs allow firms to select direct-mail prospects on the basis of data collected over the telephone. By carefully studying the response of targeted individuals to slight differences in product prices, for example, the company gains highly valuable information about the price elasticity of demand for its products. The possibilities for interactive media marketing appear to be truly enormous.

The curved band in Figure 5.10(b) again indicates the need for power terms in the equation. That pattern for residuals plotted against an independent variable indicates the need for a quadratic term in that same variable. If the plot is against the dependent variable, the indicated problem is also probably the absence of a higher-order term; that is, $Y = a + bX - cX^2$ in the model.

A megaphone plot similar to Figure 5.10(c) in all cases indicates that the variance of the residuals is not constant. The corrective action in this case is either to use a weighted least squares regression technique or to

■ Figure 5.10
## Undesirable Residual Patterns

The pattern of residuals can violate basic assumptions when (a) data are not de-trended, (b) residuals vary over time, or (c) residuals vary over the sample.

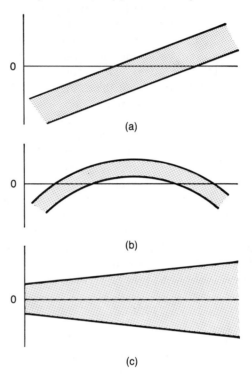

(a)

(b)

(c)

make a transformation of the dependent variable (such as changing to the logarithm of the data or using a ratio) before estimating the regression parameters.

Case 5.1

# Estimating Demand for Mrs. Smyth's Pies

In early 1990, Mrs. Smyth's Inc., a Chicago-based foods company, initiated an empirical estimation of demand for its deluxe frozen fruit pies. The firm is formulating pricing and promotional plans for the coming year, and management is interested in learning how pricing and promotional decisions might affect sales.

An analysis of earlier demand studies has led Mrs. Smyth's to hypothesize that demand for fruit pies is a linear function of the price charged, advertising and promotional activities, the price of a competing brand of frozen pies, household income, and population of the market area. A trend term is also included in the hypothesized demand function to account for the growing popularity of frozen foods over time.

Mrs. Smyth's has been marketing frozen fruit pies for several years, and its market research department has collected quarterly data for two years for six regions, including sales quantity, the retail price charged for the pies, local advertising and promotional expenditures, and the price charged by a major competing brand of frozen pies. Statistical data published by *Sales Management* magazine on population and disposable income in each of the six market areas were also available for analysis. It was therefore possible to include a wide range of hypothesized demand determinants in an empirical estimation of fruit pie demand. These data appear in Table 5.3.

The following regression equation was fitted to these data:

$$Q_{it} = a + bP_{it} + cA_{it} + dPX_{it} + eY_{it} + fPop_{it} + gT_{it} + u_{it}. \quad \textbf{5.26}$$

Here, $Q$ is the quantity of pies sold during the $t$th quarter; $P$ is the retail price in cents of Mrs. Smyth's frozen pies; $A$ represents the dollars (in thousands) spent for advertising and promotional activities; $PX$ is the price, measured in cents, charged for competing pies; $Y$ is dollars (in thousands) of disposable income per household; Pop is the population of the market area (in thousands of persons); and $T$ is the trend factor $(1988–1 = 1, \ldots , 1989–4 = 8)$. The subscript $i$ indicates the regional market from which the observation was taken, whereas the subscript $t$ represents the quarter during which the observation occurred. Least squares estimation of the regression equation on the basis of the 48 data observations (eight quarters of data for each of the six areas) resulted in the estimated regression coefficients and other statistics given in Table 5.4.

The individual coefficients for the Mrs. Smyth's pie-demand regression equation can be interpreted as follows: The intercept term, $-4{,}516.291$, has no economic meaning in this instance; it lies far outside the range of observed data and obviously cannot be interpreted as the demand for Mrs. Smyth's frozen fruit pies when all the independent variables take on zero values. The coefficient for each independent variable indicates the marginal relationship between that variable and sales of the pies, holding constant the effect of all the other variables in the demand function. For example, the $-35.985$ coefficient for $P$, the price charged for Mrs. Smyth's pies, indicates that when we hold constant the effects of all other demand variables, each 1¢ increase in price causes quarterly sales to decline by roughly 36 pies. Similarly, the 203.713 coefficient for $A$, the advertising and promotion variable, indicates that for each $1,000 (1-unit) increase in advertising during the quarter,

■ Table 5.3

## Mrs. Smyth's Frozen Fruit Pies Market Demand Data
## for Six Regional Markets, 1988–1 to 1989–4

| | Year –Quarter | Quantity | Price (cents) | Advertising ($ in thousands) | Competitor's Price (cents) | Income ($ in thousands) | Population (thousands) | Time |
|---|---|---|---|---|---|---|---|---|
| Atlanta, Ga. | 1989–4 | 27,500 | 550¢ | $10.0 | 375¢ | $41.5 | 2,650 | 8 |
| | 1989–3 | 25,000 | 600 | 7.5 | 375 | 40.5 | 2,500 | 7 |
| | 1989–2 | 25,000 | 575 | 10.0 | 375 | 40.0 | 2,450 | 6 |
| | 1989–1 | 25,000 | 575 | 5.0 | 400 | 39.5 | 2,350 | 5 |
| | 1988–4 | 27,500 | 525 | 10.0 | 400 | 39.5 | 2,300 | 4 |
| | 1988–3 | 22,500 | 500 | 7.5 | 325 | 39.0 | 2,250 | 3 |
| | 1988–2 | 25,000 | 525 | 7.5 | 375 | 39.5 | 2,150 | 2 |
| | 1988–1 | 22,500 | 600 | 5.0 | 425 | 39.5 | 2,150 | 1 |
| Baltimore, Md. | 1989–4 | 27,500 | 600 | 5.0 | 425 | 40.0 | 2,300 | 8 |
| | 1989–3 | 25,000 | 600 | 5.0 | 400 | 39.5 | 2,300 | 7 |
| | 1989–2 | 27,500 | 525 | 10.0 | 425 | 39.5 | 2,250 | 6 |
| | 1989–1 | 25,000 | 550 | 5.0 | 400 | 39.0 | 2,200 | 5 |
| | 1988–4 | 22,500 | 600 | 5.0 | 400 | 39.0 | 2,250 | 4 |
| | 1988–3 | 22,500 | 550 | 5.0 | 375 | 39.0 | 2,200 | 3 |
| | 1988–2 | 22,500 | 625 | 5.0 | 400 | 39.0 | 2,200 | 2 |
| | 1988–1 | 22,500 | 600 | 7.5 | 400 | 38.5 | 2,150 | 1 |
| Chicago, Ill. | 1989–4 | 32,500 | 600 | 5.0 | 400 | 46.0 | 6,200 | 8 |
| | 1989–3 | 32,500 | 550 | 15.0 | 375 | 45.5 | 6,150 | 7 |
| | 1989–2 | 27,500 | 600 | 5.0 | 375 | 45.0 | 6,100 | 6 |
| | 1989–1 | 22,500 | 600 | 10.0 | 350 | 44.5 | 6,150 | 5 |
| | 1988–4 | 30,000 | 550 | 5.0 | 375 | 45.0 | 6,200 | 4 |
| | 1988–3 | 30,000 | 575 | 15.0 | 350 | 44.5 | 6,250 | 3 |
| | 1988–2 | 25,000 | 600 | 5.0 | 450 | 44.5 | 6,100 | 2 |
| | 1988–1 | 27,500 | 575 | 5.0 | 375 | 44.0 | 6,050 | 1 |
| Denver, Colo. | 1989–4 | 35,000 | 500 | 15.0 | 400 | 47.5 | 1,600 | 8 |
| | 1989–3 | 32,500 | 575 | 10.0 | 400 | 47.0 | 1,650 | 7 |
| | 1989–2 | 32,500 | 550 | 7.5 | 425 | 47.0 | 1,600 | 6 |
| | 1989–1 | 30,000 | 600 | 12.5 | 400 | 46.5 | 1,550 | 5 |
| | 1988–4 | 27,500 | 550 | 5.0 | 350 | 46.0 | 1,550 | 4 |
| | 1988–3 | 25,000 | 600 | 5.0 | 325 | 46.5 | 1,500 | 3 |
| | 1988–2 | 27,500 | 575 | 10.0 | 350 | 47.0 | 1,450 | 2 |
| | 1988–1 | 30,000 | 550 | 10.0 | 425 | 46.5 | 1,450 | 1 |
| Erie, Penn. | 1989–4 | 17,500 | 600 | 2.5 | 375 | 35.5 | 300 | 8 |
| | 1989–3 | 17,500 | 625 | 2.5 | 375 | 35.0 | 290 | 7 |
| | 1989–2 | 15,000 | 600 | 5.0 | 375 | 34.5 | 285 | 6 |
| | 1989–1 | 17,500 | 575 | 2.5 | 350 | 34.5 | 270 | 5 |
| | 1988–4 | 15,000 | 625 | 2.5 | 325 | 34.0 | 265 | 4 |
| | 1988–3 | 17,500 | 575 | 2.5 | 375 | 34.0 | 270 | 3 |
| | 1988–2 | 15,000 | 575 | 5.0 | 350 | 34.0 | 275 | 2 |
| | 1988–1 | 17,500 | 575 | 2.5 | 400 | 34.0 | 280 | 1 |
| Fort Lauderdale, Fl. | 1989–4 | 27,500 | 625 | 5.0 | 400 | 46.0 | 1,500 | 8 |
| | 1989–3 | 27,500 | 625 | 12.5 | 350 | 46.0 | 1,450 | 7 |
| | 1989–2 | 27,500 | 625 | 5.0 | 450 | 45.0 | 1,300 | 6 |
| | 1989–1 | 25,000 | 625 | 5.0 | 375 | 44.5 | 1,450 | 5 |
| | 1988–4 | 30,000 | 550 | 7.5 | 425 | 44.5 | 1,350 | 4 |
| | 1988–3 | 30,000 | 575 | 12.5 | 425 | 44.0 | 1,100 | 3 |
| | 1988–2 | 27,500 | 600 | 12.5 | 400 | 43.5 | 1,050 | 2 |
| | 1988–1 | 25,000 | 575 | 10.0 | 400 | 43.5 | 1,025 | 1 |

■ Table 5.4

## Estimated Demand Function for Mrs. Smyth's Frozen Fruit Pies

|  | Coefficient (1) | Standard Error of Coefficient (2) | t-statistic (1) ÷ (2) = (3) |
|---|---|---|---|
| Intercept | −4,516.291 | 4,988.242 | −0.91 |
| Price(P) | −35.985 | 7.019 | 5.13 |
| Advertising (A) | 203.713 | 77.292 | 2.64 |
| Competitor price (PX) | 37.960 | 7.065 | 5.37 |
| Income (Y) | 777.051 | 66.423 | 11.70 |
| Population (Pop) | 0.256 | 0.125 | 2.04 |
| Time (T) | 356.047 | 92.288 | 3.86 |

Coefficient of determination = $R^2$ = 0.93
Standard error of estimate = S.E.E. = 1,442

roughly 204 additional pies were sold. The 37.960 coefficient for the competitor-price variable indicates that demand for Mrs. Smyth's pies rises by roughly 38 pies with every 1¢ increase in competitor prices. The 777.051 coefficient for the Y variable indicates that, on average, a $1,000 (1-unit) increase in the average disposable income per household for a given market leads to roughly a 777-unit increase in quarterly pie demand. Similarly, a 1,000 person (1-unit) increase in the population of a given market area leads to a small 0.256-unit increase in quarterly pie demand. Finally, the 356.047 coefficient for the trend variable indicates that pie demand is growing in a typical market by roughly 356 units per quarter. This means that Mrs. Smyth's is enjoying a secular growth in pie demand, perhaps as a result of the growing popularity of Mrs. Smyth's products or of frozen foods in general.

These individual coefficients provide useful estimates of the expected marginal influence on demand following a 1-unit change in each respective variable. However, they are only estimates. For example, it would be very unusual for a 1¢ increase in price to cause exactly a −35.985-unit change in the quantity demanded. The actual effect could be more or less. For decision-making purposes, it would be helpful to know if the marginal influences suggested by the regression model are stable or instead tend to vary widely over the sample analyzed.

In general, if we knew with certainty that $Y = a + bX$, then a 1-unit change in X would always lead to a b-unit change in Y. If $b > 0$, X and Y will be directly related; if $b < 0$, X and Y will be inversely related. If no relation at all holds between X and Y, then $b = 0$. Although the true parameter b is unobservable, its value is estimated by the regression coefficient $\hat{b}$. If $\hat{b} = 10$, a 1-unit change in X will increase Y by 10 units.

This effect might appear to be large, but it will be statistically significant only if it is stable over the entire sample. To be statistically reliable, $\hat{b}$ must be large relative to its degree of variation over the sample.

In a regression equation, there is a 68-percent probability that b lies in the interval $\hat{b}$ ± one standard error (or standard deviation) of the coefficient $\hat{b}$. There is a 95-percent probability that b lies in the interval $\hat{b}$ ± two standard errors of the coefficient. There is a 99-percent probability that b is in the interval $\hat{b}$ ± three standard errors of the coefficient. When a coefficient is at least twice as large as its standard error, we can reject the hypothesis that the true parameter b equals zero at the 95-percent confidence level. This leaves us with only a 5-percent chance of concluding incorrectly that $b \neq 0$ when in fact $b = 0$. When a coefficient is at least three times as large as its standard error (standard deviation), our confidence level rises to 99 percent and the chance of error falls to 1 percent.

Thus, a significant relation between X and Y is typically indicated whenever a coefficient is at least twice as large as its standard error; significance is even more likely when a coefficient is at least three times as large as its standard error. The independent effect of each independent variable on sales is measured using a two-tail t-statistic where:

$$t\text{-statistic} = \frac{\hat{b}}{\text{Standard error of } \hat{b}}.$$

This t-statistic is a measure of the number of standard errors between $\hat{b}$ and a hypothesized value of zero. If the sample used to estimate the regression parameters is large (for example, n > 30), the t-statistic follows a normal distribution and properties of a normal distribution can be used to make confidence statements concerning the statistical significance of $\hat{b}$. Hence $t = 1$ implies 68-percent confidence, $t = 2$ implies 95-percent confidence, $t = 3$ implies 99-percent confidence, and so on. For small sample sizes (for example, $d.f. = n - k < 30$), the t-distribution deviates from a normal distribution, and a t-table should be used for testing the significance of estimated regression parameters.

In Mrs. Smyth's frozen fruit pie demand equation, each coefficient is more than twice as large as its standard error. Therefore, we can reject the hypothesis that each of the independent variables is unrelated to pie demand with 95-percent confidence. The coefficients suggest an especially strong relation between pie demand and the P, PX, Y, and T variables. Each of these coefficients is over three times as large as its underlying standard error and therefore is statistically significant at the 99-percent confidence level.

The coefficient of determination ($R^2$) indicates that the regression model has explained 93 percent of the total variation in pie demand. This is a very satisfactory level of explanation for the model as a whole.

Another regression statistic, the standard error of the estimate (S.E.E.) is used to predict values for the dependent variable *given* values for the various independent variables. Thus, it is helpful in determining a range within which we can predict values for the dependent variable with varying degrees of statistical confidence. Although our best estimate of the value for the dependent variable is $\hat{Y}$, the value predicted by the regression equation, we use the standard error of the estimate to determine just how accurate our prediction $\hat{Y}$ is likely to be.

Assuming the standard errors are normally distributed about the regression equation, there is a 68-percent probability that actual observations of the dependent variable $Y$ will lie within the range $\hat{Y} \pm$ one standard error of the estimate. The probability that an actual observation of $Y$ will lie within two standard errors of its predicted value increases to 95 percent, and there is a 99-percent chance that an actual observed value for $Y$ will lie in the range $\hat{Y} \pm$ three standard errors.[8] It is obvious that greater predictive accuracy is associated with smaller standard errors of the estimate.

To illustrate use of the standard error of the estimate, assume that Mrs. Smyth's wishes to project the next quarter's sales of frozen fruit pies in the Baltimore, Md. market. The company expects an average price for its pies of $6.00 (600¢) and promotional expenditures of $5,000 ($5.0 thousand). The prices of competing pies are expected to decline slightly to $4.00 (400¢); disposable income per household is $40,000 ($40.0 thousand); population in the market area is 2.3 million (2,300 thousand) persons; the quarter for which demand is being forecast is the ninth quarter in the model. Inserting the appropriate unit values into the demand equation results in an estimated demand of:

$$Q = -4,516.291 - 35.985(600) + 203.713(5.0) + 37.960(400)$$
$$+777.051(40.0) + 0.2556(2,300) + 356.047(9)$$
$$= 24,970 \text{ pies.}$$

Although 24,970 is our best estimate of pie demand for Baltimore during the coming period, it is highly unlikely that precisely this number of pies will actually be sold. Either more or less may be sold, depending on the effects of other factors not explicitly accounted for in our pie demand estimation model. The standard error of the estimate is a very useful statistic because it allows us to construct a range or confidence interval within which actual sales are likely to fall. For example, sales can be projected to fall within a range of $\pm 2$ standard errors of the 24,970 expected sales level with a confidence level of 95 percent. The standard error of the estimate for the Mrs. Smyth's pie demand-estimation model is roughly 1,442 pies. Therefore, an interval of $\pm$ 2(1,442) or $\pm 2,884$ pies around the expected sales of 24,970 pies represents the 95-percent confidence interval. This means that one can predict with a 95-percent

---

[8]The standard error of the estimate is essentially equivalent to a standard deviation; it is the standard deviation of the dependent variable.

probability of being correct that sales of Mrs. Smyth's pies during the next quarter in the Baltimore area will lie in the range from 22,086 to 27,854 pies. Assuming that the hypothesized values for the various independent variables are correct, there is only a 5-percent chance that actual sales in the Baltimore market during the coming period will fall outside this range. Similarly, there is a 99-percent chance that actual sales will fall in the range of 24,970 ± 3(1,442), or between 20,644 and 29,296 pies, and only a 1-percent chance that actual sales will fall outside this range.

Mrs. Smyth's could forecast the total demand for its pies by forecasting sales in each of the six market areas, then summing these area forecasts to obtain an estimate of total pie demand. Using the demand estimation model results in Table 5.4 and data from each individual market from Table 5.3, it would also be possible to construct a confidence interval for total pie demand based on the standard error of the estimate.

## SUMMARY

In this chapter we examined a variety of techniques for empirically estimating demand relations. At the outset we described the *identification problem* and demonstrated that it can be a serious obstruction to statistical demand estimation. The identification problem results from the close interrelation among many economic variables, and it can be overcome only if one has enough prior information to identify and separate the individual relations so that shifts in a function can be distinguished from movements along the function.

Next, we considered the use of consumer interview and market experiment techniques for demand estimation in situations in which the data necessary for statistical analysis are not available. These techniques can provide valuable information about some important demand relations. However, because of the high costs and severe limits on the information that can be obtained from these techniques, statistical demand estimation is typically employed for empirical demand studies.

Because least squares *regression analysis* is by far the most widely used statistical estimating procedure in demand analysis, this technique was examined in some detail. The emphasis was on the specification of the regression model and the interpretation and use of the estimated parameters and associated regression statistics. Several problems that are frequently encountered in regression analysis were also examined. The chapter concluded with an example of the use of a regression model for empirically estimating a product's demand function.

The regression techniques introduced in this chapter are also widely used in empirical cost estimation. We shall therefore refer back to this material when cost studies are considered in Chapter 9.

## Questions

5.1 What is the identification problem?

5.2 Why is the identification problem often serious for demand estimation?

5.3 Why might a firm's customers be unwilling or unable to provide accurate demand information?

5.4 What are some possible advantages that might cause a firm to give demand–related information to its suppliers?

5.5 Describe some of the advantages and disadvantages of market experiments.

5.6 What criteria must be met if regression-based analysis is to accurately estimate demand relations?

5.7 How do linear and log-linear models differ in terms of their underlying assumptions about the nature of demand elasticities?

5.8 Does the use of regression analysis solve the identification problem in demand estimation?

5.9 Can you see any problems for demand estimation that may occur when analysts develop models purely on the basis of "goodness of fit" measured in terms of high $t$-statistics, high $R^2$, or both?

5.10 In the market study of the demand for oranges cited in the chapter, why do you suppose a lower cross-price elasticity existed between California oranges and Florida oranges than between the varieties of Florida oranges? Can these cross-price elasticity relations have anything to do with the lower price elasticity observed for California oranges?

## Problems

5.1 Identify each of the following as *true* or *false* and explain why.

A. The effect of a $1 change in price is constant, but the elasticity of demand will vary along a linear demand curve.

B. In practice, price and quantity tend to be individually rather than simultaneously determined.

C. A demand curve is revealed if prices fall while supply conditions are held constant.

D. The effect of a $1 change in price will vary, but the elasticity of demand is constant along a log-linear demand curve.

E. Consumer interviews are a useful means for incorporating subjective information into demand estimation.

5.2 Identify each of the following as *true* or *false* and explain why.

A. A parameter is a population characteristic that is estimated by a coefficient derived from a sample of data.

B. A one-tail $t$-test is used to indicate whether or not the independent variables as a group explain a significant share of demand variation.

C. Given values for independent variables, the estimated demand relation can be used to derive a predicted value for demand.

D. A two-tail *t*-test is an appropriate means for testing direction (positive or negative) of the influences of independent variables.

E. The coefficient of determination shows the share of total variation in demand that cannot be explained by the regression model.

5.3 LapTop Computers, Inc., is a leading supplier of high-quality IBM-compatible personal computers. Average price and annual unit sales data for the Model 386 high-speed laptop machine are as follows:

| | 1985 | 1986 | 1987 | 1988 | 1989 |
|---|---|---|---|---|---|
| Price($) | $9,000 | $8,000 | $6,000 | $5,000 | $3,000 |
| Units sold | 25,000 | 50,000 | 100,000 | 125,000 | 175,000 |

A. Complete the following table, and use these data to derive intercept and slope coefficients for the implied linear demand curve.

| Year | Price | Quantity | ΔPrice | ΔQuantity | Slope = ΔP/ΔQ |
|---|---|---|---|---|---|
| 1985 | $9,000 | 25,000 | | | |
| 1986 | 8,000 | 50,000 | | | |
| 1987 | 6,000 | 100,000 | | | |
| 1988 | 5,000 | 125,000 | | | |
| 1989 | 3,000 | 175,000 | | | |

B. Assuming that demand conditions are held constant, use the preceding data to plot the revealed linear demand curve.

5.4 Business is booming for Consulting Services, Inc. (CSI), a leading supplier of data-processing consulting services. The company can profitably employ technicians as quickly as they can be trained. The average hourly rate billed by CSI for trained technician services and the number of billable hours (output) per quarter during the past six quarters are as follows:

| | Q-1 | Q-2 | Q-3 | Q-4 | Q-5 | Q-6 |
|---|---|---|---|---|---|---|
| Hourly rate ($) | $20 | $25 | $30 | $35 | $40 | $45 |
| Billable hours | 2,000 | 3,000 | 4,000 | 5,000 | 6,000 | 7,000 |

Quarterly demand and supply curves for CSI services are:

$$Q_D = 6,000 - 200P + 2,000T, \quad \text{(Demand)}$$
$$Q_S = -2,000 + 200P, \qquad\qquad \text{(Supply)}$$

where $Q$ is output, $P$ is price, $T$ is a trend factor, and $T = 1$ during $Q-1$ and increases by one unit per quarter.

A. Express each demand and supply curve in terms of price as a function of output.

B. Plot the quarterly demand curves for the last six quarterly periods. (Hint: Let $T = 1$ to find the Y-intercept for Q-1, $T = 2$ for Q-2, and so on.)

C. Plot the CSI supply curve on the same graph.

D. What is this problem's relation to the identification problem?

5.5 Digital Logic, Inc., is a major producer of high-technology microwave and digital electronics components. During recent years, the rapid pace of innovation has caused a dramatic lowering of costs and selling prices for an important product, the U-2 timing device. Annual data on price and unit sales for a recent five-year period are as follows:

|  | 1986 | 1987 | 1988 | 1989 | 1990 |
|---|---|---|---|---|---|
| Price($) | $9 | $8 | $7 | $6 | $5 |
| Units sold (000) | 500 | 1,000 | 1,500 | 2,000 | 2,500 |

Annual demand and supply curves for the U-2 switch are as follows:

$$Q_D = 5,000 - 500P, \qquad\qquad \text{(Demand)}$$
$$Q_S = -5,000 + 500P - 1,000T, \quad \text{(Supply)}$$

where $Q$ is output(000), $P$ is price, $T$ is a trend factor, and $T = 1$ during 1986 and increases by one unit per year.

A. Express each demand and supply curve in terms of price as a function of output.

B. Plot the quarterly supply curves for the 1986–90 period. (Hint: Let $T = 1$ to find the Y-intercept for 1986, $T = 2$ for 1987, and so on.)

C. Plot the company's demand curve on the same graph.

D. What is this problem's relation to the identification problem?

5.6 Distinctive Designs, Inc., imports and distributes dress and sports watches. At the end of the company's fiscal year, brand manager Karla Wallace has asked you to evaluate sales of the sports-watch line using the following data:

| Month | Number of Sports Watches Sold, Q | Sports-Watch Advertising Expenditures, A | Sports-Watch Price, P | Dress-Watch Price, $P_D$ |
|---|---|---|---|---|
| July | 4,500 | $10,000 | $26 | $50 |
| August | 5,500 | 10,000 | 24 | 50 |
| September | 4,500 | 9,200 | 24 | 50 |
| October | 3,500 | 9,200 | 24 | 46 |
| November | 5,000 | 9,750 | 25 | 50 |
| December | 15,000 | 9,750 | 20 | 50 |
| January | 5,000 | 8,350 | 25 | 50 |
| February | 4,000 | 7,850 | 25 | 50 |
| March | 5,500 | 9,500 | 25 | 55 |
| April | 6,000 | 8,500 | 24 | 51 |
| May | 4,000 | 8,500 | 26 | 51 |
| June | 5,000 | 8,500 | 26 | 57 |

In particular, Wallace has asked you to estimate relevant demand elasticities. Remember that to estimate the required elasticities, you should consider months only when the other important factors considered in the preceding table have not changed. Also note that by restricting your analysis to consecutive months, changes in any additional factors not explicitly included in the analysis are less likely to affect estimated elasticities. Finally, the average arc elasticity of demand for each factor is simply the average of monthly elasticities calculated during the past year.

A. Indicate whether there was or was not a change in each respective variable for each month pair during the past year.

| Month Pair | Sports-Watch Advertising Expenditures, A | Sports-Watch Price, P | Dress-Watch Price, $P_D$ |
|---|---|---|---|
| July–Aug. | _____ | _____ | _____ |
| Aug.–Sept. | _____ | _____ | _____ |
| Sept.–Oct. | _____ | _____ | _____ |
| Oct.–Nov. | _____ | _____ | _____ |
| Nov.–Dec. | _____ | _____ | _____ |
| Dec.–Jan. | _____ | _____ | _____ |
| Jan.–Feb. | _____ | _____ | _____ |
| Feb.–March | _____ | _____ | _____ |
| March–April | _____ | _____ | _____ |
| April–May | _____ | _____ | _____ |
| May–June | _____ | _____ | _____ |

   B. Calculate and interpret the average arc advertising elasticity of demand for sports watches.

   C. Calculate and interpret the average arc price elasticity of demand for sports watches.

   D. Calculate and interpret the average arc cross-price elasticity of demand between sports and dress watches.

5.7 In the chapter, we considered a regression-based analysis of demand for Mrs. Smyth's frozen fruit pie. The estimated demand function and relevant market data can be used to estimate point demand elasticities for the Baltimore, Maryland, market. Estimate and interpret each of the following elasticities and comment on their use in Mrs. Smyth's planning process:

   A. price elasticity.

   B. advertising elasticity.

   C. cross-price elasticity.

   D. income elasticity.

5.8 The Industrial Products Corporation (IPC), a major distributor of industrial machinery, has hired a consultant to estimate the demand function for a major product. Using a regression analysis of monthly data covering the past ten years, the consultant estimated the following function:

$$Q_y = -12,400 - 0.9P_y + 50A + 300S - 35i + 0.5P_x,$$
$$\phantom{Q_y =}(10,000)\quad(0.33)\quad(21)\quad(66)\quad(8.1)\quad(0.19)$$
$$R^2 = 0.85, \quad \text{Standard Error of the Estimate} = 27.$$

Here $Q$ is the quantity demanded (measured in units), $P_y$ is price in dollars, $A$ is advertising by IPC (in hundreds of dollars), $S$ is a service quality variable measured by the amount IPC spends for service-department staff (measured in thousands of dollars), $i$ is the prime interest rate measured in percent, and $P_x$ is the price in dollars of a competing line of equipment. Standard errors for each coefficient are shown in parentheses.

   A. What percentage of the variability in demand has not been explained by this equation?

   B. During the current period, $P_y$ = $2,200, IPC advertising is $20,000, expenditures for service quality are $15,000, the interest rate is 15 percent, and $P_x$ is $2,500. What is the demand curve facing IPC?

   C. Assuming that IPC changes its price to $2,400 (but that all else remains unchanged from Part B), what is the 95-percent confidence-level range for estimated demand?

   D. IPC is considering spending an added $5,000 on advertising. What would this expenditure do to the demand curve facing IPC?

   E. Would the $5,000 in Part D be better spent if used to expand the service-department staff? Explain briefly.

5.9  Colorful Tile, Inc., is a rapidly growing chain of ceramic tile outlets that caters to the do-it-yourself home remodeling market. In 1989, 33 stores were operated in small- to medium-sized metropolitan markets. An in-house study of sales by these outlets revealed the following (standard errors in parentheses):

$$Q = 5 - 5P + 1.5A + 0.5I + 0.2HF,$$
$$\phantom{Q = 5 -} (3) \quad (1.8) \quad (0.7) \quad (0.2) \quad (0.1)$$
$$R^2 = 0.93, \quad \text{Standard Error of the Estimate} = 6.$$

Here, $Q$ is tile sales (in thousands of cases); $P$ is tile price (per case); $A$ is advertising expenditures (in thousands of dollars); $I$ is disposable income per household (in thousands of dollars); and $HF$ is household formation (in hundreds).

A.  Fully evaluate and interpret these empirical results on an overall basis.
B.  Is quantity demanded sensitive to "own" price?
C.  Austin, Texas, was a typical market covered by this analysis. During 1989 in the Austin market, price was $5, advertising was $40,000, income was an average $20,000 per household, and the number of household formations was 5,000. Calculate and interpret the relevant advertising point elasticity.
D.  Assume that the preceding model and data are relevant for the coming period. Estimate the probability that the Austin store will make a profit during 1990 if total costs are projected to be $300,000.

5.10 Getaway Tours, Inc., has estimated the following multiplicative demand function for packaged holiday tours in the East Lansing, Michigan, market using quarterly data covering the past four years (16 observations):

$$Q_y = 10P_y^{-1.10}P_x^{0.5}A_y^{3.8}A_x^{2.5}I^{1.85},$$
$$R^2 = 0.80, \quad \text{Standard Error of the Estimate} = 20.$$

Here $Q_y$ is the quantity of tours sold, $P_y$ is average tour price, $P_x$ is average price for some other good, $A_y$ is tour advertising, $A_x$ is advertising of some other good, and $I$ is per-capita disposable income. The standard errors of the exponents in the preceding multiplicative demand function are:

$$b_{P_y} = 0.04, \ b_{P_x} = 0.35, \ b_{A_y} = 0.5, \ b_{A_x} = 0.9, \text{ and } b_I = 0.45.$$

A.  Is tour demand elastic with respect to price?
B.  Are tours a normal good?
C.  Is $X$ a compliment or substitute good?
D.  Given your answer to Part C, can you explain why the demand effects of $A_y$ and $A_x$ are both positive?

# Selected References

Alexeev, Michael. "Market vs. Rationing: The Case of Soviet Housing." *Review of Economics and Statistics* 70 (August 1988): 414–420.

Baltagi, Badi H., and Dan Levin. "Estimating Dynamic Demand for Cigarettes Using Panel Data: The Effects of Bootlegging, Taxation and Advertising Reconsidered." *Review of Economics and Statistics* 68 (February 1986): 148–155.

Callasch, H. Frederick. "Price Elasticities of Demand at Retail and Wholesale Levels: An Automotive Example." *Business Economics* 19 (January 1984): 61–62.

Crafton, Steven M., and George E. Hoffer. "Estimating a Transaction Price for New Automobiles." *Journal of Business* 54 (October 1981): 611–621.

Froyen, Richard T., and Roger N. Ward. "Demand Variability, Supply Shocks and the Output-Inflation Tradeoff." *Review of Economics and Statistics* 67 (February 1985): 9–15.

Gahvari, Firoz. "Demand and Supply of Housing in the U.S., 1929–1978." *Economic Inquiry* 24 (April 1986): 333–347.

Happel, Stephen K. "The Effect of Adverse Publicity on Sales: A Case Study." *Managerial and Decision Economics* 6 (December 1984): 257–259.

Hirschey, Mark. "Intangible Capital Aspects of Advertising and R&D Expenditures." *Journal of Industrial Economics* 30 (June 1982): 275–390.

Holak, Susan L., and Srinivas K. Reddy. "Effects of a Television and Radio Advertising Ban: A Study of the Cigarette Industry." *Journal of Marketing* 50 (October 1986): 219–227.

Kaempher, William H., and Raymond T. Brastow. "The Effect of Unit Fees on the Consumption of Quality." *Economic Inquiry* 24 (April 1985): 341–348.

Kessides, Ioanis, N. "Advertising, Sunk Costs, and Barriers to Entry." *Review of Economics and Statistics* 68 (February 1986): 84–95.

Leamer, Edward E. "Let's Take the Con Out of Econometrics." *American Economic Review* 73 (March 1983): 31–43.

McCrohan, Kevin F. "A Consumer Expenditure Approach to Estimating the Size of the Underground Economy." *Journal of Marketing* 50 (April 1986): 48–60.

McQuiston, Daniel H. "Novelty, Complexity, and Importance as Causal Determinants of Industrial Buyer Behavior." *Journal of Marketing* 53 (April 1989): 66–79.

Neslin, Scott A., and Robert W. Shoemaker. "Using a Natural Experiment to Estimate Price Elasticity: The 1974 Sugar Shortage and the Ready-to-Eat Cereal Market." *Journal of Marketing* 47 (Winter 1983): 44–57.

Perreault, William D., Jr., and Laurence E. Leigh. "Reliability of Nominal Data Based on Qualitative Judgments." *Journal of Marketing Research* 26 (May 1989): 135–148.

Seater, John J. "Testing Equilibrium Models of the Business Cycle." *Review of Economics and Statistics* 67 (November 1985): 670–675.

Smith, Vernon L. "Theory, Experiment and Economics." *Journal of Economic Perspectives* 3 (Winter 1989): 151–170.

Weinberger, Marc G., and Harlan E. Spotts. "A Situational View of Information Content in TV Advertising in the U.S. and U.K." *Journal of Marketing* 53 (January 1989): 89–94.

Witt, Stephen F., and S. Raymond Johnson. "An Econometric Model of New Car Demand in the U.K." *Managerial and Decision Economics* 7 (March 1986): 19–23.

# Forecasting

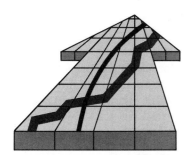

Two key functions of management for any organization are *planning* and *control*. The firm must plan for the future. Planning for the future involves the following activities:

1. Determine the product and geographic markets in which the firm can earn the highest returns.
2. Forecast the level of demand in these markets under different conditions of price, promotional activities, competition, and general economic activity.
3. Forecast the cost of producing different levels of output under conditions of changing technology, wage rates, and raw materials prices.
4. Decide on the optimum operating plan—that is, the value-maximizing plan.
5. Engage in capital acquisition programs, labor hiring and training programs, and so forth to implement the plan.

Once the plan has been determined, it must be carried out in the *control*, or *operating*, phase of enterprise activity. Planning and control are closely related; in practice, they are often inseparable. Operating procedures, or the process of control, must be geared to the firm's plans. If forecasts about demand, the cost of inputs, technology, and other factors that go into the plan are seriously in error, then the plan will be of little use and the control phase will probably break down.

In view of forecasting's key role in managerial decisions, it is not surprising that managerial economics emphasizes it. In this chapter we describe and illustrate several forecasting techniques employed in managerial decision making.

# FORECASTING METHODOLOGIES

Many techniques are available for forecasting economic variables. They range from simple, often somewhat naïve, and relatively inexpensive procedures to methods that are quite complex and very expensive. Some forecasting techniques are basically quantitative; others are qualitative. Forecasting techniques can be divided into the four following categories:

1. Qualitative analyses
2. Time-series analysis and projection
3. Econometric methods
4. Input–output analysis

It is impossible to state that one of these forecasting approaches is superior to the others. The best one for a particular task depends on the specific forecasting problem. Some important factors that must be considered include:

1. The distance into the future that one must forecast.
2. The lead time available for making decisions.
3. The level of accuracy required.
4. The quality of data available for analysis.
5. The nature of relationships included in the forecasting problem.
6. The cost and benefits associated with the forecasting problem.

Some techniques—for example, certain time-series, barometric, and survey methodologies—are well-suited for short-term projections. Others require more lead time and are therefore more useful for long-run forecasting. Within each class of forecasting technique, the level of sophistication also varies. Typically, the greater the level of sophistication, the higher the cost. If the required level of accuracy is low, less sophisticated methods may provide adequate results at minimal cost. Therefore, the choice of an appropriate forecasting methodology depends upon both the underlying characteristics of the forecasting problem and the level of accuracy required.

To determine an appropriate level of forecast accuracy, one must compare the costs and benefits of increased accuracy. When forecast accuracy is low, the probability of significant forecasting error is high, as is the chance of making suboptimal managerial decisions. Conversely, when forecast accuracy is high, the probability of substantial forecasting error is reduced and the chance of making erroneous managerial decisions is low. Thus, it is reasonable to require a relatively high level of forecast accuracy when the costs of forecast error are high. When only minor costs result from forecast error, only inexpensive and typically less precise methods can be justified.

In the material that follows, we examine both the advantages and limitations of various forecasting techniques. By understanding the strengths and weaknesses of various forecasting methodologies, managers can select an appropriate method or combination of methods to generate required forecast values.

# QUALITATIVE ANALYSES

**qualitative analysis**
A nonquantitative method of forecasting based on opinion.

**Qualitative analysis** can be a highly useful forecasting technique if it allows for the systematic collection and organization of data derived from unbiased, informed opinion. However, qualitative methods can produce biased results when specific individuals dominate the forecasting process through reputation, force of personality, or strategic position within the organization.

## Expert Opinion

The most basic form of qualitative analysis used in forecasting is *personal insight*. Here an informed individual uses personal or organizational experience as a basis for developing future expectations. Although this approach is highly subjective, the reasoned judgment of informed individuals often provides valuable insight. When the informed opinion of several individuals is relied upon, the approach is called forecasting through *panel consensus*. The panel consensus method assumes that several experts can arrive at forecasts that are superior to those that individuals generate. Direct interaction among experts is used in the panel consensus method with the hope that resulting forecasts embody all available objective and subjective evidence.

Although the panel consensus method often results in forecasts that embody the collective wisdom of consulted experts, it can sometimes be unfavorably affected by the force of personality of one or a few key individuals. A related approach, the *delphi method*, has been developed to counter this disadvantage. In the delphi method, members of a panel of experts individually receive a series of questions relating to the underlying forecasting problem. Responses are analyzed by an independent party, who then tries to elicit a consensus opinion by providing feedback to the panel members in a manner that prevents direct identification of individual positions. This method helps limit the steamroller or bandwagon problems of the basic panel consensus approach.

## Survey Techniques

Survey techniques constitute another important forecasting tool, especially for short-term projections. Designing surveys that provide unbiased and reliable information is a challenging and often difficult task. When properly carried out, however, survey research can provide managers with valuable information that would otherwise be unobtainable.

Surveys generally use interviews or mailed questionnaires asking business firms, government agencies, and individuals about their future plans. Business firms plan and budget virtually all their expenditures in advance of actual purchases or production. Surveys asking about capital budgets, sales budgets, and operating budgets can thus provide much useful information for forecasting. Government units also prepare formal budgets well before the actual spending is done, and surveys of budget material, congressional appropriations hearings, and the like can provide a wealth of information to the forecaster. Finally, even individual consumers usually plan expenditures for such major items as automobiles, furniture, housing, vacations, and education well ahead of the purchase date, so surveys of consumer intentions often accurately predict future spending on consumer goods.

Survey information may be all that is obtainable in certain forecasting situations, as, for example, when a firm is attempting to project the demand for a new product. Although they sometimes serve as an alternative to quantitative forecasting techniques, surveys frequently supplement rather than replace quantitative analysis. Their value in this role stems from two factors. First, a nonquantifiable psychological element is inherent in most economic behavior, and surveys and other qualitative methods are especially well-suited to picking up this phenomenon. Second, quantitative models generally assume stable consumer tastes, and if these tastes are actually changing, survey data may reveal the changes.

## Surveys for Forecasting Various Classes of Expenditures

Surveys useful for forecasting business activity in various sectors of the U.S. economy are published periodically by private and governmental sources. Some of the most widely used are:

**Plant and Equipment Expenditures**   Surveys of businesses' intentions to expand plant and equipment are conducted by the U.S. Department of Commerce, the Securities and Exchange Commission, the National Industrial Conference Board, McGraw-Hill, *Fortune* magazine, and various trade associations, such as the Edison Electric Institute and the American Gas Association.

**Inventory Changes and Sales Expectations**   The U.S. Department of Commerce and private organizations such as McGraw-Hill, Dun and Bradstreet, *Fortune*, *Business Week*, and the National Association of Purchasing Agents all regularly survey business expectations about future sales levels and plans for inventory changes. These surveys, although not nearly as accurate as those for long-term investment, provide a useful check on other forecasting methods.

**Consumer Expenditures**   The consumer intentions surveys of the Census Bureau, the University of Michigan Research Center, and the Sindlinger-National Industrial Conference Board all provide information on planned purchases of specific products, such as automobiles, housing, and appliances. In addition, these surveys often indicate consumer confidence in the economy and, therefore, spending expectations in general.

Attempts are being made to quantify all aspects of survey data and to incorporate this information directly into forecasting models. Although some success is being achieved with these attempts, a great deal of judgment is still required. Forecasting is becoming more scientific, but it still contains elements of art.

## TIME-SERIES ANALYSIS AND PROJECTION

**time-series methods**
Methods of forecasting that use historical data as the basis for projections.

**Time-series methods** are based on the assumption that future events will follow an established path or, alternatively, that past patterns of economic behavior prevail sufficiently to justify using historical data to predict the future. The economic forecaster using time-series techniques looks at the historical pattern of a variable and then projects, or forecasts, that it will continue moving along the path described by its past movement.

The many variations of forecasting by trend projection are all predicated on a continuation of the past relation between the variable being projected and the passage of time, so all of them employ time-series data. An economic time series is a sequential array of the values of an economic variable. Weekly, monthly, or annual series of data on sales and costs, personal income, population, labor force participation rates, and gross national product (GNP) are all examples of economic time series.

All time series, regardless of the nature of the economic variable involved, can be described by the four following characteristics:

1. *Secular trend:* the long-run increase or decrease in the series.
2. *Cyclical fluctuations:* rhythmic variations in the economic series.
3. *Seasonal variation:* variations caused by weather patterns and/or social habits that produce an *annual* pattern in the time series.
4. *Irregular or random influences:* unpredictable shocks to the system, such as wars, strikes, natural catastrophes, and so on.

These four patterns are illustrated in Figure 6.1. Figure 6.1a shows secular and cyclical trends in sales of women's clothing and Figure 6.1b shows (1) the seasonal pattern superimposed over the long-run trend (which, in this case, is a composite of the secular and cyclical trends) and (2) random fluctuations around the seasonal curve.

Time-series analysis can be as simple as projecting or extrapolating the unadjusted trend. Applying either graphic analysis ( by *eye* fitting) or least squares regression techniques, one can use historical data to determine the average increase or decrease in the series during each time period and then project this rate of change into the future. Time-series analysis can also be considerably more complex and sophisticated, allowing examination of seasonal and cyclical patterns as well as the basic trend.

Since extrapolation techniques assume that a variable will follow its established path, the problem is to determine the appropriate trend curve. In theory, one could fit any complex mathematical function to the

■ Figure 6.1

## Time-Series Characteristics: (a) Secular Trend and Cyclical Variation in Women's Clothing Sales; (b) Seasonal Pattern and Random Fluctuations

(a) The cyclical pattern in sales varies significantly from the normal secular trend.
(b) Seasonal patterns, random fluctuations, and other influences cause deviations around the cyclical pattern of sales.

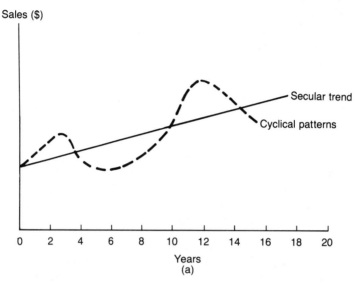

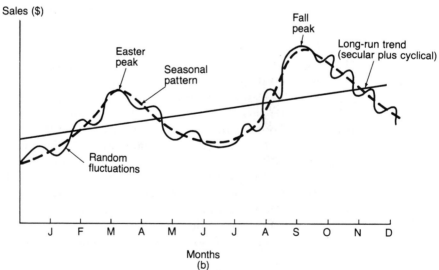

historical data and extrapolate to estimate future values. In practice, however, one typically finds linear, simple power, or exponential curves used for economic forecasting.

Selection of the appropriate curve is guided by both empirical and theoretical considerations. Empirically, it is a question of finding the curve that best fits the historical movement in the data. Theoretical considerations intervene when logic dictates that a particular pattern of future events should prevail. For example, output in a particular industry may have been expanding at a constant rate historically, but because of known resource limitations, one might use a declining growth-rate model to reflect the slowdown in growth that must ultimately prevail.

## Trend Analysis

A simple trending procedure is illustrated in Figure 6.2, which displays the fifteen years of total sales data for General Cereals, Inc. given in Table 6.1, along with a curve representing a linear relation between sales and time over the 1976 to 1990 period.

The linear relation between firm sales and time illustrated in Figure 6.2 can be written as:

$$S_t = a + b \times t. \qquad \textbf{6.1}$$

The coefficients of this equation were estimated using General Cereals' sales data and the least squares regression method as follows (standard errors in parentheses):

$$\begin{array}{cc} S_t = \$759.52 + \$363.39t & R^2 = 0.94 \\ (231.42) \quad (25.45) & \end{array} \qquad \textbf{6.2}$$

Although a linear trend projection for firm sales is relatively naïve, an important trend element is obvious in General Cereals' sales data. Using the linear trend equation estimated over the 1976 to 1990 period, we can forecast firm sales for future time periods. To do so, it is important to realize that in this model, $t = 1$ for 1976, $t = 2$ for 1977, and so on. This means that $t = 0$ in the 1975 base period. To forecast sales in any future period we simply subtract 1975 from the year in question to determine a relevant value for $t$.

For example, a sales forecast for 1995 using Equation 6.2 would be

$$t = 1995 - 1975 = 20$$
$$S_{1995} = \$759.52 + \$363.39(20)$$
$$= \$8,027 \text{ million.}$$

Similarly, a sales forecast for General Cereals' sales in the year 2000 would be calculated as:

$$t = 2000 - 1975 = 25$$
$$S_{2000} = \$759.52 + \$363.39(25)$$
$$= \$9,844 \text{ million.}$$

■ Figure 6.2

## Total Sales Revenue for General Cereals, Inc., 1976–1990

Sales data points lie in a pattern around the fitted regression line, indicating that the slope of the sales–time relation may not be constant.

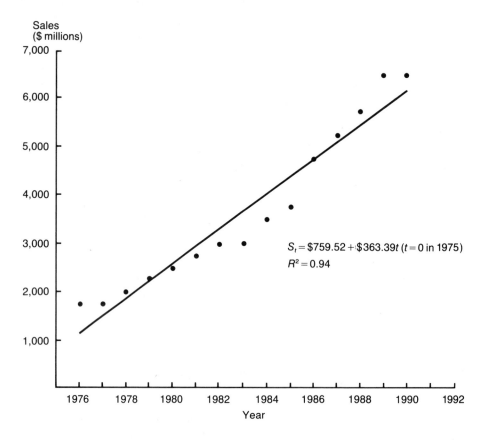

Note that these sales projections are based upon a linear trend line, which implies that sales increase by a constant dollar amount each year. In this example, General Cereals' sales are projected to grow by $363.39 million per year. However, there are important reasons for believing that the true trend for General Cereals' sales is nonlinear and that the forecasts generated by this constant change model will be relatively poor estimates of actual values. To see why a linear trend relation may not be accurate, consider the relation between the actual sales data and the linear trend shown in Figure 6.2. Remember that the least squares regression line minimizes the sum of squared residuals between actual and fitted values over the sample data. As is typical, actual data points lie above and below the fitted regression line. Note, however, that the pat-

■ Table 6.1
## Total Sales Revenue for General Cereals, Inc., 1976–1990

|  | Sales (millions of dollars) | Time Period |
|---|---|---|
| 1990 | $6,500 | 15 |
| 1989 | 6,500 | 14 |
| 1988 | 5,750 | 13 |
| 1987 | 5,250 | 12 |
| 1986 | 4,750 | 11 |
| 1985 | 3,750 | 10 |
| 1984 | 3,500 | 9 |
| 1983 | 3,000 | 8 |
| 1982 | 3,000 | 7 |
| 1981 | 2,750 | 6 |
| 1980 | 2,500 | 5 |
| 1979 | 2,250 | 4 |
| 1978 | 2,000 | 3 |
| 1977 | 1,750 | 2 |
| 1976 | 1,750 | 1 |

tern of differences between actual and fitted values varies dramatically over the sample period. Differences between actual and fitted values are generally positive in both early (1976 to 1978) and later (1988 to 1990) periods, whereas they are negative in the intervening 1981 to 1985 period. These differences suggest that the slope of the sales–time relation may not be constant but rather generally increasing over the 1976 to 1990 time period. What sales growth assumption is appropriate for forecasting purposes under these circumstances?

A model structure that captures the increasing annual sales growth pattern described in the 1976 to 1990 General Cereals sales data is the constant rate of change model, also called the constant growth rate or proportional change model. This model is appropriate for forecasting when sales appear to change over time by a constant proportional amount rather than by a constant absolute amount.

The constant rate of change model involves determining the average historical rate of change in a variable and projecting that *rate* into the future. This is essentially identical to the compounding of value model used in finance.[1] For example, if a firm is projecting its sales five years into the future and if it has determined that sales are increasing at an annual rate of 10 percent, the projection would simply involve multiplying the 10-percent compound value interest factor for five years by cur-

[1]The section entitled "Future Value (or Compound Value)" in Appendix A at the back of the text provides more material on proportional growth models.

rent sales. Assuming current sales are $1 million, the forecast of sales five years hence would be:

$$\text{Sales in Year 5} = \text{Current Sales} \times (1 + \text{Growth Rate})^5$$
$$= \$1,000,000 \times (1.10)^5$$
$$= \$1,000,000 \times 1.611$$
$$= \$1,611,000.$$

More generally, the constant rate of change projection model can be stated as follows:

$$\text{Value } t \text{ Years in the Future} = \text{Current Value} \times (1 + \text{Rate of Change})^t.$$

Just as one can estimate the constant annual change in an economic time series by fitting historical data to a linear regression model of the form $Y = a + bt$, one can also estimate the annual growth rate in a constant rate of change projection model using the same technique. In this case, the growth rate is estimated using linear regression by fitting historical data to the logarithmic transformation of the basic model. For example, if one were to formulate a constant growth rate model for firm sales, it would take the form:

$$S_t = S_0 \times (1 + g)^t. \qquad \textbf{6.3}$$

Here sales $t$ years in the future is assumed to equal current sales, $S_0$, compounded at a growth rate, g, for a period of $t$ years. Taking logarithms of both sides of Equation 6.3 results in the expression:

$$\ln S_t = \ln S_0 + \ln (1 + g) \times t. \qquad \textbf{6.4}$$

Note that Equation 6.4 is an expression of the form:

$$Y_t = a + bt,$$

where $Y_t = \ln S_t$, $a = \ln S_0$, and $b = \ln (1 + g)$; hence, its coefficients, $\ln S_0$ and $\ln (1 + g)$, can be estimated using the least squares regression technique.

Applying this technique to the General Cereals' sales data in Table 6.1 for the 1976 to 1990 period results in the following regression (standard errors in parentheses):

$$\ln S_t = \underset{(0.03)}{7.30} + \underset{(0.003)}{0.102\, t,} \qquad R^2 = 0.99 \qquad \textbf{6.5}$$

or, equivalently, by transforming this estimated equation back to its original form:

$$S_t = [\text{Antilog } 7.30] \times [\text{Antilog } 0.102]^t = \$1,480.30(1.107^t). \qquad \textbf{6.6}$$

In this model, $1,480.30 million is the adjusted level of sales for $t = 0$ (1975, because the first year of data used in the regression estimation, $t = 1$, was 1976), and 1.107 equals one plus the average annual rate of growth, meaning that General Cereals' sales increased by 10.7 percent annually from 1976 to 1990.[2]

To forecast sales in any future year using this model, we again subtract 1975 from the year being forecast to determine $t$. Thus, a constant growth model forecast of sales in 1995 is:

$$t = 1995 - 1975 = 20$$
$$S_{1995} = \$1,480.30 \, (1.107^{20})$$
$$= \$11,305 \text{ million.}$$

Similarly, a constant growth model forecast of General Cereals' sales in the year 2000 is:

$$t = 2000 - 1975 = 25$$
$$S_{2000} = \$1,480.30 \, (1.107^{25})$$
$$= \$18,759 \text{ million.}$$

The importance of selecting the correct structural form for a trending model can be demonstrated by comparing the sales projections that result from the two models we have examined. Recall that with the constant change model, sales were projected to be \$8 billion in 1995 and \$9.8 billion in 2000. Compare these sales forecasts with the \$11.3 billion in 1995, and \$18.8 billion in 2000 projected by the constant growth rate model. Notice that the difference in the near-term forecasts (1995) is smaller than the difference in the longer-term (2000) projections. This points up the fact that if an economic time series is growing at a constant rate rather than increasing by a constant dollar amount, forecasts based on a linear trend model will tend to be less accurate the further out into the future one projects.

Of course, the pattern of future sales for General Cereals, and therefore the reasonableness of a linear trend projection using either the constant change model or constant growth model, remains a matter for conjecture. Whether or not the company will be able to maintain its rapid pace of growth depends on a host of factors both within and beyond the com-

---

[2]Another frequently used form of the constant growth rate model is based on a continuous (as opposed to annual) compounding assumption. This model is expressed by the exponential equation:

$$Y_t = Y_0 e^{gt},$$

the logarithmic equivalent of which is:

$$\ln Y_t = \ln Y_0 + gt.$$

Thus, with the exponential growth assumption, the regression model's estimate of the slope coefficient, $g$, is a direct estimate of the continuous rate of growth. For example, in General Cereals' sales regression model, Equation 6.5, the coefficient 0.102 ($= 10.2$ percent) is a direct estimate of the continuous compounding growth rate for General Cereals' sales.

## 6.1  **Managerial Application**

Forecasting AIDS Epidemiology and Economic Consequences

AIDS, acquired immune deficiency syndrome, is the final stage of the disease caused by the human immunodeficiency virus (HIV). In most victims, HIV causes a deterioration in the immune system by killing a class of white blood cells called "T4 helpers." After a period of five to ten years, too few of these T4 helper cells remain, and the HIV victim succumbs to an opportunistic infection such as pneumonia. During the period between HIV infection and the onset of AIDS, victims are infectious, asymptomatic carriers. Because HIV alters the victim's genetic material and is highly prone to mutation, finding a cure is extremely difficult and any vaccine is likely to be ineffective in a substantial minority of those vaccinated. Moreover, no natural immunity has been observed. So far, the disease is fatal for nearly everyone who gets it. For all of these reasons, AIDS has become the most dreaded disease in the world today. Public officials are confronted with a complex forecasting problem in the field of epidemiology.

Epidemiology is the study of epidemics and epidemic diseases. In the study of AIDS, a key issue is estimating the spread of the disease, its frequency, and its distribution. With a long incubation period, the number of asymptomatic carriers can be considerably greater than the number of AIDS victims. Given the five- to ten-year lag between the victim's infection and the onset of AIDS symptoms, a simple extrapolation of AIDS growth curves would give a highly unreliable indication of the number of future AIDS victims. As a result, medical researchers and social scientists are turning to mathematical models and computers in the effort to improve forecasts of the human and economic costs of AIDS.

A mathematical model of the spread of

*continued*

Source: Peter J. Denning, "Computer Models of AIDS Epidemiology," *American Scientist*, July–August 1987, 347–350; Maggie Mahar, "Pitiless Scourge," *Barron's*, March 13, 1989, 6–26; and Marilyn Chase, "U.S. Weighs New Programs to Fight AIDS," *The Wall Street Journal*, June 7, 1989, B4.

pany's control. Successfully managing rapid growth over extended periods is extraordinarily difficult and is rarely observed in practice. In fact, the sales pattern shown in Figure 6.2 might describe a company experiencing phases of rapid growth (1970s), maturity (1980s), and then decline (1990s). Individual products often display such a sales pattern, as do some firms and industries. Therefore, in applying the various trend projection methods in forecasting, it is important to establish the similarity in growth opportunities between the historical and forecast periods. Prudence suggests that one limit the forecast horizon to a relatively short time frame.

**Managerial Application** *continued*

disease was first proposed in the early 1900s by Sir Donald Ross, who advocated the approach as essential for understanding the epidemiology of malaria. Ross found that malaria was transmitted by mosquitos from infected to uninfected subgroups of the human population. Though he did not know the number of infected humans and carriers, Ross discovered that there was a critical mosquito bite rate below which the disease would die out. By controlling the mosquito population, malaria would disappear.

Ross' mathematical approach is being used to model the spread of AIDS. In early 1989, there were about 80,000 known cases of AIDS in the United States, and researchers estimated that there were approximately 1.5 to 2.0 million HIV carriers. This was based on the assumption of an average eight-year incubation period and a 20- to 30-percent morbidity rate (morbidity is the probability of an infected person developing clinical symptoms of AIDS). The estimated number of HIV carriers would rise with a longer incubation period and fall with a shorter one. The number of AIDS cases and deaths will rise and fall with the disease's morbidity.

The Surgeon General's forecast of 73,000 new AIDS cases in 1991 (compared with 15,600 in 1986) has been criticized as being overly optimistic. If AIDS morbidity is in fact 70 to 100 percent, as some researchers believe, there may be as many as 200,000 new AIDS cases in 1991. At that rate, deaths due to the AIDS epidemic would be comparable to losses suffered during World War II when combat and noncombat deaths to U.S. servicemen totaled 100,000 per year. Even under "optimistic" scenarios, AIDS is expected to be the leading cause of death for persons in the 25 to 44 age group by 1991. Treatment may cost between $10 and $50 billion per year and will have a dramatic influence on hospital care, health and life insurance, employee benefits, and public services. The fact that AIDS strikes primarily young people in their most productive years intensifies its economic impact.

It is noteworthy that mathematical models and computer simulations already play an important role in focusing current research efforts and data collection. These methods may suggest how the human suffering and economic costs of AIDS can be effectively controlled.

Although trend projections can provide very adequate estimates for some forecasting purposes, a number of serious shortcomings in the technique limit its usefulness in many situations. One problem is that simple trend projection techniques lack the ability to predict cyclical turning points or other short-term fluctuations. Another is that trend projections implicitly assume that the historical relations involved in the time series will continue into the future. This is not always the case. There are many examples of the disastrous effects of using this forecasting method just prior to economic recessions in 1975, 1980, and 1982. Finally, trend analysis entails no analysis of causal relations and hence offers no help in analyzing either why a particular series moves as it does or what the effect of a particular policy decision would be on the future movement of the series.

### Seasonal and Cyclical Variations

Many important economic time series are regularly influenced by seasonal and cyclical variations. Figure 6.1 illustrated how such variations can influence demand patterns for a typical consumer product. It is worthwhile to consider these influences further, since the treatment of seasonal and cyclical variations plays an important role in time-series analysis and projection.

New housing starts constitute an important economic time series that is regularly influenced by seasonal and cyclical variations. Table 6.2 provides data on the number of new, privately owned housing units started in the United States during a recent 20-year period, 1968 to 1987. Thousands of housing units started are reported in Table 6.2a, and seasonally adjusted annual rates are shown in Table 6.2b. From Table 6.2a it is clear that there is an important seasonal element in the total variation of housing starts. Quite understandably, housing starts tend to be high in the months of May, June, and July and relatively low in Novem-

■ Table 6.2
## New Privately Owned Housing Units Started, 1968–1987

| (a) | Unadjusted Monthly Data (thousands) | | | | | | | | | | | | |
|---|---|---|---|---|---|---|---|---|---|---|---|---|---|
| | Jan. | Feb. | March | April | May | June | July | Aug. | Sept. | Oct. | Nov. | Dec. | Total |
| 1987 | 102.7 | 98.2 | 135.4 | 151.9 | 153.8 | 157.5 | 144.4 | 136.4 | 144.6 | 131.4 | 112.5 | 93.4 | 1,562.2 |
| 1986 | 111.2 | 102.5 | 143.8 | 182.8 | 180.9 | 177.3 | 164.8 | 155.7 | 145.0 | 150.1 | 111.1 | 110.8 | 1,736.0 |
| 1985 | 101.8 | 88.0 | 136.3 | 175.8 | 170.2 | 163.2 | 160.7 | 160.7 | 147.7 | 173.0 | 120.9 | 114.7 | 1,713.0 |
| 1984 | 102.7 | 120.2 | 124.7 | 159.6 | 165.8 | 167.0 | 145.8 | 136.0 | 136.6 | 140.8 | 115.8 | 92.8 | 1,607.8 |
| 1983 | 84.0 | 87.2 | 124.3 | 122.1 | 161.5 | 160.1 | 148.0 | 159.8 | 139.6 | 147.8 | 122.1 | 103.2 | 1,559.7 |
| 1982 | 41.6 | 45.6 | 78.2 | 84.1 | 98.8 | 91.1 | 95.4 | 82.5 | 106.4 | 110.5 | 99.8 | 75.9 | 1,009.9 |
| 1981 | 78.5 | 65.5 | 95.3 | 109.5 | 97.9 | 93.0 | 87.7 | 74.3 | 71.5 | 75.9 | 55.0 | 52.7 | 956.8 |
| 1980 | 68.0 | 72.7 | 78.0 | 85.6 | 80.7 | 103.4 | 107.0 | 113.0 | 121.4 | 152.7 | 112.9 | 95.7 | 1,191.1 |
| 1979 | 73.9 | 84.5 | 152.9 | 142.3 | 170.5 | 173.1 | 144.5 | 145.4 | 144.7 | 152.6 | 106.9 | 91.6 | 1,582.9 |
| 1978 | 75.6 | 84.7 | 141.9 | 163.9 | 174.6 | 172.8 | 154.6 | 156.0 | 149.2 | 158.0 | 158.6 | 102.5 | 1,692.4 |
| 1977 | 81.3 | 112.5 | 173.6 | 182.2 | 201.3 | 197.6 | 189.8 | 194.0 | 177.7 | 193.1 | 154.8 | 129.2 | 1,987.1 |
| 1976 | 72.5 | 89.9 | 118.4 | 137.2 | 147.9 | 154.2 | 136.6 | 145.9 | 151.8 | 148.4 | 128.1 | 108.6 | 1,539.5 |
| 1975 | 56.1 | 54.7 | 80.2 | 97.9 | 116.1 | 110.3 | 119.3 | 117.3 | 111.9 | 123.6 | 96.2 | 76.1 | 1,159.7 |
| 1974 | 84.5 | 109.4 | 124.8 | 159.5 | 149.0 | 147.6 | 126.6 | 111.1 | 98.3 | 96.7 | 75.1 | 55.1 | 1,337.7 |
| 1973 | 146.6 | 138.0 | 200.0 | 205.0 | 234.0 | 202.6 | 202.6 | 197.2 | 148.4 | 147.1 | 133.3 | 90.4 | 2,045.2 |
| 1972 | 149.1 | 152.2 | 203.9 | 211.6 | 225.8 | 223.1 | 206.5 | 228.6 | 203.0 | 216.5 | 185.7 | 150.5 | 2,356.5 |
| 1971 | 110.6 | 102.2 | 167.9 | 201.1 | 198.5 | 193.8 | 194.3 | 204.5 | 173.8 | 179.7 | 173.7 | 152.1 | 2,052.2 |
| 1970 | 66.4 | 74.3 | 114.7 | 128.4 | 125.0 | 135.2 | 140.8 | 128.7 | 130.9 | 140.9 | 126.9 | 121.4 | 1,433.6 |
| 1969 | 101.5 | 90.1 | 131.9 | 159.0 | 155.5 | 147.3 | 125.2 | 124.9 | 129.3 | 123.4 | 94.6 | 84.1 | 1,466.8 |
| 1968 | 80.5 | 84.6 | 126.6 | 162.0 | 140.9 | 137.9 | 139.8 | 136.6 | 134.3 | 140.8 | 127.1 | 96.4 | 1,507.6 |

ber, December, and January. The obvious source of such variation is the weather. In many northern states, it is difficult if not impossible to maintain a high level of housing starts during colder winter months. After adjusting for the seasonal element in housing starts, a regular pattern of cyclical variations becomes apparent. Seasonally adjusted annual data in Table 6.2b show that housing starts declined precipitously in 1974, 1979, and 1981. These declines preceded the economic downturns of 1975, 1980, and 1982, respectively, illustrating why housing starts are considered a leading economic indicator.

Although housing starts are an obvious and classic example of economic data subject to seasonal and cyclical variations, they are by no means a unique case. For example, economic activity in the clothing, recreation, travel, automobile, and related industries are all affected by such variations. As a result, controlling for seasonal and cyclical variations is an important aspect of time-series analysis and projection. For many economic projections, an analysis of seasonal and cyclical fluctuations can vastly improve forecasting results, especially for short-run forecasting.

■ Table 6.2
*continued*

| (b) | Seasonally Adjusted Annual Rates (thousands) | | | | | | | | | | | |
|------|------|------|------|------|------|------|------|------|------|------|------|------|
| | Jan. | Feb. | March | April | May | June | July | Aug. | Sept. | Oct. | Nov. | Dec. |
| 1987 | 1,816 | 1,838 | 1,730 | 1,643 | 1,606 | 1,586 | 1,598 | 1,585 | 1,685 | 1,523 | 1,637 | 1,399 |
| 1986 | 2,004 | 1,923 | 1,887 | 1,945 | 1,848 | 1,842 | 1,786 | 1,800 | 1,689 | 1,657 | 1,637 | 1,813 |
| 1985 | 1,849 | 1,647 | 1,849 | 1,851 | 1,693 | 1,684 | 1,673 | 1,737 | 1,653 | 1,784 | 1,654 | 1,882 |
| 1984 | 1,898 | 1,886 | 1,948 | 1,911 | 1,818 | 1,826 | 1,736 | 1,706 | 1,638 | 1,606 | 1,600 | 1,630 |
| 1983 | 1,632 | 1,706 | 1,592 | 1,549 | 1,779 | 1,743 | 1,793 | 1,873 | 1,679 | 1,672 | 1,730 | 1,694 |
| 1982 | 853 | 880 | 920 | 935 | 1,020 | 913 | 1,173 | 1,026 | 1,148 | 1,156 | 1,355 | 1,296 |
| 1981 | 1,547 | 1,246 | 1,306 | 1,360 | 1,140 | 1,045 | 1,041 | 940 | 911 | 873 | 837 | 910 |
| 1980 | 1,389 | 1,273 | 1,040 | 1,044 | 938 | 1,184 | 1,277 | 1,411 | 1,482 | 1,519 | 1,550 | 1,532 |
| 1979 | 1,727 | 1,469 | 1,800 | 1,750 | 1,801 | 1,910 | 1,764 | 1,788 | 1,874 | 1,710 | 1,522 | 1,548 |
| 1978 | 1,779 | 1,762 | 2,028 | 2,182 | 2,018 | 2,092 | 2,089 | 1,983 | 2,014 | 2,001 | 2,111 | 2,052 |
| 1977 | 1,527 | 1,943 | 2,063 | 1,892 | 1,971 | 1,893 | 2,058 | 2,020 | 1,949 | 2,042 | 2,042 | 2,142 |
| 1976 | 1,262 | 1,452 | 1,427 | 1,405 | 1,468 | 1,508 | 1,410 | 1,546 | 1,753 | 1,662 | 1,680 | 1,824 |
| 1975 | 1,032 | 904 | 993 | 1,005 | 1,121 | 1,087 | 1,226 | 1,260 | 1,264 | 1,344 | 1,360 | 1,321 |
| 1974 | 1,453 | 1,784 | 1,553 | 1,571 | 1,415 | 1,526 | 1,290 | 1,145 | 1,180 | 1,100 | 1,028 | 940 |
| 1973 | 2,481 | 2,289 | 2,365 | 2,084 | 2,266 | 2,067 | 2,123 | 2,051 | 1,874 | 1,677 | 1,724 | 1,526 |
| 1972 | 2,494 | 2,390 | 2,334 | 2,249 | 2,221 | 2,254 | 2,252 | 2,382 | 2,481 | 2,485 | 2,421 | 2,366 |
| 1971 | 1,828 | 1,741 | 1,910 | 1,986 | 2,049 | 1,026 | 2,083 | 2,158 | 2,041 | 2,128 | 2,182 | 2,295 |
| 1970 | 1,108 | 1,322 | 1,364 | 1,230 | 1,280 | 1,396 | 1,506 | 1,401 | 1,531 | 1,589 | 1,621 | 1,944 |
| 1969 | 1,769 | 1,705 | 1,561 | 1,524 | 1,583 | 1,528 | 1,368 | 1,358 | 1,507 | 1,381 | 1,229 | 1,327 |
| 1968 | 1,344 | 1,498 | 1,472 | 1,532 | 1,384 | 1,393 | 1,561 | 1,501 | 1,527 | 1,579 | 1,690 | 1,618 |

*Source: For years 1968 to 1983: Standard & Poor's Statistical Service, Basic Statistics, Building and Building Materials 50, no. 12, 137 (December 1984), sec. 2. (New York: Standard & Poor's Corporation). For years 1984 to 1987: Standard & Poor's Statistical Service, Current Statistics 54, 5, 18, (May 1988), sec. 1. (New York: Standard & Poor's Corporation).*

There are several techniques for estimating seasonal variations. A simple one examines the ratio of actual monthly data to the trend projection. For example, if monthly sales data for a product indicate that, on the average, December sales are 20 percent above the trend line, a seasonal adjustment factor of 1.20 can be applied to that trend projection to forecast sales in that month. Likewise, if it is found that February sales have on average been 15 percent below the trend, an adjustment factor of 0.85 would be applied in projecting February sales. To illustrate, annual sales might be forecast at $1.2 million, or $100,000 a month. When the seasonal factor is introduced, however, December sales would be projected at $120,000 ($= $100,000 \times 1.20$) and February sales at $85,000 ($= $100,000 \times 0.85$). Production, inventory, and financing requirements could be scheduled accordingly.

Determination of cyclical patterns is very similar to that for seasonal patterns. Here the interest is on rhythmic patterns that occur over a period of years. Although a few industries appear to exhibit rhythmic oscillations that repeat with enough regularity to be considered cycles (home construction is frequently cited), these are probably the exception rather than the rule. In addition, statistical problems make any breakdown of a time series into trend and cyclical components tenuous at best. Most analysts today recognize that both secular trends and cycles are typically generated by a common causal mechanism, and, therefore, separation of the two leads to ambiguous forecasts. Moreover, the timing, size, and duration of cycles change over time, making cyclical adjustments difficult.

The Box-Jenkins technique is one among a group of newer methods for time-series analysis that provide a sophisticated approach to analyzing the various components—trend, seasonal, cyclical, and random—that make up an economic time series. These techniques enable one to analyze complex patterns that exist in an ordered data set. For some forecasting applications they provide a substantial improvement over simpler extrapolation procedures.

## Barometric Methods

Although cyclical patterns in most economic time series are so erratic that they make simple projection a hazardous short-term forecasting technique, there is evidence that a relatively consistent relation exists between the movements of *different* economic variables over time. In other words, even though a single economic series may not exhibit a consistent pattern over time, it is often possible to find a second series (or group of series) whose movement correlates closely to that of the first. Should the forecaster have the good fortune to discover an economic series that *leads* the one being forecast, the leading series can be used as a barometer for forecasting short-term change, just as a meteorologist uses changes in a mercury barometer to forecast changes in the weather.

There is evidence that the barometric, or leading indicator, approach to business forecasting is nearly as old as business itself. More than 2,000 years ago, merchants used the arrival of trading ships as indicators of business activity. Over 100 years ago, Andrew Carnegie is reported to have used the number of smoking industrial chimneys to forecast business activity and hence the demand for steel. Today, the barometric approach to forecasting has been refined considerably, primarily through the work of the National Bureau of Economic Research and the U.S. Department of Commerce. *Business Conditions Digest*, a monthly publication of the Department of Commerce, provides extensive data on a large number of business indicators. Table 6.3 lists eleven leading, four roughly coincident, and seven lagging economic indicators of business cycle peaks those data contain.

**barometric methods**

Lead and lag relationships between economic variables used to project directional changes in the variable of interest.

**Barometric Forecasting** **Barometric methods** of forecasting are based on observation of relations among economic time series. Changes in some series appear to be consistently related to changes in one or more other series. The theoretical basis for some of these leads and lags is obvious. For example, building permits issued precede housing starts, and orders for plant and equipment lead production in durable goods

■ Table 6.3
## Leading, Coincident, and Lagging Economic Indicators of Business Cycle Peaks

*Eleven Leading Indicators*
Average workweek for production, manufacturing workers
Average weekly initial claims for state unemployment insurance
New orders for consumer goods and materials
Vendor performance measured by companies receiving slower deliveries
Contracts and orders for plant and equipment
New building permits for private housing units
Change in unfilled factory orders for durable goods
Change in sensitive materials prices
Index of stock prices for 500 common stocks
Money supply
Index of consumer expectations

*Four Roughly Coincident Indicators*
Employees on nonagricultural payrolls
Personal income minus transfer payments
Index of total industrial production
Manufacturing and trade sales

*Seven Lagging Indicators*
Average duration of unemployment
Ratio of constant-dollar inventories to sales for manufacturing and trade
Labor cost per unit of manufacturing output
Average prime rate charged by banks
Commercial and industrial loans outstanding
Ratio of consumer installment credit to personal income
Change in prices for consumer services

## 6.2 **Managerial Application**

The Stock Market as an Economic Forecaster

During the stock market crash of 1987, the Dow Jones Industrial Average (DJIA) dropped by 508 points in a single day and by 983 points in a little over two months. Many business leaders, economists, and politicians wondered whether the economy would also crash.

Between 1929 and 1987, there were nine occasions when the DJIA fell by 25 percent or more. Four of these crashes were followed by strong economic booms. Three were followed by economic downturns or recessions. Only one, the crash of 1929, was followed by a severe economic depression. Based on past history, the chance appeared to be roughly one in nine that the crash of 1987 would portend a severe economic depression.

Until the crash of 1987, the most famous crash on Wall Street occurred during 1929.

In two months' time, the DJIA lost 48 percent of its value. As everyone knows by now, this signaled the start of the Great Depression. At the time, however, analysts foresaw a return to prosperity and the economy continued to grow. Unfortunately, the initial decline was followed by three more waves of selling. Overall, the DJIA fell 89 percent between September 3, 1929 and July 8, 1932. Thousands of people were wiped out financially and millions lost their jobs. At the depths of the Depression, unemployment stood at more than 25 percent, and GNP had declined substantially.

Between the crashes of 1929 and 1987, seven market crashes occurred. On average, they lasted 16 months and represented a decline of 35 percent in the DJIA. Recent declines were quite typical. For example, the "Nixon Slide" from December 3, 1968 to

*continued*

See: Jack Willoughby, "The Stock Market Is a Lousy Economic Forecaster," *Forbes*, November 30, 1987, 32–33; and Douglas R. Sease, "Recession Ahead? Stock Market May Not Tell," *The Wall Street Journal*, May 8, 1989, C1, C2.

industries. Each of these indicators directly reflects plans or commitments for the activity that follows. Other barometers are not so directly related to the economic variables they forecast. An index of common stock prices, for example, is a good leading indicator of general business activity. Although the causal linkage here is not readily apparent, stock prices reflect aggregate profit expectations by business managers and investors and hence a composite expectation of the level of business activity.

Barometric methods of forecasting require the identification of an economic time series that consistently leads the series being forecast. Once

**Managerial Application** *continued*

May 26, 1970 saw the DJIA fall by 36 percent. The conglomerate merger wave of the 1960s ended with a bang, and several leading Wall Street firms were forced out of business. As in 1987, prophets of doom such as economist John Kenneth Galbraith likened the state of the economy to 1929. Though the economy did indeed slip into recession, the stock market took off on a more than two-year advance to new highs—that is, from January 11, 1973 until December 6, 1974, when a severe 23-month bear market saw the DJIA fall by 45 percent. At that time, an OPEC oil price surge brought on a severe economic recession and caused investors to pull money out of stocks. So sharp was the decline on Wall Street that investors in "Nifty Fifty" growth stocks such as Avon and Polaroid lost as much as 90 percent of their investments.

The most recent stock market crash prior to 1987 occurred between September 21, 1976 and February 28, 1978. A 27-percent drop reflected investor fears that the economic expansion started in the spring of 1975 had grown tired and that the return of Democrats to the White House might unleash government spending and a round of inflation. Interestingly, even though Carter did defeat Ford, government spending rose, and inflation ballooned, through it all, the economy continued to prosper.

Of course, changes in the stock market have important economic implications in their own right. As stock prices fall, investors in stocks and bonds experience a substantial loss in wealth, as do beneficiaries of pension funds and insurance companies. If worried consumers and businesses cut back on spending following a stock market crash, their caution can itself cause a downturn in economic activity. Thus, the stock market is not only an important reflection of changes in economic activity, but also an important causal factor.

What will be the full economic fallout from the stock market crash of 1987? Like the crash of 1973 to 1974, it might portend a severe economic recession. Like the crash of 1968 to 1970, it might indicate a relatively mild pending recession. Or, like the crash of 1976 to 1978, it may reflect nothing more than a correction of the market's previous excesses on the upside. Only in the early 1990s, and with the benefit of 20–20 hindsight, will the full economic implications of the crash of 1987 become obvious.

this relation is established, forecasting directional changes in the lagged series involves keeping track of movement in the leading indicator. In practice, several problems prevent such an easy solution to the forecasting problem. First, few series *always* correctly indicate changes in another economic variable. Even the best leading indicators of general business conditions forecast directional changes with only 80- to 90-percent accuracy. Second, even the indicators that have good records of forecasting directional changes generally fail to lead by a consistent period. If a series is to be an adequate barometer, it must not only indicate directional changes but must also provide a relatively constant lead time. Few series meet the test of lead-time consistency. Finally, baro-metric forecasting suffers in that, even when leading indicators prove to consistently indicate directional changes with stable lead times, they provide very little information about the magnitude of change in the forecast variable.

**Composite and Diffusion Indexes**    Two techniques that have been used with some success in partially overcoming the difficulties in baro-metric forecasting are composite indexes and diffusion indexes. *Composite indexes* are weighted averages of several leading indicators. Combining individual series into a composite index results in a series with less random fluctuation, or *noise*. The smoother composite series has less tendency to produce false signals of change in the predicted variable.

*Diffusion indexes* are similar to composite indexes. Here, instead of combining a number of leading indicators into a single standardized index, the methodology consists of noting the percentage of the total number of leading indicators that are rising at a given point in time. For example, if all of the eleven leading indicators have proved to be rela-tively reliable leading indicators of heavy equipment sales, a diffusion, or *pressure*, index would show the percentage of those indicators that is increasing at the present time. If 7 are rising, the diffusion index would be 7/11, or 64 percent; with only 3 rising, the index would register 27 percent. Forecasting with diffusion indexes typically involves projecting an increase in the economic variable if the index is above 50 (that is, when more than one-half or six of the individual leading indicators are rising) and a decline when it is below 50.

Even with the use of composite and diffusion indexes, the barometric forecasting technique is a relatively poor tool for estimating the magni-tude of change in an economic variable. Thus, although it represents a considerable improvement over simple extrapolation techniques for short-term forecasting, in which calling the turning points is necessary, the barometric methodology is not the solution to all forecasting problems.

# ECONOMETRIC METHODS

**econometric methods**

Forecasting methods that combine economic theory with mathematical and statistical tools to analyze economic relations.

**Econometric methods** of forecasting combine economic theory with mathematical and statistical tools to analyze economic relations. Econ-ometric forecasting techniques have several distinct advantages over al-ternative methods. For one, they force the forecaster to make explicit assumptions about the linkages among the variables in the economic system being examined. In other words, the forecaster must deal with *causal* relations. This process reduces the probability of logical incon-sistencies in the model and thus increases the reliability and acceptabil-ity of the results.

A second advantage of econometric methods lies in the consistency of the techniques from period to period. The forecaster can compare forecasts with actual results and use the insights gained to improve the model. That is, by feeding past forecasting errors back into the model, one can develop new parameter estimates that should improve future forecasting results.

The type of output provided by econometric forecasts is another major advantage of this technique. Since econometric models provide estimates of actual values for forecasted variables, these models indicate not only the direction of change but also the magnitude of change. This is a notable improvement over the barometric approach, which provides little information about the magnitude of expected changes.

Perhaps the most important advantage of econometric models relates to their basic characteristic of *explaining* economic phenomena. In the vast majority of business forecasting problems, management has a degree of control over some of the variables in the relationship being examined. For example, in forecasting sales of a product, the firm must take into account the price it will charge, the amount it has spent and will spend on advertising, and many other variables over which it may or may not have any influence. Only by thoroughly understanding the interrelations involved can management hope to forecast accurately and to make optimal decisions as it selects values for controllable variables.

## Single-Equation Models

Many managerial forecasting problems can be adequately addressed with single-equation econometric models. The first step in developing an econometric model is to express the economic relations in the form of equations. For example, in constructing a model for forecasting regional demand for portable personal computers, one might hypothesize that computer demand ($C$) is determined by price ($P$), disposable income ($I_d$), population (Pop), interest rates ($i$), and advertising expenditures ($A$). A linear model expressing this relation would be written as follows:

$$C = a_0 + a_1P + a_2I_d + a_3\text{Pop} + a_4i + a_5A. \qquad \textbf{6.7}$$

The next step in econometric modeling is to estimate the parameters of the system, or values of the $a$s in Equation 6.7. The most frequently used technique for parameter estimation is the application of least squares regression analysis with either time-series or cross-section data.

Once the coefficients of the model have been estimated, forecasting with a single-equation model consists of obtaining values for the independent variables in the equation and then evaluating the equation with those values. This means that an econometric model used for forecasting purposes must contain independent or explanatory variables whose values for the forecast period can be readily obtained.

## Multiple-Equation Systems

Although forecasting problems can often be analyzed adequately with a single-equation model, in many cases the interrelationships among economic variables are so complex that they require the use of multiple-equation systems. In these systems, we refer to variables whose values are determined within the model as *endogenous*, meaning originating from within, and those determined outside, or external to, the system as *exogenous*. The values of endogenous variables are determined with the model; the values of exogenous variables are given externally. Endogenous variables are equivalent to the dependent variable in a single-equation system; exogenous and predetermined variables are equivalent to the independent variables.

Multiple-equation econometric models are composed of two basic kinds of equations—identities and behavioral equations. Identities, or definitional equations, express relations that are true by definition. The statement that profits ($\pi$) are equal to total revenue ($TR$) minus total cost ($TC$) is an example of an identity:

$$\pi = TR - TC. \qquad \textbf{6.8}$$

Profits are *defined* by the relation expressed in Equation 6.8.

The second group of equations encountered in econometric models, behavioral equations, reflect hypotheses about how the variables in a system interact with one another. Behavioral equations may indicate how individuals and institutions are expected to react to various stimuli, or they may be technical, as, for example, a production function that indicates the relationships in the production system.

Perhaps the easiest way to illustrate the use of multiple-equation systems is to examine a simple three-equation model of equipment and related software sales for a personal computer retailer. As you recall, in Equation 6.7 we expressed a single-equation model that might be used to forecast regional demand for portable personal computers. However, total revenues for a typical retailer would include not only sales of personal computers but also sales of software programs (including computer games) and sales of peripheral equipment (video display terminals, printers, and so on). Although actual econometric models used to forecast total sales revenue from these items might include several equations and many important economic variables, the simple system described in this section should suffice to provide insight into the multiple-equation approach without being so complex as to become confusing. The three equations are:

$$S_t = b_0 + b_1 TR_t + u_1 \qquad \textbf{6.9}$$

$$P_t = c_0 + c_1 C_{t-1} + u_2 \qquad \textbf{6.10}$$

$$TR_t = S_t + P_t + C_t, \qquad \textbf{6.11}$$

where $S$ is software sales, $TR$ is total revenue, $P$ is peripheral sales, $C$ is personal computer sales, $t$ is the current time period, $t - 1$ is the previous time period, and $u_1$ and $u_2$ are error, or residual, terms.

Equations 6.9 and 6.10 are behavioral hypotheses. The first hypothesizes that current-period software sales are a function of the current level of total revenues; the second hypothesizes that peripheral sales depend on previous-period personal computer sales. The last equation in the system is an identity. It defines total revenue as being equal to the sum of software, peripheral equipment, and personal computer sales.

The stochastic disturbance terms in the behavioral equations, $u_1$ and $u_2$, are included because the hypothesized relations are not exact. In other words, other factors that can affect software and peripheral sales are not accounted for in the system. So long as these stochastic elements are random and their expected values are zero, they do not present a barrier to empirical estimation of system parameters. However, if the error terms are not randomly distributed, parameter estimates will be biased and the reliability of model forecasts will be questionable. Furthermore, large error terms, even if they are distributed randomly, will tend to reduce forecast accuracy.

Empirical estimation of the parameters for multiple equation systems (the *bs* and *cs* in Equations 6.9 and 6.10) often requires the use of statistical techniques that go beyond the scope of this text. We can, however, illustrate the use of such a system for forecasting purposes after the parameters have been estimated.

To forecast next year's software and peripheral sales and total revenue for the firm represented by our illustrative model, we must express S, P, and TR in terms of those variables whose values are known (or can be estimated) at the moment the forecast is generated. In other words, each endogenous variable ($S_t$, $P_t$, and $TR_t$) must be expressed in terms of the exogenous and predetermined variables ($C_{t-1}$ and $C_t$). Such relations are called reduced-form equations, because they reduce complex simultaneous relations to their most basic and simple form. Consider the manipulations of equations in the system necessary to solve for TR via its reduced-form equation.

Substituting Equation 6.9 into 6.11—that is, replacing $S_t$ with Equation 6.9—results in[3]

$$TR_t = b_0 + b_1 TR_t + P_t + C_t.$$  **6.12**

A similar substitution of Equation 6.10 for $P_t$ produces:

$$TR_t = b_0 + b_1 TR_t + c_0 + c_1 C_{t-1} + C_t.$$  **6.13**

Collecting terms and isolating TR in Equation 6.13 gives

$$(1 - b_1)TR_t = b_0 + c_0 + c_1 C_{t-1} + C_t,$$

or alternately:

$$\begin{aligned} TR_t &= \frac{b_0 + c_0 + c_1 C_{t-1} + C_t}{(1 - b_1)} \\ &= \frac{b_0 + c_0}{(1 - b_1)} + \frac{c_1}{(1 - b_1)} C_{t-1} + \frac{1}{(1 - b_1)} C_t. \end{aligned}$$  **6.14**

---

[3]The stochastic disturbance terms (us) have been dropped from the illustration because their expected values are zero. The final equation for TR, however, is stochastic in nature.

Equation 6.14 now relates current total revenues to previous- and current-period personal computer sales. Assuming that data on previous-period personal computer sales can be obtained and that current-period personal computer sales can be estimated using Equation 6.7, Equation 6.14 provides us with a forecasting model that takes into account the simultaneous relations expressed in our simplified multiple-equation system. Of course, in real-life situations, it is possible, perhaps even likely, that personal computer sales depend upon the price, quantity, and quality of available software and peripheral equipment. Then $S$, $P$, and $C$, along with other important factors, may all be endogenous, involving a large number of relations in a highly complex multiple-equation system. Untangling the important but often subtle relations involved in such a system makes forecasting with multiple-equation systems one of the most challenging and intriguing subjects in managerial economics.

# INPUT–OUTPUT ANALYSIS

**input–output analysis**

Uses interindustry linkages to show how an increase or a decrease in the demand for one industry's output will affect all sectors of an economy.

A forecasting method known as **input–output analysis** provides perhaps the most complete examination of all the complex interrelations within an economic system. Input–output analysis shows how an increase or a decrease in the demand for one industry's output will affect other industries. For example, an increase in the demand for trucks will lead to increased production of steel, plastics, tires, glass, and other materials. The increase in demand for these materials will have secondary effects. The increase in demand for glass will lead to a further increase in the demand for steel, as well as for trucks used in the manufacture of glass and steel, and so on. Input–output analysis traces through all these interindustry relations to provide information about the total impact on all industries of the original increase in the demand for trucks.

Input–output forecasting is based on a set of tables that describes the linkages among all the component parts of the economy. The construction of input–output tables is a formidable task; fortunately, such tables are available for the United States from the Office of Business Economics, U.S. Department of Commerce. To use the tables effectively, one must understand their construction. Accordingly, the construction of these tables, as well as their use, is examined in this section.

## Input–Output Tables

The starting point for constructing input–output tables is the set of accounts on which the nation's gross national product (GNP) is based; the basic accounts are listed in Table 6.4.[4] The table shows that GNP is equal to the sum of the national income accounts, items 1 through 9, or, alternatively, to the sum of the final product flows to consuming sectors, items 10 through 13.

---

[4]GNP is the value at final point of sale of all goods and services produced in the economy during a year.

■ Table 6.4

## List of National Income and Product Accounts Used to Construct GNP

---

*National Income Accounts*

1. Compensation of employees
2. Proprietors' income
3. Rental income of persons
4. Corporate profits and inventory valuation adjustment
5. Net interest        } Gross National Product
6. Business transfer payments
7. Indirect business tax and nontax liability
8. Less: Subsidies less current surplus of government enterprises
9. Capital consumption allowances

*Final Product Accounts*

10. Personal consumption expenditures
11. Gross private domestic investment
12. Net export of goods and services   } Gross National Product
13. Government purchases of goods and services

---

Input–output tables break down the income and the product account data and provide information about interindustry transactions. Table 6.5 is an example of a simplified input–output table. It is a matrix of the same gross national product data contained in Table 6.4 but with the addition of a (shaded) section showing interindustry transactions as well. Although the illustrated input–output table has only eight industry classifications, actual U.S. input–output tables are far more complex, containing over 500 separate industry classifications. The industry-to-industry flows in the shaded area depict the input–output structure of the economy. For example, the manufacturing row, row 4, shows the sales by manufacturing firms to other manufacturing firms, to other industries, and also to final users. Thus, cell 4, 2 shows sales from manufacturers to mining companies; cell 4, 4 from manufacturers to other manufacturers; and cell 4, 7 from manufacturers to service firms such as banks, entertainment companies, and the like. The manufacturing column, column 4, shows the sources of goods and services purchased by manufacturers for production, as well as the value added in their production of output. For example, cell 2, 4 shows manufacturing firms' purchases from mining companies; cell 6, 4 shows manufacturing firms' purchases from the transportation industry.

Since interindustry sales are included in the value of products sold to various final consumers, they must be omitted from the measurement of total gross national product. That is, to avoid double counting, producer-to-producer sales must be excluded from the determination of GNP. The same is true when calculating GNP using the national income accounts;

■ Table 6.5

# Input–Output Flow Table

|  |  | Interindustry Transactions |  |  |  |  |  |  |  | Final Markets (National Product Accounts) |  |  |  |
|---|---|---|---|---|---|---|---|---|---|---|---|---|---|
|  |  | Agriculture (1) | Mining (2) | Construction (3) | Manufacturing (4) | Trade (5) | Transportation (6) | Services (7) | Other (8) | Persons (9) Personal consumption expenditures (Account 10) | Investors (10) Gross private domestic investment (Account 11) | Foreigners (11) Net exports of goods and services (Account 12) | Government (12) Government purchases of goods and services (Account 13) |
| Interindustry Transactions | Agriculture (1) |  |  |  |  |  |  |  |  |  |  |  |  |
|  | Mining (2) |  |  |  | 2, 4 |  |  |  |  |  |  |  |  |
|  | Construction (3) |  |  |  |  |  |  |  |  |  |  |  |  |
|  | Manufacturing (4) |  | 4, 2 |  | 4, 4 |  |  | 4, 7 |  |  |  |  |  |
|  | Trade (5) |  |  |  |  |  |  |  |  |  |  |  |  |
|  | Transportation (6) |  |  |  | 6, 4 |  |  |  |  |  |  |  |  |
|  | Services (7) |  |  |  |  |  |  |  |  |  |  |  |  |
|  | Other (8) |  |  |  |  |  |  |  |  |  |  |  |  |
| Value Added (National Income Accounts) | Employees (9) | Compensation of employees (Account 1) |  |  |  |  |  |  |  |  |  |  |  |
|  | Owners of business and capital (10) | Profit-type income and capital consumption allowances (Accounts 2, 3, 4, 5, 6, 9) |  |  |  |  |  |  |  |  |  |  |  |
|  | Government (11) | Indirect business taxes, current surplus of government enterprises, and so forth (Accounts 7, 8) |  |  |  |  |  |  |  |  |  |  |  |

Gross national product

interindustry transactions must be eliminated to avoid redundancy. Accordingly, the entire shaded area of Table 6.5 is ignored in determining GNP. GNP is calculated either as the total of all the cells shown in the Final Markets columns or as the total of cells in the Value Added rows.

## Use of Input–Output Analysis

Input–output analysis has a variety of applications, ranging from forecasting the sales of an individual firm to probing the implications of national economic policies. The major contribution of input–output analysis is that it facilitates measurement of the effects on all industrial sectors of changes in the activity of any one sector.

The usefulness of input–output analysis can be illustrated by considering the effect of an increase in consumer demand for passenger cars. The first effect of the change in demand is an increase in the output of the automobile industry; there are further effects, however. The increase in auto output requires more steel production, which in turn requires more chemicals, more iron ore, more limestone, and more coal. Auto production also requires other products for which demand will increase, including upholstery fabrics, synthetic fibers, plastics, and glass. There will still be further reactions; for example, the production of synthetic fibers and other chemicals will lead to increased demand for electricity, containers, and transportation services. Input–output analysis traces this intricate chain reaction through all industrial sectors and measures the effects, both direct and indirect, on the output of each of the affected industries.

The industry outputs derived in this way can be used for estimating related industry requirements. For example, with supplementary data, the estimated output of each industry can be translated into requirements for employment or for additional plants and equipment. Or, bolstered by information on the geographic distribution of industries, input–output analysis can also shed light on the regional implications of changes in national GNP.

Recognizing the unique ability of input–output analysis to account completely for the complex interaction among industries, many businesses have been guided in their decision making by this analysis. For example, input–output has been used to evaluate market prospects for established products, to identify potential markets for new products, to spot prospective shortages in supplies, to add new dimensions and greater depth to the analysis of the economic environment in which the firms can expect to operate, and to evaluate investment prospects in various industries.

Input–output analysis has also been employed in the decision-making processes of government agencies at every level. A notable federal application has been in the study of long-term growth of the economy and its implications for labor force requirements. Input–output analysis has also been used to calculate the effect of U.S. exports and imports on employment in various industries and regions. A number of state and local governments have sponsored the construction of input–output tables for use in evaluating the effects of different types of economic development. Others have used input–output analysis to study the industrial impact of alternative tax programs. In some states, input–output analysis is a central element in large-scale systems for forecasting demographic and economic variables, and it also serves as an aid in planning land use, expenditure and revenue programs, industrial development, and so on.

Many regions throughout the country have been increasingly concerned about the adequacy of water resources. Input–output analysis is being used as part of a total system to measure industrial requirements for water. The analysis is particularly helpful in identifying activities that generate important demands for water, not only as direct users but also because their suppliers of materials, power, and other inputs also require water.

## Forecasting with Input–Output Tables

It should be obvious that the data required to construct an input–output system are numerous, and the analytical task of tracing the intricate interrelations is immense. Because of the enormous costs of constructing and maintaining input–output tables, individual firms, even the largest ones, typically rely on U.S. Department of Commerce tables instead of constructing their own. But firms can and do extend the published tables and apply them to their own unique situations.

To use input–output tables, it is necessary to understand thoroughly the nature of an input–output system. To facilitate such an understanding, we trace through a very simple hypothetical economy containing only three producing sectors. Table 6.6 provides the basic national accounting data for this hypothetical system. The upper section contains the detailed interindustry relationships necessary for construction of input–output tables; the lower section gives the national income and product accounts that make up GNP.

Table 6.7 shows all of this information reformulated in an input–output matrix for the system. The Producers rows contain information about the distribution of output. For example, Industry *A* produces and sells a total of $130 billion, with $10 billion going to other firms in Industry *A*, $2 billion to Industry *B*, $50 billion to Industry *C*, $40 billion to individuals for personal consumption, and $28 billion to the government. As is shown in the Producers columns, firms in Industry *A* buy $10 billion of goods and services from other *A* firms and $3 billion from *B* firms, pay $100 billion in wages, and have $17 billion left for depreciation and profits. Gross national product can be obtained from the input–output table by summing either the Value Added section or the Final Markets section. Cells in the producer-to-producer section of the matrix are eliminated to avoid double counting.

For forecasting purposes, two additional types of matrices are constructed from the Producers section of Table 6.7. One is the percentage distribution of gross output matrix, which indicates where each industry sells its products and thus how dependent it is on various sectors of the

■ Table 6.6
## National Accounting Data for a Hypothetical Economy (billions of dollars)

### Industry Production Accounts

| | Receipts | | Expenses + Profits | |
|---|---|---|---|---|
| Industry A | Sales to Industry A | $ 10 | Purchases from Industry A | $ 10 |
| | Sales to Industry B | 2 | Purchases from Industry B | 3 |
| | Sales to Industry C | 50 | Wages (employee compensation) | 100 |
| | Sales to persons | 40 | Depreciation | 10 |
| | Sales to government | 28 | Profits | 7 |
| | | $130 | | $130 |
| Industry B | Sales to Industry A | $ 3 | Purchases from Industry A | $ 2 |
| | Sales to Industry C | 15 | Purchases from Industry C | 25 |
| | Sales to persons | 30 | Wages (employee compensation) | 25 |
| | Sales to government | 20 | Depreciation | 8 |
| | Sales to exports | 2 | Profits | 10 |
| | | $ 70 | | $ 70 |
| Industry C | Sales to Industry B | $ 25 | Purchases from Industry A | $ 50 |
| | Sales to persons | 65 | Purchases from Industry B | 15 |
| | | | Wages (employee compensation) | 20 |
| | | | Profits | 5 |
| | | $ 90 | | $ 90 |

### National Income and Product Accounts

| | | | | |
|---|---|---|---|---|
| | Wages | $145 | Personal consumption expenditures | $135 |
| | Profits | 22 | Government | 48 |
| | Depreciation | 18 | Exports | 2 |
| | | $185 | | $185 |

system. Table 6.8 shows the percentage distribution matrix for this hypothetical economy. Each element in that table is found by dividing the corresponding element in Table 6.7 by its row total. For example, the 8 percent in element A,A was found by dividing the $10 billion of sales that Industry A makes for itself by the $130 billion total sales of that industry. The 4 percent in cell B,A indicates that Industry B sells 4 percent of its output to Industry A.

Other input–output matrices derived from the producer-to-producer sector of Table 6.7, the *direct* and *total requirements* tables, are especially useful when individual firms are making demand forecasts. Table 6.9 is the direct requirements table for the hypothetical economy. The entries in each column show the dollar inputs required directly from

■ Table 6.7

## Input–Output Matrix for a Hypothetical Economy (billions of dollars)

|  |  | Producers | | | Final Markets | | | |
|---|---|---|---|---|---|---|---|---|
|  |  | **A** | **B** | **C** | **Personal Consumption** | **Government** | **Exports** | **Row Totals** |
| Producers | A | 10 | 2 | 50 | 40 | 28 |  | 130 |
|  | B | 3 |  | 15 | 30 | 20 | 2 | 70 |
|  | C |  | 25 |  | 65 |  |  | 90 |
| Value Added | Wages | 100 | 25 | 20 |  |  |  | 145 |
|  | Profit plus depreciation | 17 | 18 | 5 | 40 |  |  | 40 |
|  | Column total | 130 | 70 | 90 | 135 | 48 | 2 |  |

GNP = $185

GNP = $185

■ Table 6.8

## Percentage Distribution of Gross Output

|  | Percentage Sales to Each Consuming Sector | | | | | | |
|---|---|---|---|---|---|---|---|
| Producing Industry | Industry **A** | Industry **B** | Industry **C** | Persons | Government | Export | Total |
| A | 8 | 1 | 38 | 31 | 22 | 0 | 100 |
| B | 4 | 0 | 21 | 43 | 29 | 3 | 100 |
| C | 0 | 28 | 0 | 72 | 0 | 0 | 100 |

■ Table 6.9

## Direct Requirements per Dollar of Gross Output

|  | Producing Industry | | |
|---|---|---|---|
| Supplying Industry | **A** | **B** | **C** |
| A | 0.08 | 0.03 | 0.56 |
| B | 0.02 | 0.00 | 0.17 |
| C | 0.00 | 0.36 | 0.00 |

■ Table 6.10
## Total Requirements (Direct plus Indirect) per Dollar of Output for Final Consumption

| | Producing Industry | | |
|---|---|---|---|
| Supplying Industry | *A* | *B* | *C* |
| *A* | 1.09 | 0.27 | 0.66 |
| *B* | 0.03 | 1.07 | 0.19 |
| *C* | 0.01 | 0.39 | 1.07 |

each industry given in the rows to produce $1 of output. Industry *C*, for example, requires direct inputs costing $0.56 from Industry *A* and $0.17 from Industry *B* to produce an additional $1 of output. These direct requirements figures are found by dividing each element in the industry columns in Table 6.7 by the column total. Thus, the 0.08 figure for the first-row, first-column element in Table 6.9 is found by dividing the $10 billion of purchases among Industry *A* firms by the $130 billion total found in the first column of Table 6.7.

The direct requirements matrix in Table 6.9 permits systematic examination of all of the interrelations among the various industries and final demand sectors. For example, assume that Industry *A* is expected to produce $1 million of output for sale to final consumers. Using the first column of Table 6.9, we can see that Industry *A* will use $80,000 ($1,000,000 × 0.08) of its own production in the process of manufacturing the $1 million of output for final consumption. Thus, the industry must actually produce a minimum of $1.080 million of output. Production of $1.080 million of output by *A* also requires $21,600 ($1,080,000 × 0.02) of input from Industry *B*. As shown by the 0.00 element in the last row of the first column, Industry *A* requires no direct inputs from Industry *C*.

Calculating the total effect of the original $1 million final demand for *A*'s output requires further analysis. Note that Industry *A* requires $21,600 in inputs from Industry *B*. To meet this requirement, *B* needs inputs of $648 ($21,600 × 0.03) from Industry *A* and $7,776 ($21,600 × 0.36) from Industry *C*. These requirements, in turn, must be fed back into the system to determine the second-round effects, which in turn produce further reactions as the cycle continues. Each successive reaction is smaller than the preceding one, and the reactions converge on the final effects of the original demand.

Table 6.10 presents the *total requirements*—direct plus indirect—for the hypothetical economy.[5] Each column in the table shows the inputs

---

[5] The total requirements tables provide the solution values, or the values on which the chain reaction converges.

## 6.3  **Managerial Application**
Economic Forecasting: The Art and the Science

Accurate forecasts of future aggregate economic activity would be extremely valuable to firms making hiring, inventory, and other investment decisions. Similarly, consumers making purchase and career decisions, for example, would find accurate forecasts of short-term and long-term economic trends extremely useful. The fact that most firms and consumers base important decisions on their expectations about the pace of future economic activity creates a substantial demand for economic forecasts. So extensive is this demand that the supply of economic forecasting services has exploded during recent years. For example, a wide variety of newsletters offering economic forecasts are now available. Moreover, economic forecasts by government economists and others are prominently featured on television and radio and in the print media. This high level

of business and consumer interest, and the resulting media coverage, give rise to an extraordinary level of visibility for the few hundred economists who provide forecasting services.

This high level of visibility has focused attention on both the strong points and the limitations of economic forecasting. In terms of limitations, the accuracy of economic forecasts is sometimes criticized. Very high levels of forecast accuracy are often sought. For example, will real economic growth next year be 2.0 percent or 2.5 percent? The difference, although rather small, can be very important for sectors such as capital equipment, for which business conditions are closely related to the level of aggregate economic activity. Sometimes we forget that the degree of forecast accuracy we seek is demanding indeed.

*continued*

See: Alfred L. Malabre, Jr. and Lindley H. Clark, Jr., "Changes in Economy Cause Much Confusion Among Economists," *The Wall Street Journal*, March 27, 1989, A1, A5; and Karen Pennar, "Inflation Stages a Comeback," *Business Week*, April 3, 1989, 32–33.

required, both direct and indirect, by the producing industry; each row shows the demand that supplying industries can expect per dollar of final consumption demand. To continue our illustration of a $1 million final consumer demand for the output of Industry *A*, we see that, in order to produce the $1 million to meet the final demand, Industry *A* production must total $1.09 million; Industry *B* must produce $0.03 million, and Industry *C* must produce $0.01 million. In total, production must amount to $1.13 million to supply $1 million of final output of Product *A*, with the $0.13 million being the input product required to produce the $1 million final output.

**Managerial Application** *continued*

Many don't understand why disagreement among forecasting economists is common and why this disagreement sometimes produces widely divergent economic forecasts. Both are valid reasons for concern, yet these criticisms sometimes reflect too little appreciation of the nature and scope of economic forecasting. Forecasting aggregate economic activity is an extraordinarily difficult problem. In the real world, "all else held equal" doesn't hold very often, if ever. To forecast the future course of GNP, for example, one must be able to accurately predict the future pattern of government spending, tax and monetary policy, consumer and business spending, dollar strength against foreign currencies, weather, and so on. Although typical patterns can be inferred on the basis of past trends, unexpected atypical departures often have important economic consequences that complicate economic forecasting.

Given the uncertainties involved, it seems reasonable that different forecasting economists would accord differing importance to a wide variety of economic influences. Just as individual forecasters assess different probabilities to an increase in government spending, they might interpret the likely consequences differently. Thus, forecasters' judgment is reflected not only in the interpretation they give to the data generated by complex computer models but also in the models themselves. Computers may generate economic forecasts, but they do so on the basis of programs written by economists.

Given their usefulness and resulting high visibility, it is not surprising that economic forecasts and the methodology of economic forecasting generate a great deal of controversy. In fact, the success of economic forecasting is responsible, at least in part, for some of its failures. We have come to expect a nearly unattainable level of forecast accuracy. At the same time, we forget that forecasts can, by themselves, have important economic consequences. When consumers and businesses cut back on spending in reaction to the forecast of an impending mild recession, for example, they change the basis for the forecasters' initial prediction. By their behavior, they may also cause a steeper recession. This is the forecaster's dilemma: The future as we know it doesn't exist. In fact, it can't.

---

This illustration of the construction and use of input–output tables indicates the versatility of the technique in a variety of forecasting situations. It should be apparent that a large part of that versatility depends on the detail contained in the basic input–output matrix. That is, the finer the industry distinctions in the input–output tables, the more valuable they are for forecasting purposes.

The 1982 input–output table for the U.S. economy, completed by the Bureau of Economic Analysis of the Department of Commerce, segments the industrial sector of the system into 537 industry categories. This compares with a classification into 496 and 367 separate industries for successively earlier input–output tables. The greater detail provided by these latest tables increases their value to managerial decision makers and should lead to greater use of the techniques of input–output analysis for industry and firm forecasting purposes.

# JUDGING FORECAST RELIABILITY

**forecast reliability**

Reliability is measured by the consistency of forecast and actual data.

One of the most challenging aspects of forecasting is judging the reliability of forecasts obtained from various models. How well do various methodologies deal with specific forecasting problems? In comparing forecast and actual values, how close is close enough? Is **forecast reliability** over one sample or time period necessarily transferable to other samples and time periods? Each of these questions is fundamentally important and must be adequately addressed prior to the implementation of any successful forecasting program.

Ideally, to test predictive capability, a model generated from data of one sample or period is used to forecast data for some alternative sample or period. Thus, the reliability of a model for predicting firm sales, such as that shown in Equation 6.2, can be tested by examining the relation between forecast and actual data for years beyond 1990, given that the model was generated using data from the 1976 to 1990 period. However, it is often desirable to test a model without waiting for new data to become available. In such instances, one can divide the available data into two subsamples, called a test group and a forecast group. The forecaster then estimates a forecasting model using data from the test group and uses the resulting model to forecast the data of interest in the forecast group. A comparison of forecast and actual values can then be conducted to test the stability of the underlying cost or demand relationship.

In analyzing a model's forecast capability, the correlation between forecast and actual values is of substantial interest. The formula for the simple correlation coefficient, $r$, for forecast and actual values, $f$ and $x$, respectively, is:

$$r = \frac{\sigma_{fx}}{\sigma_f \sigma_x},$$    **6.15**

where $\sigma_{fx}$ is the covariance between the forecast and actual series, and $\sigma_f$ and $\sigma_x$ are the sample standard deviations of the forecast and actual series, respectively. Most computer system statistical packages and many hand-held calculators can readily provide these data, making the calculation of $r$ a relatively simple task. Generally speaking, correlations between forecast and actual values in excess of 0.99 (99 percent) are highly desirable and indicate that the forecast model being considered constitutes an effective tool for analysis. However, in cross-sectional analysis, in which the important trend element in most economic data is held constant, a correlation of 99 percent between forecast and actual values would be quite rare. When unusually difficult forecasting problems are being addressed, correlations between forecast and actual data of 90 percent or 95 percent may prove to be satisfactory. On the other hand, in critical decision situations, forecast values may have to be estimated at very precise levels. In such instances, forecast and actual data may have to exhibit an extremely high level of correlation, 99.5 percent or 99.75 percent, in order to generate a high level of confidence in forecast reliability. In summary, the correlation between forecast and actual values necessary to reach a threshold reliability acceptance level depends in large part on the difficulty of the forecasting problem being analyzed and the cost of forecast error.

Further evaluation of a model's predictive capability can be made through consideration of a measure called the sample mean forecast error, which provides a useful estimate of the average forecast error of the model. It is sometimes called the root mean squared forecast error and is denoted by the symbol $U$. The sample mean forecast error is calculated as:

$$U = \sqrt{\frac{1}{n} \sum_{i=1}^{n} (f_i - x_i)^2}, \qquad \textbf{6.16}$$

where $n$ is the number of sample observations, $f_i$ is a forecast value, and $x_i$ is the corresponding actual value. The deviations between forecast and actual values are squared in the calculation of the mean forecast error to prevent positive and negative deviations between forecast and actual values from canceling one another out. The smaller the sample mean forecast error, the greater the accuracy one can associate with the forecasting model.

## Case 6.1

# Forecasting Sales for the Delta Equipment Company

The Delta Equipment Company, headquartered in San Francisco, California, manufactures tools and light equipment used in the residential and commercial construction industries. One of the key functions of Delta's Department of Financial Planning and Control is to identify important trends in demand so that working capital and investment funds can be efficiently allocated. A first step in Delta's long-range planning process is developing a model for forecasting the company's level of overall sales activity during coming periods.

Deriving an accurate sales forecasting model for the company is complicated by the fact that both company-specific and economy-wide influences have important effects on Delta's business. The company is not highly diversified, and sales growth therefore tends to be somewhat variable. During the last quarter of 1988, the most recent data available,

■ Table 6.11

**Seasonally Adjusted Annual Sales for the Delta Equipment Company and Related Data, 1979–1 to 1988–4**

| Year–Quarter | Sales (seasonly adjusted annual rate, $ millions) | Building Permit Applications (thousands) | Interest Rates (percent) | Time Period |
|---|---|---|---|---|
| 1988–4 | $725.0 | 3,200 | 9.25% | 40 |
| 1988–3 | 750.0 | 3,300 | 9.00 | 39 |
| 1988–2 | 750.0 | 3,350 | 9.00 | 38 |
| 1988–1 | 775.0 | 3,400 | 8.75 | 37 |
| 1987–4 | 725.0 | 3,450 | 8.50 | 36 |
| 1987–3 | 700.0 | 3,300 | 8.25 | 35 |
| 1987–2 | 700.0 | 3,250 | 8.25 | 34 |
| 1987–1 | 750.0 | 3,200 | 7.50 | 33 |
| 1986–4 | 750.0 | 3,150 | 7.50 | 32 |
| 1986–3 | 625.0 | 2,800 | 8.25 | 31 |
| 1986–2 | 625.0 | 2,850 | 8.50 | 30 |
| 1986–1 | 625.0 | 2,700 | 9.50 | 29 |
| 1985–4 | 575.0 | 2,650 | 9.50 | 28 |
| 1985–3 | 600.0 | 2,600 | 9.50 | 27 |
| 1985–2 | 600.0 | 2,500 | 10.50 | 26 |
| 1985–1 | 500.0 | 2,450 | 10.75 | 25 |
| 1984–4 | 525.0 | 2,650 | 10.25 | 24 |
| 1984–3 | 550.0 | 2,850 | 9.75 | 23 |
| 1984–2 | 575.0 | 2,800 | 9.50 | 22 |
| 1984–1 | 625.0 | 2,800 | 9.50 | 21 |
| 1983–4 | 575.0 | 2,750 | 9.00 | 20 |
| 1983–3 | 550.0 | 2,500 | 9.25 | 19 |
| 1983–2 | 525.0 | 2,450 | 8.50 | 18 |
| 1983–1 | 500.0 | 2,300 | 8.00 | 17 |
| 1982–4 | 475.0 | 2,300 | 8.00 | 16 |
| 1982–3 | 450.0 | 2,150 | 9.25 | 15 |
| 1982–2 | 425.0 | 2,050 | 12.25 | 14 |
| 1982–1 | 400.0 | 1,950 | 12.75 | 13 |
| 1981–4 | 375.0 | 1,850 | 11.75 | 12 |
| 1981–3 | 350.0 | 1,600 | 15.00 | 11 |
| 1981–2 | 325.0 | 1,750 | 15.00 | 10 |
| 1981–1 | 300.0 | 1,700 | 14.50 | 9 |
| 1980–4 | 350.0 | 1,800 | 13.75 | 8 |
| 1980–3 | 425.0 | 1,850 | 9.00 | 7 |
| 1980–2 | 400.0 | 1,750 | 9.75 | 6 |
| 1980–1 | 275.0 | 1,600 | 13.50 | 5 |
| 1979–4 | 300.0 | 1,700 | 12.00 | 4 |
| 1979–3 | 300.0 | 1,800 | 9.75 | 3 |
| 1979–2 | 325.0 | 1,850 | 9.50 | 2 |
| 1979–1 | 350.0 | 1,900 | 9.25 | 1 |

Delta's total sales revenue was at a seasonally adjusted annual rate of $725.0 million per year. Delta's business has grown rapidly during the last decade, but it tends to be interest-rate sensitive; seasonal, with sales rising during the spring and summer months; and cyclical, with sales rising during economic expansions and falling during economic recessions. In an effort to boost growth prospects and reduce business-cycle risk, the company underwent a dramatic restructuring during the early 1980s, introducing a new line of tools for residential and commercial construction to supplement its traditional lines of business in light equipment manufacturing. As a result, historical factors may influence future growth less than is true for many companies.

A visual scan of Delta's sales data for the ten-year 1979–1 to 1988–4 period in Table 6.11 suggests that both the constant change and constant growth models have the potential to provide a high level of descriptive accuracy and forecast reliability. This stems from the fact that Delta's sales have more than doubled during the last decade and therefore embody a strong trend element. For illustration, Delta sales data are shown in Figure 6.3, along with a simple linear regression model of the data.

■ Figure 6.3
## Seasonally Adjusted Annual Sales for Delta Equipment Company, 1979–1 to 1988–4

The constant growth model projects a strong upward trend in seasonally adjusted sales, but actual growth does not appear to be constant.

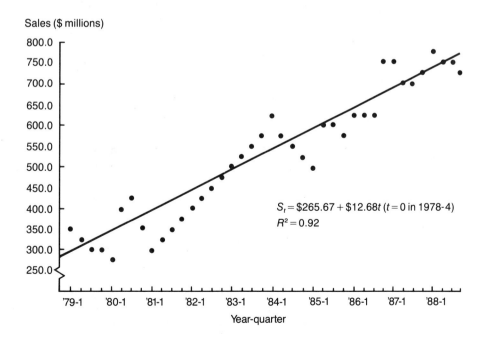

$S_t = \$265.67 + \$12.68t \ (t = 0 \text{ in } 1978\text{-}4)$
$R^2 = 0.92$

Note that the coefficient of determination ($R^2$) for this constant change model is quite high at 0.92, implying that 92 percent of sales variation over time is explained by the linear sales–time relation.

In the process of developing a sales forecasting model for Delta, it would be helpful to contrast the forecast capability of simple trend projections of seasonally adjusted company sales using the constant change and constant growth rate models with a simple econometric model. While the simple trend projection models may or may not provide an acceptable basis for forecasting future sales, depending on Delta's desired level of forecast accuracy, the constant change and constant growth rate models offer useful benchmarks for evaluating the comparative value of the econometric model alternative.

When developing an econometric forecast model, it is important to include all important economic factors that influence the company's business. The model can explicitly control for the effects of seasonal factors by seasonally adjusting Delta's sales. It can account for cyclical fluctuations related to changes in overall business conditions, at least in part, by incorporating a measure of residential and commercial construction activity. Data on building permit applications is appropriate for this purpose. Unlike data on GNP, for example, changes in permit applications will account for changes in economic activity but will be unaffected by general inflationary influences. The sensitivity of Delta's sales to changes in overall economic conditions can also be captured by considering the effects of credit market conditions. Changes in interest rates, as measured by changes in yields on 90-day short-term Treasury bills, can have an important influence on sales, because Delta's primary customers are in the capital goods sector and tend to be interest-rate sensitive. By incorporating both permit applications and T-bill interest rates in the econometric forecast model, we have adopted measures of economic activity and interest rates, respectively, that are both convenient and widely accessible. Real-world data on these and related measures can easily be obtained from government publications such as the *Economic Report of the President* and *Federal Reserve Bulletin* and from business publications such as *Barron's, Business Week, Fortune,* and *The Wall Street Journal.* Finally, the secular trend in sales, in part reflecting the increasing importance of Delta's rapidly growing sales to the residential construction industry, can be incorporated by supplementing the range of economic variables in the model with a simple trend factor. It is important to recognize, however, that the sales effects captured by this trend factor will reflect more general inflationary influences along with the secular growth in demand for Delta's products.

By incorporating a time factor in the econometric model, we are, in essence, building on the basic sales–time trend projection model shown in Figure 6.3. We hope that by adding economic variables, we will increase the proportion of the total variation in sales explained by the model. If economic activity and interest rates are indeed related to changes in Delta's sales, then the econometric model will result in a significant increase in $R^2$. However, because the variables employed in the econometric forecast model are imperfect proxies for Delta's business conditions, and given the influence of irregular or random shocks, the simple econometric model described previously may or may not constitute an improved forecasting tool. At a minimum, it will be interesting to learn whether this approach is a significant improvement over the more basic constant change and constant growth models. The answer to this question should provide a reasonable basis for further analysis.

In addition to seasonally adjusted company sales data, Table 6.11 gives data on building permit applications, interest rates, and a simple trend factor from the first quarter of 1979 to the fourth quarter of 1988. Therefore, 40 quarters (ten years) of company and economywide data are available for analysis.

To provide a meaningful basis for forecast model valuation, an estimation (or test) period must be sufficiently long to include a wide variety of economic conditions. Similarly, the forecast period over which the accuracy of the forecast model is judged must be sufficiently long to allow the analyst to consider the model's accuracy under both favorable and unfavorable economic conditions. For exploratory purposes, we will adopt the five-year 1979–1 to 1983–4 period, covering a total of 20 observations, as our estimation period. This time frame includes periods of robust and weak economic conditions along with widely variable interest rates. These are the data used to generate coefficient estimates for the three forecast models under consideration. We will adopt the five-year 1984–1 to 1988–4 period, also covering a total of 20 observations, as our forecast or "hold-out" period. These are the data used to evaluate the accuracy of the alternative forecast models being considered.

Table 6.12 shows ordinary least squares results for the constant change and constant growth models that relate Delta sales to the time trend factor, as well as for the econometric model relating sales to building permit applications, interest rates, and time (a trend factor). Note the changes in overall explanatory power ($R^2$) for each model over each time period. Whereas the constant change and constant growth models describe 92 and 89 percent, respectively, of the total variation in sales over the entire 1979–1 to 1988–4 period, both models offer only modest levels of explanatory power over the 1979–1 to 1983–4 period. As indicated by the coefficient of determination ($R^2$), each is able to explain less than three-quarters of the total variation in Delta's sales over the subperiod. In contrast, the econometric model is able to explain 97 percent of the total variation in sales over the entire period and 94 percent of total variation within the subperiod. This relative superiority of the simple econometric approach stems from its ability to reflect, at least in part, cyclical factors related to changes in economic conditions and interest rates.

■ Table 6.12

## Constant Change, Constant Growth, and Simple Econometric Models of Seasonally Adjusted Annual Sales for the Delta Equipment Company, 1979–1 to 1988–4 (*t*-statistics in parentheses)

*Descriptive Models: 1979–1 to 1988–4 (40 observations)*

| | | |
|---|---|---|
| Constant change model | $S = 265.673 + 12.681t$<br>$(18.13) \quad (20.36)$ | $R^2 = 0.92$ |
| Constant growth model | $\ln S = 5.699 + 0.025t$<br>$(169.94) \quad (17.80)$ | $R^2 = 0.89$ |
| Simple econometric model | $S = 228.609 + 0.112BPA - 10.768i + 6.297t$<br>$(2.82) \quad (3.55) \quad (-3.11) \quad (4.59)$ | $R^2 = 0.97$ |

*Forecast Models: 1979–1 to 1983–4 (20 observations)*

| | | |
|---|---|---|
| Constant change model | $S = 262.763 + 12.951t$<br>$(11.77) \quad (6.95)$ | $R^2 = 0.73$ |
| Constant growth model | $\ln S = 5.643 + 0.032t$<br>$(99.72) \quad (6.68)$ | $R^2 = 0.71$ |
| Simple econometric model | $S = 270.778 + 0.085BPA - 11.355i + 8.063t$<br>$(2.27) \quad (1.72) \quad (-2.78) \quad (3.87)$ | $R^2 = 0.94$ |

*Notes:*

$S$ = Delta sales revenue (seasonally adjusted annual rate, $ in millions)
$BPA$ = Building permit applications (thousands)
$i$ = 90-day Treasury bill interest rate (percent)
$t$ = Time period (1979–1 to 1988–4 = 40).

As a preliminary test of forecast model accuracy, regression results for the 1979–1 to 1983–4 estimation period provide interesting test models with which to forecast firm sales over the subsequent 1984–1 to 1988–4 forecast period. Specifically, building permit applications, interest rates, and time-period data from the 1984–1 to 1988–4 period will be plugged into the constant change, constant growth, and econometric models as appropriate to generate forecast values for Delta sales over the 1984–1 to 1988–4 forecast period. The comparison of these forecast values with actual sales values will show how successfully each forecast model could have predicted sales, provided that Delta had at its disposal accurate forecasts of changes in economic conditions and interest rates.

Table 6.13 shows a detailed forecast analysis for Delta Equipment Company sales during the 1984–1 to 1988–4 period. The average level of sales forecast error is $43.4 million for the constant change model, $130.2 million for the constant growth model, and $33.5 million for the econometric model. The forecast superiority for the constant change model over the constant growth model is consistent with the constant change model's relatively higher level of explained variation ($R^2$) over

■ Table 6.13

## Delta Equipment Company Sales Forecast Analysis 1984–1 to 1988–4

| Year–Quarter | Actual Sales, $S_t$ | Constant Change Forecast, $f_{1t}$ | Squared Forecast Error, $(f_{1t} - S_t)^2$ | Constant Growth Forecast, $f_{2t}$ | Squared Forecast Error, $(f_{2t} - S_t)^2$ | Simple Econometric Forecast, $f_{3t}$ | Squared Forecast Error, $(f_{3t} - S_t)^2$ |
|---|---|---|---|---|---|---|---|
| 1988–4 | $725.0 | $781.0 | $3,114.0 | $1,006.3 | $79,109.6 | $760.3 | $1,243.6 |
| 1988–3 | 750.0 | 767.9 | 318.7 | 974.6 | 50,433.3 | 763.5 | 183.3 |
| 1988–2 | 750.0 | 754.9 | 24.0 | 943.9 | 37,589.8 | 759.7 | 94.6 |
| 1988–1 | 775.0 | 742.0 | 1,092.3 | 914.2 | 19,364.1 | 758.8 | 264.0 |
| 1987–4 | 725.0 | 729.0 | 16.0 | 885.4 | 25,716.9 | 757.8 | 1,074.4 |
| 1987–3 | 700.0 | 716.0 | 257.5 | 857.5 | 24,800.5 | 739.8 | 1,584.4 |
| 1987–2 | 700.0 | 703.1 | 9.6 | 830.5 | 17,024.2 | 727.5 | 755.8 |
| 1987–1 | 750.0 | 690.1 | 3,582.5 | 804.3 | 2,950.9 | 723.7 | 692.0 |
| 1986–4 | 750.0 | 677.2 | 5,300.6 | 779.0 | 840.5 | 711.4 | 1,491.4 |
| 1986–3 | 625.0 | 664.2 | 1,540.1 | 754.5 | 16,759.5 | 665.1 | 1,604.2 |
| 1986–2 | 625.0 | 651.3 | 691.3 | 730.7 | 11,172.0 | 658.4 | 1,115.6 |
| 1986–1 | 625.0 | 638.3 | 178.0 | 707.7 | 6,836.9 | 626.2 | 1.5 |
| 1985–4 | 575.0 | 625.4 | 2,539.3 | 685.4 | 12,187.8 | 613.9 | 1,514.7 |
| 1985–3 | 600.0 | 612.4 | 154.8 | 663.8 | 4,072.1 | 601.6 | 2.6 |
| 1985–2 | 600.0 | 599.5 | 0.3 | 642.9 | 1,841.0 | 573.7 | 692.3 |
| 1985–1 | 500.0 | 586.5 | 7,488.8 | 622.7 | 15,045.4 | 558.5 | 3,426.5 |
| 1984–4 | 525.0 | 573.6 | 2,360.7 | 603.0 | 6,091.8 | 573.2 | 2,318.5 |
| 1984–3 | 550.0 | 560.6 | 113.1 | 584.1 | 1,159.9 | 587.8 | 1,426.2 |
| 1984–2 | 575.0 | 547.7 | 746.1 | 565.7 | 87.2 | 578.3 | 10.8 |
| 1984–1 | 625.0 | 534.7 | 8,148.0 | 547.8 | 5,952.2 | 570.2 | 2,999.9 |

Average:

$\bar{S}_t = \$652.5$  $\bar{f}_1 = \$657.8$  $U_1^2 = \$1,883.8$  $\bar{f}_2 = \$755.2$  $U_2^2 = \$16,951.8$  $\bar{f}_3 = \$665.5$  $U_3^2 = \$1,124.8$

Average forecast error:  $U_1 = \$43.4$  $U_2 = \$130.2$  $U_3 = \$33.5$

Correlation between forecast and actual series:  $r_{S,f_1} = 0.835$  $r_{S,f_2} = 0.835$  $r_{S,f_3} = 0.860$

*Note: For simplicity, the forecast and squared forecast error data have been rounded to the first decimal point. However, the actual calculations were done using a computer program that rounded values to the fourth decimal point. In row one, for example, you might calculate the first squared forecast error value for the constant change model as $(\$725.0 - \$781.0)^2 = -\$56.0^2$, or $3,136.0$, whereas the actual value is $(\$725.0 - \$780.8030)^2 = -\$55.8030^2$, or $3,113.9784$ rounded to $3,114.0$.*

each sample period. Similarly, the fact that the econometric model adds to the explanatory power of the constant change model explains why the average forecast error for the econometric model is the best of the three forecast models. In terms of relative magnitude, the average forecast errors are 6.7 percent of average actual sales for the constant change model, 20.0 percent for the constant growth model, and 5.1 percent for the econometric model. These data reflect underlying correlations between actual and forecast values of 0.835 for the constant change and constant growth models and 0.860 for the econometric model.

These correlations between actual and forecast values are quite modest, and they would be unsatisfactory for many forecasting purposes. However, depending on Delta's requirements for forecast precision, the accuracy of the econometric model (the best-performing of the three models) may or may not be acceptable for forecasting working capital and investment capital requirements. At a minimum, the econometric approach would seemingly provide the basis for further and more detailed analysis. Experimentation with additional economic variables and alternate functional specifications might offer further marginal improvements in forecast accuracy.

# SUMMARY

Managerial decision making requires forecasts of many future events. In this chapter we examined several techniques for economic forecasting. These included qualitative analysis, time-series analysis and projection, econometric models, and input–output methods.

All of these forecasting procedures have particular strengths and shortcomings. The appropriate method for a given forecasting problem will depend on such factors as the distance into the future being forecasted, the lead time available, the accuracy required, the quality of data available for analysis, and the nature of the economic relations involved in the forecasting problem. When little quantitative information is available, *qualitative analysis* must be relied upon to form the basis for forecasts. *Time-series methods* are appropriate for forecasting in those situations when it is thought that the historical pattern of the economic series being analyzed provides the best clues about future movement of the variable. *Barometric methods* use consistent lead and lag relationships between economic variables to project directional changes in the time series. Although it is difficult to forecast the magnitude of a change using these procedures, they have proved to be useful for predicting turning points in economic activity. Composite and diffusion indexes combine various leading indicators, thereby reducing random fluctuations and providing a smoother series, which reduces the generation of false signals.

*Econometric methods* move beyond pure forecasting to provide estimates of important relations that affect the outcomes in an economic system. This explanatory characteristic of econometric methods allows them to determine the effect on the economic variable being examined of changes in specific key variables such as product price, advertising, consumer incomes, and so on. Specification of these important interrelations allows econometric methods to forecast economic conditions under a variety of assumptions. *Input–output analysis* is another forecasting tool that focuses on the many linkages in an economic system. By tracing the flows between sectors, input–output analysis provides a basis for examining how changes in one sector of the economy will affect other sectors. It is useful for examining aggregate requirements for such key resources as energy, labor, water, and so on.

An important aspect of forecasting is testing the reliability of forecasts obtained from various basic forecasting techniques. Two statistics used in reliability analysis are the simple correlation between forecast and actual values and the average forecast error.

## Questions

6.1 What is the Delphi method? Describe its main advantages and limitations.

6.2 Describe the main advantages and limitations of survey data.

6.3 What is trend projection, and why is this method often employed in economic forecasting?

6.4 What is the basic shortcoming of trend projection that barometric approaches improve on?

6.5 What advantage do diffusion and composite indexes provide in the barometric approach to forecasting?

6.6 Explain how the econometric-model approach to forecasting could be used to examine various "what if" questions about the future.

6.7 Describe the data requirements that must be met if regression analysis is to provide a useful basis for forecasting.

6.8 Would a linear regression model of the advertising–sales relation be appropriate for forecasting the advertising levels at which threshold or saturation effects become prevalent?

6.9 Cite some examples of forecasting problems that might be addressed using input–output analysis.

6.10 What are the main characteristics of accurate forecasts?

## Problems

6.1 Rent-A-Car, Inc., provides daily auto rental service to individuals while their own cars are being repaired. Annual sales revenue has grown rapidly from \$2.5 million to \$10 million during the past five-year period.

A. Calculate the five-year growth rate in sales using the constant rate of change model with annual compounding.

B. Calculate the five-year growth rate in sales using the constant rate of change model with continuous compounding.

C. Compare your answers to parts A and B, and discuss any differences.

6.2 Mr. Ed's BBQ is a small restaurant featuring Texas-style barbecue. Wilbur Post, owner of Mr. Ed's, is concerned about the restaurant's erratic revenue pattern during recent years.

A. Complete the following table showing annual sales data for Mr. Ed's during the 1985–90 period.

| Year (1) | Sales (2) | Current Sales ÷ Previous Period Sales (3) | Growth Rate (4) = [(3) − 1] × 100 |
|---|---|---|---|
| 1985 | $250,000 | — | — |
| 1986 | 200,000 | | |
| 1987 | 400,000 | | |
| 1988 | 500,000 | | |
| 1989 | 500,000 | | |
| 1990 | 250,000 | | |

    B. Calculate the geometric average annual rate of growth for the five-year period 1985–1990. (*Hint:* Calculate this growth rate using 1985 and 1990 data.)

    C. Calculate the arithmetic average annual rate of growth for the 1985–1990 period. (*Hint:* This is the average of Column 4 figures.)

    D. Discuss any differences in your answers to parts B and C.

6.3 Environmental Designs, Inc., produces and installs energy-efficient window systems in commercial buildings. During the past ten years, sales revenue has increased from $25 million to $65 million.

    A. Calculate the company's growth rate in sales using the constant rate of change model with annual compounding.

    B. Derive a five-year and ten-year sales forecast.

6.4 The change in the quantity of Product *A* demanded in any given week is inversely proportional to the change in sales of Product *B* in the previous week. That is, if sales of *B* rose by *X* percent last week, sales of *A* can be expected to fall by *X* percent this week.

    A. Write the equation for next week's sales of *A*, using the symbols *A* = sales of Product *A*, *B* = sales of Product *B*, and *t* = time. Assume that there will be no shortages of either product.

    B. Last week, 100 units of *A* and 90 units of *B* were sold. Two weeks ago, 75 units of Product *B* were sold. What would you predict the sales of *A* to be this week?

6.5 John Elwell, a quality-control supervisor for Micro Devices, Inc., is concerned about unit labor cost increases for the assembly of electrical snap-action switches. Costs have increased from $80 to $100 per unit over the previous three years. Elwell thinks that importing switches from foreign suppliers at a cost of $115.90 per unit may soon be desirable.

    A. Calculate the company's unit labor cost growth rate using the constant rate of change model with continuous compounding.

    B. Forecast when unit labor costs will equal the current cost of importing.

6.6 To convince the loan officer at a local bank of the viability of your new store, Fashionable Styles Ltd., you would like to generate a sales forecast. You assume that next-period sales are a function of current income, advertising, and advertising by a competing retailer.

A. Write an equation for predicting sales if you assume that the percentage change in sales is twice as large as the percentage change in income and advertising but that it is only one-half as large as, and of the opposite sign of, the percentage change in competitor advertising. Use the symbols $S$ = sales, $Y$ = income, $A$ = advertising, and $CA$ = competitor advertising.

B. During the current period, sales total $500,000, income is $18,360 per capita, advertising is $24,000, and competitor advertising is $66,000. Previous-period levels were $18,000 (income), $30,000 (advertising), and $60,000 (competitor advertising). Forecast next-period sales.

6.7 P. J. Maguire, manager of product packaging at Lawncare Products, Inc., is evaluating the cost effectiveness of a preventive maintenance program in his department. He believes that the monthly downtime of the packaging line caused by equipment breakdown is related to the hours spent each month on preventive maintenance.

A. Write an equation to predict next month's downtime using the symbols $D$ = downtime, $M$ = preventive maintenance, $t$ = time, $a_0$ = constant term, $a_1$ = regression slope coefficient, and $u$ = random disturbance. Assume that downtime in the forecast (next) month decreases by the same percentage as preventive maintenance increased during the month preceding the current one.

B. If 40 hours were spent last month on preventive maintenance and this month's downtime was 500 hours, what should downtime be next month if preventive maintenance this month is 50 hours? Use the equation developed in Part A.

6.8 Toys Unlimited Ltd. must forecast sales for a popular adult trivia game to avoid stockouts or excessive inventory charges during the coming Christmas season. In percentage terms, the company estimates that game sales fall at double the rate of price increases and that they grow at triple the rate of customer traffic increases. Furthermore, these effects seem to be independent.

A. Write an equation for estimating the Christmas-season sales, using the symbols $S$ = sales, $P$ = price, $T$ = traffic, $t$ = time, and $u$ = a random disturbance term.

B. Forecast this season's sales if Toys Unlimited sold 10,000 games last season at $15 each, this season's price is anticipated to be $16.50, and customer traffic is expected to rise by 15 percent over previous levels.

6.9 Mid-Atlantic Cinema, Inc., runs a chain of movie theaters in the east-central states and enjoys great success with a "Tuesday Night at the Movies" promotion. By offering half off its regular $6 admission price, average nightly attendance has risen from 500 to 1500 persons. Popcorn and other concession revenues tied to attendance have also risen dramatically. Historically, MidAtlantic has found that 50 percent of all moviegoers buy a $2 cup of buttered popcorn. Eighty percent of these popcorn buyers, plus 40 percent of the moviegoers that do not buy popcorn, each spend an average of $1.25 on soda and other concessions.

A. Write an expression describing total revenue from tickets plus popcorn plus other concessions.

B. Forecast total revenues for both regular and special Tuesday-night pricing.

C. Forecast the total profit contribution earned for the regular and special Tuesday-night pricing strategies if the profit contribution is 25 percent on movie-ticket revenues, and 80 percent on popcorn and other concession revenues.

6.10 G. B. Strother Industries, based in Seattle, Washington, manufactures a wide range of parts for the aircraft equipment industry. The company is currently evaluating the merits of building a new plant to fulfill a recent contract with the federal government. The alternatives to expansion are to use additional overtime, to reduce other production, or both. The company will add new capacity only if the economy appears to be expanding. Therefore, forecasting the general pace of economic activity for the United States is an important input to the decision-making process. The firm has collected data and estimated the following relations for the U. S. economy:

$$\text{Last year's total profits} = \$300 \text{ billion;}$$
$$\text{(all corporations) } P_{t-1}$$

$$\text{This year's government} = \$1,000 \text{ billion;}$$
$$\text{expenditures } G$$

$$\text{Annual consumption} = \$100 \text{ billion} + 0.75Y + u;$$
$$\text{expenditures } C$$

$$\text{Annual investment expenditures } I = \$430 \text{ billion} + 0.9P_{t-1} + u;$$

$$\text{Annual tax receipts } T = 0.2 \text{ GNP;}$$

$$\text{National income } Y = \text{GNP} - T:$$

$$\text{Gross national product (GNP)} = C + I + G.$$

Forecast each of the preceding variables through the simultaneous relations expressed in the multiple equation system. Assume that all random disturbances average out to zero.

## Selected References

Armstrong, J. Scott. "Research on Forecasting: A Quarter Century Review, 1960–1984." *Interfaces* 16 (January–February 1986): 89–109.

Beaumont, Chris, Essam Mahmoud, and Victor E. McGee. "Microcomputer Forecasting Software: A Survey." *Journal of Forecasting* 4 (July–September 1984): 305–311.

Bowden, Roger J. "Feedback Forecasting Games: An Overview." *Journal of Forecasting* 8 (April-June 1989): 117–127.

Bullard, Clark W., and Anthony V. Sebald. "Monte Carlo Sensitivity Analysis of Input-Output Models." *Review of Economics and Statistics* 70 (November 1988): 708–712.

Clemen, Robert T. "Extraneous Expert Information." *Journal of Forecasting* 4 (October–December 1984): 329–348.

Cohen, Rochelle, and Fraser Dunford. "Forecasting for Inventory Control: An Example of When 'Simple' Means 'Better.'" *Interfaces* 16 (November–December 1986): 95–99.

Diamantopoulos, Adamantios, and Brian Mathews. "Factors Affecting the Nature and Effectiveness of Subjective Revision in Sales Forecasting: An Empirical Study." *Managerial and Decision Economics* 10 (March 1989): 51–60.

Feldman, Stanley J. "Structural Change in the United States: Changing Input-Output Coefficients." *Business Economics* 20 (January 1985): 39–54.

Feldman, Stanley J., David McClain, and Karen Palmer. "Sources of Structural Change in the United States, 1964–78: An Input-Output Perspective." *Review of Economics and Statistics* 69 (August 1987): 503–510.

Gardner, Everette S., Jr. "Exponential Smoothing: The State of the Art." *Journal of Forecasting* 4 (January–March 1985): 1–28.

Guerard, John B., Jr., and Carl R. Beidleman. "Composite Earnings Forecasting Efficiency." *Interfaces* 17 (September–October 1987): 103–113.

Kling, John L. "Predicting the Turning Points of Business and Economic Time Series." *Journal of Business* 60 (April 1987): 201–238.

Leontief, Wassily. *Input-Output Economics.* New York: Oxford University Press, 1985.

Mathews, Brian P., and A. Diamantopoulos. "Judgmental Revision of Sales Forecasts: A Longitudinal Extension." *Journal of Forecasting* 8 (April-June 1989): 129–140.

Patterson, K. D. "Modeling Price Expectations." *Applied Economics* 21 (March 1989): 413–426.

Raa, Thijsten. "An Alternative Treatment of Secondary Products in Input-Output Analysis: Frustration." *Review of Economics and Statistics* 70 (August 1988): 535–538.

Seyhun, H. Nejat. "The Information Content of Aggregate Insider Trading." *Journal of Business* 61 (January 1988): 1–24.

Stockton, David J., and James E. Glassman. "An Evaluation of the Forecast Performance of Alternative Models of Inflation." *Review of Economics and Statistics* 69 (February 1987): 108–117.

Ulvila, Jacob W. "Decision Trees for Forecasting." *Journal of Forecasting* 4 (October–December 1985): 377–385.

Willis, Raymond E. *Guide to Forecasting for Planners and Managers.* Englewood Cliffs, NJ: Prentice–Hall, 1987.

# Production

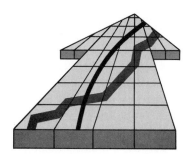

**G**iven the demand for its product, how does a firm determine the optimal level of output? Given several alternative production methods, how does the firm choose one? How will investment in new manufacturing equipment affect labor productivity and the unit costs of production? If the firm undertakes an expansion program to increase productive capacity, will its cost per unit be higher or lower after the expansion? These questions are critically important to the firm, and answers, or at least insights useful for managerial decision making are provided by the study of production.

Production is concerned with the way in which resources (inputs) are employed to produce a firm's products (outputs). The concept of production is quite broad and encompasses both the manufacture of physical goods and the provision of services. Production analysis focuses on the efficient use of inputs to create outputs. It examines the technical and economic characteristics of systems used to provide goods and services, with the aim of determining the optimal manner of combining inputs so as to minimize costs.

It is worth emphasizing that the term *production* refers to more than the physical transformation of resources. Production involves all the activities associated with providing goods and services. Thus, the hiring of workers (from unskilled labor to top management), personnel training, and the organizational structure used to maximize productivity are all part of the production process. The acquisition of capital resources and their efficient employment are also parts of production, as are the design and use of appropriate accounting control systems.

In addition to providing an important foundation for understanding costs and cost/output relations, production theory enhances one's comprehension of the integrated nature of the firm. Perhaps no other single topic in managerial economics so clearly lays out the interrelations among the various factors employed by the firm and among the functional components (for example, the output/revenue and output/cost components) in our valuation model of the firm.

# PRODUCTION FUNCTIONS

**production function**

A descriptive statement that relates inputs to outputs, showing the maximum output that can be produced with a given amount of inputs.

A **production function** is a descriptive statement that relates inputs to outputs. It specifies the maximum possible output that can be produced for a given amount of inputs or, alternatively, the minimum quantity of inputs necessary to produce a given level of output. Production functions are determined by the technology available. That is, the input/output relation for any production system is a function of the technological characteristics of the plant, equipment, labor, materials, and so on employed by the firm. Any improvement in technology, such as the addition of a process control computer that permits a manufacturing company to produce a given quantity of output with fewer raw materials and less energy and labor, or a training program that increases the productivity of labor, results in a new production function.

The basic properties of production functions can be illustrated by examining a simple two-input, one-output system. Consider a production process in which various quantities of two inputs, $X$ and $Y$, can be used to produce a product, $Q$. The inputs $X$ and $Y$ might represent resources such as labor and capital or energy and raw materials. The product $Q$ could be physical items such as television sets, cargo ships, or breakfast cereal, but it could also be a service such as medical care, education, or banking.

The production function for this system can be written as the following general relation:

$$Q = f(X, Y). \hspace{2cm} \textbf{7.1}$$

Table 7.1 is a tabular representation of such a two-input, single-output production system. Each element in the table shows the maximum quantity of $Q$ that can be produced with a specific combination of $X$ and $Y$. The table shows, for example, that 2 units of $X$ and 3 units of $Y$ can be combined to produce 49 units of output; 5 units of $X$ coupled with 5 units of $Y$ results in 92 units of output; 4 units of $X$ and 10 units of $Y$ produce 101 units of $Q$, and so on. The units of input could represent *hours* of labor, *dollars* of capital, *cubic feet* of natural gas, *tons* of raw materials, and so on. Similarly, units of $Q$ could be *numbers* of television sets or cargo ships, *cases* of cereal, *patient days* of hospital care, customer *transactions* of a banking facility, and so on.

The production function described in Table 7.1 can also be displayed graphically as in Figure 7.1. There the height of the bars associated with

■ Table 7.1
## A Representative Production Table

| Units of Y Employed | Output Quantity | | | | | | | | | |
|---|---|---|---|---|---|---|---|---|---|---|
| 10 | 52 | 71 | 87 | 101 | 113 | 122 | 127 | 129 | 130 | 131 |
| 9 | 56 | 74 | 89 | 102 | 111 | 120 | 125 | 127 | 128 | 129 |
| 8 | 59 | 75 | 91 | 99 | 108 | 117 | 122 | 124 | 125 | 126 |
| 7 | 61 | 77 | 87 | 96 | 104 | 112 | 117 | 120 | 121 | 122 |
| 6 | 62 | 72 | 82 | 91 | 99 | 107 | 111 | 114 | 116 | 117 |
| 5 | 55 | 66 | 75 | 84 | 92 | 99 | 104 | 107 | 109 | 110 |
| 4 | 47 | 58 | 68 | 77 | 85 | 91 | 97 | 100 | 102 | 103 |
| 3 | 35 | 49 | 59 | 68 | 76 | 83 | 89 | 91 | 90 | 89 |
| 2 | 15 | 31 | 48 | 59 | 68 | 72 | 73 | 72 | 70 | 67 |
| 1 | 5 | 12 | 35 | 48 | 56 | 55 | 53 | 50 | 46 | 40 |
| | 1 | 2 | 3 | 4 | 5 | 6 | 7 | 8 | 9 | 10 |

Units of X Employed

each input combination indicates the output produced. The tops of the output bars map the production surface for the system.

The discrete production data shown in Table 7.1 and Figure 7.1 can be generalized by assuming that the underlying production function is continuous. A continuous production function is one in which inputs can be varied in a continuous fashion rather than incrementally, as in the preceding example.

The three-dimensional diagram in Figure 7.2 is a graphic illustration of a continuous production function for a two-input, single-output system. Following the $X$ axis outward indicates that increasing amounts of Input $X$ are being used; going out the $Y$ axis represents an increasing usage of $Y$; and moving up the $Q$ axis means that larger amounts of output are being produced. The maximum amount of $Q$ that can be produced with each combination of Inputs $X$ and $Y$ is represented by the height of the production surface above the input plane. $Q^*$, for example, is the maximum amount of output that can be produced using the combination $X^*$, $Y^*$ of the inputs.

## Returns to Scale

**returns to scale**
The relation between output and variation in all inputs taken together.

In studying production functions, two types of relations between inputs and outputs are of interest for managerial decision making. One is the relation between output and the variation in *all inputs* taken together. This is known as the **returns to scale** characteristic of a production system. Returns to scale play an important role in managerial decisions. They affect the optimal scale, or size, of a firm and its production facili-

■ Figure 7.1
## Representative Production Surface

This discrete production function illustrates the output level resulting from each combination of Inputs $X$ and $Y$.

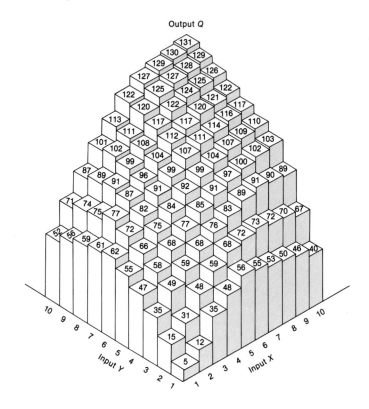

ties. They also affect the nature of competition in an industry and thus are important in determining the profitability of investment in a particular economic sector.

## Returns to a Factor

**returns to a factor**

The relation between output and variation in only one of the inputs employed.

The second important relation in a production system is that between output and variation in only *one of the inputs* employed. The terms *factor productivity* and **returns to a factor** denote this relation between the quantity of an individual input (or factor of production) employed and the output produced. Factor productivity is the key to determining the optimal combination, or proportions of inputs, that should be used to produce a product. That is, factor productivity provides the basis for efficient resource employment in a production system. Because an understanding of factor productivity will aid in our examination of returns to scale, we examine this relation first.

■ Figure 7.2
## A Continuous Production Function for a Two-Input, Single-Output System

In a continuous production function, inputs can be varied continuously.

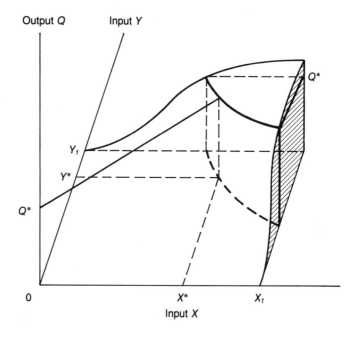

# TOTAL, MARGINAL, AND AVERAGE PRODUCT

The economic concept known as factor productivity or returns to a factor is important in the process of determining optimal input combinations for a production system. Because the process of optimization entails an analysis of the relation between the total and marginal values of a function, it will prove useful to introduce the concepts of total, average, and marginal products for the resources employed in a production system.

### Total Product

**total product**

The total output that results from employing a specific quantity of resources in a production system.

The term **total product** denotes the total output from a production system. It is synonymous with Q in Equation 7.1. Total product is a measure of the total output or product that results from employing a specific quantity of resources in a production system.

The total product concept is used to describe the relation between output and variation in only one input in a production function. For example, suppose that Table 7.1 represents a production system in which Y is a capital resource and X represents a labor input. If a firm is

■ Table 7.2

**Total Product, Marginal Product, and Average Product
of Factor *X*, Holding *Y* = 2**

| Input Quantity (*X*) | Total Product of the Input (*Q*) | Marginal Product of Input *X* ($MP_x = \partial Q/\partial X$) | Average Product of Input *X* ($AP_x = Q/X$) |
|:---:|:---:|:---:|:---:|
| 1 | 15 | +15 | 15.0 |
| 2 | 31 | +16 | 15.5 |
| 3 | 48 | +17 | 16.0 |
| 4 | 59 | +11 | 14.8 |
| 5 | 68 | + 9 | 13.6 |
| 6 | 72 | + 4 | 12.0 |
| 7 | 73 | + 1 | 10.4 |
| 8 | 72 | − 1 | 9.0 |
| 9 | 70 | − 2 | 7.8 |
| 10 | 67 | − 3 | 6.7 |

operating with a given level of capital (say, *Y* = 2), then the relevant production function for the firm in the short run is represented by the row in Table 7.1 corresponding to that level of fixed capital.[1] Operating with two units of capital, the output (total product) from the system will depend on the quantity of labor (*X*) employed. This total product of *X* can be read from the *Y* = 2 row in Table 7.1. It is also shown in column 2 of Table 7.2 and is illustrated graphically in Figure 7.3.

More generally, the total product of a production factor can be expressed as a function relating output to the quantity of the resource employed. Continuing the example, the total product of *X* is given by the production function:

$$Q = f(X|Y = 2).$$

This equation relates the output quantity *Q* (the total product of *X*) to the quantity of Input *X* employed, fixing the quantity of *Y* at two units. One would, of course, obtain other total product functions for *X* if the factor *Y* were fixed at levels other than two units.

Figure 7.4 illustrates the more general concept of the total product of an input as the schedule of output obtained as that input increases, *holding constant the amounts of the other inputs employed.* (In Figure 7.4 we are once again assuming a continuous production function where inputs can be varied in a continuous fashion rather than discretely, as in the preceding example.) Now suppose we fix, or hold constant, the

[1]In economic terminology the *short run* is a period of time during which at least one resource in a production system is fixed; that is, the quantity of that resource is constant regardless of the quantity of output produced. This concept is further developed in Chapter 8.

■ Figure 7.3

**Total, Average, and Marginal Product
for Input X, Given Y = 2**

(a) Holding $Y$ at two units, total production first rises but then falls as the amount of $X$ employed grows. (b) Total product rises so long as marginal product is positive.

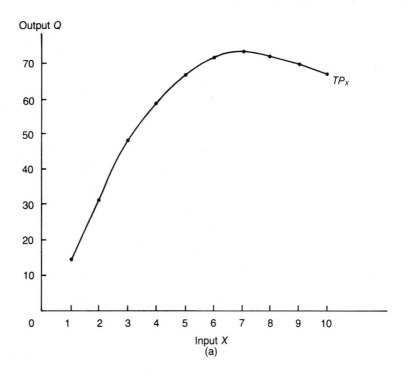

Input X
(a)

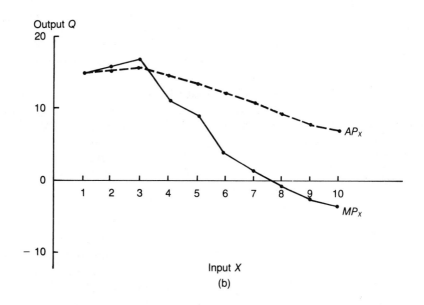

Input X
(b)

■ Figure 7.4
## Total Product Curves for *X* and *Y*

Total product curves show the increase in output following an increase in input usage.

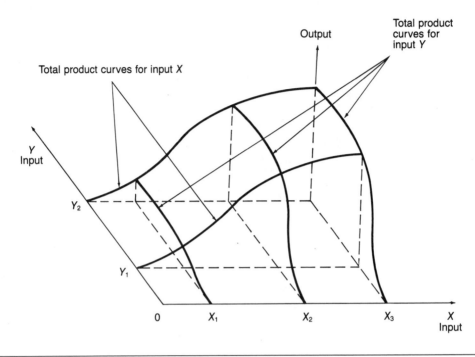

amount of Input $Y$ at the level $Y_1$. The total product curve of Input $X$, holding Input $Y$ constant at $Y_1$, originates at $Y_1$ and rises along the production surface as the use of Input $X$ is increased. Four other total product curves are shown in the figure: another for $X$, holding $Y$ constant at $Y_2$, and three for Input $Y$, holding $X$ fixed at $X_1$, $X_2$, and $X_3$, respectively.

### Marginal Product

**marginal product**

The change in output associated with a unit change in one input factor, holding other inputs constant.

Given the total product function for an input, the marginal and average products can easily be derived. The **marginal product** of a factor, $MP_X$, is the change in output associated with a one-unit change in the factor, holding other inputs constant. Accordingly, for a total product function such as that shown in Table 7.2 and Figure 7.4a, the marginal product is expressed as:

$$MP_X = \frac{\partial Q}{\partial X},$$

where $\partial Q$ is the change in output resulting from a one-unit change, $\partial X$, in the variable factor. This expression assumes that the quantity of the other input, $Y$, remains unchanged.

## Average Product

average product

Total product divided by the number of units of input employed.

A factor's **average product** is the total product divided by the number of units of input employed:

$$AP_X = \frac{Q}{X}.$$

The average product for $X$ given $Y = 2$ units is shown in column 4 of Table 7.2 and in Figure 7.3b.

For a continuous total product function, as illustrated in Figure 7.5a, the marginal product equals the slope of the total product curve, whereas the average product equals the slope of a line drawn from the origin to a point on the total product curve. The average and marginal products for Input $X$ can be determined in this manner, and these points are plotted to form the average and marginal product curves shown in Figure 7.5b.

Three points of interest, $A$, $B$, and $C$, may be identified on the total product curve in Figure 7.5a, and each has a corresponding location on the average or marginal curves. Point $A$ is the inflection point of the total product curve. The marginal product of $X$ (the slope of the total product curve) increases until this point is reached, after which it begins to decrease. This phenomenon can be seen in Figure 7.5b, as $MP_X$ is at a maximum at $A'$.

The second point on the total product curve, $B$, indicates the output at which the average and the marginal products are equal. The slope of a line from the origin to any point on the total product curve measures the average product of $X$ at that point, whereas the slope of the total product curve equals the marginal product. At Point $B$, where $X_2$ units of Input $X$ are employed, a line from the origin is tangent to the total product curve, so $MP_X = AP_X$. Note also that the slopes of successive lines drawn from the origin to the total product curve increase until Point $B$, after which their slopes decline. Thus, the average product curve rises until it reaches $B$, then declines; this feature is also shown in Figure 7.5b as Point $B'$. Here we see again that $MP_X = AP_X$ and that $AP_X$ is at a maximum.

The third point, $C$, indicates where the slope of the total product curve is zero and the curve is at a maximum. Beyond $C$ the marginal product of $X$ is negative, indicating that increased use of Input $X$ results in a *reduction* of total product. The corresponding point in Figure 7.5b is $C'$, the point where the marginal product curve intersects the $X$ axis.

## The Law of Diminishing Returns to a Factor

law of diminishing returns

As the quantity of a variable input increases, with the quantities of all other factors being held constant, the resulting increases in output eventually decrease.

The total and the marginal product curves in Figure 7.5 demonstrate the property known as the **law of diminishing returns.** This law states that as the quantity of a variable input increases, with the quantities of all other factors being held constant, the resulting *increases* in output eventually diminish. Alternatively, the law of diminishing returns states that the marginal product of the variable factor must eventually decline if enough of it is combined with some fixed quantity of one or more other

■ Figure 7.5

## Total, Marginal, and Average Product Curves:
## (a) Total Product Curve for $X$, Holding $Y = Y_1$;
## (b) Marginal Product Curve for $X$, Holding $Y = Y_1$

$MP_X$ reaches a maximum at point $A'$, where the slope of the $TP_X$ curve is greatest. $AP_X$ is at a maximum where $MP_X = AP_X$. At point $C$, $TP_X$ is at a maximum and $MP_X = 0$.

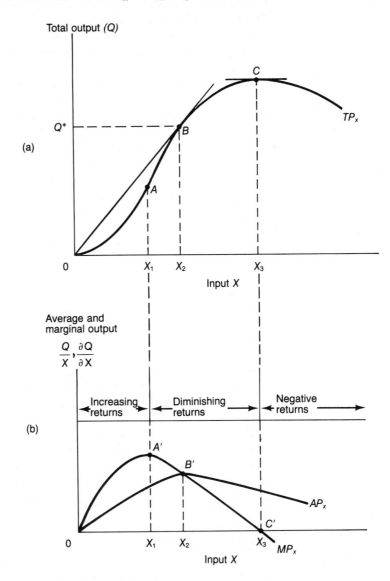

factors in a production system. The law of diminishing returns is sometimes called the law of diminishing *marginal* returns to emphasize that it deals specifically with the *marginal* product of an input.

The law of diminishing returns cannot be derived deductively. It is a generalization of an empirical observation associated with every known production system. The basis for this relation is easily demonstrated for the labor input in a production process in which a fixed amount of capital is employed.

Consider a factory with an assembly line for the production of refrigerators. If only one employee is put to work, that individual must perform each of the activities necessary to assemble refrigerators. Output from such a combination of labor and capital is likely to be quite small. In fact, it may be less than could be achieved with a smaller amount of capital because of the inefficiency of having one employee accompany the refrigerator down the assembly line rather than building it at a single station.

As additional units of labor are added to this production system—holding constant the capital input—output is likely to expand rapidly. The intensity with which the capital resource is used increases with additional labor, and increasingly efficient input combinations result. The improved use of capital resulting from the increase in labor could cause the marginal product (increase in output) of each successive employee to actually increase over some range of labor additions. This increasing marginal productivity might result from each unit of labor using a more manageable quantity of capital than is possible with less total labor input (for example, working at a single assembly station). The specialization of activity that could accompany increased labor employment is another factor that might lead to increasing returns to labor as successive units are employed.

An illustration of a production situation in which the marginal product of an input increases over some range was presented in Table 7.2. There, the first unit of labor (Input $X$) results in 15 units of production. With 2 units of labor, 31 units can be produced; the marginal product of the second unit of labor (16) exceeds that of the first (15). Similarly, addition of another unit of labor results in output increasing to 48 units, indicating a marginal product of 17 for the third unit of labor.

Eventually, enough labor will be combined with the fixed capital input that the benefits of further labor additions will not be as large as the benefits achieved earlier. When this occurs, the rate of increase in output per additional unit of labor (the marginal product of labor) will drop. Although total output will continue to increase as more units of labor are employed (the marginal product of labor is positive), the rate of increase in output will decline (the marginal product will decrease). This diminishing marginal productivity is exhibited by the fourth, fifth, sixth, and seventh units of Input $X$ in Table 7.2.

Finally, a point may be reached where the quantity of the variable input factor is so large that total output actually begins to decline with

## 7.1  **Managerial Application**
The Amazing Productivity of CAD/CAM

Computer-aided design/computer-aided manufacturing, or CAD/CAM for short, is an important new development in manufacturing. CAD systems allow research-and-development engineers to design and draw products and component parts on a computer monitor screen and then to view three-dimensional images of them from any angle. This allows the engineer to experiment inexpensively with a wide variety of possible designs. As an important part of this experimentation, the engineer runs a wide variety of computer simulations to test the strength and reliability of various designs. Thus, much product testing can take place in the design lab, and the risk of introducing an inferior design can be reduced substantially.

As the product-design phase is completed, a skeletal drawing called a "wire frame" is produced and the manufacturing phase is set to begin. Once it has taken a "look" at the CAD wire frame image, CAM equipment issues instructions to a network of integrated machine tools. On command, a prototype of the new product design is manufactured. After review and feedback from customers and marketing personnel, any final design changes are made and full-scale production can begin.

Such CAD/CAM systems not only increase quality and speed the design and manufacturing of new products, but they also allow manufacturers to quickly adjust production schedules to match changing market-demand conditions. Before CAD/CAM systems were developed, manufacturers often had a separate assembly line set up for each product line. They were reluctant to switch production from one product line to another because doing so would often entail stopping production entirely while a new production line could be set up. Be-

*continued*

See: Jim Carmichel, "New Guns the Way They Used to Be," *Outdoor Life*, May 1988, 68–75.

additional employment of that factor. In the refrigerator assembly example, this would occur when the labor force became so large that employees were getting in each other's way and hindering the manufacturing process. This happens in Table 7.2 when more than 7 units of Input $X$ are combined with 2 units of Input $Y$. The 8th unit of $X$ results in a 1-unit reduction in total output (its marginal product is $-1$), while units 9 and 10 cause output to fall by 2 and 3 units, respectively. In Figure 7.5b, the regions where the variable input factor $X$ exhibits increasing, diminishing, and negative returns have been labeled.

**Managerial Application** *continued*

sides contributing to higher labor costs, shifting production required manufacturers to maintain higher inventory levels for products temporarily taken out of production. Moreover, if a given product line was discontinued, production equipment was often removed and converted to other uses. As a result, meeting the demand that sometimes emerges following a resurgence in popularity for a discontinued item would entail the same set-up and production costs as for an entirely new product.

With CAD/CAM systems, specialized computer instructions take the place of specialized production machinery. As a result, production can quickly shift from one product line to another with little loss in labor time or effectiveness. Inventory costs can also be minimized since production set-up delays are virtually eliminated. Manufacturers can produce products "just in time" to fill customer orders. Specialized customer needs can also be met quickly by tailoring product designs to fit specific customer needs. Discontinued product lines can be quickly reintroduced to meet resurgent demand. In short, demand for 500 or 5 million items can be met quickly and efficiently.

How much does all of this wizardry cost?

In many cases, surprisingly little. Sophisticated CAD systems are often based on little more than a small network of personal computers such as the IBM PS/2 Model 70, which cost less than $7,500 each. Remington Arms, Inc., an industry leader in the small firearms market, recently spent $18 million on a 30,000 square-foot plant addition to house its new CAD/CAM flexible production system. Remington is excited about prospects for its CAD/CAM system given the small size of its overall market and the proliferation of models aimed at pleasing collectors, target shooters, and other sportsmen. Collectors and sportsmen are notoriously fickle about styling and ballistic characteristics, and demand for more than one product has surged and quickly vanished, only to return a few years later. Now, Remington can meet even limited demand for new and old products alike. In fact, the company recently announced plans to reintroduce the legendary Parker shotgun, a product that hasn't been produced in more than 40 years because it was too expensive to manufacture using standard equipment.

More than any other recent development, CAD/CAM is sure to reshape manufacturing.

 The concepts of total and marginal product and the law of diminishing returns to a factor are important in identifying efficient as opposed to inefficient input combinations. This can be illustrated with an example. Suppose Tax Advisors, Inc., has an office for processing tax returns in Lincoln, Nebraska. Table 7.3 provides information on the production function for processing tax returns in that office. As shown, if the office employs one certified public accountant (CPA), it can process one tax return per hour. Adding a second CPA increases production to four returns per hour, and with a third, output jumps to eight returns processed

■ Table 7.3
## Production Function for Tax-Return Processing

| Units of Labor Input Employed (CPAs) | Total Product of CPAs— Tax Returns Processed/Hour ($TP_{CPA} = Q$) | Marginal Product of CPAs ($MP_{CPA} = \Delta Q$) | Average Product of CPAs ($AP_{CPA} = Q/X$) |
|:---:|:---:|:---:|:---:|
| 1 | 1 | 1 | 1.00 |
| 2 | 4 | 3 | 2.00 |
| 3 | 8 | 4 | 2.67 |
| 4 | 10 | 2 | 2.50 |
| 5 | 12 | 2 | 2.40 |
| 6 | 13 | 1 | 2.17 |
| 7 | 12 | −1 | 1.71 |

per hour. Note that in this production system, the marginal product for the second CPA is three returns per hour as compared to one for the first CPA employed. The marginal product for the third CPA is four.

It is instructive to examine the source of this relative burst in productivity for the second and third CPAs. After all, a $MP_{CPA=2} = 3$ seems to indicate that the second CPA is three times as productive as the first, and $MP_{CPA=3} = 4$ says that the third CPA is even more productive. In production analysis, however, we assume that each unit of an input factor is just like all other units of that same factor, meaning that each CPA is equally competent and efficient. If individual differences in the CPA inputs do not account for the increasing productivity, what does?

Typically, it is advantages from increased specialization and better utilization of other factors in the production process that allow factor productivity to increase. As the number of CPAs increases, each can specialize, for example, in processing personal returns, partnership returns, corporate returns, and so on. Also, the additional CPAs may be better able to fully utilize computer, clerical, and other resources employed by the firm. The advantages from specialization and increased coordination among all resources cause output to rise at an increasing rate, from one to four returns processed per hour as the second CPA is employed and from four to eight returns processed as the third CPA is added.

The advantages from increased specialization and coordination are so attractive that in most instances inputs will be added at least to the point where increasing returns to each input factor are fully exploited. Thus, in practice we would not expect to see input combinations that exhibit increasing returns for any factor. Rather, input combinations in the range of diminishing returns will be commonly observed. If, for example, four CPAs could process ten returns per hour, then the marginal product of the fourth CPA ($MP_{CPA=4} = 2$) would be less than the marginal product of the third CPA ($MP_{CPA=3} = 4$) and diminishing returns to the CPA labor input would be encountered.

Finally, the irrationality of employing inputs in the negative returns range, beyond $X_3$ in Figure 7.3b, can be illustrated by noting that adding a seventh CPA would cause total output to fall from 13 to 12 returns per hour. Here the marginal product of the seventh CPA is negative one ($MP_{CPA=7} = -1$), perhaps because of problems with coordinating work among greater numbers of employees or limitations in other important inputs. Would the firm pay an additional employee's salary when that person would *reduce* the level of salable output? Obviously not, which demonstrates the irrationality of employing inputs in the range of negative returns.

# INPUT COMBINATION CHOICE

The concepts of irrational input combinations and underlying factor productivity can be more fully explored using isoquant analysis, which explicitly recognizes the potential variability of both factors in a two-input, one-output production system. This technique is introduced in the following section to examine the role of input substitutability in determining efficient input combinations.

## Production Isoquants

**isoquant**

A curve that represents all different combinations of inputs that, when combined efficiently, produce the same quantity of output.

Although one can examine the properties of production functions graphically using three-dimensional production surfaces, a two-dimensional representation using isoquants is often equally instructive and simpler to use. The term **isoquant**—derived from *iso*, meaning equal, and *quant*, from quantity—denotes a curve that represents the different combinations of inputs that, when combined efficiently, produce a specified quantity of output. Efficiency in this case refers to technological efficiency. If 2 units of $X$ and 3 units of $Y$ can be combined to produce 49 units of output, but they can also be combined less efficiently to produce only 45 units of output, the $X = 2$, $Y = 3$ input combination will lie only on the $Q = 49$ isoquant. The $X = 2$, $Y = 3$ combination resulting in $Q = 45$ is not technologically efficient, because this same input combination can produce a larger output quantity; hence, such a combination would not appear in the production function (nor on the $Q = 45$ isoquant). Production theory assumes that only the most efficient techniques are used in converting resources into products. For example, we see in Table 7.1 that 91 units of output can be produced using the input combinations: $X = 3$, $Y = 8$; $X = 4$, $Y = 6$; $X = 6$, $Y = 4$; or $X = 8$, $Y = 3$. Therefore, those four input combinations would all lie on the $Q = 91$ isoquant. Similarly, the combinations $X = 6$, $Y = 10$; $X = 7$, $Y = 8$; $X = 10$, $Y = 7$ all result in 122 units of production and, hence, lie on the $Q = 122$ isoquant.

These two isoquants are illustrated in Figure 7.6. Each point on the $Q = 91$ isoquant indicates a different combination of $X$ and $Y$ that can

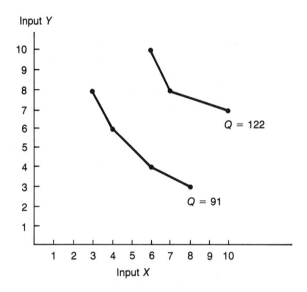

■ Figure 7.6
## Representative Isoquants from Table 7.1

Each point on an isoquant represents a different combination of Inputs $X$ and $Y$ that can be used to produce the same level of output.

produce 91 units of output. For example, 91 units can be produced with 3 units of $X$ and 8 units of $Y$, with 4 units of $X$ and 6 units of $Y$, or with any other combination of $X$ and $Y$ on the isoquant $Q = 91$. A similar interpretation can be given the isoquant for $Q = 122$ units of output.

The isoquants for the continuous production function displayed in Figure 7.2 can be located by passing a series of planes through the production surface, horizontal to the $XY$ plane, at various heights. Each plane represents a different level of output. Two such planes have been passed through the production surface shown in Figure 7.7 at heights $Q_1$ and $Q_2$. Every point on the production surface with a height of $Q_1$ above the input plane—that is, all points along curve $Q_1$— represent an equal quantity, or isoquant, of $Q_1$ units of output. The curve $Q_2$ maps out the locus of all input combinations that result in $Q_2$ units of production.

These isoquant curves can be transferred to the input surface, as indicated by the dashed curves $Q'_1$ and $Q'_2$ in Figure 7.7, then further transferred to the two-dimensional graph shown in Figure 7.8. These latter curves represent the standard form of an isoquant.

## Substituting Input Factors
The shapes of isoquants reveal a great deal about the substitutability of input factors—that is, the ability to substitute one input for another in the production process. This point is illustrated in Figure 7.9a, b, and c.

■ Figure 7.7
## Isoquant Determination for a
## Continuous Production Function

Each plane in a continuous production surface identifies an isoquant.

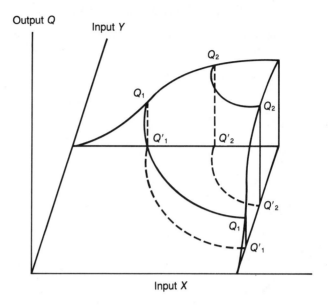

■ Figure 7.8
## Production Isoquants for a
## Continuous Production Function

Isoquants are typically C-shaped and concave to the origin.

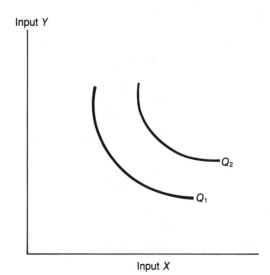

■ Figure 7.9
## Isoquants for Inputs with Varying Degrees of Substitutability: (a) Electric Power Generation; (b) Bicycle Production; (c) Dress Production

(a) Straight-line isoquants indicate perfect substitution. (b) A right-angle shape for isoquants reflects inputs that are perfect complements. (c) C-shaped isoquants indicate imperfect substitutability among inputs.

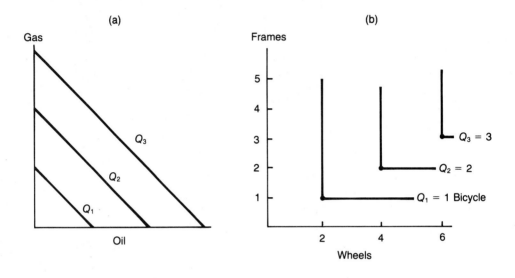

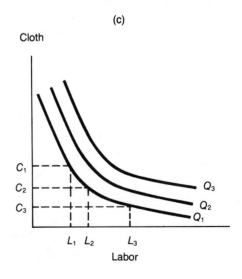

In some production systems, certain inputs can easily be substituted for one another. In the production of electricity, for example, the fuels used to power generators might represent readily substitutable inputs. Figure 7.9a shows isoquants for such an electric power generation system. The technology, a power plant with boilers equipped to burn either oil or gas, is given; various amounts of electric power can be produced by burning gas only, oil only, or varying amounts of each. Gas and oil are perfect substitutes here, and the isoquants are straight lines. Other examples of readily substitutable inputs include fish meal and soybeans to provide protein in a feed mix, energy and time in a drying process, and United Parcel Service and the U.S. Postal Service for delivery of packages. In each case, one would expect to find linear production isoquants.

At the other extreme of input substitutability lie production systems in which inputs are perfect complements for each other. In these situations, exact amounts of each input are required to produce a given quantity of output. Figure 7.9b, which illustrates the isoquants for bicycles, represents this case of complete nonsubstitutability. Exactly two wheels and one frame are required to produce a bicycle, and in no way can wheels be substituted for frames, or vice versa. Pants and coats for suits, engines and bodies for trucks, barbers and shears for haircuts, and chemicals in compounds for prescription drugs are further examples of complementary inputs. Production isoquants for complementary inputs take the shape of right angles, as indicated in Figure 7.9b.

Figure 7.9c shows an intermediate situation, that of a production process in which inputs can be substituted for each other within limits. A dress can be made with a relatively small amount of labor ($L_1$) and a large amount of cloth ($C_1$). The same dress can also be made with less cloth ($C_2$) if more labor ($L_2$) is used because the worker can cut the material more carefully and reduce waste. Finally, the dress can be made with still less cloth ($C_3$), but the worker must be so extremely painstaking that the labor input requirement increases to $L_3$. Note that although a relatively small addition of labor, from $L_1$ to $L_2$, reduces the input of cloth from $C_1$ to $C_2$, a very large increase in labor, from $L_2$ to $L_3$, is required to obtain a similar reduction in cloth from $C_2$ to $C_3$. The substitutability of labor for cloth diminishes from $L_1$ to $L_2$ to $L_3$. The substitutability of cloth for labor in the manufacture of dresses also diminishes, as can be seen by considering the quantity of cloth that must be added to replace each unit of reduced labor in moving from $L_3$ to $L_1$.

Most labor–capital substitutions in production systems exhibit this diminishing substitutability. Energy and insulation used in providing heating services also exhibit diminishing substitutability, as do doctors and medical technicians in providing health-care services.

## Marginal Rate of Technical Substitution

The slope of the isoquant provides the key to the substitutability of input factors. In Figure 7.9c, the slope of the isoquant is simply the change in

**marginal rate of technical substitution**

The amount of one input factor that must be substituted for one unit of another input factor if output is to remain unchanged.

Input $Y$ (cloth) divided by the change in Input $X$ (labor). This relation, the **marginal rate of technical substitution**[2] **($MRTS$)** of labor for cloth, provides a measure of the amount of one input factor that must be substituted for one unit of the other input factor to maintain a constant level of output. This can be stated algebraically:

$$MRTS = \frac{dY}{dX} = \frac{\Delta Y}{\Delta X} = \text{Slope of an isoquant.} \qquad \textbf{7.2}$$

The marginal rate of technical substitution is usually not constant but diminishes as the amount of substitution increases. In Figure 7.9c, for example, as more and more labor is substituted for cloth, the increment of labor necessary to replace cloth increases. Finally, at the extremes, the isoquant may even become positively sloped, indicating that the range over which the input factors may be substituted for each other is limited while the level of production remains constant.

The classic example of this case is the use of land and labor to produce a given output of wheat. As labor is substituted for land, at some point the farmers trample the wheat. As more labor is added, more land must also be added if wheat output is to be maintained. The new workers must have some place to stand.

The input substitution relation indicated by the slope of a production isoquant is directly related to the concept of diminishing marginal productivity introduced earlier. This is because the marginal rate of technical substitution is equal to $-1$ times the ratio of the marginal products of the input factors [$MRTS = -1(MP_X/MP_Y)$]. To see this, note that the loss in output resulting from a small reduction in $Y$ equals the marginal product of $Y$, $MP_Y$, multiplied by the change in $Y$, $\Delta Y$. That is:

$$\Delta Q = MP_Y \times \Delta Y. \qquad \textbf{7.3}$$

Similarly, the change in $Q$ associated with the increased use of Input $X$ is given by the expression:

$$\Delta Q = MP_X \times \Delta X. \qquad \textbf{7.4}$$

For substitution of $X$ for $Y$ along an isoquant, the absolute value of $\Delta Q$ in Equations 7.3 and 7.4 must be the same. That is, the change in output associated with the reduction in Input $Y$ must be exactly offset by the change in output resulting from the increase in Input $X$ for output to remain on the same isoquant. Thus, $\Delta Q$ in Equations 7.3 and 7.4 must be equal in size and have opposite signs. Therefore, along an isoquant:

$$-(MP_X \times \Delta X) = (MP_Y \times \Delta Y). \qquad \textbf{7.5}$$

---

[2]This term is often shortened to just the *marginal rate of substitution*.

Transposing the variables in Equation 7.5 produces:

$$-\frac{MP_X}{MP_Y} = \frac{\Delta Y}{\Delta X}$$

$$MRTS_{XY} = \text{Slope of an isoquant.}[3] \qquad \textbf{7.6}$$

Thus, the slope of a production isoquant, shown in Equation 7.2 to equal $\Delta Y/\Delta X$, is determined by the ratio of the marginal products of the inputs. Looking at Figure 7.9c we can see that the isoquant $Q_1$ has a very steep negative slope at the point $L_1C_1$. This means that when cloth is relatively abundant, the marginal product of labor is high as compared with the marginal product of cloth. On the other hand, when labor is relatively abundant at, say, point $L_3C_3$, the marginal product of labor is low relative to the marginal product of cloth.

Equation 7.6 provides a basis for examining the concept of irrational input combinations. It is irrational for a firm to combine resources in such a way that the marginal product of any input is negative, since this implies that output could be increased by using less of that resource.[4] Note from Equation 7.6 that if the inputs $X$ and $Y$ are combined in proportions such that the marginal product of either factor is negative, then the slope of the production isoquant will be positive. That is, in order for a production isoquant to be positively sloped, one of the input factors must have a negative marginal product. From this it follows that input combinations lying along a positively sloped portion of a production isoquant are irrational and would be avoided by the firm.

In Figure 7.10, the rational limits of input substitution are indicated by the points where the isoquants become positively sloped. The limits to the range of substitutability of $X$ for $Y$ are indicated by the tangencies between the isoquants and a set of lines drawn perpendicular to the $Y$

---

[3]This result can also be demonstrated by noting that along any isoquant the total differential of the production function must be zero (output is fixed along an isoquant). Thus for the production function given by Equation 7.1, setting the total differential equal to zero gives:

$$\frac{\partial Q}{\partial X}\,dX + \frac{\partial Q}{\partial Y}\,dY = 0$$

and, rearranging terms:

$$(-)\frac{\partial Q/\partial X}{\partial Q/\partial Y} = \frac{dY}{dX}.$$

Or, since $\partial Q/\partial X = MP_X$ and $\partial Q/\partial Y = MP_Y$,

$$(-)\frac{MP_X}{MP_Y} = \frac{dY}{dX} = \text{Slope of the isoquant.}$$

[4]This is technically correct only if the resource has a nonnegative cost. Thus, for example, a firm might employ additional workers even though the marginal product of labor was negative if it received a government subsidy for that employment that more than offset the cost of the output reduction.

■ Figure 7.10
## Maximum Variable Proportions for Inputs X and Y

The rational limits of substitution between Y and X occur where the isoquants become
positively sloped.

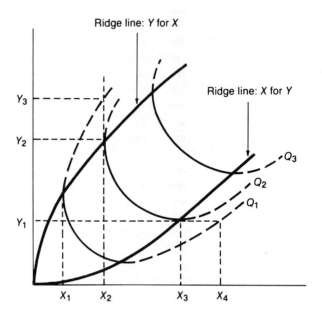

axis. Similarly, the limits of economic substitutability of $Y$ for $X$ are
shown by the tangents of lines perpendicular to the $X$ axis. The maximum and the minimum proportions of $Y$ and $X$ that would be combined
to produce each level of output are determined by the tangencies of these
lines with the production isoquants.

It is irrational for a firm to use any input combination outside these
tangents, or *ridge lines*, as they are called. Such combinations are irrational because the marginal product (the change in output resulting from
an incremental increase in an input factor) of the relatively more abundant input is negative outside the ridge lines. Addition of the last unit
of the excessive input factor actually reduces the output of the production system. Obviously, if the input factor has a positive cost, it would
be irrational for a firm to buy and employ additional units that caused
production to decrease. To illustrate, suppose a firm is currently operating with a fixed quantity of Input $Y$ equal to $Y_1$ units, as shown in Figure
7.10. In such a situation the firm would never employ more than $X_3$ units
of Input $X$, because employment of additional units of $X$ results in production of successively lower output quantities. For example, if the firm
combines $Y_1$ and $X_4$, output is equal to $Q_1$ units. By reducing usage of $X$
from $X_4$ to $X_3$, output can be increased from $Q_1$ to $Q_2$.

A similar relation is shown for Input $Y$. We see that in the area above the upper ridge line, the relative amount of $Y$ is excessive. In this area it is possible to increase production (move to a higher isoquant) by reducing the amount of $Y$ employed. For example, the input combination $X_2Y_3$ results in $Q_1$ units of output. However, by reducing the amount of $Y$ employed to $Y_2$ while holding $X$ constant at $X_2$, the firm produces a higher level of output, $Q_2$. This means that the marginal product of $Y$ is negative, since reducing its usage increases production. Thus, in the area above the upper ridge line Input $Y$ is excessive relative to Input $X$, and here $Y$'s marginal product is negative. For combinations below the lower ridge line, Input $X$ is excessive relative to the amount of Input $Y$ employed, and here $X$'s marginal product is negative. Only for input combinations lying between the ridge lines will *both* inputs have positive marginal products, and it is here (along the negatively sloped portion of the isoquant) that we must look for optimal input combinations.

# THE ROLE OF REVENUE AND COST IN PRODUCTION

To answer the question of what constitutes an optimal input combination in a production system, we must move beyond technological relations and introduce revenues and costs. In an advanced economy, productive activity results in goods that are sold rather than consumed by the producer, so we must be concerned with returns to the owners of the various input factors—labor, materials, and capital—that result from those sales. Therefore, to gain an understanding of how the factors of production should be combined for maximum efficiency, it is necessary that we shift from an analysis of *physical* productivity of inputs to an examination of their *economic* productivity, or net revenue-generating capability.

## Marginal Revenue Product

The conversion from physical to economic relations is accomplished by multiplying the marginal product of input factors by the marginal revenue resulting from the sale of goods or services produced to obtain a quantity known as the **marginal revenue product** of input:[5]

**marginal revenue product**

The economic value of a marginal unit of a particular input factor when used in the production of a specific product.

$$\text{Marginal Revenue Product of Input } X = MRP_X$$
$$= \text{Marginal Product}_X \times \text{Marginal Revenue}_Q$$
$$= MP_X \times MR_Q.$$

The marginal revenue product is the economic value of a marginal unit of a particular input factor used in the production of a specific product.

---

[5]This concept is sometimes referred to as the *value of the marginal product* of the input in perfectly competitive markets where $P = MR_Q$.

■ Table 7.4

## Marginal Revenue Product for a Single Input

| Units of Input (X) | Total Product of X (Q) | Marginal Product of X ($MP_x = \Delta Q$) | Marginal Revenue Product of X ($MP_x \times \$5$) |
|---|---|---|---|
| 1 | 3 | 3 | $15 |
| 2 | 7 | 4 | 20 |
| 3 | 10 | 3 | 15 |
| 4 | 12 | 2 | 10 |
| 5 | 13 | 1 | 5 |

For example, if the addition of one more laborer to a work force would result in the production of two incremental units of a product that can be sold for $5 per unit, the marginal product of labor is 2, and its marginal revenue product is $10 (2 × $5). Table 7.4 illustrates the marginal revenue product concept for a simple one-factor production system. The marginal revenue product values shown in column 4 of that table assume that each unit of output can be sold for $5. Thus, the marginal revenue product of the first unit of $X$ employed equals the 3 units of output produced times the $5 revenue received per unit, or $MRP_{X=1} = \$15$. The second unit of $X$ adds 4 units of production ( that is, $MP_{X=2} = 4$); hence, the $MRP$ of the second unit of $X$ is $20 (4 × $5). The marginal revenue products of the other quantities of $X$ are all determined in this manner.

### Optimal Level of a Single Input

To see how the economic productivity of an input, as defined by its marginal revenue product, is related to the use of the factor for productivity purposes, one need only consider the simple question: If the price of input $X$ in the production system depicted in Table 7.4 is $12, how many units of $X$ will a firm use? Clearly the firm will employ 3 units of $X$ because the value of adding each of these units as measured by their marginal revenue products exceeds the related cost. When 3 units of $X$ are employed, the marginal third unit causes total revenues to rise by $15 while only costing $12. At the margin, by employing the third unit of $X$, total profit rises by $3 (= $15 − $12). The fourth unit of $X$ would not be employed because the value of its marginal product ($10) would be less than the cost of employing it ($12); profit would decline by $2.

The relation between resource productivity, as measured by the marginal revenue product, and optimal employment or factor use can be generalized by referring to the basic marginal principles of profit maximization developed in Chapter 2. Recall that so long as marginal revenue exceeds marginal cost, profits must increase. In the context of production decisions, this means that if the marginal revenue product of an input (that is, the marginal revenue generated by the product's employment in a production system) exceeds its marginal cost, then profits increase as input employment increases. Similarly, when the marginal revenue product is less than the cost of the factor, marginal profit is negative, so the firm would reduce employment of that factor.

This concept of optimal resource use can be clarified by examining a simple production system in which a single variable input, L, is used to produce a single product, Q. Profit maximization requires production at a level such that marginal revenue equals marginal cost. Because the only variable factor in the system is Input L, the marginal cost of production can be expressed as:

$$MC_Q = \frac{\Delta \text{Total Cost}}{\Delta \text{Output}}$$

$$= \frac{P_L}{MP_L}.$$ **7.7**

That is, dividing $P_L$, the price of a marginal unit of L, by $MP_L$, the number of units of output gained by the employment of an added unit of L, provides a measure of the marginal cost of producing each additional unit of the product.

Since marginal revenue must equal marginal cost at the profit-maximizing output level, $MR_Q$ can be substituted for $MC_Q$ in Equation 7.7, resulting in the expression:

$$MR_Q = \frac{P_L}{MP_L}.$$ **7.8**

Equation 7.8 must hold for profit maximization because it was just shown that the right-hand side of Equation 7.8 is just another expression for marginal cost. Solving Equation 7.8 for $P_L$ results in:

$$P_L = MR_Q \times MP_L,$$

or, since $MR_Q \times MP_L$ is defined as the marginal revenue product of L:

$$P_L = MRP_L.$$ **7.9**

Equation 7.9 states the general result that a profit-maximizing firm will always employ an input up to the point where its marginal revenue product equals its cost. If the marginal revenue product exceeds the cost of the input, profits are increased by employing additional units of the factor. Similarly, when the resource's price is greater than its marginal revenue product, profit is increased by using less of the factor. Only at the level of usage where $MRP = P$ are profits maximized.

Determining the optimal level of an input can be further clarified by reconsidering our earlier Tax Advisors, Inc., example, illustrated in Table 7.3. If we again assume that three CPAs can process eight returns per hour and that employing a fourth CPA increases total output to ten

## 7.2 **Managerial Application**
Those Richer and Riskier Pay Plans

One of the most striking changes taking place in corporate America today is the dramatic reshaping of compensation plans. More than ever before, the pay of top corporate employees is contingent on firm profitability and stock-price performance.

Incentive pay plans set the compensation of top management according to how well the company achieves a number of preset objectives. Thus, in addition to salary, it becomes possible for top executives to earn thousands, if not millions, of dollars of additional incentive pay in the form of bonuses, deferred compensation, and stock options. Many boards of directors want to avoid the problems involved with measuring corporate performance using accounting data, and therefore they set incentive pay almost solely on the basis of the company's stock-price performance. The underlying logic is that by tying top-executive pay to stock-price performance, a direct incentive to maximize the value of the firm is created. Given the booming stock market of the 1980s, such incentive pay plans have resulted in an astonishing boost in pay for some top executives. Until the mid-1980s, total compensation in excess of $1 million for chief executive officers (CEOs) was a rarity reserved for a few firms at the top of the *Fortune 500*. Today, several top executives earn tens of millions of dollars per year in total compensation, and hundreds earn in excess of $1 million annually.

Proponents of this new trend in top-executive pay contend that several companies have been revitalized when management has focused on bottom-line performance. Opponents contend that such plans reflect CEOs taking unfair advantage of their positions. They cite examples of

*continued*

See: Nancy J. Perry, "Here Come Richer, Riskier Pay Plans," *Fortune*, December 19, 1988, 50–66; and Chistopher Farrell and John Hoerr, "ESOPs: Are They Good For You?," *Business Week*, May 15, 1989, 116–123.

returns, then employing a fourth CPA will reduce the marginal product of CPAs from $MP_{CPA=3} = 4$ to $MP_{CPA=4} = 2$. This describes a situation in which employment is in a range of diminishing returns to the labor factor. The optimal resource employment issue requires an answer to the question, should a fourth CPA be hired? The answer, of course, depends on whether expanding total employment will increase or decrease total profits. A fourth CPA should be hired if doing so will increase profits—otherwise not.

For simplicity, let us assume that more CPA time is the only input required to process additional tax returns and that CPAs earn $25 per

**Managerial Application** *continued*

millions of dollars in compensation being earned by top executives in the auto, steel, and other industries following wage cuts for blue-collar workers, mass layoffs, and plant closures. Although proponents admit the need for close public scrutiny, they argue that corporate restructuring is an important requirement of a vital economy and a key task facing top executives. Proponents also note that running a large modern corporation is an exceedingly complex task and requires an individual with rare management skill. They point out that top-executive pay represents a very small share of the sales and profits being earned by large companies. Moreover, stock-based rewards often accumulate over a number of years, but because they are exercised all at once, they can tend to overstate a single year's compensation.

The clearest indication that incentive pay plans are here to stay comes from the fact that they are rapidly spreading from the executive suite to the shop floor. The most widely employed form of such plans is profit sharing. Under profit sharing, employees receive a varying annual bonus based on corporate profit performance. More than 30 percent of U.S. companies employ some form of profit sharing, with most companies deferring at least some of these bonuses by putting them into employee retirement plans. Companies with 500 or fewer employees sometimes use an alternate form of profit sharing called gain sharing. Under gain sharing, all workers receive a set bonus when a specific performance target has been met. Some companies have found gain sharing to be an effective means for achieving improvements in product quality and customer service. Two newer forms of incentive pay for broad groups of employees are lump-sum bonuses and pay-for-knowledge plans. Lump-sum bonuses are one-time cash payments tied to performance that do not become a part of the employee's subsequent base pay. Pay-for-knowledge plans, perhaps the newest form of incentive pay, result in higher employee salaries following an increase in the number of tasks the employee is able to perform. Such plans have proved to be effective means for enhancing worker skills.

The design of an effective and fair incentive pay plan for top executives and other employees is a daunting challenge. What many companies have discovered is that the rewards of such plans far outweigh the risks.

hour, or roughly \$50,000 per year. If Tax Advisors, Inc., receives \$20 in revenue for each tax return prepared by the fourth CPA, the comparison of the price of labor and marginal revenue product for the fourth CPA reveals:

$$P_{CPA} < MRP_{CPA} = MR_Q \times MP_{CPA}$$

because

$$\$25 < \$40 = \$20 \times 2.$$

This implies that by employing a fourth CPA, total profits will rise by \$15 per hour (= \$40 − \$25), so the additional CPA should be hired.

Since the marginal product for the fifth CPA is also two returns per hour, the marginal revenue product remains at $40, and it follows that Tax Advisors, Inc., will choose to employ a fifth CPA as well. The marginal product for the sixth CPA position, however, is only one additional processed return. This implies that for a sixth CPA, $MRP = \$20$, which is less than the $25 per hour cost of hiring the person. The firm would incur a $5-per-hour loss by expanding hiring to that level and would, therefore, stop at an employment level of five CPAs.

To simplify this example, we have assumed that CPA time is the only variable input involved in tax-return preparation. In reality, for this product, like most, other inputs are likely to be necessary to increase output. That is, additional computer time, office supplies, and clerical support may all be required along with CPA time to increase output. If such were the case, determining the independent contribution or value of the CPA input would be more complex. If, in our example, *variable overhead* for CPA support staff and supplies equals 50 percent of sales revenue, then the relevant marginal revenue, or *net marginal revenue*, for CPA time would be only $10 per hour ($0.5 \times MR_Q$). In this instance, Tax Advisors, Inc., would find that the $20 ($= 2 \times \$10$) net marginal revenue product generated by the fourth CPA would not offset the $25 cost (wage rate). It would, therefore, employ no more than three CPAs, a level at which $MRP = 4 \times \$10 = \$40 > \$25 = P_{CPA}$. The firm will employ additional CPAs only so long as their net marginal revenue product equals or exceeds their marginal cost (price of labor).

This explains why, for example, a law firm might hire new associates at annual salaries of $80,000 when it expects them to generate $150,000 per year in gross billings, or 1,500 billable hours at a rate of $100 per hour. If variable costs are $70,000 per associate, only $80,000 is available to cover associate salary expenses. When customers pay $100 per hour for legal services, they are in fact paying for attorney time and expertise plus the support of legal secretaries, law clerks, office staff, supplies, facilities, and so on. By itself, new associate time is worth much less than $100 per hour, or $150,000 per year. The net marginal revenue of new associate attorney time, or CPA time in the preceding Tax Advisors, Inc. example, is the *marginal* value created after accounting for the variable costs of all other inputs that must be increased in order to provide service.

This relatively simple concept—that additional inputs will be employed so long as their value in production (as measured by their net marginal revenue product) exceeds their cost—provides the foundation for all production analysis. We see in the section that follows that it is the basis for determining both optimal input combinations and the profit-maximizing level of output. As is illustrated in Figure 7.7, it also underlies the demand for input factors.

## The Input Demand Function

Given data on the marginal revenue product of labor and wage rates, firms have clear incentives regarding the level of employment. If

$MRP_L > P_L$ it will pay to expand labor usage; when $MRP_L < P_L$ it will pay to cut back. If $MRP_L = P_L$, an optimal level of employment has been determined. Therefore, when an unlimited supply of labor can be employed at a given wage rate, determining the optimal level of employment involves a simple comparison of $MRP_L$ and $P_L$. However, when higher wages are necessary to expand the level of employment, this fact must be taken into account in the determination of an optimal level of employment.

To illustrate, consider the case of Micromachines, Inc. Micromachines is a high-tech company that assembles and markets Lilliputian-size machines: tiny gears and cranks the size of large specks of dust. The firm plans to introduce a new microscopic motor with the following demand conditions:

$$Q = 187{,}500 - 2{,}500P$$

or

$$P = \$75 - \$0.0004Q.$$

Motor parts are purchased from a number of independent subcontractors, and then put together at Micromachines' west coast assembly plant. Each unit of output is expected to require *two* hours of labor. Total costs for parts acquisition before assembly labor costs are as follows:

$$TC = \$250{,}000 + \$15Q.$$

Business is booming for Micromachines' established products, and the company has no excess assembly staff. To assemble this new product, the firm will need to hire and train a new staff of technical assistants. Given tight labor market conditions, Micromachines expects that an increase in employment will be possible only at higher wage rates. Based on data compiled by its director of human resources management, the firm projects the following labor supply curve in the highly competitive local labor market:

$$L_S = 10{,}000\, P_L.$$

Based on the above information, it is possible to derive Micromachines' demand curve for labor. To do so, simply note that because two hours of labor are required for each unit of output, the company's profit function can be written as:

$$\begin{aligned}
\pi &= TR - TC \\
&= (\$75 - \$0.0004Q)Q - \$250{,}000 - \$15Q - 2P_LQ \\
&= -\$0.0004Q^2 + 60Q - 2P_LQ - \$250{,}000.
\end{aligned}$$

To find Micromachines' labor demand curve, we must determine the firm's optimal level of output. The profit maximizing level of output is found by setting marginal profit equal to zero $(M_\pi = d\pi/dQ = 0)$, where:

$$d\pi/dQ = -\$0.0008Q + \$60 - 2P_L = 0.$$

This implies a direct relation between the price of labor, $P_L$, and the firm's optimal level of output:

$$2P_L = \$60 - \$0.0008Q$$

$$P_L = \$30 - \$0.0004Q.$$

It is important to recognize that this expression can be used to indicate a profit-maximizing level of output, *and* an optimal employment level. By setting $M\pi = MR - MC = 0$ we have implicitly set $MR = MC$. In terms of employment, this means we have set $MRP_L = P_L$. Therefore, Micromachines' marginal revenue product of labor is given by the expression, $MRP_L = \$30 - \$0.0004Q$.

To identify Micromachines' optimal level of employment at any given price of labor, we simply determine the amount of labor required to produce the relevant profit-maximizing level of output. Because each unit of output requires *two* units of labor, $L = 2Q$ and $Q = 0.5L$. By substitution, the firm's demand curve for labor is:

$$P_L = MRP_L$$
$$= \$30 - \$0.0004(0.5L)$$
$$= \$30 - \$0.0002L$$

or

$$L_D = 150{,}000 - 5{,}000P_L.$$

At any given wage rate, this expression will indicate Micromachines' optimal level of employment. Similarly, at any given employment level, this expression will indicate Micromachines' optimal wage rate. As can be expected, a higher wage will result in a lower level of labor demand, and the amount of labor demanded rises as the wage rate falls.

The equilibrium wage rate and employment level in the local market can be determined by setting the demand for labor equal to the supply of labor:

$$\text{Labor Demand} = \text{Labor Supply}$$
$$150{,}000 - 5{,}000P_L = 10{,}000P_L$$
$$15{,}000P_L = 150{,}000$$
$$P_L = \$10 \text{ (wage rate).}$$

To determine the equilibrium employment level, we set labor demand equal to labor supply at a wage rage of $10:

$$\text{Labor Demand} = \text{Labor Supply}$$
$$150{,}000 - 5{,}000(\$10) = 10{,}000(\$10)$$
$$100{,}000 = 100{,}000 \text{ (worker hours).}$$

This implies that Micromachines will produce 50,000 micromotors (units of output) because $Q = 0.5L = 0.5(100{,}000) = 50{,}000$ units.

Using the firm's demand curve for micromotors and total profit function, we can now calculate the optimal output price and profit levels:

$$P = \$75 - \$0.0004(50,000)$$
$$= \$55.$$
$$\pi = \$0.0004(50,000^2) + \$60(50,000) - 2(\$10)(50,000) - \$250,000$$
$$= \$750,000.$$

From this example, we see that the input demand function and the optimal level of employment can be derived by calculating the profit-maximizing level of output, then determining the amount of labor necessary to produce this output level. In our earlier Tax Advisors, Inc., example, we set $MRP_L = P_L$ to find the optimal employment level. This is similar to setting $MR = MC$ for each input. In the Micromachines, Inc., example, we incorporated labor costs directly into the profit function, and set $M\pi = 0$. Both approaches yield the same profit-maximizing result because when $M\pi = MR - MC = 0$, then $MR = MC$ and $P_L = MRP_L$. Therefore, either method can be used to determine an optimal level of employment.

Figure 7.11 shows the marginal revenue product for an input, $L$, along with its market price, $P_L^*$. Over the range to $L^*$, expanding usage of $L$ will increase total profits, since the marginal revenue product gained from employing each unit of $L$ exceeds its price. Beyond $L^*$, increased usage of $L$ will reduce profits, because the benefits gained ($MRP_L$) are less than the costs incurred ($P_L$). Only at $L^*$, where $P_L^* = MRP_L$, will total profits be maximized. Of course, if $P_L^*$ were higher, the quantity of $L$ demanded would be reduced. Similarly, if $P_L^*$ were lower, the quantity of $L$ purchased would be greater.

## Optimal Combination of Multiple Inputs

The results of preceding sections can be extended to determine the optimal proportions of multiple inputs in production systems employing several input factors. Among the several possible approaches to this task, one of the simplest involves combining technological and market relations through the use of isoquant and isocost curves. Optimal input proportions can be found graphically for a two-input, single-output system by adding a budget line or isocost curve (a line of constant costs) to the diagram of production isoquants. Each point on a budget line represents some combination of inputs, say $X$ and $Y$, whose cost equals a constant expenditure. The budget lines illustrated in Figure 7.12 are constructed in the following manner: Let $P_X = \$500$ and $P_Y = \$250$, the prices of $X$ and $Y$. For a given budget, say $B_1 = \$1,000$, the firm can purchase 4 units of $Y$ ($= \$1,000/\$250$) and no units of $X$, or 2 units of $X$ ($= \$1,000/\$500$) and none of $Y$. These two quantities represent the $X$ and $Y$ intercepts of a budget line, and a straight line connecting them identifies all combinations of $X$ and $Y$ that $\$1,000$ can purchase.

■ Figure 7.11

**The *MRP* Curve Is an Input Demand Curve**

Profits are maximized at $L^*$ where $P_L^* = MRP_L$.

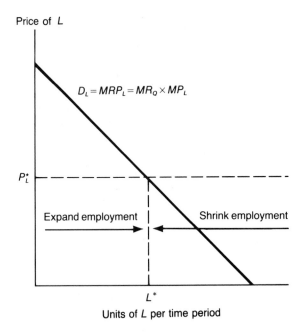

Price of $L$

$D_L = MRP_L = MR_Q \times MP_L$

$P_L^*$

Expand employment    Shrink employment

$L^*$

Units of $L$ per time period

The equation for a budget line is merely a statement of the various combinations of the inputs that can be purchased for a given dollar amount. For example, the various combinations of X and Y that can be purchased for a fixed budget, B, are given by the expression:

$$B = P_X \times X + P_Y \times Y.$$

Solving this expression for Y so that it can be graphed, as in Figure 7.12, results in:

$$Y = \frac{B}{P_Y} - \frac{P_X}{P_Y}X. \qquad \textbf{7.10}$$

Note that the first term in Equation 7.10 is the Y-axis intercept of the isocost curve. It indicates the quantity of Input Y that can be purchased with a given budget or expenditure limit, *assuming zero units of Input X are bought.* The slope of a budget line $\Delta Y/\Delta X$ equals $-P_X/P_Y$ and therefore measures the relative prices of the inputs. From this, it follows that a change in the budget level, B, leads to a parallel shift in the budget line, whereas changes in the prices of the inputs result in changes in the slope of the curve.

■ Figure 7.12
## Isocost Curves

Each point on an isocost line represents a different combination of inputs that can be
purchased for a given expenditure level.

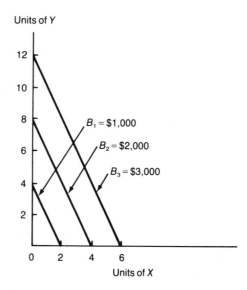

Extending the example introduced previously and illustrated in Figure 7.12 will clarify these relations. With a $1,000 budget, the $Y$-axis
intercept of the budget line has already been shown to be 4 units. Relative prices determine the slope of the budget line. Thus, in Figure 7.12
the slope of the isocost curves is given by the expression:

$$\text{Slope} = -\frac{P_X}{P_Y} = -\frac{\$500}{\$250} = -2.$$

Suppose that a firm has only $1,000 to spend on inputs for the pro-
duction of $Q$. Combining a set of production isoquants with the budget
lines of Figure 7.12 to form Figure 7.13, we find that the optimal input
combination occurs at Point $A$, the point of tangency between the budget
line and a production isoquant. At that point, $X$ and $Y$ are combined in
proportions that maximize the output attainable for expenditure $B_1$. No
other combination of $X$ and $Y$ that can be purchased for $1,000 will
produce as much output. All other $X$, $Y$ combinations along the budget
line through $X_1$, $Y_1$ must intersect isoquants representing lower output
quantities. Alternatively stated, the combination $X_1$, $Y_1$ is the least-cost
input combination that can produce output $Q_1$. All other $X$, $Y$ combinations on the $Q_1$ isoquant lie on higher budget lines. Similarly, $X_2 Y_2$ is the
least-cost input combination for producing $Q_2$, and so on. All other pos-

■ Figure 7.13
## Optimal Input Combinations

The points of tangency between the isoquant and isocost curves depict optimal input combinations at different activity levels.

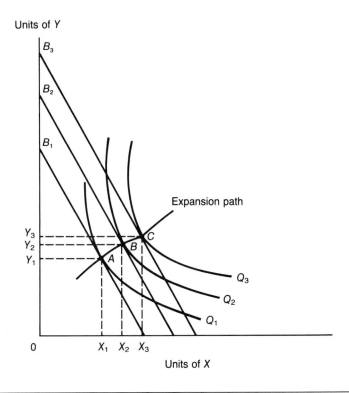

**expansion path**

Optimal input combinations for increasing output.

sible combinations for producing $Q_1$, $Q_2$, $Q_3$ are intersected by higher budget lines. By connecting points of tangency between isoquants and budget lines (Points $A$, $B$, and $C$), we identify an **expansion path** that depicts optimal input combinations as the scale of production expands.

The fact that optimal input combinations occur at points of tangency between a production isoquant and an isocost curve leads to a very important economic principle. The slope of an isocost curve was shown to equal $-P_X/P_Y$. Recall that the slope of an isoquant curve equals the marginal rate of technical substitution of one input factor for the other when production is held constant. The marginal rate of technical substitution was shown in Equation 7.6 to be given by the ratio of the marginal products of the input factors. That is, the slope of a production isoquant equals $-MP_X/MP_Y$.

At the point where inputs are combined optimally, the isocost and the isoquant curves are tangent, and, hence, their slopes are equal. Therefore, for optimal input combinations, the ratio of the prices of the inputs must be equal to the ratio of their marginal products, as is shown in Equation 7.11:

$$\frac{P_X}{P_Y} = \frac{MP_X}{MP_Y}.$$  **7.11**

Alternatively, the ratios of marginal product to price must be equal for each input:

$$\frac{MP_X}{P_X} = \frac{MP_Y}{P_Y}.$$  **7.12**

*The economic principle for least-cost combinations of inputs, as given in Equation 7.12, implies that the optimal proportions are such that an additional dollar spent on a given input adds as much to total output as would a dollar spent on any other input.* Any combination violating this rule is suboptimal in the sense that a change of inputs could result in the same quantity of output being produced for a lower cost.

The Tax Advisors, Inc., example can help illustrate these relationships. Let us assume that in addition to three CPAs, four bookkeepers are employed at a wage of $10 per hour and that $MP_{B=4} = 2$. This compares with a CPA wage of $25 per hour and $MP_{CPA=3} = 4$. Based on these assumptions, the marginal product per dollar spent is found to be:

$$\frac{MP_B}{P_B} = \frac{2}{\$10} = 0.2 \text{ (for bookkeepers)}.$$

$$\frac{MP_{CPA}}{P_{CPA}} = \frac{4}{\$25} = 0.16 \text{ (for CPAs)}.$$

This combination violates the optimal proportions rule: The ratios of marginal products to prices are not equal. The last dollar spent on the bookkeeper labor input produces ("buys") 0.2 units of output (tax-return preparations), whereas the last dollar spent on CPA time produces only 0.16 units. By transferring $1 of cost from CPA time to bookkeeper time, the firm could increase total output by 0.04 tax-return preparations per hour without increasing total cost. Expenditures on the bookkeeper input represent a better use of firm resources, and the company will reallocate resources to employ relatively more bookkeepers and relatively fewer CPAs.

It is important to recognize that the preceding analysis for determining optimal proportions of multiple inputs considers input price and input marginal product (productivity) relations only. Since the economic value of output is not considered, these data are insufficient to allow us to calculate an optimal level of total input employment. The next section again considers output value to develop the principle of optimal resource employment in production systems with multiple inputs.

## Optimal Levels of Multiple Inputs

Combining a production system's inputs in proportions that meet the conditions of Equation 7.12 insures that *any* output quantity will be produced at minimum cost. Cost minimization requires only that the ratios of marginal product to price be equal for each input—in other words, that inputs be combined in optimal proportions for a given or target level of output. Profit maximization, however, requires that a firm employ optimal input proportions *and* produce an optimal quantity of output. Thus, *cost minimization (optimal input proportions) is a necessary but not a sufficient condition for profit maximization.*

At the optimal (profit-maximizing) output level, meeting the conditions of Equation 7.12 is equivalent to employing *each* input up to the point where its marginal revenue product equals its price—the optimality condition developed in Equation 7.9. To see this, note that by the same reasoning that led to the development of Equation 7.7, the inverse of the ratios expressed in Equation 7.12 must necessarily measure the marginal cost of producing goods at any output level. That is, dividing the price of an input by the marginal product of that input is by definition the marginal cost ($MC = \Delta$Total Cost$/\Delta$Output) of producing the output that results from use of an additional unit of the input. Thus, for a two-input, single-output production system:

$$\frac{P_X}{MP_X} = MC_Q \text{ for output from a marginal unit of } X.$$

$$\frac{P_Y}{MP_Y} = MC_Q \text{ for output from a marginal unit of } Y.$$

Now, because the firm will continue employing inputs up to the point where the marginal cost of the resulting output is equal to the marginal revenue it produces (i.e., up to the point where $MC_Q = MR_Q$), the previously expressed relations result in the following system of equations at the optimal (profit-maximizing) output level:

$$\frac{P_X}{MP_X} = MR_Q \qquad\qquad \textbf{7.13}$$

and

$$\frac{P_Y}{MP_Y} = MR_Q. \qquad\qquad \textbf{7.14}$$

Rearranging produces:

$$P_X = MP_X \times MR_Q = MRP_X \qquad\qquad \textbf{7.15}$$

and

$$P_Y = MP_Y \times MR_Q = MRP_Y. \qquad\qquad \textbf{7.16}$$

Thus, *a firm's profits will be maximized when inputs are employed so that price equals marginal revenue product for each input.* The difference between cost minimization and profit maximization is that cost minimization (optimal input proportions) requires considering only the supply-related factors of input prices and marginal productivity, whereas profit maximization requires consideration of these supply-related factors *and* the demand-related marginal revenue of output. When a firm employs each input in a production system so that its *MRP* = Price, it insures that inputs are being combined in optimal proportions *and* that the total level of resource employment is optimal.

A final look at our Tax Advisors, Inc., example will illustrate these relations. Recall from our last examination of that production system that with three CPAs and four bookkeepers, the ratio of marginal products to price for these inputs indicated a need to employ more bookkeepers relative to the number of CPAs. Let us assume that hiring one more bookkeeper produces a marginal product of one tax return processed per hour ($MP_B = 1$). In addition, let us assume that with this increased employment of bookkeepers, the marginal product of the fourth CPA increases from 2 to 2.5 tax returns processed per hour. Therefore, as is typical in production, we assume that the marginal productivity of one input factor (CPAs) is enhanced when used in conjunction with more of a complementary input, bookkeepers in this case. We now have $MP_B = 1$ and $MP_{CPA} = 2.5$. With the costs of the two inputs of $P_B = \$10$ and $P_{CPA} = \$25$, we have the result that the marginal product to price ratios are equal for the two inputs:

$$\frac{MP_B}{P_B} = \frac{1}{\$10} = 0.1.$$

$$\frac{MP_{CPA}}{P_{CPA}} = \frac{2.5}{\$25} = 0.1.$$

From this we see that the combination of four CPAs and five bookkeepers is optimal from a cost-minimizing standpoint (i.e., the input *proportions* are optimal), but does it represent an optimal *level* of employment for the two inputs? (Does the resulting output level maximize profit?) To determine this, we must see if the marginal revenue products for each input equal their costs. If, as we assumed earlier, the *net* marginal revenue (NMR) per return is $10, then:

$$MRP_B = MP_B \times NMR_Q$$
$$= 1.0 \times \$10 = \$10$$
$$MRP_B = \$10 = P_B$$

and

$$MRP_{CPA} = MP_{CPA} \times NMR_Q$$
$$= 2.5 \times \$10 = \$25$$
$$MRP_{CPA} = \$25 = P_{CPA}.$$

We see that the marginal revenue product for each input equals its cost. Thus, the combination of four CPAs and five bookkeepers is an optimal *level* of employment because the resulting output quantity maximizes profit.

## 7.3　**Managerial Application**

Flexible Managers Are More Employable

During the mid-1980s, the largest companies in the U.S. economy laid off thousands of workers. Major companies such as ITT, Gulf & Western, F. W. Woolworth, General Electric, and USX, among others, made headlines as they cut employment by 75,000 to 100,000 workers *each*. Firms at the very top of the firm-size distribution, such as those found in the *Fortune 500* or *Forbes 500*, cut total employment during this period by 2 million jobs. Press coverage was intense, and commentators offered a wide variety of reasons for the decline in our nation's competitiveness. The picture that seemed to be universally portrayed was that of an inefficient and dying corporate America.

What news reports failed to point out, however, was that during this period, total civilian employment in the United States grew by more than 10 million jobs. Other successful large companies as well as small-to medium-sized corporations were quietly adding an enormous number of new job opportunities. While F. W. Woolworth shrank, Wal-Mart grew from 34,500 to 122,500 employees. Other rapidly growing firms included Sears, with around 100,000 new jobs; IBM and Digital Equipment, with roughly 50,000 new jobs each; and Federal Express, with 25,000 new jobs.

However, the real employment news of the 1980s and 1990s is the tremendous number of new job opportunities emerging in small- to medium-sized businesses. Roughly 600,000 net new jobs (additions minus deletions) were added during the mid-1980s by medium-sized employers with 20 to 99 employees. At the same time, small businesses (those businesses with 1 to 19 employees) added 1.8 million new jobs. Within these two employer-size categories, self-employ-

*continued*

See: Jonathan Clements, "The Turbulent Job Market," *Forbes*, July 13, 1987, 114–119; and Norman Alster, "What Flexible Workers Can Do," *Fortune*, February 13, 1989, 62–66.

## RETURNS TO SCALE

Thus far our discussion of production has focused on the productivity of individual inputs. A closely related topic is the question of how a proportionate increase in *all* the inputs will affect total production. This is the question of *returns to scale*, and there are three possible situations. First, if the proportional increase in all inputs is equal to the proportional increase in output, *returns to scale are constant*. For example, if a simultaneous doubling of all inputs leads to a doubling of output, then returns to scale are constant. Second, the proportional increase in output

**Managerial Application** *continued*

ment also grew by 500,000 workers, and start-ups were responsible for 700,000 new jobs. Therefore, in terms of sheer numbers, small- to medium-sized business is responsible for the recent growth in employment opportunities in the business sector. The remaining employment gains have taken place in government and in the noncorporate sector (for example, nonprofit hospitals).

Rather than being a cause for worry, recent trends in employment opportunities are characteristic of a robust and growing economic environment. Firms at the very top of the firm-size distribution, such as those making the *Fortune 500* list, tend to be in mature industries. The decline in their employment is an inevitable byproduct of this maturation. Smaller firms at an earlier point in their life cycle typically enjoy more rapid growth and are destined to supplant their larger rivals on future *Fortune 500* lists. In addition to signaling a changing of the guard among the largest firms in the U.S. economy, the job-market trends we are experiencing reflect a fundamental change in our nation's economy. Shortly after World War II, the production of industrial goods accounted for the bulk of aggregate eco-

nomic activity, and economies of scale dictated large plant sizes. Today this situation has changed dramatically. Services now account for more than two-thirds of GNP and, given the labor-intensive nature of most services, roughly three-quarters of employment opportunities.

The employment implications for today's students seem clear. Based on the statistics, most of the job opportunities that will be available to college graduates and MBAs will be with small- to medium-sized employers in the services sector instead of with industrial giants. An important difference between working for small as opposed to large employers is the relative emphasis placed on broad integrative skills rather than narrow technical expertise. Many smaller companies look for self-starters who are able to perform a wide variety of management functions. In contrast, larger companies often look for technical specialists and offer structured on-the-job training. Given the trends in today's job market, the flexible manager able to perform a large number of duties is bound to be most employable.

may be larger than that of the inputs, which is termed *increasing returns to scale*. Third, if output increases less than the proportion of input increases, we have *decreasing returns to scale*.

The returns-to-scale concept can be clarified by reexamining the production data in Table 7.1. Assume that the production system represented by those data is currently operating with 1 unit of Input X and 3 units of Input Y. Production from such an input combination would be 35 units. Suppose that we are interested in determining the effect of a 100-percent increase in the quantity of the two input factors used in the production process on the quantity of output produced. Doubling X and Y results in an input combination of X = 2 and Y = 6. Output from this input combination would be 72 units. A 100-percent increase in both $X$ and $Y$ increases output by 37 units (72 $-$ 35), a 106-percent increase (37/35 $=$ 1.06). Thus, output increases more than proportionately to the increase in the productive factors. The production system exhibits increasing returns to scale over this range of input use.

The returns to scale of a production system can vary over different levels of input use. Consider, for example, the effect of a 50-percent increase in $X$ and $Y$ from the combination $X = 2$, $Y = 6$. Increasing $X$ by 50 percent results in employment of 3 units of that factor (2 $\times$ 1.5 $=$ 3), whereas a 50-percent increase in $Y$ leads to 9 units (6 $\times$ 1.5 $=$ 9) of that input being used. The new input combination results in 89 units of production, and we see that a 50-percent increase in input factors produces only a 24-percent [(89 $-$ 72)/72 $=$ 0.24] increase in output. Since the output increase is less than proportionate to the increase in inputs, the production system exhibits decreasing returns to scale over this range of input use.

Isoquant analysis can be used to examine returns to scale for a two-input, single-output production system. Consider, in Figure 7.14, the production of $Q_1$ units of output using the input combination of $X_1Y_1$. Doubling both inputs shifts production to $Q_2$. If $Q_2$ is precisely twice as large as $Q_1$, the system is said to exhibit constant returns to scale over the range $X_1Y_1$ to $X_2Y_2$. If $Q_2$ is greater than twice $Q_1$, returns to scale are increasing, and if $Q_2$ is less than double $Q_1$, the system exhibits decreasing returns to scale.

■ Figure 7.14
## Returns to Scale

Returns to scale are measured by comparing the percentage change in output with the percentage change in all inputs.

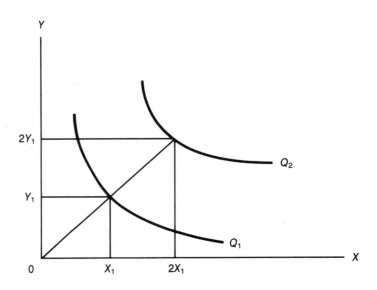

■ Figure 7.15
## Constant Returns to Scale

A production function that can be represented by a straight line from the origin indicates constant returns to scale. A given percentage change in all inputs will cause the same percentage change in output.

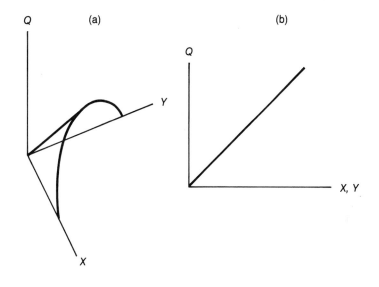

The returns to scale implicit in a given production function can also be examined in terms of two- and three-dimensional graphs, such as those drawn in Figures 7.15 through 7.18. In these graphs, the slope of a curve drawn from the origin up the production surface indicates whether returns to scale are constant, increasing, or decreasing.[6] In the production system illustrated in Figure 7.15a, for example, a curve drawn from the origin will have a constant slope, indicating that returns to scale are constant. Accordingly, the outputs for given (optimal) combinations of $X$ and $Y$ shown in Figure 7.15b are increasing exactly proportionally to increases in $X$ and $Y$. In Figure 7.16, the backbone curve from the origin exhibits a constantly increasing slope, indicating increasing returns to scale. The situation is reversed in Figure 7.17, where the production surface increases at a decreasing rate, indicating decreasing returns to scale.

A more general condition is a production function with first increasing, then decreasing returns to scale, as Figure 7.18 shows. The region of increasing returns is attributable to specialization; as output increases, specialized labor can be used and efficient, large-scale machinery can be

[6]Both inputs $X$ and $Y$ can be plotted on the horizontal axis of the (b) portions of Figures 7.15 through 7.18 because they bear constant proportions to one another. What is actually being plotted on the horizontal axis is the number of units of some fixed input combination.

■ Figure 7.16
## Increasing Returns to Scale

A curve drawn from the origin with constantly increasing slope depicts increasing returns to scale. A given percentage change in all inputs will lead to a larger percentage change in output.

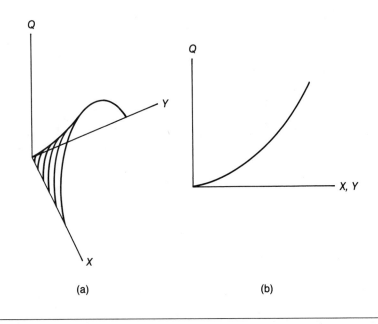

(a)                                              (b)

employed in the production process. Beyond some scale of operations, however, not only are further gains from specialization limited, but problems of coordination may also begin to increase costs substantially. When coordination expenses more than offset additional benefits of specialization, decreasing returns to scale set in.

### Output Elasticity and Returns to Scale

Even though graphic representations of returns to scale like Figures 7.15 through 7.18 are intuitively appealing, returns to scale can be more accurately determined for production functions through analysis of output elasticities. **Output elasticity,** $\epsilon_Q$, is defined as the percentage change in output associated with a 1-percent change in all inputs. Letting $\underline{X}$ represent the entire set of input factors:

**output elasticity**

The percentage change in output associated with a 1-percent change in all inputs.

$$\epsilon_Q = \frac{\text{Percentage change in output (Q)}}{\text{Percentage change in all inputs } (\underline{X})}$$

$$= \frac{\delta Q/Q}{\delta \underline{X}/\underline{X}} = \frac{\delta Q}{\delta \underline{X}} \times \frac{\underline{X}}{Q}$$

■ Figure 7.17
## Decreasing Returns to Scale

When the slope of a line drawn from the origin is constantly falling, decreasing returns to scale are indicated. A given percentage change in all inputs will lead to a smaller percentage change in output.

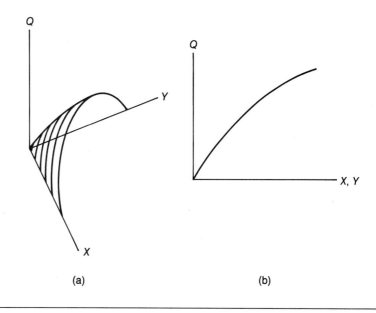

(a)          (b)

If we remember that $\underline{X}$ refers to a complete set of input factors (i.e., $\underline{X}$ = capital, labor, energy, etc.), then the following becomes clear:

| If | Then | Returns to Scale Are |
|---|---|---|
| Percentage change in $Q$ > Percentage change in $\underline{X}$ | $\epsilon_Q > 1$ | Increasing |
| Percentage change in $Q$ = Percentage change in $\underline{X}$ | $\epsilon_Q = 1$ | Constant |
| Percentage change in $Q$ < Percentage change in $\underline{X}$ | $\epsilon_Q < 1$ | Diminishing |

Therefore, returns to scale can be analyzed by examining the relationship between increases in the inputs and the quantity of output produced. For example, assume that all inputs in the unspecified production function $Q = f(X, Y, Z)$ are multiplied by the constant k. That is, all inputs are increased proportionately by the factor k (k = 1.01 for a 1-percent increase, k = 1.02 for a 2-percent increase, and so on). Then the production function can be rewritten as:

$$hQ = f(kX, kY, kZ).$$      **7.17**

■ Figure 7.18
## Variable Returns to Scale

When the slope of a line drawn from the origin varies, varying returns to scale are indicated.

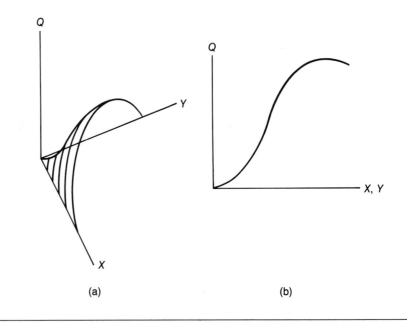

(a)                                                                (b)

---

Here $h$ is the proportional increase in $Q$ resulting from a $k$-fold increase in each input factor. From Equation 7.17, it is evident that the following relationships hold:[7]

If $h > k$, then the percentage change in $Q$ is greater than the percentage change in the inputs, $\epsilon_Q > 1$, and the production function exhibits increasing returns to scale.

If $h = k$, then the percentage change in $Q$ equals the percentage change in the inputs, $\epsilon_Q = 1$, and the production function exhibits constant returns to scale.

If $h < k$, then the percentage change in $Q$ is less than the percentage change in the inputs, $\epsilon_Q < 1$, and the production function exhibits decreasing returns to scale.

---

[7]For certain production functions called homogenous production functions, when each input factor is multiplied by a constant $k$, the constant can be completely factored out of the expression. In this case we obtain an expression of the form $hQ = k^n f(X,Y,Z)$. Here the exponent $n$ provides the key to the returns-to-scale question. If $n = 1$, then $h = k$ and the function has constant returns to scale. If $n > 1$, then $h > k$, indicating increasing returns to scale, whereas $n < 1$ indicates $h < k$ and decreasing returns to scale.

To illustrate, consider the production function $Q = 2X + 3Y + 1.5Z$. We can examine the returns to scale for this function by determining how increasing all inputs by 2 percent affects output. If, initially, $X = 1$, $Y = 2$, and $Z = 2$, output is found to be:

$$Q_1 = 2(1) + 3(2) + 1.5(2)$$

$$= 2 + 6 + 3 = 11 \text{ units.}$$

Increasing all inputs by 2 percent (letting $k = 1.02$) leads to the input quantities $X = 1.02$, $Y = 2.04$, and $Z = 2.04$, and:

$$Q_2 = 2(1.02) + 3(2.04) + 1.5(2.04)$$

$$= 2.04 + 6.12 + 3.06 = 11.22 \text{ units.}$$

Because a 2-percent increase in all inputs has led to a 2-percent increase in output ($1.02 = 11.22/11$), the system exhibits constant returns to scale.

## EMPIRICAL PRODUCTION FUNCTIONS

From a theoretical standpoint, the most appealing form of a production function might be cubic, such as the equation:

$$Q = a + bXY + cX^2Y + dXY^2 - eX^3Y - fXY^3. \qquad \textbf{7.18}$$

This form, graphed in Figure 7.18, is general in that it exhibits stages of first increasing and then decreasing returns to scale. Similarly, the marginal products of the input factors also exhibit this pattern of first increasing and then decreasing returns, as was illustrated in Figure 7.3.

Given enough input/output observations, either over time for a single firm or at a point in time for a number of firms in an industry, regression techniques can be used to estimate the parameters of the production function. Frequently, however, the data observations do not exhibit enough dispersion to indicate the full range of increasing and then decreasing returns. In these cases, simpler functional specifications can be used to estimate the production function within the range of data available. In other words, the generality of a cubic function may be unnecessary, and an alternative model specification can be used for empirical estimation. The power function described in the next section is one approximation for production functions that has proved to be extremely useful in empirical studies.

### Power Functions

One function commonly employed in production studies is the power function, which indicates a multiplicative relation between output and the various inputs and takes the form:

$$Q = aX^bY^c. \qquad \textbf{7.19}$$

Power functions have several properties that are useful in empirical research. First, power functions allow the marginal productivity of a given input to depend on the levels of *all* inputs employed, a condition that often holds in actual production systems. Second, they are linear in logarithms and thus can be easily analyzed using linear regression analysis (see Appendix 2A). That is, Equation 7.19 is equivalent to:

$$\log Q = \log a + b \log X + c \log Y. \qquad \textbf{7.20}$$

The least squares technique can be used to estimate the coefficients of Equation 7.20 and thereby the parameters of Equation 7.19. Third, power functions facilitate returns-to-scale estimation. Returns to scale are easily calculated by summing the exponents of the power function (or, alternatively, by summing the loglinear model coefficient estimates). If the sum of the exponents is less than one, diminishing returns are indicated. A sum greater than one indicates increasing returns. Finally, if the sum of the exponents is exactly one, returns to scale are constant, and the powerful tool of linear programming, described in Chapter 10, can be used to determine the optimal input/output relations for the firm.

Power functions have been employed in a large number of empirical production studies, particularly since Charles W. Cobb and Paul H. Douglas's pioneering work in the late 1920s. The impact of this work was so great that power production functions are now frequently referred to as Cobb–Douglas production functions.

## Selection of a Functional Form
## for Empirical Studies

Many other functional forms are available for empirical production study. As with empirical demand estimation, the primary determinant of the functional form used for the empirical model depends on the relation hypothesized by the researcher. In many instances, however, several plausible alternative model specifications must be fitted to the data to determine which form seems most representative of actual conditions.

Case 7.1

# Productivity in Education:
# Issues in Defining and Measuring Output

The enhancement of worker productivity is an important challenge facing managers today. Productivity enhancement is vital given the role of labor as a key input in the production of goods and services and in light of the generally increasing vigor of domestic and import competition. Of course, before incentives to enhance worker productivity can be introduced, the multiple dimensions of worker productivity must be made explicit and accurately measured. Management must be able to clearly articulate the many important dimensions of worker output and communicate this information effectively to workers.

The business and popular press is replete with examples of firms and industries that have foundered because of problems tied to the inaccurate measurement of "blue-collar" worker productivity. When worker incentives are carelessly tied to piece-rate production, mass quantities of low-quality output sometimes result. Similarly, worker incentive pay plans that emphasize high-quality output can fail to provide necessary incentives for timely delivery. What is often overlooked in discussions of worker efficiency and labor productivity is that the definition and measurement of productivity is perhaps even more difficult in the case of managers themselves and other "white-collar" workers. Problems encountered in the definition and measurement of white-collar-worker productivity can be illustrated by considering the productivity of college and university professors.

For most two-year and four-year college and university professors, teaching is a primary component of their work assignment. Faculty members have a standard teaching load, defined by the number of class hours per term, number of students taught, or a multiple of the two called "student contact hours." However, not all student contact hours are alike. For example, it is possible to generate large numbers of student contact hours per faculty member simply by offering courses in a mass lecture setting with hundreds of students per class. In other cases a faculty member might work with a very small number of students in an advanced seminar or laboratory course, generating relatively few student credit hours. The teaching "product" in each of these course settings is fundamentally similar, but few would argue with the position that numbers of students taught would be an inappropriate basis for comparing productivity of the professors teaching the different types of classes.

Additionally, no one would suggest defining teaching productivity solely in terms of the sheer quantity of students taught. Student course evaluations are typically required to provide evidence from student "customers" concerning the quality of instruction. Many schools rely on such data as an exclusive measure of teaching quality. At other schools, student course-evaluation data are supplemented by peer review of teaching methods and materials, interviews of former students, and so on. Measures of both the quantity and quality of instruction must be employed in the measurement of teaching productivity.

In addition to their important teaching role, faculty members are expected to play an active role in the ongoing administration of their academic institution. At a minimum, they participate in the peer review of faculty, in student and faculty recruiting, and in curriculum and program development. Often, faculty also play an active role on the committees that conduct the everyday management of the institution. Indeed, this faculty governance system is an important organizational difference between most academic and nonacademic institutions. Faculty members are both workers *and* management. Measuring "output" and, hence, productivity as related to these activities is very difficult.

At many schools, faculty members also play an important liaison role with external constituents. Alumni provide important financial resources to colleges and universities and appreciate programs designed for their benefit. Nondegree "short courses" are often offered on topical subjects at nominal charge for the benefit of alumni and the community at large. Similarly, faculty are asked to give lectures to local groups, interviews for the local media, and informal consulting services to local firms and organizations. Often these services are provided for free or at nominal charge as part of the faculty member's "service" function. Similarly, faculty are sometimes called on to provide service to external academic and professional organizations. Participation at national and regional academic conventions and helping in the design and writing of professional exams are typical examples of expected but unpaid services.

The preceding duties are supplemented by faculty research requirements at most four-year colleges and universities and at all graduate institutions. This requirement is fundamental to the growth and development of colleges and universities but is often misunderstood by those outside of academia. To be granted the doctoral degree, doctoral candidates must not only complete a rigorous series of courses and exams but they must also meet a dissertation requirement. A doctoral dissertation is a book-length independent study that makes an important contribution to knowledge in a scholarly discipline. In fulfilling this requirement, doctoral students demonstrate their capacity to participate in the discovery of new knowledge. A key difference between the role of university professors and that of other teachers is that professors must be intimately involved with the creation *and* dissemination of new knowledge. Thus, the research component is a key ingredient of professorial output.

Research output is extremely varied. In the physical sciences, new compounds or other physical products may result. Similarly, such research may lead to new process techniques. In most academic fields the primary research product is new knowledge, communicated in the form of research reports or other scholarly publications. As with teaching, measuring the quantity and quality of research output proves to be most challenging. Judging the value of a research product is often quite subjective, and its worth may not be recognized for years.

Given the difficulties involved with evaluating highly specialized and detailed research, many institutions consider the dollar amount of research funds awarded to an individual to be a useful indicator of the quantity and quality of research output. It is anomalous that a school's best researchers and highest-paid faculty members may be the least expensive in terms of their net costs to the institution. When established researchers are able to consistently obtain external funding in excess of incremental costs, their net employment costs can be nil. In such instances, the disadvantages to an institution of losing a "star" researcher are obvious.

Of course, just as in the case of measuring teaching quality, difficulties are encountered in measuring the quality of published research output. In most instances, the quality of published articles and books is judged in terms of the reputation of the publisher or editor, the level of readership enjoyed, and so on. Over time, the number of new research outlets has grown to keep pace with the growing level of specialization in the various disciplines. In economics, for example, there are as many as 200 possible research outlets. However, only a relative handful of these are widely read in any given subdiscipline. Competition for scarce journal space in such outlets is fierce. Acceptance rates at leading journals often average no more than 5 to 10 percent of those articles submitted. When one considers that a productive scholar is typically able to complete no more than one or two substantial research projects per year, the odds are against achieving publication of one or two first-rate journal articles per year. Thus, research productivity is usually measured in terms of both the quantity and quality of published research.

In sum, defining the role of professors at colleges and universities provides an interesting example of the difficulties involved in measuring worker productivity. Each individual academic institution must define on an ongoing basis the relative importance of the teaching, research, and service components of faculty output. Once this has been determined, the difficult task of defining and measuring faculty-member productivity on each dimension must begin.

Based on the preceding information and in light of the focus of your academic institution, answer the following questions:
A. How would you define faculty-member productivity?
B. Do you agree with the view that many elements of professorial output don't easily lend themselves to quantitative evaluation? How might you measure such productivity?
C. Would productivity clauses for professors' contracts make sense economically? What problems do you see in implementing such clauses in actual practice?
D. Reconsider your answers to Parts A through C for other service-industry occupations (for example, doctors, lawyers, and legislators). Are the issues discussed unique to academia?

## SUMMARY

In this chapter we learned that a firm's *production function* relates inputs to outputs, showing the maximum product obtainable from a given set of inputs. It is determined by the technological level of the plant and equipment employed.

Several important properties of production systems were examined, including the substitutability of inputs—a characteristic expressed by the *marginal rate of substitution*—and diminishing *returns to factor* inputs. The production function was also used to demonstrate that only those input combinations for which the *marginal products* of all input factors are positive need be analyzed to determine the optimal input proportions.

Adding prices to the analysis enabled us to specify the necessary conditions for optimality in input combination. The least-cost combination of inputs requires input proportions such that an additional dollar's worth of each input adds as much to total output as does a dollar's worth of any other input. Algebraically, this is given by the expression:

$$\frac{MP_X}{P_X} = \frac{MP_Y}{P_Y}.$$

It was also demonstrated that employment of resources up to the point where the *marginal revenue products* equaled price resulted not only in a least-cost input combination but also in a profit-maximizing activity level. Algebraically this relation is given by the expressions:

$$MRP_X = P_X,$$

and

$$MRP_Y = P_Y.$$

The question of *returns to scale* was also examined, and methods for measuring this property were illustrated. Returns to scale in production play a major role in determining market structure, a topic examined in Chapters 11 and 12.

Empirical estimation of production functions frequently uses the statistical methods of regression analysis. Although theoretical considerations indicate that cubic equations, with their greater generality, might be preferred for estimation purposes, it was shown that simpler functional forms are often quite adequate for estimation of production relations. In fact, the power function, or the Cobb–Douglas production function, is by far the most frequently encountered form in empirical work.

### Questions

7.1  Using the total product curve illustrated below:

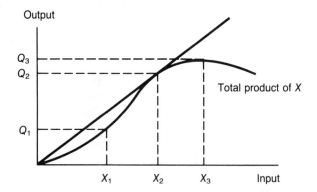

A. Describe both geometrically and verbally the marginal product and the average product associated with Output $Q_1$.
B. At what points along the curve will the marginal and the average products be maximized?
C. How could you use the related marginal product curve to identify the maximum rational quantity of input for Factor $X$, holding constant the amounts of all other inputs?

7.2 Given the following isoquant diagram (in which $L^*$ and $K^*$ indicate the optimal combination for producing Output $Q^*$ as determined by a tangency between an isocost curve and an isoquant curve):

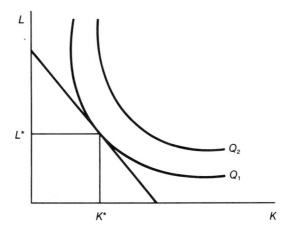

A. What would be the effect in this production system on the isocost and isoquant curves and on the optimal input combination of an increase in the relative productivity of labor, $L$?
B. What would be the effect on the curves and on the input combination referred to in Part A of a technological change that increased the productivity of capital, $K$?
C. What would be the effect of a change that proportionally increased the effectiveness of both labor and capital simultaneously?

7.3 Using a diagram of isoquant and isocost curves like those shown in Question 7.2, demonstrate that both relative input prices and factor productivity play roles in determining optimal input combinations.

7.4 Is the use of least-cost input combinations a necessary condition for profit maximization? Is it a sufficient condition? Explain.

7.5 "Output per worker is expected to increase by 10 percent during the next year. Therefore, wages can also increase by 10 percent with no harmful effects on employment, output prices, or employer profits." Discuss this statement.

7.6 Commission-based and piece rate–based compensation plans are commonly employed by businesses. Use the concepts developed in the chapter to explain this phenomenon.

7.7 "Hourly wage rates are an anachronism. Efficiency requires incentive-based pay tied to performance." Discuss this statement.

7.8  Explain why the *MP/P* relation is deficient as the sole mechanism for determining the optimal level of resource employment.

7.9  Develop the appropriate relations for determining the optimal quantities of all inputs to employ in a production system, and explain the underlying rationale.

7.10  Suppose that labor, capital, and energy inputs must be combined in fixed proportions. Does this mean that returns to scale will be constant?

## Problems

7.1  The following production table provides estimates of the maximum amounts of output possible with different combinations of two input factors, *X* and *Y*. (Assume that these are just illustrative points on a spectrum of continuous input combinations.)

| Units of Y Used | Estimated Output per Day | | | | |
|---|---|---|---|---|---|
| 5 | 210 | 305 | 360 | 421 | 470 |
| 4 | 188 | 272 | 324 | 376 | 421 |
| 3 | 162 | 234 | 282 | 324 | 360 |
| 2 | 130 | 188 | 234 | 272 | 305 |
| 1 | 94 | 130 | 162 | 188 | 210 |
| | 1 | 2 | 3 | 4 | 5 |

**Units of X Used**

A.  Do the two inputs exhibit the characteristics of constant, increasing, or decreasing marginal rates of technical substitution? How do you know?

B.  Assuming that output sells for $3 per unit, complete the following tables:

| | X Fixed at 2 Units | | | |
|---|---|---|---|---|
| Units of Y Used | Total Product of Y | Marginal Product of Y | Average Product of Y | Marginal Revenue Product of Y |
| 1 | | | | |
| 2 | | | | |
| 3 | | | | |
| 4 | | | | |
| 5 | | | | |

| | **Y Fixed at 3 Units** | | | |
|---|---|---|---|---|
| **Units of X Used** | **Total Product of X** | **Marginal Product of X** | **Average Product of X** | **Marginal Revenue Product of X** |
| 1 | | | | |
| 2 | | | | |
| 3 | | | | |
| 4 | | | | |
| 5 | | | | |

C. Assume that the quantity of $X$ is fixed at 2 units. If output sells for $3 and the cost of $Y$ is $120 per day, how many units of $Y$ will be employed?

D. Assume that the company is currently producing 162 units of output per day using 1 unit of $X$ and 3 units of $Y$. The daily cost per unit of $X$ is $120 and that of $Y$ is also $120. Would you recommend a change in the present input combination? Why or why not?

E. What is the nature of the returns to scale for this production system if the optimal input combination requires that $X = Y$?

7.2 Indicate whether each of the following statements is *true* or *false*. Explain why.

A. Decreasing returns to scale and declining average costs are indicated when $\epsilon_Q < 1$.

B. If the marginal product of capital falls as capital usage grows, the returns to capital are decreasing.

C. L-shaped isoquants describe production systems in which inputs are perfect substitutes.

D. Marginal revenue product measures the profit earned through expanding input usage.

E. The marginal rate of technical substitution will be affected by a given percentage increase in the marginal productivity of all inputs.

7.3 During recent years, computer-aided design (CAD) and computer-aided manufacturing (CAM) have become prevalent in many U.S. industries. Holding all else equal, indicate whether each of the following factors would be responsible for increasing or decreasing this prevalence. Why?

A. Rising worker pension costs

B. Technical advances in computer mainframe design

C. An increase in the nondomestic (import) share of the market

D. Falling prices for industry output

E. Computer software that is increasingly user-friendly

7.4  Determine whether the following production functions exhibit constant, increasing, or decreasing returns to scale.

A.  $Q = 0.5X + 2Y + 40Z$

B.  $Q = 3L + 10K + 500$

C.  $Q = 4A + 6B + 8AB$

D.  $Q = 7L^2 + 5LK + 2K^2$

E.  $Q = 10L^{0.5}K^{0.3}$.

7.5  W. E. Mowrey, Inc., based in St. Paul, Minnesota, manufactures and distributes dental supplies. President Walt Mowrey is reviewing the company's sales-force compensation plan. Currently, the company pays its three experienced sales staff members salaries based on years of service, past contributions to the company, and so on. Bill Michaels, a new sales trainee, is paid a more modest salary. Monthly sales and salary data for each employee are as follows:

| Sales Staff | Average Monthly Sales | Monthly Salary |
| --- | --- | --- |
| Jeanne Mooty | $160,000 | $6,000 |
| Ken Davidson | 100,000 | 4,500 |
| Anne Corrow | 90,000 | 3,600 |
| Bill Michaels | 75,000 | 2,500 |

Michaels has shown great promise during the past year, and Mowrey believes that a substantial raise is clearly justified. At the same time, some adjustment to the compensation paid to other sales personnel also seems appropriate. Mowrey is considering changing from his current compensation plan to one based on a 5-percent commission. He sees such a plan as being fairer to the parties involved and believes it would also provide strong incentives for needed market expansion.

A.  Calculate Mowrey's salary expense for each employee expressed as a percentage of the monthly sales generated by that individual.

B.  Calculate monthly income for each employee under a 5-percent of monthly sales commission-based system.

C.  Will a commission-based plan result in efficient relative salaries, efficient salary levels, or both?

7.6  The First National Bank received 3,000 inquiries following the latest advertisement describing its 30-month IRA account in the *Boston World*, a local newspaper. The most recent ad in a similar advertising campaign in *Massachusetts Business*, a regional business magazine, generated 1,000 inquiries. The newspaper ads cost $500, whereas each magazine ad costs $125.

    A. Assuming additional ads would generate similar response rates, is the bank running an optimal mix of newspaper and magazine ads? Why or why not?

    B. Holding all else equal, how many inquiries must a newspaper ad attract for the current advertising mix to be optimal?

7.7 Medical Testing Labs, Inc., provides routine testing services for blood banks in the Los Angeles area. Tests are supervised by skilled technicians using equipment produced by two leading competitors in the medical equipment industry. Records for the current year show an average of 27 tests per hour being performed on the Testlogic-1 and 48 tests per hour on a new machine, the Accutest-3. The Testlogic-1 is leased for $18,000 per month, and the Accutest-3 is leased at a rate of $32,000 per month. On average, each machine is operated 25 eight-hour days per month.

    A. Does company usage reflect an optimal mix of testing equipment?

    B. If tests are conducted at a price of $6 each while labor and all other costs are fixed, should the company lease more machines?

7.8 Ticket Services, Inc., offers ticket promotion and handling services for concerts and sporting events. The Chicago branch office makes heavy use of spot radio advertising on WNDY–AM, with each 30-second ad costing $100. During the past year, the following relation between advertising and ticket sales per event has been observed:

$$\text{Sales (units)} = 5,000 + 100A - 0.5A^2.$$

Here $A$ represents a 30-second radio spot ad, and sales are measured in numbers of tickets.

    Harry Stone, manager for the Chicago office, has been asked to recommend an appropriate level of advertising. In thinking about this problem, Stone noted its resemblance to the optimal resource employment problem he had studied in a managerial economics course that was part of his MBA program. The advertising–sales relation could be thought of as a production function, with advertising as an input and sales as the output. The problem is to determine the profit-maximizing level of employment for the input, advertising, in this "production" system. Stone recognized that to solve the problem, he needed a measure of output value. After reflection, he determined that the value of output is $2 per ticket, the net marginal revenue earned by Ticket Services (price minus all marginal costs except advertising).

    A. Continuing with Stone's production analogy, what is the "marginal product" of advertising?

    B. What is the rule for determining the optimal amount of a resource to employ in a production system? Explain the logic underlying this rule.

    C. Using the rule for optimal resource employment, determine the profit-maximizing number of radio ads.

7.9   Robert Hartly & Associates is a large human-resource management consulting firm with offices located throughout the United States. Output at the firm is measured in billable hours, which vary between partners and associates.

Partner time is billed to clients at a rate of $100 per hour, whereas associate time is billed at a rate of $50 per hour. On average, each partner generates 25 billable hours per 40-hour workweek, with 15 hours spent on promotion, administrative, and supervisory responsibilities. Associates generate an average of 35 billable hours per 40-hour workweek and spend 5 hours per week in administrative and training meetings. Variable overhead costs average 50 percent of revenues generated by partners, and, given supervisory requirements, 60 percent of revenues generated by associates.

A.  Calculate the annual (50 workweeks) net marginal revenue product of partners and associates.

B.  Assuming that partners earn $65,000 and associates earn $30,000 per year, does the company have an optimal combination of partners and associates? If not, why not? Make your answer explicit and support any recommendations for change.

7.10 Consider the following Cobb-Douglas production function for bus service in a typical metropolitan area:

$$Q = b_0 L^{b_1} K^{b_2} F^{b_3},$$

where

$Q$ = Output in millions of passenger miles;

$L$ = Labor input in worker hours;

$K$ = Capital input in bus transit hours;

$F$ = Fuel input in gallons.

Each of the parameters of this model was estimated by regression analysis using monthly data over a recent three-year period. Results obtained were as follows (standard errors in parentheses):

$$\hat{b}_0 = 1.2, \ \hat{b}_1 = 0.28, \ \hat{b}_2 = 0.63, \text{ and } \hat{b}_3 = 0.12.$$
$$(0.4) \qquad (0.15) \qquad (0.12) \qquad (0.07)$$

A.  Estimate the effect on output of a 4-percent decline in worker hours (holding $K$ and $F$ constant).

B.  Estimate the effect on output of a 3-percent reduction in fuel availability accompanied by a 4-percent decline in bus transit hours (holding $L$ constant).

C.  Calculate the returns to scale for this production system.

APPENDIX · 7 A

# A Constrained Optimization Approach to Developing the Optimal Input Combination Relationships

It was noted in Chapter 7 that the determination of optimal input proportions could be viewed either as a problem of maximizing output for a given expenditure level or, alternatively, as a problem of minimizing the cost of producing a specified level of output. In this appendix, we show how the Lagrangian technique for constrained optimization can be used to develop the optimal input proportion rule.

## Constrained Production Maximization

Consider the problem of maximizing output from a production system described by the general equation:

$$Q = f(X, Y) \qquad \text{7A.1}$$

subject to a budget constraint. The expenditure limitation can be expressed as:

$$E^* = P_X \cdot X + P_Y \cdot Y, \qquad \text{7A.2}$$

which states that the total expenditure on inputs, $E^*$, is equal to the price of Input $X$, $P_X$, times the quantity of $X$ employed, plus the price of $Y$, $P_Y$, times the quantity of that resource used in the production system. Equation 7A.2 can be rewritten in the form of a Lagrangian constraint, as developed in Chapter 2, as:

$$0 = E^* - P_X \cdot X - P_Y \cdot Y. \qquad \text{7A.3}$$

The Lagrangian function for the maximization of the production function, Equation 7A.1, subject to the budget constraint expressed by Equation 7A.3, can then be written as:

$$\text{Max } L_Q = f(X, Y) + \lambda(E^* - P_X \cdot X - P_Y \cdot Y). \qquad \text{7A.4}$$

Maximization of the constrained production function is accomplished by setting the partial derivatives of the Lagrangian expression taken with respect to $X$, $Y$, and $\lambda$ equal to zero, and then solving the resultant system of equations. The partials of Equation 7A.4 are:

$$\frac{\partial L_Q}{\partial X} = \frac{\partial f(X, Y)}{\partial X} - \lambda P_X = 0, \qquad \text{7A.5}$$

$$\frac{\partial L_Q}{\partial Y} = \frac{\partial f(X, Y)}{\partial Y} - \lambda P_Y = 0, \qquad \text{7A.6}$$

and

$$\frac{\partial L_Q}{\partial \lambda} = E^* - P_X \cdot X - P_Y \cdot Y = 0. \qquad \textbf{7A.7}$$

Equating these three partial derivatives to zero results in a set of conditions that must be met for output maximization subject to the budget limit.

Note that the first terms in Equations 7A.5 and 7A.6 are the marginal products of $X$ and $Y$ respectively. That is, $\partial f(X, Y)/\partial X$ is $\partial Q/\partial X$, which by definition is the marginal product of $X$; and the same is true for $\partial f(X, Y)/\partial Y$. Thus, those two expressions can be rewritten as:

$$MP_X - \lambda P_X = 0$$

and

$$MP_Y - \lambda P_Y = 0,$$

or, alternatively, as:

$$MP_X = \lambda P_X \qquad \textbf{7A.8}$$

and

$$MP_Y = \lambda P_Y. \qquad \textbf{7A.9}$$

Now, the conditions required for constrained output maximization, expressed by Equations 7A.8 and 7A.9, are also expressed by the ratio of equations. Thus:

$$\frac{MP_X}{MP_Y} = \frac{\lambda P_X}{\lambda P_Y}. \qquad \textbf{7A.10}$$

Cancelling the lambdas in Equation 7A.10 results in the optimality conditions developed in the chapter:

$$\frac{MP_X}{MP_Y} = \frac{P_X}{P_Y}. \qquad \textbf{7A.11}$$

For maximum production, given a fixed expenditure level, the input factors must be combined in such a way that the ratio of their marginal products is equal to the ratio of their prices. Alternatively, transposing in Equation 7A.11 to derive the expression:

$$\frac{MP_X}{P_X} = \frac{MP_Y}{P_Y},$$

we see that optimal input proportions require that the ratio of marginal product to price for all input factors must be equal.

## Constrained Cost Minimization

The relationship developed above is also derivable from the problem of minimizing the cost of producing a given quantity of output. In this case the constrained optimization problem is developed as follows. The constraint states that some level of output, $Q^*$, must be produced from the production system described by the function $Q = f(X, Y)$. Written in the standard Lagrangian format the constraint is $0 = Q^* - f(X, Y)$. The cost, or expenditure, function is given as $E = P_X \cdot X + P_Y \cdot Y$. The Lagrangian function for the constrained cost minimization problem, then, is:

$$L_E = P_X \cdot X + P_Y \cdot Y + \lambda[Q^* - f(X, Y)]. \qquad \textbf{7A.12}$$

Again, as shown above, the conditions for constrained cost minimization are provided by the partial derivatives of Equation 7A.12:

$$\frac{\partial L_E}{\partial X} = P_X - \lambda \frac{\partial (fX, Y)}{\partial X} = 0, \qquad \textbf{7A.13}$$

$$\frac{\partial L_E}{\partial Y} = P_Y - \lambda \frac{\partial (fX, Y)}{\partial Y} = 0, \qquad \textbf{7A.14}$$

and

$$\frac{\partial L_E}{\partial \lambda} = Q^* - f(X, Y) = 0. \qquad \textbf{7A.15}$$

Notice that the terms on the left-hand side in Equations 7A.13 and 7A.14 are the marginal products of $X$ and $Y$ respectively, so those expressions can be rewritten as:

$$P_X - \lambda MP_X = 0$$

and

$$P_Y - \lambda MP_Y = 0,$$

or, alternatively, as:

$$P_X = \lambda MP_X \qquad \textbf{7A.16}$$

and

$$P_Y = \lambda MP_Y. \qquad \textbf{7A.17}$$

Taking the ratio of Equation 7A.16 to Equation 7A.17 and cancelling the lambdas again produces the basic input optimality relation:

$$\frac{P_X}{P_Y} = \frac{MP_X}{MP_Y}.$$

# Problem

7A.1  Assume that a firm produces its product in a system described in the following production function and price data:

$$Q = 3X + 5Y + XY,$$
$$P_X = \$3,$$
$$P_Y = \$6.$$

Here, $X$ and $Y$ are two variable input factors employed in the production of $Q$.

A. What are the optimal input proportions for $X$ and $Y$ in this production system? Is this combination rate constant regardless of the output level?

B. It is possible to express the cost function associated with the use of $X$ and $Y$ in the production of $Q$ as Cost $= P_X X + P_Y Y$, or Cost $= \$3X + \$6Y$. Use the Lagrangian technique to determine the maximum output that the firm can produce operating under a \$1,000 budget constraint for $X$ and $Y$. Show that the inputs used to produce that level of output meet the optimality conditions derived in Part A.

C. What is the additional output that could be obtained from a marginal increase in the budget?

D. Assume that the firm is interested in minimizing the cost of producing 14,777 units of output. Use the Lagrangian method to determine what optimal quantities of $X$ and $Y$ to employ. What will be the cost of producing that output level? How would you interpret $\lambda$, the Lagrangian multiplier, in this problem?

## Selected References

Ashton, James E., and Frank X. Cook, Jr. "Time to Reform Job Shop Manufacturing." *Harvard Business Review* 67 (March–April 1989): 106–111.

Avishai, Bernard. "A CEO's Common Sense of CIM: An Interview with J. Tracy O'Rourke." *Harvard Business Review* 67 (January–February 1989): 110–117.

Banker, Rajiv D., Srikant M. Datar, and Sunder Kekre. "Relevant Costs, Congestion and Stochasticity in Production Environments." *Journal of Accounting and Economics* 10 (July 1988): 171–197.

Carson, Richard, and Peter Navarro. "A Seller's (and Buyer's) Guide to the Job Market for Beginning Economists." *Journal of Economic Perspectives* 2 (Spring 1988): 137–148.

Chew, W. Bruce. "No-Nonsense Guide to Measuring Productivity." *Harvard Business Review* 66 (January–February 1988): 110–118.

Darrow, William P. "An International Comparison of Flexible Manufacturing Systems." *Interfaces* 17 (November–December 1987): 86–91.

Eaton, Adrienne E., and Paula B. Voos. "The Ability of Unions to Adapt to Innovative Workplace Arrangements." *American Economic Review* 79 (May 1989): 172–176.

Gordon, Paul J. "What Do Professors Do?" *Business Horizons* 29 (May–June 1986): 38–43.

Griliches, Zvi. "Productivity Puzzles and R&D: Another Nonexplanation." *Journal of Economic Perspectives* 2 (Fall 1988): 9–22.

John, George, and Barton Weitz. "Salesforce Compensation: An Empirical Investigation of Factors Related to Use of Salary versus Incentive Compensation." *Journal of Marketing Research* 26 (February 1989): 1–14.

Jorgenson, Dale W. "Productivity and Economic Growth in Japan and the United States." *American Economic Review* 78 (May 1988): 217–222.

Jorgenson, Dale W. "Productivity and Postwar U.S. Economic Growth." *Journal of Economic Perspectives* 2 (Fall 1988): 23–42.

Kumpe, Ted, and Piet T. Bolwijn. "Manufacturing: The New Case for Vertical Integration." *Harvard Business Review* 66 (March–April 1988): 75–81.

Levine, Phillip B., and Olivia S. Mitchell, "The Baby Boom's Legacy: Relative Wages in the Twenty-First Century." *American Economic Review* 78 (May 1988): 66–69.

Mansfield, Edwin. "Technological Change in Robotics: Japan and the United States." *Managerial and Decision Economics* 10 (Spring 1989): 19–25.

Mefford, Robert N. "Introducing Management into the Production Function." *Review of Economics and Statistics* 63 (February 1981): 96–104.

Miller, Edward M. "A Graphical Analysis of Replacement," *Southern Economic Journal* 54 (July 1987): 206–211.

Montgomery, Edward, and William Wascher. "Creative Destruction and the Behavior of Productivity over the Business Cycle." *Review of Economics and Statistics* 70 (February 1988): 168–172.

Moriarty, Rowland T., and Gordon S. Swartz. "Automation to Boost Sales and Marketing." *Harvard Business Review* 67 (January–February 1989): 100–108.

Teece, David J. "Inter-organizational Requirements of the Innovation Process." *Managerial and Decision Economics* 10 (Spring 1989): 35–42.

# Cost Analysis

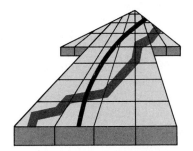

Cost analysis plays a central role in managerial economics because virtually every managerial decision requires a comparison between costs and benefits. For example, a decision to expand output requires that the increased revenues derived from added sales be compared with the higher production costs incurred. Likewise, a decision to expand capital assets requires a comparison between the revenues expected from the investment and the cost of funds required for it. The expected benefits of an advertising promotion must be compared with the costs of the program. A decision to pave the employees' parking lot or refurbish the company lunchroom requires a comparison between the projected costs and benefits expected to result from improved morale and productivity. In each case, decision analysis requires a comparison of costs and the benefits resulting from the decision.

In this chapter we examine a number of cost concepts, including alternative (or opportunity) costs, explicit versus implicit costs, marginal costs, incremental costs, and sunk costs. We also relate production costs to production functions and develop long-run and short-run cost functions suitable for empirical measurement. The materials in this chapter are useful for managerial decision making; they also help us understand how various industry structures develop and the implications of public policy that alters the structure of industry.

## RELEVANT COST CONCEPT

The term *cost* can be defined in a number of ways, and the correct definition varies from situation to situation, depending upon how the cost figure is to be used. Cost generally refers to the price that must be paid for an item. If we buy a product for cash and use it immediately, few problems arise in defining and measuring its cost. However, if the item is purchased, stored for a time, and then used, complications can arise. The problem is even more acute if the item is a long-lived asset like a machine tool or a computer that will be used at varying rates for some indeterminate period. What then is the cost of using the asset during any given period, or to produce a specific output?

The cost that should be used in a specific decision situation is called the **relevant cost.** When calculating costs for a firm's income tax returns, the law requires use of the actual dollar amount spent to purchase the labor, raw materials, and capital equipment used in production. Thus, for tax purposes, actual historical dollar outlays are the relevant costs. This is also generally true for Securities and Exchange Commission reports and for annual reports to stockholders.

For most managerial decisions, however, historical costs may not be appropriate. Typically, current and projected future costs are more relevant than historical outlays. For example, consider a construction firm that has an inventory of 1,000 tons of steel purchased at a price of $250 a ton. Steel prices now double to $500 a ton. If the firm is asked to bid on a project, what cost should it assign to the steel used in the job, the $250 historical cost or the $500 current cost? The answer is the current cost. The firm must pay $500 to replace the steel it uses, and it can sell the steel for $500 if it elects not to use it on the proposed job. Therefore, $500 is the *relevant cost* of steel for purposes of bidding on the job. Note, however, that the cost of steel for tax purposes is still the $250 historical cost.

Similarly, if a firm owns a piece of equipment that has been fully depreciated (that is, its accounting book value is zero), it cannot assume that the cost of using the machine is zero. If the machine could be sold for $1,000 now, but its market value is expected to be only $200 one year from now, the relevant cost of using the machine for one additional year is $800.[1] Again, there is little relation between the $800 true cost of using the machine and the zero cost that would be reported on the firm's income statement.

**relevant cost**

Any cost that actually affects a given decision situation and therefore should be considered in the decision process.

## OPPORTUNITY COSTS

The preceding discussion of relevant costs is based upon an alternative-use concept. Economic resources have value because they can be used to produce goods and services. When a firm uses a resource for producing a particular product, it bids against alternative users. Thus, the firm must offer a price at least as great as the resource's value in an alternative

---

[1]This statement slightly oversimplifies the fact. Actually, the cost of using the machine for one year is the current value minus the discounted present value of its value one year hence. This adjustment is necessary to account for the fact that dollars received in the future have a lower *present* worth than dollars received today.

use. The cost of aluminum used in the manufacture of airplanes, for example, is determined by its value in alternative uses. An airplane manufacturer must pay a price equal to this value or the aluminum will be used in the production of alternative goods, such as cookware, automobiles, building materials, and so on. Similarly, if a firm owns capital equipment that can be used to produce either Product *A* or Product *B*, the relevant cost of producing *A* includes the profit of the alternative Product *B* that cannot be produced because the equipment is tied up manufacturing Product *A*.

**opportunity cost**

**The value of a resource in its best alternative use.**

The term **opportunity cost** expresses this idea that the relevant cost of a resource is determined by its value in its best alternative use. In other words, opportunity cost is the value that must be foregone in using a resource for one specific purpose or in undertaking one specific activity.

## EXPLICIT AND IMPLICIT COSTS

**explicit costs**

**Out-of-pocket expenses for which there is a cash payment.**

**implicit costs**

**Noncash costs measured by the opportunity-cost concept.**

Typically, the costs of using resources in production involve both out-of-pocket or **explicit costs** and other noncash costs called **implicit costs.** Wages paid, utility expenses, payment for raw materials, interest paid to the holders of the firm's bonds, and rent on a building are all examples of explicit expenses. The implicit costs associated with any decision are much more difficult to compute. These costs do not involve cash expenditures and are therefore often overlooked in decision analysis. Since cash payments are not made for implicit costs, the opportunity-cost concept must be used to measure them. The rent a shop owner could receive on buildings and equipment if they were not used in the business is an implicit cost of the owner's own retailing activities, as is the salary that individual could receive by working for someone else instead of operating his or her own retail establishment.

An example should clarify these cost distinctions. Consider the costs associated with the purchase and operation of a Mother Baker's Pie Shop. The franchise can be bought for $25,000, and an additional $25,000 working capital is needed for operating purposes. Jones has personal savings of $50,000 that he can invest in such an enterprise; Smith, another possible franchisee, must borrow the entire $50,000 at a cost of 15 percent, or $7,500 a year. Assume that operating costs are the same no matter who owns the shop, and that Smith and Jones are equally competent managers. Does Smith's $7,500 annual interest expense mean that her costs of operating the shop are greater than those of Jones? For managerial decision purposes, the answer is no. Even though Smith has higher explicit costs because of the interest on the loan, the true financing cost, implicit as well as explicit, may well be the same for both individuals. Jones has an implicit cost equal to the amount he can earn on his $50,000 in some alternative use. If he can obtain a 15-percent return by investing in other assets of equal risk, then Jones's opportunity cost of putting his $50,000 in the pie shop is $7,500 a year. In this case,

Smith and Jones each have a financing cost of $7,500 a year. Smith's cost is explicit and Jones's is implicit.

Can we then say that the total cost of operating the shop will be identical for both individuals? Not necessarily. Just as the implicit cost of Jones's capital must be included in the analysis, so too must be the implicit cost of management. If Jones is a journeyman baker earning $35,000 a year and Smith is a master baker earning $45,000 annually, the implicit cost of management will not be equal for the two. The implicit management expense for Smith is equal to her value in her best alternative use, the $45,000 she would earn as a master baker. Jones, on the other hand, has an opportunity cost of only $35,000. Thus, Smith's relevant total costs of owning and operating the shop will be $10,000 higher than those of Jones.

## INCREMENTAL AND SUNK COSTS IN DECISION ANALYSIS

**incremental cost**

A cost that varies among the alternatives in a decision and is therefore relevant to that decision.

The relevant-cost concept also entails the idea of incremental cost. This means that for any decision, the relevant costs are limited to those that are affected by the decision. This definition of **incremental costs** as costs that vary with the decision is very much like that for the marginal concept, which was introduced as a key component in the optimization process. One must take care to recognize, however, that these two concepts, although related, differ considerably. The primary distinction is that marginal costs are always defined in terms of unitary changes in output. The incremental-cost concept is considerably broader, encompassing not only the marginal-cost concept but also cost variations that arise from any aspect of the decision problem. For example, we can speak of the incremental costs of introducing a new product line or changing the production system used to produce the current product(s) of a firm.

The incremental-cost concept means that fixed costs that will not be affected by a decision are irrelevant and should not be included in the analysis. Consider, for example, a firm that refuses to sell excess computer time for $300 an hour because it figures its cost as $350 per hour, calculated by adding a standard overhead cost of $150 an hour to an incremental operating cost of $200 an hour. The relevant cost is only $200, so the firm foregoes a $100-per-hour contribution to profit by not selling its excess time. Adding a standard allocated charge for fixed costs and overhead that are not affected by a decision entails the risk of rejecting profitable opportunities or choosing a less satisfactory alternative.

Care must also be exercised to insure against incorrectly assigning a lower incremental cost to a decision than is appropriate. This frequently happens to firms faced with temporary reductions in demand resulting in excess production capacity. Such firms often accept contracts at prices that cover operating expenses but that do not fully cover all overhead nor provide a normal profit margin. The firm accepts on the grounds that the contract price appears to exceed incremental costs and thus contributes to total overhead and profit. After accepting, other business picks up. Soon the firm is faced with turning away more profitable business or incurring higher production costs. In this situation, the true incremental costs include the increased production costs of other business or perhaps the foregone profit of business that must be turned down because of capacity constraints. It is important to remember that incremental costs include *all* costs that are affected by the decision. This means that future costs as well as current costs must be considered and opportunity costs cannot be ignored.

Inherent in the incremental-cost concept is the principle that any cost that is not affected by the decision is irrelevant to that decision. Costs that do not vary across the alternatives are called **sunk costs;** they play no role in determining the optimal course of action. For example, if a firm has unused warehouse space that will otherwise stand empty, the cost of storing a new product in it will be zero, and zero is the incremental storage cost that should be considered in deciding whether to produce the new product.

Similarly, a firm may have spent $5,000 on an option to purchase land for a new factory at a price of $100,000. Later it may be offered another equally usable site for $90,000. The $5,000 is a sunk cost; it will not be affected by the decision about which piece of property is acquired, and it should not enter into the analysis. To understand this, consider the alternatives available at the time the firm is faced with the decision to purchase the original property or to acquire the second property. If the firm proceeds with the purchase of the first property, it will have to pay a price of $100,000. The newly offered property will require an expenditure of $90,000. These are the relevant costs for the decision, and, obviously, purchase of the $90,000 property results in a $10,000 savings as compared to the original property. The $5,000 paid for the original option is an expense that will not be affected by the decision at this time. It is a sunk cost that is invariant regardless of which property is actually acquired.

Because of the frequency with which sunk costs are incorrectly treated in managerial decision making, another example should be helpful. Assume that a firm is offered a contract for $12,000 to build and install the heating and air-conditioning ducts in a new building. Labor and other operating expenses for the job are estimated to be $8,000. The firm has all the materials required to complete the work in its inventory. Assume that the materials (primarily sheet metal) originally cost the firm $5,000 but that price declines have resulted in a current market value of $3,000. The market for sheet metal is not likely to change in the near future, so no gains are expected from holding the materials in inventory. Should the firm accept the contract?

Correct analysis of this contract proposal requires us to recognize that the $5,000 original cost for the materials in inventory is a sunk cost; it will not be affected by the decision. The firm has suffered a $2,000 loss

**sunk costs**

Costs that are not affected by a specific decision and are therefore irrelevant to that decision.

## 8.1  **Managerial Application**

The Role of Time in Cost Analysis

The short run is the operating period within which at least some operating expenses are fixed. This means that previous managerial decisions have resulted in some expenses that are unavoidable during the current period. In contrast, the long run is the planning period during which the manager has complete flexibility concerning all input and output decisions. In the long run, all expense categories are subject to change, and all costs are variable.

What is often overlooked in discussions of the distinction between variable and fixed costs is the importance of timing in production decisions. For example, when workers are employed at an aging production facility, the wage bargaining power of a union can be severely compromised. If plant and equipment must be upgraded or replaced, all added plant and equipment expenditures, plus variable labor expenses, will be considered incremental costs for decision

making purposes. In this instance, company threats to abandon an entire operation must be considered viable, and wage concessions will be closely related to worker productivity. Conversely, if a company has recently built an expensive and specialized new production facility, these plant and equipment costs will often be considered fixed and irrelevant to ongoing operating decisions. Since operating decisions are made on the basis of incremental revenues and costs, managers will compare variable labor, raw material, and other input costs with the entire marginal value resulting from production. The company may thus find itself susceptible to union wage bargaining and may have to grant higher wages than would otherwise be the case.

This explains why in 1988, for example, Chrysler Corporation was willing to close an aging production facility in Kenosha, Wisconsin, that it had acquired from American

*continued*

See: Shirley Hobbs Scheibla, "Nothing to Lose but Jobs," *Barron's*, April 4, 1988, 14, 15, 56.

in inventory value regardless of whether or not it accepts the contract. The relevant materials cost is the current market value of the sheet metal ($3,000). Including this cost in the analysis leads one to the correct decision, which is to accept the contract because it results in a $1,000 gain for the firm.

In managerial decision making, care must be exercised to insure that the analysis considers only costs that are actually affected by the decision. The incremental costs associated with a given course of action can include both implicit and explicit costs. If a decision entails long-run

**Managerial Application** *continued*

Motors Corporation rather than grant wage and other concessions to members of the militant Local 72 of the United Automobile Workers union. Similarly, the massive layoffs experienced in the steel industry during the late 1970s and early 1980s reflected, at least in part, the fact that unions made high wage demands at a time when substantial expenditures for new and renovated plant and equipment were necessary.

Contractual obligations also play an important role in the distinction between variable and fixed costs. Although wages for assemblers and other blue-collar workers are often considered the classic example of variable costs, labor contracts calling for a minimum number of hours per year convert this important expense from variable to fixed costs. Thus, details of the firm's labor contract can determine whether labor costs should be treated as fixed or variable. Similarly, mortgage and lease expenses are fixed once an agreement has been signed. Before such an agreement has been reached, however, such costs are variable.

Cost categories also vary from one firm to another. Fixed costs for one company will sometimes constitute variable costs for others. This is especially true in the case of potential entrants. For example, Coors operates the largest brewery in the world in Golden, Colorado, from which it ships beverage products to markets all across the United States. Coors's substantial economies of scale in production offset the higher transportation costs of shipping to distant customers. Potential entrants to the Colorado market realize that in order to compete effectively, they must commit substantial resources for new plant and equipment, whereas plant and equipment expenses are already established and fixed for Coors; these expenses would involve a substantial additional outlay of funds and, hence, are variable costs for new competitors. Prior to entry, *all* costs are variable, even plant and equipment expenditures. However, subsequent to entry, and after the construction of production facilities, these expenses become fixed in nature.

Therefore, careful consideration of both the nature *and* timing of managerial decisions is necessary to make the important distinction between fixed and variable costs. After the decision to begin production has been made, some important cost categories become fixed. However, when the firm is entirely free to enter or exit a given market, all costs are variable.

commitments, any future costs stemming from those commitments must be accounted for. Any cost that is not affected by the decision alternatives available to a manager is a sunk cost and is irrelevant for purposes of that decision.

## SHORT-RUN AND LONG-RUN COSTS

Proper use of the relevant-cost concept for output and pricing decisions requires an understanding of the relation between a firm's cost and output, or its *cost function*. Cost functions depend on (1) the firm's produc-

**short-run cost function**

An operating cost function constrained by prior investment and other multiperiod commitments.

**long-run cost function**

A planning cost function that is not constrained by prior decisions.

**short run**

A period during which some inputs of a firm are fixed.

**long run**

A period of sufficient length that a company may alter all factors of production without restriction.

tion function and (2) input prices. The production function specifies the technical relation between inputs and the output and, when combined with the prices of inputs, determines the cost function. Two basic cost functions are used in managerial decision making: **short-run cost functions,** used in most day-to-day operating decisions, and **long-run cost functions,** typically used for long-range planning.

How does one distinguish the short run from the long run? The **short run** is defined as a period during which some inputs of a firm are fixed. In the **long run,** the firm can increase, decrease, or otherwise alter *all* factors of production without restriction. Thus, in the short run, the firm's decisions are constrained by prior capital expenditures and other commitments; in the long run, no such restrictions exist. For a public accounting firm operating out of a rented office, this period of constraint might be as short as several weeks, the time remaining on the office lease. A steel company, on the other hand, has a substantial investment in long-lived fixed assets, and the period during which its decisions will be affected by that investment is lengthy.

Both the economic life of a firm's assets and their degree of specialization will affect the period during which decisions are constrained. Consider, for example, a drugstore's purchase of an automobile for making deliveries. If the car is a standard model without modifications, it is essentially an unspecialized input factor; the car has a resale market based on the used-car market in general, and the pharmacy can sell it readily without an undue price reduction. If, however, the pharmacy has modified the car by adding refrigeration equipment for transporting perishable medicines, the car is a more specialized resource and its resale market is limited to those individuals and firms who need a vehicle with refrigeration equipment. In this case, the market price of the car might not equal its value in use to the pharmacy; hence, the short run is extended. At one extreme, a firm operating with perfectly unspecialized factors has a very brief short run; it can adjust to changes almost immediately by disposing of or purchasing assets in well-established markets. When a firm employs highly specialized factors, however, no ready market exists; the firm's short run extends for the entire economic life of the resources it currently owns.

The length of time required to order, receive, and install new assets also influences the duration of the short run. Electric utilities, for example, frequently require eight or more years to bring new generating plants on line, and this obviously extends their short-run time horizon.

In summary, the long run is a period of sufficient length to permit a company to change its productive facilities completely by adding, subtracting, or modifying assets. The short run is the period during which at least some of the firm's productive inputs cannot be altered. From this it is easy to see why long-run cost curves are often called *planning curves* and short-run curves are called *operating curves*. In the long run, plant and equipment are variable, so management can plan the most efficient physical plant, given an estimate of the firm's demand function. Once the optimal plant has been determined and the resulting investment in equipment has been made, operating decisions will be constrained by these prior decisions.

## Fixed and Variable Costs

**fixed costs**

Costs that do not vary with respect to output.

Costs that do not vary with respect to output are called **fixed costs.** Included are interest on borrowed capital, rental expense on leased plant and equipment, depreciation charges associated with the passage of time, property taxes, and salaries of employees who would not be laid off during periods of reduced activity. Since all costs are variable in the long run, the fixed-cost concept is limited to short-run analysis.

**variable costs**

Costs that vary with changes in output.

**Variable costs** vary with changes in output; they are a function of the output level. Included are such costs as raw materials, depreciation associated with the use of equipment, the variable portion of utility charges, some labor costs, sales commissions, and the costs of all other inputs that vary with output. In the long run, all costs are variable.

Such a sharp distinction between fixed and variable costs is not always realistic. A president's salary may be fixed for most purposes, but if a firm went into a severe downturn, this so-called fixed cost could certainly be reduced. Similarly, supervisors' wages are fixed within a certain range of output, but below a lower limit, supervisors might be laid off, and above an upper limit, additional supervisors would be hired. Also, the longer the duration of abnormal demand, the greater the likelihood that some "fixed" costs will actually be varied.

The recognition that some costs are fixed only if output stays within prescribed limits and that other costs can and will be varied if changed conditions are expected to persist led to the development of the *semivariable-cost* concept. In incremental cost analysis, it is essential that one consider the possibility of semivariable costs, which are fixed if incremental output does not exceed certain limits but are variable outside these bounds.

## SHORT-RUN COST CURVES

Short-run total cost curves are constructed to reflect optimal (or least-cost) input combinations for producing output *given a specific plant size.* For an existing plant, the short-run cost curve illustrates the minimum costs required to produce at various output levels and, therefore, it can be used to guide the current operating decisions of the firm.

Both fixed and variable costs affect the short-run costs of a firm. Total cost at each output level is the sum of total fixed costs (a constant) and total variable costs. Using $TC$ to represent total cost, $TFC$ for total fixed cost, $TVC$ for total variable cost, and $Q$ for the quantity of output produced, various unit costs are calculated as follows:

$$\text{Total Cost} = TC = TFC + TVC.$$

$$\text{Average Fixed Cost} = AFC = \frac{TFC}{Q}.$$

$$\text{Average Variable Cost} = AVC = \frac{TVC}{Q}.$$

$$\text{Average Total Cost} = ATC = \frac{TC}{Q} = AFC + AVC.$$

$$\text{Marginal Cost} = MC = \frac{\Delta TC}{\Delta Q} = \frac{dTC}{dQ}.$$

These cost relations are illustrated in Table 8.1 and Figure 8.1. Using the data in Table 8.1, one can both identify the various cost relationships and examine some important cost behavior. For example, note that *TFC* is invariant with increases in output and that *TVC* at each level of output equals the sum of *MC* up to that output.

Marginal cost is the change in cost associated with a *change* in output, and because fixed costs do not vary with respect to output, fixed costs do not affect marginal costs. The data also show that *AFC* declines continuously with increases in output and that *ATC* and *AVC* decline so long as they exceed *MC*, but they increase when they are less than *MC*. Thus:

$$MC = \frac{dTC}{dQ} = \frac{dTVC}{dQ}.$$

These cost relations are also shown in Figure 8.1. Figure 8.1a illustrates total cost and total variable cost curves. The corresponding unit curves appear in Figure 8.1b. Again, several important cost relations are illustrated in the figure. First, the shape of the total cost curve is deter-

■ Table 8.1

## Short-Run Cost Relations

| Q | TC | TFC | TVC | ATC | AFC | AVC | MC |
|---|---|---|---|---|---|---|---|
| 1 | $120 | $100 | $ 20 | $120.0 | $100.0 | $20.0 | $20 |
| 2 | 138 | 100 | 38 | 69.0 | 50.0 | 19.0 | 18 |
| 3 | 151 | 100 | 51 | 50.3 | 33.3 | 17.0 | 13 |
| 4 | 162 | 100 | 62 | 40.5 | 25.0 | 15.5 | 11 |
| 5 | 175 | 100 | 75 | 35.0 | 20.0 | 15.0 | 13 |
| 6 | 190 | 100 | 90 | 31.7 | 16.7 | 15.0 | 15 |
| 7 | 210 | 100 | 110 | 30.0 | 14.3 | 15.7 | 20 |
| 8 | 234 | 100 | 134 | 29.3 | 12.5 | 16.8 | 24 |
| 9 | 263 | 100 | 163 | 29.2 | 11.1 | 18.1 | 29 |
| 10 | 300 | 100 | 200 | 30.0 | 10.0 | 20.0 | 37 |

■ Figure 8.1
## Short-Run Cost Curves

(a) The productivity of variable input factors determines the slope of both the total and variable cost curves. An increase (decrease) in fixed costs shifts the total cost curve upward (downward), but it has no effect on variable cost curves. (b) Marginal cost declines to $Q_1$. Both average total cost and average variable costs fall (rise) when marginal cost is lower (higher).

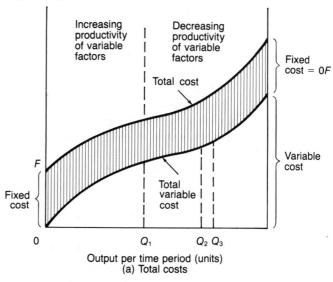

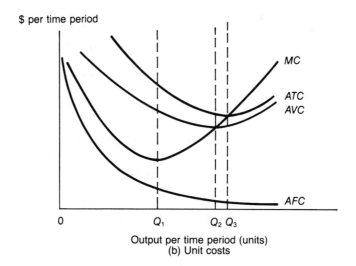

mined entirely by the total variable cost curve. That is, the slope of the total cost curve at each output level is identical to the slope of the total variable cost curve; fixed costs merely shift the total cost curve to a higher level. This means that marginal costs are totally independent of fixed cost.

Second, the shape of the total variable cost curve, and hence the total cost curve, is largely determined by the productivity of the variable input factors employed. Note that the variable cost curve in Figure 8.1 increases first at a decreasing rate up to output level $Q_1$ and then at an increasing rate. Assuming constant input factor prices, this implies that the marginal productivity of variable production inputs first increases, then decreases. In other words, the variable input factors exhibit increasing returns in the range of 0 to $Q_1$ units and diminishing returns thereafter. This relation is not unexpected. A firm's fixed factors, its plant and equipment, are designed to operate at some specific production level. Operating below that output level requires input combinations in which fixed factors are underutilized. In this output range, production can be increased more than proportionately to increases in variable inputs. At higher-than-planned output levels, however, fixed factors are being more intensively utilized, the law of diminishing returns takes over, and a given percentage increase in the variable inputs will result in a smaller relative increase in output.

This relation between short-run costs and the productivity of variable input factors is also revealed by the unit cost curves. Marginal cost declines initially over the range of increasing productivity and rises thereafter. This imparts the familiar *U* shape to the average variable cost and average total cost curves. Notice also that the marginal cost curve first declines rapidly in relation to the average variable cost curve and the average total cost curve, then turns up and intersects each of these curves at its respective minimum point.[2]

## LONG-RUN COST CURVES

In the long run, the firm has no fixed commitments; accordingly, all long-run costs are variable. Also, just as short-run cost curves assume optimal, or least-cost, input combinations for producing any level of output, *given a specific scale of plant*, long-run cost curves are constructed on the assumption that an optimal plant, *given existing technology*, is used to produce any given output level. *Existing technology* refers to the state of knowledge in the industry. If technological improvements occur, as in the development of more efficient smelting processes in a foundry, the old production and cost functions are replaced by new, possibly quite different functions.

---

[2]The relations among total, average, and marginal curves were discussed in Chapter 2, where we explained why the marginal cost curve intersects the average variable cost and the average total cost curves at their minimum points.

Long-run cost curves reveal both the nature of returns to scale and optimal, or preferred, plant sizes. Thus, long-run cost curves guide a firm's planning decisions.

## Long-Run Total Costs

If the prices of a firm's inputs are not affected by the amount of the resource purchased, a *direct* relation exists between cost and production. Consider a production function that exhibits constant returns to scale, as was illustrated in Figure 7.15. Such a production function is linear, and doubling inputs leads to doubled output. With constant input prices, doubling inputs doubles their total cost, producing a linear total cost function, as illustrated in Figure 8.2.

If a firm's production function is subject to decreasing returns to scale, as was illustrated in Figure 7.17, inputs must more than double in order to double output. Again, assuming constant input prices, the cost function associated with a production system of this kind will rise at an increasing rate, as is shown in Figure 8.3.

A production function exhibiting first increasing and then decreasing returns to scale was shown in Figure 7.18. This production function is

■ Figure 8.2
## Total Cost Function for a Production System Exhibiting *Constant* Returns to Scale

With constant returns to scale and constant input prices, an increase in all inputs will lead to a proportionate increase in total costs and output.

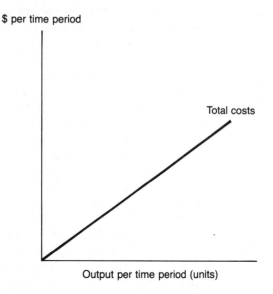

■ Figure 8.3

## Total Cost Function for a Production System Exhibiting *Decreasing* Returns to Scale

With decreasing returns to scale and constant input prices, input usage and total costs rise faster than a given increase in output.

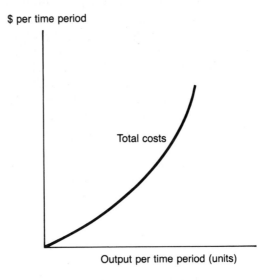

shown again along with its implied cubic cost function in Figure 8.4. Here costs increase less than proportionately with output over the range where returns to scale are increasing but more than proportionately after decreasing returns set in.

All of the direct relations between production and cost functions just described are based on constant input prices. If input prices are a function of output, owing to such factors as discounts for volume purchases or, alternatively, to higher prices with greater usage because of a limited supply of inputs, the cost function will reflect this fact. For example, the cost function of a firm that has constant returns to scale but whose input prices increase with quantity purchased will take the shape shown in Figure 8.3. Costs will rise more than proportionately as output increases. Quantity discounts, on the other hand, will produce a cost function that increases at a decreasing rate, as in the increasing returns section of Figure 8.4.

We see, then, that although cost and production are related, the nature of input prices must be examined before we attempt to relate a cost function to the underlying production function. Input prices and productivity jointly determine the total cost function.

■ Figure 8.4

## Total Cost Function for a Production System Exhibiting *Increasing,* then *Decreasing* Returns to Scale

Total cost functions often display an S-shape, reflecting varying returns to scale at various activity levels.

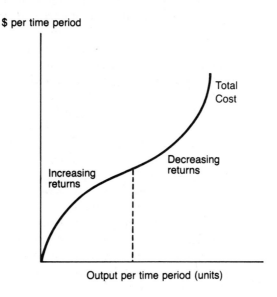

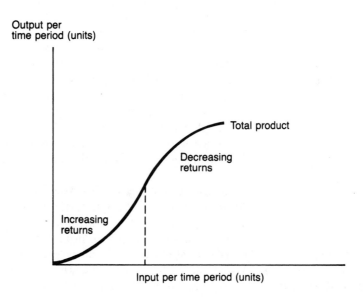

## Returns to Scale

**economies of scale**

Production or marketing advantages that lead to a decline in long-run average costs.

Many factors combine to produce the frequently encountered pattern of first increasing, then decreasing returns to scale.[3] **Economies of scale,** which cause long-run average costs to decline, result from both production and market-related factors. Specialization in the use of labor is one important factor that results in economies of scale. In the small firm, workers generally do several jobs, and their proficiency at any of them is likely to be less than that of employees who specialize in a single task. Thus, labor productivity is frequently greater in the large firm, where individuals can be hired to perform specialized tasks. This reduces the unit cost of production for a large-scale operation.

Technological factors also lead to economies of scale. As with labor, large-scale operations typically permit the use of highly specialized equipment, as opposed to the more versatile but less efficient machines used in smaller firms. Also, the productivity of equipment frequently increases with size much faster than its cost. For example, a 500,000-kilowatt electricity generator costs considerably less than two 250,000-kilowatt generators, and it also requires less fuel and fewer labor inputs when operated at capacity.

The existence of quantity discounts also leads to economies through large-scale purchasing of raw materials, supplies, and other inputs. These economies extend to the cost of capital, as large firms typically have greater access to capital markets and can acquire funds at lower rates. These factors and many more lead to increasing returns to scale and thus to decreasing average costs.

At some output level, economies of scale typically no longer hold, and average costs level out or begin to rise. Increasing average costs at high output levels are often attributed to limitations in the ability of management to coordinate an organization after it reaches a very large size. This means both that staffs tend to grow more than proportionately with output, raising unit costs, and that managements become less efficient as size increases, again raising the cost of producing a product. Although the existence of such diseconomies of scale is questioned by some researchers, the evidence indicates that diseconomies may indeed limit firm sizes in certain industries.

## Cost Elasticities and Returns to Scale

**cost elasticity**

A measure that indicates the percentage change in total costs associated with a 1-percent change in output.

Although Figures 8.2, 8.3, and 8.4 are useful for illustrating the total cost–output relation to returns to scale, it is often easier to calculate scale economies for a given production system by considering cost elasticities. **Cost elasticity,** $\epsilon_c$, measures the percentage change in total costs associated with a 1-percent change in output.

Algebraically the elasticity of cost with respect to output is:

---

[3]The terms *economies of scale* and *returns to scale* are often used interchangeably.

$$\epsilon_c = \frac{\text{Percentage Change in Total Cost (TC)}}{\text{Percentage Change in Output (Q)}}$$

$$= \frac{\partial TC/C}{\partial Q/Q}$$

$$= \frac{\partial TC}{\partial Q} \times \frac{Q}{TC}.$$

Cost elasticity is related to economies of scale as follows:

| If | | Then | Returns to Scale Are |
|---|---|---|---|
| Percentage change in $TC$ < Percentage change in $Q$ | | $\epsilon_c < 1$ | Increasing |
| Percentage change in $TC$ = Percentage change in $Q$ | | $\epsilon_c = 1$ | Constant |
| Percentage change in $TC$ > Percentage change in $Q$ | | $\epsilon_c > 1$ | Decreasing |

With a cost elasticity of less than one ($\epsilon_c < 1$), costs increase at a slower rate than output. Given constant input prices, this would imply a higher output-to-input ratio and increasing returns to scale. If $\epsilon_c = 1$, then output and costs increase proportionately, implying constant returns to scale. And finally, if $\epsilon_c > 1$, then for any increase in output, costs increase by a greater relative amount, implying decreasing returns to scale. To prevent confusion concerning cost elasticity and returns to scale, remember that an inverse relation holds between costs and scale economies and a direct relation holds between resource usage and scale economies. Thus, although $\epsilon_c < 1$ implies increasing returns to scale, because costs are increasing more slowly than output, recall from Chapter 7 that an output elasticity greater than one ($\epsilon_Q > 1$) implies increasing returns to scale, because output is increasing faster than input usage. Similarly, decreasing returns to scale are implied by $\epsilon_c > 1$ and by $\epsilon_Q < 1$. These relations are the result of the correspondence between cost functions and the underlying production functions.

## Long-Run Average Costs

Additional insight into both scale economies and the relationship between long-run and short-run costs can be obtained by examining long-run average cost (*LRAC*) curves. Since short-run cost curves relate costs and output for a specific scale of plant and long-run cost curves identify optimal scales of plant for each production level, *LRAC* curves can be thought of as an envelope of short-run average cost (*SRAC*) curves. This concept is illustrated in Figure 8.5, which shows four short-run average cost curves representing four different scales of plant. Each of the four plants has a range of output over which it is most efficient. Plant *A*, for example, provides the least-cost production system for output in the

■ Figure 8.5

## Short-Run Cost Curves for Four Scales of Plant

Short-run cost curves represent the most efficient range of output for a given plant size. The solid portion of each *SRAC* curve indicates the minimum long-run average cost for each level of output.

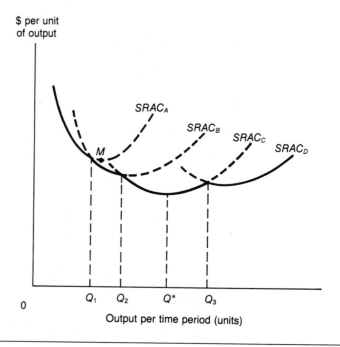

range 0 to $Q_1$ units; Plant *B* provides the least-cost system for output in the range $Q_1$ to $Q_2$; Plant *C* is most efficient for output quantities $Q_2$ to $Q_3$; and Plant *D* provides the least-cost production process for output above $Q_3$.

The solid portion of each curve in Figure 8.5 indicates the minimum long-run average cost for producing each level of output, assuming only four possible scales of plant. We can generalize this by assuming that plants of many sizes are possible, each only slightly larger than the preceding one. As shown in Figure 8.6, the long-run average cost curve is then constructed tangent to each short-run average cost curve. At each point of tangency, the related scale of the plant is optimal; no other plant will produce that particular level of output at so low a total cost. The cost systems illustrated in Figures 8.5 and 8.6 display first increasing, then decreasing returns to scale. Over the range of output produced by Plants *A*, *B*, and *C* in Figure 8.5, average costs are declining; these declining costs mean that total costs are increasing less than proportionately with output. Since Plant *D*'s minimum cost is greater than that for Plant *C*, the system exhibits decreasing returns to scale at this higher output level.

■ Figure 8.6
## Long-Run Average Cost Curve as the Envelope of Short-Run Average Cost Curves

The long-run average cost curve is the envelope of short-run average cost curves. The optimal scale for a plant is found at the point of minimum long-run average costs.

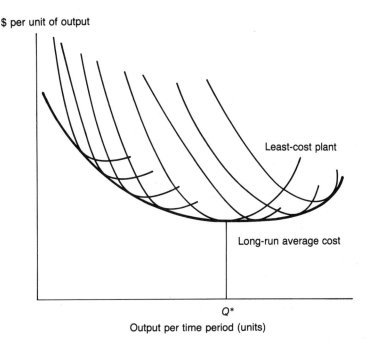

Production systems that reflect first increasing, then constant, then diminishing returns to scale result in U-shaped long-run average cost curves such as the one illustrated in Figure 8.6. Notice that with a U-shaped long-run average cost curve, the most efficient plant for each output level will typically not be operating at the point where its short-run average costs are minimized, as can be seen by referring to Figure 8.5. Plant *A*'s short-run average cost curve is minimized at Point *M*, but at that output level, Plant *B* is more efficient; that is, *B*'s short-run average costs are lower. In general, increasing returns to scale means that the least-cost plant for an output level will operate at less than full capacity. Here we define **capacity** not as a physical limitation on output but rather as the point at which short-run average costs are minimized. Only for that single output level at which long-run average cost is minimized, output $Q^*$ in Figures 8.5 and 8.6, will the optimal plant be operating at the minimum point on its short-run average cost curve. At all levels of output in the range with decreasing returns to scale (that is, at any output greater than $Q^*$), the most efficient plant will be operating at an output level slightly greater than its capacity.

**capacity**
The output level at which short-run average costs are minimized.

## 8.2 **Managerial Application**
When Large Size Is a Disadvantage

When economies of scale are substantial, larger firms are able to achieve lower costs of production or distribution than their smaller rivals. These cost advantages translate into higher and more stable profits, and a permanent competitive advantage for larger firms in some industries. Diseconomies of large-scale organizations work in the opposite direction. When diseconomies of scale are operative, larger firms suffer a cost disadvantage when compared to their smaller rivals. Smaller firms are then able to translate the benefits of small size into a distinct competitive advantage. Rather than losing profits and sales opportunities to their larger rivals, these smaller firms can enjoy higher profit rates and a gain in market share over time.

Even though the concept of diseconomies of large size is well known, it is sometimes not appreciated how common the phenomenon is in actual practice. In many sectors, smaller companies have emerged as a domi-

nant competitive force. In many industries offering business and consumer services, smaller firms are typically better able to quickly meet the specialized needs of their customers and have successfully met competition from large companies. For example, Merrill Lynch & Company is an acknowledged leader in the provision of financial services to the U.S. and many foreign governments and to institutional and retail brokerage customers. In 1989, the company had over $11 billion in revenues and more than 43,000 employees. Merrill Lynch is roughly 22 times the size of A. G. Edwards Inc., a St. Louis–based regional brokerage firm. Nevertheless, it is the performance of A. G. Edwards, not Merrill Lynch, that is the envy of the industry. A. G. Edwards has a three-year average return on stockholders' equity that exceeds 16.4 percent per year, much higher than Merrill Lynch's 10.6 percent. Similarly, its "stick to the knitting" style of management has led to a 23.1-percent aver-

*continued*

See: John A. Byrne, "Is Your Company Too Big?" *Business Week*, March 27, 1989, 84–94.

## MINIMUM EFFICIENT SCALE

The shape of long-run average cost curves is important not only because of its implications for plant scale decisions but also because of its effects on the potential level of competition in an industry. Even though U-shaped cost relations are quite common, they are not universal. In some industries, firms encounter first increasing, then constant returns to

**Managerial Application** *continued*

age annual rate of growth in sales, compared to 17.7 percent for Merrill Lynch.

Even in many sectors of industrial manufacturing, the highly flexible and customer-sensitive nature of many smaller companies has led to distinct competitive advantages. For example, although early advances in large mainframe computers were historically the domain of larger companies such as IBM, the vast majority of innovations in the computer industry during the 1980s —the personal computer, minicomputer, supercomputer, and user-friendly software —have been started or commercialized by venture-backed entrepreneurial companies.

In the past, when foreign visitors wanted to experience firsthand the latest innovations in U.S. business and administrative practice, they found it mandatory to stop and visit major corporations in Chicago, Detroit, New York, and Pittsburgh. Today, it is far more likely that they would make stops at Boston's Route 128, California's Silicon Valley, or North Carolina's Research Triangle. In many key industries, from electronics instruments to specialized steel, smaller companies have replaced larger companies in positions of industry leadership. Indeed, the trend towards a higher level of efficiency for smaller companies has become widespread. During 1989, *Business Week* magazine's review of the 1,000 largest companies in America found that the largest companies are the most profitable— as measured using return on shareholders' equity—in only 4 out of 67 industries!

In general, industries dominated by large firms tend to be those in which there are significant economies of scale, important advantages to vertical integration, and a prevalence of mass marketing. As a result, large organizations with sprawling plants emphasize large quantities of output at low production costs. Use of national media, especially TV advertising, is common. In contrast, industries in which "small is beautiful" tend to be those characterized by diseconomies of scale, considerable advantages to subcontracting for "just in time" assembly and manufacturing, and niche marketing that emphasizes the use of highly skilled individuals adept at personal selling. Small factories with flexible production schedules are common. Rather than mass quantity, many smaller companies emphasize quality. Rather than the sometimes slow-to-respond hierarchical organizations of large companies, smaller companies feature "flat" organizations with decentralized decision making and authority.

Increasingly, larger companies are finding that meeting the needs of the customer sometimes requires a dramatic downsizing of the large-scale organization.

**minimum efficient scale**
The output level at which long-run average costs are first minimized.

scale. In such instances, an L-shaped long-run average cost curve emerges, and very large plants are at no relative cost disadvantage as compared with smaller plants. Typically, the number of competitors and ease of entry will be greater in industries with U-shaped long-run average cost curves than in those with L-shaped or continuously downward-sloping long-run average cost curves. Insight into this area is gained by examining the concept of the **minimum efficient scale** (MES) plant. MES is defined as the output level at which long-run average costs are first minimized. Thus, MES will be found at the minimum point on a U-shaped long-run average cost curve (output $Q^*$ in Figures 8.5 and 8.6) and at the corner of an L-shaped long-run average cost curve.

Generally speaking, the number of competitors will be large and competition will tend to be most vigorous within industries in which the MES is small relative to total industry demand because of correspondingly small barriers to entry such as those relating to capital investment and skilled labor requirements. Competition can be less vigorous when MES is large relative to total industry output, because barriers to entry tend to be correspondingly substantial, limiting the number of potential competitors. In considering the competitive impact of a given MES level, we must always consider the overall size of the industry. Some industries are large enough to accommodate substantial numbers of very large competitors. In such instances, even though MES is large in an absolute sense, it can be quite small in a relative sense, allowing for vigorous competition. Furthermore, when the cost disadvantage of operating less than MES-size plants is relatively small, there will seldom be serious anticompetitive consequences. In summary, the barrier-to-entry effects of MES depend upon the size of the MES plant relative to total industry demand as well as the slope of the long-run average cost curve at points of less than MES-size operations.

## Transportation Costs and MES

Transportation costs play an important role in determining the efficient scale of operation. Transportation costs include terminal, line-haul, and inventory charges associated with moving output from production facilities to customers. Terminal charges consist of handling expenses necessary for the loading and unloading of shipped materials. Since terminal charges do not vary with the distance of shipment, they are as high for short hauls as for long hauls. Line-haul expenses include the equipment, labor, and fuel costs associated with moving a given commodity a specified distance. They tend to vary directly with the distance goods are shipped. Although line-haul expenses are relatively constant on a per-mile basis, they vary widely from one commodity to another. For example, it costs more to ship a ton of fresh fruit 500 miles than to ship a ton of steel a similar distance. Fresh fruit comes in odd shapes and sizes and requires more container space than a product like steel, which can be compactly loaded. Similarly, any product that is perishable, fragile, or particularly susceptible to theft (e.g., personal computers, cigarettes) will tend to have high line-haul expenses because of greater equipment, insurance, and labor expenses. Finally, there is an inventory cost component to transportation costs because of the time element involved in shipping goods. The time required for transit is extremely important, because slower forms of transport such as railroads or barges can delay receipt of sale proceeds from customers. Even though out-of-pocket expenses will be greater, air cargo or motor carrier shipments can

■ Figure 8.7
## Effect of Transportation Costs on Optimal Plant Size

High transportation costs reduce the MES plant size from $Q_A^*$ to $Q_B^*$. As transportation costs rise relative to production costs, MES plant size will fall.

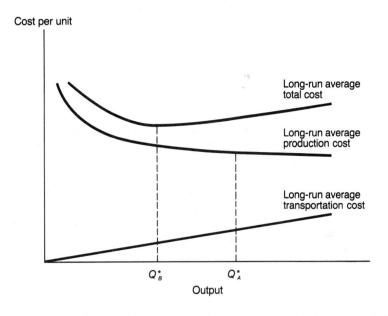

sometimes reduce the total economic costs of transportation because of their greater speed in delivery.

The relative magnitude of transportation costs can play an important role in determining optimal plant sizes. As more output is produced at a given plant, it becomes necessary to reach out to more distant customers. This can lead to increased transportation costs per unit sold. To illustrate, consider Figure 8.7. Here an L-shaped long-run average cost curve reflects average production costs that first decline and then become nearly constant. Assuming relatively modest terminal and inventory costs, greater line-haul expenses will cause transportation costs per unit to increase at a relatively constant rate. Before considering transportation costs, $Q_A^*$ would represent the MES plant size. Including transportation expenses, however, reduces the MES plant size to $Q_B^*$. In general, as transportation costs become increasingly important, MES will fall. In the extreme, when transportation costs are large in relation to production costs, as is the case with milk, gravel, cement, and many other products with high weight-to-value (or bulk-to-value) ratios, even small, relatively inefficient production facilities can be profitable when located near important markets. On the other hand, when transportation costs are relatively insignificant, as is the case for relatively low-weight, compact, high-value products such as writing pens, breakfast cereal, and electronic components, markets will be national or international in scope, and increasing returns to scale will cause output to be produced in only a few large plants.

# FIRM SIZE AND PLANT SIZE

Production and cost functions exist both at the level of the individual plant and, for multiplant firms, at the level of the entire firm. The cost function of a multiplant (or multiproduct) firm can be simply the sum of the cost functions of the individual plants, or it can be greater or smaller than this figure. To illustrate, suppose that the situation shown in Figure 8.6, a U-shaped long-run average cost curve at the plant level, holds. If demand is sufficiently large, the firm will employ N plants, each of the optimal size and each producing $Q^*$ units of output.

In this case, what will be the shape of the firm's long-run average cost curve? Figure 8.8 shows three possibilities. Each possible long-run average cost curve has important implications for the minimum efficient firm size, $Q_F^*$. First, the long-run average cost curve can be L-shaped, as in (a), if no economies or diseconomies result from combining plants. Second, costs may decline throughout the entire range of output, as in (b), if multiplant firms are more efficient than single-plant firms. Such

■ Figure 8.8
**Three Possible Long-Run Average Cost Curves for a Multiplant Firm**

(a) Constant costs characterize a multiplant facility that has neither economies nor diseconomies of scale. (b) Average costs decline if a multiplant firm is more efficient than a single-plant firm. (c) The average costs of operating several plants can eventually rise when coordinating costs overcome multiplant economies.

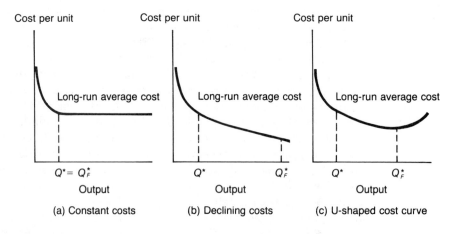

cases, when they exist, are caused by economies of multiplant operation. For example, all plants may use a central billing service, they may enjoy purchasing or distribution economies, centralized staffs of various types may serve all plants, and so on. The third possibility, shown in (c), is that costs will first decline (beyond $Q^*$, the output of the most efficient plant) and then rise. Here economies of scale for multiplant costs dominate initially, but later the cost of coordinating many operating units more than offsets these multiplant cost advantages.

All three shapes of cost curves shown in Figure 8.8 have been found in the U. S. economy, with different ones characterizing different industries. Since optimal plant and firm sizes will be identical only when multiplant economies are negligible, the magnitude of such influences must be carefully considered in evaluating the effect of scale economies on entry conditions. Both intraplant and multiplant economies can have an important effect on the minimum efficient firm size.

An example can help clarify the relation between firm size and plant size, as well as the important minimum efficient scale concept. Consider Plainfield Electronics, a New Jersey–based company that manufactures a line of large industrial control panels for a national market. Currently, the firm's production is consolidated at a single eastern-seaboard facility. Because of growth in demand for its products, a multiplant alternative to centralized production is being considered. Estimated demand, and the *single-plant* production plus transportation total cost curves for the firm are:

$$P = \$940 - \$0.02Q$$

$$TC = \$250{,}000 + \$40Q + \$0.01Q^2.$$

The profit-maximizing activity level with centralized production can be identified by locating the output level at which marginal profit is zero. (This is also the output level at which $MR = MC$). Plainfield's total profit function is:

$$\pi = TR - TC$$
$$= P \times Q - TC$$
$$= (\$940 - \$0.02Q)Q - \$250{,}000 - \$40Q - \$0.01Q^2$$
$$= -\$0.03Q^2 + \$900Q - \$250{,}000.$$

Marginal profit is:

$$M\pi = d\pi/dQ = -\$0.06Q + \$900.$$

Setting marginal profit equal to zero and solving for the related output quantity, we find:

$$M\pi = -\$0.06Q + \$900 = 0$$
$$\$0.06Q = \$900$$
$$Q = 15{,}000.$$

At $Q = 15,000$,

$$P = \$940 - \$0.02Q$$
$$= \$940 - \$0.02(15,000)$$
$$= \$640$$

and

$$\pi = -\$0.03(15,000^2) + \$900(15,000) - \$250,000$$
$$= \$6,500,000.$$

To gain insight into the possible advantages of operating multiple, smaller plants as opposed to centralized production, we can examine the average cost function for a single plant. To simplify matters, assume that multiplant production is possible under the same cost conditions described previously. That is, over the range of reasonable plant-size options, the firm's individual plant cost functions are the same with either single or multiplant operations. Also assume that there are no other multiplant economies or diseconomies of scale to contend with.

The activity level at which average cost is minimized is found by setting the first derivative of the average cost function equal to zero and solving for $Q$:

$$AC = TC/Q$$
$$= (\$250,000 + \$40Q + \$0.01Q^2)/Q$$
$$= \$250,000Q^{-1} + \$40 + \$0.01Q$$

and

$$dAC/dQ = -250,000Q^{-2} + 0.01 = 0$$
$$250,000\ Q^{-2} = 0.01$$
$$Q^{-2} = \frac{0.01}{250,000}$$
$$Q^2 = \frac{250,000}{0.01}$$
$$Q = \sqrt{25,000,000}$$
$$= 5,000.$$

Average cost is minimized at an output level of 5,000. This output level identifies the minimum efficient plant scale. Since the average cost–minimizing output level of 5,000 is far less than the single-plant profit-maximizing activity level of 15,000 units, we know that the profit-maximizing level of total output occurs at a point of rising average costs. Assuming centralized production, Plainfield would maximize profits at an activity level of $Q = 15,000$ rather than $Q = 5,000$ because market-demand conditions are such that, despite the higher average costs experienced at $Q = 15,000$, the firm can profitably supply output up to that level. Profit maximization requires consideration of both revenue and cost conditions.

Given that centralized production maximized profits at an activity level well beyond that at which average cost is minimized, it appears that Plainfield has an opportunity to reduce costs, and increase profits, by adopting the multiplant alternative. Although consideration of the single-plant $Q = 15,000$ profit-maximizing activity level and the $Q = 5,000$ average cost–minimizing activity level may appear to suggest that multiplant production with three facilities is optimal, this is incorrect. Profits were maximized at $Q = 15,000$ under the assumption of centralized production because at that activity level, both marginal revenue and marginal cost equaled $340. With multiplant production *and* each plant operating at the $Q = 5,000$ activity level, marginal cost will be lower than the $MC = \$340$ at $Q = 15,000$, and multiplant production will entail a new (and higher) profit-maximizing activity level. At $Q = 5,000$,

$$MC = dTC/dQ$$
$$= \$40 + \$0.02Q$$
$$= \$40 + \$0.02(5,000)$$
$$= \$140.$$

With multiple plants all operating at 5,000 units per year, $MC = \$140$. Therefore, it will be profitable to expand production so long as the marginal revenue obtained exceeds this minimum $MC = \$140$. This assumes, of course, that each production facility is operating at the optimal activity level of $Q = 5,000$ per plant.

The optimal multiplant activity level for the firm, assuming optimal production levels of $Q = 5,000$ at multiple plants, can be calculated by equating $MR$ to the multiplant $MC = \$140$:

$$MR = dTR/dQ = \$140 = MC$$
$$\$940 - \$0.04Q = \$140$$
$$\$0.04Q = \$800$$
$$Q = 20,000.$$

Given optimal multiplant production of 20,000 and average cost–minimizing activity levels of 5,000 for each plant, multiplant production at four facilities is suggested:

$$\frac{\text{Optimal Number of}}{\text{Plants}} = \frac{\text{Optimal Multiplant Activity Level}}{\text{Optimal Production per Plant}}$$
$$= \frac{20,000}{5,000}$$
$$= 4.$$

At $Q = 20,000$:

$$P = \$940 - \$0.02(20,000)$$
$$= \$540,$$

and

$$\pi = TR - TC$$
$$= P \times Q - 4 \times TC \text{ per plant}$$
$$= \$540(20,000) - 4[\$250,000 + \$40(5,000) + \$0.01(5,000^2)]$$
$$= \$8,000,000.$$

Given the assumed cost relations, multiplant production is much preferred to the centralized production alternative because it results in maximum profits that are \$1.5 million larger. As shown in Figure 8.9, this follows from the firm's ability to concentrate production at the minimum point on the single-plant U-shaped average cost curve.

■ Figure 8.9
## Plainfield Electronics: Single versus Multiplant Operation

In this example, profit is maximized at a production level well beyond that at which average cost is minimized for a single plant. Profits are greater with four plants because output can then be produced at minimum cost.

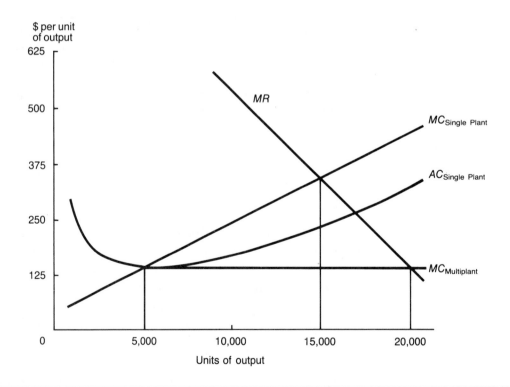

Note: *The horizontal portion of the multiplant marginal cost curve shown here is only an approximation of the actual relation. The true multiplant marginal cost curve cycles up somewhat between the 5,000-, 10,000-, 15,000-, and 20,000-unit output levels as each individual plant operates at an output level above or below 5,000 units. As can be seen from the shape of the single-plant marginal cost curve around 5,000 units, the effect would not be large.*

The multiplant cost advantages indicated in this example could stem from a variety of factors. One possibility, given that Plainfield's product is a large, heavy industrial control panel, is transportation cost savings from regional rather than centralized production. The role of distribution costs can be significant in industries in which final-product transport costs are large relative to production costs.

Finally, it is important to recognize that the optimal multiplant activity level of 20,000 units described in this example is based on the assumption that each production facility produces exactly 5,000 units of output and, therefore, $MC = \$140$. Marginal cost will only equal $\$140$ when $Q = 5,000$ or some round multiple thereof (e.g., $Q = 10,000$ from two plants, $Q = 15,000$ from three plants, and so on), and the optimal multiplant activity-level calculation is somewhat more complicated when this assumption is not met. For example, Plainfield could not produce $Q = 21,000$ at $MC = \$140$. For an output level in the 20,000 to 25,000 range, it is necessary to equate marginal revenue with the marginal cost of each plant at its optimal activity level. This reemphasizes the point that determination of the optimal multiplant activity level always depends on the comparison of relevant marginal revenues and marginal costs.

## PLANT SIZE AND FLEXIBILITY

Is the plant that can produce a given output at the lowest possible cost the optimal plant for producing that expected level of output? Not necessarily. Consider the following situation. Although actual demand for a product is uncertain, it is expected to be 5,000 units a year. Two possible probability distributions for this demand are given in Figure 8.10. Distribution *L* exhibits a low degree of variability in demand, and Distribution *H* indicates substantially higher variation in possible demand levels.

Now suppose that two plants can be employed to produce the required output. Plant *A* is quite specialized and is geared to produce a specified output at a low cost per unit. If, however, more or less than the specified output is produced (in this case 5,000 units), unit production costs rise rapidly. Plant *B*, on the other hand, is more flexible. Output can be expanded or contracted without excessive cost penalties, but unit costs are not as low as those of Plant *A* at the optimal output level. These two cases are shown in Figure 8.11.

Plant *A* is more efficient than Plant *B* between 4,500 and 5,500 units of output, but outside this range *B* has lower costs. Which plant should be selected? The answer depends on the relative cost differentials at different output levels and the probability distribution for demand. The firm should make its plant-size decision on the basis of the expected average total cost and the variability of that cost. In the example, if the demand probability distribution with the low variation, Distribution *L*, is correct, the more specialized facility will be optimal. If probability Distribution *H* more correctly describes the demand situation, the lower

■ Figure 8.10
**Probability Distributions of Demand**

Distribution *L* has a low degree of variability from the expected demand level. Distribution *H* varies substantially from the expected demand level.

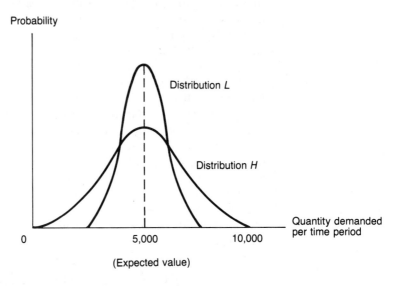

## LEARNING CURVES

For many manufacturing processes, average costs decline substantially as *cumulative* total output increases. This results from both management and labor becoming more knowledgeable about production techniques as their experience levels increase. Improvements in the use of production equipment and procedures are important in this process, as are reduced waste from defects and reduced labor requirements as workers become more proficient in their jobs.

When knowledge gained from manufacturing experience is used to improve production methods so that output is produced with increasing efficiency, the resulting decline in average costs is said to reflect the effects of the firm's **learning curve.** The learning-curve (also known as an *experience curve*) phenomenon affects average costs in a way similar to that for any technological advance that improves productive efficiency. Both involve a downward shift in the long-run average cost curve at all levels of output. That is, learning through production experience

**learning curve**
A curve that illustrates cost savings that result from production experience as total cumulative output expands.

minimum cost of the more specialized facilities will be more than offset by the possibility of very high costs of producing outside the 4,500- to 5,500-unit range; Plant *B* could have lower expected costs or a more attractive combination of expected costs and potential variation in cost.

■ Figure 8.11
## Alternative Plants for Production of Expected 5,000 Units of Output

Unit costs are lower for Plant *A* than for Plant *B* between 4,500 and 5,500 units of output. Outside this range, Plant *B* has lower unit costs.

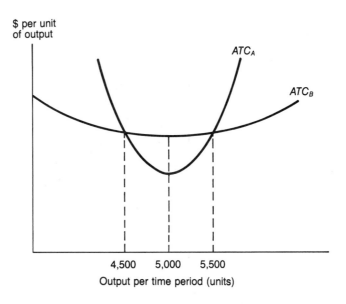

permits the firm to produce output more efficiently at each and every output level.

To illustrate, consider Figure 8.12, which shows hypothetical long-run average cost curves for periods $t$ and $t + 1$. With increased knowledge about production methods gained through the experience of producing $Q_t$ units in period $t$, long-run average costs have declined for every output level in period $t + 1$. This means that $Q_t$ units could be produced during period $t + 1$ at an average cost of *B* rather than the earlier *C*. The learning-curve cost savings is *BC*. If output were expanded from $Q_t$ to $Q_{t+1}$ between the periods, average costs would fall from *C* to *A*. This decline in average costs would reflect both the learning-curve effect, *BC*, and the effect of economies of scale, *AB*.

In order to evaluate the average-cost effect of learning or experience, it is necessary to identify carefully that portion of average-cost changes over time that is due to other factors. One of the most important of these is the effect of economies of scale. As seen before, the change in average costs experienced between periods $t$ and $t + 1$ can reflect the effects of both learning and economies of scale. This is a typical situation. Similarly, the effects of important technological breakthroughs, causing a downward shift in *LRAC* curves, and input-cost inflation, causing an

■ Figure 8.12
## Long-Run Average Cost Curve Effects of Learning

Learning will cause a downward shift from $LRAC_t$ to $LRAC_{t+1}$. An average cost decline from $C$ to $A$ reflects the effects of both learning and economies of scale.

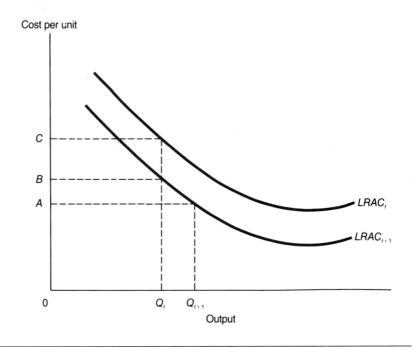

upward shift in $LRAC$ curves, must be constrained in order to examine learning-curve characteristics. Only when output scale, technology, and input prices are all held constant can the learning-curve relation be accurately represented.

   Figure 8.13 depicts the learning-curve relation suggested by Figure 8.12. Note that learning results in dramatic average-cost reductions at low total production levels but in increasingly modest savings at higher cumulative production levels. This reflects the fact that many improvements in production methods become quickly obvious and are readily adopted. Later gains often come more slowly and are less substantial.

Given this typical shape of the learning-curve relation, the learning- or experience-curve phenomenon is often characterized as a constant percentage decline in average costs as cumulative output increases. This percentage represents the proportion by which unit costs decline as the cumulative quantity of total output doubles. Suppose, for example, that average costs per unit for a new product were $100 during 1988 but fell to $90 during 1989. Furthermore, assume that these average costs are in constant dollars reflecting an accurate adjustment for input-price inflation and that an identical basic technology was used in production.

■ Figure 8.13
## Learning Curve on an Arithmetic Scale

The learning curve reflects the percentage decline in average cost as total cumulative output doubles from $Q_t$ to $2Q_t$.

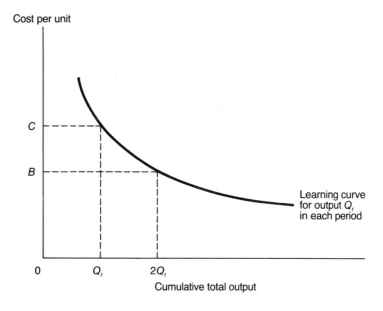

Given equal output in each period to insure that the effects of economies of scale are not incorporated in the data, the learning or experience rate, defined as the percentage by which average cost falls as output doubles, is:

$$\text{Learning Rate} = \left(1 - \frac{AC_2}{AC_1}\right) \times 100$$

$$= \left(1 - \frac{\$90}{\$100}\right) \times 100$$

$$= 10 \text{ Percent.}$$

Thus, as *cumulative* total output doubles, average cost is expected to fall by 10 percent. Continuing the example, if annual production is projected to remain constant, it will take two additional years for cumulative output to double again. Thus, one would project that average unit costs will decline to $81 (90 percent of $90) in 1991. Since the cumulative total output at that time will equal four years' production at the constant annual rate, output will again double by 1995. At that time, the learning curve will have reduced average costs to $72.90 (90 percent of $81).

Because of the frequency with which one finds the learning-curve concept described as a cause of economies of scale, it is worth repeating that although related, the two are distinct concepts. Scale economies relate to cost differences associated with different output levels during a single production period. They are specified in terms of the cost–output relation measured *along* a single *LRAC* curve. Learning curves relate cost differences to total cumulative output for a product. They are measured in terms of *shifts* in *LRAC* curves over time. These shifts result from improved production efficiencies stemming from knowledge gained through production experience. Care must be exercised to separate learning and scale effects in cost analysis.

Research in a number of industries ranging from aircraft manufacture to semiconductor memory-chip production has shown that a constant percentage savings in average costs as a result of learning or experience can be very important in some production systems. Learning or experience rates of 20 to 30 percent are sometimes reported. These high learning rates imply rapidly declining manufacturing costs as cumulative total output increases. It should be noted, however, that many learning-curve studies fail to account adequately for the expansion of annual production levels, and, therefore, reported learning or experience rates include the effects of both learning and economies of scale. Nevertheless, actual learning rates can sometimes be quite significant.

The learning-curve concept is useful for a variety of managerial decisions. Managers have found that use of the learning-curve concept substantially improves their ability to forecast production costs based on projected cumulative output. This in turn improves pricing decisions and production strategies. Managers in electronics industries have used their knowledge of the learning curve to price new products from emergent technologies. These pricing strategies explicitly account for the cost reductions expected to accompany rapid increases in total production, often resulting in attempts to maximize both market size and market share. In other instances, managers have analyzed their cost position relative to those of major competitors and concluded that, because of notable differences in total production levels, they are just chasing the competition down the experience curve and are unlikely to ever become cost competitive. This has caused some firms to drop product lines or to concentrate on narrower segments of their markets in hopes of accelerating the rate of production for one specific product, thereby increasing specialized learning and the rate at which unit costs are expected to decline. Thus, the learning curve has considerable strategic implications.

## Strategic Implications of the Learning-Curve Concept

The learning curve can often play a central role in determining a firm's long-run success or failure and therefore also plays an important role in competitive strategy. What makes the learning-curve phenomenon important for competitive strategy is its possible contribution to achieving and maintaining a dominant position in a given market. By virtue of their large relative volume, dominant firms have a greater opportunity for learning than do smaller, nonleading firms. In some instances, the market share leader may be able to "drive down" its average cost curve faster than the competition, underprice them, and permanently maintain its leadership position. Nonleading firms would then face an important and perhaps insurmountable barrier to a relative improvement in performance. Thus, where the learning-curve advantages of leading firms are important, it may be prudent for firms to relinquish nonleading positions and redeploy assets to markets in which they can achieve or maintain a dominant position.

A classic example illustrating the successful use of the learning-curve concept is provided by Texas Instruments (TI). TI is a large and highly profitable growth company headquartered in Dallas, Texas. Despite some well-publicized problems in its consumer products division (personal computers, calculators, video games), TI has long enjoyed a dominant position as a supplier in the producer products segment of the electronics industry. TI's main business is to produce semiconductor chips, a key component used to store information in computers, as well as a wide array of electronic products. With growing applications for computers and "intelligent" electronics during recent years, the demand for semiconductors is growing rapidly. A number of years ago, TI was one among a number of leading semiconductor manufacturers. At this early stage in the development of the industry, TI made the decision to price its semiconductors well below then-current production costs, given expected learning-curve advantages in the 20-percent range. TI's learning-curve strategy proved to be spectacularly successful. With a low price, volume increased dramatically. Soon TI was making so many chips that its average costs were even lower than anticipated, it could price below the competition, and dozens of competitors were knocked out of the world market. Given a relative cost advantage and strict quality controls, TI rapidly achieved a position of dominant leadership in a market that became a source of large and rapidly growing profits.

Generally speaking, in order for learning or experience to play an important role in an effective competitive strategy, two conditions must be satisfied. First, learning must be significant, resulting in average cost savings of 20 to 30 percent as cumulative output doubles. If only modest effects of learning are present, then relative product quality or customer service is likely to play a greater role in determining firm success than is a modest average cost advantage. Learning is likely to be much more important in industries with an abundance of new products or new production techniques than in mature industries with stable and well-known production methods. Similarly, learning will be important in industries producing standardized products (such as semiconductors) in which competition is based on price rather than product variety or service competition. Second, the learning-curve phenomenon must be managed. It is definitely not automatic. The beneficial effects of learning are only realized under management systems that tightly control costs and monitor potential sources of increased productive efficiency. Continuous feedback of information between production and management per-

## 8.3  **Managerial Application**

The Rush to Couple Hardware with Software

Economies of scope play an increasingly important role in helping determine the direction of corporate growth and development. Nowhere is this trend more evident than in the computer and data processing industries.

No longer confined to data processing departments, computers are now employed widely throughout business organizations by users with little or no technical computer background. These users require software systems that are simple and can be applied to a wide variety of managerial problems. In fact, "user friendliness" has become a key consideration in the development and marketing of both computer hardware and software. Increasingly, computer manufacturers have found that lack of appropriate software makes it impossible to sell hardware. Simi-

larly, providers of software have found that to address a wide market, their programs must run on hardware of a wide range of manufacturers.

The importance of software is reflected by its sales revenue. In 1987, software and services accounted for 35 percent of the total revenues generated by Digital Equipment and NCR. Similarly, software and services accounted for 32 percent of 1987 revenues at Unisys and 28 percent at Hewlett-Packard. Even at IBM, where mainframe manufacturing capability has always been a strong point, software and services accounted for 27 percent of 1987 revenues. In fact, IBM might be the most aggressive of all hardware manufacturers in terms of its recent moves to expand its involvement in the software and applications end of the busi-

*continued*

See: Anne R. Field, "Why the Hardware Giants Are Hustling into Software," *Business Week*, July 27, 1987, 53–54; and Brenton R. Schlender, "Sun Microsystems' Effort to Attract Clone Makers Finally Gets Results," *The Wall Street Journal*, January 16, 1989, 85.

sonnel is essential. To ensure the flow of useful information and a cooperative attitude among all employees, incentive pay programs that reward increased productivity are often established, allowing both employees (through their compensation) and employers (through profits) to jointly benefit through learning.

And finally, although the learning-curve phenomenon is important in new industries producing undifferentiated products, many industries do not fit this pattern. As a result, learning-curve advantages, which influence both cost conditions and competitive strategy, are an industry-specific rather than an economywide factor.

**Managerial Application** *continued*

ness. At a time of companywide cutbacks in 1987, IBM expanded its software development staff by 6,000 to a total of 27,000 employees, 7 percent of its total work force. It is noteworthy that IBM, like other leading hardware manufacturers, expects software and service revenues to account for over one-half of total company revenues by 1997.

Apple Computer, Inc. has been especially aggressive in promoting a coupling of its hardware with software for a wide range of applications. The company has a number of in-house software specialists and an independent software marketing subsidiary helping coordinate the efforts of over 6,000 independent programmers. Apple, like other major computer manufacturers, typically gets a percentage of the software revenues generated through its association with these independent software publishers.

Given the rapidly growing demand for specialized software, such revenue sharing arrangements can add up to substantial sums of money. For example, as much as 50 percent of the $1.5 billion from software applications IBM earned in 1987 came from agreements with so-called third-party software providers. Such agreements are ex-

pected to expand in importance as software continues to grow in relation to computer hardware business.

Not only are software and services important in terms of gross revenues; they make an increasingly important contribution to the bottom line as well. A basic problem facing hardware manufacturers is that recent changes in technology have made it increasingly difficult to tell one computer from another. This has forced computer manufacturers to lower prices, squeezing profit margins in the process from as high as 40 percent to the current range of 5 to 15 percent of sales. In contrast, pretax margins on software have held steady in the 15 to 25 percent range. Clearly, firms that fall behind in the software applications end of the business will also fall behind in terms of profitability.

In short, the economies of scope between computer hardware and software are so strong that distinctions between the hardware and software aspects of the business will soon become blurred, if they are not already. Today, the industry must be thought of as a hardware equipment *and* software applications industry.

# ECONOMIES OF SCOPE

**economies of scope**

A cost advantage that arises with joint production as opposed to producing each output separately.

**Economies of scope** exist for multiple outputs when the cost of joint production is less than the cost of producing each output separately. In other words, a firm will produce products that are complementary in the sense that producing them jointly costs less than producing individually. For example, suppose a regional airline offers regularly scheduled passenger service between midsize city pairs and that it expects some excess capacity. Furthermore, suppose there is a modest local demand for air parcel and small-package delivery service. Given current technology (airplane size, configuration, and so on), it is often less costly for a single airline to provide both passenger and cargo services in small regional markets than to specialize in one or the other. Thus, regional air carriers often provide both services. This can be seen as an example of economies of scope. Other examples of scope economies abound in the provision of both goods and services. Indeed, the economies-of-scope concept seems to explain best why firms produce multiple rather than single products.

An important benefit gained from economies of scope is that the concept forces management to consider both the direct and indirect benefits associated with individual lines of business. For example, on a product-line basis, some firms that offer financial services regard checking accounts and money market mutual funds as "loss leaders." That is, when one considers just the revenues and costs associated with marketing and offering checking services or running a money market mutual fund, they may just break even or yield only a marginal profit. However, successful firms like Merrill Lynch correctly evaluate the profitability of their money market mutual funds within the context of overall operations. These funds are a valuable "delivery vehicle" for the vast array of financial products and services that the firm offers. By offering money market funds on an attractive basis, Merrill Lynch establishes a working relation with an ideal group of prospective customers for stocks, bonds, tax shelters, and so on. When viewed as a delivery vehicle or marketing device, its money market mutual funds may be one of Merrill Lynch's most profitable financial product lines.

Economies of scope are also important because they permit a firm to translate superior skill or productive capability in a given product line into unique advantages in the production of complementary products. In terms of business policy, this suggests that an effective competitive strategy would emphasize the development or extension of product lines related to a firm's current stars, or areas of recognized strength. For example, PepsiCo, Inc., has long been a leader in the soft drink market. Over time, the company has gradually broadened its product line to include various brands of regular and diet soft drinks, Fritos and Doritos corn chips, Grandma's Cookies, and other snack foods. PepsiCo can no longer be considered just a soft drink manufacturer. Instead, it is a widely diversified snack foods company. In fact, well over one-half of total current profits come from non–soft drink lines. PepsiCo's snack foods product-line extension strategy was effective because it capitalized on the product development capabilities, distribution network, and marketing skills the firm had developed in its soft drink business. In the case of PepsiCo, snack foods and soft drinks are a natural fit and a good example of how a firm has been able to take the skills gained in developing one star (soft drinks) and use them to develop a second (snack foods).

In sum, the economies-of-scope concept plays an important role in managerial decision making because it offers a useful means for evaluating the potential of current and prospective lines of business. It naturally leads to definition of those areas in which the firm has a comparative advantage and thus its greatest profit potential.

# COST-VOLUME-PROFIT ANALYSIS

**cost-volume-profit analysis**

An important analytical technique used to study relations among costs, revenues, and profits.

**Cost-volume-profit analysis** (sometimes called *breakeven analysis*) is an important analytical technique used to study the relations among costs, revenues, and profits. The nature of this analysis is depicted in Figure 8.14, a basic cost-volume-profit chart composed of a firm's total cost and total revenue curves. The volume of output is measured on the horizontal axis, and revenue and cost are shown on the vertical axis. Since fixed costs are constant regardless of the output produced, they are indicated by a horizontal line. Variable costs at each output level are measured by the distance between the total cost curve and the constant fixed costs. The total revenue curve indicates the price/demand relation for the firm's product, and profits (or losses) at each output are shown by the distance between the total revenue curve and the total cost curve.

In the example depicted in Figure 8.14, fixed costs of $60,000 are represented by a horizontal line. Variable costs are assumed to be $1.80 per unit, so total costs rise by that amount for each additional unit of output produced. The product is assumed to be sold for $3 per unit.

■ Figure 8.14
## Linear Cost-Volume-Profit Chart

Output levels below the breakeven point produce losses. As output grows beyond the breakeven point, increasingly higher profits result.

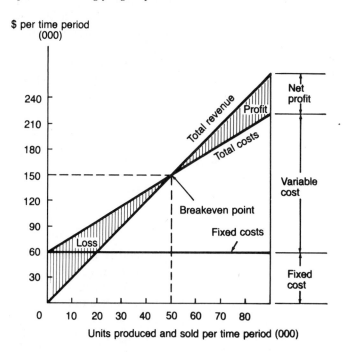

Total revenue is a straight line through the origin. The slope of the total revenue line is steeper than that of the total cost line; this follows from the fact that the firm receives $3 in revenue for every unit produced and sold, but it spends only $1.80 on labor, materials, and other variable input factors.

Up to the breakeven point, found at the intersection of the total revenue line and the total cost line, the firm suffers losses. After that point, it begins to make profits. Figure 8.14 indicates a breakeven point at a sales and cost level of $150,000, which occurs at a production level of 50,000 units.

## Algebraic Cost-Volume-Profit Analysis

Although cost-volume-profit charts provide a useful means of illustrating profit/output relationships, algebraic techniques are typically a more efficient means for analyzing decision problems. The algebra of cost-volume-profit analysis can be developed as follows. Let:

$$P = \text{Price per unit sold};$$

$$Q = \text{Quantity produced and sold};$$

$$TFC = \text{Total fixed costs};$$

$$AVC = \text{Average variable cost};$$

$$\pi_c = \text{Profit contribution}.$$

**profit contribution**

Revenue in excess of variable cost that can be used to cover fixed costs and provide profits.

**Profit contribution,** $\pi_c$, is defined as the difference between revenues and variable cost. It equals price minus average variable cost on a per-unit basis $(\pi_c = P - AVC)$. Profit contribution can be applied to cover fixed costs and then to provide profits. It is the foundation of cost-volume-profit analysis.

One useful application of cost-volume-profit analysis is in the determination of breakeven activity levels for a product. The breakeven quantity, defined as that volume of output at which total revenue $(P \times Q)$ exactly equal total costs $(TFC + AVC \times Q)$, is found as follows:

$$P \times Q = TFC + AVC \times Q$$

$$(P - AVC)Q = TFC$$

$$Q = \frac{TFC}{P - AVC}$$

$$= \frac{TFC}{\pi_c} \qquad\qquad \textbf{8.1}$$

The breakeven quantity is found by dividing the per-unit profit contribution into total fixed costs. In the example illustrated in Figure 8.14, $P = \$3$, $AVC = \$1.80$, and $TFC = \$60,000$. Profit contribution is $1.20 (= \$3.00 - \$1.80)$, and the breakeven quantity is found as follows:

$$Q = \frac{\$60,000}{\$1.20}$$

$$= 50,000 \text{ Units}.$$

A more extensive example will indicate additional uses of the concept in managerial decision making. The textbook publishing business provides a good illustration of the effective use of cost-volume-profit analysis for new product decisions. Consider the following hypothetical analysis for a college textbook:

| | |
|---|---|
| *Fixed Costs* | |
| Copyediting and other editorial costs | $ 12,000 |
| Illustrations | 32,000 |
| Typesetting | 56,000 |
| Total fixed costs | $100,000 |
| | |
| *Variable Costs per Copy* | |
| Printing, binding, and paper | $12.10 |
| Bookstore discounts | 8.00 |
| Commissions | 1.20 |
| Author's royalties | 2.20 |
| General and administrative costs | 8.50 |
| Total variable costs per copy | $32.00 |
| | |
| List price per copy | $40.00 |

The fixed costs can be estimated quite accurately; the variable costs, which are linear and which for the most part are set by contracts, can also be estimated with little error. The list price is variable, but competition keeps prices within a sufficiently narrow range to make a linear total revenue curve reasonable. The variable costs of the proposed book are $32 a copy, and the price is $40. This means that each copy sold provides $8 in profit contribution. Applying the formula of Equation 8.1, we find the breakeven sales volume to be 12,500 units:

$$Q = \frac{\$100,000}{\$8}$$

$$= 12,500 \text{ Units.}$$

Publishers can evaluate the size of the total market for a given book, the competition, and other factors. With these data as a base, they can estimate the possibilities that a given book will reach or exceed the breakeven point. If the estimate is that it will do neither, the publisher may consider cutting production costs by reducing the number of illustrations, doing only light copyediting, using a lower grade of paper, negotiating with the author to reduce the royalty rate, and so on.

    Assume now that the publisher is interested in determining how many copies must sell to earn a $20,000 profit on the text. Because profit contribution is the amount available to cover fixed costs and provide profit, the answer is found by adding the profit requirement to the book's fixed costs, then dividing by the per-unit profit contribution. The sales volume required in this case is 15,000 books, found as follows:

$$Q = \frac{\text{Fixed Costs } + \text{ Profit Requirement}}{\text{Profit Contribution}}$$

$$= \frac{\$100,000 + \$20,000}{\$8}$$

$$= 15,000 \text{ Units.}[4]$$

Consider yet another decision problem that might confront the publisher. Assume that a book club has indicated an interest in purchasing the textbook for its members and has offered to buy 3,000 copies at $27 per copy. Cost-volume-profit analysis can be used to determine the incremental effect of such a sale on the publisher's profits.

Since fixed costs do not vary with respect to changes in the number of textbooks sold, they should be ignored in the analysis. Variable costs per copy are $32, but note that $8 of this cost represents bookstore discounts. Since the 3,000 copies are being sold directly to the club, this cost will not be incurred, and hence the relevant variable cost is $24. Profit contribution per book sold to the book club then is $3 (= $27 − $24), and $3 times the 3,000 copies sold indicates that the order will result in a total profit contribution of $9,000. Assuming that these 3,000 copies would not have been sold through normal sales channels, the $9,000 profit contribution indicates the increase in profits to the publisher from accepting this order.

## Cost-Volume-Profit Analysis and Operating Leverage

Cost-volume-profit analysis is also a useful tool for analyzing the financial characteristics of alternative production systems. Here the analysis focuses on how total costs and profits vary with output as the firm operates in a more mechanized or automated manner and thus substitutes fixed costs for variable costs.

Operating leverage reflects the extent to which fixed production facilities, as opposed to variable production facilities, are used in operations. The relation between operating leverage and profit variation is clearly indicated in Figure 8.15, which contrasts three firms, A, B, and C, with differing degrees of leverage. The fixed costs of operation in Firm B are considered typical. It uses equipment, with which one operator can turn out a few or many units at the same labor cost, to about the same extent as the average firm in the industry. Firm A uses less capital equipment in its production process and has lower fixed costs, but note the steeper rate of increase in variable costs of A over B. Firm A breaks even at a lower level of operations than does Firm B. For example, at a production level of 40,000 units, B is losing $8,000, but A breaks even.

---

[4]To see that 15,000 units will indeed produce a profit of $20,000, note the following calculations:

| | |
|---|---:|
| Sales Revenue = $40 × 15,000 = | $600,000 |
| Total Cost = FC + VC = $100,000 + $32(15,000) = $100,000 + $480,000 = | 580,000 |
| Profit = Sales Revenue − Total Cost = | $ 20,000 |

## Breakeven and Operating Leverage

The breakeven point for Firm C occurs at the highest output level. Once this level is reached, profits rise at a faster rate than for Firm A or B.

### Firm A

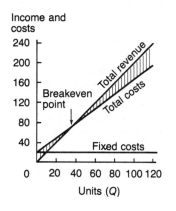

Income and costs

Selling price = $2.00
Fixed costs = $20,000
Variable costs = $1.50Q

| Units sold (Q) | Sales | Costs | Profit |
|---|---|---|---|
| 20,000 | $40,000 | $50,000 | − $10,000 |
| 40,000 | 80,000 | 80,000 | 0 |
| 60,000 | 120,000 | 110,000 | 10,000 |
| 80,000 | 160,000 | 140,000 | 20,000 |
| 100,000 | 200,000 | 170,000 | 30,000 |
| 120,000 | 240,000 | 200,000 | 40,000 |

### Firm B

Income and costs

Selling price = $2.00
Fixed costs = $40,000
Variable costs = $1.20Q

| Units sold (Q) | Sales | Costs | Profit |
|---|---|---|---|
| 20,000 | $40,000 | $64,000 | − $24,000 |
| 40,000 | 80,000 | 88,000 | − 8,000 |
| 60,000 | 120,000 | 112,000 | 8,000 |
| 80,000 | 160,000 | 136,000 | 24,000 |
| 100,000 | 200,000 | 160,000 | 40,000 |
| 120,000 | 240,000 | 184,000 | 56,000 |

### Firm C

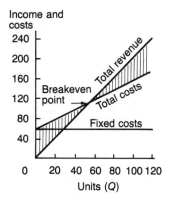

Income and costs

Selling price = $2.00
Fixed costs = $60,000
Variable costs = $1.00Q

| Units sold (Q) | Sales | Costs | Profit |
|---|---|---|---|
| 20,000 | $40,000 | $80,000 | − $40,000 |
| 40,000 | 80,000 | 100,000 | − 20,000 |
| 60,000 | 120,000 | 120,000 | 0 |
| 80,000 | 160,000 | 140,000 | 20,000 |
| 100,000 | 200,000 | 160,000 | 40,000 |
| 120,000 | 240,000 | 180,000 | 60,000 |

Firm C has the highest fixed costs. It is highly automated, using expensive, high-speed machines that require very little labor per unit produced. With such an operation, its variable costs rise slowly. Because of the high overhead resulting from charges associated with the expensive machinery, C's breakeven point is higher than that of either A or B. Once Firm C reaches its breakeven point, however, its profits rise faster than do those of the other two firms.

**Degree of Operating Leverage.**   Operating leverage can be defined more precisely in terms of how a given change in volume affects profits. For this purpose we use the degree-of-operating-leverage concept. The **degree of operating leverage** is defined as the percentage change in profit that results from a 1-percent change in units sold. Algebraically, this may be expressed as:

**degree of operating leverage**

The percentage change in profit that results from a 1-percent change in units produced and sold.

$$\text{Degree of Operating Leverage} = \frac{\text{Percentage Change in Profit}}{\text{Percentage Change in Sales}}$$

$$= \frac{d\pi/\pi}{dQ/Q}$$

$$= \frac{d\pi}{dQ} \times \frac{Q}{\pi}. \qquad \textbf{8.2}$$

The degree of operating leverage is an elasticity concept, so we could call this measure the *operating leverage elasticity of profits.* When based on linear cost and revenue curves, this elasticity measure will vary depending on the particular part of the breakeven graph that is being considered. For example, the degree of operating leverage is always greatest close to the breakeven point, where a very small change in volume can produce a very large percentage increase in profits, simply because the base profits are close to zero near the breakeven point.

For firm B in Figure 8.15, the degree of operating leverage at 100,000 units of output is 2.0, calculated as follows:[5]

$$DOL_B = \frac{\Delta\pi/\pi}{\Delta Q/Q}$$

$$= \frac{(\$41{,}600 - \$40{,}000)/\$40{,}000}{(102{,}000 - 100{,}000)/100{,}000} = \frac{\$1{,}600/\$40{,}000}{2{,}000/100{,}000}$$

$$= \frac{4\%}{2\%} = 2.$$

Here $\pi$ is profit and $Q$ is the quantity of output in units.

For linear revenue and cost relations, we can calculate the degree of operating leverage at any level of Output $Q$: The change in output is

[5]To show the calculation, we arbitrarily assume that the change in Q ($\Delta Q$) = 2,000. If we assume any other $\Delta Q$—for example, $\Delta Q$ = 1,000 or $\Delta Q$ = 4,000—the degree of operating leverage will still turn out to be 2, because we are using linear cost and revenue curves. But if we choose a base different from 100,000 units, we will find the degree of operating leverage to be different from 2.

defined as $\Delta Q$. Fixed costs are constant, so the change in profit is $\Delta Q(P - AVC)$, where $P$ = price per unit and $AVC$ = average variable cost.

The initial profit level is $Q(P - AVC) - TFC$, so the percentage change in profit is:

$$\frac{\Delta \pi}{\pi} = \frac{\Delta Q(P - AVC)}{Q(P - AVC) - TFC}.$$

The percentage change in output is $\Delta Q/Q$, so the ratio of the percentage change in profits to the percentage change in output is:

$$\frac{\Delta \pi/\pi}{\Delta Q/Q} = \frac{\Delta Q(P - AVC)/[Q(P - AVC) - TFC]}{\Delta Q/Q}$$

$$= \frac{\Delta Q(P - AVC)}{Q(P - AVC) - TFC} \times \frac{Q}{\Delta Q}.$$

After simplifying, we find:[6]

$$\text{Degree of Operating Leverage at Point } Q = \frac{Q(P - AVC)}{Q(P - AVC) - TFC}. \qquad \textbf{8.3}$$

Using Equation 8.3, we find Firm B's degree of operating leverage at 100,000 units of output to be:

$$DOL_B \text{ at } 100,000 \text{ units} = \frac{100,000(\$2.00 - \$1.20)}{100,000(\$2.00 - \$1.20) - \$40,000}$$

$$= \frac{\$80,000}{\$40,000} = 2.$$

Equation 8.3 can also be applied to Firms A and C. When this is done, we find A's degree of operating leverage at 100,000 units to be 1.67 and C's to be 2.5. Thus, with a 10-percent increase in volume, C (the firm with the most operating leverage) will experience a profit increase of 25 percent. For the same 10-percent volume gain A, the firm with the least leverage, will have only a 16.7-percent profit gain.

The calculation of the degree of operating leverage shows algebraically the same pattern that Figure 8.15 shows graphically: that the profits of Firm C, the company with the most operating leverage, are most sensitive to changes in sales volume, whereas those of Firm A, which has only a small amount of operating leverage, are relatively insensitive to volume changes. Firm B, with an intermediate degree of leverage, lies between the two extremes.

---

[6]Since $TFC = Q(AFC)$ and $AC = AVC + AFC$, where $AFC$ is average fixed cost, Equation 8.3 can be reduced further to a form that is useful in some situations:

$$DOL = \frac{Q(P - AVC)}{Q(P - AVC) - Q(AFC)}$$

$$= \frac{P - AVC}{P - AC}$$

### Limitations of Linear
### Cost-Volume-Profit Analysis

Cost-volume-profit analysis helps one understand the relations among volume, prices, and cost structure; it is also useful in pricing, cost control, and other financial decisions. However, the analysis has limitations as a guide to managerial actions.

Linear cost-volume-profit analysis is especially weak in what it implies about the sales possibilities for the firm. Any given linear cost-volume-profit chart is based on a constant selling price. Therefore, to study profit possibilities under different prices, a whole series of charts is necessary, with one chart for each price. Nonlinear cost-volume-profit analysis can be used as an alternative to this method.

Linear cost-volume-profit analysis is also deficient with regard to costs. The linear relations indicated by the chart do not hold at all output levels. As sales increase, existing plant and equipment are worked beyond capacity, thus reducing their productivity. This situation results in a need for additional workers and frequently longer work periods, which may require the payment of overtime wage rates. All of these tend to cause variable costs to rise sharply. Additional plant and equipment may be required, increasing fixed costs. Finally, over time the products sold by the firm change in quality and quantity. Such changes in product mix influence both the level and the slope of the cost function.

Although linear cost-volume-profit analysis has proved to be a useful tool for managerial decision making, care must be taken to insure that it is not used in situations in which its assumptions are violated so that the results are misleading. In short, this decision tool is like all others, in that it must be employed with a good deal of judgment.

## SUMMARY

Cost analysis plays a key role in most managerial decisions. In this chapter we introduced a number of cost concepts, showed the relation between cost functions and production functions, and examined several short-run and long-run cost analysis and estimation issues.

Although definition of relevant cost varies from one decision to another, several important concepts are common in all cost analyses. First, relevant costs are typically based on the opportunity-cost concept: the relevant cost of a resource is determined by its value in its best alternative use. Second, the relevant cost of a decision includes only those costs that are affected by the action being contemplated. This is the incremental-cost concept. If a cost is unchanged by an action, it is a sunk cost and is irrelevant to that decision. Finally, care must be taken to insure that all costs, both *explicit* and *implicit*, that are affected by a decision are included in the analysis.

Proper use of the relevant-cost concept requires an understanding of a firm's cost/output relation or its cost function. Cost functions are determined by the production function and the market-supply function for inputs. The production function specifies the technical relation between inputs and output, and the price of inputs converts this physical relation to a cost/output function.

Two basic cost functions are used in managerial decision making: *short-run cost functions*, used in most day-to-day operating decisions, and *long-run cost functions*, used for planning purposes. The *short run* is the period during which some of the firm's productive facilities are unalterable; the *long run* is a period of sufficient length to permit the company to change its production system completely by adding, subtracting, or completely modifying its assets.

In the short run, the shape of a firm's cost curves will be determined largely by the productivity of its variable input factors. Over that range of output where the marginal productivity of the variable inputs is increasing, costs will be increasing less than proportionately to output, so unit costs will be declining. Once diminishing returns to the variable factors set in, costs will begin to increase faster than output, and unit costs will begin to rise.

A similar relation holds for long-run cost curves. Here all inputs are variable, and the shape of the cost curve is determined by the presence of *economies* or *diseconomies of scale*. If economies of scale are present, the *cost elasticity* will be less than one ($\epsilon_c < 1$), and unit costs will decline as output increases. Once diseconomies of scale begin to dominate, however, $\epsilon_c > 1$, and average costs will rise.

The output level at which economies of scale cease to significantly reduce costs defines the *minimum efficient scale* (MES) of operation. MES has important implications for both plant and firm scale decisions and for industry competition.

Although a firm desires to produce its output at the minimum possible cost, uncertainty often dictates a trade-off between lower costs and production flexibility. In these cases, the firm must examine the probability distribution of demand and the relative cost differentials of alternative production techniques, then select as the optimal system the one that maximizes the value of the firm.

*Learning curves* describe the decline in average cost that can result from increased production experience. This phenomenon is an important factor in projecting future manufacturing costs in some new or rapidly growing industries. *Economies of scope* exist when complementarities in production reduce the costs of joint, as opposed to individual, production. Like learning-curve advantages, economies of scope can play an important role in long-run managerial decision making.

*Cost-volume-profit analysis* is an important tool for jointly considering fixed costs, variable costs, revenues, and profits. It can be used to study the effects of varying the *degree of operating leverage* that a firm employs and the implications of the profit-contribution concept.

## Questions

8.1 The relevant cost for most managerial decisions is the current cost of an input. The relevant cost for computing income for taxes and stockholder reporting is the historical cost. What advantages or disadvantages would you see in using current costs for tax and stock-holder-reporting purposes?

8.2   What are the relations among historical costs, current costs, and alternative opportunity costs?

8.3   What is the difference between marginal and incremental cost?

8.4   What is a sunk cost, and how is it related to a decision problem?

8.5   What is the relation between production functions and cost functions? Be sure to include in your discussion the effect of conditions in input factor markets.

8.6   Explain why $\epsilon_Q > 1$ and $\epsilon_C < 1$ both indicate increasing returns to scale. (See Chapter 7 for the definition of output elasticity.)

8.7   The president of a small firm has been concerned about rising labor and material costs, but the controller notes that average costs have not increased during the period. Is this possible? What factors might you examine to analyze this phenomenon?

8.8   Given the short-run total cost curve in Figure 8.1, explain why, (a) $Q_1$ is the minimum of the $MC$ curve, (b) $Q_2$ is the minimum of the $AVC$ curve, (c) $Q_3$ is the minimum of the $ATC$ curve, and (d) the $MC$ curve cuts the $AVC$ and $ATC$ curves at their minimum points.

8.9   Will firms in industries in which high levels of output are necessary for minimum efficient scale tend to have substantial degrees of operating leverage?

8.10  Will operating strategies of average-cost minimization and profit maximization always lead to identical levels of output?

## Problems

8.1   Using the total product curve shown below, which describes a production system in which X is the only variable input, answer the following questions relating production to costs:

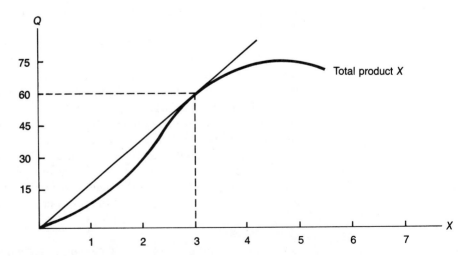

A.   Over approximately what range of input will marginal costs be falling if X is purchased in a competitive market?

B. At approximately what level of employment of Input $X$ will average variable costs be minimized?

C. If $P_X = \$25$, what is the minimum average variable cost in this production system?

D. What is the marginal cost of production at 60 units of output?

E. If the price of output is $2 per unit, is employment of 3 units of $X$ optimal for a profit-maximizing firm (assuming again that $X$ costs $25 per unit)? Explain.

8.2 Determine whether each of the following is *true* or *false*. Explain why.

A. Average cost equals marginal cost at the minimum efficient scale of plant.

B. When total fixed cost and price are held constant, an increase in average variable cost will typically cause a reduction in the break-even activity level.

C. If $\epsilon_c > 1$, diminishing returns to scale and increasing average costs are indicated.

D. When long-run average cost is decreasing, it can pay to operate larger plants with some excess capacity rather than smaller plants at their peak efficiency.

E. An increase in average variable cost will *always* increase the degree of operating leverage for firms making a positive net profit.

8.3 Indicate whether each of the following involves an *upward* or *downward shift* in the long-run average cost curve, or instead involves a *leftward* or *rightward movement along* a given curve. Also indicate whether each will have an *increasing, decreasing,* or *uncertain* effect on the level of average cost.

A. A rise in wage rates

B. A decline in output

C. An energy-saving technical change

D. A fall in interest rates

E. An increase in learning or experience

8.4 Ventura Instruments, Inc., produces precision measuring instruments that it sells to other manufacturers, who then customize and distribute the products to research laboratories. The yearly volume of output is 15,000 units. The selling price and costs per unit are as follows:

| | | |
|---|---:|---:|
| Selling price | | $250 |
| Costs: | | |
|   Direct materials | $40 | |
|   Direct labor | 60 | |
|   Variable overhead | 30 | |
|   Variable selling expenses | 25 | |
|   Fixed selling expenses | 20 | 175 |
| Unit profit before tax | | $75 |

Management is evaluating the alternative of performing the necessary customizing to allow Ventura to sell its output directly to laboratories for $300 per unit. Although no added investment is required in productive facilities, additional processing costs are estimated as follows:

| | |
|---|---|
| Direct labor | $30 per unit |
| Variable overhead | $ 5 per unit |
| Variable selling expenses | $ 2 per unit |
| Fixed selling expenses | $20,000 per year |

A. Calculate the incremental profit that Ventura would earn by customizing its instruments and marketing them directly to end users.

8.5   The Delmarva Medical Clinic, Ltd. is a medical practice serving patients in Newark, Delaware. Michael Gorby, business manager for Delmarva, has been asked by the clinic's board of directors to prepare a financial analysis of the potential of a 24-hour emergency care center. Opening such a center would require remodeling the clinic and hiring some additional staff. Estimated first-year expenses for the emergency care center are as follows:

| | |
|---|---|
| Support staff salary expense | $ 58,000 |
| Medical staff salary expense | 60,000 |
| Medical supplies | 12,000 |
| Equipment | 10,000 |
| Remodeling | 18,000 |
| Electricity, heat, and taxes | 17,000 |
| Total expenses | $175,000 |

Medical and staff salary expenses reflect additional salary and overtime costs. Supplies and remodeling expenses are above and beyond those required for normal clinic operations. Equipment costs represent a prorated share of the clinic's fixed equipment-leasing costs. Electricity costs of $2,000 reflect additional anticipated usage, and heat and taxes of $15,000 reflect an allocated share of current clinic expenses, which will not change.

A. Calculate breakeven revenue for the proposed emergency care center.

8.6   Three graduate business students are considering operating a frozen yogurt stand in the Harbor Springs, Michigan, resort area during their summer break. This is an alternative to summer employment with a local firm, where they would each earn $6,000 over the three-month summer period. A fully equipped facility can be leased at a

cost of $8,000 for the summer. Additional projected costs are $1,000 for insurance and 40¢ per unit for materials and supplies. Their frozen yogurt would be priced at $1 per unit.
  A. What is the accounting cost function for this business?
  B. What is the economic cost function for this business?
  C. What is the economic breakeven number of units for this operation? (Assume a $1 price and ignore interest costs associated with the timing of the lease payments.)

8.7 Diane Chambers is manager of the Kwik Kopy franchise in La Jolla, California. Chambers projects that by reducing copy charges from 5¢ to 4¢ each, Kwik Kopy's $600-per-week profit contribution will increase by one-third.
  A. If average variable costs are 2¢ per copy, calculate Kwik Kopy's projected increase in volume.
  B. What is Chamber's estimate of the arc price elasticity of demand for copies?

8.8 Colonial Furniture, Ltd., is contemplating production of an office desk that would sell for $800. The production of each desk would require $310 in materials and 35 hours of labor with a cost of $8 per hour. Energy, supervisory, and other variable overhead costs would amount to $60 per unit. The accounting department has derived an allocated fixed overhead charge of $75 per desk (at a projected volume of 2,000 units) to account for the expected increase in fixed costs.
  A. What is Colonial Furniture's breakeven sales volume (in units) for office desks?
  B. Calculate the degree of operating leverage (DOL) at a projected volume of 2,000 units and explain what the DOL means.

8.9 Universal Package Service (UPS) offers overnight package delivery to business customers. It has recently decided to expand its facilities to better satisfy current and projected demand. Current volume totals two million packages per month at a price of $12 each, and average variable costs are constant at all output levels. Fixed costs are $3 million per month, and profit contribution averages one-third of revenues on each delivery. After completion of the expansion project, fixed costs will double, but variable costs will decline by 25 percent.
  A. Calculate the change in UPS's monthly breakeven output level that is due to expansion.
  B. Assuming that volume remains at two million packages per month, calculate the change in the degree of operating leverage that is due to expansion.
  C. Again assuming that volume remains at two million packages per month, what is the effect of expansion on monthly profit?

8.10 Digital Disk, Inc., manufactures digital disk players at a Tampa, Florida, production facility. Given widespread consumer acceptance of the firm's products and growing acceptance of digital disk products in general, demand is growing rapidly. To better serve current and expected demand, a multiplant alternative to centralized production is being contemplated. Digital's accounting department has estimated the following demand and production cost relations for the upcoming year:

$$P = \$200 - \$0.00003Q,$$
$$TC = \$7,812,500 + \$100Q + \$0.00002Q^2.$$

A. Assuming centralized production, calculate output price and profits at the profit-maximizing activity level.
B. Calculate the output level that minimizes average cost.
C. Assume that with multiplant production, the same cost conditions as described previously hold for each individual production facility. Calculate output, price, and profit at the multiplant profit-maximizing activity level.
D. Would you describe the cost savings possible through multiplant operation as an example of economies of scale or learning-curve advantages? Why?

## Selected References

Aivazian, Varouj A., Jeffrey L. Callen, M. W. Luke Chan, and Dean C. Mountain. "Economies of Scale versus Technological Change in the Natural Gas Transmission Industry." *Review of Economics and Statistics* 69 (August 1987): 556–561.

Bernstein, Jeffrey I., and M. Ishaq Nadiri. "Interindustry R&D Spillovers, Rates of Return, and Production in High-Tec Industries." *American Economic Review* 78 (May 1988): 420–434.

Bradley, Michael, Anand Desai, and E. Han Kim. "Synergistic Gains from Corporate Acquisitions and Their Division between the Stockholders of Target and Acquiring Firms." *Journal of Financial Economics* 21 (May 1988): 3–40.

Cooper, Robin. "You Need a New Cost System When . . ." *Harvard Business Review* 67 (January-February 1989): 77–82.

Davenport, Thomas H., Michael Hammer, and Tauno J. Metsisto. "How Executives Can Shape Their Company's Information Systems." *Harvard Business Review* 67 (March-April 1989): 130–134.

Davis, David. "New Products: Beware of False Economies." *Harvard Business Review* 63 (March–April 1985): 95–101.

Geus, Arie P. De. "Planning as Learning." *Harvard Business Review* 66 (March–April 1988): 70–74.

Ghemawat, Pankaj. "Building Strategy on the Experience Curve." *Harvard Business Review* 63 (March–April 1985): 143–149.

Henderson, Bruce D. "The Application and Misapplication of the Experience Curve." *Journal of Business Strategy* 4 (Winter 1984): 3–9.

Jordan, J. S. "The Economics of Accounting Information Systems." *American Economic Review* 79 (May 1989): 140–145.

Kaplan, Robert S. "Yesterday's Accounting Undermines Production." *Harvard Business Review* 62 (July-August 1984): 95–101.

Kaplan, Robert S. "One Cost System Isn't Enough." *Harvard Business Review* 66 (January–February 1988): 61–66.

Kim, Moshe, and Giora Moore. "Economic vs. Accounting Depreciation." *Journal of Accounting & Economics* 10 (April 1988): 111–125.

Monahan, George E., and Timothy L. Smunt. "A Multilevel Decision Support System for the Financial Justification of Automated Flexible Manufacturing Systems." *Interfaces* 17 (November-December 1987): 29–40.

Pidd, Michael. *Computer Simulations in Management Science.* New York: John Wiley, 1986.

Romer, Paul M. "Growth Based on Increasing Returns Due to Specialization." *American Economic Review* 77 (May 1987): 56–62.

Ross, Marc. "Capital Budgeting Practices of Twelve Large Manufacturers." *Financial Management* 15 (Winter 1986): 15–22.

Salamon, Gerald L. "Accounting Rates of Return." *American Economic Review* 75 (June 1985): 495–504.

Sutton, Timothy G. "The Proposed Introduction of Current Cost Accounting in the U.K.: Determinants of Corporate Preference." *Journal of Accounting and Economics* 10 (April 1988): 127–149.

Wong, Jilnaught. "Economic Incentives for the Voluntary Disclosure of Current Cost Financial Statements." *Journal of Accounting and Economics* 10 (April 1988): 151–167.

# Cost Estimation

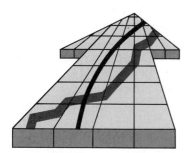

In Chapter 8, we considered how a detailed knowledge of both short-run and long-run cost functions plays an important role in managerial decision making. Short-run cost curves provide information that is useful for making operating decisions. When the marginal revenue derived from sales exceeds the marginal cost of production, an expansion in the level of output would be profitable. Conversely, when the marginal revenue derived from sales is less than the marginal cost of output, an expansion in the level of output would be unwise and would lead to lower profits.

Long-run cost curves provide information that is useful in the long-range planning process. When economies of scale and relatively low distribution costs are prevalent, an expansion in demand can often be met efficiently through an expansion in the level of output at only one or a few large production facilities. However, when a product involves only low or moderate economies of scale combined with high distribution costs, efficient production sometimes calls for smaller plants located closer to regional markets.

For costs to be properly incorporated into managerial decisions, one must have good estimates of how short-run and long-run cost curves are related to a number of important factors both within and outside the control of the firm. In this chapter, we consider various cost estimation techniques useful for obtaining such information. We begin by examining the strengths and weaknesses of statistical cost estimation techniques that rely primarily on accounting data. Accounting information provides a logical, historical perspective that is very useful, but it has limitations when it is used for estimating future costs. Imperfections in accrual accounting methods, as well as the failure to reflect current market values and opportunity costs associated with the use of various inputs, can lead to errors when costs are estimated using unadjusted accounting data. A powerful approach to statistical cost estimation involves the regression-based analysis of accounting data developed from sophisticated management information systems. Computer-generated data on product quantity, quality, and cost characteristics, when combined with familiar least squares regression methods of data analysis, constitutes a powerful low-cost tool for cost estimation. Engineering cost estimation techniques that rely on the physical relations expressed in the production function for a particular product or firm provide an alternative to statistical cost analysis based on historical data. A change in relative input prices, for example, can cause firms to change their input requirements and may thereby undermine the accuracy of engineering cost estimates. Each of the approaches examined in this chapter has its own strengths and weaknesses. Successful managers often find that accurate cost estimation requires using a combination of methods.

# SHORT-RUN COST ESTIMATION

By assuming that the firm has been operating efficiently, or at least that inefficiencies can be isolated and accounted for, it is possible to estimate cost functions by statistical analysis. Time-series and cross-sectional regression analyses are the most popular methods for estimating a firm's short-run variable cost function. Such studies regress cost on output, typically in a model that includes a number of other variables—including input prices, operating conditions, and related factors—whose effects on cost we wish to analyze or at least to account for. For estimating short-run cost relations, the total variable cost function rather than the total cost function is estimated to remove the difficult problem of allocating fixed costs to a particular production quantity. Since fixed costs do not vary with respect to output, they do not affect the average variable cost function or the marginal cost function used for short-run decision-making purposes and can therefore be safely eliminated from the analysis.

## Cost Specification and Data Preparation

Most difficulties encountered in statistical cost analysis arise from two causes: (1) errors in specification of the cost characteristics relevant to the decision and (2) problems in the collection and modification of the data to be analyzed. Thus, before examining the types of regression models actually used to estimate short-run cost functions, we should consider several caveats regarding specification, collection, and modification of cost data.

**Conceptual Problems**  Managerial decision making relates to future activities and events, so the relevant costs for managerial decisions are future costs as opposed to current or historical costs. Cost estimates based on accounting data—which record current or past costs and are thus historical—must therefore be considered only as first approximations to the relevant costs in managerial economics. These historical costs must be modified before they are used for decision-making purposes. The most typical adjustment involves setting prices of input factors, such as labor, materials, and energy, at their current or projected levels.

A second conceptual problem that occurs when accounting data are used for cost analysis stems from the failure of accounting systems to record opportunity costs. Because opportunity costs are frequently the largest and the most important costs in a short-run decision problem, cost functions derived from unadjusted accounting data can be inappropriate.

**Cost/Output Matching**  A problem may arise in the attempt to relate certain costs to output. In short-run cost analysis, only costs that vary with output should be included, but it is often difficult to distinguish between costs that are and are not related to output. Calculating the rate of economic depreciation of capital equipment is one example of this difficulty. For most depreciable assets, both time and usage determine the rate of decline in value, but only the component related to usage should be included in the estimation of the short-run cost/output relation. Typically, however, these costs are combined in accounting data on depreciation costs, and it is often impossible to separate use costs from obsolescence or time-related costs.

Semivariable costs also present a problem in cost/output matching. Some costs may not vary with output changes over certain ranges but will change once a critical level has been exceeded for a long-enough period. These cost/output relations must be accounted for if accurate short-run cost functions are to be estimated.

**Timing of Costs**  Another problem can arise from the use of accounting data in relating costs to the corresponding output. Care must be taken to adjust the data for leads and lags between cost reporting and output production. Maintenance expense provides a typical example of this problem. Production in one period often leads to higher maintenance expenses in subsequent periods. During a period of high production, recorded maintenance expenses will be unusually low because the firm's equipment is being used at full capacity, and maintenance is postponed if possible. Repairs that are made will usually be temporary in nature, aimed at getting the equipment back into production rapidly until some slack enters the production system. Without careful adjustment,

## 9.1  **Managerial Application**

Accounting Issues in Cost Estimation

The Financial Accounting Standards Board (FASB) is a nongovernmental body empowered by the Securities and Exchange Commission with responsibility for determining the nature and scope of accounting information. Started in 1973 as the logical successor to the accounting profession's Accounting Principles Board, the FASB develops new accounting standards in an elaborate process that reflects the views of accountants, business executives, security analysts, and the public. As a result, the FASB plays a key role in defining the specific information that must be incorporated in published corporate financial statements.

The FASB also plays an important role in the resolution of a broad range of important and controversial accounting issues. For example, the FASB is currently considering whether or not to require firms to use current market values rather than historical-cost book values for accounts receivables, bonds, and loan portfolios—including loans to troubled Latin American countries. This is a highly controversial issue, because the market-value approach would lead to a much different picture of corporate assets and liabilities for many companies. In some instances, money center banks would show a substantial negative net worth with a market-value treatment of debts owed by Third World countries. Similarly, some large corporations would see a dramatic decline in reported profits and a big jump in debt-equity ratios, if they were required to fully reflect the magnitude of unfunded pension liabilities.

Corporate executives typically resist the FASB's efforts to install new accounting rules, citing the higher operating expenses sometimes required to meet new guidelines. Most new standards require the capture of new data or the reworking of existing accounting information. At times, however, more subtle unspoken interests may be responsible for corporate opposition to new FASB standards. During inflationary periods, as has been the case in the United

*continued*

See: Carol J. Loomis, "Will 'FASBEE' Pinch Your Bottom Line?," *Fortune*, December 19, 1988, 93–108.

this problem can cause significant errors in statistically estimated cost functions.

**Inflation**   Price-level changes present still another problem. In time-series analysis, recorded historical data are used for statistical cost analysis, and during most periods the costs of labor, raw materials, and other items will have risen. At the same time, a generally expanding economy

**Managerial Application** *continued*

States since World War II, the use of historical book values tends to overstate net income numbers, and to understate the value
of tangible plant and equipment. As a result,
reported profit rates, such as the key return-
on-stockholders'-equity measure, can be
inflated when book-value data are used.
Because of the effects of inflation, a market-
value standard provides a more economically meaningful picture of "true" corporate
profitability, but it typically results in lower
profit rates. The fact that a market-value
standard lowers reported profits is an important concern to many executives, especially those with compensation plans tied to
reported profits.

One of the most important accounting innovations promoted by the FASB during recent years involves the new cash-flow
statements that all companies are now required to provide. By minimizing distortions that are sometimes introduced by
imperfect accrual accounting methods,
cash-flow data are intended to provide a
clearer picture of current corporate performance. Needless to say, many corporations
oppose new cash-flow reporting requirements, especially when meeting them
causes perceived (reported) performance to
falter.

On Wall Street, some observers view ongoing disputes between the FASB and the
corporate community as being based on a
rather myopic view of the information-
processing capability of both professional
and institutional investors. Clearly, the takeover and corporate restructuring boom of
the late 1980s was based on a sophisticated
awareness of corporate cash flows, an
awareness that preceded new FASB cash-
flow reporting requirements. Nevertheless,
new cash-flow statements will help individual investors by providing them with another low-cost basis for evaluating corporate
performance.

Given the wide range of important accounting issues being addressed, the role
played by the FASB has grown steadily. At
times, the public perception of the FASB
has failed to match this pace. Slowly but
surely, this is changing as the FASB's public
visibility increases. In Congressional hearings on the topic of unfunded pension fund
liabilities, for example, the role of the FASB
as an important rule-making body became
apparent to many for the first time. "I had
heard of Frisbees, but not FASBEES," con-
fessed Congressman J. J. Pickle, a Texas
Democrat. But he continued to say that in
the area of pension fund liabilities, "all at
once you have become a household word."
Although perhaps not yet a household word,
the FASB is sure to grow in importance and
visibility during the 1990s.

has caused the output of most firms to increase. Therefore output in more
recent periods is typically larger and has relatively higher cost (in nominal or current-dollar terms), so a naïve cost analysis might incorrectly
suggest that costs rise rapidly with increases in output. To remove this
bias, cost data must be deflated for price-level changes. Because factor
prices increase at different rates, composite price indexes for this deflation often do not provide satisfactory results. It is better to use an index

for each category of inputs. The problem of adjusting for price changes is further compounded by the fact that input-price changes related to increases in demand for the input when the firm's output rate increases must not be removed. Only price changes that are independent of the production system under examination should be eliminated; otherwise, the statistically estimated cost function will understate the true cost of high-level production.

A further difficulty encountered in statistical cost studies when prices fluctuate during the period of examination results from the substitution among various input factors when their relative prices change. That is, price-level changes rarely result in proportional changes in the prices of all goods and services, and, as was shown in Chapter 7, optimal input combinations depend in part on the relative prices of resources. Changes in optimal input combinations will affect the cost projections that are relevant for managerial decision analysis.

**Observation-Period Problems**   Short-run cost curves are, by definition, cost/output relations for a plant of a specific scale and technology. If the short-run curve is to be accurately estimated, the period of examination must be the one during which the product remains essentially unchanged and the plant facilities remain fixed. It should be noted that even though a firm's book value of assets remains relatively constant during the observation period, the plant may have actually changed a great deal. Consider, for example, a firm that replaces a number of obsolete, manually operated machines that have been fully depreciated with a single automated machine that it leases. The firm's production function, and hence its total cost function, undoubtedly changes substantially even though the book value of assets remains constant. The problem of changing plant and product can be minimized by limiting the length of the period over which data are analyzed. For satisfactory statistical estimation, however, the cost analyst needs an adequate sample size with a fairly broad range of outputs. This requirement tends to lengthen the necessary period of data observations and, in turn, necessitates a careful examination of a firm's total activities during the period of a cost study to achieve accurate results.

Given the need for numerous data observations over a relatively short time period, it is apparent that frequent data observations covering short production periods can improve the statistical results in empirical cost studies. Likewise, it is theoretically more satisfying to use frequent data observation points (for example, daily or weekly) so that output rates will be fairly constant *within* the observation period. At odds with this, however, is the fact that data collection and correction problems are often magnified as the length of the observation period is shortened. Although the best length for the observation period will vary from situation to situation, one month is the period most frequently used. In other words, the various elements of variable costs incurred during each month are collected and compared with output produced during the month. A total period of perhaps two to three years (24 to 36 months) can provide enough observations for statistical analysis, yet still be short enough that the plant and the product will have remained relatively unchanged. It is not possible to generalize about the best period of study for all cases, as individual circumstances must always be taken into account.

The brief examination of some of the major data problems encountered in short-run statistical cost analysis points up the importance of proper data collection within the firm. That is, the value of statistical cost analysis to the firm depends greatly on the quality of its cost accounting records. With this in mind, many firms have developed computerized management information systems in which cost and output data are recorded in sufficient detail to allow statistical analysis of their cost/output relations. It must be emphasized that, to benefit managerial decision making, these management information systems must go well beyond collecting and reporting data found in standard accounting systems. Thus, careful planning and a clear understanding of the relevant cost concepts used for various business decisions are required to establish a management information system that will provide the necessary input for proper decision analysis.

## Statistical Short-Run Cost Functions

Once data problems have been solved, cost analysts are faced with the problem of determining the proper functional form of the cost curve. A variety of linear and nonlinear models suitable for least squares regression analysis are available. If there are good theoretical or engineering reasons for using a particular model, that model will be selected. Often, however, there is no a priori reason for choosing one model over another, and in such cases the typical procedure is to fit several models to the cost/output data, then to use the one that seems to fit best in terms of the statistical tests, especially $R^2$, the coefficient of determination. In other words, if one model has an $R^2$ of 0.90, indicating that the model explains 90 percent of the variation in total variable costs, and another model has an $R^2$ of 0.95, the second model will be relied upon for operating decisions.[1]

**Linear Short-Run Cost Functions**   For a great many production systems, a linear statistical cost curve of the following form provides an adequate fit of the cost/output data:

$$C = a + bQ + \sum_{i=1}^{n} c_i X_i. \qquad\qquad \textbf{9.1}$$

[1]This assumes that the independent variables in each model are the same; only the model structure is different. Without this proviso it would be possible to artificially inflate the $R^2$ for one model merely by adding additional explanatory variables. For this reason the adjusted coefficient of determination, $\bar{R}^2$, and the $F$-test described in any basic statistics book are typically used with the coefficient of determination in evaluating regression models.

Here, $C$ refers to the total variable cost during an observation period; $Q$ is the quantity of output produced during that period; $X_i$ designates all other independent variables whose cost effects the analyst wants to account for; and $a$, $b$, and $c_i$ are the coefficients of the model as determined by the least squares regression technique. The other independent variables to be accounted for include such items as wage rates, fuel and materials costs, weather, input quality, production lot size, the product mix, and changes in product design. Including them in the model enables the analyst to better estimate the relation between cost and output.

The intercept coefficient $a$ in this model is typically irrelevant. It cannot be interpreted as the firm's fixed costs because such costs are not included in the data. Even if total costs, as opposed to total variable costs, are used as the dependent variable, the intercept coefficient $a$ may still not reflect the firm's fixed costs. This coefficient is simply the intercept of the estimated cost curve with the vertical axis. This intersection occurs at the point where output is zero and usually lies far outside the range of cost/output data observation points. As we pointed out in Chapter 5, extending the regression equation very far beyond the range of data observations is a hazardous procedure likely to result in significant error. In those limited instances in which firms or plants with very small levels of output are being considered and the measured costs are total costs, the $a$ coefficient can be taken as an estimate, albeit an imperfect one, of fixed costs. In all instances, the interpretation of individual coefficient estimates is best restricted to the relevant range of observations.

Although a linear form for the cost/output relation may be accurate for the range of available data, extrapolation far outside this range can lead to serious misstatement. Since the short run is the period during which the law of diminishing returns is operative, we would expect such distortions to be the rule at very high output levels. That is, the estimated linear relation would be taken only as an approximation (valid for limited output range) to a true curvilinear relationship. The problem of extrapolation outside the observation range is illustrated in Figure 9.1. Within the observed output range, $Q_1$ to $Q_2$, a linear function closely approximates the true cost/output relation. Extrapolation beyond these limits, however, leads to inaccurate estimates of the firm's variable costs.

Coefficient $b$ is the important one in a linear model of this type. As shown in both Figures 9.1 and 9.2, $b$ approximates both marginal costs and average variable costs within the relevant output range.

**Quadratic and Cubic Cost Functions**    Two other forms, the quadratic and the cubic, are also widely used in empirical cost studies. Figures 9.3 and 9.4 illustrate the average variable cost curve and the marginal cost curve associated with quadratic and cubic cost functions. Again, it should be emphasized that because costs that are invariant with respect to output (fixed costs) are not typically included in the empirical estimates of short-run cost curves, these curves represent variable costs

■ Figure 9.1
## Linear Approximation of the Cost/Output Function

Within the range of data observations, a linear function will often closely approximate true cost/output relations.

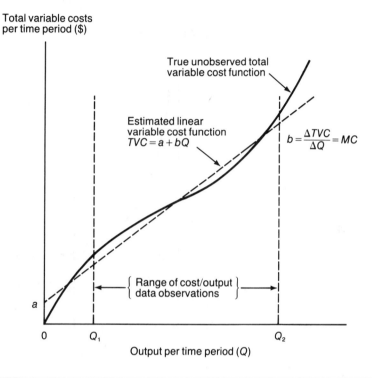

only. An estimate of the fixed costs must be added to determine the firm's short-run total cost function.

**Empirically Estimated Short-Run Cost Functions**  Many empirical studies have been undertaken to ascertain the nature of short-run cost/output relations. Studies covering industries as diverse as electric power generation, textile and steel production, and retailing have found, by and large, that both industry and firm average cost functions tend to be linear, implying constant marginal costs. These empirical findings of constant marginal cost over a wide variety of production systems may, at first, seem quite surprising. The law of diminishing productivity in microeconomic theory leads one to expect that short-run marginal costs would be increasing, imparting the traditional U shape to the average variable cost curve. Why is this not observed in empirical studies?

Although a number of explanations for this phenomenon have been hypothesized, one of the most satisfying relates to the way a modern

■ Figure 9.2

## Average Variable Cost and Marginal Cost for a Linear Cost Function: *TVC = a + bQ*

For a linear total cost function, the slope coefficient *b* estimates a constant marginal cost and average variable cost per unit.

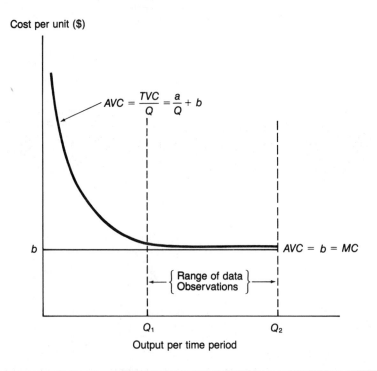

Cost per unit ($)

$AVC = \dfrac{TVC}{Q} = \dfrac{a}{Q} + b$

$AVC = b = MC$

$b$

Range of data Observations

$Q_1$          $Q_2$

Output per time period

---

*Note: If* a = 0, *AVC* = b, *a constant. However, if* a > 0, *AVC declines continuously, but at a decreasing rate as output increases, because as Q becomes larger, a/Q becomes smaller and smaller.*

production system utilizes input factors. In microeconomic theory, the quantity of the fixed factor employed in the production process is held constant in the short run, and varying quantities of the variable factor are used in conjunction with that fixed factor. The theory states that once a certain minimum level of production has been reached, additional units of the variable inputs exhibit diminishing marginal productivity because of limitations imposed by the fixed factor. In actual production systems, however, capital equipment (the fixed factor) is frequently fixed with respect to cost (that is, costs are invariant with respect to output level) but quite variable with respect to actual usage. For example, a firm producing electronic devices may vary output by changing the number of assembly stations it operates, keeping the ratio of capital (fixed factor) to labor (variable factor) it actually employs fixed over short-run produc-

■ Figure 9.3

## Average Variable Cost and Marginal Cost Curves for a Quadratic Total Variable Cost Function: $TVC = a + bQ + cQ^2$

A quadratic total cost function assumes a linear marginal cost function and a U-shaped average variable cost function.

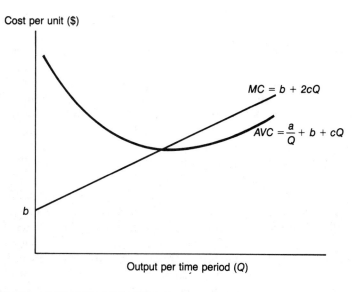

Cost per unit ($)

$MC = b + 2cQ$

$AVC = \dfrac{a}{Q} + b + cQ$

*b*

Output per time period ($Q$)

■ Figure 9.4

## Average Variable Cost and Marginal Cost Curves for a Cubic Variable Cost Function: $TVC = a + bQ - cQ^2 + dQ^3$

A cubic total cost function assumes that both marginal cost and average variable cost functions have U-shapes.

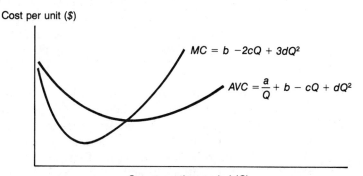

Cost per unit ($)

$MC = b - 2cQ + 3dQ^2$

$AVC = \dfrac{a}{Q} + b - cQ + dQ^2$

Output per time period ($Q$)

## 9.2  **Managerial Application**
Computer-based Cost Estimation and Control

Most manufacturing companies face major problems in cost estimation and control. Although some large, vertically integrated companies have the production capability to directly meet all of their customers' needs, many companies are often forced to "out source" with a wide range of independent suppliers. This means that independent suppliers must be relied on to provide quality components, parts, and supplies in a timely fashion so as not to impede the firm's overall operation. When companies are under pressure to adopt the latest technology, maintain high quality-control standards, *and* slash prices to remain competitive, monitoring their suppliers' cost performance becomes an important consideration.

This monitoring of suppliers' cost performance is sometimes made difficult by the fact that many such companies have not yet fully embraced modern management techniques. Buyers routinely encounter deficiencies in the statistical process controls that identify the causes of product defects

and that provide the basis for accurately estimating the cost of production. Many suppliers are even basically deficient in their ability to handle data electronically.

To address these fundamental problems, a variety of private and government organizations have recently begun to offer their services. In Cleveland, Ohio, for example, the Cleveland Advanced Manufacturing Program is one of nine technology research centers financed by the state of Ohio's $250 million Thomas Edison Program to provide a free assessment of a manufacturer's production line and cost reporting system. The National Institute of Standards has also set up regional manufacturing technology centers in Cleveland; Troy, New York; and Columbia, South Carolina. These centers transfer knowledge about advanced manufacturing and reporting systems developed by the government to smaller companies, often at little or no cost. Such cooperative ventures between private and government organizations, although still quite new,

*continued*

See: Joel Dreyfuss, "Shaping Up Your Suppliers," *Fortune*, April 10, 1989, 116–122.

tion periods. Textile mills, where the number of spindles in operation varies with output, and electricity generation plants, where the number of generators in actual use varies to increase or decrease output, provide other examples of variable employment of the "fixed" factor. Negotiated work rules also add to the fixity of capital and labor input ratios. Many labor contracts specify within narrow ranges the combinations of labor and capital equipment that can be utilized in a production system and the rate at which the capital equipment can be operated.

**Managerial Application** *continued*

seem to be becoming ever more popular.

One of the more interesting of such programs is in Wichita, Kansas. The Center for Technology Application in Wichita offers computer training and engineering advice, and it promotes close cooperation between large companies and their smaller suppliers. The Center is jointly financed by local companies, Wichita State University, and a regional agency for economic development. For example, when local tool-and-die manufacturers complained about a lack of information concerning the specification and costs of various products, the Center helped devise an inexpensive electronic method for transferring information between such companies and their suppliers. As a result, the companies and their suppliers have a much better means for estimating the costs of meeting the customers' current and future needs. New computer-controlled milling machines and computer-aided designs now allow the companies to transmit engineering concepts to sophisticated tooling machines. In the process, a dramatic improvement in product quality becomes possible. One of the most important additional benefits of new sophisticated computer-aided design/ computer-aided manufacturing systems is that they provide companies with a precise means for detailed cost estimation.

Along Massachusetts's Route 128, the accounting firm of Coopers & Lybrand has opened a manufacturing center to help local companies solve problems associated with their manufacturing and cost-reporting systems. In a recent project, the consulting firm developed a pilot system designed to allow smaller suppliers to quickly design and test manufacturing procedures. As a result, a small publisher was able to shorten the design-to-delivery cycle from fourteen to six months. Again, an important residual benefit of such computerized systems is that they allow for dramatically improved cost reporting and estimation.

During the 1990s, the use of computerized systems to control manufacturing and to act as the center of sophisticated cost-reporting systems is bound to become widespread. A few years ago, only large companies could afford the expensive mainframe computers that were required to quickly process detailed production and cost information. Today, sophisticated desktop computers are capable of providing such information at a fraction of what it used to cost. At today's prices for the computers and software systems that make sophisticated cost estimation possible, few companies, large or small, can afford *not* to employ them.

In situations such as these, the rate of utilization of each unit of the capital factor is nearly constant regardless of the production level. Since fixed and variable inputs are being used in constant proportions over wide ranges of production output, the law of diminishing marginal productivity is not observed, and the marginal cost of production remains constant.

To illustrate a regression approach to statistical analysis of short-run costs, consider the example of the Tric-E Razor Company. Weekly razor

■ Table 9.1

## Total Variable Cost and Average Variable Cost Data for the Tric-E Razor Company

| Week | Output (thousands) | Total Variable Cost (dollars) | Average Variable Cost ($ per unit) |
|------|--------------------|-------------------------------|------------------------------------|
| 1  | 27.5 | $4,750 | $172.73 |
| 2  | 30.0 | 5,000  | 166.67  |
| 3  | 32.5 | 5,750  | 176.92  |
| 4  | 40.0 | 8,500  | 212.50  |
| 5  | 10.0 | 4,250  | 425.00  |
| 6  | 27.5 | 5,500  | 200.00  |
| 7  | 30.0 | 6,000  | 200.00  |
| 8  | 32.5 | 5,750  | 176.92  |
| 9  | 35.0 | 6,000  | 171.43  |
| 10 | 37.5 | 7,000  | 186.67  |
| 11 | 40.0 | 9,250  | 231.25  |
| 12 | 10.0 | 4,000  | 400.00  |
| 13 | 12.5 | 4,250  | 340.00  |
| 14 | 15.0 | 4,500  | 300.00  |
| 15 | 22.5 | 4,250  | 188.89  |
| 16 | 25.0 | 4,750  | 190.00  |
| 17 | 12.5 | 4,250  | 340.00  |
| 18 | 15.0 | 4,250  | 283.33  |
| 19 | 17.5 | 4,500  | 257.14  |
| 20 | 20.0 | 4,750  | 237.50  |
| 21 | 22.5 | 4,500  | 200.00  |
| 22 | 25.0 | 4,500  | 180.00  |
| 23 | 35.0 | 6,750  | 192.86  |
| 24 | 37.5 | 7,750  | 206.67  |
| 25 | 17.5 | 4,250  | 242.86  |
| 26 | 20.0 | 4,250  | 212.50  |

output in thousands of units and *TVC* in dollars per week are shown for the most recent six-month period (26 observations) in Table 9.1. These data suggest the familiar S-shaped *TVC*–output relationship illustrated in Figure 9.5a. As a result, *AVC* and output have a U-shaped relationship, as shown in Figure 9.5b. Based on a simple visual scan of the data, a cubic (or third-order polynomial) regression model would seem appropriate for estimating both the *TVC* and *AVC* models. Nevertheless, it is instructive to compare the descriptive capability of these cubic models with the simpler linear and quadratic (second-order polynomial) regression models.

Table 9.2 shows least squares cost-estimation results for linear, quadratic, and cubic models for both *TVC* and *AVC* functions. Given the apparent underlying S-shaped relationship between true *TVC* and output, and the U-shaped relationship between true *AVC* and output, note

■ Figure 9.5
## Cubic Total Variable Cost and Average Variable Cost Curves for the Tric-E Razor Company

A cubic cost function provides a good description of the variation in costs experienced by the Tric-E Razor Company.

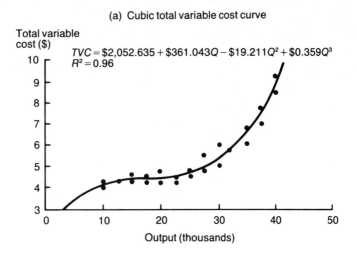

(a) Cubic total variable cost curve

Total variable cost ($)

$TVC = \$2{,}052.635 + \$361.043Q - \$19.211Q^2 + \$0.359Q^3$
$R^2 = 0.96$

Output (thousands)

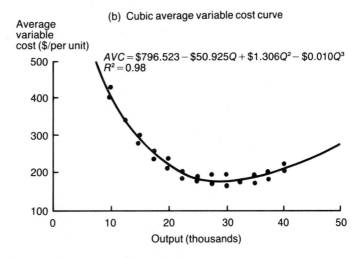

(b) Cubic average variable cost curve

Average variable cost ($/per unit)

$AVC = \$796.523 - \$50.925Q + \$1.306Q^2 - \$0.010Q^3$
$R^2 = 0.98$

Output (thousands)

the relatively greater descriptive capability displayed by the nonlinear quadratic and cubic models. The linear model is unable to describe a high proportion of the underlying variation in variable costs. The roughly one-half ($R^2 = 0.58$) to three-quarters ($R^2 = 0.75$) of variation in variable costs explained by the linear model may not form a reasonable basis for managerial decision making. On the other hand, it is quite

■ Table 9.2
## Tric-E Razor Company Cost Estimation (*t*-statistics in parentheses)

*Total Variable Cost Models*

Linear      $TVC = \$2,114.011 + \$129.670Q$      $R^2 = 0.75$
                       (5.15)        (8.44)                      S.E.E. $= \$732.97$

Quadratic    $TVC = \$6,259.366 - \$255.944Q + \$7.712Q^2$      $R^2 = 0.93$
                       (10.78)      (−5.05)       (7.72)            S.E.E. $= \$395.13$

Cubic       $TVC = \$2,052.635 + \$361.043Q - \$19.211Q^2 + \$0.359Q^3$      $R^2 = 0.96$
                       (1.60)       (2.01)       (−2.50)      (3.52)       S.E.E. $= \$323.00$

*Average Variable Cost Models*

Linear      $AVC = \$377.662 - \$5.734Q$      $R^2 = 0.58$
                       (14.25)     (−5.78)                  S.E.E. $= \$47.35$

Quadratic    $AVC = \$680.455 - \$33.901Q + \$0.563Q^2$      $R^2 = 0.97$
                       (34.41)     (−19.66)    (16.56)          S.E.E. $= \$13.46$

Cubic       $AVC = \$796.523 - \$50.925Q + \$1.306Q^2 - \$0.010Q^3$      $R^2 = 0.98$
                       (16.66)     (−7.61)      (4.57)      (−2.61)      S.E.E. $= \$12.02$

Notes:   $TVC$ = Total Variable Cost ($)
         $Q$ = Output (thousands)
     $AVC$ = Average Variable Cost ($)
   S.E.E. = Standard Error of the Estimate

possible that the roughly 95 percent of the variation in variable costs explained by the alternative quadratic and cubic cost models will form a reasonable basis for both production-related and marketing-related decisions. At a minimum, the cubic model approach seems to offer a useful starting point for a further and more detailed analysis of the variable cost–output relation.

## LONG-RUN STATISTICAL COST ESTIMATION

Statistical estimation of long-run cost curves, although similar in many respects to short-run cost estimation, is typically somewhat more complex. In the long run, all costs are variable, and the problem is to determine the shape of the least-cost production curve for plants of different sizes. Total cost curves must be estimated, and this introduces a number of additional difficulties.

As with short-run analysis, one can analyze the long-run cost/output relation by examining a single firm over a long period. In this case the assumption that plant size is held constant during the examination period is removed, and total costs are regressed against output. The basic problem with this approach is that it is almost impossible to find a situation in which the scale of a firm has been variable enough to allow statistical estimation of a long-run cost curve while technology and other extraneous conditions have remained constant. Without constant technology, the estimated cost function will bear little resemblance to the relevant long-run cost function necessary for current planning purposes.

**cross-sectional regression analysis**
A procedure for analyzing the cost experience of different-size firms (or plants) at one point in time.

Because of the difficulties encountered in using time-series data to estimate long-run cost functions, a different procedure, **cross-sectional regression analysis,** is frequently employed. This procedure compares different-size firms (or plants) at one point in time, regressing total costs against a set of independent variables. The key independent variable is again a measure of output, and other independent variables—such as regional wage rates, fuel costs, and the like—are included to account for the effect on cost of factors other than the level of output.

The use of cross-sectional analysis as opposed to time-series analysis for estimating long-run cost functions reduces some estimation problems and magnifies others. For example, since the data all represent factor prices at the same point in time, the problem of price inflation (or deflation) is removed. A new problem arises, however, because factor input prices vary in different locations; unless all the firms in the sample are located in the same region, interregional price variations may distort the analysis.

A second difficulty in cross-sectional studies can be traced to variations in accounting procedures. Differing depreciation policies among firms and varying techniques for amortizing major expenses can substantially distort their true cost/output relations.

A similar distortion in statistical cost analysis can arise if the firms examined use different means of factor payment. For example, one firm may pay relatively low wages to its employees but may have a substantial profit-sharing program. If this firm's costs are compared with those of a firm that pays higher wages but has no profit sharing, and if shared profits are not included in wage costs, it is clear that an adjustment must be made prior to estimating the cost function for the industry.

Finally, even if all of these data problems are solved so that the effects on costs of all factors other than output are held constant, a last requirement must also be met if we are to estimate accurately the long-run cost function. A basic assumption in the use of cross-sectional data is that all firms are operating at the point along the long-run curve at which costs are minimized. That is, the cross-sectional technique assumes that all firms are operating in an efficient manner and are using the most efficient plant available for producing whatever level of output they are producing. If this assumption holds, the cost/output relation found in the analysis does trace a long-run cost curve, such as that shown as *LRAC* in Figure 9.6. If this assumption is violated, however, the least squares regression line will lie above the true *LRAC* curve, and costs will be overstated.

Even more important than the uniform overstatement of average cost is the possibility that the true curvature in the long-run average cost curve may be distorted and may thereby either under- or overstate any

■ Figure 9.6
## Estimating Long-Run Average Cost Curves with Cross-Sectional Data

Cross-sectional data can be used to estimate the long-run average cost curve for an industry at a given point in time.

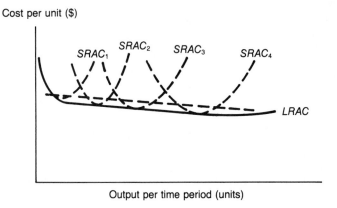

economies or diseconomies of scale in the industry being examined. For example, if the smaller firms in Figure 9.6 are operating well to the right of their optimal output, the estimated *LRAC* curve will have a downward slope much steeper than the true *LRAC* curve, and this bias will cause one to overestimate economies of scale in the industry. Similarly, scale economies may be underestimated because of a selection bias that results if small, high-cost firms fail to compete successfully, go bankrupt, and thus fail to get included in the cost study.

### Empirical Long-Run Cost Functions

The great majority of empirically estimated long-run cost functions exhibit sharply increasing returns to scale at very low output levels, but the extent of these scale economies declines as output increases, and returns quickly become constant. This means that the long-run average cost curve decreases at a decreasing rate as output increases, finally becoming horizontal. Very few studies have found evidence of decreasing returns to scale (an upturn in the average cost curve) at high output levels. These results have caused researchers to hypothesize that long-run average cost curves are more often L-shaped than U-shaped, as postulated in microeconomic theory.

### Alternative Cost Estimation Techniques

Because of the difficulty of obtaining satisfactory statistical estimates of long-run cost/output relations, several alternative means have been developed to empirically examine cost functions. Two of these, the survivor technique and the engineering technique, have proved to be useful in certain situations in which statistical cost estimation is tenuous or impossible because of the absence of adequate data or in which checks on statistical cost estimates are sought. These techniques are discussed in the following sections.

**Survivor Technique.** The survivor principle was developed by Nobel laureate George Stigler. The basic idea behind this technique is that more efficient firms—that is, those with lower average costs—will survive through time. Therefore, by examining changes in the size makeup of an industry over time, one can determine the nature of its cost/output relations.

More specifically, Stigler proposes that one classify the firms in an industry by size and calculate the share of industry output or capacity accounted for by each size class over time. If the share of one class declines over time, that size production facility is assumed to be relatively inefficient. If the relative share increases, however, firms of that size are presumed to be relatively efficient and to have lower average costs.

**survivor technique**
A method of cost analysis based on the assumption that more efficient firms are more likely to survive over time.

The **survivor technique** has been applied to examine the returns to scale of several industries. In a pioneering study, Stigler examined the distribution of steel production among firms of varying sizes.[2] Over the period 1930 to 1951, Stigler found that the percentage of industry output accounted for by the smallest and largest size classes declined, while the output share of medium-size firms increased. Stigler also applied the technique to the automobile industry. Again, he found that the smallest firms showed a continual decline in their share of total industry output. Stigler concluded from this that average costs decline with increasing size. Moreover, market-share losses by smaller firms were distributed equally among medium-size and larger firms, indicating first increasing, then constant returns to scale. In the absence of any indication of diseconomies of scale at very high output levels, he concluded that the automobile industry's long-run average cost curve is L-shaped. Following Stigler's lead, other economists have used the survivor technique to study economies of scale in banking, cement, and many other industries. Today, it is considered an especially useful approach in industry studies when individual firms are reluctant to release proprietary cost information for competitive reasons.

Although the survivor technique is a valuable tool for examining cost/output relations, it does have some severe limitations. First, it presumes that survival is directly related to minimization of long-run average costs. As is demonstrated in more detail in Chapter 11, this premise implicitly assumes that the firms examined are operating in a highly competitive market structure. If markets are protected by regulation or

[2]George J. Stigler, "The Economies of Scale," *Journal of Law and Economics* 1 (October 1958): 54–71.

## 9.3 **Managerial Application**
The Costs of Moving Headquarters

A heightened awareness of the need to maintain careful control over costs has caused several major corporations to consider the advantages of moving corporate headquarters. J. C. Penney, for example, recently spent an estimated $140 million to move from Manhattan, New York, to Dallas, Texas. Mobil Corporation, also formerly based in New York, spent between $100 and $150 million to move to Fairfax, Virginia. Other recent moves costing in excess of $10 million include International Paper's move from Manhattan to Westchester County, New York, and RJR Nabisco, Inc.'s move from Winston-Salem, North Carolina, to Atlanta, Georgia. In terms of benefits, Penney expects to save $60 million per year in operating costs by moving to Texas, and Mobil expects to save $40 million annually following its move to Virginia.

Although most corporations measure the expected benefits following a corporate move in terms of lower labor, real estate, and other operating expenses, many others are moving for less easily defined strategic benefits. Harcourt Brace Jovanovich, Inc.'s move from New York to Orlando, for example, prompted a major restructuring that led to a leaner corporate staff and higher profit margins. Similarly, RJR Nabisco's move from Winston-Salem to Atlanta is intended to help the company attract more dynamic executives and other employees with dual-career households.

Clearly, recent moves have paid off handsomely for some companies. AMR Corporation, parent company of American Airlines, Inc., reports that sick days have declined and employee commuting time has been reduced significantly following its move to

*continued*

See: Laurie Baum, "Does It Pay to Move the Corporate Headquarters?" *Business Week*, September 7, 1987, 68–69.

various barriers to entry, even inefficient smaller firms can survive for extended periods. Second, high transportation costs can make survival possible for strategically located firms despite inefficiencies. Third, in many industries, inefficient smaller firms survive by emphasizing personalized service or customized production. Successful product differentiation often makes it possible for smaller firms not only to survive but to flourish in the face of competition from larger, more cost efficient rivals.

Finally, because of the very long-run nature of the analysis, the survivor technique is particularly susceptible to the problem of distorted re-

**Managerial Application** *continued*

Dallas from New York in 1979. In addition, relocation at the hub of its airline system has made it easier for executives to travel to outlying points.

However, it is uncertain whether or not the expected savings in operating expenses and other less easily defined benefits are, on average, worth the substantial cost of moving. Professor Vickie Smith of Arizona State University contends that productivity declines dramatically when companies are in the process of considering a move. Employees become distracted when rumors circulate concerning when, where, and why a move is being contemplated. In addition, a great deal of personal wear and tear accompanies the determination of who will be invited to go along and whether or not those invited will choose to accompany the corporation to its new location. On average, relocation experts find that only 30 to 50 percent of those employees invited by the corporation agree to go along. Manville Corporation, which spent $27 million to move from New York and New Jersey to a location outside Denver, Colorado, in 1971, finds the two-hour time difference between itself and leading customers in New York to be a major headache. Sales personnel often have to call on customers from their homes at 7:30 A.M. Similarly, a series of moves in the 1970s by AM International, Inc. from Cleveland to Los Angeles to Chicago cost the company many of its senior executives and was a contributing factor to a decline that landed the company in Chapter 11 bankruptcy proceedings. Many of these costs of corporate moves go unreported and therefore are often ignored in the calculation of the net benefits to moving.

RJR Nabisco's departure, following a similar move out of Winston-Salem by Piedmont Aviation, Inc., cost that city leading corporate citizens and greatly hampered prospects for near-term growth. Citing the importance of enticing new corporate headquarters, the regional Forsyth County Development Corporation raised $1 million for industrial recruiting. Like other indirect costs of moving corporate headquarters, these expenses are often ignored. Given the many direct and indirect costs and benefits involved with moving corporate headquarters, it is not surprising that corporate relocations continue to be an important subject of concern for both corporate and public officials.

sults arising from inflation and changing technology. In many instances, inventions or innovations over time favor firms in specific size classes. Resulting changes in the distribution of industry output may reveal less about movements along industry long-run average cost curves (i.e., economies of scale) than they do about downward shifts in cost/output relations.

**Engineering Technique** The engineering method of cost analysis is based directly on the physical relations expressed in the production function for a particular product or firm. On the basis of a knowledge of the production technology involved, the optimal input combination for producing any given output quantity is determined. The cost curve is then formulated by multiplying each input in these least-cost combinations by its price and summing to develop the cost function.

**engineering technique**
A method of cost analysis based directly on the physical relations expressed in the production function for a particular product or firm.

The **engineering technique** comes the closest of any estimation procedure to reflecting the timeless nature of theoretical cost functions. It is based on currently available technology, and it alleviates the possibility of confounding results through improper data observations. That is, whereas the cost observations used for statistical cost estimation may be contaminated by any number of extraneous factors, engineering estimation avoids these complications by coupling current price quotations from suppliers with estimates of required quantities of various inputs.

The engineering method of cost estimation has proved to be useful for examining cost/output relations in such areas as oil refining, chemical production, and nuclear power generation. The engineering method of cost estimation is not without pitfalls, however, and care must be exercised to develop accurate cost functions by this method. The difficulty often comes in trying to extend engineering production functions beyond the range of existing systems or in going from pilot plant operations to full-scale production facilities. These problems are illustrated by the difficulties encountered by a major chemical company in developing a facility that made use of a new production technology. The firm completed an engineering cost study based on projected input/output relations developed from a small pilot facility. The estimated cost of constructing the new plant was $100 million and it was projected that output would have a marginal cost of approximately $100 a ton, substantially below the costs in existing facilities. Once construction got under way, however, it became clear that the projection of production relations beyond the pilot plant's size was woefully inadequate. A planned two-year construction period dragged on for five years, and construction costs ballooned to $300 million. After completion of the plant, actual marginal costs of production were $150 a ton, 50 percent greater than the estimated level. Although this is an extreme case, it does illustrate that even though the engineering method can provide a useful alternative to statistical cost estimation, it too must be applied with great care if accurate cost productions are to result.

Case 9.1

# Estimating Nursing Costs

Accurate measurement of nursing costs per patient day (a measure of output) is necessary for effective hospital management and an important concern of public officials at the federal, state, and local government levels. For example, many state Medicaid reimbursement programs base their payment rates on historic accounting measures of average costs per unit of service. However, these historic average costs may or may not be relevant to hospital management decisions. During periods of substantial excess capacity, the overhead component of average costs may become irrelevant. Conversely, when the facilities of providers are fully utilized and facility expansion becomes necessary to increase services, then all costs, including overhead, are relevant. As a result, historical average costs will provide a useful basis for planning purposes only if appropriate assumptions can be made about the relative length of periods of peak versus off-peak facility usage. From a public-policy perspective, a further potential problem arises when hospital expense reimbursement programs are based on historic average costs per day, because the care needs and nursing costs of various patient groups can vary widely. For example, if the care received by the average publicly supported Medicaid patient actually costs more than that received by non-Medicaid patients, Medicaid reimbursement based on average costs for the entire facility would be inequitable to providers and could create access barriers for some Medicaid patients.

As an alternative to historical estimation methods, one might consider using the engineering technique to estimate nursing costs. For example, the labor cost of each type of service could be estimated as the product of an estimate of the time required to perform each service times the estimated wage rate per unit of time. Multiplying this figure by an estimate of the frequency of service would provide an estimate of the aggregate cost of the service. However, a possible limitation to the accuracy of this engineering cost-estimation method is that treatment of a variety of illnesses often requires a combination of nursing services. To the extent that multiple services can be provided simultaneously, the engineering technique will tend to overstate actual costs unless the effect on costs of service "packaging" is allowed for.

Nursing cost estimation is also possible using a carefully designed regression-based approach using variable cost and service data collected at the ward, unit, or facility level. For example, weekly labor costs for registered nurses (RNs), licensed practical nurses (LPNs), and nursing aides might be related to a variety of patient services performed during some measurement period. Given sufficient variability in cost and service levels over time, useful estimates of variable labor costs become possible for each type of service and for each patient category (Medicaid, non-Medicaid, etc.). An important advantage of the regression-based approach is that it explicitly allows for the effect of service packaging on variable costs. For example, if shots and wound-dressing services are typically provided together, this will be reflected in the regression-based estimates of the variable costs per unit of shots and wound-dressing services.

Long-run costs could be estimated using either the cross-section or time-series approaches described in this chapter. Here the most common level of aggregation is the facility level. By relating total facility costs to the service levels provided by a number of hospitals, nursing homes, or out-patient care facilities during a specific period of time, useful cross-section estimates of total service costs are possible. If case mixes vary dramatically according to type of facility, then the type of facility would have to be explicitly accounted for in the regression model analyzed. Similarly, if patient mix or service-provider efficiency is expected to depend, at least in part, on the for-profit or not-for-profit organization status of the care facility, the regression model must also recognize this factor. Of course, these factors as well as price-level adjustments for inflation, among other factors, would have to be accounted for in a time-series approach to nursing cost estimation.

To illustrate a regression-based approach to nursing cost estimation, consider the following cross-section analysis of variable nursing costs conducted by the Southeast Association of Hospital Administrators (SAHA). Using confidential data provided by 40 regional hospitals, SAHA studied the relation between nursing costs per patient day and four typical categories of nursing services. These annual data appear in Table 9.3. The four categories of nursing services studied include shots, intravenous (IV) therapy, pulse taking and monitoring, and wound dressing. Each service is measured in terms of frequency per patient day. An output of 1.50 in the shots-service category means that, on average, patients received one and one-half shots per day. Similarly, an output of 0.75 in the IV-service category means that IV services were provided daily to 75 percent of a given hospital's patients, and so on. In addition to these four categories of nursing services, the not-for-profit or for-profit status of each hospital is also indicated. Using a "dummy" (or binary) variable approach, the profit status variable equals 1 for the 8 for-profit hospitals included in the study and zero for the remaining 32 not-for-profit hospitals. On an aggregate basis, average nursing costs per patient day are $123.56 for all 40 hospitals. However, average costs for the 8 for-profit hospitals in the sample were only $120.94 per patient day, or $3.28 per patient day less than the $124.22 average cost experienced by the 32 not-for-profit hospitals. By considering differences in the nursing services provided, along with the for-profit or not-for-profit status of each hospital, it becomes possible to learn whether these average cost differences are related to differences in patient mix or, perhaps, to other factors, such as efficiency or operating philosophy.

Cost estimation results, provided in Table 9.4, indicate that $R^2 = 0.84$—meaning that 84 percent of the total variation in nursing costs per patient day can be explained by the five factors studied. In terms of individual coefficient estimates, the 11.418 coefficient for the shots variable indicates an average nursing labor cost of roughly $11.42 per shot. Similarly, IV therapy results in $10.05 in nursing costs per patient day, pulse taking and monitoring costs $4.53, and wound dressing costs $18.93 per unit. Each of these four services appears to have a clear impact on nursing costs per patient day. Interestingly, a coefficient of − 2.105 for the profit-status variable indicates that, on average, nursing

■ Table 9.3

**Nursing Costs per Patient Day, Nursing Services, and Profit Status for 40 Hospitals in the Southeast**

| Hospital | Nursing Costs per Patient Day | Shots | IV | Pulse | Wound Dressing | Profit Status (1 = For-Profit, 0 = Not-For-Profit) |
|---|---|---|---|---|---|---|
| 1 | $125.00 | 1.50 | 0.75 | 2.25 | 0.75 | 0 |
| 2 | 125.00 | 1.50 | 0.75 | 2.25 | 0.75 | 0 |
| 3 | 115.00 | 1.50 | 0.50 | 2.00 | 0.50 | 1 |
| 4 | 125.00 | 2.00 | 0.75 | 2.25 | 0.75 | 0 |
| 5 | 122.50 | 1.50 | 0.50 | 2.25 | 0.75 | 0 |
| 6 | 120.00 | 1.50 | 0.75 | 2.25 | 0.75 | 1 |
| 7 | 125.00 | 1.75 | 0.75 | 2.00 | 0.50 | 0 |
| 8 | 130.00 | 1.75 | 0.75 | 2.25 | 0.75 | 0 |
| 9 | 117.50 | 1.50 | 0.50 | 2.25 | 0.50 | 0 |
| 10 | 130.00 | 1.75 | 0.75 | 3.25 | 0.75 | 0 |
| 11 | 125.00 | 1.50 | 0.75 | 3.00 | 0.50 | 0 |
| 12 | 127.50 | 1.50 | 0.75 | 2.50 | 0.75 | 0 |
| 13 | 125.00 | 1.75 | 0.75 | 2.50 | 0.50 | 0 |
| 14 | 125.00 | 1.50 | 0.50 | 2.50 | 0.75 | 0 |
| 15 | 120.00 | 1.50 | 0.75 | 2.25 | 0.50 | 0 |
| 16 | 125.00 | 1.50 | 0.50 | 2.25 | 0.75 | 0 |
| 17 | 130.00 | 1.75 | 0.75 | 2.50 | 0.75 | 0 |
| 18 | 120.00 | 1.50 | 0.50 | 2.25 | 0.50 | 0 |
| 19 | 125.00 | 1.50 | 0.75 | 2.25 | 0.75 | 0 |
| 20 | 122.50 | 1.50 | 0.50 | 2.50 | 0.75 | 0 |
| 21 | 117.50 | 1.75 | 0.50 | 2.00 | 0.50 | 1 |
| 22 | 120.00 | 1.50 | 0.50 | 2.50 | 0.50 | 0 |
| 23 | 122.50 | 1.50 | 0.75 | 2.50 | 0.75 | 1 |
| 24 | 117.50 | 1.50 | 0.50 | 2.50 | 0.50 | 0 |
| 25 | 132.50 | 1.75 | 0.75 | 2.50 | 0.75 | 0 |
| 26 | 120.00 | 1.75 | 0.50 | 2.25 | 0.50 | 1 |
| 27 | 122.50 | 1.75 | 0.50 | 2.50 | 0.50 | 0 |
| 28 | 125.00 | 1.50 | 0.75 | 2.50 | 0.75 | 0 |
| 29 | 125.00 | 1.50 | 0.50 | 2.00 | 0.75 | 0 |
| 30 | 130.00 | 1.75 | 0.75 | 2.25 | 0.75 | 0 |
| 31 | 115.00 | 1.50 | 0.50 | 2.00 | 0.50 | 0 |
| 32 | 115.00 | 1.50 | 0.50 | 2.25 | 0.50 | 0 |
| 33 | 130.00 | 1.75 | 0.75 | 2.50 | 0.75 | 0 |
| 34 | 132.50 | 1.75 | 0.75 | 3.00 | 0.75 | 0 |
| 35 | 117.50 | 1.50 | 0.50 | 2.00 | 0.50 | 1 |
| 36 | 122.50 | 1.50 | 0.50 | 2.50 | 0.75 | 0 |
| 37 | 112.50 | 1.50 | 0.50 | 2.00 | 0.50 | 0 |
| 38 | 130.00 | 1.50 | 0.75 | 3.25 | 0.75 | 0 |
| 39 | 130.00 | 1.50 | 0.75 | 3.25 | 0.75 | 1 |
| 40 | 125.00 | 1.50 | 0.75 | 3.00 | 0.75 | 1 |

■ Table 9.4

**Nursing Costs per Patient Day: Cost Estimation Results**

| Variable Name | Coefficient (1) | Standard Error of Coefficient (2) | t-Statistic (1) ÷ (2) = (3) |
|---|---|---|---|
| Intercept | 76.182 | 5.086 | 14.98 |
| Shots | 11.418 | 2.851 | 4.00 |
| IV | 10.052 | 3.646 | 2.76 |
| Pulse | 4.532 | 1.153 | 3.93 |
| Wound dressing | 18.933 | 3.370 | 5.62 |
| For-profit status | −2.105 | 0.883 | −2.38 |

Coefficient of determination = $R^2$ = 0.84
Standard error of estimate = S.E.E. = $2.21

costs per patient day are roughly $2.10 lower in for-profit than in not-for-profit hospitals after accounting for differences in patient mix as captured by the four service categories. This suggests that the efficiency or operating philosophy of for-profit hospitals may be responsible for a substantial portion of the lower nursing costs these hospitals enjoy.

Overall, despite obvious limitations, such a regression-based approach can provide useful measures of costs for both private and public decision making. In practice, nursing care cost estimation and cost reimbursement methodologies that reflect the care needs of patients can be based on a manageable number of services. In fact, Illinois, West Virginia, Ohio, and Maryland have implemented Medicaid nursing home reimbursement systems based on this concept, and several other states have similar case-mix reimbursement systems under development.

## SUMMARY

Empirical determination of a firm's cost function is a necessary requirement for optimal decision making. This chapter examined a variety of techniques for analyzing both short-run and long-run cost/output relations.

The primary statistical methodology for cost estimation is least squares regression analysis. Properly conducted time-series analysis of a single firm's cost/output relation can provide an excellent estimate of the firm's short-run variable cost function. This function indicates the nature of marginal costs and average variable costs, which are the relevant-cost concepts for short-run decision making.

Statistical estimation of long-run costs typically involves *cross-sectional regression analysis* as opposed to time-series regression analysis. Here cost/output relations for many firms of varying size are analyzed to determine the nature of the total cost function for firms of different scale.

Two major findings dominate the work of researchers in this area of cost analysis. In the short-run, the relation between cost and output appears to be best approximated by a linear function. This means that marginal costs are constant over a significant range of output for most firms. Long-run estimation has typically indicated that sharply increasing returns to scale (decreasing average costs) are available over low output ranges in most industries, giving way to constant returns (constant average costs) at higher output levels. Decreasing returns to scale (increasing average costs) appear to be the exception rather than the rule for most long-run cost functions, even at very high output quantities.

Because of the difficulties encountered in statistical cost estimation, alternative techniques of empirical analysis are frequently employed. The *survivor technique* and the *engineering technique* are two such methods commonly used for this purpose.

The survivor technique is based on the assumption that more efficient firms—those with lower average costs—will have greater probability of survival. Therefore, by examining the size makeup of an industry over time, one can determine the nature of cost/output relations.

The engineering technique is based on the physical relations expressed in a firm's production function. Using engineering estimates of input/output relationships, one determines the optimal production system and multiplies each required input by its cost to determine the cost function. This method is particularly useful for estimating cost relations for new products or plants involving new technologies for which the historical data necessary for statistical cost analysis are unavailable.

## Questions

9.1 For purposes of cost estimation, how long is the short-run time period?

9.2 Name and briefly elaborate upon three common problems encountered in short-run cost analysis.

9.3 Short-run statistical cost studies have been reported for a wide variety of industries. Long-run cost studies, on the other hand, have been restricted to a few industries. Why do you suppose so many more short-run rather than long-run studies have been conducted?

9.4 The law of diminishing productivity leads one to expect that short-run marginal (and average variable) cost curves will be U-shaped. Nevertheless, most empirical studies find constant marginal costs for many firms. Why?

9.5 What requirements must be met before a long-run cost function can be estimated?

9.6 Is a linear model appropriate for estimating the point of minimum efficient scale in an industry?

9.7 For long-run statistical cost estimation, cross-sectional analysis rather than time-series analysis is used, partly to overcome the problem of changing technology. Does the use of cross-sectional data eliminate this problem? Why or why not?

9.8  If the total cost/output relation is analyzed using regression analysis, can the intercept term be interpreted as an unbiased estimate of fixed costs?

9.9  Does the survivor technique for estimating long-run cost/output relations overcome the problem of changing technology?

9.10 Discuss the similarities between the engineering technique of cost estimation and the market-experiment approach to demand estimation.

## Problems

9.1  Assume that a linear statistical cost curve of the following form provides an adequate explanation of short-run total variable costs for a firm during a given observation period:

$$C = a + bQ + \sum_{i=1}^{n} c_i X_i.$$

Indicate whether each of the following statements is *true* or *false* and why.

A. $X_i$ designates a variety of independent variables whose nonoutput-related cost effects the analyst wants to account for.

B. A cost elasticity estimate greater than one would suggest increasing returns to scale.

C. The coefficient $b$ provides an estimate of marginal costs and average variable costs per unit.

D. The coefficient $a$ can be interpreted as the firm's fixed costs.

E. Included among relevant variable costs will be time and usage costs for most depreciable assets.

9.2  An engineering cost analysis indicates total production costs of $TC = \$500{,}000 + \$200Q - \$0.1Q^2$. Indicate whether each of the following statements is *true* or *false* and why.

A. Fixed costs equal $500,000.

B. Cost elasticities will vary with output.

C. This production system illustrates first decreasing, then increasing returns to scale.

D. If output per period doubles from 1,000 to 2,000 units, average costs will fall from $600 to $250 per unit.

E. The decline in average costs from $600 to $250 described in Part D indicates a learning-curve advantage of roughly 58 percent.

9.3  Manhattan Couriers, Inc., (MCI) provides same-day package delivery service to New York publishers at a price of $5 for each package delivered. Of this amount, $1.25 is profit contribution. MCI is considering an attempt to differentiate its service from several other competitors by providing insurance against loss caused by fire, theft, and so on. If offered, insured delivery would increase MCI's unit cost by 25 cents per package delivery. Current monthly profits are $5,000 on 12,000 package deliveries per month.

A. Assuming that average variable costs are constant at all output levels, what is MCI's total cost function before the proposed change?

B. What will be the total cost function if insured package delivery is offered?

C. Assuming that delivery prices remain stable at $5, estimate the percentage increase in deliveries necessary to maintain current profit levels.

9.4 Advanced Technology, Inc., (ATI) is evaluating a contract proposal calling for it to build and test bearings using a newly patented surface configuration. ATI would receive $1.4 million for the work. ATI's management believes that the bearings can be built and tested using existing facilities, with the exception of one piece of test equipment that can be rented at a cost of $45,000. Labor requirements are estimated at 8,000 hours, and ATI calculates labor costs at $110 per hour. This labor cost is derived by adding a 20-percent fixed overhead charge to actual direct labor costs, plus a 100-percent charge for the firm's required profit margin. This profit margin charge is the amount that management believes can be earned under normal conditions. Materials and supplies costing $250,000 will be purchased for the project, and 1,000 pounds of a specialty steel currently in inventory will be used. This steel cost $20,000 when purchased, and ATI estimates inventory carrying costs at 20 percent of initial cost. The steel has a current market value of $18,000. Finally, management has determined that resources are currently fully employed, and acceptance of this job will require turning away other available business.

ATI's cost projection for the bearing test job is as follows:

| | | |
|---|---:|---:|
| 1. Direct labor cost | | |
| (8,000 hours @ $50 per hour) | | $ 400,000 |
| 2. Direct materials: | | |
| Purchased materials | $250,000 | |
| Inventoried steel | 24,000 | 274,000 |
| Total direct labor & materials | | 674,000 |
| 3. Equipment rental | | 45,000 |
| 4. Overhead (20 percent of direct labor) | | 80,000 |
| 5. Required profit margin | | |
| (100 percent of direct labor) | | 400,000 |
| Total project cost | | $1,199,000 |

A. For each of the five cost categories in the cost estimate, determine (1) whether the cost is relevant for the decision to accept or reject the contract, (2) whether the cost is an implicit or an explicit cost, and (3) whether the cost has been properly calculated, given the information in the problem.

B. Estimate ATI's relevant cost (including all implicit as well as explicit costs) of accepting the contract.

C. How would an assumption that the economy was in a recession and that ATI didn't have enough business to keep its resources fully employed affect the relevant costs for this problem? Be specific and reestimate the costs of the job.

9.5 Power Brokers, Inc., (PBI) a discount brokerage firm, is contemplating opening a new regional office in Providence, Rhode Island. An accounting cost analysis of monthly operating costs at a dozen of its regional outlets reveals average fixed costs of $4,500 per month and average variable costs of:

$$AVC = \$59 - \$0.006Q,$$

where AVC is average variable costs (in dollars); and Q is output measured by number of stock and bond trades. A typical stock or bond trade results in $100 gross commission income, with PBI paying 35 percent of this amount to its sales representatives.

A. Estimate the trade volume necessary for PBI to reach a target return of $7,500 per month for a typical office.

B. Estimate and interpret the elasticity of cost with respect to output at the trade volume found in Part A.

9.6 Sub-Temp, Inc., offers a line of modular freezers to restaurants and other institutional buyers. Each freezer unit is self-contained and can be used individually or in tandem with additional modules of different shapes and sizes. During the current period, Sub-Temp estimates the following total cost and demand relations for its line of modular freezers:

$$TC = \$2,000,000 + \$150Q + \$0.02Q^2,$$
$$P = \$900 - \$0.03Q,$$

where TC is total cost, Q is output, and P is average price.

A. Calculate the output level at which average total cost will be minimized.

B. Estimate the profit-maximizing output level.

C. Compare and discuss your answers to Parts A and B.

9.7 The St. Thomas Winery plans to open a new production facility in the Napa Valley of California. Based on information provided by the accounting department, the company estimates fixed costs of $250,000 per year and average variable costs of:

$$AVC = \$10 + \$0.01Q,$$

where AVC is average variable cost (in dollars) and Q is output measured in cases of output per year.

A. Estimate total cost and average total cost for the coming year at a projected volume of 4,000 cases.

B. An increase in worker productivity because of greater experience or learning during the course of the year resulted in a substantial cost saving for the company. Estimate the effect of learning on average total cost if actual total cost was $522,500 at an actual volume of 5,000 cases.

9.8 Stephenson Farms, Inc., has just completed a cost study of its Wisconsin milk-production operation. By regressing total variable costs on milk production, the firm estimated the following equation:

$$\text{Cost} = \$10,500 + \$0.89Q - \$0.005Q^2.$$
$$(6,000) \quad (0.18) \quad (0.093)$$

Here $Q$ is milk production in gallons, and the numbers in parentheses are the standard errors of the coefficients. The $R^2$ for the equation was 0.87, and the standard error of the estimate was 22. Monthly observations over a two-year period were used in the study.

Interpret this estimated cost function. In other words, explain the relation between milk production and cost as depicted by this equation. Be as complete as possible.

9.9 Heavy Duty Batteries, Inc., is considering further expansion in the storage battery industry and has asked you to make an analysis of such a move's profit potential. In particular, the marketing department has suggested building a $10 million plant capable of producing two million batteries per year.

To facilitate your analysis, you consult a recent trade-association study of plants in the industry, which found the following (t-statistics in parentheses):

$$C = \$4,000 + \$18Q + \$0.001Q^2,$$
$$(12.5) \quad (6.8) \quad (5.2)$$

where

$C$ = Total Costs (in thousands of dollars);
$Q$ = Output (in thousands of batteries);
$R^2$ = 0.96;
$n$ = 39;
$F$ = 132;
S.E.E. = 2,000.

A. Define minimum efficient scale from a theoretical point of view, and discuss three aspects that determine its competitive consequences.

B. Estimate minimum efficient scale for the storage battery industry.

9.10 Logan Drill Bit, Inc., currently dominates the market for high-stress drill bits with a 40-percent market share. However, entry by new and highly sophisticated competitors is likely unless a substantial expansion program is undertaken. The time has come to expand rapidly or exit the industry. Engulf & Devour, Inc., (E & D) has made the exit alternative more palatable with an offer to purchase privately held Logan for $2 million (near current book value).

Logan has retained you to advise it in its decision about whether or not to accept the E & D offer. You have conducted an engineering cost analysis of recent Logan plant data and found the following:

$$TC = \$20 + \$5Q + \$0.25Q^2,$$

where *TC* is Total cost (in millions of dollars) and *Q* is Output (in thousands of drill bits).

Furthermore, you learn that in an average year, Logan sells 9,000 drill bits at $9,500 each. Future growth is expected to expand the market for drill bits to 96,000 units within the decade.

A. Calculate and fully interpret the current breakeven level of production.
B. Determine the output level of the minimum efficient scale (MES) plant size.
C. In light of the expected future size of the market for drill bits, how would you evaluate the future potential for competition in the industry?
D. If the current cost of capital for firms in Logan's risk class is 15 percent, should Logan expand or accept E & D's buyout offer?

## Selected References

Baldwin, John R., and Paul K. Goreckie. "The Relationship between Plant Scale and Product Diversity in Canadian Manufacturing Industries." *Journal of Industrial Economics* 34 (June 1986): 373–387.

Bernstein, Jeffrey I. "The Structure of Canadian Inter-Industry R&D Spillovers, and the Rate of Return to R&D." *Journal of Industrial Economics* 37 (March 1989): 315–328.

Black, James H. *Cost Engineering Planning Techniques for Management.* New York: Marcel Dekker, 1984.

Daughety, Andrew F., and Forrest D. Nelson. "An Econometric Analysis of Changes in the Cost and Production Structure of the Trucking Industry." *Review of Economics and Statistics* 70 (February 1988): 67–75.

Davis, David. "New Projects: Beware of False Economies." *Harvard Business Review* 63 (March–April 1985): 95–101.

Duetsch, Larry L. "Geographic Market Size and the Extent of Multiplant Operations." *Review of Economics and Statistics* 64 (February 1982): 165–167.

Hirschey, Mark, and Dean W. Wichern. "Indicators and Causes of Size Advantages in Industry." *Managerial and Decision Economics* 4 (June 1983): 64–72.

Johannes, James M., Paul D. Koch, and Robert H. Rasche. "Estimating Regional Construction Cost Differences: Theory and Evidence." *Managerial and Decision Economics* 6 (June 1985): 70–79.

Jordan, J. S. "The Economics of Accounting Information Systems." *American Economic Review* 79 (May 1989): 140–145.

Kaplan, Robert S. "Yesterday's Accounting Undermines Production." *Harvard Business Review* 62 (July–August 1984): 95–101.

Kessides, Ioannis N. "Advertising, Sunk Costs, and Barriers to Entry." *Review of Economics and Statistics* 68 (February 1986): 84–95.

Klein, Janice A. "The Human Costs of Manufacturing Reform." *Harvard Business Review* 67 (March–April 1989): 60–66.

Lieberman, Marvin B. "Market Growth, Economies of Scale, and Plant Size in the Chemical Processing Industries." *Journal of Industrial Economics* 36 (December 1987): 175–191.

Nelson, Randy A. "On the Measurement of Capacity Utilization." *Journal of Industrial Economics* 37 (March 1989): 273–286.

Oi, Walter Y. "Slack Capacity: Productive or Wasteful?" *American Economic Review* 71 (May 1981): 64–69.

Pashigian, B. Peter. "The Effect of Environmental Regulation on Optimal Plant Size and Factor Shares." *Journal of Law and Economics* 27 (April 1984): 1–28.

Prais, S. J. "Some International Comparisons of the Age of Machine-Stock." *Journal of Industrial Economics* 34 (March 1986): 261–277.

Smith, Vernon L. "Theory, Experiment and Economics." *Journal of Economic Perspectives* 3 (Winter 1989): 151–170.

Thomas, Lacy Glenn. "Advertising in Consumer Goods Industries: Durability, Economies of Scale, and Heterogeneity." *Journal of Law and Economics* 32 (April 1989): 163–193.

Thompson, Arthur A. "Strategies for Staying Cost Competitive." *Harvard Business Review* 62 (January–February 1984): 110-117.

# Linear Programming

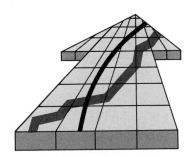

**linear programming**
An analytical technique used to solve constrained optimization problems.

inear programming is an analytical technique used to determine the optimal solution to decision problems. It is only one of a series of analytical techniques, known collectively as *mathematical programming*, that are used to solve constrained optimization problems. While more complex mathematical programming techniques are required in many decision situations, an understanding of linear programming provides a solid basis for examining the types of constrained optimization problems typically encountered in managerial economics.

Linear programming is a mathematical tool for solving maximization and minimization problems. It is particularly powerful when applied to problems for which constraints restrict the course of action available to the decision maker. Because many managerial problems are of this nature, linear programming is a very useful tool for managerial decision making.

The value of linear programming in managerial decision making can be seen by considering a few of the many types of constrained optimization problems to which it has been applied. Applications cover such diverse managerial problems as product design and product mix specification, input allocation in production systems (including job assignment of key personnel), product distribution analysis (including plant location and delivery routing), promotional mix in marketing activities, inventory and cash management, and capital budgeting (investment) decisions. Although their focuses differ considerably, each of these problems involves the allocation of scarce resources to achieve some specific goal.

In production-related decisions, firms are often faced with a variety of capacity limitations. Limited availability of skilled labor and specialized equipment, fixed plant size, and limits on raw materials or energy inputs can all constrain production. Within such capacity constraints, managers must exercise careful judgment to insure that scarce resources are used in the most efficient manner possible to produce only the products that provide the greatest returns or profits.

For example, an oil company has a specified quantity of crude oil and a fixed refinery capacity. It can produce gasoline of different octane ratings, diesel fuel, heating oil, kerosene, or lubricants. Given its crude oil supplies and refinery capacity, what mix of output should it produce? Integrated forest-products companies face a similar problem. Because they have a limited supply of logs and limited mill capacity, their problem is to determine the optimal output mix of lumber, plywood, paper, and other wood products.

A related production problem involves determining the best way of producing a given output. A firm owns two plants with which to produce its product. The plants employ somewhat different technologies, so their cost functions are different. How should production be allocated between the two plants to minimize the total cost of production, subject to these constraints: (1) both plants must, because of a union contract, operate at least 30 hours a week, and (2) at least 100,000 units of output must be produced each week to satisfy the firm's supply contracts.

In marketing, a frequently encountered issue is the optimal advertising mix among various media, where *optimal* is defined as that mix that minimizes the cost of reaching a specified number of potential customers with certain characteristics of age, income, education, and other factors.

In finance, firms may have a large number of investment opportunities but only limited funds available for investment. What set of projects will maximize the value of new long-term investments, subject to the constraint that the total capital budget not exceed some specified maximum? Moreover, firms must hold balances of cash, a nonearning asset. What is the minimum amount of cash they can hold, subject to the constraint that the probability of running short of cash must be kept below some minimum value?

None of these problem situations has a simple rule-of-thumb solution. The interrelations involved are complex, and arriving at optimal solutions requires careful analysis of the alternatives. The fact that linear programming has proved to be useful in solving such a broad range of constrained maximization and minimization problems indicates its value as a managerial decision tool.

## BASIC ASSUMPTIONS

In managerial problems, many of the production or resource constraints imposed are, in fact, inequalities rather than equalities. That is, constraints sometimes limit resource use, specifying that the amount employed must be less than or equal to ($\leq$) some fixed amount available. In other instances, constraints specify that the quantity or quality of output must be greater than or equal to (≥) some minimum requirement. Linear programming handles constraint inequalities easily, making it a useful technique with many applications in managerial economics.

A typical linear programming problem might be to maximize output subject to the constraint that no more than 40 hours of skilled labor time per week be used. Here the labor constraint would be expressed as an inequality where skilled labor ≤ 40 hours per week. This type of operating constraint means that although no more than 40 hours of skilled labor can be used, some excess capacity is permissible, at least in the short run. If 36 hours of skilled labor time were fruitfully employed during a given week, the 4 hours per week of unused labor time would be called excess capacity. This is the type of production constraint that the linear programming approach is designed for.

As the name implies, linear programming assumes all relations to be linear. What relations are involved, and how important is the assumption of linearity likely to be? Typical managerial decision problems that can be solved using the linear programming method involve revenue and cost functions and their composite, the profit function. Each of these must be linear; that is, as output increases, revenues, costs, and profits must increase linearly. For revenues to be a linear function of output, product prices must be constant. For costs to be a linear function of output, two conditions are required: returns to scale must be constant; and input prices must be constant. Constant input prices, when combined with constant returns to scale, result in a linear total cost function.

Under what conditions are product and input prices likely to be constant? In other words, when can a firm buy unlimited quantities of its inputs and sell unlimited amounts of its products without changing prices? The answer is, under conditions of pure competition. Does this mean that linear programming is applicable only for purely competitive industries and, further, only for competitive industries in which returns to scale are constant? The answer is no, because linear programming is used for decision making over limited output ranges. Frequently, the constant-returns-to-scale assumption is valid and input and product prices are approximately constant over these ranges so that the profit function can be approximated by a linear relation.

To illustrate, if an oil company is deciding the optimal output mix for a refinery with a capacity of 150,000 barrels of oil per day, it may be perfectly valid to assume that crude oil costs $15 a barrel, regardless of how much is purchased, and that the products can be sold at constant prices, regardless of the quantities offered. The firm may have to pay more for crude oil and may have to sell its output at lower prices if it tries to expand the refinery by a factor of 10, but within the range of feasible outputs (up to 150,000 barrels a day), prices are approximately constant. Further, up to its capacity limits, it is reasonable to expect that doubling crude oil inputs leads to a doubling of output; therefore, returns to scale are constant. Roughly the same conditions hold for forest-product companies, office equipment manufacturers, automobile producers, and most other firms.

We see, then, that in many instances, the linearity assumptions are valid. Even when the assumption does not hold precisely, linear approximations will seldom seriously distort the analysis.

# LINEAR PROGRAMMING AND PRODUCTION PLANNING: ONE PRODUCT

Although linear programming has been widely applied in managerial decision analysis, it has been developed most fully and is used most frequently in production decisions. Often the decision problem is to determine the least-cost combination of inputs needed to produce a particular product. In other cases, the problem may be to obtain the maximum possible output from a fixed quantity of resources. Both problems can be readily solved by linear programming. To see this more clearly, we start with a simple case and examine the problem faced by a firm that can use two inputs in various combinations to produce a single product. Then, in later sections, we examine more realistic, but necessarily more complex, cases.

## Production Processes

Assume that a firm produces a single product, $Q$, using two inputs, $L$ and $K$, which might represent labor and capital. Further, instead of the possibility of continuous substitution between $L$ and $K$, as was hypothesized in Chapter 7, assume that $Q$ can be produced using only four input combinations. In other words, four different production processes are available to the firm for making $Q$, each of which uses a different fixed combination of the two inputs, $L$ and $K$. In most industries, this is an entirely reasonable assumption, much more reasonable than continuous substitution. The four production processes, for example, might be thought of as being four different plants, each with its fixed asset configuration and each requiring a specific amount of labor to operate the equipment. Alternatively, they could be four different assembly stations or assembly lines, each using a different combination of capital equipment and labor.

The four production processes are illustrated in Figure 10.1. Process $A$ requires the combination of 15 units of $L$ and 1 unit of $K$ for each unit of $Q$ produced. Process $B$ uses 10 units of $L$ and 2 units of $K$ for each unit of output. Processes $C$ and $D$ use 7.5 units of $L$ and 3 units of $K$, and 5 units of $L$ with 5 units of $K$, respectively, for each unit of $Q$ produced. The four production processes are illustrated as rays in the figure. Each point along the production ray for Process $A$ combines $L$ and $K$ in the ratio 15 to 1, and Process Rays $B$, $C$, and $D$ are developed in the same way. Each point along a single production ray combines the two inputs

■ Figure 10.1
## Production Process Rays in Linear Programming

Points along each process ray represent combinations of Inputs $L$ and $K$ required for that production process to produce output.

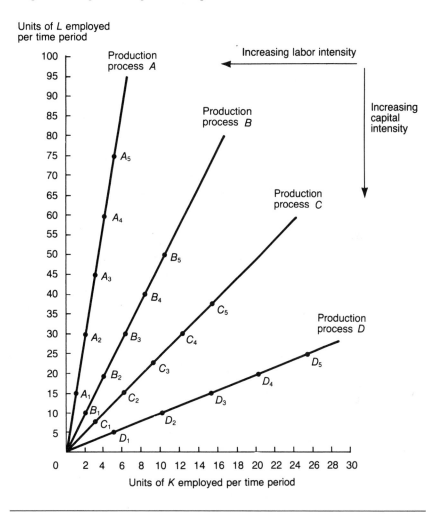

in a fixed ratio, with the ratios differing from one production process to another. If we assume that $L$ and $K$ represent labor and capital inputs, we can view the four production processes as different plants employing different production techniques. Process $A$, for example is very labor intensive in relation to the other production systems, whereas $B$, $C$, and $D$ are based on increasingly capital-intensive technologies.

Examining Process $A$, we see that Point $A_1$ indicates the combination of $L$ and $K$ that the production system requires to produce 1 unit of output. Doubling the quantities of both $L$ and $K$ doubles the quantity of

Q produced; this is indicated by the distance moved along Ray *A* from $A_1$ to $A_2$. In other words, the line segment $0A_2$ is exactly twice the length of line segment $0A_1$ and thus represents twice as much output. Further, along Production Process Ray *A*, the distance $0A_1 = A_1A_2 = A_2A_3 = A_3A_4 = A_4A_5$. Each of these line segments indicates the addition of 1 unit of output using increased quantities of *L* and *K* in the fixed ratio of 15 to 1.

Output along the ray increases proportionately with increases in the input factors. Thus, if each input is doubled, output is doubled; or if inputs increase by a factor of 10 percent, output increases in the same proportion. This follows from the linearity assumption noted previously: Each production process must exhibit constant returns to scale.

Output is measured in the same way along the three other production process rays in Figure 10.1. For example, Point $C_1$ indicates the combination of *L* and *K* required to produce 1 unit of *Q* using Process *C*. The production of 2 units of *Q* by that process requires the combination of *L* and *K* indicated at Point $C_2$, and the same is true for Points $C_3$, $C_4$, and $C_5$. Note that although the production of additional units by Process *C* is indicated by line segments of equal length, just as for Process *A*, the line segments are of different lengths between the various production systems. That is, although each production process exhibits constant returns to scale, allowing us to determine output quantities by measuring the length of the process ray in question, equal distances along *different* process rays do *not* ordinarily indicate equal output quantities.

## Production Isoquants

Joining points of equal output on the four production process rays creates a set of isoquant curves, as illustrated in Figure 10.2, where isoquants for $Q = 1,2,3,4,$ and 5 are shown. These curves have precisely the same interpretation as the isoquants developed in Chapter 7. They represent combinations of input factors *L* and *K* that can be used to produce a given quantity of output. The production isoquants in linear programming are composed of linear segments connecting the various production process rays, and the segments of the various isoquants are always parallel to one another. For example, line segment $A_1B_1$ is parallel to segment $A_2B_2$; similarly, isoquant segment $B_3C_3$ is parallel to $B_2C_2$.

The points along each segment of an isoquant between two process rays represent a combination of output from each of the two adjoining production processes. Consider Point *X* in Figure 10.2, which represents production of 4 units of *Q* using 25 units of *L* and 16 units of *K*. None of the available production processes can manufacture *Q* using *L* and *K* in the ratio 25 to 16, but that combination is possible by producing part of the output with Process *C* and part with Process *D*. In this case, 2 units of *Q* can be produced using Process *C* and 2 units using Process *D*. Production of 2 units of *Q* with Process *C* utilizes 15 units of *L* and 6 units of *K*. For the production of 2 units of *Q* with Process *D*, 10 units each of *L* and *K* are necessary. Thus, although no single production sys-

■ Figure 10.2
## Production Isoquants in Linear Programming

Each point along an isoquant represents the output level resulting from a given combination of inputs. For example, Point X depicts the production of 4 units of Q using 25 units of L and 16 units of K.

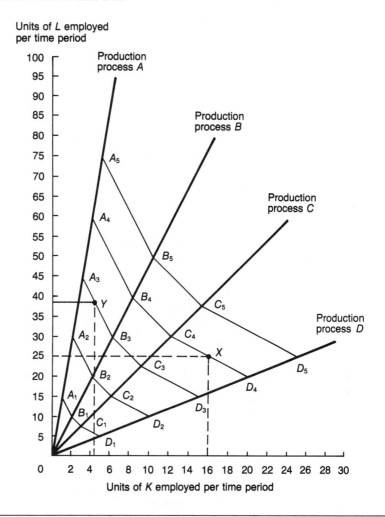

tem is available with which the firm can produce 4 units of Q using 25 units of L and 16 units of K, Processes C and D together can produce that combination.

All points lying on the production isoquant segments can be interpreted in a similar manner. Each point represents a linear combination of output using the production process systems that bound the particular segment. Point Y in Figure 10.2 provides another illustration of this. At Y, 3 units of Q are produced, using a total of 38.5 units of L and 4.3 units of $K$.[1] That input/output combination is possible through a linear combination of Processes $A$ and $B$. This can be analyzed algebraically. To produce 1 unit of $Q$ by Process $A$ requires 15 units of $L$ and 1 unit of $K$. Therefore, to produce 1.7 units of $Q$ requires 25.5 ($1.7 \times 15$) units of $L$ and 1.7 ($1.7 \times 1$) units of $K$. To produce a single unit of $Q$ by Process $B$ requires 10 units of $L$ and 2 units of $K$, so 1.3 units of $Q$ requires 13 ($10 \times 1.3$) units of $L$ and 2.6 ($2 \times 1.3$) units of $K$. Thus, Point $Y$ calls for the production of 3 units of $Q$ in total, 1.7 units by Process $A$ and 1.3 units by Process $B$, using a total of 38.5 units of $L$ and 4.3 units of $K$.

One method of determining the quantity to be produced by each production process at varying points along the isoquant is called the *relative distance method*. The relative distance method is based on the fact that the location of a point along an isoquant determines the relative shares of production for the adjacent processes. Consider Point $X$ in Figure 10.2. If Point $X$ were on Process Ray $C$, all output would be produced using Process $C$. Similarly, if $X$ were on Process Ray $D$, all output would be produced using Process $D$. Since Point $X$ lies between Process Rays $C$ and $D$, both Processes $C$ and $D$ will be used to produce the output. Process $C$ will be used relatively more than Process $D$ if $X$ is closer to Process Ray $C$ than to Process Ray $D$. Conversely, Process $D$ will be used relatively more than Process $C$ if $X$ is closer to Process Ray $D$ than to Process Ray $C$. Because Point $X$ in Figure 10.2 lies at the midpoint of the $Q = 4$ isoquant segment between $C_4$ and $D_4$, it implies production using Processes $C$ and $D$ in equal proportions. Thus, at Point $X$, $Q = 4$ and $Q_C = 2$ and $Q_D = 2$.

The relative proportions of Process $A$ and Process $B$ used to produce $Q = 3$ at Point $Y$ can be determined in a similar manner. Because $Y$ lies closer to Process Ray $A$ than to Process Ray $B$, we know that Point $Y$ entails relatively more output from Production Process $A$ than Production Process $B$. The share of total output produced using Process $A$ can be calculated by considering the distance $B_3Y$ relative to $B_3A_3$. The share of total output produced using Process $B$ can be calculated by considering the distance $A_3Y$ relative to $A_3B_3$. For example, starting from Point $B_3$, we note that the segment $B_3Y$ covers 56.6 percent of the total distance $B_3A_3$. This means that at Point $Y$, about 56.6 percent of total output is produced using Process $A$ ($Q_A = 0.566 \times 3 = 1.7$) and 43.4 percent ($= 1.0 - 0.566$) using Process $B$ ($Q_B = 0.434 \times 3 = 1.3$). Alternatively, starting from Point $A_3$, we note that the segment $A_3Y$ covers 43.4 percent

---

[1]Another assumption of linear programming is that fractional variables are permissible. In many applications, this assumption is not important. For example, in the present illustration we might be talking about labor hours and machine hours for the inputs. The solution value calling for $L = 38.5$ merely means that 38.5 hours of labor are required.

In some cases, however, inputs are large (whole plants, for example) and the fact that linear programming assumes divisible variables is important. In such cases, linear programming as described here may be inappropriate, and a more complex technique, integer programming, may be required.

of the total distance $A_3B_3$. Thus, at Point $Y$, 43.4 percent of total output is produced using Process $B$ and 56.6 percent using Process $A$. Extreme accuracy would require painstaking graphic detail, but in many instances the relative distance method can adequately approximate production intensities along isoquants.

## Least-Cost Input Combinations

Adding isocost curves to the set of isoquants permits one to determine least-cost input combinations for the production of Product $Q$. This is shown in Figure 10.3 under the assumption that each unit of $L$ costs \$3

■ Figure 10.3
## Determination of Least-Cost Production Process

The tangency between the isoquant and isocost lines at Point $B_3$ reveals the least-cost combination of inputs.

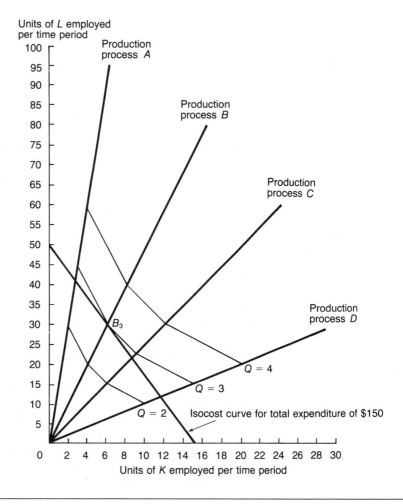

and each unit of $K$ costs \$10. The isocost curve illustrated indicates a total expenditure of \$150.

The tangency between the isocost curve and the isoquant curve for $Q = 3$ at Point $B_3$ indicates that Production Process $B$, which combines Inputs $L$ and $K$ in the ratio 5 to 1, is the least-cost method of producing $Q$. For any expenditure level, production is maximized by using Process $B$. Alternatively, Production Process $B$ is the least-cost method for producing any quantity of $Q$, given the assumed prices for $L$ and $K$.

## Optimal Input Combinations with Limited Resources

Frequently, firms faced with limited inputs during a production period may find it optimal to use inputs in proportions other than the least-cost combination. To illustrate, consider the effect of limits on the quantities of $L$ and $K$ available in our example. Specifically, assume that only 20 units of $L$ and 11 units of $K$ are available during the current production period and that the firm seeks to maximize the output of $Q$. These constraints are shown in Figure 10.4. The horizontal line drawn at $L = 20$ indicates the upper limit on the quantity of $L$ that can be employed during the production period; the vertical line at $K = 11$ indicates a similar limit on the quantity of $K$.

We can determine the production possibilities for this problem by noting that, in addition to the limitations on Inputs $L$ and $K$, the firm must operate within the area bounded by Production Process Rays $A$ and $D$. Thus, we see that combining the production possibilities with the input constraints restricts the firm to operations within the shaded area on 0PRS in Figure 10.4. This area is known as the **feasible space** in the programming problem. Any point within the space combines $L$ and $K$ in a technically feasible ratio without exceeding availability limits on $L$ and $K$.

**feasible space**

The solution space (area) in a linear programming problem that meets all the restrictions or conditions imposed by the constraints of the problem.

Because the firm is trying to maximize the production of $Q$, subject to constraints on the use of $L$ and $K$, it should operate at that point in the feasible space that touches the highest possible isoquant. This is Point $R$ in Figure 10.4, where $Q = 3$.

Although it is possible to solve problems like the foregoing example by using carefully constructed graphs, it is typically more useful to combine graphic analysis with analytical procedures to obtain accurate solutions efficiently. For example, consider Figure 10.4 again. Even if the isoquant for $Q = 3$ were not drawn, it would be apparent from the slopes of the isoquants for 2 or 4 units of output that the optimal solution to the problem must be at Point $R$. That is, it is readily apparent from the graph that the maximum production will be obtained by operating at the point where both inputs are fully employed. Because $R$ lies between Production Processes $C$ and $D$, we know that the output-maximizing production combination will use only these two production processes. We also know that all 20 units of $L$ and 22 units of $K$ will be employed, since Point $R$ lies at the intersection of the two input constraints.

■ Figure 10.4
## Optimal Input Combination with Limited Resources

Given limited resources, output is maximized at Point R because this point lies on the highest isoquant that intersects the feasible space.

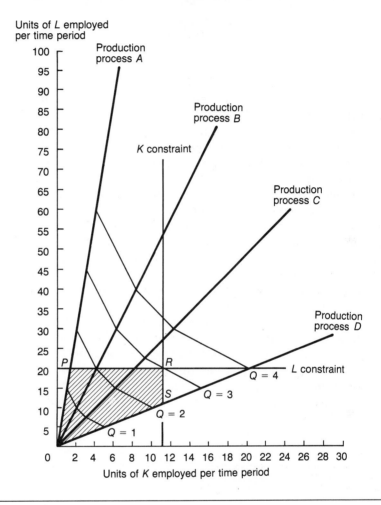

With this information from the graph, we can solve for the optimal quantities to be produced using Processes $C$ and $D$ as follows. First, recall that each unit of output produced using Process $C$ requires 7.5 units of $L$. Thus, the total $L$ required in Process $C$ will be equal to $7.5 \times Q_C$. Similarly, each unit produced using Process $D$ requires 5 units of $L$, so the total $L$ used in Process $D$ equals $5 \times Q_D$. At Point $R$, 20 units of $L$ are being used in Processes $C$ and $D$ together, and the following must hold:

$$7.5Q_C + 5Q_D = 20. \qquad \textbf{10.1}$$

## 10.1  **Managerial Application**

LP as a Tool for Financial Planning

Just a few years ago, the LP technique was thought to have fairly limited applications, primarily for problems in transportation, production scheduling, and quality control in manufacturing. Today, applications range from these production and logistics areas to personnel and financial areas.

An interesting area in which LP techniques are becoming more useful almost on a daily basis is in the field of finance. For example, consider the case of Homart Development Company, a consolidated, wholly owned subsidiary of Sears, Roebuck and Company. Homart owns and develops regional shopping centers and major office buildings. If Homart were independent, its assets would rank the company among the *Fortune 500*. The company's business covers the full range from project design through development, leasing, and management to eventual divestiture.

One of the company's most important strategic issues is scheduling projects for divestiture. In its strategic plan for 1986, for example, Homart analyzed 170 assets for possible divestiture over a period of ten years. As an alternative to its traditional procedure for project evaluation, the company designed an LP approach to the problem. The Homart LP problem has an objective of maximizing the net present value of cash proceeds from a divestiture, subject to a set of constraints on yearly returns. The decision variable indicates whether an individual project is to be sold in a given year or held instead for future divestiture. During its first year of operation, the model generated an additional profit of $40 million. This LP model is now institutionalized as a core element of the company's six-month strategic-planning cycle.

A second set of interesting finance appli-

*continued*

See: P. R. Chandy and Prakash Kharabe, "Pricing in the Government Bond Market," *Interfaces*, September–October 1986, 65–71; and James C. Bean, Charles E. Noon, and Gary J. Salton, "Asset Divestiture at Homart Development Company," *Interfaces*, January–February 1987, 48–64.

A similar relation can be developed for the use of K. Each unit of output produced from Process C requires 3 units of K, whereas Process D uses 5 units of K to produce each unit of output. The total use of K equals 11 units at Point R, and these 11 units are used in Processes C and D so that:

$$3Q_C + 5Q_D = 11. \qquad \textbf{10.2}$$

Equations 10.1 and 10.2 both must hold at Point R; therefore, by solving them simultaneously we can determine the output quantities from

**Managerial Application** *continued*

cations of LP techniques is in the area of security portfolio management. A multitude of LP programs have been developed to help investors maximize their expected rates of return on stock and bond investments, subject to a wide variety of constraints on portfolio risk, dividend and interest yields, payout levels, and so on. For example, P. R. Chandy and Prakash Kharabe have developed an LP model to help bond dealers and other investors decide whether to buy, sell, or hold government bonds. This model seeks to obtain the maximum yield for each level of risk exposure. This is especially useful to security dealers who must maintain ready inventory of government bonds of varying maturities in order to satisfy the investor demand. The Chandy and Kharabe LP model allows investors to select the proportion of the portfolio to invest in each respective security to create the highest yielding, or optimum, portfolio. It also calculates the value of alternative portfolios, allowing the portfolio manager to calculate the opportunity cost of suboptimal asset allocation.

LP software programs for sophisticated personal computers, such as those using Intel's high-speed 286 or 386 microprocessors, are now available. Although these relatively inexpensive programs sometimes require a fair amount of computer literacy, they have the potential to bring the use of LP techniques to a broad range of financial applications. Not only are such programs appropriate for determining an optimal mix of stock and bond investments, subject to a wide range of risk and return constraints, but they can also be used for many other financial planning applications. Capital budgeting and the development of an appropriate corporate strategy is made much easier when the answer to a variety of "What if?" questions can be obtained in a matter of seconds.

The greatest single barrier to the use of LP techniques in financial planning, as well as in other business applications, has been the lack of user-friendly software that can be easily applied by the nonspecialist. As more user-friendly software becomes widely available, even more rapid growth in the use of LP techniques in many new business applications is sure to follow.

Processes $C$ and $D$ at that location. Subtracting Equation 10.2 from Equation 10.1 to eliminate the variable $Q_D$ allows us to solve for $Q_C$:

$$7.5Q_C + 5Q_D = 20$$

$$\text{minus } 3.0Q_C + 5Q_D = 11$$

$$4.5Q_C \qquad = \quad 9$$

$$Q_C = \quad 2.$$

Substituting 2 for $Q_C$ in Equation 10.2 allows us to determine the output from Process D:

$$3(2) + 5Q_D = 11,$$

$$5Q_D = 5,$$

$$Q_D = 1.$$

Total output at Point R is 3 units, composed of 2 units from Process C and 1 unit from Process D.

The ability to combine graphic and analytical representations of the relations in a linear programming problem allows one to obtain precise solutions with relative ease. This approach to solving linear programming problems is developed more fully in the following section.

## LINEAR PROGRAMMING AND PRODUCTION PLANNING: MULTIPLE PRODUCTS

Many production decisions are considerably more complex than the preceding example. Accordingly, we expand our discussion, moving first to the problem of the optimal output mix for a multiproduct firm facing restrictions on productive facilities and other inputs. This problem, faced by oil refineries, cereal-processing firms, and forest-products companies, among others, is readily solved with linear programming.

Consider a firm that produces Products X and Y and uses Inputs A, B, and C. To maximize its total profits, the firm must determine the optimal quantities of each product to produce, subject to the constraints imposed by limitations on input availability. Often it is useful to structure such a linear programming problem to maximize **profit contribution,** defined as total revenue minus the variable cost of production. Fixed costs must be subtracted from the profit contribution to determine net profits. However, because fixed costs are constant, maximizing profit contribution is tantamount to maximizing profit; thus the output mix that maximizes profit contribution also maximizes net profit.

**profit contribution**

Total revenue minus variable cost.

### Specification of the Objective Function

The equation that expresses the goal of the linear programming problem is called the **objective function.** In our present example, we assume that the firm wishes to maximize total profits from the two products, X and Y, during each time period. If per-unit profit contribution (the excess of price over average variable costs) is \$12 for Product X and \$9 for Product Y, we can write the objective function as:

**objective function**

The equation that expresses the goal of a linear programming problem.

Maximize $\qquad\qquad \pi = \$12Q_X + \$9Q_Y.$ **10.3**

Here $Q_X$ and $Q_Y$ represent the quantities of each product produced. The per-unit profit contribution of X times the units of X produced and sold plus the unit contribution of Y times $Q_Y$ equals that total profit contribution, $\pi$, earned by the firm.

## Specification of the Constraint Equations

Table 10.1, which specifies the available quantities of each input, as well as their usage in the production of $X$ and $Y$, provides all the information necessary to construct the constraint relationships for this problem.

From the table we see that 32 units of Input $A$ are available in each period. We also see that 4 units of $A$ are required in the production of each unit of $X$, whereas 2 units of $A$ are necessary to produce 1 unit of $Y$. Since 4 units of $A$ are required for the production of a single unit of $X$, the total amount of $A$ used to manufacture $X$ can be written as $4Q_X$. Similarly, 2 units of $A$ are required to produce each unit of $Y$, so $2Q_Y$ represents the total quantity of $A$ used in the production of Product $Y$. Summing the quantities of $A$ used in the production of $X$ and $Y$ provides an expression for the total usage of $A$, and because this total cannot exceed the 32 units available, we can write the constraint condition for Input $A$ as:

$$4Q_X + 2Q_Y \leq 32. \qquad \textbf{10.4}$$

The constraint for Input $B$ can be determined in a like manner. One unit of Input $B$ is necessary for the production of each unit of either $X$ or $Y$, so the total amount of $B$ that will be expended is $1Q_X + 1Q_Y$. The maximum quantity of $B$ available for production in each time period is 10 units; thus, the constraint requirements associated with Input $B$ is:

$$1Q_X + 1Q_Y \leq 10. \qquad \textbf{10.5}$$

Finally, the constraint relationship for Input $C$ affects only the production of $Y$. Each unit of $Y$ requires an input of 3 units of $C$, and 21 units of Input $C$ are available. Total usage of $C$, then, is given by the expression $3Q_Y$, and the constraint can be written as:

$$3Q_Y \leq 21. \qquad \textbf{10.6}$$

Constraint equations play major roles in solving linear programming problems. One further concept must be introduced, however, before we can completely specify the linear programming problem and examine how the constraints are used to solve it.

■ Table 10.1

## Inputs Available for Production of *X* and *Y*

| Input | Quantity Available per Time Period | Quantity Required per Unit of Output | |
|---|---|---|---|
| | | X | Y |
| $A$ | 32 | 4 | 2 |
| $B$ | 10 | 1 | 1 |
| $C$ | 21 | 0 | 3 |

## Nonnegativity Requirement

Because linear programming is nothing more than a mathematical tool for solving constrained optimization problems, nothing in the technique itself insures that an answer will make economic sense. For example, in a production problem for a relatively unprofitable product, the mathematically optimal output level may be a *negative* quantity—clearly an impossible solution. Likewise, in a distribution problem, an optimal solution might include negative shipments from one point to another, another impossibility.

To prevent such nonsensical results, we must include a nonnegativity requirement. This is merely a statement that all variables in the problem must be equal to or greater than zero. Thus, for the production problem we are examining, we must add the expressions:

$$Q_X \geq 0$$

and

$$Q_Y \geq 0.$$

# GRAPHIC SPECIFICATION AND SOLUTION OF THE LINEAR PROGRAMMING PROBLEM

Having specified all the component parts of the firm's linear programming problem, we first examine this problem graphically, then analyze it algebraically. Let us begin by restating the decision problem in terms of the system of expressions for the objective function and input constraints. The firm wishes to maximize its total profit contribution, $\pi$, subject to constraints imposed by limitations on its resources. This can be expressed as:

Maximize $\qquad\qquad \pi = \$12Q_X + \$9Q_Y,$ **10.3**

subject to the following constraints:

$$\text{Input A: } 4Q_X + 2Q_Y \leq 32, \qquad \textbf{10.4}$$
$$\text{Input B: } 1Q_X + 1Q_Y \leq 10, \qquad \textbf{10.5}$$
$$\text{Input C: } \qquad 3Q_Y \leq 21, \qquad \textbf{10.6}$$

where

$$Q_X \geq 0 \text{ and } Q_Y \geq 0.$$

## Determining the Feasible Space

In Figure 10.5, the graph of the constraint equation for Input A, $4Q_X + 2Q_Y = 32$, indicates the maximum quantities of X and Y that can be produced given the limitation on the availability of Input A. A maximum of 16 units of Y can be produced if no X is manufactured; 8 units of X can be produced if the output of Y is zero. Any point along the line connecting these two outputs represents the maximum combination of X and Y that can be produced with no more than 32 units of A.

■ Figure 10.5
## Constraint Imposed by Limitations in Input *A*

The constraint equation for Input *A* represents the maximum combination of *X* and *Y* that can be produced with 32 units of *A*.

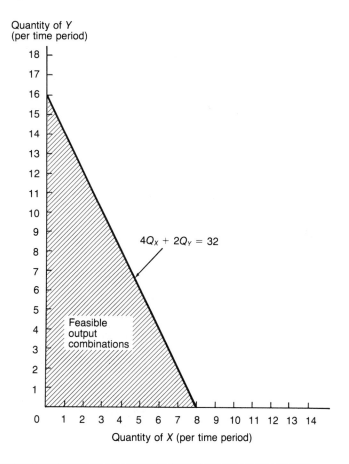

This constraint equation divides the *XY* plane into two half-spaces. Every point lying on the line or to the left of it satisfies the constraint expressed by the equation $4Q_X + 2Q_Y \leq 32$; every point to the right of the line violates that expression. Thus, only points on the constraint line or to the left of it can be in the feasible space. The shaded area of Figure 10.5 represents the feasible area as limited by the constraint on Input *A*.

In Figure 10.6 we have further limited the feasible space by adding the constraints for Inputs *B* and *C*. The constraint on Input *B* can be expressed as $Q_X + Q_Y = 10$. Thus, if no *Y* is produced, a maximum of 10 units of *X* can be produced; if output of *X* is zero, 10 units of *Y* can be manufactured. All combinations of *X* and *Y* lying on, or to the left of, the line connecting these two points are feasible with respect to utilization of Input *B*.

■ Figure 10.6
**Feasible Space**

The feasible space is reduced further by the addition of constraints on Inputs B and C. Only points within the shaded region meet all constraints.

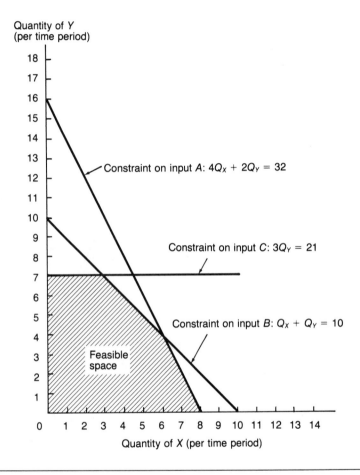

The horizontal line at $Q_Y = 7$ in Figure 10.6 represents the constraint imposed by Input C. Since C is used only in the production of Y, it does not constrain the production of X at all. Seven units of Y are, however, the maximum quantity that can be produced with the 21 units of C available.

The three input constraints, together with the nonnegativity requirement, completely define the feasible space of our linear programming problem, shown as the shaded area of Figure 10.6. Only points within this area meet all the constraints.

### Graphing the Objective Function

The objective function in our example, $\pi = \$12Q_X + \$9Q_Y$, can be graphed in the $Q_X Q_Y$ space as a series of isoprofit curves. This is illus-

■ Figure 10.7
## Isoprofit Contribution Curves

Points along the isoprofit line represent all possible combinations of X and Y that result in the same profit level.

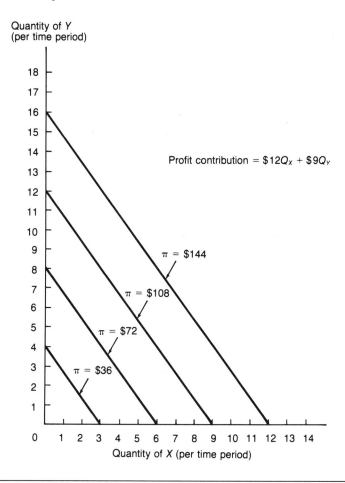

Profit contribution = $12Q_X + \$9Q_Y$

$\pi = \$144$

$\pi = \$108$

$\pi = \$72$

$\pi = \$36$

trated in Figure 10.7, where isoprofit curves for $36, $72, $108, and $144 are shown. Each isoprofit curve illustrates all possible combinations of X and Y that result in a constant total profit. For example, the isoprofit curve labeled $\pi = \$36$ identifies each combination of X and Y that results in a total profit of $36. Similarly, all output combinations along the $\pi = \$72$ curve provide a total profit contribution of $72. It is clear from Figure 10.7 that the isoprofit curves are a series of parallel lines that take on higher values as we move upward and to the right.

The general formula for isoprofit curves can be developed by considering the profit function $\pi = aQ_X + bQ_Y$, where $a$ and $b$ are the profit contributions of Products X and Y, respectively. Solving the isoprofit function for $Q_Y$ creates an equation of the following form:

$$Q_Y = \frac{\pi}{b} - \frac{a}{b} Q_X.$$

Given the individual profit contributions, $a$ and $b$, the $Q_Y$ intercept ($\pi/b$) is determined by the profit level of the isoprofit curve, whereas the slope is given by the relative profitabilities of the two products. Since the relative profitability of the products is unaffected by the output level, isoprofit curves in a linear programming problem will always be a series of parallel lines. In the example, all the isoprofit curves have a slope of $-12/9$, or $-1.33$.

## Graphic Solution of the Linear Programming Problem

Because the firm's objective is to maximize total profit, it should operate on the highest isoprofit curve obtainable. Combining the feasible space limitations shown in Figure 10.6 with the family of isoprofit curves from Figure 10.7 allows us to obtain the graphic solution to our linear programming problem. The combined graph is illustrated in Figure 10.8.

Point M in the figure indicates the solution to the problem. Here, the firm produces 6 units of X and 4 units of Y, and the total profit is $108 [($12 × 6) + ($9 × 4)], which is the maximum available under the conditions stated in the problem. No other point within the feasible spaces touches as high an isoprofit curve.

Using the combined graphic and analytical procedure introduced in the preceding section, we can obtain the result that $Q_X = 6$ and $Q_Y = 4$ at Point M as follows. At M, the constraints on Inputs A and B are both binding. That is, at M, the 32 units of Input A and 10 units of Input B are being completely utilized in the production of X and Y. Thus, Expressions 10.4 and 10.5 can be written as equations and solved simultaneously for $Q_X$ and $Q_Y$. Subtracting two times Equation 10.5 from Equation 10.4 gives:

$$4Q_X + 2Q_Y = 32$$

$$\text{minus } \underline{2Q_X + 2Q_Y = 20}$$

$$2Q_X \qquad = 12$$

$$Q_X = 6$$

Substituting 6 for $Q_X$ in Equation 10.5 results in:

$$6 + Q_Y = 10,$$

$$Q_Y = 4.$$

Notice that the optimal solution to the linear programming problem occurs at a corner of the feasible space. This is due to the linearity assumptions underlying the linear programming technique. When the objective function and all constraints are specified in linear form, the firm will always move to a point of some capacity limit—that is, to a boundary of the feasible space.

■ Figure 10.8
## Graphic Solution of the Linear Programming Problem

Point *M* is on the highest isoprofit curve that intersects the feasible space. Thus, it represents the output combination that will maximize total profit given input constraints.

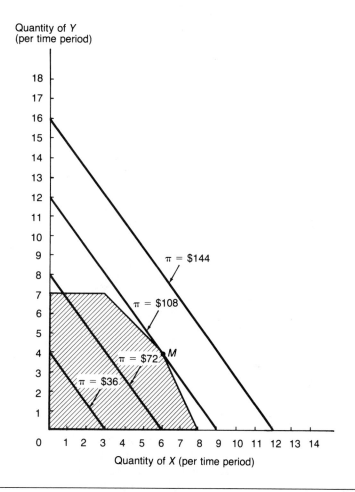

A final step is necessary to show that an optimal solution to any linear programming problem always lies at a corner of the feasible space. Because all of the relations in a linear programming problem must be linear by definition, every boundary of the feasible space is linear. Furthermore, the objective function is linear. Thus, the constrained optimization of the objective function takes place either at a corner of the feasible space, as in Figure 10.8, or at one boundary face, as is illustrated by Figure 10.9.

In Figure 10.9 we have modified the linear programming example by assuming that each unit of either *X* or *Y* produced yields a profit of $5.

■ Figure 10.9
## Graphic Solution of a Linear Programming Problem When the Objective Function Coincides with a Boundary of the Feasible Space

When the objective function coincides with the boundary of the feasible space, several different output combinations will produce maximum profits.

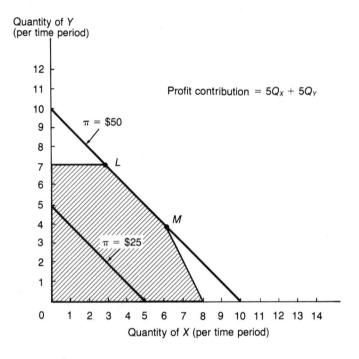

In this case, the optimal solution to the problem includes any of the combinations of $X$ and $Y$ found along Line Segment $LM$, because all of these combinations are feasible and all result in a total profit of $50. If all points along Line $LM$ provide optimal combinations of output, the combinations found at Corners $L$ and $M$ are also optimal. That is, since the firm is indifferent about whether it produces the combination of $X$ and $Y$ indicated at Point $L$ or at Point $M$, or at any point between them, either corner location provides an optimal solution to the production problem. Thus, even when the highest obtainable isoprofit curve lies along a bounding face of the feasible space, it is possible to achieve an optimal solution to the problem at a corner of the feasible space.

From this result it follows that in linear programming problems, we can limit our analysis to just the corners of the feasible space. In other words, we can ignore the infinite number of points lying within the feasible space and concentrate our efforts solely on the corner solutions.

This greatly reduces the computations necessary to solve linear programming problems that are too large to solve by graphic methods.

# ALGEBRAIC SPECIFICATION AND SOLUTION OF THE LINEAR PROGRAMMING PROBLEM

The graphic technique just described is useful to illustrate the nature of linear programming, but it can be applied only in the two-output case. Since most linear programming problems contain far too many variables and constraints to allow solution by graphic analysis, we must use algebraic methods. These algebraic techniques are especially valuable because they permit us to solve large, complex linear programming problems on computers, and this greatly extends the usefulness of the method.

### Slack Variables

**slack variables**

Variables added to a linear programming problem to account for the amount by which each constraint differs from its limit at a solution point.

To solve a linear programming problem algebraically, we must introduce one additional concept, that of **slack variables.** These variables are added to a linear programming problem to account for the amount by which each constraint differs from its limit at a solution point. One slack variable is introduced for each constraint in the problem. In our illustrative problem, the firm is faced with capacity constraints on Input Factors $A$, $B$, and $C$, so the algebraic specification of the problem contains three slack variables: $S_A$, indicating the units of $A$ that are not used in any given solution; $S_B$, representing unused units of $B$; and $S_C$, which measures the unused units of $C$.

Introducing these slack variables allows us to write each constraint relationship as an equation rather than as an inequality. Thus, the constraint on Input $A$, $4Q_X + 2Q_Y \leq 32$, can be written as:

$$4Q_X + 2Q_Y + S_A = 32. \qquad \textbf{10.7}$$

Here $S_A = 32 - 4Q_X - 2Q_Y$, which is the amount of Input $A$ not used in the production of $X$ or $Y$. Similar equality constraints can be specified for Inputs $B$ and $C$. Specifically, the equality form of the constraint on Input $B$ is:

$$1Q_X + 1Q_Y + S_B = 10, \qquad \textbf{10.8}$$

whereas for $C$ the constraint equation is:

$$3Q_Y + S_C = 21. \qquad \textbf{10.9}$$

Note that the slack variables not only allow us to state the constraint conditions in equality form, thus simplifying algebraic analysis, but also provide us with valuable information. In the production problem, for example, slack variables whose values are zero at the optimal solution indicate inputs that cause bottlenecks or are limiting factors. Slack variables with *positive* values, on the other hand, measures excess capacity in the related factor. Slack variables obviously can never take on negative values, since this would imply that the amount of the resource used exceeds the amount available. The information provided by slack variables is very important in long-range planning decisions, and it constitutes a key benefit derived from employing the linear programming technique.

## Algebraic Solution

The complete specification of our illustrative programming problem can now be stated as follows:

Maximize $\qquad\qquad\qquad \pi = \$12Q_X + \$9Q_Y,$ $\qquad\qquad$ **10.3**

subject to these constraints:

$$4Q_X + 2Q_Y + S_A = 32, \qquad\qquad \textbf{10.7}$$

$$1Q_X + 1Q_Y + S_B = 10, \qquad\qquad \textbf{10.8}$$

$$3Q_Y + S_C = 21, \qquad\qquad \textbf{10.9}$$

where

$$Q_X \geq 0, Q_Y \geq 0, S_A \geq 0, S_B \geq 0, S_C \geq 0.$$

In words, the problem is to find the set of values for Variables $Q_X$, $Q_Y$, $S_A$, $S_B$, and $S_C$ that maximizes Equation 10.3 and at the same time satisfies the constraints imposed by Equations 10.7, 10.8, and 10.9.

The problem stated in this form is underdetermined. We must obtain a simultaneous solution to the constraint equations, but there are more unknowns (five) than constraint equations (three), so we cannot obtain unique solution values. However, the requirement that the solution to any linear programming problem must occur at a corner of the feasible space provides enough information to obtain the solution. To see how, let us first state the following facts:

1. The optimal output occurs at a corner point. Accordingly, we need to examine only the corner locations of the feasible space.
2. There are a total of $M + N$ variables in the systems, where $M$ equals the number of products and $N$ equals the number of constraints. In our example, $M = 2$ because there are two variables, $X$ and $Y$, and $N = 3$ for the three constraints $A$, $B$, and $C$, for a total of five variables.
3. Each variable must be equal to or greater than zero.
4. At each corner point, the number of nonzero-valued variables is equal to the number of constraint equations.[2] Consider Figure 10.10, in which the feasible space for our illustrative problem has been regraphed. At the origin, where neither $X$ or $Y$ is produced, $Q_X$ and $Q_Y$ both equal zero. Slack exists in all inputs, however, so $S_A$, $S_B$, and $S_C$

[2]In almost all linear programming problems, the number of nonzero-valued variables in all corner solutions *exactly* equals the number of constraints in the problem. Only under a particular condition known as *degeneracy*, when more than two constraints coincide at a single corner of the feasible space, are there fewer nonzero-valued variables. This condition does not hinder the technique of solution considered in this chapter.

■ Figure 10.10
## Determination of Zero-Valued Variables at Corners of the Feasible Space

At all corner points of the feasible space, the number of nonzero-valued variables equals the number of constraint equations.

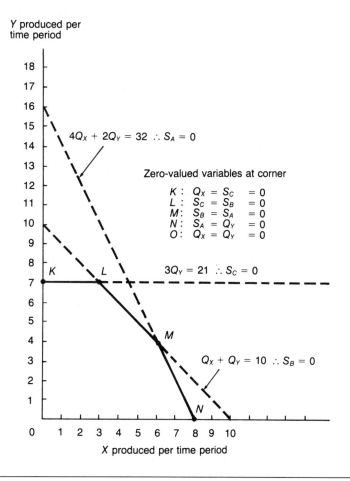

Y produced per time period

$4Q_X + 2Q_Y = 32 \therefore S_A = 0$

Zero-valued variables at corner

$K: \quad Q_X = S_C \quad = 0$
$L: \quad S_C = S_B \quad = 0$
$M: \quad S_B = S_A \quad = 0$
$N: \quad S_A = Q_Y \quad = 0$
$O: \quad Q_X = Q_Y \quad = 0$

$3Q_Y = 21 \therefore S_C = 0$

$Q_X + Q_Y = 10 \therefore S_B = 0$

X produced per time period

are all greater than zero. Now move up the vertical axis to Point K. Here $Q_X$ and $S_C$ both equal zero, because no X is being produced and Input C is being used to the fullest extent possible. However, $Q_Y$, $S_A$, and $S_B$ all exceed zero. At Point L, $Q_X$, $Q_Y$, and $S_A$ are all positive, but $S_B$ and $S_C$ are equal to zero. The remaining corners, M and N, can be examined similarly, and at each of them the number of nonzero-valued variables exactly equals the number of constraints.

We see then that the optimal solution to a linear programming problem occurs at a corner of the feasible space and that at each corner, the number of nonzero variables exactly equals the number of constraint equations. These properties enable us to rewrite the constraints as a system with three equations and three unknowns for each corner point; such a system can be solved algebraically.

Solving the constraint equations at each corner point provides values for $Q_X$ and $Q_Y$ as well as for $S_A$, $S_B$, and $S_C$. The profit contribution at each corner can be determined by inserting the values for $Q_X$ and $Q_Y$ into the objective function (Equation 10.3). The corner solution that produces the maximum profit is the solution to the linear programming problem.

The previously described procedure is followed in actual applications of linear programming. Computer programs are available that find solution values of the variables at a corner point, evaluate profits at that point, and then iterate to an adjacent corner point with a higher profit, continuing until the optimal corner point is located.

We can illustrate the technique somewhat more fully by examining the algebraic determination of the corner solutions in our present example. Although we could set any two of the variables equal to zero, it is convenient to begin by setting $Q_X$ and $Q_Y$ equal to zero and examining the solution to the programming problem at the origin. Substituting those values into the three constraint equations—10.7, 10.8, and 10.9—indicates that the three slack variables equal the total units of their respective inputs available to the firm; that is, $S_A = 32$, $S_B = 10$, and $S_C = 21$. This result is not unexpected, because at the origin neither X or Y is produced, and, therefore, none of the inputs is expended for production. The total profit contribution at the origin corner of the feasible space is zero.

Now let us examine the solution at a second corner, N in Figure 10.10, where $Q_Y$ and $S_A$ equal zero. Substituting into Constraint Equation 10.7 permits us to solve for $Q_X$:

$$4Q_X + 2Q_Y + S_A = 32$$
$$4 \times Q_X + 2 \times 0 = 32$$
$$4Q_X = 32$$
$$Q_X = 8. \qquad\qquad \textbf{10.7}$$

With the value of $Q_X$ determined, we can substitute into Equations 10.8 and 10.9 to determine values $S_B$ and $S_C$:

$$Q_X + Q_Y + S_B = 10$$
$$8 + 0 + S_B = 10$$
$$S_B = 2, \qquad\qquad \textbf{10.8}$$

and

$$3Q_Y + S_C = 21$$
$$3 \times 0 + S_C = 21$$
$$S_C = 21. \qquad\qquad \textbf{10.9}$$

The total profit contribution is:

$$\pi = \$12Q_X + \$9Q_Y$$
$$= \$12 \times 8 + \$9 \times 0$$
$$= \$96. \hspace{4cm} \textbf{10.3}$$

Next, we assign zero values to $S_B$ and $S_A$, which permits us to reach solution values for Point $M$. Substituting zero values for $S_A$ and $S_B$ in Equations 10.7 and 10.8 gives us two equations with two unknowns:

$$4Q_X + 2Q_Y + 0 = 32. \hspace{2cm} \textbf{10.7}$$
$$Q_X + Q_Y + 0 = 10. \hspace{2cm} \textbf{10.8}$$

Multiplying Equation 10.8 by two and subtracting the result from Equation 10.7 provides the value for $Q_X$:

$$4Q_X + 2Q_Y = 32 \hspace{2cm} \textbf{10.7}$$
$$\text{minus } 2Q_X + 2Q_Y = 20$$
$$2Q_X \hspace{1.5cm} = 12$$
$$Q_X \hspace{1.5cm} = 6$$

Then, substituting 6 for $Q_X$ in Equation 10.8, we find that $Q_Y = 4$. Total profit contribution in this case is \$108 [$= (\$12 \times 6) + (\$9 \times 4)$].

Similar algebraic analysis would provide the solution for the two remaining corners of the feasible space. However, rather than work through those corner solutions, we present the results in Table 10.2. Here it is apparent, just as we illustrated in the earlier graphic analysis, that the optimal solution occurs at Point $M$, where 6 units of $X$ and 4 units of $Y$ are produced. Total profit is \$108, which exceeds the profit at any other corner of the feasible space.

### Slack Variables at the Solution Point

At each corner solution, the values of the slack variables are determined by the linear programming process. For example, at the optimal solution

■ Table 10.2
## Algebraic Solution to a Linear Programming Problem

| Solution at Corner | Value of Variable | | | | | Total Profit Contribution |
|---|---|---|---|---|---|---|
| | $Q_X$ | $Q_Y$ | $S_A$ | $S_B$ | $S_C$ | |
| 0 | 0 | 0 | 32 | 10 | 21 | \$ 0 |
| N | 8 | 0 | 0 | 2 | 21 | 96 |
| M | 6 | 4 | 0 | 0 | 9 | 108 |
| L | 3 | 7 | 6 | 0 | 0 | 99 |
| K | 0 | 7 | 18 | 3 | 0 | 63 |

(Corner $M$) reached in the preceding section, $S_A$ and $S_B$ both equal zero, meaning that Inputs $A$ and $B$ are used to the fullest extent possible, but the value of $S_C$ is determined as follows. First, note that $Q_Y = 4$ at the optimal corner. Next, substitute this value into Constraint Equation 10.9 to find the solution value of $S_C$:

$$3 \times Q_Y + S_C = 21$$
$$3 \times 4 \quad + S_C = 21$$
$$S_C = \quad 9.$$

Production of the optimal combination of $X$ and $Y$ completely exhausts the available quantities of Inputs $A$ and $B$, but 9 units of Input $C$ remain unused. Thus, because Inputs $A$ and $B$ impose effective constraints on the firm's profit level, it may wish to acquire more of one or both of them in order to expand output. Input $C$, on the other hand, is in excess supply, so the firm would certainly not want more capacity of $C$; it might even attempt to reduce its purchases of $C$ during future production periods. Alternatively, if $C$ is a fixed facility, such as a computer, the firm might attempt to sell some of that excess capacity to other computer users.

### Complex Linear Programming Problems

Our illustrative linear programming problem is simple by design—we chose a problem that can be solved both graphically and algebraically so that we could first explain the theory of linear programming through the use of graphs, then rework the problem algebraically to show the symmetry between the two methods. The kinds of linear programming problems encountered in the real world, however, are quite complex, frequently involving many constraints and output variables. Such problems are too complex to solve graphically; the geometry is messy if we have three outputs, impossible for four or more. However, computer programs that use the algebraic techniques can handle large numbers of variables and constraints. Although it is not necessary for our purposes to extend the discussion to use of these computer-based solution algorithms, we call attention to them to indicate the potential problem-solving capability of the technique.

# THE DUAL IN LINEAR PROGRAMMING

**primal and dual linear programming problems**

Symmetrical pairs of maximization and minimization linear programming problem statements which describe the same constrained decision problem.

For every maximization problem in linear programming there exists a symmetrical minimization problem; for every minimization problem there exists a symmetrical maximization problem. These pairs of related maximization and minimization problems are known as the **primal and dual linear programming problems.** The symmetry or duality between constrained maximization and constrained minimization problems is a key concept in managerial economics. While the concept of duality has been implied in earlier material, explicitly examining duality in our discussion of linear programming will prove useful to show the equivalence of alternative approaches to constrained optimization.

## Duality Theory

The concept of duality is important in managerial economics for several reasons. First, duality demonstrates the symmetry between the value of a firm's products and the value of resources or inputs used in production. For example, with duality we can show that value maximization can be attained by focusing on either the revenue-generating capability and resource requirements of a firm's products, or on the cost of resources and their productivity.

In addition to providing valuable insight into the economics of optimal resource employment, duality provides the key to solving some very difficult constrained optimization problems. Because of the symmetry between primal and dual problem specifications, either one can be constructed from the other and the solution to either problem can be used to solve both. This is helpful because it is sometimes easier to obtain the solution to the dual problem than to the original or primal problem.

Finally, duality allows one to evaluate the solution of a constrained decision problem in terms of both the activities required for optimization of the firm's objective and the economic impact of the constraint conditions under which the decisions must be made. Analysis of the constraint conditions frequently provides important information for long-range planning or strategic decisions. Thus, one often sees the **primal solution** of a programming problem described as a tool for short-run operating decisions and the **dual solution** as a tool for long-run planning. Duality demonstrates the symmetry between these two activities and, therefore, the need to recognize that operating decisions and long-range planning are related.

**primal solution**

A solution that provides a basis for operating decisions.

**dual solution**

A solution that provides a basis for planning decisions.

## Imputed Values or Shadow Prices

To examine duality, we must introduce the concept of imputed values or shadow prices. In the primal programming problem discussed above, we sought the values of $Q_X$ and $Q_Y$ that would maximize the firm's profit subject to constraints on production imposed by limitations of Input Factors $A$, $B$, and $C$. Duality theory tells us that an identical operating decision would result if we instead had chosen to minimize the costs of the resources employed in producing $Q_X$ and $Q_Y$, subject to an output constraint.

The key to this duality is that the costs we are concerned with are not the acquisition costs of the inputs but rather the economic costs of using them. For a resource that is available in a fixed amount, this cost is not the acquisition cost but the opportunity cost of not being able to use it for some alternative purpose. Consider, for example, a skilled labor force employed by a firm. If the workers are fully utilized producing valuable products for the firm, then a reduction in skilled labor will reduce valuable output, and an increase in skilled labor will increase the production

## 10.2 **Managerial Application**

Karmarkar's LP Breakthrough

On a typical day, thousands of U.S. Air Force planes ferry cargo and military passengers around the globe. To keep those jets flying, the Military Airlift Command (MAC) must juggle schedules for pilots and other flight personnel. In addition, the MAC has to make literally millions of calculations to determine the most efficient flight route, cargo weight, fuel loading, and so on. After all of these details have been carefully accounted for, unexpected bad weather or emergency changes in priorities can force a complete recalculation of the entire flight plan.

Getting all of the pieces to fit together has been a classic linear programming (LP) dilemma. On one hand, if an LP computer program could help increase fuel efficiency by just 2 percent, it would be worth millions of dollars per year. On the other hand, the un-derlying complexity of the Air Force's transportation problem is so great that, until recently, it defied the capabilities of even the most sophisticated supercomputers.

In 1984, Narendra K. Karmarkar, a young scientist for AT&T Bell Laboratories, discovered an algorithm, or mathematical formula, that greatly speeds the process of solving even the most complex LP problems. In the traditional approach to solving LP problems, one corner of the feasible solution space is solved and compared to the solutions for adjacent points. If a better solution is found, the computer is instructed to move off in that direction. This iterative process continues until the program finds itself boxed in by inferior solutions. Karmarkar's algorithm employs a radically different geometric approach that finds an optimal solu-

*continued*

See: William G. Wild and Otis Port, "The Startling Discovery Bell Labs Kept in the Shadows," *Business Week*, September 21, 1987, 69–76.

of valuable output. Similarly, if some of the labor is shifted from the production of one product to another, the cost of using skilled labor in this new activity is the value of the original product that can no longer be produced. Thus, the marginal cost of a constrained resource that is fully utilized is its opportunity cost as measured by the value of the product produced.

If, on the other hand, a limited resource such as skilled labor is not fully utilized, then at least the last unit of the resource is not productive and its marginal value to the firm is zero. Acquiring an additional unit of the resource would not increase valuable output, since the firm al-

**Managerial Application** *continued*

tion more efficiently. Working from within the interior of the feasible space, the Karmarkar method avoids the tedious surface route and uses projective geometry to reconfigure the solution structure. By studying this structure, the program determines the direction in which the optimal solution is likely to lie. Then the problem structure is allowed to return to its original shape, and the program moves toward the solution, pausing at intervals to repeat the process until it finds the optimal solution.

Despite early skepticism, there is a great deal of excitement today in both the scientific and business communities concerning the potential of Karmarkar's method for solving complex LP problems. For example, AT&T is using Karmarkar's formula to forecast the most cost-effective method for meeting future demands on the telephone network linking countries with shores on the Pacific Ocean. AT&T must estimate current and future telephone demand between every pair of switching points within the network. With a ten-year horizon, the AT&T planning model includes over 42,000 variables. Considering that many variables, using

the traditional LP solution method requires four to seven hours of mainframe computer time to answer each what-if question. Karmarkar's method finds answers in just a few minutes.

The cost savings possible using the Karmarkar method make the LP approach practical in a host of new applications. AT&T is now assessing its entire long-distance telephone network in an LP problem involving 800,000 variables. A multiprocessor supercomputer from Alliant Computer Systems Corporation and a software version of Karmarkar's algorithm have been optimized for high-speed parallel processing and are expected to be installed at St. Louis's Scott Air Force Base to help solve the MAC logistics problem cited previously.

So fast have been recent developments in the area that many new and unanticipated applications are sure to emerge as software for the Karmarkar algorithm becomes available. The possibilities include a broad range of applications, from assessing risk factors in stock and bond portfolios to setting up production schedules in industrial factories.

ready has excess, or unused, units of that resource. Similarly, the firm would incur a zero opportunity cost if it utilized the currently unused units of the resource in a different activity.

Thus, the economic value, or *opportunity cost*, of a constrained resource depends upon the extent to which it is utilized. When a limited resource is fully utilized, its marginal value in use (opportunity cost) is positive. When a constrained resource is not fully utilized, its marginal value in use is zero. From this we see that minimizing the *value* of limited resources used to produce valuable output is nothing more than minimizing the opportunity costs of employing those resources for that output. Such minimization of opportunity costs is equivalent to maximizing the value of the output produced with those resources.

Since the economic value of constrained resources is determined by their value in use rather than by historical acquisition costs, we call such amounts *imputed* values or *shadow prices*. The term **shadow price** is used because it represents the price that a manager would be willing to pay for additional units of a constrained resource. Comparing the shadow price of a resource with its acquisition price indicates whether the firm has an incentive to increase or decrease the amount of the resource that it acquires in future production periods. If shadow prices exceed acquisition prices, the resource's marginal value to the firm exceeds its cost and the firm has an incentive to expand employment of the resource. If, on the other hand, the acquisition cost exceeds the shadow price, there is an incentive to reduce the employment of that resource. These relations and the importance of duality can be further clarified by considering the dual to the linear programming problem discussed previously.

**shadow price**

Imputed value that describes the opportunity cost or value in use associated with resource employment in a linear programming problem.

## The Dual Objective Function[3]

In our original or primal problem statement, in which the goal was to maximize profits, the objective function (the primal) was as follows:

### Primal Objective Function:

Maximize $\qquad\qquad \pi = \$12Q_X + \$9Q_Y.$ $\qquad\qquad$ **10.3**

In the dual problem, we seek to minimize the imputed values, or the shadow prices, of the firm's resources. Defining $V_A$, $V_B$, and $V_C$ as the shadow prices for Inputs $A$, $B$, and $C$, respectively, and $\pi^*$ as the total imputed value of the firm's fixed resources, we can write the dual objective function (the dual) as follows:

### Dual Objective Function:

Minimize $\qquad\qquad \pi^* = 32V_A + 10V_B + 21V_C.$ $\qquad\qquad$ **10.10**

Since the firm has 32 units of $A$, the total imputed value of Input $A$ is 32 times $A$'s shadow price, or $32V_A$. If $V_A$, or Input $A$'s shadow price, is found to be \$1.50 when the dual equations are solved, then the imputed value of $A$ is \$48 (= 32 × \$1.50). Inputs $B$ and $C$ are handled in the same way.

## The Dual Constraints

In the primal problem, the constraints stated that the total units of each input used in the production of $X$ and $Y$ must be equal to or less than the available quantity of the input. In the dual, the constraints state that

---

[3]Rules for constructing the dual linear programming problem from its related primal are provided in Appendix 10A at the end of this chapter.

the total value of inputs used in the production of 1 unit of X or 1 unit of Y must not be less than the profit contribution provided by a unit of these products. In other words, the shadow prices of A, B, and C times the amount of each of the inputs needed to produce a unit of X or Y must be equal to or greater than the unit profit of X or of Y. This follows from the opportunity-cost concept that underlies the determination of shadow prices. A resource can never have an opportunity cost that is less than its value in use producing one or more of the firm's products. In other words, because a firm's resources can be put to use in the production of its products, they can never have an imputed value, or opportunity cost, that is less than the value of that output. Recall that unit profit is defined as the excess of price over variable cost, that price and variable cost are both assumed to be constant, and that in our example the profit per unit of X is $12 whereas that of Y is $9. As was shown in Table 10.1, each unit of X requires 4 units of A, 1 unit of B, and 0 units of C. Therefore, the total imputed value of the resources used to produce X is $4V_A + 1V_B$. The constraint requiring that this imputed cost of producing X be equal to or greater than the profit contribution of X can be written as:

$$4V_A + 1V_B \geq 12. \qquad \textbf{10.11}$$

Moreover, because 2 units of A, 1 unit of B, and 3 units of C are required to produce each unit of Y, the second dual constraint is written as:

$$2V_A + 1V_B + 3V_C \geq 9. \qquad \textbf{10.12}$$

Because the firm produces only two products, the dual problem has but two constraint equations.

## The Dual Slack Variables

Dual slack variables can be incorporated into the problem, enabling us to express the constraint requirements as equalities. Letting $L_X$ and $L_Y$ represent the two slack variables, Constraint Equations 10.11 and 10.12 can be rewritten as:

$$4V_A + 1V_B - L_X = 12, \qquad \textbf{10.13}$$

and

$$2V_A + 1V_B + 3V_C - L_Y = 9. \qquad \textbf{10.14}$$

Here the slack variables are *subtracted* from the constraint equations, since we are dealing with greater-than-or-equal-to inequalities. The dual slack variables measure the opportunity cost associated with production of the two products X and Y. This can be seen by examining the two constraint equations. Solving Constraint Equation 10.13 for $L_X$, for example, provides:

$$L_X = 4V_A + 1V_B - 12.$$

This expression states that $L_X$ is equal to the imputed cost of producing 1 unit of X minus the profit contribution provided by that product. Thus, $L_X$, the dual slack variable associated with Product X, is a measure of the opportunity cost of producing Product X. It compares the profit contribution of Product X, $12, with the value to the firm of the resources necessary to produce it.

A zero value for $L_x$ indicates that at the margin, the imputed value of the resources required to produce a unit of $X$ is exactly equal to the profit contribution received from it. This is similar to marginal costs being equal to marginal revenue at the output level at which profits are maximized. A positive value of $L_X$ indicates that the resources used in the production of $X$ are more valuable, in terms of the profit contribution they can generate, when used to produce the other product $Y$. A nonzero value of $L_X$ measures the firm's opportunity cost (profit loss) associated with production of Product X.

The slack variable for the second dual constraint has a similar interpretation. That is, $L_Y$ is the opportunity cost of producing Product Y. It will have a value of zero if the imputed value of the resources used to produce 1 unit of $Y$ exactly equals the $9 profit contribution provided by that product. A positive value for $L_Y$ measures the opportunity loss in terms of the forgone profit contribution associated with the production of Y.

Since a firm would not choose to produce a product if the value of the resources required were greater than the value of the resulting product, it follows that a product with a positive opportunity cost will not be included in the optimal production combination in a linear programming problem. The importance of this relation is shown next, when we interpret the dual solution to our linear programming example.

## Solving the Dual Problem

The dual programming problem can be solved with the same algebraic technique that was employed to obtain the primal solution. Let us restate the equality form of the dual programming problem and examine possible corner solutions to that problem. The dual problem is expressed as:

Minimize $$\pi^* = 32V_A + 10V_B + 21V_C, \qquad \textbf{10.10}$$

subject to

$$4V_A + 1V_B - L_X = 12, \qquad \textbf{10.13}$$

and

$$2V_A + 1V_B + 3V_C - L_Y = 9, \qquad \textbf{10.14}$$

where

$$V_A, V_B, V_C, L_X, L_Y \text{ all} \geq 0.$$

Because there are only two constraints in this programming problem, the maximum number of nonzero-valued variables at any corner solution will be two. Therefore, we can proceed by setting three of the variables equal to zero and solving the constraint equations for the values of the remaining two. By comparing the value of the objective function at each feasible solution, we can determine the point at which the function is minimized. This is the dual solution.

To illustrate the process, let us first set $V_A = V_B = V_C = 0$, and solve for $L_X$ and $L_Y$:

$$4 \times 0 + 1 \times 0 - L_X = 12$$
$$L_X = -12. \qquad \textbf{10.13}$$

$$2 \times 0 + 1 \times 0 + 0 + 3 \times 0 - L_Y = 9$$
$$L_Y = -9 \qquad \textbf{10.14}$$

Since $L_X$ and $L_Y$ cannot be negative, this solution is outside the feasible set.

The values just obtained are inserted into Table 10.3 as Solution 1. All other solution values were calculated in a similar manner and used to complete Table 10.3. It is apparent from the table that not all of the solutions lie within the feasible space of our linear programming problem. Specifically, only Solutions 5, 7, 9, and 10 meet the nonnegativity requirement of the programming specification while simultaneously providing solutions in which the number of nonzero-valued variables is exactly equal to the number of constraints in the problem. Thus, these four solutions coincide with the corners of the dual problem's feasible space.

At Solution 10, the total value imputed to Inputs $A$, $B$, and $C$ is minimized. Accordingly, Solution 10 is the optimum solution, about which we can make the following observations:

1. The total imputed value of the firm's resources is exactly equal to the $108 maximum profit contribution that we found by solving the primal problem. Thus, the solutions to the primal and the dual programming problems are identical.

■ Table 10.3
## Solutions for the Dual Programming Problem

| Solution Number | Value of the Variable | | | | | Total Value Imputed to the Firm's Resources |
|---|---|---|---|---|---|---|
| | $V_A$ | $V_B$ | $V_C$ | $L_X$ | $L_Y$ | |
| 1 | 0 | 0 | 0 | −12 | −9 | a |
| 2 | 0 | 0 | 3 | −12 | 0 | a |
| 3 | 0 | 0 | b | 0 | b | a |
| 4 | 0 | 9 | 0 | −3 | 0 | a |
| 5 | 0 | 12 | 0 | 0 | 3 | $120 |
| 6 | 0 | 12 | −1 | 0 | 0 | a |
| 7 | 4.5 | 0 | 0 | 6 | 0 | $144 |
| 8 | 3 | 0 | 0 | 0 | −3 | a |
| 9 | 3 | 0 | 1 | 0 | 0 | $117 |
| 10 | 1.5 | 6 | 0 | 0 | 0 | $108 |

*a*Outside the feasible space.
*b*No real number solution.

2. The shadow price for Input $C$, $V_C$, is zero. Because the shadow price measures the *marginal* value of the input to the firm, a zero shadow price implies that the resource in question has a zero marginal value to the firm. This means that adding another unit of this input would add nothing to the firm's maximum obtainable profit. Thus, a zero shadow price for Input $C$ is consistent with our findings in the primal problem that Input $C$ is not a binding constraint. Excess capacity exists in $C$, so additional units of $C$ will not result in increased production of either $X$ or $Y$.

3. The shadow price of Input $A$ is \$1.50. A positive shadow price implies that this fixed resource imposes a binding constraint on the firm and that, if an additional unit of $A$ is added, the firm can increase its total profit by \$1.50. It would pay the firm to buy additional units of Input $A$ at any price less than \$1.50 per unit until $A$ is no longer a binding constraint. This assumes that the cost of Input $A$ *was not* deducted from the selling prices of $X$ and $Y$ to obtain the profit contribution figures used in the primal objective function. If, in fact, those costs were included in the calculation of the profit contributions, the shadow price is the amount *above* the current price of Input $A$ that the firm could afford to pay for additional units.

4. The interpretation of Input $B$'s shadow price is similar to that for $A$'s. Since $B$ imposes an effective constraint on the firm's production, an additional unit of $B$ would allow increased production of $X$ and $Y$, with total profit increasing by \$6. Thus, the firm can afford to pay up to \$6 for a marginal unit of $B$.

5. Both dual slack variables are zero. This means that the imputed value of resources required to produce a single unit of $X$ or $Y$ is exactly equal to the profit contribution provided by each of them. Thus, the opportunity cost of both $X$ and $Y$ is zero, indicating that the resources required for their production are *not* more valuable to the firm in some alternative use. Again, this is consistent with the solution of the primal problem, as both $X$ and $Y$ were produced at the optimal solution. Any product with a positive opportunity cost would be nonoptional and would not be produced.

## Use of the Dual Solution to Solve the Primal Problem

The dual solution, as we have developed it thus far, does not give us the optimal amounts of $X$ and $Y$; it does, however, provide all the information necessary to determine the optimum output mix. First, note that the dual solution informs us that Input $C$ does not impose a binding constraint on output of $X$ and $Y$. Further, it tells us that at the optimum output of $X$ and $Y$, $\pi = \pi^* = \$108$. Now consider again the three constraints in the primal problem.

$$\text{Constraint on } A: 4Q_X + 2Q_Y + S_A = 32,$$
$$\text{Constraint on } B: 1Q_X + 1Q_Y + S_B = 10,$$
$$\text{Constraint on } C: \qquad\quad 3Q_Y + S_C = 21.$$

We know that the constraints on A and B are binding, *because the dual solution found both of these inputs to have positive shadow prices.* (Recall that only resources that are fully utilized will have a nonzero marginal value in use.) Accordingly, the slack variables $S_A$ and $S_B$ are equal to zero, and the binding constraints can be rewritten as:

$$4Q_X + 2Q_Y = 32,$$

and

$$1Q_X + 1Q_Y = 10.$$

We have two equations in two unknowns, so the system can be solved for values of $Q_X$ and $Q_Y$. Multiplying the second constraint by two and subtracting from the first provides:

$$
\begin{aligned}
4Q_X + 2Q_Y &= 32 \\
\text{minus } 2Q_X + 2Q_Y &= 20 \\
\hline
2Q_X \phantom{+ 2Q_Y} &= 12 \\
Q_X &= 6
\end{aligned}
$$

and

$$
\begin{aligned}
6 + Q_Y &= 10, \\
Q_Y &= 4.
\end{aligned}
$$

These values of $Q_X$ and $Q_Y$, found after learning from the dual which constraints were binding, are identical to the values found by solving the primal problem. Further, having obtained the value for $Q_Y$, it is possible to substitute into the equation for Constraint C and solve for the amount of slack in that resource:

$$
\begin{aligned}
3Q_Y + S_C &= 21, \\
S_C &= 21 - 3 \times 4 = 9.
\end{aligned}
$$

These relations, which allow one to solve either the primal or dual specification of a linear programming problem and then quickly obtain the solution to the other, can be generalized by the two following expressions:

$$\text{Primal Objective Variable}_i \times \text{Dual Slack Variable}_i \equiv 0. \qquad \textbf{10.15}$$

$$\text{Primal Slack Variable}_j \times \text{Dual Objective Variable}_j \equiv 0. \qquad \textbf{10.16}$$

Equation 10.15 states that if an ordinary variable in the primal problem takes on a nonzero value in the optimal solution to that problem, its related dual slack variable must be zero. Only if a particular $Q_i$ is zero-valued in the solution to the primal can its related dual slack variable, $L_i$, take on a nonzero value.

A similar relation holds between the slack variables in the primal problem and their related ordinary variables in the dual, as indicated by Equation 10.16. If the primal slack variable is nonzero-valued, then the related dual variable will be zero-valued, and vice versa.

Case 10.1

# Constrained Advertising
# Cost Minimization

Constrained cost-minimization problems are frequently encountered in managerial decision making. One interesting example associated with a firm's marketing activities is the problem of minimizing advertising expenditures subject to meeting certain audience-exposure requirements. Consider, for example, a firm that is planning an advertising campaign for a new product. The goals set for the campaign include exposure to at least 100,000 individuals, with no fewer than 80,000 of those individuals having incomes of at least $50,000 annually and no fewer than 40,000 of them being single. For simplicity we will assume that the firm has only two media, radio and television, available for this campaign. One television ad costs $10,000 and is estimated to reach an audience numbering, on the average, 20,000 persons. Ten thousand of these individuals will have incomes of $50,000 or more, and 4,000 of them will be single. A radio ad, on the other hand, costs $6,000 and reaches a total audience of 10,000 individuals, all of whom have at least $50,000 in income. Eight thousand of the persons exposed to a radio ad will be unmarried. Table 10.4 summarizes these data.

## The Primal Problem

The objective is to minimize the cost of the advertising campaign. Since total cost is merely the sum of the amounts spent on radio and television ads, the objective function is:

Minimize          Cost = $6,000R + $10,000TV,

where $R$ and $TV$ represent the number of radio and television ads, respectively, that are employed in the advertising campaign.

The linear programming problem will have a total of three constraint equations: (1) the requirement for total audience exposure, (2) the income-related exposure requirement, and (3) the requirement that at least

■ Table 10.4
## Advertising Media Relations

|  | Radio | Television |
|---|---|---|
| Cost per ad | $ 6,000 | $10,000 |
| Total audience per ad | 10,000 | 20,000 |
| Audience per ad with income ≥ $50,000 | 10,000 | 10,000 |
| Unmarried audience per ad | 8,000 | 4,000 |

40,000 single persons be among those exposed to the advertising campaign.

The restriction on the minimum number of individuals that must be reached by the ad campaign can be expressed as:

$$10,000R + 20,000TV \geq 100,000.$$

This equation states that the number of persons exposed to radio ads (10,000 times the number of radio ads) plus the number exposed to television ads (20,000 times the number of television ads) must be equal to or greater than 100,000.

The two remaining constraints can be constructed similarly from the data in Table 10.4. The constraint on exposures to individuals with incomes of at least $50,000 is written:

$$10,000R + 10,000TV \geq 80,000,$$

whereas the marital status constraint is given by:

$$8,000R + 4,000TV \geq 40,000.$$

Combining the cost-minimization objective function with the three constraints—written in their equality form through the introduction of slack variables—allows us to write the programming problem as:

Minimize $\qquad$ Cost $= \$6,000R + \$10,000TV,$

subject to:

$$10,000R + 20,000TV - S_A = 100,000,$$
$$10,000R + 10,000TV - S_I = 80,000,$$
$$8,000R + 4,000TV - S_S = 40,000,$$

and

$$R, TV, S_A, S_I, S_S \geq 0.$$

Here $S_A$, $S_I$, and $S_S$ are the slack variables indicating the extent to which the minimums on total audience exposure, on exposure to individuals with incomes of at least $50,000, and on exposure to single individuals, respectively, have been exceeded. Note that the slack variables are *subtracted* from the constraint equations in this situation because we are dealing with greater-than-or-equal-to inequalities. That is, excess capacity or slack in any of the constraints implies that the audience exposure is greater than required. Thus, to make the exposures exactly equal to the required quantity, one must subtract the slack from the total.

The solution to this linear programming problem is easily obtained using the combined graphic and analytical procedure described earlier in the chapter. Figure 10.11 illustrates that solution. There the feasible space for the programming problem is delimited by the three constraint equations and the nonnegativity requirements. Addition of an isocost curve allows one to determine that costs are minimized at Point *M*,

■ Figure 10.11
**Advertising Cost-Minimization Linear
Programming Problem**

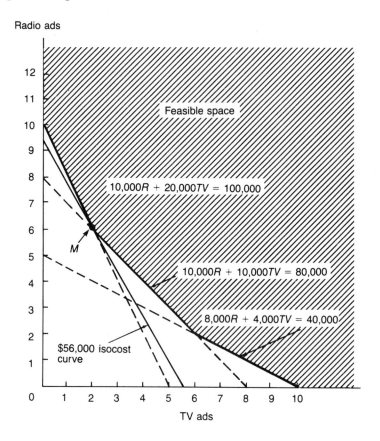

Radio ads

Feasible space

$10,000R + 20,000TV = 100,000$

$M$

$10,000R + 10,000TV = 80,000$

$8,000R + 4,000TV = 40,000$

$56,000 isocost
curve

TV ads

where the constraints on total audience exposure and exposures to individuals meeting the income requirement are binding. Recall that all
isocost curves are parallel in a linear programming problem, so one can
graph any convenient isocost curve and then just slide it to the edge of
the feasible space. Knowing that the total audience exposure and income
requirement constraints are binding allows us to solve for the problem
solution at Point $M$. With those binding constraints, the slack variables
$S_A$ and $S_I$ are both 0, and we have:

$$10,000R + 20,000TV = 100,000$$
$$\text{minus}\ \underline{10,000R + 10,000TV = \ \ 80,000}$$
$$10,000TV = \ \ 20,000$$
$$TV = 2,$$

and

$$10,000R + 20,000(2) = 100,000$$
$$10,000R = 60,000$$
$$R = 6.$$

The solution to the problem indicates that the firm should employ 6 radio and 2 television ads in its campaign in order to minimize its expenditure while meeting the audience goals set for the program. The total cost for such a campaign would be $56,000.

## The Dual Problem

The dual linear programming problem for the advertising-mix decision provides some very interesting and valuable information to the firm's management. It will prove instructive to formulate, solve, and interpret that form of the problem.

The dual programming problem in this situation will be a constrained-maximization problem, since the primal problem was a minimization problem. Also, we know that the objective function of the dual problem will be expressed in terms of shadow prices or imputed values for the constraints or restrictions in the primal problem. Thus, the dual objective function will contain three variables: (1) the imputed value, or shadow price, for the total audience exposure requirement, (2) the shadow price of the high-income audience requirement, and (3) the shadow price associated with the marital status constraint. Since the constraint limits in the primal problem become the objective function parameters in the dual, the dual objective function can be written as:

Maximize        $C^* = 100,000V_A + 80,000V_I + 40,000V_S,$

where $V_A$, $V_I$, and $V_S$ are the three shadow prices described previously.

The constraints in the dual problem are developed in terms of the objective function variables from the primal. Thus, there will be only two constraint conditions in the problem, the first associated with radio ads and the second with television ads. Both of these constraints will be of a less-than-or-equal-to nature, since the constraints in the primal were of a greater-than-or-equal-to form.

The limit on the constraint associated with radio advertising is the $6,000 coefficient of radio ads found in the objective function of the primal problem. The coefficient for the three shadow prices in the constraint equation are the numbers of exposures within each category provided by a single radio ad. The coefficient for the total audience exposure shadow price, $V_A$, therefore, will be 10,000, the number of individuals exposed to a radio ad. Similarly, the coefficient for $V_I$ is 10,000 and that for $V_S$ is 8,000. The constraint for radio ads, then, is given by:

$$10,000V_A + 10,000V_I + 8,000V_S \leq \$6,000.$$

## 10.3  **Managerial Application**
LP on the PC!

Until recently, the complexity of real-world decision problems often made it impractical for the nonspecialist to use linear programming (LP) methods. As a result, the application of LP techniques has been largely restricted to managers of the relatively few firms that employ computer programmers and have expensive mainframe computers. Instead of using more appropriate LP methods, managers of many small-to-medium sized companies still plug hypothetical financial and operating data into spreadsheet software programs, and then recalculate profit figures to see how various changes might affect the bottom line. A major problem with this popular "What if?" approach to decision analysis is the haphazard way in which various alternatives are considered. Dozens of time-consuming recalculations are often necessary before suggestions emerge that lead to a considerable improvement in operating efficiency. Even then, the

manager has no assurance that superior decision alternatives are not available.

The frustrations and limitations of the "What if?" approach to decision analysis are sure to become a thing of the past following the recent publication of What'sBest, the first truly user-friendly software program for the personal computer (PC) environment. Interestingly, the president of General Optimization, publisher of What'sBest, is Sam L. Savage, a senior lecturer with a course in linear programming at the University of Chicago's School of Business. Savage recognized the lack of necessary software as a severe impediment to both the learning and the widespread application of LP methods. Using What'sBest, both the learning and the application of LP techniques are quick and easy.

This innovative PC software comes in three versions designed to meet the needs of the personal, commercial, and professional

*continued*

See: Paul Bonner, "What's Best! Precise Modeling Utility," *PC Week*, December 24/31, 1985, 61–65; and David Sternlight, "Developing Solutions for Problems on Mac," *MacWeek*, January 10, 1989, 66–68.

The constraint associated with television advertising is constructed in the same fashion. Since each TV ad reaches a total audience of 20,000, this is the coefficient for the $V_A$ variable in the second constraint equation. The coefficients for $V_I$ and $V_S$ are 10,000 and 4,000, respectively, because these are the numbers of individuals in the income and marital categories exposed to one TV ad. With the $10,000 cost of a television ad providing a limit to the constraint, the second constraint equation for the dual problem is:

$$20,000V_A + 10,000V_I + 4,000V_S \leq \$10,000.$$

---

**Managerial Application** *continued*

user. The personal version is capable of solving a wide array of complex business LP problems involving up to 400 variable cells. For example, an LP problem that involves twenty-five variables plus an objective function and fifteen constraint conditions (sixteen equations in all) involves 400 variable cells, and could be easily handled using the personal version. The commercial version solves LP problems with up to 1,500 variable cells, and has enough capacity to meet the needs of highly sophisticated users. The professional version can be used to solve extraordinarily complex LP problems involving up to 4,000 variable cells!

Of course, the practical value of this or any new tool for managerial decision making is measured in terms of how well it actually works. Early returns on this basis are very encouraging. For example, a trucking firm has used What'sBest to optimize the route structure for a fleet of 135 trucks operating out of twenty terminals to provide overnight service throughout a dozen Midwestern states. By minimizing route mileage, the company saved $700,000 per year in operating costs and was able to avoid an outlay of $3 million for capital investment. Similarly, a 500-bed hospital was able to achieve a $1 million cost saving by optimizing its nursing schedule in light of staffing requirements. A leading natural resources company used What'sBest to develop a mix of 20 to 30 varieties of coal that maximizes energy content, minimizes customer cost, and at the same time complies with government sulphur content regulations. Other examples of practical applications include its use to help a bank decide on the best use of loanable funds, and a model to help investment bankers decide on the optimal allocation of an investment portfolio.

What makes this advance in PC software so impressive is that it makes possible the application of LP methods on a scale that previously was simply not attainable. Instead of spending substantial resources to solve only the biggest and most urgent LP problems, companies are now able to save literally millions of dollars by optimizing thousands of day-to-day problems. Rather than requiring mainframe computers and a host of programmers, all of this can be accomplished by hands-on managers using desktop computers. As new generations of LP software emerge, appreciation of the value of the LP technique as a practical tool for decision analysis may become even more widespread.

---

With the introduction of slack variables in the constraints, the dual programming problem can be stated:

Maximize $\qquad C^* = 100{,}000V_A + 80{,}000V_I + 40{,}000V_S,$

subject to

$$10{,}000V_A + 10{,}000V_I + 8{,}000V_S + L_R = \$\ 6{,}000$$

$$20{,}000V_A + 10{,}000V_I + 4{,}000V_S + L_{TV} = \$10{,}000$$

and

$$V_A, V_I, V_S, L_R, L_{TV} \geq 0.$$

**Solving the Dual**   It would be possible, although difficult, to solve the dual problem using either a three-dimensional graph or the complete enumeration technique developed earlier in this chapter. There is a much easier way to obtain the solution, because we have already solved the primal problem. Recall that the solution to both the primal and dual statements of a single linear programming problem will be complementary and that the following relations must always hold:

$$\text{Primal Objective Variable}_i \times \text{Dual Slack Variable}_i \equiv 0.$$

$$\text{Primal Slack Variable}_j \times \text{Dual Objective Variable}_j \equiv 0.$$

Thus, in this programming problem:

$$R \times L_R = 0 \text{ and } TV \times L_{TV} = 0,$$

and

$$S_A \times V_A = 0, S_I \times V_I = 0, \text{ and } S_S \times V_S = 0.$$

Because we know from the primal problem that both $R$ and $TV$ are nonzero-valued variables, $L_R$ and $L_{TV}$ in the dual problem must both be zero at the optimal solution. Further, since there was excess audience exposure in the single category in the solution to the primal—that is, $S_S \neq 0$—we know that $V_S$ in the dual must take on a value of zero in the optimal solution. This leaves only $V_A$ and $V_I$ as unknowns in the dual programming problem, and their values can be easily obtained by solving the two-equation constraint system for the two unknowns:

$$10{,}000V_A + 10{,}000V_I = \$ \ 6{,}000$$

$$20{,}000V_A + 10{,}000V_I = \$10{,}000$$

Subtracting the second constraint equation from the first results in:

$$-10{,}000V_A = -\$4{,}000,$$

$$V_A = \$0.40.$$

Substituting the value \$0.40 for $V_A$ in either constraint equation produces a value of \$0.20 for $V_I$. Finally, substituting the values for $V_A$, $V_I$, and $V_S$ into the objective function of the dual problem results in a value for $C^*$ of \$56,000 (\$0.40 × 100,000 + \$0.20 × 80,000 + \$0 × 40,000), exactly the same as the minimum cost figure obtained in the solution of the primal problem.

**Interpreting the Dual Problem Results**   The solution to the primal of our linear programming problem tells management which advertising mix meets the various goals of its marketing program at the least cost and, thereby, allows the firm to move ahead with the promotional campaign. However, the results of the dual problem are equally valuable for effective management. This is due to the fact that the dual program solution allows management to evaluate the goals that are being used to determine how best to advertise the new product.

Recall that the dual problem objective function variables (the various shadow prices) provide a measure of how the constraints affect the primal problem's objective function *at the margin*. That is, each shadow price indicates the change in the optimal solution value of the primal (and also dual) problem objective function that would accompany a marginal change in the related constraint.

Thus, in the problem we are examining, each dual problem shadow price indicates the change in total cost that would accompany a one-unit change in the various audience-exposure requirements. They are, therefore, the marginal costs of the last audience exposure gained in each of the three categories: total, with incomes $\geq$ \$50,000, and single. For example, the value of $V_A$ is the marginal cost of reaching the last individual in the total audience that is exposed to the firm's ads. In this case $V_A$ is \$0.40, indicating that if the firm were to reduce by one the number of total individuals who must come in contact with an ad, there would be a \$0.40 reduction in the \$56,000 total cost of the advertising program. Similarly, the marginal cost of increasing total audience exposure from 100,000 to 100,001 individuals is 40¢.

$V_I$, the shadow price of reaching individuals with incomes of at least \$50,000, is \$0.20, or 20¢. This means that it would cost the firm an extra 20¢ per individual to reach more persons in the high-income category.

The zero value found for $V_S$, the shadow price for the requirement on exposures to unmarried individuals, indicates that the proposed advertising campaign already reaches more than the 40,000 required individuals in this category. Thus, a small change in that constraint will have no effect on the total cost of the promotion.

By comparing these marginal costs with the benefits it expects to derive from additional audience exposures in the various classes, the firm's management is able to determine whether the goals on audience exposures are appropriate. If the expected return (profit) from one additional individual seeing an ad exceeded 40¢, it would prove profitable to design an advertising campaign for a larger audience. Likewise, if the expected return from an additional exposure to an individual in the \$50,000-and-above income class is greater than the 20¢ marginal cost of reaching one more person in that class, the lower limit on exposures to that group should be raised. In both cases, a determination that the marginal profitability of the last audience exposure is less than its marginal cost (shadow price) would indicate that the firm should reduce the size of the audience requirement for that particular category. Such a reduction would increase profits, since the costs of the advertising campaign would fall faster than the profits on lost sales.

The two slack variables in the dual problem also have an interesting interpretation. They represent the opportunity costs of using a specific advertising medium. $L_R$ is thus a measure of the inefficiency associated with using radio in the promotion, whereas the value of $L_{TV}$ indicates the added cost of including television in the media mix employed. Both $L_R$ and $L_{TV}$ were zero in the solution to the dual problem, which indicates that neither medium is cost inefficient and that, in fact, both should be included in the promotional mix. This was also what we found in the solution to the primal problem.

This example has again demonstrated the symmetry of the primal and dual specifications of a linear programming problem. Either can be used to solve the basic problem, and the interpretations of both problem statements provide valuable information for decision-making purposes.

## Postscript on the Relation of Linear Programming to the Lagrangian Technique

In an earlier section we pointed out that linear programming is used to solve maximization and minimization problems, subject to inequality constraints, just as the Lagrangian technique was used to solve optimization problems, subject to constraints that can be stated as equalities. Recall from Chapter 2 that the Lagrangian multiplier, $\lambda$, is the marginal gain in the objective function obtained by relaxing the constraints by one unit. In the preceding section we learned that the values of the dual variables, the shadow prices, measure the value of relaxing input constraints by one unit. Thus, the shadow prices are the linear programming equivalents to Lagrangian multipliers.

# SUMMARY

*Linear programming* is a technique for solving maximization or minimization problems in which inequality *constraints* are imposed on the decision maker. This kind of problem occurs frequently in both business and government, so linear programming is rapidly becoming a widely used tool in the managerial decision maker's kit.

Although linear programming has been applied to a wide variety of managerial problems, it has been developed most fully, and is used most frequently, in production problems. Accordingly, we used two production problems to explain the basic elements of the theory of linear programming. First, we presented the theory in graphic form, and then we showed that the same solution can be reached by an algebraic technique. The graphic method is useful for explaining the theory, but the algebraic method is the one used in actual practice, because it can be adapted for solution by computers and used to solve the large, complex problems actually faced by managers.

After discussing the *primal* linear programming problem, we showed that for every primal problem there exists a *dual* problem. The primal is of interest because it provides us with values for the controllable variables—the output mix in our first illustrative problem. The dual is useful because the *shadow prices* that it generates are an indication of the marginal value of adding additional capacity for each fixed input.

## Questions

10.1 Give some illustrations of managerial decision situations in which you think the linear-programming technique would be useful.

10.2 Why can't linear programming be used in each of the following situations?
  A. Strong economies of scale exist.
  B. As the firm expands output, the prices of variable factors of production increase.
  C. As output increases, product prices decline.

10.3 Do equal distances along a given production process ray in a linear programming problem *always* represent an identical level of output?

10.4 Assume that output can only be produced using Processes A and B. Process A requires Inputs L and K to be combined in the fixed ratio 2L:4K, and Process B requires 4L:2K. Is it possible to produce output efficiently using 3L and 3K? Why or why not?

10.5 Describe the relative distance method used in graphic linear programming analysis.

10.6 Is the number of isocost, isorevenue, or isoprofit lines in a typical two-input–bounded feasible space limited?

10.7 Why is the fact that the number of nonzero-valued variables exactly equals the number of constraints at corners of the feasible space so critical in linear programming?

10.8 Will maximizing a profit contribution objective function always result in also maximizing total net profits?

10.9 If the primal problem calls for determining the set of outputs that will maximize profit, subject to input constraints:
  A. What is the dual objective function?
  B. What interpretation can be given to the dual variables called the shadow prices or imputed values?
  C. What does it mean if a dual variable or shadow price equals zero?

10.10 How are the solution values for primal and dual linear-programming problems actually employed in practice?

## Problems

10.1 Indicate whether each of the following statements is *true* or *false* and explain why.
  A. Constant returns to scale and constant input prices are the *only* requirements for a total cost function to be linear.
  B. Changing input prices will *always* alter the slope of a given isocost line.
  C. In profit-maximization linear-programming problems, negative values for slack variables imply that the amount of an input resource employed exceeds the amount available.

    D. Equal distance along a given process ray indicate equal output quantities.

    E. Nonbinding constraints are constraints that intersect at the optimum solution.

10.2 Cherry Devices, Inc., assembles connectors and terminals for electronic products at a plant in New Haven, Connecticut. The plant uses labor ($L$) and capital ($K$) in an assembly-line process to produce output ($Q$), where:

$$Q = 0.025L^{0.5}K^{0.5},$$

    A. Calculate how many units of output can be produced with 4 units of labor and 400 units of capital and with 16 units of labor and 1,600 units of capital. Are returns to scale increasing, constant, or diminishing?

    B. Calculate the change in the marginal product of labor as labor grows from 4 to 16 units, holding capital constant at 400 units. Similarly, calculate the change in the marginal product of capital as capital grows from 400 to 1,600 units, holding labor constant at 4 units. Are returns to each factor increasing, constant, or diminishing?

    C. Assume now and throughout the remainder of the problem that labor and capital must be combined in the ratio 4L:400K. How much output could be produced if Cherry has a constraint of $L = 4,000$ and $K = 480,000$ during the coming production period?

    D. What are the marginal products of each factor under the conditions described in Part C?

10.3 Idaho Natural Resources, Ltd. (INR) has two mines with different production capabilities for producing the same type of ore. After mining and crushing, the ore is graded into three classes: high, medium, and low. The company has contracted to provide local smelters with 24 tons of high-grade ore, 16 tons of medium-grade ore, and 48 tons of low-grade ore each week. It costs INR $10,000 per day to operate Mine $A$ and $5,000 per day to run Mine $B$. In a day's time, Mine $A$ produces 6 tons of high-grade ore, 2 tons of medium-grade ore, and 4 tons of low-grade ore. Mine $B$ produces 2, 2, and 12 tons per day of each grade, respectively. Management's short-run problem is to determine how many days per week to operate each mine under current conditions. In the long run, management wishes to know how sensitive these decisions will be to changing economic conditions.

    A report prepared for the company by an independent management consultant addressed the company's short-run operating concerns. The consultant claimed that the operating problem could be solved using linear programming techniques by which the firm would seek to minimize the total cost of meeting contractual requirements. Specifically, the consultant recommended that INR do the following:

Minimize        Total cost = $10,000A + $5,000B

subject to

$$6A + 2B \geq 24 \quad \text{(high-grade ore constraint)},$$
$$2A + 2B \geq 16 \quad \text{(medium-grade ore constraint)},$$
$$4A + 12B \geq 48 \quad \text{(low-grade ore constraint)},$$
$$A \leq 7 \quad \text{(Mine } A \text{ operating-days in a week constraint)},$$
$$B \leq 7 \quad \text{(Mine } B \text{ operating-days in a week constraint)},$$

or, in their equality form:

$$6A + 2B - S_H = 24,$$
$$2A + 2B - S_M = 16,$$
$$4A + 12B - S_L = 48,$$
$$A + S_A = 7,$$
$$B + S_B = 7,$$

where:

$$A, B, S_H, S_M, S_L, S_A, \text{ and } S_B \geq 0.$$

Here, $A$ and $B$ represent the days of operation per week for the two mines; $S_H$, $S_M$, and $S_L$ represent excess production of high-, medium-, and low-grade ore, respectively; and $S_A$ and $S_B$ are days per week that each mine is not operated.

A graphic representation of the linear-programming problem was also provided. The graph suggests an optimal solution at Point X, where Constraints 1 and 2 are binding. Thus, $S_H = S_M = 0$ and:

$$6A + 2B - 0 = 24$$
$$\text{minus } 2A + 2B - 0 = 16$$
$$\overline{\phantom{minus } 4A = \phantom{00} 8}$$
$$A = 2 \text{ Days per Week.}$$

Substitute $A = 2$ into the high-grade ore constraint:

$$6(2) + 2B = 24$$
$$12 + 2B = 24$$
$$2B = 12$$
$$B = 6 \text{ Days per Week.}$$

A minimum total operating cost per week of $50,000 is suggested because,

$$\text{Total cost} = \$10{,}000A + \$5{,}000B$$
$$= \$10{,}000(2) + \$5{,}000(6)$$
$$= \$50{,}000.$$

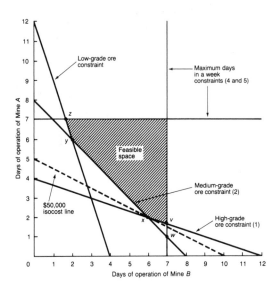

Unfortunately, the consultant's report was silent on a variety of important long-run planning issues. Specifically, INR wishes to know the following, holding all else equal:

A. How much, if any, excess production would result if the consultant's operating recommendation was followed?
B. What would be the cost effect of increasing low-grade ore sales by 50 percent?
C. What is INR's minimum acceptable price per ton if it is to renew a current contract to provide one of its customers with 6 tons of high-grade ore per week?
D. With current output requirements, how much would the cost of operating Mine *A* have to rise before INR would change its operating decision?
E. What increase in the cost of operating Mine *B* would cause INR to change its current operating decision?

10.4 Delmar Custom Homes (DCH) uses two different types of crews on home construction projects. Type *A* crews consist of master carpenters and skilled carpenters, whereas *B* crews include skilled carpenters and unskilled labor. Each home involves framing (*F*), roofing (*R*), and finish carpentry (*FC*). During recent months, *A* crews have demonstrated a capability of framing one home, roofing two, and doing finish carpentry for no more than four homes per month. Capability for *B* crews are framing three homes, roofing two, and completing finish carpentry for one during a month. DCH has agreed to build ten homes during the month of July but has subcontracted 10 percent of framing and 20 percent of finish carpentry requirements. Labor costs are $60,000 per month for *A* crews and $45,000 per month for *B* crews.

A. Formulate the linear-programming problem that DCH would use to minimize its total labor costs per month showing both the inequality and equality forms of the constant conditions.

B. Solve the linear-programming problem and interpret your solution values.

C. Assuming that DCH can both buy and sell subcontracting services at prevailing prices of $8,000 per unit for framing and $14,000 per unit for finish carpentry, would you recommend that the company alter its subcontracting policy? If so, how much could the company save through such a change?

D. Calculate the minimum increase in *A*-crew costs necessary to cause DCH to change its optimal employment combination for July.

10.5 Mary Richards is a senior loan officer with Citybank in Pittsburgh, Pennsylvania. Richards has both corporate and personal lending customers. On average, the profit contribution margin or interest-rate spread is 1.5 percent on corporate loans and 2 percent on personal loans. This return difference reflects the fact that personal loans tend to be riskier than corporate loans. Richards seeks to maximize the total dollar profit contribution earned, subject to a variety of restrictions on her lending practices. To limit default risk, Richards must restrict personal loans to no more than 50 percent of the total loans outstanding. Similarly, to ensure adequate diversification against business-cycle risk, corporate lending cannot exceed 75 percent of loaned funds. To maintain good customer relations by serving the basic needs of the local business community, Richards has decided to extend at least 25 percent of her total credit authorization to corporate customers on an ongoing basis. Finally, Richards cannot exceed her current total credit authorization of $100 million.

A. Using the inequality form of the constraint conditions, set up and interpret the linear-programming problem that Richards would use to determine the optimal dollar amount of credit to extend to corporate (*C*) and personal (*P*) lending customers. Also formulate the LP problem using the equality form of the constraint conditions.

B. Use a graph to determine the optimal solution, and check your solution algebraically. Fully interpret solution values.

10.6 The James Bond Fund is a mutual fund (open-end investment company) with an objective of maximizing income from a widely diversified corporate bond portfolio. The fund has a policy of remaining largely invested in a diversified portfolio of investment-grade bonds. Investment-grade bonds have high investment quality and receive a rating of Baa or better by Moody's, a bond rating service. The fund's investment policy states that investment-grade bonds are to be emphasized, representing at least three times the amount of junk-bond holdings. Junk bonds pay high nominal returns but have low investment quality, and they receive a rating of less than Baa from Moody's. To maintain the potential for high investor income, at least 20 percent of the fund's total portfolio must be invested in junk bonds. Like many funds, the James Bond Fund cannot use leverage (or borrowing) to enhance investor returns. As a result, total bond investments cannot equal more than 100 percent of the portfolio. Finally, the current expected return for investment-grade (I) bonds is 9 percent, and it is 12 percent for junk (J) bonds.

A. Using the inequality form of the constraint conditions, set up and interpret the linear-programming problem that the James Bond Fund would use to determine the optimal portfolio percentage holdings of investment-grade (I) and junk (J) bonds. Also formulate the problem using the equality form of the constraint conditions. (Assume that the fund managers have decided to remain fully invested and therefore hold no cash at this time.)

B. Use a graph to determine the optimal solution, and check your solution algebraically. Fully interpret solution values.

C. Holding all else equal, how much would the expected return on junk bonds have to fall to alter the optimal investment policy determined in Part B? Alternatively, how much would the return on investment-grade bonds have to rise before a change in investment policy would be warranted?

D. In anticipation of a rapid increase in interest rates and a subsequent economic downturn, the investment committee has decided to minimize the fund's exposure to bond price fluctuations. In adopting a defensive position, what is the maximum share of the portfolio that can be held in cash given the investment policies stated in the problem?

10.7  Carolina Power and Light (CP&L) is a small electric utility located in the Southeast. CP&L currently uses coal-fired capacity to satisfy its base-load electricity demand, which is the minimum level of electricity demanded 24 hours per day, 365 days per year.

CP&L currently burns both high-sulfur eastern coal and low-sulfur western coal. Each type of coal has its advantages. Eastern coal is more expensive ($50 per ton) but has higher heat-generating capabilities. Although western coal doesn't generate as much heat as eastern coal, western coal is less expensive ($25 per ton) and doesn't cause as much sulfur dioxide pollution. CP&L's base-load requirements are such that at least 2,400 million BTU's must be generated per hour. Each ton of eastern coal burned generates 40 million BTUs, and each ton of western coal burned generates

30 million BTUs. To limit sulfur dioxide emissions, the state's Environmental Protection Agency (EPA) requires CP&L to limit its total burning of sulfur to no more than 1.5 tons per hour. This affects CP&L's coal usage, because eastern coal contains 2.5 percent sulfur and western coal contains 1.5 percent sulfur. The EPA also limits CP&L particulate emissions to no more than 900 pounds per hour. CP&L emits 10 pounds of particulates per ton of eastern coal burned and 15 pounds of particulates per ton of western coal burned.

A. Set up and interpret the linear program that CP&L would use to minimize hourly coal-usage costs in light of its constraints.

B. Calculate and interpret all relevant solution values.

C. Holding all else equal, how much would the price of western coal have to rise before only eastern coal would be used? Explain.

10.8 Creative Accountants, Ltd., is a small San Francisco–based accounting partnership specializing in the preparation of individual ($I$) and corporate ($C$) income tax returns. Prevailing prices in the local market are $125 for individual tax-return preparation and $250 for corporate tax-return preparation.

Five accountants run the firm and are assisted by four bookkeepers and four secretaries, all of whom work a typical 40-hour workweek. The firm must decide how to target its promotional efforts to best use its resources during the coming tax-preparation season. Based on previous experience, the firm expects that an average of one hour of accountant time will be required for each individual return prepared. Corporate return preparation will require an average of two accountant hours and two bookkeeper hours. One hour of secretarial time will also be required for typing each individual and corporate return. In addition, variable computer and other processing costs are expected to average $25 per individual return and $100 per corporate return.

A. Set up the linear-programming problem that the firm would use to determine the profit-maximizing output levels for preparing individual and corporate returns. Show both the inequality and equality forms of the constraint conditions.

B. Completely solve and interpret the solution values for the linear-programming problem.

C. Calculate maximum possible net profits per week for the firm assuming that the accountants draw a salary of $1,500 per week, bookkeepers earn $500 per week, secretaries are paid $10 per hour, and fixed overhead (including promotion and other expenses) averages $5,000 per week.

D. After considering the preceding data, one senior accountant recommended letting two bookkeepers go while retaining the rest of the current staff. Another accountant suggested that if any bookkeepers were let go, an increase in secretarial staff

would be warranted. Which is the more profitable sugges-
tion? Why?

E. Using the equality form of the constraint conditions, set up,
solve, and interpret solution values for the dual linear-
programming problem.

F. Does the dual solution provide information useful for planning
purposes? Explain.

10.9  Designed for Sales, Inc., (DFS) is an architectural firm based in
Evanston, Illinois, that designs single-family and multifamily
housing units for real estate developers, building contractors, and
so on. DFS offers custom designs for single-family units, $Q_1$, for
$3,000 and custom designs for multifamily units (duplexes, four-
plexes, etc.), $Q_2$, for $2,000 each. Both types of output make use of
scarce drafting, artwork, and architectural resources. Each custom
design for single-family units requires 12 hours of drafting, 2 hours
of artwork, and 6 hours of architectural input. Each custom design
for multifamily units requires 4 hours of drafting, 5 hours of artwork, and 6 hours of architectural input. Currently DFS has 72
hours of drafting, 30 hours of artwork, and 48 hours of architectural services available on a weekly basis.

A. Using the equality form of the constraint conditions, set up the
primal and linear program that DFS would use to determine
the sales-revenue maximizing product mix. Also set up the
dual.

B. Solve for and interpret all solution values.

C. Would DFS's optimal product mix be different with a profit-
maximization rather than a sales revenue–maximization goal?
Why or why not?

10.10 Omaha Meat Products, Inc., (OMP) produces and markets "Cornhusker Plumpers," an extra-large frankfurter product being introduced on a test-market basis into the St. Louis, Missouri, area. This
product is similar to several others offered by OMP, and it can be
produced with currently available equipment and personnel using
any of three alternative production methods. Method $A$ requires 1
hour of labor and 4 processing-facility hours to produce 100 packages of Plumpers, one unit of $Q_A$. Method $B$ requires 2 labor hours
and 2 processing-facility hours for each unit of $Q_B$, and Method $C$
requires 5 labor hours and 1 processing-facility hour for each unit
of $Q_C$. Because of slack demand for other products, OMP currently
has 14 labor hours and 6 processing-facility hours available per
week for producing Cornhusker Plumpers. Cornhusker Plumpers
are currently being marketed to grocery retailers at a wholesale
price of $1.50 per package, and demand exceeds current supply.

A. Using the equality form of the constraint conditions, set up the
primal and dual linear programs that OMP would use to maximize production of Cornhusker Plumpers given currently
available resources.

B. Calculate and interpret all solution values.
C. Should OMP expand its processing-facility capacity if it can do so at a cost of $40 per hour?
D. Discuss the implications of a new union scale calling for a wage rate of $20 per hour.

## Selected References

Baker, Gordon L., William A. Clarke, Jr., Jonathan J. Frund, and Richard E. Wendell. "Production Planning and Cost Analysis on a Microcomputer." *Interfaces* 17 (July–August 1987): 53–60.

Bean, James C., Charles E. Noon, and Gary J. Salton. "Asset Divestiture at Homart Development Company." *Interfaces* 17 (January–February 1987): 48–64.

Best, Michael J., and Klaus Ritter. *Linear Programming: Active Set Analysis and Computer Programs.* Englewood Cliffs, NJ: Prentice-Hall, 1985.

Boquist, John A., and William T. Moore. "Estimating the Systematic Risk of an Industry Segment: A Mathematical Programming Approach." *Financial Management* 12 (Winter 1983): 11–18.

Bradbard, D. A., F. N. Ford, J. F. Cox, and W. N. Ledbetter. "The Management Science/Operations Research Industrial-Academic Interface." *Interfaces* 17 (March–April 1987): 39–48.

Cameron, Neil. *Introduction to Linear and Convex Programming.* New York: Cambridge University Press, 1985.

Chandy, P. R., and Prakash Kharabe. "Pricing in the Government Bond Market." *Interfaces* 16 (September–October 1986): 65–79.

Deniniger, Rolf A. "Teaching Linear Programming on a Microcomputer." *Interfaces* 13 (August 1983): 30–34.

Eldredge, David L. "A Cost Minimization Model for Warehouse Distribution Systems." *Interfaces* 12 (August 1982): 113–119.

Gass, Saul I. *Linear Programming,* 5th ed. New York: McGraw-Hill, 1985.

Haehling Von Lanzenauer, Christoph, Erwin Harbauer, Brian Johnston, and David H. Shuttleworth. "RRSP Flood: LP to the Rescue." *Interfaces* 17 (July–August 1987): 27–40.

Harrison, Terry P. "Micro versus Mainframe Performance for a Selected Class of Mathematical Programming Problems." *Interfaces* 15 (July–August 1985): 14–19.

Hartley, Roger. *Linear and Nonlinear Programming: An Introduction to Linear Methods in Mathematical Programming.* New York: John Wiley, 1985.

Hayes, James W. "Discount Rates in Linear Programming Formulations of the Capital Budgeting Problem." *Engineering Economist* 29 (Winter 1984): 113–126.

Render, Barry, and Ralph M. Stair, Jr. "Microcomputer Technology in Schools of Business." *Interfaces* 17 (September–October 1987): 92–102.

Ronn, Ehud I. "A New Linear Programming Approach to Bond Portfolio Management." *Journal of Financial and Quantitative Analysis* 22 (December 1987): 439–466.

Rumpf, David L., Emmanual Melachrinoudis, and Thomas Rumpf. "Improving Efficiency in a Forest Pest Control Spray Program." *Interfaces* 15 (September–October 1985): 1–11.

Schneiderjans, Marc J. *Linear Goal Programming.* Princeton, NJ: Petrocelli Books, 1984.

Sengupta, Jati K. "The Measurement of Productive Efficiency: A Robust Minimax Approach." *Managerial and Decision Economics* 9 (June 1988): 153–161.

Stensland, Gunnar, and Dag Tjøstheim. "Optimal Investments Using Empirical Dynamic Programming with Application to Natural Resources." *Journal of Business* 62 (January 1989): 99–120.

APPENDIX • 10A

# Rules for Forming the Dual Linear Programming Problem

Given the importance of duality, a list of simple rules that could be used to form the dual program to any given primal program would be useful. Four such rules exist. They are as follows:

1. Change a maximize objective to minimize and vice versa.
2. Reverse primal constraint inequality signs in dual constraints (i.e., $\geq$ to $\leq$, or $\leq$ to $\geq$).
3. Transpose primal constraint coefficients to get dual constraint coefficients.
4. Transpose objective function coefficients to get limits in dual constraints and vice versa.

Here the word *transpose* is a matrix algebra term that simply means that each row of coefficients is rearranged into columns so that row one becomes column one, row two becomes column two, and so on.

To illustrate the rules for transformation from primal and dual, consider the following simple example.

**Primal Program**

Maximize

$$\pi = \pi_1 Q_1 + \pi_2 Q_2,$$

subject to

$$a_{11}Q_1 + a_{12}Q_2 \leq r_1,$$
$$a_{21}Q_1 + a_{22}Q_2 \leq r_2,$$
$$Q_1, Q_2 \geq 0.$$

Here $\pi$ is profits and $Q$ is output. Thus, $\pi_1$ and $\pi_2$ are unit profits for $Q_1$ and $Q_2$, respectively. The resource constraints are given by $r_1$ and $r_2$. The constants in the primal constraints reflect the input requirements for each type of output. For example, $a_{11}$ is the amount of resource $r_1$ in one unit of output $Q_1$. Similarly, $a_{12}$ is the amount of resource $r_1$ in one unit of output $Q_2$. Thus, $a_{11}Q_1 + a_{12}Q_2$ is the total amount of resource $r_1$ used in production. The remaining input requirements, $a_{21}$ and $a_{22}$, have a similar interpretation. For convenience, this primal problem statement can be rewritten in matrix notation as:

**Primal Program**

Maximize $\qquad\qquad\qquad\qquad \pi = \pi_1 Q_1 + \pi_2 Q_2,$

subject to

$$\begin{bmatrix} a_{11} & a_{12} \\ a_{21} & a_{22} \end{bmatrix} \times \begin{bmatrix} Q_1 \\ Q_2 \end{bmatrix} \leq \begin{bmatrix} r_1 \\ r_2 \end{bmatrix}$$

$$Q_1, Q_2 \geq 0.$$

Matrix notation is just a convenient form of writing large numbers of equations. In going from matrix back to equation form, one just multiplies each row element by each column element. Thus, the left-hand side of the first constraint equation is $a_{11} \times Q_1$ plus $a_{12} \times Q_2$, or $a_{11}Q_1 + a_{12}Q_2$, and this sum must be less than or equal to $r_1$.

Given the expression of the primal program in matrix notation, we can now apply the four rules for transformation from primal to dual. Following these rules, we have the following:

**Dual Program**

Minimize $\qquad\qquad\qquad\qquad \pi^* = r_1 V_1 + r_2 V_2,$

subject to

$$\begin{bmatrix} a_{11} & a_{21} \\ a_{12} & a_{22} \end{bmatrix} \times \begin{bmatrix} V_1 \\ V_2 \end{bmatrix} \geq \begin{bmatrix} \pi_1 \\ \pi_2 \end{bmatrix}$$

$$V_1, V_2 \geq 0,$$

and converting from matrix back to equation form we have:

**Dual Program**

Minimize $\qquad\qquad\qquad\qquad \pi^* = r_1 V_1 + r_2 V_2,$

subject to

$$a_{11} V_1 + a_{21} V_2 \geq \pi_1,$$

$$a_{12} V_1 + a_{22} V_2 \geq \pi_2,$$

$$V_1, V_2 \geq 0.$$

Here $V_1$ and $V_2$ are the shadow prices for resources $r_1$ and $r_2$, respectively. Since $r_1$ and $r_2$ represent the quantities of the two resources available, the objective function measures the total imputed value of the resources available. Recalling the interpretation of $a_{11}$ and $a_{21}$ from the primal, we see that $a_{11}V_1 + a_{21}V_2$ is the total value of inputs used in production of one unit of output $Q_1$. Similarly, $a_{12}V_1 + a_{22}V_2$ is the total value of inputs used in production of a unit of output $Q_2$.

Finally, the primal and dual linear programming problems can be fully specified through the introduction of slack variables. Remember that with less-than-or-equal-to constraints, the left-hand side of the constraint equation must be brought up to equal the right-hand side. Thus, slack variables must be *added* to the left-hand side of such constraint equations. With greater-than-or-equal-to constraints, the left-hand side of the constraint equation must be brought down to equal the right-hand side. Thus, slack variables must be *subtracted from* the left-hand side of such constraint equations. With this, the full specification of the preceding primal and dual linear programs can be written as follows:

| **Primal Program** | **Dual Program** |
|---|---|
| Maximize $\quad \pi = \pi_1 Q_1 + \pi_2 Q_2,$ | Minimize $\quad \pi^* = r_1 V_1 + r_2 V_2,$ |
| subject to | subject to |

$$a_{11} Q_1 + a_{12} Q_2 + S_1 = r_1,$$
$$a_{21} Q_1 + a_{22} Q_2 + S_2 = r_2,$$
$$Q_1, Q_2, S_1, S_2 \geq 0,$$

$$a_{11} V_1 + a_{21} V_2 - L_1 = \pi_1,$$
$$a_{12} V_1 + a_{22} V_2 - L_2 = \pi_2,$$
$$V_1, V_2, L_1, L_2 \geq 0,$$

where $S_1$ and $S_2$ are slack variables representing excess capacity of resource $r_1$ and $r_2$, respectively. $L_1$ and $L_2$ are also slack variables; they represent the amount by which the value of resources used in the production of $Q_1$ and $Q_2$ exceeds the value of output as measured by $\pi_1$ and $\pi_2$, respectively. Thus, $L_1$ and $L_2$ measure the opportunity cost, or profit forgone, as a result of producing the last unit of $Q_1$ and $Q_2$.

Understanding these simple rules will both simplify construction of the dual, given a primal program, and facilitate the understanding and interpretation of the constraints and coefficients found in both primal and dual linear programming problems.

# Market Structure, Part I: Perfect Competition and Monopoly

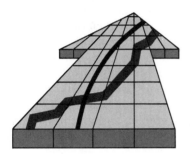

**W**e began our study of managerial economics by examining the value maximization model of the firm. That model assumes maximization of value, subject to constraints imposed by technology, resource limitations, and the economic and political environment in which the firm operates, to be the primary objective of management. This maximization process is complex and involves a wide range of factors that influence managerial decisions. Thus far, we have (1) examined the principles of economic analysis and optimization; (2) studied the characteristics of demand, including conceptual, estimation, and forecasting issues; (3) analyzed the production process, including cost analysis and estimation; and (4) considered linear programming as a methodology for optimal resource employment in the face of output quantity, output quality, and resource constraints. We are now in a position to integrate these topics to show how demand, production, and cost relations interact to determine the market structures firms face.

Market structure is described in terms of the complete array of industry characteristics that directly affect the price/output decisions made by the firm. Primary elements of market structure include the number and size distribution of actual sellers and buyers as well as potential entrants, the degree of product differentiation, the availability and cost of information about prices and output quality, and the conditions of entry and exit. Because all of these elements of market structure can have important consequences for the price/output decisions made by the firm, a careful study of market structure is necessary before value-maximizing managerial decisions can be made.

Market structure analysis is so important that we devote two full chapters to this topic. In this chapter, we consider the theories of perfect (or pure) competition and monopoly. These market structures can be viewed as the endpoints on a continuum of decreasing competition, moving from the models of perfect competition to monopolistic competition to oligopoly to monopoly. The perfect competition model describes the most vigorously competitive sectors of an economy, in which widespread price competition drives firms' profits to levels just sufficient to maintain required investment.

At the opposite end of the market structure spectrum, the monopoly model describes price/output decision making in an economic environment in which lax competitive pressures can allow even inefficient firms to survive, if not prosper. In the monopoly environment, the firm can earn above-normal (economic) profits even in the long run. Since these economic profits are sometimes derived from market power rather than innovation, superior efficiency, or other socially valued activity, monopolies are often subject to state and federal regulation, the topic of Chapter 14. In other instances in which direct government regulation is not feasible, market mechanisms such as countervailing power sometimes arise to combat the abuse of monopoly.

This examination of perfect competition and monopoly is valuable not only as a necessary backdrop for understanding managerial decision making in each of these market settings but also as a framework for understanding monopolistic competition and oligopoly. These models of market structure are the subject of Chapter 12.

## THE CONTRAST BETWEEN PERFECT COMPETITION AND MONOPOLY

**market structure**

The competitive environment in the market for a good or service.

**market**

Firms or individuals willing and able to buy or sell a particular product.

**potential entrants**

Firms or individuals who have the economic resources to enter a particular market, given sufficient economic incentives.

**Market structure** describes the competitive environment in the market for any good or service. A **market** consists of all firms and individuals who are willing and able to buy or sell a particular product. This includes firms and individuals currently engaged in buying and selling a particular product, as well as potential entrants.

A **potential entrant** is an individual or firm that poses a sufficiently credible threat of market entry to affect the price/output decisions of incumbent firms. Potential entrants play extremely important roles in many industries. Some industries with only a few active participants might at first appear to hold the potential for substantial economic profits. However, a number of potential entrants can have a substantial effect on the price/output decisions of incumbent firms. For example, IBM, Apple, Digital Equipment, and other leading computer manufacturers are viable potential entrants into the various computer components manufacturing industries, and use their threat of potential entry to obtain favorable prices from suppliers. Despite having only a relative handful of active foreign and domestic participants, computer components manufacturing is both highly innovative and vigorously price competitive. Therefore, when characterizing market structure it is important to consider the effects of both current rivals and potential entrants.

Market structure is typically characterized on the basis of four important industry characteristics: the number and size distribution of active buyers and sellers and potential entrants, the degree of product differentiation, the amount and cost of information about product price and quality, and the conditions of entry and exit. The effects of market structure are measured in terms of the prices paid by consumers, availability and quality of output, employment and career advancement opportunities, and the pace of product innovation, among other factors.

Stark differences between the perfect competition and monopoly models of buyer and seller behavior can be noted along every important dimension of market structure. We briefly characterize these differences in the next section and then elaborate on them in the rest of the chapter.

### Perfect Competition

**perfect (pure) competition**
A market structure characterized by a large number of buyers and sellers of an identical product.

**Perfect (pure) competition** is a market structure characterized by a large number of buyers and sellers of essentially the same product, where each market participant's transactions are so small that they have no influence on the market price of the product. Individual buyers and sellers are **price takers.** This means that firms take market prices as a given and devise their production strategies accordingly. Free and complete demand and supply information is available in a perfectly competitive market, and there are no meaningful barriers to entry and exit. As a result, vigorous price competition prevails, and only a normal rate of return on investment is possible in the long run. Economic profits are possible only in periods of short-run disequilibrium before rivals mount effective competitive responses.

**price takers**
Buyers and sellers whose individual transactions are so small that they do not affect market prices.

### Monopoly

**monopoly**
A market structure characterized by a single seller.

**Monopoly** is a market structure characterized by a single seller of a highly differentiated product. Because a monopolist is the sole provider of a desired commodity, the monopolist *is* the industry. The producer of every product must compete for a share of the consumer's overall market basket of goods, but monopolists face no effective competition for specific product sales from either established or potential rivals. This allows the monopolist to simultaneously determine price and output for the firm (and the industry). Substantial barriers to entry or exit often deter potential entrants and offer both efficient and inefficient monopolists the opportunity for economic profits, even in the long run.

## FACTORS THAT DETERMINE THE LEVEL OF COMPETITION

Two key conditions determine the level of competition in a given market: the number and relative size of buyers and sellers in the market, and the extent to which the product is standardized. These factors, in turn, are influenced by the nature of the product and production systems, the scope of potential entry, and buyer characteristics. These relations are described in the following sections.

## Effect of Product Characteristics on Market Structure

Good substitutes for a product will increase the degree of competition in the market for that product. To illustrate, rail service between two points is typically supplied by only one railroad. Transportation service is available from several sources, however, and railroads compete with bus lines, truck companies, barges, airlines, and private autos. The substitutability of these other modes of transportation for rail service increases the degree of competition in the transportation service market.

It is important to realize that market structures are not static. In the 1800s and early 1900s—before the introduction of trucks, buses, autos, and airplanes—railroads faced very little competition. Railroads could therefore charge excessive prices and earn monopoly profits. Because of this exploitation, laws were passed giving public authorities permission to regulate railroads' prices (a topic discussed in detail in Chapter 14). Other firms were enticed by the railroads' profits to develop competing transportation service systems, which led ultimately to a much more competitive market structure. Today, few would argue that railroads retain significant monopoly power, and public regulation of the railroads is being reduced in recognition of this fact.

The physical characteristics of a product can also influence the competitive structure of its market. A low ratio of distribution cost to total cost, for example, tends to increase competition by widening the geographic area over which any particular producer can compete. Rapid perishability of a product produces the opposite effect. Thus, in considering the level of competition for a product, the national, regional, or local nature of the market must be considered.

## Effect of Production Characteristics on Competition

When minimum efficient scale is large in relation to overall industry output, only a few firms will be able to attain the output size necessary for productive efficiency. In such instances, competitive pressures will allow only a few firms to survive in an industry. On the other hand, when minimum efficient scale is small in relation to overall industry output, many firms will be able to attain the size necessary for efficient operations. Holding all else equal, competition tends to be most vigorous when many, as opposed to only a few, efficient competitors are present in the market. This is especially true when firms smaller than minimum efficient scale face considerably higher production costs and when the construction of minimum-efficient-scale plants involves the commitment of substantial capital, skilled labor, and material resources. When construction of minimum-efficient-scale plants requires the commitment of only modest resources or when smaller firms face no important production cost disadvantages, economies of scale will have little or no effect on the competitive potential of new or entrant firms.

## Effect of Entry and Exit Conditions on Competition

Maintaining the above-normal profits or productive inefficiency of a monopolist over the long run requires substantial barriers to entry, mobility, or exit. A **barrier to entry** is any factor or industry characteristic that creates an advantage for incumbents over new arrivals. Legal rights such as patents and local, state, or federal licenses can present formidable barriers to new entry in pharmaceutical, cable television, television and radio broadcasting, and other industries. Other factors sometimes create barriers to entry, including substantial economies of scale, scope economies, large capital or skilled-labor requirements, and ties of customer loyalty created through advertising and other means.

Factors that create barriers to entry can sometimes result in compensating advantages for consumers. Even though patents can lead to monopoly profits for inventing firms, they also spur valuable new product and process development. Although extremely efficient or innovative leading firms make it difficult for new firms to enter the market and for nonleading firms to grow, they can have the favorable effect of lowering industry prices and increasing product quality. Therefore, a complete evaluation of the economic effects of entry barriers involves a consideration of both costs and benefits.

Whereas barriers to entry have the potential to impede competition by making entry or growth difficult, competitive forces can also be diminished through barriers to exit. A **barrier to exit** is any restriction on the ability of incumbents to redeploy assets from one industry or line of business to another. During the late 1980s, for example, several state governments initiated legal proceedings to impede plant closures by large employers in the steel, glass, automobile, and other industries. By imposing large fines or severance taxes or requiring substantial expenditures for worker retraining, they created significant barriers to exit.

By impeding the asset redeployment that is typical of any vigorous competitive environment, barriers to exit can dramatically increase both the costs and risk of doing business. Thus, even though one can certainly sympathize with the difficult adjustments faced by both individuals and firms affected by plant closures, government actions that create barriers to exit can have the unintended effect of impeding industrial development and market competition.

## Effect of Buyers on Competition

The degree of competition in a market is affected by buyers as well as sellers. If there are only a few buyers, there will be less competition than if there are many buyers. **Monopsony,** a market with only one buyer,

**barrier to entry**

Any advantage for industry incumbents over new arrivals.

**barrier to exit**

Any limit on asset redeployment.

**monopsony**

A market with one buyer.

## 11.1 **Managerial Application**
Barriers to Exit

Hard times have come to many towns and cities in industrial America. Factories outmoded by foreign competition and improved production methods often become burdens rather than assets to parent companies. In the face of aggressive wage and job-security demands, companies have increasingly opted to close rather than renovate these aging facilities. Until recently, workers have relied on negotiated severance benefits to bridge the gap between layoff and rehire, including payment for the retraining and relocation that often becomes necessary. However, as growth in the U.S. economy has continued to favor service rather than goods-producing sectors, and given vigorous foreign competition, the economic malaise in some sectors of industrial America

has become chronic rather than temporary. As a result, permanent plant closures have become more frequent in automobile, steel, and other basic industries, and redevelopment has been slow to replace lost employment opportunities.

Following recent plant closures, workers have begun to strike back at their former employers with the aid of state and local governments by creating substantial barriers to exit. For example, Newell Company, based in Freeport, Illinois, sent executives to Clarksburgh, West Virginia, in the summer of 1987 to inform workers that the local glass-making facility was to be idled in 12 weeks, eliminating over 900 jobs. Workers and local business leaders recoiled at the modest severance benefits offered and the

*continued*

See: Joseph B. White, "Factory Towns Start to Fight Back Angrily When Firms Pull Out," *The Wall Street Journal*, March 8, 1988, 1, 20.

exists when a single firm dominates a local labor market, when a single feed mill or livestock buyer dominates a local agricultural market, in government defense contract procurement, and in intermediate markets for certain durable consumer goods, such as the home appliances sold by major retail chains.

Monopsony is more common in factor input markets than in markets for final demand. In terms of economic efficiency, monopsony is least harmful, and can sometimes even be beneficial, in markets in which a monopsony buyer faces a monopoly or just a few sellers. For example,

**Managerial Application** *continued*

company's unwillingness to consider alternatives to plant closure. Moreover, Anchor Hocking Corporation, previous owner of the Clarksburgh facility, had benefitted from $3.5 million in state loans at interest rates of 4 percent or less during the previous decade. Workers believed that this created a moral obligation to keep the plant open. Newell, which had acquired Anchor Hocking in a hostile takeover in July 1987, argued that no commitment had been made to keep the facility open and stuck by its plant closure decision.

When the company closed the 87-year-old Clarksburgh facility in November 1987, workers and others sprang into action. Local politicians got involved, as one state legislator stood ready with a bulldozer at the factory door to block Newell from removing valuable equipment. West Virginia Governor Arch A. Moore, Jr. hit Newell with a $614.6 million breach-of-contract suit, and lawyers for the state won a federal court injunction preventing Newell from transferring equipment to other facilities. In a countermove, Newell had the case transferred to state court, and during a two-hour gap between federal and state injunctions managed to remove a $500,000 piece of transformer equipment.

In early 1988, the plant remained closed, but not on Newell's terms. The company was forced to pay an additional $1 million to aid workers. City officials pressed demands for as much as $250,000 in additional back wages, and white-collar workers challenged the company's severance package. With valuable plant machinery impounded, Newell was unable to expand its glass-making capacity at other locations and lost millions of dollars in business.

Other recent examples of local efforts to stem plant closures include a $318.3 million breach-of-contract suit by the city of Norwood, Ohio against General Motors Corporation; an effort led by rock singer Bruce Springsteen to stop closure of a Minnesota Mining and Manufacturing facility in Freehold, New Jersey; and union, business, and government efforts to resist Chrysler Corporation's closure of a Kenosha, Wisconsin, facility acquired from American Motors. Without a doubt, barriers to exit will be a controversial topic of increasing importance to business in coming years.

consider the case of the town in which one mill is the sole employer of unskilled labor. The mill is a monopsony since it is a single buyer of labor, and it may be able to use its power to reduce wage rates below competitive levels. However, if workers organize a union to bargain collectively with their employer, a single monopoly seller of labor would be created that could offset the employer's monopsony power and increase wages toward competitive market norms. Monopsony is not only accepted in such situations, it is sometimes encouraged by public policy.

# PURE COMPETITION

The market characteristics described in the preceding section determine, to a large extent, the level of competition in the market for any good or service. In this section we discuss pure competition in some detail; the monopoly market structure is discussed in the subsequent section.

Pure competition exists when the individual producers in a market have no influence on prices; they are price takers as opposed to price makers. This lack of influence on price requires the following conditions:

- *Large numbers of buyers and sellers.* Each firm in the industry produces a small portion of industry output, and each customer buys only a small part of the total.
- *Product homogeneity.* The output of each firm is perceived by customers to be essentially the same as the output of any other firm in the industry.
- *Free entry and exit.* Firms are not restricted from entering or leaving the industry.
- *Perfect dissemination of information.* Cost, price, and product quality information is known by all buyers and all sellers in the market.

These four basic conditions, which are necessary for the existence of a purely competitive market structure, are too restrictive for pure competition to be commonplace in actual markets. Although security and commodity exchanges approach the perfectly competitive ideal, imperfections occur even there. For example, the acquisition of large blocks of a firm's securities by corporate raiders clearly affects the market price of its stocks and bonds, at least in the short run. Nonetheless, some firms must make pricing decisions without any control over price, and examination of a purely competitive market structure provides insights into these pricing decisions. More importantly, a clear understanding of pure competition provides a reference point from which to analyze the more typically encountered market structures of monopolistic competition and oligopoly described in Chapter 12.

## Market Price Determination

Market price for a competitive industry is determined by aggregate supply and demand; individual firms have no control over price. A total industry demand curve for the product reflects an aggregation of the quantities that individual purchasers will buy at each price; an industry supply curve reflects the summation of the quantities that individual firms are willing to supply at different prices. The intersection of the industry supply and demand curves determines market price.

The data in Table 11.1 illustrate the process by which an industry supply curve is constructed. First, suppose each of five firms in an industry is willing to supply varying quantities of the product at different prices. Summing the individual supply quantities of these five firms at

■ Table 11.1
## Market Supply Schedule Determination

| Price ($) | Quantity Supplied by Firm | | | | | Partial Market Supply | × 1,000 = | Total Market Supply |
|---|---|---|---|---|---|---|---|---|
|  | 1 + | 2 + | 3 + | 4 + | 5 = |  |  |  |
| 1 | 5 | 0 | 5 | 10 | 30 | 50 |  | 50,000 |
| 2 | 15 | 0 | 5 | 25 | 45 | 90 |  | 90,000 |
| 3 | 20 | 20 | 10 | 30 | 50 | 130 |  | 130,000 |
| 4 | 25 | 35 | 20 | 35 | 55 | 170 |  | 170,000 |
| 5 | 30 | 55 | 25 | 40 | 60 | 210 |  | 210,000 |
| 6 | 35 | 75 | 30 | 45 | 65 | 250 |  | 250,000 |
| 7 | 40 | 95 | 35 | 50 | 70 | 290 |  | 290,000 |
| 8 | 45 | 115 | 40 | 55 | 75 | 330 |  | 330,000 |
| 9 | 50 | 130 | 45 | 65 | 80 | 370 |  | 370,000 |
| 10 | 55 | 145 | 50 | 75 | 85 | 410 |  | 410,000 |

each price determines their combined supply schedule, shown in the Partial Market Supply column. For example, at a price of $2, the output quantities supplied by the five firms are 15, 0, 5, 25, and 45 units, respectively, resulting in a combined supply of 90 units at that price. With a product price of $8, the supply quantities become 45, 115, 40, 55, and 75, for a total supply by the five firms of 330 units.

Now assume that the five firms, although representative of firms in the industry, account for only a small portion of the industry's total output. Assume specifically that there are actually 5,000 firms in the industry, each with an individual supply schedule identical to one of the five firms illustrated in the table. That is, there are 1,000 firms just like each one illustrated in Table 11.1, so the total market supply—the total quantity supplied at each price—will be 1,000 times that shown under the Partial Market Supply schedule. This supply schedule is illustrated in Figure 11.1, and adding the market demand curve to the industry supply curve, as in Figure 11.2, allows us to determine the equilibrium market price.

The market price is found by first equating the market supply and demand to find the equilibrium activity level, then substituting that quantity into either the demand or supply curve to find the market clearing price. Using the curves in Figure 11.2 we have:

$$\text{Demand} = \text{Supply}$$
$$\$40 - \$0.0001Q = -\$0.254 + \$0.000025Q$$
$$\$0.000125Q = \$40.254$$
$$Q = 322,032$$
$$P = \$40 - \$0.0001(322,032)$$
$$= \$40 - \$32.20$$
$$= \$7.80.$$

■ Figure 11.1
## Hypothetical Industry Supply Curve

Industry supply is the sum of the quantities that individual firms supply at each price.

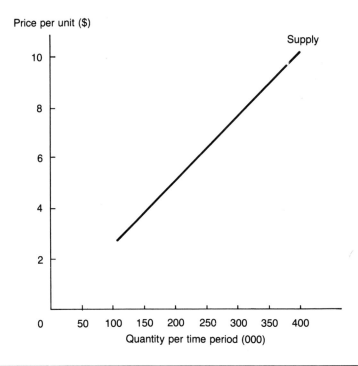

Although it is apparent from Figure 11.2 that both the quantity de-manded and supplied depend on price, a simple example should dem-onstrate the inability of an individual firm to affect price. The total demand function in Figure 11.2, which represents the summation at each price of the quantities demanded by individual purchasers, can be described by the equation:

$$\text{Quantity Demanded} = Q = 400{,}000 - 10{,}000P, \qquad \textbf{11.1}$$

or, solving for price:

$$\$10{,}000P = \$400{,}000 - Q$$
$$P = \$40 - \$0.0001Q. \qquad \textbf{11.1a}$$

According to Equation 11.1a, a 100-unit change in output would cause only a $0.0001 change in price, or, alternatively, a $0.0001 price increase (reduction) would lead to a one-unit decrease (increase) in total market demand.

The demand curve shown in Figure 11.2 is redrawn for an individual firm in Figure 11.3. The slope of the curve is −0.0001, the same as in Figure 11.2; only the scales have been changed. The intercept $7.80 is

■ Figure 11.2

## Market Price Determination in Perfect Competition

The perfectly competitive market-equilibrium price–output combination can be determined by equating the market demand and supply curves.

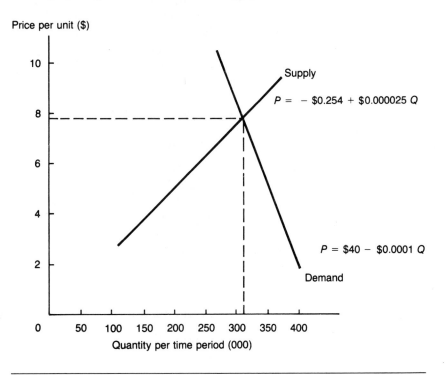

Price per unit ($)

Supply

$P = -\$0.254 + \$0.000025\ Q$

$P = \$40 - \$0.0001\ Q$

Demand

Quantity per time period (000)

---

■ Figure 11.3

## Demand Curve for a Single Firm in Perfect Competition

Firms face horizontal demand curves in perfectly competitive markets.

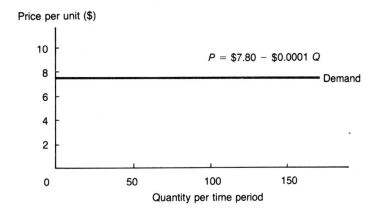

Price per unit ($)

$P = \$7.80 - \$0.0001\ Q$

Demand

Quantity per time period

---

*Note: With price constant at, say,* P*, TR = P* × Q, AR = (P* × Q)/Q = P*, *and*
MR = dTR/dQ = P*.

the going market price as determined by the intersection of the market supply and demand curves in Figure 11.2.

At the scale shown in Figure 11.3, the firm's demand curve is seen to be, for all practical purposes, a horizontal line. An output change of even 100 units by the individual firm results in only a $0.01 change in market price, and the data in Table 11.1 indicate that the typical firm would not vary output by this amount unless the market price changed by more than $10 a unit. Thus, it is clear that under pure competition, the individual firm's output decisions do not affect price in any meaningful way, and for pricing decisions, the demand curve is taken to be perfectly horizontal. That is, price is assumed to be constant irrespective of the output level at which the firm chooses to operate.

## The Firm's Price/Output Decision

Figure 11.4 illustrates the firm's price/output decision in a competitive market. We assume for simplicity that the curves graphed are those of a representative firm. Thus, the cost curves in Figure 11.4 represent an average firm in a perfectly competitive industry.

■ Figure 11.4
## Competitive Firm's Optimal Price/Output Combination

Given a horizontal demand curve, $P = MR$. Thus, short-run equilibrium occurs when $P = MR = MC$.

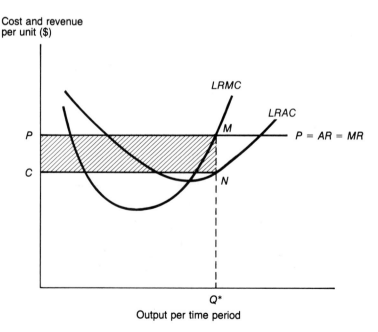

Profit maximization was shown in Chapter 2 to require that a firm operate at an output level at which marginal revenue and marginal cost are equal. With price a constant, average revenue (or price) and marginal revenue must always be equal. Therefore, to maximize profit, market price for a firm operating in a perfectly competitive industry must equal marginal cost. In the example shown in Figure 11.4, the firm chooses to operate at output level $Q^*$, where price (and hence marginal revenue) equals marginal cost, and profits are maximized.

Notice from this illustration that above-normal or economic profits may exist in the short run even under conditions of pure competition. A normal profit, defined as the rate of return just sufficient to attract the capital investment necessary to develop and operate a firm (see Chapter 1) is included as a part of economic costs. Therefore, any profit shown in a graph such as Figure 11.4 (or 11.5) is defined as economic profit and represents an above-normal rate of return. The firm incurs economic losses whenever it fails to earn a normal profit. Thus, a firm might show a small accounting profit but be suffering economic losses because these profits are insufficient to provide an adequate return to the firm's stockholders. In such instances, firms will not replace plant and equipment and will exit the industry in the long run.

In Figure 11.4 the firm produces and sells $Q^*$ units of output at an average cost of $C$ dollars; with a market price $P$, the firm earns economic profits of $P - C$ dollars per unit. Total economic profit, $(P - C)Q^*$, is shown by the shaded rectangle *PMNC*.

Over the long run, positive economic profits will attract additional firms into the industry, lead to increased output by existing firms, or both. Expanding industry supply will put downward pressure on the market price for the industry as a whole, since industry output can expand only by offering the product at a lower price. Expanded supply simultaneously pushes cost upward because of increased demand for factors of production. Long-run equilibrium will be reached when all economic profits and losses have been eliminated and each firm in the industry is operating at an output that minimizes long-run average cost (*LRAC*). The long-run equilibrium for a firm under pure competition is graphed in Figure 11.5. At the profit-maximizing output, price (or average revenue) equals average cost, so the firm neither earns economic profits nor incurs economic losses. When this condition exists for all firms in the industry, new firms are not encouraged to enter the industry nor are existing ones pressured into leaving it. Prices are stable, and each firm is operating at the minimum point on its short-run average cost curve. All firms must also be operating at the minimum cost point on the long-run average cost curve; otherwise they will make production changes, decrease costs, and affect industry output and prices. Accordingly, a stable equilibrium requires that firms operate with optimally sized plants.

The optimal price/output level for a firm in a perfectly competitive market can be further illustrated using a simple numerical example.

■ Figure 11.5
## Long-Run Equilibrium in a Competitive Market

Long-run equilibrium is reached when $Q^*$ units of output are produced at minimum $LRAC$. Thus, $P = MR = MC = AC$, and economic (excess) profits equal zero.

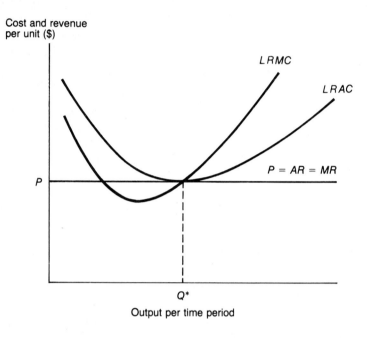

Assume that we are interested in determining the profit-maximizing activity level for the Hair Stylist, Ltd., a hair styling salon in College Park, Maryland. Given the large number of competitors, the fact that stylists routinely tailor services to meet customer needs, and the lack of entry barriers, it is reasonable to assume that the market is perfectly competitive and that the average \$20 price equals marginal revenue, $P = MR = $ \$20. Furthermore, assume that the firm's operating expenses are typical of the 100 firms in the local market and can be expressed by the following total cost function:

$$TC = \$5{,}625 + \$5Q + \$0.01Q^2,$$

where $TC$ is total cost per month (including capital costs) and $Q$ is the number of hair stylings provided.

The optimal price/output combination can be determined by setting marginal profit equal to zero, $d\pi/dQ = 0$, and solving for $Q$:

$$\pi = TR - TC$$
$$= \$20Q - \$5{,}625 - \$5Q - \$0.01Q^2$$
$$= -\$0.01Q^2 + \$15Q - \$5{,}625,$$

and

$$d\pi/dQ = -\$0.02Q + \$15 = 0$$
$$\$0.02Q = \$15$$
$$Q = 750 \text{ Hair Stylings per Month}$$

and

$$\pi = TR - TC$$
$$= \$20Q - \$5{,}625 - \$5Q - \$0.01Q^2$$
$$= \$20(750) - \$5{,}625 - \$5(750) - \$0.01(750^2)$$
$$= \$0.$$

The $Q = 750$ activity level results in a zero economic profit level ($\pi = 0$), indicating that the Hair Stylist is just able to obtain a normal or risk-adjusted rate of return on investment. (Recall that capital costs are included in the cost function.) Note also that the $Q = 750$ output level is the point at which $MR = MC$, because $\$20 = \$5 + \$0.02$ (750); and it is the point of minimum average production costs ($AC = MC = \$20$). Finally, with 100 identical firms in the industry, total industry output will be 75,000 hair stylings per month.

## The Firm's Supply Curve

Market supply curves, we have seen, are the summation of supply quantities of individual firms at various prices. We are now in a position to examine how supply schedules for individual firms are determined.

In Figure 11.6 we add the firm's average variable cost curve to the average total cost and marginal cost curves of Figure 11.4. The competitive firm's short-run supply curve will correspond to that portion of the marginal cost curve that lies above the average variable cost curve—that is, the solid portion of the marginal cost curve in Figure 11.6. Since $P = MR$ under perfect competition, the quantity supplied by the perfectly competitive firm is found at the point where $P = MC$, as long as price exceeds average variable cost.

To understand the reason for this, consider the options available to the firm. Profit maximization under pure competition requires that the firm operate at the output level at which marginal revenue equals marginal cost, if it produces any output at all. That is, the firm will either (1) produce nothing and incur a loss equal to its fixed costs or (2) produce an output determined by the intersection of the horizontal demand curve and the marginal cost curve. It will choose the alternative that maximizes profits or minimizes losses if they must be incurred. If the price is less than average variable costs, the firm should produce nothing and incur a loss equal to its total fixed cost; if the firm produces any product under this condition, its losses will increase. But if price exceeds average variable costs, then each unit of output provides some profit contribution to help cover fixed costs and provide profit; the firm should produce

■ Figure 11.6

## Competitive Firm's Short-Run Supply Curve

The perfectly competitive firm's short-run supply curve is that portion of the *MC* curve lying above the *AVC* curve.

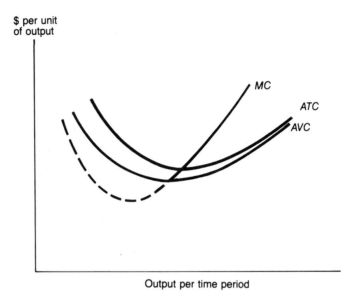

If the firm simply shuts down and terminates production, it would cease to incur variable costs, and its loss would be reduced to the level of the fixed cost loss—that is, to 100($0.60) = $60.

and sell its product, because this production reduces losses or leads to profits. Accordingly, the minimum point on the firm's average variable cost curve determines the cutoff point, or the lower limit, of its supply schedule. This is illustrated in Figure 11.7. At a very low price such as $1, *MR* = *MC* at 100 units of output. But notice that at 100 units, the firm has a total cost per unit of $2 and a price of only $1, so it is incurring a loss of $1 per unit.

Since the difference between the *ATC* and the *AVC* curves represents the fixed cost per unit of output, the total loss consists of a fixed cost component, $2.00 − $1.40 = $0.60, and a variable cost component, $1.40 − $1.00 = $0.40. Thus, the total loss is:

$$\text{Total Loss} = (100 \text{ Units}) \times (\$0.60 \text{ Fixed Cost Loss} \\ + \$0.40 \text{ Variable Cost Loss})$$

$$= \$100.$$

If the firm simply shuts down and terminates production, it would cease to incur variable costs, and its loss would be reduced to the level of the fixed cost loss—that is, to 100($0.60) = $60.

■ Figure 11.7

## Price, Cost, and Optimal Supply Decisions for a Firm under Pure Competition

The minimum point of $1.25 on the AVC curve is the lowest price level at which the firm will supply output.

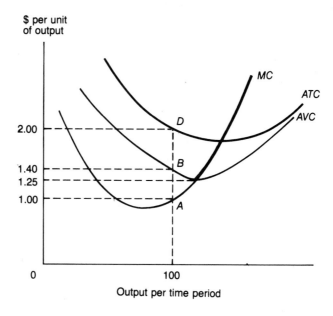

Variable cost losses will occur at any price less than $1.25, the minimum point on the AVC curve, so this is the lowest price at which the firm will operate. Above $1.25, the price more than covers variable costs. Therefore, even though total costs are not covered, it is preferable to operate and provide some contribution to cover a portion of fixed costs rather than to shut down and incur losses equal to total fixed costs.

To summarize, the perfectly competitive firm's short-run supply curve is that portion of the marginal cost curve lying above the AVC curve. When marginal cost is below average cost but above average variable cost, losses can be reduced if the firm expands production. Despite losses, firms will continue to produce when price exceeds average variable cost. Positive economic profits occur over that part of the supply function for which price (and marginal cost) exceeds average total cost.

The firm's long-run supply function is similarly determined. Since all costs are variable in the long run, a firm will choose to shut down unless total costs are completely covered. Accordingly, the portion of the firm's long-run marginal cost curve that lies above its long-run average cost curve represents its long-run supply schedule.

## 11.2  **Managerial Application**
The Difference Service Can Make

Without meaningful product differentiation, and given free entry and exit, perfectly competitive markets are characterized by relentless price competition. For this reason, firms in perfectly competitive industries are often described as price takers without opportunities for above-normal long-run profits. Nevertheless, many firms understand that combining standardized products with distinctively superior customer service can allow them to successfully exploit a market niche and fundamentally transform the profit potential of their business. Companies that serve customers best often have proved that above-normal returns can be earned in highly competitive industries.

Grocery retailing is a good example. This is a very competitive industry with low barriers to entry, readily available price and product-quality information on both branded and nonbranded merchandise, and many buyers and sellers, except in the smallest markets. Price competition is vicious, and the gross profit margin on sales is a razor-thin 1 to 2 percent, on average. Still, a number of local grocery retailers have doubled or tripled industry-average profit margins and sales-growth rates by emphasizing superior customer services.

Wegmans, a chain based in Rochester, New York, is a case in point. The company features tremendous product variety, uncrowded shopping, and speedy checkouts for customers at its huge 90,000 square foot supermarkets. In order to better serve customers, the company installed optical scanner equipment in 1974, years before the competition. A ready supply of eager, well-trained workers is ensured by Wegmans' employee development program, which in-

*continued*

See: Bro Uttal, "Companies That Serve You Best," *Fortune*, December 7, 1987, 98–108.

## MONOPOLY

Pure monopoly lies at the opposite extreme from pure competition on the market structure continuum. Monopoly exists when a single firm is the sole producer of a good that has no close substitutes; in other words, there is a single firm in the industry. Pure monopoly, like pure competition, is seldom observed. Few goods are produced by single producers, and fewer still are free from competition of close substitutes. Even public utilities are imperfect monopolists in most of their markets. Electric companies, for example, typically approach a pure monopoly in their residential lighting market, but they face strong competition from gas

**Managerial Application** *continued*

cludes 50-percent scholarships for employees with potential for college or graduate work. Company sales have been growing at a rate roughly three times the industry average of 5 percent per year.

Employee development is also emphasized at Embassy Suites, a hotel subsidiary of Holiday Corporation, headquartered in Irving, Texas. Interpersonal skills are emphasized in both hiring and training. Housekeepers that want to manage the front desk can take a company-run course on that skill. Even before a promotion becomes possible, passing grades lead to meaningful increases in pay. Workers are further motivated to emphasize service by daily reports on occupancy, profit, and customer satisfaction—all tied to monthly bonuses for all workers when goals are met or exceeded. Meanwhile, the company enjoys rapid growth and profit margins that are 2 to 2½ times that of the industry in general.

Wegmans and Embassy Suites are only two of a number of companies that successfully use distinctive customer service to transform their competitive environments. Highly profitable New York apparel manufacturer Liz Claiborne is well-known for being sensitive to retailer ordering needs so that profit-sapping markdowns are infrequent. Mail order merchants L. L. Bean, located in Freeport, Maine, and Land's End, Inc., located in Dodgeville, Wisconsin, both known for rapid service and guaranteed customer satisfaction, generate superior rates of profitability and sales growth. Automobile manufacturer American Honda ensured top-of-the-line service for customers of its new Acura line by restricting the selection of dealers to the top 25 percent of its own highly service-conscious dealer network.

These and other companies that serve customers best seem to share a number of important characteristics. They make every effort to hire, train, and motivate the right people; they invest earlier and more heavily than competitors in service-supporting technology; and they constantly strive to improve by identifying and meeting new customer needs. Unlike monopolies protected by impenetrable barriers to entry, they must keep a sharp eye on the competition. Still, the distinctive service they offer makes for hard-to-copy packages of products and services and leads to impressive profitability in traditionally low-margin industries.

and oil suppliers in the heating market. Further, in all phases of the industrial and commercial power markets, electric utilities face competition from gas- and oil-powered private generators.

Even though pure monopoly rarely exists, it is still worthy of careful examination. Many of the economic relations found under monopoly can be used to estimate optimal firm behavior in the less precise, but more prevalent, partly competitive and partly monopolistic market structures that dominate the real world. In addition, understanding monopoly market relations provides the background necessary to examine the economics of regulation, a topic of prime importance to business managers.

## Price/Output Decision under Monopoly

Under monopoly, the industry demand curve is identical to the demand curve of the firm, and because industry demand curves typically slope downward, monopolists also face downward-sloping demand curves. In Figure 11.8, for example, 100 units can be sold at a price of $10 a unit. At an $8 price, 150 units will be demanded. If the firm decides to sell 100 units, it will receive $10 a unit; if it wishes to sell 150 units, it must accept an $8 price. We see then that the monopolist can set either price or quantity, but not both. Given one, the value of the other is determined by the demand curve.

A monopolistic firm uses the same profit-maximization rule as a firm in a competitive industry: it operates at the level of output at which marginal revenue equals marginal cost. The demand curve facing the monopolistic firm, however, is not horizontal, or perfectly elastic, so marginal revenue will not coincide with price at any but the first unit of output. Marginal revenue is always less than price for output quantities greater than one because of the negatively sloped demand curve. Since the demand (average revenue) curve is negatively sloped and hence declining, the marginal revenue curve must lie below it. (This relation was examined earlier in Chapters 2, 3, and 4.)

When the monopolistic firm equates marginal revenue and marginal cost, it simultaneously determines the output level and the market price for its product. This decision is illustrated in Figure 11.9. Here the firm

■ Figure 11.8

## Firm's Demand Curve under Monopoly

The demand curve for a monopolist is the industry demand curve.

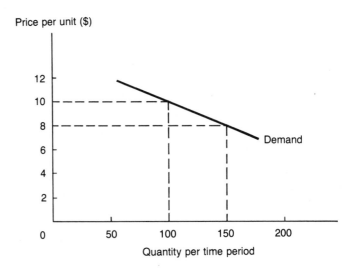

■ Figure 11.9
## Price/Output Decision under Monopoly

Monopoly equilibrium occurs where $MR = MC$. However $P > ATC$, and the firm earns economic (excess) profits.

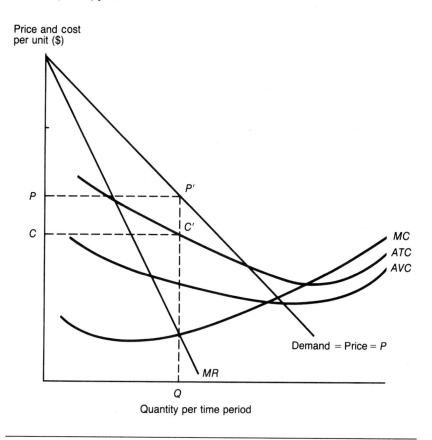

produces $Q$ units of output at a cost of $C$ per unit, and it sells this output at price $P$. Profits, which are equal to $(P - C)$ times $Q$, are represented by the area $PP'C'C$ and are at a maximum.

Q is the optimal short-run output, but the firm will engage in production only if average revenue, or price, is greater than average variable cost. This condition holds in Figure 11.9. If the price had been below the average variable cost, however, losses would have been minimized by shutting down.

 To further illustrate the solution to the price/output decision problem under monopoly, let us reconsider our earlier Hair Stylist, Ltd. example, but now we will assume that the firm has a monopoly in the College Park market (perhaps because of restrictive licensing requirements). Remember in our earlier example that each of 100 competitors had a profit-maximizing activity level of 750 hair stylings per month, for a total industry output of 75,000 hair stylings per month.

As a monopolist, the Hair Stylist would provide the total industry output. For simplicity, assume that as a monopolist, the Hair Stylist operates a chain of salons and that the cost function for each shop is the same as in the previous example. This means that by operating each shop at its average cost-minimizing activity level (750 hair stylings per month), the Hair Stylist can operate with Marginal Cost = Average Cost = $20.

Assume the industry demand curve for hair stylings in the College Park market can be written:

$$P = \$80 - \$0.0008Q.$$

The monopoly profit-maximizing activity level can be obtained by setting marginal profit equal to zero ($d\pi/dQ = 0$), or by setting marginal revenue equal to marginal cost, and solving for Q. The monopoly total revenue curve is:

$$\begin{aligned} TR &= P \times Q \\ &= (\$80 - \$0.0008Q)Q \\ &= \$80Q - \$0.0008Q^2 \end{aligned}$$

Therefore,

$$MR = dTR/dQ = \$80 - \$0.0016Q.$$

To find the profit-maximizing output level, we set $MR = MC$ and solve for Q:

$$\begin{aligned} MR &= MC \\ \$80 - \$0.0016Q &= \$20 \\ \$0.0016Q &= \$60 \\ Q &= 37{,}500 \text{ Hair Stylings per Month.} \end{aligned}$$

The resulting market price is found to be:

$$\begin{aligned} P &= \$80 - \$0.0008(37{,}500) \\ &= \$50. \end{aligned}$$

Notice that at the $Q = 37{,}500$ activity level, the Hair Stylist will operate a chain of 50 salons ($= 37{,}500/750$). Although each of these outlets will be producing $Q = 750$ hair stylings per month, a point of optimal efficiency, the benefits of this efficiency will accrue to the company in the form of economic profits rather than to consumers in the form of lower prices. Economic profit from each shop will be:

$$\begin{aligned} \pi &= TR - TC \\ &= P \times Q - AC \times Q \\ &= \$50(750) - \$20(750) \\ &= \$22{,}500 \text{ per Month.} \end{aligned}$$

With 50 shops, the Hair Stylist would earn a total economic profit of $1,125,000 per month. Note that as a monopoly, the industry will provide only 37,500 units of output, down from the 75,000 units provided in the previous case of a perfectly competitive industry. The new price of $50 per hair styling is up substantially from the perfectly competitive price of $20. Thus, the effects of monopoly appear as higher consumer prices, reduced levels of output, and the creation of substantial economic profits for the Hair Stylist, Inc. monopoly.

In general, an industry characterized by monopoly will *sell less* output *at higher prices* than would a perfectly competitive industry. From the private perspective of the ongoing monopoly firm and its stockholders, the benefits of monopoly are measured in terms of the economic profits that are possible when competition is reduced or eliminated. From a broader social perspective, however, these private benefits must be weighed against the costs borne by consumers in the forms of higher prices and reduced availability of desired products. Employees, suppliers, and others also suffer from the reduced levels of production associated with a monopoly market structure.

Nevertheless, it is important to recognize that monopoly is not always as socially harmful as indicated in the previous example. In the case of Cray Research, for example, the genius of Semore Cray and a handful of research associates created a dynamic early monopoly in supercomputers. The tremendous stockholder value created through their efforts, including millions of dollars in personal wealth for Cray and his associates, can only be viewed as a partial index of their contribution to society in general. In instances such as these, the economic profits of monopoly can be viewed as the just rewards flowing from the truly important contributions of unique firms and individuals.

## Long-Run Equilibrium under Monopoly

In the long run, a monopoly firm will continue to operate only if its price at least equals its long-run average cost. Because all costs are variable in the long run, the firm will not operate unless all costs are covered. No firm, monopolistic or competitive, will operate in the long run if it continues to suffer losses.

As was shown earlier, purely competitive firms must, in the long run, operate at the minimum point on the *LRAC* curve. This condition does not hold under monopoly. For example, consider again Figure 11.9 and assume that the *ATC* curve represents the long-run average cost curve for the firm. Here the firm will produce Q units of output at an average cost of C per unit, somewhat above the minimum point on the *ATC* curve. This firm is called a **natural monopoly,** since the market-clearing price, where $P = MC$, occurs at a point at which *long-run* average costs are still declining. In other words, market demand is insufficient to justify full utilization of even one minimum efficient scale plant. A single firm can produce the total market supply at a lower total cost than could any number of smaller firms, and competition would naturally reduce the number of competitors until only a single supplier remains. Electric

**natural monopoly**

An industry in which the market-clearing price occurs at a point at which the monopolist's long-run average costs are still declining.

## 11.3  **Managerial Application**

Investing in "Near" Monopolies

True monopoly, especially unregulated monopoly, is exceedingly rare in the U.S. economy. As a result, investment professionals have tended to focus their efforts on the next best thing: dominant companies that control 75 percent or more of their markets and seem to have permanent advantages over smaller, less well-financed rivals, and enjoy high profit margins.

Newspaper companies are an interesting example. Once a newspaper is written, the marginal cost of production is very low (only paper and ink costs), and the average cost per newspaper tends to fall continuously as the number of papers printed increases. Economies of scale typically result in local newspaper monopolies for markets with populations below 500,000 and in many larger markets, as well. Only a local

paper can offer detailed print coverage of local news, weather, and sports, and it can be the single attractive outlet for print advertising by local firms and individuals. This unique position gives local monopoly newspapers an advantage that they exploit very effectively. When a local newspaper monopoly exists, newspaper advertising tends to be very expensive when measured in terms of cost per exposure, and it is exceedingly profitable for the newspaper. For example, following the demise of *The Washington Star*, profits skyrocketed at its only competitor in the Washington, D.C., market, *The Washington Post*. Both Lee Enterprises and Gannet have profitably exploited monopolies in a variety of local newspaper markets by acquiring a large number of independent local newspapers, modernizing production

*continued*

See: Subrata N. Chakravarty and Carolyn Torcellini, "Citizen Kane Meets Adam Smith," *Forbes*, February 20, 1989, 82–85.

and gas utilities are classic examples of natural monopoly, since any duplication in production and distribution facilities would be expected to increase costs for consumers.

### Regulation of Monopoly

**underproduction**

A situation that occurs when a monopolist curtails production to a level at which marginal cost is less than price.

Natural monopolies present something of a dilemma. On the one hand, economic efficiency could be enhanced by restricting the number of producing firms to one; on the other hand, monopolies have an incentive to underproduce and can earn economic profits. **Underproduction** results when the firm curtails production to a level at which the value of the resources needed to produce an additional unit of output, as mea-

**Managerial Application** *continued*

methods, and raising prices while cutting costs. Not only are both Lee Enterprises and Gannet highly profitable, but they also have been stellar performers in terms of the total rate of return to stockholders during the 1970s and 1980s.

It is important to recognize, however, that the monopoly advantage of local newspapers is quite limited in scope. When it comes to national news, sports, the arts, or business, widely circulated national newspapers such as *The New York Times, The Wall Street Journal,* and *USA Today* enjoy a commanding relative advantage over local newspapers. Only by specializing in local news and advertising have local newspapers come to enjoy significant above-normal returns.

Radio and television are other examples of media industries that enjoy opportunities for significant above-normal returns. Restrictive government licensing gives individual stations the exclusive right to broadcast first-run network programs. Thus, hit shows can create substantial monopoly profits for the local affiliates of major networks. However, unlike local newspapers,

local radio and television monopolies are susceptible to changing licensing requirements by regulatory agencies. In addition, local television monopolies can be eroded over time by competition from cable television and other types of pay TV.

In considering the development of a monopoly investment strategy, it is not only important to recognize the risk of a future loss in monopoly power; one must also remember that the advantages of established monopoly are often already reflected in stock prices. When the market price of common stock accurately reflects the discounted net present value of future cash flows, the high returns on investment resulting from monopoly power will be reflected in high market-price/book value and price/earnings ratios. Even though early investors in growing or unrecognized monopoly power can benefit handsomely, investors in recognized monopolies earn only risk-adjusted normal rates of return on their investments. Therefore, a successful monopoly investment strategy requires discovering new, unexploited, or growing monopolies.

sured by the marginal cost of production, is less than the social benefit derived from the additional unit, as measured by price. Here social benefit is measured by the price someone is willing to pay for an additional unit of production. Under monopoly, marginal cost is clearly less than price at the firm's profit-maximizing output level. Although the resulting economic profits serve the useful function of providing incentives and helping allocate resources, it is difficult to justify above-normal profits that are the result of market power rather than exceptional performance.

How can we escape from the dilemma posed by the twin facts that monopoly can be efficient but that it can also lead to economic profits and underproduction? The answer sometimes lies in permitting monopolies to exist but regulating their prices and output quantities. The important topic of public regulation of natural monopolies is discussed in detail in Chapter 14. In other instances, market forces often emerge that effectively limit the profit potential of monopoly.

# COUNTERVAILING POWER: THE MONOPOLY/MONOPSONY CONFRONTATION

Unregulated monopoly sellers facing perfectly competitive market demand will typically limit production and offer their products to consumers at high prices. The private and social costs of this behavior are often measured by above-normal profits, inefficient production methods, and lagging rates of innovation. How is this inefficiency reduced, if not eliminated, in those instances in which direct public regulation of prices and output is not imposed? Sometimes the answer lies in the development of countervailing forces within markets.

**countervailing power**
Buyer market power that offsets seller market power, and vice versa.

**Countervailing power** is an economic influence that creates a closer balance between previously unequal sellers and buyers. The classic example is a single employer in a small town that might take advantage of the local labor force by offering less-than-competitive wages. As the single employer, the company has a monopsony in the local labor market. The workers might decide to band together and form a union, a monopoly seller in the local labor market, to offset the monopsony power of the employer.

To illustrate this classic confrontation, consider Figure 11.10, which shows the demand and supply relation in a local labor market. The downward-sloping demand for labor is simply the marginal revenue product of labor curve as discussed in Chapter 7. Remember that the marginal revenue product of labor ($MRP_L$) is simply the marginal amount of net revenue generated through employment of an additional unit of labor ($\Delta TR/\Delta L$) and is the product of the marginal product of labor ($MP_L$) and the marginal revenue of output ($MR_Q$). Thus, $MRP_L = \Delta TR/\Delta L = MP_L \times MR_Q$. $MRP_L$ tends to fall as employment expands because of the labor factor's diminishing returns. An upward-sloping supply curve reflects the fact that higher wages are typically necessary to expand the amount of labor offered. Perfectly competitive demand and supply conditions create an exact balance between demand and supply, and the competitive equilibrium wage (or price of labor), $W_C$, and employment level, $E_C$, will be observed.

A monopsony employer facing a perfectly competitive supply of labor would seek to set its marginal cost of labor, $MC_L$, equal to the marginal benefit it would derive from employment. Since the employer's marginal benefit is measured in terms of the marginal revenue product of labor, the unchecked monopsonist would set $MC_L = MRP_L$. Notice that the $MC_L$ curve exceeds the labor supply curve at each point, based on the assump-

■ Figure 11.10
## Monopoly Union and Monopsony Employer Confrontation in the Labor Market

In a perfectly competitive labor market, the equilibrium wage is at $W_C$. A monopoly union facing competitive labor demand will seek a higher wage of $W_U$. A monopsony employer facing a competitive labor supply will offer a lower wage of $W_M$.

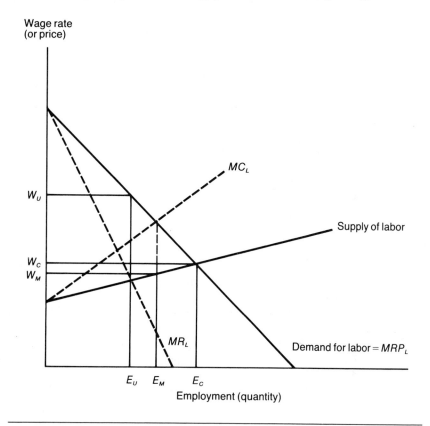

tion that wages must be increased for all workers in order to hire additional employees. (This is analogous to cutting prices for all customers in order to expand sales, causing the *MR* curve to lie below the demand curve.) Since workers need be paid only the wage rate indicated along the labor supply curve for a given level of employment, the monopsonist employer would offer employees a wage of $W_M$ and offer less than a competitive level of employment opportunities, $E_M$.

In contrast, an unchecked union, or monopoly seller of labor, could command a wage of $W_U$ if demand for labor were competitive. This solution is found by setting the marginal revenue of labor ($MR_L$) equal to the labor supply curve (marginal cost of labor to the union). However, like any monopoly seller, the union can obtain higher wages (prices)

## 11.4 **Managerial Application**

The Labor Battle in Professional Sports

Traditionally, when one thought of the classic labor confrontation between a monopoly seller of labor and a monopsony buyer of labor, the image of a labor union fighting company management in a rural one-mill town came to mind. Today, that image has been supplanted by the labor confrontation between unions and management in professional sports.

The only employer of baseball players in the United States is Major League Baseball. This association of 26 major league franchises and their owners operates in much the same way as does a large corporation with 26 different regional offices. Even though individual clubs compete with one another on the playing field, their financial competition is much different than that between true competitors. In a competitive market, the gain of one competitor comes at the expense of others. In baseball, the success of one franchise brings increased pros-

perity for all. Through revenue sharing, all clubs prospered when Hank Aaron chased and broke Babe Ruth's lifetime home-run mark, as well as when Pete Rose chased and broke Ty Cobb's lifetime record for hits. Conversely, ineptitude and poor gate sales at one franchise weaken the profit picture for everyone. Tight pennant races make for prosperity. Blowouts result in lost profits.

All baseball players are covered by a single basic labor contract negotiated through collective bargaining between the Major League Players Association (the sole union representative of the baseball players) and the owners. Thus, the player's association is a monopoly seller of baseball player talent, and the owners are a monopsony employer. During recent years, economic power in this labor market has clearly shifted from the owners toward the players. A key element of this shift has been the advent of free agency. Any baseball player with six years of major

*continued*

See: Gordon Forbes, "How NFL Players Compare to Those in Other Leagues," *USA Today*, September 28, 1987, 11C.

only by restricting employment opportunities (output) for union members. Thus, the union will be able to offer its members only the less-than-competitive employment opportunities, $E_U$, if it attempts to maximize labor income.

What is likely to occur in the case of monopoly union/monopsony employer confrontation? Typically, labor negotiation produces a compromise wage/employment outcome. Notice that this compromise has the beneficial effect of moving the labor market through countervailing

**Managerial Application** *continued*

league service is eligible to become a free agent and sign with any team, with only modest compensation in the form of draft choices due to the player's former club. While not eligible for free agency, any player with three to six years' service is eligible for impartial salary arbitration. Since free agency was developed, baseball players' salaries have exploded.

By the late 1980s, the average salary in baseball had risen to over $450,000 per year, not including substantial pensions and other fringe benefits. For example, a player with ten years' experience is eligible at 62 years of age for a maximum pension of $90,000 per year. The fact that the owners have been able to pay such salaries, and the fact that the value of baseball franchises has continued to grow rapidly, suggests that current wages are no greater than the economic worth or marginal revenue product of the players' services.

Interestingly, in professional football, where free agency is almost nonexistent, average salaries are less than $250,000 per year. Whereas all contracts are guaranteed for each player on a major league baseball roster opening day, fewer than 100 of the 1,600 professional football players have guaranteed contracts. The maximum pension at age 62 for a football player with ten years' experience is in the neighborhood of $30,000 per year, and the minimum salary for rookies is $50,000 versus $62,500 for baseball. These differences can be explained, in part, by the fact that the number of players on a team is greater for football than for baseball. On the other hand, baseball teams subsidize expensive minor league systems and don't often enjoy the level of revenues generated by successful football franchises. Thus, although marginal-revenue-product differences probably account for a major part of the differentials, at least some of the salary differences between professional players in baseball and football undoubtedly reflect the fact that the National Football League owners enjoy a relatively greater degree of monopsony power.

Similarly, relative salaries for players in the National Basketball Association and the National Hockey League reflect, in part, the balance of labor market power between monopsony owners and monopoly players' associations. In all instances, the upper bound on player salaries is the marginal revenue product generated by the player's services. The balance of power between the owners and the players will continue to determine how this revenue pie is sliced.

power away from the inefficient unchecked monopoly or monopsony solutions toward a more efficient labor market equilibrium. However, only in the unlikely event of perfectly matched monopoly/monopsony protagonists will the perfectly competitive outcome occur. Depending on the relative power of the union and the employer, either an above-market or below-market wage outcome will typically result, and employment opportunities will be somewhat below those under competitive conditions. Nevertheless, the countervailing power of a monopoly/monopsony confrontation can have the beneficial effect of improving economic efficiency from that experienced under unchecked monopoly or monopsony.

# MARKET STRUCTURE AND COMPETITIVE STRATEGY

Identifying the market structure and profit potential of any given industry can be difficult. In actual business practice, markets typically do not fall neatly within the definition of perfect competition or monopoly. Instead, market structures usually embody elements of each of these models of economic behavior. As suggested earlier, product characteristics, the local or regional limits of the market, the time necessary for reactions by established or new competitors, the pace of innovation, unanticipated changes in government regulation and tax policy, and a host of additional considerations all play important roles in defining the method and scope of competition. Among other factors, it is always helpful to consider the number of competitors, degree of product differentiation, level of information available in the marketplace, and conditions of entry when attempting to define market structure.

Table 11.2 summarizes the major characteristics typical of perfectly competitive and monopoly market structures. To develop an effective competitive strategy, it is necessary to assess the degree to which the characteristics of an individual market more or less embody elements of each. As one would expect, the probability of successful entry is greater in perfectly competitive industries. On the other hand, although entry into monopoly markets is more difficult, these markets hold the potential for substantial economic profits in the long run. The decision to enter a given industry requires careful balancing of expected costs and benefits. The search for above-normal profits is only likely to succeed when the firm can create a distinctive and valuable characteristic in the goods and services it provides.

In equilibrium, a perfectly competitive market generally offers the potential for only a normal rate of return on investment. If many equally capable competitors offer identical products, vigorous price competition tends to eliminate above-normal profits. The only exception to this rule is that superior cost efficiency can sometimes lead to superior profits, even in perfectly competitive markets. For example, a grain producer located along a river or on exceptionally fertile soil would enjoy lower-than-average irrigation and fertilizer costs, and higher profits could result. However, potential buyers would have to pay a price premium for such productive land, and subsequent investors would earn only a normal rate of return on their investment.

## Market Niche

The purchase of a business that involves a recognized monopoly is not likely to lead to above-normal rates of return. However, offering new and unique products or services can create monopoly profits, which may be

■ Table 11.2

## Summary of Perfect Competition and Monopoly (Monopsony) Market-Structure Characteristics

|  | Perfect Competition | Monopoly (Monopsony) |
|---|---|---|
| *Number of actual or potential competitors* | Many small buyers and sellers | A single seller (buyer) of a valued product |
| *Product differentiation* | None—each buyer and seller deals in an identical product | Very high—no close substitutes available |
| *Information* | Complete and free information on price and product quality | Highly restricted access to price and product-quality information |
| *Conditions of entry and exit* | Complete freedom of entry and exit | Very high barriers caused by economies of scale (natural monopoly), patents, copyrights, government franchises, or other factors |
| *Profit potential* | Normal profit in long run; economic profits (losses) in short run only | Potential for economic profits in both short and long run |
| *Examples* | Some agricultural markets (grain); commodity, stock, and bond markets; some nonspecialized input markets (unskilled labor) | Monopoly (sellers): Local telephone service (basic hook-up); municipal bus companies; gas, water, and electric utilities. Monopsony (buyers): state and local governments (roads), U.S. government (defense electronics) |

**market niche**

A specialized market segment.

protected by patents, copyrights, or other means. In many instances, these above-normal profits reflect the successful exploitation of a market niche. A **market niche** is a segment of a market that can be successfully exploited through the special capabilities of a given firm or individual. To be durable, the above-normal profits derived from a niche in the market for goods and services must not be vulnerable to imitation by competitors.

Any use of market structure as a guide to competitive strategy must address the considerable challenge posed by measurement problems encountered in defining both the magnitude and origin of above-normal rates of return. Accounting profit data derived from a historic perspective give much useful information for operating decisions and tax purposes. However, these data sometimes measure economic profits only imperfectly. For example, advertising and research and development expenditures are expensed for both reporting and tax purposes, despite the fact that each can give rise to long-term economic benefits. An "expense as incurred" treatment of advertising and research and development can lead to errors in profit measurement. Similarly, imperfections in accrual accounting methods can lead to imperfectly matched revenues and costs and, therefore, to some profit misstatement over time.

In addition to these and other obvious limitations of accounting data, business practices are often expressly intended to limit the loss of valuable trade secrets. Combined with the informational limitations of publicly available data on profitability, business practices create an information barrier that makes defining the costs and benefits of monopoly difficult for both private and public decision makers.

# SUMMARY

A *market* for goods and services consists of all firms and individuals that are willing and able to buy or sell a particular product. This includes those actively engaged in the market as well as potential entrants. A *potential entrant* is any firm or individual both willing and able to buy or sell in a market if given an economic motive for doing so. Like current participants, potential entrants often have an important influence on the vigor of competition in the marketplace.

Demand and supply relations interact to determine the market structures observed in various industries. If average cost curves quickly bottom out or begin to rise at an output level that is small in relation to overall market demand, the average cost curve for a representative firm and for the industry as a whole will have an L-shape or a U-shape, and a large number of viable competitors will typically be present. In many instances, a large number of buyers and sellers in a given market reflects homogeneous product offerings, abundant free information available in the marketplace, and complete freedom of entry and exit. The output of each individual firm is so small in relation to the overall industry that changes in the level of a firm's output have no effect on market prices. Individual firms regard market prices as a given and are sometimes called *price takers*. Such a market structure is perfectly competitive, because vigorous competition allows firms the opportunity to earn only a normal rate of return in the long run. *Perfect competition* gives rise to both efficient production of desired goods and services and equitable market prices that fairly reflect suppliers' and purchasers' value.

At the opposite end of the market-structure spectrum is *monopoly*, under which a single seller markets a valuable product. The product offered is highly differentiated, without any close substitutes. Monopoly arises in some markets with highly restricted access to information and insurmountable *barriers to entry or exit*. Barriers to entry make new entry difficult in a given industry. Barriers to exit impede the redeployment of assets from one industry or line of business to another. Both increase the cost and risk of doing business.

In monopoly, the firm *is* the industry. As such, a monopoly can simultaneously set industry prices and output so as to maximize profits. This gives rise to the potential for economic profits in the long run for both efficient and inefficient monopolists. In industries in which average costs fall continuously as firm output expands, competition will drive out individual competitors and monopoly will naturally tend to result—hence the term *natural monopoly*. The sources of monopoly are varied. When monopoly is achieved through anticompetitive behavior, it is often deemed antisocial and the worthy target of public tax and regulatory policy. In other instances, monopoly is created through the productive or innovative effort of uniquely talented individuals, and the economic profits that result are sometimes viewed as justified.

The abuse of unchecked monopoly is sometimes limited through market forces. In certain industries, buyer power sometimes offsets or balances monopoly power. *Monopsony* is a market characterized by a single buyer, and it is often an effective tool for limiting monopoly prices and profits. In such instances, monopoly/monopsony confrontation leads to an offsetting balance of *countervailing power*.

## Questions

11.1  What are the primary elements of market structure?

11.2  Describe the perfectly competitive market structure, and provide some examples.

11.3  Describe the monopoly market structure, and provide some examples.

11.4  How are barriers to entry and exit similar? How are they different?

11.5  Why is the firm demand curve horizontal in perfectly competitive markets? Does this mean that the perfectly competitive industry demand curve is also horizontal?

11.6  Why are the perfectly competitive firm and the perfectly competitive industry supply curves upward sloping?

11.7  From a social standpoint, what is the problem with monopoly?

11.8  Why are both industry and firm demand curves downward sloping in a monopoly market structure?

11.9  Give an example of monopoly in the labor market. Discuss such a monopoly's effect on wage rates and on inflation.

11.10 Describe the economic effects of countervailing power, and cite some examples of markets in which countervailing power is observed.

## Problems

11.1  Indicate whether each of the following statements is *true* or *false* and why.

A. In long-run equilibrium, every firm in a perfectly competitive industry earns zero profit. Thus, if price falls, none of these firms will be able to survive.

B. Pure competition exists in a market when all firms are price takers as opposed to price makers.

C. A natural monopoly results when the profit-maximizing output level occurs at a point where long-run average costs are declining.

D.  Downward-sloping industry demand curves characterize both perfectly competitive and monopoly markets.

E.  A decrease in the price elasticity of demand would follow an increase in monopoly power.

11.2  The City of Columbus, Ohio, is considering two proposals to privatize municipal garbage collection. First, a leading waste-disposal firm has offered to purchase the city's plant and equipment at an attractive price in return for an exclusive franchise on residential service. A second proposal would allow several individual workers and small companies to enter the business without any exclusive franchise agreement or competitive restrictions. Under this plan, individual companies would bid for the right to provide service in a given residential area. The city would then allocate business to the lowest bidder.

The city has conducted a survey of Columbus residents to estimate the amount that they would be willing to pay for various frequencies of service. The city has also estimated the total cost of service per resident. Service costs are expected to be the same whether or not an exclusive franchise is granted.

A.  Complete the following table.

| Trash Pickups per Month | Price per Pickup | Total Revenue | Marginal Revenue | Total Cost | Marginal Cost |
|---|---|---|---|---|---|
| 0 | $5.00 | | | $ 0.00 | |
| 1 | 4.80 | | | 3.75 | |
| 2 | 4.60 | | | 7.45 | |
| 3 | 4.40 | | | 11.10 | |
| 4 | 4.20 | | | 14.70 | |
| 5 | 4.00 | | | 18.00 | |
| 6 | 3.80 | | | 20.90 | |
| 7 | 3.60 | | | 23.80 | |
| 8 | 3.40 | | | 27.20 | |
| 9 | 3.20 | | | 30.60 | |
| 10 | 3.00 | | | 35.00 | |

B.  Determine price and the level of service if competitive bidding results in a perfectly competitive price/output combination.

C.  Determine price and the level of service if the city grants a monopoly franchise.

11.3  Mankato Paper, Inc., produces uncoated paper used in a wide variety of industrial applications. Newsprint, a major product, is sold in a perfectly competitive market. The following relation exists between the firm's newsprint output and total production costs:

| Total Output (tons) | Total Cost Per Ton |
|---|---|
| 0 | $ 25 |
| 1 | 75 |
| 2 | 135 |
| 3 | 205 |
| 4 | 285 |
| 5 | 375 |
| 6 | 475 |
| 7 | 600 |

A. Construct a table showing Mankato's marginal cost of newsprint production.

B. What is the minimum price necessary for Mankato to supply one ton of newsprint?

C. How much newsprint would Mankato supply at industry prices of $75 and $100 per ton?

11.4 Demand and supply conditions in the perfectly competitive market for unskilled labor are as follows:

$$Q_D = 120 - 20P, \quad \text{(Demand)}$$

$$Q_S = 10P, \quad \text{(Supply)}$$

where $Q$ is millions of hours of unskilled labor, and $P$ is the wage rate per hour.

A. Graph the industry demand and supply curves.

B. Determine the industry equilibrium price/output combination both graphically and algebraically.

C. Calculate the level of excess supply (unemployment) if the minimum wage is set at $4.50 per hour.

11.5 Farm Fresh, Inc., supplies sweet peas to canners located throughout the Mississippi River Valley. Like some grain and commodity markets, the market for sweet peas is perfectly competitive. The company's total cost per ton for processing sweet peas is given by the relation:

$$TC = \$250,000 + \$200Q + \$0.02Q^2.$$

A. Calculate the industry price necessary for the firm to supply 5,000, 10,000, and 15,000 tons of sweet peas.

B. Calculate the quantity supplied by Farm Fresh at industry prices of $200, $500, and $1,000 per ton.

11.6 New England Textiles, Inc., is a medium-sized manufacturer of blue-denim, the market for which is perfectly competitive. Its total cost function is described by the relation:

$$TC = \$25,000 + \$1Q + \$0.000008Q^2,$$

where $Q$ is square yards of blue denim produced per month.

    A. Derive the firm's supply curve, expressing quantity as a function of price.

    B. Derive the industry's supply curve if New England Textiles is one of 500 competitors.

    C. Calculate industry supply per month at a market price of $2 per square yard.

11.7 Tsuruoka, Ltd., supplies standard 256K-RAM chips to the U.S. computer and electronics industry. Like the output of its competitors, Tsuruoka's chips must meet strict size, shape, and speed specifications. As a result, the chip-supply industry can be regarded as perfectly competitive. The total cost function for Tsuruoka is:

$$TC = \$100{,}000 + \$2Q + \$0.00001Q^2,$$

where $Q$ is the number of chips produced.

    A. Calculate Tsuruoka's optimal output and profits if chip prices are stable at $3 each.

    B. Calculate Tsuruoka's optimal output and profits if chip prices rise to $6 each.

    C. If Tsuruoka is typical of firms in the industry, calculate the firm's equilibrium output, price, and profit levels.

11.8 Big Apple Music, Inc., enjoys an exclusive copyright on music written and produced by the Fab Four, a legendary British rock group. Total revenue for the group's records is given by the relation:

$$TR = \$15Q - \$0.000005Q^2.$$

Marginal costs for production and distribution are stable at $5 per unit. All other costs have been fully amortized.

    A. As a monopoly, calculate Big Apple's output, price, and profits at the profit-maximizing activity level.

    B. What record price and profit levels would prevail following expiration of copyright protection based on the assumption that perfectly competitive pricing would result?

11.9 During recent years, the Big Blue Computer Company has enjoyed substantial economic profits derived from patents covering a wide range of inventions and innovations in the personal computer field. A recent introduction, the SP/2, has proved to be especially profitable. Market demand for the SP/2 is given by the relation:

$$P = \$5{,}500 - \$0.005Q.$$

Fixed costs are nil, because research and development expenses have been fully amortized during previous periods. Average variable costs are constant at $4,500 per unit.

    A. Calculate the profit-maximizing price/output combination and economic profits if Big Blue enjoys an effective monopoly on the SP/2 because of its patent protection.

      B. Calculate the price/output combination and total economic profits that would result if competitors offer clones that make the SP/2 market perfectly competitive.

11.10 Safeguard Corporation offers a unique service; the company notifies credit card issuers after being informed that a subscriber's credit card has been lost or stolen. The Safeguard service is sold to card issuers on a one-year subscription basis. Demand and total cost relations for the service are:

$$P = \$5 - \$0.00001Q,$$

$$TC = \$50,000 + \$0.5Q + \$0.000005Q^2,$$

where $P$ is price, $Q$ is output measured in terms of the number of subscriptions in force, and $TC$ is total cost, including a risk-adjusted normal rate of return on investment.

      A. If Safeguard has a monopoly in this market, calculate the profit-maximizing price/output combination and optimal total profit.

      B. Calculate Safeguard's optimal price, output, and profits if credit card issuers effectively exert monopsony power and force a perfectly competitive equilibrium in this market.

## Selected References

Baskin, Jonathan. "Corporate Liquidity in Games of Monopoly Power." *Review of Economics and Statistics* 69 (May 1987): 312–319

Betancourt, Roger R., and John H. Y. Edwards. "Economies of Scale and the Load Factor in Electricity Generation." *Review of Economics and Statistics* 69 (August 1987): 551–556.

Clarke, Richard N. "SICs as Delineators of Economic Markets." *Journal of Business* 62 (January 1989): 17–31.

Connolly, Robert A., and Steven Schwartz. "The Intertemporal Behavior of Economic Profits." *International Journal of Industrial Organization* 3 (December 1985): 379–400.

Connolly, Robert A., Barry T. Hirsch, and Mark Hirschey. "Union Rent-Seeking, Intangible Capital and Market Value of the Firm." *Review of Economics and Statistics* 68 (November 1986): 567–577.

Cowley, Peter R. "Business Margins and Buyer/Seller Power." *Review of Economics and Statistics* 68 (May 1986): 333–337.

Domowitz, Ian, R. Glen Hubbard, and Bruce Peterson. "Market Structure and Cyclical Fluctuations in U.S. Manufacturing." *Review of Economics and Statistics* 70 (February 1988): 55–67.

Garrod, P. V., and W. Miklius. "Captive Shippers and the Success of Railroads in Capturing Monopoly Rent." *Journal of Law and Economics* 30 (October 1987): 423–442.

Harrison, Glenn W., Thomas F. Rutherford, and Ian Wooton. "The Economic Impact of the European Economic Community." *American Economic Review* 79 (May 1989): 288–294.

Karakaya, Fahri, and Michael J. Stahl. "Barriers to Entry and Market Entry Decisions in Consumer and Industrial Goods Markets." *Journal of Marketing* 53 (April 1989): 80–91.

Kessides, Ioannis N. "Advertising, Sunk Costs, and Barriers to Entry." *Review of Economics and Statistics* 68 (February 1986): 84–95.

Lapan, Harvey E., and Todd Sandler. "To Bargain or Not to Bargain: That Is the Question." *American Economic Review* 78 (May 1988): 16–21.

Martin, Stephen, "Market Power or Efficiency?," *Review of Economics and Statistics* 70 (May 1988): 331–335.

Newmark, Craig M. "Administrative Control, Buyer Concentration, and Price-Cost Margins." *Review of Economics and Statistics* 71 (February 1989): 74–79.

Shapiro, Benson P., and Thomas V. Bonoma. "How to Segment Industrial Markets." *Harvard Business Review* 62 (May–June 1984): 104–110.

Shepherd, William G. "Contestability vs. Competition." *American Economic Review* 74 (September 1984): 572–587.

Sing, Merrile. "Are Combination Gas and Electric Utilities Multiproduct Natural Monopolies?" *Review of Economics and Statistics* 69 (August 1987): 392–398.

Slade, Margaret E. "Static Profitability as a Measure of Deviations from the Competitive Norm." *Managerial and Decision Economics* 7 (June 1986): 113–118.

Thaler, Richard H. "Anomalies: The Ultimatum Game." *Journal of Economic Perspectives* 2 (Fall 1988): 195–206.

Vishwanath, Tara. "Parallel Search and Information Gathering." *American Economic Review* 78 (May 1988): 110–116.

# Market Structure, Part II: Monopolistic Competition and Oligopoly

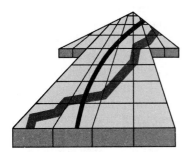

**M**onopolistic competition and oligopoly describe the market-structure environment for many firms. Both market structures embody elements of perfect competition and of monopoly. In an environment of monopolistic competition, a firm may introduce a valuable new product or process innovation that gives rise to substantial economic profits or above-normal rates of return in the short run. In the long run, entry and imitation by rivals erodes the market share of monopolistically competitive firms, and profits eventually diminish to normal levels. However, in contrast to perfectly competitive markets, the unique product characteristics of individual firms remain valued by consumers. Given the lack of perfect substitutes, monopolistically competitive firms exercise some discretion in setting prices—they are not price takers.

Oligopoly models describe markets with competition among a few firms. A handful of competitors sheltered by significant barriers to entry often have the potential for economic profits, even in the long run. With few competitors, economic incentives often exist for firms to devise illegal agreements to limit competition, fix prices, or otherwise divide markets. In fact, the history of antitrust in the United States provides numerous examples of "competitors" who illegally entered into such agreements. On the other hand, there are also some examples of markets in which vigorous competition among a small number of firms generates obvious long-term benefit to consumers. Moreover, the market discipline provided by a competitive fringe of smaller firms is sometimes sufficient to limit the potential abuse of a few large competitors.

Given the prevalence of monopolistically competitive and oligopolistic market structures, understanding their characteristics is important for analyzing how firms actually adapt to the broad range of competitive pressures faced in many industries.

# THE CONTRAST BETWEEN MONOPOLISTIC COMPETITION AND OLIGOPOLY

The major characteristics of the monopolistic competition and oligopoly market models are given here and elaborated on in the rest of the chapter.

**monopolistic competition**

A market structure characterized by a large number of sellers of differentiated products.

**Monopolistic competition** is quite similar to perfect competition in its vigorous price competition among a large number of firms and individuals. The major difference between these two models is that in monopolistic competition consumers perceive important differences between the products offered by individual firms. This gives firms at least some discretion in setting prices. However, the presence of many close substitutes limits the price-setting ability of individual firms and drives profits down to normal rates of return in the long run. As in the case of perfect competition, above-normal profits are only possible in the short-run, before rivals can take effective counter measures.

**oligopoly**

A market structure characterized by few sellers in which price/output decisions are interdependent.

Under **oligopoly,** only a few large rivals are responsible for the bulk of industry output, if not all of it. As in the case of monopoly, high to very high barriers to entry are typical. Under oligopoly, the price/output decisions of firms are interrelated in the sense that direct reactions from leading rivals can be expected. As a result, decisions of individual firms are based in part on the likely responses of competitors. This "competition among the few" involves a wide variety of price and nonprice methods of rivalry, as determined by the institutional characteristics of a particular market. Even though limited numbers of competitors give rise to a potential for economic profits, above-normal rates of return are far from guaranteed. Competition among the few can sometimes be vigorous.

# MONOPOLISTIC COMPETITION

Pure competition and pure monopoly rarely exist in actual markets. Most firms are subject to some competition, though perhaps not as vigorous as would exist under pure competition. Even though most firms compete with a large number of other firms producing highly substitutable products, many still have some control over the price of their product. They cannot sell all that they want at a fixed price, nor would they lose all their sales if they raised prices slightly. In other words, most firms face downward-sloping demand curves, signifying less-than-perfect competition.

The theory of monopolistic competition more realistically explains the actual market structure encountered by many firms. The theory retains two assumptions of a purely competitive market structure. First, each firm makes its decisions independently. That is, a price change by any one firm does not cause other firms to change their prices. (If reactions occur, then the market structure is called oligopoly, which is examined in the next section of this chapter.) Second, a large number of firms in the industry all produce the same basic product. The assumption of *completely* homogeneous products is removed, however, so each firm is assumed to be able to differentiate its product, at least to some degree, from those of rival firms.

The assumption of no direct reactions by competitors should not be misconstrued as implying independence among firms in a monopolistically competitive market. Independence is assumed in decision making, just as in a perfectly competitive market. However, each firm's demand function in such an industry is significantly affected by the existence of numerous firms producing goods that consumers view as reasonably close substitutes and the fact that many demand and cost factors have a simultaneous effect on all firms, leading frequently to similar price movements by them. This latter phenomenon causes each firm's demand to be more price inelastic than would be the case under total interfirm independence.

Product differentiation takes many forms. A tube of Crest toothpaste at a nearby drugstore is different from an identical tube available at a distant store. Since consumers evaluate products on the basis of their ability to satisfy the specific wants they have, as well as *when* and *where* they have them, products involve not only quantity, quality, and price characteristics but time and place attributes as well. Quality differentials, packaging, credit terms, or superior maintenance service, such as IBM is reputed to supply, can differentiate products, as can advertising that leads to brand-name identification. The important factor in all of these forms of product differentiation is that some consumers prefer the product of one seller to those of others.

The effect of product differentiation is to remove the perfect elasticity of the firm's demand curve. Unlike a price taker facing a horizontal demand curve, the firm determines its optimal price/output combination. The degree of price flexibility depends on the strength of a firm's product differentiation. Strong differentiation results in greater consumer loyalty and hence in more control over price. Alternatively stated, the more differentiated a firm's product, the lower the substitutability of other products for it. This is illustrated in Figure 12.1, which shows the demand curves of Firms *A* and *B*. Consumers view Firm *A*'s product as being only slightly differentiated from the bulk of the industry's output, and because many other brands are suitable replacements for its own output, Firm *A* is close to being a price taker. Firm *B*, on the other hand, has more successfully differentiated its product, and consumers are

■ Figure 12.1

## Relation between Product Differentiation and Elasticity of Demand

Firm B's steeper demand curve relative to Firm A's reflects stronger product differentiation and hence less sensitivity to price changes.

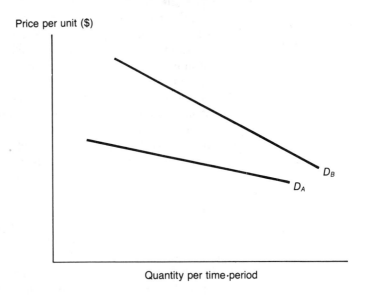

therefore less willing to substitute for B's output. Accordingly, B's demand is not so sensitive to changes in price.

## Price/Output Decisions Under Monopolistic Competition

As its name suggests, monopolistic competition embodies elements of both monopoly and perfect competition. The monopoly aspect of monopolistic competition is observed in the short run. Consider Figure 12.2. With the demand curve, $D_1$, and its related marginal revenue curve, $MR_1$, the optimum output, $Q_1$, is found at the point where $MR_1 = MC$. Short-run monopoly profits equal to the area $P_1LMATC_1$ are earned. These profits may be the result of the introduction of a patented invention, an unpatented but valuable innovation, or other factors such as an unexpected rise in demand.

With time, however, these short-run monopoly profits attract competition, and other firms enter the industry. Therefore, the competitive aspect of monopolistic competition is seen in the long run. As more firms enter and offer close (but imperfect) substitutes, the market share of the initial firm diminishes. This means that firm demand and marginal revenue curves will shift to the left, as for example, to $D_2$ and $MR_2$ in Figure 12.2. The firm's optimal output (the point where $MR_2 = MC$) shifts to

■ Figure 12.2
## Price/Output Combinations under
## Monopolistic Competition

Long-run equilibrium under monopolistic competition occurs when $MR = MC$ and $P = AC$. This typically occurs between $P_2Q_2$ (the high-price/low-output equilibrium) and $P_3Q_3$ (the low-price/high-output equilibrium).

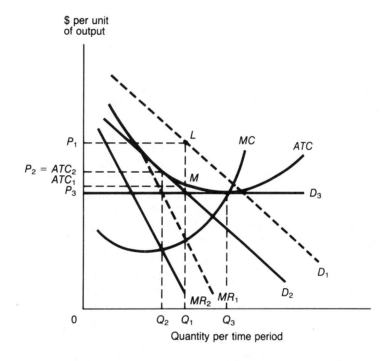

$Q_2$, and since price, $P_2$, equals $ATC_2$, economic profits are zero.[1] This price/output combination reflects the situation in which competitor entry reduces the initial firm's market share but a high degree of product differentiation remains. If new entrants offered perfect (rather than close) substitutes, firm demand in the long run would become more nearly horizontal, and the perfectly competitive equilibrium, $D_3$ with $P_3$ and $Q_3$, would be approached. In most instances, competitor entry reduces but does not eliminate product differentiation, and an intermediate price/output solution, one between $P_2Q_2$ and $P_3Q_3$, is often achieved in the long run. Such outcomes describe monopolistically competitive markets. Indeed, it is the retention of at least some degree of product differentiation that distinguishes the monopolistically competitive equilibrium from that achieved in perfectly competitive markets.

[1]Recall that the term *cost* includes a normal profit sufficient to compensate the owners of the firm for their capital investment.

## 12.1  **Managerial Application**

The Swedish Are Coming!

"Welcome to Ikea," is a greeting heard with increasing frequency all across the European continent. Ikea, a privately held furniture retailer with 77 stores in 18 countries, is already five times larger than the second-largest multinational retail chain. The company features giant stores and has been phenomenally successful. Ikea's 1987 aftertax profits hit $155 million on sales of $2.1 billion, representing an aftertax margin of 7.4 percent in a business in which margins of 1 to 2 percent are more typical. Return on equity averages an equally impressive 30-plus percent, despite employing very little financial leverage.

Until Ikea opened its first store in the southern Swedish town of Almhult in 1953, furniture retailing in Europe had been controlled by a cartel of small local shops and large department stores. Prices were high, selection quite limited, and customer service poor. Offering its own "copycat" versions of the best-selling Scandinavian designs, Ikea began selling unassembled furniture in self-service warehouse showrooms. Most importantly, prices were 30 to 50 percent below those of competing stores selling fully assembled furniture. For the first time, people of average means had the opportunity to buy quality furniture at affordable prices, and Ikea flourished.

The key objective in Ikea's marketing philosophy is to keep customers in the store until they buy something. After noticing that customers left the Almhult store empty-handed in order to get something to eat or because they were harried by young children, Ikea added a budget-priced restau-

*continued*

See: Peter Fuhrman, "The Workers' Friend," *Forbes*, March 21, 1988, 124, 128.

Note that in monopolistically competitive equilibrium, a firm will never operate at the minimum point on its average cost curve. The firm's demand curve is downward sloping, so it can be tangent to the *ATC* curve only at a point above the minimum of the *ATC* curve. Does this mean that a monopolistically competitive industry is inefficient? The answer is no, except in a superficial sense. The very existence of the downward-sloping demand curve implies that consumers value the firm's products more highly than they do products of other producers. If the number of producers were somehow reduced so that all the remaining firms could operate at their minimum cost point, some consumers

---

**Managerial Application** *continued*

rant and a children's playroom. Customers stayed in the store longer, and business boomed. All Ikea's stores have huge parking lots, easy access to expressways, and, most of all, low prices. To insure profits at rock-bottom prices, Ikea employees are cost-conscious to the point of being stingy. Foremost in Ikea's operating philosophy is the concept that no effort will be spared to keep prices to the consumer as low as possible.

Fortunately for Ingvar Kamprad, founder of Ikea, European competitors have been very slow to respond to Ikea's innovation in furniture retailing. As a result, the company has earned high profits for a much longer period of time than one might expect. Kamprad has been well rewarded for bringing a wide selection of affordable furniture to the European market. Recently, *Forbes* magazine estimated the total value of Kamprad's holdings at more than $2 billion. Like Sam Walton's success in the United States with Wal-Mart, Kamprad's success with Ikea is surprising in an industry as hotly competitive as retailing, where the value of marketing innovations typically diminishes rapidly because of quick imitation by rivals.

Few consumers in the United States have heard of Ikea, but that is expected to change in the near future. After opening eight stores in Canada during the 1976 to 1981 period, Ikea launched its U.S. operations in 1985 with a store near Philadelphia and in 1986 with a store in the Washington, D.C. suburb of Dale City, Virginia. Together the stores grossed $77 million in 1987, double what Ikea had anticipated. The company opened a third store in Baltimore during 1988 and plans ten more stores in the United States by 1992.

Suppliers and competitors both marvel at Ikea's merchandising skill. The company's in-store display is said to be second to none. However, as is typical of any firm in a monopolistically competitive industry, Ikea is especially vulnerable to imitation by competitors. Already, imitators are beginning to show up in the United States. Stør, a California-based company, has announced plans to open 30 West Coast outlets that mimic the Ikea formula, right down to the ball-filled children's playroom and red-shirted employees. Although such imitation is truly the sincerest form of flattery, it is sure to limit Ikea's profit potential in the U.S. market.

---

would clearly suffer a loss in welfare, *because the product variety they desired would no longer be available.* The higher prices and costs of monopolistically competitive industries, as opposed to perfectly competitive industries, can be seen as the economic cost of product variety. If consumers are willing to bear such costs, and often they are, then the costs must not be excessive. The success of many branded products in the face of generic competition is powerful testimony in support of this presumption.

Although the perfectly competitive and pure monopoly settings are comparatively rare in real-world markets, monopolistic competition is frequently observed. It often develops from the competitive forces that continually shape markets. For example, in 1960 a small ($37 million in sales) office-machine company, Haloid Xerox, Inc., revolutionized the copy industry with the introduction of the Xerox 914 copier. Xerography was a tremendous improvement over electrofax and other coated-paper copiers. It permitted the use of untreated paper, which produced not only a more desirable copy but one that was less expensive on a cost-per-copy basis as well. Invention of the dry copier established what is now Xerox Corporation at the forefront of a rapidly growing office-copier industry and propelled the firm to a position of virtual monopoly by 1970. However, between 1970 and 1980, the industry's market structure changed dramatically because of an influx of both domestic and foreign competition as many of Xerox's original patents expired. IBM entered the copier market in April 1970 with its Copier I model and expanded its participation in November 1972 with Copier II. Eastman Kodak made its entry into the market in 1975 with its Ektaprint model. Of course, Minnesota Mining and Manufacturing (3M) has long been a factor in the electrofax copier segment of the market. A more complete list of Xerox's recent domestic and international competitors would include at least 30 firms. The effect of this entry on Xerox's market share and profitability was dramatic. Between 1970 and 1978, for example, Xerox's share of the domestic copier market fell from 98 to 56 percent, and its return on stockholders' equity fell from 23.6 to 18.2 percent.

The monopolistic dry-copier market of 1970 has evolved into a much more competitive industry as it enters the 1990s. Because Kodak, 3M, Panasonic, and Sharp copiers are only close, rather than perfect, substitutes for Xerox machines, each company retains some price discretion, and today the industry can be described as monopolistically competitive.

The process of price/output adjustment and the concept of equilibrium in monopolistically competitive markets can be further illustrated by the following example. Assume that the Skyhawk Trailer Company, located in Toronto, Ontario, owns patents covering important design features of its Tomahawk II, an ultralight camping trailer that can safely be towed by high-mileage subcompact cars. Skyhawk's patent protection has made it very difficult for competitors to offer similar ultralight trailers. The Tomahawk II is a highly successful product, and a veritable flood of similar products can be expected within five years as Skyhawk's patent protection expires.

Skyhawk has asked its financial planning committee to identify both short- and long-run pricing and production strategies for the Tomahawk II. To facilitate the decision-making process, the committee has received the following annual demand and cost data from Skyhawk's marketing and production departments:

$$P = \$20,000 - \$15.6Q,$$
$$TC = \$400,000 + \$4,640Q + \$10Q^2,$$

where $P$ is price (in dollars), $Q$ is quantity (in units), and $TC$ is total cost, including a risk-adjusted normal rate of return on investment (in dollars).

As a first step in the analysis, we determine the optimal price/output combination if the committee were to decide that Skyhawk should take full advantage of its current monopoly position and maximize short-run profits. To find the short-run profit-maximizing price/output combination, we set the first derivative of Skyhawk's total profit function equal to zero and solve for $Q$:

$$\pi = TR - TC$$
$$= \$20{,}000Q - \$15.6Q^2 - \$400{,}000 - \$4{,}640Q - \$10Q^2$$
$$= -\$25.6Q^2 + \$15{,}360Q - \$400{,}000.$$

Therefore,

$$d\pi/dQ = -\$51.2 + \$15{,}360Q = 0$$
$$\$51.2Q = \$15{,}360$$
$$Q = 300 \text{ Units},$$
$$P = \$20{,}000 - \$15.6(300)$$
$$= \$15{,}320,$$

and

$$\pi = -\$25.6(300^2) + \$15{,}360(300) - \$400{,}000$$
$$= \$1{,}904{,}000.$$

Therefore, the financial planning committee will recommend a $15,320 price and 300-unit output level to Skyhawk management, if the firm's objective is to maximize short-run profit. Such a planning decision will result in a $1.9-million economic profit during those years when Skyhawk's patent protection effectively deters competitors.

Now let us assume that Skyhawk can maintain a high level of brand loyalty and product differentiation in the long run, despite competitor offerings of similar trailers, but that such competition will eliminate any potential for economic profits. This is consistent with a market in monopolistically competitive equilibrium, where $P = AC$ at a point above minimum long-run average costs. Skyhawk's declining market share will be reflected by a leftward shift in its demand curve to a point of tangency with its average cost curve. Although precise identification of the long-run price/output combination that might result would be very difficult, the planning committee can identify the bounds within which this price/output combination can be expected to occur.

The high-price/low-output combination point is identified by the point of tangency between the firm's average cost curve and a new demand curve reflecting a *parallel* leftward shift in demand ($D_2$ in Figure 12.2). This parallel leftward shift assumes that the firm can maintain a high degree of product differentiation. The low-price/high-output equilibrium combination is identified by the point of tangency between the average cost curve and a new horizontal firm demand curve ($D_3$ in Figure 12.2). This is, of course, the perfectly competitive market equilibrium price/output combination.

The equilibrium price/output combination that follows a parallel leftward shift in Skyhawk's demand curve can be determined by equating the slopes of the firm's original demand curve and its long-run average cost curve. That is, since a parallel leftward shift in firm demand will result in a new demand curve with an identical slope, equating the slopes of the firm's initial demand and average cost curves will identify the monopolistically competitive high-price/low-output equilibrium possibility.

To determine the slope of the average cost curve, we must find how average costs vary with respect to output. (For simplicity, assume that the previous total cost curve for Skyhawk also holds in the long run.)

$$AC = TC/Q = (\$400{,}000 + \$4{,}640Q + \$10Q^2)/Q$$
$$= \frac{\$400{,}000}{Q} + \$4{,}640 + \$10Q$$
$$= \$400{,}000Q^{-1} + \$4{,}640 + \$10Q.$$

The slope of this average cost curve is given by the expression:

$$dAC/dQ = -400{,}000Q^{-2} + 10.$$

The slope of the new demand curve is given by:

$$dP/dQ = -15.6 \text{ (same as original demand curve)}.$$

In equilibrium,

Slope of $AC$ Curve = Slope of Demand Curve
$$-400{,}000Q^{-2} + 10 = -15.6$$
$$Q^{-2} = 25.6/400{,}000$$
$$Q^2 = 400{,}000/25.6$$
$$Q = 125 \text{ Units,}$$
$$P = AC$$
$$= \frac{\$400{,}000}{125} + \$4{,}640 + \$10(125)$$
$$= \$9{,}090,$$

and

$$\pi = P \times Q - TC$$
$$= \$9{,}090(125) - \$400{,}000 - \$4{,}640(125) - \$10(125^2)$$
$$= \$0.$$

Thus, the high-price/low-output monopolistically competitive equilibrium results in a decrease in price from $15,320 to $9,090 and a fall in output from 300 to 125 units. Only a risk-adjusted normal rate of return will be earned, eliminating Skyhawk's economic profits. Of course, this long-run equilibrium assumes that Skyhawk would enjoy the same low price elasticity of demand that it experienced as a monopolist. This may or may not be the case. Typically, new entrants have the effect both of cutting a monopolist's market share and increasing the price elasticity of demand. Thus, it is reasonable to expect entry to cause both a leftward shift of and some flattening in Skyhawk's demand curve. To see the extreme limit of the demand-curve flattening process, we must consider the case of a perfectly horizontal demand curve.

The low-price/high-output (perfectly competitive) equilibrium combination occurs at the point where $P = MR = MC = AC$. This reflects the fact that the firm's demand curve is perfectly horizontal, and average costs are minimized. To find the output level of minimum average costs, we set the first derivative of the average cost function equal to zero (where $MC = AC$) and solve for $Q$:

$$AC = \$400{,}000Q^{-1} + \$4{,}640 + \$10Q.$$

Therefore,

$$dAC/dQ = -\$400{,}000Q^{-2} + \$10 = 0$$

$$Q^{-2} = \frac{\$10}{\$400{,}000}$$

$$Q^2 = 40{,}000$$

$$Q = \sqrt{40{,}000}$$

$$= 200 \text{ Units,}$$

$$P = AC$$

$$= \frac{\$400{,}000}{200} + \$4{,}640 + \$10(200)$$

$$= \$8{,}640,$$

and

$$\pi = PQ - TC$$

$$= \$8{,}640(200) - \$400{,}000 - \$4{,}640(200) - \$10(200^2)$$

$$= \$0.$$

Under this low-price equilibrium scenario, Skyhawk's monopoly price would fall in the long-run from an original $15,320 to $8,640, and output would fall from the monopoly level of 300 units to the competitive equilibrium level of 200 units per year. The company would earn only a risk-adjusted normal rate of return, and economic profits would equal zero.

## 12.2 **Managerial Application**

Monopolistic Competition in the Computer Industry

During the 1960s and 1970s, IBM was able to maintain a dominant position in the market for large mainframe computers through hundreds of design patents and a highly developed service and sales staff. Similarly, Digital Equipment Corporation (DEC) was able to achieve and maintain a leading position in the market for mid-range computers. Protection of important design features by patents made it very difficult and risky for competitors to manufacture and market computers and peripheral equipment that were compatible with IBM or DEC machines. Manufacturing risks were high not only because of the threat of patent-infringement suits but, more importantly, because an unexpected new product introduction by IBM or DEC could render obsolete entire lines of competitors' products. In fact, even some independent lessors of IBM computers were forced to leave the leasing business when unexpected technological developments by IBM drastically reduced the value of their equipment inventories. As a result, *Fortune 500* companies and other major computer users often relied exclusively on IBM or DEC for their computer needs.

All of this changed with the computer boom of the 1980s. With the advent of inexpensive and powerful new computers, hundreds of new computer applications emerged. Many of these new applications were highly specialized, making entry into the computer market possible for manufacturers able to profitably supply narrow market segments. For example, Apple successfully exploited the personal computer and educational markets with user-friendly machines and software applications; Cray revolutionized the high-speed "supercomputer" business; Compaq successfully penetrated the small- to medium-size business market.

*continued*

See: John Hillkirk, "High-Tech World Sets Product Standards," *USA Today*, May 5, 1988, 18; and *Wall Street Journal* News Roundup, "PC and Workstation Makers Square Off," *The Wall Street Journal*, January 18, 1989, B1.

Therefore, following expiration of its patent protection, management can expect that competitor entry will reduce Skyhawk's volume from 300 units per year to a level between $Q = 125$ and $Q = 200$ units per year. The short-run profit-maximizing price of \$15,320 will fall to a monopolistically competitive equilibrium price between $P = \$9,090$, the high-price/low-output equilibrium, and $P = \$8,640$, the low-price/high-

In addition, the price elasticity of demand for personal computers appeared to be far greater than anyone had previously imagined. Both foreign and domestic suppliers of low-cost "clones" of IBM equipment found a ready market for their products among first-time computer buyers. Sperry (now Unisys), Tandem, Tandy, Zenith, and many others successfully copied or imitated important design features of IBM personal computers and marketed their products to a large and rapidly growing market. These low-cost alternatives to IBM computers created vigorous price competition in the market for personal computers and reduced brand loyalty in the entire computer industry.

These and other trends in the computer industry are typical of a monopolistically competitive market structure. Computers and software are rapidly becoming standardized allowing equipment from a wide variety of manufacturers to share information. In May 1988, IBM, DEC, and 46 other leading computer manufacturers and software providers, together representing 80 percent of industry sales, joined forces to begin work on an Open Systems Interconnection (OSI) technology that would allow easy communication among all personal, mid-size, and mainframe computers. Any computer based on the OSI system will be able to send messages, share files, and exchange electronic documents with any other OSI model, regardless of the manufacturer. OSI will knock down the barriers to the free flow of information previously created by one-company proprietary standards.

Helping speed this process is the decision to require that all computers purchased by the U.S. government conform to the OSI standard by 1990. Thus, all computers will have the same basic software language and plug into networks that will have the ability to communicate worldwide. This standardization of computers and software is comparable to the nineteenth-century standardization of railroad track size to allow all trains to pass over the same tracks and the standardization of telephone equipment to permit worldwide communication. Like these previous standards, consumers can expect an important benefit. They will be able to shop widely for the best combination of hardware and software products, further increasing competition in the industry. Not only will computer applications increase, but hardware and software prices will surely continue to decline.

output equilibrium. In deciding on an optimal short-run price/output strategy, Skyhawk must weigh the benefits of high near-term profitability against the long-run cost of lost market share resulting from competitor entry. Such a decision involves consideration of current interest rates, the speed of competitor imitation, and the future pace of innovation in the industry, among other factors.

# OLIGOPOLY

The theory of monopolistic competition, while borrowing heavily from those of pure competition and pure monopoly, more accurately portrays the actual markets in which many businesses operate. It recognizes that firms often have some control over price but that their price flexibility is limited by the large number of close substitutes for their products. The theory assumes, however, that in making decisions, firms do not consider competitor reactions. Such a behavioral assumption is appropriate for some industries but inappropriate for others. When an individual firm's actions will cause its competitors to react, *oligopoly* exists.

In the United States, aluminum, automobiles, cigarettes, electrical equipment, glass, and steel are all produced and sold under conditions of oligopoly. Notice that in each of these industries a small number of firms produce all, or at least a very large percentage of, the total output. In the automobile industry, for example, General Motors, Ford, Chrysler, Honda, Toyota, Mazda, and Nissan account for almost all auto production in the United States. Even the primary competition from imported automobiles is limited to a relatively small number of firms. Aluminum production is also highly concentrated, with Alcoa, Reynolds, and Kaiser producing almost all domestic output.

Oligopoly market structures also exist in a number of other industries in which the market areas for individual firms are quite small. Examples of this type of local oligopolistic structure include many retail markets for gasoline and food. Here, only a few sellers (service stations and grocery stores) compete within a small geographic area.

It is the limited numbers of sellers that introduce interactions into the price/output decision problem under oligopoly. Consider *duopoly*, a special form of oligopoly, under which only two firms provide a particular product. For simplicity, assume that the product is homogeneous and that customers choose between the firms solely on the basis of price. Assume also that both firms charge the same price and that each has an equal share of the market. Now suppose that Firm *A* attempts to increase its sales by lowering its price. All buyers will attempt to switch to Firm *A*, and Firm *B* will lose a substantial share of its market. To retain customers, *B* will react by lowering its price. Neither firm is free to act independently; actions taken by one will lead to reactions by the other.

## Price/Output Decisions under Oligopoly

Demand curves relate the quantity of a product demanded to its price, *holding constant the effect of all other variables*. One variable that is assumed to remain fixed is the prices charged by competing firms. In an oligopolistic market structure, however, if one firm changes its price, other firms will react by changing their prices. The demand curve for the initial firm shifts position, so that instead of moving along a single demand curve as it changes price, the firm moves to an entirely new demand curve.

This phenomenon of shifting demand curves is illustrated in Figure 12.3a. Firm $A$ is initially producing $Q_1$ units of output and selling them at a price $P_1$. Demand curve $D_1$ applies here, *assuming that prices charged by other firms remain fixed.* Under this assumption, a price cut from $P_1$ to $P_2$ would increase demand to $Q_2$. Assume, however, that only a few firms operate in the market and that each has a fairly large share of total sales. If one firm cuts its price and obtains a substantial increase in volume, the other firms must lose a large part of their business. Further, they know exactly why their sales have fallen, and they react by cutting their own prices. This action shifts Firm $A$ down to the second demand curve, $D_2$, reducing its demand at $P_2$ from $Q_2$ to $Q_3$ units. The new curve is just as unstable as the old one, so knowledge of its shape is useless to Firm $A$; if it tries to move along $D_2$, competitors will react, forcing the company to yet another curve.

Shifting demand curves would present no real difficulty in making price/output decisions *if Firm A knew for sure how its rivals would react to price changes.* The reactions would just be built into the price/demand relation, and a new demand curve could be constructed to include interactions among firms. Curve $D_3$ in Figure 12.3b represents such a reaction-based demand curve; it shows how price reductions affect quantity demanded after competitive reactions have been taken into account. The problem with this approach, however, lies in the fact that each of many different theories about interfirm behavior leads to a different pricing model and thereby to different decision rules.

## Cartel Arrangements

**cartel**

Firms operating with a formal agreement setting price and output levels for their products.

**collusion**

A covert, informal agreement among firms in an industry to set prices and output levels.

In an oligopolistic market, all of the firms in an industry would benefit if they got together and set prices to maximize total industry profits. The firms could agree to set the same prices as a monopolist would and thereby could extract the maximum amount of profits from consumers. A group operating under such a formal, overt agreement is called a **cartel;** if a covert, informal agreement were reached, the firms would be operating in **collusion.** Both practices are generally illegal in the United States. Cartels are legal, however, in many parts of the world, and U.S.-based multinational corporations sometimes become involved in them in foreign markets. In addition, several important domestic markets are dominated by producer associations that operate like cartels and appear to flourish without interference from the government. Certain farm products, including milk, are prime examples of products marketed under cartel-like arrangements.

A cartel that has absolute control over all of the firms in the industry can operate as a monopoly. To illustrate, consider the situation shown in Figure 12.4. The marginal cost curves of each firm are summed horizontally to arrive at an industry marginal cost curve. Equating the cartel's total marginal cost with the industry marginal revenue curve determines the profit-maximizing output and, simultaneously, the price, $P^*$, to be charged. Once this profit-maximizing price/output level has been deter-

■ Figure 12.3
## Shifting Demand under Oligopoly

(a) A price reduction to $P_2$ by Firm A temporarily increases output to $Q_2$. As other firms reduce prices, demand shifts back from $D_1$ to $D_2$ and Firm A's output drops to $Q_3$. (b) In contrast to $D_1$ and $D_2$, the demand curve $D_3$ reflects Firm A's projections of the price reactions of competitors.

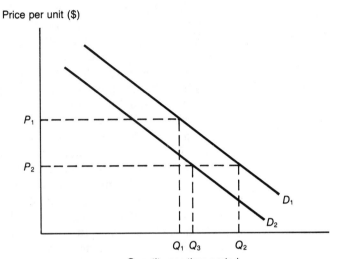

(a) Demand curves that do not explicitly recognize reactions

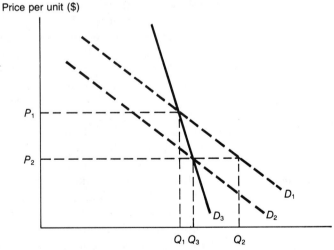

(b) Demand curve that recognizes reactions

■ Figure 12.4
## Price/Output Determination for a Cartel

Horizontal summation of the *MC* curves for each firm gives the cartel's *MC* curve. Output for each firm is found by equating its own *MC* to the industry profit-maximizing *MC* level.

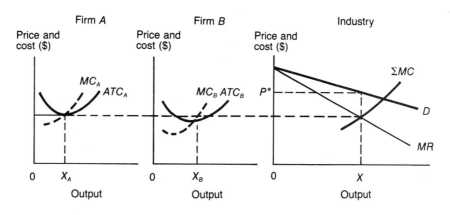

mined, each individual firm finds its output by equating its own marginal cost to the previously determined profit-maximizing marginal cost level for the industry.

Profits are often divided among firms on the basis of their individual outputs, but other allocating techniques can be used. Historical market shares, capacity as determined in a number of ways, and a bargained solution based on economic power have all been used in the past.

For numerous reasons, cartels have typically been rather short-lived. In addition to the long-run problems of changing products and of entry into the market by new producers, cartels are subject to disagreements among the members. Although firms usually agree that maximizing joint profits is mutually beneficial, they seldom agree on the equity of various profit-allocation schemes. This problem can lead to attempts to subvert the cartel agreement.

Subversion of the cartel by an individual firm can be extremely profitable to that firm. With the industry operating at the monopoly price/ output level, an individual firm's demand curve is highly elastic, provided that it can lower its price without other cartel members learning of this action and retaliating. The availability of substantial profits to a firm that cheats on the cartel, coupled with the ease with which secret price concessions can be made, makes policing cartel agreements extremely difficult.

These problems combine to make cartel survival difficult. The OPEC cartel's loss of market control in the late 1980s provides an example of a

## 12.3  **Managerial Application**
Price-Fixing in Art . . . and Garbage

Collusion in setting prices is one of the most obvious potential abuses of market power. This practice has been observed in both input and output prices. In U.S. antitrust law and policy, price-fixing is one of the few unambiguous signals of anticompetitive behavior. As such, price-fixing is strictly prohibited and subject to sharp penalty under the law. Since price-fixing is illegal, it is difficult to find managerial case studies that offer insight into the practice. However, from time to time firms and individuals are successfully prosecuted for price-fixing. Two recent cases illustrate the problem.

In an interesting case, the Justice Department found that antique dealers in the Philadelphia area routinely banded together and agreed not to bid against one another at auctions. Only one dealer in each "pool" would bid on any given antique. Then, members of the pool would gather later for a second private "knockout" session during which the items would be reauctioned, but only to pool members. Pool members then would divide the extra money paid for all items. This practice ensured that pool members could purchase desired items at the lowest possible prices, which reduced the price original owners received. In one instance, a widow from Chadds Ford, Pennsylvania, sold an antique desk for $1,325 in 1984, only to learn at the 1987 trial of one of the dealers that the desk went for $5,000 at a later knockout session.

Pooling has a long history. The practice has been documented in court cases covering a wide variety of industries, including auctions of cattle, timber, tobacco, and other commodities. Still, the practice has gone unchallenged in a number of other instances,

*continued*

See: Meg Cox, "At Many Auctions, Illegal Bidding Thrives as a Longtime Practice among Dealers," *The Wall Street Journal*, February 19, 1988, 17; and James Drummond, "Garbage Industry's Dirty Deals," *Houston Chronicle*, February 28, 1988, 5–1.

cartel that failed primarily because members could not agree on a market-sharing scheme. Pressure from new entrants attracted by relatively high oil prices added to the cartel's problems.

**price leadership**

A situation in which one firm establishes itself as the industry leader and all other firms in the industry accept its pricing policy.

## Price Leadership

A less formal but nonetheless effective means of reducing oligopolistic uncertainty is through **price leadership.** Price leadership results when one firm establishes itself as the industry leader and all other firms in the industry accept its pricing policy. This leadership may result from

**Managerial Application** *continued*

including auctions of art, antiques, and industrial products. At New York auctions for jewelry, rugs, and silver, the practice still appears to be common. Art dealers maintain that it is typical for other dealers to ask you to join their pool if they believe you will bid against them at an auction. Industrial auctioneers report that similar pools are common in commodities such as burlap and scrap metal. Dealers like them because even if they don't go home with any merchandise, at least they go home with a check. As one dealer remarked to the court, "Would you go to an auction and bid against a friend?"

Price-fixing in art even extends to industry price indexes. According to Sothebys Art Index, art appreciated at more than a 20-percent annual rate during the late 1980s, thus outperforming common stocks. However, industry experts point out that each piece of art is unique and that a category such as "Chinese ceramics" has little meaning. Moreover, works that have fallen in value don't tend to be put up for sale. Thus, even before considering commission and sales expenses, which run 30 to 50 percent, changes in Sotheby's index vastly overstate the true rate of return earned by art investors.

Price-fixing is also apparently common in a far different industry—the garbage collection business. The underlying economics of the industry make garbage collection susceptible to price-fixing and market-sharing arrangements. There are no apparent economies of scale in garbage collection. Large firms tend to be no more or less efficient than relatively small competitors. However, there are important *economies of density*. If one firm is able to collect all garbage in a given residential area, the average cost per customer will be far less than if this same amount of business is spread over a large geographic region. Firms recognize this and have repeatedly been convicted of entering into secret illegal agreements to divide territories and fix prices. For example, Browning-Ferris Industries, recognized as an innovative industry leader, has been convicted of illegally fixing prices and violating antitrust laws in two cities.

Given the potential profits associated with price-fixing and the wide range of industries in which the practice has arisen, it would appear to be one of the more serious social costs incurred in oligopolistic markets.

the size and strength of the leading firm, from cost efficiency, or as a result of the recognized ability of the leader to forecast market conditions accurately and to establish a price that produces satisfactory profits for all firms in the industry.

A typical case is price leadership by a dominant firm, usually the largest firm in the industry. Here the leader faces a price/output problem similar to a monopolist, while the other firms are price takers and essentially face a competitive price/output problem. This is illustrated in Figure 12.5, where the total market demand curve is $D_T$, the marginal cost curve of the leader is $MC_L$, and the horizontal summation of the marginal

■ Figure 12.5
## Oligopoly Pricing with Dominant-Firm Price Leadership

When the price leader has set an industry price of $P_2$, the price leader will maximize profits at $Q_1$ units of output. Price followers will supply a combined output of $Q_4 - Q_1$.

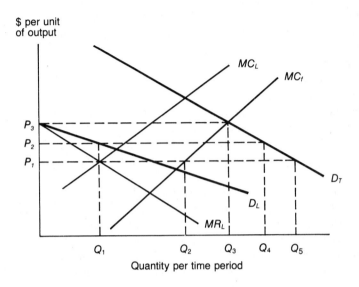

cost curves for all of the price followers is labeled $MC_f$. Because the price followers take prices as given, they choose to operate at the output level at which their individual marginal costs equal price, just as they would in a purely competitive market structure. Accordingly, the $MC_f$ curve represents the supply curve for the follower firms. This means that at price $P_3$, the followers would supply the entire market, leaving nothing for the dominant firm. At all prices below $P_3$, however, the horizontal distance between the summed $MC_f$ curve and the market demand curve represents the price leader's demand. At a price of $P_1$, for example, the price followers will provide $Q_2$ units of output, leaving demand of $Q_5 - Q_2$ for the price leader. Plotting all of the residual demand quantities for prices below $P_3$ produces the demand curve for the price leader, $D_L$ in Figure 12.5, and the related marginal revenue curve, $MR_L$.

More generally, the leader faces a demand curve of the form:

$$D_L = D_T - S_f,$$ 

**12.1**

where $D_L$ is the leader's demand, $D_T$ is total demand, and $S_f$ is the followers' supply curve found by setting price $= MC_f$ and solving for $Q_f$, the quantity that will be supplied by the price followers. Since $D_T$ and $S_f$ are both functions of price, $D_L$ is likewise determined by price.

Because the price leader faces the demand curve, $D_L$, as a monopolist, it maximizes profit by operating at the point where marginal revenue equals marginal cost; that is, where $MR_L = MC_L$. At this output level for the leader, $Q_1$, the market price is established to be $P_2$. The price followers will supply a combined output of $Q_4 - Q_1$ units. If no one challenges the price leader, a stable short-run equilibrium will have been reached.

A second type of price leadership is **barometric price leadership.** In this case, one firm announces a price change in response to what it perceives as a change in industry supply and demand conditions. This change could stem from cost increases that result from a new industry labor agreement, higher energy or material input prices, or changes in taxes, or it might result from a substantial increase or decrease in demand. With barometric price leadership, the price leader will not necessarily be the largest or dominant firm in the industry. The price-leader role may even pass from one firm to another over time. It is important, however, that the price leader accurately read the prevailing industry view of the need for price adjustment and the appropriate new price level. If a firm incorrectly assesses the desire for a price change by other firms, they may not follow its price move, and it may have to rescind or modify the announced price change to retain its market share or perhaps, if the price change involved a reduction, to prevent other firms from retaliating with even lower prices.

**barometric price leadership**

A situation in which one firm in an industry announces a price change in response to what it perceives as a change in industry supply and demand conditions and other firms respond by following the price change.

## Kinked Demand Curve

An often-noted characteristic of oligopolistic markets is that once a general price level has been established, whether through a cartel or some less formal arrangement, it tends to remain fixed for an extended period. This rigidity of prices is typically explained by yet another set of assumptions about firm behavior under conditions of price interdependence, known as the **kinked demand curve theory of oligopoly prices.**

**kinked demand curve theory of oligopoly prices**

A theory assuming that rival firms follow any decrease in price in order to maintain their respective market shares, but refrain from following increases, allowing their market share to increase at the expense of the firm making the initial price increase.

The kinked demand curve theory describes a behavior pattern in which rival firms are assumed to follow any decrease in price in order to maintain their respective market shares but to refrain from following price increases, allowing their market shares to increase at the expense of the price raiser. Thus, the demand curve facing an individual firm is kinked at the current price/output combination as illustrated in Figure 12.6. The firm is producing $Q$ units of output and selling them at a price of $P$ per unit; if it lowers its price, competing firms will retaliate by lowering their prices. The result of a price cut, therefore, is a relatively small increase in sales; that is, the demand curve associated with price reductions has very low elasticity.[2] Price increases, on the other hand, result in significant reductions in quantities demanded and in related

---

[2]The reader is referred to Figure 12.3, where the shift in demand curves that results from a price cut was explained. The curve $D_3$ in Figure 12.3b is the counterpart of the steeper segment of $D$ in Figure 12.6.

■ Figure 12.6
## Kinked Demand Curve

When price cuts are followed but price increases are not, a kink develops in the firm's demand curve. At the kink, the optimal price remains stable despite moderate changes in marginal costs.

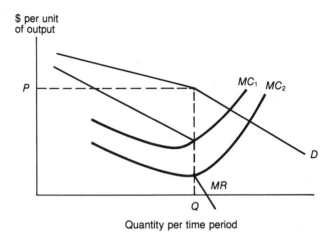

decreases in total revenue, because customers will shift to competing firms that do not follow the price increases.

Associated with the kink in the demand curve is a point of discontinuity in the marginal revenue curve. That is, the firm's marginal revenue curve has a gap at the current price/output level, which results in the rigidity of price. The profit-maximizing firm always chooses to operate at the point where marginal cost equals marginal revenue, and because of this gap in the marginal revenue curve, the price/output combination at the kink can remain optimal even though marginal cost fluctuates. Thus, as illustrated in Figure 12.6, the firm's marginal cost curve can fluctuate between $MC_1$ and $MC_2$ without causing a change in the firm's profit-maximizing price/output combination.

## NONPRICE COMPETITION

Because rival firms are likely to retaliate against price cuts, oligopolists often emphasize nonprice competitive techniques to boost demand. What does nonprice competition mean? To explain the concept, let us first assume that a firm's demand function is given by Equation 12.2:

$$Q_A = f(P_A, P_X, Ad_A, Ad_X, SQ_A, SQ_X, I, Pop, \ldots)$$
$$= a - bP_A + cP_X + dAd_A - eAd_X + fSQ_A$$
$$- gSQ_X + hI + iPop + \ldots,$$    **12.2**

where $Q_A$ is the quantity of output demanded from Firm $A$, $P_A$ is $A$'s price, $P_X$ is the average price charged by other firms in the industry, $Ad$ is advertising expenditures, $SQ$ denotes an index of styling and quality, $I$ represents income, and $Pop$ is population. The firm can control three of the variables in Equation 12.2: $P_A$, $Ad_A$, and $SQ_A$. If it reduces $P_A$ in an effort to stimulate demand, it will probably cause a reduction in $P_X$, offsetting the hoped-for effects of the initial price cut. Rather than substantially boosting sales, Firm $A$ may have simply started a price war.

Now consider the effects of changing the other controllable variables in the demand function, $Ad_A$ and $SQ_A$. Increased advertising could be expected to shift the demand curve to the right, thus enabling the firm to increase sales at a given price or to sell a constant quantity at a higher price. An improvement in styling or quality would have the same effect as a boost in the advertising budget; similar results would follow from easing credit terms, training salespersons to be more courteous, providing more convenient retail locations, or any other improvement in the product. Competitors can be expected to react to changes in nonprice variables, but the reaction rate is likely to be slower than for price changes. For one thing, these changes are generally less obvious to rival firms, at least initially, so it will take them longer to recognize that changes have occurred. Then, too, advertising campaigns have to be designed, and media time and space must be purchased. Styling and quality changes frequently require long lead times, as do training programs for salespeople, the opening of new facilities, and the like. Further, all of these nonprice activities tend to differentiate the firm's products in the minds of consumers from those of other firms in the industry, and rivals may therefore find it difficult to regain lost customers even after they have reacted. Although it may take longer to build up a reputation through nonprice competition, once the demand curve has been shifted outward, it often takes rivals longer to counteract that shift. Thus, the advantageous effects of nonprice competition are likely to be more persistent than the fleeting benefits of a price cut.

How far should nonprice competition be carried? The answer is that such activities should be carried to the point where the marginal cost of the action just equals the marginal profit produced by it. For example, suppose that services sell for $10 per unit and the variable cost per unit is $8. If less than $2 of additional expenditures will boost sales by one unit, the additional expenditure should be made.

## The Optimal Level of Advertising

Advertising is but one of the many different methods of nonprice competition employed in imperfectly competitive markets. However, promotional and selling expenses constitute a considerable share of costs in many industries, and therefore they merit special consideration. In addition to helping determine an appropriate level of promotional and selling expenses, the method for determining an optimal level of advertising illustrates the technique for determining profit-maximizing levels of expenditures for other methods of nonprice competition, such as improvements in product quality, expansions in customer service, research and development expenditures, and so on.

The rule that must be followed to determine a profit-maximizing level of expenditures for nonprice methods of competition is to set the marginal cost of the activity involved just equal to the marginal revenue or marginal benefit derived from it. This follows from the fact that, when the marginal cost of any activity equals the marginal revenue derived, the total net profit generated will be maximized. This means that the optimal level of advertising occurs at that point where the additional net revenues derived from advertising just offset the marginal advertising expenditures.

Additional or net marginal revenues per unit of output derived from advertising can be measured by the difference between marginal revenue, $MR$, and the marginal costs of production and distribution, $MC_Q$ (but not allowing for advertising expenditures), or:

$$\frac{\text{Net Marginal Revenue Derived}}{\text{from Advertising}} = \frac{\text{Marginal}}{\text{Revenue}} - \frac{\text{Marginal Cost}}{\text{of Output}}$$

$$NMR_A = MR - MC_Q. \hspace{2cm} \textbf{12.3}$$

The marginal cost of advertising, again expressed in terms of the marginal cost of selling one additional unit of output, can be written:

$$\frac{\text{Marginal Cost}}{\text{of Advertising}} = \frac{\text{Change in Advertising Expenditures}}{\text{One Unit Change in Demand}}$$

$$MC_A = \frac{\Delta \text{Advertising Expenditures}}{\Delta \text{Demand}}. \hspace{2cm} \textbf{12.4}$$

The optimal level of advertising is found where:

$$\frac{\text{Net Marginal Revenue Derived}}{\text{from Advertising}} = \text{Marginal Cost of Advertising}$$

$$MR - MC_Q = \frac{\Delta \text{Advertising Expenditures}}{\Delta \text{Demand}}$$

$$NMR_A = MC_A.$$

To illustrate, suppose that output in an individual line of business provides a profit contribution before advertising expenses of $2,500 per unit. The net marginal revenue derived from advertising that expands demand by one unit is $2,500. Marginal advertising and promotional expenditures up to this $2,500 level could then be justified. If one more unit of demand could be generated with an additional $1,000 in advertising expenditures, this additional advertising would be warranted because it makes an additional profit contribution of $1,500. On the other hand, if an additional advertising expenditure of $3,000 were necessary to expand demand by one unit, the additional advertising expenditure would reduce firm profits.

■ Figure 12.7

## Optimal Level of Advertising

A firm will expand the level of advertising up to the point where the net marginal revenue generated just equals the marginal cost of advertising.

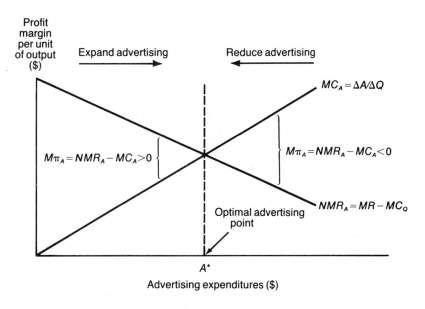

In general, it will pay to expand advertising expenditures so long as $NMR_A > MC_A$. Since the marginal profit derived from advertising is:

$$M\pi_A = NMR_A - MC_A,$$

the optimal level of advertising will occur at the point where:

$$M\pi_A = 0. \qquad \textbf{12.5}$$

This relation is illustrated in Figure 12.7. Note that so long as $NMR_A > MC_A$, $M\pi_A > 0$, and it will pay to expand the level of advertising. Conversely, when $NMR_A < MC_A$, then $M\pi_A < 0$, and it will pay to reduce the level of advertising expenditures. The optimal level of advertising is achieved when $NMR_A = MC_A$, and $M\pi_A = 0$.

## DEFINING MARKET STRUCTURE

A market consists of all individuals and firms willing and able to buy or sell competing products during a given time period. In identifying competing products the key criterion is similarity in use. Precise determination of whether or not a specific good is a distinct economic product

## 12.4  **Managerial Application**
### Concentration Is Rising in the Oil Patch

A late-1980s wave of mergers and consolidation in the oil-field service and supply industry has caused some to observe that the industry is on its way to becoming an oligopoly. Since the oil-price crash of 1986, several hundred companies have dropped from view, and some important submarkets are now dominated by as few as three or four firms. For example, four companies control virtually all of the market for the pressure pumping services typically used to complete a well. Three firms divide up 80 to 90 percent of the market for drilling mud (a lubricant used in well drilling) and 90 percent of the market for wireline and geophysical services.

The recent rise in concentration has been most striking in the geophysical and seismic sectors of the industry. Before 1986, there were at least ten major competitors in each of these areas. However, mergers involving industry leader Schlumberger, Litton Industries, Halliburton, and Gearhart Industries, among others, have sharply reduced the number of major players. Participants who remain in the industry contend that the recent increase in concentration marks only a return to more normal times, in which five or six national competitors, plus a handful of strong regional firms, dominate any particular market. High prices and the frantic pace of drilling activity during the late 1970s and early 1980s encouraged hundreds of new entrants to the industry. The sifting of the efficient from the inefficient typically occurs during downturns, such as the one endured by the industry during the late 1980s, and a reduction in the number of active competitors is both healthy and to be expected.

*continued*

See: Judith Crown, "Market Concentration Is Rising in Oil Field," *Houston Chronicle*, March 13, 1988, 5–1, 14.

involves an evaluation of cross-price elasticities for broad classes of goods. When cross-price elasticities are large and positive, goods are substitutes for one another and can be thought of as competing products in a single market. Thus, positive cross-price elasticities identify a firm's competitors. Conversely, large negative cross-price elasticities indicate complementary products. Complementary products produced by a single firm must be evaluated as a single product line serving the same market. If complementary products are produced by other companies, evaluating the potential of a given product line involves incorporating exogenous influences beyond the firm's control. When cross-price elas-

**Managerial Application** *continued*

Others say that the recent rise in concentration reflects the culmination of a long-term trend in the industry. With the exit of Gearhart and Hughes Tool, not only fringe firms and startups but also established competitors have left the market. In light of the notable losses recently borne by both the industry and major lenders, bankers and the external capital markets are likely to favor established rather than entrant firms for quite some time. It may be several years before sufficient confidence returns to spur new entry. Competition among the few may become a long-term characteristic of important parts of the business.

This has prompted concern that higher prices and equipment shortages may be in store for the oil industry when the demand for oil and oil-field services recovers. Prices have already begun to firm up in a number of sectors. Producers of tubular goods, among the hardest hit by the oil-price drop, were able to increase prices twice during 1987. Buyers are understandably worried, given that these price increases came during a still-weak oil market. They are fearful that the cost of drilling and producing oil and gas will go up faster than the rate of inflation

and thus will have an adverse impact on the level of drilling activity.

Mergers and consolidations have reduced excess capacity in the industry and therefore have helped facilitate a return to profitability. After several years of losses, higher prices were simply required to fund the necessary maintenance of equipment and new product and process development typical of a healthy industry. However, fears of a less competitive structure led the U.S. Justice Department to intervene in a 1987 merger between Baker International and Hughes Tool, requiring that the combined company divest Baker's Reed Tool Company. Without divestiture, the combined firm would have controlled 60 percent of the market for drill bits, possibly enjoying an unacceptable degree of control over prices in that important market.

Implications of the late-1980s merger wave in this industry may not be apparent for at least a decade. Not until we have gone through another period of vibrant demand for oil and oil-field services will it be clear how the productive and innovative capacity of the industry has been affected.

ticities are near zero, goods are in separate economic markets and can be separately analyzed as serving distinct consumer needs. Therefore, using cross-price elasticity criteria to disaggregate the firm's overall product line into its distinct economic components is an important task confronting the managerial decision maker.

To identify relevant economic markets and define their characteristics, firms in the United States make extensive use of economic data collected by the Bureau of the Census of the U.S. Department of Commerce. Because these data provide valuable information on economic activity across the broad spectrum of U.S. industry, we will briefly consider the method and scope of the economic censuses.

## The Economic Censuses

**economic censuses**
Data collected by the U.S. Department of Commerce that provide a comprehensive statistical profile of large segments of the U.S. economy.

The **economic censuses** provide a comprehensive statistical profile of large segments of the national economy. They are taken at five-year intervals during years ending with the digits 2 and 7—for example, 1982, 1987, 1992, and so on. Included are censuses of manufacturing, retail and wholesale trade, services, minerals, and construction. In 1982, for example, sectors covered by the economic censuses accounted for nearly 70 percent of total economic activity originating in the private sector. Principal industry groups not covered are finance, insurance, real estate, agriculture, forestry, communications, public utilities, and transportation. However, limited transportation-related information is collected, including the distance that commodities are shipped and the type of transport employed.

The economic censuses are the primary source of data concerning changes in the number and size distribution of competitors, output, and employment in the economy. They are used extensively by the government in compiling national income accounts and as a basis for current surveys of industrial production, productivity, and prices. Census data are also used extensively by government agencies in setting public policy and monitoring economic programs. Manufacturers and distributors rely on census data to analyze current and potential markets. The censuses provide data for demand and cost forecasting; market penetration analysis; layout of sales territories; allocation of advertising budgets; and locations of plants, warehouses, and retail outlets. Trade and professional associations rely on census information to learn about changes in the number, size, and geographic dispersion of firms in their industry. State and local governments and chambers of commerce use census data to assess the business climate, as well as to gauge the success of programs designed to increase business investment and employment opportunities in local areas.

A further important characteristic of the economic censuses is their coverage of geographic trends. Recent *Census of Manufacturers* surveys have measured industrial activity for legally constituted geographic units such as states, counties, and cities. Manufacturing activity levels were also provided on hundreds of SMSAs (Standard Metropolitan Statistical Areas). SMSAs are integrated economic and social units with a large volume of daily travel and communication between the central city (having 50,000 or more population) and outlying areas. Each SMSA consists of one whole county or more and may include both industrialized counties and adjoining counties that are largely residential in character. Detail for various industries is shown at the SMSA level if data for individual companies would not be disclosed and if the industry has at least 250 employees.

In addition to being a comprehensive source of information on economic activity, census data have the compelling virtues of easy access and widespread availability. Census reports can be purchased directly from the Government Printing Office at modest cost or can be consulted free of charge at most major public and college libraries. In addition, census data and reports are often republished and distributed by trade associations, business journals, magazines, and newspapers.

### The Census Classification System

Census data are collected at the establishment level—that is, at a single physical location engaged in a specific line of business. The establishment level is best suited for obtaining direct measures of output and inputs such as labor, materials, capital, and so on. It is also a useful level of aggregation for providing detailed industry and geographic tabulations. On the other hand, statistics measuring overall income and balance sheet data are best collected at the company or enterprise level. Enterprise statistics on income and balance sheet data are made available to the public by the Internal Revenue Service in its *Statistics of Income* and by the Federal Trade Commission in its *Quarterly Financial Report for Manufacturing, Mining and Trade.*

The census classification of individual establishments by sector, industry group, industry, and products is called the Standard Industrial Classification (SIC) system. Table 12.1 shows the first step in this process and illustrates how the entire scope of economic activity is subdivided into sectors described by two-digit classifications. Below the two-digit major group or sector level, the SIC system proceeds to disaggregated levels of increasingly narrowly defined activity. Currently, the SIC system proceeds from very general two-digit industry groups to very specific seven-digit product classifications. To illustrate, Table 12.2 shows the breakdown that occurs as one moves from the two-digit "food and kindred products" major group to the seven-digit "canned evaporated milk" product category. Economists generally agree that four-digit-level classifications correspond quite closely with the economic definition of a market. That is, establishments grouped at the four-digit level produce

■ Table 12.1
### Standard Industrial Classifications of Economic Activity

| Sector | Two-Digit SIC Codes |
|---|---|
| Agriculture, Forestry, and Fisheries | 01–09 |
| Mining | 10–14 |
| Contract Construction | 15–17 |
| Manufacturing | 20–39 |
| Transportation; Communication; Electric, Gas, and Sanitary Services | 40–49 |
| Wholesale and Retail Trade | 50–59 |
| Finance, Insurance, and Real Estate | 60–67 |
| Services | 70–89 |
| Public Administration | 91–97 |
| Nonclassifiable Establishments | 99 |

■ Table 12.2
## Census Classification Example

| Digit Level | Number of Classifications | Example SIC Code | Description |
|---|---|---|---|
| Two | 20 | 20 | Food and Kindred Products |
| Three | 144 | 202 | Dairy Products |
| Four | 452 | 2023 | Condensed and Evaporated Milk Industry |
| Five | 1,500 | 20232 | Canned Milk |
| Six | | | (Not currently utilized) |
| Seven | 13,000 | 2023212 | Canned Evaporated Milk |

products that are ready substitutes for one another and thus function as competitors. Therefore, managers who analyze census data to learn about the number and size distribution of actual and potential competitors focus their attention primarily on data provided at the four-digit level. For this reason, we focus our attention on four-digit-level concentration data in our discussion of market structure.

## Market Concentration

Markets fall along the continuum from perfect competition to monopoly. Where an industry falls along this continuum is important both for firms currently in the industry and those contemplating entry. Price/output strategies will vary markedly depending on the market structure encountered. In addition, profit rates are affected by the level of competitive pressures. Among the attributes describing market structure, perhaps the number and size distribution of competitors are most important. These data must be carefully considered in managerial decision making.

In addition to those directly engaged in business, both government and the public share an interest in the size distribution of firms. As is described in Chapter 14, a small number of competitors can sometimes have direct implications for regulation and antitrust policy. Thus, considerable public resources are devoted to monitoring both the size distribution and economic performance of firms in several important sectors of the economy. Data that describe these characteristics of the U.S. economy are regularly compiled and published in economic census reports published by the Department of Commerce. Among those sectors covered by the economic censuses, manufacturing is clearly the largest, accounting for approximately 20 percent of aggregate economic activity in the United States. Firm sizes in manufacturing are much larger than in other major sectors such as retail and wholesale trade, construction, services (legal, medical, etc.), and so on. Among the more than 16 million business enterprises in the United States, manufacturing is the domain of the large corporation. Thus, it provides an interesting case study for considering data that are available on the size distribution of firms.

■ Table 12.3

## A Representative Sample of Four-Digit Census Industries, 1982

| Standard Industrial Classification (SIC) Code | Description | Number of Firms | Industry Sales (millions of dollars) | Market Share (percent) | |
|---|---|---|---|---|---|
| | | | | Top Four Firms ($CR_4$) | Top Eight Firms ($CR_8$) |
| 2011 | Meat Packing Plants | 1,658 | $ 5,824.6 | 29 | 43 |
| 2043 | Cereal Breakfast Foods | 32 | 4,131.9 | 86 | a |
| 2047 | Dog, Cat, and Other Pet Food | 222 | 4,402.2 | 52 | 71 |
| 2067 | Chewing Gum | 9 | 915.3 | 95 | a |
| 2095 | Roasted Coffee | 118 | 5,826.9 | 65 | 76 |
| 2371 | Fur Goods | 503 | 419.3 | 12 | 19 |
| 2387 | Apparel Belts | 317 | 556.5 | 19 | 30 |
| 2621 | Paper Mills | 135 | 20,994.6 | 22 | 40 |
| 2711 | Newspapers | 7,520 | 21,276.3 | 22 | 34 |
| 3425 | Handsaws and Saw Blades | 119 | 487.3 | 47 | 65 |
| 3711 | Motor Vehicles and Car Bodies | 284 | 70,739.7 | 92 | 97 |
| 3721 | Aircraft | 139 | 28,024.3 | 64 | 81 |
| 3732 | Boat Building and Repairing | 1,834 | 2,369.2 | 14 | 22 |
| 3995 | Burial Caskets | 270 | 682.1 | 52 | 60 |

Note: [a] *indicates an industry with so few competitors that the Census Bureau withholds data to avoid disclosing individual company information.*

**concentration ratios**

Data in the *Census of Manufacturers* that show the percentage market share held by an industry's leading firms.

Table 12.3 shows numbers of competitors, industry sales, and leading-firm market share data for a small sample of four-digit industries taken from the 1982 *Census of Manufacturers*. Here, as is generally the case, leading-firm market shares are calculated from sales data for the top four or eight firms in an industry. These market share data are called **concentration ratios** because they measure the percentage market share held by (concentrated in) an industry's top four ($CR_4$) or eight ($CR_8$) firms. When concentration ratios are low, industries tend to be made up of many firms and competition tends to be vigorous. Industries in which the four leading firms are responsible for less than 20 percent of total industry sales (i.e., $CR_4 < 20$) are highly competitive and approximate the pure competition model. On the other hand, when concentration ratios are high, leading firms dominate following firms in terms of size, and leading firms may have more potential for pricing flexibility and economic profits. Industries in which the four leading firms control more than 80 percent of total industry sales (i.e., $CR_4 > 80$) are highly concentrated, and market structure can tend toward monopoly. However, industries with a $CR_4 < 20$ or $CR_4 > 80$ are quite rare. Three-quarters of all manufacturing activity takes place in industries with concentration ratios falling in a range where $20 \leq CR_4 \leq 80$. In terms of relative importance,

## 12.5 **Managerial Application**
World-Class Quality

Among the most important types of non-price competition are competition in product quality, new product and process development, and innovation. The Japanese and others are rightfully credited with making outstanding contributions, but U.S. companies' commanding positions in many of these areas are seldom mentioned. Much of the debate about the competitiveness of U.S. manufacturing also tends to ignore this fact. Indeed, vigorous product-quality competition is often a distinctive feature of monopolistically competitive and oligopolistic market structures.

The following list from *Fortune* covers a wide variety of products and companies that can be viewed as success stories in product quality competition. Is world-class quality developed as a result of the carrot of above-normal profits, the stick of competitive pressure, or both?

**All-electric plastics injection-molding machines:** Cincinnati Milacron
**Aluminum foil:** Reynolds Metals
**Atomic clocks:** Frequency Electronics, Hewlett-Packard
**Ball point pens:** A. T. Cross
**Balloon, laser angioplasty catheters:** C. R. Bard, Eli Lilly, Trimedyne
**Bamboo fly-fishing rods:** Walt Carpenter
**Bed sheets and towels:** Burlington Industries, Dan River, Dundee Mills,

Fieldcrest Cannon, J. P. Stevens, Springs Industries, West Point-Pepperell
**Biotech drugs:** t-PA: Genentech
**Bobcat skid-steer loaders:** Melroe
**Boots and hunting shoes:** Timberland, L. L. Bean
**Brain electrical activity mapping system:** Nicolet Instruments
**Camera film (color):** Eastman Kodak
**Central office telephone switching equipment:** AT&T
**Charcoal briquettes:** Kingsford Products
**Charge couple device image sensor:** Eastman Kodak
**Clothes dryers:** Whirlpool
**Combines:** Case IH, Deere
**Computer operating system software:** Microsoft, AT&T, IBM, Digital Equipment (MS-DOS, Unix, VM, VMS)
**Copiers:** Eastman Kodak, Xerox
**Cotton denim:** Cone Mills
**Cruising sailboats, 37 feet and under:** Pacific Seacraft
**Crystal:** Steuben Glass
**Data parallel supercomputers:** Thinking Machines
**Digital plotters:** Hewlett-Packard
**Dishwashers:** General Electric
**Distributed data base management technology:** Tandem
**Ditch Witch Trenchers:** Charles Machine Works

*continued*

Source: Partial list from Christopher Knowlton, "What America Makes Best," *FORTUNE*, March 28, 1988, 40–52. © 1988 Time Inc.

**Managerial Application** *continued*

**Drugs:** Squibb, Merck (Capoten and Vasotec)

**Hand-held cordless vacuums:** Black and Decker

**Electrodeposition primers:** PPG Industries

**Electrohydraulic servo valves:** Moog

**F-16 jet fighters:** General Dynamics

**Fast-food hamburgers:** McDonalds

**Financial, engineering, and scientific hand-held calculators:** Hewlett-Packard

**501 jeans:** Levi Strauss

**Fibers:** Du Pont

**Flashlights:** Mag Instrument

**Flutes:** Wm. S. Haynes

**FM two-way radios:** Motorola

**Frequency and time interval analyzers:** Hewlett-Packard

**Fur coats:** Peter Dion, Goldin-Feldman, Ben Kahn, Maximilian, Louis Milona

**Glass fiber for communications:** Corning Glass Works

**Gore-Tex waterproof breathable fabric:** W. L. Gore

**Handbags:** Coach Leatherware

**Hay and forage equipment:** Ford New Holland

**Heating controls:** Honeywell

**Heavy earth-moving equipment:** Caterpillar

**Ice cream and sherbet:** New York Fruit Ice

**Industrial/commercial floor sweepers, scrubbers:** Tennant

**Instant camera films:** Polaroid

**Integrated voice and data communications systems (T–1 multiplexers):** Network Equipment Technologies

**Intelsat VI satellites:** Hughes Aircraft

**Ion chromatographs:** Dionex

**Jet aircraft: 747 family of planes:** Boeing

**Jet engines:** General Electric

**Kevlar fiber:** DuPont

**Loader/backhoe:** Case IH

**Locomotives:** General Electric

**Longwall mining systems:** Joy Technologies

**Lycra spandex fiber:** Du Pont

**Magnetic resonance imaging scanners:** General Electric

**Marlboro cigarettes:** Philip Morris

**Mass spectrometers:** Finnigan

**Men's ready-to-wear suits:** Oxford Clothes

**Micro-precision machine and measuring tools:** Moore Special Tool

**Microprocessors:** (Motorola 68000 family, Intel 80X86 family) Motorola, Intel

**Microwaveable food in shelf-stable packaging: Impromptu, Top Shelf:** General Foods, Geo. A. Hormel, Continental Can

**Microwave ovens:** Litton Industries

**Minicomputers:** Digital Equipment, Hewlett-Packard, IBM

**Minisupercomputers:** Alliant Computer Systems, Convex Computer

**Multimeters:** Hewlett-Packard, John Fluke Mfg.

**Offshore drilling equipment:** Cameron Iron Works

**Oscilloscopes:** Tektronix

**Pacemakers:** Medtronic

**Paper towels:** Procter & Gamble, Scott Paper

**Personal computer applications software:** Lotus Development, Microsoft, WordPerfect

**Personal computers:** Apple Computer

**Pianos:** Steinway & Sons

**Post-it note pads:** 3M

**Power boats:** Cigarette Racing Team, Donzi Marine

**Pressure transmitters for industrial process plants:** Rosemount

*continued*

---

**Managerial Application** *continued*

**Row-crop planters:** Case IH
**Scotch S-VHS videotape:** 3M
**Scotchcal drag reduction tape:** 3M
**Sheet and strip stainless steel:** Allegheny
  Ludlum
**Soft drinks:** Coca-Cola
**Stationery:** Crane
**Stereo loudspeakers:** International Jensen,
  Allison Acoustics, Infinity Systems
**Sunglass lenses:** Corning Glass Works
**Supercomputers:** Cray Research
**Symbion J–7 and Thoratec artificial hearts:**
  Symbion, Thoratec Medical

**Tampax:** Tambrands
**Technical work stations:** Apollo, Silicon
  Graphics, Sun
**Teflon:** Du Pont
**Telephone sets:** AT&T
**Thermos vacuum containers:** Halsy Taylor/
  Thermos
**Thin-film hard disks:** Komag, Seagate
  Technology
**Tillage equipment:** Krause Plow
**Tractors, 100 hp and over:** Deere
**Washing machines:** Maytag, Whirlpool.

---

market structures that can be described as monopolistically competitive are much more common than pure competition or monopoly.

Despite the obvious attraction of concentration data as a useful source of information on the number and size distribution of current competitors, it is prudent to remain cautious in their use and interpretation. Four specific limitations are most important in terms of both business and public policy. By not recognizing these limitations, one might make incorrect judgments concerning market structure when relying on concentration ratio information.

A first serious limitation of concentration data relates to their coverage. Concentration data ignore domestic sales by foreign competitors (imports) as well as exports by domestic firms. Only data on domestic sales from *domestic production*, not total domestic sales, are reported. This means, for example, that if foreign car manufacturers have a market share of 25 percent, the four leading domestic car manufacturers account for 69 percent (= 92 percent of 75 percent) of total U.S. foreign plus domestic car sales, rather than the 92 percent as Table 12.3 suggests. Therefore, in industries in which import competition is important, concentration ratios significantly overstate the relative importance of leading domestic firms. Furthermore, although concentration is evidently falling in many sectors, it is rising in several industries in which increasing foreign competition has been responsible for the liquidation or merger of many smaller domestic firms with older, less efficient production facilities. Despite reduced numbers of domestic firms and consequent rises in concentration, the increase in foreign competition may actually be making industries such as apparel and fabricated metal products more efficient and more competitive rather than less so. The effect of foreign competition is important in many industries, but it is particularly so in manufacturing industries such as apparel, steel, automobiles, television sets, cameras, copiers, and motorcycles.

A second limitation of concentration data is that they are *national totals* whereas a relevant economic market may be national, regional, or local in scope. If high transportation costs or other product characteristics keep markets regional or local rather than national in scope, concentration ratios can significantly understate the relative importance of leading firms. For example, the leading firm in many metropolitan newspaper markets often accounts for 90 percent or more of total market advertising and subscription revenues. Thus, a national $CR_4$ level for newspapers of 22 percent in 1982 significantly understates local market power in that industry. Whereas national concentration ratios in the 20-percent range usually suggest a highly competitive market structure, the local or regional character of some markets can make national concentration figures meaningless. Other examples of products with local or regional rather than national markets include milk, bread and bakery products, commercial printing, and ready-mix concrete.

Another problem relates to the fact that concentration data provide an imperfect view of market structure by including only firms that are *currently active* in a particular industry. Recall that an economic market includes all firms willing and able to sell an identifiable product. Besides firms currently active in an industry, this includes those that can be regarded as likely potential entrants. Often the mere presence of one or more potential entrants constitutes a sufficient threat to force competitive market behavior in industries with only a handful of established competitors. Major retailers such as K mart and Sears, for example, use their positions as potential entrants into manufacturing to obtain attractive prices on a wide range of private-label merchandise such as clothing, lawn mowers, washing machines, and so on.

Finally, considering concentration data in isolation may result in misleading conclusions regarding the vigor of competition in an industry because the degree of competitiveness appears in more than one dimension. Concentration ratios measure only one element of market structure; other elements include the market shares of individual firms, barriers to entry or exit, vertical integration, and so on. Under certain circumstances, even a very few large competitors can compete vigorously. Thus, even though concentration ratios are helpful indicators of the relative importance of leading firms and perhaps the potential for market power, it must be remembered that a high level of concentration does not necessarily imply a lack of competition. In some instances, *competition among the few can be vigorous*. In addition to considering the number and size distribution of competitors as measured by concentration, firms must judge the competitive environment in light of foreign competition, transportation costs, regional product differences, likely potential entrants, advertising, customer loyalty, research and development, demand growth, and economies of scale in production, among other factors, to make accurate pricing and output decisions. All of these features of markets constitute important elements of market structure.

# COMPETITIVE STRATEGY IN IMPERFECTLY COMPETITIVE MARKETS

As was suggested in our discussion of perfectly competitive and monopoly markets, identifying the market structure and profit potential of any given industry is difficult. Product characteristics, the local or regional nature of the market, the time necessary for reactions by established or new competitors, the pace of innovation, unanticipated changes in government regulation and tax policy, and a host of additional considerations can all play important roles in defining the method and scope of competition. It is always helpful to consider the number of competitors, degree of product differentiation, level of information available in the marketplace, and conditions of entry when attempting to define market structure, but these data will seldom be definitive. Conditions of entry and exit are both subtle and dynamic, as is the role of unseen potential entrants, and this contributes to the difficulty of correctly assessing the profit potential of a current or prospective line of business.

Table 12.4 summarizes the major characteristics typical of the imperfectly competitive monopolistic competition and oligopoly market structures. To develop an effective competitive strategy, it is necessary to assess the degree to which the characteristics of an individual market embody elements of each of these market structures. Although the probability of successful entry is higher in monopolistically competitive markets, only the difficult-to-enter oligopolistic markets (like monopolistic markets) hold the potential for meaningful above-normal returns in the long run.

Firms in imperfectly competitive markets can earn economic profits (above-normal rates of return) only to the extent that they impart a valuable degree of uniqueness to their goods or services. Success, measured in terms of above-normal rates of return, requires a comparative advantage in production, distribution, or marketing that cannot easily be copied by others. Such success is difficult to achieve and often rather fleeting.

Wendy's "Where's the Beef?" advertising campaign during the early 1980s is an interesting case in point. Like other highly successful and innovative advertising campaigns, the Wendy's promotion both captured the imagination of consumers and caught competitors by surprise. Sales surged as consumers became more aware of the larger amount of meat in Wendy's hamburgers. However, this success was short-lived, as a subsequent lottery-based promotion by industry leader McDonalds caught consumers' interest. The risks of advertising as an effective form of nonprice competition in the fast food industry became even more readily

■ Table 12.4

## Summary of Monopolistic Competition and Oligopoly (Oligopsony) Market-Structure Characteristics

| | Monopolistic Competition | Oligopoly |
|---|---|---|
| *Number of actual or potential competitors* | Many sellers | Few sellers whose decisions are directly related to those of competitors |
| *Product differentiation* | Consumers perceive differences among the products of various competitors | High or low, depending on entry and exit conditions |
| *Information* | Low-cost information on price and product quality | Restricted access to price and product-quality information; cost and other data is often proprietary |
| *Conditions of entry and exit* | Easy entry and exit | High entry or exit barriers because of economies of scale, capital requirements, advertising, research and development costs, or other factors |
| *Profit potential* | Economic (above-normal) profits in short run only; normal profit in long run | Potential for economic (above-normal) profits in both short and long run |
| *Examples* | Clothing, consumer financial services, professional services, restaurants | Automobiles, bottled and canned soft drinks, investment banking, long-distance telephone service, pharmaceuticals |

apparent following the well-documented failure of Burger King's "Herb" (only a nerd wouldn't eat at Burger King) promotion. Burger King not only lost the millions of dollars it spent on an obviously ineffective advertising campaign, it also lost valuable market share to rivals with more effective advertising.

This is not to suggest that advertising and other nonprice methods of competition have not been used to great advantage by many successful firms in imperfectly competitive markets. In fact, these techniques are often the primary factor in developing a strong basis for product differentiation in the minds of consumers.

Finally, it is important to recognize that the potential for above-normal rates of return is a powerful inducement to the entry of new competitors and to the rapid growth of nonleading firms. Imitation may be the sincerest form of flattery, but it is a most effective enemy of above-normal rates of return. "Regression to the mean" is the rule rather than the exception for trends in corporate profit rates over time. During recent years, after-tax rates of return on corporate capital investment have usually been in the range of 10 to 12 percent per year. Very rarely have individual companies earned in excess of 15 to 20 percent regularly for more than a decade, and returns this high are unheard of for an entire industry with several competitors. Therefore, it seems reasonable to conclude that both price and nonprice methods of competition are often vigorous, even in imperfectly competitive industries.

Case 12.1

# Competitive Strategy at
# Columbia Drugstores, Inc.

Columbia Drugstores, Inc., based in Seattle, Washington, operates a chain of 30 drugstores in the Pacific Northwest. During recent years, Raymond Carlton, founder and president of Columbia, has become increasingly concerned with the long-run implications of competition from a new type of competitor, the so-called "hypermarket."

Long popular in France, the hypermarket is a relatively new marketing concept in the United States. Often covering more than 200,000 square feet of display space, hypermarkets allow shoppers to buy everything from groceries to prescription drugs to oil changes or haircuts. Relying on huge volume spurred by deeply discounted prices, hypermarkets have proved to be very popular with cost-conscious consumers. For example, Wal-Mart, Inc. opened a hypermarket in Garland, Texas (a Dallas suburb) in December 1987 and drew huge crowds of 60,000 customers per week during the first months of operation.

Even if this level of consumer acceptance proves to be relatively short-lived, a costly loss in walk-in traffic for area drug and grocery stores can occur. Because Columbia, like many regional drug chains, depends on such traffic for its highly profitable impulse-buying business, a serious decline in profitability can immediately follow the opening of a hypermarket in an area. Moreover, once shoppers change their regular buying habits, drugstores need to run expensive advertising campaigns to reestablish lost customer loyalty.

Columbia is especially vulnerable to hypermarket competition since all of its stores are currently located in major metropolitan areas. In fact, the effects of hypermarket competition are already being felt in eight regional markets, where hypermarkets have located within five miles of company outlets. Given the high level of success enjoyed by hypermarkets in other parts of the country, Columbia believes that in only a short time it will face a direct challenge in many, if not all, of its current markets. To devise an effective competitive strategy, Columbia must first assess the profit implications of hypermarket competition and then consider whether or not a shift in marketing strategy seems in order. For example, Columbia might shift its mix of products away from those on which it has a distinct pricing disadvantage, or it might shift its plans for expansion to smaller markets, where the hypermarket concept would prove infeasible.

To assess the effects of hypermarket competition on current profitability, Columbia asked management consultant Christine Hauschel to conduct a statistical analysis of the company's profitability in its various markets. To net out size-related influences, profitability was measured by Columbia's gross profit margin, or earnings before interest and taxes divided by sales. Columbia provided proprietary company profit, advertising, and sales data covering the last year for all 30 outlets, along with public trade association and Census Bureau data concerning the number and relative size distribution of competitors in each market, among other market characteristics.

As a first step in her study, Hauschel decided to conduct a regression-based analysis of the various factors thought to affect Columbia's profitability. First among these was the relative size of leading competitors in the relevant market, measured at the Standard Metropolitan Statistical Area (SMSA) level. Columbia's market share, $MS$, in each market area was expected to have a positive effect on profitability given the pricing, marketing, and average-cost advantages that accompany large relative size. The market concentration ratio, $CR$, measured as the combined market share of the four largest competitors in any given market, was expected to have a negative effect on Columbia's profitability given the stiff competition from large, well-financed rivals. Of course, the expected negative effect of high concentration on Columbia profitability contrasts with the positive influence of high concentration on industry profits that is sometimes observed.

Both capital intensity, $K/S$, measured by the ratio of the book value of assets to sales, and advertising intensity, $A/S$, measured by the advertising-to-sales ratio, were expected to exert positive influences on profitability. Given that profitability was measured by Columbia's gross profit margin, the coefficient on capital intensity measured Columbia's return on tangible investment. Similarly, the coefficient on the advertising variable measured the profit effects of advertising. Growth, $GR$, measured by the geometric mean rate of change in total disposable income in each market, was expected to have a positive influence on Columbia's profitability, since some disequilibrium in industry demand and supply conditions is often observed in rapidly growing areas.

Finally, to gauge the profit implications of hypermarket competition, Hauschel used a "dummy" (or binary) variable where $H = 1$ in each market in which Columbia faced hypermarket competition, and $H = 0$ otherwise. The coefficient on this variable measured the average profit-rate effect of hypermarket competition. Given the vigorous nature of hypermarket price competition, Hauschel expected the hypermarket coefficient to be both negative and statistically significant, indicating a profit-limiting influence. The Columbia profit-margin data and

■ Table 12.5

## Profit-Margin and Market-Structure Data for Columbia Drug Stores, Inc.

| Store No. | Profit Margin | Market Share | Concen- tration | Capital Intensity | Adver- tising | Growth | Hypermarket ($H=1$ if hyper- market present) |
|---|---|---|---|---|---|---|---|
| 1 | 15.0 | 25.0 | 75.0 | 10.0 | 10.0 | 7.5 | 0 |
| 2 | 10.0 | 20.0 | 60.0 | 7.5 | 10.0 | 2.5 | 1 |
| 3 | 15.0 | 40.0 | 70.0 | 7.5 | 10.0 | 5.0 | 0 |
| 4 | 15.0 | 30.0 | 75.0 | 15.0 | 12.5 | 5.0 | 0 |
| 5 | 15.0 | 50.0 | 75.0 | 10.0 | 12.5 | 0.0 | 0 |
| 6 | 20.0 | 50.0 | 70.0 | 10.0 | 12.5 | 7.5 | 1 |
| 7 | 15.0 | 50.0 | 70.0 | 7.5 | 10.0 | 0.0 | 1 |
| 8 | 25.0 | 40.0 | 60.0 | 12.5 | 15.0 | 5.0 | 0 |
| 9 | 20.0 | 10.0 | 40.0 | 10.0 | 12.5 | 5.0 | 0 |
| 10 | 10.0 | 30.0 | 60.0 | 10.0 | 12.5 | 0.0 | 0 |
| 11 | 15.0 | 20.0 | 60.0 | 12.5 | 12.5 | 7.5 | 1 |
| 12 | 10.0 | 30.0 | 75.0 | 12.5 | 10.0 | 2.5 | 0 |
| 13 | 15.0 | 50.0 | 75.0 | 7.5 | 10.0 | 5.0 | 0 |
| 14 | 10.0 | 20.0 | 75.0 | 7.5 | 12.5 | 2.5 | 0 |
| 15 | 10.0 | 10.0 | 50.0 | 7.5 | 10.0 | 2.5 | 0 |
| 16 | 20.0 | 30.0 | 60.0 | 15.0 | 12.5 | 2.5 | 0 |
| 17 | 15.0 | 30.0 | 50.0 | 7.5 | 12.5 | 5.0 | 1 |
| 18 | 20.0 | 40.0 | 70.0 | 7.5 | 12.5 | 5.0 | 0 |
| 19 | 10.0 | 10.0 | 60.0 | 12.5 | 10.0 | 2.5 | 0 |
| 20 | 15.0 | 20.0 | 70.0 | 5.0 | 12.5 | 7.5 | 0 |
| 21 | 20.0 | 20.0 | 40.0 | 7.5 | 10.0 | 7.5 | 0 |
| 22 | 15.0 | 10.0 | 50.0 | 15.0 | 10.0 | 5.0 | 1 |
| 23 | 15.0 | 40.0 | 70.0 | 7.5 | 12.5 | 5.0 | 1 |
| 24 | 10.0 | 30.0 | 50.0 | 5.0 | 7.5 | 0.0 | 0 |
| 25 | 20.0 | 40.0 | 70.0 | 15.0 | 12.5 | 5.0 | 0 |
| 26 | 15.0 | 40.0 | 70.0 | 12.5 | 10.0 | 5.0 | 1 |
| 27 | 10.0 | 20.0 | 75.0 | 7.5 | 10.5 | 2.5 | 0 |
| 28 | 15.0 | 10.0 | 60.0 | 12.5 | 12.5 | 5.0 | 0 |
| 29 | 10.0 | 30.0 | 75.0 | 5.0 | 7.5 | 2.5 | 0 |
| 30 | 10.0 | 20.0 | 75.0 | 12.5 | 12.5 | 0.0 | 0 |

related information used in Hauschel's statistical analysis are given in Table 12.5.

Regression model estimates for the determinants of Columbia's profitability are shown in Table 12.6. The coefficient of determination ($R^2$) of 0.84 means that 84 percent of the total variation in Columbia's profit-rate variability is explained by the regression model. This is a relatively high level of explanation for a cross-section study such as this, suggesting that the model will provide useful insight concerning the determinants of profitability. The intercept coefficient of 7.846 has no economic meaning since it lies far outside the relevant range of observed data. The

■ Table 12.6

# Determinants of Profitability for Columbia Drug Stores, Inc.

| Variable Name | Coefficient (1) | Standard Error of Coefficient (2) | t-Statistic (3) = (1) ÷ (2) |
|---|---|---|---|
| Intercept | 7.846 | 3.154 | 2.49 |
| Market share | 0.214 | 0.033 | 6.50 |
| Concentration | −0.203 | 0.038 | −5.30 |
| Capital intensity | 0.289 | 0.123 | 2.35 |
| Advertising | 0.722 | 0.233 | 3.09 |
| Growth | 0.842 | 0.152 | 5.56 |
| Hypermarket | −2.102 | 0.828 | −2.54 |

Coefficient of determination $= R^2 = 0.84$
Standard error of the estimate $=$ S.E.E. $= 1.872$ percent

0.214 coefficient for the market-share variable means that, on average, a 1-percent (unit) rise in Columbia's market share will lead to a 0.214-percent (unit) rise in Columbia's profit margin. Similarly, as expected, Columbia's profit margin is positively related to capital intensity, advertising intensity, and the rate of growth in the market area. Conversely, high concentration has the expected limiting influence. Because of the effects of leading-firm rivalry, a 1-percent rise in industry concentration will lead to a 0.203-percent decrease in Columbia's profit margin. This means that relatively large firms compete effectively with Columbia.

Most importantly, the regression model indicates that hypermarket competition in one of Columbia's market areas reduces Columbia's profit margin on average by 2.102 percent. Given that Columbia's rate of return on sales routinely falls in the 10- to 15-percent range, the profit-limiting effect of hypermarket competition is substantial. Looking more closely at the data, we also note that Columbia faces hypermarket competition in only one of the seven lucrative markets in which the company earns a 20- to 25-percent rate of return on sales. Both observations suggest that current and potential hypermarket competition constitutes a considerable threat to the company and one that must be addressed in an effective competitive strategy.

Of course, development of an effective competitive strategy to combat the influence of hypermarkets would involve the careful consideration of a wide range of factors related to Columbia's business. It might prove fruitful to begin this analysis by more carefully considering market characteristics for Store No. 6, the one Columbia outlet able to earn a substantial 20-percent profit margin despite hypermarket competition. For example, this analysis might suggest that Columbia, like Store No. 6, should specialize in service (e.g., prescription drug delivery) or in a slightly different mix of merchandise. On the other hand, perhaps Columbia should follow the example set by Wal-Mart in its early development and focus its plans for expansion on small- to medium-size markets. In the meantime, Columbia's still-profitable stores in major metropolitan areas could help fund future growth.

Although obviously only a first step, a regression-based study of market structure such as that described here can provide a very useful beginning to the development of an effective competitive strategy.

# SUMMARY

In this chapter, we have extended our study of market structure to consider monopolistic competition and oligopoly. These market-structure models describe the behavior of competitors in imperfectly competitive markets. They fall along the continuum between perfectly competitive and monopoly markets. As such, they help describe competitor behavior in broad sectors of our economy in which both price competition and a wide variety of methods of nonprice competition are observed.

*Monopolistic competition* describes a market structure composed of many sellers offering similar but not identical products. Because consumers perceive differences among the competitors' products, each firm has some control over the price it charges. Low-cost information on price and product quality, combined with easy entry and exit, leads to vigorous price and nonprice competition. Only normal profits are possible in long-run equilibrium. As a result, price (average revenue) and average cost are equal in equilibrium, as are marginal revenue and marginal cost. Typically, this equilibrium will occur at an average cost level higher than minimum long-run average costs, the perfectly competitive equilibrium. This differential can be viewed as the value that consumers place on the wide variety of products offered by the monopolistically competitive industry.

If only a few large firms are active in a given market, each of them will have a sizable market share, and the price/output decisions of any one competitor will have a direct, measurable influence on its rivals. This close relation is usually recognized in markets with a few leading firms, and it is reflected in ongoing decision making. *Oligopoly* is a market structure characterized by few competitors in which the decisions of each firm depend to some extent on the likely reactions of rivals. Restricted access to information on cost and product quality—combined with high to very high barriers to entry, mobility, or exit—give rise to the potential for economic profits in the long run. Product differentiation can be high (as in investment banking and cigarettes) or low (as in steel and aluminum), depending on entry, mobility, and exit conditions.

Profit-maximizing decision rules are relatively simple and straightforward in the cases of perfect competition, monopolistic competition, and monopoly. Under oligopoly, however, the rules become much more complex, almost to the point of being indeterminate. This follows from the fact that institutional considerations play an important role in defining the methods, scope, and intensity of competition in many oligopolistic markets. Since industry profits can be enhanced through cooperation by competitors in price/output decision making, interdependent decision making by individual firms is sometimes observed. *Cartels, price leadership,* and "sticky" prices as predicted by the *kinked demand curve model* have all been observed in various oligopolistic market settings over time.

More than other market structures, oligopoly markets commonly involve advertising and other nonprice methods of competition. The optimal level of advertising, or of any other type of expenditure on nonprice competition, is reached when the marginal benefit realized is just offset by the marginal cost incurred.

Knowledge about market structure is necessary for both managerial and public-policy decisions. Industry trade associations regularly publish valuable information about trends in industry growth, wage rates, research and development expenditures, and other factors. Public resources are also devoted to the regular collection and publication of data concerning the number and size distribution of competitors, market size, growth, capital intensity, investment, and so on. These public data are regularly published in *economic census* reports that offer a valuable guide to changes in the level of *industry concentration* and other important elements of the competitive environment. Industry concentration ratios measure the share of industry output that is concentrated among small groups of leading firms. High levels of industry concentration can give rise to collusion and a lessening in the vigor of competition, but this is not always the case. Competition among the few can be vigorous.

## Questions

12.1  Describe the monopolistically competitive market structure, and provide some examples.

12.2  Describe the oligopolistic market structure, and provide some examples.

12.3  Explain the process through which economic profits are eliminated in a monopolistically competitive industry versus a perfectly competitive industry.

12.4  Would you expect the demand curve for a firm in a monopolistically competitive industry to be more or less elastic after economic profits have been eliminated?

12.5  "One might expect firms in a monopolistically competitive industry to experience greater swings in the price of their products over the business cycle than those in an oligopolistic industry. However, fluctuations in profits will not necessarily follow the same pattern." Discuss this statement.

12.6　Will revenue-maximizing firms have short-run profits as large as or larger than profit-maximizing firms? If so, when? If not, why not?

12.7　Is short-run revenue maximization necessarily inconsistent with the more traditional long-run profit-maximizing model of firm behavior? Why, or why not?

12.8　Why is the four-firm concentration ratio only an imperfect measure of market power?

12.9　The statement "you get what you pay for" reflects the common perception that high prices indicate high product quality, and low prices indicate low quality. Irrespective of market-structure considerations, is this statement always correct?

12.10　"Economic profits will result whenever only a few large competitors are active in a given market." Discuss this statement.

## Problems

12.1　Indicate whether each of the following statements is *true* or *false* and why.

A. Equilibrium in monopolistically competitive markets requires that firms be operating at the minimum point on the long-run average cost curve.

B. A high ratio of distribution cost to total cost tends to increase competition by widening the geographic area over which any individual producer can compete.

C. The price elasticity of demand will tend to fall as new competitors introduce substitute products.

D. An efficiently functioning cartel would achieve the monopoly price/output combination.

E. An increase in product differentiation will tend to increase the slope of firm demand curves.

12.2　Would the following factors *increase* or *decrease* the ability of domestic auto manufacturers to raise prices and profit margins? Why?

A. Decreased import quotas

B. Elimination of uniform emission standards

C. Increased automobile price advertising

D. Increased import tariffs (taxes)

E. A rising value of the dollar, which has the effect of lowering import car prices

12.3　Soft Lens, Inc., was an early innovator in the market for extended-wear soft contact lenses. However, the company's market share has quickly eroded during the past year as some important basic patents expired. More entry and downward pressure on both prices and profits is expected during the coming year.

A. Use Soft Lens's price, output, and total-cost data to complete the following table:

| Price | Output per Week (000) | Total Revenue ($000) | Marginal Revenue ($000) | Total Cost ($000) | Marginal Cost ($000) | Average Cost ($) |
|-------|------|------|------|------|------|------|
| $20 | 0 | | | $ 3 | | |
| 19 | 1 | | | 20 | | |
| 18 | 2 | | | 36 | | |
| 17 | 3 | | | 51 | | |
| 16 | 4 | | | 65 | | |
| 15 | 5 | | | 75 | | |
| 14 | 6 | | | 84 | | |
| 13 | 7 | | | 105 | | |

B. If cost conditions remain constant, what is the monopolistically competitive high-price/low-output long-run equilibrium? (*Note:* Assume a parallel shift in the firm's demand curve.)

C. What is the monopolistically competitive low-price/high-output equilibrium? (*Note:* This is also the perfectly competitive equilibrium.)

12.4 Orthopedic Devices, Inc., (ODI) is a Toronto-based manufacturer of medical instruments used in the repair of disorders of the skeletal system and associated motor organs. During recent years, its unique R2-D2 patient monitoring system has successfully exploited a small but profitable niche in the market. R2-D2's monopoly position in this market niche is now threatened by a new competitor's announcement of the C3-PO, a monitoring device with capabilities similar to those of the R2-D2 system.

A. Complete the following table based on R2-D2's price, output, and costs per month:

| Output | Price | Total Revenue | Marginal Revenue | Total Cost | Marginal Cost |
|--------|-------|------|------|------|------|
| 1 | $ 90,000 | | | $ 80,000 | |
| 2 | 80,000 | | | 150,000 | |
| 3 | 70,000 | | | 210,000 | |
| 4 | 60,000 | | | 240,000 | |
| 5 | 50,000 | | | 275,000 | |

B. While ODI still enjoys a monopoly position, what are R2-D2's output, price, and profit at the profit-maximizing activity level?

C. What are the output, price, and profit for the R2-D2 system if a monopolistically competitive equilibrium evolves in this market following the successful introduction of the C3-PO? (Assume similar cost conditions for each firm.)

12.5  Gray Computer, Inc., located in Colorado Springs, Colorado, is a privately held producer of high-speed electronic computers with immense storage capacity and computing capability. Although Gray's market is restricted to industrial users and a few large government agencies (e.g., Department of Health, NASA, National Weather Service, etc.), the company has profitably exploited its market niche.

Glen Gray, founder and research director, has recently announced his retirement, the timing of which will unfortunately coincide with the expiration of several patents covering key aspects of the Gray computer. Your company, a potential entrant into the market for supercomputers, has asked you to evaluate the short- and long-run potential of this market. Based on data gathered from your company's engineering department, user surveys, trade associations, and other sources, the following market-demand and cost information has been developed:

$$P = \$54 - \$1.5Q,$$
$$TC = \$200 + \$6Q + \$0.5Q^2,$$

where $P$ is price (in millions of dollars); $TC$ is total labor, materials, and capital costs (in millions of dollars); and $Q$ is units (number of supercomputers).

A. Assume that these demand and cost data are descriptive of Gray's historical experience. Calculate output, price, and economic profits earned by the Gray Company as a monopolist. What is the point price elasticity of demand at this output level?

B. Calculate the range within which a long-run equilibrium price/output combination would be found for individual firms if entry eliminated Gray's economic profits. (Note: Assume that the cost function is unchanged and that the high-price/low-output solution results from a parallel shift in the demand curve while the low-price/high-output solution results from a competitive equilibrium.)

C. Assume that the point price elasticity of demand calculated in Part A is a good estimate of the relevant arc price elasticity. What is the potential overall market size for supercomputers?

D. If no other near-term entrants are anticipated, should your company enter the market for supercomputers? Why or why not?

12.6  An oil cartel has been formed by the three leading oil producers. Total production costs at various levels of oil production per day are as follows:

| Barrels per Day (millions) | Total Cost (millions of $) | | |
|---|---|---|---|
| | Arabco (*A*) | Britannia (*B*) | Cinco (*C*) |
| 0 | $ 35 | $ 50 | $ 5 |
| 1 | 40 | 75 | 25 |
| 2 | 50 | 105 | 40 |
| 3 | 65 | 140 | 65 |
| 4 | 90 | 180 | 95 |
| 5 | 125 | 225 | 130 |

A. Construct a table showing the marginal cost of production per firm.

B. From the data in Part A, determine an optimal allocation of output and maximum profits if the cartel sets $Q = 8$ and $P = \$35$.

C. Is there an incentive for individual members to cheat by expanding output when the cartel sets $Q = 8$ and $P = \$35$?

12.7 The Hand Tool Manufacturing Industry Trade Association recently published the following estimates of demand and supply relations for hammers:

$$Q_D = 60,000 - 10,000P, \quad \text{(Demand)}$$
$$Q_S = 20,000P. \quad \text{(Supply)}$$

A. Calculate the perfectly competitive industry equilibrium price/output combination.

B. Now assume that the industry output is organized into a cartel. Calculate the industry price/output combination that will maximize profits for cartel members.

C. Compare your answers to Parts A and B. Calculate the price/output effects of the cartel.

12.8 Safety Service Products (SSP) faces the following segmented demand and marginal revenue curves for its new infant safety seat:

1. Over the range of 0 to 10,000 units of output,

$$P_1 = \$60 - Q.$$

2. When output exceeds 10,000 units,

$$P_2 = \$80 - \$3Q.$$

The company's total cost function is as follows:

$$TC = \$100 + \$20Q + \$0.5Q^2,$$

where $P$ is price (in dollars), $Q$ is output (in thousands), and $TC$ is total cost (in thousands of dollars).

A. Graph the demand, marginal revenue, and marginal cost curves.
B. How would you describe the market structure of the industry in which SSP operates? Explain why the demand curve takes the shape indicated previously.
C. Calculate price, output, and profits at the profit-maximizing activity level.
D. How much could marginal costs rise before the optimal price would increase? How much could they fall before the optimal price would decrease?

12.9 Anaheim Industries, Inc., and Binghampton Electronics, Ltd., are the only suppliers to the U.S. Weather Service of an important electronic instrument. The Weather Service has established a fixed-price procurement policy, however, so $P = MR$ in this market. Total cost relations for each firm are as follows:

$$TC_A = \$7,000 + \$250Q_A + \$0.5Q_A^2 \quad \text{(Anaheim)}$$

$$TC_B = \$8,000 + \$200Q_B + \$1Q_B^2 \quad \text{(Binghampton)}$$

where $Q$ is output in units, and $MC > AVC$ for each firm.
A. What is the minimum price necessary for each firm to supply output?
B. Determine the supply curve for each firm.
C. Based on the assumption that $P = P_A = P_B$, determine industry supply curves when $P < \$200$, $\$200 < P < \$250$, and $P > \$250$.

12.10 Louisville Communications, Inc., offers 24-hour telephone answering service for individuals and small businesses in southeastern states. Louisville is a dominant, price-leading firm in many of its markets. Recently, Memphis Answering Service, Inc., and Nashville Recording, Ltd., have begun to offer services with the same essential characteristics as Louisville's service. Total cost functions for Memphis (M) and Nashville (N) services are as follows:

$$TC_M = \$75,000 - \$7Q_M + \$0.0025Q_M^2,$$

$$TC_N = \$50,000 + \$3Q_N + \$0.0025Q_N^2.$$

Louisville's total cost function is:

$$TC_L = \$300,000 + \$5Q_L + \$0.0002Q_L^2.$$

The industry demand curve for telephone answering service is:

$$Q = 500,800 - 19,600P.$$

Assume throughout the problem that the Memphis and Nashville services are perfect substitutes for Louisville's service.
A. Determine the supply curves for the Memphis and Nashville services, assuming that the firms operate as price takers.
B. What is the demand curve faced by Louisville?

    C. Calculate Louisville's profit-maximizing price and output levels. (*Hint:* Louisville's total revenue function is $TR_L = \$25Q_L - \$0.00005Q_L^2$).

    D. Calculate profit-maximizing output levels for the Memphis and Nashville services.

    E. Is the market for services from these three firms in short-run equilibrium?

## Selected References

Chalk, Andrew J. "Competition in the Brewing Industry: Does Further Concentration Imply Collusion?" *Managerial and Decision Economics* 9 (March 1988): 49–58.

Clarke, Richard N. "SICs as Delineators of Economic Markets." *Journal of Business* 62 (January 1989): 17–31.

Connolly, Robert A., and Mark Hirschey. "R&D, Market Structure and Profits: A Value-Based Approach." *Review of Economics and Statistics* 66 (November 1984): 682–686.

Connolly, Robert A., and Mark Hirschey. "Concentration and Profits: A Test of the Accounting Bias Hypothesis." *Journal of Accounting and Public Policy* 4 (Winter 1988): 313–334.

Day, George S., and Robin Wensley. "Assessing Advantage: A Framework for Diagnosing Competitive Superiority." *Journal of Marketing* 52 (April 1988): 1–20.

Domowitz, Ian, R. Glen Hubbard, and Bruce Peterson. "Market Structure and Cyclical Fluctuations in U.S. Manufacturing." *Review of Economics and Statistics* 70 (February 1988): 55–67.

Eckard, E. Woodrow, Jr., "Advertising, Competition and Market Share Instability." *Journal of Business* 60 (October 1987): 539–552.

Gatignon, Hubert, Erin Anderson, and Kristiaan Helsen. "Competitive Reactions to Market Entry: Explaining Interfirm Differences." *Journal of Marketing Research* 26 (February 1989): 44–55.

Gold, Bela. "Forces Tending to Reduce Concentration Levels in U.S. Industries." *Managerial and Decision Economics* 10 (June 1989): 115–120.

Grabowski, Henry G. "An Analysis of U.S. International Competitiveness in Pharmaceuticals." *Managerial and Decision Economics* 10 (Spring 1989): 27–33.

Hamel, Gary, Yves L. Doz, and C. K. Prahalad. "Collaborate with Your Competitors—and Win." *Harvard Business Review* 67 (January–February 1989): 133–139.

Karakaya, Fahri, and Michael J. Stahl. "Barriers to Entry and Market Entry Decisions in Consumer and Industrial Goods Markets." *Journal of Marketing* 53 (April 1989): 80–91.

Kraft, Kornelius. "Market Structure, Firm Characteristics and Innovative Activity." *Journal of Industrial Economics* 37 (March 1989): 329–336.

Lunn, John. "R&D, Concentration and Advertising: A Simultaneous Equations Model." *Managerial and Decision Economics* 10 (June 1989): 101–106.

Lustgarten, Steven, and Stavros Thomadakis. "Mobility Barriers and Tobin's q." *Journal of Business* 60 (October 1987): 519–537.

Margolis, Stephen E. "Monopolistic Competition and Multiproduct Brand Names." *Journal of Business* 62 (April 1989): 199–209.

Powell, Irene. "The Effect of Reductions in Concentration on Income Distribution." *Review of Economics and Statistics* 69 (February 1987): 75–82.

Salamon, Gerald L. "Accounting Rates of Return." *American Economic Review* 75 (June 1985): 495–504.

Schroeter, John R. "Estimating the Degree of Market Power in the Beef Packing Industry." *Review of Economics and Statistics* 70 (February 1988): 158–162.

Scott, John T., and George Pasco. "Beyond Firm and Industry Effects on Profitability in Imperfect Markets." *Review of Economics and Statistics* 68 (May 1986): 284–292.

# Pricing Practices

**markup pricing**

The common practice of setting prices to cover direct costs plus a percentage profit contribution.

hapters 11 and 12 demonstrated that, regardless of the market structure within which the firm operates, pricing for profit maximization requires careful analysis of the relation between marginal cost and marginal revenue. However, research into actual pricing practices indicates that many firms appear to set prices without any explicit analysis of marginal relations. Studies show that most firms use **markup pricing**—setting prices to cover all direct costs plus a percentage markup for profit contribution (overhead costs and profit)—instead of determining the price at which $MR = MC$. How can this apparent conflict between economic theory and observed pricing practices be reconciled?

We believe that if one thoroughly understands the procedures used for actual pricing decisions, there is no real conflict between theory and practice. Indeed, markup pricing practices are the practical means by which firms employ marginal analysis to price a wide variety of goods and services. Flexible markup pricing practices that reflect differences in marginal costs and demand elasticities are an efficient means for operating so that $MR = MC$ for each line of products sold. Similarly, peak and off-peak pricing, price discrimination, and joint product pricing practices are efficient means for operating so that $MR = MC$ for each customer or customer group and product class. In this chapter we examine each of these pricing practices, assess their value, and demonstrate the economic rationale for their use.

## MARKUP PRICING

Surveys of business practice indicate that markup pricing is by far the most widely used pricing method employed by business firms. In the most prevalent approach to markup pricing practice, firms estimate the average variable costs of producing and marketing a product, add a charge for overhead, and then add a percentage markup, or margin, for profits. The charge for indirect costs, or overhead, is usually determined by allocating these costs among the firm's products on the basis of their average variable costs. For example, if a firm's total overhead for a year was projected to be $1.3 million, and the estimated total variable costs of its planned production were $1 million, then overhead would be allocated to products at the rate of 130 percent of variable cost. Thus, if the average variable costs of a product were estimated to be $1, the firm would add a charge of 130 percent of that variable cost, or $1.30, for overhead, obtaining an estimated fully allocated average cost of $2.30. To this figure the firm might add a 30-percent markup for profits, or $0.69, to obtain a price of $2.99 per unit.

## Markup on Cost

**markup on cost**
The difference between price and cost, measured relative to cost, usually expressed as a percentage.

In general, the **markup on cost** or "*cost plus*" formula is given by the expression:

$$\text{Markup on Cost} = \frac{\text{Price} - \text{Cost}}{\text{Cost}}. \qquad \textbf{13.1}$$

**profit margin**
The difference between the price and cost of a product.

The numerator of this expression is called the **profit margin.** In the example cited above, the 30-percent markup on cost is calculated as:

$$\text{Markup on Cost} = \frac{\text{Price} - \text{Cost}}{\text{Cost}}$$

$$= \frac{\$2.99 - \$2.30}{\$2.30}$$

$$= 0.30 \text{ or } 30 \text{ Percent.}$$

Solving Equation 13.1 for price provides the expression that determines price in a cost-plus pricing system:

$$\text{Price} = \text{Cost} (1 + \text{Markup on Cost}). \qquad \textbf{13.2}$$

Continuing with the example developed above, the selling price for the product is found as:

$$\text{Price} = \text{Cost} (1 + \text{Markup on Cost})$$

$$= \$2.30(1.30)$$

$$= \$2.99.$$

## Markup on Price

Profit margins, or markups, are sometimes calculated as a percentage of price instead of cost. This alternative means of expressing profit margins can be illustrated by the **markup-on-price** formula:

**markup on price**
The difference between price and cost, measured relative to price, usually expressed as a percentage.

$$\text{Markup on Price} = \frac{\text{Price} - \text{Cost}}{\text{Price}} \qquad \textbf{13.3}$$

As in the markup-on-cost formula, the numerator of the markup-on-price formula is the profit margin. However, cost has been replaced by price in the denominator.

To convert from one markup formula to the other, simply use the following expressions:

$$\text{Markup on Cost} = \frac{\text{Markup on Price}}{1 - \text{Markup on Price}}, \qquad \textbf{13.4}$$

$$\text{Markup on Price} = \frac{\text{Markup on Cost}}{1 + \text{Markup on Cost}}. \qquad \textbf{13.5}$$

Thus, the 30-percent profit margin based on cost described in the illustration is equivalent to a 23-percent markup on price:

$$\text{Markup on Price} = \frac{0.3}{1 + 0.3} = 0.23.$$

An item with a cost of \$2.30, a 69¢ markup, and a price of \$2.99 has a 30-percent markup on cost and a 23-percent markup on price. This example illustrates the importance of being consistent in the choice of a cost or price basis when comparing markups among products or sellers.

Markup pricing is sometimes criticized as a naïve pricing technique based solely on cost considerations—and the wrong costs at that. The technique's failure to examine demand conditions, coupled with its emphasis on fully allocated accounting costs rather than marginal costs, is said to lead to suboptimal price decisions. Empirical studies, however, reject the view of markup pricing as naïve. Although inappropriate use of markup pricing formulas will lead to suboptimal managerial decisions, successful firms typically employ the method in a way that is entirely consistent with profit maximization. In fact, markup pricing can be viewed as an efficient rule-of-thumb approach to setting optimal prices. Nevertheless, it is important to be aware of both the value and limitations of the markup pricing technique to avoid potential pitfalls in its application.

## The Role of Costs in Markup Pricing

Although a variety of cost concepts are employed in markup pricing, most firms use a standard, or fully allocated, cost concept. Fully allocated costs are determined by first estimating direct costs per unit, then allocating the firm's expected indirect expenses, or overhead, assuming a standard or normal output level. Price is then determined from the resulting standard cost per unit, irrespective of short-term variations in actual unit costs.

The standard cost concept is sometimes based on historical accounting costs, and this can give rise to several problems. First, firms may fail to properly adjust historical cost data to reflect recent or expected price changes for key input factors. Unadjusted historical accounting costs may have little relevance for current decisions. The firm should estimate future costs that will be incurred during the period for which it is setting prices.

Also, accounting costs may not reflect true economic costs. The concept of opportunity costs must be employed for optimal decision making.

**peak**
Period of full capacity usage.

**off-peak**
Period of excess capacity.

The use of fully allocated costs as opposed to incremental costs can also cause errors in some pricing decisions. Fully allocated costs can be appropriate when a firm is operating at full capacity. During **peak** periods, when facilities are fully utilized, expansion would be required to further increase production. Under these conditions, an increase in production is likely to increase all plant, equipment, labor, materials, and other expenditures. Fully allocated costs are relevant for pricing purposes in such a situation. If a firm has excess capacity, as during **off-peak** periods, only those costs that actually rise with production—the incremental costs per unit—should form a basis for setting prices. Successful firms that employ markup pricing typically base prices on fully allocated costs under normal conditions, but offer price discounts or accept lower margins during off-peak periods when substantial excess capacity is available. In this way, prices can accurately reflect the effects of capacity utilization.

In some instances, output produced during off-peak periods can cost dramatically less than output produced during peak periods. When fixed costs represent a substantial share of total production costs, discounts of 30 to 50 percent for output produced during off-peak periods can often be justified on the basis of lower costs.

"Early Bird" or afternoon matinee discounts at movie theaters provide an interesting example. Except for cleaning expenses, which vary according to the number of customers, most of the operating expenses incurred at a typical movie theater are fixed. As a result, the revenue generated by adding customers during off-peak periods can significantly increase the theater's profit contribution. The fact that these off-peak customers often buy regularly priced candy, popcorn, and soda is an added bonus that can justify even lower afternoon ticket prices. Conversely, on Friday and Saturday nights when movie theaters operate at peak capacity, even a small increase in the number of customers would require an expensive expansion of facilities. Therefore, ticket prices during these peak periods reflect fully allocated costs. Similarly, McDonalds, Burger King, and many other fast-food outlets have increased their profitability substantially by introducing breakfast menus. If fixed restaurant expenses are covered by lunch and dinner business, even promotionally priced breakfast items can make a notable contribution to profits.

## The Role of Demand in Markup Pricing

Varying margins among different products sold by firms that use markup pricing methods provide clear evidence that demand analysis does, in fact, play an important role in price determination. Studies indicate that most firms differentiate their markups for different product lines on the basis of competitive pressures reflected in demand elasticities. Even though companies have always been willing to adjust prices or profit margins on specific products as market conditions varied, a high level of flexibility is now commonplace and is often a key element of competitive strategy. For example, both foreign and domestic automobile companies regularly offer rebates or special equipment packages for slow-selling models. Similarly, airlines promote different pricing schedules for various types of business and vacation travel demand. Clearly, the airline and automobile industries are examples of sectors in which competitive conditions require a careful reflection of demand and supply factors in pricing practice. However, efforts to assess cost and revenue relations among products are by no means limited to these industries. In both goods- and service-producing sectors, successful firms demonstrate the ability to quickly adjust prices to different market conditions.

Examining the margins set by a successful regional grocery store chain provides interesting evidence that demand conditions play an important role in cost-plus pricing. Table 13.1 shows the firm's typical markup on cost and markup on price for a variety of products sold in its stores.

■ Table 13.1
## Markups Charged on a Variety of Grocery Items

| Item | Markup on Cost | Markup on Price |
|------|----------------|-----------------|
| Bread–private label | 0–5 % | 0–5 % |
| Bread–brand name | 30–40 | 23–29 |
| Breakfast cereals (dry) | 5–15 | 5–13 |
| Cake mixes | 15–20 | 13–17 |
| Coffee | 0–10 | 0–9 |
| Cold cuts (processed meats) | 20–45 | 17–31 |
| Cookies | 20–30 | 17–23 |
| Delicatessen items | 35–45 | 26–31 |
| Fresh fruit–in season | 40–50 | 29–33 |
| Fresh fruit–out of season | 15–20 | 13–17 |
| Fresh vegetables–in season | 40–50 | 29–33 |
| Fresh vegetables–out of season | 15–20 | 13–17 |
| Ground beef | 0–10 | 0–9 |
| Ice cream | 15–20 | 13–17 |
| Laundry detergent | 5–10 | 5–9 |
| Milk | 0–5 | 0–5 |
| Nonprescription drugs | 35–55 | 26–35 |
| Pastries (cakes, pies, etc.) | 20–30 | 17–23 |
| Pet foods | 15–20 | 13–17 |
| Snack foods | 20–25 | 17–20 |
| Soft drinks | 0–10 | 0–9 |
| Spices | 30–60 | 23–38 |
| Soup | 0–15 | 0–13 |
| Steak | 15–35 | 13–26 |
| Toilet tissue | 10–15 | 9–13 |
| Toothpaste | 15–20 | 13–17 |

## 13.1 **Managerial Application**
Pricing Technology in Supermarkets

The vigorously price-competitive grocery industry is at the forefront of pricing technology. Already more than one-half of the nation's supermarkets use electronic scanners at checkout stations to ring up sale prices for bar-coded items. The scanners represent an important innovation in this price-sensitive industry because they allow a grocery store to avoid the costly item-by-item pricing and repricing that is necessary to keep product prices in line with rapidly changing supply and demand conditions. In addition, scanners allow the industry to employ less skilled, and therefore less costly, labor at the checkout station. Before scanners were introduced, a relatively high level of training and experience was required of checkout employees. With optical scanners,

grocery stores can use relatively unskilled labor and reduce mispricing problems. In some market areas, introduction of optical scanners allowed grocery stores to cut wage bills for checkout employees by 50 percent and more, while checkout speed and accuracy increased dramatically. These labor cost savings are in addition to other important advantages of optical scanners. Scanners integrated with a computerized inventory control system can provide a complete item-by-item sales history that is extremely valuable for market research and inventory control.

The next generation of pricing technology—electronically programmed labeling—is rapidly approaching. Instead of needing to peel outdated labels off shelves, grocery

*continued*

See: Richard Gibson, "Electronic Price Labels Tested in Supermarkets," *The Wall Street Journal*, March 31, 1988, 25.

A field manager with over 20 years' experience in the grocery business provided the authors with useful insight into the firm's pricing practices. He stated that the "price sensitivity" of an item is the primary consideration in setting margins. Staple products like bread, coffee, ground beef, milk, and soup are highly price sensitive and carry relatively low margins. Products with high margins tend to be those for which demand is less price sensitive.

Note the wide range of margins applied to different items. The 0 to 10 percent markup on cost for ground beef, for example, is substantially lower than the 15 to 35 percent margin on steak. Hamburger is a relatively low-priced meat with wide appeal to families, college students, and low-income groups whose price sensitivity is high. On the other

**Managerial Application** *continued*

store employees will soon be able to change prices electronically by plugging a hand-held computer into programmable labels clipped to store shelves or by sending data via an FM transmitter. In either case, the computer sends a price signal to a microchip embedded in the molded plastic, which then displays the new price in one-half inch liquid-crystal numerals. Currently, a clerk can change roughly 600 labels in a nine-hour period. Electronically programmed labeling can cut this time dramatically. Programmable labels will allow grocery stores to quickly cut prices to meet competitor price reductions, to eliminate oversupply of perishable items, or even to offer limited in-store specials. Like shoppers at K mart, grocery store shoppers may soon enjoy temporary specials on limited items for a few minutes during various parts of the day.

Perhaps most importantly, programmable labels lock the prices displayed on store shelves into the checkout scanner, eliminating the most vexing problem associated with the current technology. Currently, pricing errors frequently occur when prices displayed on store shelves differ from those recorded in the checkout station computer. Consumer satisfaction is greatly enhanced when displayed and charged prices match exactly.

From a consumer standpoint, the only major drawback to currently available programmable labels is that they do not provide a continuous view of price and nutritional information. A button must now be pushed in order for such data to be displayed. However, technology in the industry is rapidly changing, and the continuous display problem is sure to be solved in the near future.

The expense of the programmable labeling technology is perhaps its most important drawback from an industry viewpoint. Retrofitting an average store with the new technology currently costs in the neighborhood of $100,000. However, costs are declining and obvious long-run advantages for the merchant and consumer alike dictate that it will soon be widespread in this and related industries.

---

hand, relatively expensive sirloin, T-bone, and porterhouse steaks appeal to higher-income groups with low price sensitivity.

It is also interesting to see how seasonal factors affect the demand for grocery items like fruits and vegetables. When a fruit or vegetable is in season, spoilage and transportation costs are at their lowest levels, and high product quality translates into an enthusiastic consumer response that leads to high margins. Consumers tend to shift away from high-cost/low-quality fresh fruits and vegetables when they are out of season, thereby reducing margins on these items.

In addition to seasonal factors that affect margins over the course of a year, some market forces will affect margins within a given product class. In breakfast cereals, for example, the markup on cost for highly popular corn flakes will average only 5 to 6 percent, with brands offered by Post (General Foods Corporation) and Kellogg's competing with a variety of local store brands. However, Cheerios and Wheaties, both offered only by General Mills, Inc., enjoy a markup on cost of 15 to 20 percent. Thus, the availability of substitutes directly affects the markups on various cereals. Finally, it is interesting to note that among the wide variety of items sold in a typical grocery story, the product class with the highest margin is spices. Apparently, consumer demand for nutmeg, cloves, thyme, bay leaves, and other spices is quite insensitive to price. The manager we interviewed said that in more than 20 years in the grocery business, he could not recall a single store coupon or special offered on spices.

This retail grocery store pricing example provides valuable insight into how markup pricing rules can be used in setting an efficient pricing policy. Although the words "price elasticity" were never used in our discussions, it is clear that this concept plays a key role in the firm's markup pricing decisions. To examine those decisions further, it is necessary to develop a method for determining optimal markups in practical pricing policy.

## Markup Pricing and Profit Maximization

Clearly, demand analysis plays an important role in the markup pricing practices of successful firms. However, we need an answer to the question: How does one determine the optimal markup for products with different demand elasticities? The answer comes from careful consideration of two previously examined relations.

Recall from our analysis of demand in Chapter 4 that there is a direct relation among marginal revenue, price elasticity of demand, and the profit-maximizing price for a product. This relation was expressed in Equation 4.18 as:

$$MR = P\left(1 + \frac{1}{\epsilon_p}\right). \qquad \textbf{13.6}$$

To maximize profit, a firm must operate at the activity level at which marginal revenue equals marginal cost. But since marginal revenue always equals the right-hand side of Equation 13.6, at the profit-maximizing output level we have:

$$P\left(1 + \frac{1}{\epsilon_p}\right) = MC, \qquad \textbf{13.7}$$

or

$$P = MC\left(\frac{1}{1 + \dfrac{1}{\epsilon_p}}\right). \qquad \textbf{13.8}$$

Equation 13.8 provides a formula for the profit-maximizing price for a product in terms of its price elasticity. The equation states that the profit-maximizing price is found by multiplying marginal cost by the term:

$$\left(\frac{1}{1 + \dfrac{1}{\epsilon_p}}\right).$$

To derive the optimal markup-on-cost formula, recall from Equation 13.2 that the price established by a cost-plus method equals cost multiplied by the expression (1 + Markup on Cost). Equation 13.8 implies that marginal cost is the appropriate cost basis for cost-plus pricing and that:

$$MC(1 + \text{Markup on Cost}) = MC\left(\frac{1}{1 + \dfrac{1}{\epsilon_p}}\right).$$

By dividing each side of this expression by *MC* and subtracting 1, we find:

$$\text{Markup on Cost} = \left(\frac{1}{1 + \dfrac{1}{\epsilon_p}}\right) - 1.$$

After simplifying, the optimal (profit maximizing) markup-on-cost formula can be written:

$$\text{Optimal Markup on Cost} = \frac{-1}{\epsilon_p + 1}. \qquad \textbf{13.9}$$

The optimal markup-on-price formula can also be easily determined. Dividing each side of Equation 13.7 by *P* yields the expression:

$$\frac{MC}{P} = \left(1 + \frac{1}{\epsilon_p}\right).$$

Subtracting 1 from each side of this expression and simplifying, we find:

$$\frac{MC - P}{P} = \frac{1}{\epsilon_p}.$$

Then, multiplying each side of this expression by −1 yields:

$$\frac{P - MC}{P} = \frac{-1}{\epsilon_p}. \qquad \textbf{13.10}$$

Notice that the left-hand side of Equation 13.10 is an expression for markup on price. Thus, the optimal markup-on-price formula is:

$$\text{Optimal Markup on Price} = \frac{-1}{\epsilon_p}. \qquad \textbf{13.11}$$

Table 13.2 shows the optimal markup on marginal cost and on price for products with varying price elasticities of demand. As the table demonstrates, the more elastic the demand for a product (the more "price

■ Table 13.2

## Optimal Markup on Marginal Cost and Price at Various Price Elasticity Levels

| Price Elasticity of Demand, $\epsilon_p$ | Optimal Markup on Marginal Cost, $\dfrac{-1}{\epsilon_p + 1}$ | Optimal Markup on Price, $\dfrac{-1}{\epsilon_p}$ |
|:---:|:---:|:---:|
| −1.5 | 200.0% | 66.7% |
| −2.0 | 100.0 | 50.0 |
| −2.5 | 66.7 | 40.0 |
| −5.0 | 25.0 | 20.0 |
| −10.0 | 11.1 | 10.0 |
| −25.0 | 4.2 | 4.0 |

sensitive" it is), the smaller the optimal margin. Products with relatively less elastic demand will have higher optimal markups. In the retail grocery data, the very low markup on milk is consistent with a high price elasticity of demand for that product. Demand for fruits and vegetables during their peak seasons is considerably less price elastic, and their correspondingly higher markups reflect this lower price elasticity of demand.

We see that, far from being a naïve rule of thumb, markup pricing practices can allow a firm to arrive at optimal prices for its products in a relatively efficient manner. In fact, markup pricing might well be the optimal technique for implementing marginal analysis in pricing practice, given the high cost of information in many markets. Any attempt to more completely estimate marginal revenue and marginal cost relations for an individual product will itself increase costs. The marginal concept indicates that the firm must always weigh an added expense against the added gain and act accordingly. In its pricing policy, the firm must determine whether the added expense associated with obtaining more complete estimates of marginal relationships is more than offset by the expected gain in revenues from increased pricing precision. In many instances, markup pricing practices are efficient rules-of-thumb for setting optimal prices over broad categories of products when one considers the added expense involved in obtaining the data necessary for more detailed analysis of marginal revenues and costs for individual products.

The use of the optimal markup formulas can be further illustrated by considering the case of Bon's Boutique, a small specialty retailer located in a suburban shopping mall. In setting its initial price for a new spring line of blouses, Bon's added a 100-percent markup on cost. Costs were estimated at the $12 purchase price of each blouse plus a 50-percent allocated fixed overhead charge. Customer response was so enthusiastic that Bon's raised prices by $3 per blouse, reducing sales from 80 to 70 blouses per week. Was Bon's initial price optimal? If not, what is the optimal price?

To determine whether Bon's initial price on blouses was profit maximizing, we calculate Bon's initial price level, the price elasticity of demand, and the markup on relevant marginal cost and then apply the optimal markup formula. From the preceding data, we know that Bon's calculated cost per blouse was $18—the $12 purchase cost plus a 50-percent allocated fixed overhead charge. With a 100-percent markup on cost, Bon's initial price can be calculated from the markup-on-cost formula:

$$\text{Markup on Cost} = \frac{\text{Price} - \text{Cost}}{\text{Cost}}$$

$$1 = \frac{\text{Price} - \$18}{\$18}$$

$$\text{Price} = \$36.$$

If we assume $dQ/dP = \Delta Q/\Delta P$, then the point price elasticity of demand for blouses is:

$$\epsilon_p = \Delta Q/\Delta P \times P/Q$$
$$= [(80 - 70)/(\$39 - \$36)] \times \$36/80$$
$$= -1.5.$$

Before applying the optimal markup-on-cost formula, we must recognize that the relevant marginal cost per blouse is only the $12 purchase price. The allocated fixed overhead charge of $6 is irrelevant, since fixed overhead costs are unaffected by blouse sales. Bon's actual markup on relevant marginal costs per blouse is 200 percent, because:

$$\text{Markup on Cost} = \frac{\$36 - \$12}{\$12}$$

$$= 2 \text{ (or 200 Percent)}.$$

We can verify that this is indeed a profit-maximizing markup on cost from the optimal markup-on-cost formula:

$$\text{Optimal Markup on Cost} = \frac{-1}{\epsilon_p + 1}$$

$$= \frac{-1}{-1.5 + 1}$$

$$= 2 \text{ (or 200 Percent)}.$$

Similarly, Bon's markup on price is:

$$\text{Markup on Price} = \frac{\$36 - \$12}{\$36}$$

$$= 0.67 \text{ (or 67 Percent)}.$$

Using the optimal markup-on-price formula, we find:

$$\text{Optimal Markup on Price} = \frac{-1}{\epsilon_p}$$

$$= \frac{-1}{-1.5}$$

$$= 0.67 \text{ (or 67 Percent)}.$$

Therefore, Bon's initial $36 price on blouses was optimal, and the subsequent $3 price increase should be rescinded.

This example teaches a simple lesson. Despite consideration of inappropriate fixed overhead costs and a markup that might at first have appeared inappropriate, Bon's pricing policy is entirely consistent with profit-maximizing behavior. As is often the case, the end result of Bon's practice is an efficient pricing policy. Given the prevalence of markup pricing in everyday business practice, and the wide variety of markup rules of thumb and cost allocations typically employed, it is important that these pricing practices be carefully analyzed before they are judged suboptimal. The widespread use of markup pricing methods among highly successful firms suggests that the method is commonly employed in ways that are entirely consistent with profit-maximizing behavior.

## INCREMENTAL ANALYSIS IN PRICING

Many pricing decisions involve *incremental profit analysis*, which focuses on the relation between *changes* in revenues and costs that are due to managerial decisions. The emphasis on only the costs or revenues actually affected by the decision insures proper economic reasoning in decision analysis. That is, proper use of incremental profit analysis results in approving any action that increases net profits and in rejecting any action that reduces profits. (This statement abstracts from the possibility of changing the firm's risk posture, such as undertaking an action that might increase expected profits but that is so risky that it would raise the firm's capitalization rate to a point where the value of the firm might decline.)

**incremental analysis**
The analysis of changes in revenues and costs associated with managerial decisions.

The fact that **incremental analysis** involves only factors affected by a particular decision does not make the concept easy to apply. Proper incremental analysis requires a wide-ranging examination of the total effect of a given decision. Consider, for example, a firm's decision to introduce a new product. Incremental analysis requires that the decision be based on the net effect of changes in revenues and costs. Analysis of the effect on revenues involves an estimate of the net revenues to be received for the product, plus a study of how sales of the new product will affect the firm's other products. The new product may well compete with the firm's existing products. If so, even new products with high revenue potential when considered individually may have too small a net effect on revenue to justify their introduction. At the other extreme, a new product that complements the firm's other products can be highly profitable when judged on the basis of individual plus related product sales, even though by itself it might not appear attractive. Kodak's Instamatic camera is an example of a product introduced, at least in part, because it complemented another major component of the firm's existing product line, photographic film.

Incremental cost analysis is just as far-reaching. In addition to the direct incremental costs associated with a new product, the firm must consider any impact on the costs of existing products. For example, introduction of a new product might cause production bottlenecks that would raise the cost of other products.

Incremental analysis studies long-run as well as short-run effects. A new product may appear to generate an incremental profit in the short run because the firm has excess capacity in its existing plant and equipment. Over the long run, however, the commitment to produce a new item may require substantial investment when existing plant and equipment wear out and must be replaced. Similarly, future production may bring high opportunity costs if expansion into other product lines is restricted by the decision to produce a new product.

It is important to stress once again that incremental analysis is based on the cost and revenue changes associated with a given decision. For short-run analysis, fixed cost (overhead) is irrelevant and must not be included in incremental analysis. If the effect of the decision extends into the long run, however, fixed costs are indeed relevant and must be considered.

## An Illustration of Incremental Analysis

There are numerous examples to illustrate how firms employ incremental logic in their everyday business practice. For purposes of illustration, we consider the case of an airline deciding whether or not to add or drop a given flight. Our numbers are hypothetical, but our decision analysis reflects the actual pricing practice of a major U.S. airline. When considering adding a new flight, or dropping an existing route that appeared to be doing poorly, this airline conducted an incremental analysis along the lines illustrated in Table 13.3. The corporate philosophy was: "If revenues exceed out-of-pocket costs, put the flight on." In other words, the company compared the incremental, or out-of-pocket, costs of each proposed flight to the incremental revenues it would generate. An excess of incremental revenues over incremental costs led to a decision to add the flight. Conversely, a flight was dropped if incremental costs exceeded incremental revenues.

The out-of-pocket cost figures were obtained by circulating a proposed schedule for a new flight to every operating department and asking each to report what added expenses it would incur. Here, an alternative cost concept was used. If a ground crew was on duty and between work on other flights, the proposed flight was not charged a penny of their salary. The additional flight may even have reduced some costs. For

■ Table 13.3
## Incremental Analysis for Airline Departures

| | | |
|---|---|---:|
| Problem: | Should an extra daily flight from City $X$ to City $Y$ be added? | |
| Facts: | Fully allocated costs of this flight | $15,000 |
| | Out-of-pocket costs of this flight | 5,000 |
| | Flight should gross | 9,000 |
| Decision: | Run the flight. It will add $4,000 to gross profit by adding $9,000 to revenues and only $5,000 to costs. Overhead and other costs totaling $10,000 ($15,000 − $5,000) would be incurred whether the flight is run or not. Therefore, fully allocated costs of $15,000 are not relevant to this business decision. It is the out-of-pocket, or incremental, costs that count. | |

example, a late-night round trip flight between Colorado Springs and Denver was profitable with only a small amount of freight and *no* passenger revenues because its net cost was less than the cost for overnight parking in Colorado Springs.

On the revenue side, both the projected revenues for the flight and the effect on revenues of competing and connecting flights were considered. Several flights that failed to cover their out-of-pocket costs directly brought in passengers for connecting long-haul service. When the excess of additional revenue over cost for long-haul flights was considered, the airline earned a positive net profit on the feeder service.

Incremental analysis also extended to scheduling arrival and departure times. A proposed schedule for the Kansas City Municipal Airport, for example, had two planes landing at the same time. This was expensive for the company, because its facilities in Kansas City at that time were not sufficient to service two planes simultaneously. The airline would be forced to lease an extra fuel truck and to hire new employees at an additional monthly cost of $7,500. However, when the company began shifting around proposed departure times in other cities to avoid the congestion at Kansas City, it appeared that the company stood to lose as much as $40,000 in monthly revenues from passengers switching to competing flights leaving at more convenient hours. Needless to say, the two flights were scheduled to be on the ground in Kansas City at the same time.

## The Time Factor in Incremental Analysis
Although microeconomic theory assumes a goal of value maximization, much of it is developed around a static construct that assumes that the firm operates to maximize *short-run* profits. Implicit in this is the assumption that continual maximization of short-run profits, coupled with proper adjustments to the physical plant as technology, factor prices, and demand change, will lead to long-run profit and value maximization.

The real world is more complicated than this model suggests. Actions taken at one time affect results in subsequent periods, and wise business managers recognize this fact. Accordingly, because short-run profit maximization is seldom entirely consistent with long-run wealth maximization, firms do not focus solely on short-run profits.

An illustration will help to clarify the point. Consider a firm that sets the current price of its product below the short-run profit-maximizing level in order to expand its market rapidly. Such a policy could lead to long-run profit maximization if the firm secures a larger permanent market share. A similar policy might also forestall competitive entry into the market. From a legal standpoint, a policy of accepting less-than-maximum short-run profits could reduce the threat of antitrust suits or government regulation, again leading to long-run profit and wealth maximization.

The pricing practices of U.S. automobile manufacturers in the years just after World War II provide an example of this kind of behavior. The auto companies maintained prices on most models well below the short-run profit-maximizing level. They believed that rapid expansion in their dealership networks and in private automobile ownership would lead to higher long-run profits. There was also some concern that charging high prices during a period of extremely heavy demand might alienate customers and invite antitrust action. The subsequent rapid growth in automobile demand suggests that the industry was correct in its initial assessment and that the sacrifice of short-run profits did in fact provide substantial long-run benefits.

The correct application of incremental analysis in pricing practice requires consideration of both short-run and long-run effects on costs and revenues. More often than not, apparent conflicts between pricing practice and economic theory can be reconciled when the long-run implications of pricing decisions are better understood.

## PRICE DISCRIMINATION

Additional complexities are introduced into the pricing decision when the firm sells its products in multiple markets. The existence of more than one market or customer group gives rise to the possibility of price discrimination or differential pricing practices in various markets.

**price discrimination**
A pricing practice that sets prices in different markets that are not related to differences in costs.

**Price discrimination** exists whenever different classes of customers are charged different prices for the same product, or when differences in prices are not proportional to differences in costs for a multiproduct firm. In other words, price discrimination occurs whenever a firm's prices in different markets are not related to differentials in production and distribution costs. With price discrimination, the markup or profit margin realized varies from one customer or customer group to another.

**consumers' surplus**
The value to consumers of goods and services above and beyond the amount they pay sellers.

Price discrimination can be better understood by introducing the concept of **consumers' surplus.** Consumers' surplus is the value to consumers of goods and services above and beyond the amount they pay to

■ Figure 13.1
## An Illustration of Consumers' Surplus

Consumers' surplus is shown by the area P*AB and represents the value of output to consumers above and beyond the amount they pay to producers.

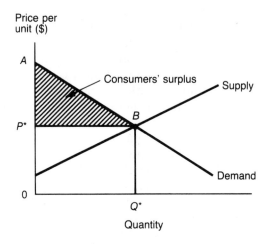

sellers. To illustrate, consider Figure 13.1, in which a market equilibrium price/output combination of $P^*$ and $Q^*$ is shown. The total value of output to consumers is given by the area under the demand curve, or area $0ABQ^*$. Since the total revenue paid to producers is price times quantity, equal to area $0P^*BQ^*$, the area $P^*AB$ represents the value of output above the amount paid to producers—that is, the consumers' surplus.

Consumers' surplus arises because individual consumers place different values on goods and services. As we proceed from Point A downward along the market demand curve, consumers with a progressively lower marginal value (utility) of consumption enter the market. A motive for price discrimination is created, because higher prices charged to consumers with high marginal values of consumption will increase revenues without affecting costs. Therefore, market power can dramatically increase profits when sellers can vary the prices they charge individual customers or customer classes and thereby "capture" the value represented by the consumers' surplus. Price discrimination will always increase profits, because it allows the firm to increase total revenue without affecting costs.

Price discrimination does not necessarily carry an evil connotation in a moral sense. It is simply a term in economics that describes a pricing practice that must be judged to be good or bad on the merits of the specific situation. In some situations, price discrimination can actually lead to lower prices for some customers and to availability of more goods and services than would otherwise be the case. For example, a municipal bus company might charge lower prices for easily identifiable consumer groups, such as the elderly and the handicapped. In such circumstances, the bus company is price discriminating in favor of elderly and handicapped riders and against its other customers. This discriminatory pricing practice serves two purposes. First, it provides elderly and handicapped customers, who may be unable to afford the usual fare, an opportunity to ride the bus. Second, because of the incremental revenues provided by the elderly and the handicapped riders, the bus company may be able to offer routes that could not be supported by revenues from full-fare customers alone, or to operate with a lower subsidy from taxpayers.

## Requirements for Profitable Price Discrimination

Two conditions are necessary for profitable price discrimination. First, different price elasticities of demand must exist in the various submarkets for a given product. Unless price elasticities differ among submarkets, there is no point in segmenting the market. With identical price elasticities and identical marginal costs, profit-maximizing pricing policy calls for the same price in all market segments. We elaborate on this point in a later section.

Second, the firm must be able to segment the market by identifying submarkets and preventing transfers among customers in different submarkets. When markets are segmented, the firm can isolate one group of buyers from another. If this is possible, the firm can sell at one price to some buyers and at a higher price to others without unauthorized trading among customers undermining its differential pricing strategy.

## Types of Price Discrimination

**first-degree price discrimination**
Charging different prices to each customer.

The extent, or *degree*, to which a firm can engage in price discrimination has been classified into three major categories. Under **first-degree price discrimination,** the firm extracts the maximum amount each and every purchaser is willing to pay for its product. The firm prices each unit of output separately at the level indicated at successive quantities along a demand curve. In effect, the demand curve becomes the firm's marginal revenue curve. Although first-degree price discrimination actually occurs in a few cases—primarily in the provision of personal services, such as legal services, medical care, and personal financial advice—the formidable demand-information requirements (the seller must know the maximum price that each buyer will pay for each unit of output) and problems of market segmentation associated with this type of price discrimination prevent its use in most situations.

**second-degree price discrimination**
Charging different prices based on customer use rates.

**Second-degree price discrimination,** a more frequently employed type of price discrimination, involves setting prices on the basis of quantity purchased. Typically, prices are *blocked*, with a high price charged for the first unit or block of units purchased by each consumer and lower prices set for successive units or blocks. Public utilities, such as electric companies, gas companies, and water companies, frequently charge block rates that are discriminatory. (Remember that for differential prices to be discriminatory in an economic sense, they cannot be related to cost differences. Therefore, block rates based strictly on different costs of service would not be classified as price discrimination.) Use of second-degree price discrimination is also somewhat limited; it can be applied only to products whose use is metered in some fashion, which explains its use by electric, gas, and water utilities. Office equipment such as copiers or time-sharing computer systems, which lend themselves to metering, are other examples of products for which second-degree price discrimination is practiced.

**third-degree price discrimination**

Charging different prices to each customer type.

The most commonly observed form of price discrimination, **third-degree price discrimination,** results when a firm separates its customers into several classes and sets a different price for each class. These customer classifications can be based on a variety of factors. A product supplier that thinks that regional markets can be isolated through control of the product distribution system may use geographical differentials. For example, in the late 1970s, General Motors set a lower price on its Chevette model in the western United States than in the rest of the country because Japanese competition made the West Coast small-car market more price-elastic than markets in other parts of the United States.

Product use provides another basis for third-degree price discrimination. IBM, Apple, Compaq, Zenith, and other major computer manufacturers routinely offer steep 20 to 30 percent discounts for corporate versus individual purchasers of personal computers. Corporate buyers who may purchase dozens, if not hundreds, of computers are understandably much more price sensitive than an individual buyer of a single PC. Educational discounts can be even more dramatic, often in excess of 30 to 40 percent off list prices. Manufacturers are especially eager to penetrate the classroom on the assumption that student users tend to become loyal future customers. Similarly, auto companies, magazine and newspaper publishers, and others prominently feature corporate and educational discounts as part of their marketing strategies.

Electric, gas, water, and telephone utilities' rate differentials between commercial and private consumers are another example of price discrimination based on product use. The utilities face very different demand elasticities in the residential and the industrial sectors of their markets. The demand for electricity from residential users is inelastic, because these customers have no good substitutes for the electricity supplied by the power utility. Industrial buyers, on the other hand, have a much more elastic demand, because many of them could generate their own power if electricity prices were to rise above the cost of operating in-plant generating equipment.

Time (either clock or calendar) provides another common basis for third degree price discrimination. Segmenting long-distance telephone rates during various hours of the day and night is one example of this type of price discrimination. Long-distance rates are higher during periods of the day when demand is greatest, especially during business hours. Movie theaters also practice price discrimination based on clock time. Calendar-time price discrimination is sometimes reflected in peak and off-peak pricing for resort facilities, airline services, and so on. Of course, lower off-peak rates sometimes only reflect lower costs of providing goods and services during off-peak hours. However, higher markups because of lower customer price sensitivity during peak periods implies price discrimination against peak customers and in favor of off-peak customers.

Age, sex, and income provide still other bases of discrimination, particularly for services as opposed to physical products. For example, lower prices for children's haircuts and movie tickets are discriminatory practices based on age; ladies'-day admission prices for sports events illustrate price discrimination based on sex. Discrimination on the bases of age, sex, and income is controversial, both popularly and legally, so this pricing practice should be thoroughly evaluated before being employed.

 An interesting illustration of price discrimination can be found in the want-ad pricing policies of local newspapers. The value of want-ad advertising varies according to the value of the item advertised. Real estate advertising has a much greater value to consumers than advertising of lower-priced household items, boats, pets, and so on. Given these differences, consumers are willing to pay much more to advertise a personal residence, for example, than to seek new homes for Whiskers and her kittens. Local newspapers satisfy the requirements necessary for profitable price discrimination, since they can easily identify the value of the item advertised and often enjoy a monopoly position in the sale of local advertising. Indeed, it is rare to find more than one newspaper company serving a local market, given the significant economies of scale in the industry.

Table 13.4 shows pricing policies during the late 1980s for local newspapers in the Madison, Wisconsin, and Denver, Colorado, markets. This comparison yields insight because of the difference in market structure. The Madison market, as is typical in the United States, is served by a single newspaper company, Madison Newspapers, Inc., with *The Wisconsin State Journal* (morning and Sunday) and *The Capital Times* (evening) editions. The Denver market, however, is served by two independent newspaper companies, *The Denver Post* and *The Rocky Mountain News*.

It is interesting to note that the monopoly position of Madison Newspapers is reflected in higher single copy and subscription prices than either the *Post* or *News*. The 40-percent price premium on daily single-copy sales and 100-percent price premium on Sunday single-copy sales in the Madison market are both dramatic, as is the 52-percent premium on daily plus Sunday subscription sales. These price differentials suggest that, by virtue of its monopoly position, Madison Newspapers en-

■ Table 13.4
## Pricing Practices and Market Shares for Local Newspapers in the Madison, Wisconsin, and Denver, Colorado, Markets

| | Madison Newspapers | Denver Post | Rocky Mountain News |
|---|---|---|---|
| *Newspaper Prices* | | | |
| Single copy—Daily | $ 0.35 | $ 0.25 | $ 0.25 |
| Single copy—Sunday | 1.00 | 0.50 | 0.50 |
| Subscription—Daily | 6.80 (mo.) | 6.25 (mo.) | 6.00 (mo.) |
| Subscription—Daily + Sunday | 11.05 (mo.) | 7.25 (mo.) | 7.25 (mo.) |
| *Want-Ad Prices (3-line ad)* | | | |
| Real estate | 18.45 (3 days) | 20.25 (3 days) | 22.95 (3 days) |
| | 39.90 (7 days) | 31.50 (7 days) | 44.10 (7 days) |
| | 67.20 (14 days) | 58.80 (14 days) | 81.90 (14 days) |
| | 139.50 (30 days) | 117.00 (30 days) | 175.50 (30 days) |
| Merchandise | 16.00 (10 days, $1,000 to $10,000 value) | 7.50 (8 days) | 11.99 (10 days) |
| | 11.00 (10 days, $100 to $1,000 value) | | |
| | 7.00 (7 days, < $100 value) | | |
| *Circulation* | | | |
| Daily (market share) | 107,000 (100%) | 213,000 (40%) | 318,000 (60%) |
| Sunday (market share) | 141,000 (100%) | 413,000 (53%) | 371,000 (47%) |

joys a substantial pricing advantage in its market when compared with the pricing discretion of either the *Post* or *News* in the Denver market.

The advantages of Madison Newspapers' monopoly position are even more apparent when we consider its want-ad pricing practices. First, note how Madison Newspapers' real estate want-ad prices are quite comparable with those charged by the *Post* and *News*, despite the fact that its overall market size is only one-third to one-half as large. This means that on a cost-per-exposure basis, Madison Newspapers' real estate want-ad prices are roughly two to three times higher than those charged by the *Post* and *News*. Moreover, although all three papers engage in price discrimination for want-ad publication, Madison Newspapers' non–real estate merchandise (auto, etc.) want-ad pricing structure is much more closely tied to the value of the item advertised than those of either the *Post* or *News*.

Just as the airline industry provided an interesting illustration of incremental analysis in pricing practice, it has often also provided an interesting basis for discussing price discrimination. Certainly rates do vary dramatically between business customers, whose travel plans change quickly and whose demand is relatively inelastic with respect to price, and vacation customers, who can establish travel plans well in advance and whose demand is typically more price elastic. However, before concluding that the higher prices charged some business customers solely reflect price discrimination, it is important to recognize that the cost of serving business customers is greater than for vacation travelers.

Business traffic is particularly heavy on Mondays, Thursdays, and Fridays. This pattern of business travel often leaves airlines with substantial unused capacity on Tuesdays and Wednesdays, as well as on Saturdays and Sundays. Given this excess capacity, the incremental cost per air traveler can be substantially lower during midweek and weekend periods. Airlines are also better able to schedule their use of airplane capacity when demand is predictable as opposed to erratic. This contributes to lower fares for restricted as opposed to unrestricted travelers. Thus, the price differentials common in airline rate structures clearly reflect the influence of cost differences, perhaps in addition to the effects of price discrimination.

## Profit Maximization under Price Discrimination

A firm that can segment its market will maximize profits by operating with marginal revenue equal to marginal cost in each market segment. This can be demonstrated by an example.

Suppose Midwest State University (MSU) wants to reduce its athletic department's operating deficit and at the same time increase student attendance at home football games. To achieve these objectives, a new two-tier pricing structure for season football tickets is being considered.

A market survey conducted by the school suggests the following market demand conditions:

| **Public Demand** | **Student Demand** |
|---|---|
| $P_P = \$225 - \$0.005Q_P$ | $P_S = \$125 - \$0.00125Q_S$ |

During recent years, the football program has run on an operating budget of $1.5 million per year. This budget covers fixed salary, recruiting, insurance, and facility-maintenance expenses. In addition to these fixed expenses, the university incurs variable ticket-handling, facility-cleaning, insurance, and security costs of $25 per season ticket. The resulting total cost and marginal cost functions are:

$$TC = \$1,500,000 + \$25Q,$$
$$MC = dTC/dQ = \$25.$$

## 13.2  **Managerial Application**
"Yield Management" in the Travel Industries

On June 16, 1988, passengers paid round-trip fares on American Airlines flight 263 between Washington, D.C., and Dallas, Texas, ranging from $158 to $1,000. Here's the breakdown: 11 first-class seats sold at $1,000 round-trip; 30 full-fare coach seats cost $760; and discount coach seats sold at fares ranging from $310 to $350 (43 seats), $270 to $308 (7 seats), $238 to $268 (38 seats) and $158 to $236 (6 seats). For example, Dallas businessman Vance Miller was able to schedule a seat only one day ahead of departure and paid a $1,000 round-trip first-class fare. Fort Worth resident Margaret Brosco was able to make her travel plans almost six weeks in advance and obtained a $158 fare. Such disparity in the prices charged to various customers, and varying rates of capacity usage, have led some to question the efficiency of the airlines' pricing practices. In fact, the prices they charge reflect a finely developed use of incremental analysis in the pricing of services for peak versus off-peak customers.

The object is not to fill a plane up but instead to maximize the fare revenue generated. Once a flight plan has been set, almost all of the costs associated with a given departure are fixed. Thus, revenue-maximizing and profit-maximizing strategies are identical. American uses computer models to predict demand for each flight. The company has 1,600 flights per day and takes reservations from as much as 330 days prior to departure right up to the last minute. Thus, it must manage roughly 150 million seats per day. At stake for American are thousands of dollars in revenue on each flight and tens of millions of dollars in revenue over the course of a year.

The key to successful "yield management" is to ensure that the right discount–full-fare mix is achieved. If there are too many discount seats on a 5 P.M. weekday

*continued*

See: Mark Rohner and Doug Carroll, "Hunting for the Cheapest Fare," *USA Today*, July 14, 1987, 8A; and Michele Manges and Jonathan Dahl, "Hotels Gamble on 'Frequent-Stay' Plans," *The Wall Street Journal*, February 27, 1989, B1.

**Managerial Application** *continued*

departure out of Chicago's O'Hare airport, which is heavily used by full-fare business travelers, American loses revenue and profits. On the other hand, deep discounts on Saturday morning departures may be necessary to maximize yield. The mix between full-fare (peak) and discount (off-peak) passengers will change constantly. Cancellations or unexpectedly slow sales can force the company to increase the number of discount fares available, sometimes right up to the time of departure. Similarly, bad weather that makes passengers too late for a connecting flight in another city can force a last-minute "fire sale" on seats reserved for connecting passengers. In all, American revises as many as 32,500 fares per day. Some move up, some move down. Restrictions on others are continually modified. The changes are so frequent that the average life span of a given fare is only five days.

Another important factor must be considered: 12 percent of the people who book a reservation on a given American flight never show up. Customers who are turned away unnecessarily represent a significant loss in revenue. To minimize this loss, American relies on computer models to indicate the optimal amount of overbooking. By selling more tickets than there are seats on a given flight, the losses associated with no shows and last-minute cancellations can be mini-mized. Without overbooking, the average number of empty seats would rise, and so would ticket prices. When more than the expected number of passengers show up, extra passengers are "bumped" to a later flight and receive free tickets or other monetary compensation in return.

How does the system work? Apparently, very well. Traffic at American and other leading airlines has exploded during recent years. Customers seem quite willing to deal with fare restrictions and other inconveniences in return for the opportunity to travel at bargain prices.

In fact, travelers may soon be able to shop for discounted hotel rooms during off-peak periods in much the same way that they now seek out bargain airline fares. The American Economic Association meets between Christmas and New Year's Day every year, a traditionally slack time in the hotel business, and obtains bargain rates for its members from Hilton Hotels. Many Ramadas now offer 30 percent off for 30-day advance-purchase hotel rooms. This new "30/30" program will help Ramada to better utilize capacity by reducing unsold rooms. Like the airline industry, the hotel business seems to have discovered the key role of incremental analysis as a means for effective yield management.

What would be the optimal football ticket prices and quantities for each market, assuming that MSU adopts a new season ticket pricing policy featuring discounts for students? To answer this question, we must realize that since $MC = \$25$, the athletic department's operating deficit will be minimized by setting $MR = MC = \$25$ in each market segment and solving for $Q$. This is also the profit-maximizing strategy for the football program. Therefore:

### Public Demand

$$TR_P = P_P \times Q_P$$
$$= (\$225 - \$0.005Q_P)Q_P$$
$$= \$225Q_P - \$0.005Q_P^2$$
$$MR_P = dTR_P/dQ_P = \$225 - \$0.01Q_P$$
$$MR_P = MC$$
$$\$225 - \$0.01Q_P = \$25$$
$$\$0.01Q_P = \$200$$
$$Q_P = 20,000,$$

and,

$$P_P = \$225 - \$0.005(20,000)$$
$$= \$125.$$

### Student Demand

$$TR_S = P_S \times Q_S$$
$$= (\$125 - \$0.00125Q_S)Q_S$$
$$= \$125Q_S - \$0.00125Q_S^2$$
$$MR_S = dTR_S/dQ_S = \$125 - \$0.0025Q_S$$
$$MR_S = MC$$
$$\$125 - \$0.0025Q_S = \$25$$
$$\$0.0025Q_S = \$100$$
$$Q_S = 40,000,$$

and,

$$P_S = \$125 - \$0.00125(40,000)$$
$$= \$75.$$

And the football program's total operating surplus (profit) will be:

$$\text{Operating Surplus (Profit)} = TR_P + TR_S - TC$$
$$= \$125(20,000) + \$75(40,000)$$
$$- \$1,500,000 - \$25(60,000)$$
$$= \$2.5 \text{ Million.}$$

To gauge the implications of this new two-tier ticket pricing practice, it is necessary to contrast these price/output and surplus levels with those that would result if MSU maintained its current policy of offering tickets to students at the same price as the general public. From the individual market demand curves, we see that:

$$Q_P = 45,000 - 200P_P \quad \text{and} \quad Q_S = 100,000 - 800P_S.$$

Therefore, under the assumption $P_P = P_S$, total demand ($Q_T$) is given as:[1]

$$Q_T = Q_P + Q_S$$
$$= 145,000 - 1,000P,$$

and

$$P = \$145 - \$0.001Q.$$

The operating surplus maximizing (profit-maximizing) uniform season ticket price is found by solving for the output level at which marginal revenue equals marginal cost for the total market:

$$TR = P \times Q$$
$$= \$145Q - \$0.001Q^2$$
$$MR = dTR/dQ = \$145 - \$0.002Q.$$

Setting marginal revenue equal to marginal cost provides:

$$MR = MC$$
$$\$145 - \$0.002Q = \$25$$
$$\$0.002Q = \$120$$
$$Q = 60,000,$$

$$P = \$145 - \$0.001(60,000)$$
$$= \$85,$$

and

$$Q_P = 45,000 - 200(\$85) \qquad Q_S = 100,000 - 800(\$85)$$
$$= 28,000 \qquad\qquad\qquad = 32,000$$

$$\text{Operating surplus (profit)} = TR - TC$$
$$= \$85(60,000) - \$1,500,000 - \$25(60,000)$$
$$= \$2.1 \text{ million.}$$

Note that the total number of tickets sold will equal 60,000 under both the two-tier and single-price policies. This results because the marginal cost of a ticket is the same in both markets. However, ticket-pricing policies featuring student discounts will both increase student attendance from 32,000 to 40,000 and maximize the football program's operating surplus at $2.5 million (rather than $2.1 million), thereby minimiz-

---

[1]This "aggregate demand curve" actually holds only for that range of prices where both the general public and students purchase tickets, i.e., at a price of $125 or less. For price above $125 only non-student purchasers will buy tickets and the Public Demand curve $P_P = \$225 - \$0.005Q_P$ represents the total market. This causes the actual Total Demand curve to be kinked at a price of $125 as shown in Figure 13.2.

## 13.3  **Managerial Application**

Do Colleges Price Discriminate?

Throughout the 1980s, college costs rose by 10 percent per year, roughly twice the rate of inflation. During the 1977 to 1987 period, average annual tuition costs at private schools jumped from $2,635 to $7,110. At most Ivy League schools, the price of a year's tuition is more than $12,000. Counting room and board and related expenses, the total bill will soon exceed $20,000 per year. Critics argue that college costs are now excessive. In 1987, William Bennet, Education Secretary in the Reagan administration, blamed colleges and universities for "charging what the market will bear."

At Franklin and Marshall College (F&M) in Lancaster, Pennsylvania, for example, tuition and fees have risen one-third faster than the average rate for private four-year colleges, to more than $15,000 per year.

Some of the money has paid for new computers and increased faculty salaries, although faculty salaries have fallen as a percentage of total spending. Following a national trend, much of the increase has gone to building administrative staff, improving student services, and increasing the endowment. James L. Powell, president of F&M, defends recent spending, noting that parent and student ratings of college quality correlate very closely with the overall level of expenditures.

The burden of higher college costs has been reduced for some by the ready availability of financial aid. Tuition plus room and board at Johns Hopkins University was $15,410 in 1987, but the average *net* cost after student aid, or tuition plus room and board and fees minus financial aid, was

*continued*

See: Harry Anderson, "Fuming over College Costs," *Newsweek*, May 18, 1987, 66–72; and Janice C. Simpson, "Rising College Costs Help Create Hot Field: Financial-Aid Planning," *The Wall Street Journal*, September 19, 1987, 19.

ing the athletic department's deficit. It is the preferred pricing policy when viewed from MSU's perspective.

Note that the price discrimination creates both "winners" and "losers." The winners following adoption of student discounts include both students and MSU. The losers are members of the public, who wind up paying higher football ticket prices or find themselves priced out of the market. It is possible that the nonstudent ticket purchasers would also be "winners" if the football program were dropped and hence tickets were unavailable for purchase at any price, without the price discrimination.

**Managerial Application** *continued*

$9,410. Nationally, the UCLA Higher Education Research Institute reports that far more than half of all students receive some form of financial aid. At some private schools, the share of students receiving financial aid approaches 90 percent.

Although some point to such statistics as proof that colleges and universities are committed to minimizing the financial burden for needy students, critics argue that schools are only engaging in a strategy of first-degree price discrimination. When a school obtains detailed data on family incomes, mortgage payments and balances, savings, and investments, it has information useful for first-degree price discrimination. By differing the amount of financial aid offered, schools can set a net price that is unique for every student. Charging the maximum each student can afford to pay is much like charging the maximum he or she is willing to pay. Moreover, as predicted by the theory of price discrimination, increases in financial aid seldom keep pace with increasing tuition and fees over the course of a student's college career. Greater school loyalty, difficulty in transferring credits, and the lack of junior college substitutes makes juniors and se-

niors more willing to pay higher net college costs than freshmen and sophomores would.

In defense of current financial aid practices, school administrators point out that many would be unable to afford college without some cross-subsidization among students. In addition, private schools must cover the full costs of education whereas public colleges and universities enjoy substantial tax-revenue income. Even the $6,000 premium paid by out-of-state students at the University of Michigan fails to cover fully allocated costs per student. The $7,700 rate for in-state students is far below average costs, and state taxpayers contribute the $9,500 per student difference. Similarly, endowment income at private colleges often supplements student tuition and fees.

However, average costs may not be relevant for pricing purposes. The *marginal* cost per student is near zero in many instances, and even very low net tuition-plus-fee income can often make a significant contribution to overhead. From an economic perspective, the pricing practices of colleges and universities appear to be quite consistent with the theory of price discrimination.

The MSU pricing problem and the concept of price discrimination can also be illustrated in graphs. Figure 13.2 shows demand curves for the general public in the first panel and for students in the second panel. The aggregate demand curve in the third panel represents the horizontal sum of the quantities demanded at each price in the public and student markets. The associated marginal revenue curve, $MR_{P+S}$, has a similar interpretation. For example, marginal revenue equals $25 at an attendance level of 20,000 in the public market and $25 at an attendance level of 40,000 in the student market. Accordingly, one point on the total marginal revenue curve will represent output of 60,000 units and mar-

■ Figure 13.2
## Price Discrimination for an Identical Product Sold in Two Markets

Price discrimination results in higher prices for market segments with low price elasticity (public) and lower prices for market segments with high price elasticity (students).

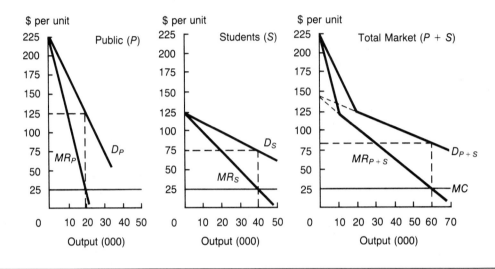

ginal revenue of $25. From a cost standpoint, it does not matter whether tickets are being sold to the public or to students; therefore, the single marginal cost curve shown in the third panel applies to both markets.

Solving this pricing problem graphically can be thought of as a two-part process. First, we must determine the profit-maximizing total output level. Profit maximization occurs at the aggregate output level at which marginal cost and marginal revenue are equal. Figure 13.2 shows a profit-maximizing output of 60,000 tickets, where marginal cost and marginal revenue both equal $25. Second, we must allocate this output between the two submarkets. Proper allocation of total output between the two submarkets can be determined graphically by drawing a horizontal line through the graphs in the first two panels at $25 to indicate that $25 is the marginal cost in *each* market at the indicated aggregate output level. The intersection of this horizontal line with the marginal revenue curve in each submarket indicates the distribution of sales and the optimal pricing structure. According to the figures, profits are maximized at an attendance (output) level of 60,000, selling 20,000 tickets to the public at a price of $125 and 40,000 tickets to students at a price of $75.

The price charged in the less-elastic public market is two-thirds higher than the price charged to students, whose demand is relatively elastic. This differential adds substantially to MSU's profits. In the nondiscrimination case, the school (organization) acts as though it faced only the single total market demand curve shown in the third panel of Figure 13.2. Profit maximization requires operation at the output level where $MR = MC$—that is, at 60,000 tickets. Here, however, the single price that would prevail is $85, the price determined by the intersection of a vertical line at 60,000 tickets with the total market demand curve, $D_{P+S}$.

Optimal price discrimination in this case, in which an identical product is being sold in two markets, requires that marginal revenues in both markets are equated not only to marginal costs but also to one another; that is, $MR_P = MR_S = MC$. This is the result of the products being indistinguishable from a "production" standpoint. If the marginal costs of production and distribution of the product in the two markets were different, profit maximization would have required equating marginal revenues to marginal costs in *each separate market*.

# MULTIPLE-PRODUCT PRICING

The basic microeconomic model of the firm assumes the firm produces a single homogeneous product. Yet most of us would be hard-pressed to name even one firm that does not produce a variety of products. Almost all firms produce at least multiple models, styles, or sizes of their output, and each of these variations is considered a separate product for pricing purposes. Although multiple-product pricing requires the same analysis as for a single product, the analysis is complicated by demand and production interrelations.

## Demand Interrelations

Demand interrelations arise because of competition or complementarity among the firm's various products. Consider, for example, a firm that produces two products. If the products are interrelated, either as substitutes or as complements, a change in the price of one will affect the demand for the other. This means that multiple-product pricing decisions must take these interrelations, perhaps among dozens of products, into account.

**Analysis of Demand Interrelations**  Demand interrelations influence the pricing decision through their effect on marginal revenue. In the case of a two-product firm, the marginal revenue functions for the products can be written as:

$$MR_A = \frac{\partial TR}{\partial Q_A} = \frac{\partial TR_A}{\partial Q_A} + \frac{\partial TR_B}{\partial Q_A}, \qquad \textbf{13.12}$$

$$MR_B = \frac{\partial TR}{\partial Q_B} = \frac{\partial TR_B}{\partial Q_B} + \frac{\partial TR_A}{\partial Q_B}. \qquad \textbf{13.13}$$

Equations 13.12 and 13.13 are general statements describing the revenue/output relations for the two products. The first term on the right-hand side of each equation represents the marginal revenue directly associated with each product. The second term illustrates the indirect marginal revenue associated with each product and the problem of demand interrelations. This term indicates the change in total revenues from the second product that is due to a change in the sales of the first. For example, $\partial TR_B/\partial Q_A$ in Equation 13.12 shows the effect on revenues generated by Product $B$ of the sale of an additional unit of Product $A$. Likewise, $\partial TR_A/\partial Q_B$ in Equation 13.13 represents the change in revenues received from the sale of Product $A$ when an additional unit of Product $B$ is manufactured and sold.

These cross-marginal revenue terms showing the demand interrelations between two products can be positive or negative, depending on the nature of the relation. For complementary products, the net effect will be positive, demonstrating that increased sales of one product will lead to increased revenues associated with the other. For competitive products the reverse is true: increased sales of one product will reduce demand for the second, and hence the cross-marginal revenue term will be negative.

This brief examination of demand interrelations demonstrates that proper price determination in the multiple-product case requires a thorough analysis of the total effect of pricing decisions on the firm's revenues. In practice, this implies that optimal pricing must be based on a proper application of incremental reasoning so that the total effect of the decision is considered.

## Production Interrelations

Just as a firm's products can be related through their demand functions, they often can also be interrelated in production. Products may be jointly produced in a fixed ratio (as, for example, in the case of cattle, where hide and beef are obtained from each animal) or in variable proportions (as in the refining of crude oil into gasoline and fuel oil). Products may compete with one another for the firm's resources, as in the case of alternative products, or they may be complementary, as when one product uses wastes generated in the production of another or when increased production of one reduces the costs of another because of economies of scale at the firm level. In each case, proper pricing decisions require consideration of production interrelations.

## Joint Products Produced in Fixed Proportions

The simplest case of joint production is that of joint products produced in fixed proportions. In this situation, it makes no sense to attempt to separate the products from a production or cost standpoint. That is, products that must be produced in fixed proportions allowing no possibility of adjusting the ratio of output are not really multiple products from a production standpoint but should be considered as a package of output. The reason for this stems from the impossibility of determining the costs for the individual products in the package. Since the products are jointly produced, all costs are incurred in the production of the *package,* and there is no economically sound way of allocating them to the individual products.

Optimal price/output determination requires analysis of the relation between the marginal revenue of the output package and its marginal cost of production. So long as the total marginal revenue of the combination (the sum of the marginal revenues obtained from each product in the package) is greater than the marginal cost of producing it, the firm gains by expanding output.

Figure 13.3 illustrates the pricing problem for two products produced in fixed proportions. The demand and the marginal revenue curves for the two products and the single marginal cost curve for production of the combined output package are shown. *Vertical* summation of the two marginal revenue curves indicates the total marginal revenue generated by the package of products. (The marginal revenue curves are summed

■ Figure 13.3
## Optimal Pricing for Joint Products Produced in Fixed Proportions

For joint products produced in fixed proportions, the optimal activity level occurs at the point where the marginal revenue derived from both products ($MR_T$) equals the marginal cost of production.

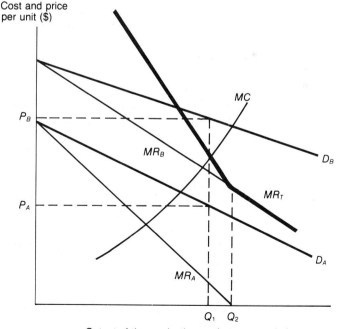

Output of the production package per period

## 13.4  **Managerial Application**
The Popularity of Sales Is Fading

In what appears to be a major shift in retail marketing strategy, some big chains are cutting back regular prices and abandoning promotional sales as an important marketing device. Spurred by the success of Wal-Mart Stores, Toys "R" Us, Circuit City Stores, and other retailers that feature "everyday low prices," many other big chains seem to be adopting a single pricing strategy for a growing list of items.

Prior to 1989, when it adopted a single pricing strategy, industry leader Sears, Roebuck & Company sold an astonishing 55 percent of its goods at "sale" prices. Like many other retailers, Sears had initially marked up goods by enough that they could be put on sale and still provide customary profit margins. However, a regular rotation of month-long specials, in addition to constant price promotions during Christmas and other peak buying seasons, sapped the

meaning from the word *sale*. Customers grew accustomed to these lower prices, and business slackened considerably during non-sale periods. In fact, Sears found that its stores were becoming fairly empty except during sales promotions. Many customers grew weary of trying to predict when Sears would run a sale on desired items and took their business to Wal-Mart and other discounters that featured "everyday low prices."

In adopting this new pricing strategy, Sears joined a growing list of retailers abandoning the sale concept. In 1989, for example, K mart Corporation expanded "everyday low prices" to 5,300 frequently purchased items, almost double the roughly 3,000 items covered previously. Similarly, Montgomery Ward & Company broadened its new low-price strategy to most areas of its stores. In mid-1989, Dayton Hudson Cor-

*continued*

See: Francine Schwadel, "The Sale Is Fading as a Retailing Tactic," *The Wall Street Journal*, March 1, 1989; and James E. Ellis, "Will the Big Markdown Get the Big Store Moving Again?" *Business Week*, March 13, 1989, 110–114.

vertically because each unit of output provides revenues from the sale of both of the joint products.) Thus, the intersection of this total marginal revenue curve ($MR_T$ in the figure) with the marginal cost curve locates the profit-maximizing output level.

The optimal price for each product is determined by the intersection of a vertical line at the profit-maximizing output quantity with the demand curves for each separate product. $Q_1$ represents the optimal quantity of the output package to be produced, and $P_A$ and $P_B$ are the prices

**Managerial Application** *continued*

poration's Target discount chain was studying the concept using market experiments in Albuquerque, New Mexico, and Knoxville, Tennessee. The trend has also expanded to smaller grocery chains and to other retailers, such as Eyelab Inc., a closely held eye-wear chain, and home-furnishings retailer Workbench, Inc.

The trend toward a single pricing policy actually started during the early 1980s. The initial success of Wal-Mart and Toys "R" Us, for example, was tied to their keeping prices low on a year-round basis. Their low prices, and those for the growing list of factory outlet stores, educated consumers about the high markups being charged by other retailers during non-sale periods. Even though sales have always been popular with consumers who seek a "bargain," many consumers came to feel cheated when they were forced to buy goods at regular prices. Thus, the trend to "everyday low prices" is, in part, an attempt to regain lost customer goodwill.

By lowering all prices, some retailers claim that they are simply being more honest with their customers. Workbench, for example, decided to cut overall prices by 15 percent while reducing the number of annual sales from six to two. Announcing its

change in pricing policy with "No Bull" buttons and fliers, the New York retailer decried competitors' "phony" pricing practices, in which they inflate regular prices so that they can artificially reduce them to "sale" prices. Warren Rubin, chairman of Workbench, decided to adopt a "fair-pricing" policy when he discovered that the share of sale merchandise had reached 85 percent of all merchandise sold. Had they been real sales, his company would have gone bankrupt.

Despite their popularity, the new "everyday low prices" policies are not expected to become universal in retailing. Some retailers contend that consumers are conditioned to expect sales at certain times of the year—after-Christmas sales, for example—and enjoy the seasonal bargains. Moreover, by offering "loss leaders," many retailers are able to move overstocked merchandise quickly and to attract new customers at the same time. Interestingly, many department stores catering to upper-middle-class customers have resisted the trend to a single pricing policy, at least so far. Customers of Dillard Department Store and Seattle's Nordstrom Inc. can still look forward to sales, although they may become less frequent than during past years.

to be charged for the individual products. To illustrate, if we are dealing with cattle, the joint package would consist of one hide and two sides of beef. $Q_1$ for the firm in question, a cattle feed lot, might be 3,000 steers, resulting in 6,000 sides of beef sold at a price of $P_A$ and 3,000 hides sold at $P_B$ per unit.

Note that the $MR_T$ curve in Figure 13.3 coincides with the marginal revenue curve for Product B at all output quantities greater than $Q_2$. This is so because $MR_A$ becomes negative at that point, and hence the firm would not sell more than the quantity of Product A represented by Output Package $Q_2$. That is, the total revenues generated by Product A are maximized at Output $Q_2$, and, therefore, sales of any larger quantity would reduce revenues and profits.

If the marginal cost curve for producing the package of output intersects the total marginal revenue curve to the right of $Q_2$, profit maximization requires that the firm raise output up to this point of intersection: price Product B as indicated by its demand curve at that point, and price Product A to maximize its total revenue. This pricing situation is illustrated in Figure 13.4, which shows the same demand and marginal revenue curves presented in Figure 13.3, along with a new marginal cost curve. The optimal output quantity is $Q_3$, determined by the intersection of the marginal cost curve and the total marginal revenue curve. Product B is sold in the amount indicated by Output Package $Q_3$ and is priced at $P_B$. The sales quantity of Product A is limited to the amount in Output

■ Figure 13.4
## Optimal Pricing for Joint Products Produced in Fixed Proportions with Excess Production of One Product

When all of by-product A cannot be sold at a price that generates positive marginal revenue, its sales will be limited to the point where $MR_A = 0$. Excess production, shown as $Q_3 - Q_2$, will be destroyed or otherwise held off the market.

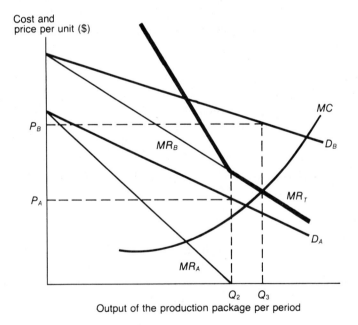

$Q_2$ and is priced at $P_A$. The excess quantity of Product *A* contained in the production, $Q_3 - Q_2$, must be destroyed or otherwise kept out of the market so that its price (and total revenue) is not lowered from that indicated at $Q_2$.

A case in point involves the joint products sliced pineapple and pineapple juice, the juice being produced as a by-product as pineapples are peeled and sliced. Some years ago, an excessive amount of juice was produced, and rather than put it on the market and depress prices, the excess was destroyed. This did not continue long, however; Dole, Del Monte, and other producers advertised heavily to shift the demand curve for juice and developed new products, such as pineapple-grapefruit juice, to create a demand for the waste product. Moreover, canning machinery was improved to reduce the percentage of product going into juice. The proportions of sliced pineapple and juice had been fixed in the short run but not in the long run.

An example of a price/output decision for two products produced in fixed proportions will help clarify these concepts.

## Case 13.1

# Joint Product Pricing at the Vancouver Paper Company

The Vancouver Paper Company, located in Vancouver, B.C., produces newsprint and packaging materials in a fixed 1:1 ratio, or one ton of packaging materials per one ton of newsprint. These two products, *A* (newsprint) and *B* (packaging materials), are produced in equal quantities because newsprint production leaves scrap materials that are useful only in the production of lower-grade packaging materials. The total and marginal cost functions for Vancouver can be written:

$$TC = \$2,000,000 + \$50Q + \$0.01Q^2,$$

where $Q$ is a composite unit of output consisting of one ton of Product *A* (newsprint) and one ton of Product *B* (packaging materials). Given current market conditions, demand curves for each product can be written as follows:

| **Newsprint** | **Packaging Materials** |
|---|---|
| $P_A = \$400 - \$0.01Q_A.$ | $P_B = \$350 - \$0.015Q_B.$ |

For each unit of $Q$ produced, the firm obtains one unit of Product *A* and one unit of Product *B* for sale to its customers. The revenue derived from the production and sale of one unit of $Q$ is composed of the revenues from the sales of one unit of Product *A* plus one unit of Product *B*.

Therefore, the total revenue function for the firm expressed as a function of $Q$ is merely the sum of the revenue functions for Products $A$ and $B$:

$$TR = TR_A + TR_B$$
$$= P_A \times Q_A + P_B \times Q_B.$$

Substituting for $P_A$ and $P_B$ results in the total revenue function:

$$TR = (\$400 - \$0.01Q_A)Q_A + (\$350 - \$0.015Q_B)Q_B$$
$$= \$400Q_A - \$0.01Q_A^2 + \$350Q_B - \$0.015Q_B^2.$$

Because one unit of Product $A$ and one unit of Product $B$ are contained in each unit of $Q$ produced, $Q_A$, $Q_B$, and $Q$ must all be equal. This allows us to substitute $Q$ for $Q_A$ and $Q_B$ to develop a total revenue function in terms of $Q$, the unit of production:

$$TR = \$400Q - \$0.01Q^2 + \$350Q - \$0.015Q^2$$
$$= \$750Q - \$0.025Q^2.$$

Note that this total revenue function assumes that all quantities of Product $A$ and $B$ that are produced are also sold. That is, it assumes no dumping or other withholding from the market of either product. Thus, it is the appropriate total revenue function if, as in Figure 13.3, the marginal revenues of both products are positive at the indicated profit-maximizing output level. When this occurs, revenues from each product contribute toward covering marginal costs.

Because the firm's total cost function for the production of these joint products was expressed in terms of $Q$, the unit of production, the profit function can be formed by combining that cost function with the total revenue function:

$$Profit = \pi = TR - TC$$
$$= \$750Q - \$0.025Q^2 - (\$2,000,000 + \$50Q + \$0.01Q^2)$$
$$= \$700Q - \$0.035Q^2 - \$2,000,000$$

The profit-maximizing output level is found where marginal profit is zero.

$$Marginal\ Profit = \frac{\partial \pi}{\partial Q} = \$700 - \$0.07Q = 0$$
$$0.07Q = 700$$
$$Q = 10,000\ units.$$

Note that at the 10,000-unit activity level the marginal revenue of each product is positive:

$$MR_A = \$400 - \$0.02Q_A \qquad\qquad MR_B = \$350 - \$0.03Q_B$$
$$= \$400 - \$0.02(10,000) \qquad\qquad = \$350 - \$0.03(10,000)$$
$$= \$200\ (at\ 10,000\ Units). \qquad\qquad = \$50\ (at\ 10,000\ Units).$$

Therefore, each product makes a positive contribution toward covering the marginal cost of production, where:

$$MC = \$50 + \$0.02Q$$
$$= \$50 + \$0.02(10,000)$$
$$= \$250.$$

There is no reason to expand or reduce production because $MR = MR_A + MR_B = MC = \$250$, and each product generates positive marginal revenues.

Prices for each product and total profits for Vancouver can be calculated from the demand and total profit functions:

$$P_A = \$400 - \$0.01Q_A \qquad P_B = \$350 - \$0.015Q_B$$
$$= \$400 - \$0.01(10,000) \qquad = \$350 - \$0.015(10,000)$$
$$= \$300, \qquad\qquad = \$200,$$

and

$$\pi = P_A Q_A + P_B Q_B - TC$$
$$= \$300(10,000) + \$200(10,000) - \$2,000,000$$
$$- \$50(10,000) - \$0.01(10,000^2)$$
$$= \$1,500,000.$$

Thus, Vancouver should produce 10,000 units of output and it should sell the resulting 10,000 units of Product A (newsprint) at a price of $300 per ton and 10,000 units of Product B (packaging materials) at a price of $200 per ton. The company would earn a total profit of $1.5 million.

The determination of a profit-maximizing activity level would be only slightly more complex if a downturn in demand for either Product A or B caused marginal revenue for one product to be negative when all output produced is sold to the marketplace.

For example, suppose that an economic recession caused the demand for Product B (packaging materials) to fall dramatically, while the demand for Product A (newsprint) and marginal cost conditions held steady. Assume new demand and marginal revenue relations for Product B of:

$$P'_B = \$290 - \$0.02Q_B$$
$$MR'_B = dTR'_B/dQ_B = \$290 - \$0.04Q_B.$$

Now, a dramatically lower price of $90 per ton [$= \$290 - \$0.02(10,000)$] would be required to sell 10,000 units of Product B. However, this price and activity level would be suboptimal.

To see why, we must again calculate the profit-maximizing activity level, assuming that all output is sold. The new marginal revenue curve for $Q$ is:

$$MR = MR_A + MR'_B$$
$$= \$400 - \$0.02Q_A + \$290 - \$0.04Q_B$$
$$= \$690 - \$0.06Q.$$

If all production were sold, the profit-maximizing level for output would be found by setting marginal revenue equal to marginal cost and solving for $Q$:

$$MR = MC$$
$$\$690 - \$0.06Q = \$50 + \$0.02Q$$
$$0.08Q = 640$$
$$Q = 8,000.$$

At $Q = 8,000$, marginal revenue and marginal cost both equal $210, since:

$$MR = \$690 - \$0.06Q \qquad MC = \$50 + \$0.02Q$$
$$= \$690 - \$0.06(8,000) \qquad = \$50 + \$0.02(8,000)$$
$$= \$210. \qquad = \$210.$$

Note, however, that the marginal revenue of Product B is no longer positive:

$$MR_A = \$400 - \$0.02Q_A \qquad MR'_B = \$290 - \$0.04Q_B$$
$$= \$400 - \$0.02(8,000) \qquad = \$290 - \$0.04(8,000)$$
$$= \$240. \qquad = -\$30.$$

Even though $MR = MC = \$210$, the marginal revenue of Product B is negative at the $Q = 8,000$ activity level. This means that the price reduction necessary to sell the last unit of Product B caused Vancouver's total revenue to decline by $30. Rather than sell Product B under such unfavorable terms, Vancouver would prefer to withhold some from the marketplace. On the other hand, Vancouver would like to produce and sell more than 8,000 units of Product A since $MR_A > MC$ at the 8,000 unit activity level. In other words, it would be profitable for the company to expand production of $Q$ just to increase sales of Product A, even if it destroyed or otherwise withheld from the market the necessary added production of Product B.

Under these circumstances, we set the marginal revenue of Product A, the only product that will be sold at the margin, equal to the overall marginal cost of production to find the profit-maximizing activity level:

$$MR_A = MC$$
$$\$400 - \$0.02Q = \$50 + \$0.02Q$$
$$\$0.04Q = \$350$$
$$Q = 8,750 \text{ Units.}$$

Thus, Vancouver should produce 8,750 units of $Q$, $Q_A$, and $Q_B$. Since this activity level is based on the assumption that only Product A will be sold at the margin and that the marginal revenue of Product A covers all the marginal costs of production, *the effective marginal cost of Product B is zero*. So long as production is sufficient to provide 8,750 units of Product A, 8,750 units of Product B will also be produced without any additional cost.

With an effective marginal cost of zero for Product B, its contribution to firm profits will be maximized by pricing the product to maximize the total revenue received. This is accomplished by setting the marginal revenue of Product B equal to zero (its effective marginal cost):

$$MR_B' = \$0$$

$$\$290 - \$0.04Q_B = 0$$

$$\$0.04Q_B = \$290$$

$$Q_B = 7,250.$$

Thus, 8,750 units of $Q$, and therefore of $Q_A$ and $Q_B$, will be produced, but only 7,250 units of Product B will be sold. The remaining 1,500 units of $Q_B$ will be destroyed or otherwise withheld from the market.

The new price and maximum total profit levels for Vancouver can now be determined as:

$$P_A = \$400 - \$0.01Q_A \qquad P_B' = \$290 - \$0.02Q_B$$

$$= \$400 - \$0.01(8,750) \qquad = \$290 - \$0.02(7,250)$$

$$= \$312.50, \qquad = \$145,$$

$$\pi = P_AQ_A + P_B'Q_B - TC$$

$$= \$312.50(8,750) + \$145(7,250) - \$2,000,000$$

$$- \$50(8,750) - \$0.01(8,750^2)$$

$$= \$582,500.$$

No other combination of production and sales levels can generate as large a profit for Vancouver.

## Joint Products Produced in Variable Proportions

Often, the firm can vary the proportions in which it produces joint products. Even the classic example of fixed proportions in the joint production of beef and hides holds only over short periods, because cattle can be bred to provide an output package with differing proportions of these two products.

When the firm can vary the proportions in which the joint output is produced, it is possible to construct separate marginal cost relations for each of the joint products. This is illustrated in Table 13.5, a schedule of

■ Table 13.5

## Cost/Output Schedule for Two Joint Products

| | | | Output of *A* | | |
|---|---|---|---|---|---|
| Output of *B* | 1 | 2 | 3 | 4 | 5 |
| 1 | $ 5 | $ 7 | $10 | $15 | $ 22 |
| 2 | 10 | 13 | 18 | 23 | 31 |
| 3 | 20 | 25 | 33 | 40 | 50 |
| 4 | 35 | 43 | 53 | 63 | 75 |
| 5 | 55 | 67 | 78 | 90 | 105 |

the total cost/output relations for two joint products, *A* and *B*. Since the marginal cost of either product is defined as the increase in total costs associated with a unit increase in that product, *holding constant the quantity of the other product produced*, the marginal costs of producing *A* can be determined by examining the data in the rows of the table, and the marginal costs of *B* are obtained from the columns. For example, the marginal cost of the 4th unit of *A*, holding the production of *B* at 2 units, is $5 (= $23 − $18); the marginal cost of the 5th unit of *B* when output of *A* is 3 units is $25 (= $78 − $53).

Optimal price/output determination for joint products in this case requires a simultaneous solution of their cost and revenue relation. The procedure can be illustrated graphically through the construction of iso-revenue and isocost curves, as in Figure 13.5. The isocost curves map out the locus of all production combinations that can be produced for a given total cost; the isorevenue curves indicate all combinations of the products that, when sold, result in a given revenue.[2] At the points of tangency between the isocost and the isorevenue curves, the marginal costs of producing the products are proportionate to their marginal revenues. The tangencies, therefore, indicate the optimal proportions in which to produce the products. Because profit equals revenue minus cost, the firm maximizes profit by operating at the tangency between the isorevenue and isocost curves whose positive difference is greatest. At that tangency, the marginal cost of producing each product just equals the marginal revenue it generates.

Point $Q^*$ in Figure 13.5 indicates the profit-maximizing combination of Products *A* and *B* in the illustrated example. Production and sale of

[2]The isorevenue relations in Figure 13.5 have been drawn as straight lines for simplicity. This implies that the products are sold in competitive markets; only if the demand curve is horizontal will prices not vary with respect to changing quantities of the two products. If pure competition does not exist and prices vary as output changes, the isorevenue curves will not be straight lines, but the optimal output combinations will still be indicated by tangencies between isocost and isorevenue curves.

■ Figure 13.5
## Optimal Price/Output Combinations for Joint Products Produced in Variable Proportions

If joint products can be produced in variable proportions, profits are maximized where $MR = MC$ for each by-product. (All values are in dollars.)

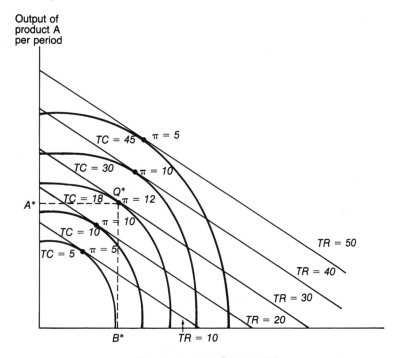

$A^*$ units of $A$ and $B^*$ units of $B$ result in a profit of 12, the maximum possible under the conditions shown.

We should note that while the preceding discussion demonstrates the possibility of determining the separate marginal costs of production for goods produced jointly in variable proportions, it is impossible to determine the individual average costs. These individual costs cannot be determined because the common costs of production—costs associated with raw materials and equipment used for both products, management expenses, and other overhead—cannot be allocated to the individual products on any economically sound basis. Therefore, any allocation of common costs that affects the price/output decision is necessarily arbitrary and possibly irrational. This point is stressed because of the frequency with which businesses and government regulatory bodies use fully allocated average costs in pricing problems of this kind.

Optimal multiple-product pricing requires a complete marginal (or incremental) analysis of the total effect of the decision on the firm's profitability. This analysis must include an examination of demand interrelations to be sure that a picture of the marginal revenue to be derived from a decision is complete. Likewise, complementarity and competition in production must be accounted for in the analysis of marginal costs. For alternative goods produced from a common production facility, this means that opportunity costs of forgone production must be considered in determining the relevant marginal costs of a decision. Linear programming has proved to be useful for cost/output analysis of this type when common facilities must be allocated among a variety of products.

# SUMMARY

This chapter examined a number of pricing topics. Markup pricing, a pricing technique that is common in practice, was shown to be closely related to marginal analysis. Proper use of markup pricing techniques requires that close attention be paid to both cost and demand considerations. The sensitivity of prices to marginal costs, coupled with the inverse relation typically observed between profit margins and the price elasticity of demand, suggest that both cost and demand considerations do indeed play major roles in markup pricing practices.

Incremental profit analysis was also shown to be a powerful tool for optimal pricing decisions. Incremental profit analysis requires that only the added costs and revenues associated with a given decision be considered. During *peak* production periods, when productive facilities are fully utilized, capacity expansion would be required to increase output. During such periods, fully allocated costs are often a close approximation to incremental costs, and they are therefore appropriate for pricing and other decision-making purposes. During *off-peak* periods, when a firm has excess capacity, fully allocated costs are seldom appropriate for decision purposes. Only output-related incremental costs are relevant in such situations.

When a firm sells its product in multiple markets, it may be able to increase profits by charging different prices to different customers, a practice known as price discrimination. To successfully engage in price discrimination, the firm must (1) face differing price elasticities of demand in various market segments and (2) be able to isolate its various submarkets to prevent transfers. Profit maximization under price discrimination requires that the firm equate marginal revenue and marginal cost in each submarket. Perfect (*first-degree*) price discrimination will maximize seller profits by eliminating all *consumers' surplus*, the unpaid-for benefit derived from consumption activities.

*Multiple-product pricing* was shown to use the same economic concepts as single-product pricing. Optimal multiple-product pricing requires that incremental revenues and incremental costs be equal for each product. The pricing analysis is complicated, however, by demand and production interrelations caused by competition or complementarity among the products' demand or production characteristics. When the demand for one product is tied to the demand for a related product or line of business, properly calculated incremental revenues will reflect both direct and indirect influences. Similarly, for joint products produced under fixed proportions, optimal prices, production, and sales levels for each product will differ according to the overall level of output. Proper use of the incremental profit concept to ensure that a pricing decision's total effect on the firm is analyzed leads to optimal pricing in the multiple-product case, just as with a single product.

## Questions

13.1  What is markup pricing?

13.2  Develop and explain the relation between the markup-on-cost and markup-on-price formulas.

13.3  Develop and explain the relation between the optimal markup on cost and the point price elasticity of demand.

13.4  Develop and explain the relation between the optimal markup on price and the point price elasticity of demand.

13.5  Discuss the role of sunk costs in pricing practice.

13.6  "One of the least practical suggestions that economists have offered to managers is that they set marginal revenues equal to marginal costs." Discuss this statement.

13.7  "Marginal cost pricing, as well as the use of incremental analysis, is looked upon with favor by economists, especially those on the staffs of regulatory agencies. With this encouragement, regulated industries do indeed employ these 'rational' techniques quite frequently. Unregulated firms, on the other hand, use marginal or incremental cost pricing much less frequently, sticking to cost-plus, or full-cost, pricing except under unusual circumstances. In my opinion, this goes a long way toward explaining the problems of the regulated firms vis-à-vis unregulated industry." Discuss this statement.

13.8  What is price discrimination?

13.9  What conditions are necessary before price discrimination is both possible and profitable? Why does price discrimination result in higher profits?

13.10 Why is it possible to determine the marginal costs of joint products produced in variable proportions but not of joint products produced in fixed proportions?

## Problems

13.1  Cliff Claven is a project coordinator at Norm Peterson & Associates, Ltd., a large Boston-based painting contractor. Claven has asked you to complete an analysis of profit margins earned on a number of recent projects. Unfortunately, your predecessor on this project was abruptly transferred, leaving you with only sketchy information on the firm's pricing practices.

A. Use the available data to complete the following table:

| Price | Marginal Cost | Markup on Cost | Markup on Price |
|---|---|---|---|
| $ 1,000 | $  500 | 100.0% | 50.0% |
| 2,000 | 750 | | |
| 3,000 | | 50.0 | |
| 5,000 | | 80.0 | |
| | 8,000 | | 20.0 |
| 15,000 | | 25.0 | |
| | 18,000 | | 10.0 |
| 25,000 | | | 4.0 |
| | 20,000 | 150.0 | |
| | 99,000 | | 1.0 |

B. Calculate the optimal markup on cost and optimal markup on price for each of the following proposed projects, based on the following estimates of the point price elasticity of demand:

| Project | Price Elasticity of Demand, $\epsilon_P$ | Optimal Markup on Cost | Optimal Markup on Price |
|---|---|---|---|
| A | −2 | | |
| B | −4 | | |
| C | −10 | | |
| D | −20 | | |
| E | −50 | | |

13.2 Payless Shoe Stores, Inc., cut prices on ladies dress shoes by 5 percent during the first quarter and enjoyed a 10-percent increase in unit sales over the period as compared to a year earlier.

A. Calculate the point price elasticity of demand for Payless shoes.

B. Calculate the company's optimal shoe price if marginal cost is $10 per unit.

13.3 Brake-Checkup, Inc., offers automobile brake analysis and repair at a number of outlets in the Philadelphia area. The company recently initiated a policy of matching the lowest advertised competitor price. As a result, Brake-Checkup has been forced to reduce the average price for brake jobs by 3 percent, but it has enjoyed a 15-percent increase in customer traffic. Meanwhile, marginal costs have held steady at $120 per brake job.

    A.  Calculate the point price elasticity of demand for brake jobs.

    B.  Calculate Brake-Checkup's optimal price and markup on cost.

13.4  TLC Lawncare, Inc., provides fertilizer and weed-control lawn services to residential customers. Its seasonal service package, regularly priced at $250, includes several chemical spray treatments. As part of an effort to expand its customer base, TLC offered $50 off its regular price to customers in the Dallas area. Response was enthusiastic, with sales rising to 5,750 units (packages) from the 3,250 units sold in the same period last year.

    A.  Calculate the arc price elasticity of demand for TLC service.

    B.  Assume that the arc price elasticity (from Part A) is the best available estimate of the point price elasticity of demand. If marginal cost is $135 per unit for labor and materials, calculate TLC's optimal markup on price and its optimal price.

13.5  Roseanne Connors, director of the Kiddie-Care Learning Center, is considering offering child-care services from 6 to 11 P.M. on weekends. Currently, the center operates only Monday through Friday between the hours of 6 A.M. and 6 P.M. At a price of $10 per night, Connors projects that parents of 15 children would take advantage of the new service. Projected costs for each hour that the center is open are as follows:

| | Costs (per hour) |
|---|---|
| Two staff members' salaries (overtime rate) | $10 (each) |
| Variable overhead (electricity, heat) | 5 |
| Allocated fixed overhead (lease expenses, insurance, etc.) | 10 |

    A.  Would the new weekend service be profitable?

    B.  Calculate the breakeven price for weekend service at a projected attendance of 15 children.

13.6  The Delta Construction Company is a building contractor serving the Gulf Coast region. The company recently bid on a new office building construction project in Mobile, Alabama. Delta has incurred bid development and job cost-out expenses of $25,000 prior to submission of the bid. The bid was based on the following projected costs:

| | |
|---|---|
| Bid development and job cost-out expenses | $   25,000 |
| Materials | 881,000 |
| Labor (50,000 hours @ $26) | 1,300,000 |
| Variable overhead (40 percent of direct labor) | 520,000 |
| Allocated fixed overhead (6 percent of total costs) | 174,000 |
| Total costs | $2,900,000 |

A. What is Delta's minimum acceptable (breakeven) contract price, assuming that the company is operating at peak capacity?

B. What is the company's minimum acceptable contract price if an economic downturn has left the company with substantial excess capacity?

13.7 The General Appliance Company manufactures an electric toaster. Sales of the toaster have increased steadily during the previous five years, and, because of a recently completed expansion program, annual capacity is now 500,000 units. Production and sales during the coming year are forecast to be 400,000 units, and standard production costs have been estimated as follows:

| | |
|---|---:|
| Materials | $ 6.00 |
| Direct labor | 4.00 |
| Variable indirect labor | 2.00 |
| Fixed overhead | 3.00 |
| Allocated cost per unit | $15.00 |

In addition to production costs, General incurs fixed selling expenses of $1.50 per unit and variable warranty repair expenses of $1.20 per unit. General currently receives $20 per unit from its customers (primarily retail department stores), and it expects this price to hold during the coming year.

After making the preceding projections, General received an inquiry about the purchase of a large number of toasters by a discount department store. The inquiry contained two purchase offers:

- *Offer 1:* The department store would purchase 80,000 units at $14.60 per unit. These units would bear the General label, and be covered by the General warranty.
- *Offer 2:* The department store would purchase 120,000 units at $14.00 per unit. These units would be sold under the buyer's private label, and General would not provide warranty service.

A. Evaluate the incremental net income potential of each offer.

B. What other factors should General consider in deciding which offer to accept?

C. Which offer (if either) should General accept? Why?

13.8 Van Conversions, Ltd., offers its custom services to both auto dealers (wholesale) and retail customers. Each conversion costs the company $1,000 in variable labor and material expenses. Demand functions for the van conversion service are as follows:

$$P_W = \$1,500 - \$0.5Q_W, \qquad \text{(Wholesale)}$$

$$P_R = \$5,000 - \$2Q_R. \qquad \text{(Retail)}$$

A.  Assuming that the company can price discriminate between its two types of customers, calculate the profit-maximizing price, output, and profit-contribution levels.

B.  Calculate point price elasticities for each customer type at the activity levels identified in Part A. Are the differences in these elasticities consistent or inconsistent with your recommended price differences in Part A? Why or why not?

13.9  Each ton of ore mined from the Baby Doe Mine in Leadville, Colorado, produces one ounce of silver and one pound of lead in a fixed 1:1 ratio. Marginal costs are $10 per ton of ore mined.

The demand curve for silver is:

$$P_S = \$11 - \$0.00003Q_S,$$

and the demand curve for lead is:

$$P_L = \$0.4 - \$0.000005Q_L,$$

where $Q_S$ is ounces of silver and $Q_L$ is pounds of lead.

A.  Calculate profit-maximizing sales quantities and prices for silver and lead.

B.  Now assume that wild speculation in the silver market has created a fivefold (or 500-percent) increase in silver demand. Calculate optimal sales quantities and prices for both silver and lead under these conditions.

13.10 Tacoma Wood Products, Inc., produces large quantities of scrap bark and sawdust as a by-product of its lumber production operations. For each thousand board feet of lumber produced, one ton of by-product is created. Lumber is sold to a national market of wholesalers, and there is a limited local demand for the by-product for use in low-grade paper production.

Total costs for Tacoma are:

$$TC = \$100 + \$10Q + \$4Q^2,$$

where $Q$ represents a unit of production consisting of one thousand board feet of lumber, a unit of $A$; and one ton of bark and sawdust by-product, a unit of $B$.

Demand curves for the two products are:

$$P_A = \$600 - \$1Q_A, \text{ (Lumber)} \qquad P_B = \$100 - \$1Q_B. \text{ (By-product)}$$

A.  What would be the optimal price/output combination for the two products, assuming that Tacoma operates as a profit-maximizing firm and that by-product can be dumped at no cost in a local landfill?

B.  Assume now that the local landfill is nearing capacity and begins charging Tacoma for dumping privileges. Calculate the maximum dumping charge that Tacoma would be willing to pay.

## Selected References

Allen, Beth, and Martin Hellwig. "Price-Setting Firms and the Oligopolistic Foundations of Perfect Competition." *American Economic Review* 76 (May 1986): 387–392.

Bellizzi, Joseph A., and Robert E. Hite. "Supervising Unethical Salesforce Behavior." *Journal of Marketing* 53 (April 1989): 36–48.

Brannman, Lance, J. Douglas Klein, and Leonard W. Weiss. "The Price Effects of Increased Competition in Auction Markets." *Review of Economics and Statistics* 69 (February 1987): 24–33.

Cauley, Stephen Day. "The Time Price of Medical Care." *Review of Economics and Statistics* 69 (February 1987): 59–68.

Crain, W. Mark, William F. Shughart II, and Robert D. Tollison. "The Convergence of Satisficing to Marginalism: An Empirical Test." *Journal of Economic Behavior and Organization* 5 (September–December 1984): 375–385.

Curry, David J., and Peter C. Riesz. "Prices and Price/Quality Relationships: A Longitudinal Analysis." *Journal of Marketing* 52 (January 1988): 36–51.

Frantzen, Dirk J. "The Cyclical Behavior of Manufacturing Prices in a Small Open Economy." *Journal of Industrial Economics* 34 (June 1986): 389–407.

Haas-Wilson, Deborah. "Tying Requirements in Markets with Many Sellers." *Review of Economics and Statistics* 69 (February 1987): 170–175.

Hill, Stephen, and Paul Blyton. "The Practice of Decision Making–Some Evidence." *Managerial and Decision Economics* 7 (March 1986): 25–28.

Knetter, Michael M. "Price Discrimination by U.S. and German Exporters." *American Economic Review* 79 (March 1989): 198–210.

Lazear, Edward P. "Retail Pricing and Clearance Sales." *American Economic Review* 76 (March 1986): 14–32.

Manes, Rene P., Francoise Shoumaker, and Peter A. Silhan. "Demand Relationships and Pricing Decisions for Related Products." *Managerial and Decision Economics* 5 (June 1984): 120–122.

Millner, Edward L., and George E. Hoffer. "Has Pricing Behavior in the U.S. Automobile Industry Become More Competitive?" *Applied Economics* 21 (March 1989): 295–304.

Oliver, Richard L., and John E. Swan. "Consumer Perceptions of Interpersonal Equity and Satisfaction in Transactions: A Field Survey Approach." *Journal of Marketing* 53 (April 1989): 21–35.

Ornstein, Stanley I., and Dominique M. Hassens. "Resale Price Maintenance: Output Increasing or Restricting? The Case of Distilled Spirits in the United States." *Journal of Industrial Economics* 36 (September 1987): 1–18.

Png, I.P.L., and D. Hirshleifer. "Price Discrimination through Offers to Match Price." *Journal of Business* 60 (July 1987): 365–383.

Rao, Vithala R. "Pricing Research in Marketing: The State of the Art." *Journal of Business* 57 (January 1984): S39–60.

Ross, Thomas W. "The Costs of Regulating Price Differences." *Journal of Business* 59 (January 1986): 143–156.

Tellis, Gerard J. "Beyond the Many Faces of Price: An Integration of Pricing Strategies." *Journal of Marketing* 50 (October 1986): 146–160.

Wong, Jilnaught. "Economic Incentives for the Voluntary Disclosure of Current Cost Financial Statements." *Journal of Accounting and Economics* 10 (April 1988): 151–167.

A P P E N D I X · 1 3 A

# Transfer Pricing

Technological advances and expanding markets brought on by a continually larger and wealthier population have, over time, led to the development of large, multi-product firms. This trend has been accelerated by financial factors—large, diversified firms have greater access to capital markets and are frequently thought to be less risky than small, undiversified companies; both these factors cause larger firms to have a lower cost of capital than smaller ones. Larger size results in increasing costs of internal communications and coordination, so if production, marketing, and financial economies of scale are to be realized, these coordination costs must be kept within reasonable bounds.

Perhaps the most significant management innovations in recent years—the establishment of divisional profit centers and decentralized operations—were designed to combat the problem of increasing costs of coordinating large-scale enterprises. Here separate profit centers are established for different products, and the individual profit centers are kept small enough so that their managers can control them without the need for excessive, expensive staffs to coordinate the various phases of the operation.

Decentralization into semiautonomous profit centers, while absolutely necessary for large-scale enterprises, creates problems of its own. Perhaps the most critical of these is that of **transfer pricing** or the pricing of products transferred between divisions. United States Steel, for example, owns coal mines and iron mines as well as steel mills, and the coal and iron divisions sell to the steel division as well as to outsiders. How much should the steel division pay for the coal and iron ore it obtains internally? Should it buy its entire requirements of these materials from the coal and iron divisions, or should it meet part of its needs from outside sources? Further, should the coal and iron divisions be expected to produce whatever amounts of coal and iron the steel division requires? Suppose the steel division offers to pay $15 a ton for coal, but the coal division can sell to outsiders for $20; should the coal divisions be required to sell to the steel mills?

The answers to these questions are critically important for at least two reasons. First, the way they are answered will influence the output of each division, hence the output of the firm as a whole. If they are answered incorrectly, the firm will not produce at the optimal level. Second, transfer prices are an important determinant of divisional profits, and since promotions, bonuses, stock options, and so on are typically based on divisional performance, if a system of transfer prices is arbitrary and inequitable, it can completely wreck morale and literally destroy the firm.

While the topic of transfer pricing is one of the more complex in managerial economics, and we cannot hope to more than scratch the

**transfer pricing:**
The pricing of products transferred among divisions of a firm.

surface in a textbook treatment of this kind, its importance dictates that we at least demonstrate the nature of the problem and point the direction toward optimal transfer rules.

## TRANSFER PRICING WITH NO EXTERNAL MARKET FOR THE INTERMEDIATE PRODUCT

The basic criterion by which to judge any internal transfer pricing scheme is the impact it will have on the operating efficiency of the firm. Optimally, a transfer pricing system will lead to activity levels in each division of the firm that are consistent with profit maximization for the entire enterprise. Alternatively stated, a well-designed transfer pricing scheme will lead to activity levels for the various decentralized divisions of a firm that are precisely identical to the activity levels that would prevail in centralized decision making without provision for divisional profit centers.

This relationship can be examined in the context of a two-division firm producing a single product. Such a case is illustrated in Figure 13A.1, which shows the demand, marginal revenue, and marginal cost curves for the entire operation of the firm.

Profit maximization requires that the firm expand its output so long as the marginal revenue of additional units is greater than their marginal costs. In terms of Figure 13A.1, this means that the firm's profits are

■ Figure 13A.1
**Profit Maximizing Price/Output Combination**

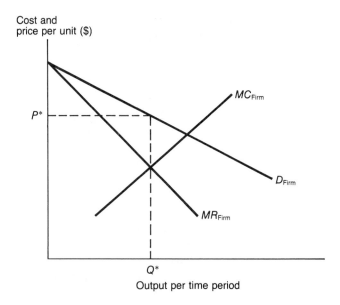

maximized at output $Q^*$, indicating a market price of $P^*$ for the firm's product.

To clarify the relationship we are developing, it will prove useful to introduce a specific set of cost and demand functions. Assume that the demand curve illustrated in Figure 13A.1 is:

$$P = \$100 - \$1Q, \qquad \textbf{13A.1}$$

and that the firm's total cost function is:

$$TC = \$70 + \$10Q + \$1.5Q^2. \qquad \textbf{13A.2}$$

The marginal revenue and marginal cost curves in Figure 13A.1 are then found as:[1]

$$MR = \$100 - \$2Q. \qquad \textbf{13A.3}$$
$$MC = \$10 + \$3Q. \qquad \textbf{13A.4}$$

Profit maximization occurs at the point where marginal revenue equals marginal cost, so the optimal output level is found as:

$$MR = MC$$
$$\$100 - \$2Q = \$10 + \$3Q$$
$$90 = 5Q$$
$$Q = 18.$$

Thus, $Q^*$ in Figure 13A.1 is 18 units and $P^*$ is \$82 (\$100 − \$18).

Consider now the situation if the firm we are examining is division-alized into a manufacturing and a distribution division. The demand curve facing the distribution division is precisely the same demand curve the firm faced initially. The total cost function of the firm is un-changed, but it can be broken down into the costs of manufacture and the costs of distribution. Assume that such a breakdown results in the divisional cost functions:

$$TC_{Mfg.} = \$50 + \$7Q + \$0.5Q^2$$

and

$$TC_{Distr.} = \$20 + \$3Q + \$1Q^2.$$

---

[1]The marginal revenue function is found as the derivative of the total revenue function; that is:

$$TR = P \times Q$$
$$= (\$100 - \$1Q)Q$$
$$= \$100Q - \$1Q^2.$$
$$MR = \frac{dTR}{dQ} = \$100 - \$2Q.$$

The marginal cost curve is given by the derivative of the total cost curve, so:

$$MC = \frac{dTC}{dQ} = \$10 + \$3Q.$$

The total cost function for the firm would be:

$$TC_{Firm} = TC_{Mfg.} + TC_{Distr.}$$
$$= \$50 + \$7Q + \$0.5Q^2 + \$20 + \$3Q + \$1Q^2$$
$$= \$70 + \$10Q + \$1.5Q^2,$$

precisely the same as Equation 13A.2. Obviously in this situation no substantive changes have taken place, and the firm should still operate at an 18-unit output level for profit maximization.

When no external market exists for the intermediate product (that is, if the manufacturing division is not able to sell its product externally), it can be shown that intrafirm transfers should take place based on prices that are set equal to the marginal costs of the transferring division—the manufacturing division in this case. This relation is shown in Figure 13A.2, which adds the net marginal revenue ($MR_{Firm} - MC_{Distr.}$) curve for the distribution division and the marginal cost curve for the manufacturing division to the revenue and cost curves illustrated in Figure 13A.1. The *net marginal revenue curve* for the distribution division is found by subtracting the marginal costs of that division from the marginal revenues generated by its marketing activities. It is essentially nothing more than a net marginal profits curve for that division prior to

■ Figure 13A.2
**Transfer Pricing with No External Market for the Intermediate Product**

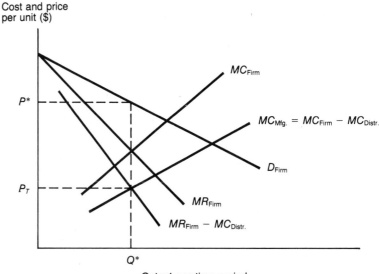

taking account of the cost of the product that has been transferred to it from the manufacturing division.

Note that in Figure 13A.2 the net marginal revenue curve for the distribution division intersects the marginal cost curve for the manufacturing division at $Q^*$, the firm's profit-maximizing activity level. This is not mere happenstance but must always occur. The reason is simple. Recall that the distribution division's net marginal revenue curve is nothing more than the firm's marginal revenue curve less the marginal cost of the distribution division. Similarly, the manufacturing division's marginal cost curve is nothing more than the firm's marginal cost curve less the marginal cost of the distribution division. If the firm's marginal revenue and marginal costs are equal at $Q^*$ units of output, then obviously the distribution division's net marginal revenue must be equal to the manufacturing division's marginal cost at the same output level. Algebraically, if:

$$MR_{Firm} = MC_{Firm},$$

then

$$MR_{Firm} - MC_{Distr.} = MC_{Firm} - MC_{Distr.} = MC_{Mfg.}.$$

This means that the correct transfer price for intermediate products for which there is no external market is the marginal cost of production. In Figure 13A.2 this transfer price is $P_T$.

Continuing with the numerical example, the net marginal revenue curve for the distribution division is given by the expression:

$$MR_{Firm} - MC_{Dist.} = \$100 - \$2Q - (\$3 + \$2Q)$$
$$= \$97 - \$4Q.$$

Equating this to the marginal cost curve of the manufacturing division results in:

$$MR_{Firm} - MC_{Distr.} = MC_{Mfg.}$$
$$\$97 - \$4Q = \$7 + \$1Q$$
$$90 = 5Q$$
$$Q = 18.$$

This result indicates once again that at an optimal activity level the net marginal revenue of the distribution division will equal the marginal cost of the manufacturing division. This leads to the profit-maximizing condition that internal transfers of intermediate products for which no external market exists must take place at marginal production costs.

It still remains to demonstrate that by setting the transfer price equal to the marginal cost of production, the two decentralized divisions will choose to operate at the firm's profit-maximizing activity level. Consider first the manufacturing division. If the firm's central management specifies that transfers are to take place at marginal manufacturing costs, then the marginal cost curve of the manufacturing division becomes its supply curve, just as the marginal cost curve is the supply curve for a firm operating as a price taker, such as a firm in pure competition. Given a transfer price, $P_T$, the manufacturing division *must* supply a quantity such that $MC_{Mfg.} = P_T$.

Now consider the distribution division. The profit function for that division can be written as:

$$
\begin{aligned}
\text{Profit} &= TR_{Firm} - TC_{Distr.}\\
&= \$100Q - \$1Q^2 - [\$20 + \$3Q + \$1Q^2 + (P_T \times Q)]\\
&= \$97Q - \$2Q^2 - \$20 - (P_T \times Q). \qquad \textbf{13A.5}
\end{aligned}
$$

Notice that in this expression we have added the term $P_T \times Q$ to the total cost function for the distribution division to account for the fact that this division must now pay a price of $P_T$ for each unit of product it receives from the manufacturing division.

Since profit maximization requires that marginal profit be zero, the profit maximization requirement for the distribution division is that the derivative of Equation 13A.5 be set to zero; that is:

$$
M\pi = \$97 - \$4Q - P_T = 0,
$$

or, solving for $P_T$, the transfer price:

$$
P_T = \$97 - \$4Q. \qquad \textbf{13A.6}
$$

Thus, profit maximization for the distribution division requires that the transfer price be equal to $\$97 - \$4Q$. Therefore, $\$97 - \$4Q$ can be considered a demand function indicating how the transfer price of the product is related to the quantity that the distribution division will seek to purchase. Note, however, that this demand function is identical to the net marginal revenue curve for the distribution division developed above.

Now if the distribution division determines the quantity it will purchase by movement along the net marginal revenue curve, and the manufacturing division is supplying output along its marginal cost curve, then the only market clearing transfer price is that price which occurs where $MR_{Firm} - MC_{Distr.} = MC_{Mfg.}$. In the example, this is at 18 units of output with a transfer price, $P_T$, equal to $\$25$ ($MC_{Mfg.} = \$7 + \$1Q = \$25$ at $Q = 18$). At a transfer price above $\$25$ the distribution division will accept fewer units of output than the manufacturing division wants to supply, while if $P_T$ is less than $\$25$, the distribution division will seek to purchase more units than the manufacturing division desires to produce. Only at a $\$25$ transfer price are the supply and demand forces in balance.

The marginal cost pricing rule can be implemented in actual practice in either of two ways. First, the distribution division could be given the manufacturing division's marginal cost curve and told that this is the supply function it must use in determining the quantity it desires to purchase internally. Alternatively, the manufacturing division could be supplied with data on the net marginal revenue curve for the distribution division and told to use this as its relevant marginal revenue curve in determining the quantity it should supply. In either case the divisions should choose to operate at Output $Q^*$, and a transfer price of $P_T = MC_{Mfg.}$ should prevail.

# TRANSFER PRICING OF A PRODUCT HAVING A COMPETITIVE MARKET

A second transfer pricing problem involves goods that can be sold externally in a competitive market. In this case, where the transferred good is sold in a competitive market, the market price of the good is also the appropriate transfer price; its use will lead to firm profit-maximizing levels of operation for all the divisions involved in the transfer.

Figure 13A.3 illustrates the economics of the competitive case. There, the demand, $D_F$, and the marginal revenue, $MR_F$, curves for the final product, $F$, are shown along with the demand, $D_T$, marginal revenue, $MR_T$, and marginal cost, $MC_T$, curves for $T$, the intermediate or trans-

■ Figure 13A.3
**Transfer Price Determination with the Intermediate Product Sold Externally in a Competitive Market: Excess Internal Demand**

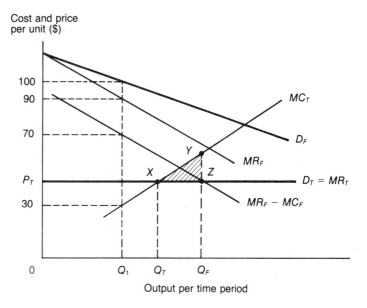

ferred product. The line $MR_F - MC_F$ represents the net marginal contribution to overhead and profits of the final product *before the transfer price is deducted.* (The area under the curve $MR_F - MC_F$ represents the total contribution *before* paying for the transferred product.) That is, $MR_F - MC_F$ shows the excess of the marginal revenue of $F$ over its marginal cost prior to a payment for the transferred good, $T$. At Output $Q_1$, for example, Product $F$ would sell at a price of $100 and would have a marginal revenue equal to $90. Since $MR_F - MC_F = \$70$, $MC_F$, *before any charge for the intermediate product,* is equal to $20. The marginal cost of the transferred product at Output $Q_1$ is $30. Since the firm earns a contribution margin of $70 on the final product at $Q_1$, and since the intermediate good costs only $30, output should be expanded beyond $Q_1$.

Profit maximization requires that both the final product and the intermediate product divisions operate at the output levels at which their marginal costs equal their marginal revenues. At any lower output level the marginal revenue obtained from sales of additional units is greater than the marginal costs of their production, and profits are increased by expanded production. At higher output levels the reverse is true; marginal costs exceed marginal revenues, and a reduction in output increases profits.

The optimal outputs for the two divisions are shown in Figure 13A.3. Division $F$ should purchase $Q_F$ units of the intermediate good, paying the market price $P_T$ for it.[2] At that point the marginal cost of producing $F$ is equal to its marginal revenue, and divisional profits—the area under the $MR_F - MC_F$ curve which lies above the horizontal line $P_T D_T$—are maximized. Division $T$ should supply $Q_T$ units of the product, the quantity at which its marginal cost equals its marginal revenue.[3] At $Q_T$ units of output its divisional profits—the area under the curve $D_T$ which lies above the curve $MC_T$—are maximized.

Note that this solution to the transfer pricing problem results in Division $F$ demanding more units of the intermediate product than Division $T$ is willing to supply at price $P_T$. This situation presents no problem to the firm: it merely indicates that profit maximization requires Division $F$ to purchase $Q_T$ units of the intermediate product internally from Division $T$ and $Q_F - Q_T$ units in the marketplace. No other solution results in as great a total profit for the firm. For example, if Division $T$ attempts to supply the entire quantity demanded by $F$, the cost to the firm would exceed the cost incurred by purchasing it in the market. The shaded triangle $XYZ$ in Figure 13A.3 indicates the excess cost, and hence the reduction in profits, that would result from such a decision.

---

[2] $D_T = MR_T$ is the relevant marginal cost of $T$ for use in producing $F$. Note that this is not the same as $MC_T$, the marginal cost of physically producing an added unit of $T$.
[3] Since the intermediate product is defined to be a purely competitive good, $MR_T = P_T$.

The use of the market price for transferring the intermediate product remains optimal even if the quantity of the intermediate product supplied by Division $T$ is greater than the demand by Division $F$ at the market price. Division $T$ merely transfers the quantity demanded by $F$ and sells the remainder in the market. This situation is depicted in Figure 13A.4.

Here, although the marginal cost of producing the intermediate product, $T$, is below the net marginal revenue obtainable from an additional unit of $F$ at the optimal quantity, $Q_F$, the marginal cost of producing $T$, *plus* the opportunity cost of not selling that additional unit in the competitive market, is greater than the net marginal revenue received from $F$. Therefore, the transfer of additional units to Division $F$ would result in lower total firm profits.

*So long as the intermediate product being transferred within the firm can be sold in a competitive market, the market price remains the proper transfer price.* Only by transferring at that price can the firm's management insure that the level of activities in both the supplying and the using divisions will be optimal for firm, as opposed to divisional, profit maximization.

■ Figure 13A.4

**Transfer Price Determination with the Intermediate Product Sold Externally in a Competitive Market: Excess Internal Supply**

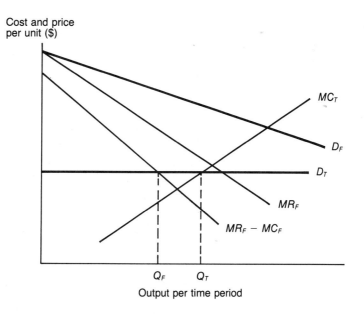

# TRANSFER PRICING WITH AN IMPERFECT EXTERNAL MARKET FOR THE INTERMEDIATE PRODUCT

Where an imperfect outside market exists for the intermediate product, transfer pricing is only slightly more complex than the case cited previously. Again, transfer pricing at marginal costs results in optimal activity levels for both the supplying and the using divisions of the firm.

This case is illustrated in Figure 13A.5. In Figure 13A.5, (a) shows the demand and the net marginal revenue curves for the final product, $F$; (b) contains the external demand and the marginal revenue curves for the intermediate product, $T$. In (c) the net marginal revenue curve for Product $F$ and the marginal revenue curve for $T$ have been horizontally summed to arrive at an aggregate net marginal revenue curve, $NMR_A$, for Product $T$. The marginal cost of producing $T$ is also shown in Figure 13A.5(c).

The profit-maximizing output of $T$ occurs where the marginal costs of producing it and the aggregate net marginal revenue obtained from it are equal: Output $Q^*$ in Figure 13A.5(c). That output is divided between internal transfers and external sales by equating the net marginal reve-

■ Figure 13A.5

**Transfer Pricing with an Imperfect Market for the Intermediate Product**

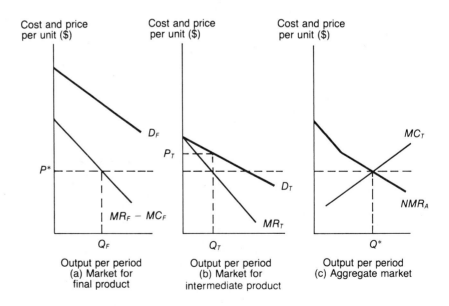

Cost and price per unit ($)

$D_F$

$P^*$

$MR_F - MC_F$

$Q_F$

Output per period
(a) Market for final product

Cost and price per unit ($)

$P_T$

$D_T$

$MR_T$

$Q_T$

Output per period
(b) Market for intermediate product

Cost and price per unit ($)

$MC_T$

$NMR_A$

$Q^*$

Output per period
(c) Aggregate market

nue in Part (a) of the figure and the marginal revenue in Part (b) to the marginal cost of the optimal output as determined in Part (c).[4] Setting an internal transfer price equal to that marginal cost, $P*$, insures that Division $F$ will demand the quantity of $T$ that leads to profit maximization not only of that division but also of the firm as a whole. The price to be charged in the external market—$P_T$ in Figure 13A.5(b)—is determined by the height of the demand curve for the product at a point directly above the intersection of the marginal revenue curve and the transfer price, or marginal cost of production.

# SUMMARY

The material we have presented on *transfer pricing* barely scratches the surface of this important but complex subject. It by no means exhausts the possible cases for intrafirm transfers of goods and services. There are, for example, situations where several internal divisions are competing for the products of yet another division, or where two or more divisions supply intermediate products to a third. Still another whole set of transfer pricing problems arises when the demand and production externalities in multiple-product firms are considered. Nonetheless, the material we have presented introduces the basic problem and demonstrates the kind of economic analysis necessary to obtain optimal solutions. To the extent that we can generalize, our analysis suggests that transfers should take place at the market price for intermediate products that are traded externally in a competitive market and at marginal cost in most other cases.

## Problems

13A.1 Heartland Agriproducts, Inc., produces agricultural products that were historically marketed through various independent distributors. Recently, Heartland made a strategic decision to integrate the production and marketing of its products. As a first step in this direction, Heartland acquired Nicholas Distribution, Inc. Nicholas previously was the sole distributor of Heartland's "Blusilo" brand grain-storage containers.

Using regional sales data for a recent year, Heartland estimates Blusilo's demand as:

$$P = \$20,000 - \$0.1Q.$$

---

[4]Note that the distribution of the intermediate product follows the same pattern as a discriminating monopolist allocating output among available segmented markets. In this case $T$ acts as a monopolist, selling part of its output in one internal market at the transfer price $P*$ and part in the external market at $P_T$.

The accounting department estimates Heartland's total production costs, $TC_P$, and Nicholas's total distribution costs, $TC_D$, for Blusilos as:

$$TC_P = \$4,000,000 + \$12,000Q + \$0.3Q^2,$$
$$TC_D = \$1,000,000 + \$4,000Q.$$

A. Given the preceding data, calculate Heartland's profit-maximizing price and output levels. Calculate Heartland's optimum profit.

B. If Heartland operates the Nicholas Distribution Division as an independent profit center, what price/output relation would describe Nicholas's "demand" for Blusilo?

C. Calculate the optimal transfer price for Blusilos between the production and distribution divisions. That is, what transfer price will result in maximum profits for Heartland?

D. Explain how Heartland would calculate an optimal intrafirm transfer price for Blusilos if a competitive external market existed.

13A.2 Computer World, Inc., imports and distributes personal computers and related products to business and individual users. The firm operates on a divisionalized basis. The importing division is responsible for packaging units purchased in the Far East and arranging for transportation to the U.S. market. The retailing division purchases products from the importing division, as well as from independent wholesalers.

Computer World is considering importing a new high-quality dot matrix printer call the Unix. In light of sales for competing products, the firm estimates the demand for Unix printers to be:

$$P = \$400 - \$0.05Q.$$

Each Unix can be purchased by the importing division for $100, with packaging and transportation costs totaling $20. The total retailing costs associated with the Unix are:

$$TC_R = \$100,000 + \$30Q + \$0.05Q^2.$$

A. Calculate optimal output, price, and total profits for the Unix, assuming that Computer World operates as a single profit center.

B. Now assume that each division operates as a separate profit center. Calculate the demand curve that the retailing division would use to determine its level of purchases from the importing division.

C. Calculate divisional output, price, and profit levels assuming that the retailing division makes its demand curve (from Part B) known to the importing division and that the importing division is allowed to set a transfer price. Assuming that each division acts to maximize divisional profits, also calculate Computer World's total profit level.

D. Again assume that Computer World operates each division as a separate profit center and that no external market exists for the Unix. What transfer price from the importing to the retailing division would assure Computer World an optimal level of Unix imports?

13A.3 Among the products manufactured and sold by the Western Electric Company (WEC) is a digital clock radio. The demand curve for this product is $P = \$610 - \$9Q$. Manufacture and sale of the radio is done by WEC's Home Products Division (HPD), with a major component part being supplied by a second division, the Electronics Specialty Division (ESD). Total cost functions for the radio and the electronic component are as follows:

$$\text{Total Cost}_{HPD} = \$3,000 + \$10Q,$$
$$\text{Total Cost}_{ESD} = \$7,000 + \$10Q + Q^2.$$

A. Assuming that there is no outside market for the component supplied by the ESD, what is the optimal quantity of product (from the firm's standpoint) that should be transferred, and what transfer price will lead to operation at this level?

B. Assume that the electronic component supplied by the ESD could be sold to an outside firm for use in another product (one that doesn't compete with WEC's) for $190. This firm will purchase up to 100 units at this price. What is the optimal transfer price in this situation? How many units will the ESD sell to the HPD? How many will it sell to the outside firm?

C. Assume now that external demand for the component manufactured by ESD is described by the function $P = \$410 - \$9.1Q$. What is the optimal transfer price? The optimal price in the external market? How many units will ESD supply to each of these two markets?

D. Explain how the following assumptions would influence the analysis of this problem: Sales of the electronic component in the external market affect sales of the radios, and production of the component by ESD affects the cost of other products of that division.

13A.4 Cambridge Electronics manufactures and sells a microprocessor that is used primarily as a control device in sophisticated manufacturing robots. Until recently, the market for this microprocessor was described by the demand curve $Q_D = 11,000 - 1.25P_D$. However, a new firm has begun manufacturing robots. This firm, Natick Instruments, uses one microprocessor of the type manufactured by Cambridge in each robot produced. Demand for Natick robots is given by the function $Q_N = 1,000 - 0.01P_N$, and Natick's cost function before accounting for the cost of the microprocessor is $TC_N = \$750,000 + \$1,000Q_N$. Thus, Cambridge's total demand is the sum of demand given by the $Q_D$ function and Natick's demand.

In addition to Cambridge, there are 50 small firms that manufacture competing microprocessors. These 50 firms each operate with a cost function $TC = \$60,000 + \$700Q + \$10Q^2$, and each acts as a price taker. Cambridge recognizes this price-taking behavior and operates as a price leader.

A. Determine the demand for microprocessors by Natick.
B. Assuming that the market cannot be segmented, determine the total domestic demand for the microprocessor.
C. Determine the aggregate microprocessor supply function for the 50 price takers.
D. Determine the demand curve faced by Cambridge in the total market.
E. Cambridge's cost function is $TC = \$200,000 + \$500Q + \$2.5Q^2$. Determine the price at which Cambridge would sell its microprocessor.
F. Assume that Cambridge acquires and operates Natick as a separate division. If there are no synergistic effects on the costs of either firm (division), what is the model that you would use to determine the optimal allocation of Cambridge's microprocessor production between transfers to Natick and the external market?
G. What transfer price would you set if each division operated as a profit center and if you wanted to maximize the firm's total profits?

# The Role of Government in the Market Economy

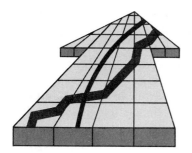

The role of government in the market economy is one of the most interesting and controversial topics in managerial economics. Examination of government's role in the marketplace is crucial to the study of managerial economics because the breadth and depth of government–business interactions have important implications for the managerial decision-making process. Government involvement in the marketplace can influence both productive efficiency and the distribution of income. Indeed, public policy often makes some tradeoff between these efficiency and equity considerations.

Although all sectors of the U.S. economy are regulated to some degree, the method and scope of regulation varies widely. For example, most companies escape price and profit restraint, except during periods of general wage-price control, but they are subject to operating regulations governing pollution emissions, product packaging and labeling, worker safety and health, and so on. On the other hand, many firms, particularly in the financial and the public utility sectors, must comply with financial regulation in addition to such operating controls. Banks, for example, have been subject to both state and federal regulation of prices (interest rates, loan fees, and so on) and financial soundness. Unlike firms in the electric power and telecommunications industries, however, banks face no explicit controls of the profits that they earn. For this reason, regulation in the financial sector (banking, insurance, securities), although more encompassing than regulation in the nonfinancial sector, is less comprehensive than the regulation of public utilities.

The growing importance of government involvement in the economy makes an examination of its causes, means, and ends an important component of managerial economics. In this chapter we analyze the role of government in the market economy by considering the economic and political rationale for regulation; grant policy, which provides firms with positive incentives for "desirable" activity; tax policy, which constrains the nature of goods and services that firms market and the production processes with which they produce them; antitrust policy, which seeks to maintain a workable level of competition in the economy; direct regulation of firms that possess substantial market power; and the recent trend toward deregulation.

# THE RATIONALE FOR REGULATION

**efficiency**

Production of what consumers demand in a least-cost fashion.

**regulation**

Government intervention in the market economy.

**equity**

Just distribution of wealth.

Both economic and political considerations enter into decisions of what and how to regulate. Economic considerations relate to cost and efficiency implications of regulatory methods. From an economic **efficiency** standpoint, a given mode of **regulation** or change in regulatory policy is desirable to the extent that benefits exceed costs. Here the question is not so much whether or not to regulate but rather what type of regulation (market competition or otherwise) is most desirable. On the other hand, **equity,** or fairness, rather than efficiency criteria must be carefully weighed when political considerations bear on the regulatory decision-making process. Here the *incidence,* or placement, of costs and benefits of regulatory decisions is considered. For example, if a given change in regulatory policy provides significant benefits to the poor, society may willingly bear substantial costs in terms of lost efficiency.

In most decisions regarding regulatory policy, the tradeoff between efficiency- and equity-related criteria is a most difficult one. Although we can't hope to resolve the conflict between economic and political rationales for regulation, it is useful to consider more carefully each argument as a basis for regulation. The material that follows addresses the question "Why *should* society regulate?" In later sections we see that some economists suggest far different reasons for the method and scope of observed regulation.

## Economic Considerations

**market failure**

The failure of a system of market institutions to sustain socially desirable activities or to eliminate undesirable ones.

Regulation of firms' production and market activities began and continues in part because of the public's perception of market imperfections. It is often believed that unregulated market activity can lead to inefficiency and waste or to market failure. **Market failure** can be described as the failure of a system of market institutions to sustain socially desirable activities or to eliminate undesirable ones.

A first type (or cause) of market failure is failure by *market structure.* For a market to realize the beneficial effects of competition, it must have many producers (sellers) and consumers (buyers), or at least the ready potential for many to enter. Some markets do not meet this condition. Consider, for example, water, power, and some telecommunications markets. If customer service in a given market area can be most efficiently provided by a single firm (a natural monopoly situation), such providers would enjoy market power and could earn economic profits by limiting output and charging high prices. As a result, utility prices and profits were placed under regulatory control, which has continued with the goal of preserving the efficiency of large-scale production while preventing the higher prices and economic profits of monopoly. When the efficiency advantages of large size are not thought to be compelling, antitrust policy limits the market power of large firms.

A second kind of market failure is failure by *incentive*. In the production and consumption of goods and services, social values and costs often differ considerably from the private costs and values of producers and consumers. Differences between private and social costs or benefits are called **externalities.** A negative externality is a cost of producing, marketing, or consuming a product that is not borne by the product's producers or consumers. A positive externality is a benefit of production, marketing, or consumption that is not reflected in the product pricing structure and, hence, does not accrue to the product's producers or consumers.

**externalities**

Differences between private and social costs or benefits.

Environmental pollution is one well-known negative externality. Negative externalities also arise when employees are exposed to hazardous working conditions for which they are not fully compensated. Similarly, a firm that dams a river or builds a solar collector to produce energy and in so doing limits the access of others to hydropower or solar power creates a negative externality.

Positive externalities can result if an increase in a firm's activity reduces costs for its suppliers, who pass these cost savings on to their other customers. The rapid growth of the computer industry has, for example, reduced input costs for both the computer and electronics industries. Economies of scale in semiconductor production made possible by increased computer demand lowered input costs for all users of semiconductors. As a result, prices have fallen for computers as well as a wide variety of "intelligent" electronic appliances, calculators, toys, and so on. Positive externalities in production can also result when a firm trains employees who later apply their knowledge in work for other firms. Similarly, positive externalities arise when an improvement in production methods is transferred from one firm to another without compensation. The dam cited previously for its potential negative externalities might also provide positive externalities by offering flood control or recreational benefits.

In short, externalities lead to a difference between the private and social costs and benefits of a given product or activity. These differences often have a notable effect on the economy. Firms that provide substantial positive externalities without compensation are unlikely to produce at the socially optimal level. Similarly, consumption activities that confer positive externalities may not reach the socially optimal level. On the other hand, negative externalities can channel too many resources to a particular activity. Producers and consumers that generate negative externalities do not pay the full cost of their activities and often continue them beyond the level that maximizes social benefits. These market imperfections or failures—instances in which the market does not provide the appropriate cost or benefit signals—provoke an active government role in the economy.

## Political Considerations

Like economic factors, political considerations play a prominent role in the design of regulatory policies.

Competition promotes efficiency by giving firms incentives to produce the types and quantities of products that consumers want. Furthermore, competitive pressures force each firm to use resources wisely to earn at least a normal profit. The market-based resource allocation system is efficient when it responds quickly and accurately to consumer preferences. *Preservation of consumer choice* or *consumer sovereignty* is an important feature of competitive markets. By encouraging and rewarding individual initiative, competition greatly enhances personal freedom. For this reason, less vigorous competitive pressure indicates diminishing consumer sovereignty. Firms with market power can limit output and raise prices to earn economic profits, whereas firms in competitive markets refer to market prices to determine optimal output quantities. Monopolies have far more discretion than firms in competitive markets. Regulatory policy can be a valuable tool with which to control monopolies, restoring control over price and quantity decisions to the public.

A second political purpose of regulatory intervention is to *limit concentration of economic and political power*. It has long been recognized that economic and political relations become intertwined and that concentrated economic power is generally inconsistent with the democratic process. Thus, the laws of incorporation, first passed during the 1850s, play an important role in the U.S. economic system. These laws allowed owners of capital (stockholders) to pool economic resources without also pooling political resources, thereby allowing big business and democracy to coexist. Of course, the large scale of modern corporations has at times diminished the controlling influence of individual stockholders. In these instances, regulatory and antitrust policy have limited the growth of large firms in order to avoid undue concentration of political power.

Important political considerations often constitute compelling justification for government intervention in the marketplace. Deciding whether a particular regulatory reform is or is not warranted is complicated by the fact that political considerations can run counter to efficiency considerations. This is not to say that policies should never be pursued when the expected benefits are exceeded by expected costs. Costs in the form of lost efficiency may sometimes be borne to achieve more equitable economic solutions.

# REGULATORY RESPONSE TO INCENTIVE FAILURES

Government intervention in the market economy responds to problems created by both positive and negative externalities in production, marketing, and consumption. In the effort to limit the frequency of market failure that is due to incentive problems, government frequently uses both grant and tax policies. In granting patents and operating subsidies, for example, government recognizes positive externalities and provides compensation to reward activities that provide such externalities. Local, state, and federal governments also levy taxes (a form of negative subsidy), along with enacting operating requirements or controls, to limit the creation of negative externalities. Although grant, tax, and operating-control policies are by no means the only government responses to incentive failures, they are among the most widely employed, and they provide a good introduction to this area of government–business interaction.

## Operating Right Grants

Regulation of operating rights is a common, though seldom discussed, method of giving firms an incentive to promote service in the public interest. Common examples would be Federal Communications Commission (FCC) control of local television and radio broadcasting rights; federal and state regulatory bodies that govern national or state chartering of banks and savings and loan institutions; and insurance commissions, which oversee insurance company licensing at the state level. In each of these instances, firms must be able to demonstrate fiscal responsibility and to provide evidence that they are meeting the needs of their service areas. Should firms fail to meet these established criteria, public franchises (in the form of broadcasting rights, charters, or licenses) can be withdrawn, or new franchises can be offered to potential competitors. Although such drastic action is rare, the mere threat of such action is often sufficient to compel compliance with prescribed regulations.

Although control of operating rights can be an effective form of regulation, it often falls short of its full potential because of imprecise operating criteria. For example, is a television station that broadcasts poorly rated local programming 20 hours per week responding better to the needs of its service area than a station that airs highly popular reruns of hit shows? How progressive an attitude must a local bank take toward electronic funds transfer services? Without clear, consistent, and workable standards of performance, operating grant regulation will be hampered by inefficiency and waste. The cost of this inefficiency is measured by the low quality and limited quantity of desired goods and services and by the excessive profits and/or high costs of firms sheltered from competition by regulatory policies.

## 14.1  **Managerial Application**

Orphan Drug Status Faces Big Changes

During the last 1980s, Genentech, a San Francisco–based leader in the biotechnology industry, and Indiana-based drug giant Eli Lilly were engaged in a race to market the next blockbuster drug. The drug, erythropoietin or EPO, is a bio-engineered anti-anemia product expected to have sales in excess of $1 billion per year during the early 1990s. EPO was developed to deal with the anemia caused by dialysis for renal disease. It also looks promising as a treatment for other types of diseases, including sickle-cell anemia. The race to market the drug was based on the fact that the winner would be eligible for a seven-year government-granted monopoly in addition to substantial tax credits granted under the Orphan Drug Act.

The act allows the Food and Drug Administration (FDA) to grant an exclusive monopoly on the production and sale of drugs used in the treatment of specific rare diseases that affect 200,000 or fewer persons. These monopoly rights are expected to provide the economic incentive necessary to make profitable the treatment of such illnesses. Much stronger than a patent monopoly, orphan drug status confers broad rights to a company for the present and future treatment of rare diseases. Current examples of medicines granted orphan drug status include AZT, which is used in the treatment of AIDS, and human growth hormones, primarily used to treat pituitary dwarfism, which prevents children from reaching a normal height. Critics contend that the act has succeeded in a manner beyond the scope of Congress's original intent.

For example, British pharmaceutical giant Wellcome PLC originally charged a wholesale price of $7,670 for AZT and estimated the average retail price to be more than $10,000 for a year's supply. Apparently in response to criticism of its high prices,

*continued*

See: Shirley Hobbs Scheibla, "Storm of the Orphans," *Barron's*, March 20, 1989, 72–73.

### Patent Grants

With patents, government grants the exclusive right to produce, use, or sell an invention or innovation for a limited period of time (17 years in the United States.) These valuable grants of legal monopoly power are intended to stimulate research and development. Without patents, competitors would quickly exploit and develop close, if not identical, substitutes for new products or processes, and inventing firms would be unlikely to reap the full benefit of their technological breakthroughs.

**Managerial Application** *continued*

the company later reduced its wholesale price to $6,130, bringing the estimated retail price for a year's treatment using the drug down to $8,000. Eli Lilly and Genentech both command prices of $10,000 to $12,000 per year for their growth-hormone drugs used to treat dwarfism in children, depending on the ages of the children being treated. Some in Congress consider this to be price gouging and want to pass a law to stop it.

When Congress passed the Orphan Drug Act, it envisioned sales of roughly $2 million per year for so-called orphan drugs. Human growth hormones now account for more than $150 million in annual sales. Many contend that such drugs should not fall within the bounds of the act. The National Commission on Rare Diseases has recommended that health professionals, institutions, and the pharmaceutical companies provide free or reduced-price drugs and services to patients who cannot afford to pay for them. In response, the growth-hormone manufacturers contend that no patient is now denied treatment because of an inability to pay.

Quite apart from difficulties associated with its orphan drug status, growth-hormone manufacturers have been criticized for selling the drugs for purposes other than the treatment of dwarfism. Although the drugs may be usefully applied to help children suffering from malnutrition, shock, and metabolic disorders, they have also been administered to short children whose parents simply want them to grow taller. In addition, weight lifters and other athletes have used them to add bulk and improve their performance. (Like steroids, the products add to an athlete's muscle.)

After growth hormones, the next lucrative product to win FDA approval under the Orphan Drug Act was AZT, the most effective treatment available for AIDS. The FDA designated AZT as an orphan drug years before Wellcome could obtain a patent, thus ensuring the company a compelling advantage over potential competition. Although AZT has been an effective treatment, recent studies show strains of the AIDS virus that are resistant to it. However, because of AZT's protection as an orphan drug, other manufacturers are precluded from developing substitutes.

Therefore, despite obvious advantages derived from the Orphan Drug Act, many people look for important changes in the act as Congress seeks to balance its important benefits with its associated costs.

Patent policy is a regulatory attempt to achieve the benefits of both monopoly and competition in the field of research and development. In granting the patent, the public confers a limited opportunity for monopoly profits to stimulate research activity and the economic growth that it creates. By limiting the patent monopoly, competition is encouraged to extend and develop the common body of knowledge.

The patent monopoly is subject to other restrictions besides the time limit. Firms cannot use patents to unfairly monopolize or otherwise limit competition. For example, in 1973 the Federal Trade Commission (FTC) charged Xerox with dominating the office-copier industry through unfair marketing and patent practices. In its complaint, the FTC alleged that Xerox, in association with Battelle Memorial Institute, a private research corporation, had created an artificial "patent barrier to competition." A final consent order in 1975 resolved the FTC's monopolization suit against Xerox. The consent order required Xerox to license competitors to use its more than 1,700 copier patents with little or no royalty charges and restricted Xerox's freedom to acquire such rights from its competitors. Partially because of this action, entry into the copier industry grew rapidly during the late 1970s.

## Subsidies

Government also responds to positive externalities by providing subsidies to private business firms. These subsidies can be indirect, like the government construction and highway maintenance grants that benefit the trucking industry. They can also take the form of direct payments, such as agricultural payment-in-kind (PIK) programs, special tax treatments, and government-provided low-cost financing.

Tax credits on business investment and depletion allowances on natural resource development are examples of tax subsidies that government sometimes gives in recognition of social benefits such as job creation, energy independence, and so on. Positive externalities associated with industrial parks induce government to provide local tax incremental or industrial revenue bond financing for such facilities. This low-cost financing is thought to provide some compensation for their external benefits.

## Tax Policies

Whereas subsidy policy gives firms positive incentives for desirable performance, tax policy contains penalties, or negative subsidies, designed to limit undesirable performance. Tax policy includes both regular tax payments and fines or penalties that may be assessed intermittently.

Local, state, or federal fines for exceeding specified weight limits on trucks, pollution taxes, and effluent charges are common examples of tax policies intended to limit negative externalities by shifting external costs of production back to firms and their customers. Determining an appropriate tax level is extremely difficult because of problems associated with estimating the magnitude of negative externalities. For example, calculating some of the social costs of air pollution, such as more frequent house painting, is relatively straightforward. Calculating the costs of increased discomfort—even death—for emphysema patients is less so. Nevertheless, regulators must consider the full range of consequences of negative externalities to create appropriate and effective incentives for pollution control.

Although tax policy may appear simply to mirror subsidy and grant policies, an important distinction should not be overlooked. If society wants to limit the harmful consequences of air pollution, for example, either subsidies for pollution reduction or taxes on pollution can provide effective incentives. Implied property rights are, however, considerably different under the two approaches. The subsidy mechanism implies a firm's right to pollute, because society pays to reduce pollution. In contrast, a system of pollution tax penalties asserts society's right to a clean environment. Firms must reimburse society for the damage caused by their pollution. The difference is a distinction in who owns the environment. Many prefer tax policy as a method for pollution reduction on the grounds that it explicitly recognizes the public's right to a clean environment.

## Operating Controls

**operating controls**
Regulation by government directive.

Operating control regulation, or control by government directive, is an important and growing form of regulation. **Operating controls** or standards are designed to limit undesirable behavior by compelling certain actions while prohibiting others. Operating control regulation that achieves 100-percent compliance creates a situation similar to that under a prohibitive tax policy. In each instance, the undesirable activity in question is completely eliminated, and no tax revenues are collected. When operating controls result in less than full compliance, operating control regulation becomes much like tax policy because fines and levies increase the costs of violators.

What kinds of operating controls are imposed on business firms? Controls over environmental pollution immediately come to mind, but businesses are also subject to many other kinds of constraints. For example, federal legislation limits automobile emissions and sets fuel efficiency and safety standards; firms handling foods, drugs, and other substances are constrained under the Pure Food and Drug Act. Working conditions are governed under various labor laws and health regulations, including provisions related to noise levels, noxious gases and chemicals, and safety standards. Antidiscrimination laws designed to protect minority groups and women can cause firms to modify their hiring and promotion policies. Wage and price controls, imposed at various times in attempts to reduce high rates of inflation, restrict firms in setting prices and affect the use of resources throughout the economic system.

Like operating grants regulation, the effectiveness of operating control regulations is often limited by vague or imprecise statutory specifications. Similarly, if the sanctions against violators are overly lenient or poorly defined, incentives for compliance lack effectiveness. Beyond the difficulties created by poorly defined regulations and sanctions, problems can also result if conflicting operating controls are imposed. For example, mandatory safety standards and pollution control requirements have increased passenger car costs by several hundred dollars. Although such costs were undoubtedly anticipated by those designing auto safety and pollution regulations, it was perhaps less obvious that these regulations would significantly reduce auto fuel efficiency. Thus, safety and pollution regulations directly conflicted with other regulations mandating increases in the fuel efficiency of cars to reduce the United States's dependence on foreign-produced oil.

Perhaps the clearest difference between operating control regulation and regulation via tax or subsidy policies is the reliance on nonmonetary incentives for compliance. There are no easy alternatives to operating control regulation in instances in which social costs are prohibitively great (e.g., nuclear disaster, ground water contamination, and so on) or difficult, if not impossible, to measure (e.g., public health, worker death, or serious injury). In some instances, however, operating control regulations can cause firms to direct their efforts toward being exempted from regulation rather than toward reducing the negative externalities of concern to society. It is not clear that operating controls are more or less effective than tax and subsidy policies in ensuring that the results of regulatory efforts are both effective and equitable. Each approach has its place.

## Who Pays for Regulation?

**tax incidence**
Point of tax collection.

**tax burden**
Economic cost of tax.

The question of who pays for regulation intended to mitigate the problems associated with failure of market incentives is an important one. Although the point of tax collection, or the **tax incidence,** of pollution charges may be a heavily polluting foundry, the economic cost of pollution taxes, or the **tax burden,** may be passed on to customers or suppliers. In fact, the question of who pays for specific regulations can seldom be determined merely by identifying the fined, taxed, or otherwise regulated party.

In general, who pays for operating control regulation depends on the elasticity of demand for the final products of affected firms. Figure 14.1 illustrates this issue by considering the theoretically polar extremes of perfectly elastic demand for final products, Figure 14.1a, and perfectly inelastic demand for final products, Figure 14.1b. Identically upward-sloping MC curves are assumed in each instance. Here, as is often the case, regulation is assumed to increase marginal costs by a fixed amount per unit. This amount, $t$, can reflect pollution taxes per unit of output or regulation-induced cost increases.

Figure 14.1a shows that good substitutes for a firm's product and highly elastic demand prevent producers from passing taxes or regulation-induced cost increases on to customers. As a result, producers (including investors, employees, and suppliers) will be forced to bear the burden of regulatory costs, at least in the short run. In these instances, falling industry rates of return on invested capital and high rates of industry unemployment will be symptomatic of regulatory influences.

Figure 14.1b shows the effect of regulation-induced cost or tax increases in the case of perfectly inelastic final-product demand. Without effective substitute products, producers can pass the burden of regulation on to customers. In contrast to the case of perfectly elastic demand,

■ Figure 14.1
## Regulatory Burden Allocation under Elastic and Inelastic Demand

(a) Highly elastic product demand places the burden of regulation-induced cost increases on producers, who must cut production from $Q_1$ to $Q_2$. (b) Low elasticity of product demand allows producers to raise prices from $P_1$ to $P_2$, and consumers bear the burden of regulation-induced cost increases.

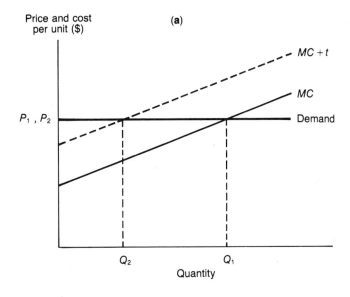

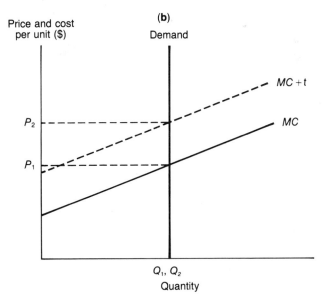

producers may encounter relatively few disadvantages because of regulation-induced cost increases.

Although the preceding analysis is greatly simplified, it points out that taxes or regulation-induced cost increases can have widely differing effects on industries if demand relationships vary. Similarly, the effect of regulation on industries with similar product-demand elasticities will vary to the extent that supply characteristics differ. For example, in industries in which marginal costs per unit are constant, per-unit taxes will increase output prices by an amount greater than in the case of rising marginal costs but by less than in the instance of falling marginal costs.

To illustrate the effects of regulation-induced cost or tax increases, let us consider the possible effects on consumers and producers of a new regulation prohibiting herbicide usage in corn production, perhaps because of fears about ground-water contamination. Assume that the industry is perfectly competitive, so the market price of $3 represents both average and marginal revenue per bushel ($P = MR = \$3$). If the marginal cost relation for each farmer, before any new regulations are imposed, can be written as:

$$MC = \$0.6 + \$0.04Q,$$

where $Q$ is bushels of corn (in thousands), then the optimal level of corn production per farm can be calculated setting $MR = MC$:

$$MR = MC$$
$$\$3 = \$0.6 + \$0.04Q$$
$$\$0.04Q = \$2.4$$
$$Q = 60(000) \text{ or } 60,000 \text{ Bushels.}$$

Given a perfectly competitive market, the supply curve for each producer is given by the marginal cost curve. From the marginal cost relation, we see that the quantity of corn supplied by each farmer is:

$$\text{Supply Price} = \text{Marginal Cost}$$
$$P = \$0.6 + \$0.04Q,$$

or

$$Q = -15 + 25P.$$

If the corn industry consists of 200,000 farmers of equal size, total industry supply can be calculated as:

$$Q_S = 200,000(-15 + 25P)$$
$$= -3,000,000 + 5,000,000P. \qquad \text{(Supply)}$$

To complete our picture of the industry prior to the new regulation on herbicides, assume that industry demand is given by the relation:

$$Q_D = 15,000,000 - 1,000,000P. \qquad \text{(Demand)}$$

In equilibrium,

$$Q_S = Q_D$$
$$-3,000,000 + 5,000,000P = 15,000,000 - 1,000,000P$$
$$6,000,000P = 18,000,000$$
$$P = \$3 \text{ per Bushel,}$$

and

$$Q_S = -3,000,000 + 5,000,000(3)$$
$$= 12,000,000(000), \text{ or } 12 \text{ Billion Bushels.}$$
$$Q_D = 15,000,000 - 1,000,000(3)$$
$$= 12,000,000(000), \text{ or } 12 \text{ Billion Bushels.}$$

Now assume that reducing herbicide usage increases the amount of tillage needed to keep weed growth controlled and causes the yield per acre to drop, resulting in a 25-percent increase in the marginal costs of corn production. For individual farmers, the effect on marginal costs is reflected as:

$$MC' = 1.25(\$0.6 + \$0.04Q)$$
$$= \$0.75 + \$0.05Q.$$

If only a few farmers in a narrow region of the country were subject to the new regulation, as would be true in the case of state or local pollution regulations, then market prices would remain stable at $3, and affected farmers would curtail production dramatically to 45,000 bushels each, because:

$$MR = MC'$$
$$\$3 = \$0.75 + \$0.05Q$$
$$\$0.05Q = \$2.25$$
$$Q = 45(000), \text{ or } 45,000 \text{ Bushels.}$$

Given a perfectly competitive industry and, therefore, a perfectly elastic demand for corn, local pollution regulations will force producers to bear the entire burden of regulation-induced cost increases.

A different situation arises when all producers are subject to the new herbicide regulation. In this instance, the revised individual-firm supply curve can be written as:

$$\text{Supply Price} = \text{Marginal Cost}$$
$$P = \$0.75 + \$0.05Q,$$

or

$$Q = -15 + 20P.$$

# 14.2 **Managerial Application**

## Supply Regulation Boosts Aspen Home Prices

Federal, state, and local rules and regulations often have an important influence on the quantity and quality of goods and services supplied to customers. Regulations governing the introduction of new drugs, automobile emissions, and airline safety are but a few examples. At times, these and other regulations can have an important effect on market demand and supply conditions.

For example, local zoning ordinances always affect the nature of competition in the real estate sector by specifying the type and location of allowed land use and construction. In many instances, such regulations stem from concerns about fire safety, floodplain control, and so forth, and they have only a minor influence on local demand and supply conditions. Similarly, restrictions designed to protect the residential or commercial nature of neighborhoods pose no significant barrier to new supply, and hence to competition, as long as they permit suffi-

cient alternative opportunities for new construction. However, when local zoning ordinances heavily restrict or effectively block new construction, the effect of even a modest increase in demand on the prices of new and existing commercial and residential units can be dramatic.

The Aspen, Colorado, real estate market is an interesting example of a situation in which the effects of modestly growing demand have been made dramatic by local regulations that result in an essentially fixed supply of new construction. In Pitkin County, where Aspen is located, 80 percent of the land is forest owned by the federal government. A "slow growth" policy adopted by the City of Aspen during the mid-1970s covers much of the remaining 20 percent. In an effective effort to restrain growth, Aspen limits building height to 28 feet, the number of bedrooms per home to five, and wood-burning fireplaces to one per residence (to limit wood-smoke pollution).

*continued*

See: Anne Kates, "Stars Unfazed by Sky-high Home Prices," *USA Today,* January 20, 1989, 2B.

Total industry supply, assuming that all 200,000 farmers remain in business (something that may not happen if the resulting changes in profit levels are substantial), will equal:

$$Q'_S = 200,000(-15 + 20P)$$

$$= -3,000,000 + 4,000,000P. \quad \text{(New Supply)}$$

The equilibrium industry price/output combination will be found where:

**Managerial Application** *continued*

A substantial amount of open space must also be preserved within each development area. Most importantly, Aspen limits the pace of overall construction to 3.5 percent per year. Only 40 to 50 residences are built each year on new sites, and another 20 to 25 new homes replace older homes torn down during the previous year. In downtown Aspen, building restrictions on commercial property for hotels and restaurants are even stricter. Here, established businesses have sometimes used local regulations to keep out unwanted new competitors.

Aspen still has only one-half of the 12,000 residents that it enjoyed as a booming silver-mining town in the 1890s, but it has recently gained popularity as a vacation spot for the rich and famous. Local residents include Don Johnson, Jack Nicholson, and Steve Walton, heir to the Wal-Mart fortune, among others. Given its housing supply restrictions, even a modest increase in demand can cause local housing prices to soar. With the new vacation interest in Aspen, the recent price appreciation enjoyed by commercial and residential real estate owners has been as breathtaking as the views of nearby Red Mountain. Typical three-bedroom subdivision homes now sell in the range of $500,000 and up. Multi-million dollar price tags are common. In early 1989, for example, the *average* price of an Aspen home approached $1 million. Without supply restrictions, average prices would be less, and the rate of price increase would clearly be reduced. In nearby Vail, Colorado, for example, similarly attractive vacation homes and condominiums can be had for hundreds of thousands of dollars less than in Aspen.

Like any market affected by an artificial restriction in supply, predicting future prices in the Aspen real estate market is extraordinarily difficult. Given the fragility of government-induced scarcity, builders must temper their demand for new construction sites knowing that prices could collapse following a general economic downturn, a change in Aspen's popularity as compared to other Colorado ski resorts, or even a slight lessening in local growth restrictions. Through its low-growth policy, local officials have perhaps unwittingly made the local real estate market much more expensive and riskier for both first-time buyers and builders. Needless to say, long-term owners have a delicate problem of their own in deciding if and when to sell.

$$Q_S' = Q_D$$
$$-3,000,000 + 4,000,000P = 15,000,000 - 1,000,000P$$
$$5,000,000P = 18,000,000$$
$$P = \$3.60 \text{ per Bushel,}$$

and

$$Q_S' = -3,000,000 + 4,000,000(3.60)$$
$$= 11,400,000(000) \text{ or } 11.4 \text{ Billion Bushels,}$$
$$Q_D = 15,000,000 - 1,000,000(3.60)$$
$$= 11,400,000(000), \text{ or } 11.4 \text{ Billion Bushels.}$$

At the new market price, each individual farm will produce 57,000 bushels of corn:

$$Q = -15 + 20(3.60)$$
$$= 57(000) \text{ or } 57,000 \text{ Bushels.}$$

Thus, industry-wide regulation of herbicides will have a smaller effect on producers because the effects of regulation are partially borne by consumers through the price increase from $3 to $3.60 per bushel. This example illustrates why state and local authorities find it difficult to regulate firms, such as farms, that operate in highly competitive national or worldwide markets. Such regulations usually initiate at the national level.

In general, regulations that affect the marginal costs of production will usually have some combination of adverse price and output effects for producers and consumers. Realizing this, some policymakers have promoted taxes or regulations with fixed or "lump sum" charges for producers. (Recall that increases in fixed costs affect neither price nor output levels for profit-maximizing firms in the short run.) Even this approach to regulation is far from painless, however, since heavily regulated producers may be forced to leave the industry in the long run, should profitability be forced below the cost of capital. It is clear that the costs of regulation must be weighed carefully against its benefits.

# REGULATORY RESPONSE TO STRUCTURAL FAILURES

In Chapters 11 and 12 we saw that monopoly or oligopoly in an industry can result in too little output and in economic profits. Regulation intended to reduce or eliminate the socially harmful consequences of such structural failures can seek to control preexisting monopoly power or to prevent its emergence. Public utility regulation, which controls the prices and profits of established monopolies, is an important example of the effort to enjoy the benefits of low-cost production by large firms while avoiding the social costs of unregulated monopoly. Tax and antitrust policies also address the problem of structural failures by limiting not only the abuse of monopoly but also its growth.

### The Dilemma of Natural Monopoly
Recall that under perfect competition, many firms produce with equal efficiency. If many small firms are viable in an industry, large firms cannot be more efficient than their smaller rivals. This condition does not necessarily hold in all industries.

In some industries, the average costs of production continue to decline as output expands. A single large firm can produce total industry output more efficiently than any group of smaller producers. Demand equals supply at a point where the long-run average cost curve for a single firm is still declining. The term *natural monopoly* describes this situation, because monopoly naturally results from the superior efficiency of a single large producer.

For example, consider Figure 14.2. Here the firm will produce Q units of output at an average cost of C per unit. Note that this cost level is above the minimum point on the long-run average cost curve, and average costs are still declining. As a monopolist, the firm can earn an economic profit equal to the rectangle PP'C'C, or Q(P − C). Local electric, gas, and water companies are the classic examples of natural monopolies, as the duplication of production and distribution facilities would greatly increase costs if more than one firm served a given area.

This situation presents something of a dilemma. Economic efficiency could be enhanced by restricting the number of firms to one, but only one firm serving a market creates the possibility of monopoly profits and inefficiency. Specifically, unregulated monopolists tend to earn economic profits or incur unnecessary costs, and to underproduce. Recall that economic profits are defined as profits so large that the firm earns a rate of return on invested capital that exceeds the risk-adjusted normal, or required, rate. Profits are useful both for allocating resources and

■ Figure 14.2
## Price/Output Decision under Monopoly

Without regulation, monopolies would charge excessively high prices and produce too little output.

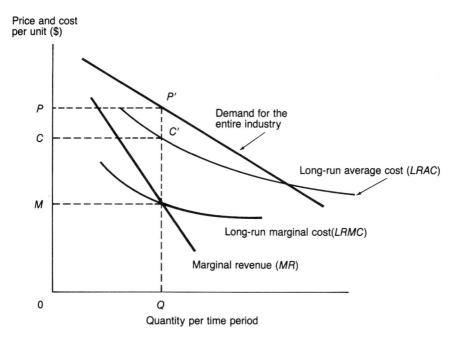

as an incentive for efficiency, but it is difficult to justify above-normal profits derived from market power rather than from exceptional performance.

Underproduction occurs when the firm curtails production to a level at which the marginal value of resources needed to produce an additional unit of output (marginal cost) is less than the benefit derived from the additional unit, as measured by the price that consumers are willing to pay for it. In other words, at outputs just greater than Q in Figure 14.2, consumers are willing to pay approximately P dollars per unit, so the value of additional units is P. However, the marginal cost of producing an additional unit is slightly less than M dollars and well below P, so cost does not equal value. Accordingly, society finds an expansion of output desirable.

Besides possibly earning economic profits and withholding production, an unregulated natural monopolist could be susceptible to operating inefficiency. In competitive markets, firms must operate efficiently to remain in business. A natural monopoly feels no pressure for cost-efficiency from established competitors. This means that the market power of the natural monopolist would permit some inefficiency and waste in production. Even though excessive amounts of operating inefficiency would surely attract new competition (new entry), substantial losses in economic efficiency may persist for extended periods in the case of natural monopoly.

How can we escape from the dilemma posed by the fact that monopoly can have the potential for greatest efficiency but that unregulated monopoly could lead to economic profits, underproduction, and resource waste? One answer is to permit natural monopolies to persist, subject to price and profit regulation.

## Utility Price Regulation

The most common method of monopoly regulation is through price controls. Price regulation typically results in (1) a larger quantity of the product being sold than would be the case with an unrestricted monopoly, (2) a reduced dollar profit, and (3) a lower rate of return on investment for the firm's owners. This situation is illustrated in Figure 14.3. A monopolist operating without regulation would produce $Q_1$ units of output and charge a price of $P_1$. If regulators set a ceiling on prices at $P_2$, the firm's effective demand curve would become the kinked curve $P_2AD$. Since price is a constant from 0 to $Q_2$ units of output, marginal revenue equals price in this range; that is, $P_2A$ is the marginal revenue curve over the output range $0Q_2$. For output beyond $Q_2$, marginal revenue is given by the original marginal revenue function. Thus, the marginal revenue curve is now discontinuous at Output $Q_2$, with a gap between Points $A$ and $L$. This regulated firm will maximize profits by operating at Output $Q_2$ and charging the ceiling price, $P_2$. Marginal revenue is greater than marginal cost up to that output but less than marginal cost beyond it.

Profits are also reduced by the regulatory action. Without price regulation, price $P_1$ is charged, a cost of $C_1$ per unit is incurred, and Output

■ Figure 14.3
## Monopoly Price Regulation: Optimal
## Price/Output Decision Making

Monopoly regulation imposes a price ceiling at $P_2$ just sufficient to provide a fair return (area $P_2AEC_2$) on investment. Under regulation, price falls from $P_1$ to $P_2$ and output expands from $Q_1$ to $Q_2$.

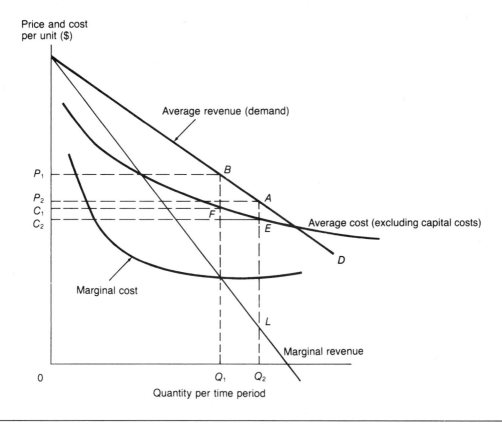

$Q_1$ is produced. Profit will be $(P_1 - C_1)(Q_1)$, which equals the area $P_1BFC_1$. With price regulation, the price is $P_2$, the cost is $C_2$, $Q_2$ units are sold, and profits are represented by the smaller area $P_2AEC_2$.

How does the regulatory authority determine a fair price? In essence, the theory is as follows. The regulatory commission plans for a fair or normal rate of return, given the risk inherent in the enterprise. The regulators also know how much capital investment will be required to produce a given output. The commission then approves prices that will earn the firm profits that, when divided by the required investment at the resultant output level, will produce the target rate of return. In the case illustrated in Figure 14.3, if the profit at Price $P_2$, when divided by the investment required to produce $Q_2$, were to produce a rate of return greater than the target, the price would be reduced until the actual and the target rates of return became equal. This treatment assumes, of course, that the cost curves in Figure 14.3 do not include equity capital costs. That is, the profit that the regulator allows is business profit, not economic profit. This treatment is the norm in public utility regulation.

To further illustrate the concept of public utility regulation, consider the case of the Malibu Beach Telephone Company, a small telephone utility serving urban customers in southern California. At issue is the rate to be charged for local telephone service (basic hookup). The monthly demand for service is given by the relation:

$$P = \$22.50 - \$0.00004Q,$$

where $P$ is service price in dollars, and $Q$ is the number of customers served. Annual total cost and marginal cost curves, excluding a normal rate of return, are given by the expressions:

$$TC = \$3,750,000 + \$70Q + 0.00002Q^2,$$
$$MC = dTC/dQ = \$70 + \$0.00004Q,$$

where cost is expressed in dollars.

In order to find the profit-maximizing level of output, we must first derive the demand and marginal revenue curves for annual service. This will give all revenue and cost relations a common annual basis. The demand curve for annual service is 12 times monthly demand:

$$P = 12(\$22.5 - \$0.000048Q)$$
$$= \$270 - \$0.00048Q,$$

and the total and marginal revenue curves for this annual demand are:

$$TR = \$270Q - \$0.00048Q^2$$
$$MR = dTR/dQ = \$270 - \$0.00096Q.$$

The profit-maximizing level of output is found by setting $MC = MR$ (where $M\pi = d\pi/dQ = 0$) and solving for $Q$:

$$MC = MR$$
$$\$70 + \$0.00004Q = \$270 - \$0.00096Q$$
$$\$0.001Q = \$200$$
$$Q = 200,000,$$

and the monthly service price is:

$$P = \$22.50 - \$0.00004(200,000)$$
$$= \$14.50 \text{ per Month (or \$174 per year).}$$

This price/output combination will result in annual total profits of:

$$\pi = \$270Q - \$0.00048Q^2 - \$3,750,000 - \$70Q - \$0.00002Q^2$$
$$= -\$0.0005Q^2 + \$200Q - \$3,750,000$$
$$= -\$0.0005(200,000^2) + \$200(200,000) - \$3,750,000$$
$$= \$16,250,000.$$

If the company has \$125 million invested in plant and equipment, the annual rate of return on investment is:

$$\text{Return on Investment} = \frac{\$16,250,000}{\$125,000,000} = 0.13 \text{ or } 13 \text{ Percent.}$$

Now let us assume that the State Public Utility Commission has decided that a 12-percent return would be fair for the level of risk taken and conditions in the financial markets. With a 12-percent return on total assets, Malibu Beach would earn business profits of:

$$\pi = \text{Allowed Return} \times \text{Total Assets}$$
$$= 0.12 \times \$125,000,000$$
$$= \$15,000,000.$$

To determine the level of output that would generate this level of total profits, we must set total profit equal to \$15 million:

$$\pi = TR - TC$$
$$\$15,000,000 = -\$0.0005Q^2 + \$200Q - \$3,750,000.$$

This implies that

$$-\$0.0005^2 + \$200Q - \$18,750,000 = 0,$$

which is a function of the form $aQ^2 + bQ - c = 0$. Solving for the roots of this equation provides the target output level. We use the quadratic equation as follows:

$$Q = \frac{-b \pm \sqrt{b^2 - 4ac}}{2a}$$
$$= \frac{-200 \pm \sqrt{200^2 - 4(-0.0005)(18,750,000)}}{2(-0.0005)}$$
$$= \frac{-200 \pm \sqrt{2,500}}{-0.001}$$
$$= 150,000 \text{ or } 250,000.$$

Because public utility commissions generally want utilities to provide service to the greatest possible number of customers at the lowest possible price, the upper figure $Q = 250,000$, is the appropriate output level. In order to induce Malibu Beach Telephone to operate at this output level, the regulatory authorities would determine the maximum allowable price for monthly service as:

$$P = \$22.50 - \$0.00004(250,000)$$
$$= \$12.50.$$

This \$12.50-per-month price will provide service to the broadest customer base possible, given the need to provide Malibu Beach with the opportunity to earn a 12-percent rate of return on its investment.

## Problems in Utility Price Regulation

**Pricing Problems**   Although the concept of price regulation is simple, many problems arise in the regulation of public utilities. First, it is impossible to exactly determine the cost and demand schedules, as well as the asset base, necessary to support a specified level of output. Utilities also serve several classes of customers, which introduces a number of different demand schedules with varying price elasticities. Therefore, many different rate schedules could produce the desired profit level. If profits of the local electric power company are too low, should rates be raised for summer (peak) or for winter (off-peak) users? Should industrial, commercial, or residential customers bear the burden of higher rates equally or unequally? Appealing to cost considerations for solutions to these problems is often of no avail, because the services provided are joint products, a factor that makes it extremely difficult, if not impossible, to separate costs and allocate them to specific classes of customers.

**Output-Level Problems**   A second problem with price regulation is that the regulators can make mistakes with regard to the optimal level and growth of service. For example, if a local telephone utility is permitted to charge excessive rates, more funds will be allocated to system expansion, and communication services will grow at a faster-than-optimal rate. Similarly, if prices allowed to natural gas producers are too low, consumers will be encouraged to use gas at a high rate, producers will not seek new gas supplies, and shortages of gas will occur. Too low a price structure for electricity will likewise encourage the use of power while discouraging the addition of new generating equipment.

**Inefficiency**   Price regulation can also lead to inefficiency. If a regulated company is guaranteed a minimum return on its invested capital, then, provided that demand conditions permit, operating inefficiencies can be offset by higher prices. To illustrate, consider the situation depicted in Figure 14.4. A regulated utility faces the demand curve $AR$ and the marginal revenue curve $MR$. If the utility operates at peak efficiency, the average cost curve $AC_1$ will apply. At a regulated price, $P_1$, $Q_1$ units will be demanded, cost per unit will be $C_1$, and profits will equal the rectangle $P_1P_1'C_1'C_1$. These profits are, let us assume, just sufficient to provide a reasonable return on invested capital.

Now suppose that another company, one with less capable managers, is operating under similar conditions. Because this management is less efficient than that of the first company, the firm's cost curve is represented by $AC_2$. If its price is set at $P_1$, it too will sell $Q_1$ units, but average cost will be $C_2$; profits will be only $P_1P_1'C_2'C_2$; and the company will be earning less than its required rate of return. In the absence of regulation, inefficiency produces low profits. Under regulation, the inefficient company can request—and probably receive—a rate increase to $P_2$. Here it

■ Figure 14.4
## Efficient and Inefficient Utility Companies

Inefficient utilities harm consumers through higher prices, $P_2$ versus $P_1$, and lower output, $Q_2$ versus $Q_1$. (Here, $AC_1$ and $AC_2$ do not include equity capital costs.)

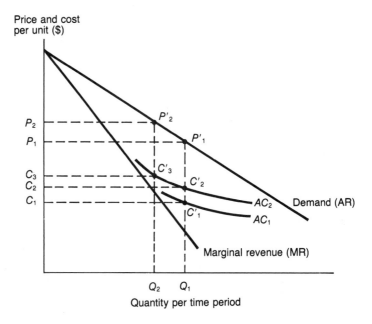

can sell $Q_2$ units of output, incur an average cost of $C_3$ per unit, and earn profits of $P_2P_2'C_3'C_3$, resulting in a rate of return on investment approximately equal to that of the efficient company. Regulation can reduce the profit incentive for efficiency.

Utility commissions can address this problem by considering efficiency performance when setting rates. For example, a particular commission might feel that 12 percent is a reasonable rate of return on stockholders' equity, but it might allow efficient companies to earn up to 12.5 percent and penalize inefficient companies by holding them to returns of less than 12 percent. The difficulty with this approach is that each utility operates in a unique setting, so it is extremely difficult to make valid comparisons. One electric company might have a cost of 2 cents per kilowatt hour, and another in the same state might have a cost of 2.5 cents. Is the first company more efficient than the second, or is the cost differential the result of differences in fuel type, plant sizes, labor costs, or depreciation charges related to construction during periods of generally lower prices? These difficulties have limited regulatory commissions' explicit use of efficiency differentials in setting profit rates for local electric utilities. However, regulators have begun to experiment with incentive-based regulation of long-distance telephone service. This innovation in regulation appears to hold substantial promise for enhanced efficiency in that industry and will be carefully evaluated in the years ahead.

**Investment Level**   A fourth problem with regulation is that it can lead to inefficient levels of investment in fixed assets. Allowed profits are calculated as a percentage of the rate base, which is approximately equal to fixed assets. If the allowed rate of return exceeds the cost of capital, it will benefit the firm to expand fixed assets and shift to capital-intensive methods of production. Conversely, if the allowed rate of return is less than the cost of capital, the firm will not expand capacity rapidly enough and will employ relatively little fixed plant but perhaps excessive amounts of fuel. Thus, regulation can lead to suboptimal input combinations.

**Regulatory Lag and Political Problems**   A related problem is that of **regulatory lag,** which is defined as the period between the time a price increase (or decrease) is appropriate and the date it becomes effective. Because of the lengthy legal proceedings these price decisions often involve, long periods can pass between the time the need for utility rate adjustments is recognized and the date they take effect.

**regulatory lag**
The period between the time a price increase (or decrease) is appropriate and the date it becomes effective.

The problem of regulatory lag is particularly acute during periods of rapidly rising prices. During the late 1960s and the 1970s, for example, inflationary pressures exerted a constant upward thrust on costs. To maintain normal profits and a fair rate of return on capital in such periods, it is necessary to raise prices expeditiously.

This is not always possible given the long delays caused by the adversarial nature of the rate-review process. Utility customers and voters exert great pressure to deny, reduce, or delay even reasonable rate increases. As elected officials or political appointees, public utility commissioners must carefully weigh consumer concerns against the needs of regulated companies to earn fair rates of return. As a result, regulatory proceedings are often lengthy.

A number of major utility companies experienced severe financial difficulties during the mid-1970s that were due at least in part to regulatory lag. The largest U.S. electric utility, Consolidated Edison (which serves New York City and the surrounding area), was almost forced into bankruptcy, and many other companies were forced to curtail construction programs because they were unable to obtain the funds necessary to purchase new plant and equipment. Profits were simply inadequate to induce investors to purchase the companies' stocks and bonds.

**Cost of Regulation**   By this time, a sixth problem with price regulation should be obvious. A great deal of careful and costly analysis must be conducted before regulatory decisions can be made. Maintaining public utility commission staffs is expensive, as are maintaining required records and processing rate cases. Ultimately, the cost of both the commissions' and the companies' regulation-related activities is borne by consumers.

Although most economists can see no reasonable alternative to utility regulation for electric, gas, local telephone, and private water companies, serious problems arise from efforts to regulate industry through price determination. Competition in the market system allocates goods and services much more efficiently. For this reason, government strives to maintain a workable level of competition in the economy through tax and antitrust policies.

## Windfall Profit Taxes

In recent years, tax policy has been used increasingly to limit perceived abuses of monopoly power and, to a lesser extent, to encourage the growth of small business. A windfall profit tax is an example of a tax policy intended to limit perceived abuses of economic power. *Normal profit* is defined as the risk-adjusted rate of return necessary to maintain investment in an industry. Economic profit is profit above and beyond necessary minimums. The term **windfall profit** commonly distinguishes economic profit that is due to firms' unexpected and unwarranted good fortune from economic profit resulting from such factors as superior operating efficiency, innovation, economies of scale, and so on.

**windfall profit**
Economic profit that is due to unexpected and unwarranted good fortune.

Windfall profit taxes have frequently been imposed during wartime both to help finance high levels of government expenditure and to reduce the substantial profits accruing to providers of critical goods and services. More recently, in 1980 the United States imposed a windfall profit tax on domestic oil company profits. The intent was to reduce oil company profits resulting from the very rapid increase in crude oil prices during the 1970s.

One of the most serious challenges to a successful windfall profit tax policy is the problem of correctly determining the magnitude of unwarranted profits. This means that prices, operating expenses, and investment policies of affected firms must be carefully scrutinized. Industry expertise is necessary to avoid potential abuses of a windfall tax policy. If firms perceive that a windfall profits tax policy is only temporary, they may incur unnecessary operating expenses or undertake unwarranted investments anticipating future benefits from such expenditures. For example, the railroad industry substantially rebuilt or replaced its right-of-way (track and related) investments during World War II. Although some reinvestment in plant and equipment was undoubtedly necessary to meet wartime demands for freight and passenger service, one can only speculate as to how much investment was undertaken simply to avoid wartime windfall profit taxes. Railroad executives obviously preferred newer plant and equipment over increased tax payments. Quite different problems may result from the windfall taxes on oil company profits. Beyond the obvious problem of defining the magnitude of windfall profits to be taxed, windfall profit taxes can increase the level of risk or uncertainty in doing business. If oil company executives perceive that profits from successful exploration activities will be taxed severely, the risk of obtaining a satisfactory return from the firm's entire drilling program could rise. Higher required profits and industry prices would naturally result. Following the collapse in worldwide oil prices in the late 1980s, it was interesting to note that many domestic oil companies, especially smaller operators, reported large aftertax losses, or even filed bankruptcy, while paying substantial windfall profit taxes. Legislative determination of economic profits can lag behind economic reality.

### Small Company Tax Preferences

During recent years, the U.S. corporate income tax system has become relatively more favorable to small business. The stated rationale is quite broad. Growth in small business is seen as being consistent with democratic principles of self-determination and individual decision making. Small firms also form an important competitive fringe in many industries, exerting downward pressure on the prices and profits of leading firms. In addition, small firms are an important source of invention and innovation. To some extent, progressive taxes are considered to partially offset the relatively high costs that regulation and government reporting requirements impose on small business.

Whatever the rationale, it is clear that small business plays an important role in the U.S. economy. The extent to which tax and other regulatory preferences enhance the competitive positions of small firms is not fully known, but their use to insure continued success of small business seems likely.

## ANTITRUST POLICY

In the late nineteenth century, a movement toward industrial consolidation developed in the United States. Industrial growth was rapid, and because of economies of scale or unfair competitive practices, oligopolistic structures emerged in several important industries. In some instances, pricing decisions were made by industry leaders who recognized that they could attain higher profits through cooperation than competition. They formed voting trusts in which voting rights to the stocks of various firms in an industry were consolidated to achieve a monopoly price/output solution. The oil and tobacco trusts of the 1880s are well-known examples.

Although profitable to the firms, the trusts were socially undesirable, and public indignation resulted in the 1890 passage of the Sherman Act, the first significant U.S. antitrust measure. Other important antitrust legislation included the Clayton Act (1914), the Federal Trade Commission Act (1914), the Robinson-Patman Act (1936), and the Celler-Kefauver Act (1950). Each of these acts was designed to prevent anticompetitive actions, the effects of which are more likely to reduce competition than to lower costs by increasing operating efficiency. In this section we present an overview of antitrust law, as well as a brief chronology of major antitrust legislation.

## Overview of Antitrust Law

**antitrust laws**

Laws designed to promote competition and prevent monopoly.

**Antitrust laws** are designed to promote competition and prevent unwarranted monopoly. These laws seek to improve economic efficiency by enhancing consumer sovereignty and the impartiality of resource allocation while limiting concentrations in both economic and political power.

There is no single antitrust statute in U.S. law. Rather, federal antitrust law is based on two important statutes, the Sherman Act and the Clayton Act, and their amendments. An important characteristic of these laws is that they broadly and somewhat vaguely ban, but never define, "restraints of trade," "monopolization," "unfair competition," and so on. By never precisely defining such key terms, the statutes left the courts to decide the specific legality or illegality of various business practices. Because of this, many principles in antitrust law rest on judicial interpretation. We must therefore consult individual court decisions (case law) in addition to statutory standards (statutory law) to assess the legality of business behavior.

## Sherman Act

The Sherman Act of 1890 was the first federal antitrust legislation. It was brief and to the point. Section 1 forbade contracts, combinations, or conspiracies in restraint of trade, which were then offenses under common law. Section 2 forbade monopolies. Both sections could be enforced through civil court actions or by criminal proceedings, with the guilty liable to pay fines or serve jail sentences. In 1974, an amendment to the Sherman Act made violations felonies rather than misdemeanors. The act now provides for $1-million maximum fines against corporations and up to $100,000 in fines and three years' imprisonment for individuals. In addition to fines and prison sentences, firms and individuals violating the Sherman Act face the possibility of paying triple damages to injured parties who bring civil suits.

However, the Sherman Act is often characterized as being too vague. Even with landmark decisions against the tobacco, powder, and oil trusts, enforcement has been sporadic. On the one hand, business people claim not to know what is legal; on the other, the Justice Department is sometimes criticized as being ignorant of monopoly-creating practices and as failing to act in a timely fashion.

Despite its shortcomings, the Sherman Act remains one of the government's main weapons against anticompetitive behavior. In 1978 a federal judge imposed some of the stiffest penalties in the history of U.S. antitrust actions on eight firms and eleven of their officers when they were convicted of violating the Sherman Act. These convictions for price fixing in the electrical wiring devices industry resulted in fines totaling nearly $900,000 and jail terms for nine of the eleven officers charged.

## Clayton Act

Congress passed two measures in 1914 to overcome weaknesses in the Sherman Act. The more important of these, the Clayton Act, addressed problems of mergers, interlocking directorates, price discrimination, and tying contracts. The other was the Federal Trade Commission Act, which outlawed unfair methods of competition in commerce and established the FTC, an agency intended to enforce the Clayton Act.

Section 2 of the Clayton Act prohibited sellers from discriminating in price among business customers unless (1) cost differentials in serving the various customers justified the price differentials or (2) the lower prices were offered in certain markets to meet competition. As a primary goal, the act sought to prevent a strong regional or national firm from employing selective price cuts to drive weak local firms out of business. Once the competitors in one market were eliminated, the national firm could charge monopoly prices and then use excess profits to subsidize cut-throat competition in other areas. The Robinson-Patman Act, passed in 1936, amended the section of the Clayton Act dealing with price discrimination. It declared specific forms of price discrimination, especially those related to chain-store purchasing practices, illegal.

Section 3 of the Clayton Act forbade tying contracts that reduce competition. A firm, particularly one with a patent on a vital process or a monopoly on a natural resource, could use licensing or other arrangements to restrict competition. One such method was the tying contract, whereby a firm tied the acquisition of one item to the purchase of another. For example, IBM once refused to sell its business machines. It only rented machines to customers and then required them to buy IBM punch cards, materials, and maintenance service. This had the effect of reducing competition in these related industries. The IBM lease agreement was declared illegal under the Clayton Act, and the company was forced to offer machines for sale and to separate leasing arrangements from agreements to purchase other IBM products.

Finally, although the Sherman Act prohibited voting trusts that lessened competition, interpretation of the act did not always prevent one corporation from acquiring the stock of competing firms and then merging them into itself. Section 7 of the Clayton Act prohibited such mergers if they were found to reduce competition. Either the Antitrust Division of the Justice Department or the FTC can bring suit under Section 7 to prevent mergers. If mergers have been consummated prior to the suit, divestiture can be ordered. The Clayton Act also prevented individuals from serving on the boards of directors of two competing companies. Two so-called competitors having common directors would obviously not compete very hard. Although the Clayton Act made it illegal for firms to merge through stock transactions when the effect would be to lessen competition, the law left a loophole. A firm could purchase the assets of a competing firm, integrate the operations into its own, and thus reduce competition. The Celler-Kefauver Act closed this loophole, making asset acquisitions illegal when the effect of such purchases was to reduce competition. By a slight change in wording, it made clear Congress' policy to attack all mergers that threatened competition, whether between buyers and sellers (vertical), between potential competitors (horizontal or product and market extension), and between entirely unrelated firms (pure conglomerate).

## Enforcement

Public enforcement of the antitrust laws is the dual responsibility of the Antitrust Division of the Department of Justice and the FTC. Generally speaking, the Justice Department concerns itself with significant or flagrant offenses under the Sherman Act, as well as with mergers for monopoly covered by Section 7 of the Clayton Act. In most instances, the Justice Department will only bring charges under the Clayton Act when broader Sherman Act violations are also involved. In addition to policing law violations, the Sherman Act also charges the Justice Department with the duty of restraining possible future violations. Thus, firms found to be in violation of the law often receive detailed federal court injunctions that regulate future business activity. In fact, "injunctive relief" (e.g., dissolution or divestiture decrees, and so on) is a much more typical outcome of Justice Department suits than are criminal penalties.

Although the Justice Department can institute civil proceedings in addition to the criminal proceedings discussed previously, civil proceedings are typically the responsibility of the FTC. The FTC is an administrative agency of the executive branch that has quasi-judicial powers with which it enforces compliance with the Clayton Act. Because the substantive provisions of the Clayton Act do not create criminal offenses, the FTC has no criminal jurisdiction. The FTC holds hearings about suspected violations of the law and issues cease and desist orders if violations are found. Cease and desist orders under the Clayton Act are subject to review by appellate courts.

## Economic Analysis in Antitrust Actions

Antitrust policy is applied if a specific business practice is thought to substantially lessen competition. Mergers are not illegal if they do not affect the vigor of competition. However, it is very difficult to accurately predict the competitive implications of a given merger. When is competition *substantially* reduced? If two firms, each with 1 percent of a market served by 100 competitors, merge, few would argue that the merger reduces competition. After the merger, 99 firms remain, and the 1-percent market-share advantage of the merged firm is not likely to be significant. However, merger of two firms that each had a substantial share of the market leaving only a few firms after the merger might affect competition. The problem lies in defining a "substantial" share of the market and quantifying a "few" remaining firms. Where should these lines be drawn?

Furthermore, if a particular merger would not itself reduce competition, but a series of similar mergers would do so, should the original merger be permitted? Assume that 20 firms, each with a 5-percent share of the market, are in competition. Suppose two of these firms merge, and a judgment made after examination of much economic evidence states that competition will suffer no harm. Approval of the merger might induce other firms to seek to merge, with the ultimate result of reduced competition. At what point should the trend toward concentration be stopped?

Market concentration is a key element in making judgments about the effect of a merger on the competitive posture of an industry, but how should an industry or a market be determined? To illustrate, suppose that two banks in lower Manhattan seek to merge. About 14,000 banks operate in the United States, and the national banking concentration ratio is low. However, the entire United States is not a relevant market for most banking services; a local area is the relevant market. But what local area? Should metropolitan New York be deemed the market? The City of New York? The Borough of Manhattan? Or lower Manhattan only? The answer depends on the nature of the banks involved. For certain classes of services, especially loans to major national corporations, the nation as a whole constitutes the market. But for personal checking-account and loan services, the local area is the relevant market.

The problem is even more complex when competing products or industries are considered. A particular bank might, for example, be the only one serving a given neighborhood, but the bank might still face intense competition from savings and loan associations, credit unions, and money market mutual funds that offer service by mail and toll-free telephone calls.

Similar problems are found in other aspects of antitrust policy. For example, given the difficulties we have noted in estimating costs for multiproduct firms, determining the presence and magnitude of price discrimination becomes difficult. A comprehensive economic cost analysis is often required to detect price discrimination, and even then the issue is often less than clear-cut.

Antitrust policy is quite complex, and its complete coverage is well beyond the scope of this text. In addition, generalizations are difficult. The fact that so many antitrust decisions are made in the courts is testimony to this point. Nevertheless, because antitrust policy does constitute a serious constraint to many business decisions, antitrust considerations are an important, if nebulous, aspect of managerial economics.

## THE REGULATED ENVIRONMENT: A SECOND LOOK

For effective decision making, managers must be aware of both the causes and the effects of regulatory processes. We have briefly addressed this need by considering economic and political factors that stimulate regulatory responses to market failures caused by incentive or structural problems. Both positive and negative aspects of current regulatory methods were briefly examined. Rather than summarizing this material immediately, however, we think that it will prove useful to look more closely at both the problems and promise of regulation. The issue is rarely one of regulation versus complete deregulation; it is more often one of how much and what kinds of regulation are most appropriate.

## Costs of Regulation

Many economists like to quote the phrase "There is no such thing as a free lunch." With respect to regulation, this can be interpreted to mean that every government program and policy has economic costs. The economic costs of regulatory policies are measured in terms of administrative burdens for regulatory agencies, deviations from optimal methods of production, and the general effect of regulation on the allocation of economic resources.

A first, and most obvious, cost of business regulation is the cost to local, state, and federal governments for supervisory agencies. Estimates for local, state, and federal expenditures for business regulation fall in the range of $3 to $5 billion per year. Interestingly, the largest regulatory budgets at the federal level are not those of traditional regulatory agencies, such as the Securities and Exchange Commission (SEC) or Interstate Commerce Commission (ICC), but those devoted to the broader regulatory activities of the Departments of Labor (for employment and job safety standards) and Agriculture (mainly for food inspection).

Although these direct costs of regulation are substantial, they may be far less than hidden or indirect costs. For example, the extensive reporting requirements of the Occupational Safety and Health Administration (OSHA) drive up administrative costs, and product prices typically increase. Similarly, consumers ultimately bear the cost of auto-emission standards mandated by the Environmental Protection Agency (EPA). In the case of auto emissions, the National Academy of Sciences and the National Academy of Engineering estimated the annual benefits of the catalytic converter at $5 billion and the annual costs at $11 billion. One might ask if the noneconomic, social advantages of this method of pollution control are sufficient to offset what appear to be significant economic disadvantages. Similarly, the economic and noneconomic benefits of regulation must be sufficient to offset considerable private costs for pollution control, OSHA-mandated noise reductions, health and safety equipment, FTC-mandated business reports, and so on.

Neither business nor the public can regard the economic costs of regulation as insignificant. Estimates of the total direct and indirect costs of these and other forms of regulation fall in the range of $100 billion per year. Given this magnitude, consideration of the total costs of regulation must play a prominent role in decisions about what and how to regulate. Where important concerns for the public's health and safety are apparent, business and government can accomplish much through cooperative

## 14.3  **Managerial Application**
Is Deregulation Working?

Consumers benefited from recent deregulation of many sectors of the U.S. economy as newly competitive and cost-conscious firms dramatically cut prices and increased product quality. Inevitably, some inefficient competitors were forced out of business. Although such losses are often viewed as the typical result of heightened competition, some concern has emerged that a loss of competitors in some previously regulated industries will stifle competition and lead to monopoly profits.

In trucking, previously regulated shippers of less-than-truckload quantities of freight operate national networks of consolidation centers surrounded by satellite terminals that offer door-to-door delivery. These networks feature sophisticated computer dispatch systems that permit the company to utilize available truck capacity efficiently. By eliminating empty backhauls, for example, the firms can dramatically cut fuel, labor, and equipment costs. Part of these cost savings pass on to customers; major companies use the rest to build their markets. Today, major trucking companies are raising their market share at the expense of smaller firms, which often find themselves unable to afford the investment necessary for efficient networking.

Similarly, major airlines have come to dominate traffic at several major airports by forming efficient "hub-and-spoke" networks. Northwest Airlines, for example, dominates the Minneapolis-St. Paul (MSP) International Airport "hub." Northwest fills its departures from the MSP airport with traffic generated by its own "spoke" or

*continued*

See: Chris Wells, "Is Deregulation Working?" *Business Week*, December 22, 1986, 50–55.

effort. The public must supervise the regulatory process to insure that government–business interactions yield policies in the public interest.

### The Size–Efficiency Problem
Natural monopoly creates a dilemma in that a single seller may achieve superior cost efficiency but may also restrict output, raise prices, and earn economic profits. This conflict between the superior efficiency of large firms and the harmful consequences of limited numbers of competitors is one of the oldest controversies in antitrust and regulatory policy. It is clear that some, perhaps many, people believe that efficiency consid-

---

**Managerial Application** *continued*

feeder flights from smaller cities across the Midwest, along with traffic fed into the company's system by commuter airlines that have operating agreements with Northwest. This captive traffic enables Northwest to increase its load factor (capacity utilization rate) and profits while making successful entry into the MSP market difficult.

Finally, changes in the FCC's deregulation of long-distance telephone service rates appear to have created a significant competitive advantage for AT&T. No longer able to get bargain rates on rental of AT&T's long-distance facilities, MCI and U.S. Sprint (AT&T's main competitors) have been forced to seek alternative means of offsetting the AT&T networking edge.

Distinguished economists such as Cornell's Alfred E. Kahn, former head of the Civil Aeronautics Board and an early proponent of deregulation, have voiced their concern. Kahn believes that recent mergers in previously regulated industries have raised concentration to the point where anticompetitive effects can be expected in some markets. Even the pro-merger Justice Department of the Reagan administration opposed the Department of Transportation's

approval of Northwest Airlines' takeover of Republic Airlines. Others have been quick to point out that competition in transportation and communication markets can be vigorous even among only a few actual and potential competitors. In the Minneapolis–St. Paul market, for example, Continental and United Airlines have proved to be formidable competitors for Northwest in the long-distance flights to large cities. Similarly, intermodal competition from passenger automobiles and intercity bus systems limits Northwest's pricing discretion on local routes, for which it may be the only scheduled airline.

In evaluating the effects of deregulation and in gauging the implications of increasing concentration for competition, it is important to remember that protecting competition is definitely not the same thing as protecting competitors. Without regulation, it is inevitable that some competitors will fall by the wayside and that concentration will rise in some markets. Although such trends must be watched closely for anticompetitive effects, they are sometimes the sign of a vigorously competitive environment.

---

erations cannot justify the sizes reached by the largest firms. However, some economists believe that the commonly observed link between leading-firm market shares (industry concentration) and profitability does derive from lower costs made possible through superior efficiency rather than from higher prices due to collusion. Research findings in this area are as controversial as they are important. They suggest the need to consider the size–efficiency issue further.

Federal legislation proposed during recent years would limit mergers between firms of a certain size, say $100 million or more in annual sales. These proposals reflect the belief that such mergers increase monopoly power and have no offsetting advantages in terms of economic efficiency. However, research on the economic causes and consequences of mergers and other corporate restructuring indicates that underutilized resources are transferred by these means to more efficient uses. Unfriendly take-overs, for example, are especially unfriendly to inefficient management, which is subsequently replaced. Perhaps one of the greatest dangers to a blanket prohibition of all mergers involving large firms is that it could protect inefficient management, or management that is insensitive to stockholder interests, against the threat of removal for unsatisfactory performance.

Although questions about merger policy are generally difficult, those related to government policy concerning the breakup of long-established firms are even more complex. The recent Justice Department cases against IBM and AT&T provide classic illustrations.

IBM did not invent the electronic computer, but it was one of the first companies to realize the enormous opportunities it presented. IBM's involvement with the computer transformed what was once a modestly successful business machines company into the dominant firm in various sectors of an expanding industry. Growing rapidly during the 1950s and 1960s, IBM became the leader in the mainframe equipment sector of the industry while playing a lesser role in peripherals and terminal equipment, software services, and other areas. In 1969, the Antitrust Divisions of the Justice Department, concerned with the potentially anticompetitive effects of IBM's market position, filed suit to break up the firm. The case foundered. Although all observers could agree that IBM was a large and highly profitable company, the sources of its success were a matter of substantial dispute. Was IBM highly profitable merely because of its leadership position (monopoly power), or was IBM a highly profitable industry leader by virtue of its ability to offer innovative products at attractive prices (efficiency)? In the first case, breaking up IBM could lead to lower prices, eliminate monopoly profits, and increase consumer welfare. In the second case, breaking up IBM would penalize the type of efficiency that competitive markets are meant to encourage. Innovation and efficiency in the industry could be blunted. Determining the source of IBM's success and the costs and benefits from a possible breakup became a problem with no obvious answer. In 1982, after more than a decade of litigation costing both sides tens of millions of dollars, the Justice Department dismissed its suit. Free from antitrust concerns, IBM clearly became more aggressive in terms of pricing and new-product development during the 1980s, with obvious benefits for users of business and personal computers.

A second interesting example of recent antitrust policy is the 1974 Justice Department suit to break up AT&T. The department argued that breaking up AT&T would stimulate competition in the telephone equipment and long-distance sectors of the industry and provide consumers with improved goods and services at lower prices. To avoid the expense and uncertainty of a prolonged antitrust case, AT&T agreed to divest itself of its local phone companies. As of January 1, 1984, a "new" AT&T was created, consisting largely of AT&T communications (long-distance phone service), AT&T information systems (computer systems), AT&T international (foreign operations), Bell Labs (research and development), and Western Electric (telephone equipment). The seven local companies created were Ameritech, Bell Atlantic, Bell South, Nynex, Pacific Telesis, Southwestern Bell, and U.S. West. Whether this reorganization of the telecommunications industry will lead to benefits for consumers remains to be seen. In the meantime, the enormous costs and risks involved make clear why such "experiments" are so rare.

## The "Capture" Problem

Our earlier examination of the "why regulate" question considered both economic and noneconomic factors that influence regulatory decisions. We noted the widely held belief that regulation is in the public interest and influences firm behavior toward socially desirable ends. This view is not universally held, however, and the compelling counterarguments must be considered.

**capture theory**

An economic theory suggesting that industry seeks regulation to limit competition and obtain government subsidies.

In the early 1970s, Nobel laureate George Stigler introduced the **capture theory** of economic regulation. According to Stigler, the machinery and power of the state are a potential resource to every industry. With its power to prohibit or compel, to take or give money, the state can and does selectively help or hurt a vast number of industries. Because of this, regulation may be actively *sought* by an industry. Stigler contends that, as a rule, regulation is acquired by industry and is designed and operated primarily for the industry's benefit. Although some regulations are undeniably onerous, these are thought to be exceptional rather than usual cases.

Stigler asserts that the types of state favors commonly sought by regulated industries include direct money subsidies, control over entry by new rivals, control over offerings of substitutes and complements, and price-fixing. Therefore, domestic "air-mail" subsidies, Federal Deposit Insurance Corporation (FDIC) regulation that reduces the rate of entry into commercial banking, suppression of margarine sales by butter producers, price-fixing in motor carrier (trucking) regulation, and American Medical Association control of medical training and licensing can be interpreted as historical examples of regulatory process control by regulated industries.

In summarizing his views on regulation, Stigler suggests that the Interstate Commerce Commission's pro-industry policies should no more be criticized than should the Great Atlantic and Pacific Tea Company (A&P) for selling groceries or politicians for seeking popular support. Current methods of enacting and carrying out regulations only make the pro-industry stance of regulatory bodies more likely. Stigler contends that the only way to get different results from regulation is to change the political process of regulator selection and to provide economic rewards to regulators who serve the public interest effectively.

## The Deregulation Movement

Growing concern with the costs and problems of government regulation gave birth in the early 1970s to a **deregulation** movement that has grown to impressive dimensions. Although it is difficult to pinpoint a single catalyst for the movement, it is hard to overlook the role played by Stigler and other economists (notably Alfred E. Kahn) who illustrated that the regulatory process can sometimes harm rather than help consumer interests.

Table 14.1 highlights some of the major steps taken toward deregulation since 1970. Although many industries have felt the effects of changing state and local regulation, changing federal regulation has been most pronounced in the financial, telecommunications, and transportation sectors. Since 1975, for example, it has been illegal for securities dealers to fix commission rates. This broke a 182-year tradition under which the New York Stock Exchange (NYSE) set minimum rates for each 100-share ("round lot") purchase. Until 1975, everyone charged the minimum rate approved by the NYSE. Purchase of 1,000 shares cost a commission of ten times the minimum, even though the overhead and work involved were roughly the same for small and large stock transactions. This system not only generated large profits for NYSE members, but it also covered the higher costs of inefficient firms. Following deregulation, commission rates tumbled, and, predictably, some of the least efficient brokerage firms merged or otherwise went out of business. Today, more than a decade later, commission rates (prices) have fallen by 50 percent or more, and the industry is noteworthy for its increasing productivity

■ Table 14.1

### Recent Major Steps toward Deregulation

| | |
|---|---|
| 1970 | Federal Reserve Board frees interest rates on large bank deposits with short maturities ($100,000 or more for six months or less). |
| 1975 | Securities and Exchange Commission prohibits fixed commissions on stock sales. |
| 1978 | Congress deregulates the airline industry. |
| 1979 | Federal Communications Commission (FCC) allows AT&T to sell unregulated services (e.g., data processing). |
| 1980 | Congress allows banks to pay interest on checking, increases competition for business loans. |
| 1980 | Congress deregulates trucking and railroads. |
| 1982 | Congress allows savings and loans to make commercial loans and related investments. |
| 1982 | Congress deregulates intercity bus services. |
| 1982 | Department of Justice and Federal Trade Commission relax merger guidelines. |
| 1984 | AT&T forced by Justice Department to divest its local phone companies. |
| 1986 | Interest rates for passbook and statement savings accounts deregulated. |
| 1989 | FCC caps AT&T's long-distance rates, deregulates its profit rate. |

and variety of new product introductions. It is also worth mentioning that during the 1975 to 1982 period, the number of sales offices in the industry increased by 80 percent, total employment rose by two-thirds, and profits increased to $1.5 billion per year, more than ten times the 1974 level. All of this may lead observers to conclude that deregulation can benefit consumers without causing any lasting damage to industry. In fact, a leaner, more efficient industry may be one of the greatest benefits of deregulation.

Despite obvious successes following deregulation, the movement has its critics. When airline ticket prices reflect the cost of service, as they must without regulation, bargain fares will be available on heavily traveled routes between major cities (e.g., New York to Los Angeles, Chicago to Miami), but relatively high fares will result for lightly traveled routes (e.g., Pittsburgh to Buffalo, New York; Kansas City to Omaha). Similarly, deregulation in the telecommunications industry caused rates for long-distance telephone calls to fall but monthly charges for local service to rise. Deregulation in the intercity bus market brought many travelers lower prices but forced Greyhound Corporation to suffer a costly strike in order to convince workers that wage levels would have to be reduced. Inefficient firms, consumers who buy goods and services whose cost is partly subsidized by other customers, and workers who take home inflated wages can all be expected to oppose efforts to continue the process of deregulation. Still, the net gains from deregulation appear to be significant.

## Rationalizing the Regulatory Process

Although some think that there is simply a question of regulation versus deregulation, this is seldom the case. Thus, it will prove valuable to consider methods of improving regulation in addition to focusing on the no-regulation alternative.

Our earlier discussion suggested that an important problem of regulation, particularly utility regulation, was that regulators seldom have the information or expertise necessary to specify, for example, the correct level of utility investment, the minimum necessary regulated carrier costs, or the optimal method of pollution control. Because technology is changing rapidly in many industries, often only those industry personnel currently working at the frontier of technology have the specialized knowledge necessary to deal satisfactorily with such issues.

One possible way to deal with the technical expertise problem of current regulation is to have more regulators focus on the preferred outcomes of regulatory processes rather than on the technical means that industry adopts to achieve those ends. The Federal Communication Commission's decision in 1989 to adopt downward-adjusting price caps for AT&T's long-distance rates rather than maintain traditional profit-rate regulation is an example of this developing trend. If AT&T is able to reduce costs faster than the FCC-mandated decline in prices, it will be able to enjoy an increase in profitability. By setting price caps that fall over time, the FCC ensures that consumers will share in expected cost savings while giving the company a positive incentive to innovate. Such innovations in regulation allow regulators to focus on defining the public interest in regulation, while industry specializes in meeting those objectives at the least cost possible. Tying regulator rewards and regulated industry profits to objective, output-oriented performance criteria could create further desirable incentives for minimizing the costs of necessary regulations.

For example, the public has a real interest in safe, reliable, and low-cost electric power. State and federal regulators who oversee the operations of utilities could develop objective standards for measuring utility safety, reliability, and cost efficiency. Tying firm profit rates to such performance-oriented criteria could stimulate real improvements in utility operations.

Competitive forces provide a persistent and socially desirable constraining influence on firm behavior. When vigorous competition is absent, government regulation can be justified through both efficiency and equity criteria. When regulation is warranted, business, government, and the public must work together to insure that regulatory processes represent not only large or special interests but also those with individually small but collectively large stakes in regulatory decisions.

## SUMMARY

The history of government involvement in the economy is both long and substantial. It is generally believed that government acts to stimulate and assist private enterprise and to regulate or control business practices so that firms operate consistently with the public interest. Although we have discussed some of the interactions between government and business throughout the text, this chapter provides a more detailed examination.

Both economic and political considerations influence decisions about what and how to regulate. *Regulation* can enhance economic *efficiency* when unrestricted market activity fails to provide the types and quantities of goods consumers demand at competitive prices. *Market failure* because of structural problems occurs when a limited number of buyers or sellers cause high prices, economic profits, or inefficiency. Market failure because of incentive problems occurs when product prices fail to reflect *externalities,* or some indirect benefits or costs of production. Inefficient levels of output and allocations of resources result. Public utility regulation is intended to limit the effects of market failure as a result of structural problems by regulating prices and profits in natural monopoly markets. If competition among a large number of firms is feasible, antitrust policy seeks to insure competitive practices. Market failure caused by incentive problems can be avoided if pollution taxes or fines adjust prices of all goods and services to reflect the full costs of production. Beyond these economic advantages, carefully designed regulations can also further the political goals of preserving consumer choice or consumer sovereignty and limiting concentration of economic and political power.

The regulatory response to incentive failures includes the supervision of operating rights (licenses), patent grants, government subsidies, taxes or fines, and operating controls. Regulation is costly. Who actually bears the burden of these costs can seldom be determined by merely considering the fined, taxed, or otherwise regulated party. All else being equal, producers (including stockholders and employees) bear the burden of regulation when final product demand is highly elastic. With inelastic demand, producers can pass the burden of regulation on to consumers.

The regulatory response to structural failures is twofold. First, when a single firm has the potential to produce output more efficiently than any group of smaller firms—a situation called natural monopoly—regulation of prices and profits insures that the monopolist acts in the public interest. The regulator sets a price lower than the profit-maximizing price in order to allow the company only a normal profit. Because regulation presents many problems, it is often thought to be preferable to limit monopoly by encouraging workable levels of competition. Thus, antitrust policy, a second approach to limiting structural failures, seeks to maintain competition. The antitrust laws deal with collusion, price discrimination, mergers, tying contracts, and other business practices that threaten competition.

Problems caused by the high and growing costs of regulation, and regulations that seem to have served industry rather than consumer interests, have helped create the recent *deregulation* movement. These problems exert a powerful influence on what and how we regulate and, therefore, on the role of government in the market economy.

## Questions

14.1 Define the term *market failure* and cite some causes. Can you also cite some examples of market failure?

14.2 What role does the price elasticity of demand play in determining the short-run effects of regulations that increase fixed costs? What if they lead to increased variable costs?

14.3 Given the difficulties encountered in regulating the various utility industries in the United States, it has been suggested that nationalization might lead to a more socially optimal allocation of resources. Do you agree? Why or why not?

14.4 Antitrust statutes in the United States have been used primarily to attack monopolization by big business. Does monopolization of the labor supply by giant unions have the same potential for misallocation of economic resources?

14.5 When will an increase in the minimum wage increase employment income for unskilled workers? When will it cause income to fall? Based on your experience, which is the more likely result?

14.6  Explain why state tax rates on personal income vary more on a state-by-state basis than do corresponding tax rates on corporate income.

14.7  Do the U.S. antitrust statutes protect competition or competitors? What is the distinction between the two?

14.8  Define *price discrimination*. When is it legal? When is it illegal? Cite some common examples of price discrimination.

14.9  Is the deregulation movement of the 1970s and 1980s consistent or inconsistent with the capture theory of economic regulation?

14.10  "Regulation is often proposed on the basis of equity considerations and opposed on the basis of efficiency considerations. As a result, the regulation versus deregulation controversy is not easily resolved." Discuss this statement.

## Problems

14.1  During each 24-hour period, coal-fired electricity generating plants emit substantial amounts of sulfur dioxide and particulate pollution into the atmosphere. Concerned citizens are appalled at the aesthetic and environmental implications of such pollution, as well as the potential health hazard to the local population.

A.  Pollution is a negative production externality and an example of market failure. What reasons might you cite for why markets fail?

B.  In analyzing remedies to the current situation, consider three general types of controls to limit pollution:

- *Regulations*—licenses, permits, compulsory standards, and so on.
- *Payments*—various types of government aid to help companies install pollution-control equipment. Aid can take the form of forgiven local property taxes, income tax credits, special accelerated depreciation allowances for pollution-control equipment, low-cost government loans, and so on.
- *Charges*—excise taxes on polluting fuels (coal, oil, and so forth), pollution discharge taxes, and others.

Review each of these methods of pollution control and do the following:

(1)  Determine the incentive structure for the polluter under each form of control.

(2)  Decide who pays for a clean environment under each form of control. (Note that each form of control has definite implications about who owns the property rights to the environment.)

(3)  Defend a particular form of control on the basis of your analysis, including both efficiency and equity considerations.

14.2 On May 2, 1989, *The Wall Street Journal* (p. B1) carried an article titled, "Do Colleges Collude on Financial Aid?" The article described the results of an annual meeting of the financial-aid officers from 23 colleges, including the eight Ivy League members and "competing" schools (e.g., Amherst, Barnard, Bryn Mawr, MIT, etc.) at which the schools compared notes on common applicants seeking financial aid. The following is an excerpt from that article:

"The schools generally refer to their annual spring meeting at Wellesley as 'financial-aid overlap.' Here's how it works.

Frank Eager, a hypothetical student, has been accepted both at Harvard, where tuition, room, and board for next fall total $19,395, and at Penn, whose costs total $19,100. Both schools agree that the Eagers qualify for financial aid, but they differ on how much. Penn figures the Eager family can afford to pay $6,000 a year for Frank's education, but Harvard arrives at a $7,000 figure. At the meeting, Penn becomes convinced that the Harvard number makes sense and increases its family-contribution amount.

As a result, Frank receives acceptance letters and financial-aid offers that would mean identical $7,000 out-of-pocket expenses for the Eagers at either school. Had the schools awarded aid independently, the Eagers might have saved $1,000 by choosing Penn. With the same family contribution, Harvard will offer a bigger aid package because its costs are higher. But the burden to the Eagers—their true price of a year's schooling—would be the same."

A. How would you determine if the "financial-aid overlap" meeting is an example of price-fixing?

B. If price-fixing does indeed occur, which laws in particular might be violated?

14.3 During recent years, U.S. car manufacturers have charged lower car prices in western states in an effort to head off competition by popular Japanese imports. Thus, subcompacts produced by GM, Ford, and others have cost consumers hundreds of dollars less in western states than in other parts of the country. This two-tier pricing scheme has raised the ire of eastern dealers, who view it as discriminatory and a violation of antitrust laws.

A. Is this pricing scheme discriminatory in the economic sense? What conditions would be necessary for it to be profitable to the auto makers?

B. Carefully describe how price discrimination could violate U.S. antitrust laws, and be sure to mention which laws in particular might be violated.

14.4 The Tobacco Products Control Act sharply curtails advertising and promotion of tobacco products in Canada. This legislation, which took effect January 1, 1989, bans all print and broadcast advertising of tobacco products in Canada. The act also orders the phase-out of all existing billboard and in-store tobacco advertising and requires stronger health warnings on tobacco packaging. Explain why this legislation is likely to *increase, decrease* or have *no effect* on the following:

A.  Consumption of tobacco products
B.  Industry advertising costs
C.  Short-run industry profits
D.  Nonadvertising methods of competition
E.  Barriers to entry.

14.5   On November 21, 1986, *The Wall Street Journal* (p. 29) carried an article titled "It'll Mean Another Two Semesters in the Red, but Who's Counting?" This article described efforts by the American Institute of Certified Public Accountants (AICPA) to require a fifth (graduate) year of study in accounting for joining the institute. The following is an excerpt from that article:

> "Technical demands have become so great on accountants that they can't get five pounds of education in a four-pound bag," explains James MacNeil, director of the AICPA's education division. He says the extra year "would help graduates understand such new complexities as leveraged leases and buyouts and new types of securities being devised by Wall Street." (Hawaii, Utah and Florida already require five years of study before taking the CPA exam, and several other states are giving the matter independent consideration.)
>
> Such arguments, however, have failed to sway many educators. "Most of the deans of the nation's 650 business schools oppose going to five years from four," says Charles Hickman, projects director for the American Assembly of Collegiate Schools of Business, based in St. Louis. "The big question raised by most deans is whether another roadblock should be raised to becoming a working accountant." Some opponents point out that since Florida imposed its five-year rule in 1983, the number of applicants for the CPA exam there has declined sharply each year.

Briefly explain the following:

A.  The causes and consequences of regulation according to the public interest theory of regulation.
B.  The causes and consequences of regulation according to the capture theory of regulation.
C.  How the preceding article supports or contradicts each.

14.6   Syzygy Medical Instruments, Inc., manufactures an innovative piece of diagnostic equipment used in medical laboratories and hospitals. The Occupational Health and Safety Administration (OSHA) has determined that additional safety precautions are necessary to bring radioactive leakage occurring during use of the machine down to acceptable levels.

Total production costs, including a normal rate of return on investment but *before* additional safeguards are installed, are:

$$TC = \$5,000,000 + \$5,000Q.$$

Market demand relations are:

$P_L = \$15,000 - \$12.5Q_L$ (Medical Laboratory Demand)

$P_H = \$10,000 - \$1Q_H.$ (Hospital Demand)

A. Assuming that the company faces two distinct markets, calculate the profit-maximizing price/output combination in each market and Syzygy's level of economic profits.
B. Describe the short- and long-run implications of meeting OSHA standards if doing so raises Syzygy's marginal cost by $1,000 per machine.
C. Calculate the point price elasticity at the initial (Part A) profit-maximizing activity level in each market. Are the differential effects on sales in each market that were seen in Part B typical or atypical?

14.7 Intergalactic Business Machines (IBM) and Compact Computer, Inc., leading competitors in the market for plug-compatible personal computers, have asked the Antitrust Division of the Justice Department for a preliminary ruling on a proposed merger. Recent operating experience of the two companies suggests the following:

$\pi_1 = \$8,000 \, Q_1 - \$1Q_1^2 - \$4,000Q_2,$ (IBM's Profit Function)

$\pi_2 = \$8,000 \, Q_2 - \$4Q_2^2 - \$1,000Q_1,$ (Compact's Profit Function)

where $\pi$ represents economic profits, $Q_1$ is IBM's output, and $Q_2$ is Compact's output.

A. Calculate maximum economic profits for each company when operated separately.
B. Calculate maximum economic profits for a merged company.
C. Calculate the net social costs or benefits from merger of the two companies. Should the Antitrust Division oppose the proposed merger?

14.8 The Woebegone Water Company is a small water utility serving rural customers in Minnesota. The company is currently engaged in a rate case with the Crow Wing County Regulatory Commission. At issue is the monthly rate to be charged for unmetered sewer and water service. The demand curve for monthly service is $P = \$40 - \$0.01Q$. This implies an annual demand curve of:

$$P = \$480 - \$0.12Q,$$

where $P$ is service price in dollars and $Q$ is the number of customers served. Total costs per year (before investment return) are described by the function:

$$TC = \$70,000 + \$80Q + \$0.005Q^2.$$

The company has assets of $2 million, and the utility commission has authorized an 11.5 percent fair rate of return on investment.

A. Calculate Woebegone's profit-maximizing price (monthly and annual), output, and rate-of-return levels.

B. Woebegone has requested a monthly price of $22. If granted, calculate Woebegone's output and total return on investment. Why are these values different from those calculated in Part A?

C. What monthly price should the commission grant if Woebegone is to be limited to an 11.5-percent rate of return?

14.9  Distinctive Fashions, Inc., is a manufacturer of fashionable dresses and evening gowns and a major employer in New York City's garment district. Distinctive's demand relation can be written as:

$$P = \$1,000 - \$0.02Q,$$

where $Q$ is the quantity of dresses demanded per year. Production of each unit of output requires 100 hours of labor, 20 hours of capital-equipment time (sewing machines, etc.), and $50 of raw materials. Distinctive has a total of 400,000 hours of capital-equipment time available in its production facility each year and can purchase all the labor and materials it desires. The capital-equipment investment by Distinctive totals $30 million, and the firm requires a 15-percent return on capital. Assume that these are the only costs incurred and that Distinctive has a profit-maximization objective.

A. You have been employed by the State Unemployment Service to evaluate the effect on employment of a proposed increase in the minimum wage. As a first step in the analysis, develop Distinctive's short-run demand curve for labor.

B. If Distinctive currently pays a wage rate of $3.35 per hour for labor, calculate the short-run impact on employment of an increase to a $4 minimum wage.

C. Calculate Distinctive's profits at the $3.35 and $4 wage levels. What are the long-run employment implications of the higher minimum wage?

14.10 The Klamath Paper Company produces corrugated boxes for industrial packaging at a plant located in Klamath Falls, Oregon. For each ton of packaging materials produced, 100 gallons of wastewater pollutant is dumped into the Klamath River. Klamath's demand and total manufacturing cost relations for corrugated boxes are:

$$P = \$6,000 - \$0.15Q,$$
$$TC = \$18,000,000 + \$2,000Q + \$0.05Q^2.$$

Both price and total manufacturing cost (which includes capital costs) are in dollars, and $Q$ is tons of output. The Oregon Department of Natural Resources (DNR) is considering various pollution-tax schemes designed to provide funding for clean-up operations as well as reduce Klamath's wastewater pollution. The DNR has determined that discharges into the river must be cut by at least 50 percent to meet new federal water-quality guidelines. Alternatively, the Klamath Water District water-treatment facility could be expanded to deal with water-treatment needs at a public cost of $25 million per year—costs that must be met through pollution charges, other taxes, or both.

A. Calculate Klamath's optimal output, price, discharge, and profit levels in light of each of the following pollution-reduction options being contemplated:

(1) No pollution taxes (disposal costs).

(2) A $2 per gallon wastewater disposal charge.

(3) Klamath being required to recycle all wastewater. Klamath calculates total recycling costs (in dollars) as:

$$TC = \$2W + \$0.000005W^2,$$

where $W$ is gallons of recycled wastewater.

(4) A $2 per gallon wastewater disposal charge on up to 500,000 gallons per year, with Klamath being required to recycle any additional wastewater.

B. Which pollution-reduction/treatment scheme is the preferred alternative?

## Selected References

Aaron, Henry. "Politics and the Professors Revisited." *American Economic Review* 79 (May 1989): 1–15.

Auerbach, Alan J., and James R. Hines, Jr. "Investment Tax Incentives and Frequent Tax Reforms." *American Economic Review* 78 (May 1988): 211–216.

Baer, Herbert. "Expanded Powers After the Crash(es)." *American Economic Review* 79 (May 1989): 156–160.

Beck, Paul J., and Michael W. Maher. "Competition, Regulation and Bribery." *Managerial and Decision Economics* 10 (March 1989): 1–12.

Brown, Charles. "Minimum Wage Laws: Are They Overrated?" *Journal of Economic Perspectives* 2 (Summer 1988): 133–146.

Clark, Don P. "Regulation of International Trade in the United States: The Tokyo Round." *Journal of Business* 60 (April 1987): 297–306.

Crandell, Robert W. "Surprises from Telephone Deregulation and the AT&T Divestiture." *American Economic Review* 78 (May 1988): 323–327.

Crandell, Robert W., and John D. Graham. "The Effect of Fuel Economy Standards on Automobile Safety." *Journal of Law and Economics* 32 (April 1989): 97–118.

Hahn, Robert W. "Economic Prescriptions for Environmental Problems: How the Patient Followed Doctor's Orders." *Journal of Economic Perspectives* 3 (Spring 1989): 95–114.

Kahn, Alfred E. "Surprises of Airline Deregulation." *American Economic Review* 78 (May 1988): 316–322.

Kane, Edward J. "Interaction of Financial and Regulatory Innovation." *American Economic Review* 78 (May 1988): 328–334.

Mayo, John W., and Joseph E. Flynn. "The Effects of Regulation on Research and Development: Theory and Evidence." *Journal of Business* 61 (July 1988): 321–336.

McFarland, Henry. "Did Railroad Deregulation Lead to Monopoly Pricing? An Application of q." *Journal of Business* 60 (July 1987): 385–400.

Peltzman, Sam. "Regulation and Health: The Case of Mandatory Prescriptions and an Extension." *Managerial and Decision Economics* 8 (March 1987): 41–46.

Pogue, Thomas F., and Larry G. Sgontz. "Taxing to Control Social Costs: The Case of Alcohol." *American Economic Review* 79 (March 1989): 235–243.

Pound, John, "The Effects of Antitakeover Amendments on Takeover Activity: Some Direct Evidence." *Journal of Law and Economics* 30 (October 1987): 353–367.

Schmalensee, Richard. "Horizontal Merger Policy: Problems and Changes." *Journal of Economic Perspectives* 1 (Fall 1987): 41–54.

Stiglitz, Joseph E. "Markets, Market Failures, and Development." *American Economic Review* 79 (May 1989): 197–203.

Wall, Richard A., and Michael Gort. "Financial Markets and the Limits of Regulation." *Managerial and Decision Economics* 9 (March 1988): 65–73.

White, Lawrence J. "Antitrust and Merger Policy: A Review and Critique." *Journal of Economic Perspectives* 1 (Fall 1987): 13–22.

# Decision Making under Uncertainty

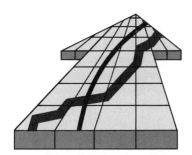

In many simple decisions, managers know with certainty the outcomes that each possible course of action will produce. A firm with $100,000 in cash that can either be invested in a 30-day Treasury bill yielding 8 percent ($658 interest for 30 days) or used to prepay a 12-percent bank loan ($986 interest for 30 days) can determine with certainty that prepayment of the bank loan will provide a $328 higher return. Similarly, a manufacturer that needs 500,000 units of an industrial fastener that it can purchase from one distributor at 74¢ per unit and from a second at 74.5¢ per unit knows with certainty that it will save $2,500 by purchasing from the first distributor.

Insight can be gained into decision problems for which events and results cannot be exactly predicted by treating the problems as though management had complete information about all possible outcomes from a given decision. Understanding the rationale for decisions under certainty conditions provides a useful framework for the somewhat more complex analysis required for decision making under uncertainty. For these reasons, much of the analysis and many of the optimality conditions developed in managerial economics assume perfect information about all events and outcomes.

In reality, however, most major managerial decisions are made under conditions of uncertainty. Managers must select a course of action from the alternatives without perfect knowledge about the occurrence of particular events or their actual effects on outcomes should they occur. The pervasiveness of uncertainty in managerial decision situations and the risk such uncertainty introduces dictate that the concepts of risk and risk analysis be explored in the study of managerial economics.

Risk analysis can be related directly to the basic valuation model underlying the microeconomic theory of the firm. When both risk levels and decision-maker attitudes toward risk taking are known, the effects of uncertainty on the basic valuation model can be reflected through adjustments to the model's numerator or denominator. The certainty equivalent method converts expected risky profit streams to their certain sum equivalents to eliminate value differences that result from different risk levels. That is, the certainty equivalent method adjusts the numerator of the basic valuation model so that present values for projects are risk adjusted and, therefore, comparable.

A second way to directly reflect uncertainty in the basic valuation model is through risk-adjusted discount rates. In this method, the interest rate in the denominator of the basic valuation model depends on the level of risk associated with a given cash flow. Thus, discounted expected profit streams once again reflect risk differences among projects and are directly comparable.

We begin this chapter by defining risk and discussing methods for measuring it. We then examine the two primary methods for adapting the basic valuation model to account for uncertainty. Finally, we discuss probability theory, decision trees, and simulation as aids to decision making under uncertainty.

# RISK IN ECONOMIC ANALYSIS

**risk**

Variation in project return or chance of loss.

Risk is defined as a hazard or peril; as an exposure to harm; and, in business, as a chance of loss.[1] Thus, **risk** refers to the possibility that some unfavorable event will occur. For example, if one buys a $1-million short-term government bond priced to yield 9 percent, the return on the investment, 9 percent, can be estimated precisely, and we say that the investment is risk free. If, however, the $1 million is invested in the stock of a company being organized to prospect for natural gas in the Gulf of Mexico, the return on the investment cannot be estimated precisely. The return could range from minus 100 percent (a complete loss) to some extremely large figure. Because of its significant danger of loss, we say that the project is risky. Similarly, sales forecasts for different products may exhibit different degrees of risk. For example, The Dryden Press may be sure that sales of a fifth edition introductory finance text will reach the projected level of 30,000 copies, but the company may be uncertain about the number of copies that it will sell of a new first-edition statistics text. The greater uncertainty associated with the sales level of the statistics text increases the chance that the firm will not profit

---

[1]Some writers distinguish between risk and uncertainty, but for our purposes this distinction is unnecessary. Accordingly, we define any decision whose outcome is less than certain as being risky, and we say that such decisions are subject to risk or uncertainty.

from publishing that book. Thus, that project's risk is greater than the risk of revising the finance text.

Risk is associated with the chance or probability of undesirable outcomes; the more likely an undesirable outcome, the riskier the decision. It is useful, however, to define risk more precisely. This more precise definition requires a step-by-step development, which occupies the remainder of this section.

## Probability Distributions

**probability**

The chance that an event will occur.

**probability distribution**

A listing of all possible outcomes with the probability that each will occur.

The **probability** of an event is defined as the chance, or odds, that the event will occur. For example, a sales manager may state, "There is a 70-percent chance that we will get an order from Delmarva Corporation and a 30-percent chance that we will not." If all possible events or outcomes are listed, and if a probability of occurrence is assigned to each event, the listing is called a **probability distribution.** For our sales example, we could set up the following probability distribution:

| Event (1) | Probability of Occurrence (2) |
|---|---|
| Receive order | 0.7 =  70% |
| Do not receive order | 0.3 =  30% |
| | 1.0 = 100% |

The possible outcomes are listed in Column 1, and the probabilities of each outcome, expressed both as decimals and percentages, appear in Column 2. Notice that the probabilities sum to 1.0, or 100 percent, as they must if the probability distribution is complete.

Risk in this very simple example can be read from the probability distribution as a 30-percent chance that the undesirable event (the firm not receiving the order from Delmarva Corporation) will occur. For most managerial decisions, however, the relative desirability of alternative events or outcomes is not so absolute. For this reason, a more general measure of the relation between risk and the probability distribution is required to incorporate risk into the decision process appropriately. The need for a more general measure of risk can be illustrated by the following situation.

Suppose that a firm is considering two investments, each calling for an outlay of $10,000. It will choose only one. Assume also that the profits on the two projects are related to the level of general economic activity in the coming year as shown in Table 15.1, a table known as a *payoff matrix*. Here we see that both projects will provide a $5,000 profit in a

■ Table 15.1

**Payoff Matrix for Projects *A* and *B***

| State of the Economy | Profits | |
|---|---|---|
| | Project *A* | Project *B* |
| Recession | $4,000 | $    0 |
| Normal | 5,000 | 5,000 |
| Boom | 6,000 | 12,000 |

normal economy, higher profits in a boom economy, and lower profits if a recession occurs. Notice also that the profits from Project *B* vary far more widely under the different states of the economy than do the profits from Project *A*. In a normal economy, both projects return $5,000 in profit. Should the economy be in a recession next year, Project *B* will produce nothing whereas Project *A* will still provide a $4,000 profit. On the other hand, if the economy is booming next year, Project *B*'s profit will increase to $12,000, but profit for Project *A* will increase only moderately to $6,000.

How, then, is one to evaluate these alternatives? Project *A* is clearly more desirable if the economy is in a recession, whereas Project *B* is superior in a boom economy. (In a normal economy the projects offer the same profit potential, and we would not favor one over the other.) To answer the question, we need to know how likely a boom, a recession, or normal economic conditions are. If we have probabilities for the occurrence of these events, we can develop probability distributions of profits for the two projects and from these obtain measures of both the expected profits and the variability of profits. These measures enable us to evaluate the projects in terms of their expected profit and the risk that the profit will deviate from the expected value.

To continue the example, assume that economic forecasts of current trends in economic indicators indicate chances of two in ten that a recession will occur, six in ten of a normal economy, and two in ten of a boom. Redefining *chances* as *probability*, we find that the probability of a recession is 0.2, or 20 percent; the probability of normal economic activity is 0.6, or 60 percent; and the probability of a boom is 0.2, or 20 percent. Notice that the probabilities add up to 1.0: 0.2 + 0.6 + 0.2 = 1.0, or 100 percent. These probabilities have been added to the payoff matrix in Table 15.1 to provide the probability distributions of profit for Projects *A* and *B* shown in Table 15.2.

If we multiply each possible outcome by its probability of occurrence and then add these products, we have a weighted average of the outcomes. The weights are the probabilities of occurrence, and the weighted average is called the *expected outcome*. Column 4 of Table 15.2 illus-

■ Table 15.2
## Calculation of Expected Values

|  | State of the Economy (1) | Probability of This State Occurring (2) | Profit Outcome if This State Occurs (3) | Expected Profit Outcome (4) = (2) × (3) |
|---|---|---|---|---|
| *Project A* | Recession | 0.2 | $ 4,000 | $ 800 |
|  | Normal | 0.6 | 5,000 | 3,000 |
|  | Boom | 0.2 | 6,000 | 1,200 |
|  |  | 1.0 |  | Expected Profit *A* $5,000 |
| *Project B* | Recession | 0.2 | $ 0 | $ 0 |
|  | Normal | 0.6 | 5,000 | 3,000 |
|  | Boom | 0.2 | 12,000 | 2,400 |
|  |  | 1.0 |  | Expected Profit *B* $5,400 |

trates the calculation of the expected profits for Projects *A* and *B*. We multiply each possible profit level (Column 3) by its probability of occurrence (Column 2) to obtain weighted values of the possible profits. Summing Column 4 of the table for each project, we obtain a weighted average of the profits under various states of the economy; this weighted average is the *expected profit* from the project.

The expected-profit calculation can also be expressed by the equation:

$$\text{Expected Profit} = E(\pi) = \sum_{i=1}^{N} \pi_i \times p_i. \qquad \textbf{15.1}$$

Here, $\pi_i$ is the profit level associated with the *i*th outcome, $p_i$ is the probability that outcome *i* will occur, and $N$ is the number of possible outcomes or states of nature. Thus, $E(\pi)$ is a weighted average of possible outcomes (the $\pi_i$ values), with each outcome's weight being equal to its probability of occurrence.

Using the data for Project *A*, we can obtain its expected profit as follows:

$$E(\pi_A) = \sum_{i=1}^{3} \pi_i \times p_i$$

$$= \pi_1 \times p_1 + \pi_2 \times p_2 + \pi_3 \times p_3$$

$$= \$4,000(0.2) + \$5,000(0.6) + \$6,000(0.2)$$

$$= \$5,000.$$

We can graph the results in Table 15.2 to obtain a picture of the variability of actual outcomes; this is shown as a bar chart in Figure 15.1. The height of each bar signifies the probability that a given outcome will

■ Figure 15.1
## Relation between State of the Economy and Project Returns

Project *B* has a greater expected return and a higher dispersion in returns (risk) than Project *A*.

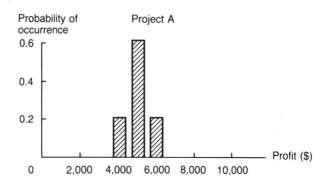

(Expected value = $5,000)

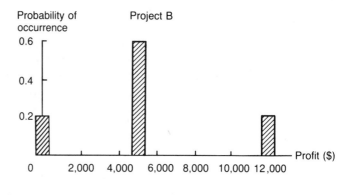

(Expected value = $5,400)

---

**expected value**

**The mean of a probability distribution.**

occur. The range of probable outcomes for Project *A* is from $4,000 to $6,000, with an average, or **expected value,** of $5,000. The expected value for Project *B* is $5,400, and the range of possible outcomes is from $0 to $12,000.

Thus far we have assumed that only three states of the economy can exist: recession, normal, and boom. Actually, the state of the economy could range from a deep depression, as in the early 1930s, to a tremendous boom, with an unlimited number of possibilities in between. Suppose that we had the information required to assign a probability to each possible state of the economy (with the sum of the probabilities still equaling 1.0) and to assign a monetary outcome to each project for each state of the economy. We would have a table similar to Table 15.2 except that it would have many more entries for "state of the economy," "probability," and "outcome if this state occurs." This table could be used to calculate expected values as shown, and the probabilities and outcomes could be approximated by the continuous curves in Figure 15.2.

Figure 15.2 is a graph of the *probability distribution of returns* on Projects *A* and *B*. In general, the tighter the probability distribution, the more likely that the actual outcome will be close to the expected value, or equivalently, the less likely that deviations of the actual outcome from the expected value will be large. Because Project *A* has a relatively tight probability distribution, its *actual* profit is more likely to be closer to its *expected* value than is that of Project *B*.

■ Figure 15.2
## Probability Distributions Showing Relation between State of the Economy and Project Returns

The actual return from Project *A* is likely to be close to the expected value. It is less likely that the actual return from Project *B* will be close to the expected value.

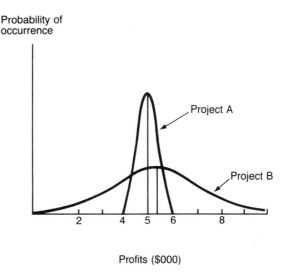

*Note:* The assumptions about the probabilities of various outcomes have changed from those in Figure 15.1. We no longer assume that the probability is zero that Project *A* will yield less than $4,000 or more than $6,000 and that Project *B* will yield less than $0 or more than $12,000. Rather, we have constructed normal distributions centered at $5,000 and $5,400 with approximately the same variability of outcome as Figure 15.1. Although the probability of obtaining exactly $5,000 was 60 percent in Figure 15.1, in Figure 15.2 it is *much smaller*. The number of possible outcomes is infinite instead of just three. With continuous distributions like Figure 15.2, it is generally more appropriate to ask the cumulative probability of obtaining *at least* some specified value than to ask the probability of obtaining exactly that value. This cumulative probability equals the area under the probability distribution curve up to the point of interest.

### Measuring Risk

Risk is a complex concept, and a great deal of controversy has surrounded attempts to define and measure it. However, a common definition and one that is satisfactory for many purposes is stated in terms of probability distributions such as those presented in Figure 15.2. This notion of risk is conveyed by the observation that *the tighter the probability distribution of possible outcomes, the smaller the risk of a given decision,* because there is a lower probability that the actual outcome will deviate significantly from the expected value. According to this definition, Project A is less risky than Project B.

To be most useful, our measure of risk should have some definite value—we need a *measure* of the tightness of the probability distribution. One such measure is the **standard deviation,** the symbol for which is $\sigma$, read *sigma*. The smaller the standard deviation, the tighter the probability distribution and, accordingly, the lower the riskiness of the alternative.[2] To calculate the standard deviation, we proceed as follows:

**standard deviation ($\sigma$)**

A measure of dispersion around the expected value in a probability distribution.

1. Calculate the expected value or mean of the distribution:

$$\text{Expected Value} = E(\pi) = \sum_{i=1}^{n} (\pi_i p_i). \qquad \textbf{15.2}$$

Here $\pi_i$ is the profit or return associated with the $i$th outcome; $p_i$ is the probability that the $i$th outcome will occur; and $E(\pi)$, the expected value, is a weighted average of the various possible outcomes, each weighted by the probability of its occurrence.

2. Subtract the expected value from each possible outcome to obtain a set of deviations about the expected value:

$$\text{Deviation}_i = \pi_i - E(\pi).$$

3. Square each deviation, multiply the squared deviation by the probability of occurrence for its related outcome, and sum these products. This arithmetic mean of the squared deviations is the variance of the probability distribution:

$$\text{Variance} = \sigma^2 = \sum_{i=1}^{n} [\pi_i - E(\pi)]^2 p_i. \qquad \textbf{15.3}$$

4. The standard deviation is found by obtaining the square root of the variance:

---

[2]Because we define risk in terms of the chance of an undesirable outcome, it would seem logical to measure risk in terms of the probability of losses, or at least of returns below the expected return, rather than by the entire distribution. Measures of below-expected returns, known as semivariance measures, have been developed, but they are difficult to analyze. In addition, such measures are unnecessary if the distribution of returns is reasonably symmetric about the expected return. For many managerial problems, this assumption of symmetry is reasonable, and thus we can use total variability to measure risk.

$$\text{Standard Deviation} = \sigma = \sqrt{\sum_{i=1}^{n} [\pi_i - E(\pi)]^2 p_i}. \qquad \textbf{15.4}$$

Calculation of the standard deviation of profit for Project A illustrates this procedure. (The calculation of the expected profit was shown previously and is therefore not repeated.)

| Deviation $[\pi_i - E(\pi)]$ | Deviation² $[\pi_i - E(\pi)]^2$ | Deviation² × Probability $[\pi_i - E(\pi)]^2 \times p_i$ |
|---|---|---|
| $4,000 - $5,000 = -$1,000 | $1,000,000 | $1,000,000(0.2) = $200,000 |
| $5,000 - $5,000 = 0 | 0 | 0(0.6) = 0 |
| $6,000 - $5,000 = $1,000 | $1,000,000 | $1,000,000(0.2) = $200,000 |
| | | Variance = $\sigma^2$ = $400,000 |

$$\text{Standard deviation} = \sigma = \sqrt{\sigma^2} = \sqrt{\$400,000} = \$632.46$$

Using the same procedure, we can calculate the standard deviation of Project B's profit as $3,826.23. Since Project B's standard deviation is larger, it is the riskier project.

This relation between risk and standard deviation can be clarified by examining the characteristics of a normal distribution as shown in Figure 15.3. If a probability distribution is normal, the actual outcome will lie within ±1 standard deviation of the mean or expected value about 68 percent of the time. That is, there is a 68-percent probability that the actual outcome will lie in the range "Expected Outcome ±1$\sigma$." Similarly, the probability that the actual outcome will be within two standard deviations of the expected outcome is approximately 95 percent, and there is a greater than 99-percent probability that the actual event will occur in the range of three standard deviations about the mean of the distribution. Thus, the smaller the standard deviation, the tighter the distribution about the expected value and the smaller the probability of an outcome that is very far from the mean or expected value of the distribution.

We should note that problems can arise when the standard deviation is used as the measure of risk. Specifically, in an investment problem, if one project is larger than another—that is, if it has a large cost and larger expected cash flows—it will normally have a larger standard deviation without necessarily being riskier. For example, if a project has expected returns of $1 million and a standard deviation of only $1,000, it is certainly less risky than a project with expected returns of $1,000 and a standard deviation of $500; the *relative* variation for the larger project is much smaller.

■ Figure 15.3
## Probability Ranges for a Normal Distribution

When returns display a normal distribution, actual outcomes will lie within ± 1 standard deviation of the mean 68.26 percent of the time, within ± 2 standard deviations 95.46 percent of the time, and within ± 3 standard deviations 99.74 percent of the time.

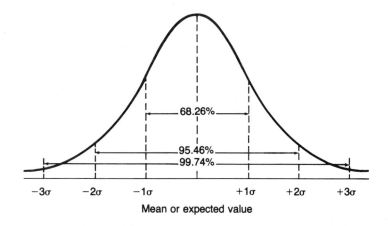

Mean or expected value

---

*Notes:*
a. The area under the normal curve equals 1.0, or 100 percent. Thus, the areas under any pair of normal curves drawn on the same scale, whether they are peaked or flat, must be equal.
b. Half of the area under a normal curve is to the left of the mean, indicating a 50-percent probability that the actual outcome will be less than the mean and a 50-percent probability that it will be greater than the mean.
c. Of the area under the curve, 68.26 percent is within ± 1σ of the mean, indicating that the odds are 68.26 percent that the actual outcome will be within the range (mean − 1σ) to (mean + 1σ).
d. For a normal distribution, the larger the value of σ, the greater the probability that the actual outcome will vary widely from, and hence perhaps be far below, the most likely outcome. Since we define "risk" as the odds of having the actual results turn out to be bad, and since σ measures these odds, we can use σ as a measure of risk.

**coefficient of variation**

A measure of relative risk obtained by dividing the standard deviation by the expected value.

One way of eliminating this problem is to calculate a measure of relative risk by dividing the standard deviation by the expected value, $E(\pi)$, to obtain the **coefficient of variation:**

$$\text{Coefficient of Variation} = \nu = \frac{\sigma}{E(\pi)}. \qquad \textbf{15.5}$$

In general, when comparing decision alternatives with costs and benefits that are not of approximately equal size, the coefficient of variation measures relative risk better than the standard deviation does.[3]

---

[3]Risk is defined here in terms of both the standard deviation and the coefficient of variation based on the *total* variability of a project's outcomes or returns. In some situations, however, a project's total variability overstates its risk. This is because projects with returns that are less than perfectly correlated with each other can be

## Use of the Standard Normal Concept

Probability distributions can be viewed as a series of *discrete values* represented by a bar chart, such as in Figure 15.1, or as a *continuous function* represented by a smooth curve, such as that in Figure 15.2. Actually, there is an important difference in the way these two graphs are interpreted: The probabilities associated with the outcomes in Figure 15.1 are given by the *heights* of the bars, whereas in Figure 15.2, the probabilities must be found by calculating the *area* under the curve between points of interest. Suppose, for example, that we have the continuous probability distribution shown in Figure 15.4. This is a normal curve with a mean of 20 and a standard deviation of 5; x could be dollars of sales, profits, or costs; units of output; percentage rates of return; or any other units. If we want to know the probability that an outcome will fall between 15 and 30, we must calculate the area beneath the curve between these points, the shaded area in the diagram.

The area under the curve between 15 and 30 can be determined by painstaking graphic analysis of this interval or, since the distribution is normal, by reference to tables of the area under the normal curve, such

■ Figure 15.4
## Continuous Probability Distribution

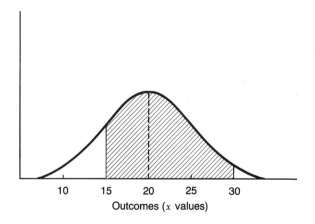

Outcomes ($x$ values)

---

combined, and the variability of the resulting combination, or "portfolio," will be less than the sum of the individual variabilities. Much of the recent work in finance is based on the idea that a project's risk should be measured in terms of its contribution to total return variability on a portfolio of assets. This contribution to overall variation is measured by a concept known as *beta*, which is related to the systematic variability or covariance of one asset's return with returns on other assets. This risk concept, like the two discussed, is based on the variability of returns, and for our purposes it is not necessary that we examine the alternative constructs more closely.

■ Table 15.3
## Area under the Normal Curve

| $z^a$ | Area from the Mean to the Point of Interest | Ordinate |
|-----|-----|-----|
| 0.0 | 0.0000 | 0.3989 |
| 0.5 | 0.1915 | 0.3521 |
| 1.0 | 0.3413 | 0.2420 |
| 1.5 | 0.4332 | 0.1295 |
| 2.0 | 0.4773 | 0.0540 |
| 2.5 | 0.4938 | 0.0175 |
| 3.0 | 0.4987 | 0.0044 |

[a] z is the number of standard deviations from the mean. Some area tables are set up to indicate the area to the left or right of the point of interest; in this book, we indicate the area between the mean and the point of interest.

as Table 15.3 or Appendix C to this book.[4] To use these tables, it is necessary only to know the mean and standard deviation of the distribution.

The distribution to be investigated must first be transformed or standardized. A **standardized variable** has a mean of zero and a standard deviation equal to one. Any distribution of revenue, cost, or profit data can be standardized with the following formula:

**standardized variable**

*A variable with a mean of zero and standard deviation equal to one.*

$$z = \frac{x - \mu}{\sigma}, \qquad \textbf{15.6}$$

where z is the standardized variable, x is the outcome of interest, and $\mu$ and $\sigma$ are the mean and standard deviation of the distribution, respectively. If the point of interest is $1\sigma$ away from the mean, then $x - \mu = \sigma$, so $z = \sigma/\sigma = 1.0$. Thus, when $z = 1.0$, the point of interest is $1\sigma$ away from the mean; when $z = 2$, the value is $2\sigma$ away from the mean, and so on.

For our example, we are interested in the probability that an outcome will fall between between 15 and 30. We first normalize these points of interest using Equation 15.6:

$$z_1 = \frac{15 - 20}{5} = -1.0, \qquad z_2 = \frac{30 - 20}{5} = 2.0.$$

[4]The area under a curve can also be determined using a method called integration. However, the equation for the normal curve is tedious to integrate, which makes the use of tables much more convenient. The equation for the normal curve is

$$f(x) = \frac{1}{\sqrt{2\pi\sigma^2}} e^{-(x-\mu)^2/2\sigma^2},$$

where $\pi$ and $e$ are mathematical constants, $\mu$ (read mu) and $\sigma$ denote the mean and standard deviation of the probability distribution, and x is any possible outcome.

The areas associated with these z values are found in Table 15.3 to be 0.3413 and 0.4773.[5] This means that the probability is 0.3413 that the actual outcome will fall between 15 and 20, and 0.4773 that it will fall between 20 and 30. Summing these probabilities shows that the probability of an outcome falling between 15 and 30 is 0.8186, or 81.86 percent.

Suppose that we had been interested in determining the probability that the actual outcome would be greater than 15. Here we would first note that the probability is 0.3413 that the outcome will be between 15 and 20, then observe that the probability is 0.5000 of an outcome greater than the mean, 20. Thus the probability is 0.3413 + 0.5000 = 0.8413, or 84.13 percent, that the outcome will exceed 15.

Some interesting properties of normal probability distributions can be seen by examining Table 15.3 and Figure 15.3, which is a graph of the normal curve. For any normal distribution, the probability of an outcome falling within plus or minus one standard deviation from the mean is 0.6826, or 68.26 percent (0.3413 × 2.0). The probability of an occurrence falling within two standards of the mean is 95.46 percent, and 99.74 percent of all outcomes will fall within three standard deviations of the mean. Although the distribution theoretically runs from minus infinity to plus infinity, the probability of occurrences beyond three standard deviations is very near zero.

An example will illustrate the use of the standard normal concept in managerial decision making. Suppose that Hastings Realty is considering a boost in advertising in an attempt to reduce a large inventory of unsold homes. The firm's management plans to make its media decision using the data shown in Table 15.4 on the expected success of television versus newspaper promotions. For simplicity, assume that the returns from each promotion are normally distributed. If the television promo-

■ Table 15.4
## Return Distributions for Television and Newspaper Promotions

|  | Market Response | Probability of Occurring ($P_i$) | Return ($R_i$) (Commission Revenues) |
|---|---|---|---|
| *Television* | Poor | 0.25 | $ 2,000 |
|  | Good | 0.50 | 6,000 |
|  | Very Good | 0.25 | 10,000 |
| *Newspaper* | Poor | 0.25 | 4,000 |
|  | Good | 0.50 | 6,000 |
|  | Very Good | 0.25 | 8,000 |

[5]The negative sign on $z_1$ is ignored, since the normal curve is symmetrical around the mean; the minus sign merely indicates that the point lies to the left of the mean.

tion costs \$4,000 while the newspaper promotion costs \$3,000, what is the probability that each will generate a profit?

To calculate the probability that each promotion will generate a profit, we must calculate the portion of the total area under the normal curve that is to the right of (greater than) each breakeven point. Using methods described earlier, we find that $E(R_{TV}) = \$6,000$, $\sigma_{TV} = \$2,828.43$, $E(R_N) = \$6,000$, and $\sigma_N = \$1,414.21$. For the television promotion, we note that the breakeven revenue level of \$4,000 is 0.707 standard deviations to the left of the expected revenue level of \$6,000 because:

$$z = \frac{x_{TV} - E(R_{TV})}{\sigma_{TV}}$$

$$= \frac{\$4,000 - \$6,000}{\$2,828.43}$$

$$= -0.707.$$

The standard normal distribution function value for $z = -0.707$ is between that for $z = -0.70$ and $z = -0.71$.

| z | Pr |
|---|---|
| -0.70 | 0.2580 |
| -0.707 | 0.2580 + a |
| -0.71 | 0.2611 |

To find the precise probability value for $z = -0.707$, we must interpolate where

$$\frac{a}{(0.2611 - 0.2580)} = \frac{(-0.707 + 0.70)}{(-0.71 + 0.70)}$$

$$\frac{a}{0.0031} = \frac{0.007}{0.01}$$

$$a = 0.0022,$$

and the probability value for $z = -0.707$ is $0.2580 + 0.0022 = 0.2602$. This means that 0.2602, or 26.02 percent, of the total area under the normal curve lies between $x_{TV}$ and $E(R_{TV})$, and it implies a profit probability for the television promotion of $0.2602 + 0.5 = 0.7602$, or 76.02 percent.

In calculating the newspaper promotion profit probability, we find:

$$z = \frac{x_N - E(R_N)}{\sigma_N}$$

$$= \frac{\$3,000 - \$6,000}{\$1,414.21}$$

$$= -2.121,$$

and the probability value for $z = -2.121$ of $0.4830 + 0.000Q = 0.4830$. This means that 0.483, or 48.3 percent, of the total area under the normal curve lies between $x_N$ and $E(R_N)$, and it implies a profit probability for the newspaper promotion of $0.483 + 0.5 = 0.983$, or 98.3 percent. In terms of profit probability, the newspaper advertisement is obviously the less risky promotion alternative.

## UTILITY THEORY AND RISK ANALYSIS

The assumption of risk aversion is basic to many decision models in managerial economics. Because this assumption is so crucial, it is appropriate to examine attitudes toward risk and discuss why risk aversion holds in general.

In theory, we can identify three possible attitudes toward risk: aversion to risk, indifference to risk, and preference for risk. **Risk aversion** characterizes individuals who prefer to avoid or minimize risk. **Risk neutrality** characterizes decision makers who focus on expected returns and disregard return dispersion (risk). **Risk seeking** characterizes decision makers who prefer risk. Given a choice between more and less risky investments with identical expected monetary returns, a risk averter will select the less risky investment and a risk seeker will select the riskier investment. Faced with the same choice, the risk-neutral investor will be indifferent between two investment projects. Some individuals prefer high-risk projects and the corresponding potential for substantial returns, especially when relatively small sums of money are involved. Entrepreneurs, innovators, inventors, speculators, and lottery ticket buyers are all examples of individuals who sometimes display risk-seeking behavior. Similarly, risk-neutral behavior is exhibited in some business decision making. However, both logic and observation suggest that business managers and investors are predominantly risk averters, especially when substantial dollar amounts are involved.

Why should risk aversion generally hold? Given two alternatives, each with the same expected dollar returns, why do most decision makers prefer the less risky one? Several explanations have been proposed, but perhaps the most satisfying one involves utility theory.

At the heart of risk aversion is the notion of a **diminishing marginal utility** for money. If an individual with no money receives $1,000, it can satisfy his or her most immediate needs. If the person then receives a second $1,000, it will obviously be useful, but the second $1,000 is not quite so necessary as the first $1,000. Thus, the value, or *utility*, of the second, or *marginal*, $1,000 is less than the utility of the first $1,000, and so on for additional increments of money. We therefore say that the marginal utility of money income or wealth diminishes.

Figure 15.5 graphs the relation between money and its utility, or value. In the figure, utility is measured in units of value or satisfaction, an index that is unique to each individual. Thus, the actual numerical values for utility have little interpretive value. Nonetheless, the concept is very important for understanding economic behavior.

Curve 15.5a describes the relation between utility and money for a risk averter. Here money has a diminishing marginal utility. This means that if the individual's wealth were to double suddenly, he or she would

---

**risk aversion**
Preference for low-risk projects to reduce loss potential.

**risk neutrality**
Project valuation based on expected returns, not risk.

**risk seeking**
Preference for high-risk projects to increase gain potential.

**diminishing marginal utility**
A condition in which the value of each additional unit is less than that of the preceding unit.

■ Figure 15.5

## Relations between Money and Its Utility

(a) Doubling wealth from Y to 2Y brings a less-than-proportional increase in utility for a risk averter. (b) Under risk neutrality, doubling wealth proportionally increases (doubles) utility. (c) For a risk seeker, doubling wealth causes a more-than-proportional increase in utility.

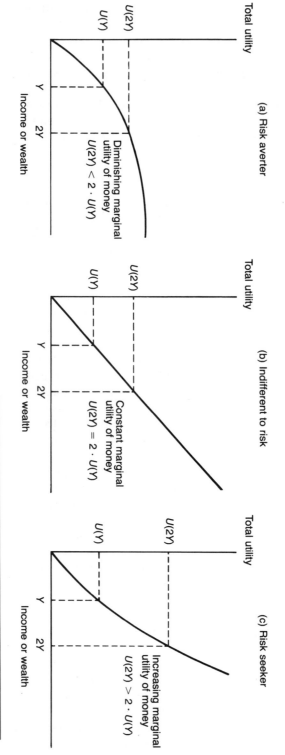

(a) Risk averter

Total utility

U(2Y)

U(Y)

Y  2Y

Income or wealth

Diminishing marginal
utility of money
U(2Y) < 2 · U(Y)

(b) Indifferent to risk

Total utility

U(2Y)

U(Y)

Y  2Y

Income or wealth

Constant marginal
utility of money
U(2Y) = 2 · U(Y)

(c) Risk seeker

Total utility

U(2Y)

U(Y)

Y  2Y

Income or wealth

Increasing marginal
utility of money
U(2Y) > 2 · U(Y)

experience an increase in utility (happiness or satisfaction), but the new level of total utility would not be twice the previous level. That is, in cases of diminishing marginal utility of money, a less-than-proportional relation holds between total utility and money. Accordingly, the utility of a doubled quantity of money is less than twice the utility of the original level. In contrast, those who are indifferent to risk perceive a strictly proportional relationship between total utility and money. Such a relation implies a constant marginal utility of money, as illustrated in Figure 15.5b. In cases of a constant marginal utility of money, the utility of a doubled quantity of money is exactly twice the utility of the original level. Finally, risk seekers perceive a more-than-proportional relation between total utility and money. In this case, the marginal utility of money increases, as shown in Figure 15.5c. With increasing marginal utility of money, the utility of doubled wealth is more than twice the utility of the original amount.

Therefore, even though total utility increases with increased money for risk averters, risk seekers, and those who are indifferent to risk, the relation between total utility and money is quite different for each group. These differences lead directly to differences in risk attitudes. Because individuals with a diminishing marginal utility for money will suffer more pain from a dollar lost than they will derive pleasure from a dollar gained, they will strongly avoid risk. Thus, they will require a very high return on any investment that is subject to much risk. In Figure 15.6, for

■ Figure 15.6
## Relation between Money and Its Utility

A risk seeker's marginal utility of money increases. A risk-indifferent individual has a constant marginal utility of money. A risk averter displays a diminishing marginal utility of money.

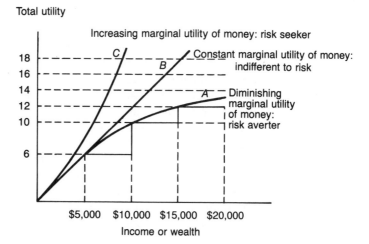

## 15.1  **Managerial Application**
Unlikely Risk Insurance

The success of state-run lotteries provides convincing evidence that many people display risk-seeking behavior, especially when small sums of money are involved. The profitability of state-run lotteries stems from the fact that ticket buyers are willing to pay $2 for a bet that has an expected return of less than $2. When only 50 percent of lottery-ticket revenues are paid out in the form of prizes, for example, each $2 ticket has an expected return of only $1. The willingness to overpay for the unlikely chance at perhaps millions of dollars stems from the fact that such opportunities are rare and lottery-ticket buyers value them highly. Many have no opportunity for hitting the jackpot in their careers. The lottery is their only chance, however remote, at a substantial sum of money.

The success of state-run lottery promotions is quite noteworthy because it is so unusual. Typically, consumers and investors display risk-averse behavior, especially when substantial sums of money are involved.

Interesting evidence of the risk-averse behavior typical of individuals is provided by travelers who routinely spend relatively small amounts to overinsure the highly unlikely risk of extremely negative or catastrophic outcomes. For example, rather than run the risk of having a vacation ruined by the theft or loss of a large amount of cash, many heed the advice of TV commercials and buy traveler's checks. This risk is very slight, however, and American Express, among others, has found the business of selling traveler's checks to be highly profit-

*continued*

See: Janis Bultman and Jan Parr, "Risky Business," *Forbes*, March 21, 1988, 98.

example, a gain of $5,000 from a base of $10,000 brings 2 units of additional satisfaction, but a $5,000 loss causes a 4-unit loss in satisfaction. A person with this utility function and $10,000 would, therefore, be unwilling to make an investment with a 50–50 chance of winning or losing $5,000, because the 9-unit expected utility of such a gamble [$E(u) = 0.5$ times the utility of $5,000 + 0.5$ times the utility of $15,000 $= 0.5 \times 6 + 0.5 \times 12 = 9$] is less than the 10 units of utility obtained by forgoing the investment and keeping the certain $10,000 current wealth. For a risk averter, the expected utility of a gamble will always be less than the utility of the expected dollar payoff.

Since an individual with a constant marginal utility for money will value a dollar gained just as highly as a dollar lost, the expected utility from a fair gamble will always exactly equal the utility of the expected

---

**Managerial Application** *continued*

able. Auto rental companies earn a large share of their total profit from selling accident insurance to motorists who are already covered on their personal auto insurance policies. Flight insurance offered in the lobbies of major airports is also very profitable for insurers. A wag is said to have remarked that coin-operated flight insurance machines are two-armed bandits. Unlike slot machines ("one-armed bandits"), they never seem to make any payoffs.

Special-risk medical insurance is another area in which consumers are willing to overinsure the very small possibility of a catastrophic outcome. The probability that each of us will die is 1.0. In other words, death from some natural or accidental cause is inevitable. However, the chance that any one of us will die from a specific disease is quite small. As a result, specific-illness medical insurance is typically a poor choice for the consumer and highly profitable for the insurance industry. The more terrible the illness, the more willing people are to buy insurance and the more profitable it becomes. For example, cancer insurance is one

of the most popular and profitable forms of specific-illness insurance on the market today.

One insurance company, Replacement Lens, Inc., has made a profitable and growing business out of a variety of special-risk insurance products. RLI got its start selling replacement contact lens insurance through eye-care professionals. Today, the company sells a broad range of special-risk insurance products. RLI offers liability insurance for officers and directors of startup companies, members of the American Psychiatric Association, and "light hazard" professionals, including social workers, nurses, and dental hygienists. One of its more unusual, and profitable, divisions in southern California insures celebrity homes against fire and commercial buildings against earthquakes. Overall, RLI's five-year average rate of return on stockholders' equity is roughly twice that of the casualty insurance industry in general.

It appears there is money to be made in providing "unlikely risk" insurance.

---

outcome. Because of this, an individual indifferent to risk can make decisions on the basis of expected monetary outcomes and need not be concerned with possible variation in the distribution of outcomes.

A second and more detailed example should clarify the relationship between utility and risk aversion. Assume that government bonds are riskless securities that currently offer a 9-percent rate of return. If an individual buys a $10,000 U.S. Treasury bond and holds it for one year, he or she will end up with $10,900, a gain of $900.

Suppose that in an alternative investment opportunity, the $10,000 would back a wildcat oil-drilling venture. If the drilling venture is successful, the investment will be worth $20,000 at the end of the year. If it is unsuccessful, the investors can liquidate their holdings and recover $5,000. There is a 60-percent chance that oil will be discovered and a

■ Table 15.5
## Expected Returns from Two Projects

| State of Nature | Drilling Operation | | | Government Bond | | |
|---|---|---|---|---|---|---|
| | Probability (1) | Outcome (2) | (3) = (1) × (2) | Probability (1) | Outcome (2) | (3) = (1) × (2) |
| Oil | 0.6 | $20,000 | $12,000 | 0.6 | $10,900 | $ 6,540 |
| No oil | 0.4 | 5,000 | 2,000 | 0.4 | 10,900 | 4,360 |
| | | | Expected value $14,000 | | | Expected value $10,900 |

40-percent chance of a dry hole or no oil. Should an investor with only $10,000 to invest choose the riskless government bond or the risky drilling operation?

To analyze this question, let us first calculate the expected monetary values of the two investments: this is done in Table 15.5. The calculation in the table is not really necessary for the government bond; the $10,900 outcome will occur regardless of what happens in the oil field. The oil-venture calculation, however, shows that the expected value of this venture ($14,000) is higher than that of the bond. Does this mean that the investor should invest in the wildcat well? Not necessarily. It depends on the investor's utility function. If an investor's marginal utility for money diminishes sharply (indicating strong risk aversion), then the utility from a producing well might not compensate for the potential loss of utility from a dry hole. If the risk-averter's utility function shown in Figure 15.6 applies, this is precisely the case. Four units of utility will be lost if no oil is found, and only three will be gained if the well produces.

Let us modify the expected monetary value calculation to reflect utility considerations. Reading from Figure 15.6, we see that this particular risk-averse investor will have 13 units of utility if he or she invests in the wildcat venture and oil is found and 6 units if no oil is found. This information is used in Table 15.6 to calculate the *expected utility* for the

■ Table 15.6
## Expected Utility of the Oil-Drilling Project

| State of Nature | Probability (1) | Monetary Outcome (2) | Associated Utility (3) | Weighted Utility (4) = (1) × (3) |
|---|---|---|---|---|
| Oil | 0.6 | $20,000 | 13.0 | 7.8 |
| No oil | 0.4 | 5,000 | 6.0 | 2.4 |
| | | | | Expected utility 10.2 |

oil investment. No calculation is needed for the government bond; its utility is 10.7 (read from Figure 15.6), regardless of the outcome of the oil venture. The investor will have 10.7 units of utility with certainty by choosing the government bond.

Because the expected utility from the wildcat venture is only 10.2 units versus 10.7 from the government bond, we see that the government bond is the preferred investment. Thus, even though the expected *monetary value* for the oil venture is higher, expected utility is greater for the bond; risk considerations dictate that the investor should buy the government bond.

# ADJUSTING THE VALUATION MODEL FOR RISK

Diminishing marginal utility leads directly to risk aversion, and risk aversion is reflected in the valuation model by which investors determine the worth of a firm. Thus, if a firm takes an action that increases its risk level, this action affects its value. To illustrate, consider the basic valuation model developed in Chapter 1:

$$V = \sum_{t=1}^{n} \frac{\pi_t}{(1 + i)^t}.$$  **15.7**

This model states that value is the discounted present worth of future profits. Under conditions of uncertainty, the profits in the numerator, $\pi$, are really the expected value of the profits each year. If the firm must choose between two alternative methods of operation—one with high expected profits and high risk and another with smaller expected profits and lower risks—will the higher expected profits be sufficient to offset the higher risk? If it will, the riskier alternative is the preferred one; if not, the low-risk procedure should be adopted.

## Certainty Equivalent Adjustments

**certainty equivalent**

The amount of money decision makers must be certain of receiving to make them indifferent between this certain sum and the expected value of a risky alternative.

A number of methods have been proposed to account for risk in the valuation model. One of these, the **certainty equivalent** approach, follows directly from the utility concept developed earlier and involves an adjustment to the numerator of the basic valuation model (Equation 15.7). Under the certainty equivalent approach, decision makers must specify the amount of money that they would have to be assured of receiving to make them indifferent between this certain sum and the expected value of a risky alternative. To illustrate, suppose that you face the following alternatives:

1. Invest $100,000. From a successful project, you receive $1 million; if it fails, you receive nothing. If the probability of success is 0.5, or 50 percent, the investment's expected payoff is $500,000 (= 0.5 × $1,000,000 + 0.5 × $0).
2. You do not make the investment and retain the $100,000.

If you find yourself indifferent between the two alternatives, $100,000 is your certainty equivalent for the risky expected return of $500,000. In other words, a certain or riskless amount of $100,000 provides exactly the same utility as the 50–50 chance to earn $1 million or $0. You are indifferent between these two alternatives.

In this example, any certainty equivalent less than $500,000 indicates risk aversion. That is, if the maximum amount that you would be willing to invest in the first alternative is less than $500,000, you are exhibiting risk-averse behavior. In general, any risky investment with a certainty equivalent less than the expected dollar value indicates risk aversion. A certainty equivalent greater than the expected value indicates risk preference. A utility of $100,000 in certain dollars equal to that of a risky expected return of $500,000 indicates a high degree of risk aversion. Each certain dollar is "worth" five times as much as each risky dollar of expected return. Alternatively, each risky dollar of expected return is only worth 20¢ in terms of certain dollars.

An expected risky sum can be converted to an equivalent certain sum using the **certainty equivalent adjustment factor,** $\alpha$, which is calculated as the ratio of a certain sum divided by an expected risky amount, where both of these dollar values provide an equivalent level of utility.

**certainty equivalent adjustment factor**

The ratio of a certain sum divided by an expected risky amount that provides equivalent utility.

$$\text{Certainty Equivalent Adjustment Factor} = \alpha = \frac{\text{Equivalent Certain Sum}}{\text{Expected Risky Sum}}. \qquad \textbf{15.8}$$

The certain sum numerator and expected return denominator can vary in dollar terms, but they provide the exact same payoff in terms of utility. In the previous investment problem, in which a certain sum of $100,000 provides the same utility as an expected risky return of $500,000, the certainty equivalent adjustment factor $\alpha = 0.2 = \$100,000/\$500,000$. This means that the "price" of one dollar in risky expected return is 20¢ in certain dollar terms.

In general, the following relationships enable us to use the certainty equivalent adjustment factor to analyze risk attitudes:

| If | | | Then | Implies |
|---|---|---|---|---|
| Equivalent certain sum | < | Expected risky sum | $\alpha < 1$ | Risk aversion |
| Equivalent certain sum | = | Expected risky sum | $\alpha = 1$ | Risk indifference |
| Equivalent certain sum | > | Expected risky sum | $\alpha > 1$ | Risk preference |

The appropriate $\alpha$ value for a given managerial decision will typically vary according to the investment's risk and the degree of the decision maker's risk aversion. Figure 15.7 shows a series of risk–return combi-

■ Figure 15.7
## Certainty Equivalent Returns

An indifference curve shows risk–return trade-offs that provide the same utility to a given individual.

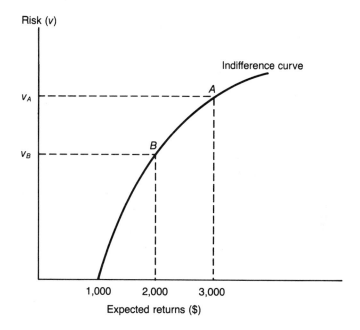

nations to which the decision maker is indifferent. For example, Point $A$ represents an investment with a perceived degree of risk $\nu_A$ and expected dollar return of $3,000. The risk–return tradeoff function, or indifference curve, shows a person who is indifferent to a certain $1,000, an expected $2,000 with risk $\nu_B$, and an expected $3,000 with risk $\nu_A$.

The indifference curve shown in Figure 15.7 can be used to construct a risk-aversion function such as the one illustrated in Figure 15.8. This conversion is obtained by dividing each risky return into its certainty equivalent return to obtain a certainty equivalent adjustment factor, $\alpha$, for each level of risk, $\nu$. For example, the certainty equivalent adjustment factor for risk level $\nu_A$ is:

$$\alpha_A = \frac{\$1,000}{\$3,000} = 0.33.$$

For risk level $\nu_B$, we have:

$$\alpha_B = \frac{\$1,000}{\$2,000} = 0.50.$$

■ Figure 15.8
## Hypothetical Risk-Aversion Function

For a risk-averse individual, the acceptable certainty equivalent adjustment factor will decline as risk increases.

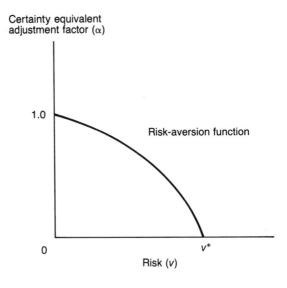

*Note:* As we have drawn it, the risk aversion function assumes that $\alpha = 0$ when $v \geq v^*$. Theoretically, $\alpha$ would never actually reach zero; rather, it would approach zero as risk became quite high.

Conceptually, $\alpha$ values could be developed for all possible levels of $v$ (risk). The range of $\alpha$ would be from 1.0 for $v = 0$ to a value close to 0 for large values of $v$, assuming risk aversion.

Given the risk-aversion function and the degree of risk inherent in any risky return, the expected risky return could be replaced by its certainty equivalent:

$$\text{Certainty Equivalent of } E(\pi_t) = \alpha E(\pi_t),$$

and Equation 15.7 could then be converted to Equation 15.9, a valuation model that explicitly accounts for risk:

$$V = \sum_{t=1}^{n} \frac{\alpha E(\pi_t)}{(1 + i)^t}. \qquad \textbf{15.9}$$

Here expected future profits, $E(\pi_t)$, are converted to their certainty equivalents, $\alpha E(\pi_t)$, and are discounted at a risk-free rate, $i$, to obtain the present value of a firm or project. With the valuation model in this form, one can appraise the effects of different courses of action with different risks and expected returns.

In order to use Equation 15.9 for real-world decision making, managers must estimate appropriate $\alpha$'s for various investment opportunities. Deriving such estimates can prove to be difficult, since $\alpha$ levels vary according to the size and riskiness of investment projects as well as according to the risk attitudes of managers and investors. In many instances, however, the record of past investments can guide the effort to determine appropriate certainty equivalent adjustment factors.

## Use of Certainty Equivalent Adjustments: An Illustration

The following example illustrates how managers use certainty equivalent adjustment factors for decision making. Assume that operations at Boulger Industries have been seriously disrupted by problems with a faulty boiler at its main fabrication facility. In fact, state fire marshals shut the facility down for an extended period recently following repeated overheating and minor explosions. The boiler problem was solved when it was discovered that a design flaw had made the pilot light safety switch inoperable.

Boulger retained the law firm of Miller and Associates to recover economic damages from the boiler manufacturer. The company has filed suit in state court for $250,000 in damages. Prior to filing suit, the Miller attorney estimated legal, expert witness, and other litigation costs of $10,000 for a fully litigated case, for which Boulger had a 10-percent chance of receiving a favorable judgment. For simplicity, assume that a favorable judgment will award Boulger 100 percent of the damages sought, whereas an unfavorable judgment will result in the firm receiving zero damages. Also assume that $10,000 is the most Boulger would be willing to pay to sue the boiler manufacturer.

In filing suit against the boiler manufacturer, Boulger has made a risky investment decision. By its willingness to bear litigation costs of $10,000, Boulger has implicitly stated that it regards the value to the firm of these out-of-pocket costs to be equivalent to the value of the risky expectation of receiving a favorable judgment against the boiler manufacturer. In other words, Boulger is willing to exchange $10,000 in certain litigation costs for the possibility of receiving a $250,000 judgment against the boiler manufacturer.

Boulger's investment decision can be characterized using the certainty equivalent adjustment method. To do this, we must first realize that the $10,000 in litigation costs will be incurred irrespective of the outcome of a fully litigated case. Therefore, this $10,000 represents a certain sum that the company must value as highly as the expected risky outcome to be willing to file suit. The expected risky outcome, or expected return from filing suit, can be calculated as:

$$\begin{aligned} \text{Expected Return} &= \text{Favorable Judgment Payoff} \times \text{Probability} \\ &\quad + \text{Unfavorable Judgment Payoff} \times \text{Probability} \\ &= \$250{,}000(0.1) + \$0(0.9) \\ &= \$25{,}000. \end{aligned}$$

To justify filing suit, Boulger's certainty equivalent adjustment factor for investment projects of this risk class must be:

$$\alpha = \frac{\text{Certain Sum}}{\text{Expected Risky Sum}}$$

$$= \frac{\text{Litigation Costs}}{\text{Expected Return}}$$

$$= \frac{\$10,000}{\$25,000}$$

$$= 0.4.$$

In words, each risky dollar of expected return from the litigation effort is worth, in terms of utility, 40¢ in certain dollars. Alternatively, $10,000 is the certain sum equivalent of the risky expected return of $25,000.

Now let us assume that after Boulger goes to court, incurring $5,000 in litigation costs, especially damaging testimony by an expert witness dramatically changes the outlook of the case in Boulger's favor. In response, the boiler manufacturer's attorney offers an out-of-court settlement in the amount of $30,000. However, Boulger's attorney recommends that the company reject this offer, estimating that it now has a 50-percent chance of obtaining a favorable judgment in the case. Should Boulger follow its attorney's advice and reject the settlement offer?

In answering this question, we must keep in mind that having already spent ("sunk") $5,000 in litigation costs, Boulger must consider as relevant litigation costs only the additional $5,000 necessary to complete litigation. These $5,000 litigation costs, plus the $30,000 out-of-court settlement offer, represent the relevant certain sum, since proceeding with the suit will require an "investment" of these additional litigation plus opportunity costs. Given the revised outlook for a favorable judgment, the expected return to full litigation is:

$$\text{Expected Return} = (\$250,000)(0.5) + (\$0)(0.5)$$

$$= \$125,000.$$

In light of Boulger's earlier decision to file suit on the basis that each dollar of expected risky return was "worth" 40¢ in certain dollars, the expected return would have a $50,000 certainty equivalent value ($125,000 × 0.4). Since this amount exceeds the settlement offer plus remaining litigation costs, the settlement offer appears to be deficient and should be rejected. On the basis of Boulger's revealed risk attitude, the out-of-court settlement offer would have to be at least $45,000 to receive favorable consideration, since at that point the settlement plus saved litigation costs of $5,000 would equal the certainty equivalent value of the expected return from continuing litigation.

From this simple example, we see that analysis of historical investment risk characteristics can prove useful as a guide to current risky investment decisions. For example, if we know a potential project's required investment and risk level, we can calculate the $\alpha$ implied by a decision to accept the investment, and we can compare it with $\alpha$'s for prior projects with similar risks. Risk-averse individuals should invest in projects if calculated $\alpha$'s are less than or equal to those for accepted historical projects in the same risk class. Further, given an estimate of expected return and risk, the maximum amount that the firm should be willing to invest in a given project can also be determined from the certainty equivalent adjustment factor. Here we can use the expected return and the $\alpha$ on prior projects with similar risk to calculate the maximum that the firm will invest in the project (certainty equivalent amount). Management will accept new projects if the level of required investment per dollar of expected return is less than or equal to that for historical projects of similar risk.

## Risk-Adjusted Discount Rates

**risk-adjusted discount rates**

The sum of the riskless rate of return plus a risk premium.

Another way to incorporate risk in managerial decision making is to adjust the discount rate, $i$—that is, the term in the denominator of the basic valuation model (Equation 15.7). Like the certainty equivalent factor, **risk-adjusted discount rates** are based on investors' trade-off between risk and return. For example, suppose that investors are willing to trade between risk and return, as shown in Figure 15.9. The curve is

■ Figure 15.9

## Relation between Risk and Rate of Return

As risk rises, investors typically demand higher expected returns to compensate for the increased risk.

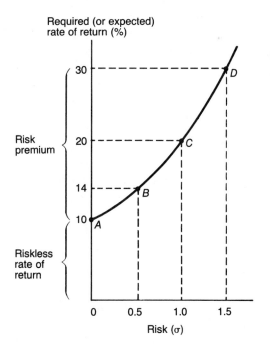

called a *market indifference curve* or a *risk–return trade-off function.* The average investor is indifferent to a riskless asset with a sure 10-percent rate of return, a moderately risky asset with a 20-percent expected return, and a very risky asset with a 30-percent expected return. As risk increases, higher expected returns on investment are required to compensate investors for the additional risk.

The difference between the expected rate of return on a particular risky asset and the rate of return on a riskless asset is called the *risk premium* on the risky asset. In the hypothetical situation depicted in Figure 15.9 the riskless rate is assumed to be 10 percent; a 4-percent risk premium is required to compensate for the level of risk indicated by $\sigma = 0.5$; and 20-percent risk premium is required for an investment with a risk of $\sigma = 1.5$.

Because required returns are related to the level of risk associated with a particular investment, we can modify the basic valuation model, Equation 15.7, to account for risk through an adjustment of the discount rate, i. Such a modification results in the valuation model:

$$V = \sum_{t=1}^{n} \frac{E(\pi_t)}{(1 + k)^t},$$    **15.10**

where k is the risk-adjusted discount rate, determined as the sum of the risk-free rate of return, $R_F$, and a required risk premium, $R_p$:

$$k = R_F + R_p.$$

In Equation 15.10, value is found as the present worth of expected future income or profits, $E(\pi_t)$, discounted at a risk-adjusted rate. Assuming that decision makers use the risk–return trade-off function shown in Figure 15.9, they would evaluate a firm or project with risk level $\sigma = 0.5$ using a 14-percent discount rate, composed of a 10-percent riskless interest rate and a 4-percent risk premium. Similarly, a riskier project with $\sigma = 1.5$ would require a risk premium of 20 percent and thus would be evaluated using a 30-percent discount rate (30 percent = 10-percent riskless rate + 20-percent risk premium).

The following example illustrates the use of risk-adjusted discount rates in managerial decision making. A&M Distributing, Inc. has to decide which of two word processing systems to purchase. One system (Project A) is specifically designed for A&M's current computer and cannot be used with those of other manufacturers; the other (Project B) is compatible with a broad variety of computer systems, including A&M's and those of competitors. The expected investment outlay is $600,000 for each alternative. Expected annual cost savings (cash inflows) over five years are $220,000 per year for Project A and $260,000 per year for Project B. The standard deviation of expected annual returns from Project A is $10,000, whereas that of Project B is $15,000. In view of this risk differential, A&M's management has decided to evaluate Project A with a 20-percent cost of capital and Project B with a 30-percent cost of capital. Which project should the company select?

We can calculate the risk-adjusted value for each project as follows:[6]

$$\text{Value}_A = \sum_{t=1}^{5} \frac{\$220{,}000}{(1.20)^t} - \$600{,}000$$

$$= \$220{,}000 \times \left( \sum_{t=1}^{5} \frac{1}{(1.20)^t} \right) - \$600{,}000$$

$$= \$220{,}000 \times 2.991 - \$600{,}000$$

$$= \$58{,}020.$$

$$\text{Value}_B = \sum_{t=1}^{5} \frac{\$260{,}000}{(1.30)^t} - \$600{,}000$$

$$= \$260{,}000 \times \left( \sum_{t=1}^{5} \frac{1}{(1.30)^t} \right) - \$600{,}000$$

$$= \$260{,}000 \times 2.436 - \$600{,}000$$

$$= \$33{,}360.$$

Because the risk-adjusted value of the safer Project *A* is larger than that for Project *B*, the firm should choose Project *A*. This choice maximizes the value of the firm.

# FURTHER TECHNIQUES FOR DECISION MAKING UNDER UNCERTAINTY

In many decision situations, the data required for incorporating risk analysis into the decision process are not readily available in a usable form. In such cases, *decision trees* and *computer simulation* help one to develop and organize risk data for decision making. We shall now examine these two decision-making techniques and the roles they play in decision making under uncertainty.

## Decision Trees

Many important decisions are not made at one point in time but rather in stages. For example, a petroleum firm considering the possibility of expanding into agricultural chemicals might take the following steps:

1. Spend $100,000 to survey supply and demand conditions in the agricultural chemical industry.

---

[6]The terms

$$\sum_{t=1}^{5} \frac{1}{(1.20)^t} = 2.991$$

and

$$\sum_{t=1}^{5} \frac{1}{(1.30)^t} = 2.436$$

are present-value-of-an-annuity interest factors. Appendix A at the end of the text explains how interest factors are calculated. Tables of interest factors for various interest rates and years (*t* values) appear in Appendix B.

## 15.2  **Managerial Application**

The Man Who Turned Down $2 Billion

One of the most celebrated court cases of our time was the legal battle in the mid-1980s between Texaco and Pennzoil. Pennzoil had entered into an agreement in principle with the Board of Directors of Getty Oil to buy the company. However, before the deal could be closed, Texaco topped the Pennzoil offer and successfully merged with Getty. Pennzoil argued that Texaco had unfairly interfered with a binding contract between itself and Getty and sued Texaco for unspecified monetary damages. Texaco argued that no such binding contract existed. The issue was clouded by the fact that Pennzoil could not have a binding contract to buy Getty under Securities and Exchange Commission rules. In conflict with SEC merger guidelines, Pennzoil still had an outstanding pub-lic tender offer at the time it was privately dealing with the board and major stockholders of Getty.

In 1984, Pennzoil offered to withdraw its lawsuit in exchange for the right to buy 37 percent of Getty from Texaco. Assured by its lawyers that the Pennzoil suit was without merit, Texaco rejected the Pennzoil offer. In 1985, a Texas court decision stunned Texaco by awarding Pennzoil a judgment in the amount of $10.3 *billion*. After the jury verdict, Texaco was forced to consider options for settlement. Texaco offered to sell 42 percent of Getty to Pennzoil to settle the case, topping Pennzoil's earlier offer. Now Pennzoil rejected settlement. Texaco appealed to the Texas Supreme Court, lost, and vowed to continue its battle to the U.S. Supreme

*continued*

See: Robert H. Mnookin, "The Mystery of the Texaco Case," *The Wall Street Journal*, November 27, 1987, 6; Allanna Sullivan and Thomas Petzinger, Jr., "Settlement Achieved, Texaco and Pennzoil Face New Challenges," *The Wall Street Journal*, December 21, 1987, 1, 10; and Caleb Solomon, "How Do You Send a $3 Billion Check if Limit Is $1 Billion?" *The Wall Street Journal*, April 7, 1988, 1.

2. If the survey results are favorable, spend $2 million on a pilot plant to investigate production methods.

3. Depending on the costs estimated from the pilot study and the demand potential from the market study, either abandon the project, build a large plant, or build a small one.

Thus, decisions are actually made in stages, with subsequent decisions depending on the results of prior decisions.

**decision tree**

A mapped-out sequence of decision points and chance events.

The sequence of events can be mapped out to resemble the branches of a tree—hence the term **decision tree.** As an example, consider Figure 15.10, which assumes that the petroleum company has completed its industry supply and demand analysis and pilot plant study and has

**Managerial Application** *continued*

Court. However, as Texaco's options for appeal narrowed, its position weakened.

Finally, faced with possible seizure of assets by Pennzoil, Texaco presented several different settlement proposals worth in the neighborhood of $2 billion each during April 1987. Pennzoil rejected them all, and demanded $4.1 billion in cash. J. Hugh Liedtke, the founder and chairman of Houston-based Pennzoil, won fame on the cover of *Fortune* magazine as "The Man Who Turned Down $2 Billion." Liedtke was apparently convinced he could get more.

In light of Pennzoil's unwillingness to budge from its $4.1 billion settlement proposal, Texaco filed for Chapter 11 bankruptcy on April 11, 1987. Under bankruptcy court protection, Texaco could delay consideration of its settlement options without the immediate threat of asset seizures. Settlement seemed to be approaching during the spring of 1987 until Texaco backed out when the SEC announced plans to file a legal brief supporting the Texaco appeal. Talks didn't resume again until the fall of 1987, when a variety of innovative "judgment

cap" proposals surfaced. Pennzoil proposed that Texaco pay a nonrefundable $1.5 billion in return for a judgment cap of $5 billion, even if the full judgment was sustained on appeal. Texaco countered with an offer of $370 million and a cap of $2 billion. Pennzoil said no.

Finally, in December 1987, Texaco and Pennzoil signed a settlement to end their dispute of nearly five years. Texaco agreed to pay Pennzoil a cash settlement in the amount of $3 billion. In four separate transactions (necessary because the Federal Reserve System could not transfer amounts of more than a billion dollars at a time), Pennzoil received the cash on April 7, 1988.

One of the riddles of the case is the question of why it took so long to settle. Robert H. Mnookin, professor of law at Stanford University, argued in November 1987 that perhaps one or both of the parties simply liked to gamble. He didn't speculate who, but press reports have noted that Pennzoil's chairman Liedtke once decorated his office with a poster of W. C. Fields—as a riverboat gambler.

determined that it should develop a full-scale production facility. The firm can build a large plant or a small one. Demand expectations for the plant's products are 50 percent for high demand, 30 percent for medium demand, and 20 percent for low demand. Depending on demand, net cash flows (sales revenue minus operating costs), all discounted to the present, will range from $8.8 million to $1.4 million for a large plant and from $2.6 million to $1.4 million for a small plant.

Because the demand probabilities are known, we can find the expected values of cash flows, as in Column 5 of Figure 15.10. Finally, we can deduct the investment outlays from the expected net revenues to obtain the expected net present value for each decision. In the example, the expected net present value is $730,000 for the large plant and $300,000 for the small one.

■ Figure 15.10
## Illustrative Decision Tree

The expected net present value of each investment alternative (Column 5) is determined by linking possible outcomes (Column 2), probabilities (Column 3), and monetary values (Column 4).

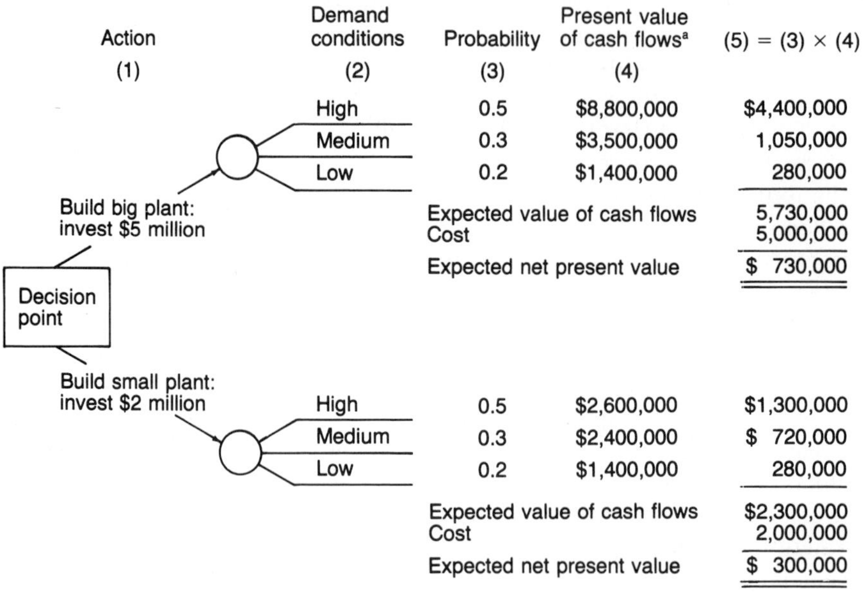

| Action (1) | Demand conditions (2) | Probability (3) | Present value of cash flows[a] (4) | (5) = (3) × (4) |
|---|---|---|---|---|
| | High | 0.5 | $8,800,000 | $4,400,000 |
| | Medium | 0.3 | $3,500,000 | 1,050,000 |
| | Low | 0.2 | $1,400,000 | 280,000 |
| Build big plant: invest $5 million | | | Expected value of cash flows | 5,730,000 |
| | | | Cost | 5,000,000 |
| | | | Expected net present value | $  730,000 |

Decision point

| | High | 0.5 | $2,600,000 | $1,300,000 |
|---|---|---|---|---|
| Build small plant: invest $2 million | Medium | 0.3 | $2,400,000 | $  720,000 |
| | Low | 0.2 | $1,400,000 | 280,000 |
| | | | Expected value of cash flows | $2,300,000 |
| | | | Cost | 2,000,000 |
| | | | Expected net present value | $  300,000 |

[a]The figures in Column 4 are the annual cash flows from operation—revenues minus cash operating costs—discounted at the firm's cost of capital.

Since the net present value of the large plant is higher, should the company decide to construct it? Perhaps, but not necessarily. Notice that the range of outcomes is greater for the large plant, with the actual net present values (Column 4, present values, in Figure 15.10 minus the investment cost) varying from $3.8 million to *minus* $3.6 million. The small plant's range runs only from $600,000 to *minus* $600,000. Because the required investment differs for the two plants, we must examine the coefficients of variation of the net present value possibilities to determine which alternative actually entails the greater risk. The coefficient of variation for the large plant's present value is 4.3, whereas that for the small plant is only 1.5.[7] Risk is greater for building the large plant.

The decision maker could take account of the risk differentials in a variety of ways. Assigning utility values to the cash flows given in Col-

[7]Using Equation 15.4 and the data on possible returns in Figure 15.10, the standard deviation of return for the large plant is $3.155 million and for the smaller is $458,260. Dividing each of these standard deviations by the expected returns for their respective plant size, as in Equation 15.5, gives the coefficient of variation.

umn 4 of Figure 15.10 would state Column 5 in terms of expected utility. The company could then choose the plant size that provided the greatest expected utility. Alternatively, a manager could calculate the present values given in Column 4 using the certainty equivalent or risk-adjusted discount rate methods. The plant that offered the larger risk-adjusted net present value would then be the optimal choice.

The decision tree illustrated in Figure 15.10 is quite simple; in actual use, the trees are frequently far more complex and involve large numbers of sequential decision points. An example of a more complex tree is illustrated in Figure 15.11. The numbered boxes represent *decision points,* instances when the management must choose among several alternatives; the circles represent *chance events,* indicating outcomes that are possible following the decisions. At Decision Point 1, the firm has three choices: invest $3 million in a large plant, invest $1.3 million in a small plant, or spend $100,000 on market research. If the large plant is built, the firm follows the upper branch, and its position has been fixed; it can only hope that demand will be high. If it builds the small plant, it follows the lower branch. If demand is low, no further action is required; if demand is high, Decision Point 2 is reached, and the firm can either do nothing or expand the plant at a cost of another $2.2 million. (If it obtains a large plant through expansion, the cost is $500,000 greater than if it had built the large plant in the first place.)

If the decision at Point 1 is to pay $100,000 for more information, the firm moves to the center branch. The research modifies the firm's information about potential demand. Initially, the probabilities were 70 percent for high demand and 30 percent for low demand. The research survey will show either favorable (positive) or unfavorable (negative) demand prospects. If they are positive, we assume that the probability for high final demand will be 87 percent and that for low demand will be 13 percent; if the research yields negative results, the odds on high final demand are only 35 percent and those for low demand are 65 percent. These results will influence the firm's decision about whether to build a large plant or a small plant.

If the firm builds a large plant and demand is high, sales and profits will be large. If, however, it builds a large plant and demand is low, sales will be low and it will incur losses. On the other hand, if it builds a small plant and demand is high, sales and profits will be lower than they could have been had a large plant been built, yet they will eliminate the chance of losses in the event of low demand. Building the large plant is therefore riskier than building the small plant. The cost of the research is, in effect, an expenditure serving to reduce the degree of uncertainty in the decision; the research provides additional information on the probability of high versus low demand, thus reducing the level of risk.

The decision tree in Figure 15.11 is incomplete because no dollar outcomes (or utility values) are assigned to the various situations. If such values are assigned, along the lines shown in the last two columns of

■ Figure 15.11
# Decision Tree with Multiple Decision Points

The decision tree allows the decision maker to illustrate the return possibilities and probabilities at each decision point.

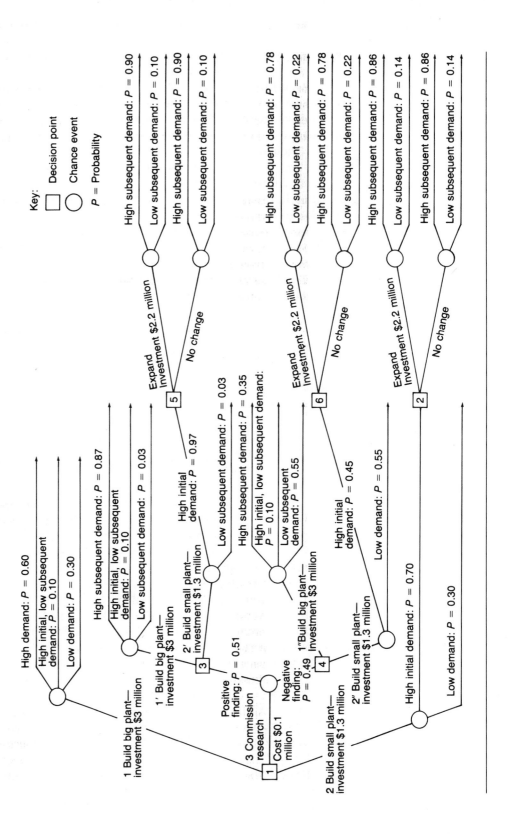

Key:

☐ Decision point

◯ Chance event

$P$ = Probability

Figure 15.10, expected values can be obtained for each of the alternative actions along with measures of the possible variability of outcomes. These values will then help the decision maker to choose among the alternatives.

## Simulation

Another technique designed to assist managers in making decisions under uncertainty is computer **simulation.** To illustrate the technique, let us consider the decision to build a new textile plant. The exact cost of the plant is not known. It is expected to be about $150 million. If no difficulties arise in construction, the cost can be as low as $125 million; however, an unfortunate series of events—strikes, unprojected increases in material costs, and technical problems—could drive the investment outlay as high as $225 million.

Revenues from the new facility, which will operate for many years, depend on population growth and personal income in the region, competition, developments in synthetic fabrics, research, and textile import quotas. Operating costs depend on production efficiency, materials, and labor-cost trends. Because both sales revenues and operating costs are uncertain, annual profits are also uncertain.

Assuming that probability distributions can be developed for each of the major cost and revenue determinants, a computer program can be constructed to simulate what is likely to occur. In effect, the computer selects one value at random from each of the relevant distributions, combines it with values selected from the other distributions, and produces an estimated profit and net present value, or rate of return on investment. This particular profit and rate of return occur only for the particular combination of values selected during the trial. The computer proceeds to select other sets of values and to compute other profits and rates of return for perhaps several hundred trials. The computer counts the number of times that each of the various rates of return results. When the computer completes its runs, it can plot the frequency with which the various rates of return occurred as a frequency distribution.

The procedure is illustrated in Figures 15.12 and 15.13. Figure 15.12 is a flow chart outlining the simulation procedure just described; Figure 15.13 illustrates the frequency distribution of rates of return generated by such a simulation for two alternative projects, $X$ and $Y$, each with an expected cost of $20 million. The expected rate of return on Investment $X$ is 15 percent and that on Investment $Y$ is 20 percent. However, these are only the average rates of return generated by the computer; simulated rates ranged from $-10$ percent to $+45$ percent for Investment $Y$ and from 5 to 25 percent for Investment $X$. The standard deviation generated for $X$ is only 4 percentage points; that for $Y$ is 12 percentage points. From this we can calculate a coefficient of variation of 0.267 for Project $X$ and 0.60 for Project $Y$. On the basis of total variability, Investment $Y$ is riskier than Investment $X$. The simulation has estimated both the expected returns on the two projects and their relative risks. A decision about which

**simulation**

A technique used to generate and analyze the distribution of project returns.

■ Figure 15.12
## Simulation for Investment Planning

Computer simulation allows detailed analysis of managerial problems involving complex cost and revenue relations.

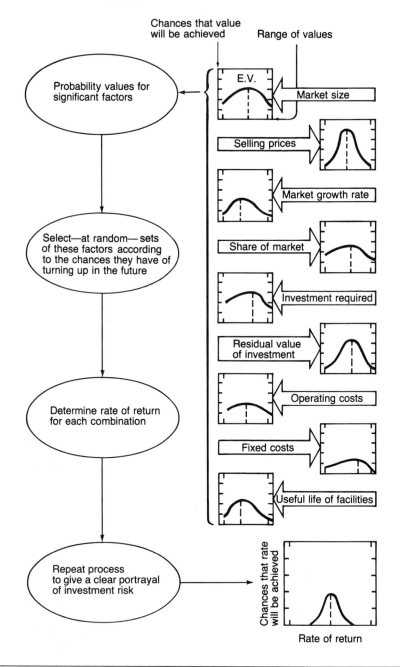

■ Figure 15.13
## Expected Rates of Return on Investments *X* and *Y*

Investments *X* and *Y* both have continuous distributions of returns around their expected values.

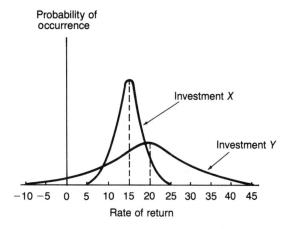

alternative to choose can now be made on the basis of one of the techniques discussed—expected utility, or present value determination that incorporates either certainty equivalents or risk-adjusted discount rates.

One final point should be made about computer simulation for risk analysis. The technique requires probability distributions for a number of variables, such as investment outlays, unit sales, product prices, input prices, and asset lives, all of which involve a fair amount of programming and machine-time costs. Full-scale simulation is expensive and therefore is used primarily for large and expensive projects such as major plant expansions or new-product decisions. In such cases, however, when a firm is deciding whether or not to accept a major undertaking involving an outlay of millions of dollars, computer simulation can provide valuable insights into the relative merits of alternative strategies.

It should also be noted that a somewhat less expensive simulation technique is available as an alternative method of analyzing the outcomes of various projects or strategies. Instead of using probability distributions for each of the variables in the problem, we can simulate the results by starting with best-guess estimates for each variable and then change the values of the variables (within reasonable limits) to see the effects of such changes on the returns generated by the project. Typically, returns are highly sensitive to some variables, less so to others. Attention is then concentrated on the variables to which profitability is most sensitive. This technique, known as sensitivity analysis, is considerably less expensive than full-scale simulation and provides similar data for decision-making purposes.

## 15.3 **Managerial Application**
How Risk Averse are Professors?

One interesting facet of risk analysis is that the professors who teach decision making under uncertainty are probably more risk averse, on average, than their students. Many professors receive only modest levels of pay. In return, they hope to be awarded tenure and a measure of job security for their contributions to the college or university community in terms of teaching, research, and service. Professors appear to be a risk-averse group, one willing to accept relatively low rates of academic pay on the basis that these returns are relatively stable.

In contrast, business undergraduates and MBA students seek employment in the business world, where rates of pay are higher and job security is far less assured. Sales personnel who depend on commission-based income bear the greatest risk and have the greatest potential for high dollar income. Salaried employees have far more assurance about their income levels but typically accept lower earning potential in return. Risks and potential returns are generally highest among smaller firms in highly competitive industries. Risks and potential returns tend to be lower in government and larger companies in regulated industries. Like the monetary returns from academia, monetary rewards in business involve a trade-off between risk and return.

We can get a glimpse of just how risk averse professors tend to be by considering how conservatively most of them invest their funds for retirement. Widely circulated academic studies of the returns to various

*continued*

See: Pamela Sebastian, "Some Academics Move to Widen Choices," *The Wall Street Journal,* August 31, 1987, 27.

### Game Theory
The decision criterion stressed throughout this book is maximization of value. Typically, value maximization is achieved through risk-adjusted valuation models as described in this chapter. Under certain circumstances, especially when the environment is viewed as being malevolent rather than neutral and when probabilities of occurrence for states of nature are difficult to assign, other decision criteria may be appropriate. These rules are perhaps most relevant in oligopoly situations, in which firms can be expected to react to the competitors' actions. Game theory is a method for dealing with such cases.

**maximin criterion**
The decision maker selects the alternative that provides the best outcome under the worst-case scenario.

### Maximin Decision Rule
One decision criterion widely discussed in the literature on decision making under uncertainty is the **maximin criterion.** This criterion states that the decision maker should select the alter-

**Managerial Application** *continued*

types of investments have shown that common stocks typically outperform bonds by a substantial margin, especially over long investment periods. For example, since 1927, the average annual rates of return are roughly 3.5 percent for short-term government bonds (money market investments), 5 percent for long-term bonds, and 10 percent for common stocks. One might naturally assume that shrewd long-term investors would put their retirement funds into stock investments.

As seen in the following table, most professors prefer low-risk bond investments (those in the Teachers Insurance and Annuity Association—TIAA) to common stock investments (those in the College Retirement Equity Fund—CREF). Fully 24 percent of the several thousand professors who participate in the TIAA–CREF retirement plan allocate all of their retirement monies to bond (TIAA) investments. Almost one-half, or 47 percent, prefer a 50–50 split. Only 3 percent allocate all of their retirement funds to common stocks (CREF). Interestingly, these preferences appear to be quite consistent across all age groups.

### Allocation of Professor's TIAA–CREF Retirement Nesteggs

| | Age Group | | | | | |
|---|---|---|---|---|---|---|
| | 29 and Under | 30–39 | 40–49 | 50–59 | 60 and Over | All Ages |
| 100 percent TIAA | 27% | 23% | 20% | 23% | 33% | 24% |
| 75 percent TIAA/25 percent CREF | 17 | 17 | 14 | 11 | 9 | 14 |
| 50 percent TIAA/50 percent CREF | 45 | 48 | 49 | 46 | 40 | 47 |
| 25 percent TIAA/75 percent CREF | 5 | 6 | 10 | 13 | 11 | 9 |
| 100 percent CREF | 3 | 3 | 4 | 4 | 4 | 3 |
| Other | 3 | 3 | 3 | 3 | 3 | 3 |

Apparently, college and university professors are a risk-averse group indeed!

native that provides the best of the worst possible outcomes. This is done by finding the worst possible (minimum) outcome for each alternative and then choosing the alternative whose worst outcome provides the highest (maximum) payoff. Hence, this criterion instructs one to maximize the minimum possible outcome.

To illustrate, consider Table 15.7, which shows the weekly profit contribution payoffs from alternative gasoline pricing strategies by Steve's U-Pumpit. Assume that Steve's has just been notified of a 3¢ reduction in the wholesale price of gas. If Steve's reduces its current self-service price by 3¢ per gallon, its weekly profit contribution will depend upon the reaction, if any, of its nearest competitor. If Steve's competitor matches the price reduction, a $2,500 profit contribution will result.

■ Table 15.7
## Weekly Profit Contribution Payoff Matrix

| | States of Nature | |
| | Competitor Reduces Price | Competitor Maintains Current Price |
| Steve's Decision Alternatives | | |
|---|---|---|
| Reduce price | $2,500 | $3,000 |
| Maintain current price | $1,000 | $5,000 |

Without any competitor reaction, Steve's would earn $3,000. If Steve's and its competitor both maintain current prices, Steve's will earn $5,000, whereas if Steve's did not match the competitor's price cut, Steve's would earn only $1,000. In our example, the worst possible outcome following a price reduction by Steve's is $2,500, but a $1,000 outcome is possible if Steve's maintains its current price. The maximin criterion requires Steve's to reduce its price, since the minimum possible outcome from this decision is greater than the minimum $1,000 payoff possible by maintaining the current price.

Although this decision criterion suffers from the obvious shortcoming of focusing on the most pessimistic outcome for each alternative, we should not dismiss it as being naïve and unsophisticated. The maximin criterion implicitly assumes a very strong aversion to risk, and we might therefore use it for decisions involving the possibility of catastrophic outcomes. When the alternatives available to the decision maker involve outcomes that endanger worker lives or the survival of the organization, for example, the maximin criterion can be an appropriate technique for decision making. Similarly, if the state of nature that prevails depends on the course of action taken by the decision maker, the maximin criterion might be appropriate. In the preceding example, one might expect that a decision by Steve's to reduce prices would cause the competitor to follow suit, resulting in the worst possible outcome for that decision alternative.

**Minimax Regret Decision Rule**   A second useful decision criterion focuses on the opportunity loss associated with a decision rather than on its worst possible outcome. This decision rule, known as the **minimax regret criterion,** states that the decision maker should minimize the maximum possible regret (opportunity cost) associated with a wrong decision *after the fact.* This criterion instructs one to minimize the difference between possible outcomes and the best outcome for each state of nature.

To illustrate this decision technique, we need to examine the concept of opportunity loss or "regret" in greater detail. In game theory, **opportunity loss** is defined as the difference between a given payoff and the highest possible payoff for the resulting state of nature. Opportunity

**minimax regret criterion**
The decision maker selects the alternative for which the maximum possible opportunity loss is smallest.

**opportunity loss**
The difference between a given payoff and the highest possible payoff in that state of nature.

■ Table 15.8

# Weekly Profit Contribution Opportunity Loss or Regret Matrix

| | States of Nature | |
|---|---|---|
| **Steve's Decision Alternatives** | **Competitor Reduces Price** | **Competitor Maintains Current Price** |
| Reduce price | $0 (= $2,500 − $2,500) | $2,000 (= $5,000 − $3,000) |
| Maintain current price | $1,500 (= $2,500 − $1,000) | $0 (= $5,000 − $5,000) |

losses result from the fact that returns actually received under conditions of uncertainty are frequently lower than the maximum return that would have been possible had perfect knowledge been available beforehand.

Table 15.8 shows the opportunity loss or regret matrix associated with Steve's gasoline pricing problem. It was constructed by finding the maximum payoff for a given state of nature in Table 15.7 and then subtracting from this amount the payoffs that would result from various decision alternatives. Opportunity loss is always a positive figure or zero, since we are subtracting each alternative payoff from the largest payoff possible in a given state of nature. For example, if Steve's competitor reduced its price, the best possible decision for that state of nature would be for Steve's to have also reduced prices. After the fact, Steve's would have no regrets had it done so. Should Steve's maintain its current price, the firm would experience a $1,500 opportunity loss or regret. To calculate this amount, subtract the $1,000 payoff associated with Steve's maintaining its current price despite a competitor price reduction from the $2,500 payoff that it would have received from matching the competitor's price reduction. Similarly, if Steve's reduced price while the competitor maintained the current price, Steve's would experience a $2,000 opportunity loss or regret after the fact.

The minimax regret criterion would cause Steve's to maintain the current retail price of gasoline, because this decision alternative minimizes the maximum regret, or opportunity loss. The maximum regret in this case is limited to the $1,500 loss that would result if the competitor reduced its current price. If Steve's were to reduce its price while the competitor maintained its current price, Steve's opportunity loss would be $2,000 per week, $500 more than the maximum regret from Steve's maintaining its current price.

**An Alternative Use of the Opportunity-Loss Concept** The opportunity loss concept can be used in yet another way in risk analysis. We have described an opportunity loss as a cost associated with uncertainty.

Therefore, the *expected opportunity loss* associated with a decision provides a measure of the expected monetary gain from the removal of all uncertainty about future events. From the opportunity loss or regret matrix, the cost of uncertainty is measured by the minimum expected opportunity loss. From the payoff matrix, the cost of uncertainty is measured by the difference between the expected payoff associated with choosing the "correct" alternative under each state of nature (which will only be known after the fact) and the highest expected payoff available from among the decision alternatives. The cost of uncertainty is the unavoidable economic loss that is due to chance. Using this concept, we are able to judge the value of reducing uncertainty by gaining additional information before choosing among decision alternatives.

Let us again examine our gasoline pricing problem to illustrate this use of opportunity loss. On the basis of the data in Table 15.8, we can calculate the expected opportunity loss of each alternative as shown in Table 15.9. Here we assume that Steve's projects a 50–50, or 50-percent, chance of a competitor price reduction. The minimum expected opportunity cost in this case is $750 and represents Steve's loss from not knowing the competitor's pricing reaction with certainty. Steve's would be better off if by an expenditure of less than $750 on information gathering, it could eliminate this uncertainty.

We must emphasize that additional expenditures on information gathering will not guarantee a higher actual profit or even that the cost uncertainty will be reduced. The opportunity-loss concept merely informs the decision maker of the expected value of removing, if possible, uncertainty about which state of nature will occur.

We often see firms engaging in activities aimed at reducing the uncertainty of various alternatives before making an irrevocable decision. For example, a food-manufacturing company will employ extensive marketing tests in selected areas to gain better estimates of sales potential before going ahead with large-scale production of a new product. Similarly, automobile manufacturers frequently install new equipment in a limited number of models to judge reliability and customer reaction before including the equipment in all models.

# SUMMARY

Risk analysis plays an integral role in the decision process for most business problems. In this chapter we defined the concept of *risk*, introduced it into the valuation model for the firm, and then examined several techniques for decision making under conditions of uncertainty.

Risk in economic analysis is characterized by variability of outcomes, and it is defined in terms of probability distributions of possible results. The tighter the distribution, the lower the variability, and hence the lower the risk. The *standard deviation* and *coefficient of variation* are two frequently used measures of risk in economic analysis.

■ Table 15.9
## Calculation of Expected Opportunity Loss

| | From the Loss Matrix | | | | | |
| | Steve's Reduces Price | | | Steve's Maintains Current Price | | |
| State of Nature | Probability of This State of Nature (1) | Opportunity Loss of This Outcome (2) | Expected Opportunity Loss (3) = (1) × (2) | Probability of This State of Nature (1) | Opportunity Loss of This Outcome (2) | Expected Opportunity Loss (3) = (1) × (2) |
|---|---|---|---|---|---|---|
| Competitor reduces price | 0.5 | $0 | $0 | 0.5 | $1,500 | $750 |
| Competitor maintains current price | 0.5 | $2,000 | $1,000 $1,000 | 0.5 | $0 | $0 $750 |

Cost of uncertainty = Minimum expected opportunity loss = $750.

| | From the Payoff Matrix | | | | | |
| | Steve's Reduces Price | | | Steve's Maintains Current Price | | |
| State of Nature | Probability (1) | Outcome (2) | (3) = (1) × (2) | Probability (1) | Outcome (2) | (3) = (1) × (2) |
|---|---|---|---|---|---|---|
| Competitor reduces price | 0.5 | $2,500 | $1,250 | 0.5 | $1,000 | $500 |
| Competitor maintains current price | 0.5 | $3,000 | $1,500 $2,750 | 0.5 | $5,000 | $2,500 $3,000 |

Expected value of a "correct" decision after the fact = $2,500(0.5) + $5,000(0.5) = $3,750.

Cost of uncertainty = Expected value of a "correct" decision − Expected value of best alternative
= $3,750 − $3,000 = $750.

The assumption of risk aversion by investors and managers is based on utility relationships. Most individuals experience *diminishing marginal utility* of money, and this leads directly to risk aversion. Investor risk aversion affects the valuation of the firm and must, therefore, be taken into account for managerial decision making. The basic valuation model can be adjusted to reflect this risk effect through the use of *certainty equivalent adjustment factors* and *risk-adjusted discount rates*.

Decision making under conditions of uncertainty is greatly facilitated by *decision trees* and *simulation*, two techniques used to structure problems and to generate data necessary for risk analysis. Decision trees map out the sequence of events in a decision problem, providing a means for examining the branching that takes place at each decision point and chance event. Simulation techniques can be used to generate frequency distributions of possible outcomes for alternative decisions and to provide inputs for expected utility, certainty equivalent, or risk-adjusted discount rate analysis.

Probability can be further employed in managerial decision making through use of the standard normal concept. Here the probability of profit or loss, for example, can be estimated by comparing the relative magnitude of a project's expected return and variance. Finally, decision making under uncertainty can be facilitated using game theory concepts. In a *maximin* strategy, the decision alternative with the least undesirable of the worst possible outcomes is chosen. In a *minimax regret* strategy, the decision alternative with the smallest maximum opportunity loss is chosen.

## Questions

15.1  Define the following terms:
    A.  Probability distribution
    B.  Expected value
    C.  Standard deviation
    D.  Coefficient of variation
    E.  Risk
    F.  Diminishing marginal utility of money
    G.  Certainty equivalent
    H.  Risk-adjusted discount rate
    I.  Decision tree
    J.  Simulation

15.2  What is the main difficulty associated with making decisions solely on the basis of comparisons of expected returns?

15.3  The standard deviation measure of risk implicitly gives equal weight to variations on both sides of the expected value. Can you see any potential limitations of this treatment?

15.4  "Utility is a theoretical concept that cannot be observed or measured in the real world. Hence, it has no practical value in decision analysis." Discuss this statement.

15.5  Graph the relation between money and its utility for an individual who buys *both* household fire insurance and state-run lottery tickets.

15.6  When the basic valuation model is adjusted using the risk-free rate, $i$, what economic factor is being explicitly accounted for?

15.7  If the expected net present value of returns from an investment project is $50,000, what is the maximum price that a risk-neutral investor would pay for it? Explain.

15.8  "Market estimates of investors' reactions to risk cannot be measured precisely, so it is impossible to set risk-adjusted discount rates for various classes of investment with a high degree of precision." Discuss this statement.

15.9  What is the value of decision trees in managerial decision making?

15.10 When is it most useful to use game theory in decision analysis?

## Problems

15.1 Identify each of the following as being consistent with *risk-averse*, *risk-neutral*, or *risk-seeking* behavior in investment-project selection. Explain why.

    A. Larger risk premiums for riskier projects

    B. Preference for smaller, as opposed to larger, coefficients of variation

    C. Valuing certain sums and expected risky sums of equal dollar amounts equally

    D. Having an increasing marginal utility of money

    E. Ignoring risk levels of investment alternatives

15.2 The certainty equivalent concept can be widely employed in the analysis of personal and business decision making. Indicate whether each of the following statements is *true* or *false* and explain why.

    A. The appropriate certainty equivalent adjustment factor ($\alpha$) indicates the minimum price in certain dollars that an individual should be willing to pay per risky dollar of expected return.

    B. An $\alpha \neq 1$ implies that a certain sum and a risky expected return of different dollar amounts provide equivalent utility to a given decision maker.

    C. If previously accepted projects with similar risk have $\alpha$s in a range from $\alpha = 0.4$ to $\alpha = 0.5$, an investment with an expected return of $150,000 is acceptable at a cost of $50,000.

    D. A project for which $NPV > 0$ using an appropriate risk-adjusted discount rate has an implied $\alpha$ factor that is too large to allow project acceptance.

    E. State lotteries that pay out 50 percent of the revenues that they generate require players who place *at least* a certain $2 value on each $1 of expected risky return.

15.3 Nancy Lopez offers free investment seminars to local PTA groups. On average, Lopez expects 1 percent of seminar participants to purchase $25,000 in tax-sheltered investments and 5 percent to purchase $5,000 in stocks and bonds. Lopez earns a 4-percent net commission on tax-shelters and a 1-percent commission on stocks and bonds.

    A. Calculate Lopez's expected net commissions per seminar if attendance averages ten persons.

15.4 Aquarius Products, Inc., has just completed development of a new line of skin-care products. Preliminary market research indicates two feasible marketing strategies: creating general consumer acceptance through media advertising, or creating distributor acceptance through intensive personal selling by company representatives. The marketing manager has developed the following estimates for sales under each alternative:

| Media Advertising Strategy | | Personal Selling Strategy | |
|---|---|---|---|
| Probability | Sales | Probability | Sales |
| 0.1 | $ 500,000 | 0.3 | $1,000,000 |
| 0.4 | 1,500,000 | 0.4 | 1,500,000 |
| 0.4 | 2,500,000 | 0.3 | 2,000,000 |
| 0.1 | 3,500,000 | | |

A.  Assume that the company has a 50-percent profit margin on sales (that is, profits equal one-half of sales revenue). Calculate expected profits for each plan.

B.  Construct a simple bar graph of the possible profit outcomes for each plan. Which plan appears to be riskier?

C.  Assume that management's utility function resembles the one illustrated in the following figure. Which strategy should the marketing manager recommend?

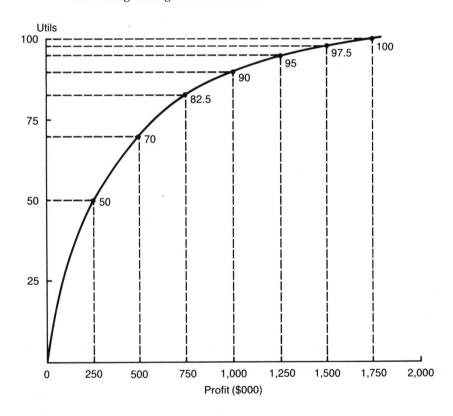

15.5  Sam Malone, marketing diretor for Nisswa Records, Inc., has just completed an agreement to rerelease a recording of The Boss's greatest hits. (The Boss had a number of hits on the rock-'n-roll charts during the early 1980s.) Preliminary market research indicates two feasible marketing strategies: (a) concentration on developing general consumer acceptance by advertising on late-night television, or (b) concentration on developing distributor acceptance through intensive sales calls by company representatives. Malone developed estimates for sales under each alternative plan and has constructed payoff matrices according to his assessment of the likelihood of product acceptance under each plan. These data are as follows:

| Strategy 1 Consumer Television Promotion | | Strategy 2 Distributor Oriented Promotion | |
| --- | --- | --- | --- |
| Probability | Outcome (Sales) | Probability | Outcome (Sales) |
| 0.32 | $ 250,000 | 0.125 | $ 250,000 |
| 0.36 | 1,000,000 | 0.750 | 750,000 |
| 0.32 | 1,750,000 | 0.125 | 1,250,000 |

A. Assuming that the company has a 50-percent profit margin on sales, calculate the expected profits for each plan.
B. Construct a simple bar graph of the possible profit outcomes for each plan. Which plan appears riskier?
C. Calculate the risk (standard deviation of the profit distribution) associated with each plan.
D. Assume that the management of Nisswa has a utility function like the one illustrated in the following figure. Which marketing strategy should Malone recommend?

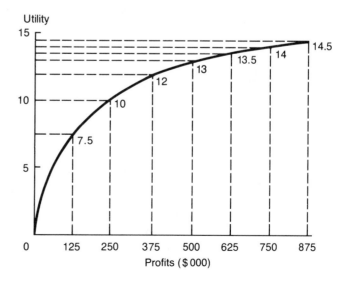

15.6  One-Hour Dryclean, Inc., is contemplating replacing an obsolete dry cleaning machine with one of two innovative pieces of equipment. Alternative 1 requires a current investment outlay of $25,373, whereas Alternative 2 requires an outlay of $24,199. The following cash flows (cost savings) will be generated each year over the new machines' four-year lives.

|  | Probability | Cash Flow |
|---|---|---|
| Alternative 1 | 0.18 | $ 5,000 |
|  | 0.64 | 10,000 |
|  | 0.18 | 15,000 |
| Alternative 2 | 0.125 | $ 8,000 |
|  | 0.75 | 10,000 |
|  | 0.125 | 12,000 |

A. Calculate the expected cash flow for each investment alternative.
B. Calculate the standard deviation of cash flows (risk) for each investment alternative.
C. The firm will use a discount rate of 12 percent for the cash flows with a higher degree of dispersion and a 10-percent rate for the less risky cash flows. Calculate the expected net present value for each investment. Which alternative should be chosen?

15.7  Tex-Mex, Inc., is a rapidly growing chain of Mexican-food restaurants. The company has a limited amount of capital for expansion and must carefully weigh available alternatives. Currently, the company is considering opening restaurants in Santa Fe or Albuquerque, New Mexico. Projections for the two potential outlets are as follows:

| City | Outcome | Annual Profit Contribution | Probability |
|---|---|---|---|
| Albuquerque | Failure | $100,000 | 0.5 |
|  | Success | 200,000 | 0.5 |
| Santa Fe | Failure | $ 60,000 | 0.5 |
|  | Success | 340,000 | 0.5 |

Each restaurant would require a capital expenditure of $700,000, plus land acquisition costs of $500,000 for Albuquerque and $1 million for Santa Fe. The company uses the 10-percent yield on riskless U.S. Treasury bills to calculate the risk-free annual opportunity cost of investment capital.

A. Calculate the expected value, standard deviation, and coefficient of variation for each outlet's profit contribution.

B. Calculate the minimum certainty equivalent adjustment factor for each restaurant's cash flows that would justify investment in each outlet.

C. Assuming that the management of Tex-Mex is risk averse and uses the certainty equivalent method in decision making, which is the more attractive outlet? Why?

15.8 Keystone Manufacturing, Inc., is analyzing a new bid to supply the company with electronic control systems. Alpha Corporation has been supplying the systems and Keystone is satisfied with its performance. However, a bid has just been received from Beta Controls, Ltd., a firm that is aggressively marketing its products. Beta has offered to supply systems for a price of $120,000. The price for the Alpha system is $160,000. In addition to an attractive price, Beta offers a money-back guarantee. That is, if Beta's systems do not match Alpha's quality, Keystone can reject and return them for a full refund. However, if it must reject the machines and return them to Beta, Keystone will suffer production delays costing the firm $60,000.

A. Construct a decision tree for this problem and determine the maximum probability that Keystone could assign to rejection of the Beta system before it would reject their offer, assuming that it decides on the basis of minimizing expected costs.

B. Assume that Keystone assigns a 50-percent probability of rejection to the Beta controls. Would Keystone be willing to pay $15,000 for an assurance bond that would pay $60,000 in the event that the Beta controls fail the quality check? (Use the same objective as in Part A.) Explain.

15.9 Speedy Business Cards, Inc., supplies customized business cards to commercial and individual customers. The company is preparing a bid to supply cards to the Nationwide Realty Company, a large association of independent real estate agents. Since paper, ink, and other costs cannot be determined precisely, Speedy anticipates that costs will be normally distributed around a mean of $20 per unit (each 500-card order) with a standard deviation of $2 per unit.

A. What is the probability that Speedy will make a profit at a price of $20 per unit?

B. Calculate the unit price necessary to give Speedy a 95-percent chance of making a profit on the order.

C. If Speedy submits a successful bid of $23 per unit, what is the probability that it will make a profit?

15.10 Sierra Mountain Bike, Inc., is a producer and wholesaler of rugged bicycles designed for mountain touring. The company is considering an upgrade to its current line by making high-grade chrome-alloy frames standard. Of course, the market response to this upgrade in product quality depends on whether its competitor also upgrades. The company's comptroller projects the following annual profits (payoffs) following resolution of the upgrade decision:

| Sierra's Decision Alternatives | States of Nature | |
|---|---|---|
| | Competitor Upgrade | No Competitor Upgrade |
| Upgrade | $1,000,000 | $1,500,000 |
| Don't upgrade | 800,000 | 2,000,000 |

A. Which decision alternative would Sierra choose given a maximin criterion? Explain.
B. Calculate the opportunity loss or regret matrix.
C. Which decision alternative would Sierra choose given a minimax regret criterion? Explain.

## Selected References

Amit, Raphael, and Joshua Livnat. "Diversification and the Risk-Return Trade-off." *Academy of Management Journal* 31 (March 1988): 154–166.

Atkinson, Scott E., and John Tschirhart. "Flexible Modeling of Time to Failure in Risky Careers." *Review of Economics and Statistics* 68 (November 1986): 558–566.

Bizer, David S., and Kenneth L. Judd. "Taxation and Uncertainty." *American Economic Review* 79 (May 1989): 331–336.

Blanchard, Oliver Jean, and N. Gregory Mankiw. "Consumption: Beyond Certainty Equivalence." *American Economic Review* 78 (May 1988): 173–177.

Boodman, David M. "Managing Business Risk." *Interfaces* 17 (March–April 1987): 91–96.

Busche, Kelly, and Christopher D. Hall. "An Exception to the Risk Preference Anomaly." *Journal of Business* 61 (July 1988): 337–346.

Crum, Roy L., and Keqian Bi. "An Observation of Estimating the Systematic Risk of an Industry Segment." *Financial Management* 17 (Spring 1988): 60–62.

Fiegenbaum, Avi, and Howard Thomas. "Attitudes Toward Risk and the Risk-Return Paradox: Prospect Theory Explanations." *Academy of Management Journal* 31 (March 1988): 85–106.

Jones, Lawrence. "A Simulation Model for Analytical Laboratory Planning." *Interfaces* 14 (November–December 1984): 80–86.

Kerr, Jeffrey L. "Diversification Strategies and Managerial Rewards: An Empirical Study." *Academy of Management Journal* 28 (March 1985): 155–179.

Lev, Benjamin, and Eugene Kwatny. "Simulation of a Regional Scheduling Problem." *Interfaces* 18 (March–April 1988): 28–44.

Luna, Robert E., and Richard A. Reid. "Mortgage Selection Using a Decision Tree Approach." *Interfaces* 16 (May–June 1986): 73–81.

Macomber, John D. "You *Can* Manage Construction Risks." *Harvard Business Review* 67 (March–April 1989): 155–165.

Merkhofer, Miley W. *Decision Science and Social Risk Management.* New York: D. Reidel Publishing, 1987.

Mukherjee, Tarun K., and Glen V. Henderson. "The Capital Budgeting Process: Theory and Practice." *Interfaces* 17 (March–April 1987): 78–90.

Pindyck, Robert S. "Risk Aversion and Determinants of Stock Market Behavior." *Review of Economics and Statistics* 70 (May 1988): 183–190.

Rose, Andrew K. "Is the Real Interest Rate Stable?" *Journal of Finance* 43 (December 1988): 1095–1111.

Sick, Gordon A. "A Certainty-Equivalent Approach to Capital Budgeting." *Financial Management* 15 (Winter 1986): 23–32.

Smith, V. Kerry, and F. Reed Johnson. "How Do Risk Perceptions Respond to Information? The Case of Radon." *Review of Economics and Statistics* 70 (February 1988): 1–8.

Thaler, Richard H., and William T. Ziemba. "Parimutuel Betting Markets: Racetracks and Lotteries." *Journal of Economic Perspectives* 2 (Spring 1988): 161–175.

# Capital Budgeting

**M**anagement faces two separate but related tasks in managing long-lived assets as it works toward the goal of maximizing the value of the firm: (1) it must use existing resources in an optimal manner; and (2) it must decide when to increase or reduce the firm's stock of resources. We have not yet explicitly separated these tasks, although our emphasis has been on the first one. Now we explicitly consider the decision to add to the stock of capital, the decision process known as *investment* or *capital budgeting.*

**capital budgeting**
The process of planning investment expenditures when returns are expected to extend beyond one year.

**Capital budgeting** consists of the entire process of planning expenditures when returns are expected to extend beyond one year. The choice of one year is arbitrary, of course, but it is a convenient cutoff for distinguishing between classes of expenditures. Obvious examples of capital outlays are expenditures for land, buildings, and equipment and for additions to working capital (e.g., inventories and receivables) associated with expansion of activities. Major advertising or promotion campaigns or a program of research and development are also likely to have impacts beyond one year and hence they come within the classification of capital budgeting expenditures.

In a very real sense, capital budgeting integrates the various elements of the firm. Although the financial manager generally has administrative control of the capital budgeting process, the effectiveness of a firm's capital investment activity depends fundamentally on inputs from all major departments. Because a sales forecast is always required, the marketing department makes a key contribution to the process. Because operating costs must be estimated, the accounting, production, engineering, and purchasing departments are also involved. The initial outlay, or investment cost, must be estimated; again engineering and purchasing typically provide input. Funds must be procured to finance the project, and obtaining these funds and estimating their cost are major tasks of the financial manager. Finally, these various estimates must be drawn together in the form of a project evaluation. Although the finance department generally writes up the evaluation report, top management sets the standards of acceptability and ultimately decides to accept or reject the project.

Our first task in this chapter is to describe the mechanics of the capital budgeting process. Then we discuss in some detail the key roles of marketing, production, and finance in the process.

## THE CAPITAL BUDGETING PROCESS

Capital budgeting is essentially an application of the proposition that a profit-maximizing firm should operate at the point where marginal revenue equals marginal cost. Applying this rule to the capital budgeting decision, marginal revenue takes the form of the rate of return on investment, and marginal cost is the firm's cost of capital.

Figure 16.1a presents this concept graphically. The horizontal axis measures the dollars of investment during a year; the vertical axis shows both the percentage cost of capital and the rate of return on projects. The boxes denote projects: Project *A*, for example, calls for an outlay of $3 million and promises a 17-percent rate of return, Project *B* requires $1 million and yields about 16 percent, and so on. The last investment, Project *E*, simply involves buying 9-percent government bonds. The investment opportunity schedule measures the yield or rate of return on each project. Figure 16.1b generalizes the concept to show a smoothed investment opportunity schedule, the curve labeled *IRR*. (The yield on a project is generally calculated as the internal rate of return (*IRR*). The process of calculating the *IRR* is explained later in this chapter.)

The curve *MCC* designates the marginal cost of capital, or the cost of each additional dollar acquired to make capital expenditures. As it is drawn in Figure 16.1a, the marginal cost of capital is constant at 10 percent until the firm has raised $8 million, after which the cost of capital begins to rise. To maximize value, the firm should accept Projects *A* through *D*, obtaining and investing $11 million, and reject *E*, the investment in government bonds. The smoothed generalized curves in Figure 16.1b indicate that the firm should invest $I^*$ dollars. At this investment level, the marginal cost of capital, the cost of the last dollar raised, is 12 percent, the same as the return on the last project accepted.

Application of the capital budgeting process is much more complex than the preceding examples would suggest. Projects do not just appear. A continuing stream of good investment opportunities results from hard thinking, careful planning, and, often, large outlays for research and development. In addition, difficult measurement problems are involved. The revenues and costs associated with particular projects must be esti-

■ Figure 16.1
## Illustrative Capital Budgeting Decision Process

(a) The rates of return of Projects A through D exceed the marginal cost of capital, and they should be accepted. However, Project E should be rejected because its marginal cost of capital is greater than its internal rate of return. (b) Point I* is the optimal investment level at which the marginal cost of capital equals the marginal return on the last project accepted.

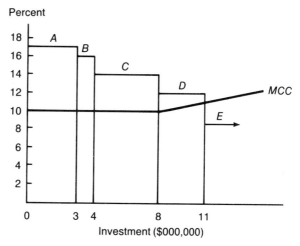

(a) Discrete investment projects

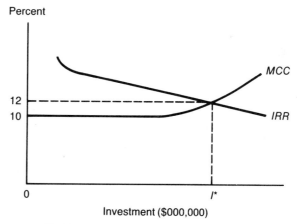

(b) Smoothed investment opportunity schedule

mated, frequently for many years into the future, in the face of great uncertainty. Finally, conceptual and empirical problems arise over the methods of calculating rates of return and the cost of capital. Managers must take action despite problems such as these, and the capital budgeting procedure described in this chapter is designed to aid in this decision process.

## Investment Proposals

The capital budgeting process begins with the generation of ideas; capital investment proposals must be created. This development of investment proposals is no small task. A firm's growth and development, even its ability to remain competitive and to survive, depend upon a constant flow of new investment ideas. Accordingly, a well-managed firm will go to great lengths to develop good capital budgeting proposals. For example, the executive vice-president of one major corporation indicated that his company takes the following steps to generate projects:

*Our R&D department is constantly searching for new products or for ways to improve existing products. In addition, our Executive Committee, which consists of senior executives in marketing, production, and finance, identifies the products and markets in which our company will compete, and the Committee sets long-run targets for each division. These targets, which are formalized in the corporate budget, provide a general guide to the operating executives who must meet them. These executives then seek new products, set expansion plans for existing products, and look for ways to reduce production and distribution costs. Since bonuses and promotions are based in large part on each unit's ability to meet or exceed its targets, these economic incentives encourage our operating executives to seek profitable investment opportunities.*

*Although our senior executives are judged and rewarded on the basis of how well their units perform, people further down the line are given bonuses for specific suggestions, including ideas that lead to profitable investments. Additionally, a percentage of our corporate profit is set aside for distribution to nonexecutive employees. Our objective is to encourage lower-level workers to keep on the lookout for good ideas, including those that lead to capital investments.*

## Project Classification

If the firm has capable and imaginative executives and employees, and if its incentive system is working properly, its personnel will advance many ideas for capital investment. Because only some ideas will be worth pursuing, project-screening procedures must be established. The first step in this screening process is to assemble a list of the proposed new investments, together with the data necessary to evaluate them.

A careful capital expenditure analysis can yield benefits, but such an evaluation is expensive. For certain types of projects, a refined analysis may be warranted; for others, cost–benefit studies will suggest a simpler procedure. Accordingly, firms frequently classify projects into the following categories:

1. *Replacement—Maintenance of Business:* Investments necessary to replace worn-out or damaged equipment;
2. *Replacement—Cost Reduction:* Investments to replace working, but obsolete, equipment;
3. *Expansion of Existing Products or Markets:* Investments to increase output of existing products or to expand outlets or distribution facilities in markets now being served;
4. *Expansion into New Products or Markets:* Investments necessary to produce a new product or to expand into a geographic area not currently served;
5. *Safety and Environmental:* Investments necessary to comply with government requirements, labor agreements, or risk-management objectives.
6. *Other:* A catch-all for investments that do not fall in one of the other categories.

Ordinarily, maintenance-type replacement decisions are the simplest to make. Assets wear out and become obsolete, and they must be replaced to continue production. The firm has a very good idea of the cost savings it obtains by replacing an old asset, and it knows the consequences of nonreplacement. Relatively simple calculations and only a few supporting documents are required for these investment decisions in profitable plants. More detailed analysis is required for cost-reducing replacements, for expansion of existing product lines, and for investments into new products or areas. Also, within each category, projects are broken down by their dollar costs: the larger the required investment, the more detailed the analysis and the higher the level of the officer who must authorize the expenditure. Thus, although a plant manager may be authorized to approve maintenance expenditures up to $10,000 on the basis of a rather limited analysis, the full board of directors may have to approve decisions that involve amounts over $1 million or expansions into new products or markets. A very detailed, refined analysis must support these latter decisions. Investments in the *Safety and Environmental* and *Other* categories are frequently treated separately from the regular capital budget because of the complexities involved in their evaluation.

## Estimating Cash Flows

**cash flow**

Cash receipts and expenditures.

The most important and often the most difficult step in capital expenditure analysis is estimating the **cash flow** associated with the project: the outflow for building and equipping the new facility and the annual cash inflows that the project will produce after it goes into operation. A great many variables influence the cash flow forecast, and many individuals and departments participate in developing it.

## 16.1  **Managerial Application**

3M: Masters of Innovation

Inventions and innovations flow out of the Minnesota Mining and Manufacturing (3M) research facilities at the rate of more than 200 per year. Many of these are modest improvements on already established products such as masking tape, coatings for highway reflectors, and sandpaper. Some are entirely new products, such as the yellow "Post-it" pads that have quickly become popular in offices everywhere. In all, the company makes more than 60,000 products that produce roughly $12 billion per year in worldwide revenues, half of which comes from abroad. 3M employs roughly 6,000 scientists and engineers, primarily in chemistry and applied science. The company is highly regarded by stock market investors and typically rates near the top of *Fortune* magazine's annual survey of the most admired corporations in America. How does 3M manage to keep innovation alive and profitable in such a large and necessarily bureaucratic organization?

Most importantly, 3M keeps its research organization relatively decentralized. Clearly defined information channels ensure that information percolates quickly and effectively from the shop floor to top management. The company depends on researchers who are close to the technology, and marketing personnel who are close to customers, to keep it informed about the performance of current products and the potential for new ones. Researchers are encouraged to spend 15 percent of their time on basic research, pursuing projects that may only pay off for the company several years in the future. To further encourage new-product introductions, each division is expected to generate 25 percent of its total annual sales from products introduced during the most recent five-year period.

*continued*

See: Russell Mitchell, "Masters of Innovation," *Business Week*, April 10, 1989, 58–63.

Although estimating cash flows for capital budgeting analysis is a difficult task, a number of key relationships help ensure an appropriate effort in this area of the capital budgeting process. First, cash flows must be constructed on an incremental basis. Only cash flows that will differ with acceptance or rejection of the project are relevant to the analysis. Second, care must be taken to include *all* incremental cash flows, including revenue and cost changes for other activities of the firm that a particular capital investment would affect. A new product's effect on the sales revenue of an existing product is an example of a frequently important

**Managerial Application** *continued*

Research and marketing personnel work closely together to shepherd each invention and innovation from the point of discovery through design and development to successful market introduction. Typically, this process takes several years. In the case of Post-it notes, for example, the design and development process took six years. This process can be shortened considerably. Some tape products take only a year to emerge. One such product that currently has 3M very excited is the first videocassette tape for Super VHS video recorders. The 3M tape improves video picture resolution by capturing 400 lines of broadcast information, versus the current industry standard of 230 lines. The company is betting that this product will gain rapid market acceptance and become the industry standard by the early 1990s.

In addition to the new product and process development, 3M depends on its research labs to protect the company from competitors' encroachment in already established markets. In 1980, for example, 3M developed the first water-activated synthetic casting tape for setting broken bones. By 1982, however, several other companies had introduced competing products. When 3M researchers found that some of these products were easier to use and had other advantages over the 3M product, they incorporated these features and other innovations in an improved 3M casting tape that is stronger and easier to use. Similarly, 3M's continuing review of existing products recently discovered a radiation leakage from a line of air ionizers used to remove dust particles from the air in factories and other industrial work settings. Rather than risk damage to its valuable reputation, the company recalled the product, despite the fact that the product posed no recognizable health hazard.

Finally, it is interesting to note that the company's R&D budget was spared when profits took an unexpected 9.5 percent downturn in 1985, partly because of the damage to 3M's overseas business from a strong dollar. Despite vigorous cost-cutting throughout the company, R&D actually rose from 4.5 percent to more than 6.5 percent of sales, more than twice the U.S. average. Obviously, the company continues to regard innovation and high standards of product quality as the bedrock of its current business, and the key to its future success.

indirect cash flow. Third, cash flows should be constructed on an after-tax basis. Fourth, depreciation should not be included among the relevant cash flows—except to account for its effect on taxes—as it is a noncash expense.

We cannot in this book fully develop the techniques and methodologies for cash flow analysis, but an examination of Tables 16.1 and 16.2 will provide an idea of what is entailed.

Table 16.1 summarizes the outlay required for an investment project to construct a facility to manufacture a new product. A total outlay of

■ Table 16.1
## Estimated Investment Requirements for Project *X*

| Capital Investment | 1995 | 1996 | 1997 | 1998 | Total |
|---|---|---|---|---|---|
| *Capital* | | | | | |
| 1. Land | $          0 | $          0 | $          0 | $          0 | $          0 |
| 2. Land improvements | 0 | 0 | 0 | 0 | 0 |
| 3. Buildings | 300,000 | 700,000 | 0 | 0 | 1,000,000 |
| 4. Process equipment | 900,000 | 1,500,000 | 0 | 0 | 2,400,000 |
| 5. Mobile equipment | 0 | 100,000 | 0 | 0 | 100,000 |
| 6. Subtotal | $1,200,000 | $2,300,000 | 0 | 0 | $3,500,000 |
| *Working Capital* | | | | | |
| 7. Accounts receivable | $          0 | $  652,500 | $238,500 | $  86,000 | $  977,000 |
| 8. Raw materials inventory | 0 | 107,500 | 52,500 | 19,000 | 179,000 |
| 9. Goods in process | 0 | 170,000 | 39,000 | 47,000 | 256,000 |
| 10. Finished materials inventory | 0 | 232,500 | 45,500 | 17,000 | 295,000 |
| 11. Operating materials and supplies | 0 | 140,500 | 12,000 | 5,000 | 157,500 |
| 12. Payables/accruals | (0) | (270,000) | (72,500) | (22,000) | (364,500) |
| 13. Net working capital | $          0 | $1,033,000 | $315,000 | $152,000 | $1,500,000 |
| Total investment (lines 6 + 13) | $1,200,000 | $3,333,000 | $315,000 | $152,000 | $5,000,000 |

$5 million is necessary—$3.5 million for land, buildings, and equipment and $1.5 million for the net investment in working capital. These expenditures will be incurred over the four years from 1995 to 1998. The plant will be constructed and equipped in 1995 and 1996, and working capital will be built up during 1996, 1997, and 1998. Since we are dealing only with cash flows and their timing, not discounted present values, the total investment outlay of $5 million is expressed in nominal dollars. In evaluating real-world investment projects, the total amount of required investment would be discounted using an appropriate cost of capital and expressed in present-value terms. Assuming investment at the beginning of each period, the present value of the total investment in this example would be expressed as $4.6 million if discounted at 10 percent, $4.5 million discounted at 12 percent, and $4.4 million discounted at 15 percent. Similarly, net cash flows for each investment period would be evaluated in present-value terms.

Table 16.2 shows a series of income statements detailing the expected cash flows during certain years of the project's anticipated 15-year life. Beginning with sales revenues, the various types of expenses and taxes are deducted to produce the net income expected from the project, as shown on the third line from the bottom. These incremental profits are before all financing charges; the cost of the capital to finance the investment project is accounted for when the cash flows are evaluated. Depre-

■ Table 16.2
## Cash Flow Analysis for Project *X*

| | Estimated Profits and Cash Flows | | | | | |
|---|---|---|---|---|---|---|
| | **1996** | **1997** | **1998** | **1999** | **2009** | **2010** |
| Gross sales, dollars | $4,336,000 | $5,203,000 | $5,781,000 | $5,781,000 | Years 2000 through 2008 not shown here | $5,781,000 | $5,781,000 |
| Less: Freight | (44,000) | (52,000) | (58,000) | (58,000) | (58,000) | (58,000) |
| Cash discounts | (17,000) | (21,000) | (23,000) | (23,000) | (23,000) | (23,000) |
| Total deductions | (61,000) | (73,000) | (81,000) | (81,000) | (81,000) | (81,000) |
| Net sales | $4,275,000 | $5,130,000 | $5,700,000 | $5,700,000 | $5,700,000 | $5,700,000 |
| Cost of sales | | | | | | |
| Variable | $2,223,000 | $2,736,000 | $3,078,000 | $3,078,000 | $3,078,000 | $3,078,000 |
| Fixed, excluding depreciation and depletion | 342,000 | 342,000 | 342,000 | 342,000 | 342,000 | 342,000 |
| Break-in costs | 333,000 | 137,000 | — | — | — | — |
| Total | 2,898,000 | 3,215,000 | 3,420,000 | 3,420,000 | 3,420,000 | 3,420,000 |
| Depreciation | 425,000 | 650,000 | 615,000 | 605,000 | 0 | 0 |
| Total cost of sales | $3,323,500 | $3,865,000 | $4,035,000 | $4,025,000 | $3,420,000 | $3,420,000 |
| Gross profit | $ 952,000 | $1,265,000 | $1,665,000 | $1,675,000 | $2,280,000 | $2,280,000 |
| Selling expenses | 228,000 | 228,000 | 228,000 | 228,000 | 228,000 | 228,000 |
| Advertising | 124,000 | 100,000 | 86,000 | 86,000 | 86,000 | 86,000 |
| Administrative | 285,000 | 285,000 | 285,000 | 285,000 | 285,000 | 285,000 |
| Provision for bad debts | 25,500 | 29,800 | 32,600 | 32,600 | 32,600 | 32,600 |
| Total: Selling and administrative | 662,500 | 642,800 | 631,600 | 631,600 | 631,600 | 631,600 |
| Net income before tax | 289,500 | 622,200 | 1,033,400 | 1,043,400 | 1,648,400 | 1,648,400 |
| Income tax (@ 34 percent) | 98,430 | 211,548 | 351,356 | 354,756 | 560,456 | 560,456 |
| Net income | 191,070 | 410,652 | 682,044 | 688,644 | 1,087,944 | 1,087,944 |
| Depreciation | 425,000 | 650,000 | 615,000 | 605,000 | 0 | 0 |
| Net cash flow | $ 616,070 | $1,060,652 | $1,297,044 | $1,293,644 | $1,087,944 | $1,087,944 |

| | |
|---|---|
| Salvage value, buildings, and machines = | 0 |
| Recovery of working capital | = $1,500,000 |
| Net cash flow, Year 15 | = $2,587,944 |

ciation, which is not a cash outlay, is added to profits to produce the bottom-line figures, the net cash flows from the project.[1]

[1]If the treatment of depreciation is not clear, recognize that net sales represent cash received and that all expenses *except depreciation* represent cash outlays during the year. In the first year, the project is expected to generate cash from net sales of $4,275,000 and to incur cash costs for taxes and all expenses shown except depreciation. Thus, $4,275,000 cash from net sales minus cash costs totaling $2,898,000 + $662,500 = $3,560,500 minus $98,430 income taxes equals $616,070. The $616,070 cash flow is, of course, also equal to net income after taxes plus depreciation.

The new plant will go into service in 1996, and it is expected to generate a net cash flow of $616,070 in that year. Cash flows are expected to climb during the next two years as the plant is broken in and the market develops, but to decline thereafter because of rising taxes caused by declining deductions for depreciation.[2]

## NET PRESENT VALUE ANALYSIS

Once cash flow estimates for a proposed investment have been generated, an evaluation must be performed to determine the worth of the project to the firm.[3] Although several methods are used to rank projects and decide whether to accept them, the economically sound approaches are all based on the discounted present value concept. Recall from Chapter 15 the basic valuation model of the firm:

$$\text{Value} = \sum_{t=1}^{n} \pi_t/(1 + k)^t$$

$$= \sum_{t=1}^{n} \frac{\text{Total Revenue}_t - \text{Total Cost}_t}{(1 + k)^t} = \sum_{t=1}^{n} \frac{\text{Net Cash Flow}_t}{(1 + k)^t}. \quad \textbf{16.1}$$

In this equation, Net Cash Flow$_t$ represents the firm's total after-tax profit plus noncash expenses such as depreciation, and $k$, which is based on an appraisal of the firm's overall riskiness, represents the average cost of capital to the firm. The value of the firm is simply the discounted present value of the difference between total cash inflows and total cash outflows. Any investment project is desirable if it increases the firm's net present value, and undesirable if accepting it causes the firm's net present value to decrease.

---

[2]The firm in our example uses accelerated depreciation for tax calculations. This causes depreciation charges (a noncash expense) to be high early in the project's life and lower later on. The high initial depreciation results in lower tax payments, hence higher cash flows during the early years.

Two other points are worth mentioning here. First, the question of what happens to the cash flows shown at the bottom of Table 16.2 can be raised. The answer is that they are available for payment of dividends and interest on capital and for reinvestment in other projects. The second point has to do with the recovery of working capital. Some amount of working capital—cash, receivables, inventories less trade credit (accounts payable), and other accruals—must be held to support sales. In the example, $1.5 million is the investment in working capital, and this investment must be maintained as long as the operations continue. Thus the $1.5 million will be needed until 2010, the year the project is expected to end. As operations are phased out during that year, inventories will be worked down, receivables will be collected without creating new ones because sales will cease, and the cash balances to operate the plant will no longer be needed. Thus, during 2010, the $1.5 million of working capital will be recovered and presumably paid to providers of capital (debt and equity) or reinvested elsewhere in the company.

[3]A knowledge of compound interest is necessary to understand this evaluation. Students who have not covered compound interest in other courses or who could use a review should read through the relevant sections of Appendix A.

The use of net present value analysis in capital budgeting involves the application of the present value model described in Equation 16.1 to individual projects rather than to the firm as a whole. In brief, the procedure is as follows:

1. Estimate the project's expected net cash flows. Depending on the nature of the project, these estimates will have a greater or lesser degree of risk. For example, the benefits from replacing a piece of equipment used to produce a stable, established product can be estimated more accurately than those from an investment in equipment to produce a new and untried product.

2. Estimate the expected cost, or investment outlay, of the project. This cost estimate will be quite accurate for purchased equipment, since cost equals the invoice price plus delivery and installation charges. Cost estimates for other kinds of projects may be highly uncertain or speculative.

**cost of capital**

A firm's cost of money; the appropriate discount rate for capital budgeting.

3. Determine an appropriate discount rate, or **cost of capital,** for the project. The cost of capital is considered in detail later in this chapter, but for now it may be thought of as being determined by the riskiness of the project—that is, by the uncertainty of the expected cash flows and the investment outlay.

4. Find the present value of the expected cash flows and subtract from this figure the estimated cost of the project.[4] The resulting figure is the **net present value (*NPV*)** of the project. If the *NPV* is greater than zero, the project should be accepted; if it is less than zero, the project should be rejected. In equation form:

**net present value (*NPV*)**

The expected cash flows of a project, discounted back to the present using an appropriate cost of capital, minus the estimated cost of the project.

$$NPV_i = \sum_{t=1}^{n} \frac{E(CF_{it})}{(1 + k_i)^t} - C_i, \qquad \textbf{16.2}$$

where $NPV_i$ is the *NPV* of the *i*th project, $E(CF_{it})$ represents the expected net cash flows of the *i*th project in the *t*th year, $k_i$ is the risk-adjusted discount rate applicable to the *i*th project, and $C_i$ is the project's investment outlay, or cost.

## *NPV* as an Application of Marginal Analysis

To see that accepting only investment projects with positive net present values is in fact an application of the marginal analysis illustrated in Figure 16.1, consider briefly the determination of the yield, or internal

---

[4]If costs are spread over several years, this fact must be taken into account. Suppose, for example, that a firm bought land in 1995, erected a building in 1996, installed equipment in 1997, and started production in 1998. One could treat 1995 as the base year, comparing the present value of the costs to the present value of the benefit stream as of that same date. Throughout this chapter, "cost" figures should be thought of as the present values of any costs that are incurred over time.

**internal rate of return**
**(IRR)**

The discount rate that equates the present value of the future returns from a project to the initial cost.

rate of return, on an investment. The **internal rate of return** is defined as that interest or discount rate that equates the present value of the future receipts of a project to the initial cost or outlay. The equation for calculating the internal rate of return is simply the *NPV* formula set equal to zero:

$$NPV_i = \sum_{t=1}^{n} \frac{E(CF_{it})}{(1 + k_i^*)^t} - C_i = 0. \qquad \textbf{16.3}$$

Here the equation is solved for the discount rate, $k_i^*$, that produces a zero net present value or causes the sum of the discounted future receipts to equal the initial cost. That discount rate is the internal rate of return earned by the project.

Because the net present value equation is a complex polynomial, it is difficult to solve for the actual internal rate of return on an investment without a computer or sophisticated calculator. For this reason trial-and-error is sometimes employed. One begins by arbitrarily selecting a discount rate. If it yields a positive *NPV*, then the internal rate of return must be greater than the interest or discount rate used, and another *higher* rate is tried. If the chosen rate yields a negative *NPV*, this implies that the internal rate of return on the project is lower than the discount rate, and the *NPV* calculation must be repeated using a *lower* discount rate. This process of changing the discount rate and recalculating the net present value continues until the discounted present value of the future cash flows equals the initial cost. The interest rate that brings about this equality is the yield, or internal rate of return on the project.[5]

Now consider again the decision rule that states that a firm should accept only projects with positive net present values when the firm's risk-adjusted cost of capital, $k_i$, is used as the discount rate. In this model, $k_i$, the risk-adjusted discount factor, is the firm's marginal cost of capital and is, therefore, the rate of interest that it must pay on the funds to invest in a project. As we have seen from the calculation of internal rates of return or yields on an investment, if the net present value of a project, calculated using the firm's cost of capital as the discount rate, is positive, this implies that the rate of return on the project is greater than the cost of capital. Likewise, if the *NPV* is negative, the implication is that the internal rate of return is less than the cost of capital. Thus the *NPV* decision technique (which limits acceptable projects to those whose net present values, using $k_i$ as the discount rate, are positive) is

---

[5]This trial-and-error procedure is a bit tedious if done by hand for a project that extends over a long time horizon. Computers and inexpensive hand-held calculators can easily provide accurate discount rates very rapidly, however, and thus the computational side of calculating internal rates of return presents no difficulty for capital budgeting analysis.

based essentially on a comparison of the marginal cost of capital and the marginal yield, or return on the investment.

## Illustration of the *NPV* Technique

To illustrate the *NPV* evaluation technique, assume that Oakdale Instruments, Inc., has two investment opportunities, each costing $100,000 and each having the expected profits shown in Table 16.3.

Let us further assume that the cost of each project is known with certainty but that the expected cash flows of Project *B* are riskier than those of Project *A*. After due consideration of the risks inherent in each project, management has determined that *A* should be evaluated with a 10-percent cost of capital and the riskier Project *B* with a 15-percent cost of capital.

Equation 16.2 can be restated as Equation 16.4, using Project *A* as an example:

$$
\begin{aligned}
NPV_A &= \sum_{t=1}^{n} \frac{E(CF_{At})}{(1 + k_A)^t} - C_A \\
&= \left[ \frac{E(CF_{A1})}{(1 + k_A)^1} + \frac{E(CF_{A2})}{(1 + k_A)^2} + \frac{E(CF_{A3})}{(1 + k_A)^3} + \frac{E(CF_{A4})}{(1 + k_A)^4} \right] - C_A \\
&= \left[ E(CF_{A1}) \left( \frac{1}{1 + k_A} \right)^1 + E(CF_{A2}) \left( \frac{1}{1 + k_A} \right)^2 + E(CF_{A3}) \left( \frac{1}{1 + k_A} \right)^3 \right. \\
&\quad \left. + E(CF_{A4}) \left( \frac{1}{1 + k_A} \right)^4 \right] - C_A \\
&= [E(CF_{A1}) (PVIF_{A1}) + E(CF_{A2}) (PVIF_{A2}) + E(CF_{A3}) (PVIF_{A3}) \\
&\quad + E(CF_{A4}) (PVIF_{A4})] - C_A.
\end{aligned}
$$

**16.4**

Values for the present value interest factors, the *PVIF* terms, are found in Appendix B. For example, $PVIF_{A1}$, the interest factor for the present value of $1 due in one year discounted at 10 percent, is 0.909; $PVIF_{A2}$, the interest factor for the present value of $1 received in two years discounted at 10 percent, is 0.826; and so on.

■ Table 16.3

## Expected Cash Flows from Projects *A* and *B*

| Year | A | B |
| --- | --- | --- |
| 1 | $50,000 | $20,000 |
| 2 | 40,000 | 40,000 |
| 3 | 30,000 | 50,000 |
| 4 | 10,000 | 60,000 |

# 16.2  **Managerial Application**

Effective Capital Budgeting for the 1990s

Corporate managements today face the serious challenge of adding value to the businesses they manage. Historically, when management thought about competition, it considered the effects of actual and potential competitors in current or future product markets. Today, management must be concerned with yet another type of competition—competition in the market for corporate control.

Stock market prices reflect the discounted net present value of a company's expected future cash flows. To the extent that management gets full value out of the assets under its control, the firm's stock price will maintain its maximum potential value. If management gets less than full value out of its assets, the stock price will be lower than its full potential value. In the rapidly changing economic environment of the 1980s, a number of companies could not achieve the synergistic and other benefits of conglomerate businesses. Similarly, the weakened control that can result when management tries to oversee a large portfolio of companies led to underutilization of corporate resources. As a result, many such firms were bought out by competitors and other outside "raiders" at high stock-price premiums. Radically restructured, they emerged as leaner, more focused, and more profitable companies. The increased stock market values made possible by higher profitability allowed both selling stockholders and buying firms or individuals to benefit from this restructuring—win-win situations for investors but not for displaced managements.

To meet the need for efficient resource utilization, managements have increasingly incorporated modern financial theory in a

*continued*

See: Walter Kiechel III, "Corporate Strategy for the 1990s," *Fortune*, February 29, 1988, 34–42.

Results of Equation 16.4 for both projects appear in tabular form in Table 16.4. Project *A*'s NPV is $8,000 and Project *B*'s is $15,000. Since both projects have positive NPVs, both earn rates of return in excess of their costs of capital; the marginal rate of return is greater than the marginal cost of capital, in the sense of Figure 16.1. If the two projects are independent, they should both be accepted, because each adds more to the value of the firm than its cost. Project *A* increases the value of the firm by $8,000 over what that value would be without the project. Project *B* increases the firm's value by $15,000. If the projects are mutually

**Managerial Application** *continued*

"value-based planning" approach to capital budgeting. Value-based planning presumes that the purpose of any investment or managerial decision is to increase the value of the firm as measured by the current market price of the company's common stock. Given the typically close relation between stock prices and cash flow data, corporate management has increasingly evaluated the profitability of investment proposals on the basis of their ability to generate net or "free" cash flows (cash flows minus investment requirements). This contrasts with more traditional approaches that focus on the effects on accounting earnings of alternative investments and managerial decisions. Attention has shifted from accounting earnings to cash flows and stock prices because some believe that accounting earnings data sometimes obscure, rather than reflect, the true economic performance of the firm. To increase the value of the firm, value-based capital budgeting simply emphasizes projects with the potential to generate maximum cash flows. These flows can then either be profitably reinvested or paid out to shareholders as dividends or stock repurchases. In either event, the maximum positive impact on the market value of the firm is achieved.

Of course, discounted cash flow analysis and cost-of-capital calculations have long been a standard tool for capital budgeting. However, with better data than ever before and powerful low-cost computing resources, the technique now achieves highly detailed levels of analysis. What is different with value-based planning in the current corporate environment is that *NPV* techniques are being increasingly applied to each separate line of business, investment, and product. Not only is the method useful for sifting the "keepers" among current products and lines of business from the "castoffs," but it also forces companies to keep in focus what Robert D. Kennedy, CEO of Union Carbide, calls the "unthinkable boundary condition." That is, "Should I sell this business? Should I buy another?"

According to Walker Lewis, chairman of the consulting firm Strategic Planning Associates, the most important task of management is to aggressively invest corporate funds. In the short-run, management must clean and prune the business to keep it lean, hungry, and efficient. In the long-run, it must carefully manage the capital budgeting process to maintain and build the core strengths of the corporation.

exclusive, *B* should be selected, because it adds more to the firm's value than *A*.

Some firms use the internal rate of return (*IRR*) approach for selecting capital investment projects rather than the *NPV* method. Under the *IRR* criterion, projects are ranked according to their *IRRs*, and projects with *IRRs* in excess of the appropriate risk-adjusted discount rate (cost of capital) are accepted. Although the *IRR* and *NPV* methods will lead to the same accept–reject decision for an individual project, they can give contradictory signals concerning choices between mutually exclusive

■ Table 16.4
**Calculating the Net Present Value (*NPV*) of Two Projects**

| Year | Expected Cash Flow | *PVIF* (10%) | PV of Cash Flow | Year | Expected Cash Flow | *PVIF* (15%) | PV of Cash Flow |
|------|------|------|------|------|------|------|------|
| 1 | $50,000 | 0.91 | $ 45,500 | 1 | $20,000 | 0.87 | $ 17,400 |
| 2 | 40,000 | 0.83 | 33,200 | 2 | 40,000 | 0.76 | 30,400 |
| 3 | 30,000 | 0.75 | 22,500 | 3 | 50,000 | 0.66 | 33,000 |
| 4 | 10,000 | 0.68 | 6,800 | 4 | 60,000 | 0.57 | 34,200 |
| | PV | | $108,000 | | PV | | $115,000 |
| | Less cost | | − 100,000 | | Less cost | | − 100,000 |
| | $NPV_A$ | | $ 8,000 | | $NPV_B$ | | $ 15,000 |

projects. That is, a given investment project might have a higher *IRR* but a lower *NPV* than an alternative project. This problem arises because the *IRR* is the implied reinvestment rate for cash flows under the *IRR* method, whereas the discount (and implied reinvestment) rate used in the *NPV* method is the firm's cost of capital. If the *IRR* for a project is very different from the cost of capital, these differing reinvestment rates can lead to differences in project ranking. In most situations, reinvestment of cash flows at a rate close to the cost of capital is more realistic; therefore, the *NPV* method is generally superior.

## OTHER ISSUES IN PROJECT EVALUATION

Ordinarily, firms operate as illustrated in Figure 16.1 and make investments up to the point where the marginal return from investment just equals the marginal cost of capital. Firms typically make investments having positive net present values, reject those with negative net present values, and choose between mutually exclusive investments on the basis of higher net present values. For many capital budgeting problems, however, the use of the *NPV* method is far more complex than the preceding description suggests. For example, the capital budgeting problem may require analysis of mutually exclusive projects with different expected lives or with substantially different initial costs. Under these conditions, the simple *NPV* approach may not select projects that maximize the value of the firm.

A complication also arises when the size of the firm's capital budget is limited. Capital rationing, as it is called, stems from a number of factors. It is sometimes a fallacy to consider that what is true of the individual parts will be true of the whole. Although individual projects might promise relatively attractive yields, combining them can create unforeseen difficulties. For example, undertaking a large number of projects simultaneously can require a very fast rate of expansion. Additional personnel requirements and organizational problems can arise that diminish overall rates of return. At some point in the capital budgeting process, management must decide what total volume of favorable projects the firm can successfully undertake without significantly reducing projected returns.

Another reason for limiting the capital budget at some firms is reluctance to engage in external financing by issuing debt or selling stock. One management, considering the plight of firms with substantial amounts of debt during economic recessions, may simply refuse to use debt financing. Another may have no objection to selling debt but may not wish to sell equity capital for fear of losing some measure of control. Still others may refuse to use any form of outside financing, considering safety and control to be more important than additional profits. Such capital rationing complicates the capital budgeting process and requires more complex tools of analysis.

## Profitability Index, or Benefit/Cost Ratio Analysis

**profitability index (*PI*)**
The benefit/cost ratio method of capital budget analysis.

A variant of *NPV* analysis that is often used in complex capital budgeting situations is called the **profitability index,** or the benefit/cost ratio method. The profitability index (*PI*) is calculated as:

$$PI = \frac{\text{PV of Cash Flows}}{\text{Cost}} = \frac{\sum_{t=1}^{n} [E(CF_{it})/(1 + k_i)^t]}{C_i}.$$   **16.5**

The *PI* shows the *relative* profitability of any project, or the present value of benefits per dollar of cost.

In *PI* analysis, a project with *PI* > 1 should be accepted, and a project with *PI* < 1 should be rejected. This means that projects will be accepted provided they return more than a dollar of discounted benefits for each dollar of cost. Thus, the *PI* and *NPV* methods always indicate the same accept–reject decisions for independent projects, since *PI* > 1 implies *NPV* > 0 and *PI* < 1 implies *NPV* < 0. However, for alternative projects of unequal size, *PI* and *NPV* criteria can give different project ranking. This can sometimes cause problems when mutually exclusive projects are being evaluated.

Table 16.5 shows *PI* and *NPV* values for two mutually exclusive projects of unequal size. The calculation of present value of cash flows for Project *B* was shown earlier in Table 16.4, and a similar calculation for Project *C* was performed. Note that the investment cost of *B* is $100,000, whereas the investment cost for *C* is $150,000. Since each project has *PI* > 1 and *NPV* > 0, both would be acceptable under either criterion. However, these projects will be ranked differently by the *PI* or *NPV* methods. Using the *PI* criterion, we would select Project *B* first. If we compute the ratio of the present value of the returns (or benefits) of each

■ Table 16.5

## Comparison of *PI* and *NPV* Rankings of Projects with Unequal Costs

|  | Project *B* | Project *C* |
|---|---|---|
| PV Cash Flow @ k = 15% | $115,000 | $170,000 |
| Cost | $100,000 | $150,000 |
| $PI = \dfrac{\text{PV Cash Flow}}{\text{Cost}}$ | 1.15 | 1.13 |
| NPV = PV Cash Flow − Cost | $ 15,000 | $ 20,000 |

project to its cost, we find *B*'s *PI* ratio to be $115,000/$100,000 = 1.15 and *C*'s ratio to be $170,000/$150,000 = 1.13. Thus, by *PI* ranking, we would select Project *B* because it produces higher discounted net returns per dollar invested. On the other hand, ranking by *NPV* would suggest selection of Project *C* before Project *B*. The *NPV* of *C* is $170,000 − $150,000 = $20,000, and the *NPV* of *B* is $115,000 − $100,000 = $15,000. Project *C* is preferable according to the *NPV* criterion because it provides the larger discounted net benefit.

Given this conflict, which project ranking method should be adopted? Alternatively stated: Is it better to use the net present value approach on an absolute basis (*NPV*) or on a relative basis (*PI*)? For a firm with substantial investment resources and a goal of maximizing shareholder wealth, the *NPV* method is better. For a firm with limited resources, however, the *PI* approach allocates scarce resources to the projects with the greatest relative effect on value. Using the *PI* method, projects are evaluated on the basis of their *NPV* per dollar of investment, avoiding a possible bias toward larger projects. In some cases, this leads to a better combination of investment projects and higher firm value. The *PI*, or benefit/cost ratio, approach has also proved to be a useful tool in public-sector decision making, where allocating scarce public resources among competing projects is a typical problem.

## STEPS IN THE CAPITAL BUDGETING PROCESS

The capital budgeting decision process has extensive information requirements. In fact, almost all of the topics covered in this book must be brought to bear on important capital budgeting decisions. Demand functions, production functions, and cost functions must all be estimated and analyzed. Market structures may have to be appraised, both to determine how competitors are likely to react to major decisions and to assess the antitrust implications of particular courses of action. Antitrust analysis is especially important if the action involves an investment in another firm or a joint venture with another company. Regulated firms are subject to special problems in their long-term investment programs, and almost all manufacturing companies consider the costs and benefits of various means for meeting pollution-control and worker health and safety requirements.

## Demand Forecasts

The first step in most capital budgeting decisions is estimating future demand. The need for this step is obvious in expansion decisions, but it is also a vital part of replacement, modernization, and pollution-control investments. A worn-out machine should not be replaced unless demand for its output will continue for some time into the future; a plant should be closed rather than equipped to control pollution if demand for the plant's output is weak.

## Cost Forecasts

Once the demand function has been estimated, the next step is to determine the operating cost function. This procedure frequently involves knowledge of production theory, input factor markets, and statistical cost estimation. Also, although we do not take up these considerations in this chapter, accurate cost analysis depends heavily on such accounting-based topics as depreciation, inventory valuation procedures, and tax considerations.

## Cash Flow Forecasts

The third step in the process is to integrate demand and cost relations to determine the optimal output level and the expected annual cash flows resulting from operation at this output. Many firms have set up systems to generate the data necessary for thorough analyses of options, and many of them construct simulation models, with demand and cost functions as key components, to evaluate major investment proposals.

## Cost of Capital

Determining the firm's cost of capital to set the appropriate discount rate is an essential part of the capital budgeting process. The cost of capital is a complex subject and is discussed in detail in finance courses; thorough treatment of the topic is beyond the scope of this book. Accordingly, we shall merely summarize some of the important elements of the cost-of-capital theory as it is developed in finance.

Firms raise funds in many forms, including long-term and short-term debt, preferred and common stock, retained earnings, and lease financing. Each source of funds has a cost, and these costs are the basic inputs in the cost of capital determination.

Capital is a necessary factor of production, and like any other factor, it has a cost. The cost of each type of capital employed by the firm is called the *component cost* of that particular capital. For example, if a firm can borrow money at 10-percent interest, the component cost of debt is 10 percent. Although firms obtain capital funds through many financial instruments, we concentrate on debt and equity capital components in this discussion of capital costs. These are the major capital resource categories, and limiting our discussion to them will enable us to examine the basic cost-of-capital concept without getting mired down in financial, accounting, and legal detail.

**component cost of debt**
The interest rate that investors require on debt issues, adjusted for taxes.

**Cost of Debt**   The **component cost of debt** is based on the interest rate that investors require on debt issues, adjusted for taxes. If a firm borrows $100,000 for one year at 10 percent interest, its before-tax dollar cost is $10,000, and its before-tax percentage cost is 10 percent. However, interest payments on debt are deductible for income tax purposes. It is necessary to account for this tax deductibility by adjusting the cost of debt to an after-tax basis. The deductibility of interest payments means, in effect, that the government pays part of a firm's interest charges. This reduces the cost of debt capital as follows:

After-tax Component Cost of Debt = (Interest Rate) × (1.0 − Tax Rate).

Assuming that the firm's marginal federal-plus-state tax rate is 50 percent, the after-tax cost of debt will be one-half the interest rate.

Note that the cost of debt applies only to *new* debt, not to the interest on old, previously outstanding debt. In other words, we are interested in the cost of new debt, or the *marginal cost of debt*. The primary importance of the cost of capital is its effect on the decision about whether to obtain capital to make new investments. The fact that the firm borrowed at high or low rates in the past is irrelevant.

**component cost of equity**
The rate of return that stockholders require on a firm's common stock.

**Cost of Equity**   The **component cost of equity** is defined as the rate of return stockholders require on a firm's common stock. Because dividends paid to stockholders are not deductible for income tax purposes (dividend payments must be made with after-tax dollars), there is no tax adjustment for the component cost of equity capital.

Although empirical estimation of the cost of equity capital is a complex and often difficult process, most methods are based on one of two relatively simple concepts. The first of these is that the cost of capital of a risky security such as a common stock consists of a riskless rate of return ($R_F$) plus a risk premium ($R_P$):

$$k_e = R_F + R_P.$$

The risk-free return is typically taken to be the interest rate on short-term U.S. government securities. Various procedures are available for estimating $R_P$ for different securities.

One frequently encountered procedure adds a premium of about four to five percentage points to the interest rate on a firm's long-term bonds so that the total risk premium on equity equals the difference between the yield on the firm's debt and that on government bonds *plus* four to five percent. For example, if government bonds yield 8 percent and a firm's bonds yield 10 percent, then cost of equity, $k_e$, would be estimated as:

$$k_e = \text{Firm Bond Rate} + 4\% \text{ to } 5\% \text{ Risk Premium}$$
$$= 10\% + 4\% \text{ to } 5\% = 14\% \text{ to } 15\%.$$

Since

$$k_e = R_F + R_P,$$

where $R_F$ = Yield on Government Bonds = 8 Percent,

$$14\% \text{ to } 15\% = 8\% + R_P$$
$$R_P = 6\% \text{ to } 7\%.$$

Analysts who use this procedure generally cite studies of historical returns on stocks and bonds and take the difference between the average yield (dividends plus capital gains) on stocks and the average yield on bonds as the risk premium of stocks over bonds. The primary difficulties with estimating risk premiums from historical returns are that (1) historical returns differ, depending on the beginning and ending dates of the estimation period, and (2) there is no reason to think that past differences in stock and bond yields precisely indicate future required risk premiums.

A second procedure for estimating $P$ is based on the capital asset pricing model (CAPM). This approach assumes that the risk of a stock depends on the sensitivity of its return to changes in the level of return on all securities in the market.

To use this procedure for estimating the required return on a stock, we proceed as follows:

- *Step 1* Estimate the riskless rate, $R_F$, generally taken to be the rate on short-term U.S. Treasury securities.

- *Step 2* Estimate the stock's risk by calculating the variability of its return relative to variability of return in the capital market as a whole. This risk index, known as the stock's **beta coefficient, β,** is a measure of the risk of one security relative to the average risk in the market, i.e., the risk of the average, stock. Thus, a stock with average risk will have a beta of 1.0; low-risk stocks will have betas less than 1.0; and high-risk stocks will have betas greater than 1.0.[6]

- *Step 3* Estimate the rate of return on the market, or average, stock. This return, $k_M$, provides a benchmark for determining how investors are pricing risk as measured by the betas of individual stocks.

**beta coefficient ($\beta$)**
A measure of the risk of one security relative to the average risk in the stock market.

---

[6]Estimation of betas is a complex task involving regressing returns for a stock on the average return to all securities. Securities analysts and investment advisory services such as *Value Line* publish estimates of betas that can be used for estimating equity capital costs.

## 16.3  **Managerial Application**

Warren Buffett: The Wizard of Omaha

In the fall of 1950, Warren Buffett entered business school at Columbia University, where he studied finance under professor Benjamin Graham. Graham was an early proponent of rational value-based investing techniques, and sought to buy portions (shares) of a business at prices below their "intrinsic value." Stocks were bargains according to Graham if they could be bought for less than two-thirds of their net working capital (current assets minus current liabilities). Graham figured that most companies could be liquidated for at least their net working capital, so a margin of safety was obtained when stocks could be obtained at these discount prices.

In 1956, Buffett returned to Omaha, Nebraska. At age 25, he assembled $105,000 in capital from family members and friends and started the Buffett Partnership Ltd. The partnership was spectacularly successful. Over 13 years, the partnership grew to $100 million in assets, earning a 29.5 percent compounded annual rate of return, and Buffett's stake grew to $25 million. In 1969, Buffett decided to dissolve the partnership and turn his attention to managing Berkshire Hathaway, an operating company he had acquired in 1965.

Operating results for Berkshire have been as impressive as Buffett's earlier stock market performance. When compared with the more typical return of 10 to 15 percent, Berkshire's 57 percent annual rate of return on stockholders' equity is amazing, especially for a widely diversified business that doesn't employ leverage. By mid-1989, the price of Berkshire stock had risen above

*continued*

See: Carol J. Loomis, "The Inside Story of Warren Buffett," *Fortune*, April 11, 1988, 26–34; and Susan Antilla, "Buffett Copycats May Be Buffeted." *USA Today*, March 27, 1989, 6B.

- *Step 4* Estimate the required rate of return on the firm's stock as:

$$k_e = R_F + \beta(k_M - R_F).$$

The value $(k_M - R_F)$ is the risk premium on the average stock. (Recall that the average stock has a beta of 1.0.) Multiplying this price of risk by the index of risk for a particular stock, $\beta$, gives us the risk premium for that stock. To illustrate, assume that $R_F = 9\%$, $k_M = 13\%$, and $\beta = 0.8$ for a given stock. The stock's required return is calculated as follows:

$$k_e = 9 + 0.8(13 - 9) = 9 + 3.2 = 12.2\%.$$

Had $\beta$ been 1.7, indicating that the stock was 70 percent more risky than the average security, $k_e$ would have been estimated as:

**Managerial Application** *continued*

$8,000 per share, roughly 800 times its price when Buffett first took control. Obviously, Buffett is as capable a business manager as he is an investor.

Berkshire's main operating divisions include a large property-and-casualty insurance company; the *Buffalo News* newspaper; Fechheimer Brothers, a Cincinnati uniform manufacturer and distributor; Omaha's Nebraska Furniture Mart; See's Candies in California; and Scott & Fetzer, a holding company that includes World Book, Kirby vacuum cleaners, and a diversified manufacturing concern. All of Berkshire's divisions are in niche businesses that enjoy strong franchises, have above-average returns on equity, have relatively modest needs for capital investment, and have the capacity to generate substantial net free cash flows. Operating managers focus on day-to-day operations and return the excess cash to Omaha. They emphasize what they do best while Buffett spends his time on capital allocation and operating performance evaluation.

At the heart of Berkshire's success is a strategy of shrewd capital allocation. Buffett does not authorize discretionary capital expenditures unless they have direct impacts on economic performance. Cost analysis and control are also important ongoing features of Berkshire's capital budgeting process. Buffett is skeptical of the effectiveness of the periodic cost-cutting programs employed at some companies. He believes that good managers monitor costs continuously. For example, with nearly $3 billion in assets, Berkshire's central office staff in Omaha consists of only 11 employees. Despite a laid-back management style, Buffett watches monthly profit figures very closely. So long as management meets operating goals, they are left alone. However, failure to meet goals receives a quick response.

When asked to summarize the key to success, Buffett merely suggests that one should be careful not to overpay, and only to invest in "good businesses." In an annual report to shareholders, Buffett once wrote: "With few exceptions, when a manager with a reputation for brilliance tackles a business with a reputation for poor fundamental economics, it is the reputation of the business that remains intact."

$$k_e = 9 + 1.7(13 - 9) = 9 + 6.8 = 15.8\%.$$

Yet another procedure for determining the cost of equity is to estimate the basic required rate of return as:[7]

$$\text{Rate of Return} = \frac{\text{Dividend}}{\text{Price}} + \text{Expected Growth Rate,}$$

$$k_e = \frac{D}{P} + g.$$

[7]The growth rate here is the growth in the price of the firm's stock, but if the dividend payout rate is constant and if the dividend capitalization rate (k) remains unchanged, earnings, dividends, and the stock price all grow at the same rate.

The rationale for this equation is that stockholder returns are derived from dividends and capital gains. If past growth rates in earnings and dividends have been relatively stable, and if investors appear to expect a continuation of past trends, then g may be based on the firm's historic growth rate. However, if the company's growth has been abnormally high or low, either because of its own unique situation or because of general economic conditions, then investors will not project the past growth rate into the future. In this case, g must be estimated in some other manner. Security analysts regularly forecast earnings growth by looking at such factors as projected sales, profit margins, and competitive factors. These forecast data can be obtained from *Business Week, Forbes,* or other sources and used as a proxy for the growth expectations of investors in general, then combined with the dividend yield expected during the coming period to estimate $k_e$ as:

$$k_e = \frac{D}{P} + \text{Growth Rate as Projected by Security Analysts.}$$

In practical work, it is best to use all of the previously described methods and then judge between them when they produce different results. People experienced in estimating equity capital costs recognize that both careful analysis and difficult judgments are required.

**Weighted Cost of Capital**   Suppose that a particular firm's after-tax cost of debt is estimated to be 6 percent (the interest rate on new debt issues is 12 percent and the firm's marginal income tax rate is 50 percent), its cost of equity is estimated to be 15 percent, and the firm has decided to finance next year's projects by selling debt. The argument is sometimes advanced that these projects cost 6 percent, because debt will be used to finance them.

This position contains a basic fallacy. In financing a particular set of projects with debt, the firm uses up some of its potential for obtaining new low-cost debt. As expansion takes place in subsequent years, at some point the firm will find it necessary to use additional equity financing or else the debt ratio will become too large. In other words, the interest rate or component cost on debt is not the firm's true opportunity cost of this kind of capital.

To illustrate, suppose that the firm has a 6-percent cost of debt and a 15-percent cost of equity. In the first year it borrows heavily, using up its debt capacity in the process, to finance projects yielding 7 percent. In the second year it has projects available that yield 13 percent, almost twice the return on first-year projects, but it cannot accept them because they would have to be financed with 15-percent equity money. To avoid this problem, the firm should be viewed as an ongoing concern, and its cost of capital should be calculated as a weighted average of the various types of funds it uses. The proper set of weights to be employed in computing the weighted average cost of capital is determined by the optimal financial structure of the firm.

In general, the risk to investors is lower on debt and higher on common stock; risk aversion, therefore, makes debt the lowest component-cost source of funds and equity the highest component-cost source. Risk increases as the percentage of total capital obtained in the form of debt increases, because the higher the debt level, the greater the probability that adverse conditions will lower earnings to the point where the firm cannot pay its interest charges or repay debt issues as they mature. The fact that interest rates on debt are lower than the expected rate of return (dividends plus capital gains) on common stock causes the overall, or average, cost of capital to the firm to decline as the percentage of capital raised as debt increases. However, the fact that more debt means higher risk offsets this effect to some extent. As a result, it is generally believed that the average cost of capital (1) declines at first as a firm moves from zero debt to some positive amount of debt, (2) hits a minimum (perhaps over a range rather than at some specific amount of debt), and then (3) rises as an increasing level of debt drives the firm's risk position beyond acceptable levels. Thus, each firm has an optimal amount of debt that minimizes its cost of capital and maximizes its value.

Figure 16.2 shows, for a hypothetical industry, how the cost of capital changes as the debt ratio increases. (The average cost of capital figures

■ Figure 16.2
## Hypothetical Cost-of-Capital Schedules for an Industry

A U-shaped weighted-average cost-of-capital curve reflects, first, lower capital costs because of the tax benefits of debt financing and, second, increasing capital costs as bankruptcy risk increases for highly leveraged firms.

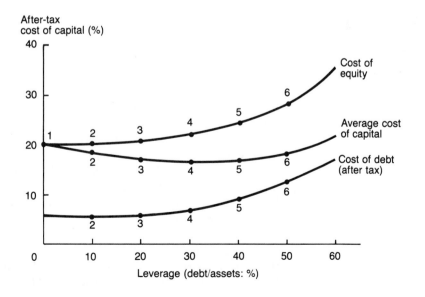

■ Table 16.6
## Calculation of Average Cost of Capital for Hypothetical Firms with Different Debt Ratios

| | | Percentage of Total (1) | Component Cost (2) | Weighted Cost (1) × (2) / 100 (3) |
|---|---|---|---|---|
| Firm 1 | Debt | 0 | 6.0 | 0.00 |
| | Equity | 100 | 20.0 | 20.00 |
| | | 100% | Average cost | 20.00% |
| Firm 2 | Debt | 10 | 6.0 | 0.60 |
| | Equity | 90 | 20.0 | 18.00 |
| | | 100% | Average cost | 18.60% |
| Firm 3 | Debt | 20 | 6.0 | 1.20 |
| | Equity | 80 | 20.0 | 16.00 |
| | | 100% | Average cost | 17.20% |
| Firm 4 | Debt | 30 | 7.0 | 2.10 |
| | Equity | 70 | 21.0 | 14.70 |
| | | 100% | Average cost | 16.80% |
| Firm 5 | Debt | 40 | 9.0 | 3.60 |
| | Equity | 60 | 22.5 | 13.50 |
| | | 100% | Average cost | 17.10% |
| Firm 6 | Debt | 50 | 12.0 | 6.00 |
| | Equity | 50 | 24.0 | 12.00 |
| | | 100% | Average cost | 18.00% |
| Firm 7 | Debt | 60 | 17.0 | 10.20 |
| | Equity | 40 | 27.5 | 11.00 |
| | | 100% | Average cost | 21.20% |

in the graph are calculated in Table 16.6.) In the figure, each dot represents one of the firms in the industry. For example, the dot labeled "1" represents Firm 1, a company with no debt. Because it is financed entirely with 20-percent equity money, Firm 1's average cost of capital is 20 percent. Firm 2 raises 10 percent of its capital as debt, and it has a 6-percent after-tax cost of debt and 20-percent cost of equity. Firm 3 also has a 6-percent cost of debt and 20-percent cost of equity, even though it uses 20 percent debt. Firm 4 has a 21-percent cost of equity and a 7-percent cost of debt. It uses 30 percent debt, and a risk premium of 1 percent has been added to the required return on equity to account for the additional risk of financial leverage. Providers of debt capital also believe that, because of the added risk of financial leverage at this debt level, they should obtain higher yields on the firm's securities. In this particular industry, the threshold debt ratio that begins to worry creditors is about 20 percent. Below 20-percent debt, creditors are unconcerned about any risk induced by debt; above 20 percent, they are aware of the higher risk and require compensation in the form of higher rates of return.

In Table 16.6, the debt and equity costs of the various firms are averaged on the basis of their respective proportions of the firm's total capital. Firm 1 has a weighted average cost of capital equal to 20 percent, Firm 2 has a weighted average cost of 18.6 percent, Firm 3 has a weighted cost of 17.2 percent, and Firm 4 has a weighted cost of 16.8 percent. These weighted costs, together with those of the other firms in the industry, are also plotted in Figure 16.2. We can see that firms with approximately 30 percent debt in their capital structure have the lowest weighted average cost of capital. Accordingly, proper calculation of the cost of capital requires that the cost of equity for a firm in the industry be given a weight of 0.70 and that of debt be given a weight of 0.30.

## The Post-Audit

**post-audit**

A comparison of actual results with those predicted in the investment proposal, plus an explanation of observed differences.

A discussion of the *post-completion audit*, or **post-audit**, is necessary in any treatment of capital budgeting. The post-audit involves (1) comparison of actual results with those predicted in the investment proposal and (2) explanation of observed differences.

The post-audit has several purposes, including the following:

1. *Improving Forecasts.* When decision makers systematically compare their projections to actual outcomes, estimates tend to improve. Conscious or subconscious biases are observed and eliminated; new forecasting methods will be sought as their need becomes apparent. People simply tend to work better if they know that their actions are being monitored.
2. *Improving Operations.* Businesses are run by people, and people can perform at higher or lower levels of efficiency. When a divisional team has made a forecast about a new installation, it is, in a sense, putting its reputation on the line. Because of the post-audit, these executives have every incentive to make it happen, to fulfill their prophecies. If costs rise above predicted levels, sales fall below expectations, and so on, then managers in production, sales, and related areas will strive to improve operations and bring results into line with forecasts.

The post-audit is a complex process. First, we must recognize that each element of the cash flow forecast is subject to uncertainty, so a percentage of all projects undertaken by any reasonably venturesome firm will prove to be unsuccessful. This fact must be considered when appraising the performances of the operating executives who submit capital expenditure requests. Second, projects sometimes fail to meet expectations for reasons beyond the control of the operating executives and for reasons that no one could realistically be expected to anticipate. For example, wage and price controls in the 1970s adversely affected many projects for which price increases had been projected; wildly fluctuating oil prices during recent years have hurt others. Third, it is often difficult to separate the operating results of one investment from those of a larger system. Fourth, if the post-audit process is not used carefully, executives may be reluctant to suggest potentially profitable but risky projects.

Because of these difficulties, some firms tend to play down the importance of the post-audit. However, observations of both businesses and governmental units suggest that the best-run and most successful organizations are those that put the greatest stress on post-audits. Accordingly, the post-audit is one of the most important elements in a good capital budgeting system.

# SUMMARY

*Capital budgeting* is the process of planning expenditures when the returns or benefits are expected to extend beyond one year. Capital budgeting decisions are among the most important that a firm's management makes because of both the size of the expenditures and the long duration of the commitments. It is a difficult process because one must deal with estimates of events that will occur some distance in the future.

Capital budgeting decision making requires integration of all the elements of the firm. Demand projections must be developed for the firm's products. Production and cost relationships have to be analyzed. Personnel requirements must be estimated. The funds necessary to support the investment project have to be procured.

Capital budgeting decisions should be made by comparing the marginal return on investment with the marginal *cost of capital*. The *net present value (NPV)* technique was shown to be a theoretically correct method for analyzing investment proposals.

For certain complex capital budgeting situations—those involving capital rationing, mutually exclusive, and closely interrelated projects—the *NPV* approach may be inappropriate for project selection. The *profitability index (PI)*, or benefit/cost ratio analysis, can sometimes improve decision making in these complex circumstances.

Calculation of the relevant *cost of capital* is a challenging problem. Proper decision making requires that a weighted average of the costs of the various types of capital employed by the firm should be used for all capital budgeting decisions.

Finally, the *post-audit* compares projected and actual results after the fact. The post-audit can provide useful information about the strengths and weaknesses of the firm's capital budgeting decision-making process, and thereby it promotes future improvements.

## Questions

16.1  Define the term *capital budgeting*.

16.2  What major steps are involved in the capital-budgeting process?

16.3  "A positive effect of R&D expenditures on the market value of the firm can be taken as evidence of an intangible capital or asset-like characteristic." Discuss this statement.

16.4 In an earlier chapter, we learned that factors should be used in proportions such that the marginal product/price ratios for all inputs are equal. For capital-management policy, this implies that the marginal net cost of debt should equal the marginal net cost of equity in the optimal capital structure. Yet we typically see firms issuing debt at interest rates substantially below the yield that investors require on the firm's equity shares. Does this mean that these firms are not operating with optimal capital structures? Explain.

16.5 Recent studies conclude that stockholders of target firms in takeover bids "win" (earn abnormal returns) and that stockholders of successful bidders do not lose subsequent to takeovers, even though takeovers usually occur at substantial premiums over pre-bid market prices. Is this observation consistent with capital market efficiency?

16.6 What characteristics make the rate of return on 90-day U.S. Treasury bills an attractive estimate of the risk-free rate of return?

16.7 How are relevant discount rates selected for *NPV* analysis?

16.8 When is *NPV* analysis appropriate? When should the profitability index (*PI*) method be used instead?

16.9 When *NPV* = 0, what is the relation between the cost of capital and the *IRR*?

16.10 What important purposes are served by the post-audit?

## Problems

16.1 Identify each of the following statements as *true* or *false*. Explain why.

A. Information costs both increase the marginal cost of capital and reduce the internal rate of return on investment projects.

B. Depreciation expenses involve no direct cash outlay, and can be safely ignored in investment-project evaluation.

C. The marginal cost of capital will be less elastic for larger than for smaller firms.

D. In practice, the component costs of debt and equity are jointly, rather than independently determined.

E. Investments necessary to replace worn-out or damaged equipment tend to have low levels of risk.

16.2 The net present value (*NPV*), profitability index (*PI*), and internal rate of return (*IRR*) methods are often employed in project valuation. Identify each of the following statements as *true* or *false*, and explain why.

A. The *IRR* method can tend to understate the relative attractiveness of superior investment projects when the opportunity cost of cash flows is below the *IRR*.

    B. A $PI = 1$ describes a project with an $NPV = 0$.

    C. Selection solely according to the $NPV$ criterion will tend to favor larger rather than smaller investment projects.

    D. When $NPV = 0$, the $IRR$ exceeds the cost of capital.

    E. Use of the $PI$ criterion is especially appropriate for larger firms with easy access to capital markets.

16.3   Indicate whether each of the following would *increase* or *decrease* the cost of capital that should be used by the firm in investment-project evaluation. Explain.

    A. Interest rates rise because the Federal Reserve System tightens the money supply.

    B. The stock market suffers a sharp decline, as does the company's stock price, without (in management's opinion) any decline in the company's earnings potential.

    C. The company's home state eliminates the corporate income tax in an effort to keep or attract valued employers.

    D. In an effort to reduce the federal deficit, Congress passes higher corporate income taxes.

    E. A merger with a leading competitor increases the company's stock price substantially.

16.4   New York City licenses taxicabs in two classes: (1) for operation by companies with fleets and (2) for operation by independent driver-owners having only one cab. The City also fixes the rates that taxis charge. For many years, no new licenses have been issued in either class. There is an unofficial market for licenses (medallions), the market value of which is currently more than $100,000.

    A. Discuss the factors determining the value of a license. To make your answer concrete, estimate numerical values for the various components that together can be summarized in a price of $100,000.

    B. What factors would determine whether a change in the fare fixed by the city would raise or lower the value of a license?

    C. Cab drivers, whether hired by companies or as owners of their own cabs, seem unanimous in opposing any increase in the number of cabs licensed. They argue that an increase in the number of cabs would increase competition for customers and drive down what they regard as an already unduly low return to drivers. Is their economic analysis correct? Who would benefit and who would lose from an expansion in the number of licenses issued at a nominal fee?

16.5   The Santa Catalina Passenger Ferry Company is contemplating leasing an additional ferryboat to expand service to Long Beach or San Diego. A financial analysis by staff personnel resulted in the following projections for a five-year planning horizon:

|  | Long Beach | San Diego |
|---|---|---|
| Cost | $200,000 | $300,000 |
| PV of expected cash flow @ k = 15% | 250,000 | 360,000 |

A. Calculate the net present value for each service. Which is more desirable according to the *NPV* criterion?

B. Calculate the profitability index for each service. Which is more desirable according to the *PI* criterion?

C. Under what conditions would either or both of the services be undertaken?

16.6 Louisiana Drilling and Exploration, Inc. (LD&E) has the funds necessary to complete one of two risky oil and gas drilling projects. The first, Permian Basin #1, involves the recovery of a well that was plugged and abandoned five years ago but that may now be profitable given improved recovery techniques. The second, Permian Basin #2, is a new on-shore exploratory well that appears to be especially promising. Based on a detailed analysis by its technical staff, LD&E projects a ten-year life for each well with annual net cash flows as follows:

| Project | Probability | Annual Cash Flow |
|---|---|---|
| Permian Basin #1 | 0.08 | $ 500,000 |
|  | 0.84 | 1,000,000 |
|  | 0.08 | 1,500,000 |
| Permian Basin #2 | 0.18 | 300,000 |
|  | 0.64 | 900,000 |
|  | 0.18 | 1,500,000 |

In the recovery-project valuation, LD&E uses an 8 percent riskless rate and a standard 12 percent risk premium. For exploratory drilling projects, the company uses larger risk premiums proportionate to project risks as measured by the project coefficient of variation. For example, an exploratory project with a coefficient of variation one and one-half times that for recovery projects would require a risk premium of 18 percent (= 1.5 × 12 percent). Both projects involve land acquisition, surface preparation, and subsurface drilling costs of $3 million each.

A. Calculate the expected value, standard deviation, and coefficient of variation for annual net operating revenues from each well.

B. Calculate the NPV for each project using the risk-adjusted discount rate method.

C. Calculate and evaluate the PI for each project.

16.7    Great Lakes Manufacturing, Inc. is considering investment in two alternative capital-budgeting projects. Project A is an investment of $75,000 to replace working but obsolete equipment. Project B is an investment of $150,000 to expand distribution facilities. Relevant cash-flow data for the two projects over their expected two-year lives are as follows:

### Project A

| Year 1 | | Year 2 | |
|---|---|---|---|
| Probability | Cash Flow | Probability | Cash Flow |
| 0.18 | $      0 | 0.08 | $      0 |
| 0.64 | 50,000 | 0.84 | 50,000 |
| 0.18 | 100,000 | 0.08 | 100,000 |

### Project B

| Year 1 | | Year 2 | |
|---|---|---|---|
| Probability | Cash Flow | Probability | Cash Flow |
| 0.50 | $      0 | 0.125 | $      0 |
| 0.50 | 200,000 | 0.75 | 100,000 |
|  |  | 0.125 | 200,000 |

A. Calculate the expected value, standard deviation, and coefficient of variation of cash flows for each project.

B. Calculate the risk-adjusted NPV for each project, using a 15-percent cost of capital for the riskier project and a 12-percent cost of capital for the less risky one. Which project is preferred using the NPV criterion?

C. Calculate the PI for each project, and rank the projects according to the PI criterion.

D. Calculate the IRR for each project, and rank the projects according to the IRR criterion.

E. Compare your answers to Parts B, C, and D, and discuss any differences.

16.8    Cunningham's Drug Store, a medium-sized drug store located in Milwaukee, Wisconsin, is owned and operated by Richard Cunningham. Cunningham's sells pharmaceuticals, cosmetics, toiletries, magazines, and various novelties. Cunningham's most recent annual net income statement is as follows:

| | | |
|---|---:|---:|
| Sales revenue | | $1,800,000 |
| Total costs | | |
| Cost of goods sold | $1,260,000 | |
| Wages and salaries | 200,000 | |
| Rent | 120,000 | |
| Depreciation | 60,000 | |
| Utilities | 40,000 | |
| Miscellaneous | 30,000 | |
| Total | | 1,710,000 |
| Net profit before tax | | $ 90,000 |

Cunningham's sales and expenses have remained relatively constant during the past few years and are expected to continue unchanged in the near future. To increase sales, Cunningham is considering using some floor space for a small soda fountain. Cunningham would operate the soda fountain for an initial three-year period and then reevaluate its profitability. The soda fountain would require an incremental investment of $20,000 to lease furniture, equipment, utensils, and so on. This is the only capital investment required during the three-year period. At the end of that time, additional capital would be required to continue operating the soda fountain, and no capital would be recovered if it were shut down. The soda fountain is expected to have annual sales of $100,000 and food and materials expenses of $20,000 per year. The soda fountain is also expected to increase wage and salary expenses by 8 percent and utility expenses by 5 percent. Because the soda fountain will reduce the floor space available for display of other merchandise, sales of non–soda fountain items are expected to decline by 10 percent.

A. Calculate net incremental cash flows for the soda fountain.

B. Assume that Cunningham has the capital necessary to install the soda fountain and places a 12-percent opportunity cost on those funds. Should the soda fountain be installed? Why or why not?

16.9 The Patriotic Press, Inc., *(PPI)* is analyzing the potential profitability of three printing jobs put up for bid by the State Department of Revenue:

| | Job A | Job B | Job C |
|---|---:|---:|---:|
| Projected winning bid (per unit) | $5.00 | $8.00 | $7.50 |
| Direct cost per unit | $2.00 | $4.30 | $3.00 |
| Annual unit sales volume | 800,000 | 650,000 | 450,000 |
| Annual distribution costs | $90,000 | $75,000 | $55,000 |
| Investment required to produce annual volume | $5,000,000 | $5,200,000 | $4,000,000 |

Assume that: (1) the company's marginal state-plus-federal tax rate is 50 percent; (2) each job is expected to have a six-year life; (3) the firm uses straight-line depreciation; (4) the average cost of capital is 14 percent; (5) the jobs have the same risk as the firm's other business; and (6) the company has already spent $60,000 on developing the preceding data. This $60,000 has been capitalized and will be amortized over the life of the project.

A. What is the expected net cash flow each year? (*Hint:* Cash flow equals net profit after taxes plus depreciation and amortization charges.)

B. What is the net present value of each project? On which project, if any, should PPI bid?

C. Suppose that PPI's primary business is quite cyclical, improving and declining with the economy, but Job A is expected to be countercyclical. Might this have any bearing on your decision?

16.10  Eureka Membership Warehouse, Inc., is a rapidly growing chain of retail outlets offering brand-name merchandise at discount prices. A security analyst's report issued by a national brokerage firm indicates that debt yielding 13 percent composes 25 percent of Eureka's overall capital structure. Furthermore, both earnings and dividends are expected to grow at a rate of 15 percent per year.

Currently, common stock in the company is priced at $30 and should pay $1.50 per share in dividends during the coming year. This yield compares favorably with the 8-percent return currently available on risk-free securities and the 14-percent average for all common stocks, given the company's estimated beta of 2.

A. Calculate Eureka's component cost of equity using both the capital asset pricing model and the dividend yield plus expected growth model.

B. Assuming a 40-percent marginal federal-plus-state income tax rate, calculate Eureka's weighted average cost of capital.

## Selected References

Agrawal, Anup, and Gershon N. Mandelker. "Managerial Incentives and Corporate Investment and Financing Decisions." *Journal of Finance* 42 (September 1987): 823–837.

Barclay, Michael J., and Clifford W. Smith, Jr. "Corporate Payout Policy: Cash Dividends versus Open-Market Repurchases." *Journal of Financial Economics* 22 (October 1988): 61–82.

Baskin, Jonathan. "An Empirical Investigation of the Pecking Order Hypothesis." *Financial Management* 18 (Spring 1989): 26–35.

Black, Fisher. "A Simple Discounting Rule." *Financial Management* 17 (Summer 1988): 7–11.

Dann, Larry Y., and Harry DeAngelo. "Corporate Financial Policy and Corporate Control: A Study of Defensive Adjustments in Asset and Ownership Structure." *Journal of Financial Economics* 20 (January/March 1988): 87–127.

Fazzari, Steven, R. Glenn Hubbard, and Bruce Peterson. "Investment, Financing Decisions, and Tax Policy." *American Economic Review* 78 (May 1988): 200–205.

Hamermesch, Daniel S. "Plant Closings and the Value of the Firm." *Review of Economics and Statistics* 70 (November 1988): 580–586.

Imhoff, Eugene A., and Jacob K. Thomas. "Economic Consequences of Accounting Standards: The Lease Disclosure Rule." *Journal of Accounting and Economics* 10 (December 1988): 277–310.

Kwan, Clarence C. Y., and Yufei Yuan. "Optimal Sequential Selection in Capital Budgeting: A Shortcut." *Financial Management* 17 (Spring 1988): 54–59.

Miller, Edward M. "The Competitive Market Assumption and Capital Budgeting Criteria." *Financial Management* 16 (Winter 1987): 22–28.

Miller, Merton H. "The Modigliani-Miller Propositions After Thirty Years." *Journal of Economic Perspectives* 2 (Fall 1988): 99–120.

Modigliani, Franco. "MM—Past, Present, and Future." *Journal of Economic Perspectives* 2 (Fall 1988): 149–158.

Mukherjee, Tarun K., and Glenn V. Henderson. "The Capital Budgeting Process: Theory and Practice." *Interfaces* 17 (March–April 1987): 78–90.

Pike, Richard, and John Sharp. "Trends in the Use of Management Science Techniques in Capital Budgeting." *Managerial and Decision Economics* 10 (June 1989): 135–140.

Schleifer, Andrei, and Robert W. Vishny. "Value Maximization and the Acquisition Process." *Journal of Economic Perspectives* 2 (Winter 1988): 7–20.

Sick, Gordon A. "A Certainty-Equivalent Approach to Capital Budgeting." *Financial Management* 15 (Winter 1986): 23–32.

Stiglitz, Joseph E. "Why Financial Structure Matters." *Journal of Economic Perspectives* 2 (Fall 1988): 121–126.

Titman, Sheridan, and Roberto Wessels. "The Determinants of Capital Structure Choice." *Journal of Finance* 43 (March 1988): 1–40.

Weaver, Samuel C., et al. "Capital Budgeting." *Financial Management* 18 (Spring 1989): 10–18.

White, Michelle J. "The Corporate Bankruptcy Decision." *Journal of Economic Perspectives* 3 (Spring 1989): 129–152.

# Compounding and the Time Value of Money

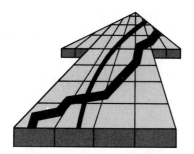

The concepts of compound growth and the time value of money are widely used in all aspects of business and economics. Compounding is the principle that underlies growth, whether it is growth in value, growth in sales, or growth in assets. The time value of money—the fact that a dollar received in the future is worth less than a dollar in hand today—also plays an important role in managerial economics. Cash flows occurring in different periods must be adjusted to their value at common point in time to be analyzed and compared. Because of the importance of these concepts in economic analysis, thorough understanding of the material on future (compound) and present values in this appendix is important for the study of managerial economics.

## FUTURE VALUE (OR COMPOUND VALUE)

Suppose that you deposit $100 in a bank savings account that pays 5-percent interest compounded annually. How much will you have at the end of one year? Let us define terms as follows:

$PV$ = Present value of your account, or the beginning amount, $100;

$i$ = Interest rate the bank pays you = 5 percent per year, or, expressed as a decimal, 0.05;

$I$ = Dollars of interest you earn during the year;

$FV_n$ = Future value, or ending amount, of your account at the end of $n$ years. Whereas $PV$ is the value now, at the *present* time, $FV_n$ is the value $n$ years into the future, after compound interest has been earned. Note also that $FV_0$ is the future value zero years into the future, which is the *present*, so $FV_0 = PV$.

In our example, $n = 1$, so $FV_n = FV_1$, and it is calculated as follows:

$$FV_1 = PV + I$$
$$= PV + (PV)(i)$$
$$= PV(1 + i). \qquad \textbf{A.1}$$

We can now use Equation A.1 to find how much the account is worth at the end of one year:

$$FV_1 = \$100(1 + 0.05) = \$100(1.05) = \$105.$$

Your account earned $5 of interest ($I = \$5$), so you have $105 at the end of the year.

Now suppose that you leave your funds on deposit for five years; how much will you have at the end of the fifth year? The answer is $127.63; this value is worked out in Table A.1.

Notice that the Table A.1 value for $FV_2$, the value of the account at the end of Year 2, is equal to

$$FV_2 = FV_1(1 + i) = PV(1 + i)(1 + i) = PV(1 + i)^2.$$

Continuing, we see that $FV_3$, the balance after three years, is

$$FV_3 = FV_2(1 + i) = PV(1 + i)^3.$$

In general, $FV_n$, the future value at the end of n years, is found as:

$$FV_n = PV(1 + i)^n. \qquad \textbf{A.2}$$

Applying Equation A.2 to our five-year, 5-percent case, we obtain

$$FV_5 = \$100(1.05)^5$$
$$= \$100(1.2763)$$
$$= \$127.63,$$

which is the same as the value in Table A.1.

■ Table A.1
## Compound Interest Calculations

| Year | Beginning Amount, $PV$ | $\times (1 + i) =$ | Ending Amount, $FV_n$ |
|---|---|---|---|
| 1 | $100.00 | 1.05 | $105.00 |
| 2 | 105.00 | 1.05 | 110.25 |
| 3 | 110.25 | 1.05 | 115.76 |
| 4 | 115.76 | 1.05 | 121.55 |
| 5 | 121.55 | 1.05 | 127.63 |

■ Table A.2

## Future Value of $1 at the End of *n* Periods: $FVIF_{i,n} = (1 + i)^n$

| Period (n) | 1% | 2% | 3% | 4% | 5% | 6% | 7% | 8% | 9% | 10% |
|---|---|---|---|---|---|---|---|---|---|---|
| 0 | 1.0000 | 1.0000 | 1.0000 | 1.0000 | 1.0000 | 1.0000 | 1.0000 | 1.0000 | 1.0000 | 1.0000 |
| 1 | 1.0100 | 1.0200 | 1.0300 | 1.0400 | 1.0500 | 1.0600 | 1.0700 | 1.0800 | 1.0900 | 1.1000 |
| 2 | 1.0201 | 1.0404 | 1.0609 | 1.0816 | 1.1025 | 1.1236 | 1.1449 | 1.1664 | 1.1881 | 1.2100 |
| 3 | 1.0303 | 1.0612 | 1.0927 | 1.1249 | 1.1576 | 1.1910 | 1.2250 | 1.2597 | 1.2950 | 1.3310 |
| 4 | 1.0406 | 1.0824 | 1.1255 | 1.1699 | 1.2155 | 1.2625 | 1.3108 | 1.3605 | 1.4116 | 1.4641 |
| 5 | 1.0510 | 1.1041 | 1.1593 | 1.2167 | 1.2763 | 1.3382 | 1.4026 | 1.4693 | 1.5386 | 1.6105 |
| 6 | 1.0615 | 1.1262 | 1.1941 | 1.2653 | 1.3401 | 1.4185 | 1.5007 | 1.5869 | 1.6771 | 1.7716 |
| 7 | 1.0721 | 1.1487 | 1.2299 | 1.3159 | 1.4071 | 1.5036 | 1.6058 | 1.7138 | 1.8280 | 1.9487 |
| 8 | 1.0829 | 1.1717 | 1.2668 | 1.3686 | 1.4775 | 1.5938 | 1.7182 | 1.8509 | 1.9926 | 2.1436 |
| 9 | 1.0937 | 1.1951 | 1.3048 | 1.4233 | 1.5513 | 1.6895 | 1.8385 | 1.9990 | 2.1719 | 2.3579 |
| 10 | 1.1046 | 1.2190 | 1.3439 | 1.4802 | 1.6289 | 1.7908 | 1.9672 | 2.1589 | 2.3674 | 2.5937 |
| 11 | 1.1157 | 1.2434 | 1.3842 | 1.5395 | 1.7103 | 1.8983 | 2.1049 | 2.3316 | 2.5804 | 2.8531 |
| 12 | 1.1268 | 1.2682 | 1.4258 | 1.6010 | 1.7959 | 2.0122 | 2.2522 | 2.5182 | 2.8127 | 3.1384 |
| 13 | 1.1381 | 1.2936 | 1.4685 | 1.6651 | 1.8856 | 2.1329 | 2.4098 | 2.7196 | 3.0658 | 3.4523 |
| 14 | 1.1495 | 1.3195 | 1.5126 | 1.7317 | 1.9799 | 2.2609 | 2.5785 | 2.9372 | 3.3417 | 3.7975 |
| 15 | 1.1610 | 1.3459 | 1.5580 | 1.8009 | 2.0789 | 2.3966 | 2.7590 | 3.1722 | 3.6425 | 4.1772 |

If an electronic calculator is handy, it is easy enough to calculate $(1 + i)^n$ directly.[1] However, tables have been constructed for values of $(1 + i)^n$ for wide ranges of $i$ and $n$. Table A.2 illustrates. Table B.1 in Appendix B contains a more complete set of compound value interest factors. Notice that we have used the term *period* rather than *year* in Table A.2. As we shall see later in the appendix, compounding can occur over periods of time different from one year. Thus, although compounding is often on an annual basis, it can be quarterly, semiannually, monthly, or for any other period.

We define the term *future value interest factor* ($FVIF_{i,n}$) to equal $(1 + i)^n$. Therefore Equation A.2 may be written as $FV_n = PV(FVIF_{i,n})$. One need only to go to an appropriate interest table to find the proper interest factor. For example, the correct interest factor for our five-year, 5-percent illustration can be found in Table A.2. We look down the Period column to 5, then across this row to the 5-percent column to find the interest factor, 1.2763. Then, using this interest factor, we find the value of $100 after five years as $FV_n = PV(FVIF_{i,n}) = \$100(1.2763) =$

---

[1]For example, to calculate $(1 + i)^n$ for $i = 5\% = 0.05$ and $n = 5$ years, we multiply $(1 + i) = (1.05)$ times $(1.05)$; multiply this product by $(1.05)$; and so on:

$$(1 + i)^n = (1.05)(1.05)(1.05)(1.05)(1.05) = (1.05)^5 = 1.2763.$$

■ Figure A.1
## Relations among Future Value Interest Factors, Interest Rates, and Time

The future value interest factor rises with increases in the interest rate and in the number of periods for interest compounding.

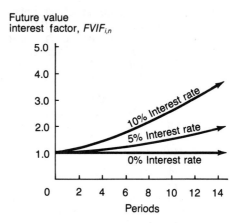

$127.63, which is identical to the value obtained by the long method in Table A.1.

### Graphic View of the Compounding Process: Growth

Figure A.1 shows how $1 (or any other initial quantity) grows over time at various rates of interest. The higher the rate of interest, the faster the rate of growth. The interest rate is, in fact, the growth rate: If a sum is deposited and earns 5 percent, then the funds on deposit grow at the rate of 5 percent per period. Similarly, the sales of a firm or the gross national product (GNP) of a country might be expected to grow at a constant rate. Projections of future sales or GNP could be obtained using the compound value process.

Future value curves could be drawn for any interest rate, including fractional rates. In Figure A.1, we have plotted curves for 0 percent, 5 percent, and 10 percent, using the data from Table A.2.

# PRESENT VALUE

Suppose that you are offered the alternative of receiving either $127.63 at the end of five years or $X$ dollars today. There is no question that the $127.63 will be paid in full (perhaps the payer is the U.S. government). Having no current need for the money, you would deposit it in a bank account that pays 5 percent interest. (Five percent is your *opportunity cost*, or the rate of interest you could earn on alternative investments of equal risk.) What value of $X$ will make you indifferent between $X$ dollars today or the promise of $127.63 five years hence?

Table A.1 shows that the initial amount of $100 growing at 5 percent a year yields $127.63 at the end of five years. Thus, you should be indifferent in your choice between $100 today and $127.63 at the end of five years. The $100 is the present value, or *PV*, of $127.63 due in five years when the applicable interest rate is 5 percent. Therefore, if $X$ is anything less than $100, you would prefer the promise of $127.63 in five years to $X$ dollars today.

In general, the present value of a sum due $n$ years in the future is the amount that, if it were invested today, would grow to equal the future sum over a period of $n$ years. Since $100 would grow to $127.63 in five years at a 5-percent interest rate, $100 is the present value of $127.63 due five years in the future when the appropriate interest rate is 5 percent.

Finding present values (or *discounting*, as it is commonly called) is simply the reverse of compounding, and Equation A.2 can readily be transformed into a present value formula:

$$FV_n = PV(1 + i)^n,$$

which, when solved for *PV*, gives

$$PV = \frac{FV_n}{(1 + i)^n} = FV_n \left[ \frac{1}{(1 + i)^n} \right]$$  **A.3**

Tables have been constructed for the term in brackets for various values of $i$ and $n$; Table A.3 is an example. For a more complete table, see Table

■ Table A.3
## Present Values of $1 Due at the End of *n* Periods

$$PVIF_{i,n} = \frac{1}{(1 + i)^n} = \left[ \frac{1}{(1 + i)} \right]^n$$

| Period (n) | 1% | 2% | 3% | 4% | 5% | 6% | 7% | 8% | 9% | 10% | 12% | 14% | 15% |
|---|---|---|---|---|---|---|---|---|---|---|---|---|---|
| 1 | .9901 | .9804 | .9709 | .9615 | .9524 | .9434 | .9346 | .9259 | .9174 | .9091 | .8929 | .8772 | .8696 |
| 2 | .9803 | .9612 | .9426 | .9246 | .9070 | .8900 | .8734 | .8573 | .8417 | .8264 | .7972 | .7695 | .7561 |
| 3 | .9706 | .9423 | .9151 | .8890 | .8638 | .8396 | .8163 | .7938 | .7722 | .7513 | .7118 | .6750 | .6575 |
| 4 | .9610 | .9238 | .8885 | .8548 | .8227 | .7921 | .7629 | .7350 | .7084 | .6830 | .6355 | .5921 | .5718 |
| 5 | .9515 | .9057 | .8626 | .8219 | .7835 | .7473 | .7130 | .6806 | .6499 | .6209 | .5674 | .5194 | .4972 |
| 6 | .9420 | .8880 | .8375 | .7903 | .7462 | .7050 | .6663 | .6302 | .5963 | .5645 | .5066 | .4556 | .4323 |
| 7 | .9327 | .8706 | .8131 | .7599 | .7107 | .6651 | .6227 | .5835 | .5470 | .5132 | .4523 | .3996 | .3759 |
| 8 | .9235 | .8535 | .7894 | .7307 | .6768 | .6274 | .5820 | .5403 | .5019 | .4665 | .4039 | .3506 | .3269 |
| 9 | .9143 | .8368 | .7664 | .7026 | .6446 | .5919 | .5439 | .5002 | .4604 | .4241 | .3606 | .3075 | .2843 |
| 10 | .9053 | .8203 | .7441 | .6756 | .6139 | .5584 | .5083 | .4632 | .4224 | .3855 | .3220 | .2697 | .2472 |

B.2 in Appendix B. For the case being considered, look down the 5-percent column in Table A.3 to the fifth row. The figure shown there, 0.7835, is the *present value interest factor* $(PVIF_{i,n})$ used to determine the present value of $127.63 payable in five years, discounted at 5 percent:

$$PV = FV_5(PVIF_{i,n})$$
$$= \$127.63(0.7835)$$
$$= \$100.$$

## Graphic View of the Discounting Process

Figure A.2 shows how the interest factors for discounting decrease as the discounting period increases. The curves in the figure were plotted with data taken from Table A.3; they show that the present value of a sum to be received at some future date decreases (1) as the payment date is extended further into the future and (2) as the discount rate increases. If relatively high discount rates apply, funds due in the future are worth very little today. Even at relatively low discount rates, the present values of funds due in the distant future are quite small. For example, $1.00 due

■ Figure A.2
### Relations among Present Value Interest Factors, Interest Rates, and Time

The present value interest factor falls with increases in the interest rate and in the number of periods prior to payment.

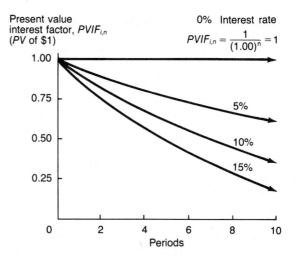

in ten years is worth about \$0.61 today if the discount rate is 5 percent. It is worth only \$0.25 today at a 15-percent discount rate. Similarly, \$1.00 due in five years at 10 percent is worth \$0.62 today, but at the same discount rate, \$1.00 due in ten years is worth only \$0.39 today.

# FUTURE VALUE VERSUS PRESENT VALUE

Notice that Equation A.2, the basic equation for compounding, was developed from the logical sequence set forth in Table A.1; the equation merely presents in mathematical form the steps outlined in the table. The present value interest factor ($PVIF_{i,n}$) in Equation A.3, the basic equation for discounting or finding present values, was found as the *reciprocal* of the future value interest factor ($FVIF_{i,n}$) for the same $i$, $n$ combination:

$$PVIF_{i,n} = \frac{1}{FVIF_{i,n}}.$$

For example, the *future value interest factor* for 5 percent over five years is seen in Table A.2 to be 1.2763. The *present value interest factor* for 5 percent over five years must be the reciprocal of 1.2763:

$$PVIF_{5\%,\ 5\ years} = \frac{1}{1.2763} = 0.7835.$$

The $PVIF_{i,n}$ found in this manner does, of course, correspond with the $PVIF_{i,n}$ shown in Table A.3.

The reciprocal relation between present value and future value permits us to find present values in two ways—by multiplying or by dividing. Thus, the present value of \$1,000 due in five years and discounted at 5 percent may be found as

$$PV = FV_n \left[\frac{1}{1+i}\right]^n = FV_n(PVIF_{i,n}) = \$1,000(0.7835) = \$783.50,$$

or as

$$PV = \frac{FV_n}{(1+i)^n} = \frac{FV_n}{FVIF_{i,n}} = \frac{\$1,000}{1.2763} = \$783.50.$$

To conclude this comparison of present and future values, compare Figures A.1 and A.2.[2] Notice that the vertical intercept is at 1.0 in each case, but future value interest factors rise, whereas present value interest factors decline.

---

[2]Notice that Figure A.2 is not a mirror image of Figure A.1. The curves in Figure A.1 approach $\infty$ as $n$ increases; in Figure A.2 the curves approach zero, not $-\infty$.

# FUTURE VALUE OF AN ANNUITY

*An annuity is defined as a series of payments of a fixed amount for a specified number of periods. Each payment occurs at the end of the period.*[3] For example, a promise to pay $1,000 a year for three years is a three-year annuity. If you were to receive such an annuity and were to deposit each annual payment in a savings account paying 4-percent interest, how much would you have at the end of three years? The answer is shown graphically as a *time line* in Figure A.3. The first payment is made at the end of Year 1, the second at the end of Year 2, and the third at the end of Year 3. The last payment is not compounded at all, the second payment is compounded for one year, and the first is compounded for two years. When the future values of each of the payments are added, their total is the sum of the annuity. In the example, this total is $3,121.60.

Expressed algebraically, with $S_n$ defined as the future value, $R$ as the periodic receipt, $n$ as the length of the annuity, and $FVIFA_{i,n}$ as the future value interest factor for an annuity, the formula for $S_n$ is:

$$S_n = R(1 + i)^{n-1} + R(1 + i)^{n-2} + \ldots + R(1 + i)^1 + R(1 + i)^0$$
$$= R[(1 + i)^{n-1} + (1 + i)^{n-2} + \ldots + (1 + i)^1 + (1 + i)^0]$$
$$= R\sum_{t=1}^{n} (1 + i)^{n-t} \text{ or } = R\sum_{t=1}^{n} (1 + i)^{t-1}$$
$$= R(FVIFA_{i,n}). \qquad \textbf{A.4}$$

■ Figure A.3
## Time Line for an Annuity: Future Value ($i$ = 4 percent)

When the interest rate is 4%, the future value of $1,000 annuity to be paid over 3 years is $3,121.60.

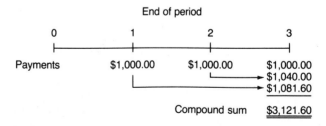

[3]Had the payment been made at the beginning of the period, each receipt would simply have been shifted back one year. The annuity would have been called an *annuity due;* the one in the present discussion, with payments made at the end of each period, is called a *regular annuity* or, sometimes, a *deferred annuity.*

■ Table A.4

## Sum of an Annuity of $1 per Period for *n* Periods

$$FVIFA_{i,n} = \sum_{t=1}^{n} (1 + i)^{t-1}$$

$$= \frac{(1 + i)^n - 1}{i}$$

| Number of Periods | 1% | 2% | 3% | 4% | 5% | 6% | 7% | 8% |
|---|---|---|---|---|---|---|---|---|
| 1 | 1.0000 | 1.0000 | 1.0000 | 1.0000 | 1.0000 | 1.0000 | 1.0000 | 1.0000 |
| 2 | 2.0100 | 2.0200 | 2.0300 | 2.0400 | 2.0500 | 2.0600 | 2.0700 | 2.0800 |
| 3 | 3.0301 | 3.0604 | 3.0909 | 3.1216 | 3.1525 | 3.1836 | 3.2149 | 3.2464 |
| 4 | 4.0604 | 4.1216 | 4.1836 | 4.2465 | 4.3101 | 4.3746 | 4.4399 | 4.5061 |
| 5 | 5.1010 | 5.2040 | 5.3091 | 5.4163 | 5.5256 | 5.6371 | 5.7507 | 5.8666 |
| 6 | 6.1520 | 6.3081 | 6.4684 | 6.6330 | 6.8019 | 6.9753 | 7.1533 | 7.3359 |
| 7 | 7.2135 | 7.4343 | 7.6625 | 7.8983 | 8.1420 | 8.3938 | 8.6540 | 8.9228 |
| 8 | 8.2857 | 8.5830 | 8.8923 | 9.2142 | 9.5491 | 9.8975 | 10.2598 | 10.6366 |
| 9 | 9.3685 | 9.7546 | 10.1591 | 10.5828 | 11.0266 | 11.4913 | 11.9780 | 12.4876 |
| 10 | 10.4622 | 10.9497 | 11.4639 | 12.0061 | 12.5779 | 13.1808 | 13.8164 | 14.4866 |

The expression in parentheses, $FVIFA_{i,n}$, has been calculated for various combinations of $i$ and $n$.[4] An illustrative set of these annuity interest factors is given in Table A.4.[5] To find the answer to the three-year, $1,000 annuity problem, simply refer to Table A.4, look down the 4-percent column to the row of the third period, and multiply the factor 3.1216 by $1,000. The answer is the same as the one derived by the long method illustrated in Figure A.3:

$$S_n = R(FVIFA_{i,n}),$$

$$S_3 = \$1,000(3.1216) = \$3,121.60.$$

Notice that for all positive interest rates, the $FVIFA_{i,n}$ for the sum of an annuity is always equal to or greater than the number of periods the annuity runs.[6]

---

[4]The third equation is simply a shorthand expression in which sigma ($\Sigma$) signifies *sum* up or add the values of *n* factors. The symbol $\sum_{t=1}^{n}$ simply says, "Go through the following process: Let $t = 1$ and find the first factor. Then let $t = 2$ and find the second factor. Continue until each individual factor has been found, and then add these individual factors to find the value of the annuity."

[5]The equation given in Table A.4 recognizes that the *FVIFA* factor is the sum of a geometric progression. The proof of this equation is given in most algebra texts. Notice that it is easy to use the equation to develop annuity factors. This is especially useful if you need the *FVIFA* for some interest rate not given in the tables (for example, 6.5 percent).

[6]It is worth noting that the entry for each period $t$ in Table A.4 equals the sum of the entries in Table A.2 up to the period $n - 1$. For example, the entry for Period 3 under the 4-percent column in Table A.4 is equal to $1.000 + 1.0400 + 1.0816 = 3.1216$.

(continued)

# PRESENT VALUE OF AN ANNUITY

Suppose that you were offered the following alternatives: a three-year annuity of $1,000 per year or a lump-sum payment today. You have no need for the money during the next three years, so if you accept the annuity, you would simply deposit the receipts in a savings account paying 4-percent interest. How large must the lump-sum payment be to make it equivalent to the annuity? The time line shown in Figure A.4 will help explain the problem.

The present value of the first receipt is $R[1/(1 + i)]$, the second is $R[1/(1 + i)]^2$, and so on. Designating the present value of an annuity of $n$ years as $A_n$ and the present value interest factor for an annuity as $PVIFA_{i,n}$, we may write the following equation:

$$
\begin{aligned}
A_n &= R\left(\frac{1}{1 + i}\right)^1 + R\left(\frac{1}{1 + i}\right)^2 + \ldots + R\left(\frac{1}{1 + i}\right)^n \\
&= R\left(\frac{1}{(1 + i)^1} + \frac{1}{(1 + i)^2} + \ldots + \frac{1}{(1 + i)^n}\right) \\
&= R\sum_{t=1}^{n}\frac{1}{(1 + i)^t} \\
&= R(PVIFA_{i,n}).
\end{aligned}
$$
A.5

■ Figure A.4
## Time Line for an Annuity: Present Value ($i$ = 4 percent)

When the interest rate is 4%, the present value of a $1,000 annuity to be paid over 3 years is $2,775.10.

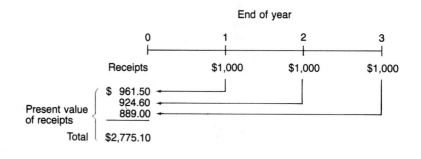

Also, had the annuity been an *annuity due*, with payments received at the beginning rather than at the end of each period, the three payments would have occurred at $t = 0$, $t = 1$, and $t = 2$. To find the future value of an annuity due, look up the $FVIFA_{i,n}$ for $n + 1$ years, then subtract 1.0 from the amount to get the $FVIFA_{i,n}$ for the annuity due. In the example, the annuity due $FVIFA_{i,n}$ is $4.2465 - 1.0 = 3.2465$, versus 3.1216 for a regular annuity. Because payments on an annuity due come earlier, it is a little more valuable than a regular annuity.

■ Table A.5
## Present Value of an Annuity of $1 per Period for *n* Periods

$$PVIFA_{i,n} = \sum_{t=1}^{n} \frac{1}{(1 + i)^t} = \frac{1 - \dfrac{1}{(1 + i)^n}}{i}$$

| Period | 1% | 2% | 3% | 4% | 5% | 6% | 7% | 8% | 9% | 10% |
|--------|------|------|------|------|------|------|------|------|------|------|
| 1 | 0.9901 | 0.9804 | 0.9709 | 0.9615 | 0.9524 | 0.9434 | 0.9346 | 0.9259 | 0.9174 | 0.9091 |
| 2 | 1.9704 | 1.9416 | 1.9135 | 1.8861 | 1.8594 | 1.8334 | 1.8080 | 1.7833 | 1.7591 | 1.7355 |
| 3 | 2.9410 | 2.8839 | 2.8286 | 2.7751 | 2.7232 | 2.6730 | 2.6243 | 2.5771 | 2.5313 | 2.4869 |
| 4 | 3.9020 | 3.8077 | 3.7171 | 3.6299 | 3.5460 | 3.4651 | 3.3872 | 3.3121 | 3.2397 | 3.1699 |
| 5 | 4.8534 | 4.7135 | 4.5797 | 4.4518 | 4.3295 | 4.2124 | 4.1002 | 3.9927 | 3.8897 | 3.7908 |
| 6 | 5.7955 | 5.6014 | 5.4172 | 5.2421 | 5.0757 | 4.9173 | 4.7665 | 4.6229 | 4.4859 | 4.3553 |
| 7 | 6.7282 | 6.4720 | 6.2303 | 6.0021 | 5.7864 | 5.5824 | 5.3893 | 5.2064 | 5.0330 | 4.8684 |
| 8 | 7.6517 | 7.3255 | 7.0197 | 6.7327 | 6.4632 | 6.2098 | 5.9713 | 5.7466 | 5.5348 | 5.3349 |
| 9 | 8.5660 | 8.1622 | 7.7861 | 7.4353 | 7.1078 | 6.8017 | 6.5152 | 6.2469 | 5.9952 | 5.7590 |
| 10 | 9.4713 | 8.9826 | 8.5302 | 8.1109 | 7.7217 | 7.3601 | 7.0236 | 6.7101 | 6.4177 | 6.1446 |

Again, tables have been worked out for $PVIFA_{i,n}$, the term in parentheses in Equation A.5. Table A.5 illustrates; a more complete listing is found in Table B.4 in Appendix B. From Table A.5, the $PVIFA_{i,n}$ for a three-year, 4-percent annuity is found to be 2.7751. Multiplying this factor by the $1,000 annual receipt gives $2,775.10, the present value of the annuity. This figure is identical to the long-method answer shown in Figure A.4:

$$A_n = R(PVIFA_{i,n}),$$

$$A_3 = \$1,000(2.7751)$$

$$= \$2,775.10.$$

Notice that the entry for each period *n* in Table A.5 is equal to the sum of the entries in Table A.3 up to and including period *n*. For example, the *PVIFA* for 4 percent, three periods as shown in Table A.5 could have been calculated by summing values from Table A.3:

$$0.9615 + 0.9246 + 0.8890 = 2.7751.$$

Notice also that for all positive interest rates, $PVIFA_{i,n}$ for the *present value* of an annuity is always less than the number of periods that an annuity runs, whereas $FVIFA_{i,n}$ for the *sum* of an annuity is equal to or greater than the number of periods.[7]

---

[7]To find the $PVIFA_{i,n}$ for an *annuity due*, look up the $PVIFA_{i,n}$ for $n - 1$ periods, then add 1.0 to this amount to obtain the $PVIFA_{i,n}$ for the annuity due. In the example, the $PVIFA_{i,n}$ for a 4-percent, three-year annuity due is 1.8861 + 1.0 = 2.8861.

# PRESENT VALUE OF AN UNEVEN SERIES OF RECEIPTS

The definition of an annuity includes the words *fixed amount*—in other words, annuities involve situations in which cash flows are *identical* in every period. Although many managerial decisions involve constant cash flows, some important decisions are concerned with uneven flows of cash. Consequently, it is necessary to expand our analysis to deal with varying payment streams.

The *PV* of an uneven stream of future income is found as the sum of the *PV*s of the individual components of the stream. For example, suppose that we are trying to find the *PV* of the stream of receipts shown in Table A.6, discounted at 6 percent. As shown in the table, we multiply each receipt by the appropriate $PVIF_{i,n}$, then sum these products to obtain the *PV* of the stream, $1,413.24. Figure A.5 gives a graphic view of the cash-flow stream.

The *PV* of the receipts shown in Table A.6 and Figure A.5 can also be found by using the annuity equation; the steps in this alternative solution process are as follows:

- *Step 1* Find *PV* of $100 due in one year:

$$\$100(0.9434) = \$94.34.$$

- *Step 2* Recognize that a $200 annuity will be received during Years 2 through 5. Thus, we can determine the value of a five-year annuity, subtract from it the value of a one-year annuity, and have remaining the value of a four-year annuity whose first payment is due in two years. This result is achieved by subtracting the *PVIFA* for a one-year,

■ Table A.6

## Present Value of an Uneven Stream of Receipts ($i = 6\%$)

| Year | Stream of Receipts | $\times PVIF_{i,n}$ = | PV of Individual Receipts |
|------|------|------|------|
| 1 | $ 100 | 0.9434 | $ 94.34 |
| 2 | 200 | 0.8900 | 178.00 |
| 3 | 200 | 0.8396 | 167.92 |
| 4 | 200 | 0.7921 | 158.42 |
| 5 | 200 | 0.7473 | 149.46 |
| 6 | 0 | 0.7050 | 0 |
| 7 | 1,000 | 0.6651 | 665.10 |
| | | PV = Sum = | $1,413.24 |

■ Figure A.5
**Time Line for an Uneven Cash Flow Stream ($i$ = 6 percent)**

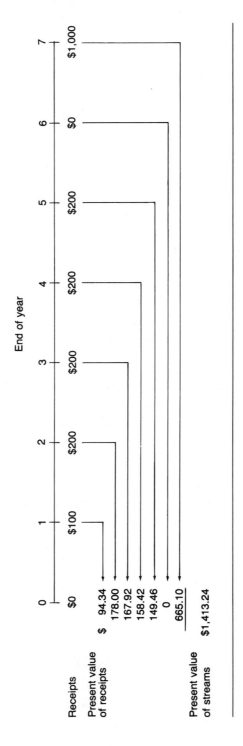

6-percent annuity from the *PVIFA* for a five-year annuity and then multiplying the difference by $200:

$$PV \text{ of the Annuity} = (PVIFA_{6\%, 5 \text{ yrs.}} - PVIFA_{6\%, 1 \text{ yr.}})(\$200)$$
$$= (4.2124 - 0.9434)(\$200)$$
$$= \$653.80.$$

Thus, the present value of the annuity component of the uneven stream is $653.80.

- *Step 3* Find the *PV* of the $1,000 due in Year 7:

$$\$1,000(0.6651) = \$665.10.$$

- *Step 4* Sum the components:

$$\$94.34 + \$653.80 + \$665.10 = \$1,413.24.$$

Either of the two methods can be used to solve problems of this type. However, the alternative (annuity) solution is easier if the annuity component runs for many years. For example, the alternative solution would be clearly superior for finding the *PV* of a stream consisting of $100 in Year 1, $200 in Years 2 through 29, and $1,000 in Year 30.

## ANNUAL PAYMENTS FOR ACCUMULATION OF A FUTURE SUM

Suppose that we want to know the amount of money that must be deposited at 5 percent for each of the next five years in order to have $10,000 available to pay off a debt at the end of the fifth year. Dividing both sides of Equation A.4 by *FVIFA*, we obtain:

$$R = \frac{S_n}{FVIFA_{i,n}}. \qquad \text{A.6}$$

Looking up the future value of an annuity interest factor for five years at 5 percent in Table A.4 and dividing this figure into $10,000, we find:

$$R = \frac{\$10,000}{5.5256} = \$1,810.$$

Thus, if $1,810 is deposited each year in an account paying 5-percent interest, at the end of five years the account will have accumulated $10,000.

## ANNUAL RECEIPTS FROM AN ANNUITY

Suppose that on September 1, 1989, you received an inheritance of $7,000. The money is to be used for your education and is to be spent during the academic years beginning September 1990, 1991, and 1992. If you place the money in a bank account paying 10-percent annual interest and make three equal withdrawals at each of the specified dates, how large can each withdrawal be so as to leave you with exactly a zero balance after the last one has been made?

The solution requires application of the present value of an annuity formula, Equation A.5. Here, however, we know that the present value of the annuity is $7,000, and the problem is to find the three equal annual payments when the interest rate is 10 percent. This calls for dividing both sides of Equation A.5 by $PVIFA_{i,n}$ to derive Equation A.7:

$$R = \frac{A_n}{PVIFA_{i,n}}. \qquad \textbf{A.7}$$

The interest factor is found in Table A.5 to be 2.4869, and substituting this value into Equation A.7, we find the three annual withdrawals to be $2,815:

$$R = \frac{\$7,000}{2.4869} = \$2,815.$$

This particular calculation is used frequently to set up insurance and pension-plan benefit schedules and to find the periodic payments necessary to retire a loan within a specified period. For example, if you want to retire in three equal annual payments a $7,000 bank loan accruing interest at 10 percent on the unpaid balance, each payment would be $2,815. In this case, the bank is acquiring an annuity with a present value of $7,000.

## DETERMINING INTEREST RATES

We can use the basic equations developed earlier to determine the interest rates implicit in financial contracts.

**Example 1**  A bank offers to lend you $1,000 if you sign a note to repay $1,610.50 at the end of five years. What rate of interest are you paying? To solve the problem, recognize that $1,000 is the PV of $1,610.50 due in five years, and solve Equation A.3 for the present value interest factor ($PVIF_{i,n}$).

$$PV = FV_n\left[\frac{1}{(1 + i)^n}\right] = FV_n(PVIF_{i,n})$$

$$\$1,000 = \$1,610.50(PVIF_{i,n} \text{ for 5 years})$$

$$\$1,000/\$1,610.50 = 0.6209 = PVIF_{i,5}. \qquad \textbf{A.3}$$

Now, go to Table A.3 and look across the row for Year 5 until you find 0.6209. It is in the 10-percent column, so you would be paying a 10-percent rate of interest.

**Example 2**  A bank offers to lend you $75,000 to buy a house. You must sign a mortgage calling for payments of $9,562.67 at the end of each of the next 25 years. What interest rate is the bank charging you?

1. Recognize that $75,000 is the *PV* of a 25-year, $9,562.67 annuity:

$$\$75,000 = PV = \sum_{t=1}^{25} \$9,562.67 \left[\frac{1}{(1 + i)^t}\right] = \$9,562.67(PVIFA_{i,n}).$$

2. Solve for $PVIFA_{i,n}$:

$$PVIFA_{i,n} = \$75,000/\$9,562.67 = 7.843.$$

3. Turn to Table B.4 in Appendix B, since Table A.5 does not cover a 25-year period. Looking across the row for 25 periods, we find 7.843 under the column for 12 percent. Therefore, the rate of interest on this mortgage is 12 percent.

# SEMIANNUAL AND OTHER COMPOUNDING PERIODS

All of the examples thus far have assumed that returns were received once a year, or annually. Suppose, however, that you put your $1,000 in a bank that offers to pay 6-percent interest compounded *semiannually*. How much will you have at the end of one year? Semiannual compounding means that interest is actually paid every six months, a fact taken into account in the tabular calculations in Table A.7. Here the annual interest rate is divided by two, but twice as many compounding periods are used, because interest is paid twice a year. Comparing the amount on hand at the end of the second six-month period, $1,060.90, with what would have been on hand under annual compounding, $1,060, shows that semiannual compounding is better from the standpoint of the saver. This result occurs because you earn interest on interest more frequently.

Throughout the economy, different types of investments use different compounding periods. For example, bank and savings and loan accounts generally pay interest quarterly, some bonds pay interest semiannually, and other bonds pay interest annually. Thus, if we are to compare securities with different compounding periods, we need to put them on a common basis. This need has led to the development of the terms *nominal*, or *stated*, *interest rate* and *effective annual*, or *annual percentage*,

■ Table A.7

## Compound Interest Calculations with Semiannual Compounding

|  | Beginning Amount (*PV*) | × (1 + *i*/2) = | Ending Amount, *FV*$_n$ |
|---|---|---|---|
| Period 1 | $1,000.00 | (1.03) | $1,030.00 |
| Period 2 | 1,030.00 | (1.03) | 1,060.90 |

*rate* (APR). The stated, or nominal, rate is the quoted rate; thus, in our example the nominal rate is 6 percent. The annual percentage rate is the rate that would have produced the final compound value, $1,060.90, under annual rather than semiannual compounding. In this case, the effective annual rate is 6.09 percent:

$$\$1,000(1 + i) = \$1,060.90,$$

$$i = \frac{\$1,060.90}{\$1,000} - 1 = 0.0609 = 6.09\%.$$

Thus, if one bank offered 6 percent with semiannual compounding, whereas another offered 6.09 percent with annual compounding, they would both be paying the same effective rate of interest. In general, we can determine the effective annual rate of interest, given the nominal rate, as follows:

- *Step 1* Find the *FV* of $1 at the end of one year, using the equation

$$FV = 1\left(1 + \frac{i_n}{m}\right)^m.$$

  Here $i_n$ is the nominal rate, and $m$ is the number of compounding periods per year.
- *Step 2* Subtract 1.0 from the result in Step 1, then multiply by 100. The final result is the effective annual rate.

**Example**   Find the effective annual rate if the nominal rate is 6 percent, compounded semiannually:

$$\text{Effective Annual Rate} = \left(1 + \frac{0.06}{2}\right)^2 - 1.0$$

$$= (1.03)^2 - 1.0$$

$$= 1.0609 - 1.0$$

$$= 0.0609$$

$$= 6.09 \text{ Percent.}$$

The points made about semiannual compounding can be generalized as follows. When compounding periods are more frequent than once a year, we use a modified version of Equation A.2:

$$FV_n = PV(1 + i)^n, \qquad \textbf{A.2}$$

$$FV_n = PV\left(1 + \frac{i}{m}\right)^{mn}. \qquad \textbf{A.2a}$$

Here $m$ is the number of times per year compounding occurs. When banks compute daily interest, the value of $m$ is set at 365, and Equation A.2a is applied.

The interest tables can be used when compounding occurs more than once a year. Simply divide the nominal, or stated, interest rate by the number of times compounding occurs, and multiply the years by the number of compounding periods per year. For example, to find the amount to which $1,000 will grow after six years with semiannual compounding and a stated 8-percent interest rate, divide 8 percent by 2 and multiply the six years by 2. Then look in Table A.2 under the 4-percent column and in the row for Period 12. You will find an interest factor of 1.6010. Multiplying this by the initial $1,000 gives a value of $1,601, the amount to which $1,000 will grow in six years at 8 percent compounded semiannually. This compares with $1,586.90 for annual compounding.

The same procedure applies in all of the cases covered—compounding, discounting, single payments, and annuities. To illustrate semiannual discounting in finding the present value of an annuity, consider the case described in the section "Present Value of an Annuity"—$1,000 a year for three years, discounted at 4 percent. With annual discounting, the interest factor is 2.7751, and the present value of the annuity is $2,775.10. For semiannual discounting, look under the 2-percent column and in the Period 6 row of Table A.5 to find an interest factor of 5.6014. This is now multiplied by half of $1,000, or the $500 received each six months, to get the present value of the annuity, $2,800.70. The payments come a little more rapidly—the first $500 is paid after only six months (similarly with other payments)—so the annuity is a little more valuable if payments are received semiannually rather than annually.

# SUMMARY

Managerial decisions often require determining the present value of a stream of future cash flows. Also, we often need to know the amount to which an initial quantity will grow during a specified time period, and at other times we must calculate the interest rate built into a financial contract. The basic concepts involved in these processes are called compounding and the time value of money.

The key procedures covered in this appendix are summarized below:

- *Future Value:* $FV_n = PV(1 + i)^n$, where $FV_n$ is the future value of an initial amount, $PV$, compounded at the rate of $i$ percent for $n$ periods. The term $(1 + i)^n$ is the future value interest factor, $FVIF_{i,n}$. Values for $FVIF$ are contained in tables.

- *Present Value:* $PV = FV_n[1/(1 + i)]^n$. This equation is simply a transformation of the future value equation. The term $[1/(1 + i)]^n$ is the present value interest factor, $PVIF_{i,n}$.

- *Future Value of an Annuity:* An annuity is defined as a series of constant or equal payments of $R$ dollars per period. The sum, or future value of an annuity, is given the symbol $S_n$, and it is found as follows:

$$S_n = R\left[\sum_{t=1}^{n}(1 + i)^{t-1}\right].$$ The term $\left[\sum_{t=1}^{n}(1 + i)^{t-1}\right]$ is the future value interest factor for an annuity, $FVIFA_{i,n}$.

- *Present Value of an Annuity:* The present value of an annuity is identified by the symbol $A_n$, and it is found as follows: $$A_n = R\left[\sum_{t=1}^{n}(1/1 + i)^{t}\right].$$ The term $\left[\sum_{t=1}^{n}(1/1 + i)^{t}\right] = PVIFA_{i,n}$ is the present value interest factor for an annuity.

# Interest Factor Tables[1]

[1]Source: Tables, "Future Value of $1 at the End of n Periods," "Present Value of $1 Due at the End of n Periods," "Future Value of an Annuity of $1 per Period for n Periods," and "Present Value of an Annuity of $1 per Period for n Periods," from *Financial Management Theory and Practice*, Fifth Edition, by Eugene F. Brigham and Louis C. Gapenski, pp. 872-879, copyright © 1988 by Holt, Rinehart and Winston, Inc., reprinted by permission of the publisher.

■ Table B.1

## Compound Sum of $1: $FVIF_{i,n} = (1 + i)^n$

| Period | 1% | 2% | 3% | 4% | 5% | 6% | 7% | 8% | 9% | 10% |
|---|---|---|---|---|---|---|---|---|---|---|
| 1 | 1.0100 | 1.0200 | 1.0300 | 1.0400 | 1.0500 | 1.0600 | 1.0700 | 1.0800 | 1.0900 | 1.1000 |
| 2 | 1.0201 | 1.0404 | 1.0609 | 1.0816 | 1.1025 | 1.1236 | 1.1449 | 1.1664 | 1.1881 | 1.2100 |
| 3 | 1.0303 | 1.0612 | 1.0927 | 1.1249 | 1.1576 | 1.1910 | 1.2250 | 1.2597 | 1.2950 | 1.3310 |
| 4 | 1.0406 | 1.0824 | 1.1255 | 1.1699 | 1.2155 | 1.2625 | 1.3108 | 1.3605 | 1.4116 | 1.4641 |
| 5 | 1.0510 | 1.1041 | 1.1593 | 1.2167 | 1.2763 | 1.3382 | 1.4026 | 1.4693 | 1.5386 | 1.6105 |
| 6 | 1.0615 | 1.1262 | 1.1941 | 1.2653 | 1.3401 | 1.4185 | 1.5007 | 1.5869 | 1.6771 | 1.7716 |
| 7 | 1.0721 | 1.1487 | 1.2299 | 1.3159 | 1.4071 | 1.5036 | 1.6058 | 1.7138 | 1.8280 | 1.9487 |
| 8 | 1.0829 | 1.1717 | 1.2668 | 1.3686 | 1.4775 | 1.5938 | 1.7182 | 1.8509 | 1.9926 | 2.1436 |
| 9 | 1.0937 | 1.1951 | 1.3048 | 1.4233 | 1.5513 | 1.6895 | 1.8385 | 1.9990 | 2.1719 | 2.3579 |
| 10 | 1.1046 | 1.2190 | 1.3439 | 1.4802 | 1.6289 | 1.7908 | 1.9672 | 2.1589 | 2.3674 | 2.5937 |
| 11 | 1.1157 | 1.2434 | 1.3842 | 1.5395 | 1.7103 | 1.8983 | 2.1049 | 2.3316 | 2.5804 | 2.8531 |
| 12 | 1.1268 | 1.2682 | 1.4258 | 1.6010 | 1.7959 | 2.0122 | 2.2522 | 2.5182 | 2.8127 | 3.1384 |
| 13 | 1.1381 | 1.2936 | 1.4685 | 1.6651 | 1.8856 | 2.1329 | 2.4098 | 2.7196 | 3.0658 | 3.4523 |
| 14 | 1.1495 | 1.3195 | 1.5126 | 1.7317 | 1.9799 | 2.2609 | 2.5785 | 2.9372 | 3.3417 | 3.7975 |
| 15 | 1.1610 | 1.3459 | 1.5580 | 1.8009 | 2.0789 | 2.3966 | 2.7590 | 3.1722 | 3.6425 | 4.1772 |
| 16 | 1.1726 | 1.3728 | 1.6047 | 1.8730 | 2.1829 | 2.5404 | 2.9522 | 3.4259 | 3.9703 | 4.5950 |
| 17 | 1.1843 | 1.4002 | 1.6528 | 1.9479 | 2.2920 | 2.6928 | 3.1588 | 3.7000 | 4.3276 | 5.0545 |
| 18 | 1.1961 | 1.4282 | 1.7024 | 2.0258 | 2.4066 | 2.8543 | 3.3799 | 3.9960 | 4.7171 | 5.5599 |
| 19 | 1.2081 | 1.4568 | 1.7535 | 2.1068 | 2.5270 | 3.0256 | 3.6165 | 4.3157 | 5.1417 | 6.1159 |
| 20 | 1.2202 | 1.4859 | 1.8061 | 2.1911 | 2.6533 | 3.2071 | 3.8697 | 4.6610 | 5.6044 | 6.7275 |
| 21 | 1.2324 | 1.5157 | 1.8603 | 2.2788 | 2.7860 | 3.3996 | 4.1406 | 5.0338 | 6.1088 | 7.4002 |
| 22 | 1.2447 | 1.5460 | 1.9161 | 2.3699 | 2.9253 | 3.6035 | 4.4304 | 5.4365 | 6.6586 | 8.1403 |
| 23 | 1.2572 | 1.5769 | 1.9736 | 2.4647 | 3.0715 | 3.8197 | 4.7405 | 5.8715 | 7.2579 | 8.9543 |
| 24 | 1.2697 | 1.6084 | 2.0328 | 2.5633 | 3.2251 | 4.0489 | 5.0724 | 6.3412 | 7.9111 | 9.8497 |
| 25 | 1.2824 | 1.6406 | 2.0938 | 2.6658 | 3.3864 | 4.2919 | 5.4274 | 6.8485 | 8.6231 | 10.834 |
| 26 | 1.2953 | 1.6734 | 2.1566 | 2.7725 | 3.5557 | 4.5494 | 5.8074 | 7.3964 | 9.3992 | 11.918 |
| 27 | 1.3082 | 1.7069 | 2.2213 | 2.8834 | 3.7335 | 4.8223 | 6.2139 | 7.9881 | 10.245 | 13.110 |
| 28 | 1.3213 | 1.7410 | 2.2879 | 2.9987 | 3.9201 | 5.1117 | 6.6488 | 8.6271 | 11.167 | 14.421 |
| 29 | 1.3345 | 1.7758 | 2.3566 | 3.1187 | 4.1161 | 5.4184 | 7.1143 | 9.3173 | 12.172 | 15.863 |
| 30 | 1.3478 | 1.8114 | 2.4273 | 3.2434 | 4.3219 | 5.7435 | 7.6123 | 10.062 | 13.267 | 17.449 |
| 40 | 1.4889 | 2.2080 | 3.2620 | 4.8010 | 7.0400 | 10.285 | 14.974 | 21.724 | 31.409 | 45.259 |
| 50 | 1.6446 | 2.6916 | 4.3839 | 7.1067 | 11.467 | 18.420 | 29.457 | 46.901 | 74.357 | 117.39 |
| 60 | 1.8167 | 3.2810 | 5.8916 | 10.519 | 18.679 | 32.987 | 57.946 | 101.25 | 176.03 | 304.48 |

*continued*

■ Table B.1
*continuing*

| Period | 12% | 14% | 15% | 16% | 18% | 20% | 24% | 28% | 32% | 36% |
|---|---|---|---|---|---|---|---|---|---|---|
| 1 | 1.1200 | 1.1400 | 1.1500 | 1.1600 | 1.1800 | 1.2000 | 1.2400 | 1.2800 | 1.3200 | 1.3600 |
| 2 | 1.2544 | 1.2996 | 1.3225 | 1.3456 | 1.3924 | 1.4400 | 1.5376 | 1.6384 | 1.7424 | 1.8496 |
| 3 | 1.4049 | 1.4815 | 1.5209 | 1.5609 | 1.6430 | 1.7280 | 1.9066 | 2.0972 | 2.3000 | 2.5155 |
| 4 | 1.5735 | 1.6890 | 1.7490 | 1.8106 | 1.9388 | 2.0736 | 2.3642 | 2.6844 | 3.0360 | 3.4210 |
| 5 | 1.7623 | 1.9254 | 2.0114 | 2.1003 | 2.2878 | 2.4883 | 2.9316 | 3.4360 | 4.0075 | 4.6526 |
| 6 | 1.9738 | 2.1950 | 2.3131 | 2.4364 | 2.6996 | 2.9860 | 3.6352 | 4.3980 | 5.2899 | 6.3275 |
| 7 | 2.2107 | 2.5023 | 2.6600 | 2.8262 | 3.1855 | 3.5832 | 4.5077 | 5.6295 | 6.9826 | 8.6054 |
| 8 | 2.4760 | 2.8526 | 3.0590 | 3.2784 | 3.7589 | 4.2998 | 5.5895 | 7.2058 | 9.2170 | 11.703 |
| 9 | 2.7731 | 3.2519 | 3.5179 | 3.8030 | 4.4355 | 5.1598 | 6.9310 | 9.2234 | 12.166 | 15.916 |
| 10 | 3.1058 | 3.7072 | 4.0456 | 4.4114 | 5.2338 | 6.1917 | 8.5944 | 11.805 | 16.059 | 21.646 |
| 11 | 3.4785 | 4.2262 | 4.6524 | 5.1173 | 6.1759 | 7.4301 | 10.657 | 15.111 | 21.198 | 29.439 |
| 12 | 3.8960 | 4.8179 | 5.3502 | 5.9360 | 7.2876 | 8.9161 | 13.214 | 19.342 | 27.982 | 40.037 |
| 13 | 4.3635 | 5.4924 | 6.1528 | 6.8858 | 8.5994 | 10.699 | 16.386 | 24.758 | 36.937 | 54.451 |
| 14 | 4.8871 | 6.2613 | 7.0757 | 7.9875 | 10.147 | 12.839 | 20.319 | 31.691 | 48.756 | 74.053 |
| 15 | 5.4736 | 7.1379 | 8.1371 | 9.2655 | 11.973 | 15.407 | 25.195 | 40.564 | 64.358 | 100.71 |
| 16 | 6.1304 | 8.1372 | 9.3576 | 10.748 | 14.129 | 18.488 | 31.242 | 51.923 | 84.953 | 136.96 |
| 17 | 6.8660 | 9.2765 | 10.761 | 12.467 | 16.672 | 22.186 | 38.740 | 66.461 | 112.13 | 186.27 |
| 18 | 7.6900 | 10.575 | 12.375 | 14.462 | 19.673 | 26.623 | 48.038 | 85.070 | 148.02 | 253.33 |
| 19 | 8.6128 | 12.055 | 14.231 | 16.776 | 23.214 | 31.948 | 59.567 | 108.89 | 195.39 | 344.53 |
| 20 | 9.6463 | 13.743 | 16.366 | 19.460 | 27.393 | 38.337 | 73.864 | 139.37 | 257.91 | 468.57 |
| 21 | 10.803 | 15.667 | 18.821 | 22.574 | 32.323 | 46.005 | 91.591 | 178.40 | 340.44 | 637.26 |
| 22 | 12.100 | 17.861 | 21.644 | 26.186 | 38.142 | 55.206 | 113.57 | 228.35 | 449.39 | 866.67 |
| 23 | 13.552 | 20.361 | 24.891 | 30.376 | 45.007 | 66.247 | 140.83 | 292.30 | 593.19 | 1178.6 |
| 24 | 15.178 | 23.212 | 28.625 | 35.236 | 53.108 | 79.496 | 174.63 | 374.14 | 783.02 | 1602.9 |
| 25 | 17.000 | 26.461 | 32.918 | 40.874 | 62.668 | 95.396 | 216.54 | 478.90 | 1033.5 | 2180.0 |
| 26 | 19.040 | 30.166 | 37.856 | 47.414 | 73.948 | 114.47 | 268.51 | 612.99 | 1364.3 | 2964.9 |
| 27 | 21.324 | 34.389 | 43.535 | 55.000 | 87.259 | 137.37 | 332.95 | 784.63 | 1800.9 | 4032.2 |
| 28 | 23.883 | 39.204 | 50.065 | 63.800 | 102.96 | 164.84 | 412.86 | 1004.3 | 2377.2 | 5483.8 |
| 29 | 26.749 | 44.693 | 57.575 | 74.008 | 121.50 | 197.81 | 511.95 | 1285.5 | 3137.9 | 7458.0 |
| 30 | 29.959 | 50.950 | 66.211 | 85.849 | 143.37 | 237.37 | 634.81 | 1645.5 | 4142.0 | 10143. |
| 40 | 93.050 | 188.88 | 267.86 | 378.72 | 750.37 | 1469.7 | 5455.9 | 19426. | 66520. | * |
| 50 | 289.00 | 700.23 | 1083.6 | 1670.7 | 3927.3 | 9100.4 | 46890. | * | * | * |
| 60 | 897.59 | 2595.9 | 4383.9 | 7370.1 | 20555. | 56347. | * | * | * | * |

* *FVIF* > 99,999.

■ Table B.2

## Present Value of $1: $PVIF_{i,n} = 1/(1 + i)^n = 1/FVIF_{i,n}$

| Period | 1% | 2% | 3% | 4% | 5% | 6% | 7% | 8% | 9% | 10% |
|---|---|---|---|---|---|---|---|---|---|---|
| 1 | .9901 | .9804 | .9709 | .9615 | .9524 | .9434 | .9346 | .9259 | .9174 | .9091 |
| 2 | .9803 | .9612 | .9426 | .9246 | .9070 | .8900 | .8734 | .8573 | .8417 | .8264 |
| 3 | .9706 | .9423 | .9151 | .8890 | .8638 | .8396 | .8163 | .7938 | .7722 | .7513 |
| 4 | .9610 | .9238 | .8885 | .8548 | .8227 | .7921 | .7629 | .7350 | .7084 | .6830 |
| 5 | .9515 | .9057 | .8626 | .8219 | .7835 | .7473 | .7130 | .6806 | .6499 | .6209 |
| 6 | .9420 | .8880 | .8375 | .7903 | .7462 | .7050 | .6663 | .6302 | .5963 | .5645 |
| 7 | .9327 | .8706 | .8131 | .7599 | .7107 | .6651 | .6227 | .5835 | .5470 | .5132 |
| 8 | .9235 | .8535 | .7894 | .7307 | .6768 | .6274 | .5820 | .5403 | .5019 | .4665 |
| 9 | .9143 | .8368 | .7664 | .7026 | .6446 | .5919 | .5439 | .5002 | .4604 | .4241 |
| 10 | .9053 | .8203 | .7441 | .6756 | .6139 | .5584 | .5083 | .4632 | .4224 | .3855 |
| 11 | .8963 | .8043 | .7224 | .6496 | .5847 | .5268 | .4751 | .4289 | .3875 | .3505 |
| 12 | .8874 | .7885 | .7014 | .6246 | .5568 | .4970 | .4440 | .3971 | .3555 | .3186 |
| 13 | .8787 | .7730 | .6810 | .6006 | .5303 | .4688 | .4150 | .3677 | .3262 | .2897 |
| 14 | .8700 | .7579 | .6611 | .5775 | .5051 | .4423 | .3878 | .3405 | .2992 | .2633 |
| 15 | .8613 | .7430 | .6419 | .5553 | .4810 | .4173 | .3624 | .3152 | .2745 | .2394 |
| 16 | .8528 | .7284 | .6232 | .5339 | .4581 | .3936 | .3387 | .2919 | .2519 | .2176 |
| 17 | .8444 | .7142 | .6050 | .5134 | .4363 | .3714 | .3166 | .2703 | .2311 | .1978 |
| 18 | .8360 | .7002 | .5874 | .4936 | .4155 | .3503 | .2959 | .2502 | .2120 | .1799 |
| 19 | .8277 | .6864 | .5703 | .4746 | .3957 | .3305 | .2765 | .2317 | .1945 | .1635 |
| 20 | .8195 | .6730 | .5537 | .4564 | .3769 | .3118 | .2584 | .2145 | .1784 | .1486 |
| 21 | .8114 | .6598 | .5375 | .4388 | .3589 | .2942 | .2415 | .1987 | .1637 | .1351 |
| 22 | .8034 | .6468 | .5219 | .4220 | .3418 | .2775 | .2257 | .1839 | .1502 | .1228 |
| 23 | .7954 | .6342 | .5067 | .4057 | .3256 | .2618 | .2109 | .1703 | .1378 | .1117 |
| 24 | .7876 | .6217 | .4919 | .3901 | .3101 | .2470 | .1971 | .1577 | .1264 | .1015 |
| 25 | .7798 | .6095 | .4776 | .3751 | .2953 | .2330 | .1842 | .1460 | .1160 | .0923 |
| 26 | .7720 | .5976 | .4637 | .3607 | .2812 | .2198 | .1722 | .1352 | .1064 | .0839 |
| 27 | .7644 | .5859 | .4502 | .3468 | .2678 | .2074 | .1609 | .1252 | .0976 | .0763 |
| 28 | .7568 | .5744 | .4371 | .3335 | .2551 | .1956 | .1504 | .1159 | .0895 | .0693 |
| 29 | .7493 | .5631 | .4243 | .3207 | .2429 | .1846 | .1406 | .1073 | .0822 | .0630 |
| 30 | .7419 | .5521 | .4120 | .3083 | .2314 | .1741 | .1314 | .0994 | .0754 | .0573 |
| 35 | .7059 | .5000 | .3554 | .2534 | .1813 | .1301 | .0937 | .0676 | .0490 | .0356 |
| 40 | .6717 | .4529 | .3066 | .2083 | .1420 | .0972 | .0668 | .0460 | .0318 | .0221 |
| 45 | .6391 | .4102 | .2644 | .1712 | .1113 | .0727 | .0476 | .0313 | .0207 | .0137 |
| 50 | .6080 | .3715 | .2281 | .1407 | .0872 | .0543 | .0339 | .0213 | .0134 | .0085 |
| 55 | .5785 | .3365 | .1968 | .1157 | .0683 | .0406 | .0242 | .0145 | .0087 | .0053 |

*continued*

■ Table B.2
*continuing*

| Period | 12% | 14% | 15% | 16% | 18% | 20% | 24% | 28% | 32% | 36% |
|---|---|---|---|---|---|---|---|---|---|---|
| 1 | .8929 | .8772 | .8696 | .8621 | .8475 | .8333 | .8065 | .7813 | .7576 | .7353 |
| 2 | .7972 | .7695 | .7561 | .7432 | .7182 | .6944 | .6504 | .6104 | .5739 | .5407 |
| 3 | .7118 | .6750 | .6575 | .6407 | .6086 | .5787 | .5245 | .4768 | .4348 | .3975 |
| 4 | .6355 | .5921 | .5718 | .5523 | .5158 | .4823 | .4230 | .3725 | .3294 | .2923 |
| 5 | .5674 | .5194 | .4972 | .4761 | .4371 | .4019 | .3411 | .2910 | .2495 | .2149 |
| 6 | .5066 | .4556 | .4323 | .4104 | .3704 | .3349 | .2751 | .2274 | .1890 | .1580 |
| 7 | .4523 | .3996 | .3759 | .3538 | .3139 | .2791 | .2218 | .1776 | .1432 | .1162 |
| 8 | .4039 | .3506 | .3269 | .3050 | .2660 | .2326 | .1789 | .1388 | .1085 | .0854 |
| 9 | .3606 | .3075 | .2843 | .2630 | .2255 | .1938 | .1443 | .1084 | .0822 | .0628 |
| 10 | .3220 | .2697 | .2472 | .2267 | .1911 | .1615 | .1164 | .0847 | .0623 | .0462 |
| 11 | .2875 | .2366 | .2149 | .1954 | .1619 | .1346 | .0938 | .0662 | .0472 | .0340 |
| 12 | .2567 | .2076 | .1869 | .1685 | .1372 | .1122 | .0757 | .0517 | .0357 | .0250 |
| 13 | .2292 | .1821 | .1625 | .1452 | .1163 | .0935 | .0610 | .0404 | .0271 | .0184 |
| 14 | .2046 | .1597 | .1413 | .1252 | .0985 | .0779 | .0492 | .0316 | .0205 | .0135 |
| 15 | .1827 | .1401 | .1229 | .1079 | .0835 | .0649 | .0397 | .0247 | .0155 | .0099 |
| 16 | .1631 | .1229 | .1069 | .0930 | .0708 | .0541 | .0320 | .0193 | .0118 | .0073 |
| 17 | .1456 | .1078 | .0929 | .0802 | .0600 | .0451 | .0258 | .0150 | .0089 | .0054 |
| 18 | .1300 | .0946 | .0808 | .0691 | .0508 | .0376 | .0208 | .0118 | .0068 | .0039 |
| 19 | .1161 | .0829 | .0703 | .0596 | .0431 | .0313 | .0168 | .0092 | .0051 | .0029 |
| 20 | .1037 | .0728 | .0611 | .0514 | .0365 | .0261 | .0135 | .0072 | .0039 | .0021 |
| 21 | .0926 | .0638 | .0531 | .0443 | .0309 | .0217 | .0109 | .0056 | .0029 | .0016 |
| 22 | .0826 | .0560 | .0462 | .0382 | .0262 | .0181 | .0088 | .0044 | .0022 | .0012 |
| 23 | .0738 | .0491 | .0402 | .0329 | .0222 | .0151 | .0071 | .0034 | .0017 | .0008 |
| 24 | .0659 | .0431 | .0349 | .0284 | .0188 | .0126 | .0057 | .0027 | .0013 | .0006 |
| 25 | .0588 | .0378 | .0304 | .0245 | .0160 | .0105 | .0046 | .0021 | .0010 | .0005 |
| 26 | .0525 | .0331 | .0264 | .0211 | .0135 | .0087 | .0037 | .0016 | .0007 | .0003 |
| 27 | .0469 | .0291 | .0230 | .0182 | .0115 | .0073 | .0030 | .0013 | .0006 | .0002 |
| 28 | .0419 | .0255 | .0200 | .0157 | .0097 | .0061 | .0024 | .0010 | .0004 | .0002 |
| 29 | .0374 | .0224 | .0174 | .0135 | .0082 | .0051 | .0020 | .0008 | .0003 | .0001 |
| 30 | .0334 | .00196 | .0151 | .0116 | .0070 | .0042 | .0016 | .0006 | .0002 | .0001 |
| 35 | .0189 | .0102 | .0075 | .0055 | .0030 | .0017 | .0005 | .0002 | .0001 | * |
| 40 | .0107 | .0053 | .0037 | .0026 | .0013 | .0007 | .0002 | .0001 | * | * |
| 45 | .0061 | .0027 | .0019 | .0013 | .0006 | .0003 | .0001 | * | * | * |
| 50 | .0035 | .0014 | .0009 | .0006 | .0003 | .0001 | * | * | * | * |
| 55 | .0020 | .0007 | .0005 | .0003 | .0001 | * | * | * | * | * |

*The factor is zero to four decimal places.

■ Table B.3

## Sum of an Annuity of $1 for *n* Periods

$$FVIFA_{i,n} = \sum_{t=1}^{n} (1 + i)^{t-1}$$

$$= \frac{(1 + i)^n - 1}{i}$$

| Number of Periods | 1% | 2% | 3% | 4% | 5% | 6% | 7% | 8% | 9% | 10% |
|---|---|---|---|---|---|---|---|---|---|---|
| 1 | 1.0000 | 1.0000 | 1.0000 | 1.0000 | 1.0000 | 1.0000 | 1.0000 | 1.0000 | 1.0000 | 1.0000 |
| 2 | 2.0100 | 2.0200 | 2.0300 | 2.0400 | 2.0500 | 2.0600 | 2.0700 | 2.0800 | 2.0900 | 2.1000 |
| 3 | 3.0301 | 3.0604 | 3.0909 | 3.1216 | 3.1525 | 3.1836 | 3.2149 | 3.2464 | 3.2781 | 3.3100 |
| 4 | 4.0604 | 4.1216 | 4.1836 | 4.2465 | 4.3101 | 4.3746 | 4.4399 | 4.5061 | 4.5731 | 4.6410 |
| 5 | 5.1010 | 5.2040 | 5.3091 | 5.4163 | 5.5256 | 5.6371 | 5.7507 | 5.8666 | 5.9847 | 6.1051 |
| 6 | 6.1520 | 6.3081 | 6.4684 | 6.6330 | 6.8019 | 6.9753 | 7.1533 | 7.3359 | 7.5233 | 7.7156 |
| 7 | 7.2135 | 7.4343 | 7.6625 | 7.8983 | 8.1420 | 8.3938 | 8.6540 | 8.9228 | 9.2004 | 9.4872 |
| 8 | 8.2857 | 8.5830 | 8.8923 | 9.2142 | 9.5491 | 9.8975 | 10.259 | 10.636 | 11.028 | 11.435 |
| 9 | 9.3685 | 9.7546 | 10.159 | 10.582 | 11.026 | 11.491 | 11.978 | 12.487 | 13.021 | 13.579 |
| 10 | 10.462 | 10.949 | 11.463 | 12.006 | 12.577 | 13.180 | 13.816 | 14.486 | 15.192 | 15.937 |
| 11 | 11.566 | 12.168 | 12.807 | 13.486 | 14.206 | 14.971 | 15.783 | 16.645 | 17.560 | 18.531 |
| 12 | 12.682 | 13.412 | 14.192 | 15.025 | 15.917 | 16.869 | 17.888 | 18.977 | 20.140 | 21.384 |
| 13 | 13.809 | 14.680 | 15.617 | 16.626 | 17.713 | 18.882 | 20.140 | 21.495 | 22.953 | 24.522 |
| 14 | 14.947 | 15.973 | 17.086 | 18.291 | 19.598 | 21.015 | 22.550 | 24.214 | 26.019 | 27.975 |
| 15 | 16.096 | 17.293 | 18.598 | 20.023 | 21.578 | 23.276 | 25.129 | 27.152 | 29.360 | 31.772 |
| 16 | 17.257 | 18.639 | 20.156 | 21.824 | 23.657 | 25.672 | 27.888 | 30.324 | 33.003 | 35.949 |
| 17 | 18.430 | 20.012 | 21.761 | 23.697 | 25.840 | 28.212 | 30.840 | 33.750 | 36.973 | 40.544 |
| 18 | 19.614 | 21.412 | 23.414 | 25.645 | 28.132 | 30.905 | 33.999 | 37.450 | 41.301 | 45.599 |
| 19 | 20.810 | 22.840 | 25.116 | 27.671 | 30.539 | 33.760 | 37.379 | 41.446 | 46.018 | 51.159 |
| 20 | 22.019 | 24.297 | 26.870 | 29.778 | 33.066 | 36.785 | 40.995 | 45.762 | 51.160 | 57.275 |
| 21 | 23.239 | 25.783 | 28.676 | 31.969 | 35.719 | 39.992 | 44.865 | 50.422 | 56.764 | 64.002 |
| 22 | 24.471 | 27.299 | 30.536 | 34.248 | 38.505 | 43.392 | 49.005 | 55.456 | 62.873 | 71.402 |
| 23 | 25.716 | 28.845 | 32.452 | 36.617 | 41.430 | 46.995 | 53.436 | 60.893 | 69.531 | 79.543 |
| 24 | 26.973 | 30.421 | 34.426 | 39.082 | 44.502 | 50.815 | 58.176 | 66.764 | 76.789 | 88.497 |
| 25 | 28.243 | 32.030 | 36.459 | 41.645 | 47.727 | 54.864 | 63.249 | 73.105 | 84.700 | 98.347 |
| 26 | 29.525 | 33.670 | 38.553 | 44.311 | 51.113 | 59.156 | 68.676 | 79.954 | 93.323 | 109.18 |
| 27 | 30.820 | 35.344 | 40.709 | 47.084 | 54.669 | 63.705 | 74.483 | 87.350 | 102.72 | 121.09 |
| 28 | 32.129 | 37.051 | 42.930 | 49.967 | 58.402 | 68.528 | 80.697 | 95.338 | 112.96 | 134.20 |
| 29 | 33.450 | 38.792 | 45.218 | 52.966 | 62.322 | 73.639 | 87.346 | 103.96 | 124.13 | 148.63 |
| 30 | 34.784 | 40.568 | 47.575 | 56.084 | 66.438 | 79.058 | 94.460 | 113.28 | 136.30 | 164.49 |
| 40 | 48.886 | 60.402 | 75.401 | 95.025 | 120.79 | 154.76 | 199.63 | 259.05 | 337.88 | 442.59 |
| 50 | 64.463 | 84.579 | 112.79 | 152.66 | 209.34 | 290.33 | 406.52 | 573.76 | 815.08 | 1163.9 |
| 60 | 81.669 | 114.05 | 163.05 | 237.99 | 353.58 | 533.12 | 813.52 | 1253.2 | 1944.7 | 3034.8 |

*continued*

■ Table B.3
*continuing*

| Number of Periods | 12% | 14% | 15% | 16% | 18% | 20% | 24% | 28% | 32% | 36% |
|---|---|---|---|---|---|---|---|---|---|---|
| 1 | 1.0000 | 1.0000 | 1.0000 | 1.0000 | 1.0000 | 1.0000 | 1.0000 | 1.0000 | 1.0000 | 1.0000 |
| 2 | 2.1200 | 2.1400 | 2.1500 | 2.1600 | 2.1800 | 2.2000 | 2.2400 | 2.2800 | 2.3200 | 2.3600 |
| 3 | 3.3744 | 3.4396 | 3.4725 | 3.5056 | 3.5724 | 3.6400 | 3.7776 | 3.9184 | 4.0624 | 4.2096 |
| 4 | 4.7793 | 4.9211 | 4.9934 | 5.0665 | 5.2154 | 5.3680 | 5.6842 | 6.0156 | 6.3624 | 6.7251 |
| 5 | 6.3528 | 6.6101 | 6.7424 | 6.8771 | 7.1542 | 7.4416 | 8.0484 | 8.6999 | 9.3983 | 10.146 |
| 6 | 8.1152 | 8.5355 | 8.7537 | 8.9775 | 9.4420 | 9.9299 | 10.980 | 12.135 | 13.405 | 14.798 |
| 7 | 10.089 | 10.730 | 11.066 | 11.413 | 12.141 | 12.915 | 14.615 | 16.533 | 18.695 | 21.126 |
| 8 | 12.299 | 13.232 | 13.726 | 14.240 | 15.327 | 16.499 | 19.122 | 22.163 | 25.678 | 29.731 |
| 9 | 14.775 | 16.085 | 16.785 | 17.518 | 19.085 | 20.798 | 24.712 | 29.369 | 34.895 | 41.435 |
| 10 | 17.548 | 19.337 | 20.303 | 21.321 | 23.521 | 25.958 | 31.643 | 38.592 | 47.061 | 57.351 |
| 11 | 20.654 | 23.044 | 24.349 | 25.732 | 28.755 | 32.150 | 40.237 | 50.398 | 63.121 | 78.998 |
| 12 | 24.133 | 27.270 | 29.001 | 30.850 | 34.931 | 39.580 | 50.894 | 65.510 | 84.320 | 108.43 |
| 13 | 28.029 | 32.088 | 34.351 | 36.786 | 42.218 | 48.496 | 64.109 | 84.852 | 112.30 | 148.47 |
| 14 | 32.392 | 37.581 | 40.504 | 43.672 | 50.818 | 59.195 | 80.496 | 109.61 | 149.23 | 202.92 |
| 15 | 37.279 | 43.842 | 47.580 | 51.659 | 60.965 | 72.035 | 100.81 | 141.30 | 197.99 | 276.97 |
| 16 | 42.753 | 50.980 | 55.717 | 60.925 | 72.939 | 87.442 | 126.01 | 181.86 | 262.35 | 377.69 |
| 17 | 48.883 | 59.117 | 65.075 | 71.673 | 87.068 | 105.93 | 157.25 | 233.79 | 347.30 | 514.66 |
| 18 | 55.749 | 68.394 | 75.836 | 84.140 | 103.74 | 128.11 | 195.99 | 300.25 | 459.44 | 700.93 |
| 19 | 63.439 | 78.969 | 88.211 | 98.603 | 123.41 | 154.74 | 244.03 | 385.32 | 607.47 | 954.27 |
| 20 | 72.052 | 91.024 | 102.44 | 115.37 | 146.62 | 186.68 | 303.60 | 494.21 | 802.86 | 1298.8 |
| 21 | 81.698 | 104.76 | 118.81 | 134.84 | 174.02 | 225.02 | 377.46 | 633.59 | 1060.7 | 1767.3 |
| 22 | 92.502 | 120.43 | 137.63 | 157.41 | 206.34 | 271.03 | 469.05 | 811.99 | 1401.2 | 2404.6 |
| 23 | 104.60 | 138.29 | 159.27 | 183.60 | 244.48 | 326.23 | 582.62 | 1040.3 | 1850.6 | 3271.3 |
| 24 | 118.15 | 158.65 | 184.16 | 213.97 | 289.49 | 392.48 | 723.46 | 1332.6 | 2443.8 | 4449.9 |
| 25 | 133.33 | 181.87 | 212.79 | 249.21 | 342.60 | 471.98 | 898.09 | 1706.8 | 3226.8 | 6052.9 |
| 26 | 150.33 | 208.33 | 245.71 | 290.08 | 405.27 | 567.37 | 1114.6 | 2185.7 | 4260.4 | 8233.0 |
| 27 | 169.37 | 238.49 | 283.56 | 337.50 | 479.22 | 681.85 | 1383.1 | 2798.7 | 5624.7 | 11197.9 |
| 28 | 190.69 | 272.88 | 327.10 | 392.50 | 566.48 | 819.22 | 1716.0 | 3583.3 | 7425.6 | 15230.2 |
| 29 | 214.58 | 312.09 | 377.16 | 456.30 | 669.44 | 984.06 | 2128.9 | 4587.6 | 9802.9 | 20714.1 |
| 30 | 241.33 | 356.78 | 434.74 | 530.31 | 790.94 | 1181.8 | 2640.9 | 5873.2 | 12940. | 28172.2 |
| 40 | 767.09 | 1342.0 | 1779.0 | 2360.7 | 4163.2 | 7343.8 | 22728. | 69377. | * | * |
| 50 | 2400.0 | 4994.5 | 7217.7 | 10435. | 21813. | 45497. | * | * | * | * |
| 60 | 7471.6 | 18535. | 29219. | 46057. | * | * | * | * | * | * |

*FVIFA > 99,999.

■ Table B.4
## Present Value of an Annuity of $1 for *n* Periods

$$PVIFA_{i,n} = \sum_{t=1}^{n} \frac{1}{(1 + i)^t} = \frac{1 - \dfrac{1}{(1 + i)^n}}{i}$$

| Number of Payments | 1% | 2% | 3% | 4% | 5% | 6% | 7% | 8% | 9% |
|---|---|---|---|---|---|---|---|---|---|
| 1 | 0.9901 | 0.9804 | 0.9709 | 0.9615 | 0.9524 | 0.9434 | 0.9346 | 0.9259 | 0.9174 |
| 2 | 1.9704 | 1.9416 | 1.9135 | 1.8861 | 1.8594 | 1.8334 | 1.8080 | 1.7833 | 1.7591 |
| 3 | 2.9410 | 2.8839 | 2.8286 | 2.7751 | 2.7232 | 2.6730 | 2.6243 | 2.5771 | 2.5313 |
| 4 | 3.9020 | 3.8077 | 3.7171 | 3.6299 | 3.5460 | 3.4651 | 3.3872 | 3.3121 | 3.2397 |
| 5 | 4.8534 | 4.7135 | 4.5797 | 4.4518 | 4.3295 | 4.2124 | 4.1002 | 3.9927 | 3.8897 |
| 6 | 5.7955 | 5.6014 | 5.4172 | 5.2421 | 5.0757 | 4.9173 | 4.7665 | 4.6229 | 4.4859 |
| 7 | 6.7282 | 6.4720 | 6.2303 | 6.0021 | 5.7864 | 5.5824 | 5.3893 | 5.2064 | 5.0330 |
| 8 | 7.6517 | 7.3255 | 7.0197 | 6.7327 | 6.4632 | 6.2098 | 5.9713 | 5.7466 | 5.5348 |
| 9 | 8.5660 | 8.1622 | 7.7861 | 7.4353 | 7.1078 | 6.8017 | 6.5152 | 6.2469 | 5.9952 |
| 10 | 9.4713 | 8.9826 | 8.5302 | 8.1109 | 7.7217 | 7.3601 | 7.0236 | 6.7101 | 6.4177 |
| 11 | 10.3676 | 9.7868 | 9.2526 | 8.7605 | 8.3064 | 7.8869 | 7.4987 | 7.1390 | 6.8052 |
| 12 | 11.2551 | 10.5753 | 9.9540 | 9.3851 | 8.8633 | 8.3838 | 7.9427 | 7.5361 | 7.1607 |
| 13 | 12.1337 | 11.3484 | 10.6350 | 9.9856 | 9.3936 | 8.8527 | 8.3577 | 7.9038 | 7.4869 |
| 14 | 13.0037 | 12.1062 | 11.2961 | 10.5631 | 9.8986 | 9.2950 | 8.7455 | 8.2442 | 7.7862 |
| 15 | 13.8651 | 12.8493 | 11.9379 | 11.1184 | 10.3797 | 9.7122 | 9.1079 | 8.5595 | 8.0607 |
| 16 | 14.7179 | 13.5777 | 12.5611 | 11.6523 | 10.8378 | 10.1059 | 9.4466 | 8.8514 | 8.3126 |
| 17 | 15.5623 | 14.2919 | 13.1661 | 12.1657 | 11.2741 | 10.4773 | 9.7632 | 9.1216 | 8.5436 |
| 18 | 16.3983 | 14.9920 | 13.7535 | 12.6593 | 11.6896 | 10.8276 | 10.0591 | 9.3719 | 8.7556 |
| 19 | 17.2260 | 15.6785 | 14.3238 | 13.1339 | 12.0853 | 11.1581 | 10.3356 | 9.6036 | 8.9501 |
| 20 | 18.0456 | 16.3514 | 14.8775 | 13.5903 | 12.4622 | 11.4699 | 10.5940 | 9.8181 | 9.1285 |
| 21 | 18.8570 | 17.0112 | 15.4150 | 14.0292 | 12.8212 | 11.7641 | 10.8355 | 10.0168 | 9.2922 |
| 22 | 19.6604 | 17.6580 | 15.9369 | 14.4511 | 13.1630 | 12.0416 | 11.0612 | 10.2007 | 9.4424 |
| 23 | 20.4558 | 18.2922 | 16.4436 | 14.8568 | 13.4886 | 12.3034 | 11.2722 | 10.3711 | 9.5802 |
| 24 | 21.2434 | 18.9139 | 16.9355 | 15.2470 | 13.7986 | 12.5504 | 11.4693 | 10.5288 | 9.7066 |
| 25 | 22.0232 | 19.5235 | 17.4131 | 15.6221 | 14.0939 | 12.7834 | 11.6536 | 10.6748 | 9.8226 |
| 26 | 22.7952 | 20.1210 | 17.8768 | 15.9828 | 14.3752 | 13.0032 | 11.8258 | 10.8100 | 9.9290 |
| 27 | 23.5596 | 20.7069 | 18.3270 | 16.3296 | 14.6430 | 13.2105 | 11.9867 | 10.9352 | 10.0266 |
| 28 | 24.3164 | 21.2813 | 18.7641 | 16.6631 | 14.8981 | 13.4062 | 12.1371 | 11.0511 | 10.1161 |
| 29 | 25.0658 | 21.8444 | 19.1885 | 16.9837 | 15.1411 | 13.5907 | 12.2777 | 11.1584 | 10.1983 |
| 30 | 25.8077 | 22.3965 | 19.6004 | 17.2920 | 15.3725 | 13.7648 | 12.4090 | 11.2578 | 10.2737 |
| 35 | 29.4086 | 24.9986 | 21.4872 | 18.6646 | 16.3742 | 14.4982 | 12.9477 | 11.6546 | 10.5668 |
| 40 | 32.8347 | 27.3555 | 23.1148 | 19.7928 | 17.1591 | 15.0463 | 13.3317 | 11.9246 | 10.7574 |
| 45 | 36.0945 | 29.4902 | 24.5187 | 20.7200 | 17.7741 | 15.4558 | 13.6055 | 12.1084 | 10.8812 |
| 50 | 39.1961 | 31.4236 | 25.7298 | 21.4822 | 18.2559 | 15.7619 | 13.8007 | 12.2335 | 10.9617 |
| 55 | 42.1472 | 33.1748 | 26.7744 | 22.1086 | 18.6335 | 15.9905 | 13.9399 | 12.3186 | 11.0140 |

*continued*

■ Table B.4
*continuing*

| Number of Pay- ments | 10% | 12% | 14% | 15% | 16% | 18% | 20% | 24% | 28% | 32% |
|---|---|---|---|---|---|---|---|---|---|---|
| 1 | 0.9091 | 0.8929 | 0.8772 | 0.8696 | 0.8621 | 0.8475 | 0.8333 | 0.8065 | 0.7813 | 0.7576 |
| 2 | 1.7355 | 1.6901 | 1.6467 | 1.6257 | 1.6052 | 1.5656 | 1.5278 | 1.4568 | 1.3916 | 1.3315 |
| 3 | 2.4869 | 2.4018 | 2.3216 | 2.2832 | 2.2459 | 2.1743 | 2.1065 | 1.9813 | 1.8684 | 1.7663 |
| 4 | 3.1699 | 3.0373 | 2.9137 | 2.8550 | 2.7982 | 2.6901 | 2.5887 | 2.4043 | 2.2410 | 2.0957 |
| 5 | 3.7908 | 3.6048 | 3.4331 | 3.3522 | 3.2743 | 3.1272 | 2.9906 | 2.7454 | 2.5320 | 2.3452 |
| 6 | 4.3553 | 4.1114 | 3.8887 | 3.7845 | 3.6847 | 3.4976 | 3.3255 | 3.0205 | 2.7594 | 2.5342 |
| 7 | 4.8684 | 4.5638 | 4.2883 | 4.1604 | 4.0386 | 3.8115 | 3.6046 | 3.2423 | 2.9370 | 2.6775 |
| 8 | 5.3349 | 4.9676 | 4.6389 | 4.4873 | 4.3436 | 4.0776 | 3.8372 | 3.4212 | 3.0758 | 2.7860 |
| 9 | 5.7590 | 5.3282 | 4.9464 | 4.7716 | 4.6065 | 4.3030 | 4.0310 | 3.5655 | 3.1842 | 2.8681 |
| 10 | 6.1446 | 5.6502 | 5.2161 | 5.0188 | 4.8332 | 4.4941 | 4.1925 | 3.6819 | 3.2689 | 2.9304 |
| 11 | 6.4951 | 5.9377 | 5.4527 | 5.2337 | 5.0286 | 4.6560 | 4.3271 | 3.7757 | 3.3351 | 2.9776 |
| 12 | 6.8137 | 6.1944 | 5.6603 | 5.4206 | 5.1971 | 4.7932 | 4.4392 | 3.8514 | 3.3868 | 3.0133 |
| 13 | 7.1034 | 6.4235 | 5.8424 | 5.5831 | 5.3423 | 4.9095 | 4.5327 | 3.9124 | 3.4272 | 3.0404 |
| 14 | 7.3667 | 6.6282 | 6.0021 | 5.7245 | 5.4675 | 5.0081 | 4.6106 | 3.9616 | 3.4587 | 3.0609 |
| 15 | 7.6061 | 6.8109 | 6.1422 | 5.8474 | 5.5755 | 5.0916 | 4.6755 | 4.0013 | 3.4834 | 3.0764 |
| 16 | 7.8237 | 6.9740 | 6.2651 | 5.9542 | 5.6685 | 5.1624 | 4.7296 | 4.0333 | 3.5026 | 3.0882 |
| 17 | 8.0216 | 7.1196 | 6.3729 | 6.0472 | 5.7487 | 5.2223 | 4.7746 | 4.0591 | 3.5177 | 3.0971 |
| 18 | 8.2014 | 7.2497 | 6.4674 | 6.1280 | 5.8178 | 5.2732 | 4.8122 | 4.0799 | 3.5294 | 3.1039 |
| 19 | 8.3649 | 7.3658 | 6.5504 | 6.1982 | 5.8775 | 5.3162 | 4.8435 | 4.0967 | 3.5386 | 3.1090 |
| 20 | 8.5136 | 7.4694 | 6.6231 | 6.2593 | 5.9288 | 5.3527 | 4.8696 | 4.1103 | 3.5458 | 3.1129 |
| 21 | 8.6487 | 7.5620 | 6.6870 | 6.3125 | 5.9731 | 5.3837 | 4.8913 | 4.1212 | 3.5514 | 3.1158 |
| 22 | 8.7715 | 7.6446 | 6.7429 | 6.3587 | 6.0113 | 5.4099 | 4.9094 | 4.1300 | 3.5558 | 3.1180 |
| 23 | 8.8832 | 7.7184 | 6.7921 | 6.3988 | 6.0442 | 5.4321 | 4.9245 | 4.1371 | 3.5592 | 3.1197 |
| 24 | 8.9847 | 7.7843 | 6.8351 | 6.4338 | 6.0726 | 5.4510 | 4.9371 | 4.1428 | 3.5619 | 3.1210 |
| 25 | 9.0770 | 7.8431 | 6.8729 | 6.4642 | 6.0971 | 5.4669 | 4.9476 | 4.1474 | 3.5640 | 3.1220 |
| 26 | 9.1609 | 7.8957 | 6.9061 | 6.4906 | 6.1182 | 5.4804 | 4.9563 | 4.1511 | 3.5656 | 3.1227 |
| 27 | 9.2372 | 7.9426 | 6.9352 | 6.5135 | 6.1364 | 5.4919 | 4.9636 | 4.1542 | 3.5669 | 3.1233 |
| 28 | 9.3066 | 7.9844 | 6.9607 | 6.5335 | 6.1520 | 5.5016 | 4.9697 | 4.1566 | 3.5679 | 3.1237 |
| 29 | 9.3696 | 8.0218 | 6.9830 | 6.5509 | 6.1656 | 5.5098 | 4.9747 | 4.1585 | 3.5687 | 3.1240 |
| 30 | 9.4269 | 8.0552 | 7.0027 | 6.5660 | 6.1772 | 5.5168 | 4.9789 | 4.1601 | 3.5693 | 3.1242 |
| 35 | 9.6442 | 8.1755 | 7.0700 | 6.6166 | 6.2153 | 5.5386 | 4.9915 | 4.1644 | 3.5708 | 3.1248 |
| 40 | 9.7791 | 8.2438 | 7.1050 | 6.6418 | 6.2335 | 5.5482 | 4.9966 | 4.1659 | 3.5712 | 3.1250 |
| 45 | 9.8628 | 8.2825 | 7.1232 | 6.6543 | 6.2421 | 5.5523 | 4.9986 | 4.1664 | 3.5714 | 3.1250 |
| 50 | 9.9148 | 8.3045 | 7.1327 | 6.6605 | 6.2463 | 5.5541 | 4.9995 | 4.1666 | 3.5714 | 3.1250 |
| 55 | 9.9471 | 8.3170 | 7.1376 | 6.6636 | 6.2482 | 5.5549 | 4.9998 | 4.1666 | 3.5714 | 3.1250 |

# Statistical Tables

■ Table C.1
## Values of the Standard Normal Distribution Function[1]

| z | 0.00 | 0.01 | 0.02 | 0.03 | 0.04 | 0.05 | 0.06 | 0.07 | 0.08 | 0.09 |
|---|------|------|------|------|------|------|------|------|------|------|
| 0.0 | .0000 | .0040 | .0080 | .0120 | .0160 | .0199 | .0239 | .0279 | .0319 | .0359 |
| 0.1 | .0398 | .0438 | .0478 | .0517 | .0557 | .0596 | .0636 | .0675 | .0714 | .0753 |
| 0.2 | .0793 | .0832 | .0871 | .0910 | .0948 | .0987 | .1026 | .1064 | .1103 | .1141 |
| 0.3 | .1179 | .1217 | .1255 | .1293 | .1331 | .1368 | .1406 | .1443 | .1480 | .1517 |
| 0.4 | .1554 | .1591 | .1628 | .1664 | .1700 | .1736 | .1772 | .1808 | .1844 | .1879 |
| 0.5 | .1915 | .1950 | .1985 | .2019 | .2054 | .2088 | .2123 | .2157 | .2190 | .2224 |
| 0.6 | .2257 | .2291 | .2324 | .2357 | .2389 | .2422 | .2454 | .2486 | .2517 | .2549 |
| 0.7 | .2580 | .2611 | .2642 | .2673 | .2704 | .2734 | .2764 | .2794 | .2823 | .2852 |
| 0.8 | .2881 | .2910 | .2939 | .2967 | .2995 | .3023 | .3051 | .3078 | .3106 | .3133 |
| 0.9 | .3159 | .3186 | .3212 | .3238 | .3264 | .3289 | .3315 | .3340 | .3365 | .3389 |
| 1.0 | .3413 | .3438 | .3461 | .3485 | .3508 | .3531 | .3554 | .3577 | .3599 | .3621 |
| 1.1 | .3643 | .3665 | .3686 | .3708 | .3729 | .3749 | .3770 | .3790 | .3810 | .3830 |
| 1.2 | .3849 | .3869 | .3888 | .3907 | .3925 | .3944 | .3962 | .3980 | .3997 | .4015 |
| 1.3 | .4032 | .4049 | .4066 | .4082 | .4099 | .4115 | .4131 | .4147 | .4162 | .4177 |
| 1.4 | .4192 | .4207 | .4222 | .4236 | .4251 | .4265 | .4279 | .4292 | .4306 | .4319 |
| 1.5 | .4332 | .4345 | .4357 | .4370 | .4382 | .4394 | .4406 | .4418 | .4429 | .4441 |
| 1.6 | .4452 | .4463 | .4474 | .4484 | .4495 | .4505 | .4515 | .4525 | .4535 | .4545 |
| 1.7 | .4554 | .4564 | .4573 | .4582 | .4591 | .4599 | .4608 | .4616 | .4625 | .4633 |
| 1.8 | .4641 | .4649 | .4656 | .4664 | .4671 | .4678 | .4686 | .4693 | .4699 | .4706 |
| 1.9 | .4713 | .4719 | .4726 | .4732 | .4738 | .4744 | .4750 | .4756 | .4761 | .4767 |
| 2.0 | .4773 | .4778 | .4783 | .4788 | .4793 | .4798 | .4803 | .4808 | .4812 | .4817 |
| 2.1 | .4821 | .4826 | .4830 | .4834 | .4838 | .4842 | .4846 | .4850 | .4854 | .4857 |
| 2.2 | .4861 | .4864 | .4868 | .4871 | .4875 | .4878 | .4881 | .4884 | .4887 | .4890 |
| 2.3 | .4893 | .4896 | .4898 | .4901 | .4904 | .4906 | .4909 | .4911 | .4913 | .4916 |
| 2.4 | .4918 | .4920 | .4922 | .4925 | .4927 | .4929 | .4931 | .4932 | .4934 | .4936 |
| 2.5 | .4938 | .4940 | .4941 | .4943 | .4945 | .4946 | .4948 | .4949 | .4951 | .4952 |
| 2.6 | .4953 | .4955 | .4956 | .4957 | .4959 | .4960 | .4961 | .4962 | .4963 | .4964 |
| 2.7 | .4965 | .4966 | .4967 | .4968 | .4969 | .4970 | .4971 | .4972 | .4973 | .4974 |
| 2.8 | .4974 | .4975 | .4976 | .4977 | .4977 | .4978 | .4979 | .4979 | .4980 | .4981 |
| 2.9 | .4981 | .4982 | .4982 | .4982 | .4984 | .4984 | .4985 | .4985 | .4986 | .4986 |
| 3.0 | .4987 | .4987 | .4987 | .4988 | .4988 | .4989 | .4989 | .4989 | .4990 | .4990 |

[1]z is the standardized variable, where $z = x - \mu/\sigma$ and x is the point of interest, $\mu$ is the mean, and $\sigma$ is the standard deviation of a distribution. Thus, z measures the number of standard deviations between a point of interest x and the mean of a given distribution. In the table above, we indicate the percentage of the total area under the normal curve between x and $\mu$. Thus, .3413 or 34.13% of the area under the normal curve lies between a point of interest and the mean when z = 1.0.

Source: Table, "Value of the Areas under the Standard Normal Distribution Function," from *Financial Management Theory and Practice*, Fifth Edition, by Eugene F. Brigham and Louis C. Gapenski, 0.880. Copyright © 1988 by Holt, Rinehart and Winston, Inc., reprinted by permission of the publisher.

■ Table C.2
## Critical $F$ Values at the 90-Percent Confidence Level ($\alpha$ = .10)[2]

*Degrees of Freedom in the Numerator (d.f. = k − 1)*

Degrees of Freedom in the Denominator (d.f. = n − k)

| | 1 | 2 | 3 | 4 | 5 | 6 | 7 | 8 | 9 | 10 | 12 | 15 | 20 | 24 | 30 | 40 | 60 | 120 | ∞ |
|---|---|---|---|---|---|---|---|---|---|---|---|---|---|---|---|---|---|---|---|
| 1 | 39.86 | 49.50 | 53.59 | 55.83 | 57.24 | 58.20 | 58.91 | 59.44 | 59.86 | 60.19 | 60.71 | 61.22 | 61.74 | 62.00 | 62.26 | 62.53 | 62.79 | 63.06 | 63.33 |
| 2 | 8.53 | 9.00 | 9.16 | 9.24 | 9.29 | 9.33 | 9.35 | 9.37 | 9.38 | 9.39 | 9.41 | 9.42 | 9.44 | 9.45 | 9.46 | 9.47 | 9.47 | 9.48 | 9.49 |
| 3 | 5.54 | 5.46 | 5.39 | 5.34 | 5.31 | 5.28 | 5.27 | 5.25 | 5.24 | 5.23 | 5.22 | 5.20 | 5.18 | 5.18 | 5.17 | 5.16 | 5.15 | 5.14 | 5.13 |
| 4 | 4.54 | 4.32 | 4.19 | 4.11 | 4.05 | 4.01 | 3.98 | 3.95 | 3.94 | 3.92 | 3.90 | 3.87 | 3.84 | 3.83 | 3.82 | 3.80 | 3.79 | 3.78 | 3.76 |
| 5 | 4.06 | 3.78 | 3.62 | 3.52 | 3.45 | 3.40 | 3.37 | 3.34 | 3.32 | 3.30 | 3.27 | 3.24 | 3.21 | 3.19 | 3.17 | 3.16 | 3.14 | 3.12 | 3.10 |
| 6 | 3.78 | 3.46 | 3.29 | 3.18 | 3.11 | 3.05 | 3.01 | 2.98 | 2.96 | 2.94 | 2.90 | 2.87 | 2.84 | 2.82 | 2.80 | 2.78 | 2.76 | 2.74 | 2.72 |
| 7 | 3.59 | 3.26 | 3.07 | 2.96 | 2.88 | 2.83 | 2.78 | 2.75 | 2.72 | 2.70 | 2.67 | 2.63 | 2.59 | 2.58 | 2.56 | 2.54 | 2.51 | 2.49 | 2.47 |
| 8 | 3.46 | 3.11 | 2.92 | 2.81 | 2.73 | 2.67 | 2.62 | 2.59 | 2.56 | 2.54 | 2.50 | 2.46 | 2.42 | 2.40 | 2.38 | 2.36 | 2.34 | 2.32 | 2.29 |
| 9 | 3.36 | 3.01 | 2.81 | 2.69 | 2.61 | 2.55 | 2.51 | 2.47 | 2.44 | 2.42 | 2.38 | 2.34 | 2.30 | 2.28 | 2.25 | 2.23 | 2.21 | 2.18 | 2.16 |
| 10 | 3.29 | 2.92 | 2.73 | 2.61 | 2.52 | 2.46 | 2.41 | 2.38 | 2.35 | 2.32 | 2.28 | 2.24 | 2.20 | 2.18 | 2.16 | 2.13 | 2.11 | 2.08 | 2.06 |
| 11 | 3.23 | 2.86 | 2.66 | 2.54 | 2.45 | 2.39 | 2.34 | 2.30 | 2.27 | 2.25 | 2.21 | 2.17 | 2.12 | 2.10 | 2.08 | 2.05 | 2.03 | 2.00 | 1.97 |
| 12 | 3.18 | 2.81 | 2.61 | 2.48 | 2.39 | 2.33 | 2.28 | 2.24 | 2.21 | 2.19 | 2.15 | 2.10 | 2.06 | 2.04 | 2.01 | 1.99 | 1.96 | 1.93 | 1.90 |
| 13 | 3.14 | 2.76 | 2.56 | 2.43 | 2.35 | 2.28 | 2.23 | 2.20 | 2.16 | 2.14 | 2.10 | 2.05 | 2.01 | 1.98 | 1.96 | 1.93 | 1.90 | 1.88 | 1.85 |
| 14 | 3.10 | 2.73 | 2.52 | 2.39 | 2.31 | 2.24 | 2.19 | 2.15 | 2.12 | 2.10 | 2.05 | 2.01 | 1.96 | 1.94 | 1.91 | 1.89 | 1.86 | 1.83 | 1.80 |
| 15 | 3.07 | 2.70 | 2.49 | 2.36 | 2.27 | 2.21 | 2.16 | 2.12 | 2.09 | 2.06 | 2.02 | 1.97 | 1.92 | 1.90 | 1.87 | 1.85 | 1.82 | 1.79 | 1.76 |
| 16 | 3.05 | 2.67 | 2.46 | 2.33 | 2.24 | 2.18 | 2.13 | 2.09 | 2.06 | 2.03 | 1.99 | 1.94 | 1.89 | 1.87 | 1.84 | 1.81 | 1.78 | 1.75 | 1.72 |
| 17 | 3.03 | 2.64 | 2.44 | 2.31 | 2.22 | 2.15 | 2.10 | 2.06 | 2.03 | 2.00 | 1.96 | 1.91 | 1.86 | 1.84 | 1.81 | 1.78 | 1.75 | 1.72 | 1.69 |
| 18 | 3.01 | 2.62 | 2.42 | 2.29 | 2.20 | 2.13 | 2.08 | 2.04 | 2.00 | 1.98 | 1.93 | 1.89 | 1.84 | 1.81 | 1.78 | 1.75 | 1.72 | 1.69 | 1.66 |
| 19 | 2.99 | 2.61 | 2.40 | 2.27 | 2.18 | 2.11 | 2.06 | 2.02 | 1.98 | 1.96 | 1.91 | 1.86 | 1.81 | 1.79 | 1.76 | 1.73 | 1.70 | 1.67 | 1.63 |
| 20 | 2.97 | 2.59 | 2.38 | 2.25 | 2.16 | 2.09 | 2.04 | 2.00 | 1.96 | 1.94 | 1.89 | 1.84 | 1.79 | 1.77 | 1.74 | 1.71 | 1.68 | 1.64 | 1.61 |
| 21 | 2.96 | 2.57 | 2.36 | 2.23 | 2.14 | 2.08 | 2.02 | 1.98 | 1.95 | 1.92 | 1.87 | 1.83 | 1.78 | 1.75 | 1.72 | 1.69 | 1.66 | 1.62 | 1.59 |
| 22 | 2.95 | 2.56 | 2.35 | 2.22 | 2.13 | 2.06 | 2.01 | 1.97 | 1.93 | 1.90 | 1.86 | 1.81 | 1.76 | 1.73 | 1.70 | 1.67 | 1.64 | 1.60 | 1.57 |
| 23 | 2.94 | 2.55 | 2.34 | 2.21 | 2.11 | 2.05 | 1.99 | 1.95 | 1.92 | 1.89 | 1.84 | 1.80 | 1.74 | 1.72 | 1.69 | 1.66 | 1.62 | 1.59 | 1.55 |
| 24 | 2.93 | 2.54 | 2.33 | 2.19 | 2.10 | 2.04 | 1.98 | 1.94 | 1.91 | 1.88 | 1.83 | 1.78 | 1.73 | 1.70 | 1.67 | 1.64 | 1.61 | 1.57 | 1.53 |
| 25 | 2.92 | 2.53 | 2.32 | 2.18 | 2.09 | 2.02 | 1.97 | 1.93 | 1.89 | 1.87 | 1.82 | 1.77 | 1.72 | 1.69 | 1.66 | 1.63 | 1.59 | 1.56 | 1.52 |
| 26 | 2.91 | 2.52 | 2.31 | 2.17 | 2.08 | 2.01 | 1.96 | 1.92 | 1.88 | 1.86 | 1.81 | 1.76 | 1.71 | 1.68 | 1.65 | 1.61 | 1.58 | 1.54 | 1.50 |
| 27 | 2.90 | 2.51 | 2.30 | 2.17 | 2.07 | 2.00 | 1.95 | 1.91 | 1.87 | 1.85 | 1.80 | 1.75 | 1.70 | 1.67 | 1.64 | 1.60 | 1.57 | 1.53 | 1.49 |
| 28 | 2.89 | 2.50 | 2.29 | 2.16 | 2.06 | 2.00 | 1.94 | 1.90 | 1.87 | 1.84 | 1.79 | 1.74 | 1.69 | 1.66 | 1.63 | 1.59 | 1.56 | 1.52 | 1.48 |
| 29 | 2.89 | 2.50 | 2.28 | 2.15 | 2.06 | 1.99 | 1.93 | 1.89 | 1.86 | 1.83 | 1.78 | 1.73 | 1.68 | 1.65 | 1.62 | 1.58 | 1.55 | 1.51 | 1.47 |
| 30 | 2.88 | 2.49 | 2.28 | 2.14 | 2.05 | 1.98 | 1.93 | 1.88 | 1.85 | 1.82 | 1.77 | 1.72 | 1.67 | 1.64 | 1.61 | 1.57 | 1.54 | 1.50 | 1.46 |
| 40 | 2.84 | 2.44 | 2.23 | 2.09 | 2.00 | 1.93 | 1.87 | 1.83 | 1.79 | 1.76 | 1.71 | 1.66 | 1.61 | 1.57 | 1.54 | 1.51 | 1.47 | 1.42 | 1.38 |
| 60 | 2.79 | 2.39 | 2.18 | 2.04 | 1.95 | 1.87 | 1.82 | 1.77 | 1.74 | 1.71 | 1.66 | 1.60 | 1.54 | 1.51 | 1.48 | 1.44 | 1.40 | 1.35 | 1.29 |
| 120 | 2.75 | 2.35 | 2.13 | 1.99 | 1.90 | 1.82 | 1.77 | 1.72 | 1.68 | 1.65 | 1.60 | 1.55 | 1.48 | 1.45 | 1.41 | 1.37 | 1.32 | 1.26 | 1.19 |
| ∞ | 2.71 | 2.30 | 2.08 | 1.94 | 1.85 | 1.77 | 1.72 | 1.67 | 1.63 | 1.60 | 1.55 | 1.49 | 1.42 | 1.38 | 1.34 | 1.30 | 1.24 | 1.17 | 1.00 |

*continued*

[2]The $F$-statistic provides evidence on whether or not a statistically significant proportion of the total variation in the dependent variable $Y$ has been explained. The $F$-statistic can be calculated in terms of the coefficient of determination as: $F_{k-1, n-k} = R^2/(k-1) \div (1 - R^2)/n - k$, where $R^2$ is the coefficient of determination, $k$ is the number of estimated coefficients in the regression model (including the intercept), and $n$ is the number of data observations. When the critical $F$-value is exceeded, we can conclude with a given level of confidence (e.g., $\alpha$ = 0.01 or 90 percent confidence) that the regression equation, taken as a whole, significantly explains the variation in $Y$.

■ Table C.2 continuing

## Critical *F* Values at the 95-Percent Confidence Level ($\alpha = .05$)

*Degrees of Freedom in the Numerator (d.f. = k − 1)*

| d.f. | 1 | 2 | 3 | 4 | 5 | 6 | 7 | 8 | 9 | 10 | 12 | 15 | 20 | 24 | 30 | 40 | 60 | 120 | ∞ |
|---|---|---|---|---|---|---|---|---|---|---|---|---|---|---|---|---|---|---|---|
| 1 | 161.4 | 199.5 | 215.7 | 224.6 | 230.2 | 234.0 | 236.8 | 238.9 | 240.5 | 241.9 | 243.9 | 245.9 | 248.0 | 249.1 | 250.1 | 251.1 | 252.2 | 253.3 | 254.3 |
| 2 | 18.51 | 19.00 | 19.16 | 19.25 | 19.30 | 19.33 | 19.35 | 19.37 | 19.38 | 19.40 | 19.41 | 19.43 | 19.45 | 19.45 | 19.46 | 19.47 | 19.48 | 19.49 | 19.50 |
| 3 | 10.13 | 9.55 | 9.28 | 9.12 | 9.01 | 8.94 | 8.89 | 8.85 | 8.81 | 8.79 | 8.74 | 8.70 | 8.66 | 8.64 | 8.62 | 8.59 | 8.57 | 8.55 | 8.53 |
| 4 | 7.71 | 6.94 | 6.59 | 6.39 | 6.26 | 6.16 | 6.09 | 6.04 | 6.00 | 5.96 | 5.91 | 5.86 | 5.80 | 5.77 | 5.75 | 5.72 | 5.69 | 5.66 | 5.63 |
| 5 | 6.61 | 5.79 | 5.41 | 5.19 | 5.05 | 4.95 | 4.88 | 4.82 | 4.77 | 4.74 | 4.68 | 4.62 | 4.56 | 4.53 | 4.50 | 4.46 | 4.43 | 4.40 | 4.36 |
| 6 | 5.99 | 5.14 | 4.76 | 4.53 | 4.39 | 4.28 | 4.21 | 4.15 | 4.10 | 4.06 | 4.00 | 3.94 | 3.87 | 3.84 | 3.81 | 3.77 | 3.74 | 3.70 | 3.67 |
| 7 | 5.59 | 4.74 | 4.35 | 4.12 | 3.97 | 3.87 | 3.79 | 3.73 | 3.68 | 3.64 | 3.57 | 3.51 | 3.44 | 3.41 | 3.38 | 3.34 | 3.30 | 3.27 | 3.23 |
| 8 | 5.32 | 4.46 | 4.07 | 3.84 | 3.69 | 3.58 | 3.50 | 3.44 | 3.39 | 3.35 | 3.28 | 3.22 | 3.15 | 3.12 | 3.08 | 3.04 | 3.01 | 2.97 | 2.93 |
| 9 | 5.12 | 4.26 | 3.86 | 3.63 | 3.48 | 3.37 | 3.29 | 3.23 | 3.18 | 3.14 | 3.07 | 3.01 | 2.94 | 2.90 | 2.86 | 2.83 | 2.79 | 2.75 | 2.71 |
| 10 | 4.96 | 4.10 | 3.71 | 3.48 | 3.33 | 3.22 | 3.14 | 3.07 | 3.02 | 2.98 | 2.91 | 2.85 | 2.77 | 2.74 | 2.70 | 2.66 | 2.62 | 2.58 | 2.54 |
| 11 | 4.84 | 3.98 | 3.59 | 3.36 | 3.20 | 3.09 | 3.01 | 2.95 | 2.90 | 2.85 | 2.79 | 2.72 | 2.65 | 2.61 | 2.57 | 2.53 | 2.49 | 2.45 | 2.40 |
| 12 | 4.75 | 3.89 | 3.49 | 3.26 | 3.11 | 3.00 | 2.91 | 2.85 | 2.80 | 2.75 | 2.69 | 2.62 | 2.54 | 2.51 | 2.47 | 2.43 | 2.38 | 2.34 | 2.30 |
| 13 | 4.67 | 3.81 | 3.41 | 3.18 | 3.03 | 2.92 | 2.83 | 2.77 | 2.71 | 2.67 | 2.60 | 2.53 | 2.46 | 2.42 | 2.38 | 2.34 | 2.30 | 2.25 | 2.21 |
| 14 | 4.60 | 3.74 | 3.34 | 3.11 | 2.96 | 2.85 | 2.76 | 2.70 | 2.65 | 2.60 | 2.53 | 2.46 | 2.39 | 2.35 | 2.31 | 2.27 | 2.22 | 2.18 | 2.13 |
| 15 | 4.54 | 3.68 | 3.29 | 3.06 | 2.90 | 2.79 | 2.71 | 2.64 | 2.59 | 2.54 | 2.48 | 2.40 | 2.33 | 2.29 | 2.25 | 2.20 | 2.16 | 2.11 | 2.07 |
| 16 | 4.49 | 3.63 | 3.24 | 3.01 | 2.85 | 2.74 | 2.66 | 2.59 | 2.54 | 2.49 | 2.42 | 2.35 | 2.28 | 2.24 | 2.19 | 2.15 | 2.11 | 2.06 | 2.01 |
| 17 | 4.45 | 3.59 | 3.20 | 2.96 | 2.81 | 2.70 | 2.61 | 2.55 | 2.49 | 2.45 | 2.38 | 2.31 | 2.23 | 2.19 | 2.15 | 2.10 | 2.06 | 2.01 | 1.96 |
| 18 | 4.41 | 3.55 | 3.16 | 2.93 | 2.77 | 2.66 | 2.58 | 2.51 | 2.46 | 2.41 | 2.34 | 2.27 | 2.19 | 2.15 | 2.11 | 2.06 | 2.02 | 1.97 | 1.92 |
| 19 | 4.38 | 3.52 | 3.13 | 2.90 | 2.74 | 2.63 | 2.54 | 2.48 | 2.42 | 2.38 | 2.31 | 2.23 | 2.16 | 2.11 | 2.07 | 2.03 | 1.98 | 1.93 | 1.88 |
| 20 | 4.35 | 3.49 | 3.10 | 2.87 | 2.71 | 2.60 | 2.51 | 2.45 | 2.39 | 2.35 | 2.28 | 2.20 | 2.12 | 2.08 | 2.04 | 1.99 | 1.95 | 1.90 | 1.84 |
| 21 | 4.32 | 3.47 | 3.07 | 2.84 | 2.68 | 2.57 | 2.49 | 2.42 | 2.37 | 2.32 | 2.25 | 2.18 | 2.10 | 2.05 | 2.01 | 1.96 | 1.92 | 1.87 | 1.81 |
| 22 | 4.30 | 3.44 | 3.05 | 2.82 | 2.66 | 2.55 | 2.46 | 2.40 | 2.34 | 2.30 | 2.23 | 2.15 | 2.07 | 2.03 | 1.98 | 1.94 | 1.89 | 1.84 | 1.78 |
| 23 | 4.28 | 3.42 | 3.03 | 2.80 | 2.64 | 2.53 | 2.44 | 2.37 | 2.32 | 2.27 | 2.20 | 2.13 | 2.05 | 2.01 | 1.96 | 1.91 | 1.86 | 1.81 | 1.76 |
| 24 | 4.26 | 3.40 | 3.01 | 2.78 | 2.62 | 2.51 | 2.42 | 2.36 | 2.30 | 2.25 | 2.18 | 2.11 | 2.03 | 1.98 | 1.94 | 1.89 | 1.84 | 1.79 | 1.73 |
| 25 | 4.24 | 3.39 | 2.99 | 2.76 | 2.60 | 2.49 | 2.40 | 2.34 | 2.28 | 2.24 | 2.16 | 2.09 | 2.01 | 1.96 | 1.92 | 1.87 | 1.82 | 1.77 | 1.71 |
| 26 | 4.23 | 3.37 | 2.98 | 2.74 | 2.59 | 2.47 | 2.39 | 2.32 | 2.27 | 2.22 | 2.15 | 2.07 | 1.99 | 1.95 | 1.90 | 1.85 | 1.80 | 1.75 | 1.69 |
| 27 | 4.21 | 3.35 | 2.96 | 2.73 | 2.57 | 2.46 | 2.37 | 2.31 | 2.25 | 2.20 | 2.13 | 2.06 | 1.97 | 1.93 | 1.88 | 1.84 | 1.79 | 1.73 | 1.67 |
| 28 | 4.20 | 3.34 | 2.95 | 2.71 | 2.56 | 2.45 | 2.36 | 2.29 | 2.24 | 2.19 | 2.12 | 2.04 | 1.96 | 1.91 | 1.87 | 1.82 | 1.77 | 1.71 | 1.65 |
| 29 | 4.18 | 3.33 | 2.93 | 2.70 | 2.55 | 2.43 | 2.35 | 2.28 | 2.22 | 2.18 | 2.10 | 2.03 | 1.94 | 1.90 | 1.85 | 1.81 | 1.75 | 1.70 | 1.64 |
| 30 | 4.17 | 3.32 | 2.92 | 2.69 | 2.53 | 2.42 | 2.33 | 2.27 | 2.21 | 2.16 | 2.09 | 2.01 | 1.93 | 1.89 | 1.84 | 1.79 | 1.74 | 1.68 | 1.62 |
| 40 | 4.08 | 3.23 | 2.84 | 2.61 | 2.45 | 2.34 | 2.25 | 2.18 | 2.12 | 2.08 | 2.00 | 1.92 | 1.84 | 1.79 | 1.74 | 1.69 | 1.64 | 1.58 | 1.51 |
| 60 | 4.00 | 3.15 | 2.76 | 2.53 | 2.37 | 2.25 | 2.17 | 2.10 | 2.04 | 1.99 | 1.92 | 1.84 | 1.75 | 1.70 | 1.65 | 1.59 | 1.53 | 1.47 | 1.39 |
| 120 | 3.92 | 3.07 | 2.68 | 2.45 | 2.29 | 2.17 | 2.09 | 2.02 | 1.96 | 1.91 | 1.83 | 1.75 | 1.66 | 1.61 | 1.55 | 1.50 | 1.43 | 1.35 | 1.25 |
| ∞ | 3.84 | 3.00 | 2.60 | 2.37 | 2.21 | 2.10 | 2.01 | 1.94 | 1.88 | 1.83 | 1.75 | 1.67 | 1.57 | 1.52 | 1.46 | 1.39 | 1.32 | 1.22 | 1.00 |

*Degrees of Freedom in the Denominator (d.f. = n − k)*

continued

■ Table C.2 continuing
## Critical *F* Values at the 99-Percent Confidence Level ($\alpha = .01$)

| d.f. | 4052 | 4999.5 | 5403 | 5625 | 5764 | 5859 | 5928 | 5982 | 6022 | 6056 | 6106 | 6157 | 6209 | 6235 | 6261 | 6287 | 6313 | 6339 | 6366 |
|---|---|---|---|---|---|---|---|---|---|---|---|---|---|---|---|---|---|---|---|
| 1 | 4052 | 4999.5 | 5403 | 5625 | 5764 | 5859 | 5928 | 5982 | 6022 | 6056 | 6106 | 6157 | 6209 | 6235 | 6261 | 6287 | 6313 | 6339 | 6366 |
| 2 | 98.50 | 99.00 | 99.17 | 99.25 | 99.30 | 99.33 | 99.36 | 99.37 | 99.39 | 99.40 | 99.42 | 99.43 | 99.45 | 99.46 | 99.47 | 99.47 | 99.48 | 99.49 | 99.50 |
| 3 | 34.12 | 30.82 | 29.46 | 28.71 | 28.24 | 27.91 | 27.67 | 27.49 | 27.35 | 27.23 | 27.05 | 26.87 | 26.69 | 26.60 | 26.50 | 26.41 | 26.32 | 26.22 | 26.13 |
| 4 | 21.20 | 18.00 | 16.69 | 15.98 | 15.52 | 15.21 | 14.98 | 14.80 | 14.66 | 14.55 | 14.37 | 14.20 | 14.02 | 13.93 | 13.84 | 13.75 | 13.65 | 13.56 | 13.46 |
| 5 | 16.26 | 13.27 | 12.06 | 11.39 | 10.97 | 10.67 | 10.46 | 10.29 | 10.16 | 10.05 | 9.89 | 9.72 | 9.55 | 9.47 | 9.38 | 9.29 | 9.20 | 9.11 | 9.02 |
| 6 | 13.75 | 10.92 | 9.78 | 9.15 | 8.75 | 8.47 | 8.26 | 8.10 | 7.98 | 7.87 | 7.72 | 7.56 | 7.40 | 7.31 | 7.23 | 7.14 | 7.06 | 6.97 | 6.88 |
| 7 | 12.25 | 9.55 | 8.45 | 7.85 | 7.46 | 7.19 | 6.99 | 6.84 | 6.72 | 6.62 | 6.47 | 6.31 | 6.16 | 6.07 | 5.99 | 5.91 | 5.82 | 5.74 | 5.65 |
| 8 | 11.26 | 8.65 | 7.59 | 7.01 | 6.63 | 6.37 | 6.18 | 6.03 | 5.91 | 5.81 | 5.67 | 5.52 | 5.36 | 5.28 | 5.20 | 5.12 | 5.03 | 4.95 | 4.86 |
| 9 | 10.56 | 8.02 | 6.99 | 6.42 | 6.06 | 5.80 | 5.61 | 5.47 | 5.35 | 5.26 | 5.11 | 4.96 | 4.81 | 4.73 | 4.65 | 4.57 | 4.48 | 4.40 | 4.31 |
| 10 | 10.04 | 7.56 | 6.55 | 5.99 | 5.64 | 5.39 | 5.20 | 5.06 | 4.94 | 4.85 | 4.71 | 4.56 | 4.41 | 4.33 | 4.25 | 4.17 | 4.08 | 4.00 | 3.91 |
| 11 | 9.65 | 7.21 | 6.22 | 5.67 | 5.32 | 5.07 | 4.89 | 4.74 | 4.63 | 4.54 | 4.40 | 4.25 | 4.10 | 4.02 | 3.94 | 3.86 | 3.78 | 3.69 | 3.60 |
| 12 | 9.33 | 6.93 | 5.95 | 5.41 | 5.06 | 4.82 | 4.64 | 4.50 | 4.39 | 4.30 | 4.16 | 4.01 | 3.86 | 3.78 | 3.70 | 3.62 | 3.54 | 3.45 | 3.36 |
| 13 | 9.07 | 6.70 | 5.74 | 5.21 | 4.86 | 4.62 | 4.44 | 4.30 | 4.19 | 4.10 | 3.96 | 3.82 | 3.66 | 3.59 | 3.51 | 3.43 | 3.34 | 3.25 | 3.17 |
| 14 | 8.86 | 6.51 | 5.56 | 5.04 | 4.69 | 4.46 | 4.28 | 4.14 | 4.03 | 3.94 | 3.80 | 3.66 | 3.51 | 3.43 | 3.35 | 3.27 | 3.18 | 3.09 | 3.00 |
| 15 | 8.68 | 6.36 | 5.42 | 4.89 | 4.56 | 4.32 | 4.14 | 4.00 | 3.89 | 3.80 | 3.67 | 3.52 | 3.37 | 3.29 | 3.21 | 3.13 | 3.05 | 2.96 | 2.87 |
| 16 | 8.53 | 6.23 | 5.29 | 4.77 | 4.44 | 4.20 | 4.03 | 3.89 | 3.78 | 3.69 | 3.55 | 3.41 | 3.26 | 3.18 | 3.10 | 3.02 | 2.93 | 2.84 | 2.75 |
| 17 | 8.40 | 6.11 | 5.18 | 4.67 | 4.34 | 4.10 | 3.93 | 3.79 | 3.68 | 3.59 | 3.46 | 3.31 | 3.16 | 3.08 | 3.00 | 2.92 | 2.83 | 2.75 | 2.65 |
| 18 | 8.29 | 6.01 | 5.09 | 4.58 | 4.25 | 4.01 | 3.84 | 3.71 | 3.60 | 3.51 | 3.37 | 3.23 | 3.08 | 3.00 | 2.92 | 2.84 | 2.75 | 2.66 | 2.57 |
| 19 | 8.18 | 5.93 | 5.01 | 4.50 | 4.17 | 3.94 | 3.77 | 3.63 | 3.52 | 3.43 | 3.30 | 3.15 | 3.00 | 2.92 | 2.84 | 2.76 | 2.67 | 2.58 | 2.49 |
| 20 | 8.10 | 5.85 | 4.94 | 4.43 | 4.10 | 3.87 | 3.70 | 3.56 | 3.46 | 3.37 | 3.23 | 3.09 | 2.94 | 2.86 | 2.78 | 2.69 | 2.61 | 2.52 | 2.42 |
| 21 | 8.02 | 5.78 | 4.87 | 4.37 | 4.04 | 3.81 | 3.64 | 3.51 | 3.40 | 3.31 | 3.17 | 3.03 | 2.88 | 2.80 | 2.72 | 2.64 | 2.55 | 2.46 | 2.36 |
| 22 | 7.95 | 5.72 | 4.82 | 4.31 | 3.99 | 3.76 | 3.59 | 3.45 | 3.35 | 3.26 | 3.12 | 2.98 | 2.83 | 2.75 | 2.67 | 2.58 | 2.50 | 2.40 | 2.31 |
| 23 | 7.88 | 5.66 | 4.76 | 4.26 | 3.94 | 3.71 | 3.54 | 3.41 | 3.30 | 3.21 | 3.07 | 2.93 | 2.78 | 2.70 | 2.62 | 2.54 | 2.45 | 2.35 | 2.26 |
| 24 | 7.82 | 5.61 | 4.72 | 4.22 | 3.90 | 3.67 | 3.50 | 3.36 | 3.26 | 3.17 | 3.03 | 2.89 | 2.74 | 2.66 | 2.58 | 2.49 | 2.40 | 2.31 | 2.21 |
| 25 | 7.77 | 5.57 | 4.68 | 4.18 | 3.85 | 3.63 | 3.46 | 3.32 | 3.22 | 3.13 | 2.99 | 2.85 | 2.70 | 2.62 | 2.54 | 2.45 | 2.36 | 2.27 | 2.17 |
| 26 | 7.72 | 5.53 | 4.64 | 4.14 | 3.82 | 3.59 | 3.42 | 3.29 | 3.18 | 3.09 | 2.96 | 2.81 | 2.66 | 2.58 | 2.50 | 2.42 | 2.33 | 2.23 | 2.13 |
| 27 | 7.68 | 5.49 | 4.60 | 4.11 | 3.78 | 3.56 | 3.39 | 3.26 | 3.15 | 3.06 | 2.93 | 2.78 | 2.63 | 2.55 | 2.47 | 2.38 | 2.29 | 2.20 | 2.10 |
| 28 | 7.64 | 5.45 | 4.57 | 4.07 | 3.75 | 3.53 | 3.36 | 3.23 | 3.12 | 3.03 | 2.90 | 2.75 | 2.60 | 2.52 | 2.44 | 2.35 | 2.26 | 2.17 | 2.06 |
| 29 | 7.60 | 5.42 | 4.54 | 4.04 | 3.73 | 3.50 | 3.33 | 3.20 | 3.09 | 3.00 | 2.87 | 2.73 | 2.57 | 2.49 | 2.41 | 2.33 | 2.23 | 2.14 | 2.03 |
| 30 | 7.56 | 5.39 | 4.51 | 4.02 | 3.70 | 3.47 | 3.30 | 3.17 | 3.07 | 2.98 | 2.84 | 2.70 | 2.55 | 2.47 | 2.39 | 2.30 | 2.21 | 2.11 | 2.01 |
| 40 | 7.31 | 5.18 | 4.31 | 3.83 | 3.51 | 3.29 | 3.12 | 2.99 | 2.89 | 2.80 | 2.66 | 2.52 | 2.37 | 2.29 | 2.20 | 2.11 | 2.02 | 1.92 | 1.80 |
| 60 | 7.08 | 4.98 | 4.13 | 3.65 | 3.34 | 3.12 | 2.95 | 2.82 | 2.72 | 2.63 | 2.50 | 2.35 | 2.20 | 2.12 | 2.03 | 1.94 | 1.84 | 1.73 | 1.60 |
| 120 | 6.85 | 4.79 | 3.95 | 3.48 | 3.17 | 2.96 | 2.79 | 2.66 | 2.56 | 2.47 | 2.34 | 2.19 | 2.03 | 1.95 | 1.86 | 1.76 | 1.66 | 1.53 | 1.38 |
| ∞ | 6.63 | 4.61 | 3.78 | 3.32 | 3.02 | 2.80 | 2.64 | 2.51 | 2.41 | 2.32 | 2.18 | 2.04 | 1.88 | 1.79 | 1.70 | 1.59 | 1.47 | 1.32 | 1.00 |

*Degrees of Freedom in the Denominator (d.f. = n − k)*

■ Table C.3
# Students' *t* Distribution[3]

| Degrees of Freedom | Area in the Rejection Region (two-tail test) | | | | | | | | | | | | |
|---|---|---|---|---|---|---|---|---|---|---|---|---|---|
| | 0.9 | 0.8 | 0.7 | 0.6 | 0.5 | 0.4 | 0.3 | 0.2 | 0.1 | 0.05 | 0.02 | 0.01 | 0.001 |
| 1 | 0.158 | 0.325 | 0.510 | 0.727 | 1.000 | 1.376 | 1.963 | 3.078 | **6.314** | **12.706** | 31.821 | **63.657** | 636.619 |
| 2 | 0.142 | 0.289 | 0.445 | 0.617 | 0.816 | 1.061 | 1.386 | 1.886 | **2.920** | **4.303** | 6.965 | **9.925** | 31.598 |
| 3 | 0.137 | 0.277 | 0.424 | 0.584 | 0.765 | 0.978 | 1.250 | 1.638 | **2.353** | **3.182** | 4.541 | **5.841** | 12.924 |
| 4 | 0.134 | 0.271 | 0.414 | 0.569 | 0.741 | 0.941 | 1.190 | 1.533 | **2.132** | **2.776** | 3.747 | **4.604** | 8.610 |
| 5 | 0.132 | 0.267 | 0.408 | 0.559 | 0.727 | 0.920 | 1.156 | 1.476 | **2.015** | **2.571** | 3.365 | **4.032** | 6.869 |
| 6 | 0.131 | 0.265 | 0.404 | 0.553 | 0.718 | 0.906 | 1.134 | 1.440 | **1.943** | **2.447** | 3.143 | **3.707** | 5.959 |
| 7 | 0.130 | 0.263 | 0.402 | 0.549 | 0.711 | 0.896 | 1.119 | 1.415 | **1.895** | **2.365** | 2.998 | **3.499** | 5.408 |
| 8 | 0.130 | 0.262 | 0.399 | 0.546 | 0.706 | 0.889 | 1.108 | 1.397 | **1.860** | **2.306** | 2.896 | **3.355** | 5.041 |
| 9 | 0.129 | 0.261 | 0.398 | 0.543 | 0.703 | 0.883 | 1.100 | 1.383 | **1.833** | **2.262** | 2.821 | **3.250** | 4.781 |
| 10 | 0.129 | 0.260 | 0.397 | 0.542 | 0.700 | 0.879 | 1.093 | 1.372 | **1.812** | **2.228** | 2.764 | **3.169** | 4.587 |
| 11 | 0.129 | 0.260 | 0.396 | 0.540 | 0.697 | 0.876 | 1.088 | 1.363 | **1.796** | **2.201** | 2.718 | **3.106** | 4.437 |
| 12 | 0.128 | 0.259 | 0.395 | 0.539 | 0.695 | 0.873 | 1.083 | 1.356 | **1.782** | **2.179** | 2.681 | **3.055** | 4.318 |
| 13 | 0.128 | 0.259 | 0.394 | 0.538 | 0.694 | 0.870 | 1.079 | 1.350 | **1.771** | **2.160** | 2.650 | **3.012** | 4.221 |
| 14 | 0.128 | 0.258 | 0.393 | 0.537 | 0.692 | 0.868 | 1.076 | 1.345 | **1.761** | **2.145** | 2.624 | **2.977** | 4.140 |
| 15 | 0.128 | 0.258 | 0.393 | 0.536 | 0.691 | 0.866 | 1.074 | 1.341 | **1.753** | **2.131** | 2.602 | **2.947** | 4.073 |
| 16 | 0.128 | 0.258 | 0.392 | 0.535 | 0.690 | 0.865 | 1.071 | 1.337 | **1.746** | **2.120** | 2.583 | **2.921** | 4.015 |
| 17 | 0.128 | 0.257 | 0.392 | 0.534 | 0.689 | 0.863 | 1.069 | 1.333 | **1.740** | **2.110** | 2.567 | **2.898** | 3.965 |
| 18 | 0.127 | 0.257 | 0.392 | 0.534 | 0.688 | 0.862 | 1.067 | 1.330 | **1.734** | **2.101** | 2.552 | **2.878** | 3.922 |
| 19 | 0.127 | 0.257 | 0.391 | 0.533 | 0.688 | 0.861 | 1.066 | 1.328 | **1.729** | **2.093** | 2.539 | **2.861** | 3.883 |
| 20 | 0.127 | 0.257 | 0.391 | 0.533 | 0.687 | 0.860 | 1.064 | 1.325 | **1.725** | **2.086** | 2.528 | **2.845** | 3.850 |
| 21 | 0.127 | 0.257 | 0.391 | 0.532 | 0.686 | 0.859 | 1.063 | 1.323 | **1.721** | **2.080** | 2.518 | **2.831** | 3.819 |
| 22 | 0.127 | 0.256 | 0.390 | 0.532 | 0.686 | 0.858 | 1.061 | 1.321 | **1.717** | **2.074** | 2.508 | **2.819** | 3.792 |
| 23 | 0.127 | 0.256 | 0.390 | 0.532 | 0.685 | 0.858 | 1.060 | 1.319 | **1.714** | **2.069** | 2.500 | **2.807** | 3.767 |
| 24 | 0.127 | 0.256 | 0.390 | 0.531 | 0.685 | 0.857 | 1.059 | 1.318 | **1.711** | **2.064** | 2.492 | **2.797** | 3.745 |
| 25 | 0.127 | 0.256 | 0.390 | 0.531 | 0.684 | 0.856 | 1.058 | 1.316 | **1.708** | **2.060** | 2.485 | **2.787** | 3.725 |
| 26 | 0.127 | 0.256 | 0.390 | 0.531 | 0.684 | 0.856 | 1.058 | 1.315 | **1.706** | **2.056** | 2.479 | **2.779** | 3.707 |
| 27 | 0.127 | 0.256 | 0.389 | 0.531 | 0.684 | 0.855 | 1.057 | 1.314 | **1.703** | **2.052** | 2.473 | **2.771** | 3.690 |
| 28 | 0.127 | 0.256 | 0.389 | 0.530 | 0.683 | 0.855 | 1.056 | 1.313 | **1.701** | **2.048** | 2.467 | **2.763** | 3.674 |
| 29 | 0.127 | 0.256 | 0.389 | 0.530 | 0.683 | 0.854 | 1.055 | 1.311 | **1.699** | **2.045** | 2.462 | **2.756** | 3.659 |
| 30 | 0.127 | 0.256 | 0.389 | 0.530 | 0.683 | 0.854 | 1.055 | 1.310 | **1.697** | **2.042** | 2.457 | **2.750** | 3.646 |
| 40 | 0.126 | 0.255 | 0.388 | 0.529 | 0.681 | 0.851 | 1.050 | 1.303 | **1.684** | **2.021** | 2.423 | **2.704** | 3.551 |
| 60 | 0.126 | 0.254 | 0.387 | 0.527 | 0.679 | 0.848 | 1.046 | 1.296 | **1.671** | **2.000** | 2.390 | **2.660** | 3.460 |
| 120 | 0.126 | 0.254 | 0.386 | 0.526 | 0.677 | 0.845 | 1.041 | 1.289 | **1.658** | **1.980** | 2.358 | **2.617** | 3.373 |
| ∞ | 0.126 | 0.253 | 0.385 | 0.524 | 0.674 | 0.842 | 1.036 | 1.282 | **1.645** | **1.960** | 2.326 | **2.576** | 3.291 |

[3]Columns in bold-face type indicate critical *t*-values for popular levels of significance for two-tail hypothesis testing. Thus, critical *t*-values for $\alpha = 0.1$ (90 percent confidence), $\alpha = 0.05$ (95 percent confidence) and $\alpha = 0.01$ (99 percent confidence) are highlighted. When the calculated *t*-statistic $= b/\sigma_b$ exceeds the relevant critical *t*-value, we can reject the hypothesis that there is no relationship between the dependent variable *Y* and a given independent variable *X*. For simple *t*-tests, the relevant number degrees of freedom (column row) is found as follows: $d.f. = n - k$, where *n* is the number of data observations and *k* is the number of estimated coefficients (including the intercept).

Source: Ya-lun Chou, *Probability and Statistics for Decision Making* (New York: Holt, Rinehart and Winston, 1972), p. 612. Reprinted by permission of the author.

# Selected Check Figures for End-of-Chapter Problems

**Case 2.1**
A. $F = 6.7$.
B. $Q = \$22.80(000)$.
C. $\pi = \$381.82(000)$.

**2.1**
B. $Q = 5$.

**2.2**
B. $Q = 5$.
C. $Q = 8$.

**2.4**
B. $ME = 5, NH = 3, VT = 2$.
C. Commission Income $= \$3,000$.

**2.5**
B. $I = 3$.
C. $I = 4$.

**2.6**
A. $Q = 500, P = \$500$,
   $\pi = \$150,000$.
B. $Q = 450, P = \$550$,
   $\pi = \$152,500$.

**2.8**
A. $Q = 6,000, MC = \$3,000$,
   $AC = \$3,000, P = \$3,600$,
   $\pi = \$3,600,000$.

B. $Q = 5,000, MC = \$2,600$,
   $AC = \$3,040, P = \$3,850$,
   $\pi = \$4,050,000$.

**2.9**
A. $Q = 400, P = \$6,000$,
   $\pi = \$400,000$.
B. $Q = 300, P = \$7,000$,
   $\pi = \$300,000$.
C. $\lambda = \$2,000$.
D. Value $= \$100,000$.

**2.10**
B. $S = 4, M = 18$.
C. $\lambda = 0.00005$.
D. $AC = \$30,000$.

**3.2**
A. $P = \$10$.
B. $P = \$1$.
C. $P = \$4, Q = 300,000$.

**3.5**
B. $P = \$10, Q = 15,000$;
   $P = \$5, Q = 35,000$;
   $P = \$0, Q = 55,000$.
C. $Q = 10,000, P = \$11.25$;
   $Q = 20,000, P = \$8.75$;
   $Q = 30,000, P = \$6.25$.

**3.6**
B. $Q = 20,000$,
   $TR = \$2,000,000$.

**3.7**
B. $P = \$50, Q = 0$;
   $P = \$60, Q = 5,000,000$;
   $P = \$70, Q = 10,000,000$.
C. $Q = 4,000,000, P = \$58$;
   $Q = 6,000,000, P = \$62$;
   $Q = 8,000,000, P = \$66$.

**3.8**
A. $Q = 2,500, MC = \$110$;
   $Q = 5,000, MC = \$120$;
   $Q = 7,500, MC = \$130$.
B. $MC = \$100, Q = 0$;
   $MC = \$125, Q = 6,250$;
   $MC = \$150, Q = 12,500$.
C. $Q = 12,500$.

**3.9**
B. $P = \$8, Q_C = 0$;
   $P = \$10, Q_C = 0$;
   $P = \$12, Q_C = 500$.
   $P = \$8, Q_P = 0$;
   $P = \$10, Q_P = 250$;
   $P = \$12, Q_P = 500$.

**3.10**
B. $P = \$5$,
   Shortage $= 31,500,000$;
   $P = \$10$,
   Shortage $= 9,000,000$;
   $P = \$15$,
   Surplus $= 13,500,000$.
C. $P = \$12, Q = 20,000,000$.

**4.1**
C. $G = 2$.

**4.2**
B. $S = 4$.
C. $G = 4$.
D. $G = 2, S = 4$.

**4.3**
B. 20¢ per util
C. $G = 2, P = \$8$;
   $G = 3, P = \$6$;
   $G = 4, P = \$4$;
   $G = 5, P = \$2$.

**4.5**
A. $Q = 600$.
B. $P = \$3$.
C. $P = \$7.50$.
D. $Q = 1,500$.
E. $\epsilon_p = -2$.

**4.6**
A. $\epsilon_p = -4$.
B. $P = \$12,500$.

**4.7**
A. $E_p = -2$.
B. $E_{PX} = -2.67$.

**4.8**
A. $E_I = 6$.
B. $E_P = -8$.

**4.9**
A. $E_{PX} = 1.5$.
B. $E_P = -3$.
C. $\Delta P = \$20$.

**4.10**
A. $E_P = -2$.
B. $\Delta P = \$2$.
C. $E_A = 1$.

**5.6**
B. $E_A = 3$.
C. $E_P = -4$.
D. $E_{PX} = 2.5$.

**5.7**
A. $\epsilon_P = -0.86$.
B. $\epsilon_A = 0.04$.
C. $\epsilon_{PX} = 0.61$.
D. $\epsilon_I = 1.24$.

**5.8**
A. 15%.
C. $\hat{Q}_Y = 612.08$ to $717.92$

**5.9**
C. $\epsilon_A = 1$.
D. $Pr = 50\%$.

**6.1**
A. $g = 32\%$.
B. $g = 28\%$.

**6.2**
B. $g = 0\%$.
C. $g = 11\%$.

**6.3**
A. $g = 10\%$.
B. $S_5 = 104,715,000 + u$,
$S_{10} = 168,610,000 + u$.

**6.4**
B. $A_t = 80 + u$.

**6.5**
A. $g = 7.4\%$.
B. $t = 2 + u$.

**6.6**
B. $S_{t+1} = \$295,000 + u$.

**6.7**
B. $D_{t+1} = 375 + u$.

**6.8**
B. $S_{t+1} = 12,500 + u$.

**6.9**
B. Regular price:
$TR = \$3,875 + u$,
Special price:
$TR = \$7,125 + u$.
C. Regular price:
$\pi = \$1,450 + u$,
Special price:
$\pi = \$3,225 + u$.

**6.10**
$I = \$700 + u$ billion.
$GNP = \$4,500 + u$ billion
$C = \$2,800 + u$ billion.
$T = \$900 + u$ billion.
$Y = \$3,600 + u$.

**7.1**
C. $Y = 3$.

**7.5**
A. Mooty = 3.75%,
Davidson = 4.5%,
Corrow = 4%,
Michaels = 3.33%.
B. Mooty = \$8,000,
Davidson = \$5,000,
Corrow = \$4,500,
Michaels = \$3,750.

**7.6**
B. $I = 4,000$.

**7.8**
C. $A = 50$.

**7.9**
A. $MRP_P = \$62,500$,
$MRP_A = \$35,000$.

**7.10**
A. $\partial Q/Q = -0.0112$.
B. $\partial Q/Q = -0.0288$.

**7A.1**
B. $X = 167, Y = 83, \lambda = 28.7$.
C. $MC = \$0.035$.
D. $Y = 83, X = 167$,
$TC = \$1,000, \lambda = 0.035$.

**8.1**
A. $X = 0$ to $X = 2$.
B. $X = 3$.
C. Minimum $AC = \$1.25$.
D. $MC = \$1.25$.

**8.4**
A. $\pi = \$175,000$.

**8.5**
A. $TR_{BE} = \$150,000$.

**8.6**
C. $Q_{BE} = 45,000$.

**8.7**
A. $\Delta Q = 20,000$.
B. $E_P = -3$.

**8.8**
A. $Q_{BE} = 1,000$.
B. $DOL = 2$.

**8.9**
A. $\Delta Q_{BE} = 250,000$.
B. $\Delta DOL = 0.4$.
C. $\Delta \pi = \$1$ million.

**8.10**
A. $Q = 1,000,000, P = \$170$,
$\pi = \$42,187,000$.
B. $Q = 625,000$.
C. $Q = 1,250,000, P = \$162.50$,
$\pi = \$46,875,000$.

**9.3**
C. $\Delta Q = 25\%$.

**9.4**
B.  $TC = \$1,193,000$.

**9.5**
A.  $Q = 1,000$.
B.  $\epsilon_C = 0.82$.

**9.6**
A.  $Q = 10,000$.
B.  $Q = 7,500$.

**9.7**
A.  $TC = \$450,000$,
    $AC = \$112.50$.
B.  Learning effect $= (\$5.50)$ or
    5%.

**9.9**
B.  $Q_{MES} = 2,000(000)$.

**9.10**
A.  $Q_{BE} = 8(000)$ or $10(000)$.
B.  $Q_{MES} = 8.944(000)$.
C.  Potential competitors $= 10.7$
    or 10.
D.  Return on Assets $= 12.5\%$.

**10.2**
A.  $L = 4, K = 400, Q = 1$;
    $L = 16, K = 1,600, Q = 4$.
B.  $\Delta MP_L = -0.0625$,
    $\Delta MP_K = -0.000625$.
C.  $Q = 1,000$.
D.  $MP_L = 0.25, MP_K = 0$.

**10.3**
A.  $S_H = 0, S_M = 0, S_L = 32$.
B.  Zero.
C.  $P = MC = \$833$.
D.  $\Delta C_A > \$5,000$.
E.  $\Delta C_B > \$5,000$.

**10.4**
B.  $A = 1, B = 4, L_F = 4$,
    $L_R = 0, L_{FC} = 0$,
    $C = \$240,000$.
C.  $\Delta TC = -\$32,000$.
D.  $\Delta C_A > \$120,000$.

**10.5**
B.  $C = \$50,000,000$,
    $P = \$50,000,000, S_D = \$0$,
    $S_B = \$100,000,000$,

$S_C = \$25,000,000, S_A = \$0$,
$\pi = \$1,750,000$.

**10.6**
B.  $I = 0.75, J = 0.25, L_I = 0$,
    $L_J = 0.05, L_L = 0, i = 0.0975$.
C.  $\Delta R_J > -3\%$.
D.  Maximum cash $= 20\%$.

**10.7**
B.  $E = 30, W = 40, S_H = 0$,
    $S_S = 0.15, S_P = 0$,
    $C = \$2,500$.
C.  $\Delta P_W = \$12.50$.

**10.8**
B.  $I = 120, C = 40, S_A = 0$,
    $S_B = 80, S_S = 0$,
    $\pi = \$18,000$.
C.  $\pi = \$1,900$.
D.  $\pi = \$5,500$.
E.  $L_I = L_C = 0, V_A = \$50$,
    $V_B = \$0, V_S = \$50$,
    $\pi^* = \$18,000$.

**10.9**
B.  $Q_1 = 5, Q_2 = 3, S_D = 0$,
    $S_A = 5, S_{AR} = 0$,
    $R = \$21,000$;
    $L_1 = L_2 = 0, V_D = \$125$,
    $V_A = \$0, V_{AR} = \$250$,
    $R^* = \$21,000$.

**10.10**
B.  $Q_A = 0, Q_B = 2, Q_C = 2$,
    $S_L = S_P = 0, Q = 4$;
    $L_A = 0.625, L_B = 0, L_C = 0$,
    $V_L = 0.125, V_P = 0.375$,
    $Q^* = 4$.
C.  $MRP = \$56.25$.

**11.2**
B.  $P = \$3.40, Q = 8$.
C.  $P = \$4.20, Q = 4$.

**11.3**
B.  $P = MC = \$50$.
C.  $P = \$75, Q = 3$;
    $P = \$100, Q = 6$.

**11.4**
B.  $P = \$4, Q = 40$.
C.  Excess supply $= 15$.

**11.5**
A. $Q = 5,000, P = \$400$;
  $Q = 10,000, P = \$600$;
  $Q = 15,000, P = \$800$.
B. $P = \$200, Q = 0$;
  $P = \$500, Q = 7,500$;
  $P = \$1,000, Q = 20,000$.

**11.6**
C. $Q_S = 31,250,000$.

**11.7**
A. $Q = 50,000, \pi = -\$75,000$.
B. $Q = 200,000, \pi = \$300,000$.
C. $Q = 100,000, P = \$4$,
  $\pi = \$0$.

**11.8**
A. $Q = 1,000,000, P = \$10$,
  $\pi = \$5,000,000$.
B. $P = MC = \$5, \pi = 0$.

**11.9**
A. $Q = 100,000, P = \$5,000$,
  $\pi = \$50,000,000$.
B. $Q = 200,000, P = \$4,500$,
  $\pi = \$0$.

**11.10**
A. $Q = 150,000, P = \$3.50$,
  $\pi = \$287,500$.
B. $Q = 100,000, P = \$1.50$,
  $\pi = \$0$.

**12.3**
B. $P = AC = \$17, Q = 3(000)$.
C. $P = AC = \$14, Q = 6(000)$.

**12.4**
B. $Q = 2, P = \$80,000$,
  $\pi = \$10,000$.
C. $Q = 4, P = \$60,000, \pi = \$0$.

**12.5**
A. $Q = 12, P = \$36$ million,
  $\pi = \$88$ million, $\epsilon_P = -2$.
B. High-price/low-output:
  $Q = 10, P = \$31$ million,
  $\pi = \$0$;
  Low-price/high-output:
  $Q = 20, P = \$26$ million,
  $\pi = 0$.

C. $Q_2 = 16.2$, high-price/
  low-output;
  $Q_2 = 23.4$, low-price/
  high-output.

**12.6**
B. $A = 4, B = 1, C = 3$,
  $\pi = \$50$ million.

**12.7**
A. $P = \$2, Q = 40,000$.
B. $P = \$3.60, Q = 24,000$.

**12.8**
C. $P = \$50, Q = 10(000)$,
  $\pi = \$150(000)$.

**12.9**
A. $P_A > \$250, P_B > \$200$.

**12.10**
C. $Q_L = 40,000, P_L = \$23$.
D. $P = \$23, Q_M = 6,000$,
  $Q_N = 4,000$.

**13.2**
A. $\epsilon_P = -2$.
B. $P = \$20$.

**13.3**
A. $\epsilon_P = -5$.
B. Optimal Markup on
  Cost $= 25\%, P = \$150$.

**13.4**
A. $E_P = -2.5$.
B. Optimal Markup on
  Price $= 40\%, P = \$225$.

**13.5**
B. $P_{BE} = \$8.33$.

**13.6**
A. $P = \$2,875,000$.
B. $P = \$2,701,000$.

**13.7**
A. $\pi_1 = \$112,000$,
  $\pi_2 = \$104,000$.

**13.8**
A. $Q_W = 500, P_W = \$1,250$,
  $Q_R = 1,000, P_R = \$3,000$,
  $\pi = \$2,125,000$.
B. $\epsilon_{PW} = -5, \epsilon_{PR} = -1.5$.

**13.9**
A. $Q_S = Q_L = 20,000$,
   $P_S = \$10.40$, $P_L = \$0.30$.
B. $Q_S = 150,000$, $P_S = \$32.50$,
   $Q_L = 40,000$, $P_L = \$0.20$.

**13.10**
A. $Q_A = 59$, $P_A = \$541$,
   $Q_B = 50$, $P_B = \$50$.
B. Maximum Disposable
   Cost = \$15.

**13A.1**
A. $Q = 5,000$, $P = \$19,500$,
   $\pi = \$5,000,000$.
C. $P_T = \$15,000$.

**13A.2**
A. $Q = 1,250$, $P = \$337.50$,
   $\pi = \$56,250$.
C. $Q = 625$, $P_I = \$245$,
   $\pi_I = \$78,125$, $P_R = \$368.75$,
   $\pi_R = -\$60,927.50$,
   $\pi = \$17,187.50$.
D. $P_T = \$120$.

**13A.3**
A. $P_T = \$69$, $Q = 29.5$.
B. $P_T = \$190$, $Q = 22.78$.
C. $Q_A = 27.8$, $Q_B = 17$,
   $P_B = \$255.30$, $P_T = \$99.60$.

**13A.4**
E. $P = \$3,380$.
G. $P_T = \$3,350$.

**14.6**
A. $Q_L = 400$, $P_L = \$10,000$,
   $Q_H = 2,500$, $P_H = \$7,500$,
   $\pi = \$3,250,000$.
B. $Q_L = 360$, $P_L = \$10,500$,
   $Q_H = 2,000$, $P_H = \$8,000$,
   $\pi = \$620,000$.
C. $\epsilon_{PL} = -2$, $\epsilon_{PH} = -3$.

**14.7**
A. $\pi_1 = \$12,000,000$, $\pi_2 = \$0$.
B. $\pi_T = \$13,250,000$.

**14.8**
A. $Q = 1,600$, $P_M = \$24$,
   $P_A = \$288$, $i = 12.5\%$.

B. $Q = 1,800$, $i = 12.25\%$.
C. $Q = 2,000$, $P_M = \$20$.

**14.9**
B. Employment Loss = 162,500.
C. $P_L = \$3.35$, $\pi = \$227,813$;
   $P_L = \$4$, $\pi = -\$718,750$.

**14.10**
A. (1) $Q = 10,000$, $P = \$4,500$,
       $D = 1,000,000$,
       $\pi = \$2,000,000$;
   (2) $Q = 9,500$, $P = \$4,575$,
       $D = 950,000$, $\pi = \$50,000$;
   (3) $Q = 7,600$, $P = \$4,860$,
       $D = 0$, $\pi = -\$3,560,000$.
   (4) $Q = 8,600$, $P = \$4,710$,
       $D = 500,000$,
       $\pi = \$760,000$.

**15.3**
A. $E(NC) = \$125$.

**15.4**
A. $E(\pi_{MA}) = \$1,000,000$,
   $E(\pi_{PS}) = \$750,000$.

**15.5**
A. $E(\pi_1) = \$500,000$,
   $E(\pi_2) = \$375,000$.
C. $\sigma_1 = \$300,000$,
   $\sigma_2 = \$125,000$.
D. $E(u_1) = 1,172$,
   $E(u_2) = 1,162.50$.

**15.6**
A. $E(CF_1) = \$10,000$,
   $E(CF_2) = \$10,000$.
B. $\sigma_1 = \$3,000$,
   $\sigma_2 = \$1,000$.
C. $NPV_1 = \$5,000$,
   $NPV_2 = \$7,500$.

**15.7**
A. $E(\pi_A) = \$150,000$,
   $\sigma_A = \$50,000$, $V_A = 0.33$,
   $E(\pi_{SF}) = \$200,000$,
   $\sigma_{SF} = \$140,000$, $V_{SF} = 0.7$.
B. $\alpha_A = 0.8$, $\alpha_{SF} = 0.85$.

**15.8**
A. $Pr = 40\%$.

**15.9**
A. $Pr = 50\%$.
B. $P = \$23.29$.
C. $Pr = 93.32\%$.

**16.5**
A. $NPV_{LB} = \$50,000$,
$NPV_{SD} = \$60,000$.
B. $PI_{LB} = 1.25, PI_{SD} = 1.2$.

**16.6**
A. $E(CF_1) = \$1,000,000$,
$\sigma_1 = \$200,000, V_1 = 0.2$,
$E(CF_2) = \$900,000$,
$\sigma_2 = \$360,000, V_2 = 0.4$.
B. $NPV_1 = \$1,192,500$,
$NPV_2 = -\$362,640$.
C. $PI_1 = 1.40, PI_2 = 0.88$.

**16.7**
A. $E(CF_{A1}) = \$50,000$,
$\sigma_{A1} = \$30,000, V_{A1} = 0.6$;
$E(CF_{A2}) = \$50,000$,
$\sigma_{A2} = \$20,000, V_{A2} = 0.4$;

$E(CF_{B1}) = \$100,000$,
$\sigma_{B1} = \$100,000, V_{B1} = 1$;
$E(CF_{B2}) = \$100,000$,
$\sigma_{B2} = \$50,000, V_{B2} = 0.5$.
B. $NPV_A = \$9,505$,
$NPV_B = \$12,570$.
C. $PI_A = 1.13, PI_B = 1.08$.
D. $IRR_A = IRR_B = 21.6\%$.

**16.8**
A. $CF = \$8,000$.

**16.9**
A. Net Cash inflow:
$A = \$1,410,000$,
$B = \$1,378,333$,
$C = \$1,156,666$.
B. $NPV_A = \$444,180$,
$NPV_B = \$159,924$,
$NPV_C = \$497,927$.

**16.10**
A. $k_e = 20\%$.
B. $k = 16.95\%$.

# Index